MAKING *America*

A HISTORY OF THE UNITED STATES

VOLUME 1 TO *1877*

CAROL BERKIN
Baruch College, City University of New York

CHRISTOPHER L. MILLER
The University of Texas—Pan American

ROBERT W. CHERNY
San Francisco State University

JAMES L. GORMLY
Washington and Jefferson College

WITH **THE HISTORY HANDBOOK**

CAROL BERKIN
BARUCH COLLEGE, CITY UNIVERSITY OF NEW YORK

BETTY S. ANDERSON
BOSTON UNIVERSITY

MAKING AMERICA: A HISTORY OF THE UNITED STATES
VOLUME 1 TO 1877, FOURTH EDITION
by Carol Berkin, Christopher L. Miller, Robert W. Cherny,
and James L. Gormly.

Copyright © 2006 by Houghton Mifflin Company. All rights reserved.

Publisher: Charles Hartford
Senior Sponsoring Editor: Sally Constable
Development Editor: Lisa Kalner Williams
Editorial Assistant: Arianne Vanni
Senior Project Editor: Bob Greiner
Editorial Assistant: Robert Woo
Senior Art and Design Coordinator: Jill Haber
Senior Photo Editor: Jennifer Meyer Dare
Senior Composition Buyer: Sarah Ambrose
Senior Manufacturing Coordinator: Marie Barnes
Senior Marketing Manager: Sandra McGuire

Text credits: pp. 54-55: Stafford Poole, *Bartolomé de las Casas, In Defense of Indians: The Defense of the Most Reverend Lord, Don Fray de las Casas, of the Order of Preachers, late Bishop of Chiapa, against the persecutors and slanderers of the peoples of the New World Discovered across the seas.* Copyright © 1974. Used with permission of Northern Illinois University Press; p 294: The Routledge Atlas of American History 4th edition by Sir Martin Gilbert.

THE HISTORY HANDBOOK, by Carol Berkin and Betty S. Anderson.

Publisher: Charles Hartford
Editor-in-Chief: Jean L. Woy
Senior Sponsoring Editor: Nancy Blaine
Editorial Associate: Annette Fantasia
Senior Project Editor: Carol Newman
Editorial Assistant: Kendra Johnson
Senior Production/Design Coordinator: Jill Haber
Senior Manufacturing Coordinator: Priscilla Bailey
Senior Marketing Manager: Sandra McGuire

Copyright © 2003 by Houghton Mifflin Company. All rights reserved.

Custom Publishing Editor: Dan Luciano
Custom Publishing Production Manager: Tina Kozik
Project Coordinator: Janell Sims

Cover image: Chippewa Indians making a birchbark canoe, 19th century engraving. *The Granger Collection*.

Printed in the United States of America.

ISBN-13: 978-0-618-70805-5
ISBN-10: 0-618-70805-7
N-05750

2 3 4 5 6 7 8 9 – CM – 07 06

Houghton Mifflin
Custom Publishing

222 Berkeley Street • Boston, MA 02116
Address all correspondence and order information to the above address.

BRIEF CONTENTS

CONTENTS

MAPS

Individual Choices

Individual Voices

It Matters

Chronologies

xvii

Figure

Tables

Authors of textbooks may dream of cheering audiences and mountains of fan mail, but this is rarely their reality. Yet there are occasional moments of glory. A colleague drops by our office to tell us she has been using our text and the students seem more prepared and more interested in class. A former student, now teaching, sends an e-mail, saying he has used our book as a basis for his first set of class lectures and discussions. Or a freshman in a survey class adds a note at the end of her exam, saying, "thanks for writing a text that isn't boring." Maybe none of this adds up to an Academy Award or a photo on the cover of *People* magazine, but comments like these do assure us that the book we envisioned a decade ago is, if not perfect, at least on the right track. And the improvements we have made in this fourth edition of *Making America* make us even more confident.

From the beginning, our goal has been to create a different kind of textbook, one that meets the real needs of the modern college student. Every history classroom reflects the rich cultural diversity of today's student body, with its mixture of native-born Americans and recent immigrants, and its significant number of serious-minded men and women whose formal skills lag behind their interest and enthusiasm for learning. As professors in large public universities located on three of the nation's borders—the Pacific Ocean, the Atlantic, and the Rio Grande—we know the basic elements both the professor and the students need in the survey text for that classroom. These elements include a historical narrative that does not demand a lot of prior knowledge about the American past; information organized sequentially, or chronologically, so that students are not confused by too many topical digressions; and a full array of integrated and supportive learning aids to help students at every level of preparedness comprehend and retain what they read.

Making America has always provided an account of the American past firmly anchored by a political chronology. In it, people and places are brought to life not only through words but also with maps, paintings, and photos. Students can see a genuine effort to communicate with them rather than impress them. And *Making America* presents history as a dynamic process shaped by human expectations, difficult choices, and often surprising consequences. With this focus on history as a process, *Making America* encourages students to think historically and to develop into citizens who value the past.

Yet, as veteran teachers, we the authors of *Making America* know that any history project, no matter how good, can be improved. Having scrawled "Revise" across the top of student papers for several decades, we impose the same demands on ourselves. For every edition, we subjected our text to the same critical reappraisal. We eliminated features that professors and students told us did not work as well as we had hoped; we added features that we believed would be more effective; and we tested our skills as storytellers and biographers more rigorously this time around. This fourth edition reflects the same willingness to revise and improve the textbook we offer to you.

The Approach

Professors and students who have used the previous editions of *Making America* will recognize immediately that we have preserved many of its central features. We have again set the nation's complex story within an explicitly political chronology, relying on a basic and familiar structure that is nevertheless broad enough to accommodate generous attention to social, economic, and diplomatic aspects of our national history. We remain confident that this political framework allows us to integrate the experiences of all Americans into a meaningful and effective narrative of our nation's development. Because our own scholarly research often focuses on the experiences of women, African Americans, and Native Americans, we would not have been content with a framework that excluded or marginalized their history. *Making America* continues to be built on the premise that all Americans are historically active figures, playing significant roles in creating the history that we and other authors narrate. We have also continued what is now a tradition in *Making America*, that is, providing pedagogical tools for students that allow them to master complex material and enable them to develop analytical skills.

Themes

This edition continues to thread the five central themes through the narrative of *Making America* that professors and students who used earlier editions will recognize. The first of these themes, the political development of the nation, is evident in the text's coverage of the creation and revision of the federal and local governments, the contests waged over domestic and diplomatic policies, the internal and external crises faced by the United States and its political institutions, and the history of political parties.

The second theme is the diversity of a national citizenry created by immigrants. To do justice to this theme, *Making America* explores not only English and European immigration but immigrant communities from Paleolithic times to the present. The text attends to the tensions and conflicts that arise in a diverse population, but it also examines the shared values and aspirations that define middle-class American lives.

Making America's third theme is the significance of regional economies and cultures. This regional theme is developed for society before European colonization and for the colonial settlements of the seventeenth and eighteenth centuries. It is evident in our attention to the striking social and cultural divergences that existed between the American Southwest and the Atlantic coastal regions as well as between the antebellum South and North.

A fourth theme is the rise and impact of large social movements, from the Great Awakening in the 1740s to the rise of youth cultures in the post–World War II generations, movements prompted by changing material conditions or by new ideas challenging the status quo.

The fifth theme is the relationship of the United States to other nations. In *Making America* we explore in depth the causes and consequences of this nation's role in world conflict and diplomacy, whether in the era of colonization of the Americas, the eighteenth-century independence movement, the removal of Indian nations from their traditional lands, the impact of the rhetoric of manifest destiny, American policies of isolationism and interventionism, or in the modern role of the United States as a dominant player in world affairs.

In this edition, however, we have added a sixth theme: American history in a global context. This new focus allows us to set our national development within the broadest context, to point out the parallels and the contrasts between our society and those of other nations. It also allows us to integrate the exciting new scholarship in this emerging field of world or global history.

Learning Features

The chapters in *Making America* follow a format that provides students essential study aids for mastering the historical material. Each chapter begins with a map and timeline that set the scene for the most significant events and developments in the narrative that follows. While the opening timeline sets significant events in a broader time frame, a chronological chart in the interior of the chapter outlines more fully the events of the given time period. On the chapter-opening page, there is a topical outline of the material students will encounter in the chapter. Then, to help students focus on the broad questions and themes, we provide critical thinking, or focus, questions at the beginning of each major chapter section. Each chapter narrative begins with "Individual Choices" that offers a brief biography of a woman or man whose life reflects or illustrates the central themes of the chapter. At the end of the chapter narrative, "Individual Voices" provides a primary source and a series of thought-provoking questions about that source. These primary sources allow historical figures to speak for themselves and encourage students to engage directly in historical analysis. Finally, each chapter concludes with a summary that reinforces the most important themes and information the student has read.

To ensure that students have full access to the material in each chapter, we provide an on-page glossary, defining terms and explaining their historically specific usage the first time they appear in the narrative. The glossary also provides brief identifications of the major historical events, people, or documents discussed on the page. This on-page glossary will help students build their vocabularies and review for tests. The glossary reflects our concern about communicating fully with student readers without sacrificing the complexity of the history we are relating.

The illustrations in each chapter provide a visual connection to the past, and their captions analyze the subject of the painting, photograph, or artifact and comment on its significance. For this edition we have selected many new illustrations to reinforce or illustrate the themes of the narrative.

New to the Fourth Edition

In this new edition we have preserved what our colleagues and their students considered the best and most useful aspects of *Making America*. We also have replaced what was less successful, revised what could be improved, and added new elements to strengthen the book—and, miraculously, we have achieved these goals without increasing the length of the text.

You will find many features that you told us worked well in the past: biographical sketches, primary sources, timelines and maps that set the scene for each chapter. You will also find new features that you told us you would like to see. For example, we have added global events to every chapter opening timeline, in recognition of the fact that citizens of the twenty-first century live in a global rather than a local setting. We have also added global focus questions to the set of questions that introduce each major section of a chapter. We believe that this attention to global developments will help students place American events in their larger context and encourage them to compare and contrast their national history with the history of other nations. The fourth edition also introduces "It Matters," a feature in each chapter that points out connections between current events and past ones. Each "It Matters" will challenge students to see the links between past and present.

Each chapter opening map is now accompanied by a focus question. This question invites students to think critically about the map and familiarizes them with the content that is to come in the chapter.

Naming in *Making America*

We have thought carefully about the names by which we have identified ethnic groups. As a general rule, we have tried to use terms that were in use among members of that group at the time under consideration. At times, however, this would have distracted readers from the topic to the terminology, and we wanted to avoid that. In such instances, we have tried to use the terms in general use today among members of that group.

Thus, we have used *African American* and *black* relatively interchangeably. The same applies to the terms *American Indian* and *Native American*. If we are writing about a particular Indian group, we have tried to use the most familiar names by which those groups prefer to be identified, for example, *Lakota* rather than *Sioux*.

Sometimes the names by which groups are identified are controversial within the group itself. Thus, in identifying people from Latin America, some prefer *Latino* and others *Hispanic*. Our usage in this regard often reflects our own regional perspective—Bob Cherny has tended to use *Latino* as that term is more widely used in California, and Chris Miller has often used *Hispanic* because that term is more widely used in Texas. In other places, we have used more specific terms; for example, we have used *Mexican* or *Mexican American* to identify groups that migrated to the United States from Mexico and because that is the usage most common among scholars who have studied those migrants in recent years.

Finally, in a few instances when we have discussed nondominant groups, we have indicated the names that such groups used for dominant groups. In some discussions of the Southwest, for example, you will encounter the term *Anglo* to indicate those people who spoke English rather than Spanish, although we are well aware that many who were (and are) called *Anglo* are not of English (or Anglo-Saxon) descent. *Anglo* has to do with language usage, from the perspective of those who spoke Spanish, rather than having to do with those English-speakers' own sense of ethnicity. Similarly, we sometimes use the term *haole* in our discussions of Hawai`i, to indicate those people whom the indigenous Hawaiians considered to be outsiders.

We the authors of *Making America* believe that this new edition will be effective in the history classroom. Please let us know what you think by sending us your views through Houghton Mifflin's web site, located at **http://college.hmco.com.**

Learning and Teaching Ancillaries

The program for this edition of *Making America* includes a number of useful learning and teaching aids. These ancillaries are designed to help students get the most from the course and to provide instructors with useful course management and presentation tools.

The **history companion**

The **Houghton Mifflin History Companion** is a collection of resources designed to complement the use of *Making America*. It is organized according to the chapters in the text and has four parts—the **Instructor Companion web site**, the **Instructor Companion CD-ROM**, the **Student Study Companion**, and the **Student Research Companion.**

The **Instructor Companion web site** and **Instructor Companion CD-ROM** features the **Instructor's Resource Manual** written by Kelly Woestman of Pittsburg State University, primary sources with instructor notes in addition to hundreds of maps, images, audio and video clips, and PowerPoint slides for classroom presentation. The Instructor Companion CD-ROM offers additional audio and video clips for classroom use, the **Test Items** written by Matthew McCoy of University of Arkansas at Fort Smith, and **HM Testing**™, a computerized version of the Test Items with flexible test-editing capabilities.

The **Student Study Companion** is a free, online study guide to accompany *Making America*. The Study Companion contains a variety of tutorial resources including the **Study Guide** written by Kelly Woestman, ACE quizzes with feedback, annotated links to history sites, chronology exercises, flashcards, and other interactivities.

The **Student Research Companion** is a free, online tool with a wealth of interactive maps and primary sources. Students can use the maps for research, classroom assignments, or review of their geography skills. Primary sources provide a real-world introduction to historical evidence. The sources include headnotes that provide pertinent background information and questions that students can answer and e-mail to their instructors.

Please contact your local Houghton Mifflin sales representative for more information about these learning and teaching tools in addition to the **Rand McNally Atlas of American History,** WebCT and Blackboard cartridges, and transparencies for United States History.

Acknowledgments

The authors of *Making America* have benefited greatly from the critical reading of this edition of the book by instructors from across the country. We would like to thank these scholars and teachers: Linda J. Cross, Tyler Junior College; John Hosmer, University High School; Dennis Judd, Cuesta College; Barbara A. Klemm, Broward Community College; Lorraine M. Lees, Old Dominion University; Matthew G. McCoy, University of Arkansas—Fort

Smith; Victoria McKain, Butler County Community College; Pamela Riney-Kehrberg, Iowa State University; Kristen L. Streater, Collin County Community College; Theman R. Taylor, Sr., The University of Central Arkansas; and Steven D. Woodsum, Brunswick High School.

Carol Berkin, who is responsible for Chapters 3 through 7, would like to thank Greg Toft, her undergraduate research assistant on this fourth edition. She also thanks the librarians at Baruch College and The Graduate Center of CUNY and the Gilder Lehrman Institute of American History for providing help in locating interesting primary sources, and colleagues and students in the Baruch history department for their ongoing, stimulating discussion of history and historical methods. She thanks her children, Hannah and Matthew, for their patience and support while she revised this book.

Christopher L. Miller, who is responsible for Chapters 1 and 2 and 8 through 15, is indebted to his students at the University of Texas—Pan American for providing the constant inspiration to innovate. Thanks, too, are due to the many students throughout the state of Texas who have participated in his fully online courses taught through the University of Texas TeleCampus. The variety of these students and the novelty of the delivery system have encouraged constant rethinking of both historical content and delivery. Online students at Lansing Community College have provided similar motivation and worthwhile feedback. Several colleagues at University of Texas—Pan American, including Charles Prather, Kenneth Buckman, Steve Rice, and the late Paul Henggeler have been particularly helpful. Colleagues on various H-NET discussion lists as always were generous with advice, guidance, and often abstruse points of information. His coauthors also proved again to be the ideal partners in an often frustrating and difficult task. Personal thanks are due to Ryan Leigh Zimmerman and Madelyn Trinity Weaver for providing a rich life away from the academy, which has made life in the academy much more bearable.

Robert W. Cherny, who is responsible for Chapters 16 through 23, wishes to thank his students who, over the years, have provided the testing ground for much that is included in these chapters, and especially to thank his research assistants who have helped with the first, second, or third edition, Randolf Arguelles, Marie Bolton, Katherine Davis, Beth Haigin, Michelle Kleehammer, Cynthia Taylor, David Winn, and Peter Gray, who helped with this fourth edition. The staff of the Leonard Library at

San Francisco State has always been most helpful; the staff of the Kansas State Historical Society was also very helpful with locating the material on Annie Diggs in Chapter 20. Among his colleagues at San Francisco State, Jerry Combs, Tony D'Agostino, Bill Issel, Paul Longmore, Barbara Loomis, Abdiel Oñate, and Jules Tygiel have provided valuable advice on particular sections. Rebecca Marshall Cherny, Sarah Cherny, and Lena Hobbs Kracht Cherny have been unfailing in their encouragement, inspiration, and support.

James L. Gormly, who is responsible for Chapters 24 through 31, would like to acknowledge the support and encouragement he received from Washington and Jefferson College. He wants to gives a special thanks to Sharon Gormly, whose support, ideas, advice, and critical eye have helped to shape and refine his chapters.

As always, this book is a collaborative effort between authors and the editorial staff of Houghton Mifflin. We would like to thank Sally Constable, senior sponsoring editor; Lisa Kalner Williams, development editor; Sandra McGuire, senior marketing manager; Bob Greiner, senior project editor; Robert Woo, editorial assistant; and Pembroke Herbert, who helped us fill this edition with remarkable illustrations, portraits, and photographs. These talented, committed members of the publishing world encouraged us and generously assisted us every step of the way.

Dear Student:

History is about people—brilliant and insane, brave and treacherous, loveable and hateful, murderers and princesses, daredevils and visionaries, rule breakers and rule makers. It has exciting events, major crises, turning points, battles, and scientific breakthroughs. We, the authors of *Making America*, believe that knowing about the past is critical for anyone who hopes to understand the present and chart the future. In this book, we want to tell you the story of America from its earliest settlement to the present and to tell it in a language and format that helps you enjoy learning that history.

This book is organized and designed to help you master your American History course. The narrative is chronological, telling the story as it happened, decade by decade or era by era. We have developed special tools to help you learn. In the next few pages, we'll introduce you to the unique features of this book that will help you to understand the complex and fascinating story of American history.

At the back of the book, you will find some additional resources. In the Appendix, you will find an annotated, chapter-by-chapter list of suggested readings. You will also find reprinted several of the most important documents in American history: the Declaration of Independence, the Articles of Confederation, and the Constitution. Here, too, are tables that give you quick access to important data on the presidents and their cabinets. In addition, you will find a complete list of glossary terms used in the book. Finally, you will see the index, which will help you locate a subject quickly if you want to read about it.

In addition, the Houghton Mifflin History Companion, available online, provides you with free exercises, quizzes, maps, and primary sources to help you study, do research, and take tests effectively. You will also be able to access the *Making America* study guide on the History Companion.

We hope that our textbook conveys to you our own fascination with the American past and sparks your curiosity about the nation's history. We invite you to share your feedback on the book: you can reach us through Houghton Mifflin's American history web site, which is located at http://college.hmco.com.

Carol Berkin, Chris Miller, Bob Cherny, and Jim Gormly

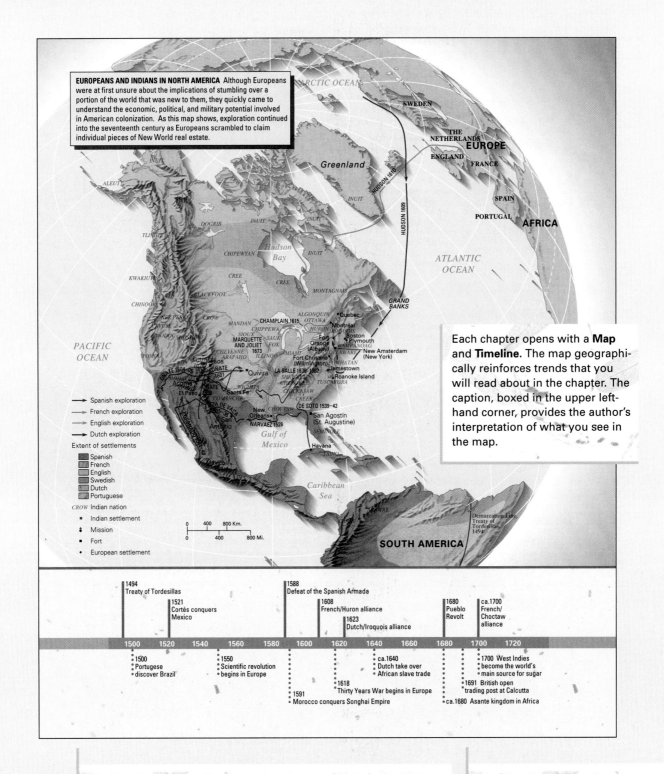

EUROPEANS AND INDIANS IN NORTH AMERICA Although Europeans were at first unsure about the implications of stumbling over a portion of the world that was new to them, they quickly came to understand the economic, political, and military potential involved in American colonization. As this map shows, exploration continued into the seventeenth century as Europeans scrambled to claim individual pieces of New World real estate.

Each chapter opens with a **Map and Timeline**. The map geographically reinforces trends that you will read about in the chapter. The caption, boxed in the upper left-hand corner, provides the author's interpretation of what you see in the map.

The timeline presents the chapter's sequence of historical happenings in a chronological fashion so that you can see what happened when. This edition of *Making America* now places events in United States history in an international context.

The **Map Focus Question,** seen on the page facing the map, asks you to analyze specific information in the map. This will prepare you for the material you will soon read in the chapter.

Individual Choices

BARTOLOMÉ DE LAS CASAS

Himself a former conquistador, Bartolomé de Las Casas was ordained as a Catholic priest in 1512 and later became one of the most vocal opponents of Spain's brutal exploitation of Native American people. He petitioned the King in 1540 and won major reforms in the way Spaniards were supposed to treat Indians, but these reforms were never well enforced

Bartolomé de Las Casas

In 1550 Spanish church officials ordered a council of learned theologians to assemble in the city of Valladolid to hear a debate over an issue so important that it challenged the entire underpinning of Spain's New World empire. At issue was the question of whether Native American Indians were human beings. Arguing that they were not was the well-respected scholar Juan Ginés de Sepúlveda. Arguing on the Indians' behalf was a former conquistador and *encomandero* named Bartolomé de Las Casas.

Born in 1474, Las Casas was the son of a small merchant in Seville. His family was privileged enough that young Bartolomé had both access and the leisure time to study at Seville's cathedral school. Like many of his contemporaries, Las Casas decided to pursue a military career, going to Granada as a soldier in 1497. Then in 1502 he embarked to the West Indies to seek his fortune in the conquest of the Americas.

Apparently Las Casas was successful as a **conquistador:** within a few years he had earned an imperial land grant with a full complement of Indian laborers. Meeting the demands of both church and king, he taught the Indians Catholicism while he exploited their labor. Eventually, however, the former came to outweigh the latter, and Las Casas's religious devotion grew in proportion. After a decade as a soldier and land baron, he became perhaps the first person to be ordained as a priest in America. His new status, however, did not prevent him from pursuing his

Individual Choices provides a portrait of an individual whose life illustrates a central theme in the chapter. Some of the individuals are famous historical figures, while others are ordinary people who played a role in shaping the events of their era. Individual Choices shows how historical events are the result of real people making real choices.

Individual Voices

Examining a Primary Source

Bartolomé de Las Casas Argues for the American Indians

In his debate with Juan Ginés de Sepúlveda before the Council of Valladolid in 1550 and 1551, Bartolomé de Las Casas repeatedly stressed the many remarkable accomplishments made by Indians, both in creating advanced civilizations of their own and in adapting to Spanish civilization. Many witnesses (most of whom had never been to America) disputed these claims, but more damaging was the argument that such accomplishments were irrelevant. Though perhaps clever, Sepúlveda argued, Indians lacked souls and therefore could never become truly civilized Christians. Like animals, then, they could be exploited but never embraced. Las Casas thought otherwise, and drew on Church doctrine to refute this claim. In the end, Las Casas's argument won the day and became the official position for the Catholic Church and the Spanish Crown.

■ *What, exactly, is Las Casas asserting in this sentence? How does this proposition set up the rest of his argument?*

Who, therefore, except one who is irreverent toward God and contemptuous of nature, has dared to write that countless numbers of natives across the ocean are barbarous, savage, uncivilized, and slow witted when, if they are evaluated by an accurate judgment, they completely outnumber all other men? ■ *This is consistent with what Saint Thomas writes: "The good which is proportionate to the common state of nature is to be found in most men and is lacking only in a few. . . . Thus it is clear that the majority of men have sufficient knowledge to guide their lives, and the few who do not have this knowledge are said to be half-witted or fools." Therefore, since barbarians of that kind, as Saint Thomas says, lack that good of the intellect which is knowledge of the truth, a good proportionate to the com-*

Individual Voices allows you to explore a primary source as a historian would. Each document is written by or is closely connected to the person featured in Individual Choices. These primary source documents include personal letters, poems, speeches, political statements, and newspaper articles. Brief introductions set the scene for each primary source, and color-coded **Exploration Points** in the margin pose provocative questions and provide interesting facts about what the document reveals.

Chronology

Partisan Tension and Jeffersonian Optimism

1796	George Washington's Farewell Address First contested presidential election: John Adams elected president, Thomas Jefferson vice president
1797	XYZ affair
1798	Quasi-War with France begins Alien and Sedition Acts Kentucky and Virginia Resolutions George Logan's mission to France
1799	Fries's Rebellion Napoleon seizes control in France
1800	Convention of Mortefontaine ends Quasi-War Jefferson and Aaron Burr tie in Electoral College Spain gives Louisiana back to France
1801	Jefferson elected president in House of Representatives; Burr vice president Judiciary Act of 1801 John Marshall becomes chief justice

War begins between American navy ships and Barbary pirates
Outdoor revival meeting at Cane Ridge, Kentucky

1802	Congress repeals all internal taxes Congress repeals Judiciary Act of 1801 French invade Santo Domingo
1803	*Marbury v. Madison* Impeachment of Justices John Pickering and Samuel Chase Louisiana Purchase
1804	Twelfth Amendment ratified Jefferson reelected
1804–1806	Lewis and Clark expedition
1806–1807	Zebulon Pike's expedition
1816	African Methodist Episcopal Church formed in Philadelphia

The **Chronology** lists the important events that we discuss in the chapter. This list reinforces the sequencing seen earlier in the chapter timeline. You can refer to this chart while reading the chapter. Afterward, you can use it to review the major events of the period.

The Politics of War

■ What problems did Abraham Lincoln and Jefferson Davis face as they led their respective nations into war?

■ How did each chief executive deal with those problems?

■ What role did European nations play during the opening years of the war?

Running the war posed complex problems for both Abraham Lincoln and Jefferson Davis. At the out-

Focus Questions begin major sections of the chapter and guide you to the most important themes in the section. These critical thinking questions help you prioritize and understand events and developments in their context. These questions also have you examine the connection of relevant moments in United States and global history.

The **On-Page Glossary** defines key terms, concepts, and vocabulary in the lower right-hand corner of the page where the term is first used in the narrative. The glossary serves as a convenient review tool, and is of special benefit to non-native speakers of English and students who need help with vocabulary. This edition of *Making America* provides a complete listing of these glossary terms in an appendix. Glossary terms are also bolded in the index, making it easier for you to relate them to their place in history.

amnesty A general pardon granted by a government, especially for political offenses.

suffrage The right to vote.

Thirteenth Amendment Constitutional amendment, ratified in 1865, that abolished slavery in the United States and its territories.

It Matters

The Nation Transformed

The Senate's decision not to remove Clinton from office reaffirmed the principle that the process of impeachment and removal of a president, or any government official, should not rest on political passions. In writing the Constitution, the drafters in Article II, Section 4, stated: "The President . . . and all civil Officials of the United States, shall be removed from Office on Impeachment for, and Conviction of, Treason, Bribery, or other high Crimes and Misdemeanors." While the Constitution does not provide a definition of "high Crimes and Misdemeanors," Congress historically has required a high standard of guilt, preventing the process from being used as a political weapon by a Congressional majority.

It Matters, a feature new to this edition, shows how a particular person, event, or theme in each chapter is relevant today. Through this feature, you will see how the past impacts the present.

Houghton Mifflin History Companion
Your primary source for Teaching and Learning
The **History Companion,** available online for **students** and on CD and online for **instructors,** provides a single source for tutorial materials and presentation materials that make teaching and learning even more dynamic. The History Companion has four components:

FOR STUDENTS:
The Student Study Companion
• ACE quizzes
• Flashcards
• Chronology exercises
• History connection exercises
• Web links and Internet resources
• Study Guide

The Student Research Companion
• Interactive maps and map exercises
• Primary sources with pedagogy and exercises

FOR INSTRUCTORS:
The Instructor Companion CD
• Test Items and HM Testing™
• Instructors Resource Manual

• Historical images in PowerPoint with notes
• Maps in PowerPoint
• Video and audio clips for classroom presentation

The Instructor Companion web site
The content from the Instructor Companion CD can also be accessed on the web site with the following exceptions:
• For security reasons, HM Testing is only available on the Instructor Companion CD.
• Many of the video clips are only available on the CD due to bandwidth concerns.

More resources will become available on the History Companion components. Please check with your local Houghton Mifflin sales representative.

Carol Berkin

Born in Mobile, Alabama, Carol Berkin received her undergraduate degree from Barnard College and her Ph.D. from Columbia University. Her dissertation won the Bancroft Award. She is now professor of history at Baruch College and the Graduate Center of City University of New York. She has written *Jonathan Sewall: Odyssey of an American Loyalist* (1974); *First Generations: Women in Colonial America* (1996); *A Brilliant Solution: Inventing the American Constitution* (2002); and *Revolutionary Mothers: Women in the Struggle for America's Independence* (2005). She has edited *Women of America: A History* (with Mary Beth Norton, 1979); *Women, War and Revolution* (with Clara M. Lovett, 1980); and *Women's Voices, Women's Lives: Documents in Early American History* (with Leslie Horowitz, 1998). She was contributing editor on southern women for *The Encyclopedia of Southern Culture* and has appeared in the PBS series *Liberty! The American Revolution* and The Learning Channel series *The American Revolution*. Professor Berkin chaired the Dunning Beveridge Prize Committee for the American Historical Association, the Columbia University Seminar in Early American History, and the Taylor Prize Committee of the Southern Association of Women Historians, and she served on the program committees for both the Society for the History of the Early American Republic and the Organization of American Historians. She has served on the Planning Committee for the U.S. Department of Education's National Assessment of Educational Progress, and chaired the CLEP Committee for Educational Testing Service.

Christopher L. Miller

Born and raised in Portland, Oregon, Christopher L. Miller received a Bachelor of Science from Lewis and Clark College and his Ph.D. from the University of California, Santa Barbara. He is currently associate professor of history at the University of Texas—Pan American. He is the author of *Prophetic Worlds: Indians and Whites on the Columbia Plateau* (1985), and his articles and reviews have appeared in numerous scholarly journals. Dr. Miller is also active in contemporary Indian affairs, having served, for example, as a participant in the American Indian Civics Project through Humboldt State University and as a member of the National Advisory Council for the Brothertown Indian Nation of New York. Professor Miller has also been active in projects designed to improve history teaching, including programs funded by the Meadows Foundation, the U.S. Department of Education, and other agencies.

Robert W. Cherny

Born in Marysville, Kansas, and raised in Beatrice, Nebraska, Robert W. Cherny received his B.A. from the University of Nebraska and his M.A. and Ph.D. from Columbia University. He is professor of history at San Francisco State University. His books include *Competing Visions: A History of California* (2005); *American Politics in the Gilded Age, 1868–1900* (1997); *San Francisco, 1865–1932: Politics, Power, and Urban Development* (with William Issel, 1986); *A Righteous Cause: The Life of William Jennings Bryan* (1985, 1994); and *Populism, Progressivism, and the Transformation of Nebraska Politics, 1885–1915* (1981). His articles on politics and labor in the late nineteenth and early twentieth centuries have appeared in journals, anthologies, and historical dictionaries and encyclopedias. In 2000, he and Ellen Du Bois co-edited a special issue of the *Pacific Historical Review* that surveyed woman suffrage movements in nine locations around the Pacific Rim. He has been an NEH Fellow, Distinguished Fulbright Lecturer at Moscow State University (Russia), and Visiting Research Scholar at the University of Melbourne (Australia). He has served as president of the Society for Historians of the Gilded Age and Progressive Era and of the Southwest Labor Studies Association and a member of the council of the American Historical Association, Pacific Coast Branch. He helped to found and continues to edit e-mail discussion lists for historians on the Gilded Age and Progressive Era (H-SHGAPE) and the history of California (H-California), both parts of H-Net, and he has served as a member of the council of H-Net (an association of more than one hundred electronic networks for scholars in the humanities and social sciences). He has also served several terms on the Academic Senate of the California State University system and has been a member of that body's executive committee.

James L. Gormly

Born in Riverside, California, James L. Gormly received a B.A. from the University of Arizona and his M.A. and Ph.D. from the University of Connecticut. He is now professor of history and chair of the history department at Washington and Jefferson College. He has written *The Collapse of the Grand Alliance* (1970) and *From Potsdam to the Cold War* (1979). His articles and reviews have appeared in *Diplomatic History, The Journal of American History, The American Historical Review, The Historian, The History Teacher,* and *The Journal of Interdisciplinary History.*

Making America

TWO WORLDS MEET For convenience sake, scholars have divided New World societies into broad culture groups, though each group was actually composed of many different, specific cultures. This map shows those culture groups and traces the routes of early explorers who opened up these new worlds to European contact and colonization.

ARCTIC OCEAN

EUROPE
ENGLAND
FRANCE

Greenland

Bering Strait

INUIT
ALEUT
HAIDA
DOGRIB
TLINGIT
CHIPEWYAN
INUIT
INUIT
INUIT
INUIT

ARCTIC

SPAIN

AFRICA

VIKINGS 1000
CABOT 1497
CARTIER 1534–35
FRENCH AND ENGLISH FISHERS
BASQUE FISHERS

NORTHWEST COAST
KWAKIUTL
CHINOOK
PLATEAU
NEZ PERCE
CAYUSE
MODOC
SHOSHONE
CROW
MANDAN
SIOUX
CHEYENNE
ARAPAHO

SUBARCTIC
CREE
CREE
MONTAGNAIS

Hudson Bay

1535
1534

GRAND BANKS

ATLANTIC OCEAN

GREAT PLAINS

BLACKFOOT

CHIPPEWA
SAUK
FOX
ILLINOIS
MIAMI

ALGONQUIN
OTTAWA
HURON
IROQUOIS
WAMPANOAG
DELAWARE
POWHATAN

VERRAZANO 1524

GREAT BASIN
POMO
NAVAHO
HOPI
ZUNI
MOHAVE
APACHE

CALIFORNIA

SOUTHWEST

WICHITA
COMANCHE

EASTERN WOODLANDS
SHAWNEE
CHEROKEE
CHICKASAW
CREEK
TUSCARORA

PACIFIC OCEAN

SOUTHEAST
CHOCTAW

COLUMBUS 1492

COLUMBUS 1493

COLUMBUS 1502–03

VESPUCCI 1499

COLUMBUS 1498

MEXICO AND MIDDLE AMERICA

Gulf of Mexico

PONCE DE LEÓN 1513
SEMINOLE

AZTEC EMPIRE
CORTES 1519–21
MAYA EMPIRE

TAINO

CARIBBEAN

Caribbean Sea

CABRILLO 1542–43

BALBOA 1510–13

ARAWAK

CARIB

AMAZON

PIZARRO 1530–33

INCA EMPIRE

SOUTH AMERICA

→ Spanish exploration
→ French exploration
→ English exploration
→ Viking exploration
→ Fishing expeditions

PLATEAU Culture area
CROW Indian nation

0 400 800 Km.
0 400 800 Mi.

---

800 Rise of the Anasazi civilization

ca. 1400 Onset of Little Ice Age

70,000–8,000 BCE Migration into Beringia

3,000 BCE Farming in central Mexico

300 CE Farming introduced to southwest North America

1000 First Viking expedition to North America

1450 Iroquois League

1492 Columbus's first voyage

10,000 BCE	2000 BCE	0	200	400	600	800	1000	1200	1400	1600

8000–6000 BCE Farming in Africa, Peru, Europe

507 BCE Roman Republic

34 CE Death of Jesus of Nazareth

1,400 BCE Iron smelting in sub-Saharan Africa

632 Death of Mohammed

962 Holy Roman Empire founded

ca. 750 Islamic trade with sub-Saharan Africa

1096–1291 Crusades

1517 Protestant Reformation begins

Making a "New" World, to 1588

1

Two Worlds Meet

Using the map on the facing page, examine the patterns of European exploration and expansion into the Western Hemisphere. How would you say that New World geography interacted with European economic, political, and diplomatic interests to influence different colonizing powers to concentrate in certain areas? What sorts of consequences would these patterns lead to?

Individual Choices

HIENWATHA

New conditions in North America led to increasing conflicts among the five northeastern Iroquois tribes during the fifteenth and sixteenth centuries. Hienwatha overcame resistance—even the murder of his family— to convince Iroquois leaders to form the Iroquois League, a political, military, and religious alliance that helped them survive massive changes and made them a major force in world diplomacy. *Newberry Library.*

Hienwatha

Things were bad, and getting worse, for the people who lived in North America's northeastern woodlands (see the chapter-opening map). For generations they had lived peacefully in their largely self-sufficient villages on the corn that the women grew and the game that the men hunted. Warfare was infrequent, and famine all but unknown. But around the time that Europeans would call 1400, a long-lasting change in the weather made corn production less dependable, and the people were forced to hunt and gather more wild foods to supplement their diets. As hunters from individual villages roamed deeper and deeper into the forests looking for food, they encountered others who, like themselves, were desperate to harvest the diminishing resources. Conflicts became common. "Everywhere there was peril and everywhere mourning," says one version of the story. "Feuds with outer nations and feuds with brother nations, feuds of sister towns and feuds of families and clans made every warrior a stealthy man who liked to kill."

In the midst of the crisis, a child who would be called Hienwatha (or Hiawatha, Maker of Rivers) was born among the woodland people. Oral accounts among the various Indian groups disagree about Hienwatha's early life. According to some sources, he was born among the Onondaga Nation sometime shortly after 1400 but came to live with the neighboring Mohawks. If so, he may well have been a war captive, taken to replace a Mohawk killed in the ever-accelerating violence that raged through the woodlands.

Having grown to adulthood among the Mohawks, the still young and unmarried outsider left his village to seek survival on his own in the woods. Food was scarce, and Hienwatha became a cannibal, killing lone travelers to eat their flesh. One day, as Hienwatha was butchering a victim, he discovered that he had a visitor. The man, a Huron Indian called Dekanahwideh (Two River Currents Flowing Together), shamed Hienwatha for his sad and dishonorable state. The stranger then told him of a spirit being called Peacemaker, who had given Dekanahwideh a vision and a mission: he was to unify all the Iroquois into a great and peaceful nation. Inspired by the stranger's words, Hienwatha vowed never to eat human flesh again and to spend his life making Dekanahwideh's vision a reality.

Hienwatha moved back among the Mohawks, married, and began telling the people about Dekanahwideh's vision and Peacemaker's message. Although many found his words inspiring, some, including Onondaga leader Tadadaho, opposed him. Tadadaho and his supporters finally attacked Hienwatha, killing his family and forcing him to flee once again into the woods.

Undaunted, Hienwatha tried to think of some way to convince his enemies among the Iroquois to accept the idea of cooperation. His solution was to weave a belt of wampum-shell strings that showed a great chain connecting the five northern Iroquois nations—Mohawk, Oneida, Onondaga, Cayuga, and Seneca. Carrying his belt, Hienwatha traveled among the five nations, telling them that they could survive only if they ceased fighting among themselves and began cooperating. He finally won over even Tadadaho, whose Onondaga Nation became the keeper of the council fires. Together Hienwatha, Dekanahwideh, Tadadaho, and the other leaders of the Five Nations created a confederation government that Europeans later would call the League of the Iroquois. Under its provisions each member nation maintained complete sovereignty in its own affairs, but all agreed fully to defend the others, share resources, and promote the confederation's overall welfare. They also vowed to carry forward Peacemaker's design by offering peace to all who would agree to live with them under the Great Tree of Peace that symbolized the new covenant. Many agreed, but many also resisted what they saw as Iroquois aggression. That included Dekanahwideh's own Huron people, who formed their own alliance system to oppose the Iroquois League.

As remarkable as Hienwatha's story is, his experience was not entirely unique. Faced with changing conditions, natural ones at first and then those brought by invading Europeans, Indians throughout the Americas struggled valiantly and creatively to restructure their societies and their lives. Sometimes the effort brought success, as it did for the Iroquois, but the new political, diplomatic, and spiritual alignments just as often triggered more struggle and war, as it did between the Iroquois and the Hurons. But whatever else might be said for the achievements of Hienwatha and his contemporary visionaries, they succeeded in reshaping America, crafting what Europeans naively—but in this one sense quite correctly—called the New World. And in the process, they helped shape the entire Atlantic world, where the making of America would soon take center stage.

INTRODUCTION

The emergency that led the Iroquois to form their confederacy was but one in a long series of unsettling events that would entirely transform their world and that of their neighbors. Nor was this the first time that America's original population had experienced upheaval in response to changing historical conditions. Having come to a highly varied and ever-changing continent **millennia** earlier, Native Americans had continually modified their environments and been modified by them, giving shape to both the physical and the human world in which America would be made.

For nearly a thousand years before the Iroquois formed their league, a combination of natural and human forces truly global in scope was having a profound impact throughout the Atlantic basin. For example, during the several centuries following the death of Mohammed in 632, the vibrant new religion that he founded, Islam, swept out of the Arabian Peninsula to conquer virtually the entire Mediterranean world. In response, native Europeans, who had themselves adopted a new and dynamic religion, Christianity, only a few centuries earlier, struck back in a series of Crusades designed to break Islamic power. At the same time, climatic changes encouraged expansion by Viking warlords out of Scandinavia southward into the European mainland and westward all the way into North America. Together these expansive societies introduced new technologies and knowledge of distant and mysterious worlds that would engender an air of restlessness throughout Europe.

One of those mysterious worlds lay to the south of the forbidding Sahara Desert in Africa. There, as in both America and Europe, people had been dealing with changing conditions by crafting societies and economies that made the most of varying environments. When Islamic trading caravans began penetrating this region in the eighth century, they found highly developed cities that could draw on massive populations and natural resources to produce goods that were in great demand throughout the evolving Atlantic world. Like Native Americans, Africans too

millennia The plural of *millennium*, a period of one thousand years.

would be drawn into the restlessness that characterized this dynamic age.

Within decades after Hienwatha convinced the Five Nations to unite, Christopher Columbus, a Genoese navigator in Spain's employ, rediscovered the **Western Hemisphere** while trying to find the hidden and distant worlds known to Islamic traders. Columbus's accident brought two historical streams together, and from that point onward, the history of each helped to form the future of both. On a global scale, this event launched a new era in human history. On a more local scale, it began a process we call *Making America.*

A World of Change

■ How did environmental changes influence the development of various societies in North America during the millennia before the emergence of the Atlantic world?

■ What forces came into play in the centuries before 1500 that would launch Europeans on a program of outward exploration?

■ What factors in sub-Saharan African history helped lead to the development of the slave trade?

Christopher Columbus's accidental encounter with the Western Hemisphere came after nearly a thousand years of increasing restlessness and dramatic change that affected all of the areas surrounding the Atlantic Ocean. After millennia of relative isolation, the natural and human environments in America were opened to the flow of people, animals, and goods from the rest of the Atlantic world. During the centuries before 1492, Christian monarchs and church leaders conducted a series of **Crusades** to wrest control of the **Holy Land** from the **Muslims.** As armies of Crusaders pushed their way into the region, they came into contact with many desirable commodities—fine silks, exotic spices, and precious stones and metals. As word spread of the finery Muslims obtained through trade with Africa and Asia, enterprising individuals began looking for ways to profit by supplying such luxuries to European consumers. At the same time, northern European **Vikings** were extending their holdings throughout many parts of Europe and westward all the way to North America. Both Crusaders and Vikings came into contact with equally restless and vibrant societies in Africa and the Western Hemisphere, lending greater impetus to continuing exploration.

American Origins

American history, both before and after Columbus's intrusion, was shaped by the peculiar landscape that had developed over millennia in the Western Hemisphere. Floating plates of the earth's crust meet along the continent's western flank, rubbing and sometimes crashing together. Like a car fender after a collision, the earth has crumpled from the impact, forming rugged mountain ranges all the way from the Arctic to the extreme tip of South America. These collisions also left gaps and weak points in the earth's crust that gave rise to volcanoes and other geological activity. The resulting upheavals constantly changed the region's face: whole mountains were created and then destroyed, rich veins of minerals formed and then were buried, and varied local habitats emerged that would house an incredible array of plant and animal species.

While upheaval was shaping the western portion of the hemisphere, erosion was the sculptor in the east. Old granite rock formations were carved by winter frosts and running water. Thousands of rivers and streams crisscrossed the flattening land, carrying the minerals eroding from higher ground to form rich and deep soil downstream. Upstream, often all that remained was bedrock with only a shallow cover of topsoil. Throughout these regions, too, different habitats supported varied life forms.

Western Hemisphere When discussing the world longitudinally (lengthwise), geographers often divide the globe into two halves (hemispheres). The **Western Hemisphere** includes North America, Mexico, Central America, and South America; the **Eastern Hemisphere** includes Europe, Asia, and Africa.

Crusades Military expeditions undertaken by European Christians in the eleventh through the thirteenth centuries to recover the Holy Land from the Muslims.

Holy Land Palestine, which now is divided between Israel, Jordan, and Syria; called the Holy Land because it is the region in which the events described in the Old and New Testaments of the Bible took place; it is sacred to Christians, Jews, and Muslims.

Muslims People who practice the religion of Islam, a monotheistic faith that accepts Mohammed as the chief and last prophet of God.

Vikings Late-medieval Danish, Swedish, and Norwegian groups who responded to land shortages and climatic conditions in Scandinavia by taking to the sea and establishing communities in various parts of western Europe, Iceland, Greenland, and North America.

Chronology

The New World

ca. 70,000–8,000 BCE	Human migration from Asia into Beringia
ca. 7000 BCE	Plant cultivation begins in North America
ca. 1400 BCE	Sub-Saharan Africans perfect iron smelting
ca. 34 CE	Death of Jesus of Nazareth and beginning of Christianity
632	Death of Mohammed and beginning of Islamic expansion
ca. 750	Islamic caravans travel to West Africa; African slave trade begins
ca. 500–1000	Rise of Hopewell culture
ca. 800–1700	Rise of Mississippian culture
ca. 1000–1400	Vikings in North America
1096–1291	The Crusades
ca. 1200	Aztecs arrive in the Valley of Mexico
ca. 1400	Beginning of Little Ice Age
ca. 1450	Hienwatha and Dekanahwideh found Iroquois League
1492	Reconquista completed / Columbus's first voyage
1500	Portuguese begin to transport and trade African slaves
1517	Martin Luther presents Ninety-five Theses
1527–1535	Henry VIII initiates English Reformation
1558	Elizabeth I becomes queen of England

Note: BCE means "before the common era."

About 2.5 million years ago, a new force came to dominate the landscape with the onset of the Great Ice Age. During the height of the Ice Age, great sheets of ice advanced and withdrew across the world's continents, and temperatures were between fifteen and twenty degrees colder than they are today. Glaciers moved southward, grinding away at the central part of North America, carving a flat corridor all the way from the Arctic Circle to the Gulf of Mexico. During the last ice advance, the Wisconsin glaciation, a sheet of ice more than 8,000 feet thick covered the northern half of both Europe and North America.

Not only did this massive ice sheet affect the underlying geology, but so much water was frozen into the glaciers that sea levels dropped as much as 450 feet. Migratory animals found vast regions closed to them by the imposing ice fields and ventured into areas exposed by the receding sea. One such region, Beringia, lay between present-day Siberia on the Asian continent and Alaska in North America (see Map 1.1). Now covered by the waters of the Bering Sea and Arctic Ocean, Beringia during the Ice Age was a dry, frigid grassland—a perfect grazing ground for animals such as giant bison and huge-tusked woolly mammoths. Hosts of predators, including large wolves and saber-toothed cats, followed them. Human populations, which until this time had been confined to the **Eastern Hemisphere,** appear to have followed as well (see page 6).

Sea levels were low enough to expose Beringia about 70,000 years ago, and the area remained above sea level more or less continually until about 10,000 years ago. Although movement southward into North America would have been difficult because of the rugged terrain and mountainous glaciers, determined people may have begun populating the continent at any time between these dates. In fact, recent archaeological finds and isolated discoveries such as that of the **Kenniwick Man** suggest that many different groups of migrating people may have arrived and

Kenniwick Man   The name given to a human skeleton discovered next to the Columbia River near Kenniwick, Washington, in 1996. The skeleton is believed to be over 9,000 years old and appears to have facial features unlike those of other ancient Indian relics.

ARCTIC
OCEAN

BERINGIA
LAND
BRIDGE

Kayuk Complex

Kogruk Complex

Flint Creek
Complex

Fort Liar
Complex

Yale

Lind
Coulee

Fort Rock
Cave

Wilson Butte
Cave

American
Falls

Eden
Lindenmeier

Scottsbluff

Starved
Rock

Gypsum
Cave

Sandia
Cave

Dent

Topenga
Complex

Lucy

Folsom

Graham
Cave

Modoc Rockshelter

Ventana Cave

Blackwater
Draw

Russell
Cave

Lehner

Cochise
Complexes

Naco

Scharbauer
('Midland')

PACIFIC
OCEAN

Frightful
Cave

ATLANTIC
OCEAN

Tequixquiác

Valsequillo

Probable coastline

Glacier

Migration route

Archaeological site

0   500   1000 Km.

0   500   1000 Mi.

MAP 1.1 First Americans Enter the New World   Although DNA evidence indicates that all early migrants to the
Western Hemisphere were genetically related, at least two cultural groups moved into North America between
70,000 and 40,000 years ago. The Old Cordilleran group, to the west of the Rocky Mountains, and the Clovis group,
to the east, left records of their passing at numerous sites, the most prominent of which are labeled here.

Although some archaeologists and many Native Americans dispute the accuracy of this forensic reconstruction, many experts consider this bust of the Kenniwick Man based on a skull discovered on the banks of the Columbia River in 1996 to be the best indication of both the deep antiquity and diversity of Old World migrations to North America during the Ice Age. *James Chatters and Thomas McClelland.*

either coexisted or succeeded each other over this 60,000-year period.

Biological evidence collected from modern Indians suggests that the majority of Native Americans are descended from three distinct migrating groups, each of which arrived at a different time. The first of these groups, called the Paleo-Indians, probably entered the continent between 30,000 and 40,000 years ago, and their descendants eventually occupied the entire area of the Western Hemisphere. The second group, collectively called the Na-Dene people, appears to have arrived very near the end of the Wisconsin era, between 10,000 and 11,000 years ago, and their descendants are concentrated in the subarctic regions of Canada and the southwestern United States. The final group, the Arctic-dwelling Inuits, or Eskimos, arrived sometime later, perhaps after Beringia had flooded again (see Map 1.1).

Even after the Ice Age came to an end, it took between 4,000 and 5,000 years for the massive glaciers to melt. During that time the melting ice kept the climate cold and damp everywhere on the continent. But by about 9,000 years ago temperatures began warming. The Ice Age creatures whose presence supplied early hunters with their primary source of meat and whose movements set the tempo for Paleo-Indian life began to die out. The hunters faced the unpleasant prospect of following the large animals into extinction if they kept trying to survive by hunting big game.

It Matters

Native Americans Shape a New World

It may be hard to imagine why understanding the original peopling of North America and how Native cultures evolved during the millennia before Columbus could possibly matter to the history of the United States or, more specifically, to how we live our lives today. Without this chapter in our history, there would likely have been no United States history at all. First and foremost, as the eminent historian Francis Jennings pointed out, if the American continent had truly been a wilderness at the time of European discovery, it would probably still be a wilderness today. Europeans in the fifteenth century lacked the tools, the organization, the discipline, and the economic resources to conquer a wilderness—such a feat would have been the equivalent of our establishing a successful colony on the moon today. But the environmental and genetic engineering conducted through the millennia of North American history created a hospitable environment into which European crops, animals, and people could easily insinuate themselves. And while the descendants of those Europeans may fool themselves into thinking that they constructed an entirely new world in North America, the fact is that they simply grafted new growth onto ancient rootstock, creating the unique hybrid that is today's America.

People everywhere in North America abandoned big-game hunting and began to explore the newly emerging local environments for new sources of food, clothing, shelter, and tools. In the forests that grew up to cover the eastern half of the continent, they developed finely polished stone tools, which they used to make functional and beautiful implements out of wood, bone, shell, and other materials. There and along the Pacific shore, people used large, heavy stone tools to hollow out massive tree trunks, making boats from which they could harvest food from inland waterways and from the sea. During this time domesticated dogs were introduced into North America, probably by newly arriving migrants from Asia. With dogs to help carry loads on land and boats

Maize (corn), which was genetically engineered by Native Americans in what is now Mexico some 7,000 years ago, became one of the staple food sources for many Indian groups in North America. This sixteenth-century illustration depicts traditional Native American agricultural practices and typical foods, including corn, squashes, and gourds. *The Pierpont Morgan Library/Art Resource, NY.*

comes from north-central Mexico, where, beginning perhaps 7,000 years ago, human intervention helped a wild strain of grass develop bigger seedpods with more nutritious seeds. Such intervention eventually transformed a fairly unproductive plant into an enormously nourishing and prolific food crop: **maize.**

Maize (corn), along with other engineered plants like beans, squash, and chilies, formed the basis for an agricultural revolution in North America, allowing many people to settle in larger villages for longer periods. Successful adaptation—including plant cultivation and eventually agriculture—along with population growth and the constructive use of spare time allowed some Indians in North America to build large, ornate cities. The map of ancient America is dotted with such centers. Along the Ohio River, a complex of sites that archaeologists call the **Adena culture** was constructed about 3,000 years ago. Large quantities of both practical and purely decorative artifacts from all over North America have been found at Adena sites. In Illinois and elsewhere in eastern North America, **Hopewell culture** took the place of Adena culture and in time was itself eclipsed by a larger **Mississippian tradition.**

Then, about 800 years ago, midwestern **mound builder** sites fell into decline, and the people who once had congregated there withdrew to separated

for river transportation, Native American people were able to make the best use of their local environments by moving around to different spots during different seasons of the year. Thus they did not establish permanent towns or villages. Rather, they followed an annual round of movement from camp to camp—perhaps collecting shellfish for several weeks at the mouth of a river, then moving on to where wild strawberries were ripening, and later in the summer relocating to fields in which maturing wild onions or sunflower seeds could be harvested.

Although these ancestors of modern Indians believed in and celebrated the animating spirits of the plants and animals that they depended on for survival, they nonetheless engaged in large-scale environmental engineering. They used fire to clear forests of unwanted scrub and to encourage the growth of berries and other plants they found valuable. In this way they produced vegetables for themselves and also provided food for browsing animals such as deer, which increased in number while other species, less useful to people, declined. They also engaged in genetic engineering. A highly significant example

maize Corn; the word *maize* comes from an Indian word for this plant.

Adena culture An early nonagricultural American Indian society centered in the Ohio River valley and spreading as far as West Virginia; it is known for having built large trading centers, where artifacts from all over North America have been found.

Hopewell culture A successor to the Adena culture also centered in the Ohio River valley and spreading as far as New York; Hopewell Indians introduced maize agriculture in about 200 BCE and built larger and more elaborate mound cities in which large-scale trading activities continued.

Mississippian tradition A culture shared by a number of American Indian societies centered in the southern Mississippi River valley; influenced by Mexican culture, it is known for its pyramid building and urban centers.

mound builder Name applied to a number of Native American societies, including the Adena, Hopewell, and Mississippian cultures, that constructed massive earthen mounds as monuments and building foundations.

villages or bands. No single satisfactory explanation accounts for why this happened, but it is interesting to note that other changes were taking place at around this time elsewhere in the Atlantic world that would have profound effects on the American story.

Change and Restlessness in the Atlantic World

During the few centuries following the death of the prophet **Mohammed** in 632, Muslim Arabs, Turks, and **Moors** made major inroads into western Asia and northern Africa, eventually encroaching on Europe's southern and eastern frontiers (see Map 1.2). During these same years, Scandinavian Vikings, who controlled the northern frontiers of Europe, began expanding southward and westward. Accomplished and fearless seamen, the Vikings swept down Europe's western shore and through Russia by river to the Mediterranean. They also began colonizing Iceland and Greenland. Then, according to Viking sagas, a captain named Bjarni Herjólfsson sighted North America in 986. Fourteen years later, Viking chieftain Leif Eriksson led an expedition to the new land, and over the decades that followed, Vikings established several American colonies.

By about the year 1000, then, the heartland of Europe was surrounded by dynamic societies that served as conduits to a much broader world. Although Europeans resented and resisted both Viking and Islamic invasion, the newcomers brought with them tempting new technologies, food items, and expansive knowledge. These contributions not only enriched European culture but also improved the quality of life. For example, new farming methods increased food production so much that Europe began to experience a population explosion. Soon Europeans would begin turning this new knowledge and these new tools against the people who brought them.

Iberians launched a **Reconquista,** an effort to break Islamic rule on the peninsula, and in 1096, European Christians launched the first in a series of Crusades to sweep the Muslims from the Holy Land. With the aid of English Crusaders, Portugal attained independence in 1147. Meanwhile in the Holy Land, hordes of Crusaders captured key points only to be expelled by Muslim counterattacks. The effort to dislodge Islamic forces from Jerusalem and other sacred sites came largely to an end in 1291, but the struggle continued in the Iberian Peninsula. By 1380 Portugal's King John I had united that country's various

principalities under his rule. In Spain, unification took much longer, but in 1469 **Ferdinand and Isabella,** heirs to the rival thrones of Aragon and Castile, married and created a united state in Spain. Twenty-three years later, in 1492, the Spanish subdued the last Moorish stronghold on the peninsula, completing the Reconquista.

Dealings with the Vikings in the north took a somewhat different turn. Although they maintained trading contacts with North America for several hundred years, the Vikings began to retreat in the middle of the 1300s. By 1450 or so, they had withdrawn entirely from their transatlantic colonies. The most likely cause of their departure was a shift in climate. Although experts disagree about the exact timing, it appears that at some time between 1350 and 1450 a significant climatic shift called the Little Ice Age began to affect the entire world. In the Arctic and subarctic, temperatures fell, snowfall increased, and sea ice became a major hazard to navigation. This shift made it impossible for the Vikings to practice the herding, farming, and trading that supported their economy in Greenland and elsewhere. Finding themselves cut off from a vibrant North Atlantic empire, Viking settlements in the British Isles, Russia, France, and elsewhere merged with local populations.

These Viking refugees often joined with their neighbors in recognizing the value of large-scale political organization. Consolidation began in France in around 1480, when Louis XI took control of five rival provinces to create a unified kingdom. Five years later in

Mohammed   Born ca. 570 into an influential family in Mecca, on the Arabian Peninsula, around 610 Mohammed began having religious visions in which he was revealed as "the Messenger of God." The content of his various visions was recorded as the Qur'an, the sacred text that is the foundation for the Islamic religion.

Moors   Natives of northern Africa who converted to Islam in the eighth century, becoming the major carriers of the Islamic religion and culture both to southern Africa and to the Iberian Peninsula (Spain and Portugal), which they conquered and occupied from the eighth century until their ouster in the late fifteenth century.

Reconquista   The campaign undertaken by European Christians to recapture the Iberian Peninsula from the Moors.

Ferdinand and Isabella   Joint rulers of Spain (r. 1469–1504); their marriage in 1469 created a united Spain from the rival kingdoms of Aragon and Castile.

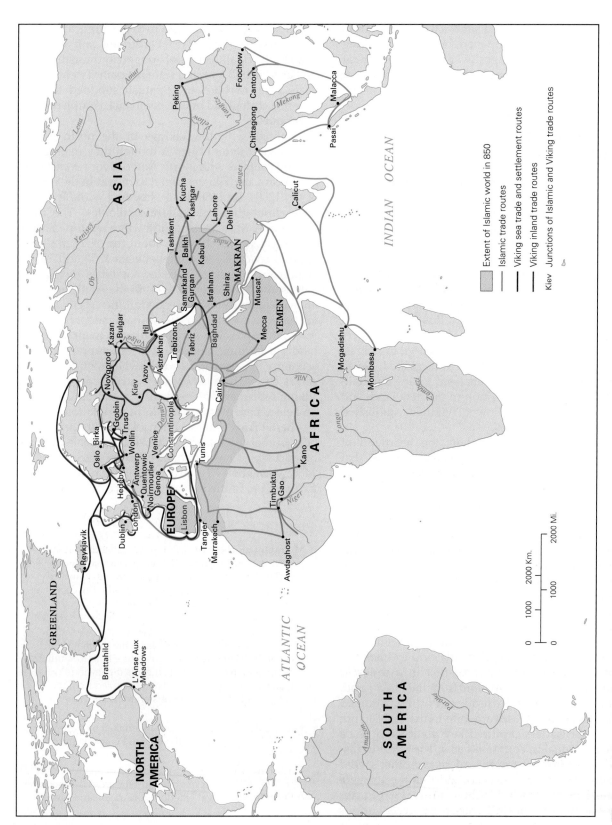

MAP 1.2 Europe and Its Neighbors, ca. 1000 Europe was not isolated during medieval times. As shown here, Viking and Islamic empires surrounded western Europe, and their trade routes crisscrossed the region, bringing far-away goods and ideas from many lands, including North America, long before Columbus "discovered" the New World.

Beginning in about the year 1000, two dynamic seafaring societies controlled the European continent's perimeters: various allied Islamic societies to the south and Vikings on all other sides. Both groups used innovative technologies and advanced geographical knowledge to continually expand their holdings, including holdings in North America. Their ships carried many new commodities as well as new knowledge into Europe, helping to create a restless, exploring spirit among Europeans. *Left: The Pierpont Morgan Library/Art Resource, NY; right: Bibliothèque Nationale, France.*

England, Henry Tudor and the House of Lancaster defeated the rival House of York in the Wars of the Roses, ending nearly a hundred years of civil war. Tudor, now styling himself King Henry VII, cemented this victory by marrying into the rival house, wedding Elizabeth of York to finally unify the English throne. As in Spain and Portugal, the formation of unified states in France and England opened the way to new expansive activity that would accelerate the creation of an Atlantic world.

The Complex World of Indian America

The world into which Vikings first sailed at the beginning of the second millennium and into which other Europeans would intrude half a millennium later was not some static realm stuck in the Stone Age. Native American societies were every bit as progressive, adaptable, and historically dynamic as those that would invade their homes. In fact, adaptive flexibility characterized Indian life throughout North America, and so the vast variety in environmental conditions that characterize the continent led to the emergence of enormous differences between various Indian groups. **Anthropologists** have tried to make

the extremely complicated cultural map of North America understandable by dividing the continent into a series of culture areas—regions where the similarities among native societies were greater than the differences. The chapter-opening map shows eleven such areas.

In the southeastern region of North America, peoples speaking Siouan, Caddoan, and Muskogean languages formed vibrant agricultural and urban societies that had ties with exchange centers farther north as well as with adventurous traders from Mexico. At places like Natchez, fortified cities housed gigantic pyramids, and farmland radiating outward provided food for large residential populations. These were true cities and, like their counterparts in Europe and Asia, were magnets attracting ideas, technologies, and religious notions from all parts of the Western Hemisphere.

Farther north, in the region called the Eastern Woodlands, people lived in smaller villages and combined agriculture with hunting and gathering. The

anthropologist   A scholar who studies human behavior and culture in the past or the present.

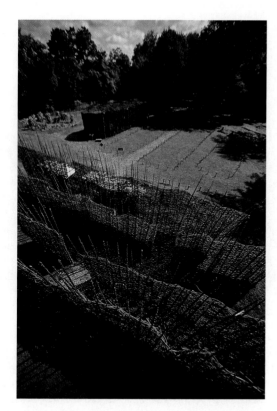

Iroquois towns consisted of rows of longhouses, often surrounded by defensive walls. This partial reconstruction of a sixteenth-century Iroquois town that stood near what is now London, Ontario, illustrates how such sites looked. The staked areas to the right of the rebuilt longhouses show where neighboring longhouses used to stand. *Richard Alexander Cooke III.*

Iroquois, for example, lived in towns numbering three thousand or more people, changing locations only as soil fertility, firewood, and game became exhausted. Before Hienwatha and the formation of the Iroquois League, each village was largely self-governed by clan mothers and their chosen male civil servants. Each town was made up of a group of **longhouses,** structures often 60 feet or more in length.

A tradition that may go back to the time when the Iroquois lived as nomadic hunters and gatherers dictated that men and women occupy different spheres of existence. The women's world was the world of plants, healing, nurturing, and order. The men's was the world of animals, hunting, war, and disorder. By late **pre-Columbian** times, the Iroquois became strongly agricultural, and because plants were in the women's sphere, women occupied places of high social and economic status in Iroquois society. Families were

matrilineal, meaning that they traced their descent through the mother's line, and matrilocal, meaning that a man left his home to move in with his wife's family upon marriage. Women distributed the rights to cultivate specific fields and controlled the harvest.

Variations on this pattern were typical throughout the Eastern Woodlands and in the neighboring Great Plains and Southwest. Agricultural village life was the dominant lifestyle in each region before Europeans came. In fact, migrants into the plains probably came from the east carrying seed corn from settlements in the Southeast and Woodlands. Groups such as the Mandans began settling on bluffs overlooking the many streams that eventually drain into the Missouri River. Living in substantial houses insulated against the cold winters, these people divided their time among hunting, crop raising, and trade. Over a five-hundred-year period, populations increased, and agricultural settlements expanded. By 1300, such villages could be found along every stream ranging southward from North Dakota into present-day Kansas.

Just as agriculturalists in the Great Plains had strong connections to the Eastern Woodlands, Indians in the Southwest were closely tied to Mexico. As early as 3,200 years ago, corn appears to have been brought into the area. But the southwestern Indians, unlike their contemporaries farther south, continued to depend extensively on hunting and food gathering for a long time after experiencing the agricultural revolution. Not until about the year 400 did Indians in this region begin building larger and more substantial houses and limiting their migrations. The greatest change, however, came during the eighth century, when a shift in climate made the region drier and a pattern of late-summer thunderstorms triggered dangerous and erosive flash floods.

There seem to have been two quite different responses to this change in climate. A group called the Anasazi expanded their agricultural ways, cooperating to build flood-control dams and irrigation canals. The need for cooperative labor meant forming larger communities, and between about 900 and 1300 the Anasazi built whole cities of multistory apartment houses along the high cliffs, safe from flooding but near their irri-

longhouse A communal dwelling, usually built of poles and bark and having a central hallway with family apartments on either side (see illustration).
pre-Columbian Existing in the Americas before the arrival of Columbus.

gated fields. In these densely populated towns Anasazi craft specialists such as potters, weavers, basket makers, and tool smiths manufactured goods for the community while farmers tended fields and priests attended to the spiritual needs of the society.

Another contingent of southwestern Indians abandoned the region, moving southward into Mexico. Here they came upon the remnants of classical city-states like Teotihuacán. One of several highly developed societies of central Mexico, Teotihuacán was the largest city-state in the Western Hemisphere, with a population of nearly 200,000. However, by around the year 600, Teotihuacán and other such societies were in decline. Over the next several hundred years, migrants from southwestern North America—so-called Chichimecs or "wild tribes"—borrowed architectural and agricultural skills from the fallen societies and built new monumental cities. The first of these, Tula, entered its heyday in about the year 1000, but a civil war two centuries later brought that civilization to an end. Shortly thereafter, another Chichimec tribe rose to prominence in central Mexico. The **Aztecs** arrived in the Valley of Mexico soon after 1200, settling on a small island in the middle of a brackish lake. From this unappealing center, a series of strong leaders used a combination of diplomacy and brutal warfare to establish a **tributary empire** that eventually ruled as many as 6 million people.

Other major changes occurred in the Southwest after 1300. During the last quarter of the thirteenth century, a long string of summer droughts and bitterly cold winters forced the Anasazi to abandon their cities. They disappeared as a people, splitting into smaller communities that eventually became the various Pueblo groups. At the same time, an entirely new population entered the region. These hunter-gatherers brought new technologies, including the bow and arrow, into the Southwest. About half of them continued to be hunter-gatherers, while the rest borrowed cultivating and home-building techniques from the Pueblos. Europeans who later entered the area called the hunter-gatherers Apaches and the settled agriculturalists Navajos.

In the balance of North America, agriculture was practiced only marginally, if at all. In areas like the Great Basin, desert conditions made agriculture too risky, and in California, the Northwest Coast, and the intermountain Plateau (see the chapter-opening map), the bounty of available wild foods made it unnecessary. In these regions, hunting and gathering remained the chief occupations.

The Nez Perces and their neighbors living in the Plateau region, for example, occupied permanent village sites in the winter but did not stay together in a single group all year. Rather, they formed task groups—temporary villages that came together to share the labor required to harvest a particular resource—and then went their separate ways when the task was done. These task groups brought together not only people who lived in different winter villages but often people from different tribes and even different language groups. In such groups, political authority passed among those who were best qualified to supervise particular activities. If the task group was hunting, the best and most senior hunters—almost always men—exercised political authority. If the task group was gathering roots, then the best and most senior diggers—almost always women—ruled. Thus among such hunting-gathering people, political organization changed from season to season, and social status depended on what activities were most important to the group at a particular time.

As these examples illustrate, variations in daily life and social arrangements in pre-Columbian North America reflected variations in climate, soil conditions, food supplies, and cultural heritages from place to place across the vast continent. But despite the enormous size of the continent and amazing variety of cultures spread across it, economic and social connections within and between ecological regions tied the people together in complex ways. For example, varieties of shell found only along the Northwest Pacific Coast passed in trade to settlements as far away as Florida, having been passed from hand to hand over thousands of miles of social and physical space.

A World of Change in Africa

Like North America, Africa was home to an array of societies that developed in response to varying natural and historical conditions. But unlike contemporary Indian groups, Africans maintained continual if perhaps only sporadic contacts with societies in

Aztecs An Indian group living in central Mexico; the Aztecs used military force to dominate nearby tribes; their civilization was at its peak at the time of the Spanish conquest.

tributary empire An empire in which subjects rule themselves but make payments, called tribute, to an imperial government in return for protection and services.

After being separated from the rest of Africa by the formation of the Sahara Desert, the Bantu people—aided perhaps by their mastery of iron-smelting technology—expanded throughout the sub-Saharan portion of the continent. This painting rendered by non-Bantu Bushmen, records a battle between themselves and Bantus. Note the relatively huge size and menacing quality of the Bantus compared with the retreating Bushmen, an indication of how the newly dominant group was perceived by its neighbors. *Private Collection.*

Europe and Asia, societies to which they had at one time been intimately linked.

Tendrils of trade between the Mediterranean and **sub-Saharan Africa** can be traced back to ancient Egypt and before, but the creation of the Sahara Desert, the product of a 1,500-year-long drought that began about 4,500 years ago, cut most of Africa off from the fertile areas of the Mediterranean coast. The people living south of the new desert were forced largely to reinvent civilization in response to changing conditions. They abandoned the wheat and other grain crops that had predominated in earlier economies, domesticating new staples such as **millet** and native strains of rice. They also abandoned the cattle and horses that had been common in earlier times, adopting sheep and goats, which were better suited to arid environments. Depending on immediate conditions, groups could establish large villages and live on a balance of vegetables, meat, and milk or, if necessary, shift over to a purely nomadic lifestyle following their herds.

Social organization tended to follow a similar adaptive strategy. The entire region was dominated by a single group of people, speakers of closely related dialects of the common Bantu language (see Map 1.3). Among these Bantu descendants and their neighbors, the social structure was based on the belief that large subgroups were descended from a common **fictive ancestor.** These larger organizations were then subdivided into

smaller and smaller groups, each independent—as a modern nuclear family might be—but tied through an elaborate family tree to hundreds or even thousands of other similar groups.

The status of each group was determined by seniority in the line of descent—those descended from the oldest offspring of the common ancestor were socially and politically superior to those descended from younger branches. This fundamental hierarchy created an organizational structure that permitted large-group cooperation and management when appropriate but also permitted each small band to function independently when conditions required. Within each group, seniority also determined political and social status: the eldest descendant of the common ancestor within each group held superior power, whereas those on the lowest branch of the family tree were treated more or less as slaves.

sub-Saharan Africa   The region of Africa south of the Sahara Desert.

millet   A large family of grain grasses that produce nutritious, carbohydrate-rich seeds used for both human and animal feed.

fictive ancestor   A mythical figure believed by a social group to be its founder and from whom all members are believed to be biologically descended.

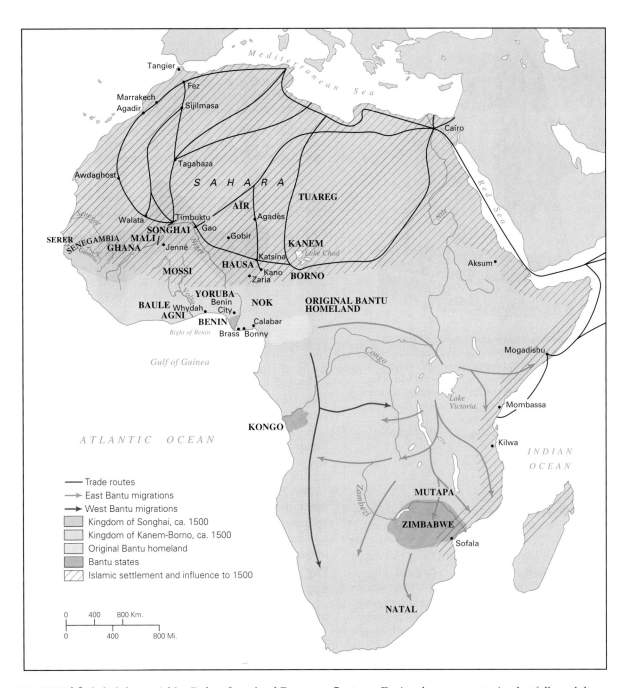

MAP 1.3 Sub-Saharan Africa Before Sustained European Contact   During the many centuries that followed the formation of the Sahara Desert, Bantu people expanded throughout the southern half of Africa. They and other groups established a number of powerful kingdoms, the capitals of which served as major trading centers among these kingdoms and for Islamic traders, who finally penetrated the desert after the year 750.

Much of the technology in place in sub-Saharan Africa can be traced to common roots that preceded the formation of the desert. Evidence suggests that pottery and simple metallurgy were part of an ancient pan-African technological tradition. However, sometime between two and three thousand years ago, sub-Saharan groups appear to have discovered iron smelting. Inventing a shaft furnace—a furnace shaped like a long tube that permitted both the high heat and air draft necessary for melting iron ore—

Introducing camels as draft animals made it possible for Arab and other traders to penetrate the forbidding Sahara Desert to open up a highly profitable trade with sub-Saharan states that were rich with gold, ivory, and other valuable commodities. This gold and diamond miniature (the sculpture is only about two-and-a-half inches tall) celebrates the riches that these animals carried out of Africa. *The Metropolitan Museum of Art, Gift of The Shaw Foundation, Inc., 1959.*

craftsmen were able to make use of abundant raw iron deposits common in southern Africa to produce tools, vessels, and weapons. This discovery may, in fact, have aided the Bantu-speakers in their extensive expansion throughout most of the continent. It certainly gave African groups an edge in carving settlements out of the jungles and grasslands. Often, large cities with elaborate social hierarchies grew in neighborhoods where iron and other ores were particularly abundant. These would then become centers for trade as well as political hubs, the seeds from which later kingdoms and empires would sprout.

These trading centers became particularly important when Islamic expansion brought new, outside sources for trade into the sub-Saharan world. The first mention of trade between Islamic adventurers and African communities stems from the eighth century, and it seems to have developed slowly over the next several hundred years. One catalyst to the trade growth was the introduction of the camel as a draft animal. Native to Asia and the Arabian Peninsula, camels were ideally suited for crossing the inhospitable desert, making it possible to establish regular

caravan routes that linked sub-Saharan trading centers with the outside world. Increasingly after 1100, metal goods—iron, gold, and precious gems—and slaves were carried across the desert by Arab, Berber, and other Muslim traders, who gave African middlemen silks, spices, and other foreign goods in exchange. This trade tended to enhance the power of African elites, leading to ever larger and more elaborate states.

Exploiting Atlantic Opportunities

▪ How did various groups of Europeans seek to exploit opportunities that arose from new discoveries leading up to and following 1492?

▪ Why did Columbus's entry into the Western Hemisphere prove to be a major turning point in the development of the Atlantic world?

▪ How did Native Americans and Africans respond initially to European expansion?

Dynamic forces in America, Europe, Africa, and beyond seemed unavoidably to be drawing the disparate societies that occupied the Atlantic shore into a complex world of mutual experience. But this process was not automatic. Enterprising people throughout the globe seized opportunities created by the spirit of restlessness and the merging of historical streams, advancing the process and giving it peculiar shape. Generally seeking profits for themselves and advancement for their own nations, tribes, or classes, those who sought to exploit the emerging new world nonetheless had enormous impact on the lives of all who occupied it. The process of outreach and historical evolution that helped to launch the American experience grew directly from these efforts at exploitation.

The Portuguese, Africa, and Plantation Slavery

The first of the European states to pull itself together was also the first to challenge Islamic dominance in both the Asian and African trade. Portugal's John I encouraged exploration by establishing a school of navigation on his kingdom's southwestern shore. Under the directorship of John's son **Henry the Navigator,**

Henry the Navigator   Prince who founded an observatory and school of navigation and directed voyages that helped build Portugal's colonial empire.

During the years before European penetration into the region, western Africa became a center for Islamic culture. Islamic scholars congregated at holy sites like the Sankoré Mosque in Timbuktu (left). Here they discussed Islamic law and wrote scholarly treatises like Sayyid al-Mukhtur ibn Ahmed ibn Abi Bakr al-Kunti al-Kabir's "An Argument for Peace," which emphasized the Qur'an's message of peace and harmony (right). Writings like these not only helped win more Africans over to Islam but also influenced Qur'anic scholarship throughout the expanding Muslim world. *Left: Photo © www.danheller.com; right: Mamma Haidara Commemorative Library, Timbuktu, Mali.*

the school sent numerous expeditions in search of new sources of wealth. By the 1430s, the Portuguese had discovered and taken control of islands off the western shore of Africa, and within thirty years Prince Henry's protégés had pushed their way to Africa itself, opening relations with the Songhai Empire.

The **Songhai Empire** was typical of the sub-Saharan trading states that emerged through Muslim contacts (see Map 1.3). As was common in the region, the Songhai state consisted of numerous smaller societies, all related through a common ancestor and organized along hierarchical lines. Society remained largely village based, with slaves at the bottom, skilled craftsmen in the middle, and a small noble class at the top. These nobles assembled in Timbuktu, a trading hub and the Songhai capital, which became a cosmopolitan center where African and Islamic influences met. Its art, architecture, and the accomplishments of its scholars impressed all who ventured there. From Timbuktu, Songhai traders shipped valuable trade goods across the Sahara by means of caravans. The Portuguese, however, offered speedier shipment and higher profits by carrying trade goods directly to Europe by sea.

By the end of the fifteenth century, Portuguese navigators had gained control over the flow of prized items such as gold, ivory, and spices out of West Africa, and Portuguese colonizers were growing sugar and other crops on the newly conquered Azores and Canary Islands. From the beginning of the sixteenth century onward, the Portuguese also became increasingly involved in slave trafficking, at first to their own plantations and then to Europe itself. By 1550, Portuguese ships were carrying African slaves throughout the world.

The Continued Quest for Asian Trade

Meanwhile, the Portuguese continued to venture outward. In 1487 Bartolomeu Dias became the first European to reach the **Cape of Good Hope** at the southern

Songhai Empire   A large empire in West Africa whose capital was Timbuktu; its rulers accepted Islam around the year 1000.

Cape of Good Hope   A point of land projecting into the Atlantic Ocean at the southern tip of Africa; to trade with Asia, European mariners had to sail around the cape to pass from the South Atlantic into the Indian Ocean.

tip of Africa. Ten years later Vasco da Gama sailed around the cape and launched the Portuguese exploration of eastern Africa and the Indian Ocean.

By the end of the fifteenth century, England, Spain, and France were vying with Portugal to find the shortest, cheapest, and safest sea route between Europe and Asia. Because of its early head start, Portugal remained fairly cautious in its explorations, hugging the coast around Africa before crossing the ocean to India. As latecomers, Spain and England could not afford to take such a conservative approach to exploration. Voyagers from those countries took advantage of technologies borrowed from China and the Arab world to expand their horizons. From China, Europeans acquired the magnetic compass, which allowed mariners to know roughly in what direction they were sailing, even when out of sight of land. An Arab invention, the **astrolabe,** which allowed seafarers to calculate the positions of heavenly bodies, also reduced the uncertainty of navigation. These inventions—together with improvements in steering mechanisms and hull design that improved a captain's control over his ship's direction, speed, and stability—made voyages much less risky.

Eager to capitalize on the new technology and knowledge, an ambitious sailor from the Italian port city of Genoa, **Christopher Columbus,** approached John II of Portugal in 1484 and asked him to support a voyage westward from Portugal, across the Atlantic, to the East Indies. The king refused when his geographers warned that Columbus had underestimated the distance. Undeterred, Columbus peddled his idea to various European governments over the next several years but found no one willing to take the risk. Finally, in 1492, Ferdinand and Isabella's defeat of the Moors provided Columbus with an opportunity.

The Spanish monarchs had just thrown off Islamic rule and added the coastal province of Granada to their holdings. They were eager to break into overseas trading, which was dominated in the east by the Arabs and in the south and west by the Portuguese. Ferdinand and Isabella agreed to equip three ships in exchange for a short, safe route to the Orient. On August 3, 1492, Columbus and some ninety sailors departed on the *Niña*, *Pinta*, and *Santa Maria* for the uncharted waters of the Atlantic. More than three months later, they finally made landfall. Columbus thought he had arrived at the East Indies, but in fact he had reached the islands we now call the **Bahamas.**

Over the next ten weeks, Columbus explored the mysteries of the Caribbean, making landfalls on the islands now known as Cuba and Hispaniola. He col-

lected spices, coconuts, bits of gold, and some native captives. He described the natives as "a loving people" who, he thought, would make excellent servants. Columbus then returned to Spain, where he was welcomed with great celebration and rewarded with backing for three more voyages. Over the next several years, the Spanish gained a permanent foothold in the region that Columbus had discovered and became aware that the area was a world entirely new to them.

England, like Spain, was jealous of Portugal's trade monopoly, and in 1497 Henry VII commissioned another Italian mariner, Giovanni Caboto, to search for a sea route to India. **John Cabot,** as the English called him, succeeded in crossing the North Atlantic, arriving in the area that Leif Eriksson had colonized nearly five hundred years earlier. Shortly thereafter, another Italian, **Amerigo Vespucci,** sailing under the Spanish flag, sighted the northeastern shore of South America and sailed northward into the Caribbean in search of a passage to the East. Finally, in 1524, Giovanni da Verrazano, sailing for France, explored the Atlantic coast of North America, charting the coastline of what later became the thirteen English mainland colonies.

A New Transatlantic World

At first, European monarchs greeted the discovery of a new world as bad news: they wanted access to the riches of Asia, not contact with some undiscovered place. As knowledge of the **New World** spread, the

---

astrolabe An instrument for measuring the position of the sun and stars; using these readings, navigators could calculate their latitude—their distance north or south of the equator.

Christopher Columbus (Cristoforo Colombo) Italian explorer in the service of Spain who attempted to reach Asia by sailing west from Europe, thereby arriving in America in 1492.

Bahamas A group of islands in the Atlantic Ocean east of Florida and Cuba.

John Cabot (Giovanni Caboto) Italian explorer who led the English expedition that sailed along the North American mainland in 1497.

Amerigo Vespucci Italian explorer of the South American coast; Europeans named America after him.

New World A term that Europeans used during the period of early contact and colonization to refer to the Americas, especially in the context of their discovery and colonization.

primary goal of exploration became finding a route around or through it—the fabled **Northwest Passage.** But gradually Europeans learned that the new land had attractions of its own.

Ambitious adventurers from Britain, France, and Iberia began exploring the fertile fishing grounds off the northern shores of North America. By 1506, such voyages became so commonplace and so profitable that the king of Portugal placed a 10 percent tax on fish imported from North America in an effort to harness this new source of wealth. But these voyages did more than feed the European imagination and the continent's appetite for seafood. It appears that these fishermen established temporary camps along the shores of North America to provide land support for their enterprises. Gradually, as the Native Americans and the fishermen came to know each other, they began to exchange goods. Europeans, even relatively poor fishermen, had many things that the Indians lacked: copper pots, knives, jewelry, woolen blankets, and hundreds of other novelties. For their part, the Indians provided firewood, food, ivory, and furs. Apparently the trade grew quickly. By 1534, when **Jacques Cartier** made the first official exploration of the Canadian coast for the French government, he was approached by party after party of Indians offering to trade furs for the goods he carried. He could only conclude that many other Europeans had come before him.

The presence of explorers such as Verrazano and Cartier and of unknown numbers of anonymous fishermen and part-time traders had several effects on the native population. The Micmacs, Hurons, and other northeastern Indian groups approached the invading Europeans in friendship, eager to trade and to learn more about the strangers. In part this response was a sign of natural curiosity, but it also reflected some serious changes taking place in the native world of North America.

As we have noted, the onset of the Little Ice Age had far-reaching effects. As the climate got colder, hunter-gatherers in the subarctic responded by withdrawing farther south, where they began to encroach on Algonquin and Iroquoian Indians. Meanwhile, the deteriorating climate made it more difficult for groups like the Iroquois to depend on their corn crops for food. Forced to rely more on hunting and gathering, the Iroquois had to expand their territory, and in doing so they came into conflict with their neighbors. As warfare became more common, groups increasingly formed alliances for mutual defense—systems like the Iroquois League. And Indians found it beneficial to welcome European newcomers into their midst—as trading partners bearing new tools, as al-

lies in the evolving conflicts with neighboring Indian groups, and as powerful magicians whose **shamans** might provide explanations and remedies for the hard times that had befallen them.

The Challenges of Mutual Discovery

■ How did Native Americans respond to increasing contact with European explorers and settlers?

■ In what ways did Europeans seek to incorporate Africans and Native Americans into their world of understanding?

■ In what ways was the world made different through the process called the Columbian Exchange?

Europeans approached the New World with certain ideas in mind and defined what they found there in terms that reflected what they already believed. American Indians approached Europeans in the same way. Both of these groups—as well as Africans—were thrown into a new world of understanding that challenged many of their fundamental assumptions. They also exchanged material goods that affected their physical well-being profoundly.

A Meeting of Minds in America

Most Europeans had a firm sense of how the world was arranged, who occupied it, and how they had come to be where they were. The existence of America—and even more the presence there of American Indians—challenged that secure knowledge. In the first stages of mutual discovery in America, most Europeans were content mentally to reshape what they found in the New World to fit with what they expected to find. Columbus expected to find India and Indians, and he believed that was precisely what he had found. Other

Northwest Passage   The rumored and much-hoped-for water route from Europe to Asia by way of North America was sought by early explorers.

Jacques Cartier   French explorer who, by navigating the St. Lawrence River in 1534, gave France its primary claim to territories in the New World.

shaman   A person who acts as a link between the visible material world and an invisible spirit world; a shaman's duties include healing, conducting religious ceremonies, and foretelling the future.

Europeans had trouble fitting American Indians into their preconceived ideas about the world. Native Americans were sometimes cast as noble savages and other times as devils. The Brazilian Indian shown in these two works illustrates the conflicting views. In one, the feather-clad Indian is shown as a wise magus paying homage to the Christ-child; in the other, an Indian devil wears the same costume while presiding over the tortures of Hell. *Left: "Adoration of the Magi" by Master of Viseu. Museu de Grao Vasco; right: "Inferno" anonymous, Portuguese. Giraudon/Art Resource, NY.*

Europeans understood that America was a new land and that the Indians were a new people, but they attempted to fit both into the cosmic map outlined in the Bible. Some Europeans assumed that the inhabitants of the new land were more pure and less corrupted than Europeans, people of God. Others viewed them as poor, ignorant savages.

Columbus's initial comments about the American Indians set the tone for many future encounters. "Of anything that they possess, if it be asked of them, they never say no," Columbus wrote; "on the contrary, they invite you to share it and show as much love as if their hearts went with it." Such writings were widely circulated in Europe and led to a perception of the Indians as noble savages, men and women free from the temptations and vanities of modern civilization.

Not all Europeans held this view of American Indians. Amerigo Vespucci, for one, found them less than noble. "They marry as many wives as they please," he explained. "The son cohabits with mother, brother with sister, male cousin with female, and any man with the first woman he meets. . . . Beyond the fact that they have no church, no religion and are not **idolaters,** what more can I say?" Much more, actually. Vespucci reported that the Indians practiced cannibalism and prostitution and decorated themselves in gaudy and "monstrous" ways.

In some ways, the arrival of Europeans may have been easier for American Indians to understand and explain than the existence of American Indians was for the Europeans. To Indians, the world was alive, animated by a spiritual force that was both universal and intelligent. This force took on many forms. Some of these forms were visible in the everyday world of ex-

idolater A person who practices *idolatry,* idol worship, a practice forbidden in the Judeo-Christian and Muslim traditions.

perience, some were visible only at special times, and some were never visible. Social ties based on fictive kinship and **reciprocal trade** linked all creatures—human and nonhuman—together into a common cosmos. These connections were chronicled in myth and were maintained through ritual, which often involved the exchange of ceremonial items believed to have spiritual value. Such objects included quartz and volcanic-glass crystals, copper, mica, shells, and other rare and light-reflecting objects. In the pre-Columbian trading world, such prized goods passed from society to society, establishing a spiritual bond between the initial givers and the eventual receivers, even though the two groups might never meet.

Europeans and European goods slipped easily into this ceremonial trading system. The trade items that the Europeans generally offered to American Indians on first contact—glass beads, mirrors, brass bells—resembled closely the items that the Indians traditionally used to establish friendly spiritual and economic relations with strangers. The perceived similarity of the trade goods offered by the Europeans led Indians to accept the newcomers as simply another new group in the complex social cosmos uniting the spiritual and material worlds.

On the other hand, Europeans perceived such items as worthless trinkets, valuing instead Indian furs and Indian land. This difference in perception became a major source of misunderstanding and conflict. To the Indians, neither the furs nor the land was of much value because by their understanding they did not "own" either. According to their beliefs, all things had innate spirits and belonged to themselves. Thus passing animal pelts along to Europeans was simply extending the social connection that had brought the furs into Indian hands in the first place. Similarly, according to Indian belief, people could not own land: the land was seen as a living being—a mother—who feeds, clothes, and houses people as long as she receives proper respect. The idea of buying or selling land was unthinkable to Indians. When Europeans offered spiritually significant objects in exchange for land on which to build, farm, or hunt, Indians perceived the offer as an effort to join an already existing relationship, and not as a contract transferring ownership.

The Columbian Exchange

Even though Europeans and American Indians saw some similarities in each other, their worlds differed greatly, sometimes in ways hidden to both groups. The natural environments of these worlds were dif-

European diseases killed many millions of Indians during the initial stages of contact because they had no immunity to such epidemic illnesses as influenza, measles, and plague. Smallpox was one of the deadliest of these imported diseases. This Aztec drawing illustrates smallpox's impact, from the initial appearance of skin lesions through death. Not only were traditional Indian medical practices unable to cure such diseases, but physical contact between shamans and patients actually helped to spread them. *Biblioteca Medicea Laurenziana.*

ferent, and the passage of people, plants, and animals among Europe, Africa, and North America wrought profound changes in all three continents. Historians call this process the **Columbian Exchange.**

Perhaps the most tragic trade among the three continents came about as the direct and unavoidable consequence of human contact. During the period leading up to the age of exploration, many Europeans lost their lives to epidemic diseases. The Black Death of the fourteenth century, for example, wiped out over a third of Europe's population. Exposure to

reciprocal trade   A system of trading in which the objective is equal exchange of commodities rather than profit.

Columbian Exchange   The exchange of people, plants, and animals between Europe, Africa, and North America that occurred after Columbus's arrival in the New World.

smallpox, measles, typhus, and other serious diseases had often had devastating results, but Europeans gradually developed resistance to infection. In contrast, the Indian peoples whom Columbus and other European explorers encountered lived in an environment in which contagious diseases were never a serious threat until the Europeans arrived. They had no **acquired immunity** to the various bacteria and viruses that Europeans carried. As a result, the new diseases spread very rapidly and were much more deadly among the native peoples than they were among Europeans.

Controversy rages over the number of Indians killed by imported European diseases. Estimates of how many people lived in America north of Mexico in 1492 run from a high of 25 million to a low of 1 million. At the moment, most scholars accept a range of from 3 to 10 million. Even if the most conservative estimate is correct, the raw numbers of people who died of smallpox, typhus, measles, and other imported diseases were enormous. In areas of early and continuing association between Europeans and Indians, between 90 and 95 percent of the native population appear to have died of disease during the first century of contact. Although the percentage was probably lower in areas where contact was infrequent and where native populations were sparse, disease took a terrible toll as it followed the lines of kinship and trade that held native North America together.

Disease, however, did not flow in only one direction. Some diseases that originated in Africa found their way to both North America and Europe and at least one, **syphilis,** may have originated in the Western Hemisphere and migrated eastward. American Indians appear to have been less debilitated physically by syphilis, to which they may have possessed partial immunity. Africans were largely unaffected by various **malarial** fevers that ravaged both European and native populations. Europeans found measles to be a mildly unpleasant childhood disease, but for both Africans and Indians it was a mass killer. The march of exchanged diseases across the North American landscape and their effects on various populations provided a constant backdrop for the continent's history.

Less immediate but perhaps equally extreme ecological effects arose from the passage of plants among Europe, North America, and Africa. The introduction of plants into the New World extended a process that had been taking place for centuries in the Old World. Trade with Asia had carried exotic plants such as bananas, sugar cane, and rice into Africa as early as 2,300 years ago. From Africa, these plants were imported to Iberian-claimed islands such as the Ca-

naries and eventually to America, where, along with cotton, indigo, coffee, and other imports, they would become **cash crops** on European-controlled plantations. Grains such as wheat, barley, and millet were readily transplanted to some areas in North America, as were grazing grasses and various vegetables, including turnips, spinach, and cabbage.

North American plants also traveled from west to east in the Columbian Exchange. Leading the way in economic importance was tobacco, a stimulant used widely in North America for ceremonial purposes and broadly adopted by Europeans and Africans as a recreational drug. Another stimulant, cocoa, also enjoyed significant popularity among Old World consumers. In addition, New World vegetables helped to revolutionize world food supplies. Remarkably easy to grow, maize thrived virtually everywhere. In addition, the white potato, tomato, **manioc,** squash, and beans native to the Western Hemisphere were soon cultivated throughout the world. Animals also moved in the Columbian Exchange. Europeans brought horses, pigs, cattle, oxen, sheep, goats, and domesticated fowl to America, where their numbers soared.

The transplanting of European grain crops and domesticated animals reshaped the American landscape. Changing the contours of the land by clearing trees and undergrowth and by plowing and fencing altered the flow of water, the distribution of seeds, the nesting of birds, and the movement of native animals. Gradually, imported livestock pushed aside native species, and imported plants choked out indigenous ones.

Probably the most important and far-reaching environmental impact of the Columbian Exchange was its overall influence on human populations. Although exchanged diseases killed many millions of Indians

---

acquired immunity   Resistance or partial resistance to a disease; acquired immunity develops in a population over time as a result of exposure to harmful bacteria and viruses.

syphilis   An infectious disease usually transmitted through sexual contact; if untreated, it can lead to paralysis and death.

malarial   Related to malaria, an infectious disease characterized by chills, fever, and sweating; malaria is often transmitted through mosquito bites.

cash crop   A crop raised in large quantities for sale rather than for local or home consumption.

manioc   Also called cassava, a root vegetable native to South America that became a staple food source throughout the tropical world after 1500.

and lesser numbers of Africans and Europeans, the transplantation of North American plants significantly expanded food production in what had been marginal areas of Europe and Africa. At the same time, the environmental changes that Europeans wrought along the Atlantic shore of North America permitted the region to support many more people than it had sustained under Indian cultivation. The overall result in Europe and Africa was a population explosion that eventually spilled over to repopulate a devastated North America.

New Worlds in Africa and America

As the Columbian Exchange redistributed plants, animals, and populations among Europe, Africa, and North America, it permanently altered the history of both hemispheres. In North America, for example, the combination of disease, environmental transformation, and immigrant population pressure changed American Indian life and culture in profound ways.

Clearly, imported disease had the most ruinous influence on the lives of Indians. Cooperative labor was required for hunting and gathering, and native groups that continued to depend on those activities faced extinction if disease caused a shortage of labor. Also, most societies in North America were **nonliterate:** elders and storytellers passed on their collective knowledge from one generation to another. Wholesale death by disease wiped out these bearers of practical, religious, and cultural knowledge. The result of this loss was confusion and disorientation among survivors. In an effort to avert extinction, remnant groups banded together to share labor and lore. Members of formerly self-sustaining kinship groups joined together in composite villages or, in some cases, intertribal leagues or confederacies. And the devastation that European diseases wrought eased the way for the deeper penetration of Europeans into North America as Indians sought alliances with the newcomers in order to gain new tools, new sources of information, and new military partners, pushing Indians into increasingly tangled relationships with Europeans.

The Columbian Exchange also severely disrupted life in Africa. Africa had long been a key supplier of labor in the Old World. The ancient Egyptians had imported slaves from Ethiopia and other regions south of the Sahara Desert, a practice that continued through Roman times. But it was Islamic traders who turned the enslavement of Africans into a thriving enterprise. When North African Muslims established

Parties of captured villagers from Africa's interior were bound together and marched to trading centers on the coast, where they were sold to European or Arab traders. The slave drivers were heavily influenced by outside contact. One of those shown here is wearing an Arab-influenced turban, while the clothing of the other is more European. Note, too, that the latter carries both a gun and a traditional African spear. *The Granger Collection.*

regular caravan routes across the desert into sub-Saharan Africa, slaves quickly became a dominant trade item, second only to gold in overall value. Perhaps as many as 4 million slaves were carried across the desert between 800 and the time the Portuguese redirected the trade in the sixteenth century.

Portuguese entry, however, revolutionized this economy. European technology, wealth, and ideas fostered the development of aggressive centralized states along the **Slave Coast** on the western shore of

nonliterate Lacking a system of reading and writing, relying instead on storytelling and mnemonic (memory-assisting) devices such as pictures.

Slave Coast A region of coastal West Africa adjacent to the Gold Coast; it was the principal source of the slaves taken out of West Africa from the sixteenth to the early nineteenth century.

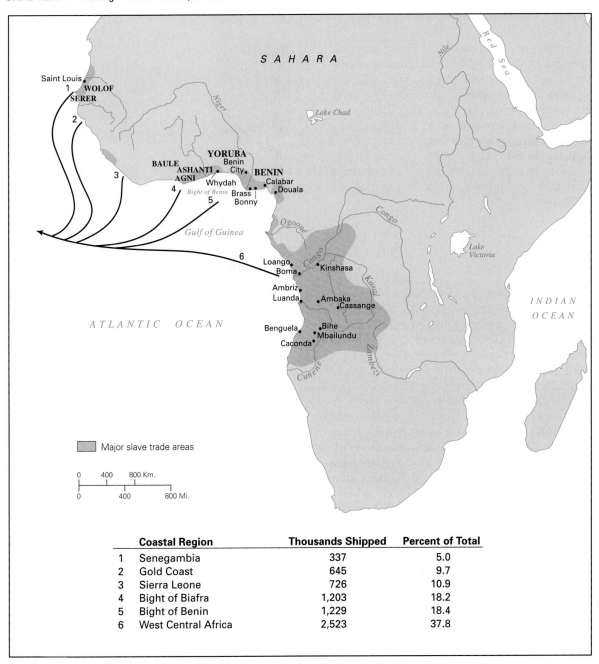

	Coastal Region	Thousands Shipped	Percent of Total
1	Senegambia	337	5.0
2	Gold Coast	645	9.7
3	Sierra Leone	726	10.9
4	Bight of Biafra	1,203	18.2
5	Bight of Benin	1,229	18.4
6	West Central Africa	2,523	37.8

MAP 1.4 Western Africa and the Atlantic Slave Trade   Africa's western shore was the major source for slaves that were transported to European colonies on the Atlantic islands, the Caribbean islands, and mainland North and South America. Powerful coastal kingdoms mounted organized raids into many inland areas to capture people who were then marched to the coast for shipment to the New World. This map shows the several regions from which slaves were extracted, and the accompanying table gives approximate numbers of people who were exported from each.

Africa's Gulf of Guinea (see Map 1.4). Armed with European firearms, aggressive tribes such as the Ashanti engaged in large-scale raiding deep into the Niger and Congo river regions. These raiders captured millions of prisoners, whom they herded back to the coast and sold to Portuguese, Spanish, Dutch, and other European traders to supply labor for mines and plantations in the New World.

It is difficult to determine the number of people sold in the West African slave trade between 1500 and

1800. The most recent estimates suggest that more than 9.5 million enslaved Africans arrived in the New World during this three-hundred-year period. And they were only a small portion of the total number of Africans victimized by the system. On average, between 10 and 20 percent of the slaves shipped to the Americas died in transit. Adding in the numbers who were shipped to other locations in the Eastern Hemisphere, who were kept in slavery within Africa, and who died during the raids and on the marches to the coast yields a staggering total.

A New World in Europe

The discovery of America and the Columbian Exchange also had staggering repercussions on life in Europe. New economic opportunities and new ideas demanded new kinds of political and economic organization. The discovery of the New World clearly forced a new and more modern society onto Europeans.

Europe's population was already rising when potatoes, maize, and other New World crops began to revolutionize food production. Populations then began to soar despite nearly continuous wars and a flood of migration to the New World. With populations on the rise and overseas empires to run, European rulers and their advisers saw that centralized states appeared to offer the most promising device for harnessing the riches of the New World while controlling ever-increasing numbers of people at home. The sons and daughters of Europe's first generation of **absolute monarchs** chose to continue the consolidation of authority begun by their parents.

As Europeans responded to social, political, and economic changes, traditional patterns of authority broke down, especially in the realm of religion. A particularly devastating blow to religious authority came from the pen of Martin Luther, a German monk. Luther preached that salvation was God's gift to the faithful. In 1517 he presented a set of arguments, the **Ninety-five Theses,** maintaining that only individual repentance and the grace of God could save sinners. The implications of this simple formula were profound: if Luther was right, then Christians could achieve salvation without the intercession of the Roman Catholic or any other church, undermining the keystone of both religious and political authority upon which order in Europe was based.

Luther's ideas took root among a generation of theologians who were dissatisfied with the corruption and superstition they found in the medieval Catholic Church, launching the period known as the **Reformation.** A Frenchman, John Calvin, further undermined the church's authority by suggesting that God had preselected only some people for salvation. Calvin called these individuals **the Elect.** For all others, no earthly effort—no good works, no prayers, no church intervention—could save them. Thus neither popes nor kings had any claim to authority, and no one held the keys to salvation except God, but happiness on earth might be attained by wresting worldly authority from the hands of kings and putting it into the hands of the Elect.

Known as **Protestantism,** the doctrines of Luther, Calvin, and others who wanted to reform the Catholic Church formed an ideology that appealed to a broad audience in the rapidly changing European world of the sixteenth century. Ever critical of entrenched authority, the new doctrines attracted lawyers, bureaucrats, merchants, and manufacturers, whose economic and political status was on the rise thanks to increased prosperity generated by the Columbian Exchange. But many in the ruling classes also found aspects of the new theology attractive. In Germany, Luther's challenge to the priesthood, and by extension to the Catholic Church itself, led many local princes to question the **divine right** to authority

absolute monarch   The ruler of a kingdom in which every aspect of national life—including politics, religion, the economy, and social affairs—comes under royal authority.

Ninety-five Theses   A document prepared by Martin Luther in 1517 protesting certain Roman Catholic practices that he believed were contrary to the will of God as revealed in Scripture.

Reformation   The sixteenth-century rise of Protestantism, with the establishment of state-sponsored Protestant churches in England, the Netherlands, parts of Germany and Switzerland, and elsewhere.

the Elect   According to Calvinism, the people chosen by God for salvation.

Protestantism   From the root word *protest*, the beliefs and practices of Christians who broke with the Roman Catholic Church; rejecting church authority, the doctrine of "good works," and the necessity of the priesthood, Protestants accepted the Bible as the only source of revelation, salvation as God's gift to the faithful, and a direct, personal relationship with God as available to every believer.

divine right   The idea that monarchs derive their authority to rule directly from God and are accountable only to God.

claimed by the ruler of the **Holy Roman Empire.** Similarly, **Henry VIII** of England, at one time a critic of Luther's ideas, found Protestantism convenient when he wanted to resist the authority of the pope and expand English national power.

Henry VIII, the son of Henry VII and Elizabeth of York, was the first undisputed heir to the English throne in several generations, and he was consumed with the desire to avoid renewed civil war by having a son who could inherit the Crown. When his wife Catherine of Aragon, daughter of Spain's Ferdinand and Isabella, failed to bear a boy, Henry demanded in 1527 that Pope Clement VII grant him a divorce and permission to marry someone else. Fearful of Spanish reprisals on Catherine's behalf, Clement refused. In desperation, Henry launched an English Reformation by seizing the Catholic Church in England, gaining complete control of it by 1535.

Henry was not a staunch believer in the views aired by Luther and others, but the idea of unifying religious and civil authority under his personal control did appeal to him. In addition, the Catholic Church owned extensive and valuable lands in England, estates that Henry could use to enhance his wealth and power. He needed Protestant support in his war against the pope's authority, so he reluctantly opened the door to Protestant practices in his newly created Church of England.

After Henry's death, his very young son—finally born to his third wife, Jane Seymour—ascended the throne as Edward VI. In the absence of a strong king, Protestants had virtual free rein, and the pace of reform quickened. Young King Edward, however, was a frail child and died after ruling for only six years. Mary, his oldest sister, succeeded him. The daughter of Henry's first wife, Mary had married Philip II of Spain and was a devout Roman Catholic. She attempted to reverse the reforming trend, cruelly suppressing Protestantism by executing several hundred leading reformers. But her brutality only drove the movement underground and made it more militant. By the time her half-sister Elizabeth, who was born and raised a Protestant, inherited the crown in 1558, the Protestant underground had become powerful and highly motivated. In fact, **Elizabeth I** spent her entire half-century reign trying to reach a workable settlement with Protestant **dissenters** that would permit them free worship without endangering her control over church and state.

Holy Roman Empire   A political entity, authorized by the Catholic Church in 1356, unifying central Europe under an emperor elected by four princes and three Catholic archbishops.

Henry VIII   King of England (r. 1509–1547); his desire to divorce his first wife led him to break with Catholicism and establish the Church of England.

Elizabeth I   Queen of England (r. 1558–1603); she succeeded the Catholic Mary I and reestablished Protestantism in England; her reign was a time of domestic prosperity and cultural achievement.

dissenter   A person who does not accept the doctrines of an established or national church.

Individual Voices

Examining a Primary Source

The Five Nations Adopt the Great Law

Pressed on all sides by radically changing conditions, five Indian nations among the Iroquoian-speaking people in the Eastern Woodlands listened to Hienwatha (Hiawatha) and joined him in embracing the message of Dekanahwideh. The Peacegiver presented a plan for government, often referred to as "The Great Law," which would become the constitution for the Iroquois League. But Dekanahwideh's vision

- *Clearly Dekanahwideh chose the image of the "great tree" for a reason. What do you see as the meaning behind this image? What do you think the four "great, long, white roots" symbolize?*

- *What is Dekanahwideh advocating in this passage? How do you suppose this advice steered Five Nations policy during the three centuries after the adoption of the Great Law?*

- *What does the Great Law suggest about the responsibility of each of the Five Nations to the confederacy as a whole? How would the scheme advocated here help the Iroquois deal with changing historical conditions?*

included much more than just peace among the Five Nations. Like similar strategies for cooperation that were being crafted by Indian groups throughout North America during this critical time, in the mid-1400s, the Great Law was a creative device that would carry the Iroquois into a new era of history.

Then Dekanahwideh said: "We have now completed arranging the system of our local councils and we shall hold our annual Confederate Council at the settlement of Thadodahho, the capitol or seat of government of the Five Nations Confederacy."

Dekanahwideh said: "Now I and you lords of the Confederate Nations shall plant a tree Ska-renj-heh-se-go-wah (meaning a tall and mighty tree) and we shall call it Jo-ne-rak-deh-ke-wah (the tree of the great long leaves)."

"Now this tree which we have planted shall shoot forth Jo-doh-ra-ken-rah-ko-wah (four great, long, white roots). These great, long, white roots shall shoot forth one to the north and one to the south and one to the east and one to the west, and we shall place on the top of it Oh-don-yonh (an eagle) which has great power of long vision, and we shall transact all our business beneath the shade of this great tree. ■ The meaning of planting this great tree, Skareh-hehsegowah, is to symbolize Ka-yah-ne-renh-ko-wa, which means Great Peace, and Jo-deh-ra-ken-rah-ke-wah, meaning Good Tidings of Peace and Power. The nations of the earth shall see it and shall accept and follow the roots and shall follow them to the tree and when they arrive here you shall receive them and shall seat them in the midst of your confederacy. ■ The object of placing an eagle on the top of the great, tall tree is that it may watch the roots which extend to the north and to the south and to the east and to the west, and whose duty shall be to discover if any evil is approaching your confederacy, and he shall scream loudly and give the alarm and all the nations of the confederacy at once shall heed the alarm and come to the rescue." ■

Summary

Making America began perhaps as long as 70,000 years ago, when the continent's first human occupants began the long process of fitting themselves to a land they would call their own. Hoping to find better conditions than they were leaving behind in Asia, they migrated across Beringia and then overcame or adapted to the ever-changing new environment in which they found themselves. Over thousands of years, they continually crafted economic strategies, social arrangements, and political systems to preserve and enhance their lives. The result was a rich and flourishing world of different cultures, linked by common religious and economic bonds.

At first, the arrival of Europeans only added another society to an already cosmopolitan sphere. The Vikings came and went, as perhaps did other non-Indians. But ultimately, the dynamic European society that arose after the Crusades and plagues of the Middle Ages became more intrusive. As a result, Native Americans faced challenges that they had never imagined: economic crises, disease, war, and the unfolding environmental changes wrought by the Europeans who followed Columbus.

In addition, influences from the New World reached out to accelerate processes that were already affecting the Old World. The flow of wealth and food out of the West was increasing populations, and this growth, with the accompanying rise of powerful kings and unified nations, led to continuing conflict over newfound resources. In Africa, strong coastal states raided weaker neighboring groups, more than doubling the flow of slaves out of Africa. This, in turn, influenced further developments in America. As disease destroyed millions of Indians, newcomers from the entire Atlantic rim poured in to replace them. These newcomers came from very different physical environments and had distinctly foreign ideas about nature. Their novel practices and ideas helped to create a new America on top of the old, rendering drastic changes to the landscape. Continuing interactions among these various newcomers, and between them and the survivors of America's original people, would launch the process of Making America.

EUROPEANS AND INDIANS IN NORTH AMERICA Although Europeans were at first unsure about the implications of stumbling over a portion of the world that was new to them, they quickly came to understand the economic, political, and military potential involved in American colonization. As this map shows, exploration continued into the seventeenth century as Europeans scrambled to claim individual pieces of New World real estate.

ARCTIC OCEAN

SWEDEN

THE NETHERLANDS

EUROPE

ENGLAND

FRANCE

SPAIN

PORTUGAL

AFRICA

Greenland

HUDSON 1610

HUDSON 1609

INUIT

INUIT

INUIT

ATLANTIC OCEAN

ALEUT

HARE

DOGRIB

TLINGIT

INUIT

INUIT

Hudson Bay

CHIPEWYAN

INUIT

GRAND BANKS

KWAKIUTL

CREE

CREE

CREE

CHINOOK

BLACKFOOT

MONTAGNAIS

PACIFIC OCEAN

NEZ PERCE

CROW

MANDAN

ALGONQUIN

OTTAWA

•Quebec

CHAMPLAIN 1615

CAYUSE

CHIPPEWA

HURON

Montréal

MODOC

SHOSHONE

SIOUX

IROQUOIS

•Boston

MARQUETTE AND JOLIET 1673

SAUK FOX

Fort Orange (Albany)

Plymouth

WAMPANOAG

POMO

CHEYENNE ARAPAHO

ILLINOIS

MIAMI

DELAWARE

New Amsterdam (New York)

NAVAHO

Taos

HOPI

ZUNI

Fort Christina (Wilmington)

POWHATAN

ONATE 1604-05

ONATE 1601

•Quivira

LA SALLE 1679-1682

•Jamestown

MOHAVE

Acoma

APACHE

ONATE 1598

SHAWNEE

•Roanoke Island

El Paso

COMANCHE

Santa Fe

CHEROKEE

TUSCARORA

WICHITA

CABEZA DE VACA 1535-36

CHICKASAW

CREEK

DE SOTO 1539-42

CORONADO 1542-43

New Orleans

CHOCTAW

San Antonio

NARVAEZ 1528

San Agostín (St. Augustine)

Gulf of Mexico

SEMINOLE

Mexico City

•Havana

TAINO

Caribbean Sea

→ Spanish exploration
→ French exploration
→ English exploration
→ Dutch exploration

Extent of settlements

Spanish
French
English
Swedish
Dutch
Portuguese

CROW Indian nation

■ Indian settlement
⚭ Mission
■ Fort
• European settlement

0   400   800 Km.
0   400   800 Mi.

ARAWAK

CARIB

Demarcation Line, Treaty of Tordesillas, 1494

SOUTH AMERICA

1494 Treaty of Tordesillas

1521 Cortés conquers Mexico

1588 Defeat of the Spanish Armada

1608 French/Huron alliance

1623 Dutch/Iroquois alliance

1680 Pueblo Revolt

ca.1700 French/Choctaw alliance

1500   1520   1540   1560   1580   1600   1620   1640   1660   1680   1700   1720

1500 Portugese discover Brazil

1550 Scientific revolution begins in Europe

ca.1640 Dutch take over African slave trade

1700 West Indies become the world's main source for sugar

1691 British open trading post at Calcutta

1591 Morocco conquers Songhai Empire

1618 Thirty Years War begins in Europe

ca.1680 Asante kingdom in Africa

A Continent on the Move, 1400–1725

Europeans and Indians in North America
Using the map on the facing page, examine the continued expansion of Europeans into the North American continent during the early colonial period and the Native Americans with whom they came into contact. In what ways did the specific groups of people that each European colonizing power encountered influence patterns of settlement and the eventual shape of the colonial world in America?

Individual Choices

BARTOLOMÉ DE LAS CASAS

Himself a former conquistador, Bartolomé de Las Casas was ordained as a Catholic priest in 1512 and later became one of the most vocal opponents of Spain's brutal exploitation of Native American people. He petitioned the King in 1540 and won major reforms in the way Spaniards were supposed to treat Indians, but these reforms were never well enforced and soon were challenged in the Spanish court. In 1550, Las Casas debated Juan Ginés de Sepúlveda, a well-respected court scholar, who insisted that Native Americans were not human and deserved no protections under law. Las Casas brought his biblical learning and his New World experience to bear, winning the debate and Catholic support for continued reforms in Spanish colonial policy. *Archivo de Indias, Seville, Spain/Bridgeman Art Library Ltd.*

Bartolomé de Las Casas

In 1550 Spanish church officials ordered a council of learned theologians to assemble in the city of Valladolid to hear a debate over an issue so important that it challenged the entire underpinning of Spain's New World empire. At issue was the question of whether Native American Indians were human beings. Arguing that they were not was the well-respected scholar Juan Ginés de Sepúlveda. Arguing on the Indians' behalf was a former conquistador and *encomandero* named Bartolomé de Las Casas.

Born in 1474, Las Casas was the son of a small merchant in Seville. His family was privileged enough that young Bartolomé had both access and the leisure time to study at Seville's cathedral school. Like many of his contemporaries, Las Casas decided to pursue a military career, going to Granada as a soldier in 1497. Then in 1502 he embarked to the West Indies to seek his fortune in the conquest of the Americas.

Apparently Las Casas was successful as a **conquistador:** within a few years he had earned an imperial land grant with a full complement of Indian laborers. Meeting the demands of both church and king, he taught the Indians Catholicism while he exploited their labor. Eventually, however, the former came to outweigh the latter, and Las Casas's religious devotion grew in proportion. After a decade as a soldier and land baron, he became perhaps the first person to be ordained as a priest in America. His new status, however, did not prevent him from pursuing his career as a conquistador; in 1513 he embarked with the Spanish force that would ravage Cuba.

Perhaps the bloodiness of the Cuba campaign or maybe just a growing Catholic conscience influenced Las Casas's next choice: he began advocating Christian rights for conquered Indians. He devised a plan that would organize Indians into farming communities under church protection, allowing them to become self-sufficient contributors to the Spanish Empire. His plan won support from the archbishop of Toledo and the Spanish Parliament. In 1519 he was given permission to start an experimental community in what is now Venezuela. But Indians in the region understandably were suspicious, and Spanish landlords were hostile; the experiment failed. Despite this setback, Las Casas remained convinced that Indians deserved full Christian recognition. He joined the Dominican order in 1523 and began writing a history of the Spanish Empire in America. As an outgrowth, he sent a series of long letters to the Council of the Indies in Madrid exposing the harsh exploitation of the natives throughout Spanish America. Las Casas then took his case personally to Spain. In 1540 he petitioned for an audience with King Charles V. As he waited for Charles to respond, he wrote a report, *Brevísima relación de la destrucción de las Indias* ("A Brief Report on the Destruction of the Indians") summarizing his experiences and views.

By the time he finally met with Charles V, Las Casas was well prepared to argue for wholesale reform of Spanish Indian policy in America. And Charles was convinced. He signed a series of new laws in 1542—the *Leyes Nuevas*—reforming the *encomienda* system and placing Indian relations under church authority.

To ensure that these reforms would be carried out, Las Casas was appointed bishop of Chiapas and sent back to the New World with forty fellow Dominicans to oversee the enforcement of the laws.

Las Casas served as bishop until 1547, when hostility from landowners in America and growing opposition to humane colonization at home prompted him to return to Spain. The chief spokesman for that growing opposition was Juan Ginés de Sepúlveda, a well-respected scholar whose star was rising in court circles. Las Casas's return prompted demands for a face-off between the two, leading to the Council of Valladolid.

The debate went on for a year, extending through 1550 into 1551. Speaking for Spanish investors and court-based politicians who, like himself, had never been to the Western Hemisphere, Sepúlveda based his argument solely on logic and Scripture. According to his view, it was impossible for Indians in the Americas to be descendants of Adam and Eve; hence they were, in his words, "as apes are to men." As such, Indians did not deserve protection from the church. Las Casas countered with firsthand evidence, drawing on his varied experiences as priest, historian, conquistador, and *encomendero* in an attempt to prove that Indians truly were human beings.

Despite Sepúlveda's great learning and his influence at court, he lost the debate: his writings were denied official recognition by the church, whereas Las Casas's were accepted. But this official victory for Las Casas was actually a failure. Though Sepúlveda's views were rejected by the church, they were embraced by conquistadors as justification for the continuing conquest and enslavement of the native population. In arguing effectively for the recognition of Indians as human beings, however, Las Casas established an undercurrent of official disapproval that served as a braking mechanism against the extreme abuse of the Native population. The resulting three-way tension— between those who would exploit the Indians, those who sought to protect them, and the Indians themselves—would shape the colonial process and would punctuate life in the Americas for generations to come.

INTRODUCTION

The debate in the Council of Valladolid in 1550 focused early attention on a situation that all European colonizers would have to face. Despite Sepúlveda's claims, the population native to the Americas *was* human. Of course, changing natural conditions and the influx of new forces such as epidemic disease had weakened them, but for centuries successful European settlement continued to require Indian cooperation. Court-based scholars like Sepúlveda might fool themselves into thinking that the Indians did not matter, but experienced veterans like Las Casas knew better. Conflicts with the Indians could spell disaster for vulnerable overseas colonies.

Conflicts with other imperial powers could lead to disaster as well. It was virtually inevitable that other nations would join Spain in seeking a share of the wealth promised by the New World. Forced into a

> **encomandero** a land owner/proprietor in the *encomienda* system, Spain's system of bonded labor in which Indians were assigned to Spanish plantation and mine owners in exchange for a tax payment and an agreement to "civilize" and convert them to Catholicism.
>
> **conquistadors** Spanish soldiers who conquered Indian civilizations in the New World.

The differences between European and Native American styles and conceptions of warfare were often striking. This scene, from the Codex Durán, illustrates a Spanish force besieged by Aztec warriors. Note the contrast in clothing, for example. For most Indian groups, warfare was a highly spiritual affair surrounded by ceremony, often involving colorful and fanciful costumes. The European battle dress, however, bespeaks a very different conception of warfare: practical and deadly. *Archivo fotografico.*

defensive posture and unable to fend off the ambitions of numerous European rivals, Spain had to watch as the Dutch and the French carved out substantial inroads into North America.

The presence of so many, and such varied, Europeans presented both challenges and exceptional opportunities for Indians. In areas where a single European power was asserting dominance, often Indians could do little but bear up under relentless economic and religious pressures. Sometimes the encounter facilitated friendship, intermarriage, and the formation of complex composite societies; sometimes it led to open hostilities and even war. But in areas where two or more European powers were contesting for control, Indians could take advantage of their pivotal position and play one side off against the other in seeking their own ends.

The constant interplay among different European traditions, a novel physical environment, and a dynamic Indian presence forged a series of new societies across the North American continent. Throughout the colonial era and beyond, these hybrid societies continued to influence historical development and to color the life of the people and the nation.

The New Europe and the Atlantic World

■ Why did European rulers promote exploration and colonization in North America?

■ How did religious and political rivalries influence the ways in which each European power approached New World colonization?

Expansion into the New World and the subsequent economic and political pressures of colonization ag-

gravated the crisis of authority in Europe. Eager to enlist political allies against Protestant dissenters, popes during this era used land grants in the New World as rewards to faithful monarchs. At the same time, Henry VIII and Elizabeth I, constantly fearful of being outflanked by Catholic adversaries, promoted the development of a powerful English navy and geographical exploration as defensive measures.

Spanish Expansion in America

Spain's entry into Atlantic exploration first sparked a diplomatic crisis between the Spanish and Portuguese. Portugal feared that Spain's intrusion might endanger its hard-won trading enterprises in Africa and the Atlantic islands. Spain, however, claimed the right to explore freely. In 1493 the pope settled the dispute by drawing a line approximately 300 miles west of Portugal's westernmost holdings. Spanish exploration, he declared, was to be confined to areas west of the line (that is, to the New World) and Portuguese activity to areas east of it (to Africa and India). A year later, Spain and Portugal updated the agreement in the **Treaty of Tordesillas**, which moved the line an additional 1,000 miles westward. Most of the Western Hemisphere fell exclusively to Spain, at least in the eyes of Roman Catholics.

Over the next several decades the Spanish monarchs recruited hardened veterans of the Reconquista

Treaty of Tordesillas   The agreement, signed by Spain and Portugal in 1494, that moved the line separating Spanish and Portuguese claims to territory in the non-Christian world, giving Spain most of the Western Hemisphere.

Chronology

New World Colonies and Native Americans

1494	Treaty of Tordesillas
1512	Creation of the *encomienda* system
1519–1521	Hernando Cortés invades Mexico
1542	de Las Casas convinces Spain to implement the Leyes Nuevas
1551	Council of Valladolid rules that American Indians are human beings with souls
1558	Elizabeth I becomes queen of England
1565	Spanish found St. Augustine in present-day Florida
1588	English defeat Spanish Armada
1598	Don Juan de Oñate destroys Ácoma pueblo
1608	French-Huron alliance
1609	Henry Hudson sails up Hudson River / Spanish found Santa Fe in present-day New Mexico
1623	Beginning of Dutch-Iroquois alliance
1627	Creation of Company of New France
1645	Dutch West India Company reorganized under Peter Stuyvesant
1680	Pueblo Revolt
1683	La Salle expedition down the Mississippi River to the Gulf of Mexico
ca. 1700	Beginning of French-Choctaw alliance

(see page 11) to lead its New World colonization efforts. **Hernando Cortés** was one such figure. In 1519 Cortés landed on the mainland of Mexico with an army of six hundred soldiers. Within three years he and his small force had conquered the mighty Aztec Empire. Although it is tempting to suppose that Cortés's victory was the product of technological superiority, his weapons made less difference in the outcome than did several other factors. More important than guns and swords were the warhorses and attack dogs that Cortés used to instill anxiety. More important than even these, however, was the Spanish philosophy of war, which emphasized hard strikes against both armed and civilian targets. This type of campaign stood in stark contrast to the Aztec art of war, which was much more ceremonial in nature and limited in scope. Cortés was also adept at cultivating diplomatic advantages. An Indian woman whom he called Doña Marina served as his translator and cultural adviser, and with her help the conquistadors gained military support from numerous tribes of Mexican Indians who resented the Aztecs' power and their continuous demands for tribute. And finally, crucially, smallpox and other European germs weakened the Aztecs during the two years in which Cortés maintained strained but peaceful relations with them.

The Spanish Crown supported many other exploratory ventures designed to bring new regions under Spain's control. In 1513 and again in 1521, Juan Ponce de León led expeditions to Florida. Following up on these voyages, Pánfilo de Narváez embarked on a colonizing mission to Florida in 1527. When his party became stranded, local Indians killed most of its members but took a few captives. One of these captives, Álvar Núñez Cabeza de Vaca, escaped with three others in 1534. The four men eventually walked all the way to Mexico, keeping detailed notes of what they saw. Cabeza de Vaca's accounts led the Spanish to send Hernando de Soto to claim the Mississippi River, and he penetrated into the heart of the mound builders' territory in present-day Louisiana and Mississippi. One year later, **Francisco Vásquez de Coronado** left

Hernando Cortés Spanish soldier and explorer who conquered the Aztecs and claimed Mexico for Spain.

Francisco Vásquez de Coronado Spanish soldier and explorer who led an expedition northward from Mexico in search of fabled cities of gold, passing through present-day New Mexico, Arizona, Colorado, Oklahoma, and Kansas, giving Spain a claim to most of the American Southwest.

Captured by Indians along the Gulf Coast of Spanish Florida, Álvar Núñez Cabeza de Vaca was made a slave. Most of his companions were afraid to resist or run away, but Cabeza de Vaca chose freedom over safety; in 1534 he led a small party of fellow captives all the way back to Mexico. His experiences and the many stories he collected from his various Indian hosts provided important intelligence for the expanding Spanish Empire. *Courtesy of Frederick Remington Art Museum, Ogdensburg, NY.*

Mexico to look for seven cities that Cabeza de Vaca had heard glittered with gold. Coronado eventually crossed what are now the states of New Mexico, Arizona, Colorado, Oklahoma, and Kansas. These explorations were but a few of the ambitious adventures undertaken by Spanish conquistadors.

Coronado never found Cabeza de Vaca's "cities of gold," but other Spaniards did locate enormous sources of wealth. In Bolivia, Colombia, and north-central Mexico, rich silver deposits rewarded the conquistadors. To the south, in present-day Peru, Francisco Pizarro in 1533 conquered the Inca Empire, an advanced civilization that glittered with gold. Enslaving local Indians for labor, Spanish officials everywhere in the New World quickly moved to rip precious metals out of the ground and from what they characterized as "heathen temples." Between 1545 and 1660, Indian and later African slaves extracted over 7 million pounds

of silver from Spanish-controlled areas, twice the volume of silver held by all of Europe before 1492. In the process, Spain became the richest nation in Europe, perhaps in the world.

Dreams of an English Eden

Given the stormy political and religious climate that prevailed during the sixteenth century, it is not surprising that Spain's early successes in the New World stirred up conflict with the other emerging states in Europe. To England, France, and other European countries, the massive flow of wealth made Spanish power a growing threat that had to be checked. The continuing religious controversies that accompanied the Reformation (see page 27) worsened the situation. Economic, religious, and political warfare was the rule throughout the century. One of the most celebrated of these early conflicts involved Spain and England.

Tension between Spain and England had been running high ever since Henry VIII had divorced his Spanish wife, Catherine of Aragon. That he quit the Catholic Church to do so and began permitting Protestant reforms in England added to the affront. Firmly wedded to the Catholic Church politically and religiously, Spain was aggressive in denouncing England. For his part, Henry was concerned primarily with domestic issues and steered away from direct confrontations with Spain or any of the other outraged Catholic countries.

The main exception to Henry's isolationism was an effort to bring Ireland and other outlying parts of his realm more firmly under his control. In 1541 Henry engineered a parliamentary change in title from "Lord of Ireland" to "King of Ireland" and used his new status to institute both religious and political reforms. He confiscated lands controlled by Irish Catholic monasteries and the estates of local lords who opposed him, channeling the money into building a stronger administrative structure. During the years to come, both Henry's heirs and the **Stuart kings** who would follow continued a systematic policy of colonization in Ireland. In the process, British authorities instituted a new set of colonial offices and encouraged generations of military adventurers, both of which would shape and advance later ventures in North America.

Stuart kings The dynasty of English kings who claimed the throne after the death of Elizabeth I, who left no heirs.

Queen Elizabeth I used her charm and intelligence to turn England into a major world power and restored order to a kingdom shaken by religious and political turmoil following the death of her father, Henry VIII. This pendant from the 1570s not only captures the queen's elegance and austere grace, but was also a powerful political statement. Note the intertwining of white and red roses—emblems of the Houses of York and Lancaster, respectively—symbolizing the unified monarchy forged by her grandfather. On the reverse is an image of a phoenix rising from the flames of its nest, symbolizing the renewal of the true monarchy. Already in her 40s by the time the "Phoenix Jewel" was crafted, it may have been the last portrait to capture Elizabeth's true age; future images of the queen always depict her as being much younger than she really was. While this may have been the product of vanity, it seems more likely that the queen wanted to diminish concerns among her subjects that aging might undermine her resolve and bring back an era of disorder. © *The British Museum.*

During the reign of Henry's younger daughter, Elizabeth, the continuing flow of New World wealth into Spain and that nation's anti-Protestant aggression led to an upturn in hostile activity. When Philip II of Spain, Elizabeth's brother-in-law and most vehement critic, sent an army of twenty thousand soldiers to root out Protestantism in **the Netherlands,** only a few miles across the English Channel from Elizabeth's kingdom, the English queen began providing covert aid to the Protestants rebels. Elizabeth also struck at Philip's most valuable and vulnerable possession: his New World empire. In 1577 Elizabeth secretly authorized English **privateer** and explorer Francis Drake to attack Spanish ships in the area reserved for Spain under the Treaty of Tordesillas. Drake carried out his task with enthusiasm, raiding

Spanish ships and seizing tons of gold and silver during a three-year cruise around the world.

Elizabeth was open to virtually any venture that might vex her troublesome brother-in-law. New World colonizing efforts promised to do that and had the potential for enriching the kingdom as well. Like the rest of Europe, sixteenth-century England was experiencing a population boom that put great stress on traditional economic institutions. Although Elizabeth's father had confiscated and redistributed large tracts of church-owned land during his reign, farmland was becoming extremely scarce, and members of both the traditional nobility and the **gentry**—a class that was becoming increasingly important because of its investments in manufacturing and trading ventures—wanted more space for expansion. A relatively small island, England could acquire more territory only by conquest or by carving it out of the New World.

Thus in 1578 Elizabeth granted her friend and political supporter Sir Humphrey Gilbert permission to found a colony in America. Gilbert claimed that John Cabot's voyages gave England a legitimate right to settle America's eastern shore, and in 1583 he set out with two hundred colonists. When the entire party was lost at sea, Gilbert's half-brother, **Sir Walter Raleigh,** petitioned the queen to take over the colonizing effort. She gladly agreed, commanding Raleigh to locate on the northern frontier of Spanish Florida, where an English settlement was sure to irritate Philip. Raleigh chose an island off the coast of present-day North Carolina. He advertised **Roanoke Island** as an "American Eden," where "the earth bringeth forth all things in abundance, as in the first Creation, without toile or labour." To honor his benefactor, he decided to call this paradise Virginia, tribute to the unwed, and thus officially virgin, queen.

---

the Netherlands/Holland/Dutch Often used interchangeably, the first two terms refer to the low-lying area in western Europe north of France and Belgium and across the English Channel from Great Britain; the Dutch are the inhabitants of the Netherlands.

privateer A ship captain who owned his own boat, hired his own crew, and was authorized by his government to attack and capture enemy ships.

gentry The class of English landowners ranking just below the nobility.

Sir Walter Raleigh English courtier, soldier, and adventurer who attempted to establish the Virginia Colony.

Roanoke Island Island off North Carolina that Raleigh sought to colonize beginning in 1585.

In 1585 Elizabeth further angered the Spanish king by openly sending an army of six thousand troops across the Channel to aid Dutch rebels. In the meantime, Philip was supporting various Catholic plots within England to subvert Elizabeth's authority and bring down the Protestant state. As tensions increased, so did Drake's piracy. In 1586 Drake intensified his campaign, not only raiding Spanish ships at sea but attacking settlements in the Caribbean. Thus by 1586, British troops were fighting the Spanish alongside Dutch rebels in Holland; Spanish spies were encouraging rebellion in England, Scotland, and Ireland; and British ships were raiding Spanish settlements in the New World. War loomed on the horizon.

The Decline of Spanish Power

Despite dreams of a New World Eden, the realities of discovery and colonization were beginning to have a severe, and in many ways negative, impact on life in Europe. The enormous inflow of wealth from the New World brought Spain power that no European country since the Roman Empire had enjoyed, but such rapid enrichment was a mixed blessing. Starting in Spain and radiating outward, prices began to climb as the growth of the money supply outpaced the growth of European economies. Too much money was chasing too few goods. Between 1550 and 1600, prices doubled in much of Europe, and **inflation** continued to soar for another half-century.

In addition, the social impact of the new wealth was forcing European monarchs to expand geographically and crack down domestically. As prices rose, the traditional landholding classes earned enormous profits from the sale of food and other necessities. Other groups fared less well. Artisans, laborers, and landless peasants—by far the largest class of people in Europe—found the value of their labor constantly shrinking. Throughout Europe, social unrest increased as formerly productive and respected citizens were reduced to poverty and begging. Overseas expansion seemed an inviting solution to the problem of an impoverished population. It was a safety valve that relieved a potentially dangerous source of domestic pressure while opening opportunities for enhancing national wealth through the development of colonies.

Sitting at the center of the new economy, Philip's Spain had the most to lose from rapid inflation and popular unrest. It also had the most to lose from New World expansion by any other European nation. Each New World claim asserted by England, France, or some other country represented the loss of a piece of treasure that Spain claimed as its own. Philip finally chose to confront building tensions by taking a desperate gamble: he would destroy England. This ploy, he thought, would effectively remove the Protestant threat, rid him of Elizabeth's ongoing harassment, and demonstrate to the rest of Europe that Spain intended to exercise absolute authority over the Atlantic world. In the spring of 1585, when tensions were at their peak, Philip began massing what was to be the largest marine force Europe had ever witnessed.

Philip wanted to attack England in the spring or summer of 1587. But Francis Drake frustrated his plans by staging a surprise attack on the Spanish port of Cádiz, disabling part of Philip's navy. The Spanish king remained resolute, however, and by the spring of 1588 he succeeded in launching an **armada** of 132 warships carrying more than three thousand cannon and an invasion force of thirty thousand men. Arriving off the shores of England in July, the so-called Invincible Armada ran up against small, maneuverable British defense ships commanded by Elizabeth's skilled pirate captains. Drake and his fleet harassed the Spanish ships, preventing them from launching a successful attack. Then a storm blowing down from the North Sea scattered the Spanish fleet, ruining Philip's expected conquest of England. Though Spanish power remained great for some time to come, the Armada disaster effectively ended Spain's near monopoly over New World colonization.

European Empires in America

■ What similarities and differences characterized Spanish, French, and Dutch patterns of empire building in North America?

■ What role did natural environments play in shaping the colonial enterprises engineered by the Spanish, the French, and the Dutch?

■ How did the colonists' experiences challenge and help to reshape imperial policies?

In the seventeenth and eighteenth centuries, Spain, France, England, and a number of lesser European nations vied for control of the Americas and for domination of the transatlantic trade. For reasons that are explained in Chapter 3, England was somewhat de-

---

inflation Rising prices that occur when the supply of currency or credit grows faster than the available supply of goods and services.

armada A fleet of warships.

layed in its colonizing efforts, and by the time it became deeply involved in New World ventures, Spain, France, and Holland had already made major progress toward establishing empires in America. These European settlements not only affected England's colonization process profoundly, but through their interactions among themselves and with the Native Americans, they also created unique societies in North America whose presence influenced the entire course of the continent's history.

The Troubled Spanish Colonial Empire

Although the destruction of the Armada in 1588 struck a terrible blow at Spain's military power and its New World monopoly, the Spanish Empire continued to grow. By the end of the seventeenth century, it stretched from New Mexico southward through Central America and much of South America into the Caribbean islands and northward again into Florida. Governing such a vast empire was difficult, and periodic efforts to reform the system usually failed. Two agencies in Spain, the House of Trade and the Council of the Indies, set Spanish colonial policy. In the colonies, Crown-appointed viceroys wielded military and political power in each of the four divisions of the empire. The Spanish colonies set up local governments as well; each town had a **cabildo secular,** a municipal council, as well as judges and other minor officials. The colonial administrators were appointed rather than elected, and most were envoys from Spain rather than native-born individuals.

Over the centuries, as the layers of bureaucracy developed, corruption and inefficiency developed as well. The Spanish government made efforts to regulate colonial affairs, sending *visitadores* to inspect local government operations and creating new watchdog agencies. Despite these safeguards, colonial officials ignored their written instructions and failed to enforce laws.

One major source of corruption and unrest stemmed from a persistent New World problem: the shortage of labor. The Spanish had adapted traditional institutions to address the demand for workers in mines and on plantations. In Spain, work was directed by **feudal** landlords, *encomenderos,* whose military service to the king entitled them to harness the labor of Spanish peasants. In New Spain, Indians took the place of the peasants in what was called the *encomienda* system. Under a law passed in 1512, administrators gave Indian workers to *encomenderos* and

required them to labor for the landlords for nine months each year. The *encomendero* paid a tax to the Crown for each Indian he received and agreed to teach his workers the Catholic faith, the Spanish language and culture, and a "civilized" vocation.

Despite some commitment to uplifting local Indians, the system in reality was brutally exploitative. As Bartolomé de Las Casas reported both to the Council of the Indies and to the king himself, landlords frequently overworked their Indian **serfs** and failed in their "civilizing" responsibilities. As the result of Las Casas's appeal, the Leyes Nuevas turned Indian relations in New Spain over to the church, and priests were assigned to enforce the laws. Among the new regulations was a stipulation that a priest accompany all expeditions to serve as witnesses that Indians were treated lawfully. For their part, the conquistadors were required to explain to Indians that they were subject to the Spanish king and to the Catholic Church, offering to absorb them peacefully. As Las Casas discovered, however, colonists often ignored even these slim protections. Some simply forged a priest's signature, anticipating that by the time the document reached administrators in faraway Madrid, no one would know the difference. Others disregarded the law altogether.

As such behavior demonstrates, Spanish colonists were seldom entirely law-abiding citizens, and a degree of tension always existed between New Spain and Old. Bureaucratic and church interference in the labor system was one source of tension. Taxes were another. Spanish colonists were taxed to support the huge and largely corrupt, unrepresentative, and self-serving imperial bureaucracy. But for many decades the wealth produced within this empire overshadowed all governing problems. The gold, silver, and copper mined by Indian and later African slaves so dazzled Spanish officials that imperial authorities took few serious steps toward practical reform until the end of the seventeenth century.

---

cabildo secular   Secular municipal council that provided local government in Spain's New World empire.

feudal   Relating to a system in which landowners held broad powers over peasants or tenant farmers, providing protection in exchange for loyalty and labor.

serfs   Peasants who were bound to a particular estate but, unlike slaves, were not the personal property of the estate owner and received traditional feudal protections.

The French Presence in America

Although France made a number of efforts to compete with Spain's New World projects during the sixteenth century, Spanish power was sufficient to prevent any major successes. For example, when a force of French Protestants established a colony in Florida in 1564, Spanish authorities sent an army to root them out. This led to increased Spanish vigilance, prompting Pedro Menéndez de Aviles to build the city of **Saint Augustine** the following year.

Unable to penetrate Spain's defenses in the south, the French concentrated their efforts farther north. A powerful incentive came from a fashion trend that seized Europe late in the sixteenth century: the broad-brimmed beaver felt hat. The felt hat's immense popularity led to the virtual extinction of fur-bearing animals in the Eastern Hemisphere by the beginning of the seventeenth century. However, early French explorers and fishermen along America's North Atlantic shore indicated that a near endless supply was ripe for the trapping in the New World (see page 21). Early in the seventeenth century, **Samuel de Champlain,** the "father of **New France,**" established trading posts in Nova Scotia and elsewhere, founded the city of Quebec, and in 1608 formed an enduring alliance with the Huron Indians. But despite these efforts and the potential profitability of the fur trade, French colonial authorities at first took little interest in overseas enterprises.

In 1627 French minister Cardinal Richelieu chartered the **Company of New France,** awarding a group of the king's favorites a charter to establish plantations in New France, but the venture failed to attract much interest. French Protestants, who might have emigrated to avoid religious persecution, were forbidden to move to the colony, and few French Catholics wanted to migrate to America. Thus the colonizing effort did not attract enough rent-paying tenants to make the envisioned estates profitable. Equally important was the fact that the few French peasants and small farmers who did venture to the New World found life in the woods and the company of Indians preferable to life as a tenant farmer. So-called *coureurs de bois,* or "runners of the woods," married Indian women and lived among the tribes, returning to the French settlements only when they had enough furs to sell to make the trip worthwhile.

Frustrated by the lack of profits, Richelieu reorganized the Company of New France in 1633, dispatching Champlain, now bearing the title Lieutenant of New France, with three ships of supplies, workmen, and soldiers who, it was hoped, would breathe new life into the colony. In its new form, the company ignored the government's demands that it establish agricultural settlements and focused instead on the

(see page 21)

IT MATTERS

The Felt Hat Fad

Changes in fashion come and go and we seldom give much thought to them as being historically significant. But the sudden popularity of felt hats in the late sixteenth century had a profound impact on not just America's history, but the history of the entire world. The flood of new wealth flowing into Europe from America permitted people of means—not just the nobility, but the landed gentry and even urban craftsmen and small business owners—to keep up with the latest fashion trends. Being in style became increasingly important to status-conscious merchants, manufacturers, and other beneficiaries of the New World boom. Demand for the beaver fur to make the felt became so steep that virtually the entire population of Old World beavers was wiped out and entire industries arose in France, the Netherlands, Great Britain, and Russia to import this "brown gold" from the Americas. Fur drew Europeans up virtually every waterway in North America, leading to the founding of many of the most prominent cities in America today. It is safe to say that without this seemingly silly fashion trend that little in the United States would be as we know it today.

Saint Augustine   First colonial city in the present-day United States; located in Florida and founded by Pedro Menéndez de Aviles for Spain in 1565.

Samuel de Champlain   French explorer who traced the St. Lawrence River inland to the Great Lakes, founded the city of Quebec, and formed the French alliance with the Huron Indians.

New France   The colony established by France in what is now Canada and the Great Lakes region of the United States.

Company of New France   Company established by Cardinal Richelieu to bring order to the running of France's North American enterprises.

coureurs de bois   Literally, "runners of the woods"; independent French fur traders who lived among the Indians and sold furs to the French.

Although this scene in Quebec was not painted until 1820, back streets in the old part of the city still looked very much as they had during the heyday of the French *coureurs de bois*. So did the people. Shops, like the one on the left, sold provisions and tools—often on credit—to the outward-bound runners of the woods, binding them to bring their next load of furs back to satisfy their debt. Thus, while the French Crown did little to encourage the fur business, it formed the core for Canada's woodland and urban economies. *Royal Ontario Museum © COM.*

continued technically to own the land and retained the power to appoint the governor and court officials in the colony.

Local authorities managed most of the colony's affairs until 1663, when the Crown began to intervene seriously in Canada. Having taken the functions of state into his own hands, young Louis XIV gave his finance minister, Jean-Baptiste Colbert, considerable authority over all monetary matters, including colonial enterprises. Seeking to make New France more efficient and to increase its contribution to the empire at large, Colbert founded the **Company of the West,** modeled on the highly successful Dutch West India Company. He also revoked the land titles held by the Company of New France, putting them directly into the king's hands, and overturned the political power of the Community of Habitants, making New France a royal colony.

Although the king reaped enormous profits from the fur trade, his colonial interests ranged beyond this single source of income. In 1673 a French expedition led by Louis Joliet and Jacques Marquette set out on a systematic exploration of New France's many waterways in search of new resources. They discovered a promising water route, but failed to follow it up. It fell to **Robert Cavelier, Sieur de La Salle,** to prove the strategic and economic value in Joliet and Marquette's discovery. In 1683 he and a party of French *coureurs de bois* and Indians retraced the earlier expedition and then followed the Mississippi River all the way to the Gulf of Mexico. La Salle immediately claimed the new territory for Louis XIV of France, naming it **Louisiana** in his honor. In 1698 the king sent settlers to the lower Mississippi Valley under the leadership of Pierre LeMoyne d'Iberville,

fur trade. Setting up posts in Quebec, Montreal, and a few more remote locations, the company became the primary outfitter of and buyer from the *coureurs de bois* and amassed huge profits by reselling the furs in Europe. After Richelieu's death in 1642, queen mother and French regent Anne of Austria acted on complaints filed by both fur trade investors and Jesuit missionaries that the Company of New France was not governing effectively. She chose to empower a new company, the **Community of Habitants of New France,** with a monopoly on the fur trade and the privilege of granting land claims. Then, in 1647, Anne approved the formation of a council that consisted of the governor, the local director of the Jesuits, the colony's military commandant, and three elected officials. Meanwhile, the Company of New France

Community of Habitants of New France Company chartered by Anne of Austria to make operations in New France more efficient and profitable; it gave significant political power to local officials in Canada.

Company of the West Company chartered by Colbert after New France became a royal colony; modeled on the Dutch West India Company, it was designed to maximize profits to the Crown.

Robert Cavelier, Sieur de La Salle French explorer who followed the Mississippi River from its origin in present-day Illinois to the Gulf of Mexico in 1683, giving France a claim to the entire river way and adjoining territory.

Louisiana French colony south of New France; it included the entire area drained by the Mississippi River and all its tributary rivers.

who in 1699 raised Louisiana's first French fort, near present-day Biloxi, Mississippi. In 1718 French authorities built the city of New Orleans to serve as the capital of the new territory.

The acquisition of Louisiana was a major accomplishment for La Salle and for France. The newly discovered river way gave the French a rich, untapped source of furs as well as an alternative shipping route, allowing them to avoid the cold, stormy North Atlantic. Also, if an agricultural venture could be started in the new territory, it might serve as an inexpensive source of supplies to support both the fur trade in Canada and France's sugar plantations in the Caribbean. But perhaps of greatest importance was Louisiana's strategic location between Spain's claims in the Southwest and the Dutch and other colonies along the eastern seaboard. Controlling this piece of real estate gave Louis considerable leverage in international diplomacy.

The Dutch Enterprise

Another source of competition to Spain's New World monopoly came from one of its former colonies: the Netherlands. The Armada disaster in 1588 had tipped the scales in favor of Dutch Protestant rebels, and the newly independent nation quickly developed a thriving commercial economy. Holland's first serious claim to American territory came in 1609, when Dutch sea captain **Henry Hudson** explored the East Coast in search of the elusive Northwest Passage (see page 21). He sailed up a large river that he hoped would lead him west to the Pacific. After realizing that he had not found the hoped-for route to the Far East, he returned to Holland and reported to his sponsor, the Dutch East India Company, that the territory surrounding this river—which he named after himself—was "pleasant with Grasse & Flowers and Goodly Trees" and that the Indians were friendly. Surely, he added, profits could be made there. Hudson's employers did not share his enthusiasm. Although the Dutch created one trading post on the Hudson River at Albany and another on Manhattan Island in 1614, the Dutch were not yet in a position to take maximum advantage of this claim.

With significant government encouragement, investors formed the **Dutch West India Company** in 1621 in order to marshal resources to expand their growing enterprises in the New World. The new company financed Dutch privateers who successfully raided Spanish and Portuguese treasure ships and, in 1634, overcame weak Spanish and Portuguese resistance to conquer a number of islands in the Caribbean.

The Dutch also pushed the Portuguese aside to take control of the transatlantic slave trade. Holland's next goal was to establish an empire on the North American mainland.

Seeking to compete with France's early efforts in the fur trade, Dutch West India Company official Peter Minuit negotiated a lease for the entire island of Manhattan from the Manhates Indians in 1626. This acquisition gave the Dutch control over the mouth of the river that Hudson had discovered and the land of "Grasses & Flowers" that it drained. Minuit's main motive, however, was to safeguard Dutch claims against those of rival European traders. For three more years, the company did nothing to attract settlers, and by 1629 only three hundred colonists had spread themselves in a thin ribbon from the capital, New Amsterdam, on Manhattan Island, upriver to Albany.

In that year, the Dutch West India Company drew up a comprehensive business plan to maximize profits and minimize dependence on local Indians for food and other support. To encourage the agricultural development necessary to support the fur industry, the company offered huge estates called **patroonships** to any company stockholder willing and able to bring fifty colonists to **New Netherland** at his own expense. In exchange, the patroons would enjoy near-feudal powers over their tenants. But few prosperous Dutchmen were interested in becoming New World barons. Rensselaerswyck, the estate of Kilian van Rensselaer, was the only patroonship to develop in accordance with the company's plan. The colony's development came to rely instead on many poorer migrants who were drawn by unofficial promises of land ownership and economic betterment.

Settlers from just about anywhere were welcome in New Netherland—the colony attracted an extremely

Henry Hudson Dutch ship captain and explorer who sailed up the Hudson River in 1609, giving the Netherlands a claim to the area now occupied by New York.

Dutch West India Company Dutch investment company formed in 1621 to develop colonies for the Netherlands in North America.

patroonship A huge grant of land given to any Dutch West India Company stockholder who, at his own expense, brought fifty colonists to New Netherland; the colonists became the tenants of the estate owner, or patroon.

New Netherland The colony founded by the Dutch West India Company in present-day New York; its capital was New Amsterdam on Manhattan Island.

Its location at the mouth of the Hudson River made the Dutch settlement of New Amsterdam a particularly important colonial trading center. Furs flowed down the river from Fort Orange (near modern Albany, New York), while guns, tools, and other trade goods traveled the other way. This etching (detail), based on a watercolor illustration painted in around 1553, captures the city's colorful vibrancy after Peter Stuyvesant and the Dutch burghers merged their power to bring order and prosperity. The weighing beam in the foreground illustrates both the prosperity and quest for order: it was used not only to weigh the loads of goods flowing through the town, but was also used as a whipping post and gallows when necessary. *Museum of the City of New York. Gift of Dr. N. Sulzberger.*

diverse population, including German and French Protestants, free and enslaved Africans, Catholics, Jews, and Muslims. In 1638 the Dutch even encouraged Swedish fur traders to create their own colony, New Sweden, within its boundaries. Local government in such a disparate community was a persistent problem. Although the Dutch West India Company was officially in charge, the actual conduct of day-to-day affairs was run by an elite group of **burghers,** men in New Amsterdam whose economic and political successes gave them significant influence. In an effort to reassert its power, the company reorganized its New World operations in 1645, appointing Peter Stuyvesant to manage all of its operations in the Western Hemisphere. Stuyvesant immediately came into conflict with the local burghers in New Amsterdam, and in 1647 he was forced to create a compromise government that gave the burghers an official

voice through a council of nine appointed representatives. Six years later, Stuyvesant and the council created a municipal government modeled on those back home in Holland. Despite this nod to democratic government, Stuyvesant ran company affairs with an iron hand, significantly tightening operations throughout the colony. In 1655 he even invaded and rooted out the Swedes, eliminating that source of dissension and competition.

burghers Town dwellers who were free from feudal obligations and were responsible for civic government during the medieval period in Europe; in New Amsterdam these were men who were not Dutch West India Company officials, but who governed civic affairs through their political influence.

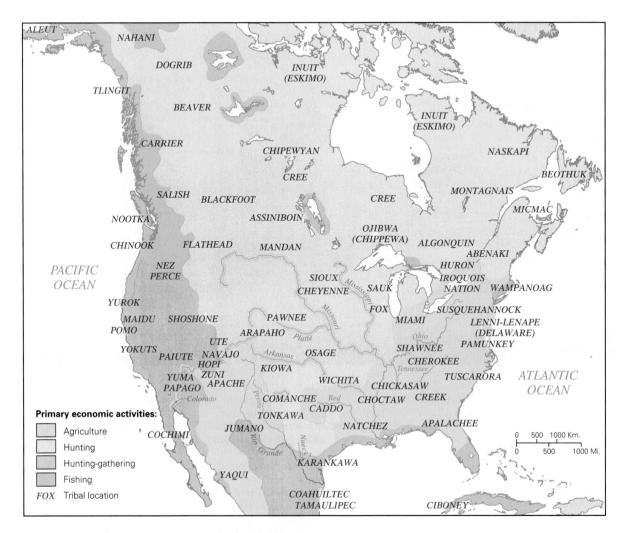

MAP 2.1 Indian Economies in North America   Indian economic activities helped to shape patterns of European settlement and investment in the New World. Regions that were primarily agricultural, like the Atlantic shoreline, lent themselves to European farming activities. Farther north and west, however, where hunting played a more prominent role in native life, the fur trade was a more attractive investment for European settlers.

Indians and the European Challenge

■ How did changes in the natural environment affect Indian societies during the early colonial period?

■ How did the arrival of Europeans influence continuing adaptations by Native American groups?

Native Americans did not sit idly by while the European powers carved out empires in North America.

Some joined the newcomers, serving as advisers and companions. Others sought to use the Europeans as allies to accomplish their own economic, diplomatic, or military goals (see Map 2.1). Still others, overwhelmed by the onset of European diseases and shifting population pressures, withdrew into the interior. The changes in native America created both obstacles and opportunities, giving shape to the patterns of expansion and conflict that characterized the colonial world.

The Indian Frontier in New Spain

Indian assistance had been critical in Spain's successful campaigns against the Aztecs and Incas. In Mexico, for example, groups who had been forced to pay tribute to the Aztec Empire gladly allied themselves with the Spanish in what the natives perceived as an opportunity to win their independence. Their hopes were soon dashed when the Spanish simply replaced the Aztecs as the new lords of a tributary empire.

Once their New World empire was firmly rooted, Spanish expansion met little native resistance until 1598, when a particularly brutal conquistador named **Don Juan de Oñate** led a large expedition to the Rio Grande region of New Mexico. When some Pueblos resisted Oñate's efforts to impose Spanish culture and religion, the conquistador chose to make an example of **Ácoma pueblo.** It took Oñate's troops three days to subdue the settlement, but Spanish steel finally overcame Ácoma clubs and stone knives. When the battle was over, Oñate ordered eight hundred Indians executed and made slaves of the nearly seven hundred survivors, mostly women and children. In addition, each male survivor over the age of 25 had one foot chopped off to prevent his escape from slavery. Two **Hopi Indians** who had been visiting Ácoma at the time of the battle had their right hands cut off and then were sent home as examples of the price of resistance.

This blatant cruelty disgusted even the most cynical authorities in New Spain, and both the church and state stepped in. Oñate was removed, and the surviving Indians were placed under joint military and religious protection. Some members of Oñate's company remained, however, founding the town of **Santa Fe** in 1609. Others scattered to set up ranches throughout the region.

Thanks in part to Las Casas's efforts, the church played a key role in developing the colonies, especially in the stark regions along Mexico's northern frontier where there were no gold mines or profitable plantations. The Franciscan order led church efforts in New Mexico and put a peculiar stamp on the pattern of Indian relations. A highly **ascetic** and disciplined order, the Franciscans were particularly offended by Pueblo religion and the Pueblo lifestyle. Indian ceremonies that involved various types of traditional religious objects smacked of idolatry to the Franciscans. Seeking to root out what they viewed as evil, the priests embarked on a wholesale effort to destroy every vestige of the Indians' religion. One priest, Fray

Thinking of themselves as agents of God and invincible, the Spanish arrogantly sought to impose their cultural and religious views on the peaceful Pueblo people of New Mexico during the seventeenth century. Much to their surprise, the Pueblos unified under a traditional leader named Popé and drove the Europeans entirely out of the region. No one knows what Popé looked like, but this sculpture by Jemez Pueblo artist Cliff Fragua is a realistic depiction of a common Pueblo man from the period. In the words of the artist, "Popé was not a trained fighter, but a man who tended gardens, hunted, and participated in the Kiva ceremonies." "My rendition of Popé depicts a simple man, one who is concerned for survival of his family, his culture, and the history and beliefs of the Pueblo People," Fragua continues. "His actions against the Spaniards were not acts of defiance, but rather, acts of survival." © *Cliff Fragua & the New Mexico Statuary Hall Commission. (This statue was selected for the National Statuary Hall in the U.S. Capitol to represent the state of New Mexico.)*

Don Juan de Oñate Spaniard who conquered New Mexico and claimed it for Spain in the 1590s.

Ácoma pueblo Pueblo Indian community that resisted Spanish authority in 1598 and was subdued by the Spanish.

Hopi Indians Indians who were related to the Comanches and Shoshones and took up residence among the Pueblo Indians as agricultural town-dwellers; their name means "peaceful ones."

Santa Fe Spanish colonial town established in 1609; eventually the capital of the province of New Mexico.

ascetic Practicing severe abstinence or self-denial, generally in pursuit of spiritual awareness.

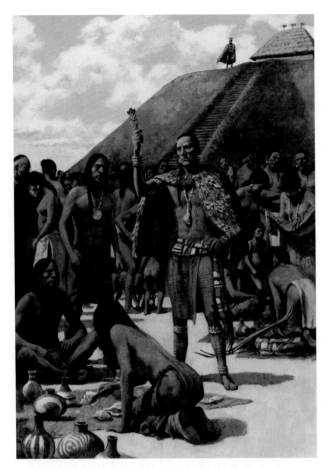

Before the arrival of European explorers like Hernando de Soto in the early 1540s, Indians in the American Southeast had lived in huge cities characterized by monumental architecture and a stratified class system with priest kings at the top, skilled craftsmen and traders in the middle, and common farmers and laborers at the bottom. This painting by archaeological reconstruction artist Tom Hall captures the bustling marketplace at Moundville, a large pre-Columbian city in present-day Alabama. Moundville appears to have begun to decline in around 1350—perhaps a consequence of climate change—and collapsed altogether following the introduction of European diseases. Scholars are unsure about what became of Moundville's survivors, but it is likely that they formed smaller villages that were easier to support in the new environment. All of the Southeastern Indian societies—the Cherokees, Choctaws, Creeks, Natchez, and many others—went through a similar transition during this period. *Tom Hall/National Geographic Society Image Collection.*

Alonso de Benavides, bragged in the 1620s that in one day he confiscated "more than a thousand idols of wood," which he then burned. The priests also interfered in the most intimate social aspects of Pueblo life, imposing foreign ideas about sexual relations and family structure, punishing most of the Pueblos' traditional practices as sinful.

After nearly a century of enduring these assaults on their most fundamental values, the Pueblos struck back. In 1680 a traditional leader named Popé led an uprising that united virtually all of the Indians in New Mexico against Spanish rule. The **Pueblo Revolt** left four hundred Spaniards dead as the rebels captured Santa Fe and drove the invaders from their land. It took almost a decade for the Spanish to regroup sufficiently to reinvade New Mexico. In 1689 troops moved back into the region and over the next several years waged a brutal war to recapture the territory. The fighting continued off and on until the end of the century, but Spanish settlers began returning to New Mexico after the recapture of Santa Fe in 1693.

Elsewhere along the northern frontier of New Spain, the unsettled nature of Indian life and the arid and uninviting character of the land made settlement unappealing to the Spaniards. Efforts at mining, raising livestock, and missionizing in Arizona and Texas were largely unsuccessful until after 1700.

The Indian World in the Southeast

Members of Spanish-exploring expeditions under would-be conquistadors such as Ponce de León and de Soto were the first Europeans to contact the mound builder societies and other Indian groups in the Southeast. Although their residential and ceremonial centers often impressed the Spaniards, these Mississippian agricultural groups had no gold and could not easily be enslaved. The conquistadors moved on without attempting to force Spanish rule or the Catholic religion on them.

Given sufficient incentive, however, the Spanish were quick to strike at Indian independence and culture. In Florida, for example, the need to protect Spanish ships from French settlers led Spain to establish garrisons such as Saint Augustine. With this and other similar military posts in place, Jesuit and Franciscan missionaries ranged outward to bring Catholicism to Indians in the region. By 1600 they had

Pueblo Revolt   Indian rebellion against Spanish authority in 1680 led by Popé; succeeded in driving the Spanish out of New Mexico for nearly a decade.

established missions from the gulf coast of Florida all the way to Georgia.

Although the Spanish presence in the region was small, its impact was enormous. The Spanish introduced European diseases into the densely populated towns in the Mississippi River region. Epidemics wiped out entire Native American civilizations and forced survivors to abandon their towns and entirely modify their ways of life. Certain groups, among them the Cherokees and Creeks, formed village-based economies that combined agriculture, hunting, and gathering. As had happened earlier in the Northeast among the Iroquois and others, this change in economy led to increasing intergroup warfare. And like the Iroquois, many southeastern groups created formal confederacies as a way of coping. One example is the **Creek Confederacy,** a union of many groups who had survived the Spanish epidemics. Internally, members created an economic and social system in which each population contributed to the welfare of all and differences were settled through athletic competition—a ballgame not unlike modern lacrosse—rather than warfare. And when new Europeans arrived in the seventeenth and eighteenth centuries, the Creeks and other confederacies found it beneficial to welcome them as trading partners and allies, balancing the competing demands of the Spanish and French, and later the English. To some degree, they took advantage of the European rivalries to advance their own interests against those of neighboring confederacies.

The Indian World in the Northeast

By the time Europeans had begun serious exploration and settlement of the Northeast, the economic and cultural changes among Eastern Woodlands Indians that had begun between 1350 and 1450 had resulted in the creation of two massive—and opposing—alliance systems. On one side were the Hurons, Algonquins, Abenakis, Micmacs, Ottawas, and several smaller tribes. On the other was the Iroquois League.

The costs and benefits of sustained European contact first fell to the Hurons and their allies. The Abenakis, Micmacs, and others who lived along the northern shore of the Atlantic were the first groups drawn into trade with the French, and it was among them that the *coureurs de bois* settled and intermarried. These family ties became firm economic bonds when formal French exploration brought these groups into more direct contact with the European trading world. Seeking advantage against the Iroquois, the Hurons and their neighbors created a great wheel of alliance with the fur trade at its hub and France as its axle.

The strong partnership between these Indians and the French posed a serious threat to the Iroquois. Having moved south out of the territory now firmly held by the Hurons when the climate first turned colder, the Iroquois Confederacy now wished to wield its combined power to reclaim the area. The presence of the French and the fur trade only made this objective all the more desirable. If they could push the Hurons and their allies out and take control of the St. Lawrence River, the French would then have to trade exclusively with the Iroquois. But the French presence also complicated the situation in that the Hurons had a ready source for guns, iron arrowheads, and other tools that gave them a military edge.

The arrival of the Dutch in the Albany area, however, offered the Iroquois an attractive diplomatic alternative. In 1623 the Dutch West India Company invited representatives from the Iroquois League to a meeting at **Fort Orange,** offering them friendship and trade. The Iroquois responded enthusiastically, but in a way that the Dutch had not anticipated. Instead of entering peacefully into the trade, the Iroquois imposed their authority over all of the Indian groups already trading with the Dutch. They began a bloody war with the **Mohicans,** who had been the Dutch traders' main source for furs in the Hudson Valley. As they had planned to do to the Hurons in the St. Lawrence Valley, by 1627 the Iroquois had driven the Mohicans out of the Hudson Valley and had taken control over the flow of furs.

Trade was so vigorous that the Iroquois soon wiped out fur supplies in their own territory and began a serious push to acquire new sources. Beginning in the late 1630s, the Iroquois Confederacy entered into a long-term aggressive war against the Hurons and their allies in New France; against the Munsees, Delawares, and other groups in the Susquehanna and Delaware River valleys to the south; and even against

Creek Confederacy   Alliance of Indians living in the Southeast; formed after the lethal spread of European diseases to permit a cooperative economic and military system among survivors.

Fort Orange   Dutch trading post established near present-day Albany, New York, in 1614.

Mohicans   Algonquin-speaking Indians who lived along the Hudson River, were dispossessed in a war with the Iroquois confederacy, and eventually were all but exterminated.

Alfred Jacob Miller based this 1837 painting of eighteenth-century mounted buffalo hunters on interviews with Shoshone Indians he met on a trip through the American West. It illustrates clearly the enormous impact the arrival of horses had on Plains Indian life. Note how few mounted men it took to drive vast numbers of animals over a cliff to their deaths. At the bottom of the cliff, women would butcher the dead animals and the meat, bones, and hides would provide food, clothing, tools, tents, and trade goods sufficient to support an entire band of Indians for some time. The arrival of the horse on the Great Plains in the late 1600s marked the beginning of 150 years of unprecedented wealth and power for the Indians in the region. *Alfred Jacob Miller, Walters Art Gallery, Baltimore.*

the Iroquois-speaking Eries to the west. Citing Hienwatha's legacy, the Iroquois justified their aggression by claiming that their conquests were simply bringing more people into the shelter of the Great Tree of Peace, expanding the confederacy to include all the northeastern Indians.

The New Indian World of the Plains

Though largely unexplored and untouched by Europeans, the vast area of the Great Plains also underwent profound transformation during the period of initial contacts. Climate change, the pressure of shifting populations, and the introduction of novel European goods through lines of kinship and trade created an altogether new culture and economy among the Indians in this region.

Before about 1400, Indians living on the plains rarely strayed far from the river ways that form the

Missouri River drainage, where they lived in villages sustained by agriculture, hunting, and gathering (see page 14). The climate cooldown that affected their neighbors to the east had a similar effect on the Plains Indians: growing seasons became shorter, and the need to hunt became greater. But at the same time, this shift in climate produced an increase in one food source: **buffalo.**

A survivor of the great ice ages, the American bison is particularly well adapted to cold climates. Unlike European cattle, which often starve when snow buries the grasses on which they graze, buffalo use their hooves to dig out the grass they need, and their efficient metabolism extracts nutrients from even poor-

buffalo   The American bison, a large member of the ox family, native to North America and the staple of the Plains Indian economy between the fifteenth and mid-nineteenth centuries.

quality pasturage. Although buffalo had long been a presence on the plains, the cold weather during the Little Ice Age spurred a massive increase in their numbers. Between 1300 and 1800, herds numbering in the millions emerged in the new environment created by the climate change.

Some groups—such as the **Caddoan**-speaking Wichitas, Pawnees, and Arikaras—virtually abandoned their agricultural villages and became hunters. Others, such as the Hidatsas, split in two: a splinter group calling themselves Crows went off permanently to the grasslands to hunt while the remainder stayed in their villages growing corn and tobacco. These and others who chose to continue their agricultural ways, the Mandans, for example, established a thriving trade with the hunters, exchanging vegetables and tobacco for fresh meat and other buffalo products.

The increase in buffalo not only provided a welcome resource for the Indians already on the Great Plains but also drew new populations to the area. As the climate farther north became unbearably severe, the Blackfeet and other Indians swept down from the subarctic Northeast to hunt on the plains. Other Algonquin-speaking Indians, including the Gros Ventres, Cheyennes, and Arapahos, soon followed. These were then joined by other northeastern groups fleeing the violence and disease that were becoming endemic in the Eastern Woodlands. Some groups, even war-weary Hurons and Iroquois, came as small parties and sought adoption among Great Plains societies. Others came en masse. The **Lakotas,** for example, once the westernmost family of Siouan agriculturalists, were pushed onto the plains by continuing pressure from the east, but they maintained close relations with their **Dakota** neighbors in Minnesota, who continued to farm and harvest wild rice and other crops. This continued tie, like that between the Crows and Hidatsas, increased both the hunters' and the farmers' chances for survival in an ever more hostile world by expanding available resources. Intergroup trade became the key to the welfare of all.

The buffalo also began to play an important role on the southern plains. There, groups such as the Apaches, Comanches, and Kiowas specialized in hunting the ever-increasing herds and then exchanging part of their kill for village-based products from their neighbors and kinsmen, the Navajos, Hopis, and Pueblos. And it was in these intergroup trades that the Plains Indians would acquire a new advantage in their efforts to expand their hunting economy: the horse.

One unintentional outcome of the Pueblo Revolt was the liberation of thousands of Spanish horses. The Pueblos had little use for these animals, but their trading partners, the Kiowas and Comanches, quickly adopted them. Horses could carry much larger loads than dogs and could survive on a diet of grass rather than taking a share of the meat. In less than a generation, horses became a mainstay of the buffalo-hunting cultures on the southern plains. And from there, horses spread quickly to other hunting people.

Northern plains dwellers such as the Shoshones quickly began acquiring horses from their southwestern kinsmen. Following a northward path along the eastern flank of the Rocky Mountains, horses were passed from one group to another in the complex trading system that had come into existence in the plains region. Well adapted to grasslands, virtually free from natural predators or diseases, and highly prized and thus well protected by their new human owners, horses greatly increased in number. By 1730, virtually all of the plains hunting peoples had some horses and were clamoring for more.

The steady demand for horses and hunting grounds created a new dynamic on the Great Plains and set a new economy into motion (see Map 2.2). After the Spanish reconquest of New Mexico, Indians could obtain horses only through warfare and trade, and both increased significantly. Surprise raids to steal horses from neighboring Indian groups and European settlements brought both honor and wealth to those who were successful. Human captives also became valuable prizes, both as replacements for individuals lost in the fighting and as items of trade. In exchange for horses, human captives might be bartered as slaves to the Spanish. Thus horse trading and slave trading became linked.

Conquest and Accommodation in a Shared New World

■ What forces shaped the day-to-day lives of settlers in New Mexico, Louisiana, and New Netherland?

■ How did settlers and American Indians adapt to changing conditions in the different regions of colonial occupation?

Caddoan   A family of languages spoken by the Wichitas, Pawnees, Arikaras, and other Plains Indians.

Lakotas/Dakotas   Subgroups of the Sioux Nation of Indians; Lakotas make up the western branch, living mostly on the Great Plains; Dakotas, the eastern branch, live mostly in the prairie and lakes region of the Upper Midwest.

MAP 2.2 Intergroup Trading on the Plains Although movies portray Plains Indians as unsophisticated hunters and warriors, Native American societies in America's midsection maintained extremely complex and cosmopolitan trading networks. As this map shows, trade routes that had existed before Europeans entered the region acquired added importance in distributing the novel technologies and ideas that the newcomers brought with them. The most important of these was horses, which were passed very quickly from group to group along these trade routes.

Old World cultures, Native American historical dynamics, and New World environmental conditions combined to create vibrant new societies in European pioneer settlements. Despite the regulatory efforts of Spanish bureaucrats, French royal officials, and Dutch company executives, life in the colonies developed in its own peculiar ways. Entire regions in what would become the United States assumed cultural contours that would shape all future developments in each.

New Spain's Northern Frontiers

Life along New Spain's northern fringe was punctuated by friction between the empire's highly organized official structure and the disorderliness common to frontier settings. For the Spanish, notions of civil order were rooted in the local community—city, town, or village—and its ruling elite. Responsibility for maintaining order belonged to the *cabildo secular*, the municipal town council composed of members of the elite or their appointees. Spain established towns in all of its New World colonies and immediately turned over local authority to a ruling *cabildo*. In Mexico, Peru, and elsewhere this practice was appropriate and usually successful, but in the high desert of New Mexico the *cabildo* system was at odds with environmental and cultural conditions.

After suppressing the Pueblo Revolt during the 1690s, Spaniards began drifting back into New Mexico. Unlike areas to the south, New Mexico offered no

San Esteban Rey, a Catholic church built at Pueblo de Ácoma in about 1642, stands as a monument to the mixing of cultures in colonial New Mexico. The building's adobe construction, rising towers, and curving corners reflect traditional Pueblo architecture, while the crosses on the top identify its European purpose. Churches like this provided an anchor for the multicultural society that emerged in the region. *Lee Marmon.*

rich deposits of gold or silver, and the climate was unsuitable for large-scale agriculture. With neither mines nor plantations to support the *encomienda* system, the basic underpinnings of the traditional ruling order never emerged. Even so, the Spanish colonial bureaucracy followed conventional imperial procedures and made Santa Fe the official municipal center for the region after its recapture from the Indians in 1693. But there were no *encomenderos* to provide wealth. The church, which was channeling money to missions, and the Spanish government, which allocated both military and civic support funds, were the only major employers in the region. Those in neither the church's nor the state's employ had to scramble for a living.

As in the days before the Pueblo Revolt, the most rewarding economic enterprise in the region was ranching. Under Pueblo control following the revolt, the small flocks of sheep abandoned by the fleeing Spanish grew dramatically. By the time the Spanish returned, sheep ranching had become a reliable way to make a living. Thus, rather than concentrating near the municipal center in Santa Fe, the population in New Mexico spread out across the land, forming two sorts of communities. South of Santa Fe, people settled on scattered ranches. Elsewhere, they gathered in small villages along streams and pooled their labor to make a living from irrigated **subsistence farming.**

Like colonists elsewhere in Spain's New World empire, the New Mexico colonists were almost entirely male. Isolated on sheep ranches or in small villages, these men sought Indian companionship and married into local populations. These marriages gave birth not only to a new hybrid population but also to lines of kinship, trade, and authority that were in sharp contrast to the imperial ideal. For example, when Navajo or Apache raiding parties struck, ranchers and villagers turned to their Indian relatives for protection rather than to Spanish officials in Santa Fe.

Far away from the imperial economy centered in Mexico City, New Mexicans looked northward for trading opportunities. Southern Plains Indians—Apaches, Comanches, Kiowas, and their kin—needed a continuous supply of horses. They could obtain them by raiding Spanish ranches, but doing so brought reprisals by ranchers and their Indian relatives. Trade was a safer option. Facing labor shortages and too poor to take advantage of traditional Spanish labor systems, New Mexicans accepted Indian slaves—especially children—in exchange for horses. Soon, these young captives became another important commodity in the already complex trading and raiding system that prevailed among the southwestern Indians and Spanish New Mexicans.

In this frontier world, unlike the rest of Spanish America, a man's social status came to depend less on his Spanish connections than on his ability to work effectively in the complicated world of kinship that prevailed in the Indian community. The people who eventually emerged as the elite class in New Mexico were those who best perfected these skills. Under their influence, Santa Fe was transformed from a traditional mission and imperial town into a cosmopolitan frontier trading center. During the next two centuries, this multiethnic elite absorbed first French and then Anglo-American newcomers while maintaining its own social, political, and economic style.

Life in French Louisiana

France's colony in Louisiana had many of the same qualities and faced many of the same problems as Spain's North American possessions. Like most European settlements, Louisiana suffered from a critical shortage of labor, leading first to dependence on the Indians and eventually to the wholesale adoption of African slavery. And like all Europeans who settled in North America, Louisianans found themselves

subsistence farming Farming that produces enough food for survival but no surplus that can be sold.

The French had difficulty persuading settlers to come to their New World province in Louisiana. As a result, the region's development depended on a mixture of various European refugees, native Indians, and imported Africans for labor. Alexander de Batz's 1735 painting gives us a good idea of what the population around New Orleans looked like at that time. As in neighboring New Mexico, a multiracial and multicultural society emerged in Louisiana that left a permanent legacy in the region. *Peabody Museum, Harvard University.*

embroiled in a complicated Native American world that usually defied European understanding.

Despite the territory's strategic location, fertile soils, and fur-bearing animals, few Frenchmen showed any interest in settling there. In the first years of the colony's existence, the population consisted primarily of three groups: military men, who were generally members of the lower nobility; *coureurs de bois* from Canada looking for new and better sources of furs; and French craftsmen seeking economic independence in the New World. The men in each group had little in common with those in the other groups, and, more important, none had knowledge of or interest in food production. In the absence of an agricultural establishment, the small number of settlers in Louisiana had to depend on imported food. At first, ships from France carried provisions to the colonies, but war in Europe frequently interrupted this source. In desperation, the colonists turned to the Indians.

The **Natchez, Chickasaws,** and **Choctaws** were all close by and well provisioned. The Chickasaws refused to deal with the French, and the Natchez, divided into quarreling factions, were sometimes helpful and sometimes hostile. But the Choctaws, locked into a war with the Chickasaws and a tense relationship with the Natchez, found the prospect of an alliance with the French quite attractive. In the realignment process, the Choctaws helped shape France's Indian policies and expansion plans. For example, af-

Natchez Indians An urban, mound-building Indian people who lived on the lower Mississippi River until they were destroyed in a war with the French in the 1720s; survivors joined the Creek Confederacy.

Chickasaw Indians An urban, mound-building Indian people who lived on the lower Mississippi River and became a society of hunters after the change in climate and introduction of disease after 1400; they were successful in resisting French aggression throughout the colonial era.

Choctaw Indians Like the Chickasaws, a mound-building people who became a society of hunters after 1400; they were steadfast allies of the French in wars against the Natchez and Chickasaws.

ter disastrous flooding along the Gulf Coast during the winter of 1719–1720, the French chose to relocate settlements onto Natchez land rather than in Choctaw territory. When the Natchez resisted French incursion, the Choctaws helped their European allies destroy the tribe—the entire Natchez Nation was either killed or exiled. The Choctaws also assisted the French in a thirty-year-long conflict with the Chickasaws, though with less success.

Despite the Choctaw alliance, which guaranteed ample food supplies and facilitated territorial acquisitions, Louisiana remained unappealing to French farmers. Recognizing the problem, the French government tried several tactics to lure settlers, occasionally resorting to some rather odd and extreme measures. For example, in the late 1690s, officials in Louisiana, aware that the absence of women was one serious deterrent to immigration, proposed that the government pay the passage of young women of good character to the colony. For several years, agents in France tried to recruit females but enlisted only twenty-four or so, who arrived in the colony in 1704. Like the noblemen and craftsmen who preceded them, these potential brides—refugees from orphanages and other public institutions—were ill suited for the primitive life offered by Louisiana and were entirely unprepared to work as farm laborers. By 1708, even officials who had been enthusiastic about the project were advising that it be discontinued. As a result, French men, like their Spanish neighbors, married Indians and, later, African slaves, creating a hybrid **creole** population.

Although Louisiana officials advised against it, the French government finally resorted to recruiting paupers, criminals, and religious or political refugees from central Europe and elsewhere to people the new land. But even with these newcomers, labor was inadequate to ensure survival, much less prosperity. Increasingly, settlers in Louisiana imported slaves to do necessary work. By 1732, slaves made up two-thirds of the population.

The Dutch Settlements

The existence of Rensselaerswyck and other great landed estates made it seem as though the New Netherland colony was prosperous and secure, but it actually was neither. Few of the wealthy stockholders in the Dutch West India Company wanted to trade their lives as successful gentleman investors for a pioneering existence on a barely tamed frontier. The economy in Holland was booming, and only the most desperate or adventurous wanted to leave. But having no one to pay their way, even the few who were willing were hard-pressed to migrate to the colony.

Desperate to draw settlers, the Dutch West India Company created an alternative to the patroonship, agreeing to grant a tract of land to any free man who would agree to farm it. This offer appealed to many groups in Europe who were experiencing hardship in their own countries but who, for one reason or another, were unwelcome in the colonies of their homelands. French Protestants, for example, were experiencing terrible persecution in France but were forbidden from going to Canada or Louisiana. Roman Catholics, Quakers, Jews, Muslims, and a wide variety of others also chose to migrate to New Netherland. Most of the colonists settled on small farms, called *bouweries* in Dutch, and engaged in the same agricultural pursuits they had practiced in Europe. Thus New Netherland was dotted with little settlements, each having its own language, culture, and internal economy.

Farming was the dominant activity among the emigrants, but some followed the example of the French *coureurs du bois* and went alone or in small groups into the woods to live and trade with the Indians. Called *bosch loopers*, these independent traders traveled through the forests, trading cheap brandy and rum for the Indians' furs, which they then sold for enormous profits. Although both tribal leaders and legitimate traders complained about the *bosch loopers'* illegal activities, company authorities could not control them.

In fact, the Dutch West India Company was unable to control much of anything in New Netherland. The incredible diversity of the settlers no doubt contributed to this administrative impotence. For example, Dutch law and company policy dictated that the Calvinistic **Dutch Reform Church** was to be the colony's official and only church. But instead of drawing everyone into one religion, the policy had the opposite effect. As late as 1642 not a single church of any

---

creole In colonial times, a term referring to anyone of European or African heritage who was born in the colonies; in Louisiana, refers to the ethnic group resulting from intermarriage by people of mixed languages, races, and cultures.

bosch loopers Dutch term meaning "woods runners"; independent Dutch fur traders.

Dutch Reform Church Calvinistic Protestant denomination; the established church in the Dutch Republic and the official church in New Netherland.

denomination had been planted. Poor leadership and unimaginative policies also contributed to the general air of disorder. Following Peter Minuit's dismissal by the company in 1631, a long line of incompetent governors ruled the colony. In the absence of any legislative assembly or other local body to help keep matters on track, for years one bad decision followed another. It took a major reorganization by the West India Company and its appointment of Peter Stuyvesant in 1645 to turn the colony around.

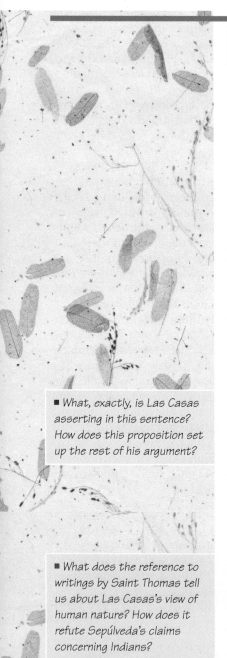

Individual Voices

Examining a Primary Source

Bartolomé de Las Casas Argues for the American Indians

In his debate with Juan Ginés de Sepúlveda before the Council of Valladolid in 1550 and 1551, Bartolomé de Las Casas repeatedly stressed the many remarkable accomplishments made by Indians, both in creating advanced civilizations of their own and in adapting to Spanish civilization. Many witnesses (most of whom had never been to America) disputed these claims, but more damaging was the argument that such accomplishments were irrelevant. Though perhaps clever, Sepúlveda argued, Indians lacked souls and therefore could never become truly civilized Christians. Like animals, then, they could be exploited but never embraced. Las Casas thought otherwise, and drew on Church doctrine to refute this claim. In the end, Las Casas's argument won the day and became the official position for the Catholic Church and the Spanish Crown.

■ *What, exactly, is Las Casas asserting in this sentence? How does this proposition set up the rest of his argument?*

■ *What does the reference to writings by Saint Thomas tell us about Las Casas's view of human nature? How does it refute Sepúlveda's claims concerning Indians?*

Who, therefore, except one who is irreverent toward God and contemptuous of nature, has dared to write that countless numbers of natives across the ocean are barbarous, savage, uncivilized, and slow witted when, if they are evaluated by an accurate judgment, they completely outnumber all other men? ■ *This is consistent with what Saint Thomas writes: "The good which is proportionate to the common state of nature is to be found in most men and is lacking only in a few. . . . Thus it is clear that the majority of men have sufficient knowledge to guide their lives, and the few who do not have this knowledge are said to be half-witted or fools." Therefore, since barbarians of that kind, as Saint Thomas says, lack that good of the intellect which is knowledge of the truth, a good proportionate to the common condition of rational nature, it is evident that in each part of the world, or anywhere among the nations, barbarians of this sort or freaks of rational nature can only be quite rare. For since God's love of mankind is so great and it is his will to save all men, it is in accord with his wisdom that in the whole universe, which is perfect in all its parts, his supreme wisdom should shine more and more in the most perfect thing: rational nature. Therefore, the barbarians of the kind we have placed in the third category are most rare, because with such natural endowments they cannot seek God, know him, call upon him, or love him. They do not have a capacity for doctrine or for performing the acts of faith or love.* ■

■ Judging from this brief excerpt from Las Casas's argument, why do you suppose he won the debate? Why would the Catholic Church have chosen to endorse and publicize his views and not Sepúlveda's?

Again, if we believe that such a huge part of mankind is barbaric, it would follow that God's design has for the most part been ineffective, with so many thousands of men deprived of the natural light that is common to all peoples. And so there would be a great reduction in the perfection of the entire universe— something that is unacceptable and unthinkable for any Christian. ■

Source: Bartolomé de las Casas, *In Defense of the Indians: The Defense of the Most Reverend Lord, Don Fray Bartolomé de las Casas, of the Order of Preachers, Late Bishop of Chiapa, Against the Persecutors and Slanderers of the Peoples of the New World Discovered Across the Seas.* Translated, edited and annotated by Stafford Poole (Dekalb, Northern Illinois University Press, © 1974). Used by permission of Northern Illinois University Press.

Summary

Spain's opening ventures in the Americas had been wildly successful, making the Iberian kingdom the envy of the world. Hoping to cash in on the bounty, other European nations challenged Spain's monopoly on American colonization, creating an outward explosion of exploring energy. Although slow to consolidate an imperial presence in North America, England was the first to confront the Spanish in force, wounding them severely. France and the Netherlands took advantage of the situation to begin building their own American empires.

For Native Americans, the entry of Europeans into their realms combined with other forces to create an air of crisis. Presented with a series of new challenges, Indians sought new ways to solve their problems and created altogether new societies. This often involved difficult choices: perhaps allying with the newcomers, resisting them, or fleeing. As different groups exercised different options, the outcome was a historically dynamic world of interaction involving all of the societies that were coming together in North America.

This dynamic interaction yielded interesting fruit. In New Spain, New France, Louisiana, New Netherland, and throughout the Great Plains, truly cosmopolitan societies emerged. Bearing cultural traits and material goods from throughout the world, these new transatlantic societies set the tone for future development in North America. As we will see in Chapter 3, societies on the Atlantic coast, too, were evolving as English colonists interacted with the land and its many occupants. The outcome of such interchange, over the centuries, was the emergence of a multicultural, multiethnic, and extraordinarily rich culture—an essential element in Making America.

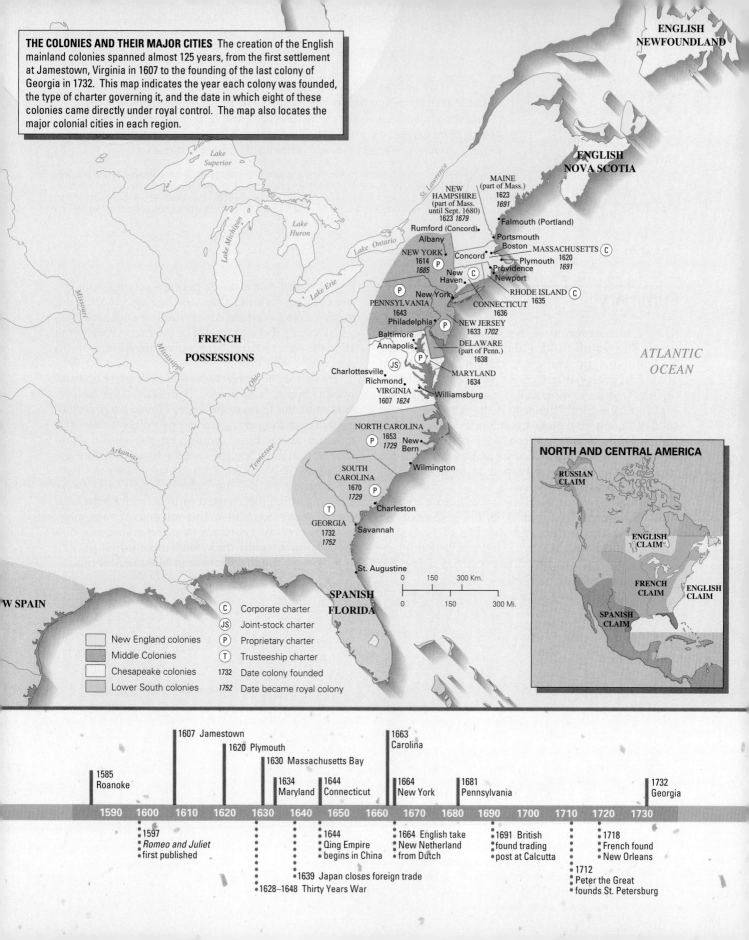

THE COLONIES AND THEIR MAJOR CITIES The creation of the English mainland colonies spanned almost 125 years, from the first settlement at Jamestown, Virginia in 1607 to the founding of the last colony of Georgia in 1732. This map indicates the year each colony was founded, the type of charter governing it, and the date in which eight of these colonies came directly under royal control. The map also locates the major colonial cities in each region.

ENGLISH
NEWFOUNDLAND

ENGLISH
NOVA SCOTIA

Lake Superior

Lake Michigan

Lake Huron

Lake Ontario

Lake Erie

St. Lawrence

MAINE
(part of Mass.)
1623
1691

NEW
HAMPSHIRE
(part of Mass.
until Sept. 1680)
1623 *1679*

Rumford (Concord)
Albany

Falmouth (Portland)
Portsmouth
Boston

NEW YORK
1614
1685 Ⓟ

Concord
New
Haven Ⓒ
Providence
Newport

Plymouth
MASSACHUSETTS Ⓒ
1620
1691

RHODE ISLAND Ⓒ
1635

Ⓟ New York

PENNSYLVANIA
1643

CONNECTICUT
1636

Philadelphia Ⓟ
NEW JERSEY
1633 *1702*

Baltimore
Annapolis

DELAWARE
(part of Penn.)
1638

ⒿⓈ
Ⓟ

Charlottesville
Richmond
VIRGINIA
1607 *1624*

MARYLAND
1634

Williamsburg

NORTH CAROLINA
1653 Ⓟ
1729   New
Bern

FRENCH
POSSESSIONS

Missouri

Mississippi

Ohio

Arkansas

Tennessee

Wilmington

SOUTH
CAROLINA
1670 Ⓟ
1729

Charleston

Ⓣ
GEORGIA
1732   Savannah
1752

St. Augustine

SPANISH
FLORIDA

W SPAIN

ATLANTIC
OCEAN

NORTH AND CENTRAL AMERICA

RUSSIAN
CLAIM

ENGLISH
CLAIM

FRENCH
CLAIM

ENGLISH
CLAIM

SPANISH
CLAIM

0   150   300 Km.

0   150   300 Mi.

Ⓒ Corporate charter
ⒿⓈ Joint-stock charter
Ⓟ Proprietary charter
Ⓣ Trusteeship charter
1732 Date colony founded
1752 Date became royal colony

☐ New England colonies
☐ Middle Colonies
☐ Chesapeake colonies
☐ Lower South colonies

1585
Roanoke

1607 Jamestown

1620 Plymouth

1630 Massachusetts Bay

1634
Maryland

1644
Connecticut

1663
Carolina

1664
New York

1681
Pennsylvania

1732
Georgia

| 1590 | 1600 | 1610 | 1620 | 1630 | 1640 | 1650 | 1660 | 1670 | 1680 | 1690 | 1700 | 1710 | 1720 | 1730 |

1597
Romeo and Juliet
first published

1644
Qing Empire
begins in China

1664 English take
New Netherland
from Dutch

1691 British
found trading
post at Calcutta

1718
French found
New Orleans

1639 Japan closes foreign trade

1628–1648 Thirty Years War

1712
Peter the Great
founds St. Petersburg

Founding the English Mainland Colonies, 1585–1732

The Colonies and Their Major Cities
Using the map on the facing page, discuss the four types of colonies created on the mainland of British North America. What differences in political participation and political institutions do you think might develop between corporate colonies and proprietary ones?

Individual Choices

NATHANIEL BACON

Nathaniel Bacon came to Virginia as a gentleman in the 1670s, but his resentment of the economic and political domination of the colony by a small group of planters transformed him into a backwoods rebel. In 1676, Bacon led an army of discontented farmers, servants, and slaves against the powerful coastal planters—and almost won. In this stained glass window, discovered and restored in the twentieth century, Bacon's social class and his commanding presence are both evident. *The Association for the Preservation of Virginia Antiquities at Bacon's Castle, Library of Virginia.*

Nathaniel Bacon

One hundred years before the English colonies of North America declared their independence, Nathaniel Bacon led a group of Virginia colonists in a rebellion against the corrupt royal governor and the elite planters who supported him. Bacon's 1670s backcountry movement came at a time when the Virginia economy was in trouble. A recent drought and a drop in the price of tobacco had diminished the fortunes of many colonists. In the backcountry, raids by the neighboring Indian tribes had led to the deaths of many farm families and their servants. Small farms were being heavily taxed, while the larger plantations, owned by Governor William Berkeley's friends, remained tax-exempt and prosperous. New arrivals to the colony, eager for land, found the governor unwilling to open the western frontier for further settlement.

In 1674 a new face arrived in the colony of Virginia. Nathaniel Bacon, a charismatic 27-year-old, had been born to privilege in Suffolk County, England, and had studied law at Cambridge. After the young Nathaniel's involvement in a series of misadventures in England, his father decided to pack him off to the colonies to keep him out of trouble. Using his father's money, Bacon was able to purchase a large plantation 40 miles up the river from the capital city of Jamestown, as well as a tract of undeveloped land in the backcountry. Bacon's social status gained him a place among the colony's elite, and within six months he was appointed to Governor Berkeley's advisory council. But Bacon's relentless ambition and his impulsiveness soon made him an unpopular figure in the wealthy planter circles.

In the spring of 1676 the militant Susquehanna Indians raided Bacon's backcountry farm, killing the overseer and three servants. Bacon, speaking for himself and his neighbors, demanded that Governor Berkeley raise a militia and rid the area of its entire Indian population. Bold and ruthless action like this would not only end the attacks but also open up more land for settlement. But the governor, who was engaged in a lucrative fur-trading business with several of the local tribes, refused. He insisted that the existing plan of building forts along the frontier would protect Bacon and his fellow backcountry friends. The angry Bacon decided to take matters into his own hands. He returned to the backcountry and raised a militia of volunteers from the area. This vigilante army began a war against not just the Susquehanna but all the Indians on the Virginia frontier. Now the equally angry Governor Berkeley stripped Bacon of his seat on the council and branded him a traitor.

After leading successful campaigns against the Indians, Bacon returned to Jamestown with forty bodyguards. He demanded that his seat on the council be restored. The intimidated Governor Berkeley gave in to this demand, but only if Bacon confessed to his crimes and asked for forgiveness. Bacon agreed—and his supporters returned home, satisfied that all was well. They were wrong. As soon as Bacon's men left the city, the governor had Bacon arrested and condemned to death for treason. Fortunately for Bacon, he had been warned of the governor's intentions and he escaped arrest.

Bacon realized that there could be no peaceful resolution to his clash with the governor and returned to the backcountry to reassemble his army. Within two weeks Bacon had recruited a force of over five hundred men. On June 23, 1676, this frontier army marched into Jamestown and demanded an audience with the governor. When Berkeley refused, Bacon ordered his troops to surround the statehouse, making prisoners of all of the political leaders in the building. Bacon then demanded that the captive legislators pass several reforms, including an act barring the governor's friends from office. Bacon also demanded that all those who participated in the rebellion receive pardons. With little choice in the matter, the colonial government agreed, and Bacon ordered his men to let the governor and his planter friends return to their homes. Allowing the governor to go free would turn out to be a crucial mistake.

Over the next several months "General" Bacon (as his troops were now calling him) and Governor Berkeley continued to fight for control of the colony. After a series of failed attempts, the governor finally reclaimed Jamestown on September 7. Within two weeks Bacon recaptured the city, but realizing that he would never be able to hold it, he took drastic steps: he burned Jamestown to the ground.

By October 20 Bacon's supporters controlled over two-thirds of Virginia. New leaders had been installed at all levels of the government, and the power of the coastal planters seemed broken. Then tragedy struck. On October 26 Nathaniel Bacon died of dysentery. Without Bacon's strong leadership the revolution soon faltered. The following spring British troops arrived to put an end to the rebellion. For the next hundred years, the royal governors of the British Crown and the wealthy coastal planters would dominate Virginia political life.

INTRODUCTION

Bacon's Rebellion reflects many of the contradictory themes and patterns of the early colonial period: the determination to create new communities and the willingness to uproot Native American communities in the process; the sense of new opportunities for success and the continuing influence of wealth and social prestige in a frontier world; and the challenge of creating a unified society in the face of the conflicting economic interests of coastal planters and backcountry farmers.

The seventeenth century saw thousands of English men and women risk the dangers of the Atlantic crossing, the hardships of frontier life, the threat of violence from other settlers and local Indian groups, and the often overwhelming sense of isolation that were all part of the colonizing experience. What motivated them? Many left England to escape religious persecution or, at the least, discrimination and harassment because of their dissenting religious views.

Puritans, Catholics, and Quakers all felt compelled to resist demands for allegiance to the Church of England. Given a choice between silence and exile, many chose to journey to what Europeans called the "New World." These English religious radicals were not alone in seeking freedom of worship. Jews, French Protestants, and German pietists also came to America to escape persecution.

Still other colonists faced the difficult choice of poverty or flight. The economic transformation of England from a feudal society to a market society disrupted the lives of the country's rural population of tenant farmers. Thrown off their land as wealthy landlords turned to sheep raising, thousands of these victims of an emerging capitalism became nomads and vagabonds, traveling from country towns to seaport cities in search of work. Desperation drove them to sign away several years of their lives to a ship captain or plantation owner in Virginia or Maryland in exchange for passage to America.

But if desperation prompted them to leave England,

It Matters

Grassroots Movements, Then and Now

Bacon's Rebellion is one of the first instances of a grassroots movement in American history. These movements often give voice to people who are not, or feel they are not, being heard by the government, or feel that their goals are not being considered by the government. Many things we take for granted today began as demands by grassroots movements, including the end to slavery, the direct election of senators, and women's suffrage. The antiwar movement of the 1960s, the environmental movements of the 1990s, and the antismoking movement of today are recent examples of grassroots movements. Often grassroots movements provide insights into changing values in American society, and, equally often, they arise as part of a cluster of reform movements.

or enemy vessels. Diseases unknown in England decimated settlements. Poor planning and simple ignorance of survival techniques destroyed others. Conflicts with local Indian populations produced violence, bloodshed, and atrocities on both sides. And though colonists lived far from the seats of power in Europe, the rivalries between English, French, Dutch, and Spanish governments spilled across the ocean, erupting in border raids and full-scale wars throughout the century.

Yet the records left by these colonists were not always tales of tragedy. New Englanders recorded the wonders of new vegetation and towering forests. New Yorkers described rolling farmlands, wide rivers, deep harbors. Virginians marveled at rich black soil, exotic flowers, and blooming plants. And throughout the colonies that emerged during the seventeenth and eighteenth centuries, settlers observed, with equal measures of amazement and contempt, the customs and appearances of a race of people entirely new to them: Native Americans.

dreams and expectations often motivated them too. These young men and woman agreed to years of servitude and backbreaking labor in the tobacco fields of the **Chesapeake**, without wages and with the most meager rations, because they hoped to acquire land when they were released from bondage. The promise of land was perhaps the most powerful appeal to more fortunate colonists as well. Families of modest means sold off their belongings and said their goodbyes to familiar faces and a familiar landscape, determined to build new and more independent lives for themselves in the colonies.

This expectation of opportunity was not the monopoly of English men and women. Dutch colonists, Swedes, Finns, and Germans also risked life and limb to reach America in order to improve their economic circumstances. Only one group of colonists, enslaved Africans, arrived on the mainland against their wills. Although their numbers were small in the seventeenth century, thousands of enslaved men, women, and children would become unwilling colonists in the decades that followed.

Colonists recorded their experiences in diaries, letters, journals, and reports to government, church, or trading company officials. These accounts dramatize the hardships and risks that settlers confronted and testify that many did not survive. Ships carrying colonists sank in ocean storms or fell victim to pirates

England and Colonization

■ What was the impact of the failure of the Roanoke Colony on England's colonizing effort?

■ What circumstances or conditions in England prompted people to migrate to America?

By the end of the century, twelve distinct colonies hugged the Atlantic coastline of English America. The thirteenth, Georgia, was founded in 1732. Although each colony had its own unique history, climate and geography produced four distinct regions: New England, the Middle Colonies, the Chesapeake, and the Lower South. The colonies within each region shared a common economy and labor system, or a similar religious heritage, or a special character that defined the population, such as ethnic diversity. And by the end of the century, as frontier outposts developed into well-established communities, certain institutions emerged in every colony. Thus, whether its founders had been religious refugees or wealthy businessmen, each colony developed a representative assembly, established courts, built houses of worship—and constructed jails. Car-

Chesapeake   The Chesapeake was the common term for the two colonies of Maryland and Virginia, both of which border on Chesapeake Bay.

Chronology

Settling the Mainland Colonies

1585	English colonize Roanoke Island		**1655**	Civil war in Maryland
1603	James I becomes king of England		**1660**	Restoration of English monarchy
1607	Virginia Company founds Jamestown		**1663**	Carolina chartered
1619	Virginia House of Burgesses meets		**1664**	New Netherland becomes New York
1620	Pilgrims found Plymouth Plantations		**1675**	King Philip's War in New England
1625	Charles I becomes king of England		**1676**	Bacon's Rebellion in Virginia
1630	Puritans found Massachusetts Bay Colony		**1681**	Pennsylvania chartered
1634	Lord Baltimore establishes Maryland		**1685**	James II becomes king of England
1635	Roger Williams founds Providence		**1686**	Dominion of New England established
1636	Anne Hutchinson banished from Massachusetts Pequot War in New England Connecticut settled		**1688**	Glorious Revolution in England
1642–1648	English civil war		**1689**	Leisler's Rebellion in New York
1649	Charles I executed Cromwell and Puritans come to power in England		**1691**	Massachusetts becomes royal colony
			1692	Salem witch trials
			1732	Georgia chartered

olinians may have thought they shared little in common with the people of Connecticut, but both sets of colonists were subject to English law, English trade policies, and English conflicts with rival nations. Separate, yet linked to one another and to what they affectionately called the "Mother Country" in crucial ways, between 1607 and 1700 the colonies transformed themselves from struggling settlements to complex societies.

England's First Attempts at Colonization

In July 1584, two small ships entered the calm waters between the barrier islands and the mainland of North Carolina. On board were a group of Englishmen, sent by the wealthy nobleman Sir Walter Raleigh with orders to reconnoiter the area and locate a likely spot for settlement. The men were impressed by the peaceful, inviting scene before them: a forest of cypress, sweet gums, pines, and flowering dogwood rising up from the sandy shores; the scent of flowers; and the gentle rustling of treetops filled with birds. The exhausted travelers could not fail to see the contrast between this exotic, lush environment, seemingly untamed by human efforts, and the carefully cultivated farmlands and pastures of their native land. But if they were awed, they were not naive. To protect themselves from unseen dangers, each man wore a suit of armor and carried weapons. Sometime that afternoon, the Englishmen got their first glimpse of the local population as three Indians approached in a canoe. It would be difficult to say which group was more amazed by what they saw. Despite all that they had read, and the many sketches they had seen, the Englishmen surely found these native people strange to behold, dressed as they were in loincloths, their bodies decorated with tattoos and adorned with necklaces and bracelets of shells. The Indians were perhaps equally astonished by the sight of strangers, encased in heavy metal on a humid summer's day.

The encounter passed without incident. Within a month, the Englishmen were gone, returning to make their report to the eagerly awaiting Raleigh. But the following year, a new group of Englishmen sank anchor off the North Carolina shore. These men, many of them soldiers recruited by Raleigh, settled on Roanoke Island. Among them was a 25-year-old historian, surveyor, and cartographer, Thomas Harriot, who published his remarkable account of his nation's first colonizing attempt, *A Briefe and True Report of the New Found Land of Virginia,* in 1588. In his *Briefe and True Report,* Harriot described the Indians the colonists encountered but failed to report the almost immediate clashes between natives and invaders. The Englishmen's unshakable sense of superiority, despite their dependence on the Indians for food, destroyed the possibility of cooperation. Before the year was over, Harriot and his shipmates returned to England.

Undaunted, Raleigh tried a second time in 1587, spending most of his remaining fortune to send over a hundred colonists to the area. Unfortunately, war with Spain made it impossible for Raleigh to send supplies to his colony for over three years. When a ship finally did reach the colony, the men on board could find no trace of the colonists. Instead they found abandoned ruins, and a single word carved into the bark of a nearby tree: "Croatan." Whether the Roanoke colonists had fled from attack by the Croatan Indians, or been rescued by them in the face of starvation, epidemic, or some other natural disaster, such as a severe drought, no one knows. News of the Roanoke mystery spread rapidly. So too did news that Sir Walter Raleigh had lost his entire fortune in his attempts at colonization. Thus, although Harriot's account stressed the possibilities for wealth and profit in America, the chilling outcome discouraged others from following Raleigh's lead.

Turmoil and Tensions in England

Although no one was willing to risk personal fortune on colonizing America, many English aristocrats believed the country needed to get rid of its numerous poor and, in their minds, dangerous men and women. Pamphlets suggested that the solution to crime and riots was to find a dumping ground for the thousands who had been displaced by the changing economy—desperate people without money or shelter, removed from their lands but having no new means of livelihood. As farmlands were turned into pastures for sheep that supplied the new woolens industries, the resentful evicted farmers carried signs reading "Sheep Eat Men."

The kings and their advisers also worried about the unrest stirred by growing demands for religious reform within the **Church of England.** The movement to "purify" the church had grown steadily, led by men and women who believed the church had kept too many Catholic rituals and customs despite its claim to be Protestant. For the seventeenth-century monarchs, the Stuart kings, this Puritan criticism smacked of treason since the king was not only head of the nation but also head of the Anglican Church. Mistrust between Puritan reformers and the Crown grew under King James I and his son Charles I, for both men were rumored to be secretly practicing Catholicism.

These economic and religious problems were not the only sources of tension in English society in the early decades of the century. A political struggle between the Crown and the legislative branch of the English government, the **Parliament,** was building to a crisis. In 1642 a civil war erupted, bringing together many of the threads of discontent and conflict. A Puritan army led by Oliver Cromwell overthrew the monarchy and in 1649 executed King Charles I. Cromwell's success established the supremacy of the Parliament. For almost a dozen years, the nation was a **Commonwealth,** a republic dominated by Puritans, merchants, and gentry rather than noblemen. Cromwell headed the government until his death in 1658, but to many English citizens his rule was as dictatorial as an absolute monarch's. In 1660 the Stuart family was invited to take the throne once again. For twenty-five years, a period called the **Restoration,** Charles II ruled the nation. But when the Crown passed to his brother James II, an avowed Catholic, a second revolution occurred. This time, no blood was

Church of England   The Protestant church established in the sixteenth century by King Henry VIII as England's official church; also known as the Anglican Church.

Parliament   The lawmaking branch of the English government, composed of the House of Lords, representing England's nobility, and the House of Commons, an elected body of untitled English citizens.

Commonwealth   The republic established after the victory of Oliver Cromwell in the English civil war; the Commonwealth lasted from 1649 until the monarchy was restored in 1660.

Restoration   The era following the return of monarchy to England, beginning in 1660 with King Charles II and ending in 1688 with the exile of King James II.

In 1616, London was a dirty, over-crowded city of some three hundred thousand people. Severe economic depression had driven thousands of rural people into the city, where they sought day labor, begged, or survived through theft and prostitution. The sight of so many poverty-stricken people persuaded many prosperous Londoners that their nation was over-populated. They hoped colonies in America could serve as "dumping grounds" for the poor. *Courtesy of the Trustees of the British Library.*

shed in England. James fled to the safety of France, and his Protestant daughter Mary and her Dutch husband, William, came to the throne of England. This **Glorious Revolution** of 1688 ended almost a century of political, ideological, and economic instability. By then, twelve American colonies were already perched on the mainland shores.

Settling the Chesapeake

■ What were the goals of the Virginia Company and of the Calvert family in creating their Chesapeake colonies? Did the colonies achieve these goals?

■ What events illustrate the racial, class, and religious tensions in the Chesapeake?

■ How did the Chesapeake colonists resolve conflicts within their communities?

Fears of financial ruin had prevented any Englishman from following in Sir Walter Raleigh's footsteps. But a new method of financing high-risk ventures, the **joint-stock company,** sparked new colonization efforts. English **entrepreneurs** had devised a way to share the burdens of potentially profitable but risky shipping deals. In a joint-stock company, merchants joined together and purchased shares in a venture. Any profits had to be shared by all, but likewise any losses would be absorbed by all. Two groups of investors realized that the same principles that were being applied to overseas commerce could also be applied to planting colonies. In 1603 both the Ply-

mouth Company and the London Company appealed to King James I for a charter to settle Virginia. The king agreed to both requests.

Although in theory these two joint-stock companies were rivals, neither worried much about its settlements intruding on the other's. Virginia was, after all, a huge and vaguely defined region, covering much of the Atlantic coast of North America and extending from one ocean to the other. The Plymouth Company chose a poor site for its colony, however. The rocky coast of Maine proved uninviting to the settlers, and sickness and Indian attacks soon sent the survivors hurrying home to England. With its sole rival out of the way, the London Company (now calling itself simply the Virginia Company) launched its enterprise. The first colonists did not set out until December 1606, heading far to the south of the ill-fated Maine colony. Here, near the Chesapeake Bay, they would create the first successful English colony in America.

Glorious Revolution   A term used to describe the removal of James II from the English throne and the crowning of the Protestant monarchs, William and Mary.

joint-stock company   A business financed through the sale of shares of stock to investors; the investors share in both the profits and losses from a risky venture.

entrepreneur   A person who organizes and manages a business enterprise that involves risk and requires initiative.

The Jamestown Colony

The 101 men and four boys sent by the Virginia Company aboard the *Susan Constant,* the *Godspeed,* and the *Discovery* had been tossed on the Atlantic waters for over five months when they at last entered the calm, broad waters of the Chesapeake Bay and made their way up a river they would name the James in honor of their king. Happy at last to feel dry land under their feet, the men disembarked on a small peninsula that jutted out into the river (see Map 3.1). They named their settlement **Jamestown.** If they had known what lay in store for them in the next decade, they might have sailed home at once.

The early years of this Jamestown colony were a seemingly endless series of survival challenges. The colonists discovered, too late, that they had encamped in an unhealthy spot. Summer brought intense heat, and the men were attacked by swarms of insects, bred in the wetlands that surrounded them. The water of the James was polluted by ocean salt water, making it dangerous to drink. One by one, the settlers fell ill, suffering typhus, malaria, or dysentery. Few of the men had any experience in wilderness survival. Indeed, most were gentlemen adventurers, hoping to discover gold and other precious metals just as the Spanish had in Central and South America. These adventurers, as one Englishman bluntly put it, "never knew what a day's labour meant." They assumed that they could enslave the local Indians and force them to do all the "labour."

Had they known more about the local Indians, they might not have relied on this solution. The Powhatan Confederacy, made up of some thirty Algonquin-speaking tribes on the coastal plains, was a powerful force in the Indian world of the east coast of North America. The chief of the Powhatans had forged this confederacy in the 1570s, in response to Spanish attempts at colonization. When the English arrived, the confederacy was led by Wahunsonacock, who effectively controlled tidewater Virginia and the eastern shore of Chesapeake Bay. Although Wahunsonacock's Powhatan tribe had only about forty warriors, he could count on the assistance of some three thousand others, drawn from member tribes such as the Pamunkeys, Mattoponis, and Arrohatecks. While the English adventurers expended their energies on a futile search for gold rather than on building shelters or stockpiling food for the winter, the Indians harvested their corn—and waited to see what this group of Europeans would do.

What the English did was not impressive. Lacking any farming skills, disorganized, and unaccustomed to following orders or working hard, the colonists soon

MAP 3.1 Early Chesapeake Settlement This map shows the location of both Indian and English colonial settlements in the early seventeenth century. As the English communities grew in number and size, conflicts between the Indians of the Powhatan Confederacy and the colonists also grew, eventually leading to warfare and considerable loss of life.

faced disease, starvation, and exposure to the elements. Temporary relief came when John Smith took command. Smith was hardly a well-liked man: he was overconfident and self-centered, full of exaggerated tales of his heroic deeds as a mercenary in exotic lands. He had narrowly escaped execution on the voyage from England for his role in organizing a mutiny. Smith did have some survival knowledge, however, and he did know how to discipline men. He established a "no work, no food" policy, and he negotiated with the Powhatans for corn and other supplies. When Smith left in 1609, the discipline and order he had established quickly collapsed. The original colonists and those who joined them the following spring remembered that winter as "the starving time." The desperate colonists burned their housing to keep warm and ate dogs, cats, mice, snakes, even shoe leather in their struggle to survive. Only sixty settlers were alive at winter's end.

The Powhatans had little sympathy for the desperate colonists. Even before Smith had departed, cooper-

Jamestown First permanent English settlement in mainland America, established in 1607 by the Virginia Company and named in honor of King James I.

ation between the two groups had begun to disintegrate, for despite all their problems, the English exhibited a sense of superiority and entitlement that alienated Wahunsonacock and his confederacy. By 1609 tension and resentment had turned to bloodshed, and raids and counterattacks defined Anglo-Indian relationships for over a decade. Wahunsonacock made several efforts to establish peace, but English encroachments on Indian lands made any lasting truce impossible. Wahunsonacock and his successor, Opechancanough, the chief of the Pamunkeys, recognized that dealing with the English colonists would require warfare, not words.

If the settlers were learning hard lessons in survival, the Virginia Company was learning hard lessons, too. The colony was hanging on by a thread, but the stockholders saw no profits. Their yearly expenses—passage for new colonists, supplies for old ones—gave them a new, more realistic understanding of the slow and costly nature of colonization. The Virginia Company seemed caught in an investor's nightmare, pumping good money after bad in hopes of delaying a total collapse. Prospects seemed bleak: the only gold the colonists had found was "fool's gold," and the investors could see nothing else of economic value in the Chesapeake.

Fortunately the investors were wrong. Tobacco, a weed native to the Americas, proved to be the colony's salvation. Pipe smoking had been a steady habit in England since the mid-sixteenth century, and Englishmen were a steady market for this "brown gold." The local strain of tobacco in Virginia was too harsh for English tastes, but one of the colonists, an enterprising young planter named John Rolfe, managed to transplant a milder strain of West Indian tobacco to the colony. This success changed Rolfe's life, earning him both wealth and the admiration of his neighbors. Rolfe made a second contribution to the colony soon afterward, easing the strained Indian-white relationships by his marriage to the same Indian princess, Pocahontas, who John Smith insisted had saved his life.

By 1612, the Virginia Colony was caught up in a tobacco craze as its settlers engaged in a mad race to plant and harvest as many acres of tobacco as possible. Yet the Virginia Company was unable to take full advantage of this unexpected windfall, for it had changed its policies in an effort to ease its financial burdens. In the beginning the company owned all the land but also bore all the costs of colonization. But by 1618, the company's new policy allowed individual colonists to own land if they paid their own immigration expenses. This **head right system** granted each

The Virginia House of Burgesses was the first representative assembly to be established in the British colonies. The legislators held their first session in a small Jamestown church, but by 1669, the tobacco planters who served in this assembly had moved into elegant quarters in the colonial capital of Williamsburg. The imposing building sent a clear message to all Virginians that government was the proper domain of gentlemen of wealth and social standing. *Library of Congress.*

male colonist a deed for 50 acres of land for himself and for every man, woman, or child whose voyage he financed. In this way the Virginia Company shifted the cost of populating and developing the colony to others. But the head rights also ended the company's monopoly on the suddenly valuable farmland.

Other important concessions to the colonists soon followed. The military-style discipline instituted by John Smith and continued by later leaders was abandoned. At the same time, a measure of self-government was allowed. In 1618 the company created an elected, representative lawmaking body called the **House of Burgesses,** which gave the landholders—tobacco

head right system The grant of 50 acres of land for each settler brought over to Virginia by a colonist.

House of Burgesses The elected lawmaking body of Virginia, established by the Virginia Company in 1618; the assembly first met in 1619.

planters—of Virginia a measure of control over local political matters. In effect, a business enterprise had finally become a colonial society.

The Virginia Company did retain one of the colony's earliest traditions: a bad relationship with the Powhatan Indians. By 1622, the English seemed to have the upper hand, for the population had grown and tobacco had brought a measure of prosperity. As Virginia planters pressed farther inland, seizing Indian land along local rivers, the new Powhatan chief, Opechanacanough, decided to strike back. On what the Christian settlers called Good Friday, he mounted a deadly attack on Jamestown, killing a quarter of the colonists in a single day. The company responded as quickly as it could, sending weapons to the Virginians. For two years, war raged between Indians and the English. Although the bloodshed became less frequent by 1625, a final peace was not reached for a decade. By that time, disease and violence had taken its toll on the Powhatans. Once over forty thousand strong, they had dwindled to fewer than five hundred people.

The Good Friday Massacre, as the English called it, brought important changes for the colony. King James I had already begun an investigation of the Virginia Company's management record—and the colony's growing profit potential. When he learned of the renewed conflict between Indians and colonists, he decided to take action. The king took away the company's charter and declared Virginia to be a royal possession.

If the king's advisers had tallied the cost in human life for the planting of this first English colony in the same manner that the company tallied expenses in pence and pounds, they would have found the outcome sobering. By 1624, only 1,275 of the 8,500 settlers who had arrived since 1607 remained alive. Fortunately, no other English colony would pay such a price for its creation.

Maryland: A Catholic Refuge

As Virginians spread out along the riverways of their colony, searching for good tobacco land, plans for a second Chesapeake colony were brewing in England. The man behind this project was not a merchant or entrepreneur, and profit was not his motive. George Calvert, the wealthy Catholic who King Charles I had just made Lord Baltimore, was motivated by a strong concern for the fate of England's dwindling number of Catholics. He envisioned a religious refuge in America, a safe haven in the face of growing harassment and discrimination against members of his faith. Calvert acquired a charter from the king that granted him a generous tract of land east and north of Chesapeake Bay. Here, Calvert planned to establish a highly traditional society, dominated by powerful noblemen and populated by obedient tenant farmers. Thus, in the 1630s, George Calvert was a reactionary thinker with a radical vision.

Calvert never realized his dream. He died before a single colonist could be recruited for his Maryland.

Baltimore was founded in 1629 and served as a shipping center for Maryland tobacco growers. By 1752, when this view was drawn, it had begun to show signs of developing into a prosperous port city. After the American Revolution, Baltimore expanded and by the 1790s boasted a population of over twenty thousand. *"Baltimore 1752," from a sketch by John Moale, Esq. Maryland Historical Society, Baltimore.*

His oldest son, Cecilius Calvert, the second Lord Baltimore, took on the task of establishing the colony. To Calvert's surprise, few English Catholics showed any enthusiasm for the project. When the first boatload of colonists sailed up the Chesapeake Bay in 1634, most of these two hundred volunteers were young Protestants seeking a better life. Calvert wisely adopted the head right system developed by the Virginia Company to attract additional settlers. The lure of land ownership, he realized, was the key to populating Maryland.

Calvert's colony quickly developed along the same lines as neighboring Virginia. Marylanders immediately turned to planting the profitable **staple crop,** tobacco, and joined the scramble for good riverfront land. Like the Virginians, these colonists used trickery, threats, and violence to pry acres of potential farmland from resisting Indians. By midcentury, the Chesapeake colonies could claim a modest prosperity, even though their populations grew slowly. But they could not claim a peaceful existence. The political crises that shook England during the mid-seventeenth century sent shock waves across the Atlantic Ocean to the American shores. These crises intertwined with local tensions among colonists or between colonists and Indians to produce rebellions, raids, and civil wars.

Troubles on the Chesapeake

In Maryland, tensions ran high between the Catholic minority, who had political influence beyond their numbers because of Lord Baltimore's support, and the Protestant majority in the colony. But with the rise to power of the Puritan leader Oliver Cromwell and his Commonwealth government in England, Calvert realized that his power to protect Maryland's Catholics was in jeopardy. Hoping to avoid any open persecution of the Catholic colonists, Calvert offered religious toleration to both Protestant and Catholic Marylanders. In 1649 he issued the innovative Toleration Act, protecting all Christians from being "troubled [or] molested . . . in respect of his or her religion." Calvert's liberal policy offended the staunchly Puritan Cromwell, who promptly repealed the act. In 1654 the Puritan-dominated Parliament went further, seizing Maryland from the Calvert family and establishing a Protestant assembly in the colony. The outcome was exactly as Calvert had feared: a wave of anti-Catholic persecution swept over Maryland.

Within a year, a bloody civil war was raging in Maryland. Protestant forces won the fiercely fought Battle of the Severn, but their victory proved futile for, once again, events in England made their impact

The ceramic jar shown above was used to store the tobacco that Europeans and Englishmen loved to smoke, sniff, or chew. Most of that tobacco was grown in Virginia and Maryland, in fields worked by slaves and servants on plantations owned by white colonists. The jar was valued both for its attractive appearance and its practical use, for it was elaborately decorated and it kept the tobacco fresh. It also served as a free advertisement for the "Carolina" brand of tobacco inside. *Colonial Williamsburg Foundation.*

felt on the colony. Oliver Cromwell died, and soon afterward the monarchy was restored. Charles II returned Maryland to the Calvert family, who had always been loyal supporters of the Stuart dynasty. Despite this reversal of fortunes, Protestants in Maryland continued their struggle, organizing unsuccessful rebellions in 1659, 1676, and again in 1681. Then, in 1689, William and Mary ascended to the throne of England in the Glorious Revolution, and Maryland's Protestants rallied once again. Led by an unlikely looking hero, the stooped and nearly crippled minister **John Coode,** colonists formed an army they called

staple crop   A basic or necessary agricultural item, produced for sale or export.

John Coode   Leader of a rebel army, the Protestant Association, that won control of Maryland in 1691.

the Protestant Association. By 1691, Coode had persuaded the Crown to make Maryland a royal colony. The story did not end here, however. In 1715 the fourth Lord Baltimore gave up the Catholic faith and joined the Church of England, leading the Crown to restore Maryland yet again to the Calverts.

Virginia was less affected by religious controversy than its neighbor. There, colonists were primarily Anglicans although small communities of Quakers, Puritans, and even members of the radical Dutch Labadist sect were scattered throughout Virginia. Religious differences, however, did not spark hostilities. Instead, the fault lines in Virginia society developed between the wealthy planters of the tidewater region and the ambitious newcomers seeking to make their fortunes in the backcountry.

The antagonism between the western, or backcountry, colonists and their more prosperous tidewater rivals was coming to a head as tobacco prices fell in the 1660s. It was in this highly volatile atmosphere that the brash young Nathaniel Bacon rose to challenge the established order of the Virginia Colony. While Bacon's rebellion ultimately failed after the death of its leader, many of the ideas behind the rebellion would resurface one hundred years later during the events leading up to the Revolutionary War.

Colonial Chesapeake Life

Every aspect of life in the Chesapeake colonies, observers noted, seemed to be shaped by tobacco. Its cultivation set rhythms of work and play in both Maryland and Virginia that were dramatically different from those in England. Planting, tending, harvesting, and drying tobacco leaves took almost ten months of the year, beginning in late winter and ending just before Christmas. In the short period between the holiday and the start of a new planting cycle, Chesapeake planters, their families, and their servants worked frantically to catch up on other, neglected farm chores. They did repairs, sewed and mended, built new cabins and sheds, cut timber and firewood. They also compressed what meager social life they had into these winter weeks, engaging—whenever possible—in hasty courtships followed by marriage.

Because tobacco quickly exhausted the soil in which it grew, planters moved frequently to new acres on their estates or to newly acquired lands farther west. Because they rarely stayed in one place very long, planters placed little value on permanent homes or on creating permanent social institutions such as schools. Throughout the century, Chesapeake colonists

sacrificed many of the familiar forms of community life to the demands of their profitable crop.

Planters engaged in an exhaustive search for a labor force large enough and cheap enough to ensure their profits. As long as poverty and social unrest plagued England, they found the workers they needed from their homeland. Over 175,000 young, single, and impoverished immigrants flooded the Chesapeake during the seventeenth century, their passages paid by the ship captain or the planter. In exchange for their transatlantic voyage, these **indentured servants** toiled for several years in the tobacco fields without pay. Planters preferred a male work force, for they shared the general European assumption that farming was a masculine activity. As a result, these colonies had an unusual population profile: men outnumbered women in most areas of Virginia and Maryland by 3 to 1. In some areas, the ratio was a remarkable 6 to 1 until the end of the century.

For these indentured servants, and often for their masters as well, life was short and brutal. They spent long, backbreaking days in the fields. Their food rations were meager, their clothing and bedding inadequate, and their shoulders frequently scarred by the master's whip. Servants wrote letters home describing their miserable existence. "People cry out day, and night," wrote one young man, who told his father that most servants would give up "any limb to be in England again."

Most servants also expressed doubts that they would survive to win their freedom. In many cases, they were correct. Disease and malnutrition took the lives of perhaps a quarter of these bound laborers. Free colonists fared little better than servants. Typhus, dysentery, and malaria killed thousands. Over one-quarter of the infants born in the Chesapeake did not live to see their first birthdays; another quarter of the population died before reaching the age of 20. Early death, the skewed ratio of men to women, and high infant mortality combined to create a **demographic disaster** that continued until the last decades of the century.

By the end of the 1600s, the labor force had become increasingly biracial. The steady supply of English

---

indentured servants Compulsory service for a fixed period of time, usually from four to seven years, most often agreed to in exchange for passage to the colonies; a labor contract called an indenture spelled out the terms of the agreement.

demographic disaster The outcome of a high death rate and an unbalanced ratio of men to women in the Chesapeake colonies.

workers dried up as economic conditions in England improved. At the same time, the cost of purchasing an African slave declined. During the next century, the shift from English servants to African slaves would be completed.

New England: Colonies of Dissenters

■ Why did English religious dissenters settle in New England?

■ What type of society did the Puritans create in Massachusetts?

■ How did the Puritan authorities deal with dissent?

While Captain John Smith was barking orders at the settlers in Jamestown, some religious dissenters in a small English village were preparing to escape King James's wrath. These residents of Scrooby Village were people of modest means, without powerful political allies or a popular cause. But they had gone one step further than the majority of Puritans, who continued to be members of the Anglican Church despite their criticisms of it. The Scrooby villagers had left the church altogether, forming a separate sect of their own. James I despised these **separatists** and declared his intention to drive them out of England—or worse.

The Scrooby separatists took James's threats seriously. In 1611 they fled to the city of Leyden in the Netherlands. They saw themselves as **Pilgrims** on a spiritual journey to religious freedom. The Dutch welcomed them warmly, but several Pilgrims feared that the comfortable life they had found in Holland was diminishing their devotion to God. By 1620, **William Bradford** was leading a small group of these transplanted English men and women on a second pilgrimage—to America.

The Plymouth Colony

The Leyden Pilgrims were joined by other separatists in England. Together, they set sail on an old, creaky ship called the *Mayflower*. On board, too, were a band of "strangers," outsiders to the religious sect who simply wanted passage to America. Crammed together in close and uncomfortable quarters, Pilgrims and strangers weathered a nightmare of violent storms and choppy waters. After nine weeks at sea, the captain anchored the *Mayflower* at Cape Cod, almost 1,000 miles north of the original Virginia destination (see Map 3.2). The exhausted passengers did not complain; they fell to the ground to give thanks. Once

The Bible was the most cherished book, and often the only book, in a colonist's home. To safeguard this treasure, many Pilgrims stored their Bibles in hand-carved boxes like this one belonging to William Bradford. This box, once decorated with the lion and unicorn symbol of England, was politicized during the American Revolution, when the British lion was scraped off. *Pilgrim Society, Pilgrim Hall Museum.*

the thrill of standing on dry land had passed, however, many of them sank into depression. The early winter landscape of New England was dreary, alien, and disturbingly empty. William Bradford's own wife, Dorothy, may have committed suicide in the face of this bleak landscape.

Talk of setting sail for Virginia spread through the ranks of the ship's crew and the passengers. Mutiny was in the air. To calm the situation, Bradford negotiated an unusual contract with every man aboard the ship—Pilgrim, crew, servant, and stranger.

This document, known as the **Mayflower Compact,** granted political rights to any man willing to remain

separatists English Protestants who chose to leave the Church of England because they believed it was corrupt.

Pilgrims A small group of separatists who left England in search of religious freedom and sailed to America on the *Mayflower* in 1620.

William Bradford The separatist who led the Pilgrims to America; he became the first governor of Plymouth Plantations.

Mayflower Compact An agreement drafted in 1620 when the Pilgrims reached America that granted political rights to all male colonists who would abide by the colony's laws.

MAP 3.2 New England Settlement in the Seventeenth and Early Eighteenth Centuries This map shows the major towns and cities of New England and their settlement dates. By the end of the seventeenth century, the region had four colonies. Colonists seeking land moved west and south toward the New York border and north toward French Canada. Those involved in trade, shipping, and crafts migrated to the seaport cities.

and to abide by whatever laws the new colony enacted. Here was an unheard-of opportunity for poor men to participate in governing themselves. All agreed, and the new colony of Plymouth Plantations began to prepare for the long winter ahead.

In Plymouth Plantations, as in Virginia, the first winter brought sickness, hunger, and death. Half of the colonists did not survive. When a Patuxet Indian, **Squanto,** came upon the remaining men and women in the spring of 1621, he found them huddled in flimsy shelters, trapped between a menacing forest and a dangerous ocean. Squanto sympathized with their confusion and their longings for home, for he had crossed the Atlantic in 1605 aboard an English trading ship and spent several years in an alien environment. He also understood what it meant to be a survivor, for the Pilgrims had settled where his own village had once stood. His entire family and tribe had been wiped out by disease carried by English traders and fishermen.

Squanto helped the colonists, teaching them how to plant corn, squash, and pumpkins. Perhaps his greatest service, however, was in helping William Bradford negotiate a peace treaty with Massasoit, leader of the local Wampanoag Indians. Agreeing that "if any did unjustly war against him, we would aid him," the Pilgrims got a similar pledge of assistance from Massasoit. The Wampanoags also agreed to spread the word to neighboring Indian communities that the Pilgrims were allies rather than enemies. The combined efforts of Squanto and Massasoit saved the Plymouth Colony, and in the fall of 1621, English settlers and Indian guests sat down together in a traditional harvest celebration of thanksgiving.

Plymouth grew slowly, its colonists earning their livings by farming, fishing, and lumbering. A few Pilgrims grew wealthy by developing a fur trade with the Indians. Unlike the Jamestown settlers, the Plymouth community worked hard for many years to preserve good relations with the local Indians. They purchased land rather than seizing it, and they proved to be strong allies when warfare broke out between Massasoit's people and their enemies. In fact, the colonists proved to be such ferocious fighters that they were known as Wotoroguenarge, or "Cutthroats."

Massachusetts Bay and Its Settlers

A second colony soon appeared beside Plymouth Plantations. In 1629 a group of prosperous Puritans, led by the 41-year-old lawyer and landowner **John Winthrop,** secured a charter for their Massachusetts Bay Company from King Charles I. These Puritans had grown increasingly worried about the government's attitude toward dissenters. The systematic harassment they suffered, coupled with a deepening economic depression in England, spurred them to set sail for New England. Advertising their colony as "a refuge for many who [God] means to save out of the general calamity," Winthrop and his colleagues had no trouble recruiting like-minded Puritans to migrate.

From the beginning, the Massachusetts Bay Colony had several advantages over Jamestown and Plymouth

Squanto A Patuxet Indian who taught the Pilgrims survival techniques in America and acted as translator for the colonists.

John Winthrop One of the founders of Massachusetts Bay Colony and the colony's first governor.

This statue of Anne Hutchinson conveys her as a courageous and determined woman. Massachusetts Bay's Puritan officials would not have approved. They considered her a dangerous heretic who overstepped her proper place as a woman by challenging the established religious and political authorities. Like Roger Williams, Anne Hutchinson was exiled from the colony for her unorthodox views. *Picture Research Consultant & Archives.*

Plantations. The colonists were well equipped and well prepared for their venture. The company had even sent an advance crew over to clear fields and build shelters for the newcomers. As religious tensions and economic distress increased in England, Massachusetts attracted thousands of settlers. This **Great Migration** continued until Oliver Cromwell's Puritan army took control of England.

While profit motivated the Virginia colonists and a desire to worship in peace prompted the Pilgrims to sail to America, the Puritans of Massachusetts were people with a mission. They hoped to create a model Christian community, a "city upon a hill" that would persuade all English men and women that Puritanism promoted godliness and prosperity. John Winthrop set out their mission in a speech to the passengers aboard the *Arabella.* "The eyes of all peoples are upon us," Winthrop warned, and, more importantly, God was watching them as well. If they abandoned or forgot their mission, the consequences would surely include divine punishment.

This sense of mission influenced the physical as well as spiritual shape of the colony. Massachusetts colonists created tight-knit farming villages and small seaport towns in which citizens could monitor one another's behavior as well as come together in prayer. This settlement pattern fit well with the realities of New England's climate and terrain, since the short growing season and the rocky soil made large, isolated plantations based on staple crops impossible. The colonists, homesick for English villages in regions such as East Anglia, did their best to reproduce familiar architecture and placement of public buildings. The result was often a hub-and-spoke design, with houses tightly clustered around a village green or common pasture, a church beside this green, and most of the fields and farms within walking distance of this village center. This design set natural limits on the size of any village because beyond a certain point— usually measured in a winter's walk to church—a farm family was considered outside the community circle. As a town's population grew and the available farmland was farther from the village green, settlers on the outer rim of the town usually chose to create a new community for themselves. The Puritans called this process of establishing a new village "hiving off."

Like Massachusetts, New Haven and the other New England settlements that followed were societies of families. Many, although not all, of the colonists arriving during the Great Migration came as members of a family. Of course, each ship carried unmarried male and female servants too, but unlike in the Chesapeake, the gender ratio in the northern colonies was never dramatically skewed. Imbalances between the sexes did occur in border towns decimated by war with the Indians or in older communities where land was scarce and the young men ventured farther west. On the whole, however, the number of men and women

Great Migration   The movement of Puritans from England to America in the 1630s, caused by political and religious unrest in England.

was roughly equal. And, unlike their Chesapeake counterparts, New Englanders never endured a demographic disaster. The cool temperatures and clean drinking water made the region an extremely healthy place for Europeans, healthier than England itself. Infant mortality was low, and most children lived to reach marriageable age and produce families of their own. A couple could expect to live a long life together and raise a family of five to seven children. One outcome of this longevity was a rare phenomenon in the seventeenth-century English world: grandparents.

Both Puritans and neighboring Pilgrims spoke of the family as "a little commonwealth," the building block on which the larger society was constructed. They set a high priority on obedience in child rearing, in part because they believed that sinfulness and disobedience were the twin results of **original sin.** Breaking a child's will was thus a necessary step toward ensuring the child's salvation. The larger society actively supported a parent's right to demand respect and a child's duty to obey. In fact, Massachusetts law made criticizing a parent a crime punishable by death. The penalty was rarely administered, but the existence of such a harsh law shows the importance of obedience within the family.

A wife was also expected to obey her husband. Puritan ministers reinforced this ideal of a **hierarchy,** or well-defined chain of command, within a family. "Wives," they preached, "are part of the House and Family, and ought to be under a Husband's Government: they should Obey their own Husbands." A husband, however, was bound by sacred obligations to care for and be respectful toward his wife. He must rule his household, he was instructed, without "rigour, haughtiness, harshness, severity; but with the greatest love, gentleness, kindness, tenderness." Marriage involved many practical duties as well. Wives were expected to strive to be "notable housewives"— industrious, economical managers of resources and skilled at several crafts. They were to spin yarn, sew, cook, bake, pickle, butcher farm animals, cure meat, churn butter, and set cheeses. In close-knit New England communities, women were able to help one another by exchanging butter for eggs, assisting with a neighbor's childbirth, or nursing the sick back to health. Husbands were expected to labor in the fields, or in the shop, in order to provide for their families.

Although obligated to be tender and loving, the husband controlled the resources of the family. This was true in all English colonies, although in the Chesapeake, early death often left the wife in charge of the family farm or shop and its profits until sons came of age. Under English law, a married woman, or

femme couverte, lost many of her legal rights because she came under the protection and governance of her husband. Married women could not acquire, sell, or bequeath property to another person. They could not sue or be sued or claim the use of any wages they earned. They could gain such basic legal rights only through special contracts made with their husbands. Puritan communities, however, frowned on any such arrangements. In the "little commonwealth" of the family, a man was the undisputed head of the household and thus had authority over all its economic resources and all its members. He also represented the family's interests in the realm of politics. No matter how wise or wealthy a woman might become, she was denied a political voice.

Government in Puritan Massachusetts

In order to create the "city upon a hill" the directors of the Massachusetts Bay Company needed, and expected, the full cooperation of all colonists. This did not mean that all colonists had an equal voice or an equal role in fulfilling this vision of a perfect community. During his speech aboard the *Arabella*, John Winthrop made it clear that the "wilderness Zion" was not intended to be an egalitarian society. Like most of his audience, Winthrop believed that it was natural and correct for some people to be rich and some to be poor—"some high and eminent in power and dignity, others mean and in subjugation." Women, children, servants, young men, and adult men without property owed obedience to others in most English communities. But in Massachusetts, there were further limitations on participation. Not even all free males with property were granted a voice in governing the colony. The first government, in fact, consisted solely of Winthrop and the eleven other stockholders of the company who had emigrated to New England. Later, the company relaxed its control and allowed a

---

original sin In Christian doctrine, the condition of sinfulness that all humans share because of Adam and Eve's disobedience to God in the Garden of Eden.

hierarchy A system in which people or things are ranked above one another.

femme couverte From the French for "covered woman"; a legal term for a married woman; this legal status limited women's rights, denying them the right to sue or be sued, own or sell property, or earn wages.

representative assembly to be elected, but the qualifications for political participation in electing these representatives or serving in the assembly were dramatically different from those set by Maryland or Virginia. No man in Massachusetts had a full political voice unless he was an acknowledged church member, not just a churchgoer. Church membership, or **sainthood,** was granted only after a person testified to an experience of "saving grace," a moment of intense awareness of God's power and a reassuring conviction of personal salvation. Thus Massachusetts made religious qualifications as important as gender or economic status in the colony's political life.

Massachusetts differed from the Chesapeake colonies in other significant ways. The colony's government enforced biblical law as well as English civil and criminal law. This meant that the government regulated a colonist's religious beliefs and practices, style of dress, sexual conduct, and personal behavior. For example, every colonist was required to attend church and to observe the Sabbath as Puritan custom dictated. The church played a role in supervising business dealings, parent-child relationships, and marital life.

In the early decades of the colony, the Puritan sense of mission left little room for religious toleration. Colonial leaders saw no reason to welcome anyone who disagreed with their religious views. English America was large, they argued, and people of other faiths could settle elsewhere. Winthrop's government was particularly aggressive against members of a new sect called the **Quakers,** who came to Massachusetts on a mission of their own—to convert Puritans to their faith. Quakers entering the colony were beaten, imprisoned, or branded with hot irons. If they returned, they were hanged. Puritan leaders showed just as little tolerance toward members of their own communities who criticized or challenged the rules of the Bay Colony or the beliefs of its church. They drove out men and women who they perceived to be **heretics,** or religious traitors, including Roger Williams and Anne Hutchinson.

Almost anyone could be labeled a heretic—even a Puritan minister. Only a year after the colony was established, the church at Salem invited **Roger Williams** to serve as its assistant minister. His electrifying sermons and his impressive knowledge of Scripture attracted a devoted following. But he soon attracted the attention of local authorities as well, for his sermons were highly critical of the colonial government. From his pulpit, Williams condemned political leaders for seizing Indian land, calling their tactics of intimidation and violence a "National Sinne." He also denounced laws requiring church attendance.

True religious faith, he said, was a matter of personal commitment. It could not and should not be compelled. "Forced religion," he told his congregation, "stinks in God's nostrils."

In 1635 John Winthrop's government banished Roger Williams from the colony. With snow thick on the ground, Williams left Salem and sought refuge with the Narragansett Indians. When spring came, many of his Salem congregation joined him in exile. Together, in 1635, they created a community called Providence that welcomed dissenters of all kinds, including Quakers, Jews, and Baptists.

Providence also attracted other Massachusetts colonists tired of the tight controls imposed on their lives by Winthrop and his colleagues. In 1644 the English government granted Williams a charter for his colony, which he eventually called Rhode Island. Within their borders, Rhode Islanders firmly established the principle of separation of church and state.

Soon after the Massachusetts authorities rid the colony of Roger Williams, a new challenge to their religious precepts and theocratic government arose. In 1634 Puritan **Anne Hutchinson,** her husband, William, and their several children emigrated to Massachusetts. The Hutchinsons made an impressive addition to the colonial community. He was a successful merchant. She had received an exceptionally fine education from her father and was eloquent, witty, and well versed in Scripture. In addition, she was clearly knowledgeable about the religious debates of the day. Like Williams, Hutchinson put little stock in the power of a minister or in any rules of behavior to assist an individual in his or her search for salvation.

---

sainthood Full membership in a Puritan church.

Quakers Members of the Society of Friends, a radical Protestant sect that believed in the equality of men and women, pacifism, and the presence of a divine "inner light" in every individual.

heretic A person who does not behave in accordance with an established attitude, doctrine, or principle, usually in religious matters.

Roger Williams Puritan minister banished from Massachusetts for criticizing its religious rules and government policies; in 1635, he founded Providence, a community based on religious freedom and the separation of church and state.

Anne Hutchinson A religious leader banished from Massachusetts in 1636 because of her criticism of the colonial government and what were judged to be heretical beliefs.

She believed that only God's grace could save a person's soul. And she declared that God made a "covenant of grace," or a promise of salvation, that did not depend on any church, minister, or worship service.

Hutchinson's opinions, aired in popular meetings at her home, disturbed the Puritan authorities. That she was a woman made her outspoken defiance even more shocking. Men like John Winthrop believed that women ought to be silent in the church and had no business criticizing male authorities, particularly ministers and **magistrates,** or government officials. A surprising number of Puritans, however, were untroubled by Hutchinson's sex. Male merchants and craftsmen who lacked political rights because they were not members of the saintly elect welcomed her attacks on these authorities. Hutchinson also attracted Puritan saints who resented the tight grip of the colonial government on their business, personal, and social lives.

In the end, none of Hutchinson's supporters could protect her against the determined opposition of the Puritan leadership. In 1637 she was arrested and brought to trial. Although she was in the last months of a troubled pregnancy, her judges forced her to stand throughout their long, exhausting, repetitive examination. Hutchinson seemed to be winning the battle of words despite her physical discomfort, but eventually she blundered. In one of her answers, she seemed to claim that she had direct communication with God. Such a claim went far beyond the acceptable bounds of Puritan belief. Triumphantly, John Winthrop and his colleagues declared her a heretic, "unfit to our society." They banished her from Massachusetts. Even after her departure, the government seemed to worry about her influence. They encouraged rumors that she was a witch and claimed that the miscarriage she suffered shortly after the trial indicated a demonic fetus.

Many Puritans who left Massachusetts did so by choice, not because they were banished. For example, in 1636 the Reverend Thomas Hooker and his entire Newton congregation abandoned Massachusetts and resettled in the Connecticut River valley. They sought freedom from Winthrop's domination, and the richer soils of the river valley attracted them. Other Puritan congregations followed these Newton families. By 1639 the Connecticut Valley towns of Hartford, Wethersfield, and Windsor had drafted their own governments, and in 1644 they united with the Saybrook settlement at the mouth of the Connecticut River to create the colony of Connecticut. In 1660 the independent New Haven community joined them.

Other Bay colonists, searching for new or better lands, made their way north to what later became Maine and New Hampshire. New Hampshire settlers won a charter for their own colony in 1679, but Maine remained part of Massachusetts until it became a state in 1820.

Indian Suppression

Although the Puritan colonists hoped to create a godly community, they were often motivated by greed and jealousy. Between 1636 and the 1670s, New Englanders came into conflict with one another over desirable land. They also waged particularly violent warfare against the Indians of the region.

When the Connecticut Valley towns sprang up, for example, Winthrop tried to assert Bay Colony authority over them. His motives were personal: he and his friends had expected to develop the valley area lands themselves someday. The Connecticut settlers ignored Winthrop's claims and successfully rebuffed his attempts to block their independence from Massachusetts. But they could not ignore the Indians of the area, who understood clearly the threat that English settlers posed to their territories and their way of life. Sassacus, leader of the Pequots, hoped that an armed struggle would break out between Winthrop and the new Connecticut towns, destroying them both. Instead, however, the two English rivals concentrated on destroying the Pequots.

By 1636, the **Pequot War** had begun, with the Indians under attack from both Massachusetts and Connecticut armies and their Indian allies, the Narragansetts and the Mohicans. Mounting a joint effort, the colonists targeted the Pequot town of Mystic Village. Although the village was defenseless and contained only civilians, Captain John Mason gave the orders for the attack. Captain John Underhill of the Massachusetts army recorded the slaughter with obvious satisfaction: "Many [Pequots] were burnt in the fort, both men, women, and children." When the survivors tried to surrender to the Narragansetts, Puritan soldiers killed them. The brutal war did not end

magistrate   A civil officer charged with administering the law.

Pequot War   Conflict in 1636 between the Pequot Indians inhabiting eastern Connecticut and the colonists of Massachusetts Bay and Connecticut: the Indians were destroyed and driven from the area.

No portrait of Metacomet, or King Philip, was painted during his lifetime. In this nineteenth-century painting, Metacomet wears traditional New England Indian clothing, yet he is armed with a European musket. This provides a stark reminder that even the bitterest enemies borrowed from one another's culture. *Library of Congress.*

settlements, the colonists retaliated by burning Indian crops and villages and selling Indian captives into slavery. By the end of the year, Metacomet had forged an alliance with the Narragansetts and several small regional tribes. Metacomet's early, devastating raids on white settlements terrified the colonists, but soon the casualties grew on both sides. Atrocities were committed by everyone involved in this struggle, which the English called King Philip's War. With the help of Iroquois troops sent by the governor of New York, the colonists finally defeated the Wampanoags. Metacomet was murdered, and his head was impaled on a stick.

Indian objections to colonial expansion in New England had been silenced. Indeed, few native peoples remained to offer resistance of any sort. Several tribes had been wiped out entirely in the war, or their few survivors sold into slavery in the Caribbean. Those who escaped enslavement or death scattered to the north and the west. The victory had cost the English dearly also. More than two thousand New England colonists lost their lives as the war spread from Plymouth to nearby settlements. And the war left a legacy of hate that prompted Indian tribes west of Massachusetts to block Puritan expansion whenever possible. The costs of New England's Indian policy prompted colonial leaders in other regions to try less aggressive tactics in dealing with local Indians. For the Wampanoags, the Narragansetts, and the Pequots, however, this decision came too late.

Change and Reaction in England and New England

Both Pilgrim and Puritan leaders had expected the broad expanse of the Atlantic Ocean to protect their colonies from the political turmoil and religious tensions that wracked seventeenth-century England. Like their Chesapeake counterparts, both were wrong. From the beginning, of course, Puritan migration to New England had been prompted by Charles I's

until all the Pequot men had been killed and the women and children sold into slavery. Connecticut claimed credit for this victory and, despite the massacre at Mystic, Massachusetts grudgingly conceded. If the Narragansett Indians believed their alliance with Winthrop provided some protection against English aggression, they were mistaken. Within five years the Puritans had assassinated the Narragansett chief, an act of insurance against problems with these Indian allies.

For almost three decades, an uneasy peace existed between New England colonists and Indians. But the struggle over the land continued. When war broke out again, it was two longtime allies—the Plymouth colonists and the Wampanoags—who took up arms against each other. By 1675, the friendship between these two groups had been eroded by Pilgrim demands for new Indian lands. Chief **Metacomet,** known to the English as King Philip, made the difficult decision to resist. When Metacomet used **guerrilla tactics** effectively, staging raids on white

Metacomet A Wampanoag chief, known to the English as King Philip, who led the Indian resistance to colonial expansion in New England in 1675.

guerrilla tactics A method of warfare in which small bands of fighters in occupied territory harass and attack their enemies, often in surprise raids; the Indians used these tactics during King Philip's War.

hostility to dissenters. When Oliver Cromwell and his Puritan armies challenged the Stuart king in 1642, Bay Colony settlers rejoiced. Many chose to return home to fight with Cromwell's armies. Throughout the decade, the Massachusetts population shrank.

Massachusetts faced a crisis in the post–civil war years. The sense of mission and the religious commitment that had accompanied its founding seemed to be declining. Few native-born colonists petitioned for full membership, or sainthood, in their local churches, perhaps because of their growing involvement with trade and commerce. And few new saints migrated to the Bay Colony after Cromwell's victory or during the Restoration era. In fact, most of the newcomers in the 1660s were not Puritans at all but Anglicans or members of other Protestant groups seeking economic opportunities. The Bay Colony leaders could not prevent them from settling, as John Winthrop had once done, for King Charles II would not allow it.

The decline in religious zeal troubled ministers and government officials alike, for it marked a sharp decline in eligible voters and officeholders. It troubled the saints, who feared their own children would never join the church and thus never become full citizens in the colony. The problem was made worse by the growing demands of prosperous non-Puritan men for an active role in the government. Some towns began to compromise, allowing men of property and good standing in the community to participate in local decision making. But the saints were not willing to set aside the church membership requirement. In 1662 they decided to introduce the **Half-Way Covenant,** an agreement that allowed the children of church members to join the church even if they did not make a convincing declaration of their own salvation. This compromise kept political power in the hands of Puritans—for the moment.

Pressures from England could not be dealt with so easily, however. Charles II cast a doubtful eye on a colony that sometimes ignored English civil law if it conflicted with biblical demands. In 1683 Charles insisted that the Bay Colony revise its charter to weaken the influence of biblical teachings and eliminate the stringent voting requirements. The Massachusetts government said no. With that, Charles revoked the charter. Massachusetts remained in political limbo until 1685, when James II came to the throne. Then conditions worsened.

In an effort to centralize administration of his growing American empire, King James II combined several of the northern colonies into one large unit under direct royal control. This megacolony, the **Do-minion of New England,** included Massachusetts, Rhode Island, Connecticut, Plymouth Plantations, and the newly acquired colonies of New Jersey and New York. James expected the Dominion to increase the **patronage,** or political favors, he could provide to his loyal supporters—favors such as generous land grants or colonial administrative appointments. He also expected to increase revenues by imposing duties and taxes on colonial goods in the vast region he now controlled.

What King James did not expect was how strongly colonists resented his Dominion and the man he chose to govern it. That man was the arrogant and greedy Sir Edmund Andros. Andros immediately offended New England Puritans by establishing the Church of England as the official religion of the new colony. Then he added insult to injury by commandeering a Puritan church in Boston for Anglican worship. Andros also alienated many non-Puritans in Massachusetts by abolishing the representative assembly there. These men had been struggling to be included in the assembly, not to have the assembly dismantled. Andros's high-handed tactics united Massachusetts colonists who had been at odds with each other. One sign of this cooperation surfaced when the Dominion governor imposed new taxes: saints and nonsaints alike refused to pay them.

When Boston citizens received news of the Glorious Revolution, they imprisoned Edmund Andros and shipped him back to England to stand trial as a traitor to the nation's new Protestant government. Massachusetts Puritans hoped to be rewarded for their patriotism, but they were quickly disappointed. Although William and Mary abolished the Dominion, they chose not to restore the Bay Colony charter. In 1691 Massachusetts became a royal colony, its governor appointed by the Crown. **Suffrage,** or voting rights, was granted to all free males who met

---

Half-Way Covenant An agreement (1662) that gave partial membership in Puritan churches to the children of church members even if they had not had a "saving faith" experience.

Dominion of New England A megacolony created in 1686 by James II that brought Massachusetts, Plymouth Plantations, Connecticut, Rhode Island, New Jersey, and New York under the control of one royal governor; William and Mary dissolved the Dominion when they came to the throne in 1689.

patronage Jobs or favors distributed on a political basis, usually as rewards for loyalty or service.

suffrage The right to vote.

the standard English **property requirement.** Church membership would never again be a criterion for citizenship in the colony.

Over the course of its sixty-year history, Massachusetts had undergone many significant changes. The Puritan ideal of small, tightly knit farming communities whose members worshiped together and shared common values and goals had been replaced for many colonists by an emerging "Yankee" ideal of trade and commerce, bustling seaport cities, diverse beliefs, and a more secular, or nonreligious, orientation to daily life. This transition increased tensions in every community, especially during the difficult years of the 1680s. Those tensions were the context for one of the most dramatic events in the region's history: the Salem witch trials.

In 1692 a group of young women and girls in Salem Village began to show signs of what seventeenth-century society diagnosed as bewitchment. They fell into violent fits, contorting their bodies and showing great emotional distress. Under questioning, they named several local women, including a West Indian slave named Tituba, as their tormentors. The conviction that the devil had come to Massachusetts spread quickly, and the number of people accused of witchcraft mushroomed. By summer, more than a hundred women, men, and children were crowded into local jails, awaiting trial. Accusations, trials, and even executions—nineteen in all—continued until the new royal governor, Sir William Phips, arrived in the colony and forbade any further arrests. Phips dismissed the court that had passed judgment based on "spectral evidence"—that is, testimony by the alleged victims that they had seen the spirits of the accused tormenting them. In January 1693, Phips assembled a new court that acquitted the remaining prisoners.

The witch trials expressed the struggle between saintly Puritan farmers of Salem Village and the town's more worldly merchants: the accusers were invariably members of the farming community; the accused were often associated with commercial activities. Nevertheless, the witch-hunts reflected the belief among people—whether farmers or merchants—that the devil and his disciples could work great harm in a community.

The Pluralism of the Middle Colonies

■ Why did the Dutch and the English encourage a multicultural population in New York?

■ What cultural and economic tensions came to a head in Leisler's Rebellion?

■ What made William Penn's vision for Pennsylvania so distinctive?

Between the Chesapeake and New England lay the vast stretch of forest and farmland called New Netherland, a Dutch colony that was home to settlers from Holland, Sweden, Germany, and France. In the 1660s, Charles II seized the area and drove the Dutch from the Atlantic coast of North America. The English divided the conquered territory into three colonies: New York, New Jersey, and Pennsylvania. Although the region changed hands, it did not change its character: the Middle Colonies remained a multicultural, commercially oriented, and competitive society no matter whose flag flew over them.

From New Amsterdam to New York

Before 1650, Europe's two major Protestant powers had maintained a degree of cooperation, and their American colonies remained on friendly terms, assisting each other, for example, in conflicts with Indians. But a growing rivalry over the transatlantic trade and conflicting land claims in the Connecticut Valley soon eroded this neighborliness. Beginning in 1652, England and Holland fought three naval wars as both nations tried to control the transatlantic trade in raw materials and manufactured goods. After each, the Dutch lost ground, and their decline made it likely that the New Netherland settlement would be abandoned.

King Charles II of England wanted New Netherland very much, and James, Duke of York (later King James II), was eager to satisfy his brother's desires. In 1664 Charles agreed to give James control of the region lying between the Connecticut and Delaware Rivers—if James could wrest it from the Dutch (see Map 3.3). The promise and the prize amounted to a declaration of war on New Netherland.

When the duke's four armed ships arrived in New Amsterdam harbor and aimed their cannon at the town, Governor Peter Stuyvesant tried to rally the local residents to resist. They refused. Life under the English, they reasoned, would probably be no worse than life under the Dutch. Perhaps it might be better. The humiliated governor surrendered the colony, and

property requirement   The limitation of voting rights to citizens who own certain kinds or amounts of property.

This portrait of Peter Stuyvesant, the governor of the Dutch colony of New Netherland, was painted by Henrick Courturier when the feisty Stuyvesant was fifty years old. Stuyvesant governed with a heavy hand, flying into a rage if colonists challenged his decisions. He was not popular, but he did bring much-needed order to the colony. *New York Historical Society.*

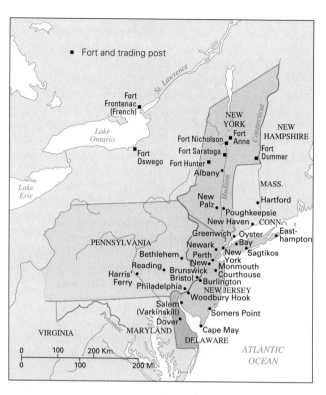

MAP 3.3 The Middle Colonies This map shows the major towns, cities, and forts in the colonies of New York, Pennsylvania (including Delaware), and New Jersey. The prosperity of the region was based on the thriving commerce of its largest cities, Philadelphia and New York, and on the commercial production of wheat.

in 1664 New Netherland became New York without a shot being fired.

James proved to be a very liberal ruler, allowing the Dutch and other European colonists to keep their lands, practice their religions, and conduct their business in their native languages. But the duke's generosity and tolerance did not extend to taxation matters. James saw his colonists much as his brother the king saw every colonist: as a source of personal revenue. James taxed New Yorkers heavily and allowed no representative assembly that might interfere with his use of the treasury. All political offices in the new colony, high or low, went to the duke's friends, creating a patronage system that impressed even King Charles.

James's colony did not develop as he had hoped, however. Settlement did not expand to the north and east as he wished. He could not enlist the aid of influential New Yorkers in his expansion plans, even though he offered them the incentive of a representative assembly in 1682. By 1685, James—now king of England—had lost interest in the colony, abandoning his schemes for its growth and abolishing the representative assembly as well.

Leisler's Rebellion

Although James viewed New York as a failure, the colony actually grew rapidly during his rule. The population doubled between 1665 and 1685, reaching fifteen thousand the year the duke ascended to the English throne. These new settlers added to the cultural diversity that had always characterized the region. The colony became a religious refuge for French

Protestants, English Quakers, and Scottish **Presbyterians.** New York's diverse community, however, did not always live in harmony. English, Dutch, and German merchants competed fiercely for control of New York City's trade and for dominance in the city's cultural life. An equally intense rivalry existed between Manhattan's merchants and Albany's fur traders. Only one thing united these competitors: a burning resentment of James's political control and the men he chose to enforce his will. Their anger increased when James created the Dominion of New England, merging New York with the Puritan colonies.

In 1689 news of the Glorious Revolution prompted a revolt in New York City similar to the one that shook Boston. **Jacob Leisler,** a German merchant, emerged as its leader. Although Leisler lacked the charisma and commanding presence that had allowed Nathaniel Bacon to rise to power in 1667, he was able to take control of the entire colony. Acting in the name of the new English monarchs, William and Mary, he not only removed Dominion officials but imprisoned several of his local opponents, declaring them enemies of Protestantism. He then called for city elections to oust James's remaining appointees. Leisler expected an era of home rule to follow his rebellion, but England's new monarchs had no intention of leaving a local merchant in charge of a royal colony. When William and Mary sent a new governor to New York, Leisler refused to surrender the reins of government. This time, the abrasive, headstrong merchant found few supporters, and eventually he was forced to step down. To Leisler's surprise, he was then arrested and charged with treason. Both he and his son-in-law were tried, found guilty, and executed. As befit traitors in the seventeenth century, the two rebels were hanged, disemboweled while still alive, and then beheaded. Afterward, their mutilated bodies were quartered. In death, Leisler became a hero and a martyr. Popular anger was so great that to quiet the discontent, the new governor had to permit formation of a representative assembly. Several of the men elected to this new legislature were ardent Leislerians, and for many years New York politics remained a battleground between home rule advocates and supporters of the royal governor and the king.

William Penn's Holy Experiment

More than most dissenting sects, Quakers had paid a high price for their strongly held convictions. Members of the Society of Friends had been jailed in England and Scotland and harassed by their neighbors throughout the empire. Quaker leaders had strong

William Penn was about 50 years old when this chalk drawing was done. Although Pennsylvania was famous for its religious tolerance and welcoming of non-English immigrants, Penn held many views in common with New England's Puritan leaders. He believed that government should impose and enforce a moral code, because drunkenness, luxury, gambling, and cursing were not only "sins against Nature" but "sins against Government." *"William Penn" by Francis Place. The Historical Society of Pennsylvania.*

motives to create a refuge for members of their beleaguered church. In the 1670s, a group of wealthy Friends purchased New Jersey from its original proprietors and offered religious freedom and generous political rights to its current and future colonists, many of whom were Puritans. The best known of these Quaker proprietors was **William Penn,** who had given up a life of privilege, luxury, and self-indulgence in Restoration society and embraced the morally demanding life of the Friends.

Penn's father, Admiral Sir William Penn, was one of England's naval heroes and a political adviser to

Presbyterians Members of a Protestant sect that eventually became the established church of Scotland but which in the seventeenth century was sometimes persecuted by Scotland's rulers.

Jacob Leisler German merchant who led a revolt in New York in 1689 against royal officials representing the Dominion of New England; he was executed as a traitor when he refused to surrender control of the colony to a governor appointed by William and Mary.

William Penn English Quaker who founded the colony of Pennsylvania in 1681.

King Charles II. The senior Penn and his son had little in common except their loyalty to the king and their willingness to provide liberal loans to support their monarch's extravagant lifestyle. Eventually, Charles rewarded the Penns' devotion. In 1681, he granted the younger Penn a charter to a huge area west of the Delaware River. This gave Penn the opportunity to create for Quakers a refuge that fully embodied their religious principles.

Penn called his new colony Pennsylvania, meaning "Penn's Woods," in memory of his father. (The southernmost section of Penn's grant, added later by Charles II, developed independent of Penn's control and in 1776 became the state of Delaware.) Like most colonial proprietors, Penn expected to profit from his charter, and he set a quitrent, or small fee, on all land purchased within his colony. But his religious devoutness ensured that he would not govern by whim. Instead, Quaker values and principles were the basis for his "holy experiment." At the heart of the Quaker faith was the conviction that the divine spirit, or "inner light," resided in every human being. Quakers thus respected all individuals. By their plain dress and their refusal to remove their hats in the presence of their social "betters," Quakers demonstrated their belief that all men and women were equal. In keeping with their egalitarian principles, Quakers also recognized no distinctions of wealth or social status in their places of worship. At the strikingly simple Quaker meeting, or worship service, any member who felt moved to speak was welcome to participate, no matter how poor or uneducated and no matter what sex or age. Although they actively sought converts, Quakers were always tolerant of other religions.

Pennsylvania's political structure reflected this **egalitarianism.** All free male residents had the right to vote during Penn's lifetime, and the legislature they elected had full governing powers. Unlike his patron, Charles II, William Penn had no intention of interfering in his colony's lawmaking process. He honored the legislature's decisions even when they disturbed or amazed him. The political quarrels that developed in Pennsylvania's assembly actually shocked Penn, but his only action was to urge political leaders not to be "so noisy, and open, in your dissatisfactions."

Penn's land policy also reflected Quaker principles. Unlike many proprietors, he wanted no politically powerful landlords and no economically dependent tenant farmers. Instead, he actively promoted a society of independent, landowning farm families. Penn also insisted that all land be purchased fairly from the Indians, and he pursued a policy of peaceful coexistence between the two cultures. William Penn took an

This sketch of a Quaker meeting highlights one of the most radical of Quaker practices: allowing women to speak in church. Most Protestant denominations, because of their reading of Saint Paul, enforced the rule of silence on women. But Quakers struck a blow at seventeenth-century gender notions by granting women an active ministerial role, a voice in church policy, and decision-making responsibilities on issues relating to the church and the family. *"The Quaker Meeting" (detail) by Egbert Van Heemskerk. The Quaker Collection, Haverford College Library.*

active role in making Pennsylvania a multicultural society, recruiting non-English settlers through pamphlets that stressed the religious and political freedoms and economic opportunities his colony offered. More than eight thousand immigrants poured into the colony in the first four years. Many did come from England, but Irish, Scottish, Welsh, French, Scandinavian, and German settlers came as well. To their English neighbors who did not speak German, newcomers from Germany such as the Mennonites and Amish were known as the "Pennsylvania Dutch" (*Deutsch*, meaning "German," would have been correct).

When William Penn died in 1717, he left behind a successful, dynamic colony. Philadelphia was already emerging as a great shipping and commercial center, rivaling the older seaports of Boston and New York City. But this success came at some cost to Penn's original vision and to his Quaker principles. The commercial orientation here, as in Puritan Massachusetts, attracted colonists who were more secular in their interests and objectives than the colony's founders.

egalitarianism   A belief in human equality.

These colonists had no strong commitment to egalitarianism. For example, many newcomers saw Penn's Indian policy as a check on their ambitions and preferred to seize land from the Indians rather than purchase it. The demand for military protection from Indians by these land-hungry farmers in the western part of the colony became a major political issue and a matter of conscience for Quakers, whose religious principles included **pacifism.** Eventually many Quakers chose to resign from the colonial government rather than struggle to uphold a holy experiment that their neighbors did not support.

The Colonies of the Lower South

■ What type of society did the founders of Carolina hope to create? How did the colony differ from their expectations?

■ Why did philanthropists create Georgia? Why did the king support this project?

William Penn was not the only Englishman to benefit from the often extravagant generosity of King Charles II. In 1663 the king surprised eight of his favorite supporters by granting them several million acres lying south of Virginia and stretching from the Atlantic to the Pacific Ocean. This gesture by Charles was both grand and calculated. France, Spain, Holland, and the Indian tribes that inhabited this area all laid claim to it, and Charles thought it would be wise to secure England's control of the region by colonizing it. The eight new colonial proprietors named their colony Carolina to honor the king's late father, who had lost his head to the Puritan Commonwealth (and whose name in Latin was Carolus; see Map 3.4).

The Carolina Colony

The proprietors' plan for Carolina was similar to Lord Baltimore's medieval dream. The philosopher John Locke helped draw up the Fundamental Constitution of Carolina, an elaborate blueprint for a society of great landowners, **yeomen** (small, independent farmers), and serfs (agricultural laborers) bound to work for their landlords. Locke later became famous for his essays on freedom and human rights (see Chapter 4)—a far cry from the social hierarchy proposed in the Carolina constitution. Like the Calverts, however, the Carolina proprietors discovered that few English people were willing to travel 3,000 miles across the ocean to become serfs. Bowing to reality, the proprietors offered the incentive of the head right system used in Virginia and Maryland decades earlier.

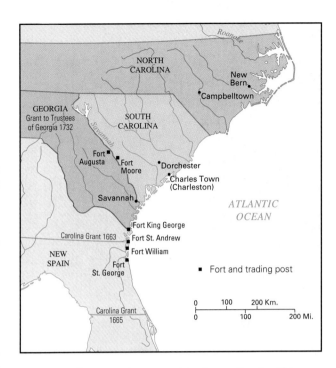

MAP 3.4 The Settlements of the Lower South This map shows the towns and fortifications of North Carolina, South Carolina, and Georgia, as well as the overlapping claims by the Spanish and the English to the territory south and west of Fort King George. The many Georgia forts reflect that colony's role as a buffer state between rice-rich South Carolina and the Spanish troops stationed in Florida.

The early settlers in Carolina, many of them relocating from the Caribbean island of Barbados, made their way to the southeastern portion of the colony, drawn there by the fine natural harbor of the port city, Charles Town (later Charleston), and its fertile surroundings. Despite the dangers of the Spanish to the south in Florida and the Yamasee Indians to the southwest, Charles Town grew rapidly, becoming the most important city in the southern colonies. These early Carolinians experimented with several money-making activities. Some established trade with the Indians of the region, exchanging English goods for deerskins and for captive victims of tribal warfare. The deerskins were shipped to England. The Indians were shipped as slaves to the Caribbean. Other colonists tapped the region's pine forests to produce

pacifism Opposition to war or violence of any kind.

yeoman Independent landowner entitled to suffrage.

The Lynch family, wealthy rice planters of South Carolina, built this elegant home on the banks of the North Santee River in the 1730s. Hopsewee Plantation is a striking example of the luxury enjoyed by the small number of elite white planters whose fortunes depended on the labor of enslaved African field workers. *Courtesy of the Hopsewee Plantation.*

naval stores—the timber, tar, resin, pitch, and turpentine that were used in building and maintaining wooden ships.

Carolinians experimented with several cash crops, including sugar cane, tobacco, silk, cotton, ginger, and olives. But none of these crops was particularly profitable. The first real success turned out to be cattle raising, a skill the settlers learned from African slaves brought into the colony by planters relocating from the West Indian sugar island of Barbados. By the 1680s, Carolina cattlemen had begun to use their profits to begin a new enterprise: rice cultivation. In 1719, when members of the Charleston planter elite wrested control of their part of Carolina from the original proprietors, the southern part of the colony, now called South Carolina, boasted the richest English colonists on the mainland.

The northern region of Carolina developed in the shadow of its southern neighbor. Bordered by the Great Dismal Swamp to the north and by smaller swamps to the south, this isolated area attracted few colonists. The land around Albemarle Sound was fertile enough, but the remaining coastline was cut off from the Atlantic by a chain of barrier islands that blocked access to oceangoing vessels. Despite all these constraints, some poor farm families and freed white indentured servants had drifted in from Virginia, searching for unclaimed land and a fresh start. They had modest success in Carolina growing tobacco and producing naval stores.

In 1729 the Albemarle colonists followed the lead of their elite neighbors around Charleston and rid themselves of proprietary rule. Then these North Carolinians went one step further: they officially separated from the rice-rich southern section of the colony. In this way, the colonists of Carolina restored to the Crown what King Charles II had once given away, for both South Carolina and North Carolina became royal colonies.

Georgia, the Last Colony

More than one hundred years after the first Jamestown colonists struggled against starvation and disease in Virginia, the last of the original thirteen colonies was established in the Lower South. In 1732 **James Oglethorpe,** a wealthy English social reformer, and several of his friends requested a charter for a colony on the Florida border. Oglethorpe's motives were philanthropic: he hoped to provide a new, moral life for many of the English men and women imprisoned for minor debts. He and his colleagues wanted no profits from the colony. King George II had other motives for granting the charter: he was anxious to create a protective buffer between the valuable rice-producing colony of South Carolina and the Spanish in Florida. The king inserted a clause in the Georgia charter requiring military service from every male settler. Thus

James Oglethorpe English philanthropist who established the colony of Georgia in 1732 as a refuge for debtors.

he guaranteed that the poor men of Georgia would protect the rich men of South Carolina.

Oglethorpe and his associates added their own special restrictions on the lives of the Georgia colonists. Although their concern about the welfare of English debtors was genuine, they believed that poverty was the outcome of a weak character or, worse, of an addiction to vice. Thus they forbade a representative assembly and denied the settlers a voice in selecting political leaders and military officers. Because they were eager to reform the character of their colonists, the trustees set other rules, including banning all alcoholic beverages to ensure that everyone worked hard and led a modest, moral life. All land grants were to be small, and no colonist could legally buy or sell property within Georgia. Slavery, the main source of labor in the southern colonies by this time, was banned, and free blacks were barred from the colony. The colonists would have to work their own fields and harvest their own crops.

Oglethorpe interviewed many imprisoned debtors, searching for members of the "deserving poor" who would benefit from Georgia. But few of these men and women met his standards. Most of the colony's settlers turned out to be South Carolinians looking for new land, and English immigrants from their society's middling ranks. These colonists did not welcome the trustees' paternalistic attitudes, and they soon challenged all the restrictive rules and regulations in the charter. They won the right to accumulate and sell land. They introduced slave labor in defiance of the trustees, and by the 1740s, illegal slave auctions were a common sight in Georgia's largest town, Savannah. By 1752, Oglethorpe and his fellow trustees had lost enthusiasm for their reform project and, with relief, returned Georgia to the king.

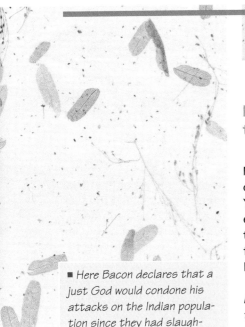

Individual Voices

Examining a Primary Source

Nathaniel Bacon: Manifesto Concerning the Troubles in Virginia, 1676

Nathaniel Bacon began his defiance of the colonial government with one specific objective: to remove the threat of Indian aggression in the backcountry of Virginia. Yet Bacon soon found himself the leader of a civil war between backcountry farmers, apprentices and servants on the one hand and the wealthy coastal planters and the royal governor on the other. Labeled a traitor by Governor Berkeley, Bacon defended himself and his actions in "The Declaration of the People." In it, he also listed his followers' many grievances against the governor.

■ Here Bacon declares that a just God would condone his attacks on the Indian population since they had slaughtered innocent colonists. Yet Bacon attacked peaceful Indians as well as those who had threatened white settlements. Do Bacon's attacks on these peaceful Indian communities suggest a larger issue of racism in the colonies?

If virtue be a sin, if piety be guilt, all the principles of morality, goodness and justice be perverted, we must confess that those who are now called rebels may be in danger of those high imputations. Those loud and several bulls would affright innocents and render the defense of our brethren and the inquiry into our sad and heavy oppressions, treason. ■ But if there be, as sure there is, a just God to appeal to; if religion and justice be a sanctuary here; if to plead the cause of the oppressed; if sincerely to aim at his Majesty's honour and die public good without any reservation or by interest; if to stand in the gap after so much blood of our dear brethren bought and sold; if after the loss of a great part of his Majesty's colony deserted and dispeopled, freely with our lives and estates to endeavour to save the remainders be treason; God Almighty judge and let guilty die. But since

■ In this section Bacon reminds his readers that the haughty tidewater planters came to Virginia as poor men, not as gentlemen, and are thus no better than his followers. Today, they would be accused of "putting on airs" or of being social climbers.

■ Bacon argues that the governor and his friends have done nothing to earn the public's trust or admiration, and have failed to provide basic protection for the citizens of the colony. One hundred years later, American revolutionaries will make the same claim against the king and Parliament of Great Britain. Do you think Bacon's claims are accurate?

we cannot in our hearts find one single spot of rebellion or treason, or that we have in any manner aimed at the subverting of the settled government or attempting of the person of any either magistrate or private man, notwithstanding the several reproaches and threats of some who for sinister ends were disaffected to us and censured our innocent and honest designs, and since all people in all places where we have yet been can attest our civil, quiet, peaceable behaviour far different from that of rebellion and tumultuous persons, let truth be bold and all the world know the real foundations of pretended guilt. We appeal to the country itself what and of what nature their oppressions have been, or by what cabal and mystery the designs of many of those whom we call great men have been transacted and carried on; but let us trace these men in authority and favour to whose hands the dispensation of the country's wealth has been committed. ■ *Let us observe the sudden rise of their estates composed with the quality in which they first entered this country, or the reputation, they have held here amongst wise and discerning men. And let us see whether their extractions and education have not been vile, and by what pretence of learning and virtue they could so soon [come] into employments of so great trust and consequence.* ■ *Let us consider their sudden advancement and let us also consider whether any public work for our safety and defence or for the advancement and propagation of trade, liberal arts, or sciences is here extant in any way adequate to our vast charge. Now let us compare these things together and see what sponges have sucked up the public treasure, and whether it has not been privately contrived away by unworthy favourites and juggling parasites whose tottering fortunes have been repaired and supported at the public charge. Now if it be so, judge what greater guilt can be than to offer to pry into these and to unriddle the mysterious wiles of a powerful cabal; let all people judge what can be of more dangerous import than to suspect the so long safe proceedings of some of our grandees, and whether people may with safety open their eyes in so nice a concern.*

Summary

After the failure of the Roanoke Colony in 1587, the English did not attempt to settle mainland America until the seventeenth century, when political conflict, economic instability, and religious persecution persuaded many English men and women that colonization might ease their national problems. Borrowing the idea of a joint-stock enterprise from English shippers, the Virginia Company financed the first successful colony at Jamestown in 1607. Between 1607 and 1732, thirteen colonies were founded on mainland America, with four distinct regions emerging: the Chesapeake, New England, the Middle Colonies, and the Lower South.

Although the Virginia Company expected to grow rich from the discovery of gold and silver, the real wealth of the first colony proved to be in agriculture.

Tobacco became known as the "brown gold" of Virginia. In 1634 the Calvert family established the second Chesapeake colony of Maryland as a refuge for English Catholics. Maryland settlers, most of whom turned out to be Protestants, chose to cultivate tobacco also. Chesapeake society was shaped by this decision. Both colonies filled with young, single males who came to America as indentured servants, working in the tobacco fields for several years in order to repay their masters for their Atlantic voyages. The demand for male field workers resulted in a skewed sex ratio. The unhealthy climate, hard labor, and poor diet produced a demographic disaster in the seventeenth-century Chesapeake. The relatively small number of women and high mortality rates prevented a traditional family structure from developing. Major conflicts among the settlers emerged in both colonies. In Maryland, Protestants and Catholics waged a long battle for control, and in Virginia, backcountry farmers rose up against the established coastal planters in 1676 in Bacon's Rebellion.

Religious dissenters seeking freedom of worship created the New England colonies. Pilgrims, or separatists, founded the first of these colonies at Plymouth in 1620. Pilgrim leader William Bradford assured the success of the colony by offering broad political rights to all the men on board the *Mayflower,* including the crew and servants, in an agreement known as the Mayflower Compact. Unlike the Chesapeake settlers, the Pilgrims established peaceful relations with the local Indians. The outcome was seventy-one years of stability in this small colony.

Puritans, who wished to "purify" the Anglican Church of all traces of Catholicism, founded Massachusetts in 1630. They expected to create a model Protestant community, a "city upon a hill," that would convince all English men and women to accept Puritan reforms. The colony's leaders required all settlers to obey biblical as well as English civil and criminal laws. Political rights were restricted to full church members, known as saints. Dissent arose, however. Roger Williams and Anne Hutchinson—both discovered that although the colony was founded for religious freedom, that freedom did not extend to everyone. Because they challenged Puritan practices or rituals or beliefs, they were exiled from Massachusetts. Roger Williams founded Rhode Island, a colony that established separation of church and state. Many colonists left Massachusetts voluntarily, exasperated by the regulation of their personal lives or seeking new land to settle. Connecticut was founded by such colonists. The Puritans ultimately lost control over Massachusetts in 1691 when the Crown revoked the charter and made it a royal colony. The tensions produced by this political change and by economic growth contributed to the Salem witch-hunts of 1691.

The region between the Chesapeake and New England, originally claimed and settled by both the Dutch and the Swedes, was "conquered" by the English in 1664. New Sweden and New Netherland became New Jersey and New York. In 1681 Quaker William Penn created the colony of Pennsylvania, known as the "holy experiment," west of New Jersey. The Middle Colonies, as they were called, were noted for their diverse populations—including Quakers, Germans, French Protestants, Dutch, Swedes, Finns, and a small community of Jews—and for their policies of religious toleration.

In the Lower South, the proprietors of Carolina expected to create a hierarchical society but discovered, as had the Calverts of Maryland, that they had to offer land under the head right system in order to attract colonists. Georgia, the last of the colonies, was founded by philanthropists who hoped to reform "worthy debtors" in English prisons. The king approved the colony because he wanted a buffer state between the Spanish-held Florida and the prosperous rice-growing colony of South Carolina.

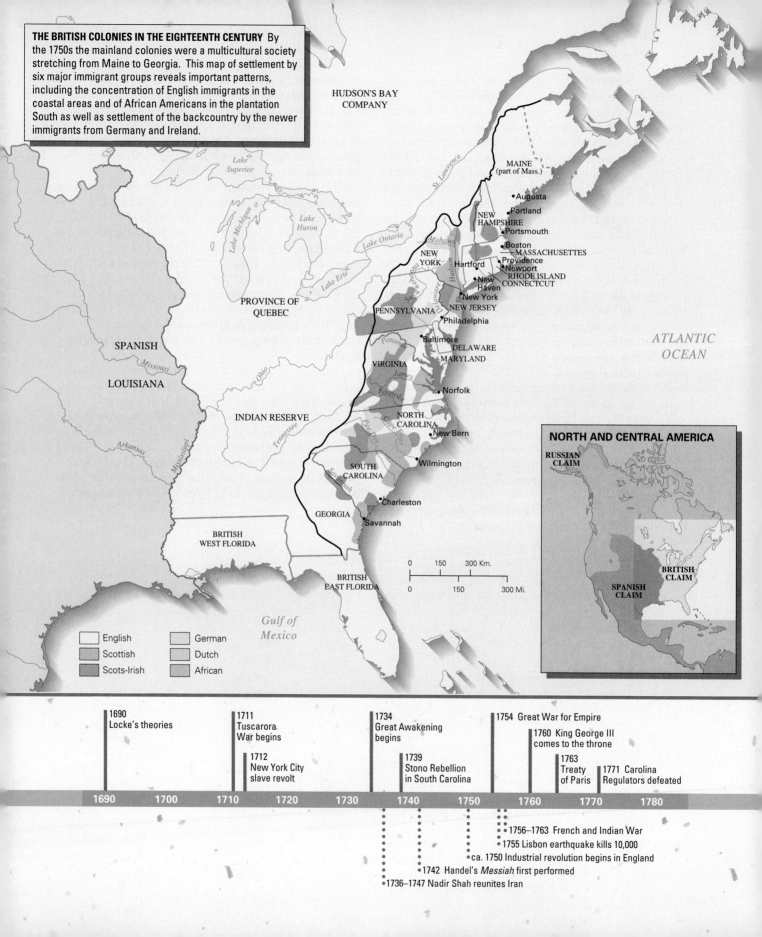

THE BRITISH COLONIES IN THE EIGHTEENTH CENTURY By the 1750s the mainland colonies were a multicultural society stretching from Maine to Georgia. This map of settlement by six major immigrant groups reveals important patterns, including the concentration of English immigrants in the coastal areas and of African Americans in the plantation South as well as settlement of the backcountry by the newer immigrants from Germany and Ireland.

HUDSON'S BAY COMPANY

Lake Superior

Lake Michigan

Lake Huron

Lake Ontario

Lake Erie

St. Lawrence

Mohawk

MAINE
(part of Mass.)

• Augusta

• Portland

NEW HAMPSHIRE

• Portsmouth

• Boston

MASSACHUSETTES

Providence

• Newport

RHODE ISLAND

CONNECTCUT

Hartford

• New Haven

NEW YORK

Hudson

Susquehanna

Delaware

• New York

PENNSYLVANIA

NEW JERSEY

• Philadelphia

PROVINCE OF QUEBEC

SPANISH

LOUISIANA

Missouri

Ohio

Tennessee

Arkansas

Mississippi

INDIAN RESERVE

Potomac

• Baltimore

DELAWARE

MARYLAND

VIRGINIA

James

Rappahannock

Roanoke

• Norfolk

NORTH CAROLINA

Cape Fear

• New Bern

Pee Dee

SOUTH CAROLINA

• Wilmington

Savannah

GEORGIA

• Charleston

Savannah

BRITISH WEST FLORIDA

BRITISH EAST FLORIDA

Gulf of Mexico

ATLANTIC OCEAN

0   150   300 Km.

0   150   300 Mi.

NORTH AND CENTRAL AMERICA

RUSSIAN CLAIM

SPANISH CLAIM

BRITISH CLAIM

English
Scottish
Scots-Irish
German
Dutch
African

1690
Locke's theories

1711
Tuscarora War begins

1712
New York City slave revolt

1734
Great Awakening begins

1739
Stono Rebellion in South Carolina

1754 Great War for Empire

1760 King George III comes to the throne

1763 Treaty of Paris

1771 Carolina Regulators defeated

| 1690 | 1700 | 1710 | 1720 | 1730 | 1740 | 1750 | 1760 | 1770 | 1780 |

1756–1763 French and Indian War

1755 Lisbon earthquake kills 10,000

ca. 1750 Industrial revolution begins in England

1742 Handel's *Messiah* first performed

1736–1747 Nadir Shah reunites Iran

The English Colonies in the Eighteenth Century, 1689–1763

4

The British Colonies in the Eighteenth Century
Using the map on the facing page, discuss immigrant settlement patterns in the mainland colonies. What role would regional economies play in determining where German, Scots-Irish, and African immigrants were concentrated?

Individual Choices

ELIZA LUCAS PINCKNEY'S GOWN

As the daughter of one prosperous South Carolina planter and the wife of another, Eliza Lucas Pinckney could afford luxury goods most colonists could not hope to enjoy. But the gown shown above was made of silk produced on her own plantation and sent to England to be woven and died. Eliza Lucas Pinckney, who became the manager of her father's three plantations when she was only a teenager, took great pride in experimenting with new crops, including silk from silkworms and the blue dye indigo. *National Museum of American History, Smithsonian Institution, Behring Center.*

Eliza Lucas Pinckney

Eliza Lucas was the daughter of a British military officer who moved his family to the colonies when she was a child. Here they settled in the new colony of South Carolina, where George Lucas acquired several thriving rice plantations. When Eliza was only sixteen, her father was recalled to active duty in the Caribbean, leaving behind a young family and an ailing wife. But George Lucas did not turn to outsiders or male relatives to take charge of his plantations while he was away; instead he turned over the daunting task to his bright, energetic daughter, Eliza. The choice may have surprised colonists who did not know Eliza, but friends and family shared her father's confidence in her. She had already shown her maturity and her organizing skills when she took over the management of the large family household from her invalid mother.

With the family's fortunes in her hands, Eliza proved her father had made the right choice. At a time when most wealthy young women in Carolina were preoccupied with thoughts of marriage and children, Eliza Lucas busied herself with planting and harvesting, paying bills, directing overseers, and selling crops. Despite her responsibilities, she did not ignore her duties as a member of her community's female social elite: she attended teas, visited the sick, and mastered the arts of dancing and music. To do all this, she set herself a grueling daily schedule. She began the day at 5:00 A.M. with two hours of reading, then toured the work in the fields, returned to the house to study music and French, and finally sat down to tutor her sister and two of the plantation's slave girls. All this was accomplished before noon. In the afternoon and evening she would do needlework, read the classics as well as the influential books of the day, and see to personal and business correspondence. One day a week, she set aside all her female duties and attended entirely to plantation business.

Under Eliza's management, the Lucas plantations prospered. From the beginning she took a bold approach, experimenting with new crops that might grow in South Carolina's climate and soil. Her father approved wholeheartedly of her unorthodox methods and assisted her in the search for potentially profitable crops. In the midst of his military duties, he found time to send her **indigo** seeds, from which blue dye could be made. He also sent her a talented indigo maker from the Caribbean island of Montserrat. It took Eliza five years of experimentation to turn a profit from indigo, but her persistence paid off. Indigo became a staple crop of South Carolina for several years.

Eliza's entrepreneurial spirit and business skills are well documented in her letters. But these letters also show the pride she took in her successes and the confidence she felt that she deserved to reap the rewards of her accomplishments. When Eliza described a "large plantation of Oaks" she had planted, she not only took credit for the project but also asserted her right to any profits in timber the grove generated. She even went so far as to insist that the oaks were "my own property, whether my father gives me the land or not." The men who worked for her would not have been surprised by such a claim, for they knew her temperament and her business skills firsthand. Eliza hired and fired the overseers, who reported directly to her, and she wrote regularly to the family's agent in London on matters of property deeds, sales of land and livestock, and the purchase of goods through local Charles Town merchants. In matters of business and legal affairs, as in other areas, Eliza's father had laid the groundwork for her expertise. He had instructed her fully on her legal rights as a single woman, or ***femme sole***, and encouraged her to make good use of the legal library left behind in her care. And she did just that. Many of her neighbors relied on her to make their wills or assist them in suing for debts. Male or female, these colonists knew less about protecting their property than this teenage girl who read law books, legal treatises, and philosophers of civil society such as John Locke.

Despite the many attempts by her father to find a suitable husband for Eliza, she stubbornly protected her independence. Believing herself too young to marry, she vowed to remain single until she was ready to live otherwise. When Eliza finally married it was to an old friend, a widower twice her age. Charles Pinckney was a leading lawyer and political figure in the colony and had acted as Eliza's mentor while her father was away. Eliza judged him to be a worthy companion for a woman of her intellect and abilities.

As Charles's wife, Eliza turned all her attention to domestic concerns, especially maternal ones, and within five years she gave birth to four children. Eliza undertook motherhood with the same energy and clarity of purpose she had shown in her years as a planter and businesswoman. She believed that the education of her children was the most important work she would ever undertake, and she prepared herself for the task well. She chose to follow John Locke's modern theories of childhood education, theories that stressed the power of nurture rather than older notions that children were burdened by original sin. Locke's advice served Eliza Lucas Pinckney well: both of her two surviving sons grew up to be political leaders during the revolutionary struggle, and her only daughter followed in Eliza's footsteps, eventually running her own plantation.

After fourteen years of marriage, Eliza was left a widow. Once again she rose to the challenge of managing a large plantation, just as she had done as a sixteen-year-old girl. She continued to manage the complex family business until her death from cancer in 1793. As a tribute to her place in colonial society, George Washington requested to be a pallbearer at her funeral.

INTRODUCTION

Despite the economic, political, intellectual, and religious ties that bound England and the colonies into a transatlantic community, many visitors to the colonies argued that Americans had a distinctive character of their own. The **unprecedented** degree of personal liberty for all except African and African American slaves struck many observers as uniquely American. The rich natural resources of the land impressed others as a key to an extraordinary American optimism. Liberty and economic opportunity drew thousands of new immigrants to the colonies every decade, not only from England but from Germany, Ireland, and France as well. Quakers and other English dissenters flocked to colonies that offered religious toleration,

> **indigo** Shrublike plant with clusters of red or purple flowers, grown on plantations in the South; it was a primary source of blue dye in the 18th century.
>
> ***femme sole*** From the French for "woman alone"; a legal term for an unmarried, widowed, or divorced woman with the legal right to own or sell property, sue or be sued, or earn wages.
>
> **unprecedented** Unheard of or novel.

The sugar-producing islands of the Caribbean were the jewels in the British empire of trade. Ship captains and ship owners made their fortunes out of the sugar or, as it was often called in the 18th century, molasses they carried from the West Indies to the mainland colonies, as well as to England and to Africa. The sugar planters lived in luxury in England, among the wealthiest men in the empire. Meanwhile, slaves labored in the cane fields in order to produce the profits these men enjoyed. *British Library; London, UK/ Bridgeman Art Library Ltd.*

such as Pennsylvania. Of course not everyone lived, as one observer insisted, "in his house like a king." The poor as well as the wealthy filled the crowded streets of Philadelphia, New York, and Boston. In western New England, land shortages in settled areas and urban unemployment were altering the social landscape. In the South, the steady flow of new immigrants to the backcountry of Virginia and the Carolinas produced subsistence-level farm families, struggling to survive. And throughout these regions of tobacco and rice production, slavery set the African and African American labor force outside the realm of economic advancement or basic personal liberties. Even so, many free white colonists would agree with Michel de Crèvecoeur, the French writer who called America "this smiling country."

Few members of the English or European elite bothered to chart these changes in American colonial life. Most continued to think of the colonies as a dumping ground for misfits and hayseeds who would struggle to survive, or not, on a violent frontier. Members of the English Parliament viewed the colonists as a constant source of problems and continued to expect the worst from them. They expected insubordinate colonial legislatures, defiant merchants who violated trade regulations, and a dangerously unstable political atmosphere in a society that gave common men such a great voice in government. To the king and his political advisers, this "smiling country" produced more gloom than sunshine. From the colonists' perspective, England and its rivals were responsible for most of the clouds on their horizon. A series of imperial wars between England and its competitors disrupted colonial life until

the 1760s, casting a long shadow over communities from Maine to Georgia. In the end, England would vanquish every rival for a North American empire, but neither the king nor the colonists could predict the surprising outcome of their nation's victory.

The English Transatlantic Communities of Trade

■ What were the main regional differences in colonial commerce?

■ In which region, and for what reasons, did new immigrants seem to have the best economic choices?

■ How were the Carolina plantation owners' profits affected by rising tensions between England and Spain and Portugal?

Although the English spoke of "the colonial trade," British America did not have a single, unified economy. Instead, four distinctive regional economies had developed on the mainland, concentrated along the Atlantic coastline and bordered on the west by the primarily **subsistence society** commonly found on the edge of white settlement. To the south, the sugar islands of the Caribbean made up a fifth unique regional economy. Each of these economies was shaped by environmental conditions, natural resources, Eng-

subsistence society A society that produces the food and supplies necessary for its survival but which does not produce a surplus that can be marketed.

Chronology

From Settlements to Societies

1690–1691	John Locke's *Essay Concerning Human Understanding* and *Two Treatises of Government*
1701	Yale College founded
1702	Queen Anne's War begins
1704	Pro-French Indians attack Deerfield, Massachusetts
1711	Tuscarora War begins in North Carolina
1712	New York City slave revolt
1715	Colonists defeat Creek and Yamasee Indians of Georgia
1734	Great Awakening spreads to New England
1739	Stono Rebellion in South Carolina
1740	King George's War begins George Whitefield begins his preaching tour
1756	Great War for Empire begins
1759	British capture Quebec
1763	Treaty of Paris ends French and Indian or Seven Years, War Paxton Boys revolt in Pennsylvania
1771	North Carolina Regulator movement defeated

lish commercial policy, the available labor force, and the available technological know-how.

Regions of Commerce

The sugar-producing islands of the West Indies were the brightest jewels in the English imperial crown. Spain had first laid claim to most of these islands, but England had gobbled up many of them when the Spanish chose to concentrate instead on the gold- and silver-mining colonies of Peru and Mexico. By the eighteenth century, the English flag flew over St. Kitts, Barbados, Nevis, Montserrat, and Jamaica. On each island, English plantation owners built fabulous fortunes on the sugar that African slaves produced. While the **absentee planters** lived in luxury in England, black slaves lived—and died in staggering numbers—on the islands, working the cane fields and tending the fires that burned day and night under the sugar vats of the "great Boiling houses."

Few mainland colonists enjoyed the wealth of this "Sugar Interest." Still, in the Lower South, planters of South Carolina and Georgia, like Eliza Lucas Pinckney, amassed considerable fortunes by growing rice in the lowlands along the Atlantic coast. By the 1730s, this American rice was feeding the people of the Mediterranean, Portugal, and Spain. By midcentury, planters were making additional profits from indigo, which Eliza Lucas Pinckney had recently introduced to the region. Other Carolinians found cattle raising a profitable enterprise. Like the sugar planters, Carolina and Georgia rice growers based their production on slave labor, but unlike the island moguls, these plantation masters never became permanent absentee landowners.

Tobacco continued to dominate the economy of the Chesapeake, although by the eighteenth century, "brown gold" was no longer the only crop Virginians and Marylanders were willing to plant. In fact, at the turn of the century, when the price of tobacco was driven down by high taxes and competition from Mediterranean sources, many **tidewater** planters chose to diversify. They began producing wheat and other grains for export. As a result, tobacco production shifted west to the area along the Potomac, the James River valley, and the **piedmont** foothills. The second major shift came in the labor force used in tobacco cultivation. By the eighteenth century, African slaves had replaced indentured servants in the fields. Planters who could afford to purchase a number of slaves

absentee planters   An estate owner who collects profits from farming or rent but does not live on the land or help cultivate it.

tidewater   Low coastal land drained by tidal streams in Maryland and Virginia.

piedmont   Land lying at the foot of a mountain range.

It Matters

Women's Roles, Then and Now

In her character and her life choices, Eliza Lucas Pinckney seems remarkably modern. Yet she lived in an era when women were assumed to be best suited for the domestic duties known as "house-wifery." Of course, Pinckney had advantages many other eighteenth-century women did not enjoy: wealth, social standing, and a father and a husband who had confidence in her abilities. Without these advantages, Pinckney might never have been able to venture outside the domestic realm. Today, Pinckney would find herself in the company of many women who are able to make careers in business, medicine, scientific research—and in an area completely closed out to Pinckney, politics. The contrast between a life that was extraordinary in the eighteenth century and ordinary in the twenty-first century prompts us to examine what changes have occurred in women's lives between the colonial era and today.

enjoyed a competitive advantage over their neighbors in both the old and the new tobacco areas because they had enough workers to plant and harvest bigger crops. This large-scale production kept tobacco the number one export of the mainland colonies.

Together, these two southern regions provided the bulk of the mainland's agricultural exports to Great Britain. By contrast, the New England regional economy depended far less on Britain as a market. Except in the Connecticut River valley, where tobacco was grown, the rocky soil of their region made large-scale farming unfeasible for New Englanders. Instead, they developed both a fishing and a lumbering industry, shipping the dried fish and timber to the West Indies. But it was shipbuilding and the ambitious **carrying trade** connected to it that dominated New England's economy. Colonists made great profits from an extensive shipping network that carried colonial exports across the Atlantic and distributed foreign goods and English manufactured products to the colonies. Some merchant-shippers—the slave traders of Newport, Rhode Island, for example—specialized in a certain commodity, but most were willing to carry any cargo that promised a profit. By the eighteenth century,

New England shipping made these colonists rivals of English merchants rather than useful sources of profit for the Mother Country.

Sandwiched between the South and New England, the colonies of New York, New Jersey, Pennsylvania, and later Delaware developed their own regional economy. The Middle Colonies combined the successes of their neighbors, creating profits from both staple-crop farming and trade. The forests of the Pocono Mountains and upper New York were a source of wood and wood products for the shipbuilding industry, and locally harvested flaxseed was exported to Ireland for its linen industry. The central crop, however, was wheat. Fortunately for the colonists of this area, the price of wheat rose steadily during the eighteenth century. The carrying trade was equally important in this region's mixed economy. Ships carrying cargoes of grain and flour milled in New York City across the Atlantic and into the Caribbean crossed paths with other colonial ships bringing manufactured goods and luxury items from Europe through the region's two major port cities, New York and Philadelphia. By 1775, Philadelphia had become the second-largest city in the British Empire.

Not everyone in Maryland grew tobacco for the market, of course, and not everyone in Massachusetts was a sailor, lumberjack, ship captain, or urban shopkeeper. The market-oriented activity was largely confined to the older coastal settlements of each region, where harbors and river ways provided the necessary transportation routes for the shipment of crops, goods, and supplies. Inland from these farms, towns, and cities, most colonies had a backcountry that was sparsely populated and farmed by European immigrants, ex-servants, or the families of younger sons from older communities. There, on what white settlers thought of as the frontier and Indians despised as the invasion line, colonists struggled to produce enough for survival. They lacked the labor force to clear the land or work sufficient acreage for a marketable crop, or they lacked the means to get that crop to market. And with no financial or political resources, they had little hope of solving either the manpower or the transport problem. As a result, this belt of subsistence economy extended like a border from Maine to western Pennsylvania, to inland Carolina, along every region of the mainland colonies. But even these backcountry

carrying trade The business of transporting goods across the Atlantic or to and from the Caribbean.

farms had a fragile link to the world of international trade, for settlers brought with them the farm tools and the basic household supplies that had been manufactured in England or imported through colonial ports.

The Cords of Commercial Empire

England's mainland colonists traded, both directly and indirectly, with many European nations and their colonies. Salt, wine, and spices reached colonial tables from southern Europe, and sugar, rum, molasses, and cotton came to their households from the West Indies. But the deepest and broadest channels in the transatlantic trade were those that connected the Mother Country and the colonies. The British purchased over half of all the crops, furs, and mined resources that colonists produced for market and supplied 90 percent of all colonial imports. Strong cords of exchange thus bound America to England, even if many colonists were second-, third-, or even fourth-generation Americans and others traced their roots to different nations and even different continents. The English mainland colonies were also bound to one another, despite a deserved reputation for dispute, disagreement, and endless rivalries. New Englanders might exchange insults with Pennsylvanians, but in the shops and on the wharfs, Pennsylvania flour, Massachusetts mackerel, Carolina rice, and scores of domestic products and produce changed hands in a lively and cheerful commerce. Domestic trade was greater in volume, although lower in value, than all foreign trade in this eighteenth-century world.

Community and Work in Colonial Society

■ How did Yankee society differ from Puritan society in early eighteenth-century New England?

■ Why did non-English settlers migrate to the British North American colonies?

■ Why did colonists in the Chesapeake and Lower South shift from indentured servants to slaves as their primary labor force? What problems faced Africans in slavery?

■ What was distinctive about life in the Middle Colonies?

■ What motivated colonists to migrate to the backcountry?

Despite the belief of many observers that there was an "American character," visitors could not fail to note striking physical and social differences as they traveled from New England to the Lower South. Moving from the carefully laid-out towns of New England, through the crowded seaport cities of the Middle Colonies, and into the isolated rural worlds of the plantation South, they could see that the Yankee culture of Connecticut was strikingly different from the elegant lifestyle and social attitudes of Charles Town planter elite.

The Emergence of the "Yankee"

In the early eighteenth century, New England's seaport towns and cities grew steadily in size and economic importance. With the rise of a profitable international commerce, the Puritan culture of the village gave way to a more secular "Yankee" culture. In this milieu, a wealthy man could rise to political prominence without any need to demonstrate his piety. Economic competition and the pursuit of profit eclipsed older notions that the well-being of the community was more important than the gains of the individual. Not merely sentiments, these changes were substantive: seventeenth-century laws regulating prices and interest rates, for example, were repealed or simply ignored. Still, some sense of obligation to the community remained in New Englanders' willingness to create and maintain public institutions such as schools and colleges. In 1701, for example, Yale College opened its doors in New Haven, Connecticut, giving the sons of elite New Englanders an alternative to Massachusetts's Harvard College, founded in 1636. And New Englanders supported newspapers and printing presses that kept their communities informed about local, regional, and even international events.

Even in more traditional New England villages, changes were evident. By the eighteenth century, many fathers no longer had enough farmland to provide adequately for all their sons. Thus many younger sons left their families and friends behind and sought their fortunes elsewhere. Some chose to go west, pushing the frontier of settlement as they searched for fertile land. Others went north, to less developed areas such as Maine. In the process, they created new towns and villages, causing the number of backcountry New England towns to grow steadily until the end of the colonial period. Still other young men abandoned farming entirely and relocated to the commercial cities of the region. Whatever their expectations, urban life often disappointed them, for inequality of wealth and opportunity went hand in hand with the overall prosperity. In Boston a growing number of poor widows

John Smibert painted his "Vew of Boston," in 1738. There are two striking feature of the town: the number of church steeples that dot the urban landscape, testimony to the importance of religion in the founding of the colony of Massachusetts, and the presence of so many ships in the busy harbor, testimony to the importance of Boston as colonial entrepot. *Courtesy of the Childs Gallery.*

and landless young men scrambled for employment and often wound up dependent on public charity. As news spread about the scarcity of farmland in the countryside and the poverty and competition for work in the cities, European immigrants to America tended to bypass New England and settle in the Middle Colonies or along the southern frontier.

Planter Society and Slavery

Southern society was changing as dramatically as New England's. By the end of the seventeenth century, the steady supply of cheap labor from England had begun to disappear. The English economy was improving, and young men who might once have signed on as indentured servants in Virginia or Maryland now chose to remain at home. Those who did immigrate preferred to indenture themselves to farmers and merchants of the Middle Colonies, where work conditions were bearable and economic opportunities were brighter. While this supply of indentured servants was declining, however, a different labor supply was beginning to increase: enslaved Africans.

Although a small number of Africans had been brought to Virginia as early as 1619, the legal differences between black workers and white workers remained vague until the 1660s. By that time, the slowly increasing numbers of African Americans elicited the different, and harsher, treatment that defined slavery in the Caribbean and South America. By midcentury, it became the custom in the Chesapeake to hold black servants for life terms, although their children were still considered free. By the 1660s, colonists turned these customs of **discrimination** into law. In 1662 Virginia took a major step toward making slavery an inherited condition by declaring that "all children born in this country shall be held bond or free according to the condition of the mother."

Slaves did not become the dominant labor force in southern agriculture until the end of the century, although southern planters were probably well aware

discrimination   Treatment based on class, gender, or racial category rather than on merit; prejudice.

of the advantages of slave labor over indentured servitude. First, a slave, bound for life, would never compete with his former master the way freed white servants did. Second, most white colonists did not believe that the English customs regulating a master's treatment of servants had to be applied to African workers. For example, Christian holidays need not be honored for African laborers, and the workday itself could be lengthened without any outcry from white neighbors. Why, then, were the early Chesapeake planters reluctant to import slaves as colonists in the Caribbean and South America had done? Two factors made them hesitate. Dutch control of the African slave trade kept purchasing prices high, and the disease environment of the Chesapeake cut human life short. Until the end of the seventeenth century, therefore, planters considered the financial investment in African laborers both too costly and too risky.

In the 1680s, however, the drawbacks to African slavery began to vanish. Mortality rates fell in the Chesapeake, and the English broke the Dutch monopoly on the slave trade. Fierce competition among English slavers drove prices down and at the same time ensured a steady supply of slaves. Under these conditions, the demand for slaves grew in the Chesapeake. Although only 5 percent of the roughly 9.5 million Africans brought to the Americas came to the North American mainland colonies, their numbers in Virginia and Maryland rose dramatically in the eighteenth century. By 1700, 13 percent of the Chesapeake population was African or of African descent. In Virginia, where only 950 Africans lived in 1660, the black population grew to 120,000 by 1756. At the end of the colonial period, blacks made up 40 percent of Virginia's population.

Colonists who could not afford to purchase African slaves now found themselves at an economic disadvantage. These poorer white Virginians and Marylanders moved west, and new immigrants to the colonies avoided the coastal and piedmont plantation society altogether. Colonial merchants and skilled craftspeople also avoided the Chesapeake, for the planters purchased goods directly from England or used slave labor to manufacture barrels, bricks, and other products. As a result, this region saw the development of few towns or cities that could provide a dense community life. The Chesapeake remained a rural society, dominated by a slaveowning class made prosperous by the labor of African Americans who lived in bondage all their lives.

If tobacco provided a comfortable life for an eighteenth-century planter, rice provided a luxurious one. The Lower South, too, was a plantation society, headed by the wealthiest mainland colonists, the rice growers of the coastal regions of Carolina and Georgia. Members of this planter elite concentrated their social life in elegant Charles Town, where they moved each summer to avoid the heat, humidity, and unhealthy environment of their lowland plantations. With its beautiful townhouses, theaters, and parks, Charles Town was the single truly cosmopolitan city of the South and perhaps the most sophisticated of all mainland cities in North America.

The prosperity that these Lower South planters enjoyed, like the prosperity of the tidewater planters, was based on the forced labor of their slaves. Indeed, the families from Barbados who settled South Carolina had never relied on indentured servants because they arrived with slaves from their Caribbean plantations. By 1708, one-half of the colonial population in Carolina was black, and by 1720, Africans and African Americans outnumbered their white masters. Farther south, in Georgia, the colonists openly defied the trustees' ban on slavery until that ban was finally lifted.

Slave Experience and Slave Culture

Most slaves brought to the mainland colonies did not come directly from Africa. Instead, these men and women were reexported to the Chesapeake or the Lower South after a short period of **seasoning** in the tropical climate of the West Indies. But all imported slaves, whether seasoned or new to the Americas, began their bondage when African slavers, often armed with European weapons, captured men, women, and children and delivered them in chains to European ships anchored along the coast of West Africa (see Map 1.2). While many of those enslaved were considered war captives, others were simply kidnap victims. The slave trader John Barbot recounted the theft of "little Blacks" who had been sent by their parents to "scare away the devouring small birds" in the family cornfield. Even before these captives reached the coast and the European slave ships waiting there, they were introduced to the horrors of slavery. Their captors treated them "severely and barbarously," beating them and inflicting wounds on their bodies. The many who died on the long march from the interior to the coast were left unburied, their bodies to be

seasoning A period during which slaves from Africa were held in the West Indies so they could adjust to the climate and disease environment of the American tropics.

Both Africans and Europeans played critical roles in the African slave trade. In this illustration, African slave drivers march their captives, wearing chains and neck-clamps, from their village. Their likely destination: European ships waiting along the west coast of Africa. *Journey of the Discovery of the Source of the Nile, New York, 1869.*

"devoured by . . . beasts of prey." As the surviving captives were branded and then put into canoes to be rowed to the waiting ships, some committed suicide, leaping overboard into the ocean waters. Slave traders tried to prevent these suicides—every death meant a smaller profit—but were not surprised by them. The slaves, they commented, dreaded life in America more than their captors dreaded hell.

The transatlantic voyage, or **middle passage,** was a nightmare of death, disease, suicide, and sometimes mutiny. The casualties included the white officers and crews of the slave ships, who died of diseases in such great numbers that the waters near Benin in West Africa were known as the "white man's grave." But the loss of black lives was far greater. Slave ships were breeding grounds for scurvy, yellow fever, malaria, dysentery, smallpox, measles, and typhus—each bringing painful death. When smallpox struck his slave ship, one European recorded that "we hauled up eight or ten slaves dead of a morning. The flesh and skin peeled off their wrists when taken hold of." Perhaps 18 percent of all the Africans who began the middle passage died on the ocean.

Until the 1720s, most Chesapeake slaves worked alone on a tobacco farm with the owner and his family or in small groups of two or three, in a system known as "gang labor." This isolation made both marriage and the emergence of a slave community almost impossible. Even on larger plantations, community formation was discouraged by the use of

"gangs" made up entirely of women and children or of men only. The steady influx of newly imported slaves, or "outlanders," during the first decades of the eighteenth century also made it difficult for African Americans to work together to create a culture in response to their disorienting circumstances. The new arrivals had to be taught to speak English and to adapt to the demands of slavery. Slowly, however, these involuntary immigrants from different African societies, speaking different languages, practicing different religions, and surviving under the oppressive conditions of slavery, did create a sense of community, weaving together African and European traditions. The result was an African American culture that gave meaning to, and a sense of identity within, the slave's oppressive world.

In the Lower South, where Eliza Lucas Pinckney ran her plantation, slaves were concentrated on large plantations where they had limited or no contact with white society. This isolation from the dominant society allowed them an earlier opportunity to develop a creole, or native, culture. In contrast to gang labor, here a "task labor" system prevailed, in which slaves were assigned certain chores to be completed within a certain time period. This alternative gave rice plan-

---

middle passage   The transatlantic voyage of indentured servants or African slaves to the Americas.

tation slaves some control over their pace of work and some opportunities to manage their free time. Local languages evolved that mixed a basic English vocabulary with words from a variety of African tongues. One of these languages, Gullah, spoken on the Sea Islands off the coast of Georgia and South Carolina, remained the local dialect until the end of the nineteenth century.

For many slaves, the bonds of community that were fostered and forged within this culture became a form of resistance to the enslavement they were forced to endure. But African Americans also developed other ways to show their hatred of slavery. The diary of Virginia planter William Byrd is filled with accounts of daily resistance: slaves who challenged orders, field hands who broke tools and staged work slowdowns, men who pretended sickness and women who claimed pregnancies, household servants who stole supplies and damaged property, and slaves of all ages who ran away to the woods for a day or two or to the slave quarters of a neighboring plantation. African Americans with families, and those who understood the odds against escape, preferred to take disruptive actions like these rather than risk almost certain death in open rebellion.

The Urban Culture of the Middle Colonies

The small family farms of Pennsylvania, with their profitable wheat crops, earned the colony its reputation as the "best poor man's country." Tenant farmers, hired laborers, and even African slaves were not unknown in eastern Pennsylvania, but the colony boasted more comfortable or middling-class farm families than neighboring New York or New Jersey. In New York great estates along the Hudson River controlled much of the colony's good land, and in New Jersey wealthy owners dominated the choicest acreage, a situation that often resulted in tensions between the landlords and their tenants.

What made the Middle Colonies distinctive was not the expansive Hudson River estates or the comfortable farmhouses in seas of wheat. The region's distinguishing feature was the dynamic urban life of its two major cities, New York and Philadelphia. Although only 3 percent of the colonial population lived in the eighteenth-century cities, they were a magnet for young men and women, widows, free African Americans and slaves, and some of the immigrant population pouring into the colonies from Europe. By 1770, Philadelphia's 40,000 residents made it

Enslaved Africans living on the Sea Islands off the Georgia and South Carolina coasts had little contact with white colonists. Although they learned English, they were able to retain many language patterns from their homeland, developing a dialect known as Gullah, which their descendants still speak today. In 1995, the American Bible Society published the Gospel of Luke in this Sea Island dialect. *Courtesy of the Penn Center, History and Culture Department, St. Helena Island, SC.*

the second-largest city in the British Empire. In the same year, 25,000 people crowded onto the tip of New York's Manhattan Island.

New York residents shared their cramped living spaces with chickens and livestock and their streets with roving packs of dogs and pigs. On the narrow cobblestone or gravel streets, pedestrians jostled one another and struggled to avoid being run down by carts, carriages, men on horseback, or cattle being driven to slaughter. Although colonial cities were usually thought to be cleaner than European cities, with better sewerage and drainage systems, garbage and excrement left to rot on the streets provided a feast for flies and scavenging animals, including free-roaming pigs.

City residents faced more serious problems than runaway carts and snarling dogs. Sailors on the ships docked at Philadelphia or New York often carried venereal diseases. These and other communicable diseases spread rapidly in overcrowded areas. Fires also raced through these cities of wooden houses, wharfs, and shops. And crime—especially robbery and assault—was no stranger in the urban environment, where taverns, brothels, and gambling houses were common.

These eighteenth-century cities offered a wide range of occupations and experiences that attracted many a farmer's daughter or son but sometimes overwhelmed a new arrival from the countryside. One farm boy wrote to his father of the "Noise and confusion and Disturbance. I must confess, the jolts of Waggons, the Ratlings of Coaches, the crying of meat for the Market, the [hollering] of negroes and the ten thousand junggles and Noises, that continually Surround us in every Part almost of the Town, confuse my Thinking."

Young men who could endure the noise and confusion sought work as **apprentices** in scores of artisan trades ranging from the luxury crafts of silver- and goldsmithing or cabinet making to the profitable trades of shipbuilding, blacksmithing, or butchering, to the more modest occupations of ropemaking, baking, barbering, or shoemaking. The poorest might find work on the docks or as servants, or they might go to sea. Young women had fewer choices because few trades were open to them. Some might become dressmakers or **milliners,** but domestic service or prostitution were more likely choices. In the Middle Colony cities, as in Boston, widowed farm wives came seeking jobs as nurses, laundresses, teachers, or seamstresses. A widow or an unmarried woman who had a little money could open a shop or set up a tavern or a boarding house.

New York City had the highest concentration of African Americans in the northern colonies. The city attracted many free African American men and women. Only perhaps 5 percent of all mainland colony African Americans were free, and those **manumitted** by their plantation masters frequently chose to remain in the South, although they faced legal and social harassment, including special taxes and severe punishments—for example, striking a white person in self-defense could cost a black man his life. Others, though, made their way to the cities of New England and the Middle Colonies, making a living as laborers and servants or sailors. In addition, although slave labor was not common in New England or on the family farms of the Middle Colonies, slaves were used on New York's docks and wharfs as manual laborers.

Life in the Backcountry

Thomas Malthus, a well-known English economist and diligent student of **demographics,** believed the eighteenth-century population explosion in the English mainland colonies was "without parallel in history." The colonial white population climbed from 225,000 in 1688 to over 2 million in 1775, and the number of African Americans reached 500,000 in the same year. Natural increase accounted for much of this growth, and over half of the colonists were under age 16 in 1775. But hundreds of thousands of white immigrants arrived during the eighteenth century, risking hunger, thirst, discomfort, fear, and death on the transatlantic voyage to start life over in America. The majority of these immigrants ended up in the backcountry of the colonies.

The migration west, whether by native-born or immigrant white colonists, gradually shifted the population center of mainland society. Newcomers from Europe and Britain, as well as descendants of original New England settlers and the younger sons of the tidewater Chesapeake, all saw their best opportunities in the sparsely settled regions of western New York, northern New England, western Pennsylvania, Virginia's Shenandoah Valley, or the Carolina backcountry. Many of these settlers were squatters who cleared a few acres and laid claim by their presence to a promising piece of land.

The westward flow of settlers was part of the American landscape throughout the century, but it became a flood after 1760. A seemingly endless train of carts, sledges, and wagons moved along Indian paths to the west, and the rivers were crowded with rafts and canoes carrying families, farm tools, and livestock. Many of these new immigrants traveled south from Pennsylvania along a wagon road that ran 800 miles from Philadelphia to Virginia, North Carolina, and Augusta, Georgia. Others chose to remain in the Middle Colonies. New York's population rose 39 percent between 1760 and 1776, and in 1769, on the day the land office opened at Fort Pitt (Pittsburgh), over twenty-seven hundred applicants showed up to register for land.

By 1760, perhaps 700,000 new colonists had made their homes in the mainland colonies. In the early

apprentice A person bound by legal agreement to work for an employer for a specific length of time in exchange for instruction in a trade, craft, or business.

milliner A maker or designer of hats.

manumit To free from slavery or bondage; to emancipate.

demographics Statistical data on population.

Few women worked in the skilled trades or crafts, although widows and daughters might manage a shop after a husband or father died. The mantua maker shown here was considered an artisan and could command a good price for her skills, which were making fancy gowns and other elaborately sewn clothing. *Courtesy of the American Antiquarian Society.*

part of the century, the largest immigrant group was the **Scots-Irish.** Later, German settlers dominated. But an occasional traveler on the wagon roads might be Italian, Swiss, Irish, Welsh, or a European Jew. Most striking, the number of British immigrants swelled after 1760, causing anger and alarm within the British government. The steady stream of young English men and women out of the country prompted government officials to consider passing laws curbing emigration. What prompted this transatlantic population shift? It was not always desperation or oppression. Many arrived with enough resources to finance their new life in the colonies. Some became indentured servants or redemptioners only to preserve those savings. While unemployment, poverty, the oppression of landlords, and crop failures pushed men and women out of Europe or Britain, it is also true that the availability of cheap land, a greater likelihood of religious freedom, and the chance to pursue a craft successfully pulled others toward the colonies.

Conflicts Among the Colonists

■ What events illustrated the tensions between races in colonial society?

■ What conflicts arose between elites and poorer colonists?

The strains of economic inequality being felt in every region of mainland British America frequently erupted into violent confrontations. At the same time, tensions between Indians and colonists continued, and tensions between black and white colonists increased as both slave and free black populations grew during the eighteenth century. In almost every decade, blood was shed as colonist battled colonist over economic opportunity, personal freedom, western lands, or political representation.

Slave Revolts, North and South

White slave masters in both the Chesapeake and the Lower South knew that a slave revolt was always a possibility, for enslaved Africans and African Americans shared with other colonists what one observer called a "fondness for freedom." Planters thus took elaborate precautions to prevent rebellions, assembling armed patrols that policed the roads and woods near their plantations. These patrols were usually efficient, and the punishment they inflicted was deadly. Even if rebels escaped immediate capture, few safe havens were available to them. Individual runaways had a hard time sustaining their freedom, but dozens of rebels from one plantation were usually doomed once whites on neighboring plantations were alerted. Despite these odds, slaves continued to seek their liberty, often timing their revolts to coincide with epidemics or imperial wars that distracted the white community.

The most famous slave revolt of the eighteenth century, the **Stono Rebellion,** took place in the midst of a yellow fever epidemic in Charles Town just as news of war between England and Spain reached the colony of South Carolina. Early on a Sunday morning in September 1739, about twenty slaves gathered at the Stono River, south of Charles Town. Their leader, Jemmy, had been born in Africa, possibly in the Congo but more likely Angola, for twenty or more of those who

Scots-Irish   Protestant Scottish settlers in British-occupied northern Ireland, many of whom migrated to the colonies in the eighteenth century.

Stono Rebellion   Slave revolt in South Carolina in 1739; it prompted the colony to pass harsher laws governing the movement of slaves and the capture of runaways.

eventually joined the revolt were Angolan. The rebels seized guns and gunpowder, killed several planter families and storekeepers, and then headed south. Rather than traveling quietly through the woods, the rebels marched boldly in open view, beating drums to invite slaves on nearby plantations to join them in their flight to Spanish Florida. Other slaves answered the call, and the Stono rebels' ranks grew to almost one hundred. But in Charleston, planters were gathering to put an end to the uprising. By late Sunday afternoon white militias had overtaken and surrounded the escaping slaves. The Stono rebels stood and fought, but the militiamen killed almost thirty of them. Those who were captured were executed. Those who escaped into the countryside were hunted down.

The Stono Rebellion terrified white South Carolinians, who hurried to make the colony's already harsh slave codes even more brutal. The government increased the slave patrols in both size and frequency. It also raised the bounties, or rewards offered for the capture of runaways, to make sure that fleeing slaves taken alive and unharmed, or brought in dead and scalped, were worth hunting down.

Hostilities between black colonists and white colonists were not confined to the South. In the crowded environment of New York City, white residents showed the same fear of slave rebellions as Carolina or Virginia planters. Their fears became reality at midnight on April 6, 1712, when two dozen blacks, armed with guns, hatchets, and swords, set fire to a downtown building. Startled New Yorkers who rushed to keep the flames from spreading were attacked by the rebels, leaving nine people shot, stabbed, or beaten to death. Six more were wounded. Militia units from as far away as Westchester were called out to quell the riot and to cut off any hope of escape for the slaves. Realizing the hopelessness of their situation, six committed suicide. Those who were taken alive suffered horrible punishment. According to the colonial governor, Robert Hunter, "some were burnt, others were hanged, one broke on the wheel, and one hung alive in chains in the town." Twenty-nine years later, the mere rumor of a conspiracy by African Americans to commit arson was enough to move white residents to violent reprisals. Despite the lack of any evidence to support the charge, 101 of the city's black residents were arrested—18 of them were hanged and 18 burned alive.

Clashes Between the Rich and the Poor

Most often, class tensions erupted into violence as tenant farmers battled landlords or their agents and backcountry farmers took up arms against the elite planters who dominated their colonial governments. New York tenant farmers had long resented the legal and economic power that manor lords wielded over their lives, and protests, labeled "land riots" by the wealthy landlords, were common throughout the century. Likewise, New Jersey landlords who tried to squeeze higher rents out of their tenants provoked bitterness—and frequent bloodshed. In January 1745, for example, tenants in Essex County, New Jersey, rioted after three of their number were arrested by local authorities. When the sheriff tried to bring one of the alleged troublemakers to the county courthouse, he was "assaulted by a great number of persons, with clubbs and other weapons," who rescued the prisoner. Later, a "multitude" armed with axes stormed the jail and rescued the remaining prisoners. Such tenant uprisings in both colonies continued during the 1750s and 1760s, as landless men expressed their resentment and frustration at their inability to acquire land of their own.

In the backcountry, settlers were likely to face two enemies: Indians and the established political powers of their own colonies. Often the clashes with the colonial government were about Indian policy. Eighteenth-century colonial legislatures and governors preferred diplomacy to military action, but western settlers wanted a more aggressive program to push Indians out of the way. Even when frontier hostilities led to bloodshed, the colonists of the coastal communities were reluctant to spend tax money to provide protection along the settlement line. In the end, bitter western settlers frequently took matters into their own hands. Bacon's Rebellion was the best example of this kind of vigilante action in the seventeenth century.

The revolt by Pennsylvania's Paxton Boys was the most dramatic eighteenth-century episode. More than most colonies, Pennsylvania's Quaker-dominated government encouraged settlers to find peaceful ways to coexist with local tribes. But the eighteenth-century Scots-Irish settlers did not share the Quaker commitment to pacifism. They demanded protection against Indian raids on isolated homesteads and small frontier towns. In 1763 frustrated settlers from Paxton, Pennsylvania, attacked a village of peaceful Conestoga Indians. Although the murder of these Indians solved nothing and could not be justified, hundreds of western colonists supported this vigilante group known as the Paxton Boys. The group marched on Philadelphia, the capital city of Pennsylvania, to press their demands for an aggressive Indian policy. With Philadelphia residents fearing their city would be attacked

Tensions between backcountry farmers and the colonial officials of North and South Carolina came to a head in the 1760s and 1770s. Calling themselves "Regulators," frontier farmers voiced their complaints about corrupt government agencies or the absence of vital services, but their protests went unheeded. By 1768, the Regulators had taken up arms against the government. Their rebellions, however, were crushed by officials like Governor Tryon of North Carolina. *Courtesy of the North Carolina Department of Archives & History, Raleigh, North Carolina.*

and looted, the popular printer and political leader Benjamin Franklin met the **Paxton Boys** on the outskirts of the city and negotiated a truce. The outcome was a dramatic shift in Pennsylvania Indian policy, illustrated by an official bounty for Indian scalps.

Vigilante action, however, was not always connected to Indian conflicts. In South Carolina, trouble arose because coastal planters refused to provide basic government services to the backcountry. Settlers in western South Carolina paid their taxes, but because their counties had no courts, they had to travel long distances to register land transactions or file lawsuits. The government provided no sheriffs either, and outlaws preyed on these communities. With the coastal planters refusing to admit any backcountry representatives to the colonial legislature, settlers could do little but complain, petition, and demand relief. In the 1760s, the farmers took matters into their own hands, choosing to "regulate" backcountry affairs themselves through vigilante action. These **Regulators** pursued and punished backcountry outlaws, dispensing justice without the aid of courts or judges.

In North Carolina, a similar power struggle led to a brief civil war. Here, a Regulator movement was organized against legal outlaws, a collection of corrupt local officials in the backcountry appointed because of their political connections to the colony's slaveholding elite. These officials awarded contracts to friends for building roads and bridges. They charged exorbitant fees to register deeds, surveys, or even the sale of cattle. And they set high poll taxes on their backcountry neighbors. The North Carolina Regula-

tors wanted these men removed, and when their demands were ignored, they mounted a taxpayers' rebellion. When tax collection dried up, the governor acted, raising a militia of twelve hundred men to march on the rebels. The showdown took place in 1771 near the Alamance River, where the governor's army easily defeated the two thousand poorly armed Regulators. Six of the movement's leaders were then hanged. The brief east-west war ended in North Carolina, but the bitterness remained. During the Revolutionary War, when most of North Carolina's coastal elite cast their lot for independence, many of the farmers of the backcountry—disgusted with colonial government—sided with England.

Reason and Religion in Colonial Society

- What political and personal expectations arose from Enlightenment philosophy?

- What was the impact of the Great Awakening on colonial attitudes toward authority?

Paxton Boys Settlers in Paxton, Pennsylvania, who massacred Conestoga Indians in 1763 and then marched on Philadelphia to demand that the colonial government provide better defense against the Indians.

Regulators Frontier settlers in the Carolinas who protested the lack or abuse of government services in their area; the North Carolina Regulators were suppressed by government troops in 1771.

Trade routes tied the eighteenth-century colonial world to parent societies across the Atlantic. The bonds of language and custom tied the immigrant communities in America to their homelands too. In addition to these economic and cultural ties, the flow of ideas and religious beliefs helped sustain a transatlantic community.

The Impact of the Enlightenment

At the end of the seventeenth century, a new intellectual movement arose in Europe: the **Enlightenment.** Enlightenment thinkers argued that reason, or rational thinking, rather than divine revelation, tradition, intuition, or established authority, was the true path to reliable knowledge and to human progress. A group of brilliant French thinkers called **philosophes,** including Voltaire, Rousseau, Diderot, Buffon, and Montesquieu, were the central figures of the Enlightenment. These philosophers, political theorists, and scientists disagreed about many issues, but all embraced the belief that nature could provide for all human wants and that human nature was basically good rather than flawed by original sin. Humans, they insisted, were rational and capable of making progress toward a perfect society if they studied nature, unlocked its secrets, and carefully nurtured the best human qualities in themselves and their children. This belief in progress and perfectibility became a central Enlightenment theme.

The Enlightenment was the handiwork of a small, intensely intellectual elite in Europe, and only the colonial elite had access to the books and essays that these philosophers produced. Elite colonists were drawn to two aspects of Enlightenment thought: its new religious philosophy of **deism** and the political theory of the "social contract." Deism appealed to colonists such as the Philadelphia scientist, writer, and political leader Benjamin Franklin and Virginia planters George Washington and Thomas Jefferson, men who were intensely interested in science and the scientific method. Deists believed that the universe operated according to logical, natural laws, without divine intervention. They thus denied the existence of any miracles after the Creation and rejected the value of prayer in this rational universe.

The most widely accepted Enlightenment ideas in the colonies were those of the English political theorist John Locke, who published his *Essay Concerning Human Understanding* in 1690 and *Two Treatises of Government* in 1691. In his political essays Locke argued that

human beings have certain natural rights that they cannot give away—or alienate—and that no one can take from them. Those rights include the right to own themselves and their own labor and the right to own that part of nature on which they have labored productively—that is, their property. However, in exchange for the government's protection of their natural rights to life, liberty, and property, people make a social contract to give up absolute freedom and to live under a rule of law. According to Locke, the government created by the **social contract** receives its political power from the consent of those it governs, and it cannot claim a divine right to rule. In Locke's scheme, the people express their will, or their demands and interests, through a representative assembly, and the government is obligated to protect and respect the natural rights of its citizens and serve their interests. If the government fails to do this, Locke said, the people have a right, even a duty, to rebel. Locke's theory was especially convincing because it meshed with political developments in England from the civil war to the Glorious Revolution that were familiar to the colonists.

Religion and Religious Institutions

Deism attracted little attention among ordinary colonists, but many eighteenth-century Americans were impressed by the growing religious diversity of their society. The waves of immigration had greatly increased the number of Protestant sects in the colonies, and colonists began to see religious toleration as a practical matter. The commitment to religious toleration did not come at an even pace, of course, nor did it extend to everyone. No colony allowed Catholics to vote or hold elective office after Rhode Island disfranchised Catholics in 1729, and even Maryland

Enlightenment An eighteenth-century intellectual movement that stressed the pursuit of knowledge through reason and challenged the value of religious belief, emotion, and tradition.

philosophe Any of the popular French intellectuals or social philosophers of the Enlightenment, such as Voltaire, Diderot, or Rousseau.

deism The belief that God created the universe in such a way that it could operate without any further divine intervention such as miracles.

social contract A theoretical agreement between the governed and the government that defines and limits the rights and obligations of each.

did not permit Catholics to celebrate Mass openly until Catholics in the city of Baltimore broke the law and founded a church in 1763. Connecticut granted freedom of worship to "sober dissenters" such as Anglicans, Quakers, and Baptists as early as 1708, but in 1750 its legislature declared it a felony to deny the **Trinity.** When colonists spoke of religious toleration, they did not mean the separation of church and state. On the contrary, the tradition of an **established church,** supported by taxes from all members of a community regardless of where they worshiped, went unchallenged in the southern colonies, where Anglicanism was established, and in Massachusetts and Connecticut, where **Congregationalism** was established.

As the diversity in churches was growing, the number of colonists who did not regularly attend any church at all was growing too. Some colonists were more preoccupied with secular concerns, such as their place in the economic community, than with spiritual ones. Others were losing their devotion to churches where the sermons were more intellectual than impassioned and the worship service was more formal than inspiring.

Into this moment stepped that group of **charismatic** preachers who, like Jonathan Edwards, denounced the obsession with profit and wealth they saw around them, condemned the sinfulness and depravity of all people, warned of the terrible punishments of eternal hellfires, and praised the saving grace of Jesus Christ. In a society divided by regional disputes, racial conflicts, and economic competition, these preachers held out a promise of social harmony based on the surrender of individual pride and a renewed love and fear of God. In voices filled with "Thunder and Lightning," they called for a revival of basic Protestant belief.

The Great Awakening

The religious revival of the eighteenth century was based as much on a new approach to preaching as on the message itself. This new-style preaching first appeared in New Jersey and Pennsylvania in the 1720s, when two **itinerant** preachers—Theodore Frelinghuysen and William Tennent Jr.—began calling the local churches to task for lack of devotion to God and for "cold" preaching. Tennent established what he called a "log college" to train fiery preachers who could spread a Christian revival throughout the colonies. Soon afterward, Jonathan Edwards spread the revival to Massachusetts. Like Frelinghuysen and Tennent, Edwards berated the lukewarm preaching

of local ministers and then turned to the task of saving lost souls. The revival, or **Great Awakening,** sparked by men like Edwards and Tennent, spread rapidly throughout the colonies, carried from town to town by the wandering ministers called "Awakeners." These preachers stirred entire communities to renewed religious devotion.

The Great Awakening's success was ensured in 1740, when **George Whitefield** toured the colonies from Charles Town to Maine. Everywhere this young preacher went, crowds gathered to hear him. Often the audiences grew so large that church sanctuaries could not hold them and Whitefield would finish his service in a nearby field or village green. His impact was electric. "Hearing him preach gave me a heart wound," wrote one colonist, and even America's most committed deist, Benjamin Franklin, confessed that Whitefield's sermons moved him. Whitefield himself recorded his effect on a crowd: "A wonderful power was in the room and with one accord they began to cry out and weep most bitterly for the space of half an hour." As the sermon progressed, the audience response became more intense: "Some of the people were as pale as death; others were wringing their hands; others lying on the ground; others sinking into the arms of their friends; and most lifting their eyes to heaven, and crying to God for mercy."

The Great Awakening did not go unchallenged. Some ministers had gladly turned over their pulpits to Awakeners. But others, angered by the criticisms of

Trinity In Christian doctrine, the belief that God has three divine aspects—Father, Son, and Holy Spirit.

established church The official church of a nation or colony, usually supported by taxes collected from all citizens, no matter what their religious beliefs or place of worship.

Congregationalism A form of Protestant church government in which the local congregation is independent and self-governing; in the colonies, the Puritans were Congregationalists.

charismatic Having a spiritual power or personal quality that stirs enthusiasm and devotion in large numbers of people.

itinerant Traveling from place to place.

Great Awakening A series of religious revivals based on fiery preaching and emotionalism that swept across the colonies during the second quarter of the eighteenth century.

George Whitefield English evangelical preacher of the Great Awakening whose charismatic style attracted huge crowds during his preaching tours of the colonies.

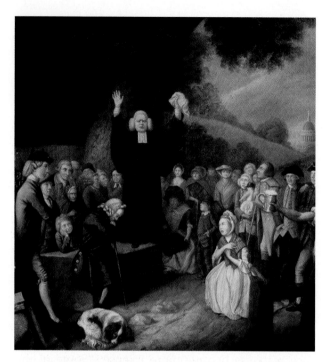

The English evangelical minister, George Whitefield, inspired awe and prompted renewed commitment to Christianity everywhere he preached. Crowds overflowed into the fields outside of colonial country churches, and men and women in his audiences often fainted or cried out in ecstasy. As the leading figure of the Great Awakening, Whitefield was loved by thousands and criticized by ministers who opposed the religious enthusiasm he represented. *Bridgeman Art Library Ltd.*

their preaching and suggestions that they themselves were unsaved, launched a counterattack against the revivalists and their "beastly brayings." Members of the colonial elite were roused to political action against a movement that constantly condemned the worldly amusements they enjoyed, such as dancing, gambling, drinking, theater, and elegant clothing. In Connecticut, for example, the assembly passed a law banning itinerant ministers from preaching outside their own parishes.

Bitter fights within congregations and denominations also developed. "Old Light" Congregationalists upheld the established service but "New Lights" chose revivalism, and "Old Side" Presbyterians battled "New Sides" over preaching styles and the content of the worship service. Congregations split, and the minority groups hurriedly formed new churches. Many awakened believers left their own **denominations** entirely, joining the Baptists or the Methodists. Anti-revivalists also left their strife-ridden churches and

became Anglicans. These religious conflicts frequently became intertwined with secular disputes. Colonists who had long-standing disagreements over Indian policy or economic issues lined up on opposite sides of the Awakening. Class tensions influenced religious loyalties, as poor colonists pronounced judgment on their rich neighbors using religious vocabulary that equated luxury, dancing, and gambling with sin.

Thus, rather than fulfilling its promise of social harmony, the Great Awakening increased strife and tension among colonists. Yet it had positive effects as well. For example, the Awakening spurred the growth of higher education. During the complicated theological arguments between Old Lights and Awakeners, the revivalists came to see the value of theological training. They founded new colleges, including Rutgers, Brown, Princeton, and Dartmouth, to prepare their clergy just as the Old Lights relied on Harvard and Yale to train theirs. One of the most important effects of the Great Awakening was also one of the least expected. The resistance to authority, the activism involved in creating new institutions, the participation in debate and argument—these experiences reinforced a sense that protest and resistance were acceptable, not just in religious matters but in the realm of politics as well.

Government and Politics in the Mainland Colonies

■ What circumstances limited a colonial governor's exercise of royal power?

■ What was the result of the struggle for power between the colonial assemblies and the colonial governors?

The English mainland colonies were part of a large and complex empire, and the English government had created many agencies to set and enforce imperial policy. Parliament passed laws regulating colonial affairs, the royal navy and army determined colonial defense, and English diplomats decided which foreign nations were friends and which were foes. But from the beginning, most **proprietors,** joint-stock

denomination A group of religious congregations that accept the same doctrines and are united under a single name.

proprietor In colonial America, a proprietor was a wealthy Englishman who received a large grant of land in America from the king or queen in order to create a new colony.

companies, and kings had also found it convenient to create local governments within their colonies to handle day-to-day affairs. Virginia's House of Burgesses was the first locally elected legislative body in the colonies, but by 1700 every mainland colony boasted a representative assembly generally made up of its wealthiest men.

In the first half of the eighteenth century, the British government decided to restructure its colonial administration, hoping to make it more efficient. Despite this reorganization, the government was notably lax in enforcing colonial regulations. Even so, colonists often objected to the constraints of imperial law and challenged the role of the king or the proprietors in shaping local political decisions. This **insubordination** led to a long and steady struggle for power between colonial governors and colonial assemblies. Over the first half of the century, the colonists did wrest important powers from the governors. But the British government remained adamant that ultimate power, or **sovereignty,** rested in the hands of king and Parliament.

Imperial Institutions and Policies

By the eighteenth century, the British government had divided responsibility for colonial regulation and management among several departments, commissions, and agencies. Even though the Lords Commissioners of Trade and Plantations had been created in 1696 to coordinate colonial **policy,** authority remained fragmented. The treasury board, for example, continued to supervise all colonial financial affairs, and its customs office collected all trade revenues. The admiralty board, however, had the authority to enforce trade regulations. The potential for conflict among all these departments, commissions, and agencies was great. But British indifference to colonial affairs helped to preserve harmony.

Parliament set the tone for colonial administration in the eighteenth century with a policy that came to be known unofficially as **salutary neglect.** Salutary, or healthy, neglect meant the government was satisfied with relaxed enforcement of most regulations as long as the colonies remained dutifully loyal in military and economic matters. As long as specific, or **enumerated,** colonial raw materials continued to flow into British hands and the colonists continued to rely on British manufactured goods, salutary neglect suited the expectations of the king, Parliament, and most government officials.

Salutary neglect did not mean that the colonists were free to do exactly as they pleased. Even in purely domestic matters the colonial governments could not operate as freely as many of them desired. The most intense political conflicts before the 1760s centered on the colonial assemblies' power to govern local affairs as they chose.

Local Colonial Government

The eighteenth-century mainland colonies remained a mixture of royal, proprietary, and corporate colonies, although the majority were held directly by the king. Whatever the form of ownership, however, the colonies were strikingly similar in the structure and operation of their governments. Each colony had a governor appointed by the king or the proprietor or, in Connecticut and Rhode Island (the two **corporate colonies**), elected to executive office. Each had a council, usually appointed by the governor, though sometimes elected by the assembly, which served as an advisory body to the governor. And each had an elected representative assembly with lawmaking and taxing powers.

The governor was the linchpin of local government because he represented royal authority and imperial interests in the local setting. In theory, his powers were impressive. He alone could call the assembly into session, and he had the power to dismiss it. He also could veto any act passed by the assembly. He had the sole power to appoint and dismiss judges, justices of the peace, and all government officials. He could grant pardons and reprieves. The governor made all land grants, oversaw all aspects of colonial trade, and conducted all diplomatic negotiations with the Indians. Because he was commander in chief of the military and naval forces of the colony, he decided what action, if any, to take in conflicts between colonists and Indians. Armed with such extensive powers, the man who sat in the English colonial governor's seat ought to have been respected—or at least obeyed.

---

insubordination Resistance to authority; disobedience.

sovereignty The ultimate power in a nation or a state.

policy A course of action taken by a government or a ruler.

salutary neglect The British policy of relaxed enforcement of most colonial trade regulations as long as the mainland colonies remained loyal to the government and profitable within the British economy.

enumerated Added to the list of regulated goods or crops.

corporate colony A self-governing colony, not directly under the control of proprietors or the Crown.

Historians are sometimes simply wrong. For over a century, experts in New York history were certain that this was a portrait of Lord Cornbury, royal governor of New York from 1702 to 1708. Cornbury, it was said, bore a striking resemblance to his cousin Queen Anne and had dressed in women's clothing in order to emphasize his connection to her authority and power. A great story, isn't it? But recently a scholar has proven that this is not Lord Cornbury. Now the task is to discover who the person in the portrait really is. *New York Historical Society.*

A closer look, however, reveals that the governor was not so powerful after all. First, in many cases he was not free to exercise his own judgment because he was bound by a set of instructions written by the board of trade. Though highly detailed and specific, these instructions often bore little relation to the realities the governor encountered in his colony. Instead, by limiting his ability to improvise and compromise, they proved more burdensome than helpful to many a frustrated governor.

Second, the governor's own skills and experience were often limited. Few men in the prime of their careers sought posts 3,000 miles from England, in the provinces. Thus governorships went to **bureaucrats** nearing the end of sometimes unimpressive careers or to younger men who were new to the rough-and-tumble games of politics. Many colonial governors were honorable and competent, but enough of them were fools, scoundrels, or eccentrics to give the office a poor reputation.

Finally, most governors served brief terms, sometimes too brief for them to learn which local issues were critical or to discern friend from foe in the colonial government. For many, the goal was simply to survive the ordeal. They were willing to surrender much of their authority to the local assemblies in exchange for a calm, uneventful, and, they hoped, profitable term in office.

Even the most ignorant or incompetent governor might have managed to dominate colonial politics had he been able to apply the grease that oiled eighteenth-century political wheels: patronage. The kings of England had learned that political loyalty could be bought on the floor of Parliament with royal favors. By midcentury, over half of the members of Parliament held Crown offices or had received government contracts. Unfortunately for the colonial governor, he had few favors to hand out. The king could also bribe voters or intimidate them to ensure the election of his supporters to Parliament, but the governor lacked this option as well. The number of eligible voters in most colonies was far too great for a governor's resources.

The most significant restraint on the governor's authority was not his rigid instructions, his inexperience, or his lack of patronage, but the fact that the assembly paid his salary. England expected the colonists to foot the bill for local government, including compensation for the governor. Governors who challenged the assembly too strongly or too often usually found a sudden, unaccountable budget crisis delaying or diminishing their allowances. Those who bent to assembly wishes could expect bonuses in the form of cash or grants of land.

While the governors learned that their great powers were not so great after all, the assemblies in every colony were making an opposite discovery: they learned they could broaden their powers far beyond the king's intent. They fought for and won more freedom from the governor's supervision and influence, gaining the right to elect their own speaker of the assembly, make their own procedural rules, and settle contested elections. They also increased their power over taxation and the use of revenues, or, in eighteenth-century parlance, their **power of the purse.**

---

bureaucrat A government official, usually appointed, who is deeply devoted to the details of administrative procedures.

power of the purse The political power that is enjoyed by the branch of government that controls taxation and the use of tax monies.

In their pursuit of power, these local political leaders had several advantages besides the governor's weakness. They came from a small social and economic elite who were regularly elected to office for both practical and social reasons. First, they could satisfy the high property qualifications set for most officeholding. Second, they could afford to accept an office that cost more to win and to hold than its modest salary could cover. Third, a habit of **deference**—respect for the opinions and decisions of the more educated and wealthy families in a community—won them office. Although as many as 50 to 80 percent of adult free white males in a colony could vote, few were considered suitable to hold office. Generations of fathers and sons from elite families thus dominated political offices. These men knew one another well, and although they fought among themselves for positions and power, they could effectively unite against outsiders such as an arrogant governor. Finally, through long careers in the legislature they honed the political, administrative, and even **oratorical** skills that would enable them to contend successfully with the royal appointees.

Conflicting Views of the Assemblies

The king and Parliament gave local assemblies the authority to raise taxes, pay government salaries, direct the care of the poor, and maintain bridges and roads. To the colonists, this division of authority indicated an acceptance of a two-tiered system of government: (1) a central government that created and executed imperial policy and (2) a set of local governments that managed colonial domestic affairs. If these levels of government were not equal in their power and scope, at least—in the minds of the colonists—they were equally legitimate. On both points, however, the British disagreed. They did not acknowledge a multilevel system. They saw a single vast empire ruled by one government consisting of king and Parliament. The colonial governments may have acquired the power to establish temporary operating procedures and to pass minor laws, but British leaders did not believe they had acquired a share of the British government's sovereign power. As the governor of Pennsylvania put it in 1726, the assembly's actions and decisions should in "no ways interfere . . . with the Legal Prerogative of the Crown or the true Legislative Power of the Mother State." "True Legislative Power" belonged with Parliament, and most British political leaders considered the assemblies to

be little more than **ad hoc** bodies, specially created to meet immediate needs and serve as surrogates, or deputies, for those with real authority.

North America and the Struggle for Empire

■ What were the diplomatic and military goals of Europeans and American Indians in North America?

■ What were the major effects of the imperial wars on the American colonists?

■ How did the English victory in 1763 affect people in North America?

During the seventeenth century, most of the violence and warfare in colonial America arose from struggles either between Indians and colonists over land or among colonists over political power and the use of revenues and resources. These struggles continued to be important during the eighteenth century. By 1690, however, the most persistent dangers to colonial peace and safety came from the fierce rivalries between the French, Spanish, and the English (see Map 4.1). Between 1688 and 1763, these European powers waged five bloody and costly wars. Most of these conflicts were motivated by politics at home, although colonial ambitions spurred the last and most decisive of them. No matter where these worldwide wars began, or what their immediate cause, colonists were usually drawn into them.

When imperial wars included fighting in America, English colonists were expected to fight without the assistance of British troops. Often the enemy the colonists faced was neither French nor Spanish but Indian, a result of the alliances Indians had formed with Europeans to advance their own interests. For example, until the mid-seventeenth century, the Huron-dominated confederacy to the north supported the French (see Map 4.2). These two allies had a strong economic bond: the French profited from the fur trade while the Hurons enjoyed the benefits of European manufactured goods. The English colonists were not without their Indian allies, however. Although

---

deference Yielding to the judgment or wishes of a social or intellectual superior.

oratorical Related to the art of persuasive and eloquent public speaking.

ad hoc Created for, or concerned with, one specific purpose; Latin for "to this [end]."

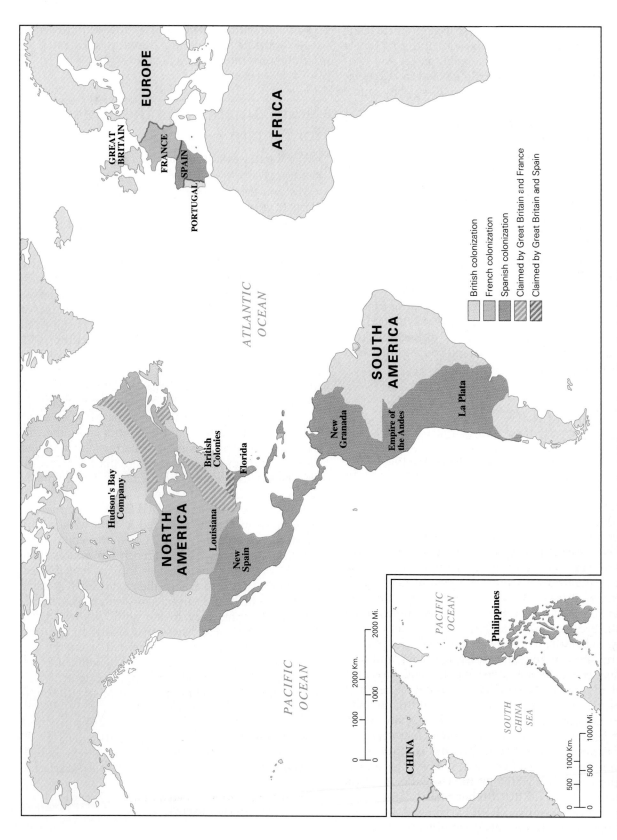

MAP 4.1 The European Empires in Eighteenth-Century America   This map shows the colonization of the Americas and the Philippines by three rival powers. It is clear from the map why British colonists felt vulnerable to attack by England's archenemies, France and Spain, until English victory in the Great War for Empire in 1763.

MAP 4.2 The Indian Confederacies This map shows the three major Indian military and political coalitions—the Huron, Iroquois, and Creek Confederacies. Unlike the squabbling English mainland colonies, these Indian tribes understood the value of military unity in the face of threats to their land and their safety and the importance of diplomatic unity in negotiating with their European allies.

the older, seventeenth-century alliances between the Wampanoags and the Plymouth settlers had ended in violence, other alliances held. Ties with the Iroquois League were carefully nurtured by the English, who appreciated the advantages of friendship with Indians living south of the Great Lakes, along crucial fur trading routes. For their part, the Iroquois were willing to cooperate with a European power who was the enemy of their perpetual rival, the Hurons. The southern English colonists turned to the **Creek Confederacy** when wars with Spain erupted. Yet the colonists' own land hunger always worked to undermine—if not unravel—these Indian alliances. Thus the southern tribes' support was unreliable, and the Iroquois, wary of the English westward expansion, often chose to pursue an independent strategy of neutrality.

The wars that raged from 1689 until 1763 were part of a grand effort by rival European nations to control the balance of power at home and abroad. The colonists often felt like pawns in the hands of the more powerful players, and resentment sometimes overshadowed their patriotic pride when England was victorious. Whatever their views on imperial diplomacy, few colonists escaped the impact of this nearly century-long struggle for power between England, France, and Spain, for periods of peace were short and the long shadow of war hung over them until Britain's major triumph in 1763.

An Age of Imperial Warfare

William and Mary's ascent to the throne in 1689 ushered in an era of political stability and religious tolerance in Britain. But it also ushered in an age of imperial warfare. Almost immediately, France took up arms against England, Holland, Sweden, and Spain in what the Europeans called the War of the League of Augsburg but which colonists called simply King William's War. With France as the enemy, New England and northern New York bore the brunt of the fighting. Because the English sent no troops to defend the border communities there, colonial armies, composed largely of untrained militia companies, and their Iroquois allies defended British interests—and their own families—in this long and vicious war. As reports of atrocities mounted, the governments of Massachusetts, Plymouth, Connecticut, and New York made a rare attempt at cooperation. They pledged to combine their resources in order to invade Canada. In the end, however, few made good on their promises of men or money, and colonial attacks on Montreal and Quebec both failed. When the war finally ended with the Treaty of Ryswick in 1697, 659 New Englanders had died in battle, in raids, or in captivity. The death toll for the Iroquois nations was higher—between 600 and 1,300. The lessons of the war were equally apparent. First, colonists paid a high price for their disunity and lack of cooperation. Second, no New Englander could ever feel secure until the French had been driven out of Canada. Third, the colonists needed the aid of the English army and navy to effectively drive the French away.

The colonists had little time to enjoy peace. Five years later, in 1702, the conflict colonists called Queen Anne's War began, once again pitting France and its now dependent ally, Spain, against England, Holland, and Austria. In this eleven-year struggle, colonists faced enemies on both their southern and northern borders. Once again, those enemies included Indians.

Creek Confederacy Alliance of the Creeks and smaller Indian tribes living in the Southeast.

Imperial wars between England and her rivals often drew the colonists and neighboring Indian tribes into conflict. Between 1711 and 1713, land-hungry North Carolinians, joined by South Carolina and Virginia militias and by Creek and Yamasee troops, turned Queen Anne's War into a brutal and successful war on the nearby Tuscarora Indians. *South Carolina Historical Society.*

Between 1711 and 1713, southern colonists were caught up in fierce warfare with the Tuscaroras, who were angered by North Carolina land seizures. The casualties were staggering. Some 150 settlers were killed in the opening hours of the war, and in the following months both sides outdid one another in cruelty. Stakes were run through the bodies of women, children were murdered, and Indian captives were roasted alive. South Carolina and Virginia sent arms and supplies to aid the North Carolina colonists, and the Creek and Yamasee Indians fought beside the white settlers against the Tuscaroras. When this war-within-a-war ended in 1713, more than a thousand Tuscaroras were dead and nearly four hundred had been sold into slavery. The survivors took refuge in the land of the Iroquois.

The war in the north was just as deadly. Indian and French raids, such as the one on Deerfield, Massachusetts, cost the lives of many New Englanders. Despite repeated calls for help, the British did not send troops to defend their northern colonies. Disappointed New Englanders raised an army of nearly thirty-five hundred men and, in 1710, triumphantly took control of the military post at Port Royal and with it all of Acadia, or as the English called it, Nova Scotia.

The war, which ended in 1713, cost New Englanders dearly. The high death toll of King William's War and Queen Anne's War was staggering: nearly one of every four soldiers in uniform had died. The financial cost was equally devastating. Four-fifths of Massachusetts revenues in 1704–1705 went for military expenses. Homeowners in Boston saw their taxes rise 42 percent between 1700 and 1713. The city's streets were filled with beggars and its homes with widows. In Connecticut and Massachusetts, colonists spoke bitterly of the Mother Country's failure to protect them. Yet this time New Englanders could see tangible gains from the imperial struggle. The English flag now flew over Nova Scotia, Newfoundland, and Hudson Bay, which meant that Maine settlers no longer had to fear enemy raids. New England fleets could fish the cod-rich waters of Newfoundland more safely. And colonial fur traders could profit from Hudson Bay's resources.

For a generation, Europeans kept the peace. In America, however, violence continued along the line of settlement, with New Englanders battling Indian allies of the French and southern colonists making war on their own former allies, the Yamasees. The short but ferociously fought Yamasee War of 1715 left four hundred of South Carolina's five thousand colonists dead in the first twelve months of fighting, a higher death rate than white Massachusetts had sustained in King Philip's War.

At the end of the 1730s, the calm in Europe was fractured. By 1740, France, Spain, and Prussia were at war with England and its ally, Austria. This war, known in the colonies as King George's War, again meant enemy attacks on both the northern and southern colonies. New Englanders, swept up in the Great Awakening, viewed the war as a Protestant crusade against Catholicism, a holy war designed to rid the continent of religious enemies. Yet when the war ended in 1748, France still retained its Canadian territories.

The Great War for Empire

Despite three major wars and countless border conflicts, the map of North America had changed very little. Colonial efforts to capture Canada or to rid the southwest of Indian enemies had not succeeded. Yet veterans of the wars, and their civilian colonial supporters, spoke with pride of the colonial armies as excellent military forces. Without assistance from British regulars or the British navy, militiamen and volunteer armies had defended their communities, defeated Indian enemies, and captured important French forts.

Many colonists remained angry and bewildered, however, by the Mother Country's military neglect. From their perspective, they were being dragged into European wars that did not concern them. Then, in 1756, the tables seemed to turn: this time, Europe was dragged into a colonial war. Westward expansion

Louisbourg was an imposing fortress capital in Nova Scotia, almost 600 miles northeast of Boston. In May of 1745, during King George's War, Massachusetts merchant William Pepperrell led four thousand New England volunteers in a successful campaign to seize Louisbourg from the French. The New Englanders hailed their victory as a Protestant triumph over Catholicism and were stunned when Britain returned the city to the enemy at war's end. *Yale University Art Gallery, Mabel Brady Garven Collection.*

deeper into North America triggered a great war for empire, referred to in Europe as the Seven Years' War and in the colonies as the French and Indian War.

The problem began in the 1740s, as the neutral zone between the French colonial empire and the British mainland settlements began to shrink. As thousands of new immigrants poured into the English colonies, the colonists pressed farther westward, toward the Ohio Valley. Virginia land speculators began to woo the Indians of the region with trading agreements. The English colonial interest in the valley alarmed the French, who had plans to unite their mainland empire, connecting Canada and Louisiana with a chain of forts, trading posts, and missions across the Ohio Valley.

Virginia's governor, Robert Dinwiddie, was troubled by French military buildup in the Ohio Valley. He warned the British that a potential crisis was developing thousands of miles from London. In 1754 Britain responded; the government agreed to send an expedition to assess French strength and warn the French to abandon a new fort on French Creek. Dinwiddie chose an inexperienced Virginia planter and colonial militia officer, Major George Washington, to lead the expedition. When Washington conveyed the warning, the French commander responded with insulting sarcasm. Tensions escalated rapidly. Dinwiddie later sent Major Washington to challenge the French at Fort Duquesne, near present-day Pittsburgh, but the French forced him to surrender.

Fearing another war, colonial political leaders knew it was time to act decisively—and to attempt cooperation. In June 1754, seven colonies sent representatives to Albany, New York, to organize a united defense. Unfortunately this effort at cooperation failed. When the Albany Plan of Union was presented to the colonial assemblies, none was willing to approve it. Instead, American colonists looked to Britain to act. This time, Britain did. Parliament sent Major General Edward Braddock, a battle-hardened veteran, to drive the French out of Fort Duquesne. Braddock's humiliating failure was only the first of many for the English in America.

English and French forces engaged each other in battle four times before war was officially declared in 1756. Soon, every major European power was involved, and the fighting spread rapidly across Europe, the Philippines, Africa, India, the Caribbean, and North America. In America, France's Indian allies joined the war more readily than England's. Iroquois tribes opted for neutrality, waiting until 1759 to throw in their lot with the English. Although Mohawks fought as mercenaries in New York and Iroquois in western Pennsylvania suppressed Delaware attacks on English colonists there, Iroquois support was erratic. In fact, some members of the League, including the Senecas, fought with the French in 1757 and 1758. Given these circumstances, a British defeat seemed likely.

In the south, the Cherokees played the French and English against each other. About 250 Cherokee warriors did sign up to fight with the Virginia militia in 1757, but as mercenaries rather than allies. By 1760, a full-scale war between colonists and Cherokees had erupted in the southern colonies. Although this Cherokee Rebellion of 1759–1761 ended in Indian defeat, the war drained off many of the southern colonial resources that might have been used against the French.

In 1756 the worried British government turned over the direction of the war to the ardent imperialist William Pitt. More than willing to take drastic steps, Pitt committed the British treasury to the largest war expenditures the nation had ever known and then put together the largest military force that North America had ever seen, combining 25,000 colonial troops with 24,000 British regulars. The fortunes of war soon reversed. By the end of 1759, the upper Ohio Valley had been taken from the French. And in August of that year, General James Wolfe took the war to the heart of French Canada: the fortress city of Quebec.

With his piercing eyes and his long red hair, the 31-year-old Wolfe looked the part of the military hero he was. Despite his eighteen years of military service, even Wolfe admitted he was daunted by the difficult

For most Americans, the English victory in the Battle of Quebec was the most dramatic event of the Seven Years' War. When Benjamin West painted "The Death of General Wolfe," he acknowledged the role Indian allies had played on both sides of this imperial struggle by adding an Indian observer to the scene. *National Gallery of Canada, Ottawa.*

task ahead of him. Quebec, heavily manned and well armed, sat on top of steep cliffs rising high above the St. Lawrence River. Inside, the formidable French general Louis-Joseph Montcalm was in command. The only possible approach was from the west of the city, across the Plains of Abraham. The problem was how to get to that battlefield.

Wolfe was uncharacteristically hesitant until he discovered a blockaded roadway running to the top of the 175-foot cliff. On the evening of September 12, forty-five hundred British soldiers climbed this diagonal path to the top. When the thoroughly surprised Montcalm saw a double line of scarlet uniforms forming on the plain at dawn, he gathered a force of more than four thousand and marched out to meet the British. The French fired several rounds, but Wolfe ordered his men to hold their fire until the enemy was within 60 yards. Then the redcoats fired, and the French turned and ran. Among the British wounded was General James Wolfe, shot through the chest. Hearing that the French were in retreat, the dying general murmured, "Now, God be praised, I will die in peace." Among the French casualties was Louis-Joseph, Marquis de Montcalm, who died the following day from internal injuries caused by a musket ball to his midsection.

Five days after the Battle of the Plains of Abraham, Quebec formally surrendered. In 1760 the city of Montreal also fell to the British. With that, the French governor surrendered the whole of New France to his enemies, and the war in North America was over. The fighting in this most global of eighteenth-century wars continued elsewhere until 1763. Spain entered the struggle as a French ally in 1761, but English victories in India, the Caribbean, and the Pacific squelched

any hopes the French had. The **Treaty of Paris** established the supremacy of the British Empire.

The Outcomes of the Great War for Empire

The war had redrawn the map of the world (see Table 4.1). The French Empire had shriveled, with nothing remaining of New France but two tiny islands between Nova Scotia and Newfoundland. Ten thousand Acadians—French colonists of Nova Scotia—were refugees of the war, deported from their homes by the English because their loyalty was suspect. These Acadians, who either relocated to France, settled in New England, or made the exhausting trek to French-speaking Louisiana, were living reminders of the French Empire's eclipse. The only other remnants of the French Empire in the Western Hemisphere were the sugar islands of Guadeloupe, Martinique, and St. Domingue, left to France because England's so-called Sugar Interest wanted no further competition in the British market. Across the ocean, France lost trading posts in Africa, and on the other side of the world, the French presence in India vanished.

The 1763 peace treaty dismantled the French Empire but did not destroy France itself. Although the nation's treasury was empty, its borders were intact.

Treaty of Paris The treaty ending the French and Indian War in 1763; it gave all of French Canada and Spanish Florida to Britain.

TABLE 4.1   Imperial and Colonial Wars

Name	Date	Participants	Treaty
In colonies: King William's War *In Europe:* War of the League of Augsburg	1688–1697	*In Europe:* France vs. England, Holland, Sweden, and Spain *In North America*: Colonists and their Iroquois allies vs. French and their Indian allies *Area:* New England and northern New York	Treaty of Ryswick (1697) *Results* Port Royal in Acadia (Nova Scotia) is returned to France France is still a presence in North America
In colonies: Queen Anne's War *In Europe:* War of the Spanish Succession	1702–1713	*In Europe:* England, Holland, and Austria vs. France and Spain *In North America:* English colonists vs. French and Spanish powers in North and South and their Indian allies	Treaty of Utrecht (1713) *Results* France renounces plans to unite with Spain under one crown England gains Caribbean islands, St. Kitts, Gibraltar, and Minorca English flag flies over Nova Scotia, New Foundland, and Hudson Bay War takes a financial toll on the colonies
War of Jenkins's Ear	1739–1740	*In Europe:* England vs. Spain *In North America:* English colonists clash with Spanish in interior regions (Georgia, South Carolina, Virginia)	None—Conflict expands into King George's War
In colonies: King George's War *In Europe:* War of the Austrian Succession	1740–1748	*In Europe:* Austria and England vs. Prussia, France, and Spain *In North America:* English colonists in New England vs. French and their Indian allies	Treaty of Aix-la-Chapelle (1748) *Results* England returns Louisbourg to French in exchange for Madras (in India)
In colonies: French and Indian War *In Europe:* Seven Years' War	1756–1763	*In Europe:* England and Prussia vs. France and Austria *In North America:* English colonists vs. French and their Indian allies *Area:* Global war; in colonies, all regions	Treaty of Paris (1763) *Results* French Empire shrinks France's presence in North America is greatly reduced France loses trading posts in Africa and exits India Britain takes Florida from Spain and Canada from France France gives up Louisiana to Spain for compensation for Florida British government is deeply in debt The borders of Britain's North American colonies are secured

France's alliance with Spain held firm, cemented by the experience of defeat. Britain was victorious, but victory did not mean Britain had escaped unharmed. The British government was deeply in debt and faced new problems associated with managing and protecting its greatly enlarged empire.

In the mainland colonies, people lit bonfires and staged parades to celebrate Britain's victory and the safety of their own borders. But the tension of being both members of a colonial society and citizens of a great empire could not be easily dismissed. The war left scars, including memories of the British military's arrogance toward provincial soldiers and lingering resentment over the quartering of British soldiers at colonial expense. The colonists were aware that the British had grounds for resentment also, particularly the profitable trade some Americans had carried on with the enemy even in the midst of the war. Suspicion and resentment, a growing sense of difference, a tug of loyalties between the local community and the larger empire—these were the unexpected outcomes of a glorious victory.

Individual Voices

Examining a Primary Source

Eliza Lucas Challenges Traditional Plantation Life

The eighteenth-century plantation world of South Carolina was a patriarchal society dedicated to the production of a single staple crop, rice. When Eliza Lucas began experimenting with indigo, figs, and hemp at Wappoo, her family plantation, it was the beginning of a new era of prosperity and diversification in the South Carolina plantation economy. As one of the few women to manage a large plantation at the time, Lucas was unique in her desire to experiment with new crops and stretch old gender roles. In her letters, Miss Lucas provides insight into the experiences of a woman succeeding in a male-dominated society. In this letter to her young niece, Lucas describes the demanding schedule she maintained in order to balance her roles as a society woman and a plantation master.

■ In this section Eliza Lucas shows us some of the ways in which she juggles her feminine and masculine roles? Do you think the men of the period spent the same amount of time devoted to learning?

■ Eliza Lucas hoped that the two African American slave girls she was educating would educate other slaves on the plantation. What arguments could be raised against this program to educate slaves? What benefits might come from the education of slaves?

Dr. Miss B.

. . . Why, my dear Miss B, will you so often repeat your desire to know how I triffle away my time in our retirement in my fathers absence. Could it afford you advantage or pleasure I should not have hesitated, but as you can expect neither from it I would have been excused; however, to show you my readiness in obeying your commands, here it is.

■ *In general then I rise at five o'Clock in the morning, read till Seven, then take a walk in the garden or field, see that the Servants are at their respective business, then to breakfast. The first hour after breakfast is spent at my musick, the next is constantly employed in recolecting something I have learned least for want of practise it should be quite lost, such as French and short hand.* ■ *After that I devote the rest of the time till I dress for dinner to our little Polly and two black girls who I teach to read, and if I have my papa's approbation (my Mamas I have got) I intend [them] for school mistres's for the rest of the negro children—another scheme you see. But to proceed, the first hour after dinner as the first after breakfast at musick, the rest of the afternoon in Needle work till candle light, and from that time to bed time read or write. 'Tis the fashion here to carry our work abroad*

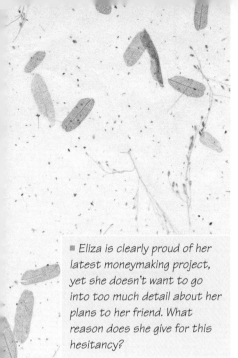

so that having company, without they are great strangers, is no interruption to that affair; but I have particular matters for particular days, which is an interruption of mine. Monday my musick Master is here. Tuesdays my friend Mrs. Chardon (about 3 mile distant) and I are constantly engaged to each other, she at our house one Tuesday—I at hers the next and this is one of the happiest days I spend at Woppoe. Thursday the whole day except what necessary affairs of the family take up is spent in writing, either on the business of the plantations, or letters to my friends. Every other Fryday, if no company, we go a vizeting so that I go abroad once a week and no oftener.

O! I had like to forgot the last thing I have done a great while. I have planted a large figg orchard with design to dry and export them. ■ *I have reconed [reckoned] my experience and the propfets [profits] to arise from these figgs, but was I to tell you how great an Estate I am to make this way, and how 'tis to be laid out you would think me far gone in romance. Your good Uncle I know has long thought I have a fertile brain at schemeing. I only confirm him in his opinion; but I own I love the vegitable world extremly. I think it an innocent and useful amusement. Pray tell him, if he laughs much at my project, I never intend to have my hand in a silver mine and he will understand as well as you what I mean. . . .*

■ Eliza is clearly proud of her latest moneymaking project, yet she doesn't want to go into too much detail about her plans to her friend. What reason does she give for this hesitancy?

Summary

Each of the colonial regions developed a unique culture and society. Each region was directly connected to Britain by a well-established pattern of trade, but trade also connected them to one another. The colonists were often at odds among themselves, yet they could and did unite when common enemies threatened.

The social and cultural diversity among the colonies developed within a common imperial structure. In many regions, society changed significantly in the eighteenth century. In New England, the outcome of increased commercial activity and a royal government was a shift from a "Puritan" culture to a more secular "Yankee" culture, despite the religious revival that Jonathan Edwards helped spark. In the South, the planter elite continued to focus on the production of staple crops but shifted from a labor force of indentured servants to one of African slaves. By midcentury, these enslaved Africans had begun to develop their own community life and their own African American culture. The Middle Colonies developed a lively urban culture, but most people who immigrated to British North America after 1700 chose to settle in the backcountry. Here opportunities were greater, although the conflict with Native Americans was a constant fact of life.

Intellectual life in the eighteenth century changed dramatically as Enlightenment ideas encouraged the expectation of progress through reliance on reason. Colonial elites affirmed John Locke's theory of natural rights as well as a skepticism about religious dogmas. The Great Awakening unleashed a second, and opposing, intellectual current. Revivalists such as Jonathan Edwards and George Whitefield spread a renewed commitment to religious salvation throughout the colonies. At the same time, "Awakeners" challenged all authority except the individual spirit, and many ordinary colonists embraced the same notion.

A similar challenge to authority emerged in politics and imperial relations. Despite England's policy of salutary neglect in governing the colonies, colonial assemblies resented royal officials and asserted their own claims to power against appointed governors and other British officials. Strains in the relationship between colonial assemblies and imperial officers ran deep.

Intense rivalry between England, France, and Spain led to five major wars between 1688 and 1763. Colonists were expected to defend their own borders in most of the wars. In the French and Indian War, however, the British played an active role in driving the French out of mainland America. The British victory in 1763 altered the colonial map of North America and changed power relations throughout the European world.

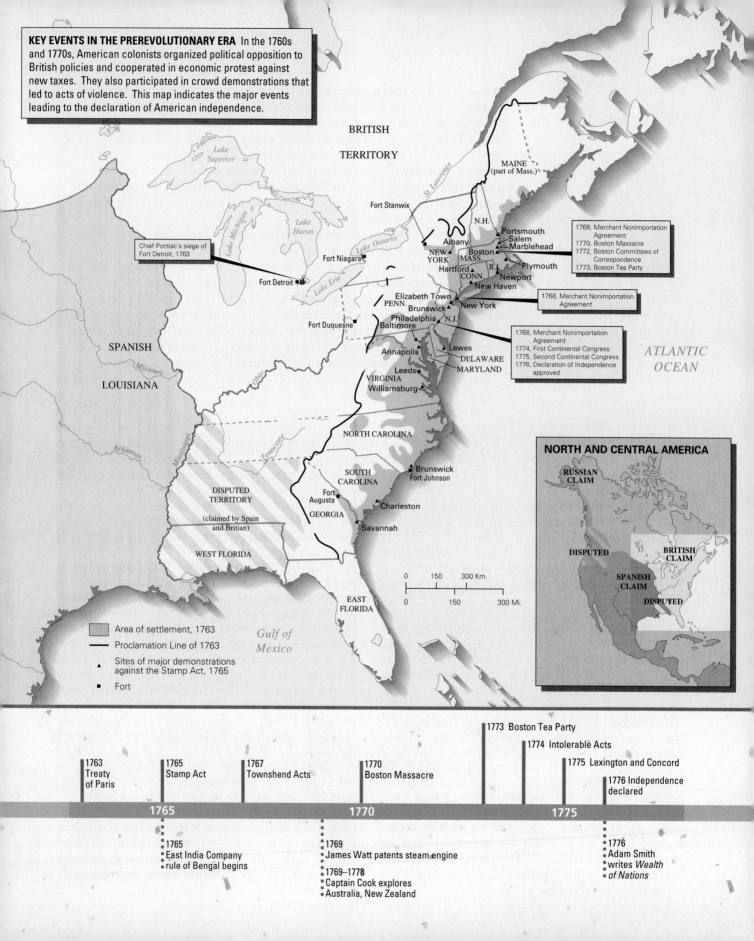

KEY EVENTS IN THE PREREVOLUTIONARY ERA In the 1760s and 1770s, American colonists organized political opposition to British policies and cooperated in economic protest against new taxes. They also participated in crowd demonstrations that led to acts of violence. This map indicates the major events leading to the declaration of American independence.

BRITISH

TERRITORY

Lake Superior

Lake Michigan

Lake Huron

St. Lawrence

MAINE (part of Mass.)

Fort Stanwix

N.H.

Albany

Lake Ontario

Fort Niagara

Chief Pontiac's siege of Fort Detroit, 1763

Fort Detroit

Lake Erie

NEW YORK

Portsmouth
Salem
Marblehead

Boston
MASS.

Hartford
CONN.

R.I.
Plymouth

Newport

New Haven

1768, Merchant Nonimportation Agreement
1770, Boston Massacre
1772, Boston Committees of Correspondence
1773, Boston Tea Party

Elizabeth Town

PENN.
Brunswick

New York

1768, Merchant Nonimportation Agreement

Fort Duquesne

Philadelphia
Baltimore

N.J.

1768, Merchant Nonimportation Agreement
1774, First Continental Congress
1775, Second Continental Congress
1776, Declaration of Independence approved

SPANISH

LOUISIANA

Missouri

Ohio

Annapolis

Lewes

DELAWARE
MARYLAND

Leeds

VIRGINIA
Williamsburg

Arkansas

Tennessee

NORTH CAROLINA

SOUTH CAROLINA

Brunswick
Fort Johnson

DISPUTED TERRITORY

(claimed by Spain and Britian)

Fort Augusta

GEORGIA

Charleston

Savannah

WEST FLORIDA

EAST FLORIDA

Gulf of Mexico

Mississippi

ATLANTIC OCEAN

NORTH AND CENTRAL AMERICA

RUSSIAN CLAIM

DISPUTED

BRITISH CLAIM

SPANISH CLAIM

DISPUTED

| 0 | 150 | 300 Km. |
| 0 | 150 | 300 Mi. |

Area of settlement, 1763

Proclamation Line of 1763

Sites of major demonstrations against the Stamp Act, 1765

Fort

1773 Boston Tea Party

1774 Intolerable Acts

1775 Lexington and Concord

1776 Independence declared

1763 Treaty of Paris

1765 Stamp Act

1767 Townshend Acts

1770 Boston Massacre

1765

1770

1775

1765 East India Company rule of Bengal begins

1769 James Watt patents steam engine

1769–1778 Captain Cook explores Australia, New Zealand

1776 Adam Smith writes *Wealth of Nations*

Deciding Where Loyalties Lie, 1763–1776

5

The Events in the Prerevolutionary Era

Using the map on the facing page, suggest the reasons for
the concentration of prerevolutionary events in New England
and the Middle Colonies. What British policies during the
1760s and early 1770s might have affected these regions more
than others?

Individual Choices

CHARLES INGLIS

This portrait of the Anglican minister and later bishop Charles Inglis reveals a proud, intelligent, self-confident gentleman. Yet Inglis, like many loyalists, was spurned by his fellow colonists after he wrote a pamphlet urging all Americans to remain loyal to the king. He risked his neighbors' ridicule, he said, because he was a true patriot and a friend to America's best interests. *National Portrait Gallery, London.*

Charles Inglis

Charles Inglis was born in Donegal, Ireland, in 1734. Like many bright young men with only modest resources, he chose a career in the ministry. He was ordained in the Anglican Church in 1758 and, perhaps to his dismay, was immediately sent across the Atlantic Ocean to begin missionary work among the Mohawk Indians of Delaware. Inglis remained among the Mohawks for almost six years. At last, in 1765, he was called to New York City to serve as assistant to the rector of the prestigious Trinity Church. Unfortunately for Inglis, New Yorkers did not esteem the Anglican Church as highly as the young cleric might have expected. Presbyterians and other dissenting sects, members of the Dutch Reformed Church, French Protestants, and even Jews populated the bustling seaport city. And in the wake of the Stamp Act and England's determination to tighten controls over colonial life, open hostility to the Church of England increased. Many of New York's leading political figures linked the church with the king's plan to oppress and tyrannize the colonists. Inglis chose to speak out in defense of both his church and his king. He antagonized local radicals by campaigning actively for the appointment of an American bishop. From Virginia to Connecticut, many American leaders saw the effort to establish a bishop in the colonies as a blow to religious freedom similar to the Crown's assaults on economic and political freedom.

By the 1770s, Inglis found himself increasingly at odds with his neighbors. Yet he chose not to be silent. He had taken an oath of loyalty to both the Anglican Church and the English Crown, and so, under the pseudonym "Papinian," he wrote pamphlets and published letters in the local newspapers in support of Parliament's right to tax the colonies and the colonists' duty to submit. When Thomas Paine published his radical *Common Sense* in 1776, Charles Inglis was one of the few conservatives who dared to repudiate this open call for revolution. In *The True Interest of America Impartially Stated in Certain Strictures on a Pamphlet Intitled Common Sense,* Inglis condemned Paine and warned of the "evils which inevitably must attend our separating" from the Mother Country. He carefully listed the advantages of a reconciliation with Great Britain and then listed the horrors that would befall the colonies if they continued on the reckless path to rebellion. He painted a portrait of "the greatest confusion, and most violent convulsions" that would be the inevitable outcome of American protest and resistance to the king's sovereignty. Pointing out the hopelessness of waging a war against the most powerful navy and army in the world, he reminded Americans that they were still "properly Britons . . . [with] . . . the manners, habits, and ideas of Britons. . . ." Those ideas, he added emphatically, did not include a republican form of government.

In 1777 Charles Inglis was named rector of Trinity Church. From his pulpit, he continued boldly to pray for the king's well-being, despite the Declaration of Independence. He would not allow the revolutionaries to constrain him; he would not let their threats silence him. He remained an outspoken loyalist even when his church was burned and his personal property was confiscated by the new state government.

Inglis was safe from personal harm throughout most of the war, for the British occupied New York City from 1776 until 1783. That year, Inglis joined thousands of other loyalists who sought refuge aboard British transport ships headed for Nova Scotia. Despite the criticism leveled against him, despite the loss of property he suffered, despite the enforced exile from what had been his home for almost two decades, Inglis refused to speak bitterly of his American enemies. "I do not leave behind me an individual," he wrote, "against whom I have the smallest degree of resentment or ill-will." Perhaps his generosity of spirit was the result of his good fortune in Canada, for in 1787 he was made the first Anglican bishop of Nova Scotia, Newfoundland, Quebec, Prince Edward Island, and Bermuda. Ironically, when he died in 1816, the United States and Britain had just ended their second war.

INTRODUCTION

During the very years that Charles Inglis was a missionary among the Mohawks, Britain and France were engaged in their final struggle for control of eastern North America. Britain's victory in 1763, would, many colonists believed, usher in a new era of economic growth, westward settlement, and cooperation between Mother Country and colonies that would continue "for Ages to come." But, like Inglis's expectations that his new post in New York City would bring him social status and respect, the colonists' hopes for harmony and good will were quickly dashed. Less than two years after the Treaty of Paris ended the war, colonists were protesting against British Indian policy and trade regulations. In the thirteen strife-filled years that followed, the colonists and the British government discovered that fundamental political differences existed between them. They found that they did not agree over the meaning of representative government or the proper division of power between Parliament and the local elected assemblies. And they found themselves in conflict over major imperial policies. English officials, for example, thought it was wise to curtail westward settlement in order to prevent costly Indian wars. American colonists, however, were certain that westward settlement would provide economic opportunity for loyal citizens. The British government and the colonists also disagreed on what obligations the colonists shared with men and women in England. The British insisted that the Americans ought to help pay the costs of maintaining the empire, but the colonists believed that this was the duty of those who remained in the Mother Country. By the 1770s, Americans who had once toasted the king and the empire drank instead to liberty and resistance to tyrants. By 1775, a new choice faced the colonists: loyalty or rebellion. And men such as Charles Inglis seemed caught in the midst of a struggle they had never anticipated and could not avoid.

The colonists who chose to protest taxation by the British government in 1765 and 1767, or to oppose the creation of courts without jury trials, or to complain of the presence of troops in their towns in peacetime did not know they were laying the groundwork for a revolution. Indeed, most of them would have been shocked at the suggestion that they were no longer British patriots. Yet events between 1763 and 1776 forced these colonists to choose between two versions of patriotism—loyalty to the king or loyalty to colonial independence—and between two visions of the future—as members of a great and powerful empire or as citizens of a struggling new nation. These events also forced Indians and African American slaves to choose an alliance with England or with the rebels, just as it forced churchmen such as Inglis and royal officials who had taken a solemn oath of allegiance to the king to decide if that oath was binding under all circumstances. The war that resulted set neighbor against neighbor, father against son, wife against husband, and slave against master. For thousands, the outcome of this crisis of loyalty was exile from home and family. For others, it meant death or injury on the battlefield, widowhood, or life as an orphan. In 1776, however, the outcome was unclear.

I t   M a t t e r s

The Right to Dissent

Charles Inglis was a man of integrity who considered himself as much an American patriot as his opponent in the pamphlet wars, Alexander Hamilton. But unlike Hamilton, Inglis believed that the protests against Parliament and the king were dangerous and unjustified and would lead to an unjust and tragic war. Throughout American history, men and women have opposed political and social choices made by the nation, including the entrance of the United States into World War I, woman suffrage, Prohibition, and the war in Vietnam. The right to dissent, guaranteed by the Constitution, has been a critical part of the American political tradition since the nation began. Examining how dissent has been offered and how it has been received is part of the historical narrative of major controversial events.

Victory's New Problems

■ Why did Prime Minister Grenville expect the colonists to accept part of the burden of financing the British Empire in 1764?

■ How did mercantile theory affect the colonies' trade with other nations?

■ Why were the colonists alarmed by Grenville's 1765 stamp tax?

■ How did the colonists protest Parliament's taxation policies?

In the midst of the French and Indian War, King George II died in his bed. Loyal subjects mourned the old king and in 1760 crowned his young grandson **George III.** At 22, the new monarch was hardworking but highly self-critical, and he was already showing the symptoms of an illness that produced **delusions** and severe depression. Although he was inexperienced in matters of state, George III meant to rule—even if he had to deal with politicians, whom he distrusted, and engage in politics, which he disliked. He chose **George Grenville,** a no-nonsense, practical man to assist him. It fell to Grenville to handle the two most pressing postwar tasks: negotiating England's victory treaty with France and its allies and designing Britain's peacetime policies.

Grenville's diplomats met with little resistance at the negotiating table. France was defeated, and it was up to the British government to decide what the spoils of war would be. England could take possession of a French Caribbean sugar island or the French mainland territory of Canada, a vast region stretching north and northwest of the English colonies. English sugar planters raised loud objections to the first option, for another sugar island would mean new competitors in the profitable English sugar markets. There was strong support, however, for adding Canada (see Map 5.1). Doing so would ensure the safety of the mainland colonies, whose people were increasingly important as consumers of English-made goods. With Canada, too, would come the rich fishing grounds off the Newfoundland coast and the fertile lands of the Ohio Valley. Such arguments in favor of Canada carried the day. By the end of 1763, George III could look with pride on an empire that had grown in physical size, on a nation that dominated the markets of Europe, and on a navy that ruled the seas.

Unfortunately, victory also brought new problems. First, the new English glory did not come cheaply. To win the war, William Pitt had spent vast sums of money, leaving the new king with an enormous war debt. English taxpayers, who had groaned under the wartime burden, now demanded tax relief, not tax increases. Second, the new Canadian territory posed serious governance problems because the Indians were unwilling to pledge their allegiance to the English king and, despite the change in flag, the French Canadians were unwilling to abandon their traditions, laws, or the Catholic Church.

Dealing with Indian and French Canadian Resistance

Both the Canadian tribes and Spain's former Indian allies along the southeastern borders of the English colonies felt threatened by Britain's victory. For decades, Indian diplomats had protected their lands by play-

---

George III   King of England (r. 1760–1820); his government's policies produced colonial discontent that led to the American Revolution in 1776.

delusion   A false belief strongly held in spite of evidence to the contrary.

George Grenville   British prime minister who sought to tighten controls over the colonies and to impose taxes to raise revenues.

Chronology

Loyalty or Rebellion?

1763 Treaty of Paris ends French and Indian War
Pontiac's Rebellion
Proclamation Line

1764 Sugar Act

1765 Stamp Act
Sons of Liberty organized
Stamp Act Congress
Nonimportation of British goods

1766 Stamp Act repealed
Declaratory Act

1767 Townshend Acts
John Dickinson's *Letters from a Farmer in Pennsylvania*

1768 Nonimportation of British goods
Massachusetts Circular Letter

1770 Boston Massacre
Townshend Acts repealed

1772 Burning of the *Gaspée*

1773 Tea Act
Boston Tea Party

1774 Intolerable Acts
First Continental Congress
Continental Association
Declaration of Rights and Grievances
Suffolk Resolves

1775 Battles of Lexington and Concord
Second Continental Congress
Olive Branch Petition
Declaration of the Causes and Necessity of Taking Up Arms

1776 Tom Paine's *Common Sense*
Declaration of Independence

ing European rivals against one another, but with the elimination of France and the weakening of Spain in mainland America, this strategy was impossible. The Creeks and Cherokees of the Southeast expected the worst—and it soon came. English settlers from the southern colonies poured into their lands, and although the Cherokees mounted full-scale resistance along the Virginia and Carolina western settlement line, the British crushed their resistance. Cherokee leaders were forced to sign treaties that opened their lands to both English settlement and military bases.

A similar invasion of Delaware and Mingo territory began in the Ohio Valley and the Great Lakes region in 1763. The British added insult to injury by raising the price of the weapons, tools, clothing, and liquor that, by now, the tribes depended on. The crisis united the Indians, who acted quickly to create an intertribal alliance known as the **Covenant Chain.** The Covenant Chain brought together Senecas, Ojibwas, Potowatomis, Hurons, Ottawas, Delawares, Shawnees, and Mingoes, all of whom stood ready to resist colonial settlers, British trading policy, and the terms of military occupation of frontier forts. Led by the Ot-

tawa chief **Pontiac,** the Indians mounted their attack on British forts and colonial settlements in the spring of 1763. By fall, their resistance had evaporated, and the Covenant Chain tribes were forced to acknowledge British control of the Ohio Valley.

The British realized that such costly victories would not ensure permanent peace in the West. As long as the "middle ground" between Indian and colonial populations continued to shrink, Indians would mount resistance. And as long as Indians resisted what Creeks bluntly called "people greedily grasping after the lands of red people," settlers would demand expensive military protection as they pushed westward. If the army did not respond, settlers were ready to take action on

Covenant Chain An alliance of Indian tribes established to resist colonial settlement in the Ohio Valley and Great Lakes region and to oppose British trading policies.

Pontiac Ottawa chief who led the unsuccessful resistance against British policy in 1763.

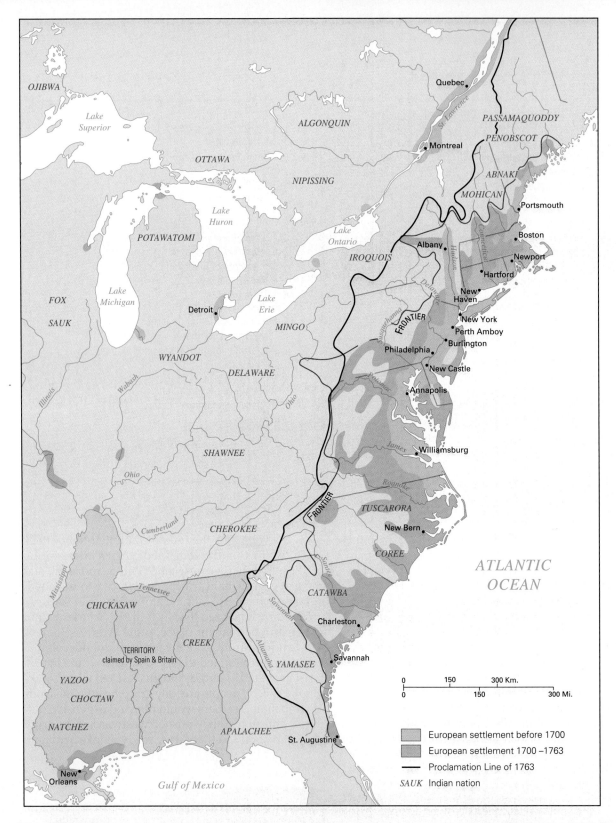

MAP 5.1 The Proclamation Line of 1763 This map shows European settlement east of the Appalachian Mountains and the numerous Indian tribes with territorial claims to the lands between the Appalachians and the Mississippi River. The Proclamation Line, which roughly follows the mountain range, was the British government's effort to temporarily halt colonial westward expansion and thus to prevent bloodshed between settlers and Indians. This British policy was deeply resented by land-hungry colonists.

Among the Iroquis nations, wampum belts were the equivalent of the written documents familiar to English and European officials. The belt above was a treaty, stating the terms and conditions under which white people were welcomed to Indian lands. The two strands of yellow signified the equality of colonist and Iroquis, or as the Oneida explained, "We will not be like Father and Son, but like Brothers." *Oneida Indian Nation.*

their own. When the Paxton Boys of western Pennsylvania avenged an Indian raid by murdering a village of innocent Conestogas (see page 100), the dangers of this type of vigilante action became painfully clear. Violence would lead to violence—unless Grenville could keep Indians and settlers at arm's length. Grenville's solution was a proclamation, issued in 1763, temporarily banning all colonial settlement west of the Appalachian Mountains.

Grenville's **Proclamation Line of 1763** outraged colonists hoping to move west and wealthy land speculators hoping to reap a profit from their western investments. With the Indian enemy reeling from defeat, settlers insisted that this was the perfect moment to cross the mountains and stake claims to the land. Most colonists simply ignored Grenville's Proclamation Line. Over the next decade, areas such as Kentucky began to fill with eager homesteaders, creating a wedge that divided northern from southern Indian tribes and increasing Indian anxiety about their own futures.

Because of their long tradition of anti-Catholic sentiment, American colonists also objected to Grenville's policy toward French-speaking Catholic Canadians. George III's advisers preferred to win over these new subjects rather than strong-arm them. Thus, to balance the French Canadians' loss of their fishing and

fur-trading industries, Grenville promised them the right to preserve their religious and cultural way of life. Britain's colonists were scandalized by this concession to the losers in the war.

Demanding More from the Colonists

Colonists were not the only ones growing discontent. In London, the king, his ministers, and many members of Parliament were impatient with colonial behavior and attitudes. Hadn't the colonists benefited more than anyone from the French defeat? asked George Grenville. And hadn't they contributed less than anyone to securing that victory? Such questions revealed the subtle but important rewriting of the motives and goals of the French and Indian War. Although Britain had waged the war to win dominance in European affairs, not to benefit the colonies, Grenville now declared that the war had been fought to protect the colonists and to expand their opportunities for settlement.

This new interpretation fit well with the government's increasing doubts about colonial commitments to the empire's trade interests. It seemed clear to Grenville that something had gone wrong in the economic relationship between England and the colonies. Colonial cities such as Boston, Philadelphia, and New York had grown considerably, yet their growth did not make England as rich as **mercantile theory** said it should. One reason was that in every colony locally produced goods competed with English-made goods. A more important reason, however, was illegal trade. Colonists seized economic opportunity wherever they found it—even in trade with England's rivals. In fact, to English amazement, colonials had continued to trade with the French Caribbean islands throughout the French and Indian War. In peacetime, colonists avoided paying **import duties** on foreign goods by

---

Proclamation Line of 1763 Boundary that Britain established in the Appalachian Mountains, west of which white settlement was banned; it was intended to reduce conflict between Indians and colonists.

mercantile theory The economic notion that a nation should amass wealth by exporting more than it imports; colonies are valuable in a mercantile system as a source of raw materials and as a market for manufactured goods.

import duties Taxes on imported goods.

bribing customs officials or landing cargoes where no customs officers were stationed.

George Grenville was often mocked for having a bookkeeper's mentality, but few laughed at what the prime minister discovered when he examined the imperial trade books. By the 1760s, the Crown had collected less than £2,000 in revenue from colonial trade with other nations while the cost of collecting these duties was over £7,000 a year. Such discoveries fueled British suspicions that the colonies were underregulated and undergoverned, as well as ungrateful and uncooperative. When the strong doubts about colonial loyalty met the reality of the British government debts and soaring expenses, something drastic could be expected to follow. And it did. In 1764 Parliament approved the reforms of colonial policy proposed by Grenville. Colonists greeted those reforms with shock and alarm.

Separately, each of Grenville's measures addressed a loophole in the proper relationship between Mother Country and colonies. For example, a **Currency Act** outlawed the use of paper money as legal tender in the colonies. In part, this was done to ensure the colonial market for English manufacturers. Although the colonists had to pay for imported English products with hard currency (gold and silver), they could use paper money to pay for locally produced goods. With paper money now banned, local manufacturers would be driven out of business.

Grenville believed the major problem was smuggling. Lawbreakers were so common, and customs officers so easily bribed, that smuggling had become an acceptable, even respectable, form of commerce. To halt this illicit traffic, Grenville set about to reform the **customs service.** In his 1764 American Revenue Act, he increased the powers of the customs officers, allowing them to use blanket warrants, called writs of assistance, to search ships and warehouses for smuggled goods. He also changed the regulations regarding key foreign imports, including sugar, wine, and coffee. This startling shift in policy, known popularly as the **Sugar Act,** revealed Grenville's practical bent. He knew that any attempt to stop the flow of French sugar into the colonies was a waste of time and resources. So he decided to make a profit for the Crown from this trade. He would lower the tax on imported sugar—but he would make sure it was collected. Until 1764, a colonist accused of smuggling was tried before a jury of his neighbors in a **civil court.** He expected, and usually got, a favorable verdict from his peers. Grenville now declared that anyone caught smuggling would be tried in a juryless **vice-admiralty court,** where a conviction was likely.

Once smuggling became too costly and too risky, Grenville reasoned, American shippers would declare their cargoes of French sugar and pay the Crown for the privilege of importing them.

The Colonial Response

Grenville's reforms were spectacularly ill timed as far as Americans were concerned. The colonial economy was suffering from a postwar **depression,** brought on in part by the loss of the British army as a steady market for American supplies and of British soldiers as steady customers who paid in hard currency rather than paper money. In 1764 unemployment was high among urban artisans, dockworkers, and sailors. Colonial merchants were caught in a credit squeeze—unable to pay their debts to British merchants because their colonial customers had no cash to pay for their purchases. These colonists were not likely to cheer a currency act that shut off a source of money or a Sugar Act that established a new get-tough policy on foreign trade. In the eyes of many colonists, the English government was turning into a greater menace than the French army had ever been.

Some colonists, however, saw these hard times and the need to tighten their belts as a welcome brake on their society's **materialism.** These Americans believed that a love of luxuries weakened people's spirit, sapped their independence, and would soon lead to the same moral decay they saw in England, where they believed extravagance and corruption infected society and tainted the nation's political leaders. After 1763, these colonists appealed to their neighbors to embrace simplicity and sacrifice. They urged prosper-

---

Currency Act   British law of 1764 banning the printing of paper money in the American colonies.

customs service   A government agency authorized to collect taxes on foreign goods entering a country.

Sugar Act   British law of 1764 that taxed sugar and other colonial imports to pay for some of Britain's expenses in protecting the colonies.

civil court   Any court that hears cases regarding the rights of private citizens.

vice-admiralty court   Nonjury British court in which a judge heard cases involving shipping.

depression   A period of drastic economic decline, marked by decreased business activity, falling prices, and high unemployment.

materialism   Excessive interest in worldly matters, especially in acquiring goods.

ous women, for example, to abandon fashion, with its "gaudy, butterfly, vain, fantastick and expensive Dresses bought from Europe," and put on the "decent plain Dresses made in their own Country." Convinced that the eighteenth-century **consumer revolution** in the colonies had eroded virtue, these colonists called for a **boycott** of all goods manufactured in England.

Other views and other proposals for action soon filled the pages of colonial newspapers. This concern suggested that Grenville's reforms had raised profound issues of liberty and the rights of citizens and of the relationship between Parliament and the colonial governments—issues that needed to be resolved. The degree to which Parliament had, or ought to have, power over colonial economic and political life required serious, public pondering. Years later, with the benefit of hindsight, Massachusetts lawyer and revolutionary John Adams stressed the importance of the Sugar Act in starting America down the road to independence. "I know not why we should blush to confess," wrote Adams, "that molasses [liquid sugar] was an essential ingredient in American independence. Many great events have proceeded from much smaller causes." But in 1764 colonists were far from agreement over the issue of parliamentary and local political powers. They were not even certain how to respond to the Sugar Act.

The Stamp Act

Did Grenville stop to consider the possibility of "great events" arising from his postwar policies? Probably not. He was hardly a stranger to protest and anger, for he had often heard British citizens grumble about taxes and assert their rights against the government. As he saw it, his duty was to fill the treasury, reduce the nation's staggering debt, arm its troops, and keep the royal navy afloat. The duty of loyal British citizens, he believed, was to obey the laws of their sovereign government. Grenville had no doubt that the measures he and Parliament were taking to regulate the colonies and their revenue-producing trade were constitutional. Some colonists, however, had doubts. Thus the next piece of colonial legislation Grenville proposed was designed not only to raise revenue but to settle the principle of parliamentary sovereignty.

The **Stamp Act** of 1765 was to be the first **direct tax** ever laid on the colonies by Parliament, and its purpose was to raise revenue by taxing certain goods and services. There was nothing startling or novel about the revenue-collecting method Grenville proposed to use. A stamp tax raised money by requiring the use of government "stamped paper" on certain goods or as

part of the cost for certain services. It was simple and efficient, and several colonial legislatures had adopted this method themselves. What was startling, however, was that Parliament would consider imposing a tax on the colonists that was not aimed at regulation of foreign trade. Up until 1765, Parliament had passed many acts regulating colonial trade. Sometimes these regulations on imports generated revenue for the Crown, and the colonists accepted them as a form of **external taxation.** But colonists expected direct taxation only from their local assemblies. If Grenville's Stamp Act became law, it would mark a radical change in the distribution of political power between assemblies and Parliament. It would be the powerful assertion of Parliament's sovereignty that Grenville intended.

Most members of Parliament saw the Stamp Act as an efficient and modest redistribution of the burdens of the empire—and a constitutional one. Colonists were certainly not being asked to shoulder the entire burden, since the estimated £160,000 in revenue from the stamped paper would cover only one-fifth of the cost of maintaining a British army in North America. Under these circumstances, Parliament saw no reason to deny Grenville's proposed tax. Thus the Stamp Act passed in February 1765 and was set to go into effect in November. The nine-month delay gave Grenville time to print the stamped paper, arrange for its shipment across the Atlantic, and appoint agents to receive and distribute the stamps in each colony. News of the tax, however, crossed the ocean rapidly and was greeted with outrage and anger. Opposition was widespread among the colonists because virtually every free man and woman was affected by a tax that required stamps on all legal documents, on newspapers and pamphlets, and even on playing cards and dice. Grenville was reaching into the pockets of

---

consumer revolution The rising market for manufactured goods, particularly luxury items, that occurred in the early eighteenth century in the colonies.

boycott An organized political protest in which people refuse to buy goods from a nation or group of people whose actions they oppose.

Stamp Act British law of 1765 that directly taxed a variety of items, including newspapers, playing cards, and legal documents.

direct tax A tax imposed to raise revenue rather than to regulate trade.

external taxation Revenue raised in the course of regulating trade with other nations.

the rich, who would need stamped paper to draw up wills and property deeds and to bring suit in court. And he was emptying the pockets of the poor, who would feel the pinch when dealing a hand of cards in a tavern or buying a printed **broadside** filled with advertising. Other segments of the colonial society would also feel the sting of the new tax. Unless colonial merchants and ship captains used stamped clearances for all shipments, the royal navy could seize their cargoes. Lawyers feared the loss of clients if they had to add the cost of the stamps to their fees. With the stamp tax Grenville united northern merchants and southern planters, rural women and urban workingmen, and he riled the most articulate and argumentative of all Americans: lawyers and newspaper publishers.

The Popular Response

Many colonists were ready to resist the new legislation. Massachusetts, whose smugglers were already choking on the new customs regulations, and whose assembly had a long history of struggle with local Crown officers, led the way. During the summer of 1765, a group of Bostonians formed a secret resistance organization called the **Sons of Liberty**. Spearheading the Sons was the irrepressible **Samuel Adams**, a Harvard-educated member of a prominent Massachusetts family who preferred the company of local working men and women to the conversation of the elite. More at home in the dockside taverns than in the comfortable parlors of his relatives, Adams was a quick-witted, dynamic champion of working-class causes. He had a genius for writing propaganda and for mobilizing popular sentiment on political and community issues. Most members of the Sons of Liberty were artisans and shopkeepers, and the group's main support came from men of the city's laboring classes who had been hard hit by the postwar depression and would suffer from the stamp tax. These colonists had little influence in the legislature or with Crown officials, but they compensated by staging public demonstrations and protests to make their opinions known.

The Sons of Liberty had been created to oppose British policies, but with class divisions widening in Boston, they sometimes added protests against local issues and local elites. Prosperous Bostonians saw a potential danger in the mobilization of lower-class crowds. For these elites, crowd protest was a double-edged sword, a useful weapon that could be deadly in the wrong hands. By January 1765, New York City also had a Sons of Liberty organization, and by Au-

gust, the Sons could be found in other cities and towns across the colonies.

Demonstrations and protests escalated, and once again Boston led the way. On August 14, shoemaker **Ebenezer McIntosh** led a crowd to protest the appointment of the colony's stamp agent, wealthy merchant Andrew Oliver. Until recently, McIntosh had headed one of two major workers' organizations in town, a **fraternal** group of artisans, apprentices, and day laborers known to the city's disapproving elite as the South End "gang." But on this August day, city gentlemen disguised themselves as workingmen and joined McIntosh's gang members as they paraded through the city streets, carrying an effigy of Oliver. The crowd destroyed the stamp agent's dockside warehouse and later broke all the windows in his home. The message was clear—and Oliver understood it well. The following day Andrew Oliver resigned as stamp agent. Boston Sons of Liberty celebrated by declaring the tree on which they hanged Oliver's effigy the "liberty tree."

Oliver's resignation did not end the protest. Customs officers and other Crown officials living in Boston were threatened with words and worse. The chief target of abuse, however, was the haughty merchant **Thomas Hutchinson,** hated by many of the ambitious younger political leaders because he monopolized appointive offices in the colony's government and by the workingmen because of his obvious disdain for ordinary people. Late one August evening, a large crowd surrounded Hutchinson's elegant brick mansion. Warned of the impending attack, Hutchinson and his family had wisely fled, escaping just before rocks began to shatter the parlor windows. By

broadside   An advertisement, public notice, or other publication printed on one side of a large sheet of paper.

Sons of Liberty   A secret organization first formed in Boston to oppose the Stamp Act.

Samuel Adams   Massachusetts revolutionary leader and propagandist who organized opposition to British policies after 1764.

Ebenezer McIntosh   Boston shoemaker whose workingman's organization, the South End "gang," became the core of the city's Sons of Liberty in 1765.

fraternal   Describes a group of people with common purposes or interests.

Thomas Hutchinson   Boston merchant and judge who served as lieutenant governor and later governor of Massachusetts; Stamp Act protesters destroyed his home in 1765.

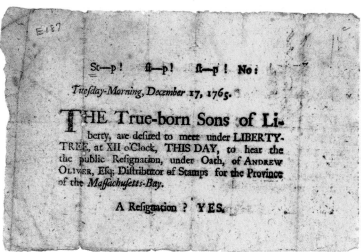

The Sons of Liberty first appeared in Boston, but this organization that united elite and working-class protesters spread quickly to other American cities. In the 1765 broadside above, the Boston Sons call a meeting to demand the resignation of local stamp agent, Andrew Oliver. Ten years later, New York's pro-British editor, James Rivington, used the illustration above while reporting that a New Brunswick mob had hanged him in effigy. The New York Sons promptly made good on the threat to Rivington, attacking his office, destroying his press, and forcing his paper to close. *Mr. Rivington: Library of Congress; Sons of Liberty Broadside: Massachusetts Historical Society.*

dawn, the house was in ruins, and Hutchinson's furniture, clothing, and personal library had been trashed.

Thomas Hutchinson was a political target of those who opposed the Stamp Act. But because he represented the privilege and power of the few and the well placed, he was also a social target of the working people in the crowd. The savage destruction of his home led many of Boston's elite to withdraw their support from popular protests of any kind. Perhaps, they reasoned, the tensions between rich and poor were more dangerous than any parliamentary reform. Like the challenge to authority of the Great Awakening, these political protests carried the seeds of social revolution.

The campaign against the stamp agents spread like a brushfire across the colonies. Agents in Connecticut, Rhode Island, Maryland, and New York were mercilessly harassed. Most stamp agents resigned. When the stamps reached colonial ports in November, only the young and conservative colony of Georgia could produce anyone willing to distribute them. Colonial governors retaliated by refusing to allow any colonial ships to leave port. They hoped this disruption of trade would persuade local merchants to help end the resistance. Their strategy back-

fired. Violence increased as hundreds of unemployed sailors took to the streets, terrorizing customs officers and any colonists suspected of supporting the king's taxation policy.

Political Debate

While the Sons of Liberty and their supporters demonstrated in the streets, most colonial political leaders were proceeding with caution. Virginia lawyer and planter **Patrick Henry** briefly stirred the passions of his colleagues in the House of Burgesses when he suggested that the Stamp Act was evidence of the king's tyranny. Not everyone agreed with him that the measure was so serious. Many did agree, however, that the heart of the matter was not stamped paper but parliamentary sovereignty versus the rights of colonial citizens. "No taxation without representation"—the principle that citizens cannot be taxed by a government unless they are represented in it—was a fundamental

Patrick Henry   Member of the Virginia House of Burgesses and American revolutionary leader noted for his oratorical skills.

Virginia planter and lawyer Patrick Henry may have acquired his oratorical brilliance from his father, a fiery Virginia preacher. Henry chose politics rather than the pulpit, and throughout the 1760s and 1770s, he stirred the House of Burgesses to resist British policy and the British king. *Colonial Williamsburg Foundation.*

assumption of free white Englishmen on both sides of the Atlantic. The crucial question was, Did the House of Commons represent the colonists even though no colonist sat in the House and none voted for its members? If the answer was no, then the Stamp Act violated the colonists' most basic "rights of Englishmen."

Stating the issue in this way led to other concerns. Could colonial political leaders oppose a single law such as the Stamp Act without completely denying the authority of the government that was responsible for its passage? Massachusetts lawyer James Otis pondered this question when he sat down to write his *Rights of the British Colonists Asserted and Proved.* Any opposition to the Stamp Act, he decided, was ultimately a challenge to parliamentary authority over the colonies, and it would surely lead to colonial rebellion and a declaration of colonial independence. He, for one, was not prepared to become a rebel.

The logic of his own argument disturbed Otis and prompted him to propose a compromise: the colonists should be given representation in the House of Commons. Few political leaders took this suggestion seriously. Even if Parliament agreed, a small contingent of colonists could be easily ignored in its decision making. Most colonial leaders thought it best to declare that American rights and liberties were under attack and to issue warnings that the assemblies

would oppose any further threats to colonial rights. They carefully avoided, however, any treasonous statements or threats of rebellion. In the most popular pamphlet of 1765, Pennsylvania lawyer Daniel Dulaney captured this combination of criticism and caution. His *Considerations on the Propriety of Imposing Taxes on the British Colonies* reaffirmed the dependence of the colonies on Great Britain. But it also reminded Parliament that Americans knew the difference between dependence and slavery.

Colonial assemblymen knew that a final question hung in the air. If Parliament asserted its right to govern the colonies directly, what powers would remain to them as members of the colonial legislatures? These men had much to lose—status, prestige, and the many benefits that came from deciding how tax monies would be allocated. In the end, the majority agreed that a firm stand had to be taken. After much debate, most assemblies followed the lead of the Virginia House of Burgesses and issued statements condemning the Stamp Act and demanding its repeal. Massachusetts reinforced this unusual show of unity among the colonies when its assembly put out a call for an intercolonial meeting of delegates to discuss the Stamp Act crisis. The call to meet was greeted with enthusiasm.

Grenville's policies appeared to be bringing about what had once seemed impossible: united political action by the colonies. Until the Stamp Act, competition among the colonial governments was far more common than cooperation. Yet in the fall of 1765 delegates from nine colonies met in New York "to consider a general and unified, dutiful, loyal and humble Representation [petition]" to the king and Parliament. The petitions this historic Stamp Act Congress ultimately produced were far bolder than the delegates first intended. They were powerful, tightly argued statements that conceded parliamentary authority over the colonies but denied Parliament's right to impose any direct taxes on them. "No taxes," the Congress said, "ever have been, or can be Constitutionally imposed" on the colonies "but by their respective Legislatures." Clearly Americans expected this tradition to be honored.

Repeal of the Stamp Act

Neither the protest in the streets nor the arguments of the Stamp Act Congress moved the king or Parliament to repeal the stamp tax. But economic pressure did. English manufacturers relied heavily on their colonial markets and were certain to be hurt by any interruption in the flow and sale of goods to America.

Thus the most powerful weapon in the colonial arsenal was a refusal to purchase English goods. On Halloween night, just one day before the stamp tax officially went into effect, two hundred New York merchants announced that they would not import any new British goods. Local artisans and laborers rallied to support this boycott. A mixture of patriotism and self-interest motivated both these groups. The merchants saw the possibility of emptying warehouses bulging with unsold goods because of the postwar depression. Unemployed and underemployed artisans and laborers saw the chance to sell their own products if the supply of cheaper English-made goods dried up. The same combination of interests existed in other colonial cities, and thus the nonimportation movement spread quickly. By the end of November, several colonial assemblies had publicly endorsed the nonimportation agreements signed by local merchants. Popular support widened as well. In many cities and towns, women publicly announced their commitment to nonimportation and vowed to spend long hours spinning and weaving their own cloth rather than purchase it ready-made from England. Their participation was crucial to the success of the boycott.

English exporters complained bitterly of the damage done to their businesses and pressured Parliament to take colonial protest seriously. Talk of repeal grew bolder and louder in the halls of Parliament. The Grenville government reluctantly conceded that enforcement of the Stamp Act had failed miserably. Even in colonies where royal officials dared to distribute the stamped paper, Americans refused to purchase it. Colonists simply ignored the hated law and continued to sue their neighbors, sell their land, publish their newspapers, and buy their playing cards as if the stamped paper and the Stamp Act did not exist.

By winter's end, Grenville was no longer prime minister. For the king's new head of state, Lord Rockingham, the critical issue was not whether to repeal the Stamp Act but how to do so without appearing to cave in to colonial pressure. After much debate and political maneuvering, the government came up with a satisfactory solution. In 1766, Great Britain repealed the Stamp Act but at the same time passed a Declaratory Act, which asserted that the colonies "have been, are, and of right ought to be subordinate unto, and dependent upon the imperial Crown and parliament of Great Britain," and thus Parliament's right to pass legislation for and raise taxes from the North American colonies was reaffirmed as absolute.

Colonists celebrated the repeal with public outpourings of loyalty to England that were as impressive as their public protests had been. There were cannon salutes, bonfires, parades, speeches, and public toasts to the king and Rockingham. In Boston, Sons of Liberty built a pyramid and covered its three sides with patriotic poetry. In Anne Arundel County, Maryland, colonists erected a "liberty pillar" and buried "Discord" beneath it. And in a spectacular but poorly executed gesture, the Liberty Boys of Plymouth, Massachusetts, tried to move Plymouth Rock to the center of town. When the famous rock on which the Pilgrims were said to have landed split in two, half of it was carried to Liberty Pole Square, where it remained until 1834.

Asserting American Rights

- Why did Charles Townshend expect his revenue-raising measures to be successful?
- What forms of resistance did the colonists use to force the repeal of Townshend's measures?
- How did the Townshend Acts affect the northern colonies' trade with the West Indies?
- What were the results of colonial resistance?

The Declaratory Act firmly asserted that Parliament had "the sole and exclusive right" to tax the colonists. This was a clear rejection of the colonial assemblies' claim to power, yet the colonists responded with indifference. Those who commented on it at all dismissed it as a face-saving device. To a degree, they were correct. But the Declaratory Act expressed the views of powerful men in Parliament, and within a year they put it to the test.

By the summer of 1766, William Pitt had returned to power within George III's government. But Pitt was old and preoccupied with his failing health. He lacked the energy to exercise the control over the government he had demonstrated during the French and Indian War. A young playboy named Charles Townshend, serving as chancellor of the exchequer, rushed in to fill the leadership void. This brash young politician wasted little time foisting a new package of taxes on the colonies.

The Townshend Acts and Colonial Protest

During the Stamp Act crisis, Benjamin Franklin had assured Parliament that American colonists accepted indirect taxation even if they violently protested a direct tax such as the Stamp Act. In other words,

Americans conceded the British government's right to any revenue arising from the regulation of colonial trade. In 1767 Townshend decided to test this distinction by proposing new regulations on a variety of imported necessities and luxuries. But the Townshend Acts were import taxes unlike any other the colonies had ever seen: they were tariffs on products made in Britain.

The Townshend Acts taxed glass, paper, paint, and lead products made in England, all part of the luxury trade. The acts also placed a three-penny tax on tea, the most popular drink among colonists everywhere and considered a necessity by virtually everyone. Townshend wanted to be certain these taxes were collected, so he ordered new customs boards established in the colonies and created new vice-admiralty courts in the major port cities of Boston, Charleston, and Philadelphia to try any cases of smuggling or tax evasion that might occur. In case Americans tried to harass customs officials, as they had so effectively done during the stamp tax protests, Townshend ordered British troops transferred from the western regions to the major colonial port cities. He knew this troop relocation would anger the colonists, but he was relying on the presence of uniformed soldiers—known as "redcoats" because of their scarlet jackets—to keep the peace. To help finance this military occupation of key cities, Townshend invoked the 1766 Quartering Act, a law requiring colonists to provide room and board, "candles, firing, bedding, cooking utensils, salt and vinegar" and a ration of beer, cider, or rum to troops stationed in their midst.

Clearly, Townshend was taking every precaution to avoid the embarrassment Grenville had suffered in the Stamp Act disaster. But he made a serious error in believing that colonists would meekly agree to pay import duties on British-made goods. When news of the new regulations reached the colonies, the response was immediate, determined, and well-organized resistance.

If the newspapers reflected popular sentiment accurately, the colonists were united in their opposition to the Townshend Acts and to the Mother Country's repressive enforcement policies. Some were incensed that the government was once again trampling on the principle of "no taxation without representation." In Boston, Samuel Adams voiced his outrage: "Is it possible to form an idea of Slavery, more compleat, more miserable, more disgraceful than that of a people, where justice is administer'd, government exercis'd, and a standing army maintain'd at the expense of the people, and yet without the least dependence upon them?" Others worried more about the economic burden of the new taxes and the quartering of the troops than about political rights. Boston lawyer Josiah Quincy Jr. asked readers of the *Boston Gazette*: "Is not the bread taken out of the children's mouths and given unto the Dogs?"

John Dickinson, a well-respected Pennsylvania landowner and lawyer, laid out the basic American position on imperial relations in his pamphlet *Letters from a Farmer in Pennsylvania* (1767). Direct taxation without representation violated the colonists' rights as English citizens, Dickinson declared. But by imposing any tax that did not regulate foreign trade, Parliament also violated those rights. Dickinson also considered, and rejected, the British claim that Americans were represented in the House of Commons. According to the British argument, colonists enjoyed "virtual representation" because the House of Commons represented the interests of all citizens in the empire who were not members of the nobility, whether those citizens participated directly in elections to the House or not. Like most Americans, Dickinson discounted virtual representation. What Englishmen were entitled to, he wrote, was *actual* representation by men they had elected to government to protect their interests. For qualified voters in the colonies, who enjoyed actual representation in their local assemblies, virtual representation was nothing more than a weak excuse for exclusion and exploitation. As one American quipped: "Our privileges are all virtual, our sufferings are real."

While political theorists set out the American position in newspaper essays and pamphlets, protest leaders organized popular resistance against acts that were clearly designed to raise revenue as well as make daily life more expensive in the colonies. Samuel Adams set in motion a massive boycott of British goods to begin on January 1, 1768. Just as before, some welcomed the chance a boycott provided to "mow down luxury and high living." But simple economics also contributed forcefully to support for the boycott. Boston artisans remained enthusiastic about any action that stopped the flow of inexpensive English-made goods to America. Small-scale merchants were also eager to see nonimportation enforced. They had little access to British credit or goods under normal circumstances, and the boycott would eliminate the advantages enjoyed by the merchant elite who did. Merchants and shippers who made their living smuggling goods from the West Indies supported the boycott because it cut out the competing English-made products. The large-scale merchants who had led the 1765 boycott were not enthusiastic, however. By 1767, their warehouses were no longer overflowing with

Massachusetts playwright, poet, and historian Mercy Otis Warren penned some of the most popular and effective propaganda for the American cause. In her plays, she portrayed pro-British officeholders as greedy, power-hungry traitors, while she praised Boston radicals as noble heroes. *"Mercy Otis Warren" by John Singleton Copley. Courtesy of the Museum of Fine Arts, Boston, bequest of Winslow Warren.*

unsold English stock, and the boycott might cut off their livelihoods. Many of these elite merchants delayed signing the agreements. Others did not sign at all.

The strongest voices raised against the boycott, and against resistance to the Townshend Acts in general, were the voices of colonists holding Crown-appointed government offices. These fortunate few—including judges and customs men—shared their neighbors' sensitivity to abuse or exploitation by the Crown. But they had sworn to uphold and carry out the programs and policies of the British government. And many of their salaries came from England. Because their careers and their identities were closely tied to the power and authority of the Crown, they were inclined to see British policymakers as well intentioned and acceptance of British policy as a patriotic duty. Jonathan Sewall, the king's attorney general in Massachusetts, was perhaps typical of these royal officeholders. Sewall had deep roots in his colonial community, for his family went back many generations and included lawyers, judges, merchants, and assemblymen. His closest friend was John Adams, cousin of Samuel Adams, and the wealthy Boston merchant and smuggler John Hancock would soon become his brother-in-law. Yet Sewall became a staunch public defender of Crown policy. In his newspaper articles he urged his neighbors to ignore the call to resistance, and he questioned the motives of the leading activists, suggesting that greed, thwarted ambition, and envy rather than high-minded principles motivated the rabble-rousers. But despite their prestige and their positions of authority, Crown officers like Sewall were no more able to prevent the boycott or slow the spread of resistance than Anglican ministers like Charles Inglis.

Just as the Sons of Liberty and the Stamp Act demonstrations brought common men into the political arena, the 1768 boycott brought politics into the lives of women. When in 1765 the inexpensive, factory-made cloth produced in England had been placed high on the list of boycotted goods, an old, neglected, and tedious domestic skill became both a real and a symbolic element in the American protest strategy. In 1768 many women responded to the challenge. Taking a bold political stance, women, including wealthy mothers and daughters, formed groups called the Daughters of Liberty and staged large public spinning bees to show support for the boycott. Wearing clothing made of "homespun" became a mark of honor and a political statement. As one male observer noted, "The ladies . . . while they vie with each other in skill and industry in their profitable employment, may vie with the men in contributing to the preservation and prosperity of their country and equally share in the honor of it." Through the boycott, politics had entered the domestic circle.

The British Humiliated

Townshend and his new taxation policy faced sustained defiance in almost every colony, but Massachusetts provided the greatest embarrassment for Parliament and the king. Massachusetts governor Francis Bernard had lost his control over local politics ever since he tried to punish the assembly for issuing a call in 1768 for collective protest, called a Circular Letter, against the Townshend Acts to other colonies. Although Bernard forced the assembly to rescind, or call back, the letter, the men chosen for the legislature in the next election simply reissued it. The helpless governor could do nothing to save face except dismiss the assembly, leaving the colony without any representative government. Bernard's ability to ensure law and order eroded rapidly after this. Throughout 1768, enforcers of the boycott roamed the streets of Boston, intimidating pro-British merchants and harassing anyone wearing British-made clothing. Boston mobs of men and women openly threatened customs officials, and the Sons of Liberty protected smuggling operations. Despite the increased number of customs officers policing the docks and wharves, the colony was doing a thriving business in smuggling foreign goods and the items listed in the hated Townshend Acts. One of the town's most notorious smugglers, the flamboyant John Hancock, grew more popular with his neighbors each time he broke the customs laws and unloaded his illegal cargoes of French and Spanish wines or West Indian sugar. When customs officers seized Hancock's vessel, aptly named the *Liberty,* in June 1768, protesters beat up senior customs men and mobs visited the homes of other royal officials. The now-desperate Governor Bernard sent an urgent plea for help to the British government.

In October 1768, four thousand troops arrived in Boston. The Crown clearly believed that the presence of one soldier for every four citizens would be enough to restore order quickly. John Adams marveled at what he considered British thickheadedness. The presence of so many young soldiers, far from home and surrounded by a hostile community, was certain to worsen the situation. Military occupation of Boston, Adams warned, made more violence inevitable. Adams was right. With time on their hands, the soldiers passed the hours courting any local women who would speak to them and pestering those who would not. They angered local dockworkers by moonlighting in the shipyards when off duty and taking jobs away from colonists by accepting lower pay. For their part, civilians taunted the sentries, insulted the soldiers, and refused the military any sign of hospitality. News of street-corner fights and tavern brawls inflamed feelings on both sides. Samuel Adams and his friends did their best to fan the flames of hatred, publishing daily accounts of both real and imaginary confrontations in which soldiers threatened the honor or endangered the safety of innocent townspeople.

The military occupation dragged on through 1769 and early 1770. On March 5, the major confrontation most people expected occurred. An angry crowd began throwing snowballs—undoubtedly laced with bricks and rocks—at British sentries guarding the customs house. The redcoats, under strict orders not to fire on civilians, issued a frantic call for help in withdrawing to safety. When Captain Thomas Preston and his men arrived to rescue the sentries, the growing crowd immediately enveloped them. How, and under whose orders, Preston's soldiers began to fire is un-

Paul Revere's engraving of the Boston Massacre appeared in newspapers the day after the confrontation between redcoats and Boston citizens. Despite the fact that Captain Preston and most of his soldiers were acquitted of wrongdoing, Revere's striking image of innocent civilians and murderous soldiers remained fixed in the popular mind. It reinforced suspicion that the British were plotting to deprive Americans of their rights and liberties. *"Boston Massacre" by Paul Revere. Library of Congress.*

known, but they killed five men and wounded eight other colonists. Four of the five victims were white laborers. The fifth, Crispus Attucks, was a free black sailor.

Massachusetts protest leaders' account of what they called the Boston Massacre appeared in colonial newspapers everywhere and included a dramatic anti-British illustration engraved by silversmith Paul Revere. A jury of colonists later cleared Preston and all but two of his men of the charges against them. But nothing that was said at their trial—no sworn testimony, no lawyer's arguments—could erase the image of British brutality against British subjects.

Even before the bloodshed of March 5, Edmund Burke, a member of Parliament known for his sympathy to the colonial cause, had warned the House of Commons that the relationship between Mother Country and colonies was both desperate and tragic. "The Americans," Burke said, "have made a discovery, or think they have made one, that we mean to oppress them; we have made a discovery, or think we have made one, that they intend to rise in rebellion. We do not know how to advance; they do not know how to retreat." Burke captured well the growing American conviction of a conspiracy or plot by Parliament to deprive the colonists of their rights and liberties. He also captured the British government's growing sense that a rebellion was being hatched. But Parliament was ready to act to ease the crisis and make a truce possible. A new minister, Frederick Lord North, was given the reins of government, and on the very day Captain Preston's men fired on the crowd at Boston, Lord North repealed the Townshend Acts and allowed the hated Quartering Act to expire. Yet Lord North wanted to give no ground on the question of parliamentary control of the colonies. For this reason, North kept the tax on tea—to preserve a principle rather than fill the king's treasury.

Success Weakens Colonial Unity

Repeal of the Townshend Acts allowed the colonists to return to the ordinary routine of their lives. But it was not true that all tensions had vanished. Troubling ones remained—and they were largely among the colonists themselves.

The economic boycott begun in 1768 exposed and deepened the growing divisions between the merchant elite and the coalition of smaller merchants, artisans, and laborers in the urban centers of the North. During the years of nonimportation, many of the wealthy merchants had secretly imported and sold British goods whenever possible. When repeal came in 1770, the demand for locally manufactured goods was still low, and artisans and laborers still faced poor economic prospects. These groups were reluctant to abandon the boycott even after repeal. But few merchants, large or small, would agree to continue it.

Many elite colonists gladly abandoned the radical activism they had shown in the 1760s in favor of social conservatism. Their fear of British tyranny dimmed, but their fear of the lower classes' clamor for political power grew. Artisans and laborers did indeed continue to press for broader participation in local politics and for more representative political machinery. The tyranny that some of them opposed was close to home. "Many of the poorer People," observed one supporter of expanded political participation, "deeply felt the Aristocratic Power, or rather the intolerable Tyranny of the great and opulent." The new political language in which these common men justified their demands made their social superiors uneasy. Their own impassioned appeals for rights and liberties were returning to haunt some of the colonial elite.

The Crisis Renewed

■ What British policies led Americans to imagine a plot against their rights and liberties?

■ How did the king hope to crush resistance in Massachusetts?

■ How did the Continental Congress respond to the Intolerable Acts?

Lord North's government took care not to disturb the calm created by the repeal of the Townshend Acts. Between 1770 and 1773, North proposed no new taxes on the colonists and made no major changes in colonial policy. American political leaders took equal care not to make any open challenges to British authority. Both sides recognized that their political truce had its limits. It did not extend to smugglers and customs men, who continued to lock horns; it did not end the bitterness of southern colonists who wished to settle beyond the Proclamation Line; nor did it erase the distrust colonial political leaders and the British government felt for each other.

Disturbing the Peace of the Early 1770s

Despite the repeal of the Townshend duties, the British effort to crack down on American smuggling continued. New England merchants whose fortunes were built on trade with the Caribbean resented the sight of customs officers at the docks and customs ships patrolling the coastline (see Map 5.2). Rhode Island merchants were especially angry and frustrated by the determined—and highly effective—customs operation in their colony. They took their revenge one June day in 1772 when the customs patrol boat, the *Gaspée*, ran aground as it chased an American vessel. That evening a band of colonists boarded the *Gaspée*, taunted the stranded customs men, and then set fire to their boat.

Rhode Islanders called the burning of the *Gaspée* an act of political resistance. The English called it an act of vandalism and appointed a royal commission to investigate. To their amazement, no witnesses came forward, and no evidence could be gathered to support any arrests. The British found the conspiracy of silence among the Rhode Islanders appalling.

Many American political leaders found the royal commission equally appalling. They were convinced that the British government had intended to bring its suspects to England for trial and thus deprive them of a jury of their peers. They read this as further evidence of the plot to destroy American liberty, and

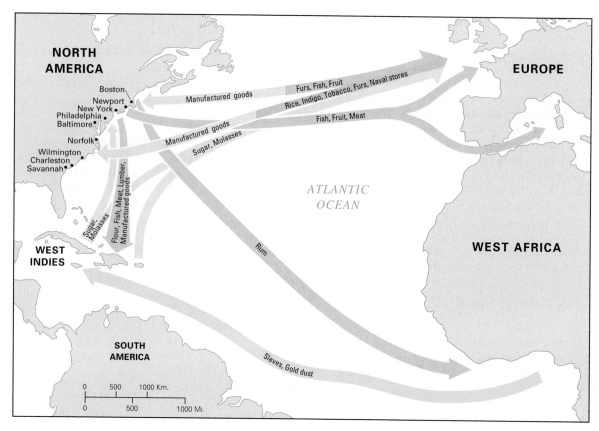

MAP 5.2 Colonial Transatlantic Trade in the 1770s This map shows the major trade routes between the British mainland colonies, West Africa, the Caribbean, and Europe and the most important export and import cargoes carried along these routes. The central role northern seaport cities played in carrying colonial agricultural products across the Atlantic and bringing British manufactured goods into the colonies is clear. Note also the role the northern colonies played in the slave trade.

they decided to keep in close contact in order to monitor British moves. Following the Virginia assembly's lead, five colonies organized a communications network called the committees of correspondence, instructing each committee to circulate detailed accounts of any questionable royal activities in its colony. These committees of correspondence were also a good mechanism for coordinating protest or resistance should the need arise. Thus the colonists put in place their first permanent machinery of protest.

The Tea Act and the Tea Party

During the early 1770s, colonial activists worked to keep the political consciousness of the 1760s alive. They commemorated American victories over British policy and observed the anniversary of the Boston Massacre with solemn speeches and sermons. The New York Sons of Liberty celebrated their founding day with dinners, endless toasts, and rituals that linked the Sons with a tradition of English radicalism. Without major British provocation, however, a revival of mass action was unlikely.

In 1773 Parliament provided that provocation. This time the government was not setting new colonial policy. It was trying to save a major commercial enterprise, the East India Tea Company. Mismanagement, coupled with the American boycott and the tendency of colonists to buy smuggled Dutch tea, had left the company in serious financial trouble. With its warehouses bursting with unsold tea, the company appealed to Parliament to rescue them.

The company directors had a plan: if Parliament allowed them to ship their tea directly to the colonial

The famous "Boston Tea Party" of December 1773 was neither secretive nor quiet. As this illustration shows, a noisy crowd gathered on the docks to cheer the men who boarded British ships to toss thousands of pounds' worth of tea into the harbor. Although the radicals donned Indian disguises, most of them were no doubt easily recognized by their supporters. Although this artist painted an all-male crowd, written accounts tell us that women were present at the Tea Party too. *Library of Congress.*

market, eliminating the English merchants who served as middlemen, they could lower their prices and compete effectively against the smuggled Dutch tea. Even with the three-penny tax on tea that remained from the Townshend era, smart consumers would see this as a bargain. Lord North liked the plan and saw in it the opportunity for vindication: Americans who purchased the cheaper English tea would be confirming Parliament's right to tax the colonies. With little debate, Parliament made the company's arrangement legal through passage of the Tea Act. No one expected the colonists to object.

Once again, British politicians had seriously misjudged the impact of their decisions. Colonists read the Tea Act as an insult, a challenge, another chilling sign of a conspiracy against their well-being and their liberty. They distrusted the arrangement, believing that the East India Tea Company would raise its prices dramatically once all foreign teas were driven off the market. And they were concerned that if other British companies marketing products in the colonies followed the East India Tea Company's example, prices for scores of products would soar. These objections, however, paled beside the colonists' immediate grasp of Lord North's strategy: purchasing cheaper English

tea would confirm Parliament's right to tax the colonies. The tea that Americans drank might be cheap, but the price of conceding the legitimacy of the tea tax was too high.

Colonists mobilized their resistance in 1773 with the skill acquired from a decade of experience. In several cities, crowds met the ships carrying the East India tea and prevented the unloading of their cargoes. They used the threat of violence to persuade ship captains to return to England with the tea still on board. As long as both the captains and the local royal officials gave in to these pressures, no serious confrontation occurred. But in Massachusetts, the most famous victim of mob violence, now Governor Thomas Hutchinson, was not willing to give in. A stalemate resulted: colonists refused to allow crews to unload the tea, but Hutchinson refused to allow the tea ships to depart without unloading. Boston activists broke the stalemate on December 16, 1773, when some sixty men, thinly disguised as Mohawk Indians, boarded the tea ships. Working calmly and methodically, they dumped 342 chests of tea, worth almost £10,000, into the waters of Boston Harbor.

The Intolerable Acts

The Boston Tea Party delighted colonists everywhere. The Crown, however, failed to see the humor in this deliberate destruction of valuable private property. The tea chests had barely settled into the harbor mud before Parliament retaliated. The king and his minister meant to make an example of everyone in Boston, the source of so much trouble and embarrassment over the past decade. Americans on the scene in England warned friends and family back home of the growing rage against the colonies. Arthur Lee, serving in London as Massachusetts's colonial agent, drew a gloomy picture of the dangers ahead in a letter to his brother. "The storm, you see, runs high," he wrote, "and it will require great prudence, wisdom and resolution, to save our liberties from shipwreck."

The four acts that Parliament passed in 1774 to discipline Massachusetts were as harsh and uncompromising as Arthur Lee predicted. The colonists called them the Intolerable Acts. The Port Act declared the port of Boston closed to all trade until the citizens compensated the East India Tea Company fully for its losses. This was a devastating blow to the colony's economy. The Massachusetts Government Act transferred much of the power of the colony's assembly to the royal governor, including the right to appoint judges, sheriffs, and members of the colonial legislature's upper house. The colony's town meetings,

The destruction of tea in Boston Harbor provoked harsh reprisals from the king and Parliament. In 1774, the British government issued a series of measures that colonists called the "Intolerable Acts." The most shocking of these was the reorganization of the Massachusetts government and the closing of the port of Boston to all trade. But instead of crushing the rebellion brewing in the colonies, the Intolerable Acts radicalized many colonists. *National Archives Image Library.*

which had served as forums for anti-British sentiment and protests, also came under the governor's direct control. A third measure, the Justice Act, allowed royal officials charged with capital crimes to stand trial in London rather than before local juries. And a new Quartering Act gave military commanders the authority to house troops in private homes. To see that these laws were enforced, the king named General Thomas Gage, commander of the British troops in North America, as the acting governor of Massachusetts.

At the same time that Parliament passed these punitive measures, the British government issued a comprehensive plan for the government of Canada. The timing of the Quebec Act may have been a coincidence, but its provisions infuriated Americans. The Quebec Act granted the French in Canada the right to worship as Catholics, retain their language, and keep many of their legal practices—all marks of a tolerance that the Crown had refused to show its English colonists. The Quebec Act also expanded the borders of Canada into the Ohio Valley at the expense of the English-speaking colonies' claim to western land. This dealt a harsh blow to Virginia planters who hoped to profit from land speculation in the region. The endorsement of Catholicism and the stifling of western expansion seemed to connect the Quebec Act to the attack on American liberty that Parliament had launched with the Intolerable Acts.

The king expected the severe punishment of Massachusetts to isolate that colony from its neighbors. But the Americans resisted this divide-and-conquer strategy. In every colony, newspaper essays and editorials urged readers to see Boston's plight as their own. "This horrid attack upon the town of Boston," said the *South Carolina Gazette,* "we consider not as an attempt upon that town singly, but upon the whole Continent." George Washington, by now an influential Virginia planter and militia officer—and a major land speculator—declared that "the cause of Boston now is and ever will be the cause of America." Indeed, the Intolerable Acts produced a wave of sympathy for the beleaguered Bostonians, and relief efforts sprang up across the colonies. The residents of Surry County, Virginia, declared they had gathered "upwards of 150 barrels of Indian corn and wheat . . . for the benefit of those firm and intrepid sons of Liberty." Throughout the year, much-needed supplies found their way to Boston despite British efforts to isolate the city.

Colonists did not stop at sympathy for the victims of the Intolerable Acts. In pamphlets and political essays, they placed these acts into the larger context of systematic oppression by the Mother Country. Political writers referred to the British government as the "enemy," conspiring to deprive Americans of their liberty, and urged colonists to defend themselves against the "power and cunning of our adversaries." This unity of sentiments, however, was more fragile than it appeared. In the cities, bitter divisions quickly developed, and artisans struggled with merchants to control the mass meetings that would make strategy choices. Samuel Adams and the radical artisans and workers of Boston suggested what might be at stake in this struggle between elites and ordinary citizens when they formed a "solemn league and covenant" to lead a third intercolonial boycott of British goods. As most Bostonians knew, the words *solemn league* referred to a pact between the Scottish Presbyterians and English Puritans who had overthrown royal government in the 1640s and beheaded a king. Adams and his allies had made their choice: armed rebellion. Yet even in crisis-torn Boston, not everyone wanted matters to go that far. And in the southern colonies, planters fearful of the social instability that resistance might bring worried that slave revolts and class antagonisms between the elite and the poorer farmers might be the ultimate outcome of escalating protest.

Creating a National Forum: The First Continental Congress

On September 5, 1774, delegates from every colony but Georgia gathered in Philadelphia for a continental congress. Few of the delegates or the people they represented thought of themselves as revolutionaries. "We want no revolution," a North Carolina delegate bluntly stated. Yet in the eyes of their British rulers, he and other colonists were treading dangerously close to treason. After all, neither the king nor Parliament had authorized the congress to which colonial assemblies and self-appointed committees had sent representatives. And that congress was intent on resisting acts of Parliament and defying the king. English men and women had been hanged as traitors for far less serious betrayals of the English government.

Some of the most articulate political leaders in the colonies attended this First Continental Congress. Conservative delegates such as Joseph Galloway of Pennsylvania hoped to slow the pace of colonial resistance by substituting petitions to Parliament for the total boycott proposed by Samuel Adams. Their radical opponents—including Samuel Adams and his cousin John, Patrick Henry, and delegates from the artisan community of Philadelphia—demanded the boycott and more. Most of the delegates were desperately searching for a third choice: a way to express their grievances and demand that injustices be corrected without further eroding their relationship with England.

The mounting crisis in Massachusetts diminished the chances of a moderate solution. Rumors spread that the royal navy was planning to bombard Boston and that General Gage was preparing to invade the countryside. Thousands of Massachusetts militiamen had begun mustering in Cambridge. The growing conflict drove many delegates into the radical camp. In this atmosphere of dread and anxiety, the Continental Congress approved the Continental Association, a boycott of all English goods to begin on December 1, 1774. The Congress also passed strong resolutions demanding the repeal of the Intolerable Acts.

The First Continental Congress had chosen radical tactics, but many delegates were torn between loyalties to two governments and their conflicting claims to power. Parliament insisted on an unconditional right to make laws for and regulate the colonies. The colonial assemblies claimed that they alone had the right to tax the colonists. Thomas Jefferson, a young Virginia planter and intellectual, tried to find a way out of this dilemma by separating loyalty to the king from resistance to Parliament. He argued that the colonists owed allegiance to the nation's king, not to Parliament, and that each colony did indeed have the right to legislate for itself. Not everyone agreed.

If no compromise could be reached, the delegates—and Americans everywhere—would have to choose where their strongest loyalties lay. Joseph Galloway believed that he had worked out the necessary compromise. In his Plan of Union, Galloway proposed a drastic restructuring of imperial relations. The plan called for a Grand Council, elected by each colonial legislature, that would share with Parliament the right to originate laws for the colonies. The Grand Council and Parliament would have the power to veto or disallow each other's decisions if necessary. A governor-general, appointed by the Crown, would oversee council operations and preserve imperial interests.

After much discussion and debate, Congress rejected Galloway's compromise by the narrowest of margins. Then it was John Adams's turn to propose a solution. Under his skillful urging and direction, the Congress adopted the Declaration of Rights and Grievances. The declaration politely but firmly established the colonial standard for acceptable legislation by Parliament. Colonists, said the declaration, would consent to acts meant to regulate "our external commerce." But they absolutely denied the legitimacy, or lawfulness, of an "idea of taxation, internal or external, for raising a revenue on the subjects of America, without their consent."

The delegates knew that the force behind the declaration came neither from the logic of its argument nor from the genius of its political reasoning. Whatever force it carried came from the unspoken but nevertheless real threat of rebellion that would occur if the colonists' demands were not met. To make this threat clearer, Congress endorsed a set of resolutions rushed to Philadelphia from Suffolk County, Massachusetts. These Suffolk Resolves called on the residents of that county to arm themselves and prepare to resist British military action. Congressional support for these resolves sent an unmistakable message that American leaders were willing to choose rebellion if politics failed.

The delegates adjourned and headed home, bringing news of the Congress's decisions with them to their families and their communities. There was nothing to do now but wait for the Crown's response. When it came, it was electric. "Blows must decide," declared King George III, "whether they are to be subject to this country or independent."

The Decision for Independence

- Could the Revolutionary War have been avoided?
- What alternatives might have kept compromise alive?
- What motivated some colonists to become loyalists and others to become patriots?

Americans were anxious while they waited for the king and Parliament to respond to the Declaration of Rights and Grievances, but they were not idle. In most colonies, a transfer of political power was occurring as the majority of Americans withdrew their support for and obedience to royal governments and recognized the authority of anti-British, patriot governments. The king might expect blows to decide the issue of colonial autonomy, but independent local governments were becoming a reality before any shots were fired.

Taking Charge and Enforcing Policies

Imperial control broke down as communities in each colony refused to obey royal laws or acknowledge the authority of royal officers. For example, when General Thomas Gage, the acting governor of Massachusetts, refused to convene the Massachusetts assembly, its members met anyway. Their first order of business was to prepare for military resistance to Gage and his army. While the redcoats occupied Boston, the rebellious assembly openly ordered the colonists to stockpile military supplies near the town of Concord (see Map 5.3).

The transition from royal to patriot political control was peaceful in communities where anti-British sentiment was strong. Where it was weak, or where the community was divided, radicals used persuasion, pressure, and open intimidation to advance the patriot cause. These radicals became increasingly impatient with dissent, disagreement, or even indecision among their neighbors. They insisted that people choose sides and declare loyalties.

In most colonial cities and towns, patriot committees arose to enforce compliance with the boycott of British goods. These committees publicly exposed those who did not obey the Continental Association, publishing violators' names in local newspapers and calling on the community to shun them. These tactics were effective against merchants who wanted to break the boycott and consumers willing to purchase English goods if they could find them. When public shaming did not work, most committees were ready to use threats of physical violence and to make good on them.

Colonists suspected of sympathizing with the British were brought before committees and made to swear oaths of support for the patriot cause. Such political pressure often gave way to violence. In Connecticut a group of patriots hauled a 70-year-old Anglican man from his bed, dragged him naked into the winter night, and beat him brutally because his loyalty to the Church of England made him suspect. In New England, many pro-British citizens, or **loyalists,** came to fear for their lives. In the wake of the Intolerable Acts, hundreds of them fled to the city of Boston, hoping General Gage could protect them from their neighbors.

The Shot Heard 'Round the World

The American situation was frustrating, but King George continued to believe that resistance in most colonies would fade if the Massachusetts radicals were crushed. In January 1775, he ordered General Gage to arrest the most notorious leaders of rebellion in that colony, Samuel Adams and John Hancock. Although storms on the Atlantic prevented the king's orders from reaching Gage until April, the general had independently decided it was time to take action. Gage planned to dispatch a force of redcoats to Concord with orders to seize the rapidly growing stockpile of weapons and arrest the two radical leaders along the way.

The patriots, of course, had their spies in Boston. Reports of the arrest orders and of suspicious troop preparations reached the militias gathered outside the occupied city. The only question was when and where Gage would attack. The Americans devised a warning system: as soon as Gage's troops began to move out of Boston, spies would signal the route with lanterns hung in the bell tower of the North Church. On April 18, 1775, riders waiting outside

loyalist An American colonist who remained loyal to the king during the Revolution.

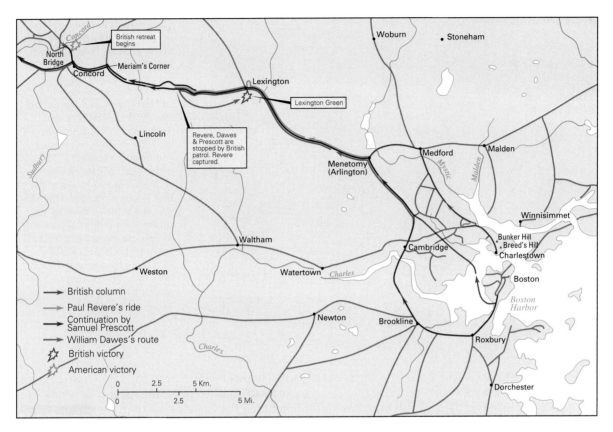

MAP 5.3 **The First Battles in the War for Independence, 1775**   This map shows the British march to Concord and the routes taken by the three Americans who alerted the countryside of the enemy's approach. Although Paul Revere was captured by the British and did not complete his ride, he is the best remembered and most celebrated of the nightriders who spread the alarm.

Boston saw one lantern, then another, flash from the bell tower. Within moments, silversmith Paul Revere and his fellow messengers rode off to give news of the British army's approach to the militia and the people living in the countryside.

Around sunrise on April 19, an advance guard of a few hundred redcoats reached the town of Lexington, where they expected to apprehend Adams and Hancock. In the pale light, they saw about seventy colonial militiamen waiting on the village green. As the badly outnumbered colonists began to disperse, eager and nervous redcoats broke ranks and rushed forward, sending up a triumphant cheer. No order came to fire, but in the confusion shots rang out. Eight Americans were killed, most of them shot in the back as they ran for safety. Nine more were wounded. Later Americans who told the story of the skirmish at Lexington would insist that the first musket fired there sounded a "shot heard 'round the world."

The British troops marched from Lexington to Concord. Surprised to find the town nearly deserted, they began a methodical search for weapons. All they uncovered were five hundred musket balls, which they dumped into a nearby pond. They then burned the town's liberty tree. Ignoring this act of provocation, the Concord **Minutemen**, in hiding nearby, waited patiently. When the moment seemed right, they swooped down on the unsuspecting British troops guarding the town's North Bridge.

The sudden attack by the Americans shocked the redcoats, who fled in a panic back toward Boston. The Minutemen followed, gathering more men along

Minutemen   Nickname first given to the Concord militia because of their speed in assembling and later applied generally to colonial militia during the Revolution.

The Pennsylvania State House in Philadelphia is best known to modern-day Americans as Independence Hall. It was here that the Declaration of Independence was debated and approved, and it was here that delegates gathered to draft a new constitution for the United States in the hot and humid summer of 1787. Although the State House boasted large windows in the East Room where the delegates met, the shutters were tightly closed—to preserve the secrecy of the debates and to prevent the huge bottlenecked flies swarming throughout the city from entering the room. *Independence National Historic Park.*

the path of pursuit. Together, these American farmers, artisans, servants, and shopkeepers terrorized the young British soldiers, firing on them at will from behind barns, stone walls, and trees. When the shaken troops reached the British encampment across the Charles River from Boston, 73 of their comrades were dead, 174 were wounded, and 26 were missing. The day after the **Battles of Lexington and Concord,** thousands of New England militiamen poured in from the surrounding countryside, dug trenches, and laid siege to Boston. As far as they and thousands of other Americans were concerned—including the loyalist refugees crowded into the city—war had begun.

The Second Continental Congress

When the Continental Congress reconvened in May 1775, it began at once to ready the colonies for war. This Second Continental Congress authorized the printing of American paper money for the purchase of supplies and appointed a committee to oversee foreign relations. It approved the creation of a Continental Army and chose George Washington, the Virginia veteran of the French and Indian War, to serve as its commander.

The Congress was clearly ready to defend Americans' rights and protect their liberties. But was it ready to declare a complete break with England? Some dele-

gates still hoped to find a peaceful solution to the crisis, despite the bloodshed at Lexington and Concord. This sentiment led the Congress to draft the **Olive Branch Petition,** which offered the king a choice: the colonists would end their armed resistance if the king would withdraw the British military and revoke the Intolerable Acts. Many delegates must have doubted the king's willingness to make such concessions, for the very next day the Congress issued a public statement in defense of the war preparations. This "Declaration of the Causes and Necessity of Taking Up Arms" boldly accused the British government of tyranny. It stopped short, however, of declaring colonial independence.

Across the Atlantic, British leaders struggled to find some negotiating points despite the king's refusal to bend. Almost two months before the battles at Lexington and Concord, Lord North had drafted a set of Conciliatory Propositions for Parliament and

---

Battles of Lexington and Concord Two confrontations in April 1775 between British soldiers and patriot Minutemen; the first recognized battles of the Revolution.

Olive Branch Petition Resolution, adopted by the Second Continental Congress in 1775 after the Battles of Lexington and Concord, that offered to end armed resistance if the king would withdraw his troops and repeal the Intolerable Acts.

the American Continental Congress to consider. North's proposals gave no ground on Parliament's right to tax the colonies, but they did offer to suspend taxation if Americans would raise funds for their own military defense. Members of Parliament who were sympathetic toward the Americans also pressed for compromise. They insisted that it made better sense to keep the colonies as a market for English goods than to lose them in a battle over raising revenue.

Cooler heads, however, did not prevail. Americans rejected Lord North's proposals in July 1775. The king, loathe to compromise, rejected the Olive Branch Petition. George III then persuaded Parliament to pass an **American Prohibitory Act** instructing the royal navy to seize American ships engaged in any form of trade, "as if the same were the ships . . . of open enemies." For all intents and purposes, King George III declared war on his colonies before the colonies declared war on their king.

The Impact of *Common Sense*

War was a fact, yet few American voices were calling for a complete political and emotional break with Britain. Even the most ardent patriots continued to justify their actions as upholding the British constitution. They were rebelling, they said, to preserve the rights guaranteed English citizens, not to establish an independent nation. Their drastic actions were necessary because a corrupt Parliament and corrupt ministers were trampling on those rights.

Although in 1764 Patrick Henry had dramatically warned the king to remember that tyrants were often deposed, few colonists had yet traced the source of their oppression to George III himself. If any American political leaders believed the king was as corrupt as his advisers and his Parliament, they did not make this view public. Then, in January 1776, Thomas Paine, an Englishman who had emigrated to America a few years earlier, published a pamphlet he called *Common Sense.* Paine's pamphlet broke the silence about King George III.

Tom Paine was a corsetmaker by trade but a political radical by temperament. As soon as he settled in Philadelphia, he became a wholehearted and vocal supporter of the colonial protest to defend colonial rights, but he preferred American political independence. In *Common Sense,* Paine spoke directly to ordinary citizens, not to their political leaders. Like the preachers of the Great Awakening, he rejected the formal language of the elite, adopting instead a plain, urgent, and emotional vocabulary and writing style designed to reach a mass audience.

Common Sense was unique in its content as well as its style. Paine made no excuses for his revolutionary zeal. He expressed no admiration for the British constitution or reverence for the British political system. Instead, he attacked the **sanctity** of the monarchy head-on. He challenged the idea of a hereditary ruler, questioned the value of monarchy as an institution, and criticized the personal character of the men who ruled as kings. The common man, Paine insisted, had the ability to be his own king and was surely more deserving of that position than most of the men who had worn crowns. Paine put it bluntly and sarcastically: "Of more worth is one honest man to society, and in the sight of God, than all the crowned ruffians that ever lived." He dismissed George III as nothing more than a "Royal Brute," and he urged Americans to establish their own republic. No wonder Charles Inglis felt compelled to respond to such radical and treasonous arguments!

Common Sense sold 120,000 copies in its first three months in print. Paine's defiance of traditional authority and open criticism of the men who wielded it helped many of his readers, both male and female, discard the last shreds of loyalty to the king and to the empire. The impact of Paine's words resounded in the taverns and coffeehouses, where ordinary farmers, artisans, shopkeepers, and laborers took up his call for independence and the creation of a republic. Political leaders acknowledged Paine's importance, although some begrudged the popular admiration lavished on this poorly educated artisan. The Harvard-trained John Adams reluctantly admitted that *Common Sense* was a "tolerable summary of the arguments I have been repeating again and again in Congress for nine months." But Adams's social snobbery led him to criticize Paine's language and his flamboyant writing style, suitable, Adams insisted, only "for an emigrant from new Gate [an English prison] or one chiefly associated with such company." Unshaken by such criticism, Tom Paine was content to see his message move so many into the revolutionary camp.

American Prohibitory Act British law of 1775 that authorized the royal navy to seize all American ships engaged in trade; it amounted to a declaration of war.

Common Sense Revolutionary pamphlet written by Thomas Paine in 1776; it attacked George III, argued against monarchy, and advanced the patriot cause.

sanctity Saintliness or holiness; the quality of being sacred or beyond criticism.

Declaring Independence

The Second Continental Congress, lagging far behind popular sentiment, inched its way toward a formal declaration of independence. But even John Adams, who had fumed at its snail's pace, took heart when the Congress opened American trade to all nations except Great Britain in early April 1776 and instructed the colonies to create official state governments. Then, on June 7, Adams's close ally in the struggle to announce independence, Virginia lawyer Richard Henry Lee, rose on the floor of the Congress and offered this straightforward motion: "That these United Colonies are, and of right ought to be, free and independent States, that they are absolved from all allegiance to the British Crown, and that all political connection between them and the State of Great Britain is, and ought to be, totally dissolved."

Lee's resolution was no more than a statement of reality, yet the Congress chose to postpone its final vote until July. The delay would give members time to win over the few fainthearted delegates from the Middle Colonies. It also would allow the committee appointed to draft a formal declaration of independence time to complete its work.

Congress had chosen an all-star group to draft the declaration, including John Adams, Connecticut's Roger Sherman, Benjamin Franklin, and New York landowner Robert Livingston. But these men delegated the task of writing the document to the fifth and youngest member of the committee, Thomas Jefferson. They chose well. The 33-year-old Virginian was not a social radical like Samuel Adams and Tom Paine. He was not an experienced politician like John Adams and Benjamin Franklin. And he lacked the reputation of fellow Virginians George Washington and Richard Henry Lee. But he had his strengths, and the committee members recognized them. Jefferson could draw on a deep and broad knowledge of political theory and philosophy. He had read the works of Enlightenment philosophers, classical theorists, and seventeenth-century English revolutionaries. And though shy and somewhat halting in his speech, Thomas Jefferson was a master of written prose. Jefferson began the **Declaration of Independence** with a defense of revolution based on "self-evident" truths about humanity's "inalienable rights"—rights that included life, liberty, and the pursuit of property. (In a later draft, the rights became "unalienable" and "property" became "happiness.") Jefferson argued that these rights were natural rather than historical. In other words, they came from the "Creator" rather than developing out of human law, government, or tradi-

In 1776, patriots everywhere celebrated independence by destroying local symbols of royal authority. New Yorkers, however, combined the practical with the symbolic, tearing down an imposing statue of King George III that had stood near the tip of Manhattan since 1770 and recycling its lead to make ammunition for the Revolutionary army. *"Pulling Down the Statue of George III" by William Walcott. Private Collection.*

tion. Thus they were broader and more sacred than the specific "rights of Englishmen." With this philosophical groundwork in place, Jefferson moved on to list the grievances that demanded that America end its relationship with Britain. He focused on the king's abuse of power rather than on the oppressive legislation passed by Parliament. All government rested on the consent of the governed, Jefferson asserted, and the people had the right to overthrow any government that tyrannized rather than protected them, that threatened rather than respected their unalienable rights.

The genius of Jefferson's Declaration was not that it contained novel ideas but that it contained ideas that were commonly accepted by America's political leaders and by most ordinary citizens as well. Jefferson gave voice to these beliefs, clearly and firmly. He also gave voice to the sense of abuse and injustice that had been growing in colonial society for several decades.

> **Declaration of Independence**   A formal statement, adopted by the Second Continental Congress in 1776, that listed justifications for rebellion and declared the American mainland colonies to be independent of Britain.

Declaring Loyalties

Delegates to the Second Continental Congress approved the Declaration of Independence on July 2, 1776, and made their approval public on July 4 (the text of the Declaration is reprinted in the Documents section at the end of this book). As John Adams was fond of saying, "The die had been cast," and Americans had to weigh loyalty to king against loyalty to a new nation. For Americans of every region, religion, social class, and race, this decision weighed heavily. In the face of such a critical choice, many wavered. Throughout the war that followed the Declaration, a surprising number of colonists clung to neutrality, hoping that the breach could be resolved without their having to participate or choose sides.

Those who did commit themselves based their decisions on deeply held beliefs and personal considerations, as well as fears. Many loyalists believed that tradition, commitment, and common sense argued for acknowledging parliamentary supremacy and the king's right to rule. These colonists had an abiding respect for the structure of the British government, with its balance between royalty, aristocracy, and the common people and its ability to preserve the rights of each group. In their judgment, the advantages of remaining within the protective circle of the most powerful nation in Europe seemed too obvious to debate. And the likelihood of swift and bloody defeat at the hands of the British army and navy seemed too obvious to risk. Many of the men who articulated the loyalist position were members of the colonial elite. They frankly admitted their fears that a revolution would unleash the "madness of the multitude." The tyranny of the mob, they argued, was far more damaging than the tyranny of which the king stood accused.

Not all colonists who chose loyalism feared the mob or revered the principles on which the British political system was based. For many, the deciding issues were economic. Holders of royal offices and merchants who depended on trade with British manufacturers found loyalty the compelling option. The loyalist ranks were also filled with colonists from the "multitude." Many small farmers and tenant farmers gave their support to the Crown when their political and economic foes—the great planters of the South or the New York manor lords—became patriots. The choice of which side to back often hinged, therefore, on local struggles and economic conflicts rather than on imperial issues.

For some of the perhaps 150,000 active loyalists, loyalism was a matter of personal character as much as conscious self-interest. Reluctance to break a solemn

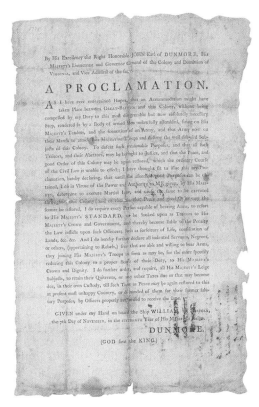

In November 1775, Virginia's royal governor, Lord Dunmore, enraged and frightened patriots by issuing this proclamation, which offered freedom to "all indentured Servants, Negroes, or others" who would help Britain squelch the impending rebellion. Thousands of enslaved men, women, and children eventually made their way to freedom behind British lines, choosing loyalism as their route to liberty. *Special Collections, University of Virginia Alderman Library.*

oath of allegiance to the king, anxiety over cutting ties with the past, fear of the chaos and violence that were a real part of revolution—any and all of these feelings could motivate a colonist to remain loyal rather than rebel.

For African Americans, the rallying call of liberty was familiar long before the Revolution began. Decades of slave resistance and rebellion demonstrated that black colonists did not need the impassioned language of a Patrick Henry or a Samuel Adams to remind them of the value of freedom. Instead, many slaves viewed the Revolution as they viewed epidemics and imperial warfare: as a potential opportunity to gain their own liberty. In the same way, free blacks saw the Revolution as a possible opportunity to win civil rights they had been denied before 1776.

African Americans had pointed out the inconsistencies of the radical position even before the Declaration of Independence. In 1773, a group of enslaved blacks in Boston petitioned the governor and the assembly for their freedom, "in behalf of all those, who . . . are held in a state of SLAVERY, within the bowels of a FREE country." There were white colonists who appreciated the injustice of a white slaveholding community in crisis over threats to its liberty. In 1774, while John Adams debated the threat of political slavery for colonial Englishmen in the First Continental Congress, his wife Abigail observed: "It always appeared a most iniquitous [sinful] scheme to me—to fight ourselves for what we are daily robbing and plundering from those who have as good a right to freedom as we have." Tom Paine agreed. Writing as "Humanus" in a Philadelphia newspaper, Paine urged white patriots to abolish slavery and give freed blacks western land grants.

Other patriots worried that slaves would seek their freedom by supporting the British in the war. The royal governor of Virginia was ready to make an offer of freedom to the colony's slaves. In 1775 Governor Dunmore expressed his intention to "arm all my own Negroes and receive all others that will come to me whom I shall declare free." Rumors of this plan horrified neighboring Maryland planters, who demanded that their governor issue arms and ammunition to protect against slave **insurrection.** Throughout the South, white communities braced themselves for a black struggle for freedom that would emerge in the midst of the colonial struggle for independence.

When Dunmore did offer freedom to "all indentured Servants, negroes or others . . . able and willing to bear Arms who escaped their masters," he was more interested in disrupting the slave-based plantation economy of his American enemies than in African American rights. Yet slaves responded, crossing into British lines in great enough numbers to create an "Ethiopian Regiment" of soldiers. These black loyalists wore a banner across their uniforms that read "Liberty to Slaves." Only six hundred to two thousand slaves managed to escape their masters in 1775–1776, but in the southern campaigns of the long war that followed, thousands of black men, women, and children made their way to the British lines. Once in uniform, black soldiers were usually assigned to work in road construction and other manual labor tasks rather than participate in combat. Perhaps as many as fifty thousand slaves gained their freedom during the war, as a result of either British policy or the disruptions that made escape possible.

Indians' responses to news of the war were far from uniform. At first, many considered the Revolution a family quarrel that should be avoided. The revolutionaries would have been satisfied to see Indians adopt this policy of neutrality. They knew they were unlikely to win Indian support given the legacy of border warfare and the actions of land-hungry settlers. As early as 1775, the Second Continental Congress issued a proclamation warning Indians to remain neutral. But the British, recognizing their advantage, made strong efforts to win Indian support. Indian leaders proceeded cautiously, however. When a British negotiator boasted to Flying Crow that British victory was inevitable, the Seneca chief was unimpressed. "If you are so strong, Brother, and they but as a weak Boy, why ask our assistance?" The chief was unwilling to commit his tribe based on issues that divided Crown and colonists but meant little to the welfare of his own people. "You say they are all mad, foolish, wicked, and deceitful—I say you are so and they are wise for you want us to destroy ourselves in your War and they advise us to live in Peace."

The British continued to press for Indian participation in the war, and many Indian tribes and confederations eventually decided that the Crown would better serve their interests and respect their rights than would the colonists. First, the British were much more likely than the colonists to be able to provide a steady supply of the manufactured goods and weapons the Indians relied on in the eighteenth century. Second, colonial territorial ambitions threatened the Indians along the southern and northwestern frontiers. Third, an alliance with the British offered some possibility of recouping land and trading benefits lost in the past. No uniformity emerged, however. Among the Iroquois, for example, conflicting choices of loyalties led pro-British Senecas to burn the crops and houses of Oneidas who had joined forces with the patriots. Among the Potowatomis, similar divisions occurred. Intertribal rivalries and Indians' concerns about the safety of their own villages often determined alignments. In the southern backcountry, fierce fighting between Indians and revolutionaries seemed a continuation of the century's many border wars. But even there, alignments could shift. Although the Cherokees began the war as British allies, a split developed, producing an internal civil war similar to the one among the Iroquois tribes.

Fewer than half of the colonists threw in their lot with the revolutionaries. Among those who did were

---

insurrection An uprising against a legitimate authority or government.

people whose economic interests made independence seem worth the risk, including artisans and urban laborers, merchants who traded outside the British Empire, large and small farmers, and many members of the southern planter elite. For these Americans, it was not simply a matter of escaping unfair taxation. A release from Britain's mercantile policies, which restricted colonial trade with other nations, held out the promise of expanded trade and an end to the risks of smuggling. Sometimes the pressure for independence came from below rather than from a colony's political leadership. For example, although Virginia's elite produced many radical spokesmen for independence such as Patrick Henry, many southern planters only reluctantly endorsed independence in order to retain their authority over the more radical ordinary farmers. Colonists affected by the Great Awakening and by its message of egalitarianism often chose the patriot side. Americans with a conscious, articulated radical vision of society—the Tom Paines and Samuel Adamses—supported the Revolution and its promise of a republic. Many who became revolutionaries shared the hope for a better life under a government that encouraged its citizens to be virtuous and to live in simplicity.

As Americans—English, European, Indian, and African American—armed themselves or fled from the violence and bloodshed they saw coming, they realized that the conflict wore two faces: this was a war for independence, but it was also a civil war. In the South, it pitted slave against master, Cherokee against Cherokee, and frontier farmer against tidewater planter. In New England, it set neighbor against neighbor, forcing scores of loyalist families to flee. In some instances, children were set against parents, and wives refused to support the cause their husbands had chosen. Whatever the outcome of the struggle ahead, Americans knew that it would come at great cost.

Individual Voices

Examining a Primary Source

Charles Inglis Calls for Reconcilation

Charles Inglis, Anglican minister and rector of New York City's Trinity Church, was one of the few loyalists who dared take issue with Thomas Paine's dramatic and powerful call to revolution, *Common Sense*. His response came in the form of a 1776 pamphlet called *The True Interest of America Impartially Stated*. In the portion of his pamphlet reprinted below, Inglis expresses horror at the prospect of breaking a sacred oath of allegiance to the Church of England and the Crown. Most loyalists who held appointed office and most Anglican ministers shared his feelings on this issue. In *The True Interest,* Inglis also predicts that the British army and navy would crush the rebellion at the cost of many American lives. His vision of the chaos, devastation, and humiliation the rebellious colonists would suffer was echoed in the private letters of loyalists everywhere. Finally, he points to the loss of property and the resulting poverty that would befall the colonies if they rose up against the Crown. Although fighting had already begun at Lexington and Concord, and the Continental Congress had started to muster an army, Inglis pleaded for the colonists to seek a reconciliation with Britain. But as John Adams was so fond of saying, "The die had been cast"; the Declaration of Independence was issued on July 4, 1776.

In many ways, Inglis proved correct. Much American blood was spilled during the Revolution and the long home-front war saw much devastation. Many of the ministers and officeholders who remained loyal saw the new state governments confiscate and sell their land and their homes. Once-wealthy loyalists such as Jonathan Sewall of Massachusetts and Joseph Galloway of Pennsylvania ended their lives in

■ *Inglis is referring to the battles in Massachusetts at Lexington, Concord, and Bunker Hill, in April and June 1775.*

■ *Although revolutionaries suffered the loss of crops, homes, and livestock, it was the loyalists who, in the end, saw their estates seized by the state governments and sold to patriotic neighbors. Do you think that confiscating their lands and possessions was justified?*

■ *Modern nations have also established colonies and fought wars to keep them. What economic advantages do colonies provide? Can you think of noneconomic reasons why colonies might be valuable?*

■ *If you were writing a response to Inglis's dire scenario, how would you refute his predictions of American defeat? What American advantages would you cite? What British disadvantages? What do you think were the most important factors in the American victory?*

exile and in poverty. Inglis was wrong, however, about the outcome of the war: in one of the greatest military upsets of Western history, the Americans brought the English to their knees.

The blood of the slain, the weeping voice of nature cries—it is time to be reconciled, it is time to lay aside those animosities which have pushed on Britons to shed the blood of Britons; ■ *it is high time that those who are connected by the endearing ties of religion, kindred and country, should resume their former friendship, and be united in the bond of mutual affection, as their interests are inseparably united. . . . By a Reconciliation with Great-Britain, Peace—that fairest offspring and gift of Heaven—will be restored. . . . What uneasiness and anxiety, what evils, has this short interruption of peace with the parent-state, brought on the whole British empire!*

Suppose we were to revolt from Great-Britain, declare ourselves Independent, and set up a Republic of our own—what would be the consequence? I stand aghast at the prospect—my blood runs chill when I think of the calamities, the complicated evils that must ensue. . . . All our property throughout the continent would be unhinged; the greatest confusion, and most violent convulsions would take place. . . . What a horrid situation would thousands be reduced to who have taken the oath of allegiance to the King; yet contrary to their oath, as well as inclination, must be compelled to renounce that allegiance, or abandon all their property in America! ■ *How many thousands more would be reduced to a similar situation; who, although they took not that oath, yet would think it inconsistent with their duty and a good conscience to renounce their Sovereign. . . .*

By a Declaration of Independency, every avenue to an accommodation with Great-Britain would be closed; the sword only could then decide the quarrel; and the sword would not be sheathed till one had conquered the other.

The importance of these colonies to Britain need not be enlarged on, it is a thing so universally known. ■ *The greater their importance is to her, so much the more obstinate will her struggle be not to lose them. . . . Great-Britain therefore must, for her own preservation, risk everything, and exert her whole strength, to prevent such an event from taking place. This being the case—Devastation and ruin must mark the progress of this war along the sea coast of America. Hitherto, Britain has not exerted her power. . . . But as soon as we declare for independency . . . ruthless war, with all its aggravated horrors, will ravage our once happy land. . . . Torrents of blood will be spilt, and thousands reduced to beggary and wretchedness. . . .* ■

Summary

The British victory over France and Spain in the Great War for Empire made Britain the most powerful European nation. Yet this victory produced new problems. The British had to govern the French population in Canada and maintain security against Indians on a greatly expanded colonial frontier. They had to pay an enormous war debt while maintaining a strong and well-equipped army and navy to keep the empire they

had won. To deal with these new circumstances, the English government chose to impose revenue-raising measures on the colonies. The outcome was growing tension between Mother Country and colonies.

The Sugar Act of 1764 tightened customs collections, the Stamp Act of 1765 placed a direct tax on legal documents, and the Townshend Acts of 1767 set import taxes on English products such as paint and tea. In response to this sharp shift in policy, the colonists chose protest, including crowd actions directed by the Sons of Liberty and boycotts of English goods. Crowds attacked royal officials, and in Boston five civilians died in the Boston Massacre, a clash with British troops. American colonists saw Parliament's revenue-raising acts as an abuse of power, and political debate began to focus on colonial rights and the possibility that the British government was threatening to curtail American liberties.

Protest led to the repeal of the acts, but political activists prepared for a quick and united response to any new crises by creating organizations such as the committees of correspondence. In 1773 the British passed the Tea Act, expecting little American opposition. The outcome was immediate protest, and in Boston a group of activists dumped thousands of pounds' worth of tea into the harbor.

Moving to punish the colonists, the English closed the port of Boston to all trade. This and other Intolerable Acts infuriated colonists, who took united action in support of Massachusetts. A new colonial forum, the First Continental Congress, met in 1774 to debate the colonies' relationship to England and to issue united protests. A Declaration of Rights and Griev-ances was sent to the king, who rejected the colonists' appeal for compromise. Instead he declared that "blows must decide."

After British troops and militiamen fought at Lexington and Concord, a Second Continental Congress began to prepare for war. Tom Paine's pamphlet *Common Sense* pushed many reluctant colonists into the revolutionary camp. Not even a reasoned rebuttal of this call to revolution, such as the one written by Charles Inglis, could halt the progress toward independence after this. In July 1776, Congress issued the Declaration of Independence, drafted by Thomas Jefferson, defending the colonists' right to resist the destruction of their liberty by a tyrannical king. In 1776 Americans faced the difficult task of choosing sides: loyalty to the Crown or revolution. Not only white colonists but African Americans and Indians had to decide whether to offer support to one side or the other or try to remain neutral in the midst of revolution. The outcome was both a war for colonial independence and a civil war that divided families and communities across America.

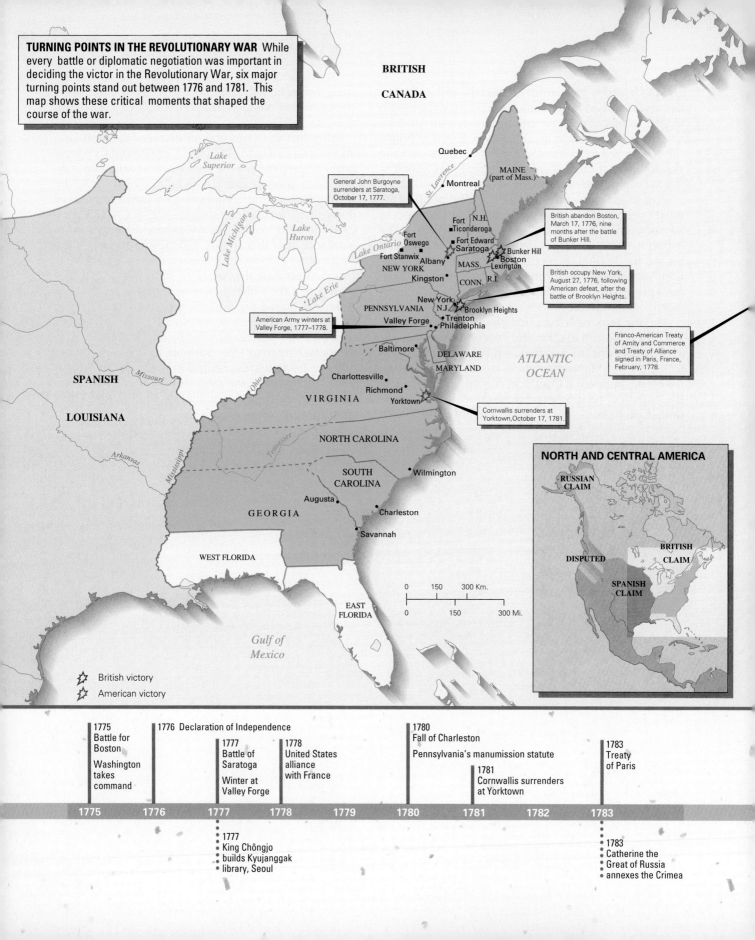

TURNING POINTS IN THE REVOLUTIONARY WAR While every battle or diplomatic negotiation was important in deciding the victor in the Revolutionary War, six major turning points stand out between 1776 and 1781. This map shows these critical moments that shaped the course of the war.

BRITISH

CANADA

Quebec

MAINE
(part of Mass.)

Montreal

General John Burgoyne surrenders at Saratoga, October 17, 1777.

Fort Ticonderoga

N.H.

British abandon Boston, March 17, 1776, nine months after the battle of Bunker Hill.

Fort Oswego

Fort Edward
Saratoga

Bunker Hill
Boston
Lexington

Fort Stanwix

Albany

MASS.

British occupy New York, August 27, 1776, following American defeat, after the battle of Brooklyn Heights.

NEW YORK

Kingston

CONN.

R.I.

New York

PENNSYLVANIA

N.J.

Brooklyn Heights

American Army winters at Valley Forge, 1777–1778.

Valley Forge

Trenton

Philadelphia

Franco-American Treaty of Amity and Commerce and Treaty of Alliance signed in Paris, France, February, 1778.

Baltimore

DELAWARE

MARYLAND

ATLANTIC OCEAN

SPANISH

LOUISIANA

Charlottesville

VIRGINIA

Richmond

Yorktown

Cornwallis surrenders at Yorktown, October 17, 1781.

NORTH CAROLINA

SOUTH CAROLINA

Wilmington

Augusta

GEORGIA

Charleston

Savannah

WEST FLORIDA

EAST FLORIDA

Gulf of Mexico

0   150   300 Km.

0   150   300 Mi.

NORTH AND CENTRAL AMERICA

RUSSIAN CLAIM

DISPUTED

BRITISH CLAIM

SPANISH CLAIM

☆ British victory
☆ American victory

Lake Superior

Lake Michigan

Lake Huron

Lake Ontario

Lake Erie

Missouri

Mississippi

Ohio

Tennessee

Arkansas

St. Lawrence

Recreating America: Independence and a New Nation, 1775–1783

Turning Points in the Revolutionary War
Using the map on the facing page, discuss the major military campaigns of the Revolutionary War. Can you explain why Burgoyne's campaign was located in New York and why Cornwallis's army was in Virginia? What role can you conclude the French played in the American victory?

Individual Choices

DEBORAH SAMPSON

Whether attracted by adventure, the promise of a pension, or the bounty soldiers received upon enlistment, Deborah Sampson decided to disguise herself as a man and enlist in the Continental Army in 1781. She served for over two years before officers discovered she was a woman and discharged her. This portrait, drawn by Joseph Stone Framingham in 1797, depicts Sampson in female dress but surrounds her with the military emblems befitting a veteran of the Revolutionary War. *Rhode Island Historical Society.*

Deborah Sampson

The Great War for Empire was still raging when Deborah Sampson was born in a small village outside Plymouth, Massachusetts, in 1760. Sampson's family tree had deep roots in New England, for her father was a descendant of two of the original Pilgrim settlers and her mother could trace her heritage back to the colony's first governor, William Bradford. Yet Deborah's parents had neither wealth nor status: the Sampsons were only a poor, struggling farm family. When Deborah was a small child, her father abandoned his wife and six children. Deborah's mother was forced to hire out some of her children, including Deborah, as servants in her neighbors' homes.

By the time the Revolutionary War began, Deborah Sampson was a tall, healthy young woman, made physically strong by years of farm work. When her term of service ended in 1779, Sampson had few choices for a next step in life. Without a dowry or an inheritance, she was unlikely to marry; without any special training, she was destined to spend her life as a servant in rural Massachusetts. But Deborah discovered another option—and chose to take it. Disguising herself as a man, she enlisted as a soldier in the Continental Army. Just as the colonies changed themselves into an independent nation, Deborah Sampson changed herself into Private Robert Shurtleff.

As a woman, Sampson might have played a role in the war by serving as a **courier** or a spy. Or she might have joined thousands of other women in the army camps, performing valuable services such as cooking, laundering, or nursing. She might have remained safely at home, knitting socks or making uniforms for the poorly clad soldiers serving under General Washington. But none of these alternatives would have given her what military service offered: the chance to see new places and have new experiences, an enlistment bonus, a pension if she survived, and a promise of land when the war ended. Thousands of poor young men risked the dangers of the battlefield for these rewards. Why not Deborah Sampson?

Perhaps patriotism also prompted her to abandon her petticoats for a uniform. Years later, when her story was published, she insisted that she had joined the army because she believed in liberty and wanted to play a meaningful part in the birth of her nation. But whatever her motives, Deborah Sampson proved herself a fine soldier and a brave one. She also managed to hide her identity for several years, even when she was wounded by a musket ball that lodged in her leg. The truth of her sex was not discovered until she was hospitalized for a fever while stationed in Philadelphia.

When the authorities realized that Private Shurtleff was actually a young woman, they dismissed her from military service at once. On October 25, 1783, eight months after the Treaty of Paris ending the war was signed, Deborah Sampson was granted an honorable discharge—and Robert Shurtleff disappeared forever.

Deborah Sampson returned to Massachusetts in November of 1783. In the spring of the following year, she married a local farmer named Benjamin Gannett and began a family. As a wife and mother, Deborah Sampson Gannett was expected to give up any role in the public sphere. Once again, however, she proved herself a rebel: in 1802 she began to travel throughout New England giving public lectures on her military career. The tales she told the crowds who flocked to hear and see her were undoubtedly full of exaggerated claims of daring battlefield exploits. Yet dressed in her uniform once again, performing a precision drill on stage that would have made Washington's drillmaster Baron von Steuben proud, Deborah Sampson demonstrated the unexpected impact of the Revolution on an ordinary American's life.

INTRODUCTION

The war that so changed Deborah Sampson's life, and the lives of most colonists, began in April 1775 as a skirmish at Concord's North Bridge. In the first months of the war, Great Britain expected an easy victory over the colonial rebels. On paper, at least, the odds against an American victory were staggering. To crush the colonial rebellion, Great Britain was ready and able to commit vast human and material resources. The well-trained and harshly disciplined British ground troops were assisted and supplied by the most powerful navy in the world, and they carried the flag of the richest imperial power of Europe. Many Indian tribes, including most of the Iroquois, allied with the British, and the Crown could expect thousands of white and black loyalists to fight beside them as well.

The American war effort was far less impressive. The Continental Congress had a nearly empty treasury, and the country's resources did not include the foundries or factories needed to produce arms, ammunition, or other military supplies. The army administration was inefficient, the population was wary of professional soldiers, and the new state governments were unwilling to raise tax monies to contribute to the Congress's war chest. Through most of the war, therefore, American officers and enlisted men could expect to be underpaid or not paid at all. They were likely to go into battle poorly equipped, often half-starved, and frequently dressed in rags. Unlike the British redcoats, these Americans had little military skill or formal military training. Most were as new to military life as Deborah Sampson.

Britain's advantage thus seemed great, but it was not absolute. To fight the war, the British had to transport arms, provisions, and men across thousands of miles of ocean. They risked delays, disasters, and destruction of supplies on the open seas. The Americans, on the other hand, were fighting on familiar terrain, and geography gave them an additional advantage: their vast, rural society could not be easily conquered even if major colonial cities were taken or an entire region were occupied. Long-standing European rivalries also worked to the advantage of the Americans and gave them valuable allies. Holland, France, and Spain all stood to gain from England's distress and were therefore willing to lend money and provide much-needed supplies to the rebellion. And in 1778, when France and Spain decided to recognize American independence formally, the war suddenly expanded into a global struggle. The support of the French navy transformed General Washington's military strategy and led eventually to the defeat of the British army at Yorktown. Even the most patriotic American had to concede that international politics, as much as military heroism or popular commitment to the Revolution, had won the colonies their independence.

No matter what eighteenth-century Americans felt about the war, no matter which side they supported or what role they played, they shared the experience of extraordinary events and the need to make extraordinary choices when the war disrupted the flow of their ordinary lives. In this most personal and immediate sense, the war was as revolutionary for them as it was for a young woman who became, for a brief but critical moment, a soldier in the name of liberty.

courier A messenger carrying official information, sometimes secretly.

American artist John Trumbull painted *The Battle of Bunker Hill* in 1786, over a decade after the bloody encounter between redcoats and American militiamen. Trumbull was a student of the famous American painter Benjamin West, who had won his reputation celebrating the English victories of the French and Indian War. Trumbull and other American students of West built their reputations by celebrating American victories in the artistic style that West taught them. *"The Death of General Warren at Bunker Hill" by John Trumbull, Yale University Art Gallery. Trumbull Collection.*

The First Two Years of War

■ What were the British and American strategies in the early years of the war?

■ What decisions and constraints kept the British from achieving the quick victory many expected?

In 1775 **Thomas Gage,** the British general serving as military governor of Massachusetts and commander of the British army of occupation there, surely wished he were anywhere but Boston. The town was unsophisticated by British standards, many of its inhabitants were unfriendly, and its taverns and lodging houses bulged at the seams with complaining loyalist refugees from the countryside. Gage's army was restless, and his officers were bored. The American encampments outside the city were growing daily, filling with local farmers and artisans after the bloodshed of Lexington and Concord. These thousands of colonial **militiamen** gathering on the hills surrounding Boston were clearly the military enemy. Yet in 1775 they were still citizens of the British Empire, not foreign invaders

or foes. Gage, like his American opponents, was caught up in the dilemmas of an undeclared war.

The Battle for Boston

With proper artillery, well placed on the hills surrounding the city, the Americans could have done serious damage to Gage's army of occupation. The problem was that the rebels had no cannon. A New Haven druggist named **Benedict Arnold** joined forces

Thomas Gage British general who was military governor of Massachusetts and commander of the army occupying Boston in 1775.

militiamen Soldiers who were not members of a regular army but ordinary citizens called out in case of an emergency.

Benedict Arnold Pharmacist-turned-military-leader whose bravery and daring made him an American hero and a favorite of George Washington until he committed treason in 1780.

Chronology

Rebellion and Independence

1775 Battle for Boston
George Washington assumes command of
Continental Army

1776 Declaration of Independence
British campaigns in South and mid-Atlantic region
George Mason's Declaration of Rights

1777 Burgoyne's New York campaign
Battle of Saratoga
Winter at Valley Forge

1778 American-French alliance

1778 British begin second southern campaign

1780 Fall of Charleston
Treason of Benedict Arnold
Pennsylvania enacts manumission statute

1781 Cornwallis surrenders at Yorktown
Loyalists evacuate United States
Articles of Confederation government established

1782 British Parliament votes to end war

1783 Treaty of Paris signed

with a Vermont farmer named Ethan Allen to solve the problem. In May 1775 their troops captured Fort Ticonderoga in New York and began the difficult task of transporting the fort's cannon across hundreds of miles of mountains and forests to Boston. By the time the artillery reached the city, however, a bloody battle between Gage and the American militia had already taken place.

In early June, Gage had issued a proclamation declaring all armed colonists traitors, but he offered **amnesty** to any rebel who surrendered to British authorities. When the militiamen ignored the general's offer, Gage decided a show of force was necessary. On June 17, 1775, under cover of cannon fire from a British warship in Boston harbor, Gage's fellow officer **William Howe** led a force of twenty-four hundred soldiers against rebel-held Breed's Hill. Despite the oppressive heat and humidity of the day, General Howe ordered his men to advance in full dress uniform, weighed down with wool jackets and heavy knapsacks. Howe also insisted on making a "proper" frontal attack on the Americans. From the top of the hill, Captain William Prescott's militiamen immediately opened fire on the unprotected redcoats. The result was a near massacre. The tables turned, however, when the Americans ran out of ammunition. Most of Prescott's men fled in confusion, and the British soldiers bayoneted the few who remained to defend their position.

Even battle-worn veterans were shocked at the carnage of the day. The British suffered more casualties that June afternoon than they would in any other

battle of the war. The Americans, who retreated to the safety of Cambridge, learned a costly lesson on the importance of an effective supply line of arms and ammunition to their fighting men. Little was gained by either side. That the battle was misnamed the **Battle of Bunker Hill** captured perfectly the confusion and the absurdity of the encounter.

Congress Creates an Army

While militiamen and redcoats turned the Boston area into a war zone, the Continental Congress took its first steps toward recruiting and supplying an army. The "regular" army that took shape was not really a national force. It was a collection of small state armies whose recruits preserved their local or regional identities. While this army was expected to follow the war wherever it led, the Continental Congress still relied on each state's militia to join in any battles that took place within its borders.

amnesty A general pardon granted by a government, especially for political offenses.

William Howe British general in command at the Battle of Bunker Hill; three years later he became commander in chief of British forces in America.

Battle of Bunker Hill British assault on American troops on Breed's Hill near Boston in June 1775; the British won the battle but suffered heavy losses.

Congress chose French and Indian War veteran **George Washington** to command the Continental forces. Washington wrote gloomily of the enormity of the task before him. Nothing he saw when he reached Massachusetts on July 3, 1775, made him more optimistic. A carnival atmosphere seemed to prevail inside the militiamen's camps. Farm-boys-turned-soldiers fired their muskets at random, often using their weapons to start fires or to shoot at geese flying overhead. In the confusion, they sometimes accidentally wounded or killed themselves and others. "Seldom a day passes but some persons are shot by their friends," Washington noted in amazement.

The camps resembled pigsties. The stench from open latrines was terrible, and rotting animal carcasses, strewn everywhere, added to the aroma. The men were dirty and infected with lice, and most soldiers were constantly scratching, trying to relieve an itch that left them covered with scabs and raw, peeling skin. General Washington was disturbed but not surprised by what he saw. He knew that the men in these camps were country boys, away from home for the first time in their lives. The chaos they created resulted from a combination of fear, excitement, boredom, inexperience, and plain homesickness, all brewing freely under poor leadership. Despite his sympathy for these young men, Washington acted quickly to reorganize the militia units, replace incompetent officers, and tighten discipline within the camps.

The British meanwhile laid plans for the evacuation of Boston, spurred in part by the knowledge that Arnold's wagon train of cannon was nearing Massachusetts. In March 1776 a fleet arrived to carry Thomas Gage, his officers, the British army, and almost a thousand loyalist refugees north to the safety of Halifax, Nova Scotia. By this time, command of His Majesty's war was in the hands of the Howe brothers—General William Howe, commander of the Breed's Hill attack, and **Richard Howe,** an admiral in the royal navy. With the help of military strategists and the vast resources of the Crown, the Howes were expected to bring the rebellion to a speedy end and restore order to the colonies.

The British Strategy in 1776

General Howe was less concerned with suppressing the radicalism of New England than the king had been. He thought the most effective strategy would be to locate areas with high concentrations of loyalists and mobilize them to secure the allegiance of their undecided and even rebellious neighbors. Howe and his advisers targeted two reputed centers of loyalist

strength. The first—New York, New Jersey, Pennsylvania—had a legacy of social and economic conflicts, such as the revolt of the Paxton Boys, that had caused many of the region's elite families to fear that independence threatened their prosperity. But loyalism was not confined to the conservative and wealthy. Its second stronghold was among the poor settlers of the Carolina backcountry. There, decades of bitter struggle between the coastal planters and the backcountry farmers had led to the Regulator movement (see page 101) and to intense loyalist sentiment among many of the embattled westerners.

General Howe's strategy had its flaws, however. First, although many people in these two regions were loyal, their numbers were never as great as the British assumed. Second, everywhere they went, British and **Hessian troops** left behind a trail of destruction and memories of abuse that alienated many Americans who might have considered remaining loyal. Howe was not likely to win over families who saw their "cattle killed and lying about the fields and pastures . . . household furniture hacked and broken into pieces . . . wells filled up and . . . tools destroyed."

Nevertheless, in 1776 Howe launched his first major military assaults in the South and the mid-Atlantic region. The campaign in the South, directed by General Henry Clinton, went badly. In North Carolina, loyalists did turn out to fight for the Crown, but the British failed to provide them the military support they needed. Poorly armed and badly outnumbered, Carolina loyalists were decisively defeated by the rebel militia on February 27 in the Battle of Moore's Creek. Rather than rush to their defense, the British abandoned their loyalist allies in favor of taking revenge on South Carolina. Clinton and an impressive fleet of fifty ships and three thousand men sailed into Charleston harbor. But the British had unexpected bad luck. As the troops started to wade ashore, they found themselves stranded on small islands surrounded by a sudden rush of tidal waters. The Americans, on the

---

George Washington Commander in chief of the Continental Army; he led Americans to victory in the Revolution and later became the first president of the United States.

Richard Howe British admiral who commanded British naval forces in America; he was General William Howe's brother.

Hessian troops German soldiers from the state of Hesse who were hired by Britain to fight in the American Revolution.

other hand, had unexpected good luck. Working frantically to defend the harbor, they constructed a flimsy fort out of local palmetto wood. To the surprise of both sides, the cannon balls fired by British ships sank harmlessly into the absorbent, pulpy palmetto stockade. The fort—and the city of Charleston—remained standing.

Embarrassed and frustrated, the British command abruptly ended its southern campaign. General Clinton, a gloomy man under the best of circumstances, sailed north, eager to escape the scene of his humiliation. The South Carolina loyalists, however, could not escape British failures. They had been denounced, mobbed, imprisoned, and sometimes tortured since 1775. Their situation grew even worse after the British withdrew.

Escape from New York

While Clinton was failing in the Carolinas, the Howe brothers were preparing a massive invasion of the mid-Atlantic region. In July 1776, Admiral Howe and General Howe sailed into New York harbor with the largest expeditionary force of the eighteenth century. With thirty thousand men, one-third of them Hessian mercenaries, this British army was larger than the peacetime population of New York City.

The Howes were not eager to demolish New York, however. Unlike most British officers, the brothers were genuinely fond of Americans, and they preferred to be agents of compromise and negotiation rather than of destruction. They hoped that a spectacular show of force and a thorough humiliation of rebel commander George Washington would be enough to bring the Americans to their senses and end the rebellion.

General Washington rushed his army south from Massachusetts to defend the city, but he had few illusions that his twenty-three thousand men, many of them sick and most of them inexperienced at war, could repel the invading British forces. In the middle of his defense preparations, Washington received a copy of the newly approved Declaration of Independence. He immediately ordered his brigades to line up on the parade grounds so that he could read Thomas Jefferson's stirring words aloud to them. He was gratified to hear the men cheer the Declaration. But privately, Washington wondered if these men would fight when they faced the enemy in battle.

For a month, the Howes made no move on the city. Finally, in the early morning of August 22, 1776, the British began their advance, landing unopposed, and moving toward the Brooklyn neck of Long Island (see Map 6.1). Just as Washington had feared, his raw and inexperienced troops quickly broke when fighting be-

MAP 6.1 The War of the North, 1775–1777 The American attempt to capture Canada and General George Washington's effort to save New York from British occupation were failures, but Washington did manage to stage successful raids in New Jersey before retreating to safety in the winter of 1777. This map details the movements of both British and American troops during the Northern Campaign, and it indicates the victories and defeats for both armies.

gan five days later. Cut off from one another, confused by the sound and sight of the attack, almost all the American troops surrendered or ran. A single Maryland regiment made a heroic stand against the landing forces but was destroyed by the oncoming British. Washington, at the scene himself, might have been captured had the Howes pressed their advantage. But they withdrew, content that they had made the American commander look foolish.

Washington took advantage of the Howes' delay to bring his troops to the safety of Manhattan Island. The safety proved temporary, for on September 15, a British attack again sent his farm-boys-turned-soldiers into flight. Angry and frustrated, Washington threw his hat to the ground and shouted, "Are these the men with whom I am to defend America!"

Washington's army fled north, with the British in hot pursuit. In a skirmish at Harlem Heights, the American commander was relieved to see his men stand their ground and win their first combat victory. He was even more relieved by the strange failure of the British to press their advantage. The British had only to follow his army into Westchester County and deliver a crushing blow, but they did not. When the redcoats finally engaged the Continentals again at White Plains, the Americans managed to retreat safely. Soon afterward, Washington took his army across the Hudson River to New Jersey and marched them farther west, across the Delaware River into Pennsylvania.

Winter Quarters and Winter Victories

Following European customs, General Howe established winter quarters for his troops before the cold set in. Redcoats and Hessians made their camps in the New York area and in Rhode Island that December, expecting Washington to make camp somewhere as well. But Washington, safe for the moment in

Most American school children are familiar with paintings of General George Washington and his Continental Army crossing the ice-covered Delaware River on December 25, 1776, in order to mount a daring surprise attack on enemy troops at Trenton, New Jersey. This painting, done in 1851 by Emanuel Leutze, recreates an event that took place 75 years earlier—and forty years before the artist was born. What role does art play in creating national myths? *The Metropolitan Museum of Art, Gift of John S. Kennedy, 1987. Photograph © The Metropolitan Museum of Art.*

Pennsylvania, was too restless to settle in just yet. Enlistment terms in his army would soon be up, and without some encouraging military success he feared few of his soldiers would reenlist. Thus Washington looked eagerly for a good target to attack—and found one. Across the Delaware, on the Jersey side, two or three thousand Hessian troops held a garrison near the town of Trenton.

On Christmas night, amid a howling storm, General Washington led twenty-four hundred of his men back across the river. Marching 9 miles through a raging blizzard, the Americans arrived to find the Hessians asleep. The surprised enemy surrendered immediately. Without losing a single man, Washington had captured nine hundred prisoners and many badly needed military supplies. Taking full advantage of the moment, Washington made a rousing appeal to his men to reenlist. About half of the soldiers agreed to remain.

The **Battle of Trenton** was a crucial victory, but Washington enjoyed his next success even more. In early January he again crossed into New Jersey from the safety of Pennsylvania and made his way toward the British garrison at Princeton. On the way, his advance guard ran into two British regiments. As both sides lined up for battle, Washington rode back and forth in front of his men, shouting encouragement and urging them to stand firm. His behavior was reckless, for it put him squarely in the line of fire, but it was also effective. When the British turned in retreat, Washington rashly rode after them, clearly delighted to be in pursuit for once in the war.

The Trenton and Princeton victories raised the morale of the Continental Army as it settled at last into its winter quarters near Morristown, New Jersey. They stirred popular support also. Americans everywhere referred to the two winter raids as a "nine-day wonder." Of course, Howe's army was still poised to march on Philadelphia when warm weather revived the war again. And Congress still had few resources to spare for Washington and his men. When Washington pleaded for supplies, Congress urged him to commandeer what he needed from civilians nearby. The general wisely refused. English high-handedness and cruelty had turned many people of the area into staunch supporters of the Revolution, and Washington had no intention of alienating them by seizing their livestock, food, or weapons.

Burgoyne's New York Campaign

In July 1777 General William Howe sailed with fifteen thousand men up the Chesapeake Bay toward Philadelphia. The Continental Congress had already fled the city, knowing that Washington could not prevent the enemy occupation. Although the Americans made two efforts to block Howe, first at Brandywine Creek and then at Germantown, the British had little problem capturing Philadelphia. The problems they did face in 1777 came not from Washington but from the poor judgment of one of their own, a flamboyant young general named **John Burgoyne.**

Burgoyne had won approval for an elaborate plan to sever New England from the rest of the American colonies. He would move his army south from Montreal, while a second army of redcoats and Iroquois, commanded by Colonel Barry St. Leger, would veer east across the Mohawk Valley from Fort Oswego. At the same time, William Howe would send a third force north from New York City. The three armies would rendezvous at Albany, effectively isolating New England and, it was assumed, giving the British a perfect opportunity to crush the rebellion.

The plan was daring and—on paper—seemed to have every chance of success. In reality, however, it had serious flaws. First, neither Burgoyne nor the British officials in England had any knowledge of the American terrain that had to be covered. Second, they badly misjudged the Indian support St. Leger would receive. Third, General Howe, no longer in New York City, knew absolutely nothing of his own critical role in the plan. Blissfully unaware of these problems, Burgoyne led his army from Montreal in high spirits in June 1777 (see Map 6.2). The troops floated down Lake Champlain in canoes and flatbottom boats and easily retook Fort Ticonderoga. From Ticonderoga, the invading army continued to march toward Albany. From this point on, however, things began to go badly for Burgoyne.

In true eighteenth-century British style, "Gentleman Johnny" Burgoyne chose to travel well rather than lightly. The thirty wagons moving slowly behind the general contained over fifty pieces of artillery for the campaign. They also contained Burgoyne's mistress, her personal wardrobe and his, and a generous supply of champagne. When the caravan encountered New York's swamps and gullies, movement

Battle of Trenton Battle on December 26, 1776, when Washington led his troops by night across the Delaware River and captured a Hessian garrison wintering in New Jersey.

John Burgoyne British general forced to surrender his entire army at Saratoga, New York, in October 1777.

In July 1777 Jane McCrea was on her way to join her loyalist fiancé, marching with General Burgoyne's army, when she was brutally murdered. The American general, Horatio Gates, accused Iroquois Indian allies of the British army of the murder. The news of McCrea's violent death added to the American army's determination to stop Burgoyne's invasion into upstate New York. This early nineteenth-century painting depicts McCrea sympathetically as a helpless, innocent victim of savagery. The fact that she was not a patriot but a supporter of King George did not seem to diminish the artist's vision of her as a martyr. Does this suggest that McCrea's politics were less important than her race and gender? *Wadsworth Atheneum.*

slowed to a snail's pace. The Americans took full advantage of Burgoyne's folly. Ethan Allen and his Green Mountain Boys harassed the British as they entered Allen's home region of Vermont. A bloody, head-on battle near Bennington further slowed Burgoyne's progress. When the general's army finally reached Albany in mid-September, neither St. Leger nor Howe were in sight.

The full support St. Leger had counted on from the Iroquois had not materialized, and he met fierce resistance as he made his way to the rendezvous point. When news reached him that Benedict Arnold and an army of a thousand Americans were approaching, St. Leger simply turned around and took his exhausted men to safety at Fort Niagara. Howe, of course, had no idea that he was expected in Albany. This left John Burgoyne stranded in the heart of New York. By mid-September 1777, his supplies dwindling, he realized his only option was to break northward through the American lines and take refuge in Canada—or surrender. On September 19, Burgoyne attacked, hoping to clear a path of retreat for his army. The elderly American general, **Horatio "Granny" Gates,** was nei-

ther bold nor particularly clever, but it took little daring or genius to defeat Burgoyne's weary, dispirited British soldiers. When Burgoyne tried once again to break through on October 7, Gates and his men held their ground. On October 17, 1777, General John Burgoyne surrendered.

News that a major British army had been defeated spread quickly on both sides of the Atlantic. It was a powerful boost to American confidence and an equally powerful blow to British self-esteem. The report also reversed the fortunes of American diplomatic efforts. Until Saratoga, American appeals to the governments of Spain, France, and Holland for supplies, loans, and military support had met with only moderate success. Now, hopes ran high that France would recognize independence and join the war effort.

Horatio "Granny" Gates Elderly Virginia general who led the American troops to victory in the Battle of Saratoga.

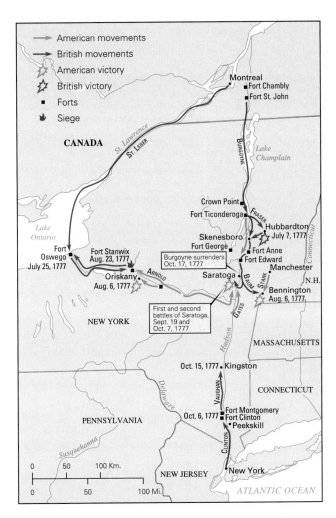

MAP 6.2 The Burgoyne Campaign, 1777 The defeat of General John Burgoyne and his army at Saratoga was a major turning point in the war. It led to the recognition of American independence by France and later by Spain and to a military alliance with both these European powers. This map shows American and British troop movement and the locations and dates of the Saratoga battles leading to the British surrender.

Winter Quarters in 1777

John Adams, who never wore a uniform, had once toasted a "short and Violent war." After Burgoyne's defeat, many Americans believed that Adams's wish was coming true. General Washington, however, did not share their optimism. French help might be coming, he pointed out, but who knew when? In the meantime, he reminded Congress the Continental Army still needed funds and supplies. Congress ignored all his urgent requests. The result was the long and dreadful winter at Valley Forge. **Valley Forge** was 20 miles from Philadelphia, where General Howe and his army were comfortably housed for the winter. Throughout December 1777, Washington's men labored to build the huts and cabins they needed. While two officers were assigned to share quarters, a dozen enlisted men were expected to crowd into a 14-by-16-foot hut. Rations were a problem from the start. Technically, each man was entitled to raw or cured meat, yet most soldiers at Valley Forge lived entirely on a diet of fire cakes, made of flour and water baked in the coals or over the fire on a stick. Blankets were scarce, coats were rare, and firewood was precious. An army doctor summed up conditions when he wrote: "Poor food—hard lodgings—cold weather—fatigue—nasty clothes—nasty cookery—vomit half my time—smoked out of my senses—the devil's in it—I can't endure it."

The doctor, however, did endure it. So did the soldiers he tended to daily, men such as the barefoot, half-naked, dirty young man who cried out in despair, "I am sick, my feet lame, my legs are sore, my body covered with this tormenting itch." While civilians mastered the steps of the latest dance craze, "the Burgoyne surrender," soldiers at Valley Forge traded the remains of their uniforms and sometimes their muskets for the momentary warmth and sense of well-being provided by liquor.

The enlisted men who survived the winter at Valley Forge were strangers to luxury even in peacetime. Like Deborah Sampson, most were from the humblest social classes: farm laborers, servants, apprentices, even former slaves. They were exactly the sort of person most Americans believed ought to fight the war. But if poverty had driven them into the army, a commitment to see the war through kept them there. The contrast between their own patriotism and the apparent indifference of the civilian population made many of these soldiers bitter. Private Joseph Plumb Martin expressed the feelings of most when he said "a kind and holy Providence" had done more to help the army while it was at Valley Forge "than did the

> **Valley Forge** Winter encampment of Washington's army in Pennsylvania in 1777–1778; because the soldiers suffered greatly from cold and hunger, the term *Valley Forge* has become synonymous with "dire conditions."

Throughout the war, both the British and the American armies settled into winter quarters until they resumed military operations in the spring. While the British usually enjoyed the comforts of urban life, in Philadelphia, Charleston, or New York, the American army made its camps in the countryside. Here, soldiers endured the snow and freezing winds in makeshift shacks or in tents, although officers often commandeered the homes of local civilians. The winter at Valley Forge was among the most brutal endured by the Continental troops, and it has come to signify the determination of the common soldiers and their commitment to the cause of independence. *Stock Montage.*

country in whose service we were wearing away our lives by piecemeal."

What these soldiers desperately needed, in addition to new clothes, good food, and hot baths, was professional military training. And that is the one thing they did get, beginning in the spring of 1778, when an unlikely Prussian volunteer arrived at Valley Forge. **Baron Friedrich von Steuben** was almost 50 years old, dignified, elegantly dressed, with a dazzling gold and diamond medal always displayed on his chest. Like most foreign volunteers, many of whom plagued Washington more than they helped him, the baron claimed to be an aristocrat, to have vast military experience, and to have held high rank in a European army. In truth, he had purchased his title only a short time before fleeing his homeland in bankruptcy and he had only been a captain in the Prussian army. A penniless refugee, von Steuben hoped to receive a military pension for his service in the American army. He had not, however, exaggerated his talent as a military drillmaster. All spring, the baron could be seen drilling

Washington's troops, alternately shouting in rage and applauding with delight. Washington had little patience with most of the foreign volunteers who joined the American cause, but he considered von Steuben a most unexpected and invaluable surprise.

In the spring of 1778, Washington received the heartening news that France had formally recognized the independence of the United States. He immediately declared a day of thanks, ordering cannon to be fired in honor of the new alliance. That day, the officers feasted with their commander, and Washington issued brandy to each enlisted man at Valley Forge. American diplomacy had triumphed; Washington hoped the combined forces of France and America would soon bring victory as well.

Baron Friedrich von Steuben   Prussian military officer who served as Washington's drillmaster at Valley Forge.

Diplomacy Abroad and Profiteering at Home

- Why did the French assist the Americans secretly in the early years of the war?
- Why did France enter the war after Saratoga?
- Besides the French, what other European power supported the American colonists' struggle against the British?
- How did the French alliance affect the war effort and wartime spending?

Like most wars, the Revolutionary War was not confined to the battlefields. Diplomacy was essential, and popular morale and support had to be sustained for any war to be won. American diplomats hoped to secure supplies, safe harbors for American ships, and if at all possible, formal recognition of independence and the open military assistance that would allow. British diplomats, on the other hand, worked to prevent any formal alliances between European powers and the American rebels. Both sides issued propaganda to ensure continued popular support for the war. General Burgoyne's defeat, and the widening of the war into an international struggle, affected popular morale in both America and Britain.

The Long Road to Formal Recognition

In 1776 England had many enemies and rivals in Europe who were only too happy to see George III expend his resources and military personnel in an effort to quell a colonial rebellion. Although these nations expected the American Revolution to fail, they were more than eager to keep the conflict going as long as possible. Before Saratoga, they preferred to keep their support for the Revolution unofficial. Thus, with the help of King Louis XVI's chief minister, the comte de Vergennes, an American entrepreneur named Arthur Lee set up a private commercial firm, supposedly for trading with France. In reality, the firm siphoned weapons and funds from France to the revolutionaries. France also agreed to open ports to American privateers and to provide French ships and seamen for raids on British commercial shipping.

The Americans hoped for more, however. In December 1776, Congress sent the printer-politician-scientist **Benjamin Franklin** to Paris in hopes of winning formal recognition of American independence. The charming and witty Franklin was the toast of Paris, adored by aristocrats and common people alike, but even he could not persuade the king to support the Revolution openly. Burgoyne's surrender changed everything. After Saratoga, the British government began scrambling to end a war that had turned embarrassing, and the French government began scrambling to reassess its diplomatic position. Vergennes suspected that the English would quickly send a peace commission to America after Burgoyne's defeat. If the American Congress agreed to a compromise ending the rebellion, France could gain nothing more. But if the French kept the war alive by giving Americans reason to hope for total victory, perhaps they could recoup some of the territory and prestige lost to England in the Seven Years' War. This meant, of course, recognizing the United States and entering a war with Britain. Vergennes knew a choice had to be made—but he was not yet certain what to do.

Meanwhile, the English government was indeed preparing a new peace offer for Congress. At the heart of the British offer were two promises that George III considered to be great concessions. First, Parliament would renounce all intentions of ever taxing the colonies again. Second, the Intolerable Acts, the Tea Act, and any other objectionable legislation passed since 1763 would be repealed. Many members of Parliament thought these overtures were long overdue. They had been vocal critics of their government's policies in the 1760s and 1770s and had refused to support the war. After Burgoyne's defeat, popular support for compromise also increased in England. The Americans, however, were unimpressed by the offers. For Congress, a return to colonial status was now unthinkable.

Benjamin Franklin knew that Congress would reject the king's offer. But he was too shrewd to relieve the comte de Vergennes's fear that a compromise was in the works. Franklin warned that France must act quickly and decisively or accept the consequences. His gamble worked, and in 1778 France and the United States signed a treaty. The pact linked French and American fates tightly together, for under its provisions neither country could make a separate peace with Great Britain. By 1779, Spain had also formally acknowledged the United States, and in 1780 the Netherlands did so too. George III had little choice but to declare war against these European nations.

Benjamin Franklin American writer, inventor, scientist, and diplomat instrumental in bringing about a French alliance with the United States in 1778 and who later helped negotiate the treaty ending the war.

The Revolution had grown into an international struggle that taxed British resources further and made it impossible for Britain to concentrate all its military might and naval power in America. With ships diverted to the Caribbean and to the European coast, Britain could no longer blockade American ports as effectively as before or transport troops to the American mainland as quickly. Above all, the entry of the French into the war opened new strategic possibilities for General Washington and his army. If the Americans could count on the cooperation of the French fleet, a British army could be trapped on American soil, cut off by French ships from supplies, reinforcements, and any chance of escape.

War and the American Public

News of the alliance with France helped release an orgy of spending and purchasing by American civilians. The conditions were ripe for such a spree in 1778. With the value of government-issued paper money dropping steadily, spending made more sense than saving. And with profits soaring from the sale of supplies to the army, many Americans had more money to spend than ever before. Also, not all of the credit that diplomats had negotiated with European allies went toward military supplies. Some of it was available for the purchase of manufactured goods. This combination of optimism, **cheap money,** and plentiful foreign goods led to a wartime spending bonanza.

Many of the goods that were imported into America in the next few years were actually British-made. American consumers apparently saw no contradiction between their strong patriotism and the purchase of enemy products. A **black market**—a network for the sale of illegally imported English goods—grew rapidly, and profits from it skyrocketed. Abandoning the commitment to "virtuous simplicity" that had led them to dress in homespun, Americans stampeded to purchase tea and other imported luxuries.

Both the government and the military succumbed to this spirit of self-indulgence. Corruption and **graft** grew common, as both high- and low-ranking officials sold government supplies for their own profit or charged the army excessive rates for goods and services. Cheating the government and the army was a game civilians could play, too. Wagoners carting pickled meat to military encampments drained the brine from the barrels to lighten their load so they could carry more. The results were spoiled meat, soldiers suffering from food poisoning—and a greater profit for the cartmen. Soldiers became accustomed to defective

The state governments, like the Continental Congress, resorted to printing paper money in order to finance the war effort. These certificates were used to pay soldiers and civilians who supplied the army with food, horses, or lodgings. Unfortunately, there was little in many of the state treasuries to back these paper certificates, and this, combined with inflation, soon made some paper money worthless. The Continental Congress's paper money declined in value faster than most. "Not worth a continental" became popular slang for anything that was worthless. *Picture Research Consultants & Archives.*

weapons, defective shoes, and defective ammunition, but many of them joined the profit game by selling off their army-issued supplies to any available buyers. Recruiters pocketed the bounties given to them to attract enlistees. Officers accepted bribes from enlisted men seeking discharges.

Popular optimism and the spending frenzy unleashed by the French treaty contrasted sharply with the financial realities facing Congress. Bluntly put, the government was broke. By 1778, both Congress and the states had exhausted their meager sources

> **cheap money** Paper money that is readily available but has declined in value.
>
> **black market** The illegal business of buying and selling goods that are banned or restricted.
>
> **graft** Misuse of one's position for profit or advantage.

of hard currency. The government met the crisis by printing more paper money. The result was rampant inflation. The value of the "continental," as the congressional paper money was called, dropped steadily with each passing day. The government's inability to pay soldiers became widely known—and enlistments plummeted. Both the state militias and the Continental Army resorted to impressment, or forced military service, to fill their ranks. Men forced to serve, however, were men more likely to mutiny or to desert. Officers did not know whether to sympathize with their unpaid and involuntary soldiers or to enforce stricter discipline upon them. Some officers executed deserters or mutineers; some ordered the men whipped. And some pardoned their men, despite the severity of their crimes. Congress acknowledged the justice of the soldiers' complaints by giving them pay raises in the form of certificates that they could redeem— after the war.

From Stalemate to Victory

■ What did France hope to achieve by coming to the aid of the struggling American army?

■ What led to General Cornwallis's surrender at Yorktown?

■ What were the most important results of the peace treaty negotiations?

The French presence in the war did not immediately alter the strategies of British or American military leaders. English generals in the North displayed caution after Burgoyne's surrender, and Washington waited impatiently for signs that the French fleet would come to his aid. The result was a stalemate. The active war shifted to the South once again in late 1778 as the British mounted a second major campaign in the Carolinas.

The War Stalls in the North

Sir Henry Clinton, now the commander of the British army in North America, knew that the French fleet could easily blockade the Delaware River and thus cut off supplies to occupied Philadelphia. So, by the time warm weather had set in, his army was on the march, heading east through New Jersey en route to New York. Clinton's slow-moving caravan, burdened by a long train of bulky supply wagons, made an irresistible target—and Washington decided to strike. Unfortunately, Washington entrusted the unreliable **General Charles Lee** with the initial attack. Lee marched his men to Monmouth, New Jersey, and as

the British approached, the Americans opened fire. Yet as soon as the British army began to return fire, Lee ordered his men to retreat. When Washington arrived on the scene, the Americans were fleeing and the British troops were closing in.

Washington rallied the retreating Americans, calling on them to re-form their lines and stand their ground. Trained by von Steuben, the men responded well. They moved forward with precision and speed, driving the redcoats back. The **Battle of Monmouth** was not the decisive victory Washington had dreamed of, but it was a fine recovery from what first appeared to be certain defeat. As for Lee, Washington saw to it that he was discharged from the army.

Monmouth was only the first of several missed opportunities that summer of 1778. In August the French and Americans launched their first joint effort, sending a combined land and naval attack against the British base at Newport, Rhode Island. At the last minute, however, French admiral D'Estaing decided that the casualty rate would be too high. He abruptly gathered up his own men and sailed to safety on the open seas. The American troops were left to retreat as best they could.

Throughout the fall and winter of 1778 Washington waited in vain for French naval support for a major campaign. Early news coming from the western front did little to improve Washington's bleak mood. In Kentucky and western Virginia, deadly Indian attacks had decimated many American settlements. The driving force behind these attacks was a remarkable British official named Harry Hamilton, who had won the nickname "Hair Buyer" because of the bounties he paid for American scalps. In October Hamilton led Indian troops from the Great Lakes tribes into the Illinois-Indiana region and captured the fort at Vincennes. The American counterattack was organized by a stocky young frontiersman, **George Rogers Clark,** whose own enthusiasm for scalping earned him the

Sir Henry Clinton General who replaced William Howe as commander of the British forces in America in 1778 after the British surrender at Saratoga.

Charles Lee Revolutionary general who tried to undermine Washington's authority on several occasions; he was eventually dismissed from the military.

Battle of Monmouth New Jersey battle in June 1778 in which Charles Lee wasted a decisive American advantage.

George Rogers Clark Virginian who led his troops to successes against the British and Indians in the Ohio Territory in 1778.

Mohawk chief Thayendanegea (Joseph Brant) believed that Iroquois lands would be lost if the Americans were victorious. He urged an Iroquois alliance with the British, fought for the British, and directed a series of deadly raids against settlements in New York. After the war—as Brant had feared—his people were forced to relocate to Canada. *"Joseph Brant" by Wilhelm von Moll Berczy, ca. 1800. National Gallery of Canada, Ottawa.*

nickname "Long-Knife." To Washington's relief, Clark and his volunteer forces managed to drive the British from Vincennes.

Border conflict with Britain's Indian allies remained a major problem, and when loyalist troops joined these Indians, the danger increased. So did the atrocities. When patriot General John Sullivan's regular army was badly defeated by Mohawk chief **Thayendanegea,** known to the Americans as Joseph Brant, and local loyalists, Sullivan took revenge by burning forty Indian villages. It was an act of violence and cruelty that deeply shocked and shamed General Washington.

Spring and summer of 1779 passed and still Washington waited for the French navy's cooperation. Fall brought the general the worst possible news: Admiral D'Estaing and his fleet had sailed for the West Indies under orders to protect valuable French possessions in the Caribbean and, if possible, to seize English possessions there. News of D'Estaing's departure spurred a new wave of discipline problems among Washington's idle troops. Mutinies and desertions increased. From his winter headquarters in Morristown Heights,

New Jersey, Washington wrote to von Steuben: "The prospect, my dear Baron, is gloomy, and the storm thickens." The real storm, however, was raging not in New Jersey but in the Carolinas.

The Second Carolinas Campaign

Since the fall of 1778, the British had been siphoning off New York–based troops for a new invasion of the South. The campaign began in earnest with the capture of Savannah, Georgia (see Map 6.3). Then, in the winter of 1779, General Henry Clinton sailed for Charleston, South Carolina, eager to avenge his embarrassing retreat in the 1776 campaign. Five thousand Continental soldiers hurried to join the South Carolina militia in defense of the city. From the Citadel, a fortification spanning the northern neck of the city's peninsula, these American forces bombarded the British with all they could find, firing projectiles made of glass, broken shovels, hatchets, and pickaxes. From aboard their ships, the British answered with a steady stream of mortar shells. On May 12, 1780, after months of deadly bombardment and high casualties on both sides, the Citadel fell. The American commander, General Benjamin Lincoln, surrendered his entire army to the British, and a satisfied General Clinton returned to New York.

Clinton left the southern campaign in the hands of **Charles Cornwallis,** an ambitious and able general who set out with more than eight thousand men to conquer the rest of South Carolina. Cornwallis and his regular army were joined by loyalist troops who were as eager to take their revenge on their enemies as Clinton had been. Since the British had abandoned the South in 1776, small, roving bands of loyalist guerrillas had kept resistance to the Revolution alive. After the British victory at Charleston, the guerrillas increased their attacks, and a bloody civil war of ambush, arson, and brutality on both sides resulted. By the summer of 1780, fortunes had reversed: the revolutionaries were now the resistance, and the loyalists were in control.

Thayendanegea Mohawk chief known to the Americans as Joseph Brant; his combined forces of loyalists and Indians defeated John Sullivan's expedition to upstate New York in 1779.

Charles Cornwallis British general who was second in command to Henry Clinton; his surrender at Yorktown in 1781 brought the Revolution to a close.

MAP 6.3 The Second Southern Campaign, 1778–1781 This map of the second attempt by Britain to crush the rebellion in the South shows the many battles waged in the Lower South before Cornwallis's encampment at Yorktown and his surrender there. This decisive southern campaign involved all the military resources of the combatants, including British, loyalist, French, and American ground forces and British and French naval fleets.

The revolutionary resistance produced legendary guerrilla leaders, including **Francis Marion,** known as the "Swamp Fox." Marion organized black and white recruits into raiding bands that steadily harassed Cornwallis's army and effectively cut British lines of communication between Charleston and the interior. While Marion did his best to trouble the British, Thomas Sumter's guerrillas and other resistance forces focused their energies on the loyalists. When these guerrillas and loyalists met head-on in battle, they honored few of the rules of war. In October 1780, for

Francis Marion South Carolina leader of guerrilla forces during the war; known as the "Swamp Fox," he harassed British forces during the second southern campaign.

In this painting, patriots stand their ground against cavalrymen led by Lieutenant Banastre Tarleton in a 1781 skirmish near Cowpens. As the painting shows, black as well as white Americans supported the revolutionary cause in the South. *"Tarleton's Cavalrymen After the Battle of Cowpens, 1781" by William Ranney. Collection of the State of South Carolina. Photograph by Hunter Clarkson, Alt Lee, Inc.*

example, in the **Battle of King's Mountain,** revolutionaries surrounded loyalist troops and picked them off one by one. As this bitter civil war continued, marauding bands terrorized civilians and plundered their farms. Often the worst damage was done by outlaws posing as soldiers.

The regular American army, under the command of the Saratoga hero, "Granny" Gates, had little success against Cornwallis. In August 1780, Gates and his men suffered a crushing defeat at Camden, South Carolina. That fall, Washington wisely replaced Gates with a younger, more energetic officer from Rhode Island, **Nathanael Greene.** The fourteen hundred Continental soldiers Greene found when he arrived in South Carolina were tired, hungry, and clothed in rags. They were also, Greene discovered, "without discipline and so addicted to plundering that the utmost exertions of the officers cannot restrain them." Greene's first steps were to ease the strains caused by civil war, raids, and plundering by offering pardons to loyalists and proposing alliances with local Indian tribes. In the end, Greene managed to win all but the Creeks away from the British.

Greene's military strategy was attrition: wear the British out by making them chase his small army across the South. He sent Virginian Daniel Morgan and six hundred riflemen to western South Carolina to tempt troops under the command of Banastre Tarleton into pursuit. Tarleton finally caught up with

Morgan on an open meadow called the Cowpens in January 1781. When the outnumbered Americans stood their ground, ready to fight, the tired and frustrated British soldiers panicked and fled. Annoyed by this turn of events, Cornwallis decided to take the offensive. Now it was Greene's turn to lead the British on a long, exhausting chase. In March 1781, the two armies finally met at Guilford Courthouse, North Carolina. Although the Americans lost the battle and withdrew, British losses were so great that Cornwallis had to rethink the southern campaign. He decided that the price of conquering the Lower South was more than he was willing to pay. Disgusted, Cornwallis ordered his army northward to Virginia. Perhaps, he mused, he would have better luck there.

Treason and Triumph

In the fall of 1780, the popular general Benedict Arnold, one of Washington's protégés, defected to the British. Although Arnold's bold plot to turn over control of

---

Battle of King's Mountain   Battle fought in October 1780 on the border between the Carolinas in which revolutionary troops defeated loyalists.

Nathanael Greene   American general who took command of the Carolinas campaign in 1780.

John Trumbull celebrates the surrender of Cornwallis at Yorktown in this painting. However, neither Cornwallis nor Washington actually participated in the surrender ceremonies. The British commander claimed illness and sent his general of the guards as his deputy. Washington, always sensitive to status as well as to protocol, promptly appointed an officer of equal rank, General Benjamin Lincoln, to serve as his deputy. *"Surrender of Lord Cornwallis" by John Trumbull. Yale University Art Gallery. Trumbull Collection.*

the Hudson River by surrendering the fort at **West Point,** New York, to the British was foiled, Arnold's treason saddened Washington and damaged American morale. Washington's unhappiness over Arnold's betrayal was eased the following spring, however, when news came that French help was at last on its way. The general sat down at a strategy session with his French counterpart, General Rochambeau, in May 1781. The results were not exactly what Washington had hoped for: he had pressed for an attack on British-occupied New York, whereas Rochambeau insisted on a move against Cornwallis in Virginia. Since the French general had already ordered Admiral de Grasse and his fleet to the Chesapeake, Washington had little choice but to concur.

Thus, on July 6, 1781, a French army joined Washington's Continental forces just north of Manhattan for the long march to Virginia. The French soldiers, elegant in their sparkling uniforms, were openly amazed and impressed by their bedraggled allies. "It is incredible," wrote one French officer, "that soldiers composed of whites and blacks, almost naked, unpaid,

and rather poorly fed, can march so well and stand fire so steadfastly."

Within a few months, General Cornwallis too would be forced to admire the American army's stamina. In July, however, the British commander was unaware that a combined army was marching toward him. His first clue that trouble lay ahead came when a force of regular soldiers, led by Baron von Steuben and the marquis de Lafayette, appeared in Virginia. Soon afterward, Cornwallis moved his army to the peninsula port of Yorktown to prepare for more serious battles ahead. The choice of **Yorktown** was one he would heartily regret.

West Point   Site of a fort overlooking the Hudson River, north of New York City.

Yorktown   Site of the last major battle of the Revolution; American and French troops trapped Cornwallis's army here, on a peninsula on the York River near the Chesapeake Bay, and forced him to surrender.

By September 1781, the French and American troops coming from New York had joined forces with von Steuben and Lafayette's men. Admiral de Grasse's fleet of twenty-seven ships, seventy-four cannon, and an additional three thousand French soldiers were in place in Chesapeake Bay. General Clinton, still in New York, had been devastatingly slow to realize what the enemy intended. In desperation, he now sent a naval squadron from New York to rescue the trapped Cornwallis. He could do little more, since most of the British fleet was in the Caribbean.

Admiral de Grasse had no trouble fending off Clinton's rescue squadron. Then he turned his naval guns on the redcoats at Yorktown. From his siege positions on land, Washington also directed a steady barrage of artillery fire against the British, producing a deafening roar both day and night. The noise dazed the redcoats and prevented them from sleeping. On October 19, 1781, Lord Cornwallis admitted the hopelessness of his situation and surrendered. Despite the stunning turn of events at Yorktown, fighting continued in some areas. Loyalists and patriots continued to make war on each other in the South for another year. Bloody warfare against the Indians also meant more deaths along the frontier. The British occupation of Charleston, Savannah, and New York continued. But after Yorktown the British gave up all hope of military victory against their former colonies. On March 4, 1782, Parliament voted to cease "the further prosecution of offensive war on the Continent of North America, for the purpose of reducing the Colonies to obedience by force." The war for independence had been won.

Winning Diplomatic Independence

What Washington and his French and Spanish allies had won, American diplomats had to preserve. Three men represented the United States at the peace talks in Paris: Benjamin Franklin, John Adams, and John Jay. At first glance, this was an odd trio. The elderly Franklin, witty and sophisticated, had spent most of the war years in Paris, where he earned a deserved reputation as an admirer of French women and French wines. Adams, competitive, self-absorbed, and socially inept, did not hide his distaste for Franklin's flamboyance. Neither man found much comfort in the presence of the prudish, aristocratic John Jay of New York. Yet they proved to be a highly effective combination. Franklin brought a crafty skill and a love of strategy to the team as well as a useful knowledge of French politics. Adams provided the backbone, for in the face of

any odds he was stubborn, determined, fiercely patriotic, and a watchdog of American interests. Jay was calm, deliberate, and though not as aggressive as his New England colleague, he matched Adams in patriotism and integrity.

European political leaders expected the Americans to fare badly against the more experienced British and French diplomats. But Franklin, Jay, and Adams were far from naive. They were all veterans of wartime negotiations with European governments, having pursued loans, supplies, and military support. And they understood what was at stake at the peace table. They knew that their chief ally, France, had its own agenda and that England still wavered on the degree of independence America had actually won at Yorktown. Thus, despite firm orders from Congress to rely on France at every phase of the negotiations, the American diplomats quickly put their own agenda on the table. They issued a direct challenge to Britain: you must formally recognize American independence as a precondition to any negotiations at all. The British commissioner reluctantly agreed. Negotiations continued for more than a year, with all sides debating, arguing, and compromising until the terms of a treaty were finally set.

In the **Treaty of Paris of 1783** the Americans emerged with two clear victories. First, although the British did not give up Canada as the Americans had hoped, the boundaries of the new nation were extensive. Second, the treaty granted the United States unlimited access to the fisheries off Newfoundland, a particular concern of New Englander John Adams. It was difficult to measure the degree of success on other issues, however, since the terms for carrying out the agreements were so vague. For example, Britain ceded the Northwest to the United States. But the treaty said nothing about approval of this transfer of power by the Indians of the region, and it failed to set a timetable for British evacuation of the forts in the territory. This lack of clarity would cause problems for the Americans. In other cases, however, the treaty's vague language worked to American advantage. The treaty contained only the most general promise that the American government would not interfere with collection of the large prewar debts southern planters owed to British merchants. The promise to urge the states to return confiscated property to loyalists was equally inexact.

> **Treaty of Paris** Treaty that ended the Revolutionary War in 1783 and secured American independence.

The peacemakers were aware of the treaty's shortcomings and its lack of clarity on key issues. But this was the price for avoiding stalemate and dangerous confrontation on controversial issues. Franklin, Adams, and Jay knew the consequences might be serious, but for the moment they preferred to celebrate rather than to worry.

Republican Expectations in a New Nation

■ How did the Revolution affect Americans' expectations regarding individual rights, social equality, and the role of women in American society?

■ What opportunities were open to African Americans during and after the Revolution?

■ What was the fate of the loyalists?

As an old man, John Adams reminisced about the American Revolution with his family and friends. Although he spoke of the war as a remarkable military event, Adams insisted that the Revolution was more than battlefield victories and defeats. The Revolution took place, Adams said, "in the hearts and the minds of the people." What he meant was that changes in American social values and political ideas were as critical as artillery, swords, and battlefield strategies in creating the new nation. "The people" were, of course, far more diverse than Adams was ever willing to admit. And they often differed in their "hearts and minds." Race, region, social class, gender, religion, even the national origin of immigrants—all played a part in creating diverse interests and diverse interpretations of the Revolution. Adams was correct, however, that significant changes took place in American thought and behavior during the war and the years immediately after. Many of these changes reflected a growing identification of the new American nation as a **republic** that ensured not only representative government but also the protection of individual rights, an educated citizenry, and an expanded suffrage.

The Protection of Fundamental Rights

The Declaration of Independence expressed the commonly held American view that government must protect the fundamental rights of life, liberty, property, and, as Jefferson put it, "the pursuit of happiness." The belief that Britain was usurping these rights was a major justification for the Revolution. Thus, whatever form Americans chose for their new, independent government, they were certain to demand the protection of these fundamental rights. This emphasis had many social consequences.

The protection of many individual rights—freedom of speech, assembly, and the press, and the right to a trial by jury—were written into the new constitutions of several states. But some rights were more difficult to define than others. While many Americans supported "freedom of conscience," not all of them supported separation of church and state. In the seventeenth century, individual dissenters such as Roger Williams and Anne Hutchinson had fought for the separation of church and state. After the Great Awakening, the same demands were made by organized dissenter communities such as the Baptists, who protested the privileges that established churches enjoyed in most colonies. When Virginia took up the question in 1776, political leaders were not in agreement. The House of Burgesses approved George Mason's Declaration of Rights, which guaranteed its citizens "the free exercise of religion," yet Virginia continued to use tax monies to support the Anglican Church. Even with the strong support of Thomas Jefferson, dissenters' demands were not fully met until 1786, when the Statute of Religious Freedom ended tax-supported churches and guaranteed complete freedom of conscience, even for atheists. Other southern states followed Virginia's lead, ending tax support for their Anglican churches.

The battle was more heated in New England. Many descendants of the Puritans wished to continue government support of the Congregational Church. Others simply wished to keep the principle of an established church alive. As a compromise, communities were sometimes allowed to decide which local church received their tax money, although each town was required to make one church the established church. New England did not separate church and state entirely until the nineteenth century.

Protection of Property Rights

Members of the revolutionary generation who had a political voice were especially vocal about the importance of private property and protection of a citizen's

republic A nation in which supreme power resides in the citizens, who elect representatives to govern them.

right to own property. In the decade before the Revolution, much of the protest against British policy had focused on this issue. For free, white, property-holding men—and for those white male servants, tenant farmers, or apprentices who hoped to join their ranks someday—life, liberty, and happiness were interwoven with the right of landownership.

The property rights of some infringed on the freedoms of others, however. Claims made on western lands by white Americans often meant the denial of Indian rights to that land. Masters' rights included a claim to the time and labor of their servants or apprentices. In the white community, a man's property rights usually included the restriction of his wife's right to own or sell land, slaves, and even her own personal possessions. Even the independent-minded Deborah Sampson lost her right to own property when she became Mrs. Gannett. And the institution of slavery transformed human beings into the private property of others.

The right to property was a principle, not a guarantee. Many white men were unable to acquire land during the revolutionary era or in the decades that followed. When the Revolution began, one-fifth of free American people lived in poverty or depended on public charity. The uneven distribution of wealth among white colonists was obvious on the streets of colonial Boston, in the rise in **almshouses** in Philadelphia, and in the growth of voluntary relief organizations that aided the homeless and the hungry in other cities and towns. For some, taking advantage of opportunities to acquire property was difficult even when those opportunities arose. Washington's Continental soldiers, for example, were promised western lands as delayed payment for their military service. But when they left the army in 1783, most were penniless, jobless, and sometimes homeless. They had little choice but to sell their precious land warrant certificates, trading their future as property owners for bread today.

Legal Reforms

Although economic inequality actually grew in the decades after the Revolution, several legal reforms were spurred by a commitment to the republican belief in social equality. Chief targets of this legal reform included the laws of **primogeniture** and **entail.** In Britain, these inheritance laws had led to the creation of a landed aristocracy. The actual threat they posed in America was small, for few planters ever adopted them. But the principle they represented remained important to republican spokesmen such as Thomas

In this portrait of Mary Harvey Champneys and her stepdaughter, Sarah Champneys, the two women pose in the respectable attire of a matron and an unmarried girl. The artist, Edward Savage, began his career making copies of paintings by more notable artists such as John Singleton Copley, but later managed to earn his living as a portraitist. In an era without photography, family portraits served as memorials as well as a display of wealth. *The Gibbes Museum of Art/Carolina Art Association.*

Jefferson, who pressed successfully for their abolition in Virginia and North Carolina.

The passion for social equality—in appearance if not in fact—affected customs as well as laws. To downplay their elite status as landowners, revolution-

almshouse A public shelter for the poor.

primogeniture The legal right of the eldest son to inherit the entire estate of his father.

entail A legal limitation that prevents property from being divided, sold, or given away.

Sheet music such as "The Ladies Patriotic Song" found its way into the parlors of many revolutionary and early republic homes. This song, which celebrates the heroes of independence, George Washington and John Adams, also celebrates what postwar society considered to be feminine virtues: beauty, innocence, and patriotic devotion. *Chicago Historical Society.*

aries stopped the practice of adding "**Esquire** (abbreviated "Esq.") after their names. (George Washington, Esq., became plain George Washington.)

Even unintentional elitist behavior could have embarrassing consequences. When General George Washington and the officers who served with him in the Revolutionary War organized the Society of the Cincinnati in 1783, they were motivated by the desire to sustain wartime friendships. The society's rules, however, brought protest from many Americans, for membership was hereditary, passing from officer fathers to their eldest sons. Grumblings that the club would spawn a military aristocracy—incompatible with republican government—drove Washington and his comrades to revise the offending society bylaws.

In some states, the principle of social equality had concrete political consequences. Pennsylvania and Georgia eliminated all property qualifications for voting among free white males. Other states lowered their property requirements for voters but refused to go as far as universal white manhood suffrage. They feared that the outcome of such a sweeping reform was unpredictable. Even women might demand a political voice.

Women in the New Republic

The war did not erase differences of class, race, region, or age for either men or women. Thus its impact was not uniform for all American women. Yet some experiences, and the memories of them, were probably shared by the majority of white and even many black women. They would remember the war years as a time of constant shortages, anxiety, harassment, and unfamiliar and difficult responsibilities. Men going off to war left women to manage farms or shops in addition to caring for large families and household duties. Women had to cope with the critical shortages of food and supplies and to survive on meager budgets in inflationary times. Many, like the woman who pleaded with her soldier husband to "pray come home," may have feared they would fail in these new circumstances. After the war, however, many remembered with satisfaction how well they had adapted to new roles. They expressed their sense of accomplishment in letters to husbands that no longer spoke of "your farm" and "your crop" but of "our farm" and even "my crop."

Many women found they enjoyed the sudden independence from men and from the domestic hierarchy that men ruled in peacetime. Even women in difficult circumstances experienced this new sense of freedom. Grace Galloway, wife of loyalist exile Joseph Galloway of Pennsylvania, remained in America during the war in an effort to preserve her husband's

Esquire   A term used to indicate that a man was a gentleman.

Tracking Changes in Gender Roles

Eighteenth-century women like Deborah Sampson and Esther DeBerdt Reed tested the limits of traditional gender roles, demonstrating bravery on the battlefield and political organizing skills during the American Revolution. But it would be over 140 years before their descendants could vote in a national election and decades more before they could serve in the military. The impact of this social change can be seen today in the accomplishments of women such as Lt. General Claudia J. Kennedy, the United States Army's first female three-star general; Sandra Day O'Connor, the first woman to become a Supreme Court justice; and Geraldine Ferraro, the first woman to be the vice-presidential nominee of a national party. Tracking major changes in gender roles and examining why those changes occurred is a critical part of the historian's task.

property. Shunned by her patriot neighbors, reduced from wealth to painful poverty, Grace Galloway nevertheless confided to her diary that "Ye liberty of doing as I please Makes even Poverty more agreable than any time I ever spent since I married." If Galloway experienced new self-confidence and liberty during wartime, not all women were so fortunate. For the victims of rape and physical attack by soldiers on either side, the war meant more traditional experiences of vulnerability. American soldiers sang songs of flirtation and of their hopes for kisses from admiring young women, but occupying armies, guerrilla bands, and outlaws posing as soldiers left trails of abuse, particularly in New Jersey, along the frontier, and in the Carolinas.

For women, just as for men, the war meant adapting traditional behavior and skills to new circumstances. Women who followed the eighteenth-century custom of joining husbands or fathers in army camps took up the familiar domestic chores of cooking, cleaning, laundering, and providing nursing care. Outside the army camps, loyalist and patriot women served as spies or saboteurs and risked their lives by sheltering soldiers or hiding weapons in their cellars. Sometimes they opted to burn their crops or destroy their homes to prevent the enemy from using them. These were conscious acts of patriotism rather than wifely duties. On some occasions, women crossed gender boundaries dramatically. Although few behaved like Deborah Sampson and disguised themselves as men, women such as **Mary Ludwig** and Margaret Corbin did engage in military combat. These "Molly Pitchers" carried water to cool down the cannon in American forts across the country; but if men fell wounded, nearby women frequently took their place in line. After the war, female veterans of combat, including Corbin, applied to the government for pensions, citing as evidence the wounds they had received in battle.

In the postwar years, members of America's political and social elite engaged in a public discussion of women's role in the family and in a republican society. Spurred by Enlightenment assertions that all humans were capable of rational thought and action and by the empirical evidence of women's patriotic commitments and behavior, these Americans set aside older colonial notions that women lacked the ability to reason and to make moral choices. They urged a new role for women within the family: the moral training of their children. This training would include the inculcating of patriotism and republican principles. Thus the republic would rely on wives and mothers to sustain its values and to raise a new generation of concerned citizens.

This new ideal, **"republican womanhood,"** reflected Enlightenment ideals, but it also had roots in economic and social changes that began before the Revolution, including the growth of a prosperous urban class able to purchase many household necessities. No longer needing to make cloth or candles or butter, prosperous urban wives and mothers had time to devote to raising children. Republican womanhood probably had little immediate impact in the lives of free ordinary women, who remained unable to purchase essential goods or to pay others to do household chores, or in the lives of African American or Indian women.

Although women's active role in the education of the next generation was often applauded as a public,

Mary Ludwig Wife of a soldier at Fort Monmouth; one of many women known popularly as "Molly Pitchers" because they carried water to cool down the cannon their husbands fired in battle.

"republican womanhood" A role for mothers that became popularized following the Revolution; it stressed women's importance in instructing children in republican virtues such as patriotism and honor.

political contribution, not simply a private, family duty, it did not lead to direct political participation for female Americans. The Constitution left suffrage qualifications to the state governments, and no state chose to extend voting rights to women. Only one state, New Jersey, failed to stipulate "male" as a condition for suffrage in its first constitution, and this oversight was soon revised.

Although American republicanism expected mothers to instill patriotism in their children, it also expected communities to provide formal education for future citizens. Arguing that a citizen could not be both "ignorant and free," several states allotted tax money for public elementary schools. Some went even further. By 1789, for example, Massachusetts required every town to provide free public education to its children. After the Revolution, *children* meant girls as well as boys.

This new emphasis on female education was a radical departure for women. Before the Revolution, the education of daughters was haphazard at best. Colleges and the preparatory schools that trained young men for college were closed to female students. A woman got what formal knowledge she could by reading her father's or her brother's books. Some women, most notably Anne Hutchinson and the Massachusetts revolutionary propagandist Mercy Otis Warren, were lucky enough to receive fine educations from the men in their family. But most women had to be content to learn domestic skills rather than geography, philosophy, or history. After the Revolution, however, educational reformers reasoned that mothers must be well versed in history and even political theory if they were to teach their children the essential principles of citizenship. By the 1780s, private academies had opened to educate the daughters of wealthy American families. These privileged young women enjoyed the rare opportunity to study mathematics, history, and geography. Although their curriculum was often as rigorous as that in a boys' preparatory school, the addition of courses in fancy needlework reminded the girls that their futures lay in marriage and motherhood.

The War's Impact on Slaves and Slavery

The protection of liberty and the fear of enslavement were major themes of the Revolution. Yet the denial of liberty was a central reality in the lives of most African Americans. As the movement for independence developed, slaves' political and military loyalties reflected their best guess as to which side offered them the greatest chance of freedom. Ironically, the desire for freedom set many of them against the Revolution. Of the fifty thousand or so slaves who won their freedom in the war, half did so by escaping to the British army. Only about five thousand African American men joined the Continental Army once Congress opened enlistment to them in 1776. Black soldiers were generally better treated by the British than by the revolutionaries. In both armies, however, African American troops received lower

The blessings of liberty and equality at the heart of the Revolution did not extend to all Americans. In New England, slavery was abolished after the war, but free blacks were not welcomed into white society. The illustration above of a celebration sponsored in 1793 by Massachusetts governor John Hancock for free African Americans was accompanied by a satiric poem that mocked blacks and what the poet saw as their crude attempts to mimic polite society. *Library Company of Philadelphia.*

As a child, Phillis Wheatley was brought from Africa and sold to a Boston couple who came to recognize and encourage her literary talent. Wheatley's patriotic poetry won approval from George Washington and praise from many revolutionary leaders. She died free but in poverty in the 1780s. *Library of Congress.*

pay than white soldiers and were often assigned to the most dangerous or menial duties.

With American victory in 1781, African American loyalist soldiers faced a difficult decision: to remain in America and risk reenslavement or to evacuate along with the British army. Many stayed, prompting a group of angry owners to complain that there was "reason to believe that a great number of slaves which were taken by the British army are now passing in this country as free men." The British transported those who chose to leave to Canada, to England, to British Florida, to the Caribbean, or to Africa. Three thousand former slaves settled initially in Nova Scotia, but the racism of their white loyalist neighbors led more than a thousand of these veterans to emigrate a second time. Led by an African-born former slave named Thomas Peters, they sailed to Sierra Leone, in West Africa, where they established a free black colony. Slaves found other routes to freedom besides military service during the war. Some escaped from farms and plantations to the cities, where they passed as free people. Others fled to the frontier, where they joined sympathetic Indian tribes. Women and children, in

particular, took advantage of wartime disruptions to flee their masters' control.

The long war affected the lives of those who remained in slavery. Control and discipline broke down when the southern campaigns dragged on, distracting slaveowners and disrupting work routines. Slave masters complained loudly and bitterly that their slaves "all do now what they please every where" and "pay no attention to the orders of the overseer." These exaggerated complaints point to real but temporary opportunities for slaves to alter the conditions under which they worked and lived.

In the northern states, the revolutionaries' demand for liberty undermined black slavery. Loyalists taunted patriots, asking, "How is it that we hear the loudest yelps for liberty among the drivers of negroes?" The question made the contradiction between revolutionary ideals and American reality painfully clear. Not all slaveowners, however, needed to be shamed by others into grappling with the hypocrisy of their position. In the 1760s and 1770s, influential political leaders such as James Otis, Thomas Paine, and Benjamin Rush campaigned against the continuation of slavery. In Boston, Phillis Wheatley, a young African-born slave whose master recognized and encouraged her literary talents, called on the revolutionaries to acknowledge the universality of the wish for freedom. "In every human breast," Wheatley wrote, "God had implanted a Principle, which we call love of freedom; it is impatient of Oppression, and pants for Deliverance. . . . I will assert, that the same Principles live in us." George Washington was among those who admired Wheatley's talents and respected her demands for black freedom, and he publicly acknowledged her as an American poet.

Free black Americans joined with white reformers to mobilize antislavery campaigns in Pennsylvania, Massachusetts, Rhode Island, and Connecticut. In Boston and Philadelphia, slaves petitioned on their own behalf to be "liberated from a state of Bondage, and made Freemen of this Community." Of course, these states were home to few slaves, and the regional economy did not depend on unfree labor. Thus it was easier there to acknowledge the truth in the slave's cry: "We have no property! . . . we have no children! . . . we have no city! . . . we have no country!"

Manumission increased during the 1770s, especially in the North. In 1780, Pennsylvania became the first state to pass an emancipation statute, making

---

manumit To free from slavery or bondage; to emancipate.

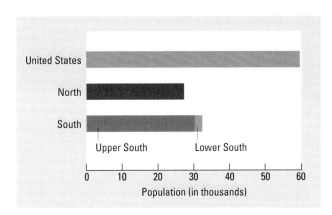

United States
North
South

Upper South　　Lower South

0　10　20　30　40　50　60
Population (in thousands)

FIGURE 6.1 Free Black Population, 1790 This graph shows the number of free African Americans in the United States in 1790, as well as their regional distribution. These almost 60,000 free people were less than 10 percent of the African American population of the nation. Although 40 percent of northern blacks were members of this free community, only about 5.5 percent of the Upper South African Americans and less than 2 percent of those in the Lower South lived outside the bounds of slavery.

manumission a public policy rather than a private matter of conscience. Pennsylvania lawmakers, however, compromised on a gradual rather than an immediate end to slavery. Only slaves born after the law was enacted were eligible, and they could not expect to receive their freedom until they had served a twenty-eight-year term of indenture. By 1804, all northern states except Delaware had committed themselves to a slow end to slavery.

Slavery was far more deeply embedded in the South, as a labor system and as a system that regulated race relations. In the Lower South, white Americans ignored the debate over slavery and took immediate steps to replace missing slaves and to restore tight control over work and life on their plantations. Manumission did occur in the Upper South. Free black communities grew in both Maryland and Virginia after the Revolutionary War, and planters openly debated the morality of slavery in a republic and the practical benefits of slave labor. They did not all reach the same conclusions. George Washington freed all his slaves on the death of his wife, but Patrick Henry, who had often stirred his fellow Virginia legislators with his spirited defense of American liberty, justified his decision to continue slavery with blunt honesty. Freeing his slaves, he said, would be inconvenient (see Figure 6.1).

The Fate of the Loyalists

Before independence was declared, white Americans loyal to the Crown experienced the isolation and disapproval of their communities. Some faced the physical danger of tarring and feathering, imprisonment, or beatings. Still others saw their property destroyed. After 1775, loyalists flocked to the safety of British-occupied cities, crowding first into Boston and later into New York City and Philadelphia. When the British left an area, the loyalists evacuated with them. More than a thousand Massachusetts loyalists boarded British ships when Boston was abandoned in 1776, and fifteen thousand more sailed out of New York harbor when the war ended in 1781. Altogether, as many as a hundred thousand men, women, and children left their American homes to take up new lives in England, Canada, and the West Indies.

Wealth often determined a loyalist's destination. Rich and influential men such as Thomas Hutchinson of Massachusetts took refuge in England during the war. But life in England was so expensive that it quickly ate up their resources and drove them into debt. Accustomed to comfort, many of these exiles passed their days in seedy boarding houses in the small cities outside London. They lost more than servants and fine clothes, however. In a society dominated by aristocrats and royalty, loyalist men who had enjoyed status and prestige in America suddenly found themselves socially insignificant, with no work and little money. Loyalists in England grew more desperately homesick each day.

When the war ended, most of the loyalists in England departed for Nova Scotia, New Brunswick, or the Caribbean. Many of these exiles were specifically forbidden to return to the United States by the new state governments. Others refused to go back to America because they equated the new republican society with mob rule. Those who were willing to adjust to the new American nation returned slowly.

Less prosperous loyalists, especially those who served in the loyalist battalions during the war, went to Canada after 1781. The separation from family and friends, as much as the bleak climate of Canada, at first caused depression and despair in some exiles. One woman who had bravely endured the war and its deprivations broke down and cried when she landed at Nova Scotia. Like the revolutionaries, these men and women had chosen their political loyalty based on a mixture of principle and self-interest. Unlike the revolutionaries, they had chosen the losing side. They lived with the consequences for the rest of their lives.

Canada became the refuge of another group of loyalists: members of the Indian tribes that had supported the Crown. The British ceded much of the Iroquois land to the United States in the Treaty of Paris, and American hostility toward "enemy savages" made peaceful postwar coexistence unlikely. Thus, in the 1780s, Mohawks, Onondagas, Tuscaroras, Senecas, Oneidas, and Cayugas along with Delawares, Tutelos, and Nanticokes created new, often multiethnic settlements on the banks of the Grand River in Ontario. These communities marked an end to the dislocation and suffering many of these refugees had experienced during the Revolution, when steady warfare depleted Indian resources and made thousands dependent on the British for food, clothing, and military supplies. A majority of the Indians who settled in Canada had already spent years in makeshift encampments near Fort Niagara after American armies destroyed their farms, homes, and villages.

Individual Voices

Examining a Primary Source

Esther DeBerdt Reed Glories in the Usefulness of Women

Deborah Sampson took the most daring path to participation in the Revolution. But other women also pushed the boundaries of women's traditional sphere by organizing to play a public role in the war effort. Wealthy Philadelphia matron Esther DeBerdt Reed, for example, helped organize women's voluntary associations to raise funds and supplies for the American army. Openly political activities by women were not always greeted favorably by the community, however. Women who expressed their patriotism through public actions were accused of overstepping the boundaries of their gender—that is, of unfeminine behavior. Reed defended her activism in "The Sentiments of an American Woman," printed in 1780. In this unusual document, she connects the patriotic women of the Revolution with heroic women of history, and she discusses female patriotism in terms that Deborah Sampson would surely have applauded.

■ *Here, Constitution does not mean a written plan of government but the natural characteristics and appropriate behaviors of women—and of men. Do you think Reed is challenging the notion that women are constitutionally, or naturally, weak and incapable of making decisions and acting on them? Or is she saying that women are decisive and competent only in times of great crisis?*

On the commencement of actual war, the Women of America manifested a firm resolution to contribute as much as could depend on them, to the deliverance of this country. Animated by the purest patriotism they are sensible of sorrow at this day, in not offering more than barren wishes for the success of so glorious a Revolution. They aspire to render themselves more really useful; and this sentiment is universal from the north to the south of the Thirteen United States. ■ *Our ambition is kindled by the fame of those heroines of antiquity, who have rendered their sex illustrious, and have proved to the universe, that, if the weakness of our Constitution, if opinion and manners did not forbid us to march to glory by the same paths as the Men, we should at least equal and sometimes surpass them in our love for the public good. I glory in all that which my sex has done great and*

■ *Male revolutionary leaders often drew analogies between their choices and actions and those of biblical heroes and leaders of the Roman republic. Why do you think Reed referred to the women of the Bible and Ancient Rome?*

■ *If you were opposed to the activities Reed was engaged in, what arguments would you make against this type of female activism?*

commendable. ■ *I call to mind with enthusiasm and with admiration, all those acts of courage, of constancy and patriotism, which history has transmitted to us: The people favoured by Heaven, preserved from destruction by the virtues, the zeal and the resolution of Deborah, of Judith, of Esther! . . . Rome saved from the fury of a victorious enemy by the efforts of Volunia, and other Roman ladies: So many famous sieges where the Women have been seen forgetting the weakness of their sex, building new walls, digging trenches with their feeble hands; furnishing arms to their defenders, they themselves darting the missile weapons on the enemy, resigning the adornments of their apparel, and their fortunes to fill the public treasury, and to hasten the deliverance of their country. . . . [We are] Born for liberty, disdaining to bear the irons of a tyrannic Government.* ■ *. . . Who knows if persons disposed to censure, and sometimes too severely with regard to us, may not disapprove our appearing acquainted even with the actions of which our sex boasts? We are at least certain, that he cannot be a good citizen who will not applaud our efforts for the relief of the armies which defend our lives, our possessions, our liberty.*

Summary

When the colonies declared their independence, many people on both sides doubted that the Americans could win the war. The British outnumbered and outgunned the Americans, and their troops were better trained and better equipped. The Americans' major advantage was logistic: they were fighting a war on familiar terrain.

The early British strategy was to invade New York and the southern colonies, where they expected to rally strong loyalist support. But this strategy proved unsuccessful, not only because they were waging war on unfamiliar territory but because they had overestimated loyalist strength and persisted in alienating would-be sympathizers. Also, Washington's hit-and-run tactics made it impossible for the British to deliver a crushing blow.

The most dramatic turning point in the war came in 1777 when British general John Burgoyne's plan to isolate New England from the rest of the rebelling colonies failed. Burgoyne was forced to surrender at Saratoga, New York. The surprising American victory led to an alliance between France and the United States and the expansion of the war into an international conflict. The British again chose to invade the South in 1778, but despite early victories, their campaign ended in disaster. American victory was assured when French and American forces defeated General Cornwallis at Yorktown, Virginia, in October 1781. Fighting continued for a time, but in March 1782, the British Parliament ended the conflict. The war for American independence had been won. The Treaty of Paris was negotiated in 1783, and to the surprise of many European diplomats, the Americans gained important concessions.

Independence from British rule was not the only outcome of the war. Victory led to transformations in American society. Individual rights were strengthened for free white men. A republican spirit changed the outlook, if not the condition, of many Americans, as customs that signaled a hierarchical society gave way to more egalitarian behavior. The wartime experiences of women such as Deborah Sampson led American intellectuals to reconsider women's "nature" and their abilities. Although full citizenship was confined to free white males, white women's capacity for rational thought was acknowledged, and their new role as the educators of their children led to expanded formal education for women. Black Americans also made some gains. Fifty thousand slaves won their freedom during the war, thousands by serving in the Continental Army. Some northerners moved to outlaw slavery, but southern slaveholders chose to preserve the institution despite intense debate. Loyalists, having made their political choices, had to live with the consequences of defeat. For most, the outcome was permanent exile from their homeland.

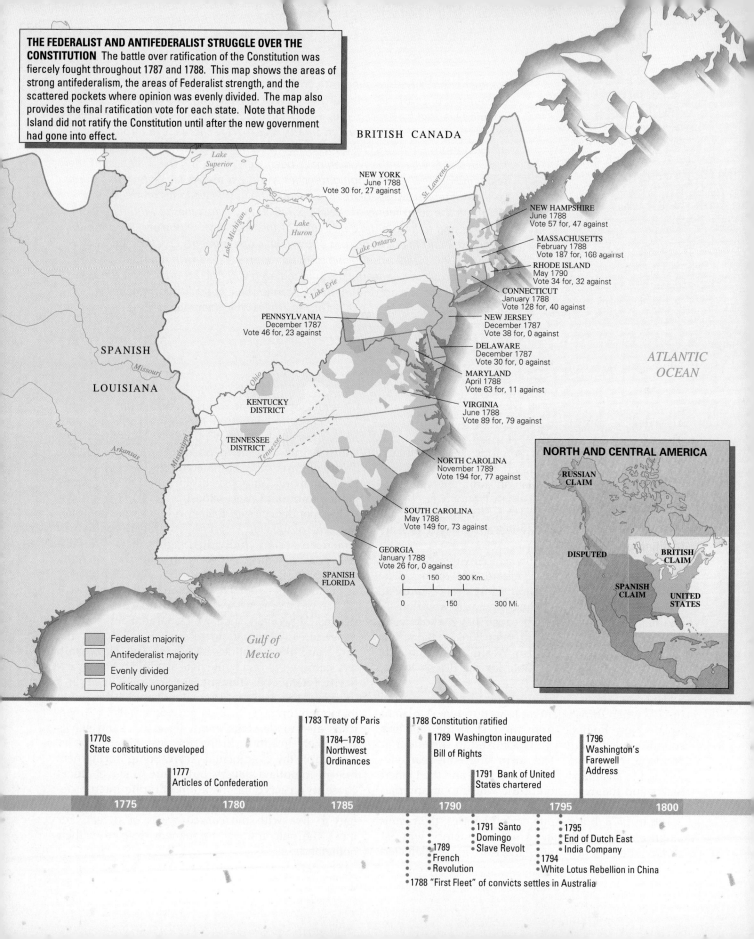

THE FEDERALIST AND ANTIFEDERALIST STRUGGLE OVER THE CONSTITUTION The battle over ratification of the Constitution was fiercely fought throughout 1787 and 1788. This map shows the areas of strong antifederalism, the areas of Federalist strength, and the scattered pockets where opinion was evenly divided. The map also provides the final ratification vote for each state. Note that Rhode Island did not ratify the Constitution until after the new government had gone into effect.

BRITISH CANADA

Lake Superior

Lake Michigan

Lake Huron

Lake Ontario

Lake Erie

St. Lawrence

SPANISH

LOUISIANA

Missouri

Ohio

KENTUCKY DISTRICT

TENNESSEE DISTRICT

Arkansas

Tennessee

Mississippi

NEW YORK
June 1788
Vote 30 for, 27 against

NEW HAMPSHIRE
June 1788
Vote 57 for, 47 against

MASSACHUSETTS
February 1788
Vote 187 for, 168 against

RHODE ISLAND
May 1790
Vote 34 for, 32 against

CONNECTICUT
January 1788
Vote 128 for, 40 against

PENNSYLVANIA
December 1787
Vote 46 for, 23 against

NEW JERSEY
December 1787
Vote 38 for, 0 against

DELAWARE
December 1787
Vote 30 for, 0 against

MARYLAND
April 1788
Vote 63 for, 11 against

VIRGINIA
June 1788
Vote 89 for, 79 against

ATLANTIC OCEAN

NORTH CAROLINA
November 1789
Vote 194 for, 77 against

SOUTH CAROLINA
May 1788
Vote 149 for, 73 against

GEORGIA
January 1788
Vote 26 for, 0 against

SPANISH FLORIDA

Gulf of Mexico

0   150   300 Km.

0   150   300 Mi.

NORTH AND CENTRAL AMERICA

RUSSIAN CLAIM

DISPUTED

BRITISH CLAIM

SPANISH CLAIM

UNITED STATES

Federalist majority

Antifederalist majority

Evenly divided

Politically unorganized

1770s
State constitutions developed

1777
Articles of Confederation

1783 Treaty of Paris

1784–1785
Northwest Ordinances

1788 Constitution ratified

1789 Washington inaugurated

Bill of Rights

1791 Bank of United States chartered

1796
Washington's Farewell Address

1775   1780   1785   1790   1795   1800

1791 Santo Domingo Slave Revolt

1789
French Revolution

1795
End of Dutch East India Company

1794
White Lotus Rebellion in China

1788 "First Fleet" of convicts settles in Australia

Competing Visions of the Virtuous Republic, 1770–1796

7

The Federalist and Antifederalist Struggle over the Constitution
Using the map on the facing page, support or challenge the idea that small states and large states had different attitudes toward ratification of the Constitution.

Individual Choices

ALEXANDER HAMILTON

Author of many of *The Federalist Papers* essays and first secretary of the treasury, Alexander Hamilton was admired for his intellectual brilliance and his political vision, even by bitter political opponents. Hamilton was a true American success story: an illegitimate son of a Scottish merchant, he immigrated to the mainland during his teenage years, where he enjoyed a meteoric career. Hamilton served as Washington's aide-de-camp, became a leader of the New York bar, and entered New York's social elite by his marriage into the Schuyler family. In 1804, a political enemy, Aaron Burr, killed Hamilton in a duel. *"Alexander Hamilton" by Charles Wilson Peale. Courtesy of the Independence National Historical Park Collection.*

Alexander Hamilton

Alexander Hamilton came into the world in 1757 without any of the attributes needed for success in the eighteenth century. He was poor, isolated on a tiny island in the Caribbean, and as John Adams once crudely put it, "the bastard brat of a Scots peddlar." But if Hamilton had few social or material resources, he had many intellectual ones. His genius and ambition catapulted him into the elite social circles of New York and into the very center of political power and influence in the new American nation. Hamilton's life was, in every respect, a tale of rags to riches.

By the time he was 13, Hamilton's brilliance had attracted the attention of influential men. His employer on the island of St. Croix paid his passage to New York, where other gentlemen saw to his education. He arrived at King's College (now Columbia University) in 1774, just as the bonds of affection and loyalty between Great Britain and the colonies were about to come permanently undone. He quickly set aside his studies to join the protests and demonstrations. His charisma was immediately evident: at 17 he could hold a crowd spellbound, delivering an extemporaneous speech against taxation and government corruption. He wrote pamphlets attacking Parliament's colonial policy that made him an overnight leader of the radical movement in New York City. When the war began, the 19-year-old Hamilton immediately took command of an artillery company. By 1777, he had found the most important mentor in his life: General George Washington. Hamilton became Washington's secretary and aide-de-camp, a protégé to the most admired man in America.

By 1780, Hamilton was married to the daughter of one of the richest, most politically prominent men in New York, General Philip Schuyler. He could have spent the rest of his life enjoying the rounds of parties and balls, fishing at his father-in-law's Hudson Valley estate, and practicing law for elite clients. But Hamilton chose to be a statesman, not simply a gentleman. He had a bold vision for his adopted country. He was convinced that it could quickly rise to be the most productive, prosperous nation in the world, rivaling its former Mother Country, England. And he had an equally bold plan to ensure that this vision became a reality.

Hamilton was a driving force behind the move to discard the Articles of Confederation and create a strong central government, empowered to set a national economic agenda, regulate trade and commerce, encourage entrepreneurial enterprises, maintain law and order, and win the respect of foreign powers through military strength and diplomacy. When the Constitution was drafted, Hamilton campaigned brilliantly for its ratification, writing many of the most effective *Federalist* essays and outmaneuvering the Antifederalists in New York's ratifying convention. In 1789 Hamilton took his place in the cabinet of the first president, his longtime mentor George Washington. As secretary of the Treasury, a post Hamilton interpreted as the prime ministership, he initiated programs to realize his vision: establishing the Bank of the United States, funding the national debt, imposing tariffs, and proposing an ambitious plan to encourage the rapid development of manufacturing in America. Although Thomas Jefferson and James Madison were soon organizing opposition to his policies and his vision, Hamilton left his mark on the nation's future.

In 1795, at the age of 37, Alexander Hamilton chose to resign from office. Despite Washington's continued confidence in him, Hamilton knew that any new programs he proposed would be blocked by his Jeffersonian opponents in the Congress. By the following year, he was back in New York City, practicing law, helping to organize the Bank of New York, and working for the abolition of slavery with fellow Federalist John Jay. Although Hamilton was an elitist, he believed in a hierarchy built on ability, not birthright. Slavery was unacceptable to him because it denied thousands of people the right to rise to power and wealth by their talent, ambition, and intelligence.

Hamilton's fiercely nationalistic politics, his commitment to a nation built on commerce and manufacturing rather than agriculture, his open admiration for England, and his vocal opposition to the French Revolution made him a controversial figure until his death in 1804. In that year, Aaron Burr, furious with Hamilton for blocking his political career, challenged Hamilton to a duel. Burr knew the emotional impact of such a challenge, for Hamilton's oldest son had been killed in a duel only three years earlier. The two men met at dawn on the cliffs of Weehawken, New Jersey—a site chosen because, after his son's death, Hamilton had helped pass a law making dueling illegal in New York. No one is certain what happened that July morning. Friends say that Burr aimed directly at his opponent and fired a fatal shot while Hamilton discharged his gun into the air. Alexander Hamilton died that afternoon.

All New York City seemed to turn out for the funeral. In a slow march to Trinity Church, Revolutionary War artillery, infantry, and militia companies, fellow military officers, clergymen, friends, and family were followed by long lines of foreign diplomats, city officers, trustees, faculty and students from Columbia College, and directors of the city's major financial institutions. Both British and French ships in the harbor fired their guns in salute. The champion of an active, strong central government, the architect of American industrialization, was dead. But, as Jefferson himself conceded, the economic direction Alexander Hamilton had chosen for the United States would not be altered.

INTRODUCTION

Between 1776 and 1783, Americans fought to create an independent nation. But what kind of nation would that be? Most free white Americans rejected the notion of an American monarchy and embraced the idea of a republic. Yet a republic could take many forms, and Americans who enjoyed a political voice disagreed on what form was best for the new nation. As a consequence, the transition from independence to nationhood generated heated debate.

How should power be divided between local and national governments? How should laws be made, and by whom? Who should be empowered to administer those laws? What programs and policies should the national government endorse? And, finally, how could the government be designed to protect the unalienable individual rights that free white Americans believed they possessed? Men such as Alexander Hamilton and James Madison knew as well as Tom Paine these questions had to be answered, and soon.

The Articles of Confederation was the nation's first effort at republican government. The Confederation, which joined the states together in friendship, guided Americans through the last years of the war and the

The men who drafted the New Jersey constitution took care to include a property qualification for voting but forgot to specify the sex of an eligible voter. Thus women who owned property had the right to vote from 1776 to 1807, when the "error" was corrected. New Jersey did not choose to grant women the vote again for over a century. *Corbis/Bettmann.*

peace negotiations. It also organized the northwest territories for settlement and established the political steps toward statehood within each territory. These were major achievements. But the Confederation government did not survive the decade of postwar adjustment, for many political leaders believed it was too weak to solve the nation's economic and social problems or set America's course for the future.

In 1787 delegates to a Constitutional Convention produced a new plan of government, the Constitution. It was fashioned from compromises between the interests of small states and large ones, between southern and northern regional interests, and between those who sought to preserve the sovereignty of the states and those who wished to increase the power of the national government. The Constitution created a strong central government with the right to regulate interstate and foreign trade and the power to tax.

Not everyone supported the adoption of this new government. Its opponents, known as Antifederalists, charged that it rejected many of the basic ideals of the Revolution, especially the commitment to local representative government and the guarantee of protection from the dangers of centralized authority. Many continued to believe that state governments were the best

guarantee that republican values would be maintained. Others feared the new government would be dominated by the wealthiest citizens. The Federalists, or pro-Constitution group, responded by arguing that the new government would save America from economic disaster, international scorn, and domestic unrest. Leading patriots of the 1760s and 1770s could be found on both sides of this debate, but the Federalists carried the day.

The adoption of the Constitution did not magically solve all America's problems. Tensions between northern and southern states were becoming as serious as those between the West and the more settled regions of the Atlantic coast. The nation was deeply divided over foreign policy and the lineup of allies and enemies in Europe. And even after the Constitution was ratified, many Americans continued to believe that strong local governments rather than an active central government best protected their liberties. Nevertheless, when President George Washington said his farewells to public life in 1796, most Americans were confident that their young nation would survive.

America's First Constitutions

■ What types of legislatures did the states create?

■ What were the major elements of the Articles of Confederation?

■ What problems arose in ratifying the Articles?

The writers of state constitutions were the first to grapple with troubling but fundamental issues—in particular, the definition of citizenship and the extent of political participation. Should women be allowed to vote? Could landless men, servants, free blacks, or apprentices enjoy a political voice? These were exactly the kinds of questions John Adams feared might arise in any discussion of voting rights, or suffrage. They raised the specter of democracy, which he considered a dangerous system. Once the question was posed, he predicted, "There will be no end of it . . . women will demand a vote, lads from twelve to twenty-one will think their rights are not enough attended to, and every man who has not a **farthing** will demand an equal voice with any other in all acts of state."

farthing   A British coin worth one-fourth of a penny and thus a term used to indicate something of very little value.

Chronology

From Revolution to Nationhood

1770s	State constitutions developed
1776	Oversight in New Jersey constitution gives property-holding women right to vote
1777	Congress adopts Articles of Confederation
1781	States ratify Articles of Confederation Cornwallis surrenders at Yorktown
1784–1785	First two Northwest Ordinances
1786	Annapolis Convention Shays's Rebellion
1787	Constitutional Convention Third Northwest Ordinance
1787–1788	States ratify U.S. Constitution
1789	First congressional elections George Washington inaugurated as first president Judiciary Act of 1789 French Revolution
1791	First Bank of the United States chartered Bill of Rights added to Constitution Alexander Hamilton's *Report on Manufactures*
1792	Washington reelected
1793	Genêt affair Jefferson resigns as secretary of state
1794	Whiskey Rebellion in Pennsylvania Battle of Fallen Timbers
1795	Congress approves Jay's Treaty Treaty of San Lorenzo
1796	Washington's Farewell Address

English political tradition supported Adams's view that political rights were not universal. Under English law, "rights" were, in fact, particular *privileges* that a group enjoyed because of special social circumstances—including age, sex, wealth, or family ties. In their first constitutions, several states extended these privileges to all free white men, a democratic reform but one that still sets special conditions of race and sex.

The state constitutions reflected the variety of opinion on this matter of democracy within a republic. At one end of the spectrum was Pennsylvania, whose constitution abolished all property qualifications and granted the vote to all white males in the state. At the other end were states such as Maryland, whose constitution continued to link the ownership of property to voting. To hold office, a Marylander had to meet even higher standards of wealth than the voters.

While constitution writers in every state believed that the legislature was the primary branch of government, they were divided over other issues. Should there be a separate executive branch? Should the legislature have one house or two? What qualifications should be set for officeholders? Again, Pennsylvania produced the most democratic answer to this question. Pennsylvania's constitution concentrated all power to make and to administer law in a one-house, or **unicameral,** elected assembly. The farmers and artisans who helped draft this state constitution eliminated both the executive office and the upper house of the legislature, remembering that these had been strongholds for the wealthy in colonial times. Pennsylvania also required annual elections of all legislators to ensure that the assembly remained responsive to the people's will. In contrast, Maryland and the other states divided powers among a governor, or executive branch, and a **bicameral** legislature, although the legislature enjoyed the broader powers. Members of the upper house in Maryland's legislature had to meet higher property qualifications than those in the lower house, or assembly. In this manner, political leaders in this state ensured their elite citizens a secure voice in lawmaking.

Pennsylvania and Maryland represented the two ends of the democratic spectrum. The remaining states fell between these poles. The constitutions of New

unicameral Having a single legislative house.
bicameral Having a legislature with two houses.

Having a Vision for the Future

In 1791, Alexander Hamilton outlined his vision for the economic future of the United States. When Hamilton predicted that manufacturing would overtake agriculture as the basis for the American economy, he knew he would be setting himself against some of the most important people in the nation. Hamilton's *Report on Manufactures* was not adopted by Congress, but the ideas set forth in it would eventually become central to the economy of the United States. Hamilton's belief that a strong central government with broad economic powers could encourage the fledgling manufacturing industries of the new country set the stage for the United States to become the economic superpower it is today.

Hampshire, North Carolina, and Georgia followed the democratic tendencies of Pennsylvania. New York, South Carolina, and Virginia chose Maryland's more conservative or traditional approach. New Jersey and Delaware took the middle ground, with at least one surprising result. New Jersey's first constitution, written in 1776, gave the vote to "all free inhabitants" who met certain property qualifications. This requirement denied the ballot to propertyless men but granted voting rights to property-holding women. A writer in the *New York Spectator* in 1797 snidely remarked that New Jersey women "intermeddl[ing] in political affairs" made that state's politics as strange as those of the "emperor of Java [who] never employs any but women in his embassies." Nevertheless, for thirty-one years, at least a few New Jersey women regularly exercised their right to elect the men who governed them. Then, in 1807, state lawmakers took away that right, arguing that "the weaker sex" was too easily manipulated by political candidates to be allowed to vote.

A state's particular history often determined the type of constitution it produced. For example, coastal elites and lowland gentry had dominated the colonial governments of New Hampshire, South Carolina, Virginia, and North Carolina. These states sought to correct this injustice by ensuring representation to small farming districts in interior and frontier regions. The memory of high-handed colonial governors and elitist

upper houses in the legislature led Massachusetts lawmakers to severely limit the powers of their first state government. The constitutions in all of these states reflected the strong political voice that ordinary citizens had acquired during the Revolution.

Beginning in the 1780s, however, many states revised their constitutions, increasing the power of the government. At the same time, they added safeguards they believed would prevent abuse. The 1780 Massachusetts constitution was the model for many of these revisions. Massachusetts political leaders built in a system of so-called checks and balances among the legislative, judicial, and executive branches to ensure that no branch of the government could grow too powerful or overstep its assigned duties. Over the opposition of many farmers and townspeople, these newer state constitutions also curbed the democratic extension of voting and officeholding privileges. Thus wealth returned as a qualification to govern, although the revised constitutions did not allow the wealthy to tamper with the basic individual rights of citizens. In seven states, these individual rights were safeguarded by a **bill of rights** guaranteeing freedom of speech, religion, and the press as well as the right to assemble and to petition the government.

The Articles of Confederation

There was little popular support for a powerful central government in the early years of the Revolution. Instead, as John Adams later recalled, Americans wanted "a Confederacy of States, each of which must have a separate government." When Pennsylvania's **John Dickinson** submitted a blueprint for a strong national government to the Continental Congress in July of 1776, he watched in wonder and dismay as his colleagues transformed his plan, called **Articles of Confederation**, into a government that preserved the rights and privileges of the states.

Members of the one-house Continental Congress agreed that the new government should also be a uni-

bill of rights   A formal statement of essential rights and liberties under law.

John Dickinson   Philadelphia lawyer and revolutionary pamphleteer who drafted the Articles of Confederation.

Articles of Confederation   The first constitution of the United States; it created a central government with limited powers, and it was replaced by the Constitution in 1788.

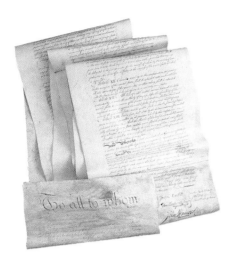

The Articles of Confederation were debated for almost as many years as they were in effect. Proposed in 1775, they were not ratified by the states until 1781. Eight years later, the Constitution replaced them. Eighteenth-century citizens hotly debated the virtues and shortcomings of the Articles, and historians have continued to disagree over the merits of this blueprint for a first American government. *The National Archives of the United States, published by Harry N. Abrams, Inc. Photograph by Jonathan Wallen.*

cameral legislature, without an executive branch or a separate judiciary. Democrats like Tom Paine and Samuel Adams praised the Articles' concentration of lawmaking, administrative, and judicial powers in the hands of an elected assembly, whereas conservatives like John Adams condemned the new government as "too democratical," lacking "any equilibrium" among the social classes.

Both Paine and Adams were eager to see a government that could protect the nation from tyranny. Paine, however, feared tyranny from above, from a power-grasping executive or an aristocratic upper house. Adams feared tyranny from below, from a majority of ordinary citizens who might exercise their will recklessly. Tyranny of any sort seemed unlikely from the proposed Confederation government since its powers were so limited. It had no authority to tax or to regulate trade or commerce. These powers remained with the state governments, reflecting the view of many Americans that the behavior of their local governments could be closely monitored. Because it had no taxing power, the Confederation had to depend on the states to finance its operations.

Dickinson's colleagues agreed that the state legislatures, not the voters themselves, should choose the members of the Confederation Congress. But they

did not agree on how many members each state should be allotted. The question boiled down to this: should the states have equal representation or **proportional representation** based on population? Dickinson argued for a one-state, one-vote rule, but fellow Pennsylvanian Benjamin Franklin insisted that large states such as his own deserved more influence in the new government. This time, Dickinson's argument carried the day, and the Articles established that each state, large or small, was entitled to a single vote when the Confederation roll was called. The same jealous protection of state power also shaped the Confederation's amendment process. Any amendment required the unanimous consent of the states.

Arguments over financial issues were as fierce as those over representation and sovereignty. How was each state's share of the federal operating budget to be determined? Dickinson reasoned that a state's contribution should be based on its population, including inhabitants of every age, sex, and legal condition (free or unfree). This proposal brought southern political leaders to their feet in protest. Because their states had large, dependent slave populations, the burden of tax assessment would fall heavily on slave masters and other free white men. In the end, state assessments for the support of the new federal government were based on the value of land, buildings, and improvements rather than on population. The Continental Congress thus shrewdly avoided any final decision on the larger question of whether slaves were property or people.

When Congress finally submitted the Articles to the states for their approval in November of 1777, the fate of the western territories proved to be the major stumbling block to **ratification.** In his draft of the Articles, Dickinson had designated the Northwest Territory as a national domain. The states with colonial charters granting them land from the Atlantic to the Pacific Oceans protested, each claiming the exclusive right to portions of this vast region bounded by the Ohio River, the Great Lakes, and the Mississippi River (see Map 7.1). New Jersey, Maryland, and other states whose colonial charters gave them no claim to western territory disagreed. While New Jersey and others eventually gave in, Maryland delegates dug in their heels, insisting that citizens of any state ought

proportional representation   Representation in the legislature based on the population of each state.

ratification   The act of approving or confirming a proposal.

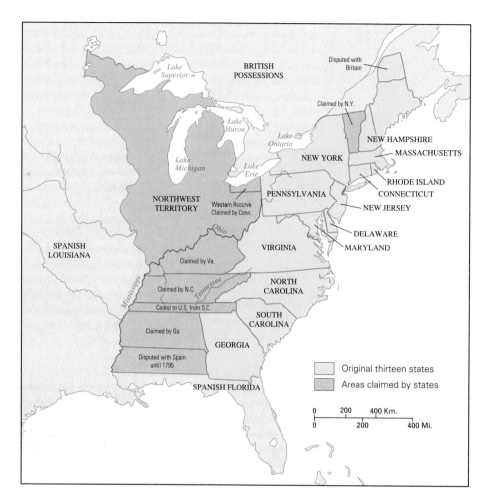

MAP 7.1 Western Land Claims After American Independence This map indicates the claims made by several of the thirteen original states to land west of the Appalachian Mountains and in the New England region. The states based their claims on the colonial charters that governed them before independence. Until this land was ceded to the federal government, new states could not be created here as they were in the Northwest Territory.

to have the right to pioneer the northwestern territories. Maryland's ultimatum—no national domain, no ratification—produced a stalemate. To resolve the problem, Virginia, which claimed the lion's share of the Northwest, agreed to cede all claims to Congress. The other states with claims followed suit and the crisis was over. In 1781 Maryland became the thirteenth and final state to ratify the Confederation government. Establishing this first national government had taken three and a half years. (The text of the Articles of Confederation is reprinted in the Documents appendix at the back of this book.)

Challenges to the Confederation

- What problems undermined the Confederation, and what changes did they produce?
- What was the impact of Shays's Rebellion on national politics?
- What gains did nationalists expect from a stronger central government?
- How did the Confederation establish relations with other nations of the world?

The members of the first Confederation Congress had barely taken their seats in 1781 when Cornwallis surrendered at Yorktown and peace negotiations began in Paris. Even the most optimistic of the Confederation leaders could see that the postwar problems of the new nation were more daunting than negotiations with French or British diplomats. The physical, psychological, and economic damage caused by the long and brutal home-front war was extensive. In New Jersey and Pennsylvania, communities bore the scars of rape and looting by the British occupying armies. In the South, where civil war had raged, a steady stream of refugees filled the cities. In Charleston, "women and children . . . in the open air round a fire without blanket or any Cloathing but what they had on" were a common sight. In many communities, livestock had vanished, and crops had been seized or ruined. In New England, a natural disaster magnified problems created by the war: insects wiped out wheat crops, worsening food shortages and the local economic depression.

After the war, economic depression spread rapidly throughout the states. Four years after the American victory, Thomas Jefferson wrote enthusiastically from France that a visit to Europe would make Americans "adore [their] country, its climate, its equality, liberty, laws, people and manners." America's unemployed sailors, debt-ridden farmers, and destitute widows and orphans would have found it difficult to share his enthusiasm.

Depression and Financial Crisis

Financial problems plagued wealthy Americans as well as poor farmers and unpaid Revolutionary War veterans. Many merchants had overextended their credit importing foreign goods after the war. Land **speculators** had also borrowed too heavily in order to grab up confiscated loyalist lands or portions of the Northwest Territory. Merchants whose fortunes depended on English markets paid a high price for an American victory that cut ties with England. Planters were hard hit when the demand for staple crops such as rice dropped dramatically after the war, and by 1786 the New England fisheries were operating at only about 80 percent of their prewar level. Not surprisingly, the English did nothing to ease the plight of their former colonists. In fact, Britain banned the sale of American farm products in the West Indies and limited the rights of American vessels to carry goods to and from Caribbean ports. These restrictions hit New England shipbuilding so hard that whole communities were impoverished.

The Confederation government did not create these economic problems, but it had little success in dealing with them. In fact, it was helpless to solve its own most pressing problem—debt. To finance the war, the Continental Congress had printed more than $240 million in paper money backed by "good faith" rather than by the hard currency of gold and silver. As doubts grew that the government could ever **redeem** these continentals for hard currency, their value fell rapidly. The scornful phrase "not worth a continental" indicated popular attitudes about the government as well as its finances. Congress was also embarrassed by the substantial debts to foreign nations it was unable to repay.

In 1781 the government turned to Philadelphia shipper and merchant **Robert Morris** for advice on how to raise funds. Morris, known as a financial wizard, came up with a solution: ask the states to approve federal **tariffs**, or import taxes, on certain foreign goods. The tariffs would provide desperately needed income for the Confederation and relieve the states from having to contribute funding many could scarcely afford. For three years, beginning in 1782, Congress sought the necessary unanimous approval for a duty of 5 percent on imported goods, payable in hard currency rather than paper money. But the plan failed because both Virginia and Rhode Island said no. To add insult to injury, some states promptly passed their own tariffs on imported goods. The failure of the tariff strategy prompted one critic of the Confederation government to comment: "Thirteen wheels require a steady and powerful regulation to keep them in good order." Until Congress could act without the unanimous consent of all states, nothing could "prevent the machine from becoming useless."

The Northwest Ordinances

Still in financial crisis, the Confederation pinned its hopes for solvency on the sale of western lands in the Northwest Territory. Here at least Congress had the

---

speculator   A person who buys and sells land or some other commodity in the hope of making a profit.

redeem   To pay a specified sum in return for something; in this case, to make good on paper money issued by the government by exchanging it for hard currency, silver or gold.

Robert Morris   Pennsylvania merchant and financial expert who advised the Continental Congress during the Revolution and served as a fundraiser for the Confederation government.

tariff   A tax on imported or exported goods.

During his years of diplomatic service in Paris, Thomas Jefferson is believed to have fallen in love with the British artist Maria Cosway. In 1788, he presented her with a miniature portrait, a replica of the model John Trumbull intended to use for his painting *The Declaration of Independence.* Cosway took this likeness of Jefferson with her to Italy where it remained until 1976, when it was given to the United States as a gift of the Italian government in honor of the 200th anniversary of American independence. *©The White House Historical Association.*

authority to act, for it could set policy for the settlement and governance of all national territories. In 1784, 1785, and 1787, a national land policy took shape in three **Northwest Ordinances.** These regulations had political significance beyond their role in raising money for the government: they guaranteed that the men and women who moved west would not be colonial dependents of the original states.

The 1784 ordinance established that five new states would be carved out of the region, each to stand on an equal footing with the older, original states. In the earliest stages of settlement, each territory would have an appointed governor. As soon as the number of eligible voters in the territory increased sufficiently, however, they could elect a representative assembly, and the territory could begin to govern itself. Once a state constitution was drafted and approved by the territory's voters, the new state could send elected representatives to the Confederation Congress. Ohio, Indiana, Illinois, Michigan, and Wisconsin each followed this path to full statehood (see Map 7.2 and the table "Ad-

mission of States into the Union" in the Tables appendix at the back of the book).

The ordinance of 1785 spelled out the terms for sale of the land. Mapmakers divided the region into five districts and subdivided each district into townships. Each township, covering 36 square miles, was broken down in a gridlike pattern of thirty-six 640-acre plots. Congress intended to auction these plots off to individual settlers rather than to land speculators, but when the original selling price of $1 per acre in hard currency proved too high for the average farm family, Congress lowered the price and lifted the ban on sales to speculators.

The ordinance of 1787 established that sixty thousand white males were needed for a territory to apply for admission as a state. Thomas Jefferson, who drafted this ordinance, took care to protect the liberties of the settlers with a bill of rights and to ban slavery north of the Ohio River. Jefferson's provisions trampled on the rights of American Indians, however, for their claims to the land were ignored in favor of white settlement.

Diplomatic Problems

The Confederation's diplomatic record was as discouraging as its financial plight. Problems with the British and the Indians arose in the West as settlers began to pour into the Northwest Territory. Although the British had agreed in the Treaty of Paris (1783) to evacuate their western forts, they refused to take any steps until the Americans honored their treaty obligations to repay their war debts and return loyalists' confiscated property. From their strongholds in the territories, the British encouraged Indian resistance by selling arms and supplies to the Shawnees, Miamis, and Delawares. These tribes, and others, denied the legitimacy of the two treaties that turned over the northwest territories to the Americans.

American claims to western lands rested on the 1784 **Treaty of Fort Stanwix** and the 1785 **Hopewell Treaties.** The former, negotiated with the remnants

---

Northwest Ordinances   Three laws (1784, 1785, 1787) that dealt with the sale of public lands in the Northwest Territory and established a plan for the admission of new states to the Union.

Treaty of Fort Stanwix   Treaty signed in 1784 that opened all Iroquois lands to white settlement.

Hopewell Treaties   Treaties signed by 1785 in which the Choctaws, Chickasaws, and Cherokees granted American settlement rights in the Southwest.

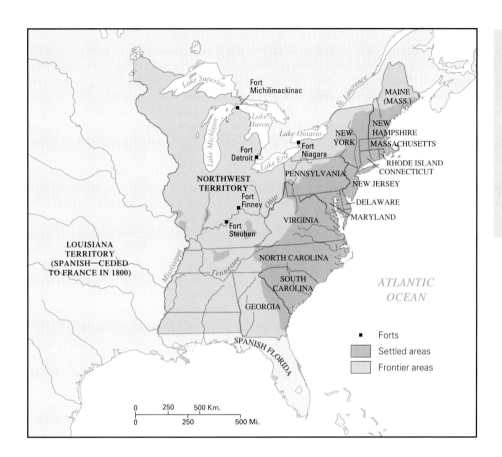

MAP 7.2 The United States in 1787 This map shows the extent of American westward settlement in 1787 and the limits placed on that settlement by French and Spanish claims west of the Mississippi and in Florida. Plans for the creation of five states in the Northwest Territory were approved by Congress in 1787, ensuring that the settlers in this region would enjoy the same political rights as the citizens of the original thirteen states.

of the Iroquois confederacy, opened all Iroquois lands to white settlement; the second, signed by Choctaw, Chickasaw, and Cherokee chiefs, granted Americans settlement rights in the Southwest. The Shawnees and their allies challenged both treaties. By what right, they asked, did those tribes speak for them? Throughout the 1780s, the Confederation and the Indians resorted to warfare rather than negotiation.

The Confederation preferred diplomacy to armed conflict when dealing with European powers. Congress sent John Adams to Great Britain, but not even this persistent and dedicated New Englander could wring any concessions from the British. The American bargaining position was weak. Commercial ties with France and Holland had not developed as rapidly after independence as some patriots had predicted, and thus American merchants remained economically dependent on England as a source of manufactured goods, and on British possessions in the Caribbean for trade. Britain had no desire to end America's economic dependency.

The Confederation had problems with allies as well as with enemies. Spain, for example, was alarmed by American settlers pouring into the land east of the Mississippi. Almost fifty thousand Americans had already moved into what would become Kentucky and Tennessee, and thousands more were eager to farm the rich, river-fed lands of the region. The Spanish government, which controlled access to the Mississippi River and the port of New Orleans, responded by banning all American traffic on the river. The Confederation appointed **John Jay,** fresh from his success as a Paris peace commissioner, to negotiate with Spain on this and other issues, but Jay could make no headway.

The Confederation had no better luck in dealing with the **Barbary pirates.** For many years, the rulers

John Jay New York lawyer and diplomat who negotiated with Great Britain and Spain on behalf of the Confederation; he later became the first chief justice of the Supreme Court and negotiated the Jay Treaty with England.

Barbary pirates Pirates along the Barbary Coast of North Africa who attacked European and American vessels engaged in Mediterranean trade.

of Algiers, Tunisia, Tripoli, and Morocco had taken advantage of their location along the Barbary Coast of North Africa to attack European vessels engaged in Mediterranean trade. Most European nations kept this piracy under control by paying blackmail or by providing armed escorts for their merchant ships. The Barbary pirates showed no mercy to American ships, which were no longer protected by the British bribes or the royal navy. In 1785 a New England ship was captured, its cargo seized, and the crew stripped and sold into slavery. Though appalled and outraged, the Confederation Congress, with no navy and no authority to create one, could do little to ensure safe passage for American ships on the Mediterranean.

A Farmers' Revolt

From the "Wild Yankees" of Pennsylvania's Susquehanna Valley to the "Liberty-Men" of Maine, eighteenth-century backcountry settlers organized to resist speculators' claims on the land and to demand that political power remain with local communities rather than state governments. After the Revolution, these rebels used the language of republicanism to defend their protests and to justify the occasional violence that erupted in their areas. "We fought for land & liberty, & it is hard if we can't enjoy either," wrote one **squatter** in response to a land speculator's claim to his farm. "Who can have a better right to the land than we who have fought for it, subdued it & made it valuable." Farmers suffering from the postwar economic depression had a long list of complaints, including high rents, and land prices, heavy taxes, debts, burdensome legal fees, and the failure of central governments to provide protection from Indian attacks and frontier bandits. These backcountry settlers often made members of the political and economic elite uneasy just as their colonial counterparts—the Regulators and the Paxton Boys—had done. When farmers in western Massachusetts began an organized protest in 1786, this uneasiness reached crisis proportions.

The farmers of western Massachusetts were among the hardest hit by the postwar depression and the rising inflation that accompanied it. Many were deeply in debt to creditors who held mortgages on their farms and lands. In the 1780s, these farmers looked to the state government for temporary relief, hoping that it would pass **stay laws** that would temporarily suspend creditors' rights to foreclose on, or seize, lands and farm equipment. The Massachusetts assembly responded sympathetically and thus aroused the anger of merchants and other creditors who were them-

selves deeply in debt to foreign manufacturers. The upper house of the state legislature, with its more elite members, sided with the creditors and blocked the passage of stay laws. The Massachusetts government then shocked the farmers by raising taxes.

In 1786 hundreds of farmers revolted. They believed they were protecting their rights and their communities as true republicans must do, but their creditors viewed their actions quite differently. To them, the farmers appeared to be dangerous rebels threatening the state with "anarchy, confusion, and total ruin." They accused **Daniel Shays,** a 39-year-old veteran of Bunker Hill, of leading the revolt.

In 1786, farmers known as Shays's rebels closed several courts and freed a number of their fellow farmers from debtors' prison. Their actions struck a chord among desperate farmers in other New England states, and the rebellion began to spread. Fear of a widespread uprising spurred the Massachusetts government to action. It sent a military force of six hundred to Springfield, where more than a thousand farmers, most armed with pitchforks rather than guns, had gathered to close the local courthouse. When the farmers were within range, the troops let loose a cannon barrage that killed four and set the remaining men to flight. Then, on February 4, 1787, four thousand troops surprised the remaining "rebels" in the village of Petersham. Although Daniel Shays managed to escape, the farmers' revolt was over.

Shays's Rebellion revealed the temper of the times. When the government did not respond to their needs, the farmers acted as they had been encouraged to act in the prerevolutionary years. They organized and they protested—and when government still did not respond, they took up arms against what they considered to be injustice. Across the country, many Americans sympathized with these farmers. But just as many did not. Abigail Adams, whose husband, John, had been labeled an irresponsible troublemaker by loyalist opponents only a decade earlier, turned this language against the leaders of the farmers' revolt. She condemned them as "ignorant, restless, des-

---

squatter   A person who settles on unoccupied land to which he or she has no legal claim.

stay laws   Laws suspending the right of creditors to foreclose on debtors; they were designed to protect indebted farmers from losing their land.

Daniel Shays   Revolutionary War veteran considered the leader of the farmers' uprising in western Massachusetts called Shays's Rebellion.

In 1786, western Massachusetts farmers began an agrarian revolt against high taxes and mortgage foreclosures that soon spread to other New England states. Most of the leaders of the uprising, known as Shays's Rebellion, were veteran officers of the American Revolution; many had participated in the protest and resistance that preceded the war itself. The government of Massachusetts crushed the rebellion, jailing some leaders and driving Daniel Shays to seek asylum in Vermont. News of the uprising prompted elite political leaders like George Washington and Alexander Hamilton to press for a more powerful central government, able to ensure "law and order" throughout the nation. *National Portrait Gallery, Washington, D.C.; Art Resource, N.Y.*

peradoes, without conscience or principles," who were persuading a "deluded multitude to follow their standards."

The revolt stirred up fears of slave rebellions and pitched battles between debtors and creditors, haves and have-nots. Above all, it raised doubts among influential political figures about the ability of either state governments or the Confederation to preserve the rule of law. To men such as George Washington, now a planter and private citizen, Shays's Rebellion was a national tragedy, not for its participants but for the reputation of the United States. When the farmers' protest began, Washington wrote to authorities in Massachusetts urging them to act fairly but decisively. "If they have real grievances," he said, the government should acknowledge them. But if not, authorities should "employ the force of government against them at once. . . . To be more exposed to the eyes of the world, and more contemptible than we already are, is hardly possible."

The Revolt of the "Better Sort"

In important ways, the Articles of Confederation embodied the desires of the revolutionary generation for a limited central government that directed diplomacy and coordinated military defense but left the major tasks of governing to local representative governments. Yet such a government was proving to have troubling costs and trying consequences. By 1786, members of the nation's elite, or the "better sort," believed the survival of the nation was in question. Washington predicted "the worst consequences from

a half-starved, limping government, always moving upon crutches and tottering at every step." For him, for Hamilton, and for others like them who thought of themselves as **nationalists,** the solution was clear. "I do not conceive we can long exist as a nation," Washington remarked, "without having lodged somewhere a power which will pervade the whole Union in as energetic a manner as the authority of the State government extends over the several states." Here was a different form of republican government to consider.

Support for a stronger national government grew in the key states of Virginia, Massachusetts, and New York. Men of wealth and political experience urged a reform agenda that included giving the central government taxing powers, devising an easier amendment process, and providing some legal means to enforce national government policies that a state might oppose. They wanted a government that could establish stable diplomatic and trade relations with foreign countries. They also wanted a national government able to preserve their property and their peace of mind. One of the driving forces behind this appeal for reform was Alexander Hamilton.

In 1786 a group of influential Virginians called for a meeting on interstate trade restrictions that placed import taxes on goods carried from state to state. The

nationalists Americans who preferred a strong central government rather than the limited government prescribed in the Articles of Confederation.

In 1876, Thomas Pritchard Rossiter painted his *Signing of the Constitution of the United States* honoring a group of statesmen that included James Madison, Alexander Hamilton, and George Washington, who presided over the Constitutional Convention. Thomas Jefferson, absent because of his duties as ambassador to France, referred to the fifty-five delegates who crafted the Constitution as a gathering of "demigods." *Signing of the Constitution of the United States by Thomas Pritchard Rossiter, 1867. Fraunces Tavern Museum.*

Confederation Congress approved a meeting of state delegates at Annapolis, Maryland, to discuss this issue. But the meeting organizers had a second agenda: to test the waters on revising the nation's constitution. Although only a third of the states participated in the Annapolis conference, nationalists were convinced that their position had substantial support. They asked Congress to call a convention in Philadelphia so that political leaders could continue to discuss interstate commerce problems—and other aspects of government reform. Some members of Congress were reluctant, but news of Shays's Rebellion tipped the balance in favor of the convention.

Creating a New Constitution

■ What major compromises did the framers make in writing the new constitution?

■ What safeguards did James Madison see in his "checks and balances" system?

Late in May 1787, George Washington called the convention to order in Philadelphia. Before him sat delegates from eleven of the thirteen states (New Hampshire's delegates did not arrive until late July), closeted behind curtained windows and locked doors in the heat and humidity of a Philadelphia summer. These secrecy precautions stemmed, they said, from

their wish to speak frankly about the nation's political and economic problems without fear that foreign governments would use that information to their advantage. They were also looking out for thier own reputations in their home states for they quickly realized they might have to make comprises that would be unpopular with their state governments. Only Rhode Island refused to participate, accusing the convention of masquerading as a discussion of interstate trade in order to drastically revise the national government. The accusation by "Rogue's Island," as critics called the smallest state, was correct. The fifty-five prominent and prosperous men did expect to make significant changes in the structure of the government. Here was another reason to keep the deliberations secret.

Most of the men gathered in that room were lawyers, merchants, or planters—Americans of social standing though not necessarily intellectual achievement. When the absent Thomas Jefferson later referred to the convention members as "demigods," he was probably thinking of the likes of 81-year-old Benjamin Franklin, whose sparkling wit and crafty political style set him apart from his colleagues despite his advanced age; or of the articulate, brilliant Alexander Hamilton of New York, whose reputation as a financial mastermind equal to the Confederation's adviser Robert Morris was well established; or of Pennsylvania's Gouverneur Morris, who was widely admired for his intelligence as well as for his literary skills, and his fellow delegate, the logical and learned James Wilson; and finally of **James Madison,** the prim Virginia planter who turned out to be the chief architect of a new constitution. Several notable men were absent. Jefferson, author of the Declaration of Independence, was abroad serving as ambassador to France. John Adams, driving force behind the influential Massachusetts constitution of 1780, was representing the United States in the same capacity in London. And the two great propagandists of the Revolution, Samuel Adams and Thomas Paine, were also absent, for both opposed any revision of the Articles of Confederation.

Revise or Replace?

Most of the delegates were nationalists, but they did not necessarily agree on how best to proceed. Should they revise the Articles or abandon them? Eventually, Edmund Randolph of Virginia, Charles Pinckney of South Carolina, William Paterson of New Jersey, and Alexander Hamilton himself would present blueprints for the new government. But it was the Virginia planter and lawyer Edmund Randolph who first captured the convention's attention with his delegation's proposal, which effectively amended the Articles of Confederation out of existence.

Although Randolph introduced the **Virginia Plan** on the convention floor, James Madison was its guiding spirit. The 36-year-old Madison was no dashing figure. He was small, frail, charmless, and a hypochondriac. But he was highly respected as a scholar of philosophy and history and as an astute political theorist, and his long service as a member of the Virginia legislature and in the Confederation Congress gave him a practical understanding of politics and government. At the convention, Madison brought all his knowledge to bear on this question: what was the best form of government for a strong republic? He concluded, as John Adams had done early in the 1780s, that the fear of tyranny should not rule out a powerful national government. Any dangerous abuse of power could be avoided if internal checks and balances were built into the republican structure.

Madison's Virginia Plan embodied this conviction. It called for a government with three distinct branches—legislative, executive, and judicial—to replace the Confederation's Congress, which was performing all three functions. By dividing power in this way, Madison intended to ensure that no individual or group of men could wield too much authority, especially for self-interested reasons. Madison's plan also gave Congress the power to **veto** laws passed by

James Madison described himself as "feeble" and "sickly" and suffered all his life from dizzy spells and stomach disorders. But this small, shy Virginia planter won the respect of his colleagues as a brilliant political theorist during the drafting of the Constitution, and later as a genius for organizing the machinery of party politics. *Library of Congress.*

the state legislatures and the right to intervene directly if a state acted to interrupt "the harmony of the United States."

The notion of a strong government able, as Madison put it, "to control the governed" but also "obliged to control itself" was endorsed by the delegates. But they were in sharp disagreement over many specific issues in the Virginia Plan. The greatest controversy swirled around representation in the legislative branch—Congress—a controversy familiar to those who had helped draft the Articles of Confederation. Madison proposed a bicameral legislature with

James Madison   Virginia planter and political theorist known as the "father of the Constitution"; he became the fourth president of the United States.

Virginia Plan   Fourteen proposals by the Virginia delegation to the Constitutional Convention for creating a more powerful central government and giving states proportional representation in a bicameral legislature.

veto   The power or right of one branch of government to reject the decisions of another branch.

membership in each house based on proportional representation. Large states supported the plan, for representation based on population worked to their advantage. Small states objected heatedly, calling for equal representation for each state. Small states argued that proportional representation would leave them helpless against a federal government dominated by the large ones. Small-state delegates threw their support behind a second proposal, the **New Jersey Plan,** which also called for three branches of government and gave Congress the power to tax and to control national commerce. This plan, however, preserved an equal voice and vote for every state within a unicameral legislature.

Debate over the two plans dragged on through the steamy days of a June heat wave. Tempers flared, and at times the deadlock seemed hopeless. Threats to walk out of the convention came from both sides. A compromise was needed to prevent distrust and hostility from destroying the convention. That compromise, hammered out by a special committee, was presented by Roger Sherman of Connecticut. Their **Great Compromise** used the idea of a two-house legislature in order to satisfy both sides. It proposed proportional representation in the lower house (the House of Representatives) and equal representation in the upper house (the Senate).

The Great Compromise resolved the first major controversy at the convention but opened the door to the next one. The delegates had to decide how the representatives to each house were to be elected. A compromise also settled this issue. State legislatures would select senators, and the eligible voters of each state would directly elect their state's representatives to the lower house. This formula allowed the delegates to acknowledge the sovereignty of the state governments but also to accommodate the republican commitment to popular elections in a representative government.

The delegates faced one last stumbling block over representation: which Americans were to be counted to determine a state's population? This issue remained as divisive as it had been when the Articles of Confederation were drafted. Southern delegates took care to argue that slaves, who composed as much as one-third and sometimes more of each plantation state's residents, should not be included in the population count on which a state's tax assessments were based. On the other hand, they insisted that these slaves should be included in the population count that determined a state's seats in the House of Representatives. Northern delegates protested, declaring that slaves should be considered property in both in-

stances. These delegates were motivated by self-interest rather than a desire for consistency, for if slaves were considered property, not people, the North would dominate the lower house.

A compromise that defied reason but made brilliant political sense settled this question. The **Three-Fifths Compromise** established that three-fifths of the slave population would be included in a state's critical headcount. A clause was then added guaranteeing that the slave trade would continue for a twenty-year period. Some southern leaders, especially in South Carolina, wanted this extension badly because they had lost many slaves during the Revolution. But not all slaveowners concurred. Virginia's George Mason, a slave owner himself, spoke passionately of the harm slavery did to his region. It not only prevented white immigration to the South, Mason said, but infected the moral character of the slave master. "Every master of slaves," Mason argued, "is born a petty tyrant." Slaveowners "bring the judgment of heaven upon a country," particularly one intended as a republic.

Drafting an Acceptable Document

The Three-Fifths Compromise ended weeks of debate over representation. No other issue arose to provoke such controversy, and the delegates proceeded calmly to implement the principle of checks and balances. For example, the president, or executive, was named commander in chief of the armed forces and given primary responsibility for foreign affairs. To balance these **executive powers,** Congress was given the right to declare war and to raise an army. Congress received the critical "power of the purse," but this power to tax and to spend the revenues raised by

---

New Jersey Plan   A proposal submitted by the New Jersey delegation at the Constitutional Convention for creating a government in which the states would have equal representation in a unicameral legislature.

Great Compromise   A proposal calling for a bicameral legislature with equal representation for the states in one house and proportional representation in the other.

Three-Fifths Compromise   An agreement to count three-fifths of a state's slave population for purposes of determining a state's representation in the House of Representatives.

executive powers   Powers given to the president by the Constitution.

taxation was checked in part by the president's power to veto congressional legislation. As yet another balance, Congress could override a presidential veto by the vote of a two-thirds majority. Following the same logic of distributing power, the delegates gave authority to the president to name federal court judges, but the Senate had to approve all such appointments.

Occasionally, as in the system for electing the president, the convention chose awkward or cumbersome procedures. For example, many delegates opposed direct popular election of the president. Some agreed with the elitist sentiments of George Mason, who said this "would be as unnatural . . . as it would [be] to refer a trial of colours to a blind man." Others simply doubted that the citizens of one state would be familiar enough with a candidate from a distant state to make a valid judgment. In an age of slow communication, few men besides George Washington had a truly national reputation. Should the president be chosen by state legislators who had perhaps worked in government with political leaders from outside their states? Delegates rose to object that this solution threatened too great a concentration of power in the legislators' hands. As a somewhat clumsy compromise, the delegates created the **Electoral College,** a group of special electors to be chosen by the states to vote for presidential candidates. Each state would be entitled to a number of electors equal to the number of its senators and representatives sitting in Congress, but no one serving in Congress at the time of a presidential election would be eligible to be an elector. If two presidential candidates received the same number of Electoral College votes, or if no candidate received a majority of the Electoral College votes, then the House of Representatives would choose the new president. This complex procedure honored the **discretion** of the state governments in appointing the electors but limited the power of individuals already holding office.

The long summer of conflict and compromise ended with a new plan for a national government. Would the delegates be willing to put their names to the document they had created in secrecy and by overreaching their authority? Benjamin Franklin fervently hoped so. Though sick and bedridden, Franklin was carried by friends to the convention floor, where he pleaded for unanimous support for the new government. When a weary George Washington at last declared the meetings adjourned on September 17, 1787, only a handful of delegates left without signing what the convention hoped would be the new American constitution.

Resolving the Conflict of Vision

- What were the Antifederalists' arguments against the Constitution? What were the Federalists' arguments in its favor?
- What was the outcome of the ratification process?

The framers of the Constitution called for special state **ratifying conventions** to discuss and then vote on the proposed change of government. They believed that these conventions would give citizens a more direct role in this important political decision. But the ratifying procedure also gave the framers two advantages. First, it allowed them to bypass the state legislatures, which stood to lose power under the new government and were thus likely to oppose it. Second, it allowed them to nominate their supporters and campaign for their election to the ratifying conventions. The framers added to their advantage by declaring that the approval of only nine states was necessary to establish the Constitution. Reluctantly, the Confederation Congress agreed to all these terms and procedures. By the end of September 1787, Congress had passed the proposed Constitution on to the states, triggering the next round of debates over America's political future.

The Ratification Controversy

As Alexander Hamilton boasted, "The new Constitution has in favor of its success . . . [the] very great weight of influence of the persons who framed it." Hamilton was correct. Men of wealth, political experience, and frequently great persuasive powers put their skills to the task of achieving ratification. But what Hamilton did not mention was that many revolutionary heroes and political leaders opposed the Constitution with equal intensity—most notably Patrick Henry, Samuel Adams, and George Clinton, the popular governor of New York. Boston's most effective revolutionary propagandist, **Mercy Otis Warren,** immediately

Electoral College A body of electors chosen by the states to elect the president and vice president; each state may select a number of electors equal to the number of its senators and representatives in Congress.

discretion The power or right to act according to one's own judgment.

ratifying conventions A meeting of delegates in each state to determine whether that state would ratify the Constitution.

Mercy Otis Warren Writer and historian known for her influential anti-British plays and essays during the pre-revolutionary era; an active opponent of the Constitution.

took up her pen to attack the Constitution and even **canvassed** her neighbors to stand firm against what she called an assault on republican values. Thus the leadership on both sides of the issue was drawn from the political elite of the revolutionary generation.

The pro-Constitution forces won an early and important victory by clouding the language of the debate. They abandoned the label "nationalists," which drew attention to their belief in a strong central government, and chose to call themselves **Federalists,** a name originally associated with a system of strong state governments and limited national government. This shrewd tactic cheated opponents of the Constitution out of their rightful name. The pro-Constitution forces then dubbed their opponents **Antifederalists.** This label implied that their adversaries were negative thinkers, pessimists, and a group lacking a program of its own.

Although the philosophical debate over the best form of government for a republic was an important one, voters considered other, practical factors in choosing a Federalist or Antifederalist position. Voters in states with a stable or recovering economy were likely to oppose the Constitution because the Confederation system gave their states greater independent powers. Those in small, geographically or economically disadvantaged states were likely to favor a strong central government that could protect them from their competitive neighbors. Thus the small states of Delaware and Connecticut ratified the Constitution quickly, but in New York and Virginia ratification was hotly contested.

To some degree, Federalist and Antifederalist camps matched the divisions between the relatively urban, market-oriented communities of the Atlantic coast and the frontier or rural communities of the inland areas. For example, the backcountry of North and South Carolina and the less economically developed areas of Virginia saw little benefit in a stronger central government, especially one that might tax them. But coastal centers of trade and overseas commerce such as Boston, New York City, and Charleston were eager to see an aggressive and effective national policy regarding foreign and interstate trade. In these urban centers, artisans, shopkeepers, and even laborers joined forces with wealthy merchants and shippers to support the Constitution as they had once joined them to make the Revolution. No generalization can explain every political choice, of course. No economic or social group was unified under the Federalist or the Antifederalist banner. On the whole, however, it can be said that the Federalists were better organized, had more resources at their dis-

posal, and campaigned more effectively than the Antifederalists.

In the public debates, the political differences between the Federalists and Antifederalists were sharply defined. Antifederalists rejected the claim that the nation was in a "critical period," facing economic and political collapse. As one New Yorker put it: "I deny that we are in immediate danger of anarchy and commotions. Nothing but the passions of wicked and ambitious men will put us in the least danger. . . . The country is in profound peace . . . and the lives, the liberty and property of individuals is protected." Nevertheless, the Federalists were successful in portraying the moment as a crisis or turning point for the young republic—and in insisting that their plan for recovery was better than no plan at all.

The Antifederalists struck hard against the dangerous elitism they believed they saw in the Constitution. They portrayed the Federalists as a privileged, sophisticated minority, ready and able to tyrannize the people if their powerful national government were ratified. Be careful, one Massachusetts man warned, because "these lawyers, and men of learning, and moneyed men, that talk so finely and gloss over matters so smoothly, to make us poor illiterate people swallow down the pill, expect to get into Congress themselves." And New York Antifederalist Melancton Smith predicted that the proposed new government would lead inevitably to rule by a wealthy, unrepresentative minority. Smith argued with simple eloquence that members of a House of Representatives who had so much power ought to "resemble those they represent . . . and be disposed to seek their true interests." But this was impossible, Smith reasoned, when the representative body was so small and the political ambitions and financial resources of the elite were so great. The Virginia revolutionary leader Richard Henry Lee was flabbergasted that his generation would even consider ratification of the Constitution. "'Tis really astonishing," he wrote to a New York opponent in the summer of 1788, "that the same people, who have just emerged from a long and cruel

---

canvass A survey that is taken.

Federalists Supporters of the Constitution; they desired a strong central government.

Antifederalists Opponents of the Constitution; they believed a strong central government was a threat to American liberties and rights.

despotism Rule by a tyrant.

war in defense of liberty, should agree to fix an elective **despotism** upon themselves and posterity."

The Antifederalists' most convincing evidence of elitism and its potential for tyranny was that the Constitution lacked a bill of rights. The proposed new national Constitution contained no written guarantees of the people's right to assemble or to worship as they saw fit, and it gave no assurances of a trial by jury in civil cases or the right to bear arms. The framers believed these rights were secure because most state constitutions contained strong guarantees of these rights. But antifederalists put the question to both voters and delegates: what did this glaring omission tell Americans about the framers' respect for republican ideals? The only conclusion, Antifederalists argued, was that the Constitution was a threat to republican principles of representative government, a vehicle for elite rule, and a document unconcerned with the protection of the people's individual liberties. Its supporters, Antifederalists warned, were "crying 'wolf'" over economic and social problems in order to seize power.

The Federalist strategy was indeed to portray America in crisis. They pointed to the stagnation of the American economy, to the potential for revolt and social anarchy, and to the contempt that other nations showed toward the young republic. They also argued that the Constitution fulfilled and could preserve the republican ideals of the Revolution far better than the Articles of Confederation. Their cause was put forward most convincingly by Alexander Hamilton, James Madison, and John Jay, who entered the newspaper wars over ratification in the key state of New York. Together, they produced a series of essays known today as the *Federalist Papers.* Although these 85 essays were all signed "Publius," Hamilton wrote 51 of them, Madison 29, and Jay 5. Their common theme was the link between American prosperity and a strong central government.

The Federalist Victory

Practical politics rather than political theory seemed to influence the outcome of many of the ratifying conventions. Delaware, New Jersey, Georgia, and Connecticut—all small states—quickly approved the Constitution. In Pennsylvania, Antifederalists in the rural western regions lost control of the convention to the Federalists and thus that state also endorsed the Constitution. In the remaining states, including Massachusetts, Virginia, and New York, the two sides were more evenly matched.

Antifederalists were in the majority in the Massachusetts convention, where most of the delegates were

The unknown artist of *The Federal Procession in New York, 1788* captured the jubilant mood of Americans as they celebrated their new Constitution with parades, bonfires, and banquets. As the "Ship of State" float indicates, New Yorkers were particularly eager to acknowledge the role of their own Alexander Hamilton in launching the new government. *Library of Congress.*

small farmers from the western counties and more than twenty of them had participated in Shays's Rebellion. The Federalists' strategy was to make political deals with key delegates, winning over Antifederalists such as Samuel Adams and John Hancock, for example, with promises to demand the addition of a bill of rights to the Constitution. Class divisions, however, turned out to be critical during the convention balloting. Men of high social and economic status voted 107 to 34 for ratification. The less wealthy delegates were more divided, voting against the Constitution by a ratio of 2 to 1. At the final count, a 19-vote margin gave the Federalists a narrow victory in Massachusetts.

After Massachusetts ratified, the fight shifted to New Hampshire. Here, too, Federalists won by a small majority. Rhode Island, true to its history of opposition to strong central authority, rejected the Constitution decisively. But Maryland and South Carolina ratified it, and the tide in favor of the new government influenced the next critical vote: that of Virginia. There, Antifederalist leaders Lee, Henry, and James Monroe focused on the absence of a bill of rights in the proposed Constitution. James Madison, and George Washington

Federalist Papers   Essays written by Alexander Hamilton, John Jay, and James Madison in support of the Constitution.

directed the Federalist counterattack. In the end, the presence of Washington proved irresistible because Virginians knew that this war hero and admired colleague was certain to be the first president of the United States if the Constitution went into effect. When the vote was taken on June 25, 1788, Virginia became the tenth state to ratify the new government.

New York's battle was equally intense. Acknowledging that the absence of a bill of rights was a major political error, Federalist leaders Jay and Hamilton made a public pledge to support its inclusion. By then, however, ten states had already ratified the Constitution, and so the new government was a **fait accompli.** Realizing this, on July 26, 1788, a majority of New York delegates voted yes on ratification.

President George Washington

The election of senators and Congress members was almost complete by February 4, 1789, when presidential electors met in each state to choose the nation's first president. Although George Washington did not seek the position, he knew the nation expected him to serve. The general was among the very few in the revolutionary generation to have a national reputation. He was hailed as the hero of the Revolution, and he looked and acted the part of the dignified, virtuous patriot. Washington became president by a unanimous vote of the Electoral College. For regional balance, New Englander John Adams was chosen vice president.

In April 1789, as Washington made his way from Virginia to his inauguration in New York City, the temporary national capital, Americans thronged to greet him with parades, sharply dressed military escorts, and choruses of church bells and cannon fire. Near Trenton, New Jersey, the scene of his first victory in the Revolutionary War, he passed through a triumphal arch 20 feet high, supported by thirteen pillars, and inscribed in gold with the date of the Battle of Trenton. As his barge took him across the Hudson River, private boats sailed alongside, their passengers singing songs composed in his honor. Thousands of supporters gathered to see him take the oath of office. Yet amid the celebration, Washington and his closest advisers knew the future was uncharted and uncertain. "We are in a wilderness," Madison observed, "without a single footstep to guide us."

Washington agreed. The new president understood that he symbolized a national experiment in government and that friends and critics of the United States would be closely watching his behavior in office. Since he was the first to hold the presidency, his every action had the potential to become a ritual and to set

George Washington was a favorite subject of portrait artists in both the 18th and 19th centuries. In 1789, soon after Washington's first inauguration, the artist John Ramage painted this miniature for Mrs. Washington. Despite the fact that Ramage had been a loyalist during the Revolutionary War, by the 1780s his miniatures were in great demand during the early national period. The portrait of Washington is only 2⅛ inches high, but the case that holds it also holds strands of the president's hair. *Christies Images, Inc.*

a precedent for those who followed. "Few . . . can realize," he wrote, "the difficult and delicate part which a man in my situation has to act. . . . I walk on untrodden ground."

Washington proceeded with caution and deliberation. He labored carefully over each of his selections to the almost one thousand federal offices waiting to be filled. He took particular care in choosing the men to head four executive departments created with approval from Congress. Naming his **protégé** Alexander Hamilton to the Treasury Department was probably Washington's easiest decision. He asked the Massachusetts military strategist Henry Knox to head the War Department and fellow Virginian Edmund Randolph to serve as attorney general. Washington chose

fait accompli An accomplished deed or fact that cannot be reversed or undone.

protégé An individual whose welfare or career is promoted by an influential person.

another Virginian, Thomas Jefferson, to be secretary of state. Over time, the president established a pattern of meeting with this **cabinet** of advisers on a regular basis to discuss policy matters. Together, they made major decisions and, as Washington expected, expressed serious disagreements that exposed him to differing viewpoints on policy.

Competing Visions Re-emerge

■ How did Alexander Hamilton's expectations for the new nation differ from those of Thomas Jefferson? What were the consequences of this conflict of vision?

■ How did the French Revolution affect Washington's diplomatic policy?

A remarkable but, as it turned out, short-lived spirit of unity marked the early days of Washington's administration. Federalists had won the overwhelming majority of seats in the new Congress, and this success enabled them to work quickly and efficiently on matters they felt had priority. But the unity was fragile. By 1792, sectional divisions were deepening, and as the government debated foreign policy and domestic affairs, two distinct groups, voicing serious differences of opinion, began to form. Alexander Hamilton's vision for America guided one group. At the heart of the other was the vision of Thomas Jefferson.

Unity's Achievements

In addition to creating the four executive departments that became the cabinet, the First Congress passed the **Judiciary Act of 1789.** This act established a Supreme Court, thirteen district courts, and three circuit courts. It also empowered the Supreme Court to review the decisions of state courts and to nullify any state laws that violated either the Constitution or any treaty made by the federal government. President Washington chose John Jay to serve as first chief justice of the Supreme Court.

The First Congress also managed to break the stalemate on the tariff issue. Southern leaders had opposed a tariff because a tax on imports added to the cost of the consumer goods that southern agriculturalists had to purchase. Northeastern leaders had favored tariff legislation because such a tax, by making foreign goods more expensive, would benefit their region's merchants and manufacturers. During Washington's first term, southerner James Madison took the lead in conducting the delicate negotiations over tariffs. The result was an import tax on certain items such as rum, cocoa, and coffee.

For several years, New York City served as the capital of the new United States. But plans were soon laid for a new capital city to be created on the banks of the Potomac River, on land donated by Virginia and Maryland. This new city was to be named Washington, in honor of the hero of the Revolution and the first president of the new nation. Although elaborate plans for elegant, tree-lined streets such as this one were drawn up, for many years visitors and residents alike described Washington, D.C., as a dismal town of muddy streets and dreadful climate. *Library of Congress.*

Madison also prodded Congress to draft the promised **Bill of Rights.** Although more than two hundred suggestions were submitted to Congress, Madison honed them down to twelve. On December 15, 1791, ten of these were added to the Constitution as the Bill of Rights, and soon after, both Rhode Island and North Carolina ratified the Constitution and joined the union. Eight of these original constitutional amendments spelled out the government's commitment to

cabinet A body of officials appointed by the president to run the executive departments of the government and to act as the president's advisers.

Judiciary Act of 1789 Law establishing the Supreme Court and the lower federal courts; it gave the Supreme Court the right to review state laws and state court decisions to determine their constitutionality.

Bill of Rights The first ten amendments to the U.S. Constitution, added in 1791 to protect certain basic rights of American citizens.

protect individual **civil liberties.** They guaranteed that the new national government could not limit free speech, interfere with religious worship, deny U.S. citizens the right to keep or bear arms, force the quartering of troops in private homes, or allow homes to be searched without proper search warrants. The amendments prohibited the government from requiring persons accused of crimes to testify against themselves, nor could it deny citizens the right to a trial by jury. The government also could not deprive a citizen of life, liberty, or property without "due process of law," or impose excessive bail, or administer "cruel and unusual punishments." The Ninth Amendment made clear that the inclusion of these protections and rights did not mean that others were excluded. The Tenth Amendment stated that any powers not given to the federal government or denied to the states belonged solely to the states or the people.

Condensed into these ten amendments was a rich history of struggle for individual rights in the face of abusive power. It was a history that recalled the experiences of colonists protesting the illegal search and seizure of cargoes in Boston harbor, the British government's insistence on quartering troops in New York homes, and the religious persecution of men and women who dissented from established churches both in England and in the colonies.

Hamilton and Jefferson's Differences

Alexander Hamilton was consumed by a bold dream: to transform agricultural America into a manufacturing society that rivaled Great Britain. His blueprint for achieving this goal called for tariffs designed to protect developing American industry rather than simply raise revenue. It also called for **subsidies,** or government financial support, for new enterprises and incentives to support new industries. And it relied on strong economic and diplomatic ties with the mercantile interests of England. Hamilton's vision had great appeal in the Northeast but few advocates in the southern states. Indeed, his ambitious development program seemed to confirm Patrick Henry's worst fears: that the new government would produce "a system which I have ever dreaded—subserviency of Southern to Northern Interests."

Virginia planters Thomas Jefferson and James Madison offered a different vision of the new nation: a prosperous, agrarian society. Instead of government tariffs designed to encourage American manufacturing, they advocated a national policy of **free trade** to keep consumer prices low. The agrarian view did not entirely rule out commerce and industry in the United States. As long as commercial society remained "a handmaiden to agriculture," Jefferson saw no danger that citizens would be exploited or lured into the love of luxury that destroyed republics. In the same fashion, Hamilton was content to see agriculture thrive as long as it did not drain away the scarce resources of the national government or stand in the way of commercial or industrial growth. Hamilton and men of similar vision around him spoke of themselves as true **Federalists.** Those who agreed with Jefferson and Madison identified themselves as **Republicans.**

The emergence of two political camps was certain to trouble even the men who played a role in creating them. The revolutionary generation believed that **factions,** or special-interest parties, were responsible for the corruption of English politics. John Adams seemed to speak for all these political leaders when he declared: "A division of the republic into two great parties . . . is to be dreaded as the greatest political evil." Yet as President Washington was quick to see, **sectionalism** fueled the growth of just such a division.

Hamilton's Economic Plan

As secretary of the Treasury, Alexander Hamilton was expected to seek solutions to the nation's **fiscal** prob-

civil liberties Fundamental individual rights such as freedom of speech and religion, protected by law against interference from the government.

subsidy Financial assistance that a government grants to an enterprise considered to be in the public interest.

free trade Trade between nations without any protective tariffs.

Federalists Political group formed during Washington's first administration; led by Alexander Hamilton, they favored an active role for government in encouraging commercial and manufacturing growth.

Republicans Political group formed during Washington's first administration; led by Thomas Jefferson and James Madison, they favored limited government involvement in encouraging manufacturing and the continued dominance of agriculture in the national economy.

faction A political group with shared opinions or interests.

sectionalism Excessive concern for local or regional interests.

fiscal Relating to finances.

lems, particularly the foreign and domestic debts hanging over America's head. His proposals were the source of much of the conflict that divided Congress in the early 1790s.

In January 1790 Hamilton submitted a *Report on Public Credit* to the Congress. In it, he argued that the public debt fell into three categories, each requiring attention: (1) foreign debt, owed primarily to France; (2) state debts, incurred by the individual states to finance their war efforts; and (3) a national debt in the form of government securities (the notorious paper continentals) that had been issued to help finance the war. To establish credit, and thus to be able to borrow money and attract investors in American enterprises, Hamilton declared that the nation had to make good on all it owed.

Hamilton proposed that the federal government assume responsibility for the repayment of all three categories of debt. He insisted the continentals be redeemed for the amount shown on the certificate, regardless of what their current value might be. And he proposed that *current* holders of continentals should receive that payment regardless of how or when they had acquired them. These recommendations, and the political agenda for economic growth they revealed, raised furious debate within Congress.

Before Hamilton's *Report on Public Credit*, James Madison had been the voice of unity in Congress. Now, Madison leapt to his feet to protest the treasury secretary's plan. The government's debt, both financial and moral, Madison argued, was not to the current creditors holding the continentals but to the *original* holders. Many of the original holders were ordinary citizens and Continental soldiers who had sold these certificates to speculators at a tremendous loss during the postwar depression. The state treasuries of New York, Pennsylvania, and Maryland were three of the largest speculators, buying up great quantities of these bonds when they were disgracefully cheap. If Hamilton's plan were adopted, Madison protested, these speculators, rather than the nation's true patriots, would reap enormous unfair profits.

Madison's emotional opposition to Hamilton's debt program came from a deep distrust of certain ways of attaining wealth. Although enslaved men and women performed the work done on Madison's plantation, the Virginia planter believed that wealth acquired by productive labor was moral whereas wealth gained by the manipulation of money was corrupt. Hamilton simply sidestepped the moral issue by explaining the difficulty of identifying and locating the original holders of the continentals. Whatever the ethical merits of Madison's argument, Hamilton

said, his solution was impractical. Congress supported Hamilton, but the vote reflected the growing rift between regions.

Madison was far from silenced, however. Next, he led the opposition to Hamilton's proposal that the federal government assume, or take over, the states' debts. Here, Hamilton's motives were quite transparent: as a fierce nationalist, he wished to concentrate both political and economic power in the federal government at the expense of the states. He knew that creditors, who included America's wealthiest citizens, would take a particular interest in the welfare and success of any government that owed them money. By concentrating the debt in the federal government, Hamilton intended to give America's elite a clear stake in America's success. Hamilton also knew that a sizable debt provided a compelling reason for raising revenue. By assuming the state debts, the federal government could undercut state governments' need for new taxes—and justify its own.

Congress saw the obvious **inequities** of the plan. Members from states such as Maryland and Virginia quickly reminded Congress that their governments had paid all their war debts during the 1780s. If the national government assumed state debts and raised taxes to repay them, responsible citizens of Maryland and Virginia would be taxed for the failure of Massachusetts or New York to honor their obligations. Although the Senate approved the assumption of state debts, members of the House strongly objected and deferred a decision. Hamilton, realizing he faced defeat, moved to break the deadlock by a behind-the-scenes compromise with Madison and his ally Jefferson. Hamilton was confident he held a valuable bargaining chip: the location of the national capital.

In 1789 the new government had made New York its temporary home until Congress could settle on a permanent site. The choice turned out to be politically delicate because of regional jealousy and competition. Hamilton was willing to put the capital right in Jefferson's backyard in exchange for the Virginian's support on assumption of state debts. The deal clearly appealed to southern regional pride, but Madison and Jefferson had deeper motives for agreeing to it. Like many good Republicans, they believed it was important to monitor the deliberations of a powerful government. But in an age of slow land travel and slower communication, it was difficult to keep watch from a distance. New Englanders also knew that "watching"

---

inequities Unfair circumstances or proceedings.

meant the chance to influence the government. "The climate of the Potomac," one New Englander quipped, would prove unhealthy, if not deadly, to "northern constitutions." Nevertheless, by trading away the capital location, Hamilton ensured the success of his assumption plan.

The year 1791 began with another controversial proposal from the secretary of the Treasury. This time, Hamilton outlined a plan for chartering a national bank. The bank, modeled on the Bank of England, would serve as fiscal agent for the federal government, although it would not be an exclusively public institution. Instead, the bank would be funded by both the government and private sources in a partnership that fit nicely with Hamilton's plan to tie national prosperity to the interests of private wealth.

Once again, James Madison led the opposition. He argued that the government had neither the express right nor the **implied power** to create a national institution such as the bank. The majority of Congress did not agree, but Madison's argument that the bank was unconstitutional did cause President Washington to hesitate over signing the congressional bill into law. As usual, Washington decided to consult advisers on the matter. He asked both Secretary of State Jefferson and the Treasury head Hamilton to set down their views.

Like Madison, Jefferson was at that time a **strict constructionist** in his interpretation of the Constitution. On February 15, 1791, he wrote of the dangers of interpreting the government's powers broadly. "To take a single step beyond the boundaries . . . specifically drawn around the powers of Congress," he warned, "is to take possession of a boundless field of power." A **broad constructionist,** Hamilton saw no such danger in the bank. He based his argument on Article 1, Section 8, of the Constitution, which granted Congress the right to "make all Laws which shall be necessary and proper" to exercise its legitimate powers. As he put it on February 23: "The powers contained in a constitution . . . ought to be construed liberally in advancement of the public good." And because it seemed obvious that "a bank has a natural relation to the power of collecting taxes," Hamilton believed there could be no reasonable constitutional argument against it. Hamilton's argument persuaded the president, and the bank was chartered on February 25, 1791. By July 4, 1791, stock in the newly established Bank of the United States was offered for sale.

Hamilton's assumption strategy and the creation of a bank were just preliminaries to the ambitious economic development program that he put forward in 1792 in his *Report on Manufactures*. But this time his package of policies for aggressively industrializing the nation—including protective tariffs and government incentives and subsidies—was too extreme to win support in Congress. Still, the Bank of the United States, which provided much-needed working **capital** for new commercial and manufacturing enterprises, and the establishment of sound national credit, which attracted foreign capital to the new nation, had gone far toward moving the economy in the direction of Hamilton's vision.

Foreign Affairs and Deepening Divisions

In 1789, just as George Washington became the first president of the United States, the **French Revolution** began. And in the years in which Hamilton was advancing his economic programs, that revolution stirred new controversy within American politics.

The first signs of serious resistance to the French monarchy came when **Louis XVI,** king of France, asked for new taxes. Reformers within the French parliament, or Estates General, refused, choosing instead to reduce the king's power and create a constitutional monarchy. Outside the halls of government, crowds took to the streets in the name of broad social reform. On July 14, 1789, Parisian radicals stormed the Bastille prison, a symbol of royal oppression, tear-

implied power   Power that is not specifically granted to the government by the Constitution but can be viewed as necessary to carry out the governing duties listed in the Constitution.

strict constructionist   A person who believes the government has only the powers specifically named in the Constitution.

broad constructionist   A person who believes the government can exercise any implied powers that are in keeping with the spirit of the Constitution.

capital   Money needed to start or sustain a commercial enterprise.

French Revolution   Political rebellion against the French monarchy and aristocratic privileges; it began in 1789 and ended in 1799.

Louis XVI   The king of France (r. 1774–1792) when the French Revolution began; he and his wife, Marie Antoinette, were executed in 1793 by the revolutionary government.

Edmund Genêt came to the United States in 1793 on a mission to recruit Americans to fight for France in that nation's war against Great Britain. Traveling from Charleston to New York, the charming, persuasive Genêt roused considerable popular support—and the wrath of President George Washington. The president viewed Genêt's unauthorized activities as an insult to American sovereignty and a threat to American foreign policy. At Washington's insistence, the French government issued a recall of "Citizen Genêt," but when news came that a warrant for Genêt's arrest had also been issued, Washington granted Genêt political asylum in America. The lively Frenchman settled in New York and married a daughter of Governor George Clinton. *Collection of the Albany Institute of History and Art. Bequest of George Genêt.*

ing down its walls and liberating its political prisoners. The crowds filling the Paris streets owed some of their political rhetoric and ideals to the American Revolution. The marquis de Lafayette acknowledged this debt when he sent his old friend President Washington the key to the Bastille. Like most Americans in these early days of the French Revolution, Washington was pleased to be identified with this new struggle for the "rights of man." Briefly, enthusiasm for the French Revolution united Hamilton's Federalists and Jefferson's Republicans.

By 1793, however, American public opinion began to divide sharply on the French Revolution. Popular support faded when the revolution's most radical party, the Jacobins, imprisoned and then executed the king and his wife. Many shocked Americans denounced the revolution completely when the Jacobins, in their **Reign of Terror** against any who opposed their policies, began marching moderate French reformers as well as members of the nobility to the guillotine to be beheaded.

Soon after eliminating their revolutionary opponents, the Jacobin government vowed to bring "liberty, equality, and brotherhood" to the peoples of Europe, by force if necessary. This campaign to spread the revolution led France into war with England, Spain, Austria, and **Prussia.** At the very least, France expected the Americans to honor the terms of the treaty of 1778, which bound the United States to protect French possessions in the West Indies from enemy attack. The enemy most likely to strike was England, a fact that suddenly made a second war between England and the United States a possibility.

American opinion on a second war with England was contradictory and complex. George Blake, a Boston lawyer and political figure, reminded his fellow citizens, "The [French] cause is half our own, and does not our policy and our honor urge us to most forcibly cherish it?" But others who continued to support the French Revolution, including Thomas Jefferson, did not want the United States to become embroiled in a European war. Many who condemned the French Revolution nevertheless were eager to use any excuse to attack the British, who still were occupying forts in the Northwest and restricting American trade in the Caribbean. Political leaders such as Hamilton who were working toward better relations with England were appalled not only by the French assault on other nations but also by the prospect of American involvement in it. While Americans struggled with these contradictory views, the French plotted to mobilize American support directly.

In 1793 the new French republic sent a diplomatic minister to the United States. When Citizen **Edmund Genêt** arrived in Charleston, he wasted no time on formal matters such as presenting his credentials as

Reign of Terror The period from 1793 to 1794 in the French Revolution when thousands of people were executed as enemies of the state.

Prussia A northern European state that became the basis for the German Empire in the late nineteenth century.

Edmund Genêt Diplomat sent by the French government to bring the United States into France's war with Britain and Spain.

an official representative from France to either the president or the secretary of state. Instead, he immediately launched a campaign to recruit Americans to the war effort. By all accounts, Genêt was charming, affable, and in the words of one observer, so humorous that he could "laugh us into the war." President Washington, however, was not amused. Genêt's total disregard for formal procedures infuriated Washington, who was undecided about whether to officially recognize the French minister. Genêt's bold attempts to provoke incidents between the United States and Spain stunned Hamilton. Even Thomas Jefferson grew uncomfortable when the Frenchman used the port of Philadelphia to transform a captured British ship into a French privateer!

On April 22, 1793, Washington decided to act. Publicly, the president issued a proclamation that declared American **neutrality** without actually using the term. While allowing Washington to avoid a formal **repudiation** of America's treaty with France, the proclamation made clear that the United States would give no military support to the French. Privately, Washington asked the French government to recall Genêt.

The Genêt affair had domestic as well as diplomatic repercussions. For the first time, George Washington came under public attack. A Republican newspaper whose editor was employed by Jefferson in the State Department questioned the president's integrity in refusing to honor the Franco-American treaty. Washington was furious with this assault on his character. Federalist newspapers struck back, insisting that Jefferson and his followers had actively encouraged the outrageous behavior of Genêt, and Federalists issued resolutions condemning Genêt. By the end of 1793, Jefferson had resigned from Washington's government, more convinced than ever that Hamilton and his supporters posed a serious threat to the survival of the American republic.

More Domestic Disturbances

Hamilton's Federalists agreed that the republic was in danger—from Jefferson's Republicans. By Washington's second term (he was reelected in 1792), both political groups were trying to rouse popular sentiment for their programs and policies and against those of their opponents. Just as in the prerevolutionary years, these appeals to popular opinion broadened participation in the debate over the future of the nation. Ordinary citizens did not always wait until their political leaders solicited their views, however. In the wake of the French Revolution and British in-

terference in the West and on the seas, organizations rose up to make demands on the government. The most troubling of these to President Washington were the **Democratic-Republican societies.**

Between 1793 and 1794, thirty-five Democratic-Republican societies were created. Made up primarily of craftsmen and men of the "lower orders," these pro-French political groups also had their share of professional men, merchants, and planters. In Philadelphia, for example, noted scientist and inventor David Rittenhouse and Alexander Dallas, secretary to the governor of Pennsylvania, were society members. In Kentucky, which had split from Virginia in 1792, local elites organized their own society, separate from the one made up of western farmers. No matter what the background of the membership, these societies shared a common agenda: to serve as a platform for expressing the public's will. They insisted that political officeholders were "the agents of the people," not their leaders, and thus should act as the people wished.

In 1794 many western farmers were dismayed over what they considered the government's indifference toward the people. Kentucky settlers fretted about the navigation of the Mississippi, while Pennsylvania and Carolina farmers resented a new federal **excise** tax on whiskey. Although the Democratic-Republican societies denied an active role in spurring a new farmers' revolt against the government, a belief that the government ought to respond to its citizens' demands did seem to motivate Pennsylvania, Carolina, and Kentucky farmers to tar and feather **excise men,** burn the barns of tax supporters, and intimidate county officials. The most determined and organized resistance came from Pennsylvania, where, in July 1794, a crowd ransacked and burned the home of the federal excise inspector and then threatened to march on Pittsburgh if the tax on whiskey were not repealed.

neutrality The policy of treating both sides in a conflict the same way and thus favoring neither.

repudiation The act of rejecting the validity or the authority of something.

Democratic-Republican societies Political organizations formed in 1793 and 1794 to demand greater responsiveness by the state and federal governments to the needs of the citizens.

excise A tax on the production, sale, or consumption of a commodity or on the use of a service within a country.

excise men Men who collected taxes on an article of trade or sale.

President Washington, haunted by the memory of Shays's Rebellion and worried that the radical spirit of the French Revolution was spreading throughout America, determined to crush this **Whiskey Rebellion** firmly. Calling up fifteen thousand militiamen, the president marched into the countryside to do battle with a few hundred citizens armed with rifles and pitchforks. In the face of such an overwhelming military force, the whiskey rebels abruptly dispersed.

Washington publicly laid the blame for the western insurrection on the Democratic-Republican societies. Federalists in Congress rushed to propose a resolution condemning those groups. Fisher Ames, an ardent Massachusetts Federalist, delivered an impassioned condemnation of the societies, accusing them of spreading "jealousies, suspicions, and accusations" against the government. They had, Ames declared, "arrogantly pretended sometimes to be the people and sometimes the [people's] guardians, the champions of the people." Instead, he said, they represented no one but themselves.

The Jeffersonians, generally believed to be sympathetic to the societies, knew it would be politically damaging to defend them in the aftermath of the Whiskey Rebellion. Instead, they worked to see a more moderate expression of disapproval emerge from Congress.

By 1796, the Democratic-Republican organizations had vanished from the American political scene. The president's public condemnation and Congress's censure undoubtedly damaged them. But improvements on the western borders also diminished the farmers' interest in protest organizations. In October 1795, Carolina planter Thomas Pinckney won the concession from Spain that Jay had been unable to obtain in earlier negotiations: free navigation of the Mississippi River. Pinckney's **Treaty of San Lorenzo** not only gave western farmers an outlet to ocean trade through the port of New Orleans but also ensured that Indian attacks would not be launched from Spanish-held territories.

Jay's Treaty

During Washington's second administration, the diplomatic crisis continued to worsen. England resented America's claim to neutrality, believing it helped France. The British, therefore, ignored American claims that "free ships made free goods" and began to seize American vessels trading with the French Caribbean islands. These seizures prompted new calls for war with Great Britain.

Anti-British emotion ran even higher when the governor of Canada actively encouraged Indian resistance to American settlement in the Northwest. Washington and the general public considered Indian relations dismal enough without such meddling, especially since efforts to crush the Miamis of Ohio had recently ended in two embarrassing American defeats. In February 1794, as General Anthony Wayne headed west for a third attempt against the Miamis, the Canadian governor's fiery remarks were particularly disturbing.

Jefferson's departure left little anti-British sentiment in the cabinet. But it remained strong in the Congress, where the House of Representatives considered restricting trade with England. Outside the government, war hysteria showed itself as mobs attacked English seamen and tarred and feathered Americans expressing pro-British views. What would Washington do?

Early in 1794, the president sent Chief Justice John Jay to England as his special **envoy.** Jay's mission was to produce a compromise that would prevent war between the two nations. Jay, however, was pessimistic. Britain wanted to avoid war with the United States, but what would British diplomats concede to his weak nation?

Jay's negotiations did resolve some old nagging issues. In the treaty that emerged, Britain agreed to evacuate the western forts although it did not promise to end support for Indian resistance to American western settlement. Britain also granted some small trade favors to America in the West Indies. For its part, the United States agreed to see that all prewar debts owed to British merchants were at last paid. Jay, a committed abolitionist, did not press for any provision compensating slaveholders for slaves lost during the Revolution. In the end, Jay knew he had given up more than he gained: he had abandoned America's demand for freedom of the seas and acknowledged

Whiskey Rebellion A protest by grain farmers against the 1794 federal tax on whiskey; militia forces led by President Washington put down this Pennsylvania uprising.

Treaty of San Lorenzo Treaty between the United States and Spain, negotiated in 1795 by Thomas Pinckney; Spain granted the United States the right to navigate the Mississippi River and use the port of New Orleans as an outlet to the sea.

envoy A government representative charged with a special diplomatic mission.

In 1794, the new federal government passed an excise tax on whiskey made from surplus American grains. Farmers in western Pennsylvania rose up in protest against what they considered an unfair assault on their livelihood. Using tactics straight out of the pre–Revolutionary War era, including tarring and feathering the "revenooer" assigned to collect the taxes, the "Whiskey Rebels" challenged the federal government's authority. President Washington met this challenge by assembling an army of almost thirteen thousand men to put down the Whiskey Rebellion. Critics declared the president's response excessive. Do you agree? *Library of Congress.*

the British navy's right to remove French property from any neutral ship.

Jay's Treaty did little to enhance John Jay's reputation or popularity. After reading it, fellow New Yorker Robert R. Livingston said bluntly: "Mr. Jay has sacrificed the essential interests of this country." In Congress, judgments on the treaty were openly **partisan.** Federalists credited Jay's Treaty with preserving the peace, but Republicans condemned it as an embarrassment and a betrayal of France. Worried that the angry debate over ratification would fan popular outrage, the president banned public discussion of the treaty. Republican congressmen, however, leaked accounts to the press. Once again, the president came under attack, and Kentucky settlers threatened rebellion, warning Washington that if he signed Jay's Treaty, "western America is gone forever—lost to the Union." The treaty finally squeaked through the Senate in the spring of 1795 with only two southern senators supporting ratification. The House debate on appropriations for the treaty was equally bitter and prolonged. In the end, however, Congress endorsed Jay's handiwork. Despite the criticism, Jay knew he had accomplished his mission, for American neutrality in the European war continued.

Jay's negotiations with England damaged the prestige and authority of Washington's administration. The president did far better, however, in military and diplomatic affairs in the West. In August 1794, Anthony Wayne's army defeated the northwestern Indians at the **Battle of Fallen Timbers.** Wayne then lived up to his reputation as "Mad Anthony" by rampaging through enemy villages, destroying all that he could. These terror tactics helped produce the **Treaty of Greenville** in August 1795. By this treaty, the Indi-

Jay's Treaty Controversial 1794 treaty negotiated between the United States and Great Britain by John Jay to ensure American neutrality in the French and English war.

partisan Taking a strong position on an issue out of loyalty to a political group or leader.

Battle of Fallen Timbers 1794 battle in which Kentucky riflemen defeated Indians of several tribes, helping to end Indian resistance in the Northwest.

Treaty of Greenville 1795 treaty in which the United States agreed to pay northwestern Indians about $10,000 for the land that later became the state of Ohio.

ans ceded most of the land that later became the state of Ohio. These victories, combined with the auspicious terms of Pinckney's Treaty of San Lorenzo, won praise for the troubled president.

Washington's Farewell

The bitter political fight over Jay's Treaty, combined with the steady and nagging criticism of his policies in the press and the hardening of party lines between Federalists and Republicans, helped George Washington make an important decision: he would not seek a third term as president. Instead, in 1796 he would return to his beloved Virginia home, Mount Vernon, and resume the life of a gentleman planter.

When Washington retired, he left behind a nation very different from the one whose independence he had helped win and whose survival he had helped secure. The postwar economic depression was over, and the war raging in Europe had produced a steadily rising demand for American foodstuffs. More fundamentally, in the fifteen years since the Revolution, the U.S. economy had moved decisively in the direction that Alexander Hamilton had envisioned. The values and expectations of a **market economy**—with its stress on maximizing profit and the pursuit of individual economic interests—had captured the imagination and shaped the actions of many white Americans. Hamilton's policies as secretary of the treasury had both reflected and advanced a growing interest in the expansion of trade, the growth of markets, and the development of American manufacturing and industry. In its political life, the republic had been reorganized and the relationships between the states and the central government redefined. The new Constitution granted greater diplomatic and commercial powers to the federal government but protected individual citizens through the Bill of Rights. America's political leaders, though convinced that factions were dangerous to the survival of the republic, had nevertheless created and begun to work within an evolving party system.

In his Farewell Address to the public, Washington expressed his thoughts on many of these changes. Although Jefferson had believed the president was a Federalist partisan, Washington spoke with feeling against parties in a republic, urging the nation to return to nonpartisan cooperation. Washington also warned

Independence sparked renewed westward migration by land-hungry Americans. The federal government took steps to legitimate these incursions into Indian homelands by persuading selected chiefs and warriors of the Northwest to cede all rights to vast tracts of this Ohio Valley land. The document above provides a sample of the eleven hundred signatures obtained in the Greenville Treaty of 1795, a treaty that ceded almost two-thirds of present-day Ohio and portions of Indiana. Many tribes protested such treaties on the grounds that the signers were not legitimate spokesmen for their people. *Library of Congress.*

America and its new leaders not to "interweave our destiny with any part of Europe" or "entangle our peace and prosperity in the toils of European ambition." An honorable country must "observe good faith and justice toward all nations," said the aging Virginian, but Americans must not let any alliance develop that draws the nation into a foreign war. The final ingredient in Washington's formula for America's success and its "permanent felicity" was the continuing virtue of its people.

market economy   An economy in which production of goods is geared to sale or profit.

Individual Voices

Examining a Primary Source

Alexander Hamilton Envisions a Prospering America

Alexander Hamilton made no effort to hide his grand vision for the new nation, even though many American leaders strongly opposed him. He had been an early and persistent advocate of a strong central government, and once it was created, he immediately proposed that it play an active role in developing the nation's economy. Hamilton's success in establishing a national bank and in funding the national debt led him to suggest an ambitious plan for government encouragement of manufacturing and industry. In his *Report on Manufactures,* which he submitted to Congress in 1791, Hamilton made a persuasive argument for the benefits of rapid economic growth in the manufacturing sector. Opposition to the report was immediate and effective, and this time, political leaders who shared Jefferson's agrarian vision for America managed to deal a crushing defeat to Hamilton. In fact, Congress refused to act on the Treasury secretary's suggestions.

■ Hamilton was well aware that the need for the national government to support manufacturing was still disputed. Why do you think he begins with the claim that most people now support this type of government involvement in the economy?

■ What arguments do you think Jefferson or Madison would use to defend the superiority of agriculture over manufacturing or commerce?

■ What were some of the "embarrassments" suffered by Americans during the war?

. . . The expediency of encouraging manufactures in the United States, which was not long since deemed very questionable, appears at this time to be pretty generally admitted. . . . ■ *It ought readily to be conceded that the cultivation of the earth—as the primary and most certain source of national supply—as the immediate and chief source of subsistence to man . . . as including a state most favourable to the freedom and independence of the human mind . . . has intrinsically a strong claim to pre-eminence over every other kind of industry.*

But, that it has a title to any thing like an exclusive predilection, in any country, ought to be admitted with great caution. That it is more productive than every other branch of Industry requires more evidence than has yet been given in support of that position. . . . ■ *To affirm, that the labour of the Manufacturer is unproductive, because he consumes as much of the produce of the land, as he adds value to the raw materials which he manufactures, is not better founded, than it would be to affirm, that the labour of the farmer, which furnishes materials to the manufacturer is unproductive, because he consumes an equal value of manufactured articles. Each furnishes a certain portion of the produce of his labor to the other. . . .*

Not only the wealth, but the independence and security of a Country, appear to be materially connected with the prosperity of manufactures. Every nation, with a view to those great objects, ought to endeavor to possess within itself all the essentials of national supply. These comprise the means of Subsistence, habitation, clothing, and defense.

The possession of these is necessary to the perfection of the body politic; to the safety as well as to the welfare of the society . . . the extreme embarrassments of the United States during the late War, from an incapacity of supplying themselves, are still matters of keen recollection. . . . ■

■ *Hamilton could not, of course, anticipate or predict the American Civil War of the 1860s, in which "adverse interests" between the North and the South played a major role.*

. . . It is not uncommon to meet with an opinion that though the promoting of manufactures may be the interest of a part of the Union, it is contrary to that of another part. The Northern & Southern regions are sometimes represented as having adverse interests in this respect. Those are called Manufacturing, these Agricultural states; and a species of opposition is imagined to exist between the Manufacturing and Agricultural interests. This idea . . . is the common error of the early periods of every country; but experience gradually dissipates it. . . . ■

Summary

After independence was declared, Americans faced the challenge of creating a new nation out of thirteen distinct states. Faced with enormous debt and still surrounded by real and potential enemies, the new nation's ability to survive seemed doubtful to many Americans and foreigners. As colonies became states, they drafted their own constitutions. Some put in place democratic forms of government whereas others built in more restrictive features such as high property qualifications for officeholding. The first national government, operating under the Articles of Confederation, reflected the states' strong desire to preserve their individual sovereignty. It also embodied the revolutionary generation's opposition to a strong centralized government with extensive powers. This Confederation government lacked basic powers: it could not raise taxes or regulate commerce, and its legislation required the unanimous approval of the states.

The Confederation could point to several achievements, however: it negotiated the peace treaty of 1783, and it established, through three Northwest Ordinances, the process by which territories achieved statehood on an equal footing with the original states. But with limited powers, the Confederation could not resolve the nation's financial problems, deal effectively with foreign nations, or ensure social order within its borders. Efforts to raise needed funds through the sale of western land resulted in renewed conflict with both the British and the Indians. Settlement on the southern frontier provoked retaliation by the Spanish. Barbary pirates seized American trading ships in the Mediterranean. Domestic violence erupted when Massachusetts farmers, hard hit by the postwar depression, rose up in revolt in Shays's Rebellion in 1786. By that time, many of the nation's elite political figures insisted that the system of national government had to be revised if the country wished to survive.

In the summer of 1787, Alexander Hamilton and other nationalists met in Philadelphia to consider a new constitution. The Constitution they produced, after long months of debate and compromise, steered a middle ground between a central government that was too powerful and one that was too weak. It established executive, legislative, and judicial branches, which could "check and balance" one another and thus safeguard the nation from tyranny. The new government was empowered both to raise taxes and regulate commerce. The new Constitution was ratified by the states in 1788 after intense battles between pro-Constitution forces, known as Federalists, and their Antifederalist adversaries. Federalist leaders such as Hamilton, Madison, and Jay campaigned tirelessly for ratification, convinced that the nation was in crisis and could not endure without the new government, and in time they prevailed. Soon after George Washington took office as the first president, serious differences in political opinion emerged. Alexander Hamilton's vision of a vigorous commercial and industrial nation came into conflict with Thomas Jefferson's hopes for an agrarian nation. These two factions disagreed over economic and foreign policy. The French Revolution intensified the divisions: while Hamilton argued against American support for the French in their war against England, Jefferson pressed the administration to align with America's fellow revolutionaries. Washington managed to steer a neutral course in this European conflict.

By the end of Washington's second term, the United States had expanded its borders, negotiated with Spain for access to the Mississippi River, and under Hamilton's guidance, established a national bank at the center of an economic system that promoted market-oriented growth. The country had survived domestic unrest and the development of political parties, which formed along largely sectional or regional lines. The departing Washington urged Americans to continue to cooperate and cautioned them not to allow competing visions of America's future to harm the new nation.

AMERICAN EXPANSION AND INDIAN LAND CESSIONS, TO 1800

Growth was a dominant characteristic of the United States during the late 1700s. As this map shows, population was becoming increasingly dense and pushing westward. At the same time, Indians were forced to withdraw, ceding large expanses of land, often under threat of violence.

BRITISH CANADA

Lake Superior

Lake Michigan

Lake Huron

MAINE
(Mass.)

St. Lawrence

VERMONT

1788
NEW YORK
Albany

Portsmouth
NEW HAMPSHIRE
Boston

Lake Ontario

1797 1788

1785
Hartford
New Haven

MASSACHUSETTS

Newport
RHODE ISLAND

Fort
Detroit

1788

Lake Erie

1784   1789

CONNECTICUT

New York

INDIANA
TERRITORY

TERRITORY
NORTH OF
OHIO RIVER

PENNSYLVANIA
Trenton
Philadelphia

NEW JERSEY

1795

Baltimore
Washington, D.C.

DELAWARE

FRENCH

Missouri

St. Louis
Vincennes

1795

Ohio

Frankfort

VIRGINIA

Richmond

MARYLAND

ATLANTIC
OCEAN

LOUISIANA

KENTUCKY

1775

1775

Arkansas

1785   1798   1791   1777

NORTH
CAROLINA   Raleigh

Mississippi

TENNESSEE

Tennessee

1798

1777

SOUTH
CAROLINA

NORTH AND CENTRAL AMERICA

RUSSIAN
CLAIM

TERRITORY
SOUTH
OF OHIO RIVER

GEORGIA   1790

Charleston

Savannah

DISPUTED

BRITISH
CLAIM

MISSISSIPPI TERRITORY

Natchez

1785

FRENCH
CLAIM

UNITED
STATES

SPANISH
POSSESSIONS

SPANISH
FLORIDA

SPANISH
CLAIM

*Gulf of
Mexico*

| 0 | 150 | 300 Km. |
| 0 | 150 | 300 Mi. |

**Population density per
square mile, 1800**

	90 or more		6–18
	45–90		2–6
	18–45		Unsettled areas

1788 Area and date of
Indian land cession

Timeline

1796
Washington retires

Adams elected

1798
Quasi-War

Alien and Sedition Acts

Kentucky and Virginia Resolutions

1801
Jefferson elected

1803 *Marbury v. Madison*

Louisiana Purchase

1804
Jefferson reelected

Lewis and Clark expedition

| 1770 | 1792 | 1794 | 1796 | 1798 | 1800 | 1802 | 1804 | 1806 |

1802 France invades Santo Domingo

1800 Spain cedes Louisiana to France

1791
Slave revolt in Santo Domingo

1799 Napoleon seizes power

1769–1795
British Empire expands into
Australia, Africa, Ceylon

1798 France invades Egypt

Second Coalition against France

The Early Republic, 1796–1804

American Expansion and Indian Land Cessions, to 1800

Using the map on the facing page, note the huge expanses of land that had come into the United States' possession and the enormous potential offered by French Louisiana, which would soon become part of the nation's public domain. What opportunities did the control of so much real estate offer to the young nation? What problems would the nation face, internally, from foreign sources, and from Native Americans as it sought to exploit this wealth?

Individual Choices

GEORGE LOGAN

The United States was caught up in a wave of patriotism when the French slighted President Adams's ambassadors in the XYZ affair. Federalists promoted a war against France, but George Logan chose to resist emotionalism and Federalist pressure by going to France to iron out the two nations' difficulties, thus ending the threat of war. *"George Logan" by Gilbert Stuart. Courtesy of the Historical Society of Pennsylvania Collection, Atwater Kent Museum of Philadelphia.*

George Logan

The very idea of the United States fighting a war presented a serious personal dilemma for George Logan. He was a loyal American with deep roots in the nation's history—his grandfather James Logan had been one of the first generation of pioneers in Pennsylvania. Like many descendants of Pennsylvania's first families, George was a Quaker and was morally opposed to war. His father, a conscientious objector during the Revolutionary War, had sent him to study medicine in Scotland and Paris while the war continued. Returning to the United States in 1780, George learned that his family was dead and that much of the considerable Logan estate had been destroyed.

Some of the family's landholdings had survived, but, Logan noted, his primary inheritance consisted of "piles of utterly depreciated paper currency." He turned to farming to support himself and then, in 1785, to politics, winning a seat in the Pennsylvania assembly. Ever a critic of Federalist economic and diplomatic strategies, he followed his friend Thomas Jefferson when the Republican faction became an opposition party.

By 1798, Logan seemed well on his way to recovering the fortune and prominence that the war had taken. But then the Federalists engineered a diplomatic crisis with France, and war again seemed inevitable. Recalling his father's frustration as the colonies were drawn into war in 1776, Logan made a fateful choice: he would risk his property, his reputation, even his life, to prevent another war.

Quietly Logan began selling off some of his land, accumulating cash to support a private peace effort. He then went to his friend Jefferson, who gave him letters of introduction to important people in France. Federalist agents learned of Logan's aims and put him under surveillance, but he slipped their noose and sailed for Germany during the summer of 1798. There he met with the marquis de Lafayette (see pages 167 and 203), who used his influence to get Logan into France and arrange an audience with French foreign minister Talleyrand.

Facing a newly formed coalition of antirevolutionary European powers including Russia, Britain, Austria, the Ottoman Empire, Portugal, Naples, and the Vatican, the last thing Talleyrand wanted was to further alienate the only other revolutionary and democratic nation in the world. Meeting with Talleyrand and other French officials in early August, Logan capitalized on this fact. He told them that most Americans supported democracy in France but warned that French seizure of American ships and other hostile actions were undermining that support. He assured them that if the French released the American sailors they were holding and ended the embargo placed on American ships, American popular support would turn back to France and force the Federalist government to end the Quasi-War. Talleyrand was convinced, assuring Logan that if Adams would send a new, official peace delegation, France would be happy to meet with it.

Logan's news was warmly received by his fellow Republicans and, surprisingly, by President Adams, who ignored his party's advice and immediately sought peace with France. Within a year, American ambassador William Vans Murray and Napoleon finalized the peace Logan had initiated. Logan had succeeded. Choosing to risk all for peace, he overcame official constraints and averted a war.

Outraged Federalists in Congress responded by passing the "Logan Act," which imposed a fine of $5,000 and a three-year prison term on any American citizen who conducted a private diplomatic mission to a foreign government. Passed after Logan's meetings with Talleyrand, the Logan Act could not be used to punish the courageous Quaker from Pennsylvania for his interference in 1798. But Logan might have been prosecuted under its provisions when, in 1810, he sailed to England in an effort to avert a war with that nation. This time Logan failed: war between the United States and England finally broke out in 1812. He then retired to his farm in Philadelphia, his name immortalized only in the federal law designed to punish the moral integrity he personified so well.

INTRODUCTION

That George Logan would undertake such a novel and highly risky venture as trying to negotiate a peace between the United States and France is a measure both of his personal Quaker faith and the nation's political state. George Washington had lent stability to a new and uncertain government, but his retirement reopened many of the divisions that had arisen during its formation. And Washington's replacement, John Adams, seemed incapable of calming these anxieties. Under his watch, the United States became involved in an undeclared war with France and saw its international reputation consistently decline.

Adams also seemed incapable of resolving deep divisions at home. Led by Alexander Hamilton, radical Federalists had tried to undermine the electoral process in 1796 and then used the war crisis to wage an internal war against their political enemies. Far from succeeding in the destruction of their critics, these Federalist efforts actually helped to crystallize opposition, giving Hamilton's key rival, Thomas Jefferson, a forum from which to assault the party in power. In 1800 these efforts backfired on the Federalists: despite trying to rig the election again, Federalists were soundly defeated in the national election and turned out of office.

Assuming the presidency in 1801, Jefferson ushered in a new era in American politics. Though there were strong undercurrents of opposition, even within his own party, Jefferson instituted a series of reforms that would launch the country on a heady, freewheeling adventure of continental expansion and global trade. His secretary of the Treasury, Albert Gallatin, implemented radical tax cuts and equally radical cuts in government spending. At the same time, Jefferson waged an aggressive foreign policy designed to restore American international trading and win new territory from the European powers that still owned large tracts along the nation's borders. His successes could be measured by a mounting federal Treasury surplus, increased national income, and expanding borders.

Under Jefferson's leadership most Americans saw significant improvement in their everyday lives, and the nation became increasingly optimistic. But for many, the promise in Jefferson's America was not as universal as it appeared. For women, Native Americans, and African Americans, life undoubtedly improved and opportunities certainly expanded, but underlying prejudices and rigid codes of public behavior prevented their full realization. Contradictions shot through the whole of Jeffersonian America, counterbalancing the enthusiastic optimism and giving peculiar shape to national life.

Conflict in the Adams Administration

- How did diplomatic affairs in Europe affect Americans in the closing years of the eighteenth century?

- How did Federalists manipulate the crisis with France in 1798 for their own political advantage?

- What steps did Republicans take to counter Federalist manipulations?

Retiring president George Washington spoke for many in 1796 when he warned of "the baneful effects of the spirit of party" in his Farewell Address. Men like Washington believed in the ideal of republican citizenship, of sacrificing personal interest for the good of the republic. To such men, all political ideas that did not correspond with their vision of the republic's welfare were dangerous, even traitorous. Strong Federalists like Hamilton were sure that the Republican faction growing up around Jefferson constituted such a danger and wanted desperately to destroy it. For their part, Republicans were equally sure that Federalists were motivated by no higher motives than personal interest. And having spent several years organizing for a confrontation, Republicans were eager to unseat the politicians responsible for suppressing the Whiskey Rebellion and for tying the United States diplomatically to England. As the two groups prepared to face off, however, new factional lines opened.

The Split Election of 1796

As the broadly accepted leader of the opposition to Hamilton and his policies, Thomas Jefferson was the Republicans' logical choice to represent them in the presidential election in 1796. Most people at the time were not surprised that Republicans chose **Aaron Burr,** a brilliant young New York attorney and member of the Senate, to balance the ticket. Though many years apart in age and from vastly different backgrounds, both Jefferson and Burr were veterans of the revolutionary struggles in 1776 and outspoken champions of democracy.

Although he styled himself a spokesman for the common man, Burr definitely was not one—his father and uncle were presidents of Princeton and Yale Colleges, respectively, and his grandfather was the famous evangelical minister Jonathan Edwards (see page 103). During the Revolutionary War, Burr accepted a commission in the Continental Army, where he found common cause with the radical democrats who had formed the Sons of Liberty (see page 126). By 1784, he had used his political connections and backing from the Sons of Liberty to win a place in the New York state assembly. In 1791 the New York Sons of Liberty, now calling themselves the Society of St. Tammany, maneuvered Burr's election to the U.S. Senate.

Meanwhile, Jefferson had returned from Paris in 1789 to join Washington's cabinet as secretary of state. He was deeply disturbed to find that the once-unified revolutionary forces he knew from 1776 had divided into what he called a "republican side" and a "kingly one," and he complained that "a preference of kingly over republican government was evidently the favorite sentiment." His own preferences put him in

This miniature portrait of John Adams painted by John Trumbull in 1792 shows the stable (some said stodgy) statesman that Americans turned to after George Washington chose to step down as president. *"John Adams" by John Trumbull, 1792. Yale University Art Gallery, Trumbull Collection.*

league with, and eventually on the same ticket as, Burr and his associates in the Society of St. Tammany, who were equally dismayed.

The apparent unity among Republicans contrasted sharply with divisions in the Federalist faction. Most Federalists assumed that Vice President Adams would succeed Washington as president, but Hamilton and some other hardcore party members doubted the New Englander's loyalty to the party. They favored **Thomas Pinckney** of South Carolina. The younger son of a prestigious South Carolina planter, Pinckney had been a prominent military figure during the Revolution and became governor of South Carolina during the late 1780s. He emerged as a major political force when he successfully negotiated the treaty with Spain that opened the Mississippi River to American commerce. This coup won Pinckney the unreserved

Aaron Burr New York lawyer and vice-presidential candidate in 1796; he became Thomas Jefferson's vice president in 1801 after the House of Representatives broke a deadlock in the Electoral College.

Thomas Pinckney South Carolina politician and diplomat who was an unsuccessful Federalist candidate for president in 1796.

Chronology

Partisan Tension and Jeffersonian Optimism

1796 George Washington's Farewell Address
First contested presidential election: John Adams
elected president, Thomas Jefferson vice president

1797 XYZ affair

1798 Quasi-War with France begins
Alien and Sedition Acts
Kentucky and Virginia Resolutions
George Logan's mission to France

1799 Fries's Rebellion
Napoleon seizes control in France

1800 Convention of Mortefontaine ends Quasi-War
Jefferson and Aaron Burr tie in Electoral College
Spain gives Louisiana back to France

1801 Jefferson elected president in House of
Representatives; Burr vice president
Judiciary Act of 1801
John Marshall becomes chief justice

War begins between American navy ships and
Barbary pirates
Outdoor revival meeting at Cane Ridge, Kentucky

1802 Congress repeals all internal taxes
Congress repeals Judiciary Act of 1801
French invade Santo Domingo

1803 *Marbury v. Madison*
Impeachment of Justices John Pickering and
Samuel Chase
Louisiana Purchase

1804 Twelfth Amendment ratified
Jefferson reelected

1804–1806 Lewis and Clark expedition

1806–1807 Zebulon Pike's expedition

1816 African Methodist Episcopal Church formed in
Philadelphia

admiration of both southerners and westerners (see page 205). Hamilton supported him, though, both because Pinckney was less associated with radical causes than was Adams and because Hamilton felt he could exercise more influence over the mild-mannered South Carolinian than he could over the stiff-necked Yankee.

Most Federalists, however, aligned behind the old warhorse from Massachusetts. A descendant of New England Calvinists (see page 27), Adams was a man of strong principles, fighting for what he believed was right despite anyone's contrary opinion. Though a thorough Federalist, he remained Thomas Jefferson's close friend: both he and his wife, Abigail, maintained a spirited correspondence with the red-haired Virginian during his stay in Paris. Like Washington, Adams was seen by many old revolutionaries as above politics, as a **statesman** whose conscience and integrity would help the new nation avoid the pitfalls of **factionalism.**

It was precisely Adams's statesmanship that led Hamilton to oppose him; the head of the radical Federalists sought to rig the election against Adams. According to the Constitution, each member of the Electoral College could cast votes for any two candidates; the highest vote getter became president, and the runner-up became vice president. Hamilton urged Pinckney supporters to cast only one vote—for Pinckney—so that Adams could not get enough votes to win the presidency. But Hamilton underestimated Pinckney's unpopularity in the North, Adams's unacceptability to southerners, and Jefferson's growing popularity among northern dissidents. Nor did the Treasury secretary expect Adams supporters to learn of the plot; when they did, they withheld votes from Pinckney to make up for the votes being withheld from Adams.

Because of the squabbling within the Federalist faction, Jefferson received the votes of disgruntled Federalist electors as well as electors within Republican ranks. He thus ended up with more votes than

statesman A political leader who acts out of concern for the public good and not out of self-interest.

factionalism In politics, the emergence of various self-interested parties (factions) that compete to impose their own views onto either a larger political party or the nation at large.

Pinckney—and only three fewer than Adams. So the nation emerged from the first truly contested presidential election with a split administration: the president and vice president belonged to different factions and held opposing political philosophies.

Never known for charm, subtlety, or willingness to compromise, Adams was ill suited to lead a deeply divided nation. Although he disavowed any monarchist sentiments in his inaugural address, the new president's aloofness did little to put Republicans' fears to rest, and he made few **conciliatory** gestures. In fact, from Washington's cabinet Adams retained Oliver Wolcott, James McHenry, and Timothy Pickering, all of whom were Hamilton men through and through. This move thoroughly angered Republicans, who had hoped Hamilton's influence would wane now that he had retired from government service to practice law. And then Adams further stung his foes by withholding an expected diplomatic appointment from James Madison. Clearly the factions were still alive and well and locked in conflict. This disunity enticed interested parties both at home and abroad to try to undermine Adams's authority and influence.

XYZ: The Power of Patriotism

One group seeking to take advantage of the divisions in the United States was the revolutionary government in France. America's minister to France, James Monroe, sympathized with the French cause, but the pro-British impact of Jay's Treaty (see pages 205–206) and the antirevolutionary rhetoric adopted by Federalists led the French to suspect American sincerity. During the election of 1796, France sought to influence American voting by actively favoring the Republican candidates, threatening to terminate diplomatic relations if the vocally pro-British Federalists won. True to its word, the revolutionary government of France broke off relations with the United States as soon as Adams was elected.

Angry at the French, Adams retaliated in 1796 by calling home the sympathetic Monroe and replacing him with devout Federalist **Charles Cotesworth Pinckney,** the older brother of Hamilton's favored candidate for the presidency. The French refused to acknowledge the hyper-Federalist Pinckney as ambassador and began seizing American ships. Faced with what was fast becoming a diplomatic crisis, and possibly a military one as well, Adams wisely chose to pursue two courses simultaneously. Asserting that the United States would not be "humiliated under a colonial spirit of fear and a sense of inferiority," he

Americans saw the XYZ affair as proof of European corruption standing in sharp contrast to American virtue. In this 1798 engraving by Charles Williams, a maidenly America is flattered to distraction by courtly Europeans while members of the French Directory prepare to plunder her wealth. *Lilly Library.*

pressed Congress in 1797 to build up America's military defenses. At the same time, he dispatched John Marshall and Elbridge Gerry to join Pinckney in Paris, where they were to arrange a peaceful settlement of the two nations' differences.

Playing a complicated diplomatic game, French foreign minister **Charles Maurice de Talleyrand-Périgord** declined to receive Pinckney and the peace delegation. As weeks passed, three businessmen residing in Paris, whose international trading profits stood at risk, offered themselves as go-betweens in solving the stalemate. According to Pinckney's report, these men suggested that if the Americans were willing to pay a bribe to key French officials and guarantee an American loan of several million dollars to

conciliatory   Striving to overcome distrust or to regain good will.

Charles Cotesworth Pinckney   Federalist politician and brother of Thomas Pinckney; he was sent on a diplomatic mission to Paris in 1796 during a period of unfriendly relations between France and the United States.

Charles Maurice de Talleyrand-Périgord   French foreign minister appointed by the revolutionary government in 1797; he later aided Napoleon Bonaparte's overthrow of that government and served as his foreign minister.

France, the three businessmen would be able to get them a hearing. Offended at such treatment, Pinckney broke off diplomatic relations. Reporting the affair to President Adams, Pinckney refused to name the would-be go-betweens, calling them only "X," "Y," and "Z."

Americans' response to the **XYZ affair** was overwhelming. France's diplomatic slight seemed a slap in the face to a new nation seeking international respect. In Philadelphia, people paraded in the streets to protest French arrogance. The crowds chanted Pinckney's reported response: "No, no, not a sixpence!" This wave of patriotism overcame the spirit of division that had plagued the Adams administration, giving the president a virtually unified Congress and country. In the heat of the moment, Adams pressed for increased military forces, and in short order Congress created the Department of the Navy and appropriated money to start building a fleet of warships. Then, on July 7, 1798, Congress rescinded all treaties with France and authorized privateering against French ships. Congress also created a standing army of twenty thousand troops and ordered that the militia be expanded to thirty thousand men. Washington added his prestige to the effort by coming out of retirement to lead the new army, with Hamilton as his second-in-command. Although running sea battles between French and American ships resulted in the sinking or capture of many vessels on both sides, Congress shied away from actually declaring war, which led to the conflict being labeled the **Quasi-War.**

The Home Front in the Quasi-War

Still disappointed over their failure to steal the presidential election, radical Federalists immediately seized upon the war as a means to crush their political enemies. In Congress, they began referring to Jefferson and his supporters as the "French Party" and accused the vice president and his faction of treason whenever they advised a moderate course. Arguing that the presence of this "French Party" constituted a danger to national security, congressional Federalists proposed a series of new laws to destroy all opposition to their political agenda.

One source of opposition was **naturalized** American citizens. The revolutionary promises of "life, liberty, and the pursuit of happiness" had drawn many immigrants to the United States. Disappointed by Hamilton's approach to government and economics,

they were drawn to Jefferson's political rhetoric—especially his stress on equal opportunity and his attacks on entrenched elites. In 1798 Federalists in Congress passed three acts designed to counter political activities by immigrants. The Naturalization Act extended the residency requirement for citizenship from five to fourteen years. The Alien Act authorized the president to deport any foreigner he judged "dangerous to the peace and safety of the United States." The Alien Enemies Act permitted the president to imprison or banish any foreigner he considered dangerous during a national emergency. The Naturalization Act was designed to prevent recent immigrants from supporting the Republican cause by barring them from the political process. The other two acts served as a constant reminder that the president or his agents could arbitrarily imprison or deport any resident alien who stepped out of line.

The other source of support for Jefferson was a partisan Republican press, which attempted to balance the biased news and criticism spewing forth from Federalist news sources. To counter this, congressional Federalists passed the Sedition Act. In addition to outlawing conspiracies to block the enforcement of federal laws, the Sedition Act prohibited the publication or utterance of any criticism of the government or its officials that would bring either "into contempt or disrepute." In the words of one Federalist newspaper, "It is patriotism to write in favour of our government, it is **sedition** to write against it." Federalists brandished the law against all kinds of criticism directed toward either the government or the president, including perfectly innocent political editorials. Not surprisingly, most of the defendants in the fifteen cases brought by federal authorities under the Sedition Act were prominent Republican newspaper editors.

XYZ affair A diplomatic incident in which American envoys to France were told that the United States would have to loan France money and bribe government officials as a precondition for negotiation.

Quasi-War Diplomatic crisis triggered by the XYZ affair; fighting occurred between the United States and France between the early summer of 1798 and the official end of the conflict in September 1800, but neither side issued a formal declaration of war.

naturalized Granted full citizenship (after having been born in a foreign country).

sedition Conduct or language inciting rebellion against the authority of a state.

Republicans complained that the **Alien and Sedition Acts** violated the Bill of Rights, but Congress and the federal judiciary, controlled as they were by Hamilton loyalists, paid no attention. Dissidents had little choice but to take their political case to the state governments, which they did in the fall of 1798. One statement, drafted by Madison, came before the Virginia legislature, and another, by Jefferson, was considered in Kentucky.

Madison and Jefferson based their **Virginia and Kentucky Resolutions** on the Tenth Amendment, contending that powers not specifically granted to the federal government under the Constitution or reserved to the people in the Bill of Rights fell to the states. By passing laws such as the Alien and Sedition Acts that were not explicitly permitted in the text of the Constitution, Congress had violated the states' rights. The two authors differed, however, in the responses they prescribed for states to take. For his part, Madison asserted that when the majority of states agreed that a federal law had violated their Tenth Amendment rights, they could collectively overrule federal authority. But Jefferson went further, arguing that each individual state had the "natural right" to **interpose** its own authority to protect its own rights and the rights of its citizens.

The Virginia and Kentucky Resolutions passed in their respective state legislatures, but no other states followed suit. Even within Kentucky and Virginia, great disagreement arose over how far state authority should extend. Nevertheless, this response to the Federalists' use of federal power brought the disputed relationship between federal law and **states' rights** into national prominence.

Another bone of contention was the methods used to finance the Quasi-War with France and the impact these methods had on various groups of Americans. Consistent with Hamilton's views on finance, tariffs and excises were to be the primary source of revenue, and they had the greatest impact on people who needed manufactured or imported items but had little hard cash. In addition, Federalists imposed a tax on land, hitting cash-poor farmers especially hard. In 1799 farmers in Northampton County, Pennsylvania, refused to pay the tax and began harassing tax collectors. Several tax resisters were arrested, but an auctioneer named John Fries, himself a Federalist, raised an armed force to break them out of jail. Later, federal troops sent by Adams to suppress what Federalists characterized as **Fries's Rebellion** arrested Fries and two of his associates. Charged with treason, the three were tried in federal court, found guilty, and condemned to death.

Settlement with France

The Federalists' seeming overreaction to French provocation and domestic protest alienated increasing numbers of Americans. Adams himself was eager to end the conflict, and when a private American citizen, George Logan, sent news from France that Foreign Minister Talleyrand was asking that a new American delegation be sent, Adams, who had grown impatient with the radical Federalist's lack of statesmanship, seized this opportunity to end the Quasi-War and regain control of his party. Telling the Federalist-dominated Congress that he would give them the details later, Adams instructed the American minister to the Netherlands, William Vans Murray, to go immediately to Paris. As rumors of negotiations began to circulate, Hamilton and his supporters became furious, all but accusing Adams of treason. This gave the president the ammunition he needed: he fired Pickering, Wolcott, and McHenry, Hamilton's primary supporters in his cabinet, and then embarrassed the Federalist judiciary by granting a presidential pardon to John Fries and his fellow Pennsylvania rebels.

Adams's diplomatic appeal to France was well timed. When Murray and his delegation arrived in Paris in November 1799, they found that whatever belligerence might have existed toward the United States had been swept away. On November 9, 1799,

---

Alien and Sedition Acts   Collectively, the four acts—Alien Act, Alien Enemies Act, Naturalization Act, and Sedition Act—passed by Congress in 1798 designed to prevent immigrants from participating in politics and to silence the anti-Federalist press.

Virginia and Kentucky Resolutions   Statements that the Virginia and Kentucky legislatures issued in 1798 in response to the Alien and Sedition Acts; they asserted the right of states to overrule the federal government.

interpose   To place a barrier between two objects or forces; to Jefferson, the principle of interposition meant that states had the right to use their sovereign power as a barrier between the federal government and the states' citizens when the natural rights of those citizens were at risk.

states' rights   The political position in favor of limiting federal power to allow the greatest possible self-government by the individual states.

Fries's Rebellion   A tax revolt by Pennsylvania citizens in 1799 that was suppressed by federal forces; leader John Fries was condemned to death for treason but received a presidential pardon from John Adams.

Napoleon Bonaparte had overthrown the government that was responsible for the XYZ affair. Napoleon was more interested in establishing an empire in Europe than in continuing an indecisive conflict with the United States. After some negotiation, Murray and Napoleon drew up and signed the Convention of Mortefontaine, ending the Quasi-War on September 30, 1800.

The "Revolution of 1800"

- What did Thomas Jefferson mean by the statement "Every difference of opinion is not a difference of principles"?
- How did Federalists respond to losing the election of 1800? What does this response reveal about their political attitudes?
- How did Jefferson's vision for America differ from that of Hamilton, Adams, and other Federalists?

According to the partisan press, the political situation in 1800 was as simple as the contrast between the personalities of the major presidential candidates. The Republican press characterized Adams as a monarchist and a **spendthrift,** charging that Adams's efforts to expand the powers of the federal government were really attempts to rob citizens of freedom and turn the United States back into a colony of England. In contrast, the Republican press characterized Jefferson as a man of the people, sensitive to the appeals of southern and western agricultural groups who felt perpetually ignored or abused by northeastern Federalists and their constituents. According to Federalist newspapers, however, Vice President Jefferson was a dangerous radical and an atheist, a man who shared French tastes for radical politics, **dandyism,** and immorality. In the eyes of the Federalists, Adams was a man whose policies and steady-handed administration would bring stability and prosperity, qualities that appealed to manufacturers and merchants in New England, as well as to Calvinists and other supporters of a conservative social and political order. The rhetoric became so hateful that even Adams and Jefferson got caught up in it—the old friends stopped speaking to each other. Nearly twenty years would pass before they renewed their friendship.

The Lesser of Republican Evils

As the election of 1800 approached, the split between the Adams and Hamilton wings of the Federalist faction widened. Both agreed on the necessity of dumping Jefferson as vice president, putting forward Charles Cotesworth Pinckney, hero of the XYZ affair, to replace

him. But Adams's behavior in the wake of George Logan's mission to France had angered the radicals; they now wanted Adams to be gone as well. Having gotten Pinckney into the Electoral College balloting, Hamilton again tried to steal the 1800 election. As before, he advised delegates to withhold votes, but this time he engaged in direct lobbying, even writing a pamphlet in which he questioned Adams's suitability for the presidency.

Hamilton's methods backfired again: Federalists cast one more vote for Adams than for Pinckney. But more important, Hamilton's scheming and his faction's consistent promanufacturing stance had so alienated southern Federalists that many chose to support Jefferson. With Jefferson pulling in the southern vote and his running mate—Burr again—pulling in the craftsmen and small-farm vote in New York, the Republicans outscored the Federalists by 16 votes in the Electoral College. But that still did not settle the election. Burr and Jefferson won the same number of electoral votes (see Map 8.1). The tie threw the election into the House of Representatives, which was still stocked with hard-line Federalists elected during the Quasi-War hysteria in 1798.

Undoubtedly many Federalists in the House wished they could overturn the election of 1800 altogether, but the Constitution specifically barred them from doing so. Instead, they faced the task of choosing between two men whom most of them viewed as being dangerous radicals bent on destroying the Federalists' hard work. Indecision was plain: in ballot after ballot over six grueling days early in 1801, neither Jefferson nor Burr could win the necessary majority.

In addition to exhaustion and frustration, two things finally combined to break the deadlock. First, Hamilton convinced several Federalists that even though Jefferson's rhetoric was dangerous, the Virginian was a gentleman of property and integrity, whereas Burr was "the most dangerous man of the community." Second, Virginia and Pennsylvania mobilized their militias, intent on preventing a "legislative usurpation"

Napoleon Bonaparte   General who took control of the French government in November 1799, at the end of France's revolutionary period; he eventually proclaimed himself emperor of France and conquered much of the continent of Europe.

spendthrift   A person who spends money recklessly or wastefully.

dandyism   Dressing and behaving in an overly ornate and flamboyant fashion.

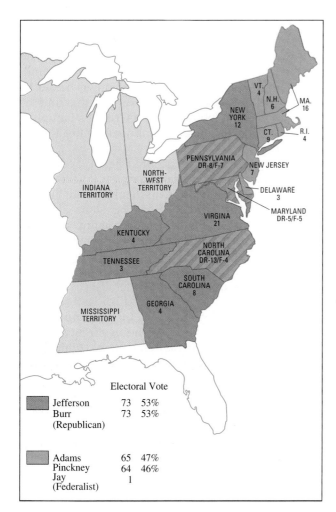

Electoral Vote

Jefferson	73	53%
Burr	73	53%
(Republican)		

Adams	65	47%
Pinckney	64	46%
Jay	1	
(Federalist)		

MAP 8.1 Election of 1800 The political partnership between Thomas Jefferson and Aaron Burr allowed the Republicans to unseat Federalist John Adams in the election of 1800. As this map shows, only New England voted as a bloc for the Federalist, while Burr's political home, New York, went entirely to Jefferson.

of the popular will. As Delaware senator James Bayard described the situation, Federalists had to admit "that we must risk the Constitution and a Civil War or take Mr. Jefferson." Finally, on the thirty-sixth ballot, on February 17, 1801, Jefferson emerged a winner.

Federalists and Republicans agreed about very little, but the threat of civil war frightened both factions equally. Not long after Jefferson's election, both parties aligned briefly to pass the **Twelfth Amendment** to the Constitution, which requires separate balloting in the Electoral College for president and vice president, thereby preventing deadlocks like the one that nearly wrecked the nation in 1800. The new electoral proce-

dure led to new sorts of political intrigues, but the manipulation that Hamilton attempted was no longer possible after the Twelfth Amendment was ratified in 1804.

Federalist Defenses and a Loyal Opposition

The Federalists had outmaneuvered themselves in the election of 1800, but they were not about to leave office without erecting some defenses for the political and economic machinery they had constructed. The Federalist-controlled judiciary, which had proved its clout during the controversy over the Alien and Sedition Acts, appeared to offer the strongest bulwark to prevent Republicans from tampering with the Constitution. Thus, during their last days in office, the Federalist **lame ducks** in Congress passed the **Judiciary Act of 1801,** which created sixteen new federal judgeships, six additional **circuit courts,** and a massive structure of **federal marshals** and clerks. President Adams then rushed to fill all these positions with loyal Federalists, signing appointments right up to midnight on his last day in office. The appointments came in such large numbers and so late in the day that **John Marshall,** Adams's secretary of state, was unable to deliver all the appointment letters before his own term ran out. But Marshall did deliver one letter promptly: the one addressed to himself, making him chief justice of the Supreme Court.

Twelfth Amendment Constitutional amendment, ratified in 1804, that provides for separate balloting in the Electoral College for president and vice president.

lame duck An officeholder who has failed to win, or is ineligible for, reelection but whose term in office has not yet ended.

Judiciary Act of 1801 Law that the Federalist Congress passed to increase the number of federal courts and judicial positions; President Adams rushed to fill these positions with Federalists before his term ended.

circuit court A court of appeals that has the power to review and either uphold or overturn decisions made by lower courts; in terms of authority, these stand between federal district courts and the Supreme Court.

federal marshal A law enforcement officer who works directly for the federal district court; each district court has one marshal, who in turn employs a staff of deputies to carry out orders from the court.

John Marshall Virginia lawyer and politician whom President Adams made chief justice of the Supreme Court; his legal decisions helped shape the role of the Supreme Court in American government.

Painted while he was at the height of his power and influence, this portrait of Chief Justice John Marshall captures the jurist's imposing presence—he would dominate the Supreme Court and American constitutional law for over thirty years after his appointment in 1801, setting many precedents that remain in force today. *Boston Athenaeum.*

Considering the ill will evident in the Alien and Sedition Acts and the presidential electioneering, Jefferson's inaugural address was oddly conciliatory. "We are all Republicans; we are all Federalists," Jefferson said, seeming to abandon partisan politics and align himself with those who had recently labeled him a "brandy-soaked defamer of churches" and a "contemptible hypocrite." In his mind, all Americans shared the same fundamental principles—the principles of 1776. But even Jefferson considered the election of 1800 a revolution—"as real a revolution in the principles of our government as that of 1776 was in its form."

Jefferson was right in many respects about the revolutionary nature of the election of 1800. Although his inaugural address preached kinship between Federalists and Republicans, the new president repeatedly criticized his opponents for their lack of faith in democracy and the American people. Unlike the Federalists, Jefferson was unalterably opposed to using the power of government against those who opposed his political position. "If there be any among us who would wish to dissolve this Union or to change its republican form," he said, "let them stand undisturbed as monuments of the safety with which error of opinion may be tolerated, where reason is left free to combat it."

As a result of Jefferson's reassuring address, the nation began to share the president's view that "every difference of opinion is not a difference of principles." Even extreme Federalists such as Fisher Ames came to understand that a "party is an association of honest men for honest purposes, and when the State falls into bad hands, is the only efficient defense; a champion who never flinches, a watchman who never sleeps." Ames went on to describe how a loyal **opposition party** should behave. "We are not to revile or abuse magistrates, or lie even for good cause," he said. "We must act as good citizens, using only truth, and argument, and zeal to impress them." With parties such as these, a system of loyal opposition could become a permanent part of a republican government without risk to security or freedom. And in keeping with the two-party spirit and Jefferson's philosophical commitment to free speech, Congress let the Sedition Act and the Alien Acts expire in 1801 and 1802 and did not seek to replace them. It also repealed the Naturalization Act, replacing its fourteen-year probationary interval with a five-year naturalization period.

Confident in Americans' ability to reason, Jefferson outlined a plan for a "wise and frugal government" that would seek "equal and exact justice to all men of whatever state or persuasion, religious or political." He would, he said, support state governments "in all their rights" but would not tear down the federal structure or fail to pay its debts.

Jefferson's Vision for America

Jefferson had a strong, positive vision for the nation, and the party made every effort to put his policies

opposition party   A political party opposed to the party or government in power.

It Matters

The "Revolution of 1800"

Beginning with debates over the ratification of the Constitution and continuing with ever-increasing stridency through the Quasi-War, fears over the disloyalty of opposition party members set the tone for all political discourse in the infant United States. For example, in 1798, Representative John Rutledge shouted from the House floor that all who were critical of the Federalist administration "believe it to be their duty to do all in their power to overturn the whole system, to effect which, they may think a French army and a French invasion necessary." To which Republican John Nicholas replied: "More evil is to be apprehended in this country from the votaries of despotism, than from the votaries of France," accusing Federalists of seeking to "subvert all the liberties of our country." Yet despite this violent—and heartfelt—rhetoric, Federalist leaders like Alexander Hamilton came to agree with Jefferson that "every difference of opinion is not a difference of principles," and peacefully turned the reins of government over to the Republicans in 1800. This was the real "Revolution of 1800": the creation of the two-party political tradition that continues to allow the peaceful transit of power through elections rather than fostering foreign invasion or subverting liberties to put forward a political agenda.

into effect. He embraced a specific notion of proper political, economic, and social behavior. The greatest dangers to a republic, he believed, were (1) high population density and the social evils it generated and (2) the concentration of money and power in the hands of a few. Accordingly, Jefferson wanted to steer America away from the large-scale, publicly supported industry so dear to Hamilton and toward an economy founded on yeoman farmers—men who owned their own land, produced their own food, and were beholden to no one. Such men, Jefferson believed, could make political decisions based solely on pure reason and good sense.

But Jefferson was not naive. He knew Americans would continue to demand the comforts and luxuries found in industrial societies. His solution was simple. In America's vast lands, he said, a nation of farmers could produce so much food that "its surplus [could] go to nourish the now perishing births of Europe, who in return would manufacture and send us in exchange our clothes and other comforts." Overpopulation and **urbanization**—the twin causes of corruption in Europe—would not occur in America, for here, Jefferson said, "the immense extent of uncultivated and fertile lands enables every one who will labor, to marry young, and to raise a family of any size."

Making such a system work, however, would require a radical change in economic policy. The government would have to let businesses make their own decisions and succeed or fail in a marketplace free of government interference. In an economy with absolutely free trade and an open marketplace, the iron law of **supply and demand** would determine the cost of goods and services. This view of the economy was a direct assault on mercantilist notions of governments controlling prices and restricting trade to benefit the nation-state.

Jefferson believed that, given the shortage of raw materials and foodstuffs in war-torn and overcrowded Europe and its oversupply of manufactured items, free trade in a truly open international economy would benefit the United States. If the European nations could be convinced to drop trade restrictions and let the marketplace decide the value of goods, the principles of supply and demand would ensure profits for American producers and shippers.

Republicanism in Action

■ How did Republicans deal with the defenses that Federalists put in place in 1801? What successes did they have?

■ What policies did Jefferson pursue to carry out his vision for the country? What obstacles did he encounter?

When Jefferson assumed office, he ushered a new spirit into national politics and the presidency. A combination of circumstances moved him to lead a

urbanization The growth of cities in a nation or region and the shifting of the population from rural to urban areas.

supply and demand The two factors that determine price in an economy based on private property: (1) how much of a commodity is available (supply) and (2) how many people want it (demand).

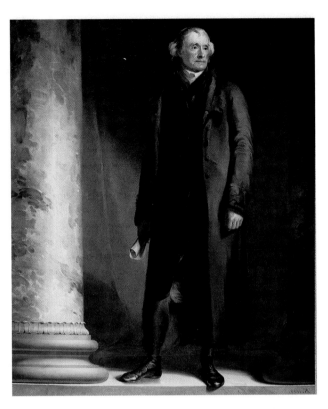

Suffering a lifelong sensitivity to cold as well as a dislike for formality, Thomas Jefferson usually chose to dress practically, in fairly plain clothes that kept him warm. This 1822 portrait by Thomas Sully captures the former president in his customary greatcoat, unadorned suit, and well-worn boots. *"Thomas Jefferson" by Thomas Sully. West Point Museum, United States Military Academy, West Point, N.Y.*

much simpler life than his predecessors in office had led. For one thing, he was the first president to be inaugurated in the new national capital, the still largely uncompleted Washington City, which afforded quite different and much more limited **amenities.** Washington lacked the taverns, **salons,** and entertaining social circles that both previous capitals, New York and Philadelphia, had offered. Personal preferences also moved him in a simpler direction. He refused, for example, to ride in a carriage, choosing to go by horseback through Washington's muddy and rutted streets. He continued to give parties as he had done in Paris, but he sat his guests at a round table so that no one might be seen as more important than the others. He abandoned the fashion of wearing a wig, letting his red hair stand out, and he sometimes entertained with startling informality, wearing frayed slippers and work clothes.

But this show of simplicity and his conciliatory inaugural address were somewhat misleading. Jeffer-

son was a hardworking politician and administrator whose main objective was to turn the nation around with all possible speed. He quickly launched a program to revamp the American economy and give the United States a place in the international community. Along the way, he captured many Americans' affection and their political loyalty but also alienated those who did not share his vision or who lacked his zeal.

Assault on Federalist Defenses

Aware of the purpose behind the Judiciary Act of 1801 and Adams's midnight appointments, Republicans chose to wage an aggressive partisan war to reverse Federalist control of the justice system. In January 1802, Republicans in Congress proposed the repeal of the 1801 Judiciary Act, arguing that the new circuit courts were outrageously expensive and unnecessary. Federalists countered that if Congress repealed the act, it would in effect be terminating judges for reasons other than the "high crimes and misdemeanors" mentioned in the Constitution, thereby violating the separation of powers. Congress proceeded anyway, replacing the Judiciary Act of 1801 with the Judiciary Act of 1802, and awaited the response of the Federalist courts.

The **constitutionality** of the new Judiciary Act was never tested, but the power of the judicial branch to interpret and enforce federal law did become a major issue the following year. On taking office, Jefferson's secretary of state, James Madison, held back the appointment letters that John Marshall had been unable to deliver before the expiration of his term. One jilted appointee was William Marbury, who was to have been **justice of the peace** for the newly created District of Columbia (see page 199). Marbury, with the support of his party, filed suit in the Supreme Court.

amenities Conveniences, comforts, and services.
salon A gathering place, generally in a private home, where people came together to discuss their common interests; in the eighteenth and early nineteenth centuries, these were often the places where politicians gathered to discuss philosophy and policy issues.
constitutionality Accordance with the principles or provisions of the Constitution.
justice of the peace The lowest level of judge in some state court systems, usually responsible for hearing small claims and minor criminal cases; because Washington, D.C., is a federal territory rather than a state, the justice of the peace for that district is a federal appointee.

Marbury v. Madison was Chief Justice Marshall's first major case, and in it he proved his political as well as his judicial ingenuity. Marshall was certain that the Judiciary Act of 1789 required Madison to deliver the appointment letter, but the chief justice was keenly aware that if he ordered Madison to deliver it and Madison refused, the Court did not have the power to enforce the order. In such a direct confrontation between the executive and judicial branches, Marshall was sure to lose. Rather than risking a serious blow to the dignity of the Supreme Court, Marshall ruled in 1803 that the Constitution contained no provision for the Supreme Court to issue such orders as the Judiciary Act of 1789 required and that therefore the law was unconstitutional.

This decision put Jefferson and Madison in a difficult political position. On one hand, the authors of the Virginia and Kentucky Resolutions were on record for arguing that the states and not the courts should determine the constitutionality of federal laws. But political realities forced them to accept Marshall's decision in this case if they wanted to block Adams's handpicked men from assuming lifetime appointments in powerful judicial positions. Although this **precedent** for **judicial review** did not immediately invalidate the principles set forth in Jefferson's and Madison's earlier **manifestos,** it established the standard that federal courts, rather than states, could decide the constitutionality of acts of Congress.

Marshall's decision in *Marbury v. Madison* gave the Republicans the power to withhold undelivered letters of appointment from the Adams administration, but it gave them no power to control the behavior of judges whose appointments were already official. Thus, in the aftermath of the Marbury decision, Republican radicals in Congress decided to take aim at particularly partisan Federalist judges.

John Pickering of New Hampshire was an easy first target. An alcoholic who suffered from mental illness, he was known to rave incoherently both on and off the bench, usually about the evils of Jefferson and republicanism. No one, not even staunch Federalists, doubted that the besotted man was incompetent, but it was far from certain that he had committed the "high crimes and misdemeanors" for which he was **impeached** in 1803. Whether he had or not, the Senate found him guilty and removed him from office.

Emboldened by that easy victory and armed with a powerful precedent, radical Republicans took on Supreme Court justice Samuel Chase. Chase was notorious for making partisan decisions—such as condemning John Fries to death—and for using the federal bench as an anti-Republican soapbox. Unlike Picker-

ing, Chase defended himself very competently, making the political motivations behind the impeachment effort obvious to all observers. In the end, both Federalists and many Republicans voted to dismiss the charges, returning Chase to his position on the Supreme Court. The Republican radicals' failure to impeach Chase reinforced Jefferson's authority in calling for conciliation. The radicals now had little choice but to accept Jefferson's more moderate position or bolt the party.

Implementing a New Economy

One area of general agreement among Republicans was the determination to tear down Hamilton's economic structure and replace it with a new one more consistent with Jefferson's vision. Responsibility for planning and implementing this economic policy fell to Treasury Secretary **Albert Gallatin.** Gallatin's first effort as secretary of the Treasury was to try to settle the nation's debts. His ambitious goal was to make the United States entirely debt free by 1817. With Jefferson's approval, Gallatin implemented a radical course of budget cutting, going so far as to close several American embassies overseas to save money. At home, Gallatin and Jefferson pared administrative costs by reducing staff and putting an end to the fancy receptions and other social events that President Adams had so enjoyed. The administration cut the military by half, reducing the army from four thousand to twenty-five hundred men and the navy from twenty-five ships to a mere seven.

But Gallatin's cost cutting did much more than just reduce the national budget. First, Gallatin was able to

---

Marbury v. Madison   Supreme Court decision (1803) declaring part of the Judiciary Act of 1789 unconstitutional, thereby establishing an important precedent in favor of judicial review.

precedent   An event or decision that may be used as an example in similar cases later on.

judicial review   The power of the Supreme Court to review the constitutionality of laws passed by Congress and by the states.

manifesto   A written statement publicly declaring the views of its author.

impeach   To formally charge a public official with criminal conduct in office; once the House of Representatives has impeached a federal official, the official is then tried in the Senate on the stated charges.

Albert Gallatin   Treasury secretary in Jefferson's administration; he favored limited government and reduced the federal debt by cutting spending.

Although Jefferson's efforts to stop Barbary pirate depredations against American shipping in the Mediterranean were largely a failure, the struggle provided a wonderful training ground for future military leaders. Young naval commander Stephen Decatur was one such figure. In the course of the fighting, Decatur boarded a pirate ship and engaged in hand-to-hand fighting against the crew, eventually winning the fight even though he had already been wounded by a bullet through his arm. *Naval Historical Foundation.*

mask the firing of loyal Federalists still employed in civil service in a seemingly nonpartisan appeal to fiscal responsibility. He accomplished another ideological goal by reducing the overall federal presence, putting more responsibilities onto the states, where his and Jefferson's philosophy said they belonged. In addition, Gallatin's plan called for a significant change in how the government raised money. In 1802 the Republican Congress repealed all **internal taxes,** leaving customs duties and the sale of western lands as the sole sources of federal revenue. With this one sweeping gesture, Gallatin struck a major blow for Jefferson's economic vision by tying the nation's financial future to westward expansion and foreign trade. But this vision would soon face serious challenges.

Threats to Jefferson's Vision

One threat to Jefferson's commitment to foreign trade came from pirates who patrolled the northern coast of Africa from Tangier to Tripoli, controlling access to the Mediterranean Sea. Ever since gaining independence, the United States had in effect been bribing the Barbary pirates not to attack American ships (see page 189). By 1800, fully a fifth of the federal budget was earmarked for this purpose, a cost Gallatin wished to see eliminated as he tried to balance the nation's books. To Jefferson, principle was as important as financial considerations. Jefferson decided on war.

Asserting presidential privilege as commander in chief, he dispatched navy ships to the Mediterranean in 1801.

The war that followed was a fiasco from anyone's point of view. After some indecisive engagements between the American fleet and the pirates, Jefferson's navy suffered a major defeat with the capture of a prize warship, the *Philadelphia,* and its entire crew. A bold but unsuccessful attempt to invade Tripoli by land across the Libyan Desert led only to a threat to kill the crew of the *Philadelphia* and other hostages. The war dragged along until 1805, when the United States finally negotiated peace terms, agreeing to pay $60,000 for the release of the hostages and accepting the pirates' promise to stop raiding American shipping.

In the meantime, France and Spain posed a serious threat to Jefferson's dream of rapid westward expansion. As settlers continued to pour into the region between the Appalachian Mountains and the Mississippi River, the commercial importance of that inland waterway increased. Whoever controlled the mouth of the Mississippi—the place where it flows past New Orleans and into the Gulf of Mexico and the open

> **internal taxes** Taxes collected directly from citizens, like Alexander Hamilton's various excise taxes (see page 204), as opposed to tariffs or other taxes collected in connection with foreign trade.

With backing from the French, François Dominique Toussaint L'Ouverture (center) led his fellow slaves in a revolt against their French and Spanish masters, driving the Europeans from the West Indian island of Santo Domingo in 1791. Emperor Napoleon Bonaparte double-crossed Toussaint in 1802, sending a French army to seize the island. Although Toussaint was captured, his army defeated the French, creating the republic of Haiti in 1804. *"Toussaint L'Ouverture" by William Edouard Scott. Amistad Research Center, Tulane University, New Orleans, AFAC Collection.*

seas—would have the power to make or break the interior economy.

In accordance with the Treaty of San Lorenzo (1795) (see page 205), Spain had granted American farmers the right to ship cargoes down the Mississippi without paying tolls, and had given American merchants permission to **transship** goods from New Orleans to Atlantic ports without paying export duties. In 1800, however, Napoleon had traded some of France's holdings in southern Europe to Spain in exchange for Spain's land in North America. The United States had no agreement with France concerning navigation on the Mississippi, so the deal between Spain and France threatened to scuttle American commerce on the river. Anxiety over this issue turned to outright panic when, preparatory to the transfer of the land to France, Spanish officials suspended free trade in New Orleans.

Jefferson responded on two fronts. Backing away from his usual anti-British position, he announced, "The day France takes possession of New Orleans we must marry ourselves to the British fleet and nation," and he dispatched James Monroe to talk with the British about a military alliance. He also had Monroe instruct the American minister to France, Robert Livingston, that he could spend as much as $2 million to try to purchase New Orleans and as much adjacent real estate as possible.

Napoleon may have been considering the creation of a Caribbean empire when he acquired Louisiana from Spain. Rich with sugar, the island of **Santo Domingo** was strategically well placed to serve as a hub for French exploitation of the North American interior. France and Spain had shared ownership of the island until an army under the leadership of a former slave named **François Dominique Toussaint L'Ouverture** liberated the French half in 1791 and the Spanish half ten years later. With backing from the French, Toussaint made himself president of the unified nation, but in 1802 Napoleon betrayed him by sending an invasion force to reclaim Santo Domingo. Americans feared that the French army's next destination would be New Orleans.

The French army was able to defeat and capture Toussaint, but no more. The rebels' military skills and yellow fever, malaria, and other tropical diseases destroyed the French force. Stymied in the Caribbean, Napoleon turned his full attention back to extending his holdings in Europe and was seeking funds to finance a continental war. Thus, by the time Monroe and Livingston entered into negotiations with the French in 1803, Napoleon had instructed Foreign Minister Talleyrand to offer the whole of Louisiana to the Americans for $15 million.

transship   The practice of shipping cargo to a secondary port and then transferring it to other ships for transport to a final destination; cargos from up the Mississippi River were shipped by barge to New Orleans and then loaded onto ocean-going vessels to be carried to American ports along the Atlantic coast.

Santo Domingo   Caribbean island (originally named Hispaniola by Christopher Columbus and also known as Saint Domingue) shared by the modern nations of Haiti and the Dominican Republic.

François Dominique Toussaint L'Ouverture   Black revolutionary who liberated the island of Santo Domingo, only to see it reinvaded by the French in 1802.

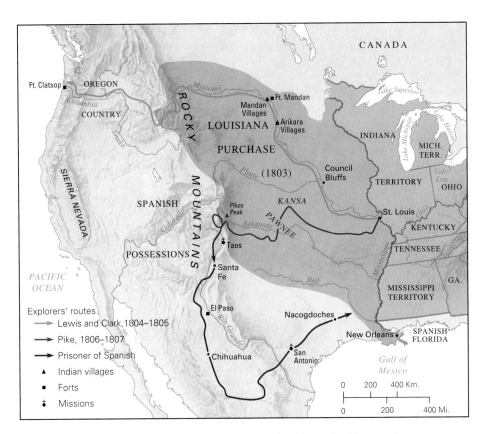

MAP 8.2 Louisiana Purchase and American Exploration   As this map shows, President Jefferson added an enormous tract of land to the United States when he purchased Louisiana from France in 1803. The president was eager to learn as much as possible about the new territory and sent two exploration teams into the West. In addition to collecting information, Lewis and Clark's and Pike's expeditions sought to commit Indian groups along their paths to alliances with the United States and to undermine French, Spanish, and British relations with the Indians, even in those areas that were not officially part of the United States. In Pike's case, this covert intelligence assignment led to his arrest by Spanish authorities and eventual expulsion from their territory.

Pushing Westward

Although Livingston and Monroe had been authorized to spend only $2 million for the purchase of Louisiana, they jumped at the deal offered by Talleyrand, hoping that President Jefferson would approve. The president not only approved but was overjoyed. The deal contained three important benefits for Jefferson and the nation. It removed one European power—France—from the continent and saved Jefferson from having to ally the United States with Britain. It secured the Mississippi River for shipments of American agricultural products to industrial Europe. And it doubled the size of the United States, opening uncharted new expanses for settlement by yeoman farmers.

The **Louisiana Purchase** was immensely popular among most Americans, but it raised significant constitutional questions that helped to keep party divisions alive. The framers of the Constitution had made

> **Louisiana Purchase**   The U.S. purchase of Louisiana from France for $15 million in 1803; the Louisiana Territory extended from the Mississippi River to the Rocky Mountains.

The winter that the Lewis and Clark expedition spent among the Mandan Indians proved to be a learning experience for both the explorers and the Native Americans. This painting by nineteenth-century artist C. M. Russell captures one of those experiences as leaders among the Hidatsa Indians encounter their first African American—William Clark's servant York. Puzzled by his color, the quizzical Indians rubbed at York's skin to see if the color would come off. *Montana Historical Society.*

no provision for the acquisition of new territories by the United States. Opponents of the Louisiana Purchase—mostly northeastern Federalists who feared the dilution of their political and economic power—asserted that the nation was prohibited from extending westward beyond its then-current boundaries without specific constitutional authorization. Ignoring the constitutional issue, Jefferson submitted the purchase to Congress for ratification in November 1803, winning an overwhelming majority. He later defended this action: "Strict observance to the written laws is doubtless one of the high duties of a good citizen, but it is not the highest. The laws of necessity, of self-preservation, of saving our country when in danger, are of a higher obligation."

Even before the Louisiana Purchase, "laws of necessity" had led Jefferson to exert presidential power in an unusual way. Although Spanish, French, and American fur traders, outlaws, and soldiers of fortune had crisscrossed Louisiana over the years, little systematic exploration had been done. When rumors of the land transfer between France and Spain began circulating, Jefferson started preparations to send his private secretary, **Meriwether Lewis,** and a small party into the territory to take a look at the land (see Map 8.2). In a series of confidential letters, Jefferson informed Lewis that the party was to pretend to be on a scientific mission, and the president issued false papers to that effect. Their primary mission, however, was to note the numbers of French, Spanish, and other agents in the area, along with the numbers and condition of the Indians, and to chart major water-

ways and other important strategic sites. They were also to open the way for direct dealings between the Indians and the United States, undermining the Indians' relations with the Spanish and French whenever possible. Early in 1803, months before Congress authorized the Louisiana Purchase, the president sought and received a secret congressional **appropriation** granting the funds necessary to finance the mission.

Lewis, his co-commander **William Clark,** and the rest of the Corps of Discovery set out by boat in the spring of 1804. Pushing its way up the Missouri River, the party arrived among the Mandan Indians (see pages 14; 49) in present-day North Dakota in the late fall. They chose to winter among the Mandans, a decision that may have ensured the expedition's success. The Mandans were a settled agricultural group who had been farming along the upper Missouri for over a thousand years. Unlike many of their neighbors, they had resisted the temptation to abandon their villages for mounted buffalo hunting

Meriwether Lewis Jefferson aide who was sent to explore the Louisiana Territory in 1803; he later served as its governor.

appropriation Public funds authorized for a specific purpose.

William Clark Soldier and explorer who joined Meriwether Lewis as co-leader on the expedition to explore the Louisiana Territory; he was responsible for mapmaking.

when horses had arrived on the northern plains after 1700. Their villages, which offered food and shelter for the wandering hunting tribes, soon became hubs in the evolving Plains trading and raiding system (see pages 49; 50). By wintering with the Mandans, the expedition came into contact with many of the Indian and European groups that participated in the complex economy of the West. Lewis and Clark acted on Jefferson's secret instructions by learning all they could from the Mandans and their visitors about the fur trade, the nature of military alliances, and the tribes that lived farther west.

One particularly important contact Lewis and Clark made during the Mandan winter was with a French trapper named Charbonneau and his Shoshone wife, **Sacajawea.** Between the two of them, Sacajawea and Charbonneau spoke several of the languages understood by the Indians in the Far West and possessed knowledge about the geography and the various peoples in the area. With their help, Lewis and Clark were able to make contact with the Shoshones, who aided them in crossing the Rocky Mountains. From there, the expedition passed from Indian group to Indian group along a chain of friendship. The Nez Perce Indians, for example, were allied to the Shoshones and accepted the party hospitably. The Nez Perces then sent word down the Columbia River that these men were allies, ensuring their safe and speedy passage. Following this chain of Indian hospitality, the expedition finally reached the Pacific Ocean in November 1805.

While many Native American groups genuinely welcomed Lewis and Clark, others remained dubious about the newcomers. On the return trip, part of the expedition ventured off its original outward course to explore new territory and encountered a party of **Piegan Indians.** Allied closely with trading interests in Canada and involved in sporadic war with the Shoshones, the Piegans afforded the party no special diplomatic status, attempting to steal a gun from them while they slept. The Americans thwarted the theft and, in the melee that followed, were able to fight the Piegans off long enough to make a strategic retreat. Years later, Piegan Indians and their allies in the northern Rockies cited this encounter as justification for continuing hostilities toward Americans and their Indian trading partners.

Europeans in the interior were also skeptical of American "scientific" parties. In 1806 Lieutenant Zebulon M. Pike set out on a venture to explore the territory between the Missouri and Red Rivers south of Lewis and Clark's route. The Pawnee and Kansa Indians in the region received Pike with great reserve,

pointing out that the Spanish had recently sent an army through their territory demanding Indian allegiance. Undaunted, Pike continued his journey by following the trail left by the Spanish force, eventually arriving in what is now Colorado (see Map 8.2). From there, he pushed southward, venturing into New Mexico. Though he claimed that this trespass was an innocent navigational error, his party nonetheless was captured by a Spanish army detachment and held for three months. Pike and his men were finally escorted back to the United States and set free with a warning to stay out of Spanish lands and Spanish affairs.

Challenge and Uncertainty in Jefferson's America

■ How did the life of the average American change during Jefferson's presidency?

■ What place did Native Americans and African Americans have in the America Jefferson envisioned? How did each of these groups respond to these roles?

Jefferson's policies not only put the nation on a new road politically and economically but also brought a new spirit into the land. The Virginian's commitment to opportunity and progress, to openness and frugality, offered a stark contrast in approach and style to the policies of his predecessors. The congressional elections of 1802 and the presidential election in 1804 proved Jefferson's popularity and the Republican Party's strong appeal. Nevertheless, some disturbing social and intellectual undercurrents began to surface during his second term. National expansion strained conventional social institutions as white farmers, entrepreneurs, and adventurers seized the opportunities that Republican economic and expansion policies offered. Adding to the strain was the fact that the Jeffersonian spirit was more of a promise than a commitment and that Jefferson's vision for the republic excluded many.

The Heritage of Partisan Politics

The popularity of Jefferson's party was abundantly clear in 1804. Jefferson had won an extremely narrow

Sacajawea Shoshone woman who served as guide and interpreter on the Lewis and Clark expedition.

Piegan Indians The branch of the Blackfoot Indians who resided in areas of what is now Montana during the late eighteenth and early nineteenth centuries.

victory in 1800, and his Republican Party had won significant but hardly overwhelming majorities in Congress. The congressional elections of 1802, however, had virtually eclipsed Federalist power, and Federalists faced the presidential election of 1804 with dread. Former president John Adams commented, "The power of the Administration rests upon the support of a much stronger majority of the people throughout the Union than the former administrations ever possessed since the first establishment of the Constitution."

Despite an abiding faith in the emerging two-party system, staunch Federalist congressman Fisher Ames withdrew from public life, followed by John Jay and other prominent leaders. Some traditional Federalists, however, continued to fight. The party tapped former vice-presidential candidate Charles Cotesworth Pinckney to head the 1804 presidential ticket. For the vice presidency, the Federalists chose Rufus King, a defender of the notion of loyal opposition and the two-party system.

Federalists had trouble identifying issues on which to build a viable platform. Hoping to capitalize on **anti-expansionist** fears in New England and sentiments favoring states' rights in the South, the Federalists focused their campaign on Jefferson's acquisition of Louisiana. In a direct appeal to Yankee **frugality,** Federalists charged that Jefferson had paid too much for the new territory and was attempting to use the region to build a unified agrarian political faction. Pinckney accused Jefferson of violating his own political principles by exerting a federal power not explicitly granted in the Constitution. Some Republicans shared this view, but no one could question Jefferson's overall success in accomplishing the party's goals. During his first administration, Jefferson had eliminated internal taxes, stimulated westward migration, eliminated the hated Alien and Sedition Acts, and rekindled hope in the hearts of many disaffected Americans.

At the same time, he had proved that he was no threat to national commerce or to individual affluence. Despite Federalist fears, the economy continued to grow at the same rate during Jefferson's tenure in office as it had under the Federalists. In the process, those who engaged in international trade amassed enormous fortunes. Such economic growth permitted Jefferson to maintain a favorable **balance of payments** throughout his first administration, a feat the Federalists had never achieved. And with Gallatin's help, Jefferson had proved his fiscal responsibility by building up a multimillion-dollar Treasury surplus.

The enormous scope of Jefferson's successes and the limited scope of his opponent's platform helped swing the election of 1804 firmly over to the Republi-cans. Jefferson won 162 electoral votes to Pinckney's 14, carrying every state except Connecticut and Delaware.

Westward Expansion and Social Stress

Eastern Federalists and other critics of Jefferson's vision had some justification for their concerns about the rapid growth of the West. A baby boom had followed the Revolution, and as new territories opened in the West, young people streamed into the region at a rate that alarmed many. This had an unsettling effect on communities in the East. During the eighteenth century, older people maintained authority by controlling the distribution of land to their children. With only so much worthwhile land to go around, sons and daughters lived with and worked for their parents until their elders saw fit to deed property over to them. As a result, children living in the East generally did not become independent—that is, they did not become church members, marry, or operate their own farms or businesses—until they were in their thirties. Economic opportunities available on the frontier, however, lessened young people's need to rely on their parents for support and lowered the age at which they began to break away. During the early part of the nineteenth century, the age at which children attained independence fell steadily. By the 1820s, children were joining churches in their teens and marrying in their early to mid-twenties. Breathing the new air of independence, intrepid young people not only migrated west but also challenged their parents' authority at home. Obviously social and political traditionalists were upset. Business interests in the East were also upset as they witnessed westward expansion drawing off population, which in time would drive up the price of labor and reduce profits.

Conditions out west were even less stable as rapid growth put enormous stress on conventional institutions. The population of Ohio, for example, grew from 45,000 in 1800 to 231,000 in 1810, and similar

---

anti-expansionist   One opposed to the policy of expanding a country by acquiring new territory.

frugality   An unwillingness to spend money for unnecessary things; by stereotype, New Englanders (Yankees) supposedly have an ingrained tendency to frugality.

balance of payments   The difference between a nation's total payments to foreign countries and its total receipts from abroad.

The Mississippi River drainage system was the only reliable transportation route for Americans moving into the West during the early 1800s. Farmers moved produce to market on keelboats like the one depicted here. Above decks, cargo and livestock endured weather and exposure to mosquitoes and other river menaces. Below decks, however, there was a cabin-like environment where people could eat, drink, and sleep in comfort during the often long trip downriver. One problem with this mode of transport was that the current on the giant river made upstream travel impossible during much of the year, so boats like this one were often sold for lumber after they reached New Orleans. *Miriam and Ira D. Wallach Division of Art, Prints and Photographs, The New York Public Library. Astor, Lenox and Tilden Foundations; Musee d'Histoire Naturelle, Le Havre, France.*

rates of growth occurred in the new states of Tennessee and Kentucky and in territories from Louisiana north to Michigan and west to Missouri. Authorities in the West found these increases challenging as they tried to deal with the practical matters of maintaining governments, economies, and peaceful relations among the new settlers and between the settlers and neighboring Indians.

Most of the people who moved west looked forward to achieving the agrarian self-sufficiency that Jefferson advocated, but life in the West was far from what Jefferson had hoped it would be. Inexpensive, reliable transportation was impossible in the vast, rugged interior, and Jefferson's notion of breadbasket America trading with industrial Europe was doomed without it. No navigable streams ran eastward from America's interior across the Appalachians to the Atlantic, and the ridges of those mountains made road building extremely difficult.

Only two reliable routes existed for transporting produce from the interior to shipping centers in the East. The Ohio-Mississippi-Missouri drainage system provided a reliable watercourse, and huge cargoes flowed along its stream. Shipping goods on the Mississippi, however, was a dangerous and expensive operation. Because of the river's strong current, loads could be shipped only one way—downstream. Rafts were built for the purpose and then were broken up and sold for lumber in New Orleans. Shippers had to return home by foot on the **Natchez Trace.** On both legs of the journey, travelers risked attack by river

Natchez Trace A road connecting Natchez, Mississippi, with Nashville, Tennessee; it was commercially and strategically important in the late eighteenth and early nineteenth centuries.

Evangelical denominations gained ever wider followings during the early nineteenth century as the uncertainties accompanying rapid expansion took their toll on national self-confidence. Mass baptisms like this one painted by Russian tourist Pavel Svinin celebrated the emotional moment of conversion and the individual's rebirth as a Christian. *"A Philadelphia Anabaptist Immersion During a Storm" by Pavel Svinin. The Metropolitan Museum of Art, Rogers Fund, 1942. (42.95.20. Photograph © 1979 The Metropolitan Museum of Art.)*

pirates, Indians, and sickness. Moreover, it was virtually impossible for shippers to take manufactured goods back with them because of the condition of the roads and the distances involved. The other river route—the St. Lawrence River, flowing east from the Great Lakes to the northern Atlantic—presented similar problems. In addition, that river passed through British Canada and therefore was closed to American commercial traffic.

As a result of geographical isolation and the rapid pace of settlement, the economy in the West became highly localized. Settlers arriving with neither food nor seed bought surplus crops produced by established farmers. The little capital that was generated in this way supported the development of local industries in hundreds of farming villages. Enterprising craftsmen ranging from **coopers** to **wheelwrights** produced hand-manufactured items on demand. As long as people kept moving into an area, local economies boomed. But when new arrivals slowed and then stopped, the market for surplus crops and local manufactures collapsed, and the economy went bust. Swinging from boom to bust and back again became a way of life in newly settled areas.

Along with economic instability, social instability was also common. The odd mixture of ethnic, religious, and national groups found in western villages did little to bring cohesiveness to community life.

The Religious Response to Social Change

The changes taking place in the young republic stirred conflicting religious currents. One was liberalism in religious thought. The other was a new **evangelicalism.**

Born of the Enlightenment (see page 102) in France, Scotland, and England, liberal religious thought emphasized the connection between **rationalism** and faith. To rationalists like both Jefferson and Adams, the possibility that a being as perfect as God might behave irrationally was unthinkable. In fact, for such

cooper   A person who makes or repairs wooden barrels.

wheelwright   A person who makes or repairs wheels for carts, wagons, or other vehicles.

evangelicalism   A Protestant religious persuasion that emphasizes the literal truth of the Gospels and salvation through faith alone; in the early nineteenth century, it became infused with increasing amounts of romantic emotionalism and an emphasis on converting others.

rationalism   The theory that the exercise of reason, rather than the acceptance of authority or spiritual revelation, is the only valid basis for belief and the best source of spiritual truth.

men, the more plain, reasonable, and verifiable religious claims were, the more likely it was that they emanated from God. Less perfect than God, it was man who had cluttered the plain revealed truth with irrational claims and insolvable mysteries. For his part, Jefferson was so convinced of this logic that he edited his own version of the Bible, keeping only the moral principles and the solid historical facts and discarding anything supernatural.

This liberal creed led many, including Jefferson, to abandon organized religion altogether. Not all liberals were so quick to bolt organized worship however. John Adams, for example, continued to adhere to New England Congregationalism, but he and others used their influence to promote a young and more liberal clergy who sought to insert a heavy dose of rationalism into the old Puritan structure. Rejecting such traditional mysteries as the **Trinity** and the literal divinity of Christ, a so-called **Unitarian** movement emerged and expanded inside Congregational churches during the years just before and following the American Revolution. Liberal influence within Congregationalism became so prominent in New England that Unitarians were able to engineer the election of their own **Henry Ware** as the senior professor of theology at Harvard College, formerly the educational heart of orthodox Calvinist America. Though outraged, more traditional Congregationalists did little immediately to oust liberals from their churches. In the decades to come, however, doctrinal disagreements between the parties would lead to outright religious war.

While deism and Unitarianism were gaining strong footholds in eastern cities, disorder, insecurity, and missionizing activities were helping to foster a very different kind of religious response in the West. Although Methodists, Baptists, Presbyterians, and evangelical Congregationalists disagreed on many specific principles, they all emphasized the spirited preaching that could bring about the emotional moment of conversion—the moment of realization that without the saving grace of God, every soul is lost. Each of these denominations concentrated on training a new, young ministry and sending it to preach in every corner of the nation. In this way, another religious awakening swept across America, beginning in Cane Ridge, Kentucky, in 1801 and spreading throughout the South and West.

The new evangelicalism stressed the individual nature of salvation but at the same time emphasized the importance of Christian community. Looking back to the first generation of Puritans in America,

the new evangelicals breathed new life into the old Puritan notion of God's plan for the universe and the leading role that Americans were to play in its unfolding. As early nineteenth-century Presbyterian divine Lyman Beecher put it, "It was the opinion of [Jonathan] Edwards that the millennium would commence in America . . . all providential signs of the times lend corroboration to it."

Early nineteenth-century evangelicals formed official **synods,** councils, and conventions as well as hundreds of voluntary associations designed to carry out what they characterized as God's plan for America. These organizations helped counterbalance the forces of extreme individualism and social disorder by providing ideological underpinnings for the expansive behavior of westerners and a sense of mission to ease the insecurities produced by venturing into the unknown. They also provided an institutional framework that brought some stability to communities in which traditional controls were lacking. These attractive features helped evangelicalism to sweep across the West. During the early nineteenth century, it became the dominant religious persuasion in that region.

The Problem of Race in Jefferson's Republic

Jefferson's policies enabled many Americans to benefit from the nation's development, but they certainly did not help everyone. Neither Native Americans nor African Americans had much of a role in Jefferson's republic, and each group was subject to different forms of unequal treatment during the Jeffersonian era.

A slaveholder himself, Jefferson expressed strong views about African Americans. In his *Notes on the*

Trinity   The Christian belief that God consists of three divine persons: Father, Son, and Holy Spirit.

Unitarianism   A religion that denies the Trinity, teaching that God exists only in one person; it also stresses individual freedom of belief and the free use of reason in religion.

Henry Ware   Liberal Congregationalist who was elected senior theologian at Harvard College in 1805, making Unitarianism the dominant religious view at the previously Calvinist stronghold.

synod   An official governing council of a religious denomination that makes decisions on theological matters and matters of church law.

Benjamin Bannaker's
PENNSYLVANIA, DELAWARE, MARY-
LAND, AND VIRGINIA
ALMANAC,
FOR THE
YEAR of our LORD 1795;
Being the Third after Leap-Year.

BANNAKER.

PHILADELPHIA:
Printed for WILLIAM GIBBONS, Cherry Street

Born a free man in Maryland, Benjamin Banneker took full advantage of the educational opportunities that were offered to him and quickly displayed that he was a mathematical prodigy. Under the tutelage of businessman and gentleman scientist Joseph Ellicott, Banneker eventually became so proficient at trigonometry and calculus that he was invited to join the engineering team that helped to lay out the nation's capital at Washington, D.C., and published his own almanac of astronomical predictions. In doing so, he challenged prevailing stereotypes concerning the intellectual abilities possess by African Americans. He even engaged in a spirited correspondence with Thomas Jefferson himself, asserting that the president needed to revise his attitudes about race. *Courtesy of the American Antiquarian Society.*

State of Virginia (1781), Jefferson asserted that blacks were "inferior to whites in the endowments both of body and mind." Even when presented with direct evidence of superior black intellectual accomplishments, Jefferson remained unmoved. When the well-respected African American mathematician, astronomer, and engineer Benjamin Banneker sent a copy of an almanac he had prepared to Jefferson, the then secretary of state replied, "No body wishes more than I do to see such proofs as you exhibit, that nature has given to our black brethren, talents equal to those of the other colors of men." However, he refused to acknowledge that Banneker's work provided such proofs. "I have a long letter from Banneker," Jefferson later told his friend Joel Barlow, "which shows him to have had a

mind of very common stature indeed." He went on to suggest that the almanac had actually been written by a white engineer who was intent on "puffing" Banneker's reputation.

Jefferson was convinced, and stated publicly on many occasions, that the white and black races could not live together without inevitably polluting both. This was the key reason for what little opposition he voiced to slavery and for his continued involvement in various projects to remove African Americans by colonizing them in Africa. And yet despite this attitude, many of his contemporaries believed that he kept a slave mistress, Sally Hemings, by whom he fathered several children, a contention that modern DNA evidence has demonstrated as credible. Even so, almost no documentary evidence about the relationship exists despite the fact that hundreds of the nation's most prolific writers (and gossips) passed through Jefferson's home regularly. Circumstantial evidence, however, suggests that their relationship was an exclusive one and lasted for a long period of time. And traditions passed down through generations of Sally Hemings's descendants claim that theirs was a romantic, even sentimental, bond.

Given his belief in racial inequality, it would seem contradictory that Jefferson could have had a long-term affectionate relationship with an African American woman. If so, it reflects equally deep-seated contradictions that shot through American society at the time. Truly a man of his century and his social class, Jefferson was convinced that women, like slaves, existed to serve and entertain men. Thus his entanglement with Hemings, who probably was the half-sister of Martha Wayles Skelton, Jefferson's deceased wife, would have seemed no more unequal or unnatural than his marriage to Martha. But while the relationship may have seemed perfectly natural behind closed doors, the race code to which Jefferson gave voice in his various publications and official utterances defined it as entirely unacceptable in public. This rigid separation between public and private behavior led Jefferson to keep the relationship secret, and his friends and family—even most of his political enemies—joined him in a conspiracy of silence. This, too, was reflective of broader social ambiguities, contradictions that defined the sex lives of masters and slaves in Jefferson's South.

Throughout the Jeffersonian era, the great majority of African Americans lived in that South, and most of them were slaves. But from the 1790s onward, the number of free blacks increased steadily. Emancipation did not bring equality, however, even in northern states. Many states did not permit free blacks to testify in court, vote, or exercise other fundamental freedoms accorded to whites. Public schools often refused admission to black children. Even churches were often closed to blacks who wished to worship.

Some African Americans began to respond to systematic exclusion and to express their cultural and social identity by forming their own institutions. In Philadelphia, tension between white and free black Methodists led former slave Richard Allen to form the Bethel Church for Negro Methodists in 1793. Two years later, Allen became the first black deacon ordained in America. Ongoing tension with the white Methodist hierarchy, however, eventually led Allen to secede from the church and form his own **African Methodist Episcopal Church** (Bethel) in 1816. Similar controversies in New York led black divine James Varick to found an African Methodist Episcopal Church (Zion) in that city in 1821.

African American leadership was not confined to religious and intellectual realms. **James Forten,** for example, a free-born African American, followed up on his experience as a sailor in the Revolutionary navy with a career as a sailmaker in Philadelphia. Despite both overt and subtle racial discrimination, he acquired his own company in 1798, eventually becoming a major employer of both African American and white workers. Though himself a Quaker, Forten often cooperated with Richard Allen but did not subscribe to projects designed to separate the races, working consistently—even to the point of petitioning Congress and the Pennsylvania assembly—to pass laws ensuring desegregation and equal treatment. In cooperation with other African American entrepreneurs, such as Boston's Paul Cuffe, Forten invested expertise, capital, and personal influence in an effort to create jobs for black city-dwellers and opportunities for budding black businessmen. Despite these efforts, the overall racial atmosphere in Jefferson's America significantly limited the number of African American leaders who would attain positions of wealth or influence.

Jefferson thought differently of Native Americans than he did of African Americans. He considered Indians to be "savages" but was not convinced that they were biologically inferior to Europeans: "They are formed in mind as well as in body, on the same module with the 'Homo Sapiens Europaeus,'" he said. Jefferson attributed the differences between Indians and Europeans to what he termed the Indians' cultural retardation. He was confident that if whites lifted Indians out of their uncivilized state and put them on an equal footing with Europeans, Indian populations

would grow, their physical condition would improve, and they would be able to participate in the yeoman republic on an equal footing with whites.

Jefferson's Indian policy reflected this attitude. Jefferson created a series of government-owned trading posts at which Indians were offered goods at cheap prices. He believed that Indians who were exposed to white manufactures would come to agree that white culture was superior and would make the rational decision to adopt that culture wholesale. At the same time, both the government and right-minded philanthropists should engage in instructing Native Americans in European methods of farming, ensuring that these former "savages" would emerge as good, Republican-voting frontier farmers. Until this process of **acculturation** was complete, however, Jefferson believed the Indians, like children, should be protected from those who would take advantage of them or lead them astray. Also like children, the Indians were not to be trusted to exercise the rights and responsibilities of citizenship. Thus Indian rights were not protected by the Constitution but were subject to the whims of the Senate—which drafted and ratified Indian treaties—and of the army—which enforced those treaties.

The chief problem for Jeffersonian Indian policy was not the Indians' supposed cultural retardation but their rapid modernization. Among groups such as the Cherokees and Creeks, members of a rising new elite—often the offspring of European fathers and Indian mothers—led their people toward greater prosperity and diplomatic independence. Alexander McGillivray of the Creeks, for example, deftly manipulated American, French, and Spanish interests to Creek advantage while building a strong economic base founded on both communally and privately owned plantations. In similar fashion, the rising Cherokee elite in 1794 established a centralized government that

African Methodist Episcopal Church   African American branch of Methodism established in Philadelphia in 1816 and in New York in 1821.

James Forten   African American entrepreneur with a successful sailmaking business in Philadelphia who provided leadership for black business enterprises and advocated both racial integration and equal rights during the Jeffersonian era.

acculturation   Changes in the culture of a group or an individual as a result of contact with a different culture.

began pushing the Cherokees into a new era of wealth and power.

Although Jefferson might have greeted such acculturation with enthusiasm, the Indians' white neighbors generally did not. Envisioning all-out war between the states and the Indians—war that his reduced government and shrunken military was helpless to prevent—Jefferson advanced an alternative. Having acquired Louisiana, Jefferson suggested the creation of large reserves to which Indians currently residing within states could relocate, taking themselves out of state jurisdictions and removing themselves from the corrupting influence of the "baser elements" of white society. Although he did not advocate the use of force to move Indians west of the Mississippi, he made every effort to convince them to migrate. This idea of segregating Native Americans from other Americans formed the basis for Indian policy for the rest of the century.

Individual Voices

Examining a Primary Source

Congress Debates George Logan's Mission to France

Even before any official news had reached Washington, rumors were flying about George Logan's trip to France to negotiate an end to the diplomatic crisis that was plaguing the nation. Less than a month after Logan had set off for Europe, Federalists in Congress proposed a new law that would make any such efforts at unofficial peacemaking a federal crime. Republican representative Albert Gallatin urged patience: wait for the president to present the facts to Congress as he had promised to do. But the Federalists persisted, leading Gallatin to ask why they were so eager to criminalize Logan's actions. In a moment of heated candor, Massachusetts Federalist Harrison G. Otis blurted out the answer, revealing what was really at work inside the radical circle.

- **What is Otis saying here? What does he perceive as the motive behind the Republican criticism of a bill to outlaw acts like Logan's?**

- **This speech is quoted from The Debates and Proceedings in the Congress of the United States, the official record of Congress from 1789 through 1824. In this source, speeches were generally reported in the third person; hence Otis is referred to as "he."**

- **What is Otis saying was the actual motivation for proposing this bill? What conclusions can you draw from this statement about the nature of partisan politics in 1798? To what extent is such political practice in play today?**

Again: it is insisted that the secret of the resolution on the table, was to perpetuate the division of party, and that, although but few real causes of dissension remain, yet we are determined to throw down the gauntlet and excite the greatest possible irritation. ■ *This accusation he denied.* ■ *He did not believe that the resolution was introduced with any such design; but if such had been the object of the mover, the blame would not attach to him or to his friends. They might even then have justified themselves upon principles of self-defence. He appealed to the whole House that, within a few days after the commencement of this session, they were threatened with a notice that motions might be expected in favor of repealing the Alien and Sedition acts; which could owe their origin to no other intention but that of inflaming the public mind, and of persevering in the endeavor to expose the Administration and its friends to odious imputations. Therefore we should stand acquitted, if, instead of giving time to our adversaries to furnish their weapons, and carry war into our borders, we had seized this occasion to strike the first blow.* ■

Summary

Americans faced a difficult choice in 1796: to continue in a Federalist direction with John Adams or to move into new and uncharted regions of democracy with Thomas Jefferson. Factionalism and voter indecision led to Adams's election as president and Jefferson's as vice president. The split outcome frightened Federalists, and they used every excuse to make war on their political opponents. Diplomatically, they let relations with France sour to the point that the two nations were at war in all but name. At home, they used repressive measures such as the Alien and Sedition Acts to try to silence opponents, and they imposed tariffs and taxes that were hateful to many. Reminded of what they had rebelled against in the Revolution, in 1800 the American people decided to give Jefferson and the Republican faction a chance.

Although Jefferson would call the election "the revolution of 1800," even hard-line Federalists such as Hamilton were sure that the general direction in government would not change. Just to be safe, however, Federalists stacked the court system so that Republicans would face insurmountable constraints if they tried to change government too much. At the same time, they organized themselves into a true political party, an ever-present watchdog on the activities of their rivals.

Jefferson's inaugural address in 1801 seemed to announce an end to partisan warfare, but both Madison and hard-line Republicans in Congress attempted to restrict Federalist power in the court system. The Republican program, however, was not entirely negative. Jefferson looked toward a future in which most Americans could own enough land to produce life's necessities for themselves and would be beholden to no one and thus free to vote as their consciences and rationality dictated. To attain this end, Jefferson ordered massive reductions in the size of government, the elimination of internal federal taxes, and rapid westward expansion, including the purchase of the vast territory called Louisiana. For some the outcome was a spirit of excitement and optimism, but not everyone was so hopeful. Many were unsure and fearful of the new order's novelty and of the stresses that rapid expansion engendered; social change disrupted lives and communities.

Jefferson clearly wanted most Americans to share in the bounty of an expanded nation, but not all were free to share equally. For American Indians, the very success of Jefferson's expansion policy meant a contraction in their freedom of action. African Americans also found that the equality Jefferson promised to others was not intended for them, though many like Benjamin Banneker and Paul Cuffe grasped for it anyway. As to women, Jefferson himself observed, "The appointment of a woman to office is an innovation for which the public is not prepared, nor am I"; they were encouraged to play an active role in the new nation but were expected to do so only through their roles as wives and mothers.

AMERICAN EXPANSION AND POPULATION GROWTH, 1820 As the United States and Britain came closer and closer to war, many shared the hope that an American victory would open up new opportunities for territorial and economic expansion. As this map shows, these hopes were well founded. Breaking the power of Indian groups along the northwestern frontier and removing the British from the Great Lakes ushered in an era of optimism following the War of 1812, fostering a new wave of population growth as new states and territories joined the nation.

CANADA

OREGON COUNTRY

British Treaty Line of 1818

Missouri

RED RIVER BASIN CESSION (1818)

Lake Superior

MICHIGAN TERRITORY 1818

Lake Huron

Lake Michigan

Spanish Treaty Line of 1814

MISSOURI TERRITORY 1812

L. Ontario

MAINE 1820

VT.

N.H. Portsmouth

NEW YORK

Albany

Boston

MASS.

Hartford

Newport R.I. CONN.

Detroit

L. Erie

PENNSYLVANIA

Philadelphia

New York

Trenton N.J.

Ft. Wayne

OHIO

Baltimore

DEL.

ILLINOIS 1818

INDIANA 1816

Ohio

Washington D.C.

MD.

Vincennes

Frankfort

St. Louis

MISSOURI* (1821)

KENTUCKY

VIRGINIA

Richmond

Norfolk

TENNESSEE

NORTH CAROLINA

Raleigh

SPANISH POSSESSIONS

ARKANSAS TERRITORY 1819

Memphis

SOUTH CAROLINA

GEORGIA

Charleston

Spanish Treaty Line of 1819

MISSISSIPPI 1817

ALABAMA 1819

Savannah

LOUISIANA 1812

Natchez

St. Augustine

New Orleans

FLORIDA TERRITORY (ceded by Spain, 1819)

ATLANTIC OCEAN

PACIFIC OCEAN

Gulf of Mexico

Population density per square mile, 1820

90 or more

45–90

18–45

6–18

2–6

Unsettled areas

* Missouri organized a state government in 1820.

0   200   400 Km.

0   200   400 Mi.

| 1794 Eli Whitney obtains patent for cotton gin | 1808 Embargo Economic depression | 1810 First Vincennes conference between Harrison and Tecumseh | 1812 War declared against England | 1813 Fort Mims massacre First mechanized textile factory | 1814 Treaty of Ghent | 1815 Battle of New Orleans |

1809 Fort Wayne Treaty

| 1790 | 1800 | 1808 | 1809 | 1810 | 1811 | 1812 | 1813 | 1814 | 1815 |

1804 Napoleon crowned emperor in France

1809 Franco-Russian Alliance

1813 2,400 power looms operate in England

1814 Defeat of Napoleon

1814–1815 Congress of Vienna

Increasing Conflict and War, 1805–1815

9

American Expansion and Population Growth, 1820

Using the map on the facing page, and comparing it to the opening map for Chapter 8 (see page 210), examine the twin dynamics of population growth and westward expansion that characterized this era. How did these twin dynamics influence American political and diplomatic decision making and social life for all Americans between Jefferson's second presidential administration and the years immediately following the War of 1812?

Individual Choices

TECUMSEH

Coming of age in the years when his people were facing their greatest challenge from invading Europeans, Tecumseh followed in his father's footsteps by becoming an influential war leader among the Shawnee people. And following his mother's influence, a Creek Indian who had married across tribal lines, he persistently emphasized the unity between all Native American people. Both influences would lead him to undertake heroic efforts to preserve what remained of the Indians' territory in the years following the American Revolution. But neither his war skills nor his diplomatic skills would win the day. Killed fighting American aggression in the War of 1812, Tecumseh's dismembered body foreshadowed the dismemberment of the Indian nations. According to many experts, this particular portrait, a composite of several sketches, comes closest to capturing what this inspiring Indian leader actually looked like at the peak of his career. *Benson J. Lossing,* The Pictorial Field Book of the War of 1812.

Tecumseh

In the opening days of the nineteenth century, most Americans believed the native people in the continent's interior were an odd survival from the Stone Age who lived in isolated tribes constantly warring among themselves and were doomed to extinction. It was only fair, then, that more progressive people like themselves deserved the Indians' land and inevitable that they would acquire it. Tecumseh knew better, and few did as much to try to stop the loss of Indian land that whites deemed inevitable.

Tecumseh's entire life stood in stark contrast to dominant white theories about Indian life. Although he was born among the Shawnee Indians in Ohio in around 1768, Tecumseh's mother was actually a Creek Indian from Alabama. His parents had met when his father had visited the Creeks in the 1750s. In the sophisticated Indian world of the American interior, such visitations were common, as were intergroup marriages. Because of their cosmopolitan connections, the children of such marriages often attained positions of high authority.

A combination of his family connections and a distinguished military career led to Tecumseh's emergence as war chief in the late 1780s. It was in this capacity that he helped defeat American general Arthur St. Clair in 1791. American vengeance came in 1794 when General "Mad" Anthony Wayne crushed an intertribal Indian army that included Tecumseh and his Shawnee warriors at the Battle of Fallen Timbers. Wayne then forced the Indians to sign the Treaty of Greenville, ceding a huge tract of land to the United States. In exchange, the American government promised to protect the Indians from further incursions.

This promise was not kept. In the years that followed, American agents used a combination of bribery, coercion, and outright violence to convince **civil chiefs** to cede more land. Seeking to stop these new invasions, Tecumseh approached war chiefs with a bold plan to stop American expansion once and for all. What he had in mind was a vast alliance system in which the warriors from all tribes along the American frontier would agree to stop civil chiefs from selling land and commit their military might to turn back any American armies that sought to push the Indians out. Joining Tecumseh was his younger brother, Tenskwatawa, the Shawnee Prophet. According to the Prophet, if the Indians gave up white ways and white goods, stopped selling their land, and resumed their traditional lives, the whites would vanish from their world. Taken together, the messages from the two brothers reinforced each other and proved quite compelling. Tecumseh began traveling throughout the frontier, inviting warriors from all tribes to join his expanding alliance.

Bent on continuing expansion, white leaders like Indiana territorial governor William Henry Harrison found the formation of a solid line of Indian resistance frightening. Harrison continually attacked both Tecumseh and the Prophet, trying to discredit them in the eyes of potential followers. For their part, the Prophet and

Tecumseh became increasingly strident in their insistence that Indian people should live out their own lives on their own land.

Abandoning argument and character assassination, Harrison resorted to violence, leading an army to invade the brothers' headquarters at Prophetstown on Tippecanoe Creek in November 1811. With Tecumseh absent seeking new allies, the Prophet attempted to save his village and the promise of his vision, but Harrison's forces overcame a spirited defense and burned the town, destroying its winter food supply. By the time Tecumseh reached Tippecanoe in January, few of his followers remained, and his carefully crafted alliance system was in the process of unraveling. Thinking first of the survivors' welfare, Tecumseh traveled extensively into British territory and among the various tribes in the West, seeking emergency relief supplies to replace what Harrison's forces had destroyed.

It was while he was in the process of raising that relief that war again broke out, this time between the United States and Great Britain. In Canada at the time, Tecumseh quickly learned that American troops were marching through Indian country, harassing villages and confiscating necessary food supplies. With his hopes for a unified Indian barrier to American expansion crushed, he decided that the only hope for the Shawnees' future lay in a British victory. He immediately delivered what was left of his alliance to the British. Tecumseh soon joined Colonel Henry Proctor in commanding an army of twelve hundred Indians from various tribes and nine hundred British regular troops. This joint force enjoyed great success against the Americans, but at the Battle of the Thames, on October 5, 1813, Tecumseh's forces were overrun and Tecumseh was shot. After the battle, triumphant American troops mutilated his body and left it lying on the field.

When Tecumseh died, hopes for a unified Indian resistance died with him, and his mutilated body foreshadowed the future for the Indian land base. Stinging from military defeats and with no more strong voices urging common cause, the once-cosmopolitan world of the Indian interior became what whites imagined it to be: isolated tribes constantly warring among themselves, each scrambling to salvage some small portion of land and dignity. Expansionists like Harrison used this desperation to play one group off against another, carving piece after piece out of the Indian domain until, by 1850, virtually no Indians remained in the territory Tecumseh had tried to preserve.

INTRODUCTION

Tecumseh's situation in Indiana reflected many of the more troubling problems that beset the nation during the opening decades of the nineteenth century. Sitting at the juncture of three worlds—the dynamic republican world of Jeffersonian America, the European imperial world in Canada, and his own Native American world—Tecumseh perceived that unless something happened soon, all three worlds were heading for a crisis.

Jefferson had set an ambitious agenda for the country that was extremely popular with many Americans, but it created serious stresses within the nation and across the world. Along the Atlantic frontier, imperial powers such as Great Britain and France challenged Jefferson's commitment to open trade and freedom of the seas. A war of words, blustering threats, and some open confrontations pushed the United States increasingly toward crisis and triggered economic disaster. Along the western frontier, a variety of Indian

> **civil chiefs** In many Native American societies, leadership was shared among different classes of chiefs, each of which was responsible for specific political tasks; civil chiefs generally were responsible for overseeing domestic affairs, while war chiefs were responsible for diplomacy.

groups opposed Jefferson's vision of rapid westward expansion. Here too, verbal and some armed conflicts engendered an air of crisis. And to many, including Harrison, these seemed not to be isolated phenomena. Convinced that a conspiracy was afoot between Indian dissidents like Tecumseh and imperial agents from Great Britain and France, an increasing number of Jeffersonians demanded aggressive action.

Try as they might to ease the growing tensions, neither Jefferson and his successor, James Madison, nor Federalist and Republican dissidents could stem the tide of crisis. Harrison finally took matters over the edge: his attack on Prophetstown precipitated a general call for a war that would set the nation on a new course altogether.

Troubling Currents in Jefferson's America

■ How did varying interests between regions of the country complicate Jefferson's political situation during his second term as president?

■ What impact did European politics have on the American economy between 1804 and 1808?

Jefferson's successes, culminating in his victory in the 1804 election, seemed to prove that Republicans had absolute control over the nation's political reins. But factions that would challenge Jefferson's control were forming. A small but vocal coalition of disgruntled Federalists threatened to secede from the Union. Even within his own party, Jefferson's supremacy eroded and dissidents emerged. Diplomatic problems also joined domestic ones to trouble Jefferson's second administration.

Emerging Factions in American Politics

The Federalists' failure in the election of 1804 nearly spelled the troubled party's demise. With the West and the South firmly in Jefferson's camp, disgruntled New England Federalists found their once-dominant voice being drowned out by those who shared Jefferson's rather than Hamilton's view of America's future (see page 230). Proclaiming that "the people of the East cannot reconcile their habits, views, and interests with those of the South and West," Federalist leader Timothy Pickering advocated radical changes in the Constitution that he thought might restore balance. Among other things, northeasterners demanded

much stricter standards for admitting new states in the West and the elimination of the Three-Fifths Compromise. Pickering brought together a tight political coalition called the Essex Junto to press for these changes.

Regional fissures began to open inside Jefferson's party as well. Throughout Jefferson's first administration, some within his party, especially those from the South, criticized the president for turning his back on republican principles by expanding federal power and interfering with states' rights. One of Jefferson's most vocal critics was his cousin John Randolph.

The two Virginia Republicans clashed on the eve of the 1804 election over the Yazoo affair. This complicated legal tangle had begun back in 1794 when a group of politically well-connected land speculators succeeded in using bribes and other questionable methods to secure over 40 million acres of land from the State of Georgia for a mere five hundred thousand dollars. Georgia voters were outraged and in the next election threw the corrupt state congressmen who were responsible for the deal out of office. When the new state legislature convened in 1796, it overturned the previous sale, but in the meantime, much of the land had already been sold to individual farmers, who had already taken possession. Georgia ordered these individuals to move off the disputed land, offering them financial compensation, but many refused, taking the matter to court. The political and legal infighting continued until 1802, when Georgia finally joined the other original states in ceding its western

secede To withdraw formally from membership in a political union; threats of secession were used frequently during the early nineteenth century to bring attention to political issues.

Essex Junto Junto—A group of political conspirators who seek power outside of the regular political process—composed of radical Federalists in Essex County, Massachusetts, who at first advocated constitutional changes that would favor New England politically and later called for New England and New York to secede from the United States.

John Randolph Virginia Republican politician who was a cousin of Thomas Jefferson; he believed in limited government and objected to several of Jefferson's policies.

Yazoo affair Corrupt deal in which the Georgia legislature sold a huge tract of public land to speculators for a low price but later overturned the sale; the basis for the Supreme Court case of *Fletcher v. Peck*, discussed in more detail in Chapter 10, which in 1810 established the sanctity of civil contracts over state legislation.

Chronology

Domestic Expansion and International Crisis

1794	Eli Whitney patents cotton gin
1803	Britain steps up impressment Renewal of war between France and Britain
1804	Duel between Alexander Hamilton and Aaron Burr Jefferson reelected
1805	Beginning of Shawnee religious revival
1806	Napoleon issues Berlin Decree
1807	Burr conspiracy trial Founding of Prophetstown *Chesapeake* affair
1808	Embargo of 1808 goes into effect Economic depression begins James Madison elected president
1809	Non-Intercourse Act Fort Wayne Treaty Chouteau brothers form Missouri Fur Company
1810	Macon's Bill No. 2 Vincennes Conference between Harrison and Tecumseh Formation of War Hawk faction
1811	United States breaks trade relations with Britain Second Vincennes Conference between Harrison and Tecumseh Battle of Tippecanoe and destruction of Prophetstown
1812	United States declares war against England United States invades Canada James Madison reelected
1813	Fort Mims massacre Battle of Put-in-Bay Embargo of 1813 First mechanized textile factory, Waltham, Massachusetts Battle of the Thames
1814	Battle of Horseshoe Bend Napoleon defeated British capture and burn Washington, D.C. Battle of Plattsburgh Treaty of Ghent
1815	Battle of New Orleans Treaty of Fort Jackson Portage des Sioux treaties
1819	Treaty of Edwardsville
1825	Prairie du Chien treaties

lands to the United States as part of the compromise necessary to gain ratification for the Constitution (see pages 185–186). With Jefferson's approval, Georgia included the disputed Yazoo lands with other claims, turning the state conflict into a federal one and involving the national government in a matter that Randolph and others believed should have been worked out by the state.

In 1806 Jefferson again irritated Randolph by approaching Congress for a $2 million appropriation to be used to win French influence in convincing Spain to sell Florida to the United States. Citing these and other perceived violations of Republican principles, Randolph announced, "I found I might co-operate or be an honest man." Randolph chose honesty, splitting with Jefferson to form a third party, the **Tertium Quid,** fracturing the Republican united political front.

A second fissure in the party opened over controversial vice president Aaron Burr's political scheming. Upset that Burr had not conceded the presidency immediately after the tied Electoral College vote in 1800, Jefferson snubbed him throughout his first four years in office and then dropped him as his vice-presidential nominee in 1804. But Burr's political failures constituted an opportunity for the Essex Junto: Pickering offered to help Burr become governor of

Tertium Quid Republican faction formed by John Randolph in protest against Jefferson's plan for acquiring Florida from Spain; the name is Latin and means a "third thing," indicating Randolph's rejection of both the Federalist and Republican Parties.

New York if Burr would deliver the state to the northern confederacy and support secession. Burr agreed, but mainstream New York Federalists were furious, especially Alexander Hamilton. During the New York state election in the spring of 1804, Hamilton was quoted by the press as saying that Burr was "a dangerous man, and one who ought not to be trusted with the reins of government." Burr lost the election in a landslide, wrecking the junto's scheme and pushing himself into an even greater personal and political crisis. Never willing to accept defeat gracefully, Burr demanded that Hamilton retract his statements. When Hamilton refused, Burr challenged him to a duel. An excellent shot, the vice president put a bullet directly through Hamilton's liver, wounding him gravely. Hamilton soon died.

Killing Hamilton did not solve Burr's problem: he was indicted for murder and fled. While in hiding, he made contact with James Wilkinson, with whom he struck up some sort of business deal. A former Revolutionary War commander who had become a freelance adventurer, Wilkinson was employed simultaneously by Spain and the United States, each of which thought he represented their interests. Wilkinson's real loyalties and intentions remain mysterious. At one point, he told Spanish officials that he and Burr intended to establish an independent republic in the Mississippi Valley, but Burr informed the British that they intended to carve a republic out of Spanish territory. Once Congress reconvened in the fall of 1804, Burr became immune, as president of the Senate, from prosecution for killing Hamilton and emerged from hiding. He then used his political connections to gain an appointment for Wilkinson to be governor of the Louisiana Territory, providing an institutional foundation for whatever plot they had hatched.

When Burr's vice-presidential term expired in 1805, he ventured west, sailing down the Mississippi to recruit associates. Rumors of intrigue soon surfaced, and federal authorities became interested late in 1806 when they received a letter from Wilkinson implicating Burr in a "deep, dark, wicked, and wide-spread conspiracy" against the United States. Learning that Wilkinson had turned him in, Burr tried to reach Spanish Florida but was captured early in 1807 and put on trial for treason.

Burr's trial was a circus, an open arena for Jefferson and his critics to air their views on such touchy subjects as presidential power, westward expansion, and national loyalty. Presiding over the case, Chief Justice John Marshall, no friend to Jefferson, made it clear that he believed Burr was a victim, not the perpetrator, of a conspiracy. Jefferson, however, asserted his belief that Burr was guilty, and the president was determined to have him prosecuted to the full extent of the law. Using the powers of his office, Jefferson offered pardons to conspirators who would testify against Burr, and he leaked information that would make his former vice president look guilty. He also refused to honor a **subpoena** issued by Marshall requiring the president to appear in court and to produce official presidential documents that might have a bearing on the case. In this instance, Jefferson embarrassed the chief justice by recalling that Marshall had supported George Washington's assertion of presidential privilege when the first president refused to present key papers to Congress relating to Jay's Treaty (see pages 205–206). Marshall backed down, and neither Jefferson nor his executive papers appeared in court.

But Marshall struck back in his own way. The chief justice instructed the jury that the Constitution defined *treason* as "levying war against the United States or adhering to their enemies" and that a guilty verdict required direct evidence from two witnesses. Because Burr had not waged war, and because neither Spain nor Britain was at the moment an enemy of the United States, the jury acquitted the former vice president, to the glee of Jefferson's critics.

The Problem of American Neutrality

Internal tensions in American politics were matched by growing stress in the nation's diplomatic and economic relations. Jefferson's economic successes had been the product of continuing warfare in Europe. With their fleets engaged in naval battles, their people locked in combat, and their lands crisscrossed by opposing armies, Europeans needed American ships and the fruits of American labor, especially food. American neutrality assured continued prosperity as long as the contending parties in Europe agreed to the diplomatic principle of neutrality.

Americans immediately grasped at this opportunity. An upsurge in European campaigning in 1803 helped raise the total value of American exports by over 65 percent. A significant proportion of the in-

---

subpoena A writ, or order, requiring an individual to appear in court to give testimony.

The impressment of sailors into the British navy from American ships was one of the more prominent causes of the War of 1812. This 1790 engraving shows an American sailor being seized at gunpoint while those who might try to assist him are elbowed aside. *Library of Congress.*

crease came from the shipment of foreign goods to foreign markets by way of neutral American ports: sugar from the Caribbean, for example, frequently passed through the United States on its way to Europe. These so-called **reexports** rose in value from $14 million in 1803 to $60 million in 1807, prompting a rapid growth in earnings for American shipping. In 1790, net income from shipping amounted to a mere $5.9 million; by 1807 the volume had surged to $42.1 million.

Prospects seemed bright for America's economic and diplomatic future and for Jefferson's dream of agricultural America feeding overcrowded, war-torn Europe. But politicians in both England and France cared about their own military victories, not about American prosperity. Their decisions, especially those relating to neutral shipping, disrupted American trade and created an atmosphere of hostility.

Another source of tension was a British law that empowered the king's warships to engage in **impressment.** For decades, British sailors had protested the exceedingly cruel conditions and low pay in His Majesty's navy by jumping ship in American ports

and enlisting as merchant sailors on American vessels. Strapped for mariners by renewed warfare, England pursued a vigorous policy of reclaiming British sailors after 1803, even if they were on neutral American ships and, more provocatively, even if they were citizens of the United States. It is estimated that the British abducted as many as eight thousand sailors from American ships between 1803 and 1812. The loss of so many seamen hurt American shippers economically, but it wounded American pride even more. Like the XYZ affair, impressment seemed to be a direct denial of the United States' status as a legitimate nation.

reexports Products shipped from one nation to another by way of a third; during wartime, neutral nations can be used as third parties to carry goods to combatants.

impressment Procedure permitted under British maritime law that authorized commanders of warships to force English civilian sailors into military service.

Economic Warfare

Pressure on American neutrality increased after 1805, when a military deadlock emerged in the European war: Britain was supreme at sea, and France was in control on the continent of Europe. Stuck in a stalemate, both sides used whatever nonmilitary advantages were available in an effort to tip the balance in their favor. Thus the war changed from one of military campaigning to one of diplomatic and economic maneuvering. Seeking to close off foreign supplies to England, in November 1806 Napoleon issued the Berlin Decree, barring ships that had anchored at British harbors from entering ports controlled by France. The British Parliament responded by issuing a series of directives that permitted neutral ships to sail to European ports only if they first called at a British port to pay a transit tax. It was thus impossible for a neutral ship to follow the laws of either nation without violating the laws of the other. All this European blustering, however, had little immediate effect on the American economy. From the issuance of the Berlin Decree to the end of 1807, American exports and shipping rose more than they had risen during any similar period.

But such good fortune was not to last. Seeking to break France's dependence on America as a source for food and other supplies, Napoleon sought an alliance with Russia, and in the spring of 1807 his diplomatic mission succeeded. Having acquired an alternative source for grain and other foodstuffs, Napoleon immediately began enforcing the Berlin Decree, hoping to starve England into submission. The British countered by stepping up enforcement of their European blockade and aggressively pursuing impressment to strengthen the royal navy.

The escalation in both France's and Britain's economic war efforts quickly led to confrontation with Americans and a diplomatic crisis. A pivotal event occurred in June 1807. The British **frigate** *Leopard,* patrolling the American shoreline, confronted the American warship *Chesapeake.* Even though both ships were inside American territorial waters, the *Leopard* ordered the American ship to halt and hand over any British sailors on board. When the *Chesapeake*'s captain refused, the *Leopard* fired several **broadsides,** crippling the American vessel, killing three sailors, and injuring eighteen. The British then boarded the *Chesapeake* and dragged off four men, three of whom were naturalized citizens of the United States. Americans were outraged.

Americans were not the only ones galvanized by British aggression. Shortly after the *Chesapeake* affair, word arrived in the United States that Napoleon had

responded to Britain's belligerence by declaring a virtual economic war against neutrals. In the **Milan Decree,** he vowed to seize any neutral ship that so much as carried licenses to trade with England. What was worse, the Milan Decree stated that ships that had been boarded by British authorities—even against their crew's will—would be subject to immediate French capture.

Many Americans viewed the escalating French and English sanctions as insulting treachery that cried out for an American response. The *Washington Federalist* newspaper observed, "We have never, on any occasion, witnessed . . . such a thirst for revenge." If Congress had been in session, the legislature surely would have called for war, but Jefferson stayed calm. War with England or France or, worse still, with both would bring Jefferson's whole political program to a crashing halt. He had insisted on inexpensive government, lobbied for American neutrality, and hoped for renewed prosperity through continuing trade with Europe. War would destroy his entire agenda. But clearly Jefferson had to do something.

Believing that Europeans were far more dependent on American goods and ships than Americans were on European money and manufactures, Jefferson chose to violate one of his cardinal principles: the U.S. government would interfere in the economy to force Europeans to recognize American neutral rights. In December 1807, the president announced the **Embargo Act,** which would, in effect, close all American foreign trade as of January 1 unless the Europeans agreed to recognize America's neutral rights to trade with anyone it pleased.

Berlin Decree Napoleon's order declaring the British Isles under blockade and authorizing the confiscation of British goods from any ship found carrying them.

frigate A very fast warship, rigged with square sails and carrying from thirty to fifty cannon on two gun decks.

broadside The simultaneous discharge of all the guns on one side of a warship.

Milan Decree Napoleon's order authorizing the capture of any neutral vessels sailing from British ports or submitting to British searches.

Embargo Act Embargo (a government-ordered trade ban) announced by Jefferson in 1807 in order to pressure Britain and France to accept neutral trading rights; it went into effect in 1808 and closed down all U.S. foreign trade.

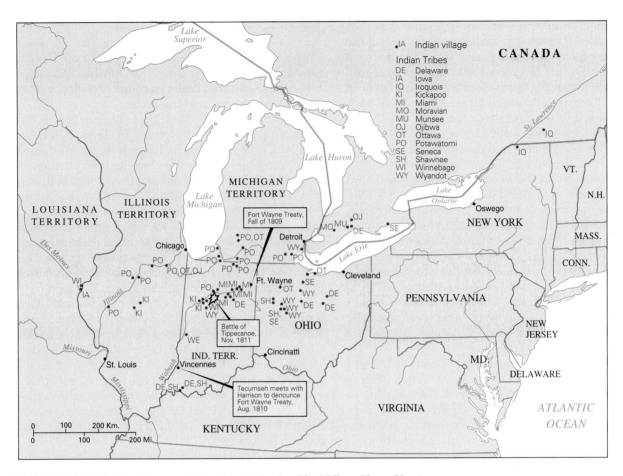

MAP 9.1 Indian Territory, ca. 1812 Frontier leaders like William Henry Harrison were very worried about unified Indian resistance in the years leading up to the War of 1812, and this map shows why. Strong Indian groups, some of which were allied with Tecumseh, formed a nearly solid frontier line on the nation's western borders. Harrison's efforts and the War of 1812 virtually destroyed this constraint on American expansion.

Crises in the Nation

▪ How did Jefferson's economic and Indian policies influence national developments after 1808?

▪ How did problems in Europe contribute to changing conditions in the American West?

▪ What did the actions of frontier politicians such as William Henry Harrison do to bring the nation into war in 1812?

Jefferson's reaction to European aggression immediately began strangling American trade and with it America's domestic economic development. In addition, European countries still had legitimate claims on much of North America, and the Indians who continued to occupy most of the continent had enough military power to pose a serious threat to the United States if properly motivated (see Map 9.1). While impressment, blockade, and embargo paralyzed America's Atlantic frontier, a combination of European and Indian hostility along the western frontier added to the air of national emergency. The resulting series of domestic crises played havoc with Jefferson's vision of a peaceful, prosperous nation.

Economic Depression

Although Jefferson felt justified in suspending free trade to protect neutral rights, the result was the worst economic depression since the founding of the British colonies in North America. Critics such as John Randolph pronounced Jefferson's solution worse than the problem—like trying "to cure corns by cutting off the toes." And while Jefferson's "damn-bargo," as critics called it, was only halfheartedly enforced, the economy slumped disastrously. Taken together, all American exports fell from $109 million to $22 million, and net earnings from shipping fell by almost 50 percent. During 1808, earnings from legitimate business enterprise in America declined to less than a quarter of their value in 1807.

The depression shattered economic and social life in many eastern towns. It has been estimated that thirty thousand sailors were thrown out of work and that as many as a hundred thousand people employed in support industries were laid off. During 1808 in New York City alone, 120 businesses went bankrupt, and the combination of unemployment and business failure led to the imprisonment of twelve hundred New Yorkers for debt. New England, where the economy had become almost entirely dependent on foreign trade, was hit harder still. In light of Jefferson's policies and the collapsing economy, the extremism expressed by the Essex Junto three years earlier began to sound reasonable.

New Englanders screamed loudest about the impact of the embargo, but southerners and westerners were just as seriously affected by it. The economy of the South had depended on the export of staple crops like tobacco since colonial times and was rapidly turning to cotton. There, embargo meant near-death to all legitimate trade. In response to the loss of foreign markets, tobacco prices fell from $6.75 per hundredweight to $3.25, and cotton from 21 to 13 cents per pound. In the West, wholesale prices for agricultural products spiraled downward also. Overall, the prices of farm products were 16 percent lower between 1807 and 1811 than they had been between 1791 and 1801. At the same time, the price of virtually every consumer item went up. For example, the price of building materials—hardware, glass, and milled lumber—rose 11 percent during the same period, and the price of textiles climbed 20 percent. In fact, the only consumer item that did not go up in price was the one item farmers did not need to buy: food. Faced with dropping incomes and soaring costs, farmers probably felt the trade restrictions more profoundly than others.

Rather than blaming their problems on the Republican administration, however, disaffected farmers directed their anger at the British. Frontiersmen believed, rightly or wrongly, that eliminating British interference with American trade would restore the boom economy that had drawn so many of them to the edge of American settlement. Thus westerners banded together to raise their voices in favor of American patriotism and war against Britain.

Political Upheaval

Despite the escalating crisis in the country, Jefferson remained popular and powerful, but like Washington, he chose to step down from the presidency after serving two terms, making it clear to party officials that he favored James Madison to replace him in the upcoming presidential election of 1808. Although Madison and Jefferson had much in common and were longtime friends, they seemed very different from each other. Few could say they knew Madison well, but those who did found him captivating: a man of few words but of piercing intellect and unflinching conviction. Those less well acquainted with him thought the quiet Virginian indecisive: where Jefferson tended to act on impulse, Madison approached matters of state as he approached matters of political philosophy—with caution, patience, and reason.

Riding his reputation as a brilliant political thinker and his status as Jefferson's chosen successor, Madison easily defeated his Federalist opponent, Charles Cotesworth Pinckney. But the one-sided results disguised deep political divisions in the nation at large. Federalist criticism of Jefferson's policies, especially of the embargo, was finding a growing audience as the depression deepened, and in the congressional election in 1808 the Republicans lost twenty-four seats to Federalists.

Internal dissent also weakened the Republican Party. Dissatisfied with Jefferson's policies, both southern and northeastern party members contested Madison's succession. The Tertium Quid challenged Jefferson's authority in the **party caucus** and tried to secure the nomination for the stately and conservative **James Monroe.** Jefferson managed to hold the party's southern wing in line, but northeasterners, stinging under the pressure of the embargo, bucked the decision of the party caucus and nominated their own presidential candidate: New Yorker George Clinton. Although Clinton polled only six electoral votes for the presidency, his nomination was a sign of growing divisions over the problems that the United States faced in 1808.

party caucus A meeting of members of a political party to decide on questions of policy or leadership or to register preferences for candidates running for office.

James Monroe Republican politician from Virginia who served in diplomatic posts under George Washington, John Adams, and Thomas Jefferson; he later became the fifth president of the United States.

During Madison's first two years in office, lack of any progress toward resolving the nation's woes seemed to confirm critics' perception of his indecisiveness. Despite that, Republicans actually made gains in the congressional elections in 1810: they regained fourteen of the seats they had lost in the House in 1808 and picked up two additional Senate seats. But this was no vote of confidence in Madison. Though the new congressmen were Republicans, sixty-three of them did not support Madison or his commitment to a conciliatory policy toward the British. These new members of Congress were mostly very young, extremely patriotic, and represented frontier constituents who were being ravaged by the agricultural depression. In the months to come, their increasingly strident demands for aggressive action against England earned them the nickname **War Hawks.**

The Rise of the Shawnee Prophet

A key reason for War Hawk militancy was the unsettled conditions along the western frontier. Relations with Indians in the West had been peaceful since the Battle of Fallen Timbers in 1794. The Shawnees and other groups had been thrown off their traditional homelands in Ohio by the Treaty of Greenville (see page 206) and forced to move to new lands in Indiana. There, food shortages, disease, and continuing encroachment by settlers caused many young Indians to lose faith in their traditional beliefs and in themselves as human beings.

In the midst of the crisis, one disheartened, diseased alcoholic rose above his afflictions to lead the Indians into a brief new era of hope. Tecumseh's younger brother Lalawethika had bragged that he would play an influential role in his people's affairs (his name meant "Noisemaker"). But his prospects had declined along with those of his people. Lacking his brother's training as a warrior, Lalawethika felt increasingly hopeless, turned to alcohol, and finally in 1805 became critically ill. He claimed that he remembered dying and meeting the Master of Life, who showed him the way to lead his people out of degradation and commanded him to return to the world of the living so he could tell the Indians what they must do to recover their dignity. He then awoke, cured of his illness. Launching a full-fledged religious and cultural revival designed to teach the ways revealed to him by the Master of Life, he adopted the name Tenskwatawa ("the Way"). Whites called him **"The Prophet."**

Blaming the decline of his people on their adoption of white ways, the Prophet taught them to go back to their traditional lifestyle—to discard whites' clothing, religion, and especially alcohol—and live as their ancestors had lived. He also urged his followers to unify against the temptations and threats of white exploiters and hold on to what remained of their lands. If they followed his teachings, the Prophet insisted, the Indians would regain control of their lives and their lands, and the whites would vanish from their world. In 1807 the Prophet established a religious settlement, Prophetstown, on the banks of Tippecanoe Creek in Indiana Territory. This community was to serve as a center for the Prophet's activities and as a living model for revitalized Indian life. The residents of Prophetstown worked together using traditional forms of agriculture, hunting, and gathering.

Although the Prophet preached a message of ethnic pride, nonviolence, and passive resistance, as white settlers continued to pressure his people, he began to advocate more forceful solutions to the Indians' problems. In a speech to an intertribal council in April 1807, he suggested for the first time that warriors unite to resist white expansion. Although he did not urge his followers to attack the whites, he made it clear that the Master of Life would defend him and his followers if war were pressed on them.

Prophecy and Politics in the West

While Tenskwatawa continued to stress spiritual means for stopping white aggression, his brother **Tecumseh** pushed for a more political course of action. Seven years older than the Prophet, Tecumseh had always inclined more toward politics and warfare. Known as a brave fighter and a persuasive political orator, Tecumseh traveled throughout the western frontier, working out political and military alliances designed to put a stop to white expansion once and for all. Although

War Hawks   Members of Congress elected in 1810 from the West and South who campaigned for war with Britain in the hopes of stimulating the economy and annexing new territory.

The Prophet   Shawnee religious visionary who called for a return to Indian traditions and founded the community of Prophetstown on Tippecanoe Creek in Indiana.

Tecumseh   Shawnee leader and brother of the Prophet; he established an Indian confederacy along the frontier that he hoped would be a barrier to white expansion.

Although they had enormous respect for each other, Indiana territorial governor William Henry Harrison and Tecumseh were both ferocious when it came to defending their political and diplomatic positions. This painting of their confrontation at the 1810 peace conference held at Vincennes makes this point clearly. The two never actually came to blows at this meeting or at another held one year later, but they never were able to find common ground. Tecumseh's refusal to compromise his people's rights to their land would eventually lead to renewed warfare and his own death. *Cincinnati Museum Center.*

he did not want to start a war against white settlers, Tecumseh exhorted Indians to defend every inch of land that remained to them. In 1807 he warned Ohio governor Thomas Kirker that they would do so with their lives.

Tecumseh's plan might have brought about his brother's goals. Faced by a unified defensive line of Indians stretching along the American frontier from Canada to the Gulf of Mexico, the United States probably would have found it virtually impossible to expand any farther, and the Indian confederacy would have become a significant force in America's future. The very brilliance of Tecumseh's reasoning and his success at organizing Indian groups caused a great deal of confusion among whites. Various white officials were convinced that the Shawnee leader was a spy either for the French or for the British and that his activities were an extension of some hidden plot by one European power or another. Though wrong, such theories helped to escalate the air of crisis in the West and in the nation at large.

Indiana governor William Henry Harrison had good reason to advance the impression of a conspiracy between Tecumseh and the British. Harrison and men like him believed the United States had the right to control all of North America and, accordingly, to brush aside anything standing in the way by any means available (see Map 9.1). Britain and the Indians were thus linked in their thinking. Both were seen as obstacles to national destiny—and many War Hawks prayed for the outbreak of war between the United States and

the British with the Indians in between. Such a war would provide an excuse for attacking the Indians along the frontier to break up their emerging confederation and dispossess them of their land. In addition, a war would justify invading and seizing Canada, fulfilling what many considered a logical but frustrated objective of the American Revolution. At the same time, taking Canada from the British would open rich timber, fur, and agricultural lands for American settlement. More important, it would secure American control of the Great Lakes and St. Lawrence River—potentially a very valuable shipping route for agricultural produce from upper New York, northern Ohio, and the newly opening areas of the **Old Northwest.**

Choosing War

With the nation reeling from the economic squeeze of the embargo, Congress replaced it with the **Non-Intercourse Act** early in 1809. The new law forbade

---

Old Northwest The area of the United States referred to at the time as the Northwest Territory, it would eventually be broken into the states of Indiana, Illinois, Michigan, and Wisconsin.

Non-Intercourse Act Law passed by Congress in 1809 reopening trade with all nations except France and Britain and authorizing the president to reopen trade with them if they lifted restrictions on American shipping.

trade only with England and France and gave the president the power to reopen trade if either of the combatants lifted its restrictions against American shipping. Even though this act was much less restrictive than the embargo, American merchants were relieved when it expired in the spring of 1810. At that point, Congress passed an even more permissive boycott, **Macon's Bill No. 2.** According to this new law, merchants could trade with the combatants if they wanted to take the risk, but if either France or England lifted its blockade, the United States would stop trading with the other.

Hoping to cut England off from needed outside supplies, Napoleon responded to Macon's Bill in August by sending a letter to the American government promising to suspend French restrictions on American shipping. In secret, however, the French emperor issued an order to continue seizing American ships. Despite Napoleon's devious intentions, Madison sought to use the French peace overture as a lever: he instructed the American mission in London to tell the British that he would close down trade with them unless they joined France in dropping trade restrictions. Sure that Napoleon was lying, the British refused, backing the president into a diplomatic corner. In February 1811, the provisions of Macon's Bill forced Madison to close trading with Britain for its failure to remove economic sanctions, stepping up tensions all around.

Later in the year, events in the West finally triggered a crisis. The underlying origin of the problem was an agreement, the Fort Wayne Treaty, signed in the fall of 1809 between the United States and representatives of the Miami, Potawatomi, and Delaware Indians. In return for an outright bribe of $5,200 and individual **annuities** ranging from $250 to $500, civil chiefs among these three tribes sold over 3 million acres of Indian land in Indiana and Illinois—land already occupied by many other Indian groups.

In August 1810, Tecumseh met with Governor Harrison in Vincennes, Indiana, to denounce the Fort Wayne Treaty. Harrison insisted that the agreement was legitimate. Speaking for those whose lands had been sold out from under them, Tecumseh said, "They want to save that piece of land, we do not wish you to take it. . . . I want the present boundary line to continue. Should you cross it, I assure you it will be productive of bad consequences." But Harrison refused to budge.

The Vincennes meeting convinced the Indians that they must prepare for a white attack. The Prophet increasingly preached the Master of Life's commitment to support the faithful in a battle against the whites.

It Matters

The Battle of Tippecanoe

Americans today largely accept unthinkingly that although Indians are an extremely interesting part of American history, they never really mattered. This modern dismissal of Indian significance is entirely incorrect. Throughout the years leading up to the Battle of Tippecanoe, Harrison warned officials in Washington that if Tecumseh's activities were allowed to continue unchecked, the combined military force he might assemble would be sufficient to stop American westward expansion altogether. This was not baseless exaggeration. As Harrison himself said of Tecumseh, "He is one of those uncommon geniuses, which spring up occasionally to produce revolutions and overturn the established order of things." We will never know how close Tecumseh came to overturning the established order. We do know, however, that he spent a considerable amount of time during 1810 and 1811 traveling throughout the frontier drumming up support. We know, too, that he experienced considerable success. Historians disagree about whether he could have succeeded in stopping American expansion, but there is no question that such a unified force along the American frontier would have compelled politicians like Jefferson to reconsider their policies. In either case, America today would be a profoundly different place had Harrison not destroyed Prophetstown and undermined the growing Indian confederacy.

Tecumseh traveled up and down the American frontier, enlisting additional allies into his growing Indian confederacy. Meanwhile, Harrison grew more and more eager to attack the Indians before they could unite fully. He got his chance when a second peace conference, also held at Vincennes in the summer of

Macon's Bill No. 2 Law passed by Congress in 1810 that offered exclusive trading rights to France or Britain, whichever recognized American neutral rights first.

annuity An allowance or income paid annually.

1811, also failed. Citing the failed peace effort and sporadic skirmishes between frontier settlers and renegade bands of Indians, none of whom were directly connected to Tecumseh, Harrison ordered an attack. On November 7, in the so-called **Battle of Tippecanoe,** an army of enraged frontiersmen burned Prophetstown. Then, having succeeded in setting the Indian frontier ablaze, Harrison called for a declaration of war against the Indians and the British.

Headlining Harrison's call for war, a Kentucky newspaper proclaimed, "The war on the Wabash is purely BRITISH, the SCALPING KNIFE and TOMAHAWK of British savages, is now, again devastating our frontiers." Coming as it did while Congress was already embroiled in debate over economic sanctions and British impressment, the outbreak of violence on the frontier was finally enough to push Madison into action. Still hoping for some sort of peaceful resolution, the president chose his words carefully when he told Congress, "We behold . . . on the side of Great Britain, a state of war against the United States; and on the side of the United States, a state of peace toward Britain." As chairman of the House Foreign Relations Committee, however, **John C. Calhoun** was less circumspect: "The mad ambition, the lust of power, and the commercial avarice of Great Britain have left to neutral nations an alternative only between the base surrender of their rights, and a manly vindication of them." He then introduced a war bill in Congress.

When the vote was finally cast in 1812, the war bill passed by a vote of 79 to 49 in the House and 19 to 13 in the Senate. Although they seemed to have the most to lose from continued indecisive policies, representatives from the heavily Federalist regions that depended the most on overseas trade—Massachusetts, Connecticut, and New York, for example—voted against war, whereas strongly Republican western and southern representatives voted in favor.

The Nation At War

■ What geographic and economic factors impeded American war efforts against Great Britain and Britain's Indian allies?

■ How did events in Europe influence the war in America?

■ To what extent were Americans' objectives in going to war accomplished?

The nation was dreadfully unprepared when the breach with England finally came. With virtually no army or navy, the United States was taking a terrible risk in engaging what was fast becoming the most awesome military power in the world. Not surprisingly, defeat and humiliation were the main fruits of American efforts as the two nations faced off.

The Fighting Begins

Despite years of agitation, the war's actual arrival in 1812 caught the United States terribly unprepared. Republican cost cutting had virtually disbanded the military during Jefferson's first term in office. Renewed fighting with pirates in the Mediterranean and building tensions in the Atlantic had forced Republicans to increase military spending, but the navy still had fewer than twenty vessels, and the army could field fewer than seven thousand men. And for all its war fever, Congress balked at appropriating new funds even after war had been declared. Thus the first ventures in the war went forward with only grudging financial support.

In line with what the War Hawks wanted, the first military campaign was a three-pronged drive toward Canada and against the Indians (see Map 9.2). One force, commanded by Harrison, was successful in raiding undefended Indian villages but was unable to make any gains against British troops. Farther east, a force led by Major General Stephen Van Rensselaer was defeated by a small British and Indian army. Meanwhile, the third force, commanded by Henry Dearborn, lunged at Montreal but nervously withdrew back into U.S. territory after an inconclusive battle against the British.

American sailors fared much better during the war's opening days. Leading the war effort at sea were three frigates: the *Constitution* (popularly known as **Old Ironsides**), the *President,* and the *United States.* In mid-August, the *Constitution* outmaneuvered and eventually sank what the British described as "one of our stoutest frigates," the H.M.S. *Guerrière.* The *United States,* under the command of Stephen Decatur, enjoyed a victory against the British frigate the H.M.S.

Battle of Tippecanoe Battle near Prophetstown in 1811, where American forces led by William Henry Harrison defeated the followers of the Shawnee Prophet and destroyed the town.

John C. Calhoun Congressman from South Carolina who was a leader of the War Hawks and the author of the official declaration of war in 1812.

Old Ironsides Nickname of the U.S.S. *Constitution,* the forty-four-gun American frigate whose victory over the *Guerrière* bolstered sagging national morale during the War of 1812.

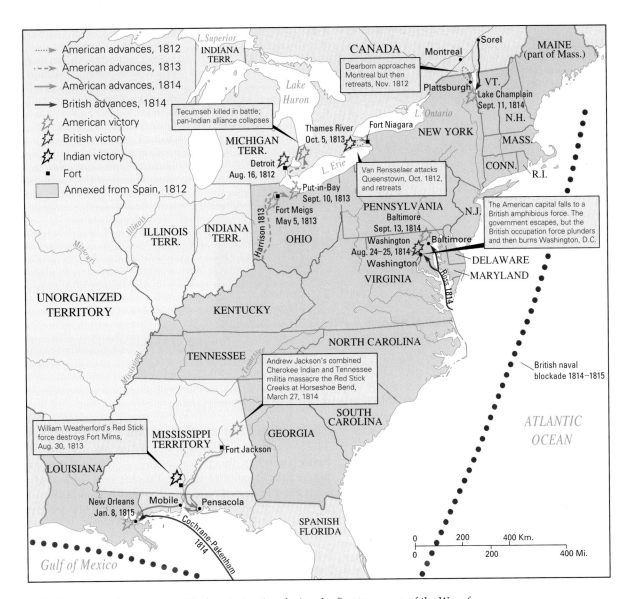

MAP 9.2 The War of 1812 The heaviest action during the first two years of the War of 1812 lay along the U.S./Canadian border. In 1814 the British sought to knock the United States out of the war by staging three offensives: one along the northern frontier at Platts-burgh, New York; one into the Chesapeake; and a third directed at the Mississippi River at New Orleans. All three offensives failed.

Macedonian. Enduring thirty broadsides fired by the *Macedonian*, Decatur's gunners splintered the British ship with seventy broadsides of their own. Though no stranger to the horrors of war, Decatur was shocked by what he found when he boarded the crippled vessel: "fragments of the dead scattered in every direction, the decks slippery with blood, and one continuous agonizing yell of the unhappy wounded." American privateers also enjoyed success, capturing

450 British merchant ships valued in the millions during the first six months of the war.

American naval victories were all that kept the nation's morale alive in 1812. Former Treasury secretary Albert Gallatin summarized the nation's humiliating military efforts: "The series of misfortunes," he wrote to Jefferson, "exceeds all anticipations made even by those who had least confidence in our inexperienced officers and undisciplined men." The land war had

Naval victories like the sinking of the H.M.S. *Guerrière* by the U.S.S. *Constitution,* shown here in an 1812 painting by Michael Felice Corne, were the only things keeping American morale alive during the disastrous first year of the War of 1812. *"Constitution & Guerrière" by Michael Felice Corne. The New Haven Colony Historical Society, gift of Mrs. S. Galpin.*

been, as another politician would recall, a "miscarriage, without even the heroism of disaster." Vowing to reverse the situation, Congress increased the size of the army to fifty-seven thousand men and offered a $16 bonus to encourage enlistments.

Thus in 1812 Madison stood for reelection at a time when the nation's military fate appeared uncertain and his own leadership seemed shaky. Although the majority of his party's congressional caucus supported him for reelection, nearly a third of the Republican congressmen—mostly those from New York and New England—rallied around New Yorker De-Witt Clinton, nephew and political ally of Madison's former challenger George Clinton. Like his uncle, De-Witt Clinton was a Republican who favored Federalist economic policies and agreed with New England Federalists that the war was unnecessary. Most Federalists supported Clinton, and the party did not field a candidate of its own.

When the campaign was over, the outcome was nearly the same as the congressional vote on the war bill earlier in the year. New York and New England rallied behind Clinton. The South and West continued to support Madison, the Republicans, and war. Madison won but was in no position to gloat. His share of electoral votes had fallen from 72 percent in 1808 to 58.9 percent. At the same time, Republican Party strength in the House dropped by over 13 percent, in the Senate by about 8 percent.

The War Continues

When military campaigning resumed in the spring of 1813, it appeared that the U.S. Army would fare as badly as it had the previous fall. Fighting resumed when British colonel Henry Proctor and Tecumseh, with a joint force of nine hundred British soldiers and twelve hundred Indians, laid siege to Harrison's command camped at Fort Meigs on the Maumee Rapids in Ohio. An army of twelve hundred Kentucky militiamen finally arrived and drove the enemy off, but they were so disorganized that they lost nearly half their number in pursuing the British and Indian force. Harrison was shocked, proclaiming the Kentuckians' "excessive ardour scarcely less fatal than cowardice." Having escaped virtually unscathed, Proctor and Tecumseh continued to harass American forces through the summer. Then, with winter approaching, the British and Indians withdrew to Canada. Harrison, who had been busy raising additional troops, decided to pursue.

No doubt Harrison's new effort would have proved as fruitless as his earlier ones, but an unexpected event turned the odds in his favor. One key problem plaguing Harrison and other commanders in the field was that the British controlled the Great Lakes and so could depend on an uninterrupted supply line. In contrast, American forces and their supplies moved along undeveloped roads and were easy targets for

Choosing to side with the British against the United States in the War of 1812, Tecumseh joined British commander Henry Proctor in leading a joint force of Indians and British regulars. On October 5, 1813, their force was attacked by an army led by Tecumseh's old rival William Henry Harrison. As shown in this painting of the battle, a penetrating cavalry charge (upper left) broke the British line while the Indian forces continued fighting. In the melee, Tecumseh was shot and died on the field. In this romanticized view, we see him, gun down and tomahawk raised as a bullet from a mounted officer's pistol moves unerringly toward him. *Library of Congress.*

Indian and British attackers. **Oliver Hazard Perry,** a young naval tactician, had been given command of a small fleet assigned to clear the lakes of British ships. After months of playing hide-and-seek among the shore islands, British and American ships met in battle at Put-in-Bay in September 1813. Two hours of cannon fire left Perry's **flagship,** the *Lawrence,* nearly destroyed, and 80 percent of the crew lay dead or wounded. Perry refused to surrender. He slipped off his damaged vessel and took command of another ship standing nearby. What remained of his command then sailed back into the heart of the British force and after three hours of close combat subdued and captured six British ships. Perry immediately sent a note to Harrison stating, "We have met the enemy and they are ours."

Buoyed by this news, Harrison's army closed in on Proctor and Tecumseh at the Thames River, about 50 miles northeast of Detroit, on October 5. The British force faced a piercing cavalry charge and lacking naval support was soon forced to surrender. The Indians held out longer, but when word spread that Tecumseh had been killed, they melted into the woods,

leaving the body of their fallen leader to be torn apart by the victorious Americans.

Another war front had also opened farther south during 1813. Although the Creek Confederacy as a whole wished to remain neutral, one faction calling themselves the Red Sticks had allied with Tecumseh in 1812. In the summer of 1813, Red Stick leader William Weatherford led a force against Fort Mims, killing all but about thirty of the more than three hundred occupants. The so-called Fort Mims massacre enraged whites in the Southeast. In Tennessee, twenty-five hundred militiamen rallied around **Andrew Jackson,**

Oliver Hazard Perry American naval officer who led the fleet that defeated the British in the Battle of Put-in-Bay during the War of 1812.

flagship The ship that carries the fleet commander and bears the commander's flag.

Andrew Jackson General who defeated the Creeks at Horseshoe Bend in 1814 and the British at New Orleans in 1815; he later became the seventh president of the United States.

a young brawler and Indian fighter. Already called "Old Hickory" because of his toughness, Jackson made a bold promise: "The blood of our women & children shall not call for vengeance in vain." In the course of that summer and fall, Jackson's frontier ruffians fought multiple engagements against the Red Stick Creeks, driving them into hiding.

While these battles raged on land, the British shut down American forces at sea. Embarrassed by the success of Old Ironsides and the other American frigates, the British admiralty ordered that "the naval force of the enemy should be quickly and completely disposed of" and sent sufficient ships to do the job. The American naval fleet and **merchant marine** found themselves bottled up in port by the world's strongest navy.

The Politics of War

The war had wound down for the winter by the time Congress reconvened in December 1813, but the outlook was not good. Disappointed that American forces had not knocked the British out of the war, Republican representative William Murfree spoke for many when he said, "The result of the last campaign disappointed the expectations of every one." President Madison tried to be optimistic. Recalling the victories during the year, he said, "The war, with its **vicissitudes,** is illustrating the capacity and destiny of the United States to be a great, a flourishing, and a powerful nation."

Madison's optimism seemed justified later in December when the British offered to open direct peace negotiations with the Americans. The president quickly formed a peace commission, but until its work was done, Madison and Congress still had to worry about the practical issues of troops and money, both of which were in critically short supply.

Despite increases in army pay and bonuses for new recruits, enlistments were falling off in 1813. Congressional Republicans responded by adding further enticements for new recruits, including grants of 160 acres of land in the western territories. Congress also authorized the president to extend the term of enlistment for men already in service. By 1814, Congress had increased the size of the army to more than sixty-two thousand men but had not figured out how to pay for all the changes.

Presenting the federal budget for 1814, Treasury Secretary William Jones announced that the government's income would be approximately $16 million, but its expenses would amount to over $45 million. Traditional enemies of internal taxes, the Republicans faced a dilemma. Shortly after convening, members

of Congress had passed a set of new taxes and could not imagine explaining another increase to their constituents. So congressional Republicans decided to borrow instead, authorizing a $35 million deficit.

Adding to the money problem was the fact that, to this point in the war, the United States had permitted neutral nations to trade freely in American ports, carrying American exports to England and Canada and English goods into eastern ports. As a result of this flourishing trade, American currency was flooding out of the United States at an alarming rate, weakening the nation's economy. At the same time, American food was rolling directly into British military commissaries, strengthening the enemy's ability and will to fight.

In a secret message to Congress, the president proposed an absolute embargo on all American ships and goods—neither was to leave port—and a complete ban on imports that were customarily produced in Great Britain. Federalists, especially those from New England, screamed in protest. They called the proposal "an engine of tyranny, an engine of oppression," no different, they said, from the Intolerable Acts imposed on American colonies by Britain in 1774 (see pages 135–137). But congressional Republicans passed the embargo a mere eight days after Madison submitted it.

The **Embargo of 1813** was the most far-reaching trade restriction bill ever passed by Congress. It confined all trading ships to port, and even fishing vessels could put to sea only if their masters posted sizable **bonds.** Government officials charged with enforcing the new law had unprecedented **discretionary powers.** The impact was devastating: the embargo virtually shut down the New England and New York economies, and it severely crippled the economy of nearly every other state.

New British Offensives

While Congress debated matters of finance and trade restrictions, events in Europe were changing the en-

merchant marine   A nation's commercial ships.

vicissitudes   Sudden or unexpected changes encountered during the course of life.

Embargo of 1813   An absolute embargo on all American trade and British imports.

bond   A sum of money paid as bail or security.

discretionary powers   Powers to be used at one's own judgment; in government, powers given to an administrative official to be used without outside consultation or oversight.

Although the British were successful in capturing the United States capital, defenders stalled the invasion long enough for the government to escape. In frustration, the British pillaged the deserted city and then burned the public buildings. The Capitol Building was badly damaged and all of the books in the Library of Congress, which was housed in the building, were destroyed. *"The Capitol," watercolor 1814, by George Munger. Photo by Israel Sack.*

tire character of the war. On March 31, 1814, the British and their allies took Paris, forcing Napoleon to abdicate his throne. Few in America mourned the French emperor's fall. Jefferson wrote, "I rejoice . . . in the downfall of Bonaparte. This scourge of the world has occasioned the deaths of at least ten millions of human beings." Napoleon's defeat, however, left the United States as Great Britain's sole military target. Republican Joseph Nicholson expressed a common lament when he observed, "We should have to fight hereafter not for 'free Trade and sailors rights,' not for the Conquest of the Canadas, but for our national Existence."

As Nicholson feared, a flood of combat-hardened British veterans began arriving in North America, and the survival of the United States as an independent nation was indeed at issue. By the late summer of 1814, British troop strength in Canada had risen to thirty thousand men. From this position of power, the British prepared a chain of three offensives to bring the war to a quick end.

In August 1814, twenty British warships and several troop transports sailed up Chesapeake Bay toward Washington, D.C. The British arrived outside Washington at midday on August 24. The troops defending the city could not withstand the force of hardened British veterans, but they delayed the invasion long enough for the government to escape. Angered at being foiled, the British sacked the city, torching most of the buildings. They then moved on toward the key port city of Baltimore.

At Baltimore, the British navy had to knock out Fort McHenry and take the harbor before the army could take the city. On September 13, British ships armed with heavy **mortars** and rockets attacked the

mortar A portable, muzzle-loading cannon that fires large projectiles at high trajectories over a short range; traditionally used by mobile troops against fixed fortifications.

fort. Despite the pounding, when the sun rose on September 14, the American flag continued to wave over Fort McHenry. The sight moved a young Georgetown volunteer named **Francis Scott Key,** who had watched the shelling as a prisoner aboard one of the British ships, to record the event in a poem that was later set to music and became the national anthem of the United States. Having failed to reduce the fort, the British were forced to withdraw, leaving Baltimore undisturbed.

While this strike at the nation's midsection was raging, Sir George Prevost, governor-general of Canada, massed ten thousand troops for an invasion in the north. The British force arrived just north of Plattsburgh, New York, on September 6, where it was to join the British naval fleet that controlled Lake Champlain. However, a small American flotilla under the command of Lieutenant Thomas Macdonough outmaneuvered the imposing British armada and forced a surrender on September 11. Prevost had already begun his attack against the defenders at Plattsburgh, but when he learned that the British lake fleet was defeated and in flames, he lost his nerve and ordered his men to retreat.

On yet another front, the British pressed an offensive against the Gulf Coast designed to take pressure off Canada and close transportation on the Mississippi River. The defense of the Gulf Coast fell to Andrew Jackson and his Tennesseans. Having spent the winter raising troops and collecting supplies, in March 1814 Jackson and his army of four thousand militiamen and Cherokee volunteers resumed their mission to punish the Red Stick Creeks. Learning that the Red Sticks had established a camp on the peninsula formed by a bend in the Tallapoosa River, Jackson led his men on a forced march to attack. On March 27 in what was misleadingly called the **Battle of Horseshoe Bend,** Jackson's force trapped the Creeks and slaughtered nearly eight hundred people, destroying Red Stick opposition and severely crippling Indian resistance in the South.

After the massacre at Horseshoe Bend, Jackson moved his army toward the Gulf of Mexico, where a British offensive was in the making. Arriving in New Orleans on December 1, he found the city ill prepared to defend itself. The local militia, consisting mostly of French and Spanish residents, would not obey American officers. "Those who are not for us are against us, and will be dealt with accordingly," Jackson proclaimed. He turned increasingly to unconventional sources of support. Free blacks in the city formed a regular army corps, and Jackson created a special unit of black refugees from Santo Domingo under the

command of Colonel Jean Baptiste Savary. White citizens protested Jackson's arming of runaway slaves, but he ignored their objections. "Legitimate citizens" protested too when Jackson accepted a company of river pirates under the command of **Jean Lafitte,** awarding them a blanket pardon for all past crimes. "Hellish Banditti," Jackson himself called them, but the pirate commander and the general hit it off so well that Lafitte became Jackson's constant companion during the campaign.

Having pulled his ragtag force together, Jackson settled in to wait for the British attack. On the morning of January 8, 1815, it came. The British force, commanded by General Edward Pakenham, emerged from the fog at dawn, directly in front of Jackson's defenses. Waiting patiently behind hastily constructed barricades, Jackson's men began firing cannon, rifles, and muskets as the British moved within range. According to one British veteran, it was "the most murderous fire I have ever beheld before or since." Pakenham tried to keep his men from running but was cut in half by a cannonball.

When it was all over, more than two thousand British troops had been killed or wounded in the **Battle of New Orleans,** while a mere seventy-one Americans fell. This was by far the most successful battle fought by American forces during the War of 1812. But ironically, it was fought after the war was over.

The War's Strange Conclusion

While the British were closing in on Washington in the summer of 1814, treaty negotiations designed to end the war were beginning in Ghent, Belgium. Confident that their three-pronged attack against the United States would soon knock the Americans out of

---

Francis Scott Key Author of "The Star-Spangled Banner," which chronicles the British bombardment of Fort McHenry in 1814; Key's poem, set to music, became the official U.S. national anthem in 1931.

Battle of Horseshoe Bend Battle in 1814 in which Tennessee militia massacred Creek Indians in Alabama, ending Red Stick resistance to white westward expansion.

Jean Lafitte Leader of a band of pirates in southeast Louisiana; he offered to fight for the Americans at New Orleans in return for the pardon of his men.

Battle of New Orleans Battle in the War of 1812 in which American troops commanded by Andrew Jackson destroyed the British force attempting to seize New Orleans.

The nearly miraculous American victory in the Battle of New Orleans—fought two weeks after the Americans and British had signed a peace treaty—helped launch a new era in American nationalism. And, as this illustration from a popular magazine shows, it made Andrew Jackson, shown waving his hat to encourage his troops, a national hero of greater-than-human proportions. *Library of Congress.*

the war, the British delegates were in no hurry to end it by diplomacy. They refused to discuss substantive issues, insisting that all of the matters raised by Madison's peace commission were nonnegotiable.

At that point, however, domestic politics in England began to play a deciding role. After nearly a generation of armed conflict, the English people were war-weary, especially the taxpayers. As one British official put it, "Economy & relief from taxation are not merely the War Cry of Opposition, but they are the real objects to which public attention is turned." The failures at Plattsburgh and Baltimore made it appear that at best the war would drag on at least another year, at an estimated cost to Britain of an additional $44 million. Moreover, continuation of the American war was interfering with Britain's European diplomacy. Trying to arrive at a peace settlement for Europe at the **Congress of Vienna,** a British official commented, "We do not think the Continental Powers will continue in good humour with our Blockade of the whole Coast of America." Speaking for the military, the **Duke of Wellington** reviewed British military successes and failures in the American war and advised his countrymen, "You have no right . . . to demand any **concession** . . . from America."

In the end, the **Treaty of Ghent,** completed on December 24, 1814, simply restored diplomatic relations between England and the United States to what they had been prior to the outbreak of war. The treaty said nothing about impressment, blockades, or neutral trading rights. Neither military action nor diplomatic

finagling netted Canada for the War Hawks. And the treaty did nothing about the alleged conspiracies between Indians and British agents. Although Americans called the War of 1812 a victory, they actually won none of the prizes that Madison's war statement had declared the nation was fighting for.

Peace and the Rise of New Expectations

■ How did events during the War of 1812 help to move the American economy in new directions after peace was restored?

■ What impact did changes in the economy have on the institution of slavery and on the lives of slaves?

Congress of Vienna Conference between ambassadors from the major powers in Europe to redraw the continent's political map after the defeat of Napoleon; it also sought to uproot revolutionary movements and restore traditional monarchies.

Duke of Wellington The most respected military leader in Great Britain at this time, Wellington was responsible for the defeat of Napoleon.

concession In diplomacy, something given up during negotiations.

Treaty of Ghent Treaty ending the War of 1812, signed in Belgium in 1814; it restored peace but was silent on the issues over which the United States and Britain had gone to war.

Despite repeated military disasters, loss of life, and diplomatic failure, the war had a number of positive effects on the United States. Just to have survived a war against the British was enough to build national confidence, but to have scored major victories such as those at Plattsburgh, Baltimore, and especially New Orleans was truly worth boasting about. Americans emerged from the conflict with a new sense of national pride and purpose. And many side effects from the fighting itself gave Americans new hopes and plans.

New Expectations in the Northeastern Economy

Although trading interests in the Northeast suffered following Jefferson's embargo and were nearly ruined by the war and Madison's embargo, a new avenue of economic expansion opened in New England. Cut off from European manufactured goods, Americans started to make more textiles and other items for themselves.

Samuel Slater, an English immigrant who had been trained in manufacturing in Britain, introduced the use of machines for spinning cotton yarn to the United States in 1790. His mill was financially successful, but few others tried to copy his enterprise. Even with shipping expenses, tariffs, and other added costs, buying machine-made British cloth was still more practical than investing large sums at high risk to build competing factories in the United States. And after 1800, Jefferson's economic policies discouraged such investment. But his embargo changed all that. After it went into effect in 1808, British fabrics became increasingly unavailable and prices soared. Slater and his partners moved quickly to expand their spinning operations to fill the void. And now his inventiveness was widely copied.

Another entrepreneur, Francis Cabot Lowell, went even further than Slater. Left in the lurch economically by the embargo, Lowell ventured to England in 1810. While there, he engaged in wholesale industrial espionage, observing British textile-manufacturing practices and machinery and making detailed notes and sketches of what he saw. Returning to the United States just before war broke out in 1812, Lowell formed the Boston Manufacturing Company. In 1813 the company used the plans Lowell had smuggled back to the United States to build a factory in Waltham, Massachusetts. The new facility included spinning machines, power looms, and all the equipment necessary to **mechanize** every stage in the production of finished cloth, bringing the entire process under one roof. Like Slater's innovations, Lowell's too were soon duplicated by economically desperate New Englanders.

The spread of textile manufacturing was astonishing. Prior to 1808, only fifteen cotton mills of the sort Slater had introduced had been built in the entire country. But between the passage of the embargo and the end of 1809, eighty-seven additional mills had sprung up, mostly in New England. And when war came, the pace increased, especially when Lowell's idea of a mechanized textile factory proved to be highly efficient and profitable. The number of people employed in manufacturing increased from four thousand in 1809 to perhaps as many as a hundred thousand in 1816. In the years to come, factories in New England and elsewhere supplied more and more of the country's consumer goods.

New Opportunities in the West

But business growth was not confined to the Northeast. Following the war, pioneers poured into the West in astounding numbers. The population of Ohio had already soared from 45,000 in 1800 to 231,000 in 1810, but it more than doubled again by 1820, reaching 581,000. Indiana, Illinois, Missouri, and Michigan experienced similar growth. Most of those who flooded into the newly opened West were small farmers, but subsistence agriculture was not the only economic opportunity that drew expectant Americans into the region. Big business, too, had great expectations for finding new wealth in the West.

One of the designs behind the Lewis and Clark and the Zebulon Pike expeditions had been to gain entry for the United States into the burgeoning economy in North America's interior (see pages 227–228). That economy was complex, with many commodities being traded, and few entirely understood all of its intricacies. There was one facet, though, that was well known and very desirable to entrepreneurs: the brown gold of beaver, mink, and other animal furs.

Even before the War of 1812, individual fur traders had tried to break the monopoly wielded by the English and Canadians over the trade along the northern frontier and by the Spanish and French farther south. One particularly visionary businessman had already put a plan in motion before the war to create a continent-wide trading network. John Jacob Astor, a German immigrant who had arrived in the United

---

mechanize   To substitute machinery for human labor.

Generally, when we think of the Far West in the early nineteenth century, especially the fur trade, we think of wild adventures experienced by colorful men who had little thought for responsibilities or wealth. Attractive though that image may be, the fact is that the early American fur trade was big business and the entrepreneurs who succeeded at it became true captains of industry. Here we see the home that fur profits built for the Chouteau family in St. Louis, a considerable mansion by any standards. *"St. Louis the Fourth City, 1764–1909" by Walter B. Stevens. S. J. Clarke Publishing Co. , 1909.*

States in 1783, announced that he intended to establish "a range of Posts or Trading houses" along the route that Lewis and Clark had followed from St. Louis to the Pacific (see Map 8.2).

Another visionary entrepreneur sought a similar fortune in the Southwest. Auguste Chouteau was French by birth, but like many frontiersmen, he changed nationalities as frequently as the borderlands changed owners. Chouteau had helped to found the town of St. Louis and had been instrumental in establishing that city as the capital for a fur-trading empire. He, his brother Pierre, and an extended family of business partners used intermarriage to create a massive kinship network that included important French, Spanish, and Indian connections. With kinship ensuring cooperative trading partners, the Chouteau brothers were able to extend their reach deep into the Missouri region and establish trade between St. Louis and the Spanish far western trading capital at Santa Fe (see page 51). As Americans began to penetrate the area, the Chouteau brothers took the change in stride, inviting William Clark of the Corps of Discov-

ery and fur entrepreneur Andrew Henry to join forces with them in founding the Missouri Fur Company in 1809.

The war disrupted both Astor's and the Missouri Fur Company's operations, but when the war was over, the fur business resumed with increasing vigor. Pierre Chouteau and his various American partners pushed continually farther into the West, using their strategy of forming traditional Indian trading partnerships, often rooted in intermarriage, to expand business. Chouteau also used his kin partnerships and capital from the fur trade to branch into other businesses. He was a cofounder of the Bank of Missouri and served as its president for a number of years. He also operated flour mills and distilleries and speculated in real estate. Members of his extended family later helped to found Kansas City, pioneered mining in Colorado, and financed railroad building in the Dakotas.

The joint efforts of individual farmers and business tycoons such as Astor and the Chouteaus opened the West and proved to the satisfaction of many that

Following the War of 1812 and the death of Tecumseh, aggressive American expansionists put great pressure on Indians living on the eastern side of the Mississippi River to move farther west. In location after location, American Indian agents and their military escorts set up treaty negotiations designed to acquire ever-increasing amounts of land that would accommodate ambitious would-be farmers. This painting captures one of the largest of these, the Prairie du Chien conference of 1825, at which the Sauk, Fox, Chippewa, and other Indians in Illinois, Wisconsin, and Michigan ceded huge portions of land in hopes of winning peace. *Wisconsin Historical Society.*

great fortunes and good lives could be had on the frontier. Though the promise was nearly always greater than the reality, the allure of the West was unmistakable. And after the War of 1812, the nation's aspirations became more and more firmly tied to that region's growth and development.

But American westward expansion posed a terrible threat to Native Americans. When Harrison's soldiers burned Prophetstown and later killed Tecumseh, they wiped out all hopes for a pan-Indian confederacy. In addition, the civil war among the Creeks, followed by Jackson's victories against the Red Stick faction, removed all meaningful resistance to westward expansion in the South. Many Indian groups continued to wield great power, but accommodationist leaders such as those who formed the Cherokee government suggested that cooperation with federal authorities was the best course.

Collaboration between the United States and Native Americans helped to prevent renewed warfare, but at enormous cost to the Indians. Within a year of the Battle of Horseshoe Bend, Jackson forced the Creeks to sign the Treaty of Fort Jackson, which confiscated over 20 million acres of land from the Creek Confederacy. A similar but more gradual assault on Indian landholding began in the Northwest in 1815. In a council meeting at Portage des Sioux in Illinois Territory, the United States signed peace accords with the various tribes that had joined the British during the war. Both sides pledged that their earlier hostilities would be "forgiven and forgotten" and that all the agreeing parties would live in "perpetual peace and friendship." The northwestern Indians, however, possessed some 2 million acres of prime real estate between the Illinois and Mississippi Rivers—land that the United States government had already given away as enlistment bonuses to white war volunteers. Moving the Indians off that land as quickly as possible thus became a matter of national priority.

Over the next several years, **federal Indian agents** used every tactic they could think of to coerce groups like the Kickapoo Indians into ceding their lands. Finally, in 1819, the Kickapoo Nation signed the Treaty of Edwardsville, turning over most of the land the United States had demanded. Having secured this massive tract, government agents then turned their attention to the vast holdings of more distant tribes—the Sauk, Fox, Chippewa, and Dakota Indians in western Illinois, Wisconsin, and Michigan. As they had done with the Kickapoos, American negotiators used bribery, threat, and manipulation of local tensions to pursue their goal, eventually winning an enormous cession of land in the Prairie du Chien treaties of 1825.

A Revolution in the Southern Economy

Indian dispossession and westward expansion also promised great economic growth for the South. In the years before the War of 1812, the southern economy had been sluggish, and the future of the region's single-crop agricultural system was doubtful. Tobacco, the mainstay of the South's economy, was no longer the glorious profit maker it had been during the colonial period. Sea Island cotton, rice, sugar, and other products continued to find markets, but they grew only in limited areas. However, the technological and economic changes that came in the war's wake pumped new energy into the South. In only a few decades, an entirely new South would emerge.

The mechanization of the British textile industry in the late eighteenth century created an enormous new demand for cotton. Southern planters had been growing the fibrous plant since colonial times, but soil and climatic conditions limited the growing area for the sort of **long-staple cotton** that could be harvested and sold economically. Large areas of the South and Southwest had proved suitable for growing **short-staple cotton,** but the time and labor required to pick the sticky seeds from the compact **cotton bolls** made the crop unprofitable. In 1793 a young Yale College graduate, **Eli Whitney,** was a guest at a plantation in Georgia, where he learned about the difficulty of removing the seeds from short-staple cotton. In a matter of weeks, Whitney helped to perfect a machine that allowed a small and unskilled work force to quickly comb out the seeds without damaging the fibers. He obtained a **patent** for the cotton gin (short for "cotton engine") in 1794 and set up a factory in New Haven, Connecticut, to manufacture the machine. Whitney's engine, though revolutionary in its impact, was a relatively simple mechanism, and despite his patent, other manufacturers and individual planters stole the design and built their own cotton gins.

The outcome of Whitney's inventiveness was the rapid spread of short-staple cotton throughout inland South Carolina and Georgia. Then, just as it seemed that the southern economy was about to bloom, embargo and war closed down exports to England. Although some cotton growers were able to shift sales from England to the rising new factories in New England, a true explosion of growth in cotton cultivation had to await war's end.

With the arrival of peace and the departure of the British naval blockade, cotton growing began to spread at an astounding rate. The massacre of the Red Stick Creeks removed the final major threat of Indian resistance in the South, and southerners rushed into frontier areas, spreading cotton agriculture into Alabama and Mississippi and then into Arkansas, northern Louisiana, and eastern Texas. From 1815 onward, the South's annual cotton crop grew by leaps and bounds. By 1840, annual exports reached nearly a million and a half bales, and increasing volumes were consumed within the United States by the mushrooming textile factories in the Northeast.

federal Indian agents Government officials who were responsible for negotiating treaties with Native American groups; at this time they were employed by the War Department.

long-staple cotton A variety of cotton with long and loosely packed pods of fiber that is easy to comb out and process.

short-staple cotton A variety of cotton with short and tightly packed pods of fiber in which the plant's seeds are tangled.

cotton boll The pod of the cotton plant; it contains the plant's seeds surrounded by the fluffy fiber that is spun into yarn.

Eli Whitney American inventor and manufacturer; his perfecting of the cotton gin revolutionized the cotton industry.

patent A government grant that gives the creator of an invention the sole right to produce, use, or sell that invention for a set period of time.

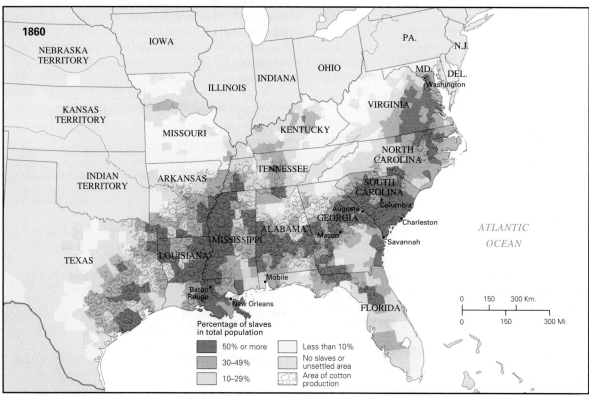

MAP 9.3 Cotton Agriculture and Slave Population Between 1820 and 1860, the expansion of cotton agriculture and the extension of slavery went hand in hand. As these maps show, cotton production was an isolated activity in 1820, and slavery remained isolated as well. By 1860, both had extended westward.

Reviving and Reinventing Slavery

Before the emergence of cotton, when the South's agricultural system was foundering, many southerners began to question the use of slaves. In 1782 Virginia made it legal for individual masters to free their slaves, and many did so. In 1784 Thomas Jefferson proposed (but saw defeated) a land ordinance that would have prohibited slavery in all of the nation's territories after 1800. Some southern leaders advocated abolishing slavery and transporting freed blacks to Africa. But the booming southern economy after the War of 1812 required more labor than ever. As a result, African American slavery expanded as never before.

Viewed side by side, a map showing cotton agriculture and one showing slave population would appear nearly identical (see Map 9.3). In the 1820s, when cotton production was most heavily concentrated in South Carolina and Georgia, the greatest density of slaves occurred in the same area. During the 1840s, as cotton growing spread to the West, slavery followed. By 1860, both cotton growing and slavery would appear on the map as a continuous belt stretching from the Carolinas through Georgia and Alabama and on to the Mississippi River.

The virtually universal shift to cotton growing throughout the South brought about not only the expansion and extension of slavery but also substantial modifications to the institution itself. The wide variety of economic pursuits in which slave labor had been employed from the colonial period onward led to varied patterns in slave employment. In many parts of the South, slaves traditionally exercised a great deal of control over their work schedules as they completed assigned tasks (see page 96). But the cotton business called for large gangs of predominantly unskilled workers, and increasingly slaves found themselves regimented like machines in tempo with the demands of cotton production.

At the same time, as northeastern factories were able to provide clothing, shoes, and other manufactured goods at ever more attractive prices and western farmers shipped cheap pork and grain into southern markets, plantation managers found it more practical to purchase such goods rather than to pro-

The invention of the cotton gin and the spread of cotton agriculture throughout the American South created an enormous new demand for slave workers and changed the nature of their work. A handful of slaves could process large amounts of fiber using the revolutionary new machine, but it took armies of field workers to produce the raw cotton. *Library of Congress.*

duce them. Thus slaves who formerly had performed various skilled tasks such as milling and weaving found themselves pressed into much less rewarding service as brute labor in the cotton fields. To a large extent, then, specialized manufacturing in the North and large-scale commercial food production in the West permitted an intensified cotton industry in the South and helped foster the increasing dehumanization of the peculiar labor system that drove it.

Individual Voices

Examining a Primary Source

Tecumseh Describes American Indian Policy Under William Henry Harrison

Between 1808 and 1811, Shawnee political spokesman Tecumseh and Indiana Territory governor William Henry Harrison engaged in a running war of words. In the course of these discussions, Tecumseh became increasingly frustrated at Harrison's apparent ignorance of political and social organization among the various groups of Indians in the American interior. He repeatedly explained that though relations among the various Indians were complex, they nevertheless constituted a single people and not a patchwork of separate nations. Finally, at a conference in Vincennes on August 20, 1810, Tecumseh lost his temper and accused Harrison of intentionally misunderstanding the nature of Native American intergroup relations as part of a larger effort to defraud the Indians of their land. The original handwritten transcript of this speech contains many abbreviations as well as some unusual spelling and punctuation. The excerpt that follows has been modernized for easier reading.

■ *What exactly is Tecumseh charging Harrison and his agents of doing? What does this suggest about Tecumseh's understanding of the nature of Indian organization and Harrison's misunderstandings about it?*

■ *Why would Tecumseh insist that warriors rather than village chiefs decide policy toward the United States?*

■ *The Wea Indians, a small Miami Indian group, did not sign the Fort Wayne Treaty but later were pressured by Harrison and his accomplice, Winamac, to give their approval. A political headman among the Potawatomi Indians, Winamac worked closely with Harrison, using threats and bribes to convince many of his peers to sign away their lands.*

■ *What did Tecumseh propose to do if Harrison persisted in conducting Indian policy and land acquisition as he had done at Fort Wayne? Why do you think Tecumseh chose this particular approach?*

You try to force the red people to do some injury. It is you that is pushing them on to do mischief. You endeavor to make distinctions. You wish to prevent the Indians to do as we wish them to: unite and let them consider their land as the common property of the whole. You take tribes aside and advise them not to come into this measure. . . .

The reason I tell you this is [that] you want by your distinctions of Indian tribes in allotting to each a particular tract of land to make them to war with each other. You never see an Indian come and endeavor to make the white people do so. You are continually driving the red people when at last you will drive them into the great Lake where they can't either stand or work. ■

You ought to know what you are doing with the Indians. Perhaps it is by direction of the President to make those distinctions. It is a very bad thing and we do not like it. Since my residence at Tippecanoe, we have endeavored to level all distinctions to destroy village chiefs by whom all mischief is done; it is they who sell our land to the Americans [so] our object is to let all our affairs be transacted by Warriors. ■

This land that was sold and the goods that were given for it was only done by a few. The treaty was afterwards brought here and the Weas were induced to give their consent because of their small numbers. The treaty at Fort Wayne was made through the threats [by] Winamac, ■ *but in future we are prepared to punish those chiefs who may come forward to propose to sell their land. If you continue to purchase [land from] them, it will produce war among the different tribes, and at last I do not know what will be the consequences to the white people. . . .*

I now wish you to listen to me. If you do not it will appear as if you wished me to kill all the chiefs that sold you the land. I tell you so because I am authorized by all the tribes to do so. I am at the head of them all. I am a Warrior and all the Warriors will meet together in two or three moons from this. Then I will call for those chiefs that sold you the land and shall know what to do with them. If you do not restore the land, you will have a hand in killing them. ■

Summary

After Jefferson's triumphal first four years in office, factional disputes at home and diplomatic deadlocks with European powers began to plague the Republicans. Although the Federalists were in full retreat, many within Jefferson's own party rebelled against some of his policies. When Jefferson stepped down in 1808, tapping James Madison as his successor, Republicans in both the Northeast and the South bucked the president, supporting George Clinton and James Monroe, respectively.

To a large extent, the Republicans' problems were the outcome of external stresses. On the Atlantic frontier, the United States tried to remain neutral in the wars that engulfed Europe. On the western frontier, the Prophet and Tecumseh were successfully unifying dispossessed Indians into an alliance devoted to stopping U.S. expansion. Things went from bad to worse when Jefferson's use of economic sanctions gave rise to the worst economic depression since the beginnings of English colonization. The embargo strangled the economy in port cities, and the downward spiral in agricultural prices threatened to bankrupt many in the West and South.

The combination of economic and diplomatic constraints brought aggressive politicians to power in 1808 and 1810. Men such as William Henry Harrison expected that war with England would permit the United States finally to realize independence—forcing freedom of the seas, eliminating Indian resistance, and justifying the conquest of the rest of North America. Despite Madison's continuing peace efforts, southern and western interests finally pushed the nation into war with England in 1812.

Although some glimmering moments of glory heartened the Americans, the war was mostly disastrous. But after generations of fighting one enemy or another, the English people demanded peace. When their final offensive in America failed to bring immediate victory in 1814, the British chose to negotiate. Finally, on Christmas Eve, the two nations signed the Treaty of Ghent, ending the war. From a diplomatic point of view, it was as though the war had never happened: everything was simply restored to pre-1812 status.

Nevertheless, in the United States the war created strong feelings of national pride and confidence, and Americans looked forward to even better things to come. In the Northeast, the constraints of war provoked entrepreneurs to explore new industries, creating the first stage of an industrial revolution in the country. In the West, the defeat of Indian resistance combined with bright economic opportunities to trigger a wave of westward migration. In the South, the economy was revolutionized by the cotton gin and the growing demand for fiber among English and then American manufacturers. Throughout the country, economic progress promised to improve life for most Americans, but as before, both African Americans and Native Americans would bear much of the cost.

TRANSPORTATION IN AMERICA As this map shows, before 1820, roads and trails crisscrossed the United States. However, most of the roads shown here were little more than dirt tracks, with no bridges and few accommodations for travelers. It was impossible to ship large loads of goods along such roads, limiting economic expansion.

CANADA

OREGON COUNTRY

Ft. La Reine
Ft. Charles
Ft. St. Pierre
Ft. Kaministiquia

Mandan Villages
Arikara Villages

St. François Xavier

Montreal

MICHIGAN TERR.
Ft. Pontchartrain (Detroit)

Ft. Frontenac
Ft. Niagara

Portland
Boston
Worcester
Providence

ILLINOIS TERR.
Ft. St. Joseph
Ft. St. Louis
Ft. Crèvecoeur
Ft. Orléans

Sandusky
Pittsburgh Road
Forbes

Albany
New York

MOHAWK TRAIL
GREAT GENESEE ROAD
BOSTON POST ROAD

Philadelphia
Lancaster
Baltimore
Washington

San Francisco Bay

Pawnee Village

LOUISIANA TERRITORY

Cahokia
St. Louis

INDIANA TERR.

Chillicothe

Independence

Ft. Massiac

Shawnee Village

Staunton
Richmond
Williamsburg

SANTA FE TRAIL

ALTA CALIFORNIA

San Francisco
Monterey

OLD SPANISH TRAIL

Colorado

Oraibi
Zuñi
Acoma

Taos
Santa Fe
Albuquerque

Arkansas

Red

Comanche Village

Cumberland Gap
Nashville

AVERY'S TRACE
WILDERNESS ROAD
WARRIOR'S PATH

Charlotte

GREAT TRADING PATH

Raleigh

WESTERN ROAD

VIRGINIA ROAD
CAPE FEAR ROAD
POST ROAD

Wilmington

Santa Barbara
San Gabriel
Los Angeles
San Diego

Mojave Villages

Yuma Villages

Casa Grande (ruins)
Tubac

NEW SPAIN

TRAIL

El Paso

CHIHUAHUA TRAIL

Rio Grande

Caddodachos

Arkansas Post

MISSISSIPPI TERR.

ORLEANS TERR.

Ft. Toulouse

NICKAJACK TRAIL
CHICKASAW TRAIL
NATCHEZ TRACE

Apalachicola Fort

CHARLESTON PATH

Charleston

Savannah

ATLANTIC OCEAN

PACIFIC OCEAN

BAJA CALIFORNIA

Loreto

Chihuahua

San Juan Baptista

Nacogdoches
Natchitoches

San Antonio
La Bahia

Laredo
Mier
Reinosa
Serralvo
Matamoros

Natchez
New Orleans

TRADER'S PATH

Pensacola

SURVEYED TRAIL

MAIN TRAIL

St. Augustine

SPANISH FLORIDA

Tampa Bay

Gulf of Mexico

Queretaro
Mexico City
Veracruz

Inland waterways
Roads
Trails
• Towns, camps, and missions
■ Forts
■ Indian villages
States
Territories

0 200 400 Km.
0 200 400 Mi.

1807
First steamboat

1815
Cumberland Road started

1819 Economic panic
1820 Missouri Compromise
1823 Monroe Doctrine
1825 Erie Canal completed
1828 Jackson elected

1832
Bank War
Nullification crisis
Worcester v. Georgia
Jackson reelected

1838
Trail of Tears

1810   1815   1820   1825   1830   1835   1840

1808
Britain takes over Sierra Leone in Africa

1814
Defeat of Napoleon

1818
Britain becomes dominant in India

1821
Mexico gains independence from Spain

1829
Russia begins conquest of Central Asia

1834
Abolition of slavery in British Empire

The Rise of a New Nation, 1815–1836

10

Transportation in America

Using the map on the facing page, note the severe constraints that geography and the lack of an organized transportation system placed on American economic and physical expansion. What efforts would individuals, states, and the federal government have to make in order to make Americans' expectations for continuing growth a reality? What expected and unexpected outcomes would flow from these efforts?

Individual Choices

JOHN C. CALHOUN

As a young congressman in the years bracketing the War of 1812, John C. Calhoun was celebrated as a leading American nationalist. But in the years following the economic panic of 1819 and the sectional crisis in Missouri, Calhoun chose to abandon nationalism in favor of states' rights and southern sectionalism. As vehement in his new sentiments as he had been in his earlier ones, Calhoun became a virtual patron saint among states' rights advocates for generations to come. *National Portrait Gallery/Art Resource, NY.*

John C. Calhoun

The prosperity that followed the War of 1812 seemed to justify the nationalistic optimism that had guided the young War Hawks during the years before the war. Now dominant in Congress, these same young men joined Presidents Madison and Monroe in pushing for a carefully balanced economic system that supposedly would lead to increasing prosperity for the whole nation. Instead, unfounded economic optimism led to overspeculation, and in 1819 the bubble burst, setting off a six-year depression. Viewing the economic wreckage and shocked by solutions proposed by his political allies, former War Hawk John C. Calhoun made a fateful choice that would nearly tear the nation apart.

Little in Calhoun's background would have suggested that he would emerge as a controversial and divisive figure. A political prodigy, at age 29 he had been elected to the U.S. House of Representatives, where he joined forces with other up-and-coming legislators as part of the hyperpatriotic War Hawk faction. After the War of 1812 he continued to act as a dedicated nationalist, working closely with Henry Clay to build the American System—Clay's plan for a national market economy. Calhoun drafted specific bills necessary to the program; won House support for chartering a new national bank, spending federal funds for transportation development, and creating the nation's first protective tariff package; and convinced President Madison of the program's constitutionality. Calhoun quickly established a reputation as a solid nationalist; his admiring colleague John Quincy Adams found him to be "above all sectional and factious prejudices more than any other statesman of this Union with whom I have ever acted."

But in the wake of the economic Panic of 1819, Calhoun began entertaining serious "sectional and factious prejudices." To a large extent this was because of proposals on the part of his northeastern colleagues to use tight credit and higher tariffs as a way of fighting off the effects of the depression. While these solutions made sense to manufacturers and some other beneficiaries of the postwar boom, they threatened to strangle the growing cotton industry that was fast becoming the centerpiece in the economy of the South. But population growth in the Northeast and increasing economic specialization in parts of the West gave protariff forces all the votes they needed to promote their political agenda in Congress. Soon, Calhoun came to believe, the Northeast would emerge as a tyrannical mother country, and the rest of the nation would become its oppressed and dependent colonies.

Seeing incoming president Andrew Jackson as being perhaps even more nationalistic than his predecessors, and fearing extension of northeastern domination, in 1828 Calhoun drafted a pamphlet called *The South Carolina Exposition and Protest*. Drawing on ideas enunciated years before by James Madison and Thomas Jefferson in their Virginia and Kentucky Resolutions, Calhoun argued that the federal union was nothing more than a convenient mechanism for carrying out the collective will of the states. As such, its sovereignty was not superior to that of the states. More importantly, if a state determined that a federal law violated the basic rights of its citizens, a popular assembly could declare that law null—having no legal force—within its borders. This doctrine became known as nullification.

The crisis itself centered on a hodgepodge of tariff legislation passed by Congress in 1828. By 1832, the so-called Tariff of Abominations had so alienated South Carolinians that they chose to act on Calhoun's nullification principle: a popular assembly declared the tariff null. Jackson responded by building up federal forces in South Carolina and demanding that Congress pass a "force bill" that would allow him to use federal troops to establish martial law in the state. South Carolina in turn mobilized its militia to defend its sovereignty. And Calhoun, the once-proud nationalist, resigned as Jackson's vice president to stand with his state for the principle of nullification.

Though civil war was avoided in 1832—cooler heads in Congress were able to craft a temporary solution to the tariff conflict—Calhoun's decision to apply his considerable political talent to the cause of sectionalism helped bring the nation to the very brink of war. In the years to come, Calhoun would continue to fan the flames of sectionalism. By the time of his death in 1850, Calhoun had become a virtual patron saint for the southern cause, and most people had forgotten that this paragon of sectionalism had at one time been an equally rabid nationalist. The transformations that unsettled the nation turned Calhoun completely around. And his new legacy would affect the nation every bit as profoundly as had his earlier one.

INTRODUCTION

Though certainly more talented than many Americans and more powerful than most, John C. Calhoun nonetheless was typical of his generation in many ways. Like most of his contemporaries he was angered by British invasions of American sovereignty and lobbied for war in 1812. Following the war he embraced the spirit of national unity and good feelings to promote economic consolidation, leading Congress to revolutionize public finance laws in order to encourage expansive growth. And these policies succeeded: the United States experienced an exciting growth spurt after 1815. But when the speculative bubble burst in 1819, the optimism and unity that had characterized the country faltered.

Calhoun was also typical of a growing number of Americans in his views on politics. Like his fellow prodigies Henry Clay and William Henry Harrison, Calhoun had made politics a career from very early in life. Of course, Calhoun, Clay, and Harrison were property owners, and their families had always exercised political rights, but during the 1820s more and more Americans gained those same rights and took politics every bit as seriously as Calhoun and his privileged colleagues. In this highly charged atmosphere, matters of state became for the first time in the nation's history a topic for debate among people from all regions and from a broad cross-section of occupations and communities. As for Calhoun, politics for these newly enfranchised voters was not some gentleman's game but a form of personal combat designed to make their own lives better and to test their wills and their loyalties. To such highly motivated men, even the risk of civil war was an acceptable price for claiming their personal and sectional rights.

An "Era of Good Feelings"

■ What were the sources for Americans' optimism as they emerged from the War of 1812?

■ What steps did the American government take to capitalize on this optimism?

■ How did new developments in the nation influence foreign affairs?

■ How did events in North Africa and Europe influence developments in the United States?

---

market economy An economic system based on the buying and selling of goods and services, in which prices are determined by the forces of supply and demand.

James Madison had been the butt of jokes and the cause of dissension within his own party during the War of 1812, but he emerged from the war a national hero with considerable political clout. Although his fellow Republicans may have considered his wartime policies indecisive, after the war Madison immediately seized the political initiative to inaugurate vigorous new diplomatic and domestic programs. His successor, James Monroe, then picked up the beat, pressing on with a new nationalistic Republican agenda. The nationalism that arose after the war seemed to bring political dissension to a close. Commenting on the decline of partisan politics, a Federalist newspaper in Boston proclaimed the dawn of an **"Era of Good Feelings."**

The "American System" and New Economic Direction

The nation was much more unified politically in 1815 than it had been for years. The war's outcome and the growth that began to take place immediately following the peace settlement had largely silenced Madison's critics within the Republican Party. And during the waning days of the war, extreme Federalists had so embarrassed their party that they were at a severe political disadvantage.

The Essex Junto was primarily responsible for the Federalists' embarrassment. The junto had capitalized on the many military blunders and growing national debt to cast Republicans in a bad light and was drawing increasing support in the Northeast. In mid-December 1814 the Essex Junto staged the Hartford Convention, voting to secede from the union unless Congress repealed the Embargo of 1813 and passed the slate of constitutional reforms the junto had been pushing since its formation (see page 242). However, news of the Treaty of Ghent, which ended the War of 1812, and of the American victory in the Battle of New Orleans caused many to view the Federalists' efforts as either foolish or treasonous, and party popularity underwent a steep decline.

Facing no meaningful opposition, Madison chose in December 1815 to launch an aggressive new domestic policy. He challenged Congress to correct the economic ills that had caused the depression and helped to propel the nation into war. He also encouraged the states to invest in the nation's future by financing transportation systems and other internal improvements. Former critics such as DeWitt Clinton, Henry Clay, and John C. Calhoun quickly rallied behind the president and his nationalistic economic and political agenda.

Clay took the lead. He had come to Congress as one of the War Hawks in 1810 and had quickly become the dominant voice among the younger representatives. Born in Virginia in 1777, Clay had moved at the age of 20 to the wilds of Kentucky to practice law and carve out a career in politics. He was fantastically successful, becoming Speaker of the Kentucky state assembly when he was only 30 years old and winning a seat in the House of Representatives four years later. He became Speaker of the House during the prewar crisis. Now aligning himself firmly with the new economic agenda, Clay became its champion, calling it the **American System.**

What congressional Republicans had in mind was to create a national market economy. In the colonial period and increasingly thereafter, local market economies grew up around the trading and manufacturing centers of the Northeast. Individuals in these areas produced single items for cash sale and used the cash they earned to purchase goods produced by others. Specialization was the natural outcome. Farmers, for example, chose to grow only one or two crops and to sell the whole harvest for cash, which they used to buy various items they had once raised or made for themselves. Calhoun and others wanted to see such interdependence on a much larger scale. They envisioned a time when whole regions would specialize in producing commodities for which geography, climate, and the temperament of the people made each locale most suitable. Agricultural regions in the West, for example, would produce food for the industrializing Northeast and the fiber-producing South. The North would depend on the South for efficiently produced cotton, and both South and West would depend on the Northeast for manufactured goods. Improved transportation systems would make this flow of goods possible, and a strong national currency would ensure orderly trade between states. Advocates of the American System were confident that the balance eventually established among regions would free the nation as a whole from economic dependence on manufacturing centers in Europe.

Era of Good Feelings   The period from 1816 to 1823, when the decline of the Federalist Party and the end of the War of 1812 gave rise to a time of political cooperation.

American System   An economic plan sponsored by nationalists in Congress; it was intended to capitalize on regional differences to spur U.S. economic growth and the domestic production of goods previously bought from foreign manufacturers.

Clay and his cohorts recognized that one of the first steps in bringing all this about would have to be a national banking authority. True, Republicans had persistently opposed Alexander Hamilton's Bank of the United States (see page 202) and had killed it in 1811 by not renewing its initial twenty-year charter. During the war, however, bankers, merchants, and foreign shippers had chosen not to accept the paper currency issued by local and state banks. The postwar call for a unified national economy prompted Republicans to press again for a national currency and for a national bank to regulate its circulation. In 1816 Calhoun introduced legislation chartering a Second Bank of the United States, which Congress approved overwhelmingly. The Second Bank had many of the same powers and responsibilities as Hamilton's bank. Congress provided $7 million of its $35 million in opening capital and appointed one-fifth of its board of directors. The Second Bank opened for business in Philadelphia on January 1, 1817.

Proponents also saw improvements in transportation and communications as essential. Access to reliable transportation by means of the Great Lakes and the Ohio and Mississippi Rivers had been one of the principal planks in the War Hawk platform in 1812, and poor lines of supply and communication had spelled disaster for American military efforts during the war itself. Announcing that they would "bind the republic together with a perfect system of roads and canals," Republicans in Congress put forward a series of proposals designed to improve transportation and communications.

Finally, Calhoun took the lead in advocating **protective tariffs** to help the fledgling industries that had hatched during the war. Helped by the embargoes, American cotton-spinning plants had increased rapidly between 1808 and 1815. But with the return of open trade at war's end, British merchants dumped accumulated inventories of cotton and woolen cloth onto the U.S. market below cost in an effort to hamper further American development. Although some New England voices protested tariffs as unfair government interference, most northeasterners supported protection. Most southerners and westerners, however, remained leery of its impact on consumer prices. Still, shouting with nationalistic fervor about American economic independence, westerners such as Clay and southerners such as Calhoun were able to raise enough support to pass Madison's proposed **Tariff of 1816,** opening the way for continued tariff legislation in the years to come.

The popularity of these measures was apparent in the outcome of the 1816 elections. Madison's handpicked successor, fellow Virginian James Monroe, won by a decisive electoral majority: 184 votes to Federalist Rufus King's 34. Congressional Republicans enjoyed a similar sweep, winning more than three-fourths of the seats in the House of Representatives and the Senate. Presented with such a powerful mandate and the political clout necessary to carry it out, Republicans immediately set about expanding on the new nationalistic agenda.

The Transportation Problem

In the years before the War of 1812, travel on the nation's roads was a wearying experience. People who could afford transportation by stagecoach were crammed into an open wagon bouncing behind four horses on muddy, rutted, winding roads. Stagecoaches crept along at 4 miles per hour—when weather, equipment, and local **blue laws** permitted them to move at all. And the enjoyment of such dubious luxury did not come cheaply: tolls for each mile of travel equaled the cost of a pint of good whiskey.

Recognizing the need for more and better roads, entrepreneurs sought to profit by building private **turnpikes** between heavily traveled points. In 1791, for example, a private company opened a 66-mile-long road between Philadelphia and Lancaster, Pennsylvania, hoping to make money on tolls. Between that time and the outbreak of war in 1812, private companies invested millions of dollars to construct several thousand miles of turnpikes.

Despite such private efforts, it was clear to many after the war that only the large-scale resources available to state and federal governments could make a practical difference in the transportation picture. Immediately after the war, Calhoun introduced legislation in Congress to finance a national transportation program. Congress approved, but Madison vetoed the bill, stating that the Constitution did not authorize federal spending on projects designed to benefit the states. But Calhoun finally won Madison's support by convincing the president that a government-funded national road between Cumberland, Maryland, and Wheeling, Virginia, was a military and postal necessity and therefore the initial federal expenditure of $30,000 for the **Cumberland Road** was permissible under the Constitution. That constitutional hurdle cleared, actual construction began in 1815.

Although people and light cargoes might move efficiently along the proposed national road, water transportation remained the most economical way to

protective tariff   Tax on imported goods intended to make them more expensive than similar domestic goods, thus protecting the market for goods produced at home.

Tariff of 1816   First protective tariff in U.S. history; its purpose was to protect America's fledgling textile industry.

blue laws   Local legislation designed to enforce Christian morality by forbidding certain activities, including traveling, on Sunday.

turnpike   A road on which tolls are collected at gates set up along the way; private companies hoping to make a profit from the tolls built the first turnpikes.

Cumberland Road   The initial section of what would be called the "National Road," a highway built with federal funds; this section stretched from Cumberland, Maryland, to Wheeling, Virginia. Later the road would be extended to Vandalia, Illinois, and beyond.

Before the transportation revolution, traveling was highly risky and uncomfortable. This painting shows a rather stylish stagecoach, but its well-dressed passengers are clearly being jostled. Note how the man in the front seat is bracing himself, while the man behind him loses his hat under the wheels. *"Travel by Stagecoach Near Trenton, New Jersey" by John Lewis Krimmel. The Metropolitan Museum of Art, Rogers Fund, 1942 (42.95.11). Photograph © 1984 The Metropolitan Museum of Art.*

ship bulky freight. Unfortunately, with few exceptions, navigable rivers and lakes did not link up conveniently to form usable transportation networks. Holland and other European countries had solved this problem by digging canals to expand the areas served by waterways. Before the War of 1812, some Americans had considered this solution, but enormous costs and engineering problems had limited canal construction to less than 100 miles. After the war, however, the entry of the state and federal governments into transportation development opened the way to an era of canal building.

New York State was most successful at canal development. In 1817 the state started work on a canal that would run more than 350 miles from Lake Erie at Buffalo to the Hudson River at Albany. Aided by Governor DeWitt Clinton's unswerving support and the gentle terrain in western New York, engineers planned the **Erie Canal.** Three thousand workers dug the huge ditch and built the **locks,** dams, and **aqueducts** that would transport barges carrying freight and passengers across the state. This vision became reality when the last section of the canal was completed and the first barge made its way from Buffalo to Albany and then on to New York City in 1825.

Canals were really little more than extensions of natural river courses, and fighting the currents of the great rivers that they connected remained a problem.

Pushed along by current and manpower, a barge could make the trip south from Pittsburgh to New Orleans in about a month. Returning north, against the current, took more than four months, if a boat could make the trip at all. As a result, most shippers barged their freight downriver, sold the barges for lumber in New Orleans, and walked back home along the **Natchez Trace,** a well-used path that eventually became another national road.

In 1807 Robert Fulton wedded steam technology borrowed from England with his own boat design to prove that steam-powered shipping was possible. Steam-driven water wheels pushed his 160-ton ship, the *Clermont,* upstream from New York City to Albany in an incredibly quick thirty-two hours. Unfortunately,

Erie Canal A 350-mile canal stretching from Buffalo to Albany; it revolutionized shipping in New York State.

lock A section of canal with gates at each end, used to raise or lower boats from one level to another by admitting or releasing water; locks allow canals to compensate for changes in terrain.

aqueduct An elevated structure raising a canal to bridge rivers, canyons, or other obstructions.

Natchez Trace A road connecting Natchez, Mississippi, with Nashville, Tennessee; it evolved from a series of Indian trails.

the design of the *Clermont* required deep water and large amounts of fuel to carry a limited **payload,** demands that rendered what many called "Fulton's Folly" impractical for most of America's rivers. After the war, however, Henry M. Shreve, a career boat pilot and captain, began experimenting with new designs and technologies. Borrowing the hull design of the shallow-draft, broad-beamed keelboats that had been sailing up and down inland streams for generations, Shreve added two lightweight high-compression steam engines, each one driving an independent side wheel. He also added an upper deck for passengers, creating the now-familiar multistoried steamboats of southern lore. Funded by merchants in Wheeling, Virginia—soon to be the western terminus for the Cumberland Road—Shreve successfully piloted one of his newly designed boats upriver, from Wheeling to Pittsburgh. Then, in 1816, he made the first successful run south, all the way to New Orleans.

Legal Anchors for New Business Enterprise

President Madison had raised serious constitutional concerns when Henry Clay and his congressional clique proposed spending federal money on road development. Though Calhoun was able to ease the president's mind on this specific matter, many constitutional issues needed clarification if the government was going to play the economic role that nationalists envisioned.

In 1819 the Supreme Court took an important step in clarifying the federal government's role in national economic life. The case arose over an effort by the state of Maryland to raise money by placing **revenue stamps** on federal currency. When a clerk at the Bank of the United States' Baltimore branch, James McCulloch, refused to apply the stamps, he was indicted by the state. In the resulting Supreme Court case, *McCulloch v. Maryland* (1819), the majority ruled that the states could not impose taxes on federal institutions and that McCulloch was right in refusing to comply with Maryland's revenue law. But more important, in rejecting Maryland's argument that the federal government was simply a creation of the several states and was therefore subject to state taxation, Chief Justice John Marshall wrote, "The Constitution and the laws made in pursuance thereof are supreme: that they control the constitution and laws of the respective states, and cannot be controlled by them." With this, Marshall declared his binding opinion that federal law was superior to state law in all matters.

Marshall demonstrated this principle again and reinforced it five years later in the landmark case of *Gibbons v. Ogden* (1824). In 1808 the state of New York had recognized Robert Fulton's accomplishments in steamboating by granting him an exclusive contract to run steamboats on rivers in that state. Fulton then used this monopoly power to sell licenses to various operators, including Aaron Ogden, who ran a ferry service between New York and New Jersey. Another individual, Thomas Gibbons, was also running a steamboat service in the same area, but he was operating under license from the federal government. When Ogden accused Gibbons of violating his contractual monopoly in a New York court, Gibbons took refuge in federal court. It finally fell to Marshall's Supreme Court to resolve the conflict. Consistent with its earlier decision, the Court ruled in favor of Gibbons, arguing that the New York monopoly conflicted with federal authority and was therefore invalid. In cases of interstate commerce, it ruled, Congress's authority "is complete in itself" and the states could not challenge it.

But it was going to take more than federal authority and investment to revolutionize the economy. Private money would be needed as well, and that too required some constitutional clarification. At issue were contracts, the basis for all business transactions, and their security from interference by either private or public challengers.

One case from before the war was important in clarifying how federal authorities would deal with matters of contract. The issue was the Yazoo affair, in which the Georgia state legislature had contracted to sell vast tracts of land to private investors (see page 242). The decision by the legislature to overturn that contract led to a great deal of political fuss, but it created a legal problem also: could a state legis-

---

payload   The part of a cargo that generates revenue, as opposed to the part needed to fire the boiler or supply the crew.

revenue stamps   Stickers affixed to taxed items by government officials indicating that the tax has been paid.

McCulloch v. Maryland   Supreme Court case (1819) in which the majority ruled that federal authority is superior to that of individual states and that states cannot control or tax federal operations within their borders.

Gibbons v. Ogden   Supreme Court case (1824) in which the majority ruled that the authority of Congress is absolute in matters of interstate commerce.

lature dissolve an executed contract? This came before Marshall's Court in 1810 with the case of *Fletcher v. Peck* (1810). In this case, the Court ruled that even if the original contract was fraudulently obtained, it still was binding and that the state legislature had no right to overturn it. Nor, it ruled in a later case, could a state modify a standing contract. That case, *Dartmouth College v. Woodward* (1819), involved Dartmouth College's founding charter, which specified that new members of the board of trustees were to be appointed by the current board. In 1816 the New Hampshire state legislature tried to take over the college by passing a bill that would allow the state's governor to appoint board members. The college brought suit, claiming that its charter was a legal contract and that the legislature had no right to abridge it. Announcing the Court's decision, Marshall noted that the Constitution protected the sanctity of contracts and that state legislatures could not interfere with them.

These and other cases helped ease the way for the development of new business ventures. With private contracts and federal financial bureaus safe from state and local meddling and the superiority of Congress in interstate commerce established, businesses had the security they needed to expand into new areas and attempt to turn Clay's dream of a national market economy into a reality. And private investors knew that their involvement in often risky ventures was protected, at least from the whims of politicians.

James Monroe and the Nationalist Agenda

While Congress and the courts were firmly in the hands of forward-looking leaders, the presidency passed in 1816 to the seemingly stolid James Monroe. Personally conservative, Monroe nonetheless was a strong nationalist as well as a graceful statesman. He had served primarily as a diplomat during the contentious period that preceded the War of 1812, and as president he turned his diplomatic skills to the task of calming political disputes. He was the first president since Washington to take a national goodwill tour, during which he persistently urged various political factions to merge their interests for the benefit of the nation at large.

Monroe's cabinet was well chosen to carry out the task of smoothing political rivalries while flexing nationalistic muscles. He selected John Quincy Adams, son and heir of Yankee Federalist John Adams, as secretary of state because of his diplomatic skill and to

This portrait of James Monroe, painted as he entered the White House in 1816, captures the president's conservative bearing. His clothing, for example, is much more typical of the revolutionary years than of the nineteenth century. His conservatism endeared him to many who were tired of political strife. *"James Monroe" by John Vanderlyn. National Portrait Gallery, Smithsonian Institution/Art Resource, NY.*

win political support in New England. Monroe tapped southern nationalist John C. Calhoun for secretary of war and balanced his appointment with that of southern states' rights advocate William C. Crawford as secretary of the Treasury. With his team assembled, Monroe launched the nation on a course designed to increase its control over the North American continent and improve its position in world affairs.

> *Fletcher v. Peck* Supreme Court case (1810) growing out of the Yazoo affair in which the majority ruled that the original land sale contract rescinded by the Georgia legislature was binding, establishing the superiority of contracts over legislation.
>
> *Dartmouth College v. Woodward* Supreme Court case (1819) in which the majority ruled that private contracts are sacred and cannot be modified by state legislatures.

Madison had already taken steps toward initiating a more aggressive diplomatic policy, setting the tone for the years to come. Taking advantage of U.S. involvement in the War of 1812, Barbary pirates (see page 189) had resumed their raiding activity against American shipping. In June 1815, Madison ordered a military force back to the Mediterranean to put an end to those raids. Naval hero Stephen Decatur returned to the region with a fleet of ten warships. Training his guns on the port of Algiers itself, Decatur threatened to level the city if the pirates did not stop raiding American shipping. The Algerians and the rest of the Barbary pirates signed treaties ending the practice of exacting **tribute.** They also released all American hostages and agreed to pay compensation for past seizures of American ships. Celebrating the victory, Decatur gave voice to a militant new American nationalism, proclaiming, "Our Country! In her intercourse with foreign nations may she always be in the right; but our country, right or wrong."

As though in direct response to Decatur's pronouncement, Monroe maintained Madison's firm stand as he attempted to resolve important issues not settled by earlier administrations. Secretary of State Adams began negotiating for strict and straightforward treaties outlining America's economic and territorial rights.

The first matter Adams addressed was the Treaty of Ghent (1814)—specifically, the loose ends it had left dangling. One problem had been the **demilitarization** of the Great Lakes boundary between the United States and British Canada. In the 1817 Rush-Bagot Agreement, both nations agreed to cut back their Great Lakes fleets to only a few vessels. A year later, the two nations drew up the Convention of 1818: the British agreed to honor American fishing rights in the Atlantic, to recognize a boundary between the Louisiana Territory and Canada at the 49th parallel, and to occupy the Oregon Territory jointly with the United States.

With these northern border issues settled, Adams set his sights on defining the nation's southern and southwestern frontiers. Conditions in Spanish Florida were extremely unsettled. Pirates and other renegades used Florida as a base for launching raids against American settlements and shipping, and runaway slaves found it a safe haven in their flight from southern plantations. By December 1817, matters in the Florida border region seemed critical. Reflecting on the situation there, General Andrew Jackson wrote the president advocating the invasion of Spanish Florida. "Let it be signified to me through any channel . . . that the possession of the Floridas would be desirable to the United States, and in sixty days it will be accomplished."

A short time later, Secretary of War Calhoun ordered Jackson to lead a military expedition into southern Georgia. Jackson's orders read that he was to patrol the border to keep raiders from crossing into the United States and runaway slaves from going out, but he later claimed that Monroe secretly authorized him to invade Florida. Jackson crossed the border, forcing the Spanish government to flee to Cuba. Spain vigorously protested, and Secretary of War Calhoun and others recommended that the general be severely disciplined. Adams, however, saw an opportunity to settle the Florida border issue. He announced that Jackson's raid was an act of self-defense that would be repeated unless Spain could police the area adequately. Fully aware that Spain could not guarantee American security, Adams knew that the Spanish would either have to give up Florida or stand by and watch the United States take it by force. Understanding his country's precarious position, Spanish minister Don Luis de Onís chose to cede Florida in the **Adams-Onís Treaty** of 1819. The United States got all of Florida in exchange for releasing Spain from $5 million in damage claims resulting from border raids. Spain also relinquished all previous claims to the Oregon Country in exchange for acknowledgment of its claims in the American Southwest.

Spain's inability to police its New World territories also led to a more general diplomatic problem. As the result of Spain's weakness, many of its colonies in Latin America had rebelled and established themselves as independent republics. Fearful of the anticolonial example being set in the Western Hemisphere, most members of the Congress of Vienna (see page 259) seemed poised to help Spain reclaim its overseas empire. Neither England, which had developed a thriving trade with the new Latin American republics, nor the United States felt that Europe should be allowed to intervene in the affairs of the Western Hemisphere. In 1823 British foreign minister George Canning proposed that the United States and England form an alliance to end European meddling in Latin America.

tribute　A payment of money or other valuables that one group makes to another as the price of security.

demilitarization　The removal of military forces from a region and the restoration of civilian control.

Adams-Onís Treaty　Treaty between the United States and Spain in 1819 that ceded Florida to the United States, ended any Spanish claims in Oregon, and recognized Spanish rights in the American Southwest.

Most members of Monroe's cabinet supported allied action, but Adams protested that America would be reduced to a "cock-boat in the wake of the British man-of-war." Instead, he suggested a **unilateral** statement to the effect that "the American continents by the free and independent condition which they have assumed, and maintain, are henceforth not to be considered as subject for future colonization by any European power."

Monroe remained undecided. He trusted Adams's judgment but did not share the secretary of state's confidence in the nation's ability to fight off European colonization without British help. Monroe nevertheless conceded the nationalistic necessity for the United States to "take a bolder attitude . . . in favor of liberty." The president's indecision finally vanished in November 1823 when he learned that the alliance designed to restore Spain's colonies was faltering. With the immediate threat removed, Monroe rejected Canning's offer and in his annual message in December announced that the United States would regard any effort by European countries "to extend their system to any portion of this hemisphere as dangerous to our peace and safety." He went on to define any attempt at European intervention in the affairs of the Western Hemisphere as a virtual act of war against the United States and at the same time promised that the United States would steer clear of affairs in Europe.

The **Monroe Doctrine,** as this statement was later called, was exactly the proud assertion of principle "in favor of liberty" that Monroe had hoped for. It immediately won the support of the American people. The Monroe Doctrine, like Decatur's "Our country, right or wrong" speech, seemed to announce the arrival of the United States on the international scene. Both Europeans and Latin Americans, however, thought it was a meaningless statement. Rhetoric aside, the policy depended on the British navy and on Britain's informal commitment to New World autonomy.

Dynamic Growth and Political Consequences

■ How did the global economic situation contribute to American economics between 1815 and 1820?

■ How did postwar economic optimism help lead to economic panic in 1819?

■ How did economic growth and panic contribute to sectional conflict and political contention?

During the **Napoleonic wars,** massive armies had drained Europe's manpower, laid waste to crops, and tied up ships, making European nations dependent on America. After those wars ended in 1815, Europeans continued to need American food and manufactures as they rebuilt a peacetime economy. Encouraged by a ready European market and expanding credit offered by the Second Bank of the United States and by various state banks, budding southern planters, northern manufacturers, and western and southwestern farmers embarked on a frenzy of speculation. They rushed to borrow against what they were sure was a golden future to buy equipment, land, and slaves.

Although all shared the same sense of optimism, entrepreneurs in the North, West, and South had different ideas about the best course for the American economy. As the American System drew the regions together into increasing mutual dependency, the tensions among them increased as well. As long as economic conditions remained good, there was little reason for conflict, but when the speculative boom collapsed, sectional tensions increased dramatically.

The Panic of 1819

Earlier changes in federal land policy had contributed to the rise of speculation. In 1800 and again in 1804, Congress had passed bills lowering the minimum number of acres of federal land an individual could purchase and the minimum price per acre. After 1804 the minimum purchase became 160 acres and the minimum price, $1.64 per acre. The bill also permitted farmers to pay the government in **installments**. For most Americans, the minimum investment of $262.40 was still out of reach, but the installment option encouraged many to take the risk and buy farms they could barely afford.

Land speculators complicated matters considerably. Taking advantage of the new land prices, they too jumped into the game, buying land on credit. Unlike farmers, however, speculators never intended to put the land into production. They hoped to subdivide

---

unilateral   Undertaken or issued by only one side and thus not involving an agreement made with others.

Monroe Doctrine   President Monroe's 1823 statement declaring the Americas closed to further European colonization and discouraging European interference in the affairs of the Western Hemisphere.

Napoleonic wars   Wars in Europe waged by or against Napoleon Bonaparte between 1803 and 1815.

installment   Partial payments of a debt to be made at regular intervals until the entire debt is repaid.

THE REMEMBRANCER,

OR

DEBTORS PRISON RECORDER.

"HE WHO'S ENTOMB'D WITHIN A PRISON'S WALLS
ENDURES THE ANGUISH OF A LIVING DEATH"

VOL. I.   NEW-YORK, SATURDAY, APRIL 8, 1820.   No. 1.

THE
DEBTORS PRISON RECORDER
IS ISSUED FROM THE PRESS OF
CHARLES N. BALDWIN,
AND PUBLISHED BY
JOHN B. JANSEN,
No. 15 Chatham-street,
NEW-YORK,
At two dollars per annum, payable quarterly in advance.

Persons at a distance may have the paper regularly forwarded to them by mail, provided they forward the requisite advance, *post paid.*

TO THE PUBLIC.

THE chief object of this publication will be to spread before an enlightened public the deplorable effects resulting from the barbarous practice of imprisonment for debt—to exhibit the misery of its wretched victims, and the unfeeling conduct of unpitying creditors. By these means, " with truth as its guide, and justice for its object," it will, it is hoped, gradually prepare the minds of the community for the entire abolition of a law which exists a dishonor to the precepts of Christianity, and as a blot on the statute book.

It will be published weekly, in an octavo form, each number to consist of eight pages, comprising a succinct and correct history of the interesting incidents which daily occur in the debtors prison—a correct Journal of prisoners received and discharged from time to time, with such remarks as may grow out of peculiar persecution or other causes; nor will it neglect to announce the number of those who are supplied with food from that inestimable body, the Humane Society, to whom the profits of this publication will be faithfully applied, as a small testimonial of the gratitude felt by the unfortunate inmates of the prison, for their distinguished beneficence. It will contain interesting extracts from the latest European and American publications. In its columns will be found a variety of communications on various interesting subjects, from gentlemen without the prison walls, who have kindly volunteered their services to furnish us with essays on the ARTS and SCIENCES, criticisms on the DRAMA, POETRY, &c.

This work will be edited, and its matter carefully revised by several prisoners, who, if they cannot themselves enjoy the benefits of their labor, may at least feel a pleasure in the reflection that after ages will bestow a pitying tear on their sufferings, and bless them for the exertions made to rescue their country from the only vestage of feudal tyranny remaining in a land that boasts of freedom.

The small pittance paid for its perusal, will, it is beleived, procure for it the patronage of a generous public, who will be amply remunerated in performing a duty subserving the great and benign ends of Charity, while in return they are furnished with a species of reading not to be met with in any other publication.

Before the adoption of modern bankruptcy laws, it was not uncommon for people to be put in prison when they could not pay their debts. One impact of the Panic of 1819 was a huge upturn in such imprisonments. Responses varied: creditors stinging from gross losses insisted on vigorous enforcement of debtor laws, but many who were thrown out of work by forces beyond their control protested. Newspapers like *The Remembrancer, or Debtors Prison Recorder,* which began publication with this issue on April 8, 1820, called for reform in debtor laws and also reported gruesome stories about the sufferings of previously respectable people who found themselves in debtors' prison through no fault of their own. Debtors Prison Recorder, *Vol. 1., No. 1, New York, Saturday, April 8, 1820.*

and sell it to people who could not afford to buy 160-acre lots directly from the government. Speculators also offered installment loans, pyramiding the already huge tower of debt.

Banks—both relatively unsupervised state banks and the Second Bank of the United States—then added to the problem. Farmers who bought land on credit seldom had enough cash to purchase farm equipment, seed, materials for housing, and the other supplies necessary to put the land to productive use.

So the banks extended liberal credit on top of the credit already extended by the government and by land developers. Farmers thus had acreage and tools, but they also had an enormous debt.

Two developments in the international economy combined to undermine the nation's tower of debt. The economic optimism that fed the speculative frenzy rested on profitable markets. But as the 1810s drew to a close and recovery began in Europe, the profit bandwagon began to slow, and optimism to slip. Not only was Europe able to supply more of its own needs, but Europeans were also importing from other regions of the globe. Led by Great Britain, European nations were establishing colonies in Asia, Africa, and the Pacific. In addition, the recent independence of many of Europe's Latin American colonies deprived the Europeans of the gold and silver that had driven international economics since the discovery of America. Europe became less and less dependent on American goods and, at the same time, less and less able to afford them. Thus the bottom began to fall out of the international market that had fueled speculation within the United States.

Congress noted the beginning of the collapse late in 1817 and tried to head off disaster by tightening credit. The government stopped installment payments on new land purchases and demanded that they be transacted in hard currency. The Second Bank of the United States followed suit in 1818, demanding immediate repayment of loans in either gold or silver. State banks then followed and were joined by land speculators. Instead of curing the problem, however, tightening credit and recalling loans drove the economy over the edge. The speculative balloon burst, leaving nothing but a mass of debt behind. This economic catastrophe became known as the **Panic of 1819.**

Six years of economic depression followed the panic. As prices declined, individual farmers and manufacturers, unable to repay loans for land and equipment, faced **repossession** and imprisonment for debt. In Cincinnati and other agricultural cities, bankruptcy sales were a daily occurrence. In New England and the West, factories closed, throwing both employees and owners out of work. In New York and other manufacturing and trading cities, the ranks of the unem-

Panic of 1819 A financial panic that began when the Second Bank of the United States tightened credit and recalled government loans.

repossession The reclaiming of land or goods by the seller or lender after the purchaser fails to pay installments due.

ployed grew steadily. The number of **paupers** in New York City nearly doubled between 1819 and 1820, and in Boston thirty-five hundred people were imprisoned for debt. Shaken by the enormity of the problem, John C. Calhoun observed in 1820: "There has been within these two years an immense revolution of fortunes in every part of the Union; enormous numbers of persons utterly ruined; multitudes in deep distress."

Economic Woes and Political Sectionalism

Despite Monroe's efforts to merge southern, northern, and nationalist interests during the Era of Good Feelings, the Panic of 1819 drove a wedge between the nation's geographical sections. The depression touched each of the major regions differently, calling for conflicting solutions. For the next several years, the halls of Congress rang with debates rooted in each section's particular economic needs.

Tariffs were one proven method for handling economic emergencies, and as the Panic of 1819 spread economic devastation throughout the country, legislators from Pennsylvania and the Middle Atlantic states, southern New England, and then Ohio and Kentucky began clamoring for protection. Others disagreed, turning tariffs into the issue that would pit region against region more violently than any other during these years.

Farmers were split on the tariff issue. Irrespective of where they lived, so-called yeoman farmers favored a free market that would keep the price of the manufactures they had to buy as low as possible. In contrast, the increasing number of commercial farmers—those who had chosen to follow Henry Clay's ideas and were specializing to produce cash crops of raw wool, hemp, and wheat—joined mill owners, factory managers, and industrial workers in supporting protection against the foreign dumping of such products. So did those westerners who were producing raw minerals such as iron and tin that were in high demand in the industrializing economy.

Southern commercial farmers, however, did not join with their western counterparts in favoring protection. After supporting the protective Tariff of 1816, Calhoun and other southerners became firm opponents of tariffs. Their dislike of protection reflected a complex economic reality. Britain, not the United States, was the South's primary market for raw cotton and its main supplier of manufactured goods. Protective tariffs raised the price of the latter as well as the possibility that Britain might enact a **retaliatory tariff** on cotton imports from the South. If that happened, southerners would pay more for manufactures but receive less profit from cotton.

When, in 1820, northern congressmen proposed a major increase in tariff rates, small farmers in the West and cotton growers in the South combined to defeat the measure. Northerners then wooed congressmen from the West, where small farmers were begging for relief from high land prices and debt. The northerners supported one bill that lowered the minimum price of public land to $1.25 per acre and another that allowed farmers who had bought land before 1820 to pay off their debts at the reduced price. The bill also extended the time over which those who were on the installment plan could make payments. Then, in 1822, northerners backed a bill authorizing increased federal spending on the Cumberland Road, an interest vital to westerners. Such **blandishments** finally had the desired outcome. In 1824 western congressmen joined with northern manufacturing interests to pass a greatly increased tariff.

This victory demonstrated an important new political reality. Of the six western states admitted to the Union after 1800, three—Ohio, Indiana, and Illinois—were predominantly farming states, split between commercial and nonspecialized farming. The other three—Louisiana, Mississippi, and Alabama—were increasingly dominated by cotton growing. As long as northern commercial interests could pull support from Ohio, Indiana, and Illinois, the balance of power in Congress remained relatively even. But new expansion in either the North or South had the potential to tip the political scale. As all three regions fought to implement specific solutions to the nation's economic woes, the regional balance of power in Congress became a matter of crucial importance.

The Missouri Compromise

The delicate balance in Congress began to wobble immediately in 1819 when Missouri Territory applied for statehood. New York congressman James Tallmadge Jr.

paupers   A term popular in the eighteenth and nineteenth centuries to describe poor people; cities like New York and Boston often registered paupers so as to provide local relief.

retaliatory tariff   A tariff on imported goods imposed neither to raise revenue nor control commerce but to retaliate against tariffs charged by another nation.

blandishment   The use of flattery or manipulation to convince others to support a particular project or point of view.

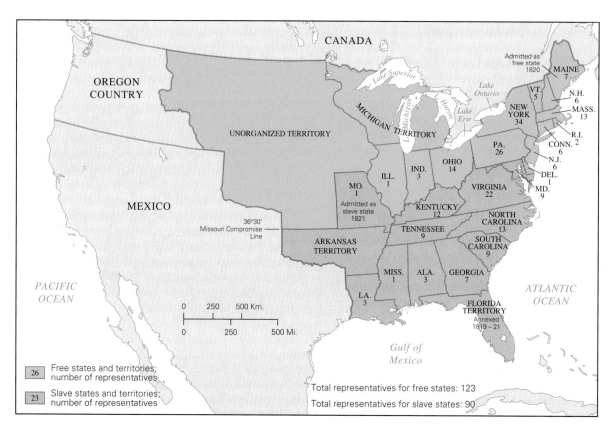

MAP 10.1 Missouri Compromise and Representative Strength The Missouri Compromise fixed the boundary between free and slave territories at 36°30′ north latitude. This map shows the result both in geographical and political terms. While each section emerged from the compromise with the same number of senators (24), the balance in the House of Representatives and Electoral College tilted toward the North.

realized that if Missouri was admitted as a free state, its economy would resemble the economies of states in the Old Northwest, and its congressmen would be susceptible to northern political deal making. This realization led Talmadge to propose that no new slaves be taken into Missouri and that those already in the territory be emancipated gradually. Southerners likewise understood that if Missouri was admitted as a slave state, its economy would resemble the economies of the southern states and its congressional **bloc** would undoubtedly support the southern position on tariffs and other key issues. They unified to oppose the **Tallmadge Amendment.**

Both sides in the debate were deeply entrenched, but in 1820 Henry Clay suggested a compromise. Late in 1819, Maine had separated from Massachusetts and applied for admission to the United States

as a separate state. The compromise proposed by Clay was to admit Missouri as a slave state and Maine as a free state. Clay also proposed that after the admission of Missouri, slavery be banned forever in the rest of the Louisiana Territory above 36°30′ north latitude, the line that formed Missouri's southern border (see Map 10.1). With this provision, Congress approved

> **bloc** A group of people united for common action.
> **Tallmadge Amendment** An amendment to a statehood bill for Missouri proposed by New York congressman James Tallmadge Jr. that would have banned slavery from the new state; it created a deadlock in Congress that necessitated the Missouri Compromise.

the **Missouri Compromise,** and the issue of slavery in the territories faded for a while.

The Missouri crisis was more than a simple debate over economic interests and congressional balances. Although economic issues had caused the conflict, slavery—its expansion and, for a few, its very existence—had become part of a struggle between sections over national power. For former Federalists such as Rufus King, the crisis offered an opportunity to use the slavery issue to woo northerners and westerners away from the traditionally southern-centered Republican coalition. Thus DeWitt Clinton and other northeastern dissidents joined with former Federalists to criticize their party's southern leadership and challenge Monroe's dominance. Wise to this political "party trick," Jefferson observed that "King is ready to risk the union for any chance of restoring his party to power and wriggling himself to the head of it." Still, the "trick" was an effective one: from 1820 onward, opportunistic politicians would attempt to use slavery to their own advantage.

New Politics and the End of Good Feelings

Conducted in the midst of the Missouri crisis, the presidential election of 1820 went as smoothly as could be: Monroe was reelected with the greatest majority ever enjoyed by any president except George Washington. Despite economic depression and sectional strife, the people's faith in Jefferson's party and his handpicked successors remained firm. As the election of 1824 approached, however, it became clear that the nation's continuing problems had broken Republican unity and destroyed the public's confidence in the party's ability to solve domestic problems.

Approaching the end of his second term, Monroe could identify no more gentleman Republicans from Virginia to carry the presidential torch. Although he probably favored John Quincy Adams as his successor, the president carefully avoided naming him as the party's **standard-bearer,** leaving that task to the Republican congressional caucus. If Monroe was hoping that the party would nominate Adams, he was disappointed when the southern-dominated party caucus tapped Georgia states' rights advocate William Crawford as its candidate. Certainly Clay and Adams were disappointed: each immediately defied party discipline by deciding to run against Crawford without the approval of the caucus. Encouraged by the apparent death of the caucus system for nominating presiden-

tial candidates, the Tennessee state legislature chose to put forward its own candidate, Andrew Jackson.

The election that followed was a painful demonstration of how deeply divided the nation had become. Northern regional political leaders rallied behind Adams, southern sectionalists supported Crawford, and northwestern commercial farmers and other backers of the American System lined up behind Clay. But a good portion of the American people—many of them independent yeoman farmers, traditional craftsmen, and immigrants—defied their political leaders by supporting the hero of New Orleans: Jackson.

The source of Jackson's political popularity is something of a mystery because the Tennessean remained almost entirely silent during the campaign. But his posture as a man of action—a doer rather than a talker—and the fact that he was a political outsider certainly played key roles. For whatever combination of reasons, once the ballots were cast, it became apparent that this groundswell of popular enthusiasm was a potent political force. Though a political **dark horse,** Jackson won the popular election, but the Electoral College vote was another matter (see Map 10.2). Jackson had 99 electoral votes to Adams's 84, Crawford's 41, and Clay's 37, but that was not enough to win the election. Jackson's opponents had a combined total of 162 of the 261 electoral votes cast. Thus Jackson won a **plurality** of electors but did not have the "majority of the whole number of electors" required by the Constitution. The Constitution specifies that in such cases, a list of the top three vote getters be passed to the House of Representatives for a final decision.

By the time the House had convened to settle the election, Crawford, the third-highest vote getter, had suffered a disabling stroke, so the list of candidates had only two names: John Quincy Adams and Andrew Jackson. Because Clay had finished fourth, he was not

---

Missouri Compromise Law proposed by Henry Clay in 1820 admitting Missouri to the Union as a slave state and Maine as a free state and banning slavery in the Louisiana Territory north of latitude 36°30′.

standard-bearer The recognized leader of a movement, organization, or political party.

dark horse A political candidate who has little organized support and is not expected to win.

plurality In an election with three or more candidates, the number of votes received by the winner when the winner receives less than half of the total number of votes cast.

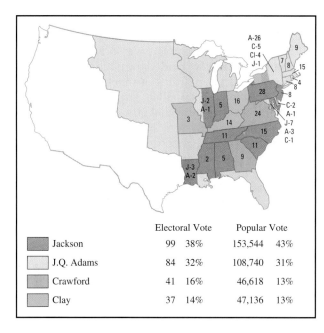

		Electoral Vote		Popular Vote	
	Jackson	99	38%	153,544	43%
	J.Q. Adams	84	32%	108,740	31%
	Crawford	41	16%	46,618	13%
	Clay	37	14%	47,136	13%

MAP 10.2 Election of 1824   This map showing the 1824 presidential election illustrates how divided the nation had become politically. William Crawford, the official Republican Party nominee, placed third in the Electoral College. The two most successful candidates, Andrew Jackson and John Quincy Adams, represented no political party. Speaker of the House Henry Clay, who finished fourth, played a key role in the outcome. Under his leadership, the House elected Adams.

in contention in the **runoff election.** As Speaker of the House, however, he was in a particularly strategic position to influence the outcome, and friends of both hopefuls sought his support. Adams's and Clay's views on tariffs, manufacturing, foreign affairs, and other key issues were quite compatible. Clay therefore endorsed Adams, who won the House election and in 1825 became the nation's sixth president.

Jackson and his supporters were outraged. They considered Clay a betrayer of western and southern interests, calling him the "Judas of the West." Then when Adams named Clay as his secretary of state—the position that had been the springboard to the presidency for every past Republican who held it—Jacksonians exploded. Proclaiming Adams's election a "corrupt bargain," Jackson supporters withdrew from the party of Jefferson, bringing an end to the one-party system that had emerged under the so-called **Virginia Dynasty** and dealing the knockout blow to the Era of Good Feelings.

The "New Man" in Politics

■ What factors helped change Americans' political options during the mid-1820s?

■ How did the election of Andrew Jackson in 1828 reflect those new options?

Since Washington's day the presidency had been considered an office for gentlemen and statesmen. The first several presidents had tried to maintain an air of polite dignity while in office, and voters were generally pleased with that orderly approach. But with the massive social changes taking place after the War of 1812, the conduct of national politics changed drastically. New voters from new professions with radically varying political and economic views began making demands. Many felt isolated from a political system that permitted the presidency to pass from one propertied gentleman to another. Clearly, changing times called for political change, and the American people began to press for it in no uncertain terms.

Adams's Troubled Administration

John Quincy Adams may have been the best-prepared man ever to assume the office of president. The son of revolutionary giant and former president John Adams, John Quincy had been born and raised in the midst of America's most powerful political circles. By the time of his controversial election in 1825, Adams had been a foreign diplomat, a U.S. senator, a Harvard professor, and an exceptionally effective secretary of state. Adams conducted himself in office as his father had, holding himself above partisan politics and refusing to use political favors to curry support. As a result, Adams had no effective means of rallying those who might have supported him or of pressuring his opponents. Thus, despite his impressive résumé, Adams's administration was a deeply troubled one.

Adams's policy commitments did nothing to boost his popularity. The new president promised to increase tariffs to protect American manufacturing and

runoff election   A final election held to determine a winner after an earlier election has eliminated the weakest candidates.

Virginia Dynasty   Term applied to the U.S. presidents from Virginia in the period between 1801 and 1825: Jefferson, Madison, and Monroe.

to raise funds necessary to pay for "the improvement of agriculture, commerce, and manufactures." He also wanted the Second Bank of the United States to stabilize the economy while providing ample loans to finance new manufacturing ventures. And he advocated federal spending to improve "the elegant arts" and advance "literature and the progress of the sciences, ornamental and profound." High sounding though Adams's objectives were, Thomas Jefferson spoke for many when he observed that such policies would establish "a single and splendid government of an aristocracy . . . riding and ruling over the plundered ploughman and beggared yeomanry." Jefferson's criticism seemed particularly apt in the economic turmoil that followed the Panic of 1819. Moreover, the increase in federal power implied by Adams's policies frightened southerners, and this fear, combined with their traditional distaste for tariffs, virtually unified opposition to Adams in the South.

Led by John C. Calhoun, Adams's opponents tried to manipulate tariff legislation to undercut the president's support. Calhoun proposed that Congress should propose an unprecedented increase in tariff rates. Northeastern Jacksonians should then voice support for the increase while Jackson supporters in the West and South opposed them. Calhoun and his colleagues envisioned a win-win situation: northeastern Jacksonians would win increasing support from manufacturing interests in their region by appearing to support tariffs; southern and western Jackson supporters could take credit for sinking tariff increases, cementing support in their districts; and Adams, who had promised increases as part of his political agenda, would appear ineffectual and his support undermined. But Calhoun and his fellow conspirators had miscalculated: when the tariff package came to the floor in May 1828, key northeastern congressmen engineered its passage. The resulting **Tariff of Abominations** was not what Calhoun had expected, but it served his ends by establishing tariff rates that were unpopular with almost every segment of the population, and the unpopular president would bear the blame.

Democratic Styles and Political Structure

Adams's demeanor and outlook compounded his problems. He seemed more a man of his father's generation than of his own. The enormous economic and demographic changes that occurred during the first decades of the nineteenth century created a new political climate, one in which Adams's archrival Andrew Jackson felt much more at ease than did the stiff Yankee who occupied the White House.

One of the most profound changes in the American political scene was an explosion in the number of voters. Throughout the early years of the republic's history, voting rights were limited to white men who held real estate. In a nation primarily of farmers, most men owned land, so the fact of limited suffrage raised little controversy. But as economic conditions changed, a smaller proportion of the population owned farms, and while bankers, lawyers, manufacturers, and other such men often were highly educated, economically stable, and politically concerned, their lack of real estate barred them from political participation. Not surprisingly, such elite and middle-class men urged suffrage reform. In 1800 only three of the sixteen states—Kentucky, Vermont, and New Hampshire—had no property qualifications for voting, and Georgia, North Carolina, and Pennsylvania permitted taxpayers to vote even if they did not own real property. By 1830, only five of the twenty-four states retained property qualifications, nine required tax payment only, and ten made no property demands at all. Of course, all of the states continued to bar women from voting, no matter how much property they may have owned, and most refused the ballot to African Americans, whether free or slave. Still, the raw number of voters grew enormously and rapidly. In the 1824 election, 356,038 men cast ballots for the presidency. Four years later, more than three times that number of men voted.

Complementing the impact of the expanding **electorate** were significant changes in the structure of politics itself. Key among them was the method for selecting members of the Electoral College (see page 195). Gradually, state after state adopted the popular election of electors until, by 1828, state legislatures in only two states continued to appoint them. At the same time, more and more government jobs that had traditionally been appointive became elective. Thus more voters would vote to fill more offices and could

Tariff of Abominations Tariff package designed to win support for anti-Adams forces in Congress; its passage in 1828 discredited Adams but set off sectional tension over tariff issues.

electorate The portion of the population that possesses the right to vote.

As suffrage requirements loosened, politicians began canvassing for votes among common people. This painting by George Caleb Bingham captures the spirit of the new politics, showing an office seeker drumming up support from people on the street. *"Canvassing for a Vote,"* *1852, by George Caleb Bingham. The Nelson Gallery–Atkins Museum of Art, Kansas City, MO (purchase: Nelson Trust), 54-9.*

affect the political process in new, profound ways. In addition, states increasingly dropped property qualifications for officeholding as well as voting, opening new opportunities for breaking the gentlemanly monopoly on political power.

Political opportunists were not slow to take advantage of the new situation. Men such as New Yorker **Martin Van Buren** quickly came to the fore, organizing political factions into tightly disciplined local and statewide units. A longtime opponent of Governor DeWitt Clinton's faction in New York, Van Buren molded disaffected Republicans into the so-called Bucktail faction. In 1820 the Bucktails used a combination of political patronage—the ability of the party in power to distribute government jobs—**influence peddling,** and fiery speeches to draw newly qualified voters into the political process and swept Clinton out of office.

Many new voters were gratified at finally being allowed to participate in politics but sensed that their participation was not having the impact it should. They resented the "corrupt bargain" that had denied the presidency to the people's choice—Andrew Jackson—in the election of 1824. Voters in upstate New York and elsewhere pointed at organizations such as the **Masons,** claiming that they used secret signs and rituals to ensure the election of their own members,

thus maintaining the supremacy of political parties and thwarting the popular will. In the fall of 1826, William Morgan, a bricklayer and Mason from Canandaigua, New York, decided to publish some of the organization's lesser secrets. Morgan was promptly arrested—charged with owing a debt of $2.69—and jailed. What happened after that remains a mystery. Some unknown person paid Morgan's debt, and he was released. But as he emerged from jail, he was seized, bound and gagged, and dragged into a carriage that whisked him out of town. He was never seen again.

Morgan's disappearance caused a popular outcry, and political outsiders demanded a complete investigation. When no clues turned up, many assumed that

Martin Van Buren   New York politician known for his skillful handling of party politics; he helped found the Democratic Party and later became the eighth president of the United States.

influence peddling   Using one's influence with people in authority to obtain favors or preferential treatment for someone else, usually in return for payment.

Masons   An international fraternal organization with many socially and politically prominent members, including a number of U.S. presidents.

a Masonic conspiracy was afoot. Within a year, opportunistic young politicians, including New Yorkers Thurlow Weed and William Seward and Pennsylvanian **Thaddeus Stevens,** had harnessed this political anxiety by forming a new party: the **Antimasonic Party.** Based exclusively on the alienation felt by small craftsmen, farmers, and other marginalized groups, the Antimasons had no platform beyond their shared faith in conspiracies and opposition to them. The Antimasonic Party was, in effect, a political party whose sole cause was to oppose political parties.

What was happening in New York was typical of party and antiparty developments throughout the country. As the party of Jefferson dissolved, a tangle of political factions broke out across the nation. This was precisely the sort of petty politics that Adams disdained, but the chaos suited a man like Jackson perfectly. So, while the Antimasons were busy pursuing often highly fanciful conspiracy theories, Van Buren was busy forging with the hero of New Orleans an alliance that would fundamentally alter American politics.

The Rise of "King Andrew"

Within two years of Adams's election, Van Buren had brought together northern outsiders like himself, dissident southern Republicans like John C. Calhoun, and western spokesmen like **Thomas Hart Benton** of Missouri and John H. Eaton of Tennessee into a new political party. Calling themselves Democratic-Republicans—**Democrats** for short—this party railed against the neofederalism of Clay and Adams's National Republican platform. The Democrats called for a return to Jeffersonian simplicity, states' rights, and democratic principles. Behind the scenes, however, they employed the tight organizational discipline and manipulative techniques that Van Buren had used to such good effect against the Clintonians in New York. Lining up behind the recently defeated popular hero Andrew Jackson, the new party appealed to both opportunistic political outsiders and democratically inclined new voters. In the congressional elections of 1826, Van Buren's coalition drew the unqualified support of both groups, unseating enough National Republicans to gain a twenty-five-seat majority in the House of Representatives and an eight-seat advantage in the Senate.

Having Andrew Jackson as a candidate was probably as important to the Democrats' success as their ideological appeal and tight political organization. In many ways, Jackson was a perfect reflection of the new voters. Like many of them, he was born in a log cabin under rustic circumstances. His family had faced more than its share of hardships: his father had died two weeks before Andrew's birth, and he had lost his two brothers and his mother during the Revolutionary War. In the waning days of the Revolution, at the age of 13, Jackson joined a mounted militia company and was captured by the British. His captors beat their young prisoner and then let him go, a humiliation he would never forgive.

At the end of the war, Jackson set out to make his own way in the world. Like many of his contemporaries, he chose the legal profession as the route to rapid social and economic advancement. In 1788 he was appointed **public prosecutor** for the North Carolina district that later split off to become Tennessee. Driven by an indomitable will and a wealth of native talent, Jackson became the first U.S. congressman from the state of Tennessee and eventually was elected to the Senate. He also was a judge on the Tennessee Supreme Court. Along the way, Jackson's exploits established his solid reputation as a heroic and natural leader. Even before the War of 1812, his toughness had earned him the nickname "Old Hickory" (see pages 255–256). Also, in the popular view, it was Jackson's brashness, not Adams's diplomacy, that had finally won Spanish Florida for the United States.

Jackson's popular image as a rough-hewn man of the people was somehow untarnished by his political alliance with business interests, his activities as a land speculator, and his large and growing personal fortune and stock of slaves. In the eyes of frontiersmen,

Thaddeus Stevens   Opportunistic politician who was one of the founders of the Antimasonic Party; he later became a leader of the "Conscience Whigs" and later still became one of the key organizers of the Republican Party. During and after the Civil War, he was the leader of the Radical Republican faction in Congress.

Antimasonic Party   Political party formed in 1827 to capitalize on popular anxiety about the influence of the Masons; it opposed politics-as-usual without offering any particular substitute.

Thomas Hart Benton   U.S. senator from Missouri and legislative leader of the Democrats; he was a champion of President Jackson and a supporter of westward expansion.

Democrats   Political party that brought Andrew Jackson into office; it recalled Jeffersonian principles of limited government and drew its support from farmers, craftsmen, and small businessmen.

public prosecutor   A lawyer appointed by the government to prosecute criminal actions on behalf of the state.

During the nineteenth century many practical and purely decorative items were used to advertise political candidates. This campaign pendant for Andrew Jackson and the thread box depicting John Quincy Adams are good examples. The pictures themselves give insight into the public images of the two candidates: Jackson appears to be flamboyant and romantic, whereas Adams seems stern and conservative. *Collection of Janice L. and David J. Frent.*

small farmers, and to some extent urban working-men, he remained a common man like them. Having started with nothing, Jackson seemed to have drawn from a combination of will, natural ability, and divine favor to become a man of substance without becoming a snob.

Caricature and image making rather than substantive issues dominated the election campaign of 1828. Jackson supporters accused Adams of being cold, aristocratic, and corrupt in bowing to speculators and special interests when defining his tariff and land policies. Adams supporters charged Jackson with being a dueler, an insubordinate military adventurer, and an uncouth backwoodsman whose disregard for propriety had led him to live with a woman before she divorced her first husband.

The characterization of Adams as cold was accurate, but charges of corruption were entirely untrue, though Adams's refusal to respond led many to believe them. The charges against Jackson were all too true, but voters saw them as irrelevant. Rather than

damaging Jackson's image, such talk made him appear romantic and daring. When all was said and done, the Tennessean polled over a hundred thousand more popular votes than did the New Englander and won the vast majority of states, taking every one in the South and West (see Map 10.3).

As if in response to his supporters' desires and his opponents' fears, Jackson swept into the White House on a groundswell of unruly popular enthusiasm. Ten thousand visitors crammed into the capital to witness Jackson's inauguration on March 4, 1829. Showing his usual disdain for tradition, Jackson took the oath of office and then pushed through the crowd and

caricature An exaggerated image of a person, usually enhancing their most uncomplimentary features.

special interest A person or organization that seeks to benefit by influencing legislators to support particular policies.

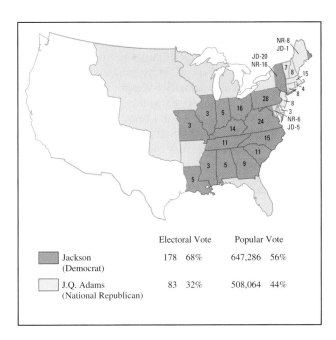

	Electoral Vote		Popular Vote	
Jackson (Democrat)	178	68%	647,286	56%
J.Q. Adams (National Republican)	83	32%	508,064	44%

MAP 10.3 Election of 1828 This map shows how the political coalition between Andrew Jackson and Martin Van Buren turned the tables in the election of 1828. Jackson's Democratic Party won every region except Adams's native New England.

mounted his horse, galloping off toward the White House followed by a throng of excited onlookers. When they arrived, the mob flowed behind him into the presidential mansion, where they climbed over furniture, broke glassware, and generally frolicked. The new president was finally forced to flee the near-riot by climbing out a back window. Clearly a boisterous new spirit was alive in the nation's politics.

Launching Jacksonian Politics

That he was a political outsider was a major factor in Jackson's popularity. Antimasons and others were convinced that politics consisted primarily of conspiracies among political insiders, and Jackson curried their support by promising **retrenchment** and reform in the federal system. In the process he initiated a personal style in government unlike that of any of his predecessors in office and alienated many both inside and outside Washington.

Retrenchment was first on the new president's agenda. Jackson challenged the notion that government work could be carried out best by an elite core of professional civil servants. Such duties, Jackson declared, were "so plain and simple that men of intel-

ligence may readily qualify themselves for their performance." And in order to keep such men from becoming entrenched, Jackson promised to institute regular rotation in office for federal bureaucrats: appointments in his administration would last only four years, after which civil servants would have to return to "making a living as other people do."

Like many of Jackson's policies, this rotation system was designed to accomplish more than a single goal. Because no new party had come to power since Jefferson's election in 1800, Jackson inherited some ten thousand civil servants who owed their jobs to Republican patronage. Rotation in office gave the president the excuse to fire people whom he associated with the "corrupt bargain" and felt he could not fully trust. It also opened up an unprecedented opportunity for Jackson to reward his loyal supporters by placing them in the newly vacated civil service jobs. The Jacksonian adage became "To the victor belong the **spoils,**" and the Democrats made every effort to advance their party's hold on power by distributing government jobs to loyal party members.

Patronage appointments extended to the highest levels in government. Jackson selected cabinet members not for their experience or ability but for their political loyalty and value in satisfying the various factions that formed his coalition. The potential negative impact of these appointments was minimized by Jackson's decision to abandon his predecessors' practice of regularly seeking his cabinet members' advice on major issues: the president called virtually no cabinet meetings and seldom asked for his cabinet's opinion. Instead, he surrounded himself with an informal network of friends and advisers. This so-called **Kitchen Cabinet** worked closely with the president on matters of both national policy and party management.

Jackson's relationship with everyone in government was equally unconventional. He was known to rage, pout, and storm at suspected disloyalty. Earlier presidents had at least pretended to believe in the equal distribution of power among the three branches of government, but Jackson avowed that the executive

retrenchment In government, the elimination of unnecessary jobs or functions for reform or cost-cutting purposes.

spoils Jobs and other rewards for political support.

Kitchen Cabinet President Jackson's informal advisers, who helped him shape both national and Democrat Party policy.

should be supreme because the president was the only member of the government elected by all the people. He made it clear that he would stand in opposition to both private and congressional opponents and was not above threatening military action to get his way. Reflecting his generally testy relationship with the legislative branch, he vetoed twelve bills in the course of his administration, three more than all his predecessors combined. Nor did he feel any qualms about standing up to the judiciary. Such arrogant assertions of executive power led Jackson's opponents to call the new president "King Andrew."

The Reign of "King Andrew"

■ What was President's Jackson role in shaping U.S. Indian policy? How does his background account for his policy choices?

■ How did conditions in each region of the country influence the national divisions reflected in the nullification crisis and the Bank War?

Jackson had promised the voters "retrenchment and reform." He delivered retrenchment, but reform was more difficult to arrange. Jackson tried to implement reform in four broad areas: (1) the nation's banking and financial system, (2) internal improvements and public land policy, (3) Indian affairs, and (4) the collection of revenue and enforcement of federal law. The steps that Jackson took appealed to some of his supporters but strongly alienated others. Thus, as Jackson tried to follow through on his promise to reform the nation, he nearly tore the nation apart.

Jackson and the Bank

The Second Bank of the United States, chartered in 1816, was an essential part of Clay and Calhoun's American System. In addition to serving as the depository for federal funds, the Second Bank issued national currency, which could be exchanged directly for gold, and it served as a national clearing-house for notes issued by state and local banks. In that capacity, the Second Bank could regulate currency values and credit rates and help to control the activities of state banks by refusing to honor their notes if the banks lacked sufficient gold to back them. The Second Bank could also police state and local banks by calling in loans and refusing credit—actions that had helped bring on the Panic of 1819 and had made the Second Bank very unpopular.

In 1823 **Nicholas Biddle** became president of the Second Bank. An able administrator and talented econ-

omist, Biddle enforced firm and consistent policies that restored some confidence in the bank and its functions. But many Americans still were not ready to accept the notion of an all-powerful central banking authority. The vast majority of opponents were Americans who did not understand the function of the Second Bank, viewing it as just another instrument for helping the rich get richer. These critics tended instinctively to support the use of hard currency, called **specie.** Other critics, including many state bankers, opposed the Second Bank because they felt that Biddle's controls were too strict and that they were not receiving their fair share of federal revenues. Speculators and debtors also opposed the bank: when they gambled correctly, they could benefit from the sort of economic instability the bank was designed to prevent.

Hoping to fan political turmoil in the upcoming presidential election, Jackson's opponents in Congress proposed to renew the bank's twenty-year charter four years early, in 1832. They hoped that Biddle's leadership had established the bank as a necessary part of the nation's economy, even in critics' minds, and that Democratic Party discipline would break down if the president tried to prevent the early renewal of the charter. They were partially right—Congress passed the renewal bill, and Jackson vetoed it—but the anticipated rift between Jackson and congressional Democrats did not open. The president stole the day by delivering a powerful veto message geared to appeal to the mass of Americans on whose support his party's congressmen depended. Jackson denounced the Second Bank as an example of vested privilege and monopoly power that served the interests of "the few at the expense of the many" and injured "humbler members of society—the farmers, the mechanics, and laborers—who have neither the time nor the means of securing like favors to themselves." And Jackson went even further, asserting that foreign interests, many of which were seen as enemies to American rights, had used the bank to accumulate large blocks of American securities.

Although the charter was not renewed, the Second Bank could operate for four more years on the basis of its unexpired charter. Jackson, however, wanted to kill the Second Bank immediately, to "deprive the conspirators of the aid which they expect from it money

> **Nicholas Biddle** President of the Second Bank of the United States; he struggled to keep the bank functioning when President Jackson tried to destroy it.
>
> **specie** Coins minted from precious metals.

Published in 1833, this political cartoon entitled "The Diplomatic Hercules [Andrew Jackson] Attacking the Political Hydra [The Second Bank of the United States]" illustrates why the Bank War enhanced rather than hurt Jackson at the polls. Many voters saw the bank as a monster that used its tentacles of complicated financial policy to choke common people while enriching the speculators and merchants who supported it. *New York Historical Society.*

and power." The strategy Jackson chose was to withdraw federal funds and redeposit the money in state banks. Although this move was illegal, Jackson nonetheless ordered Treasury Secretary Louis McLane to withdraw the federal funds. When he refused, the president fired and replaced him with William J. Duane, who also refused to carry out Jackson's order. Jackson quickly fired him too and appointed Kitchen Cabinet member Roger B. Taney to head the Treasury Department. Stepping around the law rather than breaking it, Taney chose not to transfer federal funds directly from the Second Bank to state banks, but instead simply kept paying the government's bills from existing accounts in the Second Bank while placing all new deposits in so-called **pet banks.**

Bank president Biddle was not going to give up without a fight. Powerless to stop Taney's diversion of federal funds, Biddle sought to replace dwindling assets by raising interest rates and by calling in loans owed by state banks. In this way, the banker believed, he would not only head off the Second Bank's collapse but also trigger a business panic that might force the government to reverse its course. "Nothing but the evidence of suffering . . . will produce any effect," Biddle said as he pushed the nation toward economic instability. Biddle was correct that there would be "evidence of suffering," but the full effect of the **Bank War** would not be felt until after the reign of "King Andrew" had ended.

Jackson and the West

Although Jackson was a westerner, his views on federal spending for roads, canals, and other internal im-

provements seemed based more on politics than on ideology or regional interest. For example, when Congress passed a bill calling for federal money to build a road in Kentucky—from Maysville, on the Ohio border, to Lexington—Jackson vetoed it, claiming that it would benefit only one state and was therefore unconstitutional. But three practical political issues influenced his decision. First, party loyalists in places such as Pennsylvania and New York, where Jackson hoped to gain support, opposed federal aid to western states. Second, Lexington was the hub of Henry Clay's political district, and by denying aid that would benefit that city, Jackson was putting his western competitor in political hot water. Finally, Jackson's former congressional district centered on Nashville—already the terminus of a national road and therefore a legitimate recipient of federal funds. Thus Jackson could lavish money on his hometown while seeming to stand by strict constitutional limitations on federal power.

Disposing of the **public domain** was the other persistent problem Jackson faced. By the time he came to

pet banks   State banks into which Andrew Jackson ordered federal deposits to be placed to help deplete the funds of the Second Bank of the United States.

Bank War   The political conflict that occurred when Andrew Jackson tried to destroy the Second Bank of the United States, which he thought represented special interests at the expense of the common man.

public domain   Land owned and controlled by the federal government.

Throughout the West, people without money simply camped on publicly owned land. This painting by George Caleb Bingham captures one such family as they pause outside their log cabin. Western politicians like Thomas Hart Benton argued that such "squatters" had a legitimate right to claim the land they settled and fought for legislation protecting squatters' rights. *"The Squatters" by George Caleb Bingham, 1850. Courtesy of Museum of Fine Arts, Boston.*

power, land policy had become a major factor in sectional politics. Although the price of $1.25 per acre for public land established in the wake of the Panic of 1819 was a significant improvement over the previous price, it was still too high for many hopeful farmers. Abandoning his predecessors' notion that public land sales should profit the government, Jackson took the position that small farmers should be able to buy federal land for no more than it cost the government to **survey** the plot and process the sale.

Jackson thus directed Congress that "public lands shall cease as soon as practicable to be a source of revenue," and western Jacksonians responded immediately. One of them, Senator Thomas Hart Benton of Missouri, proposed in 1830 that the price of government land be dropped gradually from $1.25 to just 25 cents an acre and that any lands not sold at that price simply be given away. He also suggested that squatters—anyone who was currently settled illegally on public land—be given the first chance to buy the tract where they were squatting when the government offered it for sale.

Such measures pleased Jackson's western supporters but frightened easterners and southerners. His

supporters in the East and South feared that migration would give the West an even bigger say in the nation's economic and political future. In addition, southerners were concerned that Congress would replace revenues lost from the sale of public land by raising tariffs, threatening the South's economic relationship with Europe. Northerners were afraid that as people moved west, the drain on population would drive up the price of labor, increasing the cost of production and lowering profits. The result was nearly three years of debate in Congress. A frustrated Henry Clay, desperate to save any scrap of his economic plans for the nation, suggested that the distribution of public land be turned over to the states. Congress, relieved to have the matter taken out of its hands, passed Clay's bill in 1833, but Jackson vetoed it, taking another slap at Clay and affirming that the distribution of the public domain was a federal matter.

Jackson and the Indians

At the end of the War of 1812, the powerful Cherokees, Choctaws, Seminoles, Creeks, and Chickasaws—the so-called **Five Civilized Tribes**—numbered nearly seventy-five thousand people and occupied large holdings within the states of Georgia, North and South Carolina, Alabama, Mississippi, and Tennessee. These Indians had embraced Jefferson's vision of acculturation but were seen as an obstruction to westward migration, especially by grasping planters on the make who coveted Indian land for cotton fields. A similar situation prevailed in the Northwest. Though neither as numerous nor as Europeanized as the Civilized Tribes, groups such as the Peorias, Kaskaskias, Kickapoos, Sauks, Foxes, and Winnebagos were living settled and stable lives along the northern frontier.

Throughout the 1820s, the federal government tried to convince tribes along the frontier to move farther west. Promised money, new land, and relief from white harassment, many Indian leaders agreed. Others, however, resisted, insisting that they stay where they were. The outcome was terrible factionalism within Indian societies as some lobbied to sell out and move west while others fought to keep their lands.

survey   To determine the area and boundaries of land through measurement and mathematical calculation.

Five Civilized Tribes   Term used by whites to describe the Cherokee, Choctaw, Seminole, Creek, and Chickasaw Indians, many of whom were planters and merchants.

Playing on this factionalism, federal Indian agents were able to extract land cessions that consolidated the eastern tribes onto smaller and smaller holdings. One such transaction, the 1825 Treaty of Indian Springs, involved fraud and manipulation so obnoxious that President Adams overturned the ratified treaty and insisted on a new one.

Adams's protective attitude did not extend to all Indians, however. The Prairie du Chien treaties (see page 263) called for the gradual removal of the northwestern tribes to the west side of the Mississippi. Drawn by the presence of gold and rich soil, impatient white miners and farmers moved onto the treaty lands even before the Indians left. In 1827 the Winnebagos, under Red Bird, resisted this invasion by raiding mining settlements in what was still legally Indian territory. White miners called for federal troops to assist their militia companies in suppressing Winnebago resistance. Despite the illegality of the miners' actions, the Adams administration complied, driving Red Bird and his people out of the disputed region.

Adams at least paid lip service to honest dealings with the Indians and the sanctity of treaties. Jackson scoffed at both. In 1817 he had told President Monroe, "I have long viewed treaties with the Indians an absurdity not to be reconciled to the principles of our government." As president, Jackson advocated removing all the eastern Indians to the west side of the Mississippi, by force if necessary (see Map 10.4). Following Jackson's direction, Congress passed the **Indian Removal Act** in 1830, appropriating the funds necessary to purchase all of the lands held by Indian tribes east of the Mississippi River and to pay for their resettlement in the West.

It did not take Jackson long to begin implementing his new authority. Like the Winnebagos, the Sauk and Fox Indians also resisted violations of the Prairie du Chien treaties. When white farmers penetrated Sauk Indian territory during the summer of 1831, the Jackson administration authorized federal troops to forcibly move the entire band of more than a thousand Indian men, women, and children across the Mississippi. During the following spring, however, one Sauk leader, **Black Hawk,** led a party back "home." Harassed by Illinois militia units, Black Hawk's resistance force clung to their territory until federal troops marched in from Illinois and Missouri, killing more than three hundred Indians and capturing Black Hawk.

At the same time, whites were exerting similar pressure on the southern tribes. The case of the Cherokees provides an excellent illustration of the new, more aggressive attitude toward Indian policy. Having allied with Jackson against the Creeks in 1813, the Cherokees emerged from the War of 1812 with their lands pretty well intact, and a rising generation of progressive leaders pushed strongly for the tribe to embrace white culture. In the early 1820s the Cherokees created a formal government with a bicameral legislature, a court system, and a professional, salaried civil service. In 1827 the tribe drafted and ratified a written constitution modeled on the Constitution of the United States. In the following year the tribe began publication of its own newspaper, the *Cherokee Phoenix*, printed in both English and Cherokee, using the alphabet devised earlier in the decade by tribal member **George Guess (Sequoyah).**

Rather than winning the acceptance of their white neighbors, however, those innovations led to even greater friction. From the frontiersmen's point of view, Indians were supposed to be dying out, disappearing into history, not founding new governments and competing successfully for economic power. Thus in 1828 the Georgia legislature **annulled** the Cherokee constitution. In the following year, gold was found on Cherokee land. As more than three thousand greedy prospectors violated tribal territory, the state of Georgia extended its authority over the Cherokees and ordered all communal tribal lands seized.

That was the first in a series of laws that the Georgia legislature passed to make life as difficult as possible for the Cherokees in hopes of driving them out of the state. When Christian missionaries living with the tribe protested the state's actions and encouraged the Cherokees to seek federal assistance, Georgia passed a law that required teachers among the Indians to obtain licenses from the state—a law expressly designed to eliminate the missionaries' influence. When two missionaries, Samuel Austin Worcester and Elizur Butler, refused to comply, a company of

Indian Removal Act   Law passed by Congress in 1830 providing for the removal of all Indian tribes east of the Mississippi and the purchase of western lands for their resettlement.

Black Hawk   Sauk leader who brought his people back to their homeland in Illinois; he was captured in 1832 when U.S. troops massacred his followers.

George Guess (Sequoyah)   Cherokee silversmith and trader who created an alphabet that made it possible to transcribe the Cherokee language according to the sounds of its syllables.

annul   To declare a law or contract invalid.

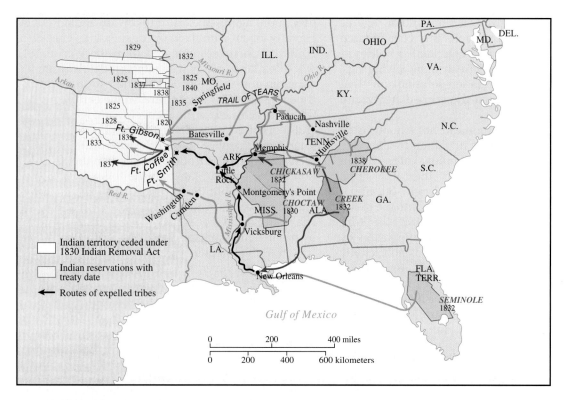

MAP 10.4 Indian Removal The outcome of Andrew Jackson's Indian policy appears clearly on this map. Between 1830 and 1835, all of the Civilized Tribes except Osceola's faction of Seminoles were forced to relocate west of the Mississippi River. Thousands died in the process. © Martin Gilbert, *The Routledge Atlas of American History,* Fourth Edition, ISBN: 0415281512 HB & 0415281520 PB.

Georgia militia invaded their mission in the heart of Cherokee country, arrested the teachers, and marched them off to jail.

Two notable lawsuits came out of the combined efforts of the missionaries and Cherokees to get justice. In the first case, *Cherokee Nation v. Georgia* (1831), the Cherokees claimed that Georgia's action in extending authority over them and enforcing state law within Cherokee territory was illegal because they were a sovereign nation in a treaty relationship with the United States. The U.S. Supreme Court refused to hear this case. Speaking for the Court, Chief Justice John Marshall stated that the Cherokee Nation was neither a foreign nor a domestic state but was a "domestic dependent nation" and as such had no standing in federal court.

As American citizens, however, Worcester and Butler did have legitimate standing under federal law, and in 1832 Marshall was able to render a decision in the case of *Worcester v. Georgia.* In this case, the Court ruled that the Cherokee Nation was a distinct political community recognized by federal authority and that Georgia did not have legitimate power to pass laws regulating Indian behavior or to invade Indian land. He thus declared all the laws Georgia had passed to harass the Cherokees null and void and ordered the state to release Worcester and Butler from jail.

Cherokee Nation v. Georgia Supreme Court case (1831) concerning Georgia's annulment of all Cherokee laws; the Supreme Court ruled that Indian tribes did not have the right to appeal to the federal court system.

Worcester v. Georgia Supreme Court case (1832) concerning the arrest of two missionaries to the Cherokees in Georgia; the Court found that Georgia had no right to rule in Cherokee territory.

When white farmers began moving into territory that legally belonged to the Sauk and Fox Indians during the summer of 1831, Andrew Jackson's Department of War chose to remove the Indians by force rather than the renegade frontiersmen. Black Hawk chose to resist by moving his band back to their homeland to plant crops in the spring of 1832. Harassed by Illinois militia, the Sauk band attempted to flee back across the Mississippi River but were headed off by federal troops and massacred at the Battle of Bad Axe: the official report noted that 150 Indians were killed—though it acknowledged that number was too low "as a large proportion were slain in endeavoring to swim to the islands" and their bodies lost—while 40, including Black Hawk, were captured. *Chicago Historical Society.*

It Matters

Worcester v. Georgia

It would be easy to conclude that Andrew Jackson's refusal to enforce the Supreme Court's decision in *Worcester v. Georgia* was an important first step in the decline of Indian power and sovereignty. In the long run, however, this landmark case became the foundation for American Indian survival. Emphasizing that Indians had once lived as truly sovereign nations, the Court declared that their relationship with the United States was as government to government and that the Constitution defined this relationship as exclusive: "The Cherokee nation, then, is a distinct community occupying its own territory, with boundaries accurately described." Within that territory local and state laws had no power and no one could enter without Indian permission. "The whole intercourse between the United States and this nation, is, by our constitution and laws, vested in the government of the United States." In the twentieth and twenty-first centuries Native Americans have used this recognition of national sovereignty successfully in the courts to revitalize their communities and have become a powerful economic and political force in today's America.

Although the Cherokees had grounds for celebration, their joy was short-lived. Jackson refused to use any federal authority to carry out the Court's order. When the Cherokees and their sympathizers pressed Jackson on the matter, he claimed that he was powerless to help and that the only way the Indians could get protection from the Georgians was to relocate west of the Mississippi.

Under this sort of pressure, tribal unity broke down. The majority of Cherokees stood fast with their stalwart leader John Ross, fighting Georgia through the court system. But another faction emerged advocating relocation. Preying on the division, federal Indian agents named the dissenters as the true representatives of the tribe and convinced them to sign the **Treaty of New Echota** (1835), in which the minority faction sold the last 8 million acres of Cherokee land in the East to the U.S. government for $5 million.

Treaty of New Echota Treaty in 1835 by which a minority faction gave all Cherokee lands east of the Mississippi to the U.S. government in return for $5 million and land in Indian Territory.

It is easy to gloss over the brutality and dehumanization that were an essential part of removing the Cherokees and other Indians from the Southeast during the 1830s, but this last remaining landmark provides gruesome testimony to the actualities of the "Trail of Tears." This blockhouse at the former site of Fort Marr in Tennessee was one of four corner guard towers that were connected by high walls that contained Indians waiting to be transported to Indian Territory. Such confinement often lasted for months, during which time food, fresh water, adequate shelter, and sanitary facilities were either minimal or not supplied at all. Armed sentinels in the blockhouses could shoot through specially drilled gun ports if the Indian detainees ever protested their inhumane treatment. *© Copyright 1994–2003 by Golden Ink. All Rights Reserved. Used with permission.*

A similar combination of pressure, manipulation, and outright fraud led to the dispossession of all the other Civilized Tribes. During the winter of 1831–1832, the Choctaws in Mississippi and Alabama became the first tribe to be forcibly removed from their lands to a designated Indian Territory between the Red and Arkansas Rivers in what is now Oklahoma. They were joined by the Creeks in 1836 and by the Chickasaws in 1837. John Ross and the other anti-treaty Cherokee leaders continued to fight in court and to lobby in Congress, but in 1838 federal troops rounded up the entire Cherokee tribe and force-marched them to Indian Territory. Like all of the Indian groups who were forcibly removed from their native lands, the Cherokees suffered terribly. In the course of the long trek, which is known as the **Trail of Tears** (see Map 10.4), nearly a fourth of the twenty thousand Cherokees who started the march died of disease, exhaustion, or heartbreak.

The only one of the Civilized Tribes to abandon legal defenses and adopt a policy of military resistance was the Seminoles. Like the other tribes, the Semi-

Trail of Tears Forced march of the Cherokee people from Georgia to Indian Territory in the winter of 1838, during which thousands of Cherokees died.

noles were deeply divided. Some chose peaceful relocation; others advocated rebellion. After the conciliatory faction signed the Treaty of Payne's Landing in 1832, a group led by Osceola broke with the tribe, declaring war on the protreaty group and on the United States. After years of guerrilla swamp fighting, Osceola was finally captured in 1837, but the antitreaty warriors fought on. The struggle continued until 1842, when the United States withdrew its troops, having lost fifteen hundred men during the ten-year conflict. Eventually, even the majority of Osceola's followers agreed to move west, though a small faction of the Seminoles remained in Florida's swamps, justly proud that they were neither conquered nor dispossessed by the United States.

The Nullification Crisis

Southern concerns about rising tariffs during the debate over western lands reflected the South's abiding political and economic posture during the Jackson administration. For years, southerners had complained that tariffs discriminated against them. From their point of view, they were paying at least as much in tariffs as the North and West but were not getting nearly the same economic benefits.

This matter had come to a head in 1829 when the impact of the ill-considered Tariff of Abominations (1828) began to be felt throughout the nation. The new tariffs roused loud protest from states such as South Carolina, where soil exhaustion and declining prices for agricultural produce were putting strong economic pressure on men who were deeply invested in land and slaves. Calhoun, who took office as Jackson's vice president in 1829, spearheaded the protest.

Though it guarded the author's identity, the South Carolina legislature published Calhoun's *South Carolina Exposition and Protest* in 1828, fanning the flames of sectionalism. Calhoun's nullification sentiments reflected notions being expressed throughout the nation. And as Calhoun's pamphlet circulated to wider and wider audiences, nationalists such as Clay and Jackson grew more and more anxious about the potential threat to federal power. The test came in 1830, when Senator Robert Y. Hayne of South Carolina and Senator Daniel Webster of Massachusetts entered into a debate over Calhoun's ideas. Hayne zealously supported Calhoun; Webster appealed to nationalism. Many have maintained that Hayne's speech was better argued than Webster's, but what mattered was how the president and the nation viewed the debate. Jackson soon made his position clear. At a political banquet, he offered the toast, "Our Federal Union—It must be preserved," indicating that he would brook no nullification arguments. Calhoun, who was sitting near the president, then rose and countered Jackson's toast with one of his own: "The Union—next to our liberty most dear." For Jackson, who valued loyalty above all else, his vice president's insubordination was inexcusable. Still, two years passed before the crisis finally came.

In 1832 nullification advocates in South Carolina called for a special session of the state legislature to consider the matter of state versus federal power. The convention met in November and voted overwhelmingly to nullify the despised tariff. The legislature also elected Hayne, nullification's most prominent spokesman, as governor and named Calhoun as his replacement in the Senate. The vice president, who realized that he would not be Jackson's running mate in the coming election, finally admitted writing the *Exposition and Protest* and resigned from the vice presidency to lead the pro-nullification forces from the Senate floor.

Jackson quickly proved true to his toast of two years before. Bristling that nullification violated the Constitution and was "destructive of the great object for which it was formed," Jackson immediately reinforced federal forts in South Carolina and sent warships to guarantee the tariff's collection. He also asked Congress to pass a "force bill" giving him the power to invade the rebellious state if doing so proved necessary to carry out federal law. In hopes of placating southerners and winning popular support in the upcoming election, Congress passed a lowered tariff, but it also voted to give Jackson the power he requested.

South Carolina nullifiers immediately called a new convention, which withdrew its nullification of the previous tariff but passed a resolution nullifying the force bill. Because Jackson no longer needed the force bill to apply federal law and collect the new tariff, he chose to ignore this action. Thus there was no real resolution to the problem, and the gash over federal versus states' rights remained unhealed. The wound continued to fester until it was finally cauterized thirty years later by civil war.

Osceola Seminole leader in Florida who opposed removal of his people to the West and led resistance to U.S. troops; he was captured by treachery while bearing a flag of truce.

nullification Refusal by a state to recognize or enforce a federal law within its boundaries.

Daniel Webster Massachusetts senator and lawyer who was known for his forceful speeches and considered nullification a threat to the Union.

Individual Voices

Examining a Primary Source

John C. Calhoun Justifies the Principle and Practice of Nullification

■ What is the significance of Calhoun's assertion that the federal union is a "union of States" and "not of individuals"?

■ How does Calhoun's description of the process by which the Constitution was ratified justify his claims concerning the rights of a statewide convention to declare federal laws null and void?

■ The expression "meum and tuum" is Latin for "mine and thine." Here Calhoun is saying that a citizen's claim that the government has wrongly taken his or her property—a conflict between "mine and thine"—would be an appropriate matter to take to court. In cases, however, where all citizens believe themselves deprived by the government, it falls to the state and not to the courts to act on their behalf.

■ On what basis does Calhoun justify the expulsion of federal authorities from a state? What assumptions is he making about federal rights versus states' rights?

After resigning from the vice presidency in 1832 over the nullification crisis, John C. Calhoun was appointed by the South Carolina legislature to fill a vacancy in its U.S. Senate delegation. One year later, in February 1833, Calhoun stood before the Senate defending South Carolina's actions and the principle of nullification. In a brief statement, Calhoun summarized his views and attempted to justify his home state's act of disobedience in refusing to comply with federal tariff laws.

The people of Carolina believe that the Union is a union of States, and not of individuals; that it was formed by the States, and that the citizens of the several States were bound to it through the acts of their several States; that each State ratified the Constitution for itself, and that it was only by such ratification of a State that any obligation was imposed upon its citizens. ■ *Thus believing, it is the opinion of the people of Carolina that it belongs to the State which has imposed the obligation to declare, in the last resort, the extent of this obligation, as far as her citizens are concerned; and this upon the plain principles which exist in all analogous cases of compact between sovereign bodies. On this principle the people of the State, acting in their sovereign capacity in convention, precisely as they did in the adoption of their own and the Federal Constitution, have declared, by the ordinance, that the acts of Congress which imposed duties under the authority to lay imposts, were acts not for revenue, as intended by the Constitution, but for protection, and therefore null and void.* ■ *. . . It ought to be borne in mind that, according to the opinion which prevails in Carolina, the right of resistance to the unconstitutional acts of Congress belongs to the State, and not to her individual citizens; and that, though the latter may, in a mere question of* meum and tuum, ■ *resist through the courts an unconstitutional encroachment upon their rights, yet the final stand against usurpation rests not with them, but with the State of which they are members; and such act of resistance by a State binds the conscience and allegiance of the citizen. . . .*

   The Constitution has admitted the jurisdiction of the United States within the limits of the several States only so far as the delegated powers authorize; beyond that they are intruders, and may rightfully be expelled; and that they have been efficiently expelled by the legislation of the State through her civil process, as has been acknowledged on all sides in the debate, is only a confirmation of the truth of the doctrine for which the majority in Carolina have contended. ■

Summary

With the end of the War of 1812, President Madison and the Republicans promoted a strong agenda for the nation. Joining with former critics such as Henry Clay and John C. Calhoun, Madison pushed for a national market economy by sponsoring federal legislation for a national bank, controlled currency, and tariff protection for American industry. In addition, Madison gave free rein to nationalists such as Stephen Decatur, John Quincy Adams, and Andrew Jackson, who succeeded in enhancing the nation's military reputation and expanding its sphere of influence.

While the nation moved forward in accomplishing its diplomatic goals, the Republicans' economic agenda suffered from a lack of viable transportation and communication systems. Expecting quick and enormous profits, New York built the Erie Canal, the first successful link between the increasingly urban and manufacturing East and the rural, agricultural West. Convinced finally that transportation improvements were necessary for national defense and for carrying out the work of the government, Madison and his successors joined with state officials to begin the process of building a truly national system of roads and canals.

But what had begun as an age of optimism closed in a tangle of conflict and ill will. A much-hoped-for prosperity dissolved in the face of shrinking markets, resulting in economic panic in 1819 and a collapse in the speculative economy. Economic hard times, in turn, triggered increased competition between the nation's geographical sections, as leaders wrestled for control over federal power in an effort to rid particular areas of economic despair. Supporters of the American System tried to craft a solution, but their compromise did not entirely satisfy anyone. And in the sea of contention that swelled around the Missouri Compromise, the Era of Good Feelings collapsed.

Meanwhile, distressed by what seemed an elite conspiracy to run American affairs, newly politicized voters swept the gentlemanly John Quincy Adams out of office and replaced him with the more exciting and presumably more democratic Andrew Jackson. Backed by a political machine composed of northern, western, and southern interests, Jackson had to juggle each region's financial, tariff, and Indian policy demands while trying to hold his political alliance and the nation together. The outcome was a series of regional crises—the Bank War, nullification, and Indian removal—that alienated each region and together constituted a crisis of national proportions.

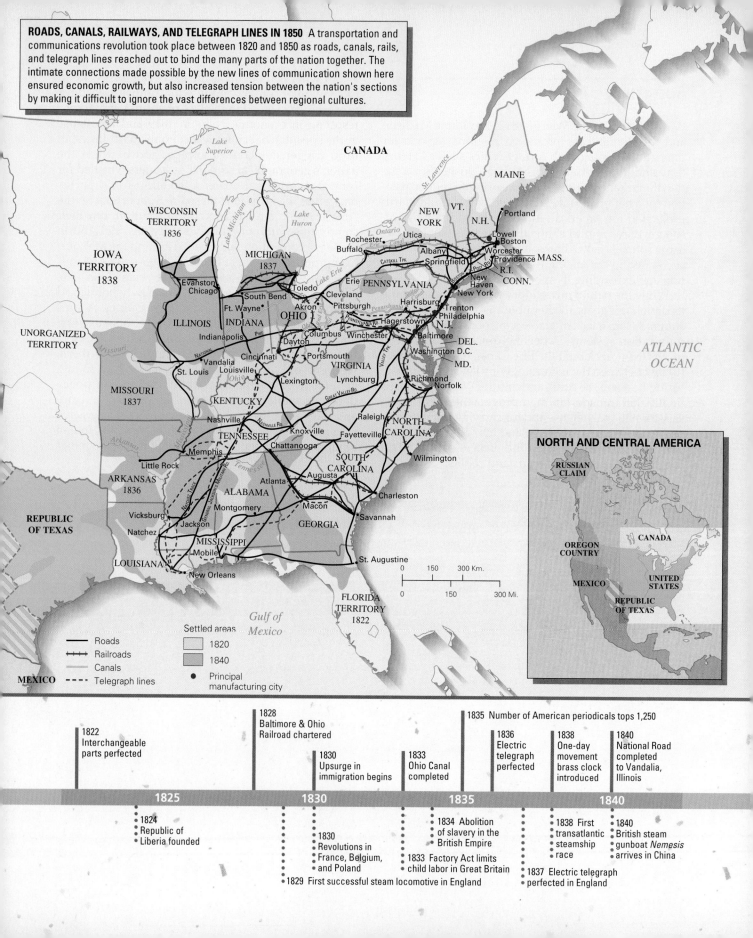

ROADS, CANALS, RAILWAYS, AND TELEGRAPH LINES IN 1850 A transportation and communications revolution took place between 1820 and 1850 as roads, canals, rails, and telegraph lines reached out to bind the many parts of the nation together. The intimate connections made possible by the new lines of communication shown here ensured economic growth, but also increased tension between the nation's sections by making it difficult to ignore the vast differences between regional cultures.

CANADA

Lake Superior

WISCONSIN TERRITORY 1836

IOWA TERRITORY 1838

Lake Michigan

MICHIGAN 1837

Lake Huron

MAINE

Portland

NEW YORK

VT.

N.H.

Rochester
Buffalo
L. Ontario
Utica
Albany
Springfield
Lowell
Boston
Worcester
Providence
MASS.
R.I.
New Haven
CONN.
New York

UNORGANIZED TERRITORY

Evanston
Chicago
South Bend
Ft. Wayne
ILLINOIS
INDIANA
Indianapolis

Toledo
Cleveland
Akron
OHIO
Columbus
Dayton

Erie
PENNSYLVANIA
Pittsburgh
Harrisburg
Trenton
Philadelphia
N.J.
Hagerstown
Winchester
Baltimore
DEL.
Washington D.C.
MD.

Lake Erie

St. Louis
Vandalia
Cincinnati
Louisville
Ohio R.
Lexington
Portsmouth
VIRGINIA
Lynchburg
Richmond
Norfolk

ATLANTIC OCEAN

MISSOURI 1837

KENTUCKY

Nashville
TENNESSEE
Knoxville
Chattanooga
Raleigh
Fayetteville
NORTH CAROLINA

Little Rock
Memphis

ARKANSAS 1836

Atlanta
Augusta
SOUTH CAROLINA
Wilmington

REPUBLIC OF TEXAS

Vicksburg
Natchez
Jackson
ALABAMA
Montgomery
Macon
Charleston

LOUISIANA
Mobile
MISSISSIPPI
GEORGIA
Savannah

New Orleans
St. Augustine

Gulf of Mexico

FLORIDA TERRITORY 1822

0   150   300 Km.

0   150   300 Mi.

MEXICO

Settled areas
1820
1840

Roads
Railroads
Canals
Telegraph lines

● Principal manufacturing city

NORTH AND CENTRAL AMERICA

RUSSIAN CLAIM

OREGON COUNTRY

CANADA

MEXICO

UNITED STATES

REPUBLIC OF TEXAS

1822 Interchangeable parts perfected

1828 Baltimore & Ohio Railroad chartered

1830 Upsurge in immigration begins

1833 Ohio Canal completed

1835 Number of American periodicals tops 1,250

1836 Electric telegraph perfected

1838 One-day movement brass clock introduced

1840 National Road completed to Vandalia, Illinois

1825   **1830**   **1835**   **1840**

1824 Republic of Liberia founded

1830 Revolutions in France, Belgium, and Poland

1829 First successful steam locomotive in England

1834 Abolition of slavery in the British Empire

1833 Factory Act limits child labor in Great Britain

1838 First transatlantic steamship race

1837 Electric telegraph perfected in England

1840 British steam gunboat *Nemesis* arrives in China

The Great Transformation, 1828–1840

11

Roads, Canals, Railways, and Telegraph Lines in 1850

Compare the map on the facing page with the opening map for Chapter 10, noting the changes that took place in transportation and communications systems. In what ways did these changes in transportation and communications change traditional patterns of economics, politics, and culture within the United States? How might they have facilitated greater tension as well as cooperation between different regions in the country?

Individual Choices

Helen Jewett

Anonymity was something virtually unknown to most people in early America. In the villages where most people lived, everyone knew everyone, and strangers were viewed with suspicion. But increasingly during the 1830s the rise of new cities brought hordes of strangers together, making anonymity a very real factor in many people's lives. And in a city full of strangers, it was not only easier to hide an identity but also easier to invent one. In urban centers such as Boston, Philadelphia, and, most notoriously, New York, enterprising people could break social conventions, class restrictions, and other limitations on their ambitions by concocting new identities. Many undoubtedly got away with it, disappearing among the thousands of other faceless strangers. Others, however, came to public attention, and a few became objects of lurid fascination. Helen Jewett was one of those few.

Jewett's story begins with that of a little girl named Dorcas Doyen, the daughter of a poor and drunken Maine shoemaker. Dorcas's mother died when she was 10 years old, and her father decided to put her out as a domestic servant. After working for three years in a modest household, Dorcas was hired as a house servant by Maine's chief justice. While living in the judge's home, young Dorcas was exposed to a genteel lifestyle that she could never have known in her father's rustic cabin, and she worked very hard at trying to blend into her new environment. Her employers encouraged her desire to "better herself," giving her fashionable clothes to wear and access to books and the leisure time for reading. She was so successful in her efforts that visitors often mistook her for one of the judge's own daughters.

But Dorcas Doyen was not one of the judge's daughters and, given her background, could never aspire to the lifestyle to which she was so eagerly becoming accustomed. As a teenager rapidly approaching womanhood, Dorcas faced the unpleasant reality that as long as she remained in the relatively closed, face-to-face village world of rural Maine, she could never be anything more than a daughter of poverty, the serving girl that everyone knew her to be. Hemmed in by an apparent lack of choices, at age 17 she disappeared from the judge's house, taking with her some of her books and stylish clothes and all of the gracious manners she had acquired over the years. Dorcas Doyen was never seen again.

Almost immediately after Dorcas disappeared, a woman named Maria B. Benson established herself in the city of Portland, Maine. Her beauty, charm, and wit soon allowed Miss Benson to become a much-sought-after companion by the upwardly mobile young men in the city, who lavished her with gifts and showered her with cash. Though no one in polite society at the time would have used such an expression, Maria Benson was a high-class call girl, and a successful one, but three years later she disappeared from Portland, never to be seen again.

Not long after Maria vanished, a woman named Helen Jewett turned up in New York City. Beautiful and cultured, she quickly took up residence in one of the most

HELEN JEWETT

Blessed with natural beauty and a quick mind, Helen Jewett became a very successful prostitute in New York City. Although she had been born in poverty and had no valid claim to genteel status, she passed herself off as the dishonored daughter of an elite family. Called "confidence men" and "painted women" by contemporaries, such pretenders used the anonymity possible in newly emerging American cities in the 1830s to insinuate themselves into polite social circles. The press coverage of Helen Jewett's grisly murder brought attention to these unsavory types, and her death was used as a moral lesson illustrating the costs that might accompany sneaking through social barriers. *Courtesy of the American Antiquarian Society.*

fashionable brothels in America's most fashionable city. There she entertained a following of educated, economically comfortable young clerks and junior managers who were putting off marriage while launching their careers. Whenever asked about her background, Jewett told her clients that she was a victim of circumstances. She claimed that she had been born into a respectable New England family. Orphaned at an early age, she had been adopted by a kindly local judge who raised her in genteel elegance. He had even sent her to an elite boarding school. There, however, she fell in with the reckless son of a wealthy merchant, who took advantage of her innocence by seducing and then abandoning her. Homeless and friendless, deserted on the cruel streets of New York, she turned to the only profession open to a dishonored woman.

This story line, so similar to plots in the best-selling sentimental novels of the time, explained the anomaly of a cultured and intelligent woman who made her living by disreputable means. "Soiled" and yet still genteel, she slipped through the cracks of social convention, living out a polite existence despite her fallen condition. And she probably would have continued this successful life if horror had not intervened. Late on the night of April 10, 1836, the fallen but fashionable Helen Jewett was murdered, literally hacked to death with an ax and then set on fire. The sparkling quality of Jewett's life and the gruesome nature of her death made her murder an overnight media sensation—newspapers scrambled for the latest tidbits about the death, and life, of this conventionally contradictory young woman. In the end, none of the investigations yielded definitive evidence about who killed her, but it was not long before they unearthed the truth about her identity: Helen Jewett, once also known as Maria Benson, was actually Dorcas Doyen.

In the terminology of the time, Dorcas Doyen had chosen to become a "painted woman," a pretender to social status that she could not otherwise legitimately claim. Becoming a prostitute apparently was an acceptable price to pay in order to escape the stifling constraints to which her birth and early life would have condemned her in the village world of rural Maine. And it all came about because the new economy that was emerging in America was creating peculiar urban spaces in which such masquerades were possible. Moralistic journalists were quick to point out that her deception caused her grisly death. Nevertheless, her story revealed not only the risks but also the expanding range of choices that were coming into being in a new, modern, and urbanizing America.

INTRODUCTION

Helen Jewett might be considered an exceptional woman in any era, but all the more so in the early nineteenth century. At a time when expectations for women increasingly constrained their public roles—confining them, at least ideally, to positions as mothers, teachers, and churchgoers at the high end of the social spectrum or factory workers or domestic servants at the lower end—her decision to become a prostitute certainly stands out. But in a way, her experience typifies much broader patterns in American life during this period. Like many in her generation, she followed the economic opportunities that were fleeing the countryside and concentrating in the newly arising cities. She also made a conscious choice to forego marriage and childbearing in exchange for a career. And like so many of her contemporaries, her success in that career was itself a product of changing times: the anonymity that came with the rise of cities permitted prostitution to thrive, just as the deferral of marriage for the sake of personal development may have encouraged upwardly mobile young men to seek out women like her. At the same time, the worsening of conditions for working people certainly provided an incentive for young Dorcas Doyen to create a false identity for herself that would allow her to transcend her lowly origins. She came to the city to make something

Networks of improved roads made travel much easier in the 1820s and 1830s than it had been earlier in the century but led to a new complication: traffic jams. This picture of the Fairview Inn in 1829 illustrates the problem, as riders, wagons, and herds of animals all crowd for space on the road outside Baltimore. *"The Fairview Inn, 1829" by Thomas Coke Ruckle. Maryland Historical Society.*

new and better of herself—transforming herself in line with the great transformation happening around her.

But the urbanization that was taking place in the northeastern section of the country was only one manifestation of the upheaval that was affecting the nation at large. As cotton production continued to offer staggering profits for efficient and lucky southern planters, that industry and its various features—especially slavery—underwent significant growth and change. That in turn affected the everyday lives of everyone of every race in the ever-expanding Cotton Belt.

These drastic changes in the Northeast and South reinforced each other. Factory development led to increased demand for cotton, while increased efficiency in cotton growing added to manufacturing profitability. The expanding transportation networks that allowed goods and people to move around the country fed this upsurge. Despite resistance by many, the United States was rapidly being knit into a single nation, a process that would reward many but which created a whole new catalog of problems.

The Transportation Revolution

■ What technological innovations contributed to the development of new transportation systems during the era between 1828 and 1840?

■ How did the exchange of scientific knowledge between Europe and the United States contribute to America's changing transportation systems?

■ How did newly emerging networks of transportation and communication change the lives of Americans in the North, West, and South?

To pull together the sort of integrated national market economy that leaders such as Henry Clay envisioned, Americans had to find ways to overcome the vast distances and difficult terrain that separated the various regions of the country. Directly after the War of 1812, politicians and inventive entrepreneurs established new transportation routes and technologies, but much more was needed. A truly integrated economy required intersecting networks of transportation and communications that could channel the produce of the West and South into the industrializing North, and the manufactures of the North into the markets of the South and West.

Extending the Nation's Roads

Both government and private enterprise embarked on road-building projects after the War of 1812. Between 1815 and 1820, the so-called National Road snaked its way across the Cumberland Gap in the Appalachian Mountains and wound from the Atlantic shore to the Ohio River at Wheeling, Virginia. Then, in 1822, a political deal between northeastern congressmen and their western colleagues extended funding and further extended the road (see page 281). By 1838 this state-of-the-art highway—with its evenly graded surface, gravel pavement, and stone bridges—had been pushed all the way to Vandalia, Illinois. Within a few more years, it reached St. Louis, the great jumping-off point for the Far West.

At the same time, a series of other roads were beginning to merge into a transportation network. The Natchez Trace (see page 275) also enjoyed federal patronage, as did the so-called Military Road con-

Chronology

The Dawn of Modernization

1822	John H. Hall perfects interchangeable parts for gun manufacturing
1828	Baltimore and Ohio Railroad
1830	Steam locomotive *Tom Thumb* beaten in race by stagecoach horse
1830–1840	Ten-year immigration figure for United States exceeds 500,000
1833	Ohio Canal completed
1834	Main Line Canal from Philadelphia to Pittsburgh completed

1835	Number of U.S. periodicals exceeds 1,250, with combined circulation of 90 million
1836	Samuel F. B. Morse invents electric telegraph Bronson Alcott's *Conversations with Children on the Gospels* Murder of Helen Jewett
1838	National Road completed to Vandalia, Illinois First mass-produced brass clock

necting Nashville even more directly to New Orleans. The Nashville Road, in turn, connected Nashville to Knoxville, where a traveler could pick up the Great Valley Road to Lynchburg, Virginia, and from there the Valley Turnpike, which connected with the Cumberland Road. Eventually towns from Portland, Maine, to Saint Augustine, Florida, and from Natchez, Mississippi, to New Haven, Connecticut, were linked by intersecting highways (see the chapter-opening map). Increasing numbers of people used these new roads to head west looking for new opportunities. Farmers, craftsmen, fur hunters, and others already settled in the West used them too, moving small loads of goods to the nearby towns and small cities that always sprang up along the unfolding transportation routes. But the new roads did little to advance large-scale commerce. Heavy and bulky products were too expensive to move: at a minimum, hauling a ton of freight along the nation's roads cost 15 cents a mile. At that rate, the cost of shipping a ton of oats from Buffalo to New York City amounted to twelve times the value of the cargo.

A Network of Canals

But the new roads also linked rural America to an ever-expanding network of waterways that made relatively inexpensive long-distance hauling possible. Completed in 1825, the Erie Canal revolutionized shipping (see page 275): transporting a ton of oats

from Buffalo to Albany fell from $100 to $15, and the transit time dropped from twenty days to just eight. All of New York State celebrated. Businessmen in New York City were particularly happy. During the early nineteenth century, the flood of goods from America's interior made New York City the most important commercial center in the nation.

The spectacular success of the Erie Canal prompted businessmen, farmers, and politicians throughout the country to promote canal building. State governments offered exclusive charters to canal-building companies, giving them direct financial grants, guaranteeing their credit, and easing their way in every possible manner. The result was an explosion in canal building that lasted through the 1830s (see the chapter-opening map).

Pennsylvania's experiences were typical. Jealous of New York's success, Pennsylvania projected a massive system of canals, roads, and natural waterways designed to make Philadelphia the commercial center of the Western Hemisphere. Central to Pennsylvania's plan was the **Main Line Canal,** connecting the Delaware and Schuylkill Rivers at Philadelphia with the Ohio River at Pittsburgh. The problem was that a mountain range more than 2,000 feet high separated

Main Line Canal Ambitious canal-building enterprise by the state of Pennsylvania to connect the Delaware River at Philadelphia with the Ohio River at Pittsburgh.

The Allegheny Portage Railroad was an engineering marvel for its time, carrying canal boats over the Allegheny Mountains as part of the Main Line Canal system. This painting by Karl Bodmer illustrates how the portage system worked. Canal barges were floated onto submerged railcars. The railcars were attached to a cable, and steam winches pulled them up an incline. Four inclines later the canal boats were hauled across the mountain's peak and then lowered down another five inclines and into the water on the opposite side. *"View of Mauch Chunk, Pennsylvania with Railroad" by Karl Bodmer, 1832. Maximilian-Bodmer Collection, Joslyn Art Museum.*

the two cities. The Main Line Canal would have needed locks five times the size of those used on the Erie Canal—an engineering feat beyond the abilities of even the most skilled designers in the country. Engineering veterans of the New York effort finally resorted to a **portage** railroad over the Allegheny Mountains.

Completed in 1834, the **Allegheny Portage Railroad** permitted canal boats to make the trip across the mountains. On each side of the mountains, canal boats were floated onto submerged railcars. The railcars were attached to a cable, and steam winches pulled them up a series of inclined planes. At the top of one incline, horses (later locomotives) towed the railcars over level ground to the next incline. After being pulled up five steep inclines, the railcars—still carrying the canal boats with their passengers and cargo—were carefully lowered down the inclines, and the boats were placed in the canal to continue their trips by water.

The portage railroad was an engineering marvel, but it was expensive to build and was only one of several massive projects necessary to complete Pennsylvania's "Golden Link to the West." Engineers designed and built tunnels, aqueducts, and enormous locks, all at outrageous cost. By the time the Main Line system was completed, anyone intent on migrating to the West could travel at a good speed and in relative comfort all the way from Philadelphia to Pittsburgh, but the tolls alone cost as much as 6 acres of prime farmland. In the long run, the Main Line Canal was a

dismal financial failure, never earning investors one cent of profit.

Despite Pennsylvania's bad experience, nearly every state in the North and West undertook some canal building between 1820 and 1840. States and private individuals invested more than $100 million on nearly 3,500 miles of canals during the heyday of canal building. One of the most important examples was Ohio's canal system. Seeking to complete a circuit of inland waterways, Ohio began building a canal connecting Cleveland on Lake Erie with Portsmouth on the Ohio River. After the **Ohio Canal** was completed in 1833, it became possible for a merchant in New York to ship manufactured goods up the Hudson River to Albany, along the Erie Canal to Buffalo, along the shore of Lake Erie to Cleveland, on the Ohio Canal to Portsmouth, then down the Ohio and Mississippi Rivers all the way to New Orleans without the cargo ever leaving the water. And with Henry Shreve's successful experiments with steamboats (see

portage The carrying of boats or supplies overland between two waterways.

Allegheny Portage Railroad A rail line that carried canal boats over the Allegheny Mountains as part of the Main Line Canal system.

Ohio Canal A canal connecting Cleveland to Portsmouth, completing a network of waterways linking the Hudson River, the Great Lakes, and the Mississippi River system.

Surprisingly enough, the first steam locomotive manufactured in the United States did not go into service in the rapidly modernizing Northeast but rather in the equally, though differently, modernizing South. The *Best Friend of Charleston* was commissioned by the Charleston and Hamburg Railroad to haul cotton and other bulky freight as well as passengers in South Carolina. *Southern Railroad Image Archive.*

page 276), meat, grain, ore, and other western products could move just as easily in the other direction.

But this new mobility did not come cheaply. Canals like those in Ohio and neighboring Indiana cost as much as $20,000 to $30,000 a mile to build, and financing was always a problem. Hoping for large profits, entrepreneurs such as John Jacob Astor invested heavily in canal building. Before 1836, careful investors could make a 15 to 20 percent **return on capital** in canal building, but after that, most canal companies faced bankruptcy, as did the states that had helped finance them.

Steam Power

Steam power took canal building's impact on inland transportation a revolutionary step further. After Shreve's pioneer voyage in 1816, the cost of shipping a ton of goods down American rivers fell annually. By 1840, the price had declined from an average of 1¼ cents a mile to less than half a cent, and the cost of upstream transport from over 10 cents a mile to less than a cent. In addition, steamboats could carry bulky and heavy objects that could not be hauled upstream for any price by any other means. The impact of steam technology on the economies of the South and West was staggering. The presence of dependable transportation on the Mississippi drew cotton cultivation farther into the nation's interior, western farmers flooded into the Ohio Valley, and fur trappers and traders pressed up the Missouri River.

Steam technology also had applications in areas without navigable rivers. Towns lacking water routes

to the interior began losing revenue from inland trade to canal towns such as Albany and Philadelphia. Predictably, entrepreneurs in places like Baltimore looked for other ways to move cargo. In fact, demands from Baltimore merchants spurred Maryland to take the lead in developing a new transportation technology: the steam railroad. In 1828 the state chartered the **Baltimore and Ohio Railroad** (B&O). The B&O soon demonstrated its potential when inventor Peter Cooper's steam locomotive *Tom Thumb* sped 13 miles along B&O track. Steam railroading, however, did not seem destined to succeed. In 1829, England's Liverpool and Manchester Railway drew attention and investment by pitting horse-drawn and steam-drawn trains against each other. The steam engines won easily. When Cooper tried the same stunt in the following year, however, the horse won. The B&O abandoned steam power, replacing it with coaches pulled along the rails by horses.

Despite the B&O's failure, South Carolina chose to invest in steam technology and chartered a 136-mile rail line from Charleston to Hamburg. Here, the first full-size American-built locomotive, the *Best Friend of Charleston*, successfully pulled cars until the engine exploded, taking much of the train and many of its

return on capital   The yield on money that has been invested in an enterprise or product.

Baltimore and Ohio Railroad   First steam railroad commissioned in the United States; it resorted to using horse-drawn cars after a stagecoach horse beat its pioneer locomotive in a race.

passengers with it. Rather than giving up on the idea of steam power, however, the Charleston and Hamburg Railroad had the engine rebuilt and began putting "buffer" cars filled with cotton bales between the engine and the other cars to protect passengers and cargoes from boiler explosions. Massachusetts followed this practice as well, as it tried to compete with New York by building a railroad from Boston to Albany.

Although rail transport enjoyed some success during this early period, it could not rival water-based transportation systems. By 1850 individual companies had laid approximately 9,000 miles of track, but not in any coherent network. Rails were laid with little or no standardization of track size, and the distance between tracks varied from company to company. As a result, railcars with their loads could not be transferred from one company's line to another's. Other problems also plagued the fledgling industry. Boiler explosions, fires, and derailments were common because pressure regulators, spark arresters, and brakes were inadequate. And in state capitals, investors who hoped to profit from canals, roads, and steam shipping lobbied to prevent legislatures from supporting rail expansion.

The Information Revolution

Distance impaired not only American commerce but also the conduct of the republic itself. Since the nation's founding, American leaders had expressed the fear that the continent's sheer size would make true federal democracy impractical. Voting returns, economic data, and other information crucial to running a republic seemed to take an impossibly long time to circulate, and the problem promised to get worse as the nation grew. During the 1790s, for example, it took a week for news to travel from Virginia to New York City and three weeks for a letter to get from Cincinnati to the Atlantic coast. This difficulty led Thomas Jefferson and others to speculate that the continent would become a series of allied republics, each small enough to operate efficiently given the slow speed of communication. The transportation revolution, however, made quite a difference in how quickly news got around. After the Erie Canal opened, letters posted in Buffalo could reach New York City within six days and might get to New Orleans within two weeks.

As the nation expanded, and as economics and social life became more complicated, Americans felt growing pressure to keep up with news at home and in the nation's new territories. The revolution in transportation helped them do so by making the transport of printed matter faster and cheaper. At the same time,

revolutions in printing technology and paper production significantly lowered the cost of printing and speeded up production. Organizations such as the American Bible Society and the American Tract Society joined newspaper and magazine publishers in producing a literal flood of printed material. In 1790 the 92 newspapers being published in America had a total **circulation** of around 4 million. By 1835 the number of periodicals had risen to 1,258, and circulation had surpassed 90 million.

The explosion in the volume and velocity of communications was enhanced by a true revolution in information technology that was in its starting phases. In the mid-1830s, both Samuel F. B. Morse in the United States and Charles Wheatstone and William Cooke in Great Britain began experimenting with the world's first form of electronic communication: the **electric telegraph.** Morse won the contest, perfecting his version in 1836. Simple in design, Morse's transmitter consisted of a key that closed an electrical circuit, thereby sending a pulse along a connected wire. Morse developed a code consisting of dots (short pulses) and dashes (longer pulses) that represented letters of the alphabet. With this device a skilled operator could quickly key out long messages and send them at nearly the speed of light. Over the next several years, Morse worked on improvements to extend the distance that the impulses would travel along the wires. Finally, in 1843, Congress agreed to finance an experimental telegraph line from Washington, D.C., to Baltimore. Morse sent his first message on the experimental line on May 24, 1844. His message, "What hath God wrought!" was a fitting opening line for the telecommunications revolution.

The New Cotton Empire in the South

■ Why did living conditions for southerners—black and white—change after 1820?

■ How did elite white southerners respond to the change? What were the impacts of their response on slaves, free blacks, and poor whites?

circulation   The number of copies of a publication sold or distributed.

electric telegraph   Device invented by Samuel F. B. Morse in 1836 that transmits coded messages along a wire over long distances; the first electronic communications device.

It was the South that was first to take advantage of expanding transportation systems, especially steam power. The South exploded outward, seeking new lands on which to grow the glamour crop of the century: cotton. In 1820 cotton was being grown heavily in parts of Virginia, South Carolina, and Georgia. With Shreve's shallow-draft steamboats in place, within a matter of decades, the cotton empire had expanded to include most of Alabama, Mississippi, and Louisiana and extensive portions of eastern Texas, Kentucky, Tennessee, Arkansas, and southern Missouri. The new dependence on a single crop changed the outlook and experiences not just of large planters but also of the slaves, free blacks, and poor whites whose labor made cotton king.

A New Birth for the Plantation System

Few images have persisted in American history longer than that of courtly southern planters in the years before the Civil War. Throughout the nineteenth and much of the twentieth centuries, songs and stories immortalized the myth of a wealthy and well-mannered southern aristocracy upholding a culture of romantic chivalry. Charming though this image is, it is not accurate.

Statistics from the antebellum South suggest that the great planters of popular myth were a tiny minority of the overall southern white population. By far the largest class of slaveholders—nearly three-quarters of the total—was the "farmer" class, people who owned between 80 and 160 acres of land and fewer than ten slaves. Next on the social ladder came a "gentry" class—about 15 percent of the slaveholding population—people who owned up to 800 acres and between ten and twenty slaves. The rest, about 12 percent of slaveholders, were true planters, possessing more than 800 acres and more than twenty slaves. Taken together, all three classes constituted less than one-third of white southerners. Though few in number, slaveholders in general, and the planter class in particular, controlled the biggest share of productive land and labor. As a result, their economic, political, and social importance was far out of proportion to the size of their population, and their legend equally inflated.

Even among the handful of true southern planters, the aristocratic manners and trappings of the idealized plantation were unusual. The rapidly rising cotton economy brought a new sort of man to the forefront. These new aristocrats were generally not related to the old colonial plantation gentry. Most had begun their careers as land speculators, financiers, and rough-and-tumble yeoman farmers who had capitalized on both ruthlessness and lucky speculations in the burgeoning cotton market to amass large landholdings and armies of slaves. Describing his master's cultural interests, one former slave recalled, "My master's habits were such as were common enough among the dissipated planters of the neighborhood; and one of their frequent practices was to assemble on Saturday or Sunday . . . and gamble, run horses, or fight game-cocks, discuss politics, and drink whisky and brandy and water all day long."

This is not to say that the image of grand plantations and lavish aristocratic living is entirely false. The owners of cotton plantations made an excellent living from the labor of their slaves. Although they often complained of debt and poor markets, it appears that large-scale planters could expect an annual return on capital of between 8 and 10 percent—the equivalent of what the most successful northern industrialists were making. Agricultural profits in non-cotton-producing areas were significantly lower, but even there slavery netted white landowners major profits. The enormous demand for workers in the heart of the Cotton Belt (see Map 9.3) created a profitable interstate trade in slaves, especially after Congress outlawed the importation of slaves from abroad in 1808. Although an unknown number of slaves continued to be smuggled in, mostly from the nearby Caribbean islands, most came to the Cotton Belt from the plantations of former tobacco, rice, and sugar growers who now went into the business of breeding and selling slaves. Thus even planters who did not grow cotton came to have a significant investment in its cultivation and in the labor system that was its cornerstone.

The increasing demand for slaves had a terribly unsettling effect on social stability in the plantation world. Whereas generations of slaves had coexisted with generations of slave owners on the traditional plantations in the colonial South, now the appeal of quick profits led planters in places like Virginia and Maryland to sell off their slaves, often breaking up

---

chivalry The code of honor among medieval knights that was central to the romantic self-image among southern planters.

antebellum The decades before the Civil War, the period from 1815 to 1860; Latin for "before the war."

Cotton Belt The region in the southeastern United States in which cotton is grown.

Despite the popular image that antebellum planters lived lives of idle luxury in great mansions, most actually lived in modest homes and worked alongside their employees and slaves, as this 1838 painting by an anonymous artist shows. *"Ye Southern Planter" 1838. Private collection.*

families and deeply rooted social connections in the process. This fragmentation of slave society helped to further dehumanize an already dehumanizing institution and drove a deeper wedge between the races.

The enormous profits earned from cotton in the 1840s and 1850s permitted some planters—or, more often, the children of successful cotton capitalists—to build elegant mansions and to affect the lifestyle that they associated with a noble past. Voracious readers of romantic literature, planters assumed what they imagined were the ways of medieval knights, adopting courtly manners and the nobleman's **paternalistic** obligation to look out for the welfare of social inferiors, both black and white. Women decked out in the latest gowns flocked to formal balls and weekend parties. Young men were sent to academies where they could learn the twin aristocratic virtues of militarism and honor. Young women attended private "seminaries" where they were taught, in the words of one southern seminary mistress, "principles calculated to render them useful and rational companions." Courtship became highly ritualized, an imitation of imagined medieval court manners.

Practical concerns, however, always threatened to crack this romantic veneer. Although huge profits might be made in cotton planting, successful ventures required major capital investment. If land suitable for cotton could be purchased directly from the federal government, it might be had for as little as 25 cents an acre, but efficient planting called for huge blocks of land, and planters often had to pay a premium to get them. Contrary to popular perception, slave labor was not cheap. At the height of the slave trade, a healthy male field hand in his mid-twenties sold for an average of $1,800. Younger and older men or those in less than perfect health sold for less, but even a male child too young to work in the fields might cost anywhere from $250 to $500.

Often planters purchased slaves and fields on credit and genuinely feared that their carefully constructed empires and lifestyles might collapse in an instant. Aristocratic parents sought to use marriage as a means of adding to family and economic security. "As to my having any sweethearts that is not thought of," one young southern woman complained. "Money is too much preferred, for us poor Girls to be much caressed."

Even those girls whose fortunes earned caresses faced a strange and often difficult life. Planters' wives bore little resemblance to their counterparts in popular fiction. Far from being frail, helpless creatures, southern plantation mistresses carried a heavy burden of responsibility. A planter's wife was responsible for all domestic matters. She supervised large staffs of

paternalistic Treating social dependents as a father treats his children, providing for their needs but denying them rights or responsibilities.

Slave life in the antebellum South presented an array of complex and often contradictory sides, as these two images illustrate. On the left, a parlor scene shows two young house slaves in absolute subjugation—one even serves as a footstool for his mistress. The nicely framed daguerreotype on the right, however, depicts slaves in a very different light; this couple either had the means to bear the cost of the expensive photograph or their owner thought highly enough of them to do so. These are but two striking images of a complex evolving world that emerged in the cotton South, the legacy of which we continue to live with today. *Ohio State University Libraries (left); Maryland Historical Society Library, Special Collections Department, Cased Photo #156 (right).*

slaves, organized and ran schools for the children on the plantation, looked out for the health of everyone, and managed all plantation operations in the absence of her husband. All those duties were complicated by a sex code that relegated southern women to a peculiar position in the plantation hierarchy—between white men and black slaves. On the one hand, southern white women were expected to exercise absolute authority over their slaves. On the other, they were to be absolutely obedient to white men. "He is master of the house," said plantation mistress Mary Boykin Chesnut about her husband. "To hear [him] is to obey." This contradiction put great pressure on southern women, adding severe anxiety to their other burdens. "All the comfort of my life depends upon his being in a good humor," Chesnut remarked. And while in some respects planters treated their slaves like machines, slaves were nonetheless human—and sexual—beings, a fact that produced even more stress for plantation mistresses. Like Thomas Jefferson before them (see page 234), antebellum planters found that their power over slave women afforded them sexual as well as financial benefits. One southerner rationalized this situation, saying, "The intercourse which takes place with enslaved females is less depraving in its effects [on white men] than when it is carried on with females of their own caste." As a result, a partic-

ularly beautiful young slave woman, who like Sally Hemings might herself have been the daughter of such a relationship, could bring as much as $5,000 at auction. Constrained as they were by the region's strict rules of conduct, the wives of these men generally were powerless to intercede. Though some may not have minded release from sexual pressures, they had to be mindful of slave concubines and their children, both of whom occupied an odd place in the domestic power structure. It is little wonder, then, that Chesnut concluded her observations about southern womanhood with the statement, "There is no slave . . . like a wife."

Life Among Common Southern Whites

Federal census figures for the early nineteenth century reveal that fully two-thirds of free southern families owned no slaves, and among the minority who did, half owned fewer than five. A small number of these families owned stores, craft shops, and other urban businesses in Charleston, New Orleans, Atlanta, and other southern cities. Some were attorneys, teachers, doctors, and other professionals. The great majority, however, were proud small farmers who owned, leased, or simply squatted on the land they farmed.

Often tarred with the label "poor white trash" by their planter neighbors, and described as shiftless, idle backcountry rabble, these people were often productive stock raisers and farmers. They concentrated on growing and manufacturing by hand what they needed to live, but all aspired to end up with small surpluses of grains, meat products, and other commodities that they could sell either to neighboring plantations or to merchants for export. Many of these small farmers tried to grow cotton in an effort to raise cash, though they generally could not do so on a large scale. Whatever cash they raised they usually spent on necessary manufactures, as well as on land and slaves.

These small farmers had a shaky relationship with white planters. On the one hand, many wanted to join the ranks of the great planters, hoping they could transform their small holdings into cotton empires. On the other hand, they resented the aristocracy and envied the planters' exalted status and power. They also feared the expansion of large plantations, which often forced small holders to abandon their hard-won farms and slaves.

Although they seldom rebelled openly against their social superiors, common white people often used the power of the ballot box to make their dissatisfactions known. For despite the enormous power of the plantation elite, they were greatly outnumbered by the lesser class of whites, who had the power to wreck the entire social and economic structure if they became sufficiently disgruntled. Thus the *noblesse oblige* practiced by aristocrats toward poorer whites was as much a practical necessity as it was a romantic affectation.

Large-scale planters also used racial tensions as a device for controlling their contentious neighbors. Although they were not above taking slave concubines or trusting African Americans with positions of authority on plantations, the white elite nonetheless emphasized white superiority and common cause when conversing with their poorer farmer neighbors. They pointed out that although poor farmers may have felt underprivileged when compared with their wealthier counterparts, they at least were spared the most demeaning of work: a still-lower class bore that burden. Thus what freedoms and privileges poor whites enjoyed were afforded by the existence of slavery. And should slavery ever end, planters avowed, whether because of poor white political maneuverings or outside pressures, it would be the farmers who would have the most to lose.

Free Blacks in the South

Caught in the middle between southern planters, slaves, and poor white farmers, African Americans in the South who were not slaves often faced extreme discrimination. Some communities of free blacks could trace their origins back to earliest colonial times, when Africans, like Europeans, served limited terms of indenture. The majority, however, had been freed recently because of diminishing plantation profits during the late 1700s. Most of these people lived not much differently from slaves, working for white employers as day laborers.

Mounting restrictions on free blacks during the first half of the nineteenth century limited their freedom of movement, economic options, and the protection they could expect to receive by law. In the town of Petersburg, Virginia, for example, when a free black woman named Esther Fells irritated her white neighbor, he took it upon himself to whip her for disturbing his peace. The sheriff did not arrest the assailant but instead took Mrs. Fells into custody, and the court ordered that she be given fifteen more lashes for "being insolent to a white person." Skin color left free African Americans open to abuses and forced them to be extremely careful in their dealings with their white neighbors.

Still, some opportunities were available for a handful of free blacks who had desirable skills. In the Upper South—Delaware, Maryland, and Virginia—master carpenters, coopers, painters, brick masons, blacksmiths, boatmen, bakers, and barbers hired young African American boys as apprentices. Those who could stick out their apprenticeship might make an independent living. The situation was different for African American girls. They had few opportunities as skilled laborers. Some became seamstresses and washers, others became cooks, and a few grew up to run small groceries, taverns, and restaurants. Folk healing, **midwifery,** and prostitution also led to economic independence for some black women.

It is worth noting that perhaps as many as 10 percent of free southern African American heads of household were slaveowners, but by itself this statistic may be somewhat misleading. Many free black men were

---

noblesse oblige   The belief that members of the elite are duty-bound to treat others charitably, especially those of lower status than themselves.

midwifery   The practice of assisting women in childbirth.

forced to buy their wives and children in order to re-unite families and often were prevented by restrictive slave codes from legally freeing them. Still, a good many people of African descent owned plantations and gangs of slave laborers, though these possessions seldom earned them entry into local elite circles.

Living Conditions for Southern Slaves

Slaveowners' enormous economic investment in their human property played a significant role in the treatment slaves received. Damaging or, worse, killing a healthy slave resulted in a significant financial loss. But to maintain profitability, slaveholders had to keep productivity levels high. This need led southern states to write increasingly harsh **slave codes** during the late eighteenth and early nineteenth centuries, giving slaveowners virtual life-and-death control over their human chattel. A delicate balance between power and profit shaped planters' policies toward slaves and set the tone for slave life. Like the vital machines in northern factories, slaves received the minimum maintenance required to keep them in proper working order.

As to the work itself, cotton planting led to increasing concentration in the tasks performed by slaves. A survey of large and medium-size plantations during the height of the cotton boom shows that the majority of slaves (58 percent of the men and 69 percent of the women) were employed primarily as **field hands.** Of the rest, only 2 percent of slave men and 17 percent of slave women were employed as **house slaves.** The remaining 14 percent of slave women were employed in nonfield occupations such as sewing, weaving, and food processing. Seventeen percent of slave men were employed in nonfield activities such as driving wagons, piloting riverboats, and herding cattle. Another 23 percent were managers and craftsmen.

The percentage of slave craftsmen was much higher in cities, where slave artisans were often allowed to hire themselves out on the open job market in return for handing part of their earnings over to their owners. In Charleston, Norfolk, Richmond, and Savannah, slave artisans formed guilds. Feeling threatened by their solidarity, white craftsmen appealed to state legislatures and city councils for restrictions on slave employment in skilled crafts. Such appeals, and the need for more and more field hands, led to a decline in the number of slave artisans during the 1840s and 1850s.

With the possible exception of sexual exploitation, no area of slave existence has captured the imagina-

Although slaves increasingly were being used in the burgeoning cotton industry during the antebellum years, some continued to practice skilled trades throughout the South. Horace King, for example, was a civil engineer who designed and built bridges and public buildings, including sections of the Alabama state capitol building. *Collection of the Columbus Museum, Columbus, Georgia; Museum purchase.*

tion as much as violence. The image of sadistic white men beating slaves permeates the dark side of the southern myth. Such behavior, however, though not unknown, was far from typical. Slaves were money, and injuring slaves was expensive behavior that most slaveowners could not afford. Still, given the need to keep up productivity, slaveowners were not shy about using measured force. "I always punish according to the crime," one plantation owner declared. "If it is a

slave codes Laws that established the status of slaves, denying them basic rights and classifying them as the property of slaveowners.

field hands People who do agricultural work such as planting, weeding, and harvesting.

house slaves People who did domestic work such as cleaning and cooking.

This early photograph, taken on a South Carolina plantation before the Civil War, freezes slave life in time, giving us a view of what slave cabins looked like, how they were arranged, how the largest majority of slaves dressed, and how they spent what little leisure time they had. *Collection of William Gladstone.*

Large one I give him a genteel flogging with a strop, about 75 Lashes I think is a good whipping." Noting the practical limitations even to this "genteel" form of discipline, he continued, "When picking cotton I never put on more than 20 stripes and very frequently not more than 10 or 15." But not all plantation owners were gentle or even practical when it came to discipline. The historical record is filled with accounts of slaveowners who were willing to take a financial loss by beating slaves until they became useless or even died.

In keeping with demands for profitability, housing for slaves was seldom more than adequate. Generally, slaves lived in one-room log cabins with dirt floors and a fireplace or stove. Mindful of the need to maintain control and keep slaves productive, slaveowners tried to avoid crowding people into slave quarters. As one slaveowner explained, "The crowding [of] a number into one house is unhealthy. It breeds contention; is destructive of delicacy of feeling, and it promotes immorality between the sexes."

Though not all planters shared this view, census figures suggest that the average slave cabin housed five or six people.

Though not crammed fifty to a house, as were workers in some New York slums, slave quarters were not particularly comfortable. The cabins had windows, but generally only wooden shutters and no glass. The windows let in flies in summer and cold in winter, but closing the shutters shut out the light. When the shutters were closed against flies and cold, the most reliable source of light was an open fireplace or stove, which was also used for heat and cooking. Ever-present fires increased the danger of cabins burning down, especially because chimneys were generally made of sticks held together with dried mud. As one slave commented, "Many the time we have to get up at midnight and push the chimney away from the house to keep the house from burning up."

As in the cabin homes of common southern whites, furnishings in slave houses were usually fairly crude and often were crafted by the residents themselves.

Bedding generally consisted of straw pallets stacked on the floor or occasionally mounted on rough bedsteads. Other furnishings were equally simple—rough-hewn wooden chairs or benches and plank tables.

Clothing was very basic. One Georgia planter outlined the usual yearly clothing allowance for slaves: "The proper and usual quantity of clothes for plantation hands is two suits of cotton for spring and summer, and two suits of woolen for winter; four pair of shoes and three hats." On some plantations, slave women spun, wove, and sewed cotton fabric called osnaburg. This material was durable, but rough and uncomfortable to wear. As one slave complained, the material was "like needles when it was new." Women generally wore simple dresses or skirts and blouses made from the scratchy osnaburg. Children often went naked in the summer and were fitted with long, loose-hanging osnaburg shirts during the colder months.

It appears that the slave diet, like slave clothing and housing, was sufficient to maintain life but not particularly pleasing. One slave noted that there was "plenty to eat sich as it was," but in summer flies swarmed all over the food. Her master, she said, would laugh about that, saying the added protein provided by the flies "made us fat." Despite justified complaints, the fact is that the average slave diet was rich by comparison with the diet of many other Americans. Slaves in the American South ate significantly more meat than workers in the urban North. In addition to meat, slaves consumed milk and corn, potatoes, peas and beans, molasses, and fish. Generally the planter provided this variety of food, but owners also occasionally permitted slaves to hunt and fish and to collect wild roots, berries, and vegetables. Theft also added to the quantity and variety of foods available in the slave quarters.

Although the diet provided to slaves kept them alive and functioning, the southern diet in general lacked important nutrients, and diet-related diseases plagued southern communities. Slaves were also subject to hernia, pneumonia, and **lockjaw,** of which each, in its way, was the product of slaves' working and living conditions. Because of the lack of proper sanitation, slaves also suffered from dysentery and **cholera.**

One major public health risk that was **endemic** among slaves was in the realm of circulatory disease. Recent research reveals that slave children were generally undernourished because slaveowners would not allocate ample resources to feed people who did not work. Once children were old enough to work, however, they had access to a very high-calorie diet.

Such early malnutrition followed by an instant transition to a high-calorie and often high-fat diet may well have led to the high incidence of heart attacks, strokes, and similar ailments among slaves found in the historical record. And given the balance-sheet mentality among plantation owners, this phenomenon may not have been unwelcome. Old people who could not work hard were, like children, a liability; thus having slaves die from circulatory disease in middle age saved planters from unnecessary expenditures later on.

Most of what we know about living conditions for slaves comes from relatively large plantations in the Cotton Belt. Although most slaves lived under such circumstances, a very large minority lived on small farms in communities of between five and ten, or sometimes just one or two slaves. It appears that slaves on such farms were usually not much better off than slaves on large plantations. Economic life for southern farmers was always difficult; they lived a hand-to-mouth existence, often short of food, clothing, and housing. Small farmers saw slaves as vehicles for social and economic advancement; they were willing to starve, overwork, or sell their slaves if doing so meant economic betterment for their own families. When all was going well, slaves might be treated like members of the farmer's family—much as apprentices might be considered members of a northern craftsman's family. But when conditions were not good, slaves were the first casualties.

Whether on large plantations or small farms, the burden of slavery was a source of constant stress for both slaves and masters in the newly evolving South. The precarious nature of family life, the ever-present threat of violence, and the overwhelming sense of powerlessness weighed heavily on slaves. And among masters, the awareness that they often were outnumbered and thus vulnerable to organized slave rebellion was a source of anxiety. Locked into this fear- and hate-laden atmosphere, everyone in the cotton South was drawn into what would become a long-lasting legacy of racial tension and distrust.

lockjaw   A popular name for tetanus, an often fatal disease resulting primarily from deep wounds.

cholera   An infectious disease of the small intestines whose bacteria is often found in untreated water.

endemic   Present among a particular group or groups of people or geographical area.

The Manufacturing Boom

- How did the process of manufacturing change in the United States after 1820? How did this change affect the nature of work?

- In what ways did the American system of manufacturing change the traditional patterns of trade between the United States and the rest of the world?

- How did the developing factory system affect the lives of artisans, factory owners, and middle-class Americans?

Although the South changed radically during the opening years of the nineteenth century, one thing persisted: the economy remained rooted in people's homes. Before the 1820s, households in the North also produced most of the things they used. For example, more than 60 percent of the clothing that Americans wore was spun from raw fibers and sewn by women in their own homes. Some householders even crafted sophisticated items—furniture, clocks, and tools—but skilled **artisans** usually made such products. These craftsmen, too, usually worked in their homes, assisted by family members and an extended family of artisan employees: **apprentices** and **journeymen.**

Beginning with the cotton-spinning plants that sprang up during the War of 1812, textile manufacturing led the way in pushing production in a radical new direction (see page 260). From 1820 onward, manufacturing increasingly moved out of the home and into factories, and cities began to grow up around the factories. The intimate ties between manufacturers and workers were severed, and both found themselves surrounded by strangers in the new urban environments. "In most large cities there may be said to be two nations, understanding as little of one another, having as little intercourse, as if they lived in different lands," said Unitarian minister William Ellery Channing in 1841. "This estrangement of men from men, of class from class, is one of the saddest features of a great city."

The "American System of Manufacturing"

The transition from home manufacturing to factory production did not take place overnight, and the two processes often overlapped. Pioneer manufacturers such as Samuel Slater relied on home workers to carry out major steps in the production of textiles. Using what was called the **putting-out system,** cotton spinners supplied machine-produced yarn to individual households, where families then wove fabric on their own looms during their spare time. Such activities pro-

vided much-needed cash to farm families, enabled less productive family members (like the elderly or children) to contribute, and gave entire families worthwhile pastimes during lulls in the farming calendar.

But innovations in manufacturing soon began displacing such home crafting. The factory designs pioneered by Francis Cabot Lowell and his various partners were widely copied during the 1820s and 1830s. Spinning and weaving on machines located in one building significantly cut both the time and the cost of manufacturing. Quality control became easier because the tools of the trade, owned by the manufacturer rather than by the worker, were standardized and employees were under constant supervision. As a result, the putting-out system for turning yarn into cloth went into serious decline, falling off by as much as 90 percent in some areas of New England. Even home production of clothes for family use slid into decline. Women discovered that spending their time producing cheese or eggs or other marketable items could bring in enough cash to purchase clothing and still have money left over. Throughout the 1830s and 1840s, ready-made clothing—often cut, machine-sewn, and finished by semiskilled workers in factory settings—became standard wearing apparel.

A major technological revolution helped to push factory production into other areas of manufacturing as well during these years. In traditional manufacturing, individual artisans crafted each item one at a time, from the smallest part to the final product. A clockmaker, for example, either cast or carved individually by hand all of the clock's internal parts. As a result, the mechanisms of a clock worked together only in the clock for which they had been made. If that clock ever needed repair, new parts had to be custom-made for it. The lack of **interchangeable parts**

---

artisan A person whose primary employment is the specialized production of hand-manufactured items; a craftsperson.

apprentice A person who is bound by contract to a craftsman, providing labor in exchange for learning the skills associated with the craft.

journeyman A person who has finished an apprenticeship in a trade or craft and is a qualified worker in the employ of another.

putting-out system Manufacturing system through which machine-made components were distributed to individual families who used them to craft finished goods.

interchangeable parts Parts that are identical and which can be substituted for one another.

As American industry became increasingly mechanized in the decades after 1820, suitable mill sites—places with solid foundations for factory buildings and reliable water flow for powering machinery—became highly prized. Often long stretches of riverbanks would sprout factory after factory. This was the case in Brandywine Village near the present site of Wilmington, Delaware, which became the leading mechanized, flour-producing center in the United States during the early nineteenth century. *Historical Society of Delaware Collection.*

made manufacturing extremely slow and repairs difficult, and it limited employment in the manufacturing trades to highly skilled professionals.

While serving as ambassador to France, Thomas Jefferson had encountered the idea of standardizing parts, so that a wheel from any given clock could be used in any other similar clock. Eli Whitney, perfecter of the cotton gin (see page 265), was the first American to propose the large-scale use of interchangeable parts—for a gun-manufacturing scheme in 1798. Whitney's efforts failed because he lacked money and pre-

cision machine tools. But a quarter-century later, in 1822, one of Whitney's partners in this pioneering venture, John H. Hall, brought together the necessary skill, financing, and tools to prove that manufacturing guns from interchangeable parts was practical. Within twenty years this "American system of manufacturing," as it was called, was being used to produce a wide range of products—farm implements, padlocks, sewing machines, and clocks. Formerly, clocks had been a status symbol setting apart people of means from common folks; however, using standardized

It Matters

Manufacturing and the Revolution in Time

Before the 1830s, complex manufactured items like guns and clocks were extremely expensive, generally beyond the means of most Americans. The manufacturing revolution changed all that. In 1838, Chauncey Jerome introduced the first mass-produced brass clock at a price that virtually any American could afford, and the clocks sold by the thousands. The distribution of clocks and the means by which they were produced reinforced each other. Factory production required a much greater degree of regimentation than had individual hand manufacturing: the efforts of armies of workers, clerks, managers, shippers, and others essential to industry had to be coordinated if factories were going to function effectively. No longer living at their place of work, all of these employees, from the highest to the lowest in status, needed to have a reliable way of telling time. Jerome's clocks provided that reliability, contributing to a revolution in the way Americans began thinking about time itself. Increasingly people looked to mechanical devices rather than to natural ones—the transit of the sun, the changing of seasons—to punctuate their lives, and industry profited accordingly. As American society has become increasingly complex, we have become even more dependent on time management and various devices for implementing it. As we look at our day planner or electronic personal information manager, we are participating in a world that was born in 1838 with the introduction of cheap brass clocks.

New Workplaces and New Workers

With machines now producing standardized parts for complex mechanisms such as clocks, the worker's job was reduced to simply assembling premade components. The centuries-old **guild** organization for artisans—preserved in the hierarchical system of apprentices, journeymen, and master craftsmen—rapidly fell away as extensive training in the manufacturing arts became irrelevant.

At first, owners found they had to use creative means to attract workers into the new factories. Some entrepreneurs developed **company towns.** In New England these towns resembled traditional New England villages. Families recruited from the economically depressed countryside were installed in neat row houses, each with its own small vegetable garden. The company employed each family member. Women worked on the production line. Men ran heavy machinery and worked as **millwrights,** carpenters, haulers, or as day laborers dredging out the **millraces.** Children did light work in the factories and tended gardens at home.

Lowell's company developed another system at its factories. Hard-pressed to find enough families to leave traditional employment and come to work in the factories, Lowell recruited unmarried farm girls. The company built dormitories to house these young working women, offering cash wages and reasonable prices for room and board, as well as cultural events and educational opportunities. Because most of the girls saw factory work as a transitional stage between girlhood and marriage, Lowell assured them and their families that the company would strictly control the moral atmosphere so that the girls' reputations would remain spotless.

Not everyone was convinced that factory work, even under strict supervision, was appropriate for

parts, pioneer manufacturers like Seth Thomas and Chauncey Jerome revolutionized clock making to the point where virtually all Americans could afford them. Not only that, Thomas's and Jerome's breakthroughs produced clocks so inexpensive and reliable that even the British and Europeans began importing them. This reversed the long-standing pattern of manufactures moving exclusively from Europe to America, a trend that would grow in the years to come.

guild An association of craftspeople with the same skills who join together to protect their mutual interests.

company town A town built and owned by a single company; its residents depend on the company not only for jobs but for stores, schools, and housing.

millwright A person who designs, builds, or repairs mills or mill machinery.

millrace The channel for the fast-moving stream of water that drives a mill wheel.

young women. "Few of them ever marry," Boston journalist Orestes A. Brownson incorrectly reported. "Fewer still ever return to their native places with reputations unimpaired." Others, however, even the young women themselves, defended the system. In a letter to the editor, one young woman attacked Brownson personally. "And now, if Mr. Brownson is a man . . . let him come among us: let him make himself as well acquainted with us as our pastors and superintendents are; . . . he would not see worthy and virtuous girls consigned to infamy, because they work in a factory."

In New York, Philadelphia, and other cities, immigrant slums offered opportunistic manufacturers an alternative source of labor. In the shoe industry, for example, one family would make soles, while a neighboring family made heels, and so forth. This type of operation was not as efficient as large shoe factories, but the money that urban manufacturers saved by not building factories and by paying rock-bottom wages to desperate slum-dwellers made it possible for the companies to compete successfully in the open market.

The combination of machine production and a growing pool of labor proved economically devastating to workers. No longer was the employer a master craftsman or a paternalistic entrepreneur who felt some responsibility to look out for his workers' domestic needs. Factory owners were obligated to investors and bankers and had to squeeze the greatest possible profit out of the manufacturing process. They kept wages low, regardless of the workers' cost of living. As the swelling supply of labor allowed employers to offer lower and lower wages, increasing numbers of working people faced poverty and squalor.

Immigration supplied much of this labor. Between 1820 and 1830 slightly more than 151,000 people immigrated to the United States. In the decade that followed, that number increased to nearly 600,000; between 1840 and 1850, well over a million and a half people moved to the United States from abroad (see Map 11.1). This enormous increase in immigration changed not only the **demographic** but also the cultural and economic face of the nation. The flood of immigrants collected in the port and manufacturing cities of the Northeast, where they joined Americans fleeing financial depression in the countryside after the economic panics of 1819 (see page 280) and 1837 (discussed in Chapter 12). Adding to the resulting brew were former master craftsmen, journeymen, and apprentices who no longer had a secure place in the changing economy. Together, though seldom cooperatively, these groups helped to form a new social class in America.

Nearly half of all the immigrants who flooded into the United States between 1820 and 1860 came from Ireland—a nation beset with poverty, political strife, and, after a devastating blight began killing the potato crop in 1841, starvation. For centuries Ireland had been a colony in the British Empire, and Irish immigrants had few marketable skills or more money than the voyage to America cost. They arrived penniless, many of them speaking not English but Gaelic, and most had little or no chance of finding employment.

Similar conditions beset many members of the second most numerous immigrant group: the Germans. Radical economic change and political upheaval in Germany were putting both peasants and skilled craftsmen to flight. Like Irish peasants, German farmers arrived in America destitute and devoid of opportunities. Trained German craftsmen had a better chance of finding employment, but the changeover from handicraft to industrial production—the very change that in many cases had driven them from Germany— was also taking place in America. And like the Irish, few spoke English well.

Not only were the new immigrants poor and often unskilled, but also most were culturally different from native-born Americans. Religion was their most notable cultural distinction: the majority were Roman Catholics. Their Catholicism separated them from most Americans, who claimed to be Protestant whether they worshiped actively or not. It also made them suspect in the minds of people steeped in anti-Catholic sentiments handed down from earlier generations of Lutheran, Presbyterian, Quaker, and other immigrants who had fled Catholic persecution. In religion, then, as well as in language, dress, and eating and drinking habits, the new immigrants were very different from the sorts of people whose culture had come to dominate American society.

Poverty, cultural distinctiveness, and a desire to live among people who understood their ways and spoke their language brought new immigrants to neighborhoods where their countrymen had already found places to live. In New York, Philadelphia, and other cities, people with the same culture and religion built churches, stores, pubs or beer halls, and other familiar institutions that helped them cope with the shock of transplantation from Europe and gave them a chance to adapt gradually to life in the United States. They also started fraternal organizations and clubs to overcome the loneliness, isolation, and powerlessness they were experiencing.

Because the new immigrants were poor, housing in their neighborhoods was often substandard, and living conditions were crowded, uncomfortable, and unsanitary. Desperate for work and eager to make their own way in their new country, these fresh immigrants were willing to do nearly anything to earn money. Lacking the resources to buy farms and lacking the skills to enter professional trades, they were the perfect work force for the newly evolving industrial economy. As the flow of immigrants increased, the traditional labor shortage in America was replaced by a **labor glut,** and the social and economic status of all workers declined accordingly.

Living Conditions in Blue-Collar America

Working conditions for **blue-collar workers** in factories reflected the labor supply, the amount of capital available to the manufacturing company, and the

---

demographic The statistical distribution of subpopulations (ethnic groups, for example) among the larger population of a community or nation.

labor glut Oversupply of labor in relation to the number of jobs available.

blue-collar workers Workers who wear work clothes, such as coveralls and jeans, on the job; their work is likely to involve manual labor.

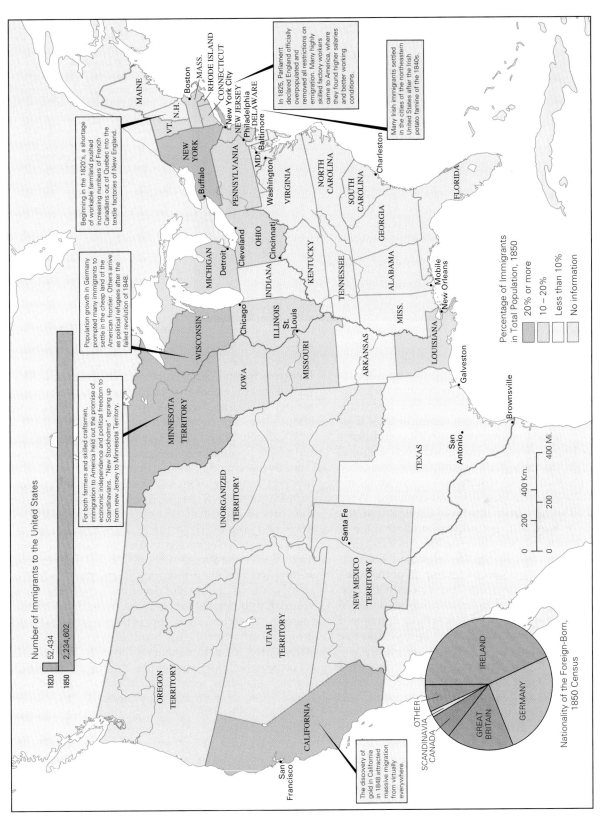

Number of Immigrants to the United States

1820 — 52,434

1850 — 2,234,602

Beginning in the 1820's, a shortage of workable farmland pushed increasing numbers of French Canadians out of Quebec into the textile factories of New England.

In 1825, Parliament declared England officially overpopulated and removed all restrictions on emigration. Many highly skilled factory workers came to America, where they found higher salaries and better working conditions.

Many Irish immigrants settled in the cities of the northeastern United States after the Irish potato famine of the 1840s.

Population growth in Germany prompted many immigrants to settle in the cheap land of the American frontier. Others arrive as political refugees after the failed revolution of 1848.

For both farmers and skilled craftsmen, immigration to America held out the promise of economic independence and political freedom to Scandinavians. "New Stockholms" sprang up from new Jersey to Minnesota Territory.

The discovery of gold in California in 1848 attracted massive migration from virtually everywhere.

Percentage of Immigrants in Total Population, 1850

- 20% or more
- 10 – 20%
- Less than 10%
- No information

Nationality of the Foreign-Born, 1850 Census

IRELAND • GERMANY • GREAT BRITAIN • CANADA • SCANDINAVIA • OTHER

MAP 11.1 Origin and Settlement of Immigrants, 1820–1850 Immigration was one of the most important economic, political, and social factors in American life during the antebellum period. As this map shows, with the exception of Louisiana, immigration was confined almost exclusively to areas where slavery was not permitted. This gave the North, Northwest, and California a different cultural flavor than the rest of the country and also affected the political balance between those areas and the South.

Working-class neighborhoods like the infamous Five Points District in New York, shown in this anonymous 1829 picture, were filthy, unhealthy, and crime-ridden. Reformers sought to help by changing workers' habits and morals but seldom addressed their economic plight. *"Five Points District," artist unknown, ca. 1829. Courtesy of Mr. and Mrs. Screven Lorillard. Photograph by Josh Nefsky.*

personal philosophy of the factory owner. Girls at Lowell's factories described an environment of familiar paternalism. Factory managers and boarding-house keepers supervised every aspect of their lives in much the same manner that authoritarian fathers saw to the details of life on traditional New England farms. As for the work itself, one mill girl commented that it was "not half so hard as . . . attending the dairy, washing, cleaning house, and cooking." What bothered factory workers most was the repetitive nature of the work and the resulting boredom. One of Lowell's employees described the tedium. "The time is often apt to drag heavily till the dinner hour arrives," she reported. "Perhaps some part of the work becomes deranged and stops; the constant friction causes a belt of leather to burst into a flame; a stranger visits the room, and scans the features and dress of its inmates inquiringly; and there is little else to break the monotony."

She went on to note that daydreaming provided relief from the boredom and the ear-shattering noise of the machinery. But daydreaming in front of fast-moving equipment could have disastrous consequences for what a New Jersey magazine called "the human portion of the machine." Inattentive factory workers were likely to lose fingers, hands, or whole arms to whirring, pounding, slashing mechanisms. Not a few lost their lives. Though managers may have wanted to make factories safer, investors vetoed any additional costs that safety devices might have

incurred. Samuel Slater, for example, complained bitterly to his investors after a child was chewed up in a factory machine. "You call for yarn but think little about the means by which it is to be made."

Gradually Slater's and Lowell's well-meaning paternalism became rare as factory owners withdrew from overseeing day-to-day operations. The influx of laborers from the depressed countryside and of foreign immigrants wiped out both decent wages and the sorts of incentives the early manufacturing pioneers had employed. Not only did wages fall but laborers were also expected to find their own housing, food, and entertainment. Soon hulking **tenements** sprang up, replacing the open fields and clusters of small homes that once had dominated the urban landscape. Large houses formerly occupied by domestic manufacturers and their apprentices were broken up into tiny apartments by profit-hungry speculators who rented them to desperate laborers. Cellars and attics became living spaces like the rest of the building. In cities like New York, laborers lived 50 to a house in some working-class areas. As population densities reached 150 people an acre in such neighborhoods, sewage disposal, drinking water, and trash removal became difficult to provide. Life in such con-

tenement　An urban apartment house, usually with minimal facilities for sanitation, safety, and comfort.

ditions was grossly unpleasant and extremely un-healthy: epidemics of typhus, cholera, and other crowd diseases swept through the slums periodically.

Investigating living and working conditions, a *New York Tribune* reporter found conditions deplorable. "The floor is made of rough plank laid loosely down, and the ceiling is not quite so high as a tall man," he reported. "The walls are dark and damp and the miserable room is lighted only by a shallow sash partly projecting above the surface of the ground and by the light that struggles from the steep and rotting stairs." In this dark and tiny space, he observed, "often lives the man and his work bench, the wife, and five or six children of all ages; and perhaps a palsied grandfather and grandmother and often both. Here they work, here they cook, they eat, they sleep, they pray."

Life and Culture Among a New Middle Class

Large-scale manufacturing not only changed industrial work but also introduced demands for a new class of skilled managerial and clerical employees. Under the old system of manufacturing, the master craftsman or his wife had managed the company's accounts, hired journeymen and apprentices, purchased raw materials, and seen to the delivery of finished products. The size of the new factories made such direct contact between owners, workers, and products impossible. To fill the void, a new class of professionals came into being. In these days before the invention of the typewriter, firms such as Lowell's Boston Manufacturing Company employed teams of young men as clerks. These clerks kept accounts, wrote orders, and drafted correspondence, all in longhand using **quill pens.** As elite owners such as Lowell and his partners became wrapped up in building new factories, pursuing investors, and entering new markets, both clerical and manufacturing employees were increasingly supervised by professional managers.

One distinguishing characteristic of the new **white-collar workers** was their relative youth. These young people, many of them the sons and daughters of rural farmers, had flocked to newly emerging cities in pursuit of formal education. They stayed to seek employment away from the economic instability and **provincialism** of the farm. The experience of Elizabeth Yale Hancock, a country girl from upstate New York, was fairly typical. After attending public school in Champlain, Elizabeth transferred to the Plattsburgh Academy. She studied there full-time for two terms before taking a job teaching at a public school while con-

tinuing classes at the academy part-time. She then went to the Female Seminary in Buffalo, where she enrolled in college-level classes. While pursuing her studies there, she worked as a nanny and resident tutor. Finally graduating from the seminary, Elizabeth took a job as a teacher at a select school.

Men too attended school when and where they could get financial assistance and then settled down where they could find employment and the company of others like themselves. And, as Elizabeth Hancock's experience indicates, women joined men in moving into new professions. While middle-class men found employment as clerks, bookkeepers, and managers, middle-class women parlayed their formal education and their gender's perceived gift for nurturing children into work as teachers. It became acceptable for women to work as teachers for several years before marriage, and many avoided marriage altogether to pursue their hard-won careers.

Middle-class men and women tended to put off marriage as long as possible while they established themselves socially and economically. They also tended to have fewer children than their parents had had. In the new urban middle-class setting, parents felt compelled to send their children to school so that they could take their place on the career ladder chosen by their parents. Adding nothing to family income, children thus became economic liabilities rather than assets, and middle-class adults used a combination of late marriage and various forms of birth control to keep families small.

A lack of traditional ties affected the lives of both married and unmarried middle-class people. Many unmarried men and women seeking their fortunes in town boarded in private homes or rooming houses. After marriage, middle-class men and women often moved into private town homes, isolating themselves and their children from perceived dangers in the faceless city but also cutting them off from the comforting sociability of traditional country life. Accordingly, these young people crafted new urban structures that might provide the missing companionship and guidance.

quill pen A pen made from the shaft of a feather; the end of the quill is sharpened with a knife and then dipped in ink.

white-collar workers Workers able to wear white shirts on the job because they do no grubby manual labor.

provincialism The limited and narrow perspective thought to be characteristic of people in rural areas.

Obviously some sought the company of women like Helen Jewett. Most, however, found companionship in **voluntary associations.** Students in colleges and universities formed a variety of discussion groups, preprofessional clubs, and benevolent societies. After graduation, groups such as the Odd Fellows and the Masons brought people together for companionship. Such organizations helped enforce traditional values through rigid membership standards stressing moral character, upright behavior, and, above all, order.

The *Odd Fellows' Manual* summarized the philosophy of these organizations well. "In the transaction of our business we pursue strict parliamentary rules, that our members may be qualified for any public stations to which they may be called by their fellow-citizens," the manual asserts. "And when business has been performed, we indulge in social intercourse, and even in cheerful and innocent hilarity and amusement. But all in strict order and decorum, good fellowship and prudence are constantly to be kept in view." In such clubs, people could discuss the latest books or world affairs with others of similar education and lifestyle in an affable setting. As the *Odd Fellows' Manual* went on to say, "Exercise yourself in the discussions of your Lodge not for the purpose of mere debate, contention, or 'love of opposition,' but to improve yourself in suitably expressing your sentiments." Young people also created and joined professional and trade groups. These associations served a social function, but they also became forums for training novices and for setting standards for professional methods and modes of conduct.

Members of the new middle class also used their organizing skills to press for reforms. While the elite class of factory owners and financiers generally formed the leadership for such organizations as the American Tract Society, the American Bible Society, and the American Board of Commissioners for Foreign Missions—each a multimillion-dollar reforming enterprise—young middle-class men and women provided the rank and file of charity workers.

In addition to their youth, another characteristic that prevailed among this newly forming class was deep anxiety. Although their education and skills earned them jobs with greater prestige than those of the average worker, these clerks and supervisors could be laid off or demoted to working-class status at any time. Also, because of the anonymity in the new cities, it was virtually impossible to know if a stranger was truly a member of one's own class or an imposter who might use the trappings of gentility to take advantage of the new urban scene. Such suspicions led to a very strict set of rules for making social connections, and

the wary atmosphere also helps to explain the fascination with a woman like Helen Jewett, whose life, and especially whose death, illustrated the dangers posed by and to pretenders to middle-class gentility.

Social Life for a Genteel Class

The changes in lifestyle that affected working-class and middle-class Americans were in large part an outcome of changes in the daily lives of those who owned and operated manufacturing businesses. In earlier years, when journeymen and apprentices had lived with master craftsmen, they were in effect members of a craftsman's extended family. The master craftsman/owner exercised great authority over his workers but felt obligated to care for them almost as a parent would have done. Such working arrangements blurred the distinction between employee and employer. Crammed together in the same household, owner and workers shared the same general lifestyle, kept the same hours, ate the same food, and enjoyed the same leisure activities. The factory system ended this relationship. The movement of workers out of the owners' homes permitted members of the emerging elite class to develop a **genteel** lifestyle that set them off from the army of factory workers and lesser number of clerks. Genteel families aimed at the complete separation of their private and public lives. Men in the manufacturing elite class spent their leisure time in new activities. Instead of drinking, eating, and playing with their employees, business owners began to socialize with one another in private clubs and in church and civic organizations. Instead of attending the popular theater, elite patrons began endowing opera companies and other highbrow forms of entertainment.

The lives of the factory owners' wives also changed. The mistress of a traditional manufacturing household had been responsible for important tasks in the operation of the business. Genteel women, in contrast, were expected to leave business dealings to men. Ensconced in private houses set apart from the new centers of production and marketing, genteel women found themselves with time on their hands. To give themselves something to do, they sought areas of ac-

voluntary association   An organization or club through which individuals engage in voluntary service, usually associated with charity or reform.

genteel   The manner and style associated with elite classes, usually characterized by elegance, grace, and politeness.

Voluntary associations and fraternal organizations sprang up by the hundreds in the new urban America that was emerging in the 1830s and 1840s. These organizations provided companionship and, more importantly, a sense of order for the newly emerging middle class. The Odd Fellows was one prominent example. This sheet music cover, from a piece entitled "The Oddfellows March," is but one piece of evidence of the enormous cultural contributions that these organizations made to emerging modern American life. *Maryland Historical Society.*

tivity that would provide focus and a sense of accomplishment without imperiling their elite status by involving them in what was now perceived as the crass, masculine world of commerce. Many found outlets for their creative energies in fancy needlework, reading, and art appreciation societies. But some wished for more challenging activities. Sarah Huntington Smith, for example, a member of Connecticut's elite, spoke for many when she complained in 1833, "To make and receive visits, exchange friendly salutations, attend to one's wardrobe, cultivate a garden, read good and entertaining books, and even attend religious meetings for one's own enjoyment; all this does not satisfy me."

One activity that consumed genteel women was motherhood. Magazines and advice manuals, which began appearing during the 1820s and 1830s, rejected the traditional adage of "spare the rod, spoil the child," replacing it with an insistence on gentle nurturing. One leader in this movement was author and teacher Bronson Alcott. Alcott denied the concept of **infant depravity** that had so affected Puritan parents during the colonial era and led them to break their children's will, often through harsh measures (see page 71). Instead, he stated emphatically that "the child must be treated as a free, self-guiding, self-controlling being."

Alcott was equally emphatic that child rearing was the mother's responsibility. As his wife, Abigail, wrote of family management in Alcott's household, "Mr. A aids me in general principles, though nobody can aid me in the detail." And, according to Alcott, women should feel especially blessed for having such an opportunity.

Books like Alcott's *Conversations with Children on the Gospels* (1836–1837) flooded forth during these years and appealed greatly to isolated and underemployed women. Many adopted the advertised **cult of domesticity** completely. Turning inward, these women centered their lives on their homes and children. In doing so, they believed they were performing an important duty for God and country and fulfilling their most important, perhaps their only, natural calling.

Other genteel women agreed with the general tone of the domestic message but widened the woman's supposedly natural sphere outward, beyond the nursery, to encompass the whole world. They banded together with like-minded women to get out into the world in order to reform it. "I want to be where every arrangement will have unreserved and constant reference to eternity," Sarah Huntington Smith explained. Smith herself chose to become a missionary. Others during the 1830s and 1840s involved themselves in a variety of reform movements, such as founding Sunday schools or opposing alcohol abuse. These causes let them use their nurturing and purifying talents to improve what appeared to be an increasingly chaotic and immoral society, the world represented by Helen Jewett.

infant depravity The idea that children are naturally sinful because they share in the original sin of the human race but have not learned the discipline to control their evil instincts.

cult of domesticity The belief that women's proper role lies in domestic pursuits.

Individual Voices

Examining a Primary Source

The Press "Remembers" Helen Jewett

The United States in 1836 was rapidly becoming more modern. One measure of its emerging modernity, a feature with which we are all too familiar today, was the rise of a sensationalist press. The murder of Helen Jewett (really Dorcas Doyen) presented an irresistible opportunity for this new medium. Although a few responsible newspapers printed factually based stories about the victim's early life, sensationalist newspapers seeking larger sales and plumped-up reputations for being investigative published ever more exaggerated accounts of Jewett's life and death. The *New York Herald*, for example, continued to print romanticized stories about Jewett even after it became generally known that her early life was rather unremarkable and that the charming Miss Jewett was a fictional creation by an intelligent and inventive woman who was intent on shaping her life on her own terms. The following is taken from a story printed in the *Herald* on April 12, 1836.

■ *Although it was generally known that young Dorcas was actually hired as a serving girl in Judge Weston's household, this story suggests that she was a guest or companion in the justice's home. Why would a news writer choose to "revise" the facts?*

Her private history is most remarkable—her character equally so. . . . In Augusta, Maine, lived a highly respectable gentleman, Judge Western [sic], by name. Some of the female members of his family pitying the bereaved condition of young Dorcas invited her to live at the Judge's house. At that time Dorcas was young, beautiful, innocent, modest, and ingenuous. Her good qualities and sprightly temper won the good feelings of the Judge's family. She became a chere-amie of his daughters—a companion and a playmate. . . . ■

■ *How does the account of the seduction of the teenage Dorcas add to the story? Why might this version have had more appeal than the truth for popular audiences?*

After having continued at the Academy for some time, Dorcas, during the summer of 1829, went to spend the vacation at a distant relative's at Norridgewock, a town on the Kennebeck river, about 28 miles above Augusta. Dorcas was then sixteen years of age—and one of the most lovely, interesting, black eyed girls, that ever appeared in that place.

In this town, in the course of visiting, she became acquainted with a young man, by the name of H—— Sp——y, a fine youth, elegant and educated, since said to be a Cashier in one of the banks of Augusta. After a short acquaintance with him, all was gone that constitutes the honor and ornament of the female character. . . . ■

■ *Aspasia was the mistress of Pericles, the foremost Athenian statesman of classical Greece. Despite a disreputable background, Aspasia used her intelligence and wit to charm the political elite of Athens in the fifth century BCE. Though charming, she frequently was the target of public attacks that painted her as a common harlot.*

She returned after a short season to Augusta. Her situation soon became known in the Judge's family. A quarrel ensued. She left her protector, after having in a moment of passion lost all the rules of virtue and morality.

After having recovered from her first lapse from the path of virtue, she retreated to Portland, took the name of Maria B. Benson, and became a regular Aspasia ■ *among the young men, lawyers, and merchants.* ■

■ *Whom does the writer want the audience to blame for Dorcas Doyen's descent into prostitution? Why?*

Summary

Although seemingly the most old-fashioned region of the country, the South that emerged during the years leading up to 1840 was a profoundly different place than it had been before the War of 1812. As an industrial revolution overturned the economies in Great Britain and the American Northeast, economic options for southerners changed radically. Although they clothed their new society in romanticized medieval garb, they were creating an altogether new kind of economy and society. The efficient production of cotton by the newly reorganized South was an essential aspect of the emerging national market economy and a powerful force in the Great Transformation.

Change in the North was more obvious. As factories replaced craft shops and cities replaced towns, the entire fabric of northern society seemed to come unraveled. The new economy and new technology created wonderful new opportunities but also imposed serious constraints. A revamped social structure replaced the traditional order as unskilled and semiskilled workers, a new class of clerks, and the genteel elite carved out new lives. The new cities also developed a dark underside where the tawdry glamour that characterized Helen Jewett's life often led to grotesque death. As in the South, the outcome was a remarkable transformation in the lives of everyone in the region.

Tying these two regions together was a new network of roads, waterways, and communications systems that accelerated the process of change. After 1840, it was possible to ship goods from any one section of the country to any other, and people in all sections were learning more about conditions in far distant parts of the growing country. Often this new information promised prosperity, but it also made more and more people aware of the enormity of the transformation taking place and the glaring differences between the nation's various regions. The twin outcomes would be greater integration in the national economy and increasing tension between mutually dependent participants in the new marketplace.

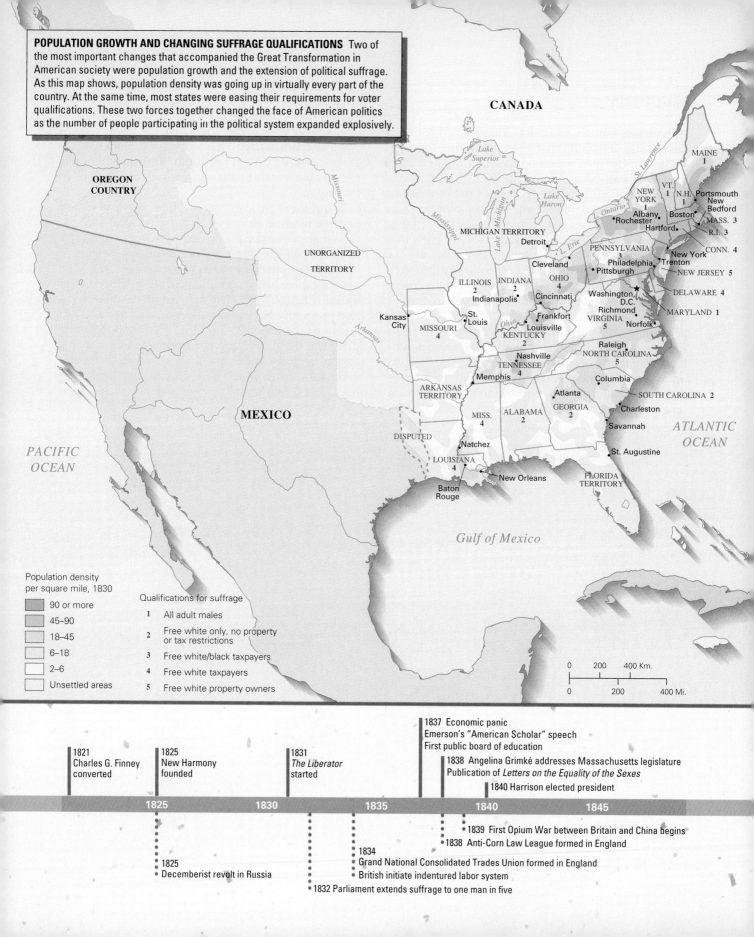

POPULATION GROWTH AND CHANGING SUFFRAGE QUALIFICATIONS Two of the most important changes that accompanied the Great Transformation in American society were population growth and the extension of political suffrage. As this map shows, population density was going up in virtually every part of the country. At the same time, most states were easing their requirements for voter qualifications. These two forces together changed the face of American politics as the number of people participating in the political system expanded explosively.

CANADA

OREGON COUNTRY

UNORGANIZED TERRITORY

MICHIGAN TERRITORY

Lake Superior

Lake Huron

Lake Michigan

L. Ontario

L. Erie

MAINE
1

VT.
1

N.H.
1

NEW YORK
1

Portsmouth
New Bedford

MASS. 3

R.I. 3

Albany
Rochester
Boston
Hartford

CONN. 4

PENNSYLVANIA
3

Philadelphia
Pittsburgh

New York
Trenton

NEW JERSEY 5

Detroit

Cleveland

OHIO
4

Washington,
D.C.

DELAWARE 4

MARYLAND 1

ILLINOIS
2

INDIANA
2

Indianapolis

Cincinnati

Frankfort

Louisville

Richmond

Norfolk

VIRGINIA
5

Kansas City

St. Louis

MISSOURI
4

KENTUCKY
2

Ohio

Nashville

TENNESSEE
4

Raleigh

NORTH CAROLINA
5

Columbia

SOUTH CAROLINA 2

ARKANSAS TERRITORY

Memphis

MISS.
4

ALABAMA
2

GEORGIA
2

Atlanta

Charleston

Savannah

Missouri

Mississippi

Arkansas

MEXICO

DISPUTED

Natchez

LOUISIANA
4

New Orleans

Baton Rouge

FLORIDA TERRITORY

St. Augustine

PACIFIC OCEAN

ATLANTIC OCEAN

Gulf of Mexico

Population density per square mile, 1830

- 90 or more
- 45–90
- 18–45
- 6–18
- 2–6
- Unsettled areas

Qualifications for suffrage

1   All adult males

2   Free white only, no property or tax restrictions

3   Free white/black taxpayers

4   Free white taxpayers

5   Free white property owners

0   200   400 Km.

0   200   400 Mi.

1821 Charles G. Finney converted

1825 New Harmony founded

1831 *The Liberator* started

1837 Economic panic
Emerson's "American Scholar" speech
First public board of education

1838 Angelina Grimké addresses Massachusetts legislature
Publication of *Letters on the Equality of the Sexes*

1840 Harrison elected president

1825   1830   1835   1840   1845

1839 First Opium War between Britain and China begins

1838 Anti-Corn Law League formed in England

1834 Grand National Consolidated Trades Union formed in England
British initiate indentured labor system

1825 Decemberist revolt in Russia

1832 Parliament extends suffrage to one man in five

Responses to the Great Transformation, 1828–1840

12

Population Growth and Changing Suffrage Qualifications

Using the map on the facing page, note the increasing concentration of population in certain areas and also the rules that controlled voting on a regional basis. How would these two factors manifest themselves in the presidential election of 1840? How was the face of American politics changed?

Individual Choices

ANGELINA GRIMKÉ

Born in the South to a prominent slaveholding family,
Angelina Grimké moved to
the North to distance herself
from an institution she hated.
When she discovered that
northerners were no more
sympathetic about the plight
of slaves than southerners
and would not give abolition
a free hearing, she chose to do
something about it. She
toured the Northeast, speaking first to groups of women
and then to large mixed audiences. She capped her tour by
becoming the first woman to
address the Massachusetts
state legislature. Her courage
won new respect both for
abolitionists and for women.
Library of Congress.

Angelina Grimké

On March 22, 1838, Boston newspapers reported an unprecedented historical event. On the day before, a young woman had become the first of
her gender to address a committee of the Massachusetts state legislature.
The young woman was Angelina Emily Grimké, and her speech was a
ringing condemnation of slavery.

Many thought it odd that a woman barely out of her twenties would
stand before the legislature to speak on any subject, but to speak so
boldly on a topic so controversial was odder still. And more than just odd,
to speak out against slavery, even in Boston, was dangerous. And that
was precisely why Angelina Grimké had chosen to do it.

Born in 1808, Angelina was the thirteenth child of Judge John
Faucheraud Grimké and his wife, Mary Smith Grimké. Both of Angelina's
parents were descendants of old South Carolina aristocratic families and
members in good standing of the state's social and political elite. But
Angelina was never comfortable in this environment of carefree gentility. Raised
mostly by her older sister Sarah, young Angelina was extremely serious-minded.
When presented for confirmation in her parents' Episcopal faith, she refused,
saying, "If, with my feelings and views as they now are, I should go through that
form, it would be acting a lie. I cannot do it."

Sarah, too, was uncomfortable with plantation life and Episcopalian ritual.
While on a trip to Philadelphia she became attracted to Quakerism and brought
this new faith home. But being a Quaker in antebellum South Carolina was anything but easy—the Society of Friends in Charleston consisted of but two old men.
Sarah finally chose to leave her family and move to Pennsylvania, where she could
practice her faith. Angelina, too, eventually converted to the Quaker faith and, in
1829, followed her sister to Philadelphia.

One of the Quaker principles that attracted Sarah and Angelina was its rejection of slavery. Though raised in a slaveholding family, several of the Grimké children opposed the institution. Their brother Thomas, for example, was one of the
key organizers of the American Colonization Society, which labored to free slaves
and return them to Africa. Most of their Quaker friends, too, supported colonization and the Colonization Society's gradual approach, but this was not acceptable
to Angelina. Just before leaving South Carolina, she had written about slavery in
her diary: "May it not be laid down as an axiom, that the system must be radically
wrong which can only be supported by transgressing the laws of God."

In fact, Angelina was at first disappointed and then angered by northern indifference to the slavery issue. Even in Quaker circles, conservative leaders sought to
maintain peace in congregations by prohibiting the discussion of slavery. And non-
Quakers treated those who vocally attacked the institution with outright hostility.
In 1834 riots had broken out in New York and Philadelphia when abolitionist
speakers had tried to give public addresses. Finally, in the late summer of 1835,
after a year of repeated outbreaks, William Lloyd Garrison published an appeal in

The Liberator calling for the citizens of Boston to stop mob violence and give abolitionist speakers a fair hearing. His courage in standing up to the mobs was like a personal call for Angelina. Although she tried to resist the temptation, she felt compelled to write a letter to Garrison praising his stand.

"The ground upon which you stand is holy ground," she wrote. "Never—never surrender it. If you surrender it, the hope of the slave is extinguished." Garrison was so moved by the letter that he immediately published it, casting a spotlight on its young female author. "I had some idea it might be published," Angelina wrote in her diary, "but did not feel at liberty to say it must not be. . . ." Friends, family members, even her sister Sarah begged Angelina to withdraw the letter, but she refused. "I cannot describe the anguish of my soul," she wrote. "Nevertheless I could not blame the publication of the letter, nor would I have recalled it if I could."

As to the danger, she had written to Garrison, "If persecution is the means which God has ordained for the accomplishment of this great end, EMANCIPATION; then . . . I feel as if I could say, LET IT COME; for it is my deep, solemn deliberate conviction, that this is a cause worth dying for. . . ."

From that point, there was no turning back. In 1836 she wrote an *Appeal to the Christian Women of the South,* calling for them to stand up and put an end to the institution of slavery. In the following year she addressed an *Appeal to the Women of the Nominally Free States.* Then she accepted an invitation from the American Anti-Slavery Society to begin a lecture tour, speaking at first only to groups of women, but eventually to large mixed audiences. The acclaim she won finally led to her appearance at the state house in Boston, where the committee not only listened to her arguments but invited her back for an additional session. "The chairman," she reported, "was in tears almost the whole time that I was speaking."

Angelina's choice and the wide acceptance she gained through her eloquence made it easier from then on for abolitionist speakers to win the hearing Garrison had begged for. And the precedent she set, first in speaking to large audiences of men and women together and then in addressing the Massachusetts legislature, proved to women that they could and should publicly proclaim their ideas, even on dangerous subjects.

INTRODUCTION

Standing before the Massachusetts state legislature in 1838, Angelina Grimké was violating nearly every standard for behavior that applied to her generation. The daughter of a southern plantation family, she nonetheless opposed slavery and was willing to declare her opinions publicly. As a woman, she was taking a step that no other of her sex had yet done by testifying about this controversial issue in the halls of government. A person of deep faith and unswerving commitment, she felt she had to speak out. And in that, she stood with many in her generation. Changing conditions wrought by the so-called Great Transformation in the nation's economy and society prompted unusual responses by many. In 1838 Grimké stood alone at the podium, but she was not alone in spirit.

In her many speeches and written works, Grimké gave voice to both a growing anxiety and a growing hopefulness that was sweeping over America. She and many of her fellow Christians shared with transcendentalists, socialists, and other communitarians a belief in human perfectibility that drove them all into a frenzy of work and experimentation. In northern cities, on southern plantations, and at western revival meetings, members of all social classes were crafting cultural expressions designed to give meaning to their lives and lend shape to a society that seemed to be losing all direction. At the same time, ambitious politicians were re-creating the art of politics in line with new economic and cultural imperatives. A new, modern, and much more complicated America clearly was in the making.

Toward an American Culture

■ To what extent were American cultural expressions influenced by international forces?

■ How did developments in American arts and letters reflect the spirit of change during the Jacksonian era?

■ What other cultural consequences emerged from this dynamic era?

As Angelina Grimké's life illustrates, profound changes were taking place during the first decades of the nineteenth century that were altering traditional relationships between individuals and society. Both frontiersmen and city-dwellers became increasingly self-reliant, giving rise to a widespread commitment to individualism. The changing economic, social, and political systems that came to maturity in the Jacksonian era, as well as the character of the popular president himself, helped to fix this individualistic creed as a dominant force in an evolving American culture.

Traditional community ties based on close-knit, longtime social and family relationships could not survive in towns and villages where migrating opportunity seekers came and went. Nor could such ties develop and thrive in the growing trading and manufacturing centers where throngs of strangers massed to seek a better living. Instead, as visiting French nobleman **Alexis de Tocqueville** observed, Americans seemed to be "animated by the most selfish **cupidity.**" Indeed, a new world of opportunity seemed open to those with the talent, desire, and good luck to pursue it. As Tocqueville also observed, "The government of democracy brings the notion of political rights to the level of the humblest citizens, just as the dissemination of wealth brings the notion of property within the reach of all the members of society."

Romanticism and Genteel Culture

Underlying the new mood in American thought and culture was a philosophical attitude sweeping across the Atlantic. **Romanticism,** the European philosophers' rebellion against Enlightenment reason (see page 102), stressed the heart over the mind, the wild over the controlled, the mystical over the rational. The United States, with its millions of acres of wilder-

Giving voice to the Romantic sentimentalism that rapidly was setting the tone for middle-class culture in early nineteenth-century America, women writers like Lydia Sigourney became virtual overnight celebrities, selling thousands of books to newly emerging urban consumers. This early daguerreotype, by African American photographer Augustus Washington, captures Sigourney at the height of her popularity and influence. *Watkinson Library, Trinity College, Hartford, Connecticut.*

ness, teeming populations of wild animals, and colorful frontier myths, was the perfect setting for romanticism to flower. Uniting individualism and romanticism, many of the era's leading intellectuals emphasized the positive aspects of life in the United States, cele-

Alexis de Tocqueville French traveler and historian who toured the United States in 1831 and wrote *Democracy in America,* a classic study of American institutions and the American character.

cupidity The extreme desire for wealth; greed.

romanticism Artistic and intellectual movement characterized by interest in nature, emphasis on emotion and imagination over rationality, and rebellion against social conventions.

Chronology

Modernization and Rising Stress

1806	Journeyman shoemakers' strike in New York City
1821	Charles G. Finney experiences a religious conversion
1823	James Fenimore Cooper's *The Pioneers*
1825	Thomas Cole begins Hudson River school of painting Robert Owen establishes community at New Harmony, Indiana
1826	Shakers have eighteen communities in the United States
1828	Weavers protest and riot in New York City Andrew Jackson elected president
1829	Grand jury in Rochester, New York, declares alcohol most prominent cause of crime
1830	Joseph Smith Jr. publishes Book of Mormon
1831	Nat Turner's Rebellion William Lloyd Garrison begins publishing *The Liberator*
1832	Jackson reelected
1833	Lydia Sigourney publishes bestsellers *Letters to Young Ladies* and *How to Be Happy*
1834	Riot in Charlestown, Massachusetts, leads to destruction of Catholic convent

	George Bancroft publishes volume 1 of his American history Formation of National Trades' Union Formation of Whig Party
1835	Five Points riot in New York City
1836	Congress passes the gag rule Martin Van Buren elected president
1837	Horace Mann heads first public board of education Panic of 1837 Ralph Waldo Emerson's "American Scholar" speech
1838	Emerson articulates transcendentalism Angelina Grimké addresses Massachusetts state legislature on evils of slavery Sarah Grimké publishes *Letters on the Equality of the Sexes and the Condition of Women*
1839	Mormons build Nauvoo, Illinois
1840	Log-cabin campaign William Henry Harrison elected president
1841	Brook Farm established
1842	*Commonwealth v. Hunt*
1843	Dorothea Dix advocates state-funded insane asylums

brating it in forms of religious, literary, and artistic expression. In the process, they launched new forms of thought and presentation that won broad recognition among the genteel and middle classes.

Romanticism and individualism had their earliest impact in the religious realm. Reeling under the shock of social change that was affecting every aspect of life, many young people sought a religious anchor to bring themselves some stability. Many, especially in the rising cities in the Northeast, found a voice in New Englander **Ralph Waldo Emerson.**

Emerson was pastor of the prestigious Second Unitarian Church in Boston when tragedy struck: his young wife, Ellen Louisa, died in 1831. Emerson ex-

perienced a religious crisis and, looking for new inspiration, traveled to Europe. There he met the famous Romantic poets William Wordsworth and Thomas Carlyle, who influenced him to seek truth in nature and spirit rather than in rationality and order. Emerson combined this Romantic influence with his already strong Unitarian leaning, creating a new

Ralph Waldo Emerson   Philosopher, writer, and poet whose essays and poems made him a central figure in the transcendentalist movement and an important figure in the development of literary expression in the United States.

philosophical creed called **transcendentalism.** Recovered from his grief, he returned to the United States to begin a new career as an essayist and lecturer, spreading the transcendentalist message.

"Historical Christianity has fallen into the error that corrupts all attempts to communicate religion," Emerson told the students at the Harvard Divinity School in 1838. "It has dwelt, it dwells, with noxious exaggeration about the person of Jesus. Men have come to speak of revelation as somewhat long ago given and done, as if God were dead." But Emerson believed that God was far from dead. "The world is not the product of manifold power," Emerson taught, "but of one will, of one mind; and that one mind is everywhere active, in each ray of the star, in each wavelet of the pool." This being the case, Emerson went on, "The prayers and even the dogmas of our church, are . . . wholly insulated from anything now extant in the life and business of the people." Only through direct contact with the **transcendent** power in the universe could men and women know the truth. "It cannot be received at second hand," Emerson insisted, but only through the independent working of the liberated mind.

Although Emerson emphasized **nonconformity** and dissent in his writings, his ideas were in tune with the cultural and economic currents of his day. In celebrating the individual, Emerson validated the surging individualism of Jacksonian America. In addition, because each person had to find his or her own path to knowledge, Emerson could extol many of the disturbing aspects of modernizing America as potentially liberating forces. Rather than condemning the "selfish cupidity" that Tocqueville said characterized Jacksonian America, Emerson stated that money represented the "prose of life" and was, "in its effects and laws, as beautiful as roses."

Emerson not only set the tone for American philosophical inquiry but also suggested a bold new direction for American literature. In 1837 he issued a declaration of literary independence from European models in an address at Harvard University entitled "The American Scholar." Young American writers responded enthusiastically. During the twenty years following this speech, Henry David Thoreau, Walt Whitman, Henry Wadsworth Longfellow, and other writers and poets refined the transcendentalist gospel, emphasizing the uniqueness of the individual and the role of literature as a vehicle for self-discovery. "I celebrate myself, and sing myself," Whitman wrote. They also carried the Romantic message, celebrating the primitive and the common. Longfellow wrote of the legendary Indian chief Hiawatha (Hienwatha; see page 4) and sang the praise of the village blacksmith.

In "I Hear America Singing," Whitman conveyed the poetry present in the everyday speech of mechanics, carpenters, and other common folk.

Perhaps the most radical of the transcendentalists was Emerson's good friend and frequent houseguest **Henry David Thoreau.** Emerson and his other followers made the case for self-reliance, but Thoreau embodied it, camping on the shore of Walden Pond near Concord, Massachusetts, where he did his best to live independent of the rapidly modernizing market economy. "I went to the woods because I wished to live deliberately," Thoreau wrote, "and not, when I came to die, discover that I had not lived."

Like Thoreau, a number of women were also seeking meaning through their writing. Sarah Moore Grimké, elder sister of abolitionist Angelina Grimké, published a well-received essay on women's rights called *Letters on the Equality of the Sexes and the Condition of Women* in 1838. Margaret Fuller picked up on the same theme in her *Woman in the Nineteenth Century* (1845), after demonstrating her own equality by editing the highly influential transcendentalist magazine *The Dial* as well as serving as chief literary critic for the *New York Tribune.*

But the most popular women writers of the day were those who were most successful at communicating the sentimentalized role for the new genteel woman. **Lydia Sigourney** was one of the first American women to carve out an independent living as a writer. Her first book, *Moral Pieces, in Prose and Verse,* was published in 1815. By 1830 she was a regular contributor to over thirty popular magazines. Like many critics, Edgar Allan Poe dismissed her work as shallow and **mawkish,** but he actively solicited her writing

---

transcendentalism   A philosophical and literary movement asserting the existence of God within human beings and in nature and the belief that intuition is the highest source of knowledge.

transcendent   Lying beyond the normal range of experience.

nonconformity   Refusal to accept or conform to the beliefs and practices of the majority.

Henry David Thoreau   Writer and naturalist and friend of Ralph Waldo Emerson; his best-known work is *Walden* (1854).

Lydia Sigourney   Nineteenth-century Romantic and sentimental author who was one of the first women in American history to make a living as a professional writer.

mawkish   Mushy, exaggerated, and insincere sentimentality.

This 1827 painting by Thomas Cole, capturing a scene from James Fenimore Cooper's *Last of the Mohicans,* illustrates the Romantic mood current during the early nineteenth century. In line with artistic romanticism, nature dwarfs all else. Even a large Indian camp seems insignificant in size, lost in an exaggerated image of the mountains in the Hudson River region of New York. *"Last of the Mohicans" by Thomas Cole. Fenimore House Museum, New York State Historical Association, Cooperstown, NY.*

for his own magazine, the *Southern Literary Messenger.* In 1833 she published two bestsellers, *How to Be Happy* and *Letters to Young Ladies,* both of which emphasized Christian activism and the domestic ideal. Catharine Beecher was another woman writer who enjoyed enormous success for her practical advice guides aimed at making women more effective homemakers. The novels of women writers E. D. E. N. Southworth and Susan Warner were among the most popular books published in the first half of the nineteenth century.

Other authors joined Sigourney, Southworth, and Warner in pushing American literature in Romantic directions. James Fenimore Cooper and Nathaniel Hawthorne each helped to popularize American themes and scenes in their writing. Even before Emerson's "American Scholar," Cooper had launched a new sort of American novel and American hero. In *The Pioneers* (1823), Cooper introduced Natty Bumppo, also called Hawkeye, a frontiersman whose honesty, independent-mindedness, and skill as a marksman

represented the rough-hewn virtues so beloved by Romantics and popularly associated with the American frontier. Altogether, Cooper wrote five novels featuring the plucky Bumppo, and they all sold well.

Nathaniel Hawthorne explored a different but equally American literary theme: the tension between good and evil. In *Twice-Told Tales* (1837), Hawthorne presented readers with a collection of moral **allegories** stressing the evils of pride, selfishness, and secret guilt among puritanical New Englanders. He brought these themes to fruition in his novel *The Scarlet Letter* (1850), in which adulteress Hester Prynne overcomes shame to gain redemption while her secret lover, Puritan minister Arthur Dimmesdale, is destroyed by his hidden sins.

allegory A story in which characters and events stand for abstract ideas and suggest a deep, symbolic meaning.

George Bancroft did for American history what novelists like Cooper did for American literature. A prominent Jacksonian, Bancroft set out to capture in writing the unique nature of the American experience. His history of the United States from the first settlement of the continent through the American Revolution eventually filled ten volumes, published between 1834 and 1874. From Bancroft's perspective, Jacksonian democracy was the perfect form for human government and was the product of the complex history of the American nation. Focusing on strong leaders who carried out God's design by bringing liberty into the world, Bancroft made clear that the middle-class qualities of individualism, self-sufficiency, and a passionate love of liberty were the essence of the American experience and the American genius. Bancroft's history became the definitive work of its kind, influencing generations of American students and scholars in their interpretations of the nation's past.

The drive to celebrate American scenes and the young nation's uniqueness also influenced the visual arts during this period. **Neoclassicism** had dominated the art scene during the late eighteenth century and first decades of the nineteenth. Influenced by Enlightenment rationalism, neoclassical artists brought to their painting and sculpture the simple, logical lines found in Greek and Roman art. They often used classical imagery in their portrayals of contemporary figures and events. Horatio Greenough's statue of George Washington, for example, presented the nation's first president wrapped in a toga, looking like a Greek god.

After 1825, however, classical scenes were gradually being replaced by American ones. Englishman Thomas Cole came to the United States in 1818 hoping to find a romantic paradise. Disappointed by the neoclassical art scene in Philadelphia, Cole began traveling into the American interior. In the Hudson River valley Cole found the paradise he was seeking, and he began painting romantically exaggerated renderings of these locales. The refreshing naturalness and Americanness of Cole's landscapes attracted a large following, and other artists took up the style. This group of landscapists is known as the **Hudson River school,** after the area where most of its members painted.

Another movement in American art that reflected the temper of the time is exemplified by the paintings of George Caleb Bingham. Bingham was born in Virginia and educated for a time in Pennsylvania before he went west to Missouri. There he painted realistic pictures of common people engaged in everyday activities. The flatboatmen, marketplace-dwellers, and electioneering politicians in Bingham's paintings were

artistic testimony to the emerging democratic style of America in the Jacksonian period (see illustrations on pages 286 and 292).

Culture Among Workers and Slaves

Most genteel people in the antebellum era would have denied that working people, whether the wage-earning immigrants in northern cities or slaves in the South, had a "culture." But each of these groups crafted viable cultures that suited their living and working conditions and were distinct from the genteel culture of their owners or supervisors.

Wretched living conditions and dispiriting poverty encouraged working-class people in northern cities to choose social and cultural outlets that were very different from those of upper- and middle-class Americans. Offering temporary relief from unpleasant conditions, drinking was the social distraction of choice among working people. Whiskey and gin were cheap and available during the 1820s and 1830s as western farmers used the new roads and canals to ship distilled spirits to urban markets. In the 1830s, consumers could purchase a gallon of whiskey for 25 cents.

Even activities that did not center on drinking tended to involve it. While genteel and middle-class people remained in their private homes reading Sigourney or Hawthorne, working people attended popular theaters cheering entertainments designed to appeal to their less polished tastes. **Minstrel shows** featured fast-paced music and raucous comedy. Plays, such as Benjamin Baker's *A Glance at New York in 1848,* presented caricatures of working-class "Bowery B'hoys" and "G'hals" and of the well-off-Broadway "pumpkins" they poked fun at. To put the audience in the proper mood, theater owners sold cheap drinks in the lobby or in basement pubs. Alcohol was also usually sold at sporting events that drew large work-

neoclassicism   A revival in architecture and art in the eighteenth and nineteenth centuries inspired by Greek and Roman models and characterized by order, symmetry, and simplicity of style.

Hudson River school   The first native school of landscape painting in the United States (1825–1875); it attracted artists rebelling against the neoclassical tradition.

minstrel show   A variety show in which white actors made up as blacks presented jokes, songs, dances, and comic skits.

Slave artisans often fashioned beautiful and functional items that incorporated both European and African design motifs, creating a unique material culture in the American South. A potter, now known only as Dave, crafted enormous storage jars (some examples of his work hold 30 gallons or more) that he inscribed with original poetry. Slave women often used needlework as a means of self-expression, as exemplified by this Star of Bethlehem quilt, crafted by a slave in Texas known only as Aunt Peggy. *Storage jar: Collection of McKissick Museum, University of South Carolina; quilt: Cincinnati Art Museum. Gift of Mrs. Cletus T. Palmer.*

ing-class audiences—bare-knuckle boxing contests, for instance, where the fighting was seldom confined to the boxing ring.

Stinging from their low status in the urbanizing and industrializing society, angry about living in hovels, and freed from inhibitions by hours of drinking, otherwise rational workingmen often pummeled one another to let off steam. And in working-class neighborhoods, where police forces were small, fistfights often turned into brawls and then into riots pitting Protestants against Catholics, immigrants against the native-born, and whites against blacks.

Working-class women experienced the same dull but dangerous working conditions and dismal living circumstances as working-class men, but their lives were even harder. Single women were particularly bad off. They were paid significantly less than men but had to pay as much and sometimes more for living quarters, food, and clothing. Marriage could reduce a woman's personal expenses—but at a cost. While men

congregated in the barbershop or candy store drinking and socializing during their leisure hours, married women were stuck in tiny apartments caring for children and doing household chores.

Like their northern counterparts, slaves fashioned for themselves a culture that helped them to survive and to maintain their humanity under dehumanizing conditions. The degree to which African practices endured in America is remarkable, for slaves seldom came to southern plantations directly from Africa. What evolved was a truly unique African American culture.

Traces of African heritage were visible in slaves' clothing, entertainment, and folkways. Often the plain garments that masters provided were upgraded with colorful headscarves and other decorations similar to ornaments worn in Africa. Hairstyles often resembled those characteristic of African tribes. Music, dancing, and other forms of public entertainment and celebration also showed strong African roots. Musical instruments were copies of traditional ones, modified only by the use of New World materials. And stories that were told around the stoves at night were a New World adaptation of African trickster tales. Other links to Africa abounded. Healers among the slaves used African ceremonies, Christian rituals, and both imported and native herbs to effect cures. Taken together, these survivals and adaptations of African traditions provided a strong base underlying a solid African American culture.

Abiding family ties helped to make possible this cultural continuity. Slave families endured despite kinship ties made fragile by their highly precarious life. Children could be taken away from their parents, husbands separated from wives at the whim of masters. And anyone might be sold at any time. Families that remained intact, however, remained stable. When families did suffer separation, the extended family of grandparents and other relatives offered emotional support and helped maintain some sense of continuity. Another African legacy, the concept of fictive kinship (see page 16) also contributed to family stability by turning the whole community of slaves into a vast network of aunts and uncles.

Within families, the separation of work along age and gender lines followed traditional patterns. Slave women, when not laboring at the assigned tasks of plantation work, generally performed domestic duties and tended children, while the men hunted, fished, did carpentry, and performed other "manly" tasks. Children were likely to help out by tending family gardens and doing other light work until they were old enough to join their parents in the fields or learn skilled trades.

Slaves' religion, like family structure, was another means for preserving unique African American traits. White churches virtually ignored the religious needs of slaves before the mid-eighteenth century. During the Great Awakening (see page 103), however, many white evangelicals turned their attention to the spiritual life of slaves. "Your Negroes may be ignorant and stupid as to divine Things," evangelical Samuel Davies told slaveowners, "not for Want of Capacity, but for Want of Instruction; not through their Perverseness, but through your Negligence." In the face of slaveowners' negligence, evangelical Presbyterians, Baptists, and Methodists took it upon themselves to carry the Christian message to slaves.

Though the designation Baptist or Methodist would suggest that the Christianity practiced by slaves resembled the religion practiced by southern whites, it differed in significant ways. Slave preachers untrained in white theology often equated Christian and African

religious figures, creating unique African American religious symbols. Ceremonies too combined African practices such as group dancing with Christian prayer. The merging of African musical forms with Christian lyrics gave rise to a new form of Christian music: the spiritual. Masters often encouraged such worship, thinking that the Christian emphasis on obedience and meekness would make slaves more productive and more peaceful servants. Some, however, discouraged religion among their slaves, fearing that large congregations of slaves might be moved to rebellion. Thus some religious slaves had to meet in secret to practice their own particular form of Christianity.

Radical Attempts to Regain Community

To many of all classes, society seemed to be spinning out of control as modernization rearranged basic lifestyles during the antebellum period. Some religious groups and social thinkers tried to ward off the excesses of Jacksonian individualism by forming utopian communities that experimented with various living arrangements and ideological commitments. They hoped to strike a new balance between self-sufficiency and community support.

A wealthy Welsh industrialist, Robert Owen, began one of the earliest experiments along these lines. In 1825 he purchased a tract of land on the Wabash River in Indiana called New Harmony. Believing that the solution to poverty in modern society was to collect the unemployed into self-contained and self-supporting villages, Owen opened a textile factory in which own-

---

trickster tales   Stories that feature as a central character a clever figure who uses his wits and instincts to adapt to changing times; a survivor, the trickster is used by traditional societies, including African cultures, to teach important cultural lessons.

extended family   A family group consisting of various close relatives as well as the parents and children.

spiritual   A religious folk song originated by African Americans, often expressing a longing for deliverance from the constraints and hardships of their lives.

utopian   Idealistic reform sentiment based on the belief that a perfect society can be created on Earth and that a particular group or leader has the knowledge to actually create such a society.

New Harmony   Utopian community that Robert Owen established in Indiana in 1825; economic problems and discord among members led to its failure two years later.

On one of his western tours, artist Karl Bodmer paused to paint this view of New Harmony, Welsh philanthropist Robert Owen's experimental utopian community in Indiana. Like many similar communities, this peaceful commune was destroyed by a combination of internal dissension and pressure from suspicious and often jealous outsiders. *"View of New Harmony" by Karl Bodmer, 1833. Maximilian-Bodmer Collection, Joslyn Art Museum.*

ership was held communally by the workers and decisions were made by group consensus. Even though the community instituted innovations like an eight-hour workday, cultural activities for workers, and the nation's first school offering equal education to boys and girls, New Harmony did not succeed. Owen and his son, Robert Dale Owen, were outspoken critics of organized religion and joined their close associate Frances (Fanny) Wright in advocating radical causes. These leanings made the Owenites unpopular with more traditional Americans, and when their mill experienced economic hardship in 1827, New Harmony collapsed.

A more famous experiment, **Brook Farm,** had its origin in the transcendentalist movement but later flirted with **socialistic** ideas like those practiced at New Harmony. The brainchild of George Ripley, Brook Farm was designed to "prepare a society of liberal, intelligent and cultivated persons, whose relations with each other would permit a more wholesome and simple life than can be led amidst the pressure of our competitive institutions." To carry out this enter-

prise Ripley set up a joint-stock company, selling the initial twenty-four shares of stock for $500 each. Most of the stockholders were transcendentalist celebrities such as Nathaniel Hawthorne and Ralph Waldo Emerson. Rather than living and working at the site as Ripley had hoped they would, most just dropped in from time to time. Disappointed, in 1844 Ripley adopted a

Frances (Fanny) Wright Infamous nineteenth-century woman who advocated what at the time were considered radical causes, including racial equality, equality for women, birth control, and open sexuality.

Brook Farm An experimental farm based on cooperative living; established in 1841, it first attracted transcendentalists and then serious farmers before fire destroyed it in 1845.

socialist Practicing socialism, the public ownership of manufacturing, farming, and other forms of production so that they benefit society rather than produce individual or corporate profits.

new constitution based on the socialist ideas of Frenchman Charles Fourier. **Fourierism** emphasized community self-sufficiency, the equal sharing of earnings among members of the community, and the periodic redistribution of tasks and status to prevent boredom and elitism. With this new disciplined ideology in place, Brook Farm began to appeal to serious artisans and farmers, but a disastrous fire in 1845 cut the experiment short. Other Fourierist communities were also founded during this period—nearly a hundred such organizations sprang up from Massachusetts to Michigan—and although none achieved Brook Farm's notoriety, all shared the same unsuccessful fate.

Some communal experiments were grounded in various religious beliefs. The **Oneida Community,** established in central New York in 1848, for example, reflected the notions of its founder, John Humphrey Noyes. Though educated in theology at Andover and Yale, Noyes could find no church willing to ordain him because of his strange belief that his followers could escape sin through faith in God, communal living, and group marriage. Unlike Brook Farm and New Harmony, the Oneida Community was very successful financially, establishing thriving logging, farming, and manufacturing businesses. It was finally dissolved as the result of local pressures directed at the "free love" practiced by its members.

Economically successful communes operated by the **Shakers,** an offshoot of the Quakers, tried to sidestep the Oneida Community's problems by banning sex altogether. Founded in Britain in 1770 and then transported to America in 1774, the sect grew slowly at first, but in the excitement of the early nineteenth century, it expanded at a more vigorous rate. By 1826 eighteen Shaker communities had been planted in eight states. Throughout the Jacksonian era and after, the Shakers established communal farms and grew to a population of nearly six thousand. The Shaker communities succeeded by pursuing farming activities and the manufacture and sale of furniture and handcrafts admired for their design and workmanship. But like the Oneida Community, the Shakers' ideas about marriage and family stirred up controversy. In a number of cases, converts deserted husbands or wives in order to join the organization, often bringing their children with them. This led to several highly publicized lawsuits. Controversy also raged over the practice in some areas of turning orphaned children or other public **wards** over to the Shakers. Like most such experiments, the Shaker movement went into decline after 1860, though vestiges of it remain operative today.

The group that was most successful at joining the religious fervor of the Second Great Awakening with the inclination to communalism was a peculiarly American movement founded by New York farmer **Joseph Smith Jr.** Smith's story is surrounded by a haze of religious zeal and myth, but he reported that in 1827 an angel named Moroni led him to a set of golden plates inscribed in a strange hieroglyphic language. Church tradition holds that Smith and a series of secretaries worked for nearly two years to translate the writing on the plates. The result of their effort was the Book of Mormon, first printed and available for purchase in 1830.

Although the Book of Mormon greatly resembled the books of the Old Testament and purported to be a truly ancient document, it captured many of the themes that most appealed to Americans during the restless Jacksonian era. In line with Romantic literature, the Book of Mormon evoked a mythic past. In adventure passages that rival Cooper's, Smith's testament traces the history of America back to the migrations of several Old World groups during biblical times. According to the Book of Mormon, one group, the Lamanites, sank into barbarity and became the forefathers of the American Indians. Another group, the Nephites, tried to return the Lamanites to the true religion but failed and was nearly destroyed by the Lamanites. Finally, only two Nephites remained: Mormon and his son Moroni. In the year 384, they buried the golden plates chronicling America's hidden past and its place in God's unfolding plan for the universe. Moroni, in the form of an angel, waited for a true spiritual descendant to whom he might reveal

Fourierism Social system advanced by Frenchman Charles Fourier, who argued that people were capable of living in perfect harmony under the right conditions, which included communal life and republican government.

Oneida Community A religious community established in central New York in 1848; its members shared property, practiced group marriage, and reared children under communal care.

Shakers A mid-eighteenth-century offshoot of the Quakers, founded in England by Mother Ann Lee; Shakers engaged in spirited worship, including dancing and rhythmic shaking, hence their name, and practiced communal living and strict celibacy.

ward A child who is legally put into the care of someone other than a parent.

Joseph Smith, Jr. Founder of the Church of Jesus Christ of Latter-day Saints, also known as the Mormon Church, who transcribed the Book of Mormon and led his congregation westward from New York to Illinois; he was later murdered by an anti-Mormon mob.

the plates and their truths. Smith proclaimed that he was that descendant.

In 1830 Smith founded the Church of Jesus Christ of Latter-day Saints—also called the Mormon Church, after the prophet Mormon. Announcing that he had experienced a revelation that called for him to establish a community "on the borders by the Lamanites," Smith led his congregation as a unit out of New York in 1831 to settle in the northeastern Ohio village of Kirtland. There the people known as Mormons thrived for a while, stressing notions of community, faith, and hard work. The Mormons tended to be clannish, however, keeping to themselves and excluding others, making outsiders suspicious. In addition, the tight discipline practiced by the Mormon community not only made them more prosperous than most surrounding farms and villages but also gave them considerable political clout as church members engaged in **block voting**.

There, too, economic pressure, internal dissension, and religious persecution convinced Smith to lead his followers farther west into Missouri. Again the Mormons faced serious resentment from frontiersmen. Smith then decided to relocate his congregation to the Illinois frontier, founding the city of Nauvoo in 1839. Continuing conversions to the new faith brought a flood of Mormons to Smith's Zion in Illinois. In 1844 Nauvoo, with a population of fifteen thousand Mormons, dwarfed every other Illinois city.

Reactions to Changing Conditions

■ How did Americans deal with the stresses created by rapid change during the Jacksonian era?

■ What were the cultural consequences of their actions?

In the grasping, competitive conditions that were emerging in the dynamic new America, an individual's status, reputation, and welfare seemed to depend exclusively on his or her economic position. The combination of rapid geographical expansion and unprecedented opportunities in business produced a highly precarious social world for all Americans. Desperate for some stability, many pushed for various reforms to bring the fast-spinning world under control.

A Second Great Awakening

Popular religion was a major counterbalance to the modernizing tendencies that shocked many Americans as the Great Transformation progressed. While some were drawn to transcendentalism and a hand-

ful chose to follow radical communitarian leaders, others sought solace within existing, mainstream denominations. Beginning in the 1790s both theologians and popular preachers sought to create a new Protestant creed that would maintain the notion of Christian community in an atmosphere of increasing individualism and competition.

Mirroring tendencies in the political and economic realms, Protestant thinking during the opening decades of the nineteenth century emphasized the role of the individual. Preachers such as Jonathan Edwards and George Whitefield had moved in this direction during the Great Awakening of the 1740s, but many Protestant theologians continued to share the conviction that salvation was a gift from God that individuals could do nothing to earn (see page 103). Timothy Dwight, Jonathan Edwards's grandson, took the first step toward liberalizing this position in the 1790s, but it fell to his students at Yale College, especially Nathaniel Taylor, to create a new theology that was entirely consistent with the prevailing secular creed of individualism. According to this new doctrine, God offers salvation to all, but it is the individual's responsibility to seek it. Thus the individual has "free will" to choose or not choose salvation. Taylor's ideas struck a responsive chord in a restless and expanding America. Hundreds of ordained ministers, licensed preachers, and **lay exhorters** carried the message of individual empowerment to an anxious populace.

Unlike Calvinist Puritanism, which characterized women as the weaker sex, the new evangelicalism stressed women's spiritual equality with—and even spiritual superiority to—men. Not surprisingly, young women generally were the first to respond to the new message: during the 1820s and 1830s, women often outnumbered men by two to one in new evangelical congregations. The most highly effective preachers of the day took advantage of this appeal, turning women into agents spreading the word to their husbands, brothers, and children.

Charles Grandison Finney was one of the most effective among the new generation of preachers. A former schoolteacher and lawyer, Finney experienced a soul-shattering religious conversion in 1821. Declaring that "the Lord Jesus Christ" had retained him "to

block voting The practice by organized groups of people to coordinate their voting so that all members vote the same way, thereby enhancing the group's political influence.

lay exhorter A church member who preaches but is not an ordained minister.

After becoming the president of Oberlin College, evangelist Charles G. Finney reenacted the traveling tent revivals that had brought him into national prominence as the leading spokesman for the new evangelicalism that arose during the Second Great Awakening. *Oberlin College Archives, Oberlin, Ohio.*

plead his cause," Finney performed on the pulpit as a spirited attorney might argue a case in court. A religious revival "is not a miracle, or dependent on a miracle in any sense," Finney announced, to the shock of conservative Calvinists. Arguing for souls was like moving a judge to make the right decision in a lawsuit—the result of effective persuasion. Seating those most likely to be converted on a special "anxious bench," Finney focused on them as a lawyer might a jury. The result was likely to be dramatic. Many of the targeted people fainted, experienced bodily spasms, or cried out in hysteria. Such dramatic presentations and results brought Finney enormous publicity, which he and an army of imitators used to gain access to communities all over the West and Northeast. The result was a nearly continuous season of religious revival. The **Second Great Awakening** spread from rural community to rural community like a wildfire until, in the late 1830s, Finney carried the fire into Boston and New York.

Revival meetings were remarkable affairs. Usually beginning on a Thursday and continuing until the following Tuesday, they drew together huge crowds who listened to spirited preaching in the evenings and engaged in religious study, conversation, and wrenching soul searching during the daylight hours.

Second Great Awakening   An upsurge in religious fervor that began around 1800 and was characterized by revival meetings.

revival meeting   A meeting for the purpose of reawakening religious faith, often characterized by impassioned preaching and emotional public testimony by converted sinners.

At one such meeting, as many as twenty-five thousand people listened to forty different preachers. As one witness proclaimed, there were "loud ejaculations of prayer . . . some struck with terror . . . others, trembling weeping and crying out . . . fainting and swooning away."

The new revivals led to the breakdown of traditional church organizations and the creation of various Christian denominations. **Evangelical sects** such as the Presbyterians, Baptists, and Methodists split into groups who supported the new theology and those who clung to more traditional notions. Church splits also occurred for reasons that now seem petty. One Baptist congregation, for example, split over the hypothetical question of whether it would be a sin to lie to marauding Indians in order to protect hidden family members. Those who said lying to protect one's family was no sin formed a separate congregation of so-called Lying Baptists. Those who said lying was sinful under any circumstances gathered as Truth-Telling Baptists.

In the face of such fragmentation, all denominations voiced concern that state support of any one church would give that denomination an artificial advantage in the continuing competition for souls. Oddly, those most fervent in their Christian beliefs joined deists and other Enlightenment-influenced thinkers in arguing steadfastly for the continued and even more stringent separation of church and state. This, in turn, added to the spirit of competition as individual congregations vied for voluntary contributions to keep their churches alive.

Even though religious conversion had become an individual matter and competition for tithes a genuine concern, revivalists did not ignore the notion of community. In fact, preachers like Finney put great emphasis on creating a single Christian community to stand in opposition to sin. One proclaimed deep impatience with "Old Church Hipocrites who think more of their particular denomination than Christ Church." Finney himself wrote that during his revivals, "Christians of every denomination generally seemed to make common cause, and went to work with a will, to pull sinners out of the fire." As one Finney convert wrote to his sister, "We are either marching toward heaven or towards hell. How is it with you?"

"I know this is all algebra to those who have never felt it," Finney said. "But to those who have experienced the agony of wrestling, prevailing prayer, for the conversion of a soul, you may depend on it, that soul . . . appears as dear as a child is to the mother who brought it forth with pain." This intimate connection forged bonds of mutual responsibility, giving a generation of isolated individuals something to rally around, a common starting point for joint action. According to the new theology, it was the convert's duty to carry the message of the free gift of salvation to the multitudes still in darkness. Another strong goad to Christian activism at this time was the rise of **postmillennialism** among Second Great Awakening theologians and other believers. Understanding it to be their divine commission to bring on the return of Christ by converting and perfecting the world, postmillennialists threw themselves into what they believed was God's design for them. Evangelicalism and postmillennialism together formed the core for an activist ideology by which new congregations, missionary societies, and a thousand other benevolent groups rose up to lead America and the world in the continuing battle against sin.

Free and Slave Labor Protests

While the new forms of religion appealed to many northern workers and southern slaves, others in both groups blamed their miseries not on sin but on their exploitation by others. In view of their grim working and living conditions, it is not surprising that some manufacturing workers and slave laborers protested their situations. In both cases, the most skilled and well educated took the lead in making their dissatisfaction with the new modes of production known to factory owners and plantation masters.

The first organized labor strike in America took place in 1806, when a group of journeyman shoemakers stopped work to protest the hiring of unskilled workers to perform some tasks that higher-paid journeymen and apprentices had been doing. The strike failed when a New York court declared the shoemakers' actions illegal, but in the years to come many other journeymen's groups would try the same tactic. In large part they were reacting to the mechanization that threatened their jobs and their social position. In addition, they bemoaned their loss of power to set hours, conditions, and wages for the work they

evangelical sects   Protestant groups that emphasized the sole authority of the Bible and the necessity of actively striving to convert others.

postmillennialism   The tenet in some Christian theology teaching that Christ will return to Earth after religious activists have succeeded in converting all people to Christianity and following a thousand years under their godly rule.

performed; industrialization robbed them of their status as independent contractors and forced many to become wage laborers.

Instead of attacking or even criticizing industrialization, however, journeymen simply asked for what they believed was their fair piece of the pie: decent wages and working conditions and some role in decision making—all of which they had traditionally possessed. Throughout the industrializing cities of the Northeast and the smaller manufacturing centers of the West, journeymen banded together in **trade unions:** assemblies of skilled workers grouped by specific occupation. During the 1830s, trade unions from neighboring towns merged with one another to form the beginnings of a national trade union movement. In this way, house carpenters, shoemakers, handloom weavers, printers, and comb makers established national unions through which they attempted to enforce uniform wage standards in their industries. In 1834 journeymen's organizations from a number of industries joined to form the **National Trades' Union,** the first labor organization in the nation's history to represent many different crafts.

The trade union movement, however, accomplished little during the antebellum period. Factory owners, bankers, and others who had a vested interest in keeping labor cheap and, in their view, making it more efficient used every device available to prevent unions from gaining the upper hand. Employers countered the national trade unions by forming associations to resist union activity. They also used the courts to keep organized labor from disrupting business.

Despite such efforts, a number of strikes affected American industries during the 1830s. In 1834 women working in the textile mills in Lowell, Massachusetts, closed down production in response to a 25 percent reduction in their wages. And they proved their organizational skills and economic clout again two years later when they struck over an increase in boarding house rates. Such demonstrations of power by workers frightened manufacturers, and gradually over the next two decades, employers replaced native-born women in the factories with immigrants, who were less liable to organize successfully and, more important, less likely to win approval from sympathetic judges or consumers.

Still, workers won some small victories in the battle to organize. A significant breakthrough finally came in 1842 when the Massachusetts Supreme Court decided in the case of *Commonwealth v. Hunt* that Boston's journeymen boot makers were within their rights to organize "in such manner as best to subserve their own interests" and to call strikes. By that time, however, economic changes had so undermined labor's ability to withstand the rigors of strikes and court cases that legal protection became somewhat meaningless.

Not all labor protests were as peaceful as the shoemakers' strike. In 1828, for example, immigrant weavers protested the pitiful wages paid by Alexander Knox, New York City's leading textile employer. Storming Knox's home to demand higher pay, the weavers invaded and vandalized the house and beat Knox's son and a cordon of police guards. The rioters then marched to the garret and basement homes of weavers who had refused to join the protest and destroyed their looms.

Not all the riots that occurred in American cities during these years were directly related to working conditions. Notable were ethnic riots that shook New York, Philadelphia, and Boston during the late 1820s and 1830s. In 1834, for example, rumors began circulating in Boston that innocent girls were being held captive and tortured in a Catholic convent in nearby Charlestown. A Protestant mob stormed the building, leaving it a heap of smoldering ashes. A year later, in New York's notoriously overcrowded and lawless Five Points District, roving gangs of native-born Protestant and immigrant Irish Catholic men battled in the streets. The ethnic tension evident in these and other riots was the direct result of declining economic power and terrible living conditions—and worker desperation. Native-born journeymen blamed immigrants for lowered wages and loss of status. Immigrants simmered with hatred at being treated like dirt by their native-born coworkers.

Unlike workers in the North, who at least had some legal protections and civil rights, slaves had nothing but their own wits to protect them against a society that classed them as disposable personal property. Slaves were skilled at the use of **passive resistance.** Clever strategies for getting extra food, clothing, and other supplies were passed on from generation to generation. Slaves often stole food, not because they were hungry but because its unexplainable disappearance flustered their masters. Farm ani-

> **trade union** A labor organization whose members work in a specific trade or craft.
>
> **National Trades' Union** The first national association of trade unions in the United States; it was formed in 1834.
>
> **passive resistance** Resistance by nonviolent methods.

mals also disappeared mysteriously, tools broke in puzzling ways, people fell ill from unknown diseases, and workers got lost on the way to fields—all these events were subtle signs of slaves' discontent. Slaves also used flattery and trickery, convincing whites that slave-initiated improvements were really the master's idea.

The importance of passive resistance was evident in the folk tales and songs that circulated among slaves. Perhaps the best-known example is the stories of Br'er—that is, Brother—Rabbit, a classic trickster figure who uses deceit to get what he wants. In one particularly revealing tale, Br'er Rabbit is caught by Br'er Fox, who threatens Rabbit with all sorts of horrible tortures. Rabbit begs Br'er Fox to do anything but throw him into the nearby briar patch. Seizing on Rabbit's apparent fear, Fox unties Br'er Rabbit and pitches him deep into the middle of the briar patch, expecting to see the rabbit struggle and die amid the thorns. Br'er Rabbit, however, scampers away through the briars, calling back over his shoulder that he was born and bred in a briar patch and laughing at Br'er Fox's gullibility. Such stories taught slaves how to deal cleverly with powerful adversaries.

Not all slave resistance was passive. Perhaps the most common form of active resistance was running away (see Map 12.1). The number of slaves who escaped may never be known, though some estimate that an average of about a thousand made their way to freedom each year. Most of these lived in **border states,** where freedom lay perhaps only a few miles away from the slave quarters. Large numbers also escaped from Texas and other states where the nearby Mexican border or the Indian frontier promised protection and relative freedom.

Of all the slaves who made the run to freedom during the reign of King Cotton, fully a third were artisans, wagoners, boat pilots, and other specially skilled and privileged slaves, and more than 80 percent were men between the ages of 16 and 35. Young men were not likely to be burdened with family responsibilities and had the physical strength to resist capture, and artisans, almost all of whom were men, had viable economic options in the free world and the relative liberty to move around without constant supervision. But running away was always a dangerous gamble. One former slave recalled, "No man who has never been placed in such a situation can comprehend the thousand obstacles thrown in the way of the flying slave. Every white man's hand is raised against him—the patrollers are watching for him—the hounds are ready to follow on his track."

Anti-Catholic and anti-immigrant feelings often caused rioting in American cities during the 1830s and 1840s. In 1834, street violence escalated into a full-fledged riot in Massachusetts, leading to the burning of a Catholic convent in Charlestown, a Boston suburb. This engraving, which adorned the covers of a number of pamphlets that purported to tell the true lurid story of the events surrounding the fire, shows the convent ablaze as fire companies try in vain to smother the flames. Though the most notorious event of this kind that occurred during this era, this riot was anything but exceptional. *The Nun of St. Ursula: Burning of the Convent by Harry Hazel.*

Besides the undeniable appeal of freedom, some more immediate factors seem to have prompted slaves to risk running away. Frederick Douglass, who later became a famous abolitionist leader, was a skilled craftsman who ran away because he finally grew tired of turning his wages over to his master. Most contemporary observers thought that fear of punishment for some crime was the most common motivation for flight. Some slaves, however, reported that they ran not because they had done something that merited punishment but to keep themselves from doing so. "They didn't do something and run," one former slave reported. "They run before they did it, 'cause they knew that if they struck a white man there wasn't going to be a nigger. In them days they run to keep from doing something." Yet another strong motivation for running was to keep families together or to reunite, if only for a short time. Advertisements for runaway slaves often contained such comments as "He is no doubt trying to reach his wife."

border states   The slave states of Delaware, Maryland, Virginia, Kentucky, and Missouri, which shared a border with states in which slavery was illegal.

MAP 12.1 Escaping from Slavery Running away was one of the most prominent forms of slave resistance during the antebellum period. Success often depended on help from African Americans who had already gained their freedom and from sympathetic whites. Beginning in the 1820s an informal and secret network called the Underground Railroad provided escape routes for slaves who were daring enough to risk all for freedom. The routes shown here are based on documentary evidence, but the network's secrecy makes it impossible to know if they are drawn entirely accurately.

The most frightening form of slave resistance was open and armed revolt. Despite slaveholders' best efforts, slaves planned an unknown number of rebellions during the antebellum period, and many of them were actually carried out. The most serious and violent of these uprisings was the work of a black preacher, Nat Turner. After years of planning and organization, in 1831 Turner led a force of about seventy slaves in a predawn raid against the slaveholding households in Southampton County, Virginia. It took four days for white forces to stop the assault. During that time, the slaves slaughtered and mutilated fifty-

No pictures of famed slave revolt leader Nat Turner are known to exist, but this nineteenth-century painting illustrates how one artist imagined the appearance of Turner and his fellow conspirators. White southerners lived in terror of scenes such as this and passed severe laws designed to prevent African Americans from ever having such meetings. *Granger Collection.*

five white men, women, and children. Angry, terrified whites finally captured and executed Turner and sixteen of his followers.

In the wake of Nat Turner's Rebellion, fear of slave revolts reached paranoid levels in the South, especially in areas where slaves greatly outnumbered whites. After reading about and seeing a play depicting a slave insurrection, Mary Boykin Chesnut gave expression to the fear that plagued whites in the slave South: "What a thrill of terror ran through me as those yellow and black brutes came jumping over the parapets! Their faces were like so many of the same sort at home. . . . How long would they resist the seductive and irresistible call: 'Rise, kill, and be free!'"

Frightened and often outnumbered, whites felt justified in imposing stringent restrictions and using harsh methods to enforce them. Southern courts and legislatures clapped stricter controls on the freedoms granted to slaves and to free blacks. In most areas, free African Americans were denied the right to own guns, buy liquor, hold public assemblies, testify in court, and vote. Slaves were forbidden to own any private property, to attend unsupervised worship services, and to learn reading and writing. Also, codes that prevented slaves from being unsupervised in towns virtually eliminated slaves as independent urban craftsmen after 1840. In many areas of the South, white citizens formed local vigilance committees, bands of armed men who rode through the countryside to overawe slaves and dissuade them from attempting to escape or rebel. Local authorities pressed court clerks, ship captains, and other officials to limit the freedom of blacks. White critics of slavery—who had been numerous, vocal, and well respected before the birth of King Cotton—were harassed, prosecuted, and sometimes beaten into silence.

The Middle Class and Moral Reform

Witnessing the squalor and violence in working-class districts and the deteriorating condition for slaves led many genteel and middle-class Americans to push for reforms. The missionary activism that accompanied the Second Great Awakening dovetailed with this reformist inclination. The Christian benevolence movement gave rise to hundreds of voluntary societies ranging from maternal associations designed to improve child rearing to political lobby groups aiming at outlawing alcohol, Sunday mail delivery, and other perceived evils. Such activism drew them together in common causes and led to deep friendships and a shared sense of commitment—antidotes to the alienation and loneliness common in the competitive world of the early nineteenth century.

As traditional family and village life broke down in the new America, voluntary societies pressed for public intervention to address social problems. The new theology reinforced the reforming impulse by emphasizing that even the most depraved might be saved if proper means were applied. This idea had immediate application in the realm of crime and punishment. Reformers characterized criminals not as evil but as lost and in need of divine guidance. In Auburn, New York, an experimental prison system

vigilance committees Groups of armed private citizens who use the threat of mob violence to enforce their own interpretation of the law.

Christian benevolence A tenet in some Christian theology teaching that the essence of God is self-sacrificing love and that the ultimate duty for Christians is to perform acts of kindness with no expectation of reward in return.

Prison reformers insisted that idleness was symptomatic of the criminal personality and insisted that only a combination of exhausting physical exercise, solitary confinement, and silence were necessary to affecting rehabilitation. At the experimental prison in Auburn, New York, officials erected a huge step-wheel, chaining prisoners and forcing them to climb for extended periods of time, seeking to instill discipline. © *Collection of the New York Historical Society.*

put prisoners to work during the day, condemned them to absolute silence during mealtimes, and locked them away in solitary confinement at night. Reformers believed that this combination of hard work, discipline, and solitude would put criminals on the path to productive lives and spiritual renewal.

Mental illness underwent a similar change in definition. Rather than viewing the mentally ill as hopeless cases doomed by an innate spiritual flaw, reformers now spoke of them as lost souls in need of help. Dorothea Dix, a young, compassionate, and reform-minded teacher, advocated publicly funded asylums for the insane. She told the Massachusetts state legislature in 1843: "I tell what I have seen. . . . Insane persons confined within the Commonwealth, in cages, closets, cellars, stalls, pens! Chained, naked, beaten with rods, and lashed into obedience!" For the balance of the century, Dix toured the country pleading the cause of the mentally ill, succeeding in winning both private and public support for mental health systems.

A hundred other targets for reform joined prisons and asylums on the agenda of middle-class Christian activists. Embracing their Puritan ancestors' strict observance of the Sabbath, newly awakened Christians insisted on stopping Sunday mail delivery and demanded that canals be closed on Sundays. Some joined Bible and tract societies that distributed Christian literature; others founded Sunday schools or op-

erated domestic missions devoted to winning either the irreligious or the wrongly religious (as Roman Catholics were perceived to be) to the new covenant of the Second Great Awakening.

Many white-collar reformers acted in earnest and were genuinely interested in forging a new social welfare system. A number of their programs, however, seemed more like social control because they tried to force people to conform to a middle-class standard of behavior. For example, reformers believed that immigrants should willingly discard their traditional customs and beliefs and act like Americans. Immigrants who chose to cling to familiar ways were suspected of disloyalty. This aspect of benevolent reform was particularly prominent in two important movements: public education and temperance.

Before the War of 1812, most Americans believed that education was the family's or the church's re-

Dorothea Dix Philanthropist, reformer, and educator who was a pioneer in the movement for specialized treatment of the mentally ill.

irreligious Hostile or indifferent to religion.

temperance Moderation or abstinence in the consumption of alcoholic drinks.

sponsibility and did not require children to attend school. Many people depended on the apprenticeship system rather than on schools to provide the rudiments of reading, writing, and figuring. But as the complexity of economic, political, and cultural life increased during the opening decades of the nineteenth century, **Horace Mann** and other champions of education pushed states to introduce formal public schooling.

Like his contemporary Charles G. Finney, Mann was trained as a lawyer, but unlike Finney, he believed that ignorance, not sin, lay at the heart of the nation's problems. "If we do not prepare children to become good citizens," Mann proclaimed, "if we do not enrich their minds with knowledge, then our republic must go down to destruction, as others have gone before it." Democracy could continue only where there was equality, and, Mann believed, public education was "a great equalizer of the conditions of men—the balance wheel of the social machinery."

Mann and Massachusetts took the lead in formalizing schooling in 1837, when the state founded the country's first public board of education, with Mann at its head. Seizing control of Massachusetts's educational establishment, Mann immediately extended the school year to a minimum of six months, organized a state teachers' association, and increased teacher salaries. Gradually the state board changed the curriculum in Massachusetts schools to emphasize "practical" education, replacing classical learning and ministerial training with courses such as arithmetic, practical geography, and physical science.

Education reformers were interested in more than "knowledge." Mann and others were equally concerned that new immigrants and the children of the urban poor be trained in Protestant values and middle-class habits. Thus the books used in public schools emphasized virtues such as promptness, perseverance, discipline, and obedience to authority. In Philadelphia and other cities where Roman Catholic immigrants concentrated, Catholic parents resisted the cultural pressure applied on their children by Protestant-dominated public school boards. They supported the establishment of **parochial schools**—a development that aggravated the strain between native-born Protestants and immigrant Catholics.

Another source of such tension was a Protestant crusade against alcohol. Drinking alcohol had always been common in America and before the early nineteenth century was not broadly perceived as a significant social problem. Unhealthy drinking water, the absence of affordable alternatives like coffee and tea, and the desire for an escape from difficult and un-

comfortable surroundings had turned the United States into what one historian has termed "the alcoholic republic." But during the 1820s and 1830s, three factors contributed to a new, more ominous perception.

One was the increasing visibility of drinking and its consequence, drunkenness, as populations became more concentrated in manufacturing and trading cities, especially by immigrants and others in the working class. In Rochester, New York, for example, a town that went through the throes of modernization in the late 1820s, the number of drinking establishments multiplied rapidly as the population grew. Anyone with a few cents could get a glass of whiskey at grocery stores, either of two candy stores, barbershops, or even private homes—all within a few steps of wherever a person might be. By 1829 this proliferation of public drinking led the county grand jury sitting in Rochester to conclude that strong drink was "the cause of almost all of the crime and almost all of the misery that flesh is heir to."

The second factor was alcohol's economic impact in a new and more complex world of work. Factory owners and managers recognized that workers who drank often and heavily, on or off the job, threatened the quantity and quality of production. Owners and supervisors alike rallied around the temperance movement as a way of policing the undisciplined behavior of their employees, both in and out of the factory. By promoting temperance, these reformers believed they could clean up the worst aspects of city life and turn the raucous lower classes into clean-living, self-controlled, peaceful workers, increasing their productivity and business profits.

The third factor was a social and religious one. Like most of the reform movements, the temperance movement began in churches touched by the Second Great Awakening. Drunkenness earned special condemnation from reawakened Protestants, who believed that people were responsible not only for their sins but also for their own salvation. A person whose reason was besotted by alcohol simply could not rise to the demand. Christian reformers, therefore, believed that temperance was necessary not only to preserve the nation but also to win people's souls.

Horace Mann Educator who called for publicly funded education for all children and was head of the first public board of education in the United States.

parochial school A school supported by a church parish; in the United States, the term usually refers to a Catholic school.

Opposition to Slavery

Although some people had always had doubts about the morality of slavery, little organized opposition to it appeared before the American Revolution. During the Revolution, many Americans saw the contradiction between slavery and the "unalienable rights" of "life, liberty, and the pursuit of happiness." By the end of the Revolution, only Georgia and South Carolina continued to allow the importation of slaves, while Massachusetts specifically prohibited slavery altogether and Pennsylvania had begun to phase it out gradually. Even the plantation states showed increasing flexibility in dealing with slavery, as some elite southerners began to realize the unprofitability, though generally not the immorality, of the institution. After Virginia authorized owners to free their slaves in 1782, Delaware and Maryland soon did likewise. By the mid-1780s, most states, including those in the South, had active antislavery societies. In 1807, when Congress voted to outlaw permanently the importation of slaves in the following year, little was said in defense of slavery as an institution. But after 1815, the morality of slavery had begun to emerge as a national issue.

Public feeling about slavery during these years is reflected in the rise of the **American Colonization Society,** founded in 1817. This society was rooted in economic pragmatism, humanitarian concern for slaves' well-being, and a belief that blacks were not equal to whites and therefore the two races could not live together. Such ideas prompted the organization to propose that if slaveowners emancipated their slaves, or if funds could be raised to purchase their freedom, the freed slaves should immediately be shipped to Africa. Others noted that because many slaves had embraced Christianity, they might be agents in the extension of enthusiastic religious conversion. Theologian Samuel Hopkins, who believed slavery to be a sin, pointed out that God had allowed it "so that blacks could embrace the gospel in the New World and then bear the glad tidings back to Africa."

Although the American Colonization Society began in the South, its policies were particularly popular in the Northeast and West. In eastern cities, workers fearful for their jobs lived in dread of either enslaved or free blacks flooding in, lowering wages, and destroying job security. In western states such as Indiana and Illinois, farmers feared that competition could arise from a slaveholding aristocracy. In both regions, white supremacists argued that the extension of slavery beyond the Mississippi River and north

Not all African Americans supported the idea of transporting free-born and liberated slaves to Africa. Paul Cuffe believed that the opportunity should be encouraged. The son of a former slave and an American Indian woman, Cuffe became a sailor. He eventually purchased his own ship and then a fleet of ships, becoming a very successful Boston-area merchant and whaler. He supported many efforts to promote the welfare of American Americans, even supplying money and ships to transport freed slaves who wished to leave the United States to live in the former slave colony of Liberia in Africa. This portrait of a "Black Sailor" is thought to be the mature Paul Cuffe. *Christie's Images, Inc.*

of the **Mason-Dixon Line** would eventually lead to blacks mixing with the white population, a possibility they found extremely distasteful. Of course slaves had little to say about this strategy, but African Americans who were not slaves generally did not share their white neighbors' enthusiasm for the colonization movement. A few though, like Paul Cuffe (see

American Colonization Society   Organization founded in 1817 to end slavery gradually by assisting individual slave owners to liberate their slaves and then transporting them to Africa.

Mason-Dixon Line   The boundary between Pennsylvania and Maryland; it marked the northern division between free and slave states before the Civil War.

page 235), supported the idea of a black homeland in Africa for free African Americans who chose to go.

Most preachers active in the Second Great Awakening supported the idea of colonization, but a few individuals pressed for more radical reforms. The most vocal leader among the antislavery forces during the early nineteenth century was **William Lloyd Garrison.** A Christian reformer from Massachusetts, Garrison in the late 1820s concentrated all his energies in the antislavery cause. In 1831 he founded the nation's first prominent abolitionist newspaper, *The Liberator.* In it he advocated immediate emancipation for African Americans, with no compensation for slaveholders. In the following year, Garrison founded the New England Anti-Slavery Society and then, in 1833, branched out to found the national American Anti-Slavery Society.

At first, Garrison stood alone. Some Christian reformers joined his cause, but the majority held back. For the same reasons that they supported colonization, most northern whites detested the notion of immediate emancipation, and radical **abolitionists** at this early date were almost universally ignored or, worse, attacked when they denounced slavery. Throughout the 1830s, riots often accompanied abolitionist rallies, and angry mobs stormed stages and pulpits to silence abolitionist speakers. Still, support for the movement gradually grew. In 1836 petitions flooded into Congress demanding an end to the slave trade in Washington, D.C. Not ready to engage in an action quite so controversial, Congress passed a **gag rule** that automatically **tabled** any petition to Congress that addressed the abolition of slavery. The rule remained in effect for nearly a decade.

Despite this official denial by the national Congress, a neglect shared by many state assemblies, not all governments remained closed to the discussion of slavery. In Massachusetts, for example, the state legislature held hearings in 1838 to explore the slavery issue. Like many others who before had remained silent, Angelina Grimké spoke up in an effort to bring the problem of slavery to the attention of the nation at large.

The Whig Alternative to Jacksonian Democracy

■ What did Jackson's opponents hope to accomplish when they built their coalition to oppose the Democrats?

■ Did the coalition accomplish their purposes? Why or why not?

The same fundamental structural changes that led to such social and cultural transformations had an enor-mous impact on politics as well. Although Andrew Jackson was quite possibly the most popular president since George Washington, not all Americans agreed with his philosophy, policies, or political style. As the Bank War illustrates (see page 291), men like Henry Clay and Daniel Webster, who inherited the crumbling structure of Jefferson's Republican Party, continually opposed Jackson in and out of Congress but seemed unable to overcome sectional differences and culture wars enough to challenge Jackson's enormous national power. Gradually, however, anger over Jackson's policies and anxiety about change forged cooperation among the disenchanted, who coalesced into a new national party.

The End of the Old Party Structure

The end of Jackson's first term in office, 1832, was a landmark year in the nation's political history. In the course of that single year, the Seminoles declared war on the United States, Jackson declared war on the Second Bank, South Carolina declared war on the binding power of the Constitution, and the Cherokees waged a continuing war in the courts to hold on to their lands. The presidential election that year reflected the air of political crisis.

Henry Clay had started the Bank War for the purpose of creating a political cause to rally Jackson's opponents. The problem was that Jackson's enemies were deeply divided among themselves. Clay opposed Jackson because the president refused to support the American System (see pages 272–274) and used every tool at his disposal to attack Clay's economic policies. Southern politicians like Calhoun, however, feared and hated Clay's nationalistic policies as much as they did Jackson's assertions of federal power. And

William Lloyd Garrison   Abolitionist leader who founded and published *The Liberator,* an antislavery newspaper.

abolitionist   An individual who supported national legislation outlawing slavery, either gradually or immediately, with or without compensation to slave owners.

gag rule   A rule that limits or prevents debate on an issue.

table   Action taken by a legislative body (Congress, for example) to postpone debate on an issue until a positive vote to remove the topic from the table is taken.

political outsiders like the Antimasons distrusted all political organizations. These divisions were underscored in the 1832 election.

The Antimasons (see page 287) kicked off the anti-Jackson campaign in September 1831 when they held the nation's first nominating convention in Baltimore. Thurlow Weed's skillful political manipulation had pulled in a wide range of people who were disgusted with what Jefferson had called "political party tricks," and the convention drew a broad constituency. Using all his charm and influence, Weed cajoled the convention into nominating William Wirt, a respected lawyer from Maryland, as its presidential candidate.

Weed and Wirt fully expected that when the Republicans met in convention later in the year, they would rubber-stamp the Antimasonic nomination and present a united front against Jackson. But the Republicans, fearful of the Antimasons' odd combination of **machine politics** and antiparty paranoia, nominated Clay as their standard-bearer. The Republicans then issued the country's first formal **party platform,** a ringing document supporting Clay's economic ideas and attacking Jackson's use of the spoils system (see page 289).

Even having two anti-Jackson parties in the running did not satisfy some. Distrustful of the Antimasons and put off by Clay's nationalist philosophy, southerners in both parties refused to support any of the candidates. They finally backed nullification (see page 297) advocate John Floyd of Virginia.

Lack of unity spelled disaster for Jackson's opponents. Wirt and Floyd received votes that might have gone to Clay. But even if Clay had gotten those votes, Jackson's popularity and the political machinery that he and Van Buren controlled would have given the victory to Jackson. The president was reelected with a total of 219 electoral votes to Clay's 49, Wirt's 7, and Floyd's 11. Jackson's party lost five seats in the Senate but gained six in the House of Representatives. Despite unsettling changes in the land and continuing political chaos, the people still wanted the hero of New Orleans as their leader.

The New Political Coalition

If one lesson emerged clearly from the election of 1832, it was that Jackson's opponents needed to pull together if they expected to challenge the growing power of "King Andrew." Imitating political organizations in Great Britain, Clay and his associates began calling Jackson supporters Tories—supporters of the king—and calling themselves Whigs. The antimonar-

BORN TO COMMAND.

OF VETO MEMORY.

HAD I BEEN CONSULTED.

KING ANDREW THE FIRST.

Calling themselves Whigs after the English political party that opposed royal authority, Henry Clay, John C. Calhoun, and Daniel Webster joined forces to oppose what they characterized as Andrew Jackson's kingly use of power. This lithograph from 1834 depicting Jackson in royal dress stepping on the Constitution expresses their view quite vividly. *New York Historical Society.*

chial label stuck, and the new party formed in 1834 was called the **Whig Party.**

The Whigs eventually absorbed all the major factions that opposed Jackson. At the heart of the party were Clay supporters: advocates of strong government and the American System in economics. The nullifiers in the South, however, quickly came around when Clay and Calhoun found themselves on the

machine politics   The aggressive use of influence, favors, and tradeoffs by a political organization, or "machine," to mobilize support among its followers.

party platform   A formal statement of the principles, policies, and promises on which a political party bases its appeal to the public.

Whig Party   Political party that came into being in 1834 as an anti-Jackson coalition and that charged "King Andrew" with executive tyranny.

same side in defeating Jackson's appointment of Van Buren as American minister to England. This successful campaign, combined with Calhoun's growing awareness that Jackson was perhaps more dangerous to his constituents' interests than was Clay, led the southerner and his associates back into Clay's camp. The Antimasons also joined the Whig coalition. Disgusted by Jackson's use of patronage and back-alley politics—not to mention the fact that the president was a Mason—they overcame their distrust of Clay's party philosophy. A final major group to rally to the Whigs was the collection of Christian reformers whose campaigns to eliminate alcohol, violations of the Sabbath, and dozens of other perceived evils had become increasingly political during the opening years of the 1830s. Evangelicals disapproved of Jackson's personal lifestyle, his views on slavery, his Indian policy, and his refusal to involve government in their moral causes. The orderly and sober society that Clay and the Whigs envisioned appealed to such people.

The congressional elections in 1834 provided the first test for the new coalition. In this first electoral contest, the Whigs won nearly 40 percent of the seats in the House of Representatives and more than 48 percent in the Senate. Clearly cooperation was paying off.

Van Buren in the White House

Jackson had seemed to be a tower of strength when he was first elected to the presidency in 1828, but by the end of his second term, he was aging and ill. Nearly 70 years old and plagued by various ailments, Old Hickory decided to follow Washington's example and not run for a third term. Instead, Jackson used all the power and patronage at his command to ensure that Martin Van Buren, his most consistent loyalist, would win the presidential nomination at the Democratic Party convention.

If Jackson personified the popular charisma behind Democratic Party success, Van Buren personified its political machinery. A skilled organizer, his ability at creating unlikely political alliances had earned him the nickname "the Little Magician." Throughout Jackson's first term, Van Buren had headed up the Kitchen Cabinet (see page 289) and increasingly became Jackson's chief political henchman. In 1832 Jackson had repaid his loyalty by making him vice president, with the intention of launching him into the presidency.

Meanwhile, Clay and his Whig associates were hatching a plot to deny the election to the Democrats. Instead of holding a convention and thrashing out a platform, the Whigs let each region's party organiza-

tion nominate its own candidates. Whig leaders, especially experienced political manipulator Thurlow Weed, hoped a large number of candidates would confuse voters and throw the election into the House of Representatives, where skillful political management and Van Buren's unpopularity might unseat the Democrats. As a result, four **favorite sons** ran on the Whig ticket. Daniel Webster of Massachusetts represented the Northeast. Hugh Lawson White, a Tennessean and former Jackson supporter, ran for the Southwest. South Carolina nullifier W. P. Mangum represented the South. William Henry Harrison, former governor of Indiana Territory and victor at the Battle of Tippecanoe in 1811, was tapped to represent the Northwest.

Weed underestimated the Democrats' hold on the minds of the voters. Van Buren captured 765,483 popular votes—more than Jackson had won in the previous election—but his performance in the Electoral College was significantly weaker than Jackson's had been. Van Buren squeaked by with a winning margin of less than 1 percent, but it was a victory, and the presidential election did not go to the House of Representatives. House Democrats lost thirty-seven seats to Whigs. In the Senate, however, Democrats increased their majority to more than 62 percent. Even with that slight edge, Van Buren could expect trouble getting Democratic policies through Congress. This handicap was worsened by a total collapse in the economy just weeks after he took office.

The **Panic of 1837** was a direct outcome of the Bank War and Jackson's money policies, but it was Van Buren who would take the blame. The crisis had begun with Nicholas Biddle's manipulation of credit and interest rates in an effort to discredit Jackson and have the Second Bank rechartered in spite of the president's veto (see page 291). Jackson had added to the problem by removing paper money and credit from the economy in an effort to win support from hardmoney advocates. Arguing that he wanted to end "the monopoly of the public lands in the hands of speculators and capitalists," Jackson had issued the **Specie Circular** on August 15, 1836. From that day

> **favorite son** A candidate nominated for office by delegates from his or her own region or state.
>
> **Panic of 1837** An economic collapse that came as the result of Andrew Jackson's fiscal policies and led to an extended national economic depression.
>
> **Specie Circular** Order issued by President Jackson in 1836 stating that the federal government would accept only specie—gold and silver—as payment for public land; one of the causes of the Panic of 1837.

forward payment for public land had to be made in specie.

The contraction in credit and currency had the same impact in 1836 as it had in 1819: the national economy collapsed. By May 1837, New York banks were no longer accepting any paper currency, and soon all banks had adopted the policy of accepting specie only. Unable to pay back or collect loans, buy raw materials, or conduct any other sort of commerce, hundreds of businesses, plantations, farms, factories, canals, and other enterprises spiraled into bankruptcy by the end of the year. More than a third of the population was thrown out of work, and people who were fortunate enough to keep their jobs found their pay reduced by as much as 50 percent. Fledgling industries and labor organizations were cast into disarray, and the nation sank into both an economic and an emotional depression.

As credit continued to collapse through 1838 and 1839, President Van Buren tried to address the problems. First, he extended Jackson's hard-money policy, which caused the economy to contract further. Next, in an effort to keep the government solvent, Van Buren cut federal spending to the bone, shrinking the money supply even more. Then, to replace the stabilizing influence lost when the Second Bank was destroyed, he created a national treasury system endowed with many of the powers formerly wielded by the bank. The new regional treasury offices accepted specie only in payment for federal lands and other obligations and used that specie to pay federal expenses and debts. As a result, specie was sucked out of local banks and local economies. While fiscally sound by the wisdom of the day, Van Buren's decisions only made matters worse for the average person and drove the last nail into his political coffin.

The Log-Cabin and Hard-Cider Campaign of 1840

The Whigs had learned their lesson in the election of 1836: only a unified party could possibly destroy the political machine built by Jackson and Van Buren. As the nation sank into depression, the Whigs lined up behind a single candidate for the 1840 election, determined to use whatever means were necessary to break the Democrats' grip on the voters.

Once again, Henry Clay hoped to be the party's nominee, but Thurlow Weed convinced the party that William Henry Harrison would have a better chance in the election. Weed chose Harrison because of his distinguished military record and because the gen-

Democrats tried to discredit Whig candidate William Henry Harrison by characterizing him as a backwoods hick. This strategy backfired when romantically inclined American voters rallied around the image Whigs painted of their candidate as a simple, honest, and hospitable frontiersman. In this cartoon, Harrison is shown dispensing hard cider to his supporters (which actually was done at campaign events), while Van Buren and Jackson wince at the taste of this simple, poor man's drink and plot to turn off the flow of Harrison's hospitality. *Boston Athenaeum.*

eral, who had been a political lion thirty years earlier, had been out of the public eye for a long time and had few enemies left. For Harrison's running mate, the party chose **John Tyler,** a Virginia senator who had

> **John Tyler**   Virginia senator who left the Democratic Party after conflicts with Andrew Jackson; he was elected vice president in 1840 and became president when William Henry Harrison died in office.

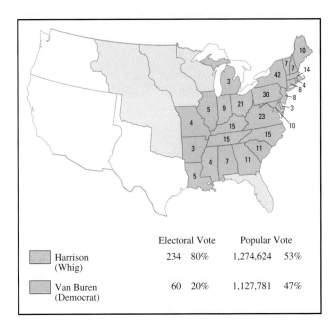

	Electoral Vote		Popular Vote	
Harrison (Whig)	234	80%	1,274,624	53%
Van Buren (Democrat)	60	20%	1,127,781	47%

MAP 12.2 Election of 1840 Although the difference in popular votes between William Henry Harrison and Martin Van Buren was small in the election of 1840, Harrison won a landslide victory in the Electoral College. This map shows why. After floundering through several elections, the Whig Party was finally able to organize a national coalition, giving it solid victories in all of the most populous regions of the country. Only the Far West, which was still sparsely settled, voted as a block for Van Buren.

It Matters

The Log-Cabin and Hard-Cider Campaign

Political pundits revel in criticizing modern electioneering for its abundant use of spin, exaggeration, and mudslinging. But these qualities are certainly nothing new. As early as 1800, opposing Federalists and Republicans had resorted to name calling and political spin as they campaigned for John Adams or Thomas Jefferson, respectively. But something certainly changed with the election of 1840. By 1840, volunteer statesmen had been virtually replaced as candidates by professional politicians. And as political parties became more complex and coordinated, a corp of professional political managers also emerged. Now the outcome of an election meant more than a change in ideological tilt; it often meant that candidates and their ever-expanding staffs would be out of work. It is little wonder, then, that what is often called the first *modern* election in American history was so nasty. In fact, it set the style for presidential campaigning that continues today.

bolted from Jackson's Democratic Party during the Bank War. Weed clearly hoped that the Virginian would draw votes from the planter South while Harrison carried the West and North.

Although the economy was in bad shape, the Whig campaign avoided addressing any serious issues. Instead, the Whigs launched a smear campaign against Van Buren. Although he was the son of a lowly tavern keeper, the Whig press portrayed him as an aristocrat whose expensive tastes in clothes, food, and furniture were signs of dangerous excess during an economic depression. Harrison really was an aristocrat, but the Whigs played on the Romantic themes so popular among their genteel and middle-class constituents by characterizing him as a simple frontiersman—a Natty Bumppo—who had risen to greatness through his own efforts. Whig claims were so extravagant that the Democratic press soon satirized Harrison in political cartoons showing a rustic hick rocking on the porch of a log cabin swilling hard cider. The

satire backfired. Whig newspapers and speechmakers seized on the image and sold Harrison, the longtime political insider, as a simple man of the people who truly lived in a log cabin.

Van Buren had little with which to retaliate. Harrison had a fairly clean and certainly a distinguished political and military career behind him. Tyler, too, was well respected. And Van Buren had simply not done a good job of addressing the nation's pressing economic needs. Voters, from former Antimasons to Christian reformers, cried out for change, and Van Buren could not offer them one. The combination of political dissatisfaction and campaign hype brought the biggest voter turnout to that time in American history: nearly twice as many voters came to the polls in 1840 as had done so in 1836. And while Harrison won only 53 percent of the popular vote, Weed's successful political manipulations earned the Whigs nearly 80 percent of the electoral votes, sweeping the Democrats out of the White House (see Map 12.2).

Individual Voices

Examining a Primary Source

Angelina Grimké Corrects Catharine Beecher on Women's Activism

Her letter to William Lloyd Garrison and then her unprecedented testimony in the Massachusetts state legislature made Angelina Grimké a national celebrity. Many famous people began corresponding with her, including fellow abolitionist and frequent writer on women's issues Catharine Beecher. Despite Beecher's expectation that she and Grimké would agree on most matters, the two were often at odds. In fact, their correspondence reveals many of the strains that beset the nation (and the nation's women) during this difficult era. In the excerpt that follows, from an October 1827 letter, Grimké responds to a statement made by Beecher in an earlier letter.

■ In the first paragraph of this passage, Grimké quotes from one of Catharine Beecher's earlier letters. What does Beecher seem to be saying about the extent to which women should be advocates for abolitionism? What limits to such activism do her words imply?

Thou sayest, when a woman is asked to sign a petition, or join an Anti-Slavery Society, it is "for the purpose of contributing her measure of influence to keep up agitation in Congress, to promote the excitement of the North against the iniquities of the South, to coerce the South by fear, shame, anger, and a sense of odium, to do what she is determined not to do." Indeed! Are these the only motives presented to the daughters of America, for laboring in the glorious cause of Human Rights? . . . ■

■ What sort of action does Grimké advocate in response to perceived evils such as slavery? How does her view differ from Beecher's?

But I had thought the principal motives urged by abolitionists were not these; but that they endeavored to excite men and women to active exertion—first, to cleanse their own hands of the sin of slavery, and secondly, to save the South, if possible, and the North, at any rate, from the impending judgments of heaven. The result of their mission in this country, cannot in the least affect the validity of that mission. ■ *Like Noah, they may preach in vain; if so, the destruction of the South can no more be attributed to them, than the destruction of the antediluvian* ■ *world to him. "In vain," did I say? Oh no! The discussion of the rights of the slave has opened the way for the discussion of other rights, and the ultimate result will most certainly be, "the breaking of every yoke," the letting the oppressed of every grade and description go free, an emancipation far more glorious than any the world has ever yet seen, and introduction into that "liberty wherewith Christ hath made his people free."* ■

■ Antediluvian is a term not heard much today. It refers to the time period before the Great Flood described in the Bible (ante means "before"; diluvian means "flood").

■ What does Grimké see as the appropriate goal for abolitionism? How might this explain her willingness to risk public ridicule and even physical danger by speaking out against slavery?

Summary

William Henry Harrison inherited an excitingly dynamic but deeply troubled country. An economic crisis triggered by Andrew Jackson's Specie Circular was worsened by Van Buren's treasury system, and both were compounded by Nicholas Biddle's manipulations. The emerging new party system promised great exhilaration and political sport but not much in the way of solutions. Still, Americans were caught up in the new politics as never before: nearly twice as many men voted in the 1840 election as had done so in any other presidential contest.

Political participation was only one of the many ways in which Americans responded to the many unsettling changes that had been taking place as part of the Great Transformation. Different economic classes responded by creating their own cultures and by adopting specific strategies for dealing with anxiety. Some chose violent protest, some passive resistance. Some looked to heaven for solutions and others to earthly utopias. And out of this complex swirl, something entirely new and unexpected emerged: a new America, on its way to being socially, politically, intellectually, and culturally modern.

In the election of 1840, a man who had become a national figure by fighting against Indian sovereignty and for westward expansion swept a new sentiment into national politics. Increasingly Americans came to believe that the West would provide the solutions to the problems ushered in during the Great Transformation. In the short term, this notion led to an exciting race by Americans toward the Pacific. But different visions about how the West would solve the nation's problems soon added to the ever-growing air of crisis.

GEOGRAPHICAL EXPANSION AND POPULATION GROWTH During the 1840s, population growth and westward expansion were celebrated as never before in American history. This map shows the result. By 1850 population density was increasing in most of the settled portions of the country and huge new regions were coming under American control.

CANADA

Treaty Line 1846

Fort Vancouver
Columbia
Portland

OREGON TERRITORY 1848

Treaty Line of 1842

Lake Superior

Treaty Line of 1842

MAINE 1842

Oregon Country 1846

R O C K Y

OREGON TRAIL

UNORGANIZED TERRITORY

Missouri

MINNESOTA TERRITORY 1849

Lake Michigan

Lake Huron

Portland
N.H.
Boston
MASS.
R.I.
CONN.

NEW YORK
Albany
Syracuse
Rochester
Buffalo

VT.

WISCONSIN 1848
Milwaukee

MICHIGAN
Detroit

L. Erie

LASSEN'S TRAIL

Snake

OREGON

Fort Laramie

Fort Laramie TRAIL

IOWA 1846
MORMON TRAIL

Chicago

ILLINOIS
Nauvoo

Cleveland

Erie
PENNSYLVANIA
Philadelphia
Pittsburgh
Baltimore

New York
Trenton

NEW JERSEY
DELAWARE
MARYLAND

Sutter's Fort

CALIFORNIA TRAIL

UTAH TERRITORY 1850
Salt Lake City

SALT LAKE TO LOS ANGELES TRAIL

Fort Kearney

MISSOURI

St. Louis

INDIANA

OHIO
Cincinnati

Washington, D.C.
Richmond
VIRGINIA

Sutter's Mill
San Francisco

Evansville

Frankfort
Louisville

Norfolk

CALIFORNIA 1850

OLD SPANISH TRAIL

Colorado

Independence

Missouri Compromise Line, 36°30' N

Ohio

KENTUCKY

Raleigh

Los Angeles

Mexican Cession 1848

NEW MEXICO TERRITORY 1850
Santa Fe

Santa Fe TRAIL

CIMARRON CROSSING TRAIL

SANTA FE TRAIL

Arkansas

Nashville

Tennessee

NORTH CAROLINA

TENNESSEE

SOUTH CAROLINA

SANTA FE TRAIL

ARKANSAS

Atlanta

Charleston

Red

Texas Annexation 1845

MISS.

ALABAMA

GEORGIA
Columbus

Savannah

PACIFIC OCEAN

Chihuahua

TEXAS 1845

Natchez

LOUISIANA

New Orleans

FLORIDA 1845

St. Augustine

ATLANTIC OCEAN

Rio Grande

Nueces

Baton Rouge

MEXICO

Gulf of Mexico

— Western trail
━ Treaty or cession boundary

Population density per square mile, according to the United States Census, 1850

▨ 90 or more
▨ 45–90
▨ 18–45
▨ 6–18
☐ 2–6
☐ Unknown

0   200   400 Km.
0   200   400 Mi.

Timeline

1820 Missouri Compromise

1821 Austin settles families in Texas

1835 Texas Revolution

1843 First wagon train into Oregon

1845 United States annexes Texas

1846 War with Mexico

1848 Gold discovered in California
Treaty of Guadelupe Hidalgo

1820   1825   1830   1835   1840   1845   1850   1855

1837 Queen Victoria crowned in England

1842 Britain annexes Hong Kong

1848 Revolutions in France, Germany, Hungary and Italy
Communist Manifesto published

1847 France conquers Algeria

1846 Corn Laws repealed in England

Westward Expansion and Manifest Destiny, 1841–1848

Geographical Expansion and Population Growth
Compare the map on the facing page with the opening maps
for Chapter 8 and Chapter 12, noting the trends in population
growth and concentration. How might these trends have
contributed to the popularity of manifest destiny during the
1840s and the similarities and/or differences between how
various regions in the country defined it?

Individual Choices

LORENZO DE ZAVALA

Lorenzo de Zavala fought against tyranny in his native Mexico. When the government he helped establish after a successful revolution against Spain refused to create a democracy, Zavala moved to Texas. In 1835 he joined the Texas Revolution against Mexico and was elected vice president of the Republic of Texas. *"Lorenzo de Zavala" by C. E. Proctor. Archives Division, Texas State Library. Photograph by Eric Beggs.*

Lorenzo de Zavala

Although Lorenzo de Zavala was a physician by training, his heart persistently pulled him into politics. An ardent federalist, he was elected to the Mérida city council in his native Yucatán, in southern Mexico, when he was only 23 years old. Then in 1814 he was elected as a delegate to the Spanish parliament. He never assumed his seat: the young liberal was imprisoned by Spain's King Ferdinand VII for expressing antimonarchical sentiments. Gaining his release in 1817, Zavala returned to Yucatán.

Zavala chafed at Spanish rule, and as revolutionary movements broke out in all parts of Mexico in 1820, he again entered politics, winning election as the secretary of the Yucatán assembly. From this position, he assisted the Mexican independence movement. Shortly after it succeeded in 1821, he was elected to the Mexican constituent congress, serving there and in the national senate until 1827, when he was appointed provincial governor.

By 1829, Zavala was having doubts about Mexico's future. The independent government had proved far from stable, and the ruling authorities seemed just as reactionary as the Spaniards. The liberals' pleas to allocate farmland to peasants, for example, were continually refused by the government. Seeking some way to help the peasants, Zavala resigned his governorship and secured an empresario grant to settle five hundred poor Mexican families in Texas.

For the next several years, Zavala traveled and wrote a history of the revolutionary movement in Mexico, which he published in 1831. Then, finding himself in Paris in 1833, Zavala returned to public service and politics by accepting a post as Mexico's ambassador to France. In the following year, Antonio López de Santa Anna pushed his way into power, suspending the constitution, dissolving the national congress, and assuming dictatorial control. Watching events unfold from his post in Paris, Zavala became increasingly disaffected by Santa Anna. In 1835 he resigned as ambassador and sailed for Texas, where he hoped to join with others in ousting Santa Anna and restoring the constitution. When Stephen F. Austin called for a "general consultation of the people" to consider appropriate responses to Santa Anna's aggression in the fall of 1835, Zavala sought and won a seat.

Like many settlers in Texas—whether they were originally from the United States, Europe, or Mexico—Zavala wanted reform but not necessarily independence. Thus he agreed with the Consultation's decision in November 1835 to form a provisional government using the Mexican constitution of 1824—a document he had helped write—as a legal foundation. But when Santa Anna declared all members of the Consultation traitors and ordered troops into Texas, Zavala gave up hope of a peaceful settlement. On March 2, 1836, he chose to join his colleagues in signing a declaration of independence, and then threw himself into the task of writing a constitution for Texas. The resulting document was an interesting hybrid: a mixture of Zavala's and James Madison's views concerning liberal federalism.

The Texas Consultation ratified the new constitution on March 16, 1836. Then, in recognition of Zavala's strong political voice and the significant role he had played in launching the revolution, the Consultation unanimously elected him vice president of the Republic of Texas.

The revolution and the establishment of the Texas Republic represented a victory for views that Zavala and many Mexican-born Texans had held for a lifetime. Throughout his political career, Zavala had fought for reform in Mexico, helping to win independence from Spain and pushing for liberal federalism. His expectations had been dashed by the tyranny of self-interested political factions, which had created such instability that Santa Anna had been able to bully his way to the top and suspend constitutional government. For Zavala and many others, the choice was clear: if Mexico could not be reformed, they would rally behind a new state where their ideals might become reality. The Republic of Texas became the seat for their dreams.

INTRODUCTION

Lorenzo de Zavala was but one of many westerners who found themselves in unexpected situations during the first half of the nineteenth century. In various regions of the American West, different ecological conditions, ideological commitments, Native American populations, and national claims created a series of complex settings. After William Henry Harrison's election to the presidency in 1840, the nation's political and cultural focus would tilt progressively westward. As transportation systems extended the American frontier, and as industrialization generated new capital, adventurous speculators would invest in the newly opened West. Expecting to find a wide-open land of opportunity, multitudes of Americans quickly followed. Many who hoped to move west, and more who saw in the West a fertile ground for expanding the political and ideological values they held dear, adopted a faith in the nation's **manifest destiny** to control the whole of the North American continent.

Had he lived to see it, Zavala would no doubt have been both surprised and disappointed when the United States fought a war with Mexico over westward expansion. But without doubt he would have celebrated the fact that the war once again forced the United States to confront the inconsistency between its promise of freedom and the reality of slavery. Even so, the divisive wedges that the slavery debate drove into the heart of the political nation would have disheartened this loyal Tejano. Instead of engaging in the sort of mature and rational discussion that Zavala would have advocated, Americans used slavery as a playing piece in an increasingly bitter game of sectional politics.

The Complicated Worlds of the West

■ How did most Americans imagine "the West"? To what extent were their imaginings accurate?

■ Who generally were the first pioneers to move into the West? How did they and those who followed actually move westward and establish communities there?

Americans entertained conflicting images about what they might find in the newly opening West. Many were convinced that most of the region was a vast wasteland, inhospitable to human civilization. Others were certain that it was a world full of promise. Enterprising capitalists often led the way in systematic exploration, looking for furs, gold, and other sources of quick profit. But it did not take long before a wide variety of others followed. Whether they expected a wasteland, a paradise, or something in between, what all of these newcomers to the West did find was a natural and cultural world that was much more complex than anything they had imagined.

Western Myths and Realities

Two views of the West, tied to Americans' earlier explorations there, dominated the popular imagination in the 1840s. One, traceable to Zebulon Pike's expedition in 1806–1807, envisioned the West as a "great American desert" unsuitable for habitation by any

manifest destiny Term first used in the 1840s to describe the right and duty of the United States to expand westward.

but the hardiest and most primitive Indians. The other, traceable to the Lewis and Clark expedition, imagined a region rich in resources. Common to both was the notion that the West, whether desert or paradise, was largely unoccupied: a virgin land free for the taking.

Realities in the **Far West** were much more complex than the myths suggested. Indeed, vast areas of the region had extremely dry and fragile **ecologies** largely unfit for the sort of economic exploitation nineteenth-century Americans desired. At the other extreme, some regions were so wet that their rain forests were virtually impassable by horse or vehicle. And all over the West, in areas large and small, thousands of local ecologies stood between the two extremes. But none of it was virgin land.

For thousands of years, various Indian groups had extracted a rich living from the many different environments in the Far West. Through the twin strategies of geographic mobility and intergroup trading, Indians had taken advantage of the West's diversity, receiving what each ecological zone had to offer. Like Europeans, Indians managed and exploited resources, but this flexible approach to the complicated and often fragile ecology of the Far West provided an excellent living and did minimal damage (see page 13). If the land appeared to expansionists in the United States to be unoccupied, it was only because they would not, or could not, recognize a system of land use that was foreign to them.

With the arrival of Spanish, French, Russian, and other Europeans, the already complex world of inter-relations in the West became even more complicated. Indians on the Great Plains used the mobility provided by European horses to expand not just their hunting range but also their trading range. Goods from the Plains made their way regularly to Spanish settlements in New Mexico, and replacement horses, guns, and other European goods flooded northward in return. This was the world into which early western entrepreneurs such as John Jacob Astor and Auguste Chouteau had entered earlier in the century (see pages 260–261). No unexploited land or great American desert could have supported their monumental visions of an inland empire providing rare furs to genteel consumers in the eastern states and Europe. What both men did was tap into an already sophisticated trading world, and both became extremely wealthy and influential as a result.

In the rough-and-tumble world of the Missouri fur trade, men earned respect through ability and toughness alone. Jim Beckwourth, a former slave from Virginia, had both, and was widely recognized as one of the era's leading mountain men. *Courtesy of the Colorado Historical Society.*

Western Enterprises

The image of the solitary trapper braving a hostile environment and even more hostile Indians is the stuff of American adventure novels and movies. Although characters such as Christopher "Kit" Carson and Jeremiah "Crow Killer" Johnson really did exist, these men were merely advance agents for an **extractive industry** geared to the efficient removal of animal pelts.

What drew men like Carson and Johnson into the Far West in the 1830s and 1840s was an innovation in the fur business instigated by a former Astor employee and one-time partner of Chouteau, William Henry Ashley. Taking advantage of the presence of large numbers of underemployed young men seeking fortune and adventure in the West, Ashley broke

Far West In North America, the lands west of the Mississippi River.

ecology Relating to the interactive relationships between organisms (animals, plants, microorganisms, etc.) and the physical environment in which they are found.

extractive industry An industry, such as fur trapping, logging, or mining, that removes natural resources from the environment.

Chronology

Expansion and Crisis

1820	Missouri Compromise
1821	Stephen F. Austin settles Americans in Texas William Becknell opens Santa Fe Trail
1831	Nez Perce and Flathead delegation ask whites to live among them
1834	Mexican government begins seizure of California mission lands
1835	Texas Revolution begins
1836	Rebellion in California against Mexican rule
1838	Senate rejects annexation of Texas Armed confrontation between Maine and New Brunswick
1839	John Sutter founds New Helvetia
1840	Split between moderates and radicals in American Anti-Slavery Society
1841	John Tyler becomes president Congress passes preemption bill
1842	Elijah White named federal Indian agent for Oregon
1843	First wagon train into Oregon Oregon adopts First Organic Laws
1844	James K. Polk elected president Murder of Joseph Smith
1845	United States annexes Texas Term "manifest destiny" coined
1846	War with Mexico begins Oregon boundary established; United States and Britain end joint occupancy California declares itself a republic
1847	Whitman massacre Mormons arrive in Utah
1848	Gold discovered in California Treaty of Guadalupe Hidalgo Zachary Taylor elected president

the long tradition of depending exclusively on Indian labor for collecting furs. In 1825 he set up the highly successful rendezvous system. Under this arrangement, individual trappers—white adventurers like Carson and Johnson, African Americans such as James Beckwourth, and a large number of Indians—combed the upper Missouri, trapping, curing, and packing furs. Each hunter carved out his own territory in the western Rocky Mountains and enforced his claim through a combination of mutual respect and violence. Once each year Ashley conducted a fur rendezvous in the mountains, where the trappers brought their furs and exchanged them for goods. Pioneer missionary Pierre Jean de Smet called these gatherings "one of the most picturesque features of early frontier life in the Far West."

Ashley's, Chouteau's, and Astor's strategies for extracting wealth from the Far West were successful and made these men very rich and important. But the success of their complex business inadvertently led to its decline. The expansion in international commerce

flowing out of the fur trade helped open the way for importing vast amounts of silk from Asia. Soon silk hats became a fashion rage among luxury-loving consumers in both America and Europe, displacing the beaver hats that had consumed most American furs. In addition, the efficiency with which these gigantic organizations extracted fur from the western wilderness virtually wiped out beaver populations in the Rocky Mountains. Through the 1830s and 1840s, the beaver business slowed to a near standstill.

Many beaver hunters stayed in the West, however, becoming founding members of new communities. As early as 1840, fur trapper Robert "Doc" Newell reportedly told his companion Joe Meek, "Come, we are all done with this life in the mountains—done with wading in Beaver-dams, and freezing or starving alternately—done with Indian trading and Indian fighting. The fur trade is dead in the Rocky Mountains, and it is no place for us now, if ever it was." The two men then headed to the Willamette Valley in Oregon to become settlers. The great captains in the fur

This painting by Alfred Jacob Miller captures the color and spirit of the annual fur rendezvous and shows the wide variety of colorful people the event brought together—not only Indians and mountain men, but sightseeing English lords like William Drummond Steward (shown here on his white horse). *"Encampment on Green River" by Alfred Miller. Joslyn Art Museum, Omaha, Nebraska. Gift of the Enron Foundation.*

industry came to similar conclusions, pulling their capital out of trapping and diverting it to more attractive ventures: banks, mills, real estate, and the burgeoning canal and rail systems.

Often the first people to join the former fur trappers in settling the West were not rugged yeoman farmers but highly organized and well-financed land speculators and developers. From the earliest days of the republic, federal public land policy favored those who could afford large purchases and pay in cash. Liberalization of the land laws during the first half of the nineteenth century put smaller tracts—for less money and on credit terms—within reach of more citizens, but speculators continued to play a role in land distribution by offering often even smaller tracts and more liberal credit (see page 292). This was particularly true as states granted rights-of-way, first to canal companies and then, increasingly, to railroad developers as a way of financing internal improvements. Land along transportation routes was especially valuable, and developers could often turn an outright grant into enormous profits.

A third group of expectant fortune hunters was lured into the Far West by the same magnet that had drawn the Spanish to the American Southwest: gold.

Since colonial times, Americans had persistently hunted precious metals, usually without much success. The promise of gold continued to draw people westward, however, onto Winnebago lands in 1827 and into Cherokee territory in 1829 (see page 293). But the most impressive case of gold fever would not strike until 1848, when a group of laborers digging a millrace in northern California found flakes and then chunks of gold. Despite efforts to suppress the news, word leaked out, and by mid-May 1848 men were rushing from all over California and Oregon into the Sierra foothills northeast of Sacramento to prospect for gold. By September, news reached the East that the light work of panning for gold in California could yield $50 a day, two months' wages for an average northern working-man. In 1849 more than a hundred thousand **forty-niners** took up residence in California.

As in earlier gold rushes, most of these fortune hunters did not discover gold, but many of them stayed to establish trading businesses, banks, and

forty-niners Prospectors who streamed into California in 1849, after the discovery of gold northeast of New Helvetia in 1848.

farms. Others moved on, still seeking their fortunes. But eventually they too, for the most part, settled down to become shopkeepers, farmers, and entrepreneurs.

Moving Westward

Distinct waves of Americans pushed westward into the areas opened by gold seekers, fur trappers, and land speculators. All of these migrants were responding to promises of abundant land in America's interior. But different groups were reacting to very different conditions in the East, and those differences gave shape to their migrations and to the settlements they eventually created.

The underlying cause for most westward migration was the hope of economic opportunity. "To make money was their chief object," one young pioneer woman in Texas commented; "all things else were subsidiary to it." Like her family, many settlers went to the Southwest to improve their fortunes by taking advantage of rising cotton prices in hopes of becoming prosperous inland planters. Many, too, were pushed by economic forces to seek new lives in the West, especially after the panics of 1819 and 1837. New England Yankees, for example, were edged out of the Northeast by two forces. First, the long-established New England tradition of dividing family holdings equally among adult children had created a significant shortage of workable farms in the region. Second, innovations in spinning and weaving made large-scale wool processing economical, creating a new demand for this fiber. Starting after 1824, a sheep-raising craze swept New England, especially in the Connecticut River valley. Sheep required little labor but a lot of land, and people who had the capital to amass large herds soon began buying out their less fortunate neighbors. Between 1825 and 1840, sheep displaced people throughout much of the New England countryside. Thus young people in New England faced a choice between moving into cities or trying to establish New England–style farming in new areas. A significant number opted to migrate westward.

The image of the independent frontier farmer fleeing the restrictions of civilized life and hewing out a living with an ax, a hoe, and single-minded self-sufficiency is a persistent myth in American history, but the true picture is less romantic. Most people went west not solo but as part of a larger community and often as the result of organized land development efforts. In Texas, for example, most migrants in the 1820s and 1830s came in large groups under the direction of men such as **Stephen F. Austin** and Martín de León. The Spanish government in Mexico gave these *empresarios*

land grants and the right to assess fees in exchange for encouraging settlement in Spain's northern New World colonies. Austin's father, Moses Austin, was the first Anglo-American *empresario*. On January 17, 1821, Spanish authorities gave him permission to settle three hundred American families within a 200,000-acre tract between the Brazos and Colorado Rivers. Following his father's death, the younger Austin took over the enterprise and in the aftermath of the Panic of 1819 was able to offer families large plots of land for a filing fee of only 12½ cents an acre. "I am convinced," he exclaimed, "that I could take on fifteen hundred families as easily as three hundred if permitted to do so."

Beginning with Austin's first overland party in the winter of 1821, migrants to Texas generally traveled in small-to-medium-size groups. Some of them ventured overland, others by boat. One settler, Jared E. Groce, transported an entire plantation from Georgia to Texas—fifty wagons full of personal belongings and more than a hundred slaves—but that was unusual. More typical was the experience of a young woman named Rabb. She traveled in a family group of seven adults and eight children, who found and settled with other relatives when they arrived in Texas. Even those few who arrived alone seldom stayed that way. "Those of us who have no families of our own, reside with some of the families in the settlement," one young migrant observed. "We remain here notwithstanding the scarcity of provisions, to assist in protecting the settlement."

Migration to Oregon also involved group effort but followed a different pattern. The first permanent Anglo-American settlements in the Pacific Northwest were begun by missionaries carrying the Second Great Awakening's message of Christianity and Americanism to the Indians, who welcomed and in some cases had even invited them. These missionaries encouraged mass migration to the new territory. "Who will come & possess the land, who?" Henry H. Spalding wrote from his mission station in Oregon, urging farmers, mechanics, and additional missionaries to rush westward immediately. Missionaries all over the Northwest repeated his summons, which echoed in the religious and secular newspapers and magazines that enjoyed wide circulation during the 1830s and 1840s. Coming on the heels of the Panic of

Stephen F. Austin American colonizer in Texas and leading voice in the Texas Revolution.

empresario In the Spanish colonies, a person who organized and led a group of settlers in exchange for

Although modern movies and traditional folklore portray early Texas as a barely settled cowboy frontier, the region actually was attractive because vast areas in its eastern and central regions could support large-scale cotton, sugar, and other lucrative plantation businesses. This painting from 1845 captures the more genteel side of Texas life during the pioneer era. *Texas Memorial Museum, The University of Texas, Austin.*

1837, these calls appealed strongly to people eager for economic opportunity in familiar cultural surroundings. Thus, when the Methodist Church issued a call for a "great reinforcement" for its mission in Oregon, it received a flood of applications, and three separate reinforcements arrived in Oregon by ship in 1840. But large-scale immigration did not begin until 1843, when missionary Marcus Whitman led the first major emigration along what would later be called the **Oregon Trail.**

Every spring thereafter for decades, families from all over the East gathered in Missouri to start the overland trek. "Probably there were sixty-five or seventy, or possibly more than that, wagons in our train, and hundreds of loose cattle and horses," one young woman pioneer reported, and that was just one of the wagon trains on the trail that summer. "We were not allowed to travel across the plains in any haphazard manner," she continued. "No family or individual was permitted to go off alone from the company."

Although trail life was novel for most of the Oregon-bound emigrants, the division in domestic labor re-mained much as it had been at home. "Everybody was supposed to rise at daylight, and while the women were preparing breakfast, the men rounded up the cattle, took down the tents, yoked the oxen to the wagons and made everything ready for an immediate start after the morning meal was finished." Even social customs remained the same. "Life on the plains was a primitive edition of life in town or village," the same pioneer woman remarked. "We were expected to visit our neighbors when we paused for rest. If we did not, we were designated as 'high-toned' or 'stuck-up.' . . . Human nature is the same the world over. Bickerings and jealousies arose just as they would have done in a settlement of the same size."

And so life went on during the six months it took to cross the more than 2,000 miles separating the set-

Oregon Trail The overland route from St. Louis to the Pacific Northwest followed by thousands of settlers in the 1840s.

Though highly idealized, this painting of an emigrant wagon train settling down for the night on the Oregon Trail does capture many accurate details. Notice, for example, the division of labor: women are washing, cooking, and tending to small children while men are drawing water, herding animals, and preparing to hunt for food. Diaries kept by actual emigrants confirm this was the way life was on the trail. *The Corcoran Gallery of Art, Washington, D.C. Gift of Mr. & Mrs. Lansdell K. Christie.*

tled part of the nation and the **Oregon Country.** Once in Oregon, families arriving in the wagon trains tended to settle in rings around the already existing missions, which soon became the hubs for New England–style villages in the Pacific Northwest.

Another migration pattern led toward the **Great Basin.** Despite their growth in numbers and prosperity, Joseph Smith's community of Mormons in Nauvoo, Illinois, continued to be victims of religious and economic persecution. On June 27, 1844, Joseph Smith was murdered by a mob in neighboring Carthage, Illinois. The remaining church leaders concluded that the Mormons would never be safe until they moved far from mainstream American civilization. **Brigham Young,** Smith's successor, decided to search for a safe refuge beyond the Rocky Mountains and led sixteen hundred Mormons out of Nauvoo. After establishing

a base camp in Iowa, Young put together a contingent of 146 young men and women and set out for the Far West, laying out roads, building bridges, and planting crops so that the main body of the church could

Oregon Country The region to the north of Spanish California extending from the crest of the Rocky Mountains to the Pacific Coast.

Great Basin A desert region of the western United States including most of Nevada and parts of Utah, California, Idaho, Wyoming, and Oregon.

Brigham Young Mormon leader who took over in 1844 after Joseph Smith's death and guided the Mormons from Illinois to Utah, where they established a permanent home for the church.

follow in comfort. On July 24, 1847, Young's party finally pushed into the valley of the **Great Salt Lake.** Young immediately assigned some followers to begin an irrigation project and sent others on to California to buy livestock. The rest of the congregation soon arrived, and within a matter of weeks the Mormon community had become a thriving settlement of nearly two thousand.

Despite their differences, pioneers shared one fundamental problem: hard cash was always in short supply. Frontier farmers in every region of the West lived on a shoestring, barely making ends meet when conditions were good and falling into debt when weather or other hazards interrupted farming. Still, those who were lucky and exercised careful management were able to carve out excellent livings. Strongly centralized authority and a deeply felt sense of community helped the Mormons, for example, to overcome even bad luck and deficient skills. Many in other communities, however, had to sell out to satisfy creditors or saw their land repossessed for debts. Pulling up stakes again, they often moved to new lands exhausted of furs and opened to settlement by merchant-adventurers and Indian agents.

Many pioneers had no legal claim to their lands. People bankrupted by unscrupulous speculators or by their own misfortune or mismanagement often settled wherever they could find a spread that seemed unoccupied. Thousands of squatters living on unsold federal lands were a problem for the national government when the time came to sell off the public domain. Always with an eye to winning votes, western politicians frequently advocated "squatter rights," as Thomas Hart Benton had done in 1830 (see page 294). Western congressmen finally maneuvered the passage of a **preemption bill** in 1841, allowing squatters to settle on unsurveyed federal land. Of course, this right did not guarantee that they would have the money to buy the land once it came on the market, or that they would make profitable use of it in the meantime. Thus shoestring farming, perpetual debt, and an uncertain future continued to challenge frontier farmers.

The Social Fabric in the West

■ What challenges did various communities in the West have to face?

■ What cultural arrangements helped settlers deal with these challenges?

■ Why did distinctly different western societies develop in the Far West?

Although migrants to places such as Texas, Oregon, and Utah headed for and found strange new lands, most had no intention of carving out a new social order in the West. Rather, they intended to re-create the society they were leaving behind. The physical and cultural environments into which they moved, however, forced change on them. The West, after all, was not an unpopulated place, and pioneers had to accommodate themselves to the geography and people they found there. Thus the different origins and eventual destinations of various migrants resulted in some significant differences in the cultures and societies of the Far West. The result was not one frontier but a patchwork of frontier areas.

The New Cotton Country

Migrants to cotton country in the Mississippi Valley and beyond brought a particular lifestyle with them. Often starting out as landless herders, migrating families carved out claims beyond the **frontier line** and survived on a mixture of raised and gathered food until they could put the land into agricultural production. The Indians who preceded them in the Mississippi Valley unintentionally simplified life for these families; the Indians had already cleared large expanses of land for agriculture. Removal of the Indians to the Far West and the continuing devastation of Indian populations by disease meant that southern frontiersmen could plant corn and cotton quickly and reap early profits with minimal labor.

Although some areas were cleared and extremely fertile, others were swampy, rocky, and unproductive. In these less desirable locales, settlers were allowed to survey their own claims. The result was odd-shaped farms, differences in the quality of land owned by neighboring farmers, and the re-creation of the southern class system in the new lands. Those fortunate enough to get profitable lands might become

Great Salt Lake   A shallow, salty lake in the Great Basin near which the Mormons established a permanent settlement in 1847.

preemption bill   A temporary law that gave squatters the right to buy land they had settled on before it was offered for sale at public auction.

frontier line   The outer limit of agricultural settlement bordering on areas still under Indian control or unoccupied.

great planters; those not so fortunate had to settle for lesser prosperity and lower status.

During the pioneer phase of southern frontier life, all the members of migrating families devoted most of their time to the various tasks necessary to keep the family alive. Even their social and recreational lives tended to center on practical tasks. House building, planting, and harvesting were often done in cooperation with neighbors. Such occasions saw plenty of food and homemade whiskey consumed, and at day's end, music and dancing often lasted long into the night. Women gathered together separately for large-scale projects such as group quilting. Another community event for southwestern settlers was the periodic religious revival, which brought people from miles around to revival meetings that might last for days (see pages 342–343). Here they could make new acquaintances, court sweethearts, and discuss the common failings in their souls and on their farms.

Westering Yankees

For migrants to areas such as Michigan and Oregon, the overall frontier experience differed in many respects from that in the Mississippi Valley. In the Old Northwest, Indians had also cleared the land for planting, easing the task for incoming farmers. As arriving whites pushed out the Winnebagos and others, pioneers snatched up the Indians' deserted farms. In this region, professional surveyors had already carved the land into neat rectangular lots before it was sold. These surveys generally included provision for a township, where settlers quickly established villages similar to those left behind in New England, in which they re-created the social institutions they already knew and respected—first and foremost, law courts, churches, and schools. These institutions helped to prevent the sort of social distinctions that developed so quickly along the southern frontier. That is not to say that all northern frontiersmen fared equally, but class differences among them were not so vast or so obvious as between members of the slaveholding elite and their poorer neighbors.

Conditions in the Oregon Country resembled those farther east in most respects, but some significant differences did exist. Most important, the Indians in the Oregon Country had never practiced agriculture—their environment was so rich in fish, meat, and wild vegetables that farming was unnecessary—and they still occupied their traditional homelands and outnumbered whites significantly. Although

both of these facts might have had a profound impact on life in Oregon, early pioneers were bothered by neither. Large open prairies flanking the Columbia, Willamette, and other rivers provided abundant fertile farmland. And the Indians helped rather than hindered the pioneers.

Much like the Indians in colonial New England, groups such as the Nez Perces, Cayuses, and Kalapuyas welcomed whites. In fact, in 1831 the Nez Perces, who had hosted Lewis and Clark in 1805 (see page 229), and the Flatheads issued an appeal for whites to come live among them, spurring the rush of missionaries who opened the Oregon Country for American settlement. Although occasional tensions arose between white settlers and Indians, no serious conflict took place until the winter of 1847, when a combination of disease, white population pressure, and factionalism within the tribe led a group of Cayuse Indians to kill missionaries Marcus and Narcissa Whitman. The Whitman massacre triggered the Cayuse War and led to a concerted effort by white Americans in the Oregon Country to remove Indians.

Like their southwestern counterparts, pioneers in both the Old and the Pacific Northwest cooperated in house building, annual planting and harvesting, and other big jobs, but a more sober air prevailed at these gatherings among the descendants of New England Puritans. Religious life was also more solemn. Religious revivals swept through Yankee settlements during the 1830s and 1840s, but the revival meetings tended to be held in churches at the center of communities rather than in outlying campgrounds. As a result, they were usually briefer and less emotional than their counterparts in the Southwest and strongly reinforced the Yankee notion of village solidarity.

The Hispanic Southwest

The physical and cultural environment in California differed greatly from the Pacific Northwest, and frontier life in California was in many ways unique. One major reason for the difference was that Spain had colonized California and the Spanish had left a lasting cultural imprint.

Although they could assert a claim extending back to the mid-1500s, systematic Spanish exploration into what is now the state of California did not begin until 1769. Prompted in part by Russian expansion into Spanish-claimed territory, Gaspar de Portolá, the governor of Baja California, led an expedition northward and established garrisons at San Diego and Monterey.

Using Indian labor, Franciscan missionaries transformed the dry California coastal hill country into a blooming garden and built a long string of missions in which to celebrate their religion. This painting of Mission San Gabriel conveys the beauty and the awesome size of these mission establishments. *Courtesy of the Santa Barbara Mission Archive-Library.*

Junípero Serra, a Franciscan monk, accompanied Portolá's expedition and established a mission, San Diego de Alcalá, near the present city of San Diego. Eventually Serra and his successors established twenty-one missions extending from San Diego to the town of Sonoma, north of San Francisco.

The mission system provided a framework for Spanish settlement in California. Established in terrain that resembled the hills of Spain, the missions were soon surrounded by groves, vineyards, and lush farms. California Indians were harnessed for the labor needed to create this new landscape, but not willingly: the missionaries often forced them into the missions, where they became virtual slaves. The death rate from disease and harsh treatment among the mission Indians

was terrible, but their labor turned California's coastal plain into a vast and productive garden.

The Franciscans continued to control the most fertile and valuable lands in California until after Mexico won independence from Spain. Between 1834 and 1840, however, the Mexican government seized the mission lands in California and sold them off to private citizens living in the region. An elite class of

Junípero Serra Spanish missionary who went to California in 1769; he and his successors established near the California coast a chain of missions that depended on Indian labor.

Spanish-speaking Californians snatched up the rich lands. Taking advantage of continuing turmoil in the Mexican government and the distance between California's fertile coast and Mexico City, these landholding **Californios** amassed a great degree of political and economic power. Never numbering more than about a thousand people, this Hispanic elite class eventually owned some 15 million acres of California's richest land. In 1836 the Californios and non-Hispanic newcomers together rebelled against Mexico to make one of their own, Juan Bautista Alvarado, governor. The landholding elite never ended California's official relationship with Mexico but continued to run their own affairs.

At first, the Californios welcomed outsiders as neighbors and trading partners. Ships from the United States called at California ports regularly, picking up cargoes of beef **tallow**, cow hides, and other commodities to be shipped around the world, and settlers who promised to open new lands and business opportunities were given generous grants and assistance. **John Sutter,** for example, received an outright grant of land extending from the Sierra foothills southwest to the Sacramento Valley, where in 1839 he established a colony called New Helvetia.

People of many races and classes could be found strolling the lanes in New Helvetia and in other northern California settlements. Farther south, however, in the heartland of Spanish California, the Hispanic landholding elite resented intrusions by lower-class Mexicans and other newcomers. Thus, although new pioneers had been instrumental in elevating him to power, Governor Alvarado worried constantly about their designs and motivations. His henchmen arrested a number of American and British citizens on the suspicion that they were plotting to overthrow his government.

A similar but more harmonious pattern of interracial cooperation existed in other Spanish North American provinces. In 1821 trader William Becknell began selling and trading goods along the Santa Fe Trail from St. Louis to New Mexico. By 1824, the business had become so profitable that people from all over the frontier moved in to create a permanent Santa Fe trade. As had taken place in St. Louis, an elite class emerged in Santa Fe from the intermingled fortunes and intermarriages among Indian, European, and American populations, and a strong kinship system developed. Thus, based on kinship, the Hispanic leaders of New Mexico, unlike those of California, consistently worked across cultural lines, whether to fight off Texan aggression or eventually to lobby for **annexation** to the United States.

Intercultural cooperation also characterized the early history of Texas settlement. Spanish and then Mexican officials aided the empresarios, hoping that the aggressive Americans would form a frontier line between southern Plains Indians and prosperous silver-mining communities south of the **Rio Bravo.** Tensions rose, however, as population increased. Despite the best efforts of the Mexican government to encourage Hispanics to settle in Texas, fully four-fifths of the thirty-five hundred land titles perfected by the empresarios went to non-Hispanics, most of whom were impoverished but hopeful frontiersmen from the southern United States.

In Texas, economic desperation combined with cultural insensitivity and misunderstanding to create the sort of tensions that were rare in New Mexico. As a result of the relative lack of harmony and the enormous stretches of land that separated ethnic groups in Texas, both **Texians** and **Tejanos** tended to cling to their own ways.

The Mormon Community

Physical and cultural conditions in the Great Basin led to a completely different social and cultural order in that area. Utah is a high-desert plateau where water is scarce and survival depends on careful management. The tightly knit community of Mormons was perfectly suited to such an inhospitable place, and their social order responded well to the hostile environment.

Mormons followed a simple principle: "Land belongs to the Lord, and his Saints are to use so much as they can work profitably." The church measured off

Californios   Spanish colonists in California in the eighteenth and nineteenth centuries.

tallow   Hard fat obtained from the bodies of cattle and other animals and used to make candles and soap.

John Sutter   Swiss immigrant who founded a colony in California; the discovery of gold on his property in the Coloma Valley, northeast of New Helvetia (Sacramento) in 1848 attracted hordes of miners who seized his land, leaving him financially ruined.

annexation   The incorporation of a territory into an existing political unit such as a neighboring country.

Rio Bravo   The Spanish and then Mexican name for the river that now forms the border between Texas and Mexico; the Rio Grande.

Texians   Non-Hispanic settlers in Texas in the nineteenth century.

Tejanos   Mexican settlers in Texas in the nineteenth century.

With two wives and several children to help share the burden of work, this Mormon settler was in a good position to do well, even in the harsh conditions that prevailed in the near-desert environment of Utah. Sensitive to disapproval from more traditional Christians, families like this tended to associate exclusively with other Mormons and pressured outsiders to leave as quickly as possible. *Denver Public Library, Western History Division.*

plots of various sizes, up to 40 acres, and assigned them to settlers on the basis of need. Thus a man with several wives, a large number of children, and enough wealth to hire help might receive a grant of 40 acres, but a man with one wife, few children, and little capital might receive only 10. The size of a land grant determined the extent to which the recipient was obligated to support community efforts. When the church ordered the construction of irrigation systems or other public works, a man who had been granted 40 acres had to provide four times the amount of labor as one who had been granted 10 acres. Like settlers elsewhere, the Mormons in Utah joined in community work parties, but cooperation among them was more rigidly controlled and formal. As on other frontiers, when the system worked it was because it was well suited to natural conditions.

Mormons had their own peculiar religious and social culture, and because of their bad experiences in Missouri and Illinois, they were unaccepting of strangers. The General Authorities of the church made every effort to keep Utah an exclusively Mormon so-ciety, welcoming all who would embrace the new religion and its practices but making it difficult for non-Mormons to stay in the region. The one exception was the American Indian population. Because Indians occupied a central place in Mormon sacred literature (see pages 340–341), the Mormons practiced an accepting and gentle Indian policy. Like other missionaries, Mormons insisted that Indians convert to their religion and lifestyle, but the Mormon hierarchy used its enormous power in Utah to prevent private violence against Indians whenever possible.

The Triumph of "Manifest Destiny"

■ What forces in American life contributed to the concept of manifest destiny?

■ To what extent did the actions taken by American settlers in Oregon and Texas reflect the ideal of manifest destiny?

■ What were the global implications of manifest destiny?

Economic opportunity was the primary reason for

westward movement before the Civil War erupted in 1861, but cultural and religious concerns also pushed people west, following migrants they knew personally or people whose religious views and cultural values resembled their own. Political ideology, too, promoted westward expansion. The idea that proved most influential in opening the West was not new, but it received a name only in 1845: manifest destiny.

The Rise of Manifest Destiny

To some extent, manifest destiny can be traced back to the sense of mission that had motivated colonial Puritans (see page 71). Like John Winthrop and his Massachusetts Bay associates, many early nineteenth-century Americans believed they had a duty to go into new lands. During the antebellum period, romantic nationalism, land hunger, and Second Great Awakening evangelicalism shaped this sense of divine mission into a new and powerful commitment to westward expansion. As the American Board of Commissioners for Foreign Missions noted in its annual report for 1827, "The tide of emigration is rolling westward so rapidly, that it must speedily surmount every barrier, till it reaches every habitable part of this continent." The power of this force led many to conclude that the westward movement was not just an economic process but was part of a divine plan for North America and the world.

Not surprisingly, the earliest and most aggressive proponents of expansion were Christian missionary organizations whose many magazines, newsletters, and reports were the first to give it formal voice. Politicians, however, were not far behind. Democratic warhorse and expansion advocate Thomas Hart Benton of Missouri borrowed both the tone and content of missionary rhetoric in his speeches promoting generous land policies, territorial acquisition, and even overseas expansion. In 1825, for example, Benton argued in favor of American colonization of the Pacific coast for two reasons: it would bring "great and wonderful benefits" not only to the Indians but also to the Chinese and Japanese; and it would allow "science, liberal principles in government, and true religion [to] cast their lights across the intervening sea."

Expansion to the North and West

One major complication standing in the way of the nation's perceived manifest destiny was the fact that Spain, Britain, Russia, and other countries already owned large parts of the continent. The continued presence of the British, for example, proved to be a constant source of irritation. During the War of 1812, the War Hawks had advocated conquering Canada and pushing the British from the continent altogether (see page 250). Although events thwarted this ambition, many continued to push for that objective by either legal or extralegal means.

One confrontation flared in 1838. The United States and Britain had been disputing Maine's boundaries since the Treaty of Paris in 1783. Growing impatient, Canadian loggers moved into the disputed region during the winter of 1838–1839 and began cutting trees. American lumberjacks resolved to drive them away, and fighting soon broke out. The Canadian province of New Brunswick and the state of Maine then mobilized their militias, the American Congress nervously called up fifty thousand men in case of war, and President Van Buren ordered in **Winfield Scott.** Once on the scene, General Scott was able to calm tempers and arrange a truce, but tension continued to run high.

Another source of dispute between the United States and Great Britain was the **Oregon Question.** The vast Oregon tract had been claimed at one time or another by Spain, Russia, France, England, and the United States (see Map 13.1). By the 1820s, only England and the United States continued to contest for its ownership. At the close of the War of 1812, the two countries had been unable to settle their claims, and in 1818 had agreed to joint occupation of Oregon for ten years (see page 278). They extended this arrangement indefinitely in 1827, with the **proviso** that either country could end it with one year's notice.

Oregon's status as neither British nor American was a problem even before wagon trains of Americans began pouring into the region. In 1841 wealthy American pioneer Ewing Young died without leaving a will. Because the Oregon Country had no laws, no guidelines existed on who was entitled to inherit his property. Finally, Methodist missionary officials

---

Winfield Scott Virginia soldier and statesman who led troops in the War of 1812 and the War with Mexico; he was still serving as a general at the start of the Civil War.

Oregon Question The question of the national ownership of the Pacific Northwest; the United States and England renegotiated the boundary in 1846, establishing it at 49° north latitude.

proviso A clause making a qualification, condition, or restriction in a document.

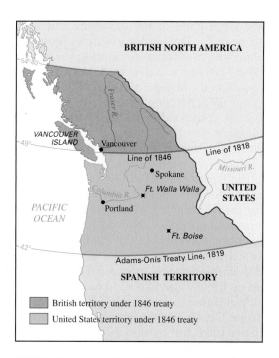

MAP 13.1 Oregon Territory   This map shows the changing boundaries and shifting possession of the Oregon Country. As a result of Polk's aggressive stance and economic pressures, Britain ceded all land south of the 49th parallel to the United States in 1846.

created a **probate court** and instructed it to follow the statutes of the state of New York. At the same time, the missionaries appointed a committee to frame a constitution and draft a basic code of laws. Opposition from the British put an end to this early effort at self-rule, but the movement continued.

Two years later, Americans in Oregon began agitating again, this time supposedly because of wolves preying on their livestock. Settlers in the Willamette Valley held a series of "Wolf Meetings" in 1843 to discuss joint protection and resolved to create a civil government. They called a constitutional convention for May 2. Although the British tried to prevent the convention, the assembly passed the **First Organic Laws** of Oregon on July 5, 1843, making Oregon an independent republic in all but name. Independence, however, was not the settlers' long-term goal. The document's preamble announced that the code of laws would continue in force "until such time as the United States of America extend their jurisdiction over us."

Revolution in Texas

Questions about the nation's southwestern borders were quite different from boundary disputes in the Northeast and Pacific Northwest. Unlike the situation in northern Maine and the Oregon Country, the matter of ownership in the Southwest was fairly clear. The area including present-day Texas, New Mexico, Arizona, California, Nevada, and portions of Colorado, Oklahoma, Kansas, and Wyoming belonged to Spain prior to Mexico's successful revolution in 1821. After that revolution, common precedent dictated that it belonged to Mexico, despite Spain's continued protest to the contrary. But owning this vast region and controlling it were two different matters. The distance and rough terrain separating the capital in Mexico City from the northern provinces made governing the region problematic. Moreover, large areas of Texas and New Mexico were home to strong and independent Indian groups such as the Comanches, who made the extension of both settlement and law difficult.

Although the Spanish and then the Mexican government had invited Anglo-Americans to settle in the Southwest, these pioneers generally ignored Mexican customs, including their pledge to practice Roman Catholicism, and often disregarded Mexican law. This was particularly the case after 1829, when Mexico began attaching duties to trade items moving between the region and the neighboring United States. Mexico also abolished importing slaves. Bad feelings grew over the years, but the distant and politically unstable Mexican government could do little to enforce laws, customs, or faith. In addition, despite the friction between cultures in Texas, many Tejanos—men such as Lorenzo de Zavala—were disturbed by the corruption and political instability in Mexico City and were as eager as their Texian counterparts to participate in the United States' thriving cotton market.

Assuming responsibility for forging a peaceful settlement to the problems between settlers in Texas and the Mexican government, Stephen F. Austin went to

probate court   A court that establishes the validity of wills and administers the estates of people who have died.
First Organic Laws   A constitution adopted by American settlers in the Oregon Country on July 5, 1843, establishing a government independent from Great Britain and requesting annexation by the United States.

Mexico City in 1833. While Austin was there, **Antonio López de Santa Anna** seized power after a series of revolutions and disputed elections. A former supporter of federalism and a key figure in the adoption of a republican constitution in 1824, Santa Anna had come to the conclusion that Mexico was not ready for democracy. Upon assuming power, he suspended the constitution, dismissed congress, and set himself up as the self-declared "Napoleon of the West."

Throughout Mexico, former revolutionaries and common citizens who had anticipated democracy were outraged by Santa Anna's actions. To the south, in Yucatán and elsewhere, provinces openly rebelled. The same potential existed along the northern frontier as well. Trying to avoid an open break, Austin met with Santa Anna in 1834 and presented several petitions advocating reforms and greater self-government in Texas, but Santa Anna made it clear that he intended to exert his authority over the region. On his arrival back in Texas in 1835, Austin declared, "War is our only recourse." At a banquet given in his honor early in September, Austin announced to the mixed Tejano and Texian audience, "The constitutional rights and the security and peace of Texas—they ought to be maintained; and jeopardized as they now are, they demand a general consultation of the people." He was immediately made chairman of a committee to call for a convention of delegates from all over Texas. Members of the group that convened followed Austin's terminology, referring to themselves as the "Consultation."

Mexican officials, viewing the unrest in Texas as rebellion against their authority, issued arrest warrants for all the Texas troublemakers they could identify and **deployed** troops to San Antonio. Austin's committee immediately sent out word for Texans to arm themselves. The **Texas Revolution** started quickly thereafter when the little town of Gonzales refused to surrender a cannon to Mexican officials on September 29, 1835, and a battle ensued several days later (see Map 13.2).

After the battle in Gonzales and several other small encounters, the Texas Consultation formed itself into a provisional government in November 1835 and adopted the Mexican federalist constitution of 1824, recently suspended by Santa Anna, as its legal foundation. Angered by the rebellion, Santa Anna personally led the Mexican army into Texas, arriving in San Antonio on February 23, 1836. Knowing that Santa Anna was on his way, Texas commander William Travis had moved his troops into the **Alamo.** On March 6 Santa Anna ordered an all-out assault and despite sustaining staggering casualties was able

MAP 13.2 Texas Revolution   This map shows troop movements and the major battles in the Texas Revolution, as well as the conflicting boundary claims made by Texans and the Mexican government. The Battle of San Jacinto and the Treaty of Velasco ended the war, but the conflicting land claims continued when Mexico repudiated the treaty.

to capture the former mission. Most of the post's defenders were killed in the assault, and Santa Anna executed those who survived the battle, including

Antonio López de Santa Anna   Mexican general who was president of Mexico when he led an attack on the Alamo in 1836; he again led Mexico during its war with the United States in 1846–1848.

deploy   To position military resources (troops, artillery, equipment) in preparation for action.

Texas Revolution   A revolt by American colonists in Texas against Mexican rule; it began in 1835 and ended with the establishment of the Republic of Texas in 1836.

Alamo   A fortified Franciscan mission at San Antonio; rebellious Texas colonists were besieged and annihilated there by Santa Anna's forces in 1836.

Following the Battle of San Jacinto, Mexican president Antonio López de Santa Anna was captured while trying to escape disguised as a private. Texas forces brought him to Sam Houston, who had been wounded in the battle, in order to convey his formal surrender. A month later, the captured president signed the Treaty of Valasco, granting Texas its independence in exchange for his own release and return to Mexico. *Texas State Library and Archives Commission.*

former American congressman and frontier celebrity Davy Crockett.

While Santa Anna was subduing San Antonio, Texas rebels elsewhere were occupied with consolidating the revolution. On March 2, a convention met at Washington-on-the-Brazos and issued a declaration of independence. The convention adopted a constitution written by former Mexican revolutionary and federalist Lorenzo de Zavala, ratifying it on March 16. On the following day, David G. Burnet was elected president of the new republic, and Zavala was elected vice president. **Sam Houston** had earlier been named commander of the army.

Despite the loss at the Alamo, Texans continued to underestimate Santa Anna's strength and his resolve to put down the rebellion. After a series of defeats, however, the Texans scored a stunning victory on April 21. Santa Anna had ordered his army to pause at the San Jacinto River. Arriving in the vicinity undetected, Houston's force of just over nine hundred formed up quietly and attacked. In just eighteen minutes, 630 Mexican soldiers lay dead. Disguised in a private's uniform, Santa Anna attempted to escape but was captured and brought to Houston. In exchange

for his release, in May 1836 the Mexican president signed the **Treaty of Velasco,** officially recognizing Texas's independence and acknowledging the Rio Grande as the border between Texas and Mexico. Santa Anna then returned to Mexico and was immediately deposed as president. The new government repudiated the treaty with Texas, but was in no immediate position to do anything about it.

As in Oregon, many leaders in Texas hoped their actions would lead to swift annexation by the United States. In 1838 Houston, by then president of the Republic of Texas, invited the United States to annex Texas. Because all of Texas lay below the Missouri Compromise line (see page 281–283), John Quincy Adams, elected to the House of Representatives after his loss

Sam Houston   American general and politician who fought in the struggle for Texas's independence from Mexico and became president of the Republic of Texas.

Treaty of Velasco   Treaty that Santa Anna signed in May 1836 after his capture at the San Jacinto River; it recognized the Republic of Texas but was later rejected by the Mexican congress.

in the presidential election of 1828, **filibustered** for three weeks against the acquisition of such a massive block of potential slave territory. Seeking to avoid national controversy, Congress refused to ratify the annexation treaty.

The Politics of Manifest Destiny

Although Adams was typical of one wing of the Whig coalition, he certainly did not speak for the majority of Whigs on the topic of national expansion. The party of manufacturing, revivalism, and social reform inclined naturally toward the blending of political, economic, and religious evangelicalism that was manifest destiny. William Henry Harrison himself, the united party's first national candidate, was a colorful figure in American westward expansion. He had been a prominent War Hawk and Indian fighter in the years leading up to the War of 1812 (see pages 250–252), and his political campaign in 1840 celebrated the simple pleasures and virtues of frontier life, appealing to a westering population. When Harrison died soon after taking office in 1841, his vice president, John Tyler, picked up the torch of American expansionism.

Tyler was a less typical Whig than even Adams. A Virginian and a states' rights advocate, he had been a staunch Democrat until the nullification crisis, when he bolted the party in protest against Jackson's strong assertion of federal power (see page 297). As president, Tyler seemed still to be more Democrat than Whig. Although he had objected to Jackson's use of presidential power, like Old Hickory, Tyler as president was unyielding where political principles were concerned. He vetoed high protective tariffs, internal improvement bills that he perceived as unnecessary, and attempts to revive the Second Bank of the United States. In fact, during Tyler's administration, Whigs accomplished only two moderate goals: they eliminated Van Buren's hated treasury system (see page 354), and they passed a slightly higher tariff. Tyler's refusal to promote Whig economic policies led to a general crisis in government in 1843, when his entire cabinet resigned over his veto of a bank bill.

Tyler did share his party's desire for expansion, however. He assigned his secretary of state, Daniel Webster, to negotiate a treaty with Britain to settle the Maine matter once and for all. The resulting **Webster-Ashburton Treaty** (1842) gave more than half of the disputed territory to the United States and finally established the nation's northeastern border with Canada. Tyler also adopted an aggressive stance on the Oregon Question by appointing a federal Indian agent

for the region in 1842—an act of doubtful legality in view of the mutual occupation agreement between the United States and Great Britain. His appointee, former missionary Elijah White, was one of the organizers of the Wolf Meetings and helped draft the First Organic Laws. Historians have speculated that Tyler also encouraged Marcus Whitman to help guide a large party of immigrants into Oregon in 1843 as a way of bolstering the U.S. claim to the region.

Tyler also pushed a forceful policy toward Texas and the Southwest. In 1842 Sam Houston repeated his invitation for the United States to annex Texas, only to be rebuffed by Secretary of State Webster, a New Englander who shared Adams's views. When Webster resigned with the other cabinet officers in 1843, however, Tyler replaced him with fellow Virginian Abel P. Upshur, who immediately reopened the matter of Texas annexation.

Negotiations between Houston's representatives and Tyler's secretary of state—Upshur at first, then, after Upshur's death, John C. Calhoun—led to a treaty of annexation on April 11, 1844. In line with the repudiated Treaty of Velasco, the annexation document named the Rio Grande as the southern boundary of Texas. Annexation remained a major arguing point between proslavery and antislavery forces, however, and the treaty failed ratification in the Senate. The issue of Texas annexation then joined the Oregon Question as a major campaign issue in the presidential election of 1844.

Expansion and the Election of 1844

As the Whigs and the Democrats geared up for a national election, it became clear that expansion would be the key issue. This put the two leading political figures of the day, Democrat Martin Van Buren and Whig Henry Clay, in an uncomfortable position. Van Buren was on record as opposing the extension of slavery and was therefore against the annexation of Texas. Clay, the architect of the American System (see page 272), was opposed to any form of uncontrolled

filibuster To use obstructionist tactics, especially prolonged speechmaking, in order to delay legislative action.
Webster-Ashburton Treaty Treaty that in 1842 established the present border between Canada and northeastern Maine.

This campaign banner celebrating the candidacy of James K. Polk and George M. Dallas on the Democratic ticket carries a subtle message conveying the party's platform. Surrounding Polk's picture are twenty-five stars, one for each state in the Union. Outside the corner box, a twenty-sixth star stands for Texas, which Polk promised to annex. *Collection of David J. and Janet L. Frent.*

expansion, especially if it meant fanning sectional tensions, and he too opposed immediate annexation of Texas. Approaching the election, both issued statements to the effect that they would back annexation only with Mexico's consent.

Clay's somewhat ambiguous stance on expansion contrasted sharply with Tyler's efforts to advance the cause of manifest destiny. However, President Tyler's constant refusal to support the larger Whig political agenda led the party to nominate Clay anyway. Van Buren was not so lucky. The strong southern wing of the Democratic Party was so put off by Van Buren's position on slavery that it blocked him, securing the nomination of Tennessee congressman **James K. Polk.**

The Democrats based their platform on the issues surrounding Oregon and Texas. They implied that the regions rightfully belonged to the United States, stating "that the re-occupation of Oregon and the re-annexation of Texas at the earliest practicable period are great American measures." Polk vowed to stand up to the British by claiming the entire Oregon Country up to 54°40′ north latitude and to defend the territorial claims of Texas. The Democrats played up both regions to appeal to the manifest destiny sentiments of both northerners and southerners. For his part,

Clay continued to waffle on expansionism, emphasizing economic policies instead.

The election demonstrated the people's commitment to manifest destiny. Clay was a national figure, well respected and regarded as one of the nation's leading statesmen, whereas Polk was barely known outside Tennessee. Still, Polk polled forty thousand more popular votes than Clay and garnered sixty-five more electoral votes. Seeing the election as a political barometer, outgoing president Tyler prepared a special message to Congress in December 1844 proposing a **joint resolution** annexing Texas. Many congressmen who had opposed annexation could not ignore the clear mandate given to manifest destiny in the presidential election, and the bill to annex Texas passed in February 1845, just as Tyler prepared to turn the White House over to his Democratic successor.

James K. Polk   Tennessee congressman who was a leader of the Democratic Party and the dark-horse winner of the presidential campaign in 1844.

joint resolution   A formal statement adopted by both houses of Congress and subject to approval by the president; if approved, it has the force of law.

Though Polk was not well known, he was a seasoned politician. Often called "Young Hickory" because of his political resemblance to Andrew Jackson, Polk had entered politics in Tennessee as a very young man, serving fourteen years in Congress and two years as governor of the state. Like Jackson, Polk was tenacious, seldom willing to surrender when locked into political struggles. He supported Jacksonian political notions, disavowing protective tariffs and national banks while embracing expansionism.

Holding to the position he had taken prior to the election, in his annual message for 1845 Polk asked Congress to end the joint occupation of Oregon. Referring to the largely forgotten Monroe Doctrine (see page 278–279), the president insisted that no nation other than the United States should be permitted to occupy any part of North America and urged Congress to assert exclusive control over the Oregon Country even if doing so meant war.

Neither the United States nor Britain intended to go to war over Oregon. The only issue—where the border would be—was a matter for the bargaining table, not the battlefield. Recalling the rhetoric that had gotten him elected, Polk insisted on 54°40′. The British lobbied for the Columbia River as the boundary, but their position softened quickly. The fur trade along the Columbia was in rapid decline and had become unprofitable by the early 1840s. As a result, in the spring of 1846, the British foreign secretary offered Polk a compromise boundary at the 49th parallel. The Senate recommended that Polk accept the offer, and a treaty settling the Oregon Question was ratified on June 15, 1846. Sectional politics, however, delayed the admission of Oregon as a territory for a few years.

Expansion and Sectional Crisis

- On what bases did some Americans support and other Americans oppose the war with Mexico?
- How did expansionism and economics help shape Americans' positions on slavery in the 1840s?

Slavery lay at the heart of the significant political controversy that accompanied expansion. Although only a few radicals totally opposed slavery, many people in the North and West strongly opposed its expansion. For them this was less a moral than an economic issue. The expansion of slavery meant open economic competition with slaves or slaveholders for jobs and profits. Southerners, in contrast, demanded that slavery be allowed to expand as far as economic opportunity permitted. And, not surprisingly, southerners

believed the nation's manifest destiny was to expand into areas where cotton would grow and slavery would be most profitable. Given these strong economic motives, the congressional gag rule passed in 1836 (see page 351) could not prevent the debate over expansion from turning into a debate over slavery.

The Texas Crisis and Sectional Conflict

Whatever President Polk chose to do about Texas would have promoted a political crisis, but action of some sort could not be avoided. In annexing Texas, Tyler and Calhoun had offended the Mexican government, which still considered Texas a province. When Congress adopted the joint resolution annexing Texas and establishing the Rio Grande as its southern border, Mexico's popular press linked the event with an uprising in New Mexico in 1837 and continued restlessness in California, raising fears of an American conspiracy against Mexican sovereignty. The press demanded that Mexico sever diplomatic relations with the United States. The government did so immediately, threatening war. Polk added to the tension, and seemed to confirm Mexican fears, by declaring that the entire Southwest should be annexed.

Polk sought his objectives peacefully but prepared to use force in case Mexico rejected his overtures. Late in 1845, the president dispatched John Slidell to Mexico City to negotiate the boundary dispute. He also authorized Slidell to purchase New Mexico and California if possible. At the same time, Polk dispatched American troops to Louisiana, ready to strike if Mexico resisted Slidell's offers. And he notified the American consul in California, Thomas O. Larkin, that the Pacific fleet had orders to seize California ports if war broke out with Mexico. If American citizens in the region then wished to rebel against Mexico, the president said, the United States would support them and invite them to join the Union.

Nervous but bristling over what seemed to be preparations for war, and rightfully upset that Polk had disregarded the break in diplomatic relations by sending an emissary, the Mexican government refused to receive Slidell. In January 1846, Slidell sent word to the president that his mission was a failure. Receiving that report, Polk ordered **Zachary Taylor** to

Zachary Taylor American general whose defeat of Santa Anna at Buena Vista in 1847 made him a national hero and the Whig choice for president in 1848.

MAP 13.3 The Southwest and the Mexican War When the United States acquired Texas, it inherited the Texans' boundary disputes with Mexico. This map shows the outcome: war with Mexico in 1846 and the acquisition of the disputed territories in Texas as well as most of Arizona, New Mexico, and California through the Treaty of Guadalupe Hidalgo.

lead troops from New Orleans toward the Rio Grande. Shortly thereafter, an American military party led by **John C. Frémont** entered California's Salinas Valley. By April, the Mexican government had had enough. On April 22, Mexico proclaimed that its territory had been violated by the United States and declared war. Two days later, Mexican troops engaged a detachment of Taylor's army at Matamoros on the Rio Grande, killing eleven and capturing the rest. When news reached Washington of Taylor's battle at Matamoros, Polk immediately called for war. Although the nation was far from united on the issue, Congress agreed on May 13, 1846 (see Map 13.3).

The outbreak of war disturbed many Americans. In New England, for example, protest ran high. Tran-

scendentalist Henry David Thoreau was an outspoken critic and chose to be jailed rather than pay taxes that would support the war. It was not expansion as such that troubled Thoreau, but the connection between Texas annexation and slavery. To southerners, the broad stretch of land lying south of 36°30′ (the Missouri Compromise line) represented both economic and political power. The adoption of proslavery constitutions in newly acquired territories would

John C. Frémont Explorer, soldier, and politician who explored and mapped much of the American West and Northwest; he later ran unsuccessfully for president.

ensure the immigration of friendly voters and the installation of congenial governments, which would strengthen the South's economic and political interests in Congress. Northerners were perturbed by these implications but saw something even more alarming in the southern expansion movement. Since the Missouri Compromise (1820), some northerners had come to believe that a slaveholding **oligarchy** controlled life and politics in the South. Abolitionists warned that this "Slave Power" sought to expand its reach until it controlled every aspect of American life. Many viewed Congress's adoption of the gag rule in 1836 and the drive to annex Texas as evidence of the Slave Power's influence. Thus debates over Texas pitted two regions of the country against each other in what champions of both sides regarded as mortal combat.

Serious political combat began in August 1846 when David Wilmot, a Democratic representative from Pennsylvania, proposed an amendment to a military appropriations bill specifying that "neither slavery nor involuntary servitude shall ever exist" in any territory gained in the War with Mexico. The **Wilmot Proviso** passed in the House of Representatives but failed in the Senate, where equal state representation gave the South a stronger position. At Polk's request, Wilmot refused to propose his proviso when the House reconsidered the war appropriations bill, but Van Buren Democrats defied Polk by attaching the amendment again, and the House approved it once more. Again the Senate rejected the amended bill. In opposing the amendment, John C. Calhoun (reelected to the Senate after serving as Tyler's secretary of state) argued that any territory acquired in the war would belong to all the American people, and that for Congress to forbid any citizen from taking slaves into the area would violate the constitutional protection of life, liberty, and property. The House finally decided in April to appropriate money for the war without stipulating whether or not slavery would be permitted.

War with Mexico

While all this political infighting was going on in Washington, D.C., a real war was going on in the Southwest. In California, American settlers rallied in open rebellion in the Sacramento Valley. The rebels captured the town of Sonoma in June 1846 and declared themselves independent. They crafted a flag depicting a grizzly bear and announced the birth of the Bear Flag Republic. Rushing to Sonoma, Frémont's force joined the Bear Flag rebels and began to march south toward Monterey. The little army arrived on July 19, only to find that the Pacific fleet had

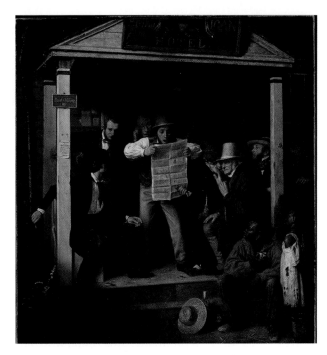

Slaves look on in obvious interest as men gathered at the post office devour the latest news from the front in the war with Mexico. One newspaperman in Baltimore reported, "The news from the army on the Rio Grande has caused more general excitement in this city than has before taken place, perhaps during the present generation." *"War News from Mexico" by Richard Caton Woodville, 1848. The Manogian Foundation © 1996. Board of Trustees, National Gallery of Art, Washington, D.C.*

already acted on Polk's orders and seized the city. The Mexican forces were in full flight southward.

To round out the greater southwestern strategy, Polk ordered Colonel Stephen Kearny to invade New Mexico on May 15. After leading his men across 800 miles of desert to Santa Fe, Kearny found a less-than-hostile enemy force facing him. Members of the interracial upper class of Santa Fe had already expressed interest in joining the United States. Given the opportunity, they surrendered without firing a shot.

oligarchy A small group of people or families who hold power.

Wilmot Proviso Amendment to an appropriations bill in 1846 proposing that any territory acquired from Mexico be closed to slavery; it was defeated in the Senate.

Within a short time, all of the New Mexico region and California were securely in the hands of U.S. forces. Zachary Taylor in Texas, however, faced more serious opposition. Marching across the Rio Grande, Taylor headed for the Mexican city of Monterrey, which he attacked in September 1846. He managed to capture the city, but only at the cost of agreeing to let the enemy garrison pass unmolested through his lines. From Monterrey, Taylor planned to turn southward toward Mexico City and lead the main attack against the Mexican capital, but politics intervened.

After Taylor's successful siege at Monterrey, Polk began to perceive the popular general as a political threat. In an attempt to undermine Taylor's political appeal, Polk turned the war effort over to Winfield Scott, ordering Scott to gather an army at the port of Tampico, on the Gulf of Mexico. Drawing men from Taylor's and other forces, Scott was then to sail down to Veracruz, from which the army was to move inland to take Mexico City (see Map 13.3).

Polk complicated the military situation by plotting with deposed Mexican president Santa Anna, who had been exiled to Cuba after his defeat at San Jacinto. In secret correspondence with the president, Santa Anna promised that he would end the war and settle the border dispute in Polk's favor if Polk would help him return to Mexico. The American president agreed to sneak Santa Anna back into Mexico, where he soon resumed the presidency. Going back on his agreement, however, Santa Anna also picked up his sword and vowed to resist American territorial expansion into the disputed territory. Thus, while Scott and Taylor were realigning the American forces, Mexico's most able general resumed command of the army and chose to strike.

Planning to crush Taylor's remaining force and then wheel around to attack Scott, Santa Anna and his numerically superior army encountered Taylor at Buena Vista in February 1847. Tired and dispirited from forced marching across the desert, the Mexican army was in no shape to fight, but Santa Anna ordered an attack anyway. Tactically speaking, the **Battle of Buena Vista** was a draw, but it was a strategic victory for the Americans: Taylor's fresher troops stalled Santa Anna's forces, permitting Scott's forces to capture Veracruz on March 9. His eyes firmly on a quick victory, Scott moved relentlessly toward Mexico City. By May 15, however, Scott had run into trouble. Many of his troops were serving under twelve-month enlistments, which had just expired. Feeling they had no obligation to stay, nearly a third of his army went home, leaving the general powerless to proceed. Finally, after three months of waiting, Scott received

supplies and reinforcements and resumed his march on Mexico City. After a crushing assault, Scott and his force routed the Mexican defenders and captured the city on September 13, 1847.

With Mexico City, all of Texas, New Mexico, and California in American hands, the direction of treaty talks should have been fairly predictable. Scott's enormous success, however, caused Santa Anna's government to collapse, leaving no one to negotiate with American peace commissioner Nicholas Trist. After a month had passed with no settlement, Polk concluded that Trist was not pressing hard enough and removed him as peace commissioner. But by the time Polk's orders arrived, the Mexican government had elected a new president and on November 11 told Trist that Mexico was ready to begin negotiations. When Trist received Polk's removal order, he ignored it and pressed on with negotiations. Finally, on February 2, 1848, Trist and the Mexican delegation signed the **Treaty of Guadalupe Hidalgo,** granting the United States all the territory between the Nueces River and the Rio Grande and between there and the Pacific. In exchange, Trist agreed that the United States would pay Mexico $15 million, and he committed the United States to honoring all claims made by Texans for damages resulting from the war.

Polk was very angry when he heard the terms of the treaty. Although the United States had obtained everything it had gone to war for, Polk felt that Scott's sweeping victory at Mexico City should have netted the United States more territory for less money. Political realities in Washington, however, prevented Polk from trying to get a more aggressive treaty ratified by the Senate. Although the president had strong support for his own position in favor of annexing all of Mexico, many antislavery voices loudly protested bringing so much land south of the Missouri Compromise line into the Union. Others opposed the annexation of Mexico because they feared that the largely Roman Catholic population might be a threat to Protestant institutions in the United States. Still others, many of whom had opposed the war to begin with, had moral objections to taking any territory by

Battle of Buena Vista   Battle in February 1847 during which U.S. troops led by Zachary Taylor forced Santa Anna's forces to withdraw into the interior of Mexico.

Treaty of Guadalupe Hidalgo   Treaty (1848) in which Mexico gave up Texas above the Rio Grande and ceded New Mexico and California to the United States in return for $15 million.

An American private, Samuel E. Chamberlain, made this drawing of the Battle of Buena Vista. Present at the battle, Chamberlain watched as Mexican forces overran an artillery emplacement. The Americans eventually turned the tide, and the battle came out a draw. Even so, troops under Santa Anna were forced to retreat into the Mexican interior, spoiling the general's hope for a quick and easy victory against the invading Americans. *"Battle of Buena Vista" by Samuel Chamberlain, 1847. San Jacinto Museum of History Association.*

force. Perhaps more convincing than these arguments, however, was the fact that the war had cost a lot of money, and congressmen were unwilling to allocate more if peace was within reach. Thus Polk submitted the treaty Trist had negotiated, and the Senate approved it by a vote of 38 to 14.

Politicizing Slavery

The American victory in the War with Mexico was an enormous shot in the arm for American nationalism and manifest destiny, but it also brought the divisive issue of slavery back into mainstream politics to a degree unknown since the Missouri Compromise. Opposed to slavery expansion for both political and ethical reasons, David Wilmot had broken a gentlemen's agreement among congressmen to skirt around slavery issues, firmly wedding American expansion and slavery in the minds of many. Even a largely unpolitical nonconformist like Henry David Thoreau found the connection obvious, and protested the war for that reason.

Of course, being opposed to the expansion of slavery was not the same thing as opposing the institution of slavery itself, and antislavery sentiments were still not widespread among the American people during the 1840s. However, as the debates over the Mexican War indicate, abolitionist voices were getting louder and more politically insistent. Despite strong and sometimes violent opposition, the abolition movement had continued to grow, especially among the privileged and educated classes in the Northeast. Throughout the 1830s, evangelicals increasingly stressed the sinful nature of slavery and broke away from the **gradualism** of the American Colonization Society (see page 350). Driven by their postmillennialism (see page 343), men and women steeped in evangelical zeal joined

gradualism   The belief that slavery in the United States should be abolished gradually, by methods such as placing territorial limits on slavery or settling free blacks in Africa.

Sojourner Truth was a remarkable woman for her time, or for any time. One anecdote claims that a white policeman in New York state demanded that she identify herself. Using her cane to thrust herself upright to her full six feet of height, she boomed out the same words that God used to identify himself to Moses: "I am that I am." The policeman was unnerved and scurried away. Showing such bravery and pride in both her race and sex, it is little wonder that she commanded great respect in both antislavery and women's rights circles throughout her lifetime. *Sophia Smith Collection, Smith College.*

with William Lloyd Garrison and Angelina Grimké in urging the immediate, uncompensated liberation of slaves.

Garrison, however, consistently alienated his followers. Calling the Constitution "a covenant with death and an agreement with hell," Garrison burned a copy of it, telling his followers, "so perish all compromises with tyranny," and he urged them to have no dealings with a government that permitted so great an evil as slavery. Citing the reluctance of most organized churches to condemn slavery outright, Garrison urged his followers to break with them as well. He also offended many of his white evangelical supporters by associating with and supporting free black advocates of abolition.

During the 1830s, even moderates within the abolition movement had celebrated **Frederick Douglass, Sojourner Truth,** and other African American abolitionists, welcoming them as members of the American Anti-Slavery Society. But more insistent black voices frightened white abolitionists. African American abolitionist David Walker cried, "The whites want slaves, and want us for their slaves, but some of them will curse the day they ever saw us." Walker advocated that African Americans should "kill or be killed." Another black spokesman, Henry Highland Garnet, proclaimed, "Strike for your lives and liberties. Now is the day and hour. Let every slave in the land do this and the days of slavery are numbered. Rather die freemen than live to be slaves."

Garrison's sentiments mobilized some, but most of his followers were more conservative. In 1840 this and other controversial issues caused many of those moderates to bolt from Garrison's American Anti-Slavery Society to form the more temperate American and Foreign Anti-Slavery Society. This new group forged strong ties with mainstream politicians and church leaders who, while opposed to any extension of slavery and sympathetic to moderate abolitionist proposals, had been relatively silent because of Garrison's reputation for radicalism.

Issues in the Election of 1848

Efforts by moderate antislavery supporters meshed with the political aspirations of both those who opposed slavery's expansion primarily for political and economic reasons and those who were motivated by purely ethical concerns to bring limited abolitionism into the political mainstream. Hoping to cash in on the popular attention created by debates over slavery during the War with Mexico, moderates in 1840 challenged both Whig and Democrat ambivalence by forming a third political party: the **Liberty Party.**

Specifically disavowing Garrison's radical aims, Liberty Party leaders argued that slavery would even-

Frederick Douglass   Abolitionist and journalist who escaped from slavery in 1838 and became an influential lecturer in the North and abroad.

Sojourner Truth   Abolitionist and feminist who was freed from slavery in 1827 and became a leading preacher against slavery and for the rights of women.

Liberty Party   The first antislavery political party; it was formed in Albany, New York, in 1840.

It Matters

The Moderate Split in the Abolition Movement

It is fitting to herald bold leaders like William Lloyd Garrison, celebrating their deep commitment to ethical causes and their willingness to engage in radical action to accomplish their goals. In doing so, we often ignore more moderate voices speaking to those same goals. In the case of abolitionism, however, one of the key events in moving the cause out of obscurity and bringing it into mainstream public attention was the split between radicals and moderates in 1840. By disavowing Garrison's growing radicalism, moderates were able to forge solid alliances with political, business, and religious leaders throughout the North and West as well as with British and other international slavery opponents, who would, together, make the elimination of slavery part of everyday conversation. According to Nobel Prize–winning author Robert William Fogel, it was this broad proliferation of abolitionist discourse, along with its unflinching refusal to go away, that eventually caused slavery's demise.

tually die on its own if it could be confined geographically. In addition, the Liberty Party called for the abolition of slavery in Washington, D.C., and in all the territories where it already existed. Though certainly more popular than Garrison's radical appeals, this moderate message drew little open political support: in 1840 Liberty Party presidential candidate James G. Birney had garnered only about 7,000 out of the nearly 2.5 million votes cast. But in 1844, when he again ran on the Liberty Party ticket, he won 62,000 popular votes. Clearly a moderate antislavery position was becoming more acceptable.

Even in the face of such evidence, both major parties continued to practice the politics of avoidance. Suffering ill health, Polk chose not to run for a second term in 1848, leaving the Democrats scrambling for a candidate. They chose Lewis Cass of Michigan—a longtime moderate on slavery issues—as their presidential candidate and balanced the ticket with General William Butler of Kentucky. The Whigs hoped to ride a wave of nationalism following the War with Mexico by running military hero Zachary Taylor, a Louisianan and a slaveholder, for president and moderate New Yorker Millard Fillmore for vice president.

During the election campaign, Cass tried to avoid offending anyone by suggesting that the federal government withdraw entirely from the slavery question. He advanced instead a policy of **popular sovereignty,** which would permit the territories to choose for themselves whether or not to admit slavery. Taylor refused to go even that far, echoing Calhoun's opinion that no one had the authority to control slavery in the territories.

As in 1840 and again in 1844, it took a third party to cut to the heart of the issues. A number of northern Democrats who had supported the Wilmot Proviso felt that Cass's and the Democratic Party's position on slavery was too weak-kneed. Casting about for alternatives, they joined with a number of northern Whigs who could not support the slaveholding Taylor and with former members of the Liberty Party, which had collapsed after its failure in 1844, to promote the candidacy of antislavery advocate Martin Van Buren. Adopting the slogan "Free soil, free speech, free labor, and free men," this northern antislavery coalition dubbed itself the **Free-Soil Party.** Even more than the Liberty Party before it, the Free-Soil Party avoided taking a radical stand on the issue of slavery itself but was firm about excluding slavery from the territories.

The two major parties split more than 2.5 million votes almost evenly—Taylor polled 1,360,000 to Cass's 1,220,000 and won the presidency with 163 electoral votes to Cass's 127. The Free-Soilers, however, made a stronger showing than their predecessors had made. When the votes were counted, Van Buren had won almost 300,000, nearly 10 percent of the total votes cast, but no electoral votes. Congress remained split between Whigs and Democrats, though many northern Whigs were leaning in a Free-Soil direction. Sectional issues had not yet fragmented the political system, but large cracks were now visible.

popular sovereignty The doctrine that the people of a territory had the right to determine whether slavery would exist within their territory.

Free-Soil Party A political party that opposed the extension of slavery into any of the territories newly acquired from Mexico.

Individual Voices

Examining a Primary Source

Lorenzo de Zavala Predicts the Spread of Liberal Democracy

Lorenzo de Zavala spent his entire adult life working for expanding freedoms in his native Mexico. Working at first within the Spanish Empire and then as both an elected and appointed administrative official in the independent Mexican republic, Zavala constantly chafed at what he characterized as the unnatural impositions that governments placed on a rational and freedom-loving citizenry. Having fled the military dictatorship that emerged in Mexico in the late 1820s, Zavala traveled extensively and recorded his views about government and his hopes for Mexico's future.

■ What is Zavala suggesting here about human nature and cultural adaptation? Based on this reasoning, why would he have opposed Mexican policies in Texas?

■ To whom and to what is Zavala referring in this passage? What does this say about his reasons for supporting revolution in Texas?

■ These seven Mexican states are the northernmost—that is, closest to the United States. The six states that follow all occupy the Mexican interior.

■ Zavala seems to be describing a process not unlike that which U.S. expansionists would call "manifest destiny." Is Zavala espousing manifest destiny? How do his views compare with those expressed by others at this time?

I have set forth my opinions concerning that beautiful and rich portion of land known formerly as the province of Texas. . . . Once the way was opened to colonization, as it should have been, under a system of free government, it was necessary that a new generation should appear within a few years and populate a part of the Mexican republic, and consequently that this new population should be entirely heterogeneous with respect to the other provinces or states of the country. Fifteen or twenty thousand foreigners distributed over the vast areas of Mexico, Oaxaca, Veracruz, etc., scattered among the former inhabitants cannot cause any sudden change in their ways, manners and customs. Rather they adopt the tendencies, manners, language, religion, politics and even the vices of the multitude that surrounds them. An Englishman will be a Mexican in Mexico City, and a Mexican an Englishman in London. ■

The same thing will not happen with colonies. Completely empty woods and lands, uninhabited a dozen years ago, converted into villages and towns suddenly by Germans, Irish, and North Americans, must of necessity form an entirely different nation, and it would be absurd to try to get them to renounce their religion, their customs and their deepest convictions. ■ *What will be the result?*

I have stated it many times. They will not be able to subject themselves to a military regime and ecclesiastical government such as unfortunately have continued in Mexican territory in spite of the republican-democratic constitutions. . . . When a military leader tries to intervene in civil transactions, they will resist, and they will triumph. They will organize popular assemblies to deal with political matters as is done in the United States and in England. They will build chapels for different faiths to worship the Creator according to their beliefs. . . . Within a few years this fortunate conquest of civilization will continue its course through other states toward the south, and those of Tamaulipas, Nuevo Leon, San Luis, Chihuahua, Durango, Jalisco, and Zacatecas ■ *will be the freest ones in the Mexican confederation. Meanwhile, those of Mexico, Puebla, Veracruz, Oaxaca, Michoacan and Chiapas will have to experience for some time the military and ecclesiastical influence.* ■

Summary

During the first half of the nineteenth century, the westward movement of Americans steadily gained momentum. Some successful entrepreneurs such as William Henry Ashley made enormous profits from their fur-trading empires. Land speculators and gold seekers, too, helped open areas to settlement. Such pioneers were usually followed by distinct waves of migrants who went west in search of land and opportunity. In Texas, Oregon, California, Utah, and elsewhere in the West, communities sprang up like weeds. Here they interacted—and often clashed—with one another, with those who had prior claims to the land, and with the land itself. As a result, a variety of cultures and economies developed in the expansive section of the country.

Outside the West, conflicting views about the country's manifest destiny promoted an air of crisis for the nation at large. Northerners wanted a West that would be free for diversified economic development. Southerners wanted to sow every suitable acre with cotton. And people from each region tried to use expansion to add to their power in Congress, hoping to further their economic and political demands—tariff, tax, and internal improvement measures that would favor their section of the country.

In the course of the debate, one issue—slavery—began to eclipse all others in symbolizing the differing demands made by the North and South. For northerners, the idea of going to war to win Oregon was acceptable because it was geographically unsuitable for slavery, but the idea of going to war to acquire Texas was quite another matter. The possibility of more southern senators and representatives filled northerners with dread. Nevertheless, the nation chose to fight a war with Mexico in 1846–1848, and won, gaining California and vast territories in the Southwest. Though the value of much of this territory was questionable, the discovery of gold in California in 1848 made it a prize well worth political contention.

Meanwhile, voices challenging slavery's moral implications gained a wider audience. Radical abolitionists, especially William Lloyd Garrison, still labored for acceptance, but by separating themselves from Garrison's radicalism and aligning with like-minded politicians, moderate abolitionists brought their cause into the political mainstream. The limited success enjoyed by the Liberty Party and then by the Free-Soil Party demonstrated that opposition to slavery's expansion was becoming more acceptable in the North, but it still was not popular enough to shatter the existing political party system. Though not broken, national unity certainly was experiencing severe stress as the nation continued to move westward.

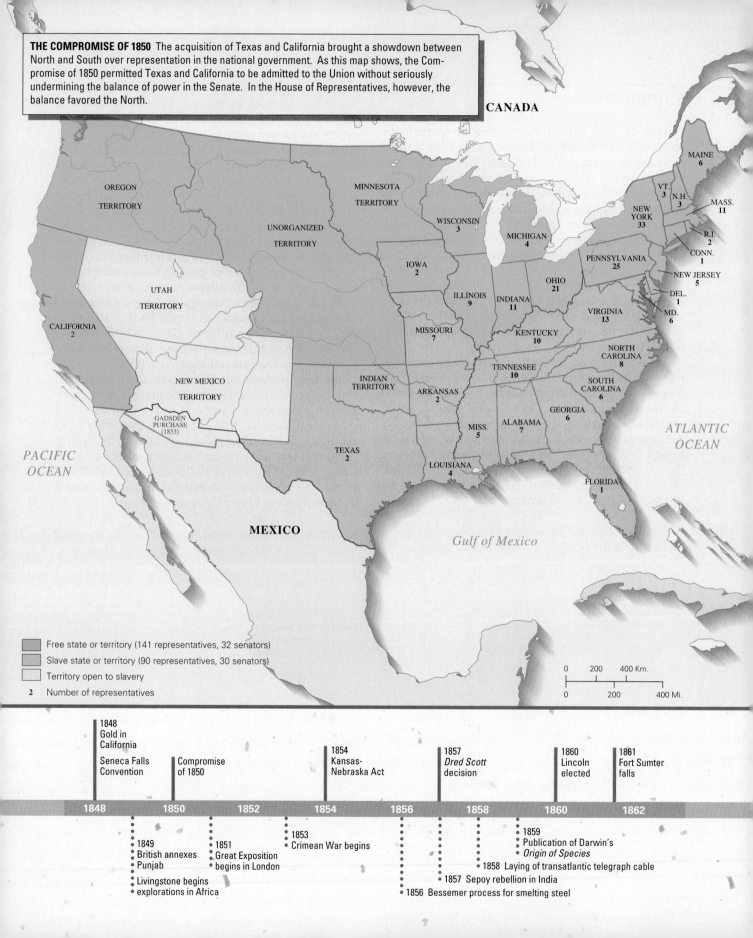

THE COMPROMISE OF 1850 The acquisition of Texas and California brought a showdown between North and South over representation in the national government. As this map shows, the Compromise of 1850 permitted Texas and California to be admitted to the Union without seriously undermining the balance of power in the Senate. In the House of Representatives, however, the balance favored the North.

CANADA

OREGON TERRITORY

MINNESOTA TERRITORY

UNORGANIZED TERRITORY

WISCONSIN 3

MICHIGAN 4

MAINE 6

VT. 3

N.H. 3

NEW YORK 33

MASS. 11

R.I. 2

CONN. 1

NEW JERSEY 5

DEL. 1

MD. 6

UTAH TERRITORY

IOWA 2

ILLINOIS 9

INDIANA 11

OHIO 21

PENNSYLVANIA 25

CALIFORNIA 2

MISSOURI 7

KENTUCKY 10

VIRGINIA 13

NORTH CAROLINA 8

NEW MEXICO TERRITORY

INDIAN TERRITORY

ARKANSAS 2

TENNESSEE 10

SOUTH CAROLINA 6

GADSDEN PURCHASE (1853)

GEORGIA 6

MISS. 5

ALABAMA 7

TEXAS 2

LOUISIANA 4

FLORIDA 1

PACIFIC OCEAN

MEXICO

ATLANTIC OCEAN

Gulf of Mexico

■ Free state or territory (141 representatives, 32 senators)

■ Slave state or territory (90 representatives, 30 senators)

□ Territory open to slavery

2 Number of representatives

0   200   400 Km.

0   200   400 Mi.

1848 Gold in California

Seneca Falls Convention

Compromise of 1850

1854 Kansas-Nebraska Act

1857 *Dred Scott* decision

1860 Lincoln elected

1861 Fort Sumter falls

1848   **1850**   **1852**   **1854**   **1856**   **1858**   **1860**   **1862**

1853 Crimean War begins

1849 British annexes Punjab

1851 Great Exposition begins in London

1859 Publication of Darwin's *Origin of Species*

1858 Laying of transatlantic telegraph cable

Livingstone begins explorations in Africa

1857 Sepoy rebellion in India

1856 Bessemer process for smelting steel

Sectional Conflict and Shattered Union, 1848–1860

14

The Compromise of 1850

Use the map on the facing page to analyze patterns of political representation between the three major sections of the country: the North, West, and South. Given the patterns of population growth and density noted on the opening map for Chapter 13, what expectations would reasonable people from each region of country have entertained as the result of the compromise?

Individual Choices

Frederick Douglass

Although he was born a slave, Frederick Douglass gave a lot of thought to freedom while growing up in Baltimore, Maryland, during the 1820s. As a young boy he cultivated white friends, both for their companionship and because they were willing to teach him to read and write, but he was struck by the difference in their status. He would tell them, "You will be free as soon as you are twenty-one, *but I am a slave for life!*"

But escaping was not an easy thing to do, as he learned in 1834. He and two other slaves hit upon a plan to steal a canoe and paddle into Chesapeake Bay, drifting out of Maryland and into freedom. But their plan was betrayed; Douglass and his colleagues were arrested and dragged off to jail. Douglass was sure that he would be gravely punished for trying to escape—his master threatened to sell him to a cotton plantation in Alabama—but instead he was made an apprentice ship caulker.

Working as an apprentice, Douglass observed that he was "kept in such a perpetual whirl of excitement, I could think of nothing, scarcely, but my life; and in thinking of my life, I almost forgot my liberty." He soon became a master caulker, earning the highest wages in the yard. "I was now of some importance to my master," Douglass recalled. "I was bringing him from six to seven dollars per week." His productivity earned him a lot of freedom: he made his own contracts, set his own work schedule, and collected his own earnings. But he also remembered his liberty. "I have observed this in my experience of slavery," Douglass commented, "that whenever my condition was improved, instead of its increasing my contentment, it only increased my desire to be free."

In 1838 Douglass decided that he would again try to escape. He chose not to contact any of the white organizations that helped slaves to escape to the North because he believed that in seeking applause, such organizations undermined their purpose. "The *underground railroad* . . . by their open declarations, has been made most emphatically the *"upper-ground railroad,"* Douglass observed, pointing out that such advertisement actually made it easier for masters to track runaway slaves. He chose instead to depend on personal friends for help. He had become engaged to a free black woman named Anna Murray, who sold a featherbed and other property to finance his escape. He also contacted a retired black sailor from whom he secured seaman's protection papers, legal documents entitling black sailors to pass unmolested through slave territory.

Bearing cash and the borrowed papers, Douglass disguised himself as a sailor and boarded a train heading north out of Baltimore on September 3, 1838. Switching from train to ferry boat, ferry boat to steamship, steamship back to train, and finally train back to ferry boat, Douglass made his way northward, arriving in New York City early on the morning of September 4. Although he had a couple of close calls—he ran into two men who knew he was not a sailor, one of whom apparently did not notice him and another who chose not to turn him in—Douglass's escape had succeeded.

FREDERICK DOUGLASS

Working as a skilled craftsman in the shipyards of Baltimore, Frederick Douglass remained, nonetheless, a slave and was forced to turn his hard-earned wages over to his owner. Seeking economic self-sufficiency and personal freedom, he chose to escape from slavery in 1838 to seek employment as a free man in Massachusetts. Facing the constraint of severe racial discrimination, Douglass had difficulty making a living until abolitionist William Lloyd Garrison heard him speak at an antislavery rally. Garrison promoted Douglass as a lecturer and he soon became recognized as one of the most effective abolitionist activists in the country. Postcards like this one, which presents a daguerreotype of Douglass looking his most imposing and severe, were used to advertise his appearances and to promote the abolitionist cause. Douglass continued to be a leader in the African American rights movement until his death in 1895. *Art Institute of Chicago.*

Douglass now had what the white boys he had known in his younger days also enjoyed: he was free. But the color of his skin still deprived him of equality. Moving to the town of New Bedford, Massachusetts, where he hoped to earn a living in the boatyards, Douglass found that "such was the strength of prejudice against color, among the white caulkers, that they refused to work with me, and of course I could get no employment." For three years he was forced to do odd jobs to keep himself and his wife alive. "There was no work too hard—none too dirty," he recalled.

But in 1841 Douglass found a new profession and a new life. Attending an antislavery conference in Nantucket, Douglass was cajoled by a white abolitionist to speak about his experiences. "It was a severe cross," Douglass recalled, "but I took it up reluctantly." Famed abolitionist William Lloyd Garrison heard Douglass's speech, declaring that "Patrick Henry, of revolutionary fame, never made a speech more eloquent in the cause of liberty." Garrison was so moved that he offered to support Douglass as a lecturer in the antislavery cause. Douglass accepted, lending a thundering voice to the cause of racial equality for the next fifty years.

INTRODUCTION

Though not a politician, Frederick Douglass certainly was not immune to the political wrangling going on around him. Like many Americans, Douglass's life was in a state of constant upheaval as politicians engaged in abstract power games that had all-too-real consequences.

Struggles over tariffs, coinage, internal improvements, public land policy, and dozens of other practical issues intersected in complicated ways with the overinflated egos of power-hungry politicians to create an air of political contention and national crisis. The discovery of gold in California followed by a massive rush of Americans into the new territory added greed to the equation. Then strong-willed men such as Jefferson Davis and Stephen A. Douglas threw more fuel on the fire as they fought over the best—that is, most profitable and politically advantageous—route for a transcontinental railroad that would tie California's wealth to the rest of the nation. The halls of Congress rang with debate, denunciation, and even physical violence.

Beneath it all lurked an institution that Frederick Douglass knew all too well: slavery. In a changing society rife with the problems of expansion, immigration, industrialization, and urbanization, political leaders tried either to seek compromise or to ignore the slavery question altogether. In reality, they could do neither. As the nation's leaders wrestled with a host of new issues, the confrontation between northern and southern societies peaked. Although many people wanted peace and favored reconciliation, ultimately both sides rejected compromise, leading to the end of the Union and the beginning of America's most destructive and deadly war.

New Political Options

■ How did the presidential election in 1848 help to foster political dissent?

■ How did events in Europe help to push the American economy forward during the 1850s? In what ways did this contribute to growing political tensions?

■ What new political options affected the political system during the 1850s? In what ways?

The presidential election in 1848 had celebrated American expansion and nationalism, but at the same time it revealed a strong undercurrent of dissent. The political system held together during the election, and the existing parties managed to maintain the politics of avoidance, but the successes enjoyed by Free-Soil challengers were evidence that significant problems churned under the surface. It was clear to many that the nation's political system was not meeting their economic and ideological needs, and they began looking for new options. Efforts at compromise might save the nation from the immediate consequences of growth, modernization, and sectional tension, but crisis clearly was in the air.

Disaffected Voices and Political Dissent

It did not take long after the election of 1848 for cracks in the system to become more prominent. In an effort to compete with Democrats in northeastern cities, the Whigs had tried to win Catholic and immigrant voters away from the rival party. The strategy backfired. Not only did the Whigs not attract large numbers of immigrants, but they alienated two core groups among their existing supporters. One such group was artisans, who saw immigrants as the main source of their economic and social woes. The other was Protestant evangelicals, to whom Roman Catholic Irish and German immigrants symbolized all that was wrong in the world and threatening to the American republic. Whig leaders could do little to address these voters' immediate concerns, and increasing numbers left the Whig Party to form state and local coalitions more in tune with their hopes and fears.

One of the most prominent of these locally oriented groups was the anti-Catholic, anti-immigrant **Know-Nothings.** This loosely knit political organization traced its origins back to secret **nativist** societies that had come into existence during the ethnic tension and rioting in Philadelphia, Boston, and New York in the 1830s. These secret fraternal groups at first dabbled in politics by endorsing candidates who shared their **xenophobic** views. Remaining underground, they told their members to say "I know nothing" if they were questioned about the organization or its political intrigues, hence the name Know-Nothings.

Increasingly after 1848, these secretive groups became more public and more vocal. To the artisans and others who formed the core of the Know-Nothing movement, the issues of slavery and sectionalism that seemed to dominate the national political debate were nothing but devices being used by political insiders and the established parties to divert ordinary Americans from real issues of concern. The Know-Nothings pointed instead at immigration, loss of job security, urban crowding and violence, and political corruption as the true threats to American liberties. They built a platform charging that immigrants were part of a Catholic plot to overthrow democracy in the United States. Seeking to counter this perceived threat, they contended that "Americans must rule America" and urged a twenty-one-year naturalization period, a ban against naturalized citizens holding public office, and the use of the Protestant Bible in public schools.

Know-Nothings from different regions disagreed about many things, but they all agreed that the Whig and Democratic Parties were corrupt and that the only hope for the nation lay in scrapping traditional politics and starting anew. Like the Antimasonic movement in the 1820s (see pages 287; 352), in which many Know-Nothing leaders got their start in politics, the Know-Nothing Party expressed antiparty sentiments, alleging wholesale voter fraud and government corruption by both major parties. As future president Rutherford B. Hayes noted, the people were expressing a "general disgust with the powers that be."

Many Know-Nothings had deep ties with the evangelical Protestant movement and indeed represented one dimension of Christian dissent, but not all Protestant dissenters shared their single-mindedness. Many evangelical reformers believed the nation was beset by a host of evils that imperiled its existence. Progress without Christian principles and individual morality, they thought, posed a great danger for the United States, and they viewed slavery, alcohol, Catholicism, religious heresy, and corrupt government as threats to the nation's moral fiber. In their efforts to create moral government and to direct national destiny, these reformers advocated social reform through both religious and political action. Temperance was one of the more prominent topics of their political concern (see page 349). The war on alcohol had made great gains since the 1830s: thirteen states had enacted laws prohibiting the manufacture and sale of liquor. Overall, however, progress seemed slow, and like Know-Nothings and others, temperance advocates became increasingly impatient with the traditional political parties.

Another group that was growing impatient with traditional politics brought an altogether new voice to the American scene. Having assumed the burden of eliminating sin from the world back in the 1830s (see page 325), many evangelical women had rallied around reform causes. Their growing prominence in the abolition movement, for example, had led William Lloyd Garrison to insist that they play a more equal role. In 1840 he proposed that a woman be elected to the executive committee of the American Anti-Slavery Society. And later that year women were members of Garrison's delegation to the first World Anti-Slavery Convention in London. British antislavery advocates,

---

Know-Nothings Members of anti-Catholic, anti-immigrant organizations who eventually formed themselves into a national political party.

nativist Favoring native-born inhabitants of a country over immigrants.

xenophobic Fearful of or hateful toward foreigners or those seen as being different.

Chronology

Toward a Shattered Union

1848   Seneca Falls Convention
Zachary Taylor elected president
Immigration to United States exceeds 100,000

1850   Compromise of 1850

1852   First railroad line completed to Chicago
Harriet Beecher Stowe's *Uncle Tom's Cabin*
Franklin Pierce elected president
Whig Party collapses
Know-Nothing Party emerges

1853   Gadsden Purchase

1854   Republican Party formed
Kansas-Nebraska Act
Ostend Manifesto

1855   Proslavery posse sacks Lawrence, Kansas
Pottawatomie Massacre

1856   James Buchanan elected president
Demise of Know-Nothing Party

1857   *Dred Scott* decision
Proslavery Lecompton constitution adopted
in Kansas

1858   Lincoln-Douglas debates
Minnesota admitted to Union

1859   Oregon admitted to Union
John Brown's raid on Harpers Ferry

1860   Abraham Lincoln elected president
Crittenden compromise fails

1861   Confederate States of America formed
Fort Sumter shelled
Federal troops occupy Maryland and Missouri
Confederate troops occupy east Tennessee

---

however, like most of their American counterparts, considered the presence of women inappropriate and refused to seat them.

Angelina Grimké was one of the first to announce the frustration women were feeling (see pages 330–331). In her speech before the Massachusetts state assembly in 1838, she had asked, "Are we aliens, because we are women? Are we bereft of citizenship because we are mothers, wives and daughters of a mighty people? Have women no country—no interests staked in public weal—no liabilities in the common peril—no partnership in a nation's guilt and shame?" In that same year, her sister Sarah went further, writing a powerful indictment against the treatment of women in America and a call for equality. In *Letters on the Equality of the Sexes and the Condition of Woman,* Sarah proclaimed, "The page of history teems with woman's wrongs . . . and it is wet with woman's tears." Women must, she said, "arise in all the majesty of moral power . . . and plant themselves, side by side, on the platform of human rights, with man, to whom they were designed to be companions, equals and helpers in every good word and work."

Like Sarah Grimké, many other women began backing away from male-dominated causes and began ad-

vancing their own cause. In 1848 two women who had been excluded from the World Anti-Slavery Convention, **Lucretia Mott** and **Elizabeth Cady Stanton,** called concerned women to a convention at Seneca Falls, New York, to discuss their common problems. At Seneca Falls, they presented a Declaration of Sentiments, based on the Declaration of Independence, citing "the history of repeated injuries and usurpations on the part of man toward woman, having in direct object the establishment of an absolute tyranny over her." The convention adopted eleven resolutions relating to equality under the law, rights to control property, and other prominent gender issues. A twelfth resolution, calling for the right to vote, failed to receive unanimous endorsement.

Lucretia Mott   Quaker minister who founded the Philadelphia Female Anti-Slavery Society (1833) and co-organized the Seneca Falls Women's Rights Convention in 1848.

Elizabeth Cady Stanton   Pioneering woman suffrage leader, co-organizer of the first Women's Rights Convention, held in Seneca Falls, New York, in 1848.

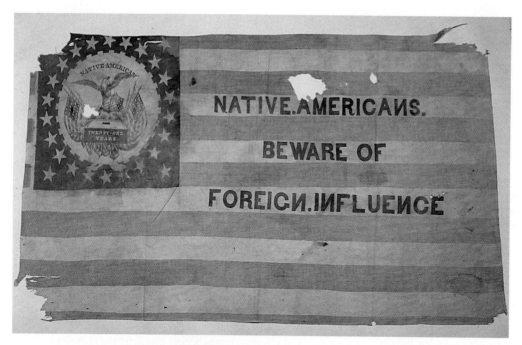

Convinced that slavery and other sectional issues were blinding Americans to the true dangers stemming from uncontrolled immigration and foreign influence, the Know-Nothing Party ran Millard Fillmore for president in 1856. Banners like this one warned Americans and solicited their votes. Fillmore succeeded in getting 21 percent of the popular vote. *Milwaukee County Historical Society.*

While none of these movements alone was capable of overturning the ruling political order, they were symptomatic of serious problems perceived by growing numbers of citizens. Though there were serious differences in the problems that each of these groups emphasized, they shared a number of perceptions in common. All that was missing was a catalyst that could bind them together into a unified dissenting force.

The Politics of Compromise

While Know-Nothings, evangelicals, and women attacked the political parties from outside, problems raised by national expansion were continuing to erode party unity from within. Immediately after Zachary Taylor's election in 1848, California's future became a new divisive issue.

California presented a peculiar political problem. Once word reached the rest of the nation that California was rich with gold, politicians immediately began grasping for control over the newly acquired territory. Although large parts of the area lay below the 36°30′ line that the Missouri Compromise had set for slavery expansion, that legislation had applied only

to territory acquired in the Louisiana Purchase. This left wide open the question of slavery in the new territories acquired from Great Britain and Mexico in the previous decade.

Having been primarily responsible for crafting the earlier compromise (see pages 281–283), Henry Clay took it upon himself to find a solution to the new situation. Clay was convinced that any successful agreement would have to address all sides of the issue. He thus proposed a complex **omnibus** bill to the Senate on January 20, 1850. California would enter the Union as a free state, but the slavery question would be left to popular sovereignty in all other territories acquired through the Treaty of Guadalupe Hidalgo (see page 382). The bill also directed Texas to drop a continuing border dispute with New Mexico in exchange for federal assumption of Texas's public debt. Then, to appease abolitionists, Clay called for an end to the slave trade in Washington, D.C., and balanced that with a

omnibus Including or covering many things; an omnibus bill is a piece of legislation with many parts.

CONGRESSIONAL SCALES,
A TRUE BALANCE.

The question of how a war with Mexico might unbalance the nation politically weighed heavily on people's minds as the nation entered the 1850s. In this cartoon, lithographer Nathaniel Currier—who later would found the famous graphic art company Currier and Ives—illustrates the problem. Trying himself to balance the Wilmot Proviso against Southern Rights, the president seeks to keep congressional representatives from the North and the South in balance as well. *Library of Congress.*

clause popular with southerners: a new, more effective **fugitive slave law.**

Though Clay was trying to please all sectional interests, the omnibus bill satisfied no one; Congress debated it without resolution for seven months. Despite appeals to reason by Clay and Daniel Webster, Congress remained hopelessly deadlocked. Finally, in July 1850, Clay's proposals were defeated. The 73-year-old political veteran left the capital tired and dispirited, but **Stephen A. Douglas** of Illinois set himself to the task of reviving the compromise. Using practical economic arguments and backroom political arm twisting, Douglas proposed each component of Clay's omnibus package as a separate bill, steering each forward toward a comprehensive compromise. Finally, in September, Congress passed the **Compromise of 1850.**

Silenced by the political machinations of their mainstream colleagues, both antislavery and evangelical Whigs chafed at the provision that allowed slave catchers to follow runaway slaves into the North.

fugitive slave law   Law providing for the return of escaped slaves to their owners.

Stephen A. Douglas   Illinois senator who tried to reconcile northern and southern differences over slavery through the Compromise of 1850 and the Kansas-Nebraska Act.

Compromise of 1850   Plan intended to reconcile North and South on the issue of slavery; it recognized the principle of popular sovereignty and included a strong fugitive slave law.

Striking back, they increasingly joined forces with African Americans to seek solutions outside the political realm. Throughout the 1850s, both white and African American activists sought to help slaves escape from the South on the **Underground Railroad.** This covert network provided hiding places and aid for runaway slaves along routes designed to carry them from southern plantations through American territory made hostile by the fugitive slave law and on to safety in Canada. Individuals like **Harriet Tubman** made frequent excursions into the South. Along with Frederick Douglass and others, she also delivered lectures on their life in slavery to white audiences across the North, increasing northern awareness of the plight of slaves and stirring hostility toward the fugitive slave provisions of the Douglas package.

The Compromise of 1850 did little to relieve underlying regional differences and only aggravated political dissent. That slaveowners could pursue runaway slaves into northern states and return them into bondage brought slavery too close to home for many northerners. Nor did southerners find any reason to celebrate: admission of another nonslave state further drained their power in the Senate, and slavery had gained no positive protection, either in the territories or at home. Still, the compromise created a brief respite from the slavery-extension question at a time when the nation's attention increasingly needed to focus on other major changes in national life.

A Changing Political Economy

In the years following the Compromise of 1850, American economic and territorial growth continued to play a destabilizing role in both national and regional development. Most notably, during the 1850s industrial growth accelerated, further altering the nation's economic structure. By 1860 less than half of all northern workers made a living from agriculture as northern industry became more concentrated. Steam began to replace water as the primary power source, and factories were no longer limited to locations along rivers and streams. The use of interchangeable parts became more sophisticated and intricate. In 1851, for example, Isaac Singer devised an assembly line using this technology and began mass-producing sewing machines, fostering a boom in ready-made clothing. As industry expanded, the North became more reliant on the West and South for raw materials and for the food consumed by those working in northeastern factories.

Railroad development stimulated economic and industrial growth. Between 1850 and 1860, the number of miles of railroad track in the United States increased from 9,000 to more than 30,000. The vast majority of these lines linked the Northeast with the Midwest, carrying produce to eastern markets and eastern manufactures to western consumers. In 1852 the Michigan Southern Railroad completed the first line into Chicago from the East, and by 1855 that city had become a key transportation hub linking regions farther west with the eastern seaboard.

Developing this transportation system was difficult. A lack of bridges over major rivers, particularly over the Ohio, impeded rail traffic. Because there still was no standard **rail gauge**—at least twelve different measurements were used—cargo frequently had to be carted from one rail line to another. Despite these problems, railroads quickly became an integral part of the expanding American economy. Western farmers who had previously shipped their products downriver to New Orleans now sent them much more rapidly by rail to eastern industrial centers. The availability of reliable transportation induced farmers to cultivate more land, and enterprising individuals started up related businesses such as warehouses and **grain elevators,** simplifying storage and loading along railroad lines. Mining boomed, particularly the iron industry; the railroads not only transported ore but also became a prime consumer.

Building a railroad required huge sums of money. In populous areas, where passenger and freight traffic was heavy, the promise of a quick and profitable return on investment allowed railroads to raise sufficient capital by selling company stock. In sparsely settled regions, however, where investment returns were much slower, state and local governments loaned money directly to rail companies, financed them indirectly by purchasing stock, or extended state tax exemptions. The most crucial aid to railroads, however, was federal land grants.

The federal government, which owned vast amounts of unsettled territory, gave land to developers who

Underground Railroad   The secret network of northerners who helped fugitive slaves escape to Canada or to safe areas in free states.

Harriet Tubman   One of the most famous and most effective of the many African American "conductors" on the Underground Railroad; she is thought to have been personally responsible for leading at least three hundred slaves into freedom.

rail gauge   The distance between train tracks.

grain elevator   A building equipped with mechanical lifting devices and used for storing grain.

AN EXPRESS FREIGHT SHIPMENT OF 30 COACHES, APRIL 15, 1868
BY ABBOT, DOWNING & CO., CONCORD, N.H. TO WELLS, FARGO CO., OMAHA, NEB.

The expansion of railroads facilitated transportation in a number of ways. Not only could western farmers get their produce to market and buy bulky manufactured goods delivered by train, but other modes of transportation were made easier. This illustration shows thirty stagecoaches built by a New Hampshire firm being hauled in a single load to the Wells Fargo Company in Omaha, Nebraska, which, in turn, used them to haul passengers and small freight to places the trains did not go. *New Hampshire Historical Society, Concord.*

then leased or sold plots of ground along the proposed route to finance construction. In 1850 one such federal proposal made by Illinois senator Stephen A. Douglas resulted in a 2.6-million-acre land grant to Illinois, Mississippi, and Alabama for a railroad between Chicago and Mobile. Congress also invested heavily in plans for a transcontinental railroad and on March 4, 1853, appropriated $150,000 to survey potential routes across the continent.

While Americans were enjoying the rail boom, events in Europe were creating new markets for American produce. Several years of bad weather helped spur crop failures throughout the region. In the face of rising public protest over the high cost of food, in 1846 the British Parliament repealed the Corn Laws, which had outlawed the importation of grain since 1804. Two years later, revolutions spread throughout much of continental Europe, followed by the outbreak of several wars. During the 1850s, the price of grain rose sharply in world markets. Railroads allowed western farmers to ship directly to eastern seaports and on to Europe. Meanwhile, technological advances in farm-

ing equipment enabled American farmers to harvest enough grain to meet world demand.

Using the steel plow devised in 1837 by **John Deere,** farmers could cultivate more acres with greater ease. The mechanical reaper invented in 1831 by **Cyrus McCormick** allowed a single operator to harvest as much as fourteen field hands could by hand. Railroads distributed these new pieces of heavy equipment at a reasonable cost. The combination of greater production potential and speedy transportation prompted westerners to increase farm size and concentrate on cash crops. The outcome of these developments was a vast increase in the economic and political power of the West.

John Deere   American industrialist who pioneered the manufacture of steel plows especially suited for working hard-packed prairie soil.

Cyrus McCormick   Virginia inventor and manufacturer who developed and mass-produced the McCormick reaper, a machine that harvested grain.

Cyrus McCormick's mechanical reaper, shown here in an 1846 advertisement from *The Cultivator* magazine, was one of the technological wonders of its time, permitting a single farmer to harvest as much grain as fourteen field hands could using conventional tools. *State Historical Society of Wisconsin.*

Western grain markets provided the foodstuffs for American industrialization, and Europe provided much of the labor. Factories employed unskilled workers for the most part, and immigrants made up the majority of that labor pool as food shortages, poverty, and political upheaval drove millions from Europe, especially from Ireland and Germany (see page 320). Total immigration to the United States exceeded 100,000 for the first time in 1848, and in 1851, 221,000 people migrated to the United States from Ireland alone. In 1852 the number of German immigrants reached 145,000. Many of these newcomers, particularly the Irish, were not trained in skilled crafts and wound up settling in the industrial urban centers of the Northeast, where they could find work in the factories.

This combination of changes set the stage for political crisis. Liberalized suffrage rules transformed naturalized immigrants into voters, and both parties courted them, adding their interests to the political pot. Meanwhile, a mechanized textile industry hungry for southern fiber lent vitality to the continued growth of the cotton kingdom and the slave labor system that gave it life. Northern political leaders visualized an industrial nation based on free labor, but that view ran counter to the southern elites' ideals of **agrarian capitalism** based on slavery. In the West, most continued to believe in the Jeffersonian ideal of an agricultural nation of small and medium-size farms and could not accept either industrial or cotton capitalism as positive developments.

Political Instability and the Election of 1852

Dynamic economic progress improved material life throughout the nation, but it also raised serious questions about what course progress should take. As one clear-sighted northern minister pointed out in 1852, the debate was not about whether America should pursue progress but about "different kinds and methods of progress." Contradictory visions of national destiny were about to cause the breakdown of the existing party system.

Slavery seemed to loom behind every debate, but most Americans, even southerners, had no personal investment in the institution. Two-thirds of southerners owned no slaves, tolerating the institution but having only fleeting contact with the great plantations and the peculiar labor system operating on them. North-

agrarian capitalism A system of agriculture based on the efficient, specialized production of crops intended to generate profits rather than subsistence.

erners, too, were largely indifferent. Men like young Illinois state congressman **Abraham Lincoln** believed the institution was wrong but were not inclined to do anything about it. What mattered to these people was not slavery but autonomy—control over local affairs and over their own lives.

The slavery question challenged notions of autonomy in both the North and the South. In their widely disseminated rhetoric, abolitionists expanded the specter of the Slave Power conspiracy (see page 381), especially in the aftermath of the Compromise of 1850. Growing numbers perceived this conspiracy as intent on imposing southern ways onto all parts of the country and installing southern elites or their sympathizers in seats of power in every section of the nation. Whether they were farmers in western states like Illinois or artisans in Pennsylvania, common people were jealous of their own local institutions and would resist a southern takeover. Nor would common people in the South accept interference from outsiders, and the ever more vigorous antisouthern crusade by northern radicals alarmed them as well.

The Compromise of 1850 momentarily eased regional fears, but sectional tensions still smoldered beneath the surface. These embers flamed anew in 1852 with the publication of *Uncle Tom's Cabin* by **Harriet Beecher Stowe.** Stowe portrayed the darkest inhumanities of southern slavery in the first American novel to include African Americans as central characters. *Uncle Tom's Cabin* sold three hundred thousand copies in its first year. Adapted for the stage, it became one of the most popular plays of the period. The book stirred public opinion and breathed new life into antislavery sentiments, leading Free-Soilers and so-called **conscience Whigs** to renew their efforts to limit or end slavery. When these activists saw that the Whig Party was incapable of addressing the slavery question in any effective way, they began to look for other political options.

Superficially, the Whigs seemed well organized and surprisingly unified as a new presidential election approached. They passed over Millard Fillmore, who had advanced into the presidency when Zachary Taylor died in office in July 1850, in favor of General Winfield Scott, Taylor's military rival in the War with Mexico. The Democrats remained divided through forty-nine ballots, unable to decide between Lewis Cass of Michigan, Stephen A. Douglas of Illinois, and **James Buchanan** of Pennsylvania. They finally settled on the virtually unknown **Franklin Pierce** of New Hampshire, who pledged to live by and uphold the Compromise of 1850 and keep slavery out of politics. This promise was enough to bring Martin Van

Harriet Beecher Stowe's novel *Uncle Tom's Cabin* was historic for a number of reasons. Not only did it help to fire up northern antislavery sentiments, but it also was the first American novel that featured African American characters in prominent roles. It was issued in various editions with many different covers, but most of them featured the lead character, Uncle Tom—another first in American publishing. This particular cover, from an early "Young Folks' Edition" of the book, depicts the stooped old man with his young, sympathetic white mistress. *Collection of Picture Research Consultants & Archives.*

Buren back to the Democrats, and he brought many Free-Soilers back with him. Many others, though, abandoned Van Buren and joined forces with conscience Whigs.

Abraham Lincoln Illinois lawyer and politician who argued against popular sovereignty in debates with Stephen Douglas in 1858; he lost the senatorial election to Douglas but was elected president in 1860.

Harriet Beecher Stowe American novelist and abolitionist whose novel *Uncle Tom's Cabin* fanned antislavery sentiment in the North.

conscience Whigs Members of the Whig Party who supported moderate abolitionism, as opposed to cotton Whigs, members who opposed abolitionism.

James Buchanan Pennsylvania senator who was elected president in 1856 after gaining the Democratic nomination as a compromise candidate.

Franklin Pierce New Hampshire lawyer and Democratic politician nominated as a compromise candidate and elected president in 1852.

Scott was a national figure and a distinguished military hero, but Pierce gathered 254 electoral votes to Scott's 42. This one-sided victory, however, revealed more about the disarray in the Whig Party than it did about Pierce's popularity or Democratic Party strength. Splits between "cotton" and "conscience" groups splintered Whig unity. Regional tension escalated as Free-Soil rhetoric clashed with calls for extending slavery. Confrontations between Catholics and Protestants and between native-born and immigrant laborers caused bitter animosity. In the North, where immigration, industrialization, and antislavery sentiment were most prevalent and economic friction was most pronounced, massive numbers of voters, believing the Whigs incapable of addressing current problems, deserted the party.

Increasing Tension Under Pierce

The Democratic Party and Franklin Pierce, its representative in the White House, were also not immune to the pressures of a changing electorate. Pierce was part of the **Young America Movement,** which, as a whole, tried to ignore the slavery issue, advocating romantic and aggressive nationalism, manifest destiny, and republican revolutions throughout the Americas. In line with the Young America agenda, Pierce emphasized expansion; choosing a route for a transcontinental railroad became the keystone in his agenda for the nation.

Southerners knew that a railroad based in the South would channel the flow of gold from California through their region and would also open new areas for settlement and allow cotton agriculture to spread beyond the waterways that had proved so necessary to its expansion so far. Eventually the new territories would become states, increasing the South's national political power.

That model of development was totally unacceptable to several groups: to northern evangelicals, who viewed slavery as a moral blight on the nation; to Free-Soil advocates, who believed the spread of slavery would degrade white workers; and to northern manufacturers, who wanted to maintain dominance in Congress to ensure continued economic protection. In May 1853, only two months after assuming office, Pierce inflamed all of these groups by sending James Gadsden, a southern railroad developer, to Mexico to purchase a strip of land lying below the southern border of the New Mexico Territory. Any rail line built westward from a southern city would have to cross that land as it proceeded from Texas to California, and Pierce and his southern supporters

wanted to make sure that it was part of the United States. The **Gadsden Purchase,** signed on December 30, 1853, added 29,640 square miles of land to the United States for a cost of $10 million. It also finalized the southwestern border of the United States.

Rather than enhancing Pierce's reputation as a nationalist, the Gadsden Purchase fed the perception that he was a southern sympathizer promoting the extension of slavery. It also led to a more serious sectional crisis. The Gadsden Purchase prompted proponents of a southern route for the transcontinental railroad, led by Secretary of War **Jefferson Davis,** to push for government sponsorship of the project. Rooted politically in Chicago and having invested his own money in rail development, Illinois senator Stephen A. Douglas rose to the challenge. He used his position as chairman of the Senate's Committee on Territories to block Davis's effort to build a transcontinental railroad through the South and pushed for a route westward from Chicago. This route passed through territory that had been set aside for a permanent Native American homeland and thus had not been organized into a federal territory. To rectify this problem, Douglas introduced a bill on January 4, 1854, incorporating the entire northern half of Indian Territory into a new federal entity called Nebraska.

Douglas knew that he would need both northern and southern support to get his bill through Congress, so he tried to structure the legislation so as to alienate neither section. Fearful that the bill would spark yet another debate over slavery, Douglas sought to silence possible opposition by proposing that the matter be left to popular sovereignty within the territory itself—let the voters of Nebraska decide. Noting that the proposed territory was above the Missouri Compromise line, southerners pointed out that Congress might prohibit popular sovereignty from functioning. Douglas responded that the Compromise of

> **Young America Movement** A political movement popular among young voters during the 1840s and early 1850s that advocated free-market capitalism, national expansionism, and American patriotism; a strong force within the Democratic Party, Young America leaders tried to avoid antislavery debates and other divisive controversies.
>
> **Gadsden Purchase** A strip of land in present-day Arizona and New Mexico that the United States bought from Mexico in 1853 to secure a southern route for a transcontinental railroad.
>
> **Jefferson Davis** Secretary of war under Franklin Pierce; he later became president of the Confederacy.

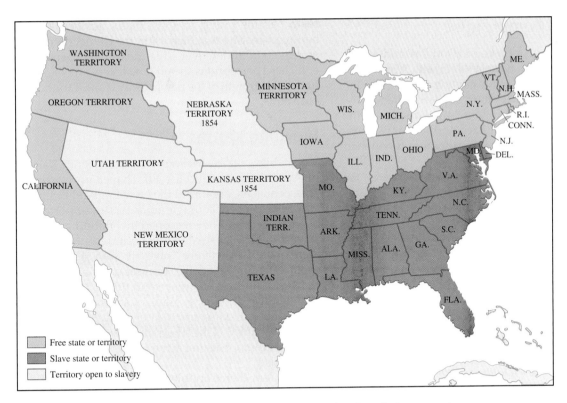

MAP 14.1 The Kansas-Nebraska Act This map shows Stephen Douglas's proposed compromise to resolve the dilemma of organizing the vast territory separating the settled part of the United States from California and Oregon. His solution, designed in part to win profitable rail connections for his home district in Illinois, stirred a political crisis by repealing the Missouri Compromise and replacing it with popular sovereignty.

1850 superseded the 1820 Missouri Compromise, but he finally supported an amendment to his original bill dividing the territory in half—Nebraska in the north and Kansas in the south (see Map 14.1). Assuming that popular sovereignty would lead to slavery in Kansas and a system of free labor in Nebraska, Douglas calculated that both northerners and southerners would be satisfied and support the bill.

Toward a House Divided

■ How did various political coalitions react to the Kansas-Nebraska Act?

■ What was the effect of these various reactions on the national political climate?

Once again slavery threatened national political stability. In the North, opponents of the bill formed local coalitions to defeat it. On January 24, 1854, a group of

Democrats including Salmon P. Chase, Gerrit Smith, Joshua Giddings, and **Charles Sumner** published "The Appeal of the Independent Democrats in Congress, to the People of the United States." They called the bill an "atrocious plot" to make Nebraska a "dreary region of despotism, inhabited by masters and slaves." On February 28, opponents of the Kansas-Nebraska bill met in Ripon, Wisconsin, and recommended the formation of a new political party. Similar meetings took place in several northern states as opposition to the bill grew. In the wake of these meetings, the existing party system would collapse and a new one would arise to replace it.

Charles Sumner Massachusetts senator who was brutally beaten by a southern congressman in 1856 after delivering a speech attacking the South.

A Shattered Compromise

Despite this strong opposition, Douglas and Pierce rallied support for the **Kansas-Nebraska Act** in Congress. On May 26, 1854, after gaining approval in the House of Representatives, the bill passed the Senate, and Pierce soon signed it into law. Passage of the Kansas-Nebraska Act crystallized northern antislavery sentiment. To protest, many northerners threatened **noncompliance** with the fugitive slave law of 1850. As Senator William Seward of New York vowed, "We will engage in competition for the virgin soil of Kansas, and God give the victory to the side which is stronger in numbers as it is in right."

Antislavery forces, however, remained divided into at least three major groups. The Free-Soil contingent opposed any extension of slavery but did not necessarily favor abolishing the institution. The other two groups—Garrisonians and evangelicals—wanted immediate abolition but disagreed on many particulars. William Lloyd Garrison and his followers believed that slavery was the primary evil facing the nation, and they embraced anyone who held that position. Evangelicals agreed that slavery was evil, but they believed it was one among many vices undermining the virtuous republic. All three groups constantly agitated against slavery and what they perceived as southern control of national politics. They weakened the Democratic Party's strength in the North but could not bring themselves to align behind a single opposition party.

Talk of expansion also threatened Democratic unity in the South. Many southerners believed that extending slavery was necessary to prevent northern domination. Increased northern wealth and continued conflict over the expansion of slavery convinced many southern Democrats that northern manufacturing and commercial power threatened to reduce the South to a "colony" controlled by northern bankers and industrialists.

Some southerners attempted to neutralize this perceived threat by acquiring colonies of their own in the Caribbean and Central America. Although all these efforts were the work of a few power-hungry individuals, many northerners believed them to be part of the Slave Power conspiracy. President Pierce unintentionally aggravated this sentiment by pushing to acquire Cuba, which he hoped to purchase from Spain. The Spanish, however, were unwilling to negotiate, and in October 1854 three of Pierce's European ministers met in Ostend, Belgium, and secretly drafted a statement outlining conditions that might justify taking Cuba by force. When the so-called **Ostend Mani-festo** became public in 1855, many northerners felt betrayed, fearing that Pierce and the Democratic Party approved of undercover adventurism to expand slavery. These perceptions stirred antislavery anxieties and fueled the growth of the newly formed anti-Democratic coalitions.

Bleeding Kansas

Meanwhile, political friction was about to ignite Kansas. In April 1854, abolitionist Eli Thayer of Worcester, Massachusetts, organized the New England Emigrant Aid Society to encourage antislavery supporters to move to Kansas. They reasoned that flooding a region subject to popular sovereignty with right-minded residents could effectively "save" it from slavery. This group eventually sent two thousand armed settlers to Kansas, founding Lawrence and other communities. With similar designs, proslavery southerners, particularly those in Missouri, also encouraged settlement in the territory. Like their northern counterparts, these southerners came armed and ready to fight for their cause.

President Pierce appointed governors in both Kansas and Nebraska and instructed them to organize elections for territorial legislatures. As proslavery and antislavery settlers vied for control of Kansas, the region became a testing ground for popular sovereignty. When the vote came on March 30, 1855, a large contingent of armed slavery supporters from Missouri—so-called border ruffians—crossed into Kansas and cast ballots for proslavery candidates. According to later Senate investigations, 60 percent of the votes cast were illegal. These unlawful ballots gave proslavery supporters a large majority in the Kansas legislature. They promptly expelled all abolitionist legislators and enacted the Kansas Code—a group of laws meant to drive all antislavery forces out of the territory. Antislavery advocates refused to acknowledge the validity of the election or the laws. They organized their own free-state government and drew up an alternative constitution, which they submitted to the voters.

Kansas-Nebraska Act   Law passed by Congress in 1854 that allowed residents of Kansas and Nebraska territories to decide whether to allow slavery within their borders.

noncompliance   Failure or refusal to obey a law or request.

Ostend Manifesto   Declaration by American foreign ministers in 1854 that if Spain refused to sell Cuba, the United States might be justified in taking it by force.

Though no one would deny that their cause was noble, many of the men who flocked to Kansas to resist the expansion of slavery were no less violent than their proslavery adversaries. This photograph taken in 1859 shows a gang of armed antislavery men who had just broken an accomplice (John Doy, seated) out of jail in neighboring St. Joseph, Missouri. Like proslavery border ruffians, many of these men also served in guerrilla bands during the Civil War, and some went on to careers as famous outlaws after the war was over. *Kansas State Historical Society.*

Bloodshed soon followed. Attempting to bring the conflict to conclusion, proslavery territorial judge Samuel LeCompte called a grand jury of slavery supporters that indicted members of the free-state government for treason and sent a **posse** of about eight hundred men armed with rifles and five cannon to Lawrence. There they "arrested" the antislavery forces and sacked the town, burning buildings and plundering shops and homes. But the violence did not end there. Hearing news of the "Sack of Lawrence," **John Brown,** an antislavery zealot, vowed to "fight fire with fire." Reasoning that at least five antislavery supporters had been killed since the conflict erupted, he and seven others abducted five proslavery men living along the Pottawatomie River south of Lawrence and murdered them. The "Pottawatomie Massacre" triggered a series of episodes in which more than two hundred men were killed. Much of the violence was the work of border ruffians and zealots like Brown, but to many people in both the North and the South, the events symbolized the "righteousness" of their cause.

The Kansas issue also led to violence in Congress. During the debates over the admission of the territory, Charles Sumner, a senator from Massachusetts, delivered an abusive and threatening speech against proslavery advocates. In particular, he made insulting remarks about South Carolina and its 60-year-old senator Andrew Butler. Butler was out of town, but Butler's nephew, Representative Preston Brooks, accosted Sumner and nearly beat him to death with a cane. Though **censured** by the House of Representatives, Brooks was overwhelmingly reelected by his

posse A group of people usually summoned by a sheriff to aid in law enforcement.

John Brown Abolitionist who fought proslavery settlers in Kansas in 1855; he was hanged for treason after seizing the U.S. arsenal at Harpers Ferry in 1859 as part of an effort to liberate southern slaves.

censure To issue an official rebuke, as by a legislature to one of its members.

home district and openly praised for his actions—he received canes as gifts from admirers all over the South.

Meanwhile the presidential election of 1856 was approaching. The Pierce administration's actions, southern expansionism, and the Kansas-Nebraska controversy swelled the ranks of dissenters like those who had convened in Ripon. Now formally calling themselves the **Republican Party,** these northern and western groups began actively seeking support. Immigration also remained a major issue, but the Know-Nothings, despite their success at the local and state levels, split over slavery at their initial national convention in 1855. Disagreement over a **plank** dealing with the Kansas-Nebraska Act caused most northerners to bolt from the convention. Some formed an anti-slavery group called the Know-Somethings, but many joined Republican coalitions. In 1856 the remaining Know-Nothings reconvened and nominated former president Millard Fillmore as the party's standard-bearer. John C. Frémont, a moderate abolitionist who had achieved fame as the liberator of California (see pages 380–381), got the Republican nomination. The few remaining Whigs endorsed Fillmore at their convention, while some former Know-Nothings met separately and endorsed Frémont. The Democrats rejected both Pierce and Douglas and nominated James Buchanan from Pennsylvania, selecting John C. Breckinridge of Kentucky as Buchanan's running mate to balance the ticket between the North and the South.

The election became a contest for party survival rather than a national referendum on slavery. Buchanan received 45 percent of the popular vote and 163 electoral votes. Frémont finished second with 33 percent of the popular vote and 114 electoral votes. Fillmore received 21 percent of the popular vote but only 8 electoral votes. Frémont's surprisingly narrow margin of defeat demonstrated the appeal of the newly formed Republican coalition to northern voters. The Know-Nothings, fragmented over slavery, disappeared and never again attempted a national organization.

Bringing Slavery Home to the North

On March 4, 1857, James Buchanan became president of the United States. The 65-year-old Pennsylvanian had begun his political career in Congress in 1821 and owed much of his success to southern support. His election came at a time when the nation needed strong leadership, but Buchanan seemed unable to provide it. During the campaign, he had emphasized national

In attempting to win his freedom, Dred Scott unintentionally set a legal process in motion that would deny Congress's right to control the extension of slavery. This 1858 painting captures Scott's resolution and strength of character. *"Dred Scott" by Louis Schultze, 1881. Missouri Historical Society.*

unity, but he proved incapable of achieving a unifying compromise. His attempt to preserve the politics of avoidance only strengthened radicalism in both the North and the South. **Regionalism** colored all political issues, and every debate became a contest between competing social, political, and economic ideologies.

Though Buchanan's shortcomings contributed to the rising crisis, an event occurred within days of his inauguration that sent shock waves through the al-

Republican Party Political party formed in 1854 that opposed the extension of slavery into the western territories.

plank One of the articles of a political platform.

regionalism Loyalty to the interests of a particular region of the country.

ready troubled nation. **Dred Scott,** a slave once owned by John Emerson, resided in Missouri, a slave state. But between 1831 and 1833, Emerson, an army surgeon, had taken Scott with him during various postings, including stints in Illinois and Wisconsin, where the Missouri Compromise banned slavery. Scott's attorney argued that living in Illinois and Wisconsin had made Scott a free man. When, after nearly six years in the Missouri courts, the state supreme court rejected this argument in 1852, Scott, with the help of abolitionist lawyers, appealed to the United States Supreme Court. In a 7-to-2 decision, the Court ruled against Scott. Chief Justice Roger B. Taney, formerly a member of Andrew Jackson's Kitchen Cabinet and a stalwart Democrat (see page 289), argued that in the eyes of the law slaves were not people but property; as such, they could not be citizens of the United States and had no right to petition the Court. Taney then ignited a political powder keg by ruling that Congress had no constitutional authority to limit slavery in a federal territory, thereby declaring the Missouri Compromise unconstitutional.

While southerners generally celebrated the decision, antislavery forces and northern evangelical leaders called the *Dred Scott* decision a mockery of justice and a crime against a "higher law." Some radical abolitionists argued that the North should separate from the Union. Others suggested impeaching the Supreme Court. Already incensed by events in Kansas, antislavery leaders predicted that the next move by the Slave Power conspiracy would be to get the Supreme Court to strike down antislavery laws in northern states.

Meanwhile, the Kansas issue still burned. The fact that very few slaveholders actually moved into the territory did nothing to deter proslavery leaders, who met in Lecompton, Kansas, in June 1857 to draft a state constitution favoring slavery. When the **Lecompton constitution** was submitted for voters' approval, antislavery forces protested by refusing to vote, so it was easily ratified. But when it was revealed that more than two thousand nonresidents had voted illegally, both Republicans and northern Democrats in Congress roundly denounced it. The Buchanan administration joined southerners in support of admitting Kansas to the Union as a slave state and managed to push the statehood bill through the Senate, but the House of Representatives rejected it. Congress then returned the Lecompton constitution to Kansas for another vote. This time Free-Soilers participated in the election and defeated the proposed constitution. Kansas remained a territory.

The Kansas controversy proved a hard pill for Douglas to swallow. He believed in popular sovereignty

It Matters

The *Dred Scott* Case

If one had to point to a single event that, perhaps more than any other, made civil war inevitable in the United States, it was the Taney Court's decision in *Dred Scott v. Sanford*. More than anything else, this decision revealed the shortsightedness of Federalists when they had cobbled together the Three-Fifths Compromise as a way of rushing a new Constitution out for state ratification. The mere mention of slavery in the Constitution would have given defenders of the institution an argument for its legitimacy, but to have made it integral to the basic representative structure of government gave them an iron defense. However, the Court's opinion went far beyond just legitimizing slavery. According to Justice Taney's argument, no state could "introduce any person, or description of persons, who were not intended to be embraced in this new political family, which the constitution brought into existence, but were intended to be excluded from it." Because no state at the time of ratification had included African Americans as citizens, then no one of African descent could become a citizen of the United States. Ever! It would take the Thirteenth and Fourteenth Amendments to the Constitution to reverse Taney's opinion and remove the errors that the Federalists' haste had inserted in that document in the first place.

but could not support the fraudulent election that brought the Lecompton constitution to Congress for approval. And the *Dred Scott* decision had virtually nullified his pet solution by ruling that even popular sovereignty could not exclude slavery from a state or territory. Still entertaining presidential ambitions,

Dred Scott   Slave who sued for his liberty in the Missouri courts, arguing that four years on free soil had made him free; the Supreme Court's 1857 ruling against him negated the Missouri Compromise.

Lecompton constitution   State constitution written for Kansas in 1857 at a convention dominated by proslavery forces; it would have allowed slavery, but Kansas voters rejected it.

Douglas sought a solution that might win him both northern and southern support in a run for the office in 1860. His immediate goal, however, was reelection to the Senate.

Illinois Republicans selected Abraham Lincoln to run against Douglas for the Senate in 1858. Born on the Kentucky frontier in 1809, Lincoln had accompanied his family from one failed farm to another, picking up schooling in Indiana and Illinois as opportunities arose. As a young man he worked odd jobs—farm worker, ferryman, flatboatman, surveyor, and store clerk—and was a member of the Illinois militia during the Black Hawk War in 1832 (see page 293). Two years after the war, Lincoln was elected to the Illinois legislature and began a serious study of law. He was admitted to the Illinois state bar in 1836. A strong Whig, Lincoln followed Henry Clay's economic philosophy and steered a middle course between the "cotton" and "conscience" wings of the Whig Party. Lincoln acknowledged that slavery was evil but contended that it was the unavoidable consequence of black racial inferiority. The only way to get rid of the evil, he believed, was to prevent the expansion of slavery into the territories, forcing it to die out naturally, and then make arrangements to separate the two races forever, either by transporting them to Africa or creating a segregated space for them in the Americas.

Lincoln was decidedly the underdog in the contest with Douglas and sought to improve his chances by challenging the senator to a series of debates about slavery and its expansion. Douglas agreed to seven debates in various parts of the state. During the debate at Freeport, Lincoln asked Douglas to explain how the people of a territory could exclude slavery in light of the *Dred Scott* ruling. Douglas's reply became known as the **Freeport Doctrine.** Slavery, he said, needed the protection of "local police regulations." In any territory, citizens opposed to slavery could elect representatives who would "by unfriendly legislation" prevent the introduction of slavery. Lincoln did not win Douglas's Senate seat, but the debate drew national attention to the Illinois race, and Lincoln won recognition as an up-and-coming Republican force.

Radical Responses to Abolitionism and Slavery

Southerners bristled at claims by Lincoln and others that slavery was immoral. Charles C. Jones and other southern evangelical leaders, for example, offered a religious defense of slavery. Such apologists argued that whites had a moral responsibility to care for blacks and instruct them in the Christian faith. Those who claimed that the Bible condoned slavery pointed out that the Israelites practiced slavery and that when Jesus walked among slaves he never mentioned freedom. The apostle Paul, they argued, even commanded slaves to obey their masters.

Many southerners, like some of their Republican opponents, were less interested in the slave than in how slavery affected white society and white labor. When the Republicans argued that slavery defiled labor, southern apologists countered that slavery was a "mudsill," or foundation, supporting democracy. Southerners contended that whites in the South enjoyed a greater degree of freedom than northern whites because slaves did all the demeaning work, freeing whites for more noble pursuits. Moreover, southern lawyer George Fitzhugh argued, both the North and the South relied equally on a subjugated work force: southerners on **chattel slavery** and northerners on **wage slavery.** Fitzhugh charged that poor northern whites were a "mudsill" as surely as slaves were in the South. The only meaningful difference between wage slaves and southern slaves, Fitzhugh concluded, was that northerners accepted no responsibility for housing and feeding their work force, condemning laborers to suffer at below-subsistence conditions.

These ideas infuriated northerners as much as antislavery arguments angered southerners because they challenged deeply held cultural and social values. Northern radicals increasingly called for the violent overthrow of slavery, and Kansas zealot John Brown moved to oblige them. In 1857 Brown came to the East, where he convinced several prominent antislavery leaders to finance a daring plan to raise an army of slaves in an all-out insurrection against their masters. Brown and a small party of followers attacked the federal arsenal at **Harpers Ferry,** Virginia, on October 16, 1859, attempting to seize weapons. The

---

Freeport Doctrine Stephen Douglas's belief, stated at Freeport, Illinois, that a territory could exclude slavery by writing local laws or regulations that made slavery impossible to enforce.

chattel slavery The bondage of people who are considered to be the movable personal property of their owners.

wage slavery The bondage of workers who, though legally free, are underpaid, trapped in debt, and living in extreme poverty.

Harpers Ferry Town in present-day West Virginia and site of the U.S. arsenal that John Brown briefly seized in 1859.

Seeing himself as an avenging angel, John Brown, shown here in an 1856 photograph, used the same terrorist tactics employed by border ruffians in Kansas. A year after this picture was taken, Brown began a two-year campaign to raise funds, volunteers, and political support for starting a massive armed slave uprising in Virginia, He finally struck at the federal armory at Harpers Ferry, Virginia, on October 16, 1859, where he and his force of volunteers were quickly overcome and arrested. He was hanged for treason on December 2, 1859. *Boston Athenaeum.*

arsenal proved an easy target, but no slaves joined the uprising. Local citizens surrounded the arsenal, firing on Brown and his followers until federal troops commanded by Colonel **Robert E. Lee** arrived. On October 18, Lee's forces battered down the barricaded entrance and arrested Brown. He was tried, convicted of treason, and hanged on December 2, 1859.

Brown's raid on Harpers Ferry captured the imagination of radical abolitionists. Republican leaders denounced it, but other northerners proclaimed Brown a martyr. Church bells tolled in many northern cities on the day of his execution. In New England, Ralph Waldo Emerson proclaimed Brown "that new saint." Such reactions caused many appalled southerners— even extreme moderates—to seriously consider **secession.** In Alabama, Mississippi, and Florida, state legislatures resolved that a Republican victory in the

upcoming presidential election would provide sufficient justification for such action.

The Divided Nation

■ How did the realignment of the political party system during the 1850s contribute to the conduct and results of the presidential election in 1860?

■ Why did the election results have the political effects that they did?

The Republicans were a new phenomenon on the American political scene: a purely regional political party. Rather than making any attempt to forge a national coalition, the party drew its strength and ideas almost entirely from the North. The Republican platform—"Free Soil, Free Labor, and Free Men"— stressed the defilement of white labor by slavery and contended that the Slave Power conspiracy was eroding the rights of free whites everywhere. By taking up a cry against "Rum, Romanism, and Slavery," the Republicans drew former Know-Nothings and temperance advocates into their ranks. The Democrats hoped to maintain a national coalition, but as the nation approached a new presidential election, their hopes began to fade.

The Dominance of Regionalism

During the Buchanan administration, Democrats found it increasingly difficult to achieve national party unity. Facing Republican pressure in their own states, northern Democrats realized that any concession to southern Democratic demands for extending or protecting slavery would cost them votes at home. In April 1860, as the party convened in Charleston, South Carolina, each side was ready to do battle for its political life.

The fight began when northern supporters of Stephen A. Douglas championed a popular sovereignty position. Southern radicals demanded a plank calling for the legal protection of slavery in the territories. After heated debates, neither side would compromise. When the delegates finally voted, the Douglas forces carried the day. Disgusted delegates from eight

Robert E. Lee   A Virginian with a distinguished career in the U.S. Army who resigned to assume command of the Confederate army in Virginia when the Civil War began.

secession   Withdrawal from the United States.

southern states walked out of the convention. Shocked, the remaining delegates adjourned the convention; they would reconvene in Baltimore in June. Most southern delegates boycotted the Baltimore proceedings, and Douglas easily won the Democratic presidential nomination. Moderate southerner Herschel V. Johnson of Georgia was his running mate. Hoping to attract moderate voters from both the North and the South, the party's final platform supported popular sovereignty and emphasized allegiance to the Union.

The southern Democratic contingent met one week later, also in Baltimore, and nominated Vice President John C. Breckinridge of Kentucky as its presidential candidate and Joseph Lane of Oregon as his running mate. The southern Democrats' platform vowed support for the Union but called for federal protection of the right to own slaves in the territories and for the preservation of slavery where it already existed.

In May 1860, a group of former Whigs and Know-Nothings along with some disaffected Democrats convened in Baltimore and formed the **Constitutional Union Party.** They nominated John Bell, a former southern Know-Nothing and wealthy slaveholder from Tennessee, for president and Edward Everett of Massachusetts, a former Whig leader, as his running mate. Hoping to resurrect the politics of compromise, the party resolved to take no stand on the sectional controversy and pledged to uphold the Constitution and the Union and to enforce the laws of the nation.

Having lost most of its moderates to the Constitutional Union coalition and having virtually no southerners in its ranks to start with, the Republican convention faced few ideological divisions, but personality conflicts were rife. The front-runner for the Republican nomination appeared to be William Seward of New York. A former Whig and longtime New York politician, Seward had actively opposed any extension of slavery during the early 1850s but had switched to the popular-sovereignty position during the Kansas controversy. Several other Republican favorites—Salmon P. Chase of Ohio, Simon Cameron of Pennsylvania, and Edward Bates of Missouri—agreed with Seward's position but sought their own nominations. Eventually, however, Illinois favorite son Abraham Lincoln emerged as Seward's major competition. Many delegates considered Seward too radical. Moreover, he and his campaign manager, Thurlow Weed (see page 287), had earned the distrust of many prominent Republicans for their political wheeling and dealing. Lincoln, in contrast, had a reputation for integrity and had not seriously alienated any of the Republican factions. He won the nomination on the third ballot.

The Election of 1860

The 1860 presidential campaign began as several separate contests. Lincoln and Douglas competed for northern votes; the Republicans were not even on the ballot in the **Deep South.** Douglas proclaimed himself the only national candidate but received most of his support from northerners who feared the consequences of a Republican victory. By the same token, Breckinridge and the southern Democrats expected no support in the North. Bell and the Constitutional Unionists attempted to campaign in both regions but attracted mostly southern voters anxious to stave off the crisis of disunion.

Slavery and sectionalism were the key issues. Even when a congressional investigation revealed evidence of graft, bribery, and shady dealings in the Buchanan administration, Republicans linked these charges to the supposed Slave Power conspiracy. The slaveholding elite, they contended, not only had attempted to subvert liberty but had used fraudulent means to keep the Democratic Party of Buchanan—and Douglas—in power. "Honest Abe Lincoln," the man of the people, would lead the fight against the forces of slavery and corruption. This argument drew in many northern voters, including a lot of former Know-Nothings.

Sensing that Lincoln would win the North, Douglas launched a last-ditch effort to win the election and hold the Union together by pushing his campaign into the South. Douglas and his forces tried unsuccessfully to form a coalition between moderate Democrats and Constitutional Unionists. Already in poor health, Douglas all but exhausted himself trying to prevent disunion.

As the election drew near, the likelihood of a Republican victory deeply alarmed southerners. Even moderate southerners started to believe that the Republicans intended to crush their way of life and to enslave southern whites economically while freeing southern blacks. Northern qualms were aroused as well when the pro-Democrat *New York Herald* contended that the election of Lincoln would bring "hundreds of thousands" of slaves north to compete with

---

Constitutional Union Party Political party that organized on the eve of the Civil War with no platform other than preservation of the Constitution, the Union, and the law.

Deep South The region of the South farthest from the North, usually said to comprise the states of Alabama, Florida, Georgia, Louisiana, Mississippi, and South Carolina.

Four candidates representing four different parties vied for the presidency in the election of 1860. As this political cartoon makes clear, the *Dred Scott* case set the agenda for the election. Here Scott provides the music as each of the four presidential candidates dances with a partner who symbolizes his perceived political orientation. John C. Breckinridge (upper left) dances with fellow southern Democrat James "Buck" Buchanan, illustrating his alignment with southern proslavery hard-liners. John H. Bell (lower right) dances with a Native American, symbolizing his nativist Know-Nothing affiliations, suggesting avoidance of the slavery issue. Meanwhile, Stephen A. Douglas (lower left) escorts a disheveled Irishman, suggesting his alignment with northeastern urban interests including immigrants and other "undesirables." Finally, Abraham Lincoln (upper right) is seen with an African American woman, an obvious reference to his party's perceived abolitionist leanings. *Lilly Library.*

whites for jobs, resulting in "African amalgamation with the fair daughters of the Anglo-Saxon, Celtic, and Teutonic races."

Seeking to counter such scare tactics, national Republican leaders forged a platform that advocated limits on slavery's expansion but contained no planks seeking an end to slavery in areas where it already existed. They also called for higher tariffs (to appeal to northern industrialists) and for internal improvements and public lands legislation (to appeal to westerners). Particularly in the Midwest, party leaders worked hard to portray themselves as "the white man's party." In line with the position Lincoln had taken in his 1858 debates with Douglas, Republicans argued that excluding slavery meant excluding blacks from competition with whites. These tactics alienated a few abolitionists but persuaded many northerners and westerners to support the party.

On November 6, 1860, Abraham Lincoln was elected president of the United States with 180 electoral votes—a clear majority—but only 40 percent of the popular vote. Lincoln carried all the northern states, California, and Oregon (see Map 14.2). Douglas finished second with 29 percent of the popular vote but just 12 electoral votes. He won only Missouri. Bell won the 39 electoral votes of Virginia, Kentucky, and Tennessee. Breckinridge, as expected, carried the Deep South but tallied only 72 electoral votes and 18 percent of the popular vote nationwide. For the first time in American history, a purely regional party held the presidency. The Republicans, who had made no effort to win votes in the South,

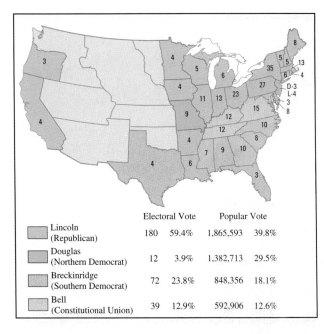

	Electoral Vote		Popular Vote	
Lincoln (Republican)	180	59.4%	1,865,593	39.8%
Douglas (Northern Democrat)	12	3.9%	1,382,713	29.5%
Breckinridge (Southern Democrat)	72	23.8%	848,356	18.1%
Bell (Constitutional Union)	39	12.9%	592,906	12.6%

MAP 14.2 Election of 1860 The election of 1860 confirmed the worst fears expressed by concerned Union supporters during the 1850s: changes in the nation's population made it possible for one section to dominate national politics. As this map shows, the Republican and southern Democratic Parties virtually split the nation, and the Republicans were able to seize the presidency.

also swept congressional races in the North and secured a large majority in the House of Representatives for the upcoming term.

The First Wave of Secession

After the Republican victory, southern sentiment for secession snowballed, especially in the Deep South. The Republicans were a "party founded on a single sentiment," stated the *Richmond Examiner*: "hatred of African slavery." The *New Orleans Delta* agreed, calling the Republicans "essentially a revolutionary party." But this party now controlled the national government. To a growing number of southerners, the Republican victory was proof that secession was the only alternative to political domination.

Calls for secession had been heard for decades, and most Republicans did not believe that the South would actually leave the Union. Seward had ridiculed threats of secession as an attempt "to terrify or alarm" the northern people. Lincoln himself believed that the "people of the South" had "too much sense" to launch an "attempt to ruin the government." During the campaign, he had promised "no interference by

the government, with slaves or slavery within the states," and he continued to urge moderation.

In a last-ditch attempt at compromise, **John J. Crittenden** proposed a block of permanent constitutional amendments—amendments that could never be repealed—to the Senate on December 18, 1860. He suggested extending the Missouri Compromise line westward across the continent, forbidding slavery north of the line, and protecting slavery to the south. Crittenden's plan also upheld the interstate trade in slaves and called for compensation to slaveowners who were unable to recover fugitive slaves from northern states. Although this plan seemed to favor the South, it had some appeal in the North, especially among businessmen who feared that secession would cause a major depression. Thurlow Weed, Seward's political adviser, seemed ready to listen to such a compromise, but Lincoln was "inflexible on the territorial question." The extension of the Missouri Compromise line, Lincoln warned, would "lose us everything we gained by the election." He let senators and congressmen know that he wanted no "compromise in regard to the extension of slavery." The Senate defeated Crittenden's proposals by a vote of 25 to 23. The Kentuckian then proposed putting the measure to a vote of the people, but Congress rejected that idea as well.

Meanwhile, on December 20, 1860, delegates in South Carolina met to consider seceding from the Union. South Carolina had long been a hotbed of resistance to federal authority, and state officials determined to take action to protect slavery before the newly elected Republican administration came to power. Amid general jubilation, South Carolina delegates voted unanimously to dissolve their ties with the United States. Just as the radicals hoped, other southern states followed. During January 1861, delegates convened in Mississippi, Florida, Alabama, Georgia, and Louisiana and voted to secede.

On February 4, 1861, delegates from the six seceding states met in Montgomery, Alabama, and formed the provisional government for the **Confederate States of America.** During the several weeks that followed,

John J. Crittenden Kentucky senator who made an unsuccessful attempt to prevent the Civil War by proposing a series of constitutional amendments protecting slavery south of the Missouri Compromise line.

Confederate States of America Political entity formed by the seceding states of South Carolina, Georgia, Florida, Alabama, Mississippi, and Louisiana in February 1861; Texas, Virginia, Arkansas, Tennessee, and North Carolina joined later.

the provisional congress drafted a constitution, and the six Confederate states ratified it on March 11, 1861.

The Confederate constitution emphasized the "sovereign and independent character" of the states and guaranteed the protection of slavery in any new territories acquired. It allowed tariffs solely for the purpose of raising government revenue and prohibited government funding of internal improvements. It also limited the president and vice president to a single six-year term. A cabinet composed of six executive department heads rounded out the executive branch. In all other respects, the Confederate government was identical to that in the United States. In fact, the U.S. Constitution was acknowledged as the supreme law in the Confederacy except in those particulars where it conflicted with provisions in the Confederate Constitution.

While this process was under way, the Confederate cause got a significant boost when Texas, which had been holding back, declared itself part of the new nation. Despite unionist pleas from Governor Sam Houston, the heavily populated cotton-growing region in the eastern part of the state opted to join neighboring Louisiana in rebellion, and the rest of the population followed suit. The Confederacy now numbered seven states.

Responses to Disunion

Even as late as March 1861, not all southerners favored secession. John Bell and Stephen Douglas together had received more than 50 percent of southern votes in 1860, winning support from southerners who desired compromise and had only limited stakes in upholding slavery. These "plain folk" joined together with some large planters, who stood to suffer economic loss from disunion, in calls for moderation and compromise. And the border states, which were less invested in cotton and had numerous ties with the North, were not strongly inclined toward secession. In February, Virginia had called for a peace conference to meet in Washington in an effort to forestall hostilities, but this attempt, like Crittenden's effort, also failed to hold the Union together.

The division in southern sentiments was a major stumbling block to the election of a Confederate president. Many moderate delegates to the constitutional convention refused to support radical secessionists, believing them to be equally responsible with the Republicans for initiating the crisis. The convention remained deadlocked until two prosecession Virginia legislators nominated Mississippi moderate Jefferson Davis as a compromise candidate.

Davis appeared to be the ideal choice. Austere and dignified, he had not sought the job but seemed extremely capable of handling it. A West Point graduate, he served during the War with Mexico, was elected to the Senate soon afterward, then left the Senate in 1851 to run unsuccessfully for governor in Mississippi. After serving as secretary of war under Franklin Pierce, he returned to the Senate in 1857. Although Davis had long championed southern interests and owned many slaves, he was no romantic, fire-eating secessionist. Before 1860 he had been a strong **Unionist,** arguing only that the South be allowed to maintain its own economy, culture, and institutions, including slavery. He had supported the Compromise of 1850. When he had fought for a southern route for a transcontinental railroad as secretary of war, he believed that it would benefit the South economically, but he also felt that it would tie the whole nation more firmly together. Like many of his contemporaries, however, Davis had become increasingly alarmed by the prospect of declining southern political power. Immediately after Mississippi's declaration of secession, Davis resigned his Senate seat and threw in with the Confederacy.

To moderates like Davis, the presidential election of 1860 was simply a forceful demonstration of a fact already in evidence: unless the South took a strong stand against outside interference, the region would no longer be able to control its own internal affairs. The initial northward tilt in the Senate created by California's admission in 1850 had been aggravated in 1858 by the admission of Minnesota and by Oregon's statehood in 1859. Southerners, Davis believed, needed to act in concert to convince northerners to either leave the South alone or face the region's withdrawal from the nation. "To rally the men of the North, who would preserve the government as our fathers found it," Davis proclaimed, "we . . . should offer no doubtful or divided front."

Elected provisional president of the Confederate States of America unanimously on February 9, 1861, Davis addressed the cheering crowds in Montgomery a week later and set forth the Confederate position: "The time for compromise has now passed," he said. "The South is determined to maintain her position, and make all who oppose her smell Southern powder and feel Southern steel." In his inaugural address several days later, he stressed a desire for peace but reiterated that the "courage and patriotism of the

Unionist Loyal to the United States of America.

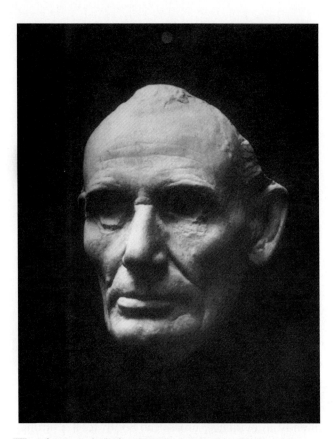

A few months before being nominated by the Republican Party as its presidential candidate, Abraham Lincoln permitted Illinois artist Leonard Volk to cast the future president's face in plaster. Preserved for all these years, this casting and the many reproductions that have been struck from it remain the most accurate picture we have of Lincoln before the secession crisis tore the nation apart. Captured in time, we can see the noble and serious man whose unflinching determination saw the nation through its worst historical crisis. As the many hundreds of photographs and other images of Lincoln during his presidency attest, he would never look this young and confident again. *Picture History.*

Confederate States" would be "found equal to any measure of defense which honor and security may require."

Northern Democrats and Republicans alike watched developments in the South with dismay. President Buchanan argued that secession had no constitutional validity and that any state leaving the Union did so unlawfully. He confused the issue, however, by stating his belief that the federal government had no constitutional power to "coerce a State" to remain in the Union. He blamed the crisis on "incessant and violent agitation on the slavery question," chiding northern states for disregarding fugitive slave laws and calling for a constitutional amendment protecting slavery.

Waiting to assume the office he had just won, Lincoln wrestled with the twin problems of what he would do about secession and slavery. African American abolitionist Frederick Douglass summed up Lincoln's dilemma. "Much as I value the current apparent hostility to Slavery," Douglass stated, "I plainly see that it is less the outgrowth of high and moral conviction against Slavery, as such, than because of the trouble its friends have brought upon the country." The South had divided the nation by seceding, and as Douglass indicated, many northerners were much more concerned about the breakup of the nation and potential hostilities between the North and the South than they ever had been about slavery. Lincoln wrote, "My opinion is that no state can, in any way, lawfully get out of the Union, without the consent of the others." He attempted to clarify his position in a letter to Alexander H. Stephens, who would soon become vice president of the Confederacy. Trying to reassure him that "a republican administration" would not "directly or indirectly, interfere with their slaves, or with them, about their slaves," the president-elect still refused to consider any compromise on disunion or the extension of slavery.

Before he could do anything else, Lincoln first had to unite his party. In an attempt to appease all the Republican factions, he chose his cabinet with great care. His vice president, the moderate Hannibal Hamlin of Maine, had supported Lincoln but was also a friend of William Seward and had been chosen to balance the ticket factionally. Lincoln continued this balancing act by appointing to his cabinet his four main rivals for party control. Seward received the job of secretary of state. Moderate Edward Bates of Missouri became attorney general. Although many Republicans considered Simon Cameron of Pennsylvania to be "destitute of honor and integrity," in the interest of appeasing Cameron's supporters and maintaining party unity, Lincoln reluctantly named him secretary of war. Salmon P. Chase of Ohio, a longtime politician and sometime radical on the slavery question, became secretary of the Treasury. Despite Lincoln's evenhandedness, his political balancing act was not easy to maintain. Chase and Seward, for instance, had a long history of political infighting and hated each other. That Lincoln would appoint Chase to any position so angered Seward that he threatened to resign, and Lincoln had to persuade him to remain.

The Nation Dissolved

- What problems confronted Abraham Lincoln and Jefferson Davis in March 1861?
- How did their actions contribute to the escalating national crisis?

Abraham Lincoln was inaugurated on March 4, 1861. In his inaugural address he repeated themes that he had been stressing since the election: no interference with slavery in states where it existed, no extension of slavery into the territories, and no tolerance of secession. "The Union," he contended, was "perpetual." The Constitution, according to its **Preamble,** had been written to form a "more perfect union," and no state could withdraw. Lincoln believed that the nation remained unbroken, and he pledged to see "that the laws of the Union be faithfully executed in all the States." This policy, he continued, necessitated "no bloodshed or violence, and there shall be none, unless it is forced upon the national authority. The power confided in me will be used to hold, occupy, and possess the property and places belonging to the government, and to collect the duties and imposts." If war came, he argued, it would be over secession, not slavery, for the federal government had a duty to maintain the Union by any means, including force.

Lincoln, Sumter, and War

Lincoln's first presidential address drew mixed reactions. Most Republicans found it firm and reasonable, applauding its tone. Union advocates in both the North and the South thought the speech held promise for the future. Even former rival Stephen Douglas stated, "I am with him." Moderate southerners commended Lincoln's "temperance and conservatism" and believed the speech was all "any reasonable Southern man" could have expected. Confederates and their sympathizers, however, branded the speech a "Declaration of War." Lincoln had hoped the address would foster a climate of reconciliation, show his commitment to maintaining the Union, and demonstrate his determination to find a peaceful solution, for he desperately needed time to organize the new government and formulate a plan of action. But such luxuries were not forthcoming.

Even before Lincoln assumed office, South Carolina officials had ordered the state militia to seize two federal forts—Fort Moultrie and Castle Pinckney—and the federal arsenal at Charleston. In response, Major Robert Anderson had moved all federal troops from Charleston to **Fort Sumter,** an island stronghold in Charleston Harbor. The Confederate congress determined that "immediate steps be taken to obtain possession" of forts still under U.S. control and demanded that President Buchanan remove all federal troops from the sovereign territory of the Confederacy. Despite his sympathy for the southern cause, Buchanan had announced that Fort Sumter would be defended "against all hostile attacks, from whatever quarter." On January 9, 1861, a Charleston Harbor **battery** fired on a supply ship, the *Star of the West,* as it attempted to reach the fort. Buchanan denounced the action but did nothing.

Immediately after taking office in March, Lincoln received a report from Fort Sumter that supplies were running low. Under great pressure from northern public opinion to do something without starting a war, he responded cleverly. He informed South Carolina governor Francis Pickens of his peaceful intention to send unarmed boats carrying food and supplies to the besieged fort. Lincoln thus placed the Confederacy in a no-win position: if Pickens accepted the resupply of federal forts he would lose face, but firing on an unarmed ship would be sufficiently dishonorable to justify stronger federal action. After studying the situation, Confederate officials determined to beat Lincoln to the punch. President Davis ordered the Confederate commander at Charleston, General P. G. T. Beauregard, to demand the evacuation of Sumter and, if the federals refused, to "proceed, in such a manner as you may determine, to reduce it." On April 11, while the supply ships were still on their way, Beauregard called on Anderson to surrender. When Anderson rejected the ultimatum on the following day, shore batteries opened fire on the island fortress. After a thirty-four-hour artillery battle, Anderson surrendered. Neither side had inflicted casualties on the other, but civil war had officially begun.

Across the North, newspapers contrasted the president's resolute but restrained policy with the violent aggression of the Confederates, and the public rallied behind the Union cause. In New York City, where southern sympathizers had once vehemently criticized abolitionist actions, a million people attended a

Preamble An introductory paragraph in a formal document setting out its underlying justification and purpose.

Fort Sumter Fort at the mouth of the harbor of Charleston, South Carolina; it was the scene of the opening engagement of the Civil War in April 1861.

battery An army artillery unit, usually supplied with heavy guns.

In this vivid engraving, South Carolina shore batteries under the command of P. G. T. Beauregard shell Fort Sumter, the last federal stronghold in Charleston Harbor, on the night of April 12, 1861. Curious and excited civilians look on from their rooftops, never suspecting the horrors that would be the outcome of this rash action. *Library of Congress.*

Union rally. Even northern Democrats rallied behind the Republican president, hearkening to Stephen Douglas's statement that "there can be no neutrals in this war, only patriots—or traitors." Spurred by the public outcry and confident of support, Lincoln called for seventy-five thousand militiamen to be mobilized "to maintain the honor, the integrity, and the existence of our National Union, and the perpetuity of popular government." Northern states responded immediately and enthusiastically. Across the Upper South and the border regions, however, the call to arms meant that a decision had to be made: whether to continue in the Union or join the Confederacy.

Choosing Sides in Virginia

The need for southern unity in the face of what he saw as northern aggression pushed Jefferson Davis to employ a combination of political finesse and force to create a solid southern alignment. He selected his cabinet with this in mind, choosing one cabinet member from each state except his own Mississippi and appointing men of varying degrees of radicalism. But unity among the seven seceding states was only one of Davis's worries. A perhaps more pressing concern was alignment

among the eight slave states that remained in the Union. These states were critical, for they contained more than half of the entire southern population (two-thirds of its white population), possessed most of the South's industrial capacity, produced most of its food, and raised more than half of its horses. In addition, many experienced and able military leaders lived in these states. If the Confederacy was to have any chance of survival, the human and physical resources of the whole South were essential.

It was not Davis's appeal for solidarity but Lincoln's call to mobilize the militia that won most of the other slave states for the Confederate cause. In Virginia, Governor John Letcher refused to honor Lincoln's demand for troops, and on April 17 a special convention declared for secession. Voters in Virginia overwhelmingly ratified this decision in a popular referendum on May 23. By then Letcher had offered **Richmond** as a site for the new nation's capital. The Confederate congress accepted the offer in order to strengthen ties with Virginia and because facilities in Montgomery were less than adequate.

Not all Virginians were flattered by becoming the seat for the Confederacy. Residents of the western portion of the state had strong Union ties and long-standing political differences with their neighbors east of the Allegheny Mountains. Forty-six counties called mass Unionist meetings to protest the state's secession, and in a June convention at Wheeling, they elected their own governor, Francis H. Pierpoint, and drew up a constitution. The document was ratified in an election open only to voters willing to take an oath of allegiance to the Union. Eastern Virginians considered the entire process illegal, but the West Virginia legislature finally convened in May 1862 and requested admission to the United States.

For many individuals in the Upper South, the decision to support the Confederacy was not an easy one. Virginian Robert E. Lee, for example, was deeply devoted to the Union. A West Point graduate and career officer in the U.S. Army, he had a distinguished record in the war with Mexico and as superintendent of West Point. General Winfield Scott, commander of the Union forces, called Lee "the best soldier I ever saw in the field." Recognizing his military skill, Lincoln offered Lee field command of the Union armies, but the Virginian refused, deciding that he should serve his

Richmond Port city on the James River in Virginia; already the state capital, it became the capital of the Confederacy.

native state instead. Lee agonized over the decision but told a friend, "I cannot raise my hand against my birthplace, my home, my children." He resigned his U.S. Army commission in April 1861. When he informed Scott, a personal friend and fellow Virginian, of his decision, Scott replied, "You have made the greatest mistake of your life, but I feared it would be so." Scott chose to remain loyal to the Union.

A Second Wave of Secession

Influenced by Virginia and by Lee's decision, three other states joined the Confederacy. Arkansas had voted against secession in March, hoping that bloodshed might be averted, but when Lincoln called for militia units, Governor Henry M. Rector answered, "None will be furnished. The demand is only adding insult to injury." The state then called a second convention and on May 6 seceded from the Union. North Carolinians had also hoped for compromise, but moderates turned secessionist when Secretary of War Simon Cameron **requisitioned** "two regiments of militia for immediate service" against the Confederacy. Governor John W. Ellis replied, "I regard the levy of troops made by this administration for the purpose of subjugating the states of the South [to be] in violation of the Constitution and a gross usurpation of power." North Carolina seceded on May 20.

Tennessee, the eleventh and final state to join the Confederacy, was the home of many moderates, including John Bell, the Constitutional Union candidate in 1860. Eastern residents favored the Union, and those in the west favored the Confederacy. The state's voters at first rejected disunion overwhelmingly, but after the fighting began, Governor Isham C. Harris and the state legislature initiated military ties with the Confederacy, forcing another vote on the issue. Western voters carried the election, approving the agreement and seceding from the Union on June 8. East Tennesseans, who remained loyal Unionists, tried to divide the state much as West Virginians had done, but Davis ordered Confederate troops to occupy the region, thwarting the effort.

Trouble in the Border States

Four slave states remained in the Union, and the start of hostilities brought political and military confrontation in three of the four. Delaware quietly stayed in the Union. Voters there had given Breckinridge a plurality in 1860, but the majority of voters disapproved of secession, and few of the state's citizens owned slaves. Maryland, Missouri, and Kentucky, however,

Like the citizens in western Virginia, people in eastern Tennessee remained faithful to the Union. Men like those shown here swore allegiance to the United States flag and tried to split the state in two—one rebel and the other loyal—but Confederate troops put a stop to their efforts. *Library of Congress.*

each contained large, vocal secessionist minorities and appeared poised to bolt to the Confederacy.

Maryland was particularly vital to the Union, for it enclosed Washington, D.C., on the three sides not bordered by Virginia. If Maryland were to secede, the Union would be forced to move its capital. Maryland voters had overwhelmingly supported Breckinridge in 1860, and southern sympathizers controlled the legislature. But Governor Thomas Hicks, a Unionist, refused to call a special legislative session to consider secession.

On April 6, a Massachusetts regiment responding to Lincoln's call for troops passed through Baltimore on the way to the capital. A mob confronted the soldiers, and rioters attacked the rear companies with bricks, bottles, and pistols. The soldiers returned fire. When the violence subsided, twelve Baltimore residents and four soldiers lay dead, and dozens more

requisition To demand for military use.

were wounded. Secessionists reacted violently, destroying railroad bridges to keep additional northern troops out of the state. In effect, Washington, D.C., was cut off from the North.

Lincoln and General Scott ordered the military occupation of Baltimore and declared **martial law.** The state legislature finally met and voted to remain neutral. Lincoln then instructed the army to arrest suspected southern sympathizers and hold them without formal hearings or charges. When the legislature met again and appeared to be planning secession, Lincoln ordered the army to surround Frederick, the legislative seat—just as Davis had dispatched Confederate troops to occupy eastern Tennessee. With southern sympathizers suppressed, new state elections were held. The new legislature, overwhelmingly Unionist, voted against secession.

Kentucky had important economic ties to the South but was strongly nationalistic. Like Kentuckians Henry Clay and John Crittenden, most in the state favored compromise. The governor refused to honor Lincoln's call for troops, but the state legislature voted to remain neutral. Both the North and the South honored that neutrality. Kentucky's own mili-

tia, however, split into two factions, and the state became a bloody battleground where even members of the same family fought against one another.

In Missouri, Governor Claiborne F. Jackson, a former proslavery border ruffian, pushed for secession arguing that Missourians were bound together "in one brotherhood with the States of the South." When Unionists frustrated the secession movement, Jackson's forces seized the federal arsenal at Liberty and wrote to Jefferson Davis requesting artillery to support an assault on the arsenal at St. Louis. Union sympathizers, however, fielded their own forces and fought Jackson at every turn. Rioting broke out in St. Louis as civilians clashed with soldiers, and mob violence marred the nights. Jackson's secessionist movement sent representatives to the Confederate congress in Richmond, but Union forces maintained nominal control of the state and drove prosouthern leaders into exile.

> **martial law** Temporary rule by military authorities, imposed on a civilian population in time of war or when civil authority has broken down.

Individual Voices

Examining a Primary Source

Frederick Douglass: What to the Slave Is the Fourth of July?

■ To whom is Douglass referring here? Who did he consider his constituency to be?

■ Ironically, Douglass's statement predicted one of Roger Taney's points in the Dred Scott decision five years later. "In the opinion of the court, the legislation and histories of the times, and the language used in the declaration of independence, show, that neither the class of persons who had been imported as slaves, nor their descendants, whether they had become free or not, were then acknowledged as a part of the people, nor intended to be included in the general words used in that memorable instrument."

After escaping from slavery and then experiencing continuing denigration in the North, Frederick Douglass eventually became a very effective speaker for the abolition cause. Always very direct, Douglass often said things to white audiences that they *really* did not want to hear. In 1852 the Ladies' Anti-Slavery Society of Rochester invited Douglass to speak at their Fourth of July celebration. They were extremely shocked by what he said.

Fellow-citizens, pardon me, allow me to ask, why am I called upon to speak here today? What have I, or those I represent, to do with your national independence? ■ *Are the great principles of political freedom and of natural justice, embodied in that Declaration of Independence, extended to us? and am I, therefore, called upon to bring out humble offering to the national altar, and to confess the benefits and express devout gratitude for the blessings resulting from your independence to us? . . .*

But such is not the state of the case. I say it with a sad sense of the disparity between us. I am not included within the pale of this glorious anniversary! ■

■ *What is Douglass's point in denying connection to the holiday about which he had been invited to speak?*

■ *Douglass is quoting here from Psalm 137, which he had recited in full earlier in the speech. This Psalm, which relates to the fall of Israel and the Babylonian Captivity, is cited again when Douglass discusses the fate of nations that defy God. What point was Douglass making in citing this Psalm?*

Your high independence only reveals the immeasurable distance between us. The blessings in which you, this day, rejoice, are not enjoyed in common. The rich inheritance of justice, liberty, prosperity and independence, bequeathed by your fathers, is shared by you, not by me. The sunlight that brought life and healing to you, has brought stripes and death to me. This Fourth [of] July is yours, not mine. ■ *. . .*

Fellow-citizens; above your national, tumultuous joy, I hear the mournful wail of millions! whose chains, heavy and grievous yesterday, are, to-day, rendered more intolerable by the jubilee shouts that reach them. If I do forget, if I do not faithfully remember those bleeding children of sorrow this day, "may my right hand forget her cunning, and may my tongue cleave to the roof of my mouth!" ■ *To forget them, to pass lightly over their wrongs, and to chime in with the popular theme, would be treason most scandalous and shocking, and would make me a reproach before God and the world.*

Summary

As the Compromise of 1850 failed to alleviate regional tension and debates over slavery dominated the political agenda, the Whig Party, strained by fragmentation among its factions, disintegrated. Two completely new groups—the Know-Nothings and the Republicans—competed to replace the Whigs. A series of events—including the Kansas-Nebraska Act and the *Dred Scott* decision—intensified regional polarization, and radicals on both sides fanned the flames of sectional rivalry.

The new regional political coalitions of the 1850s more accurately reflected the changed composition of the electorate, but their intense commitment to regional interests left them far less able than their more nationally oriented predecessors to achieve compromise. Even the Democratic Party could not hold together, splitting into northern and southern wings. By 1859, the young Republican Party, committed to restricting slavery's expansion, seemed poised to gain control of the federal government. Fearing that the loss of political power would doom their way of

life, southerners recoiled in terror. Neither side felt it could afford to back down.

With the election of Abraham Lincoln in 1860, six southern states withdrew from the Union. Last-minute efforts at compromise, such as the Crittenden proposal, failed, and on April 12, 1861, five weeks after Lincoln's inauguration, Confederate forces fired on federal troops at Fort Sumter in Charleston Harbor. Certain that secession was illegal, Lincoln's constituency expected action, but the president's options were limited by the varied ideologies of his supporters. Similarly, Jefferson Davis and the newly created Confederacy faced problems resulting from disagreement about secession. But Lincoln believed that he had to call the nation to arms, and this move forced wavering states to choose sides. Internal divisions in Virginia, Tennessee, Maryland, Kentucky, and Missouri brought further violence and military action. Before summer, a second wave of secession finally solidified the lineup, and the boundary lines, between the two competing societies. The stakes were set, the division was complete: the nation was poised for the bloodiest war in its history.

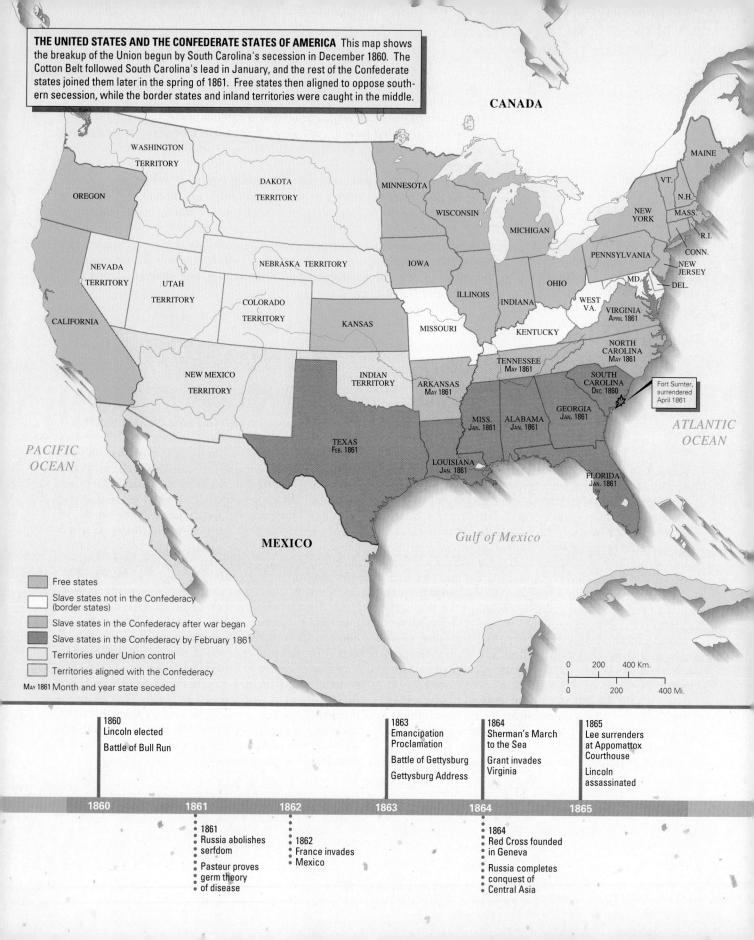

THE UNITED STATES AND THE CONFEDERATE STATES OF AMERICA This map shows the breakup of the Union begun by South Carolina's secession in December 1860. The Cotton Belt followed South Carolina's lead in January, and the rest of the Confederate states joined them later in the spring of 1861. Free states then aligned to oppose southern secession, while the border states and inland territories were caught in the middle.

CANADA

WASHINGTON TERRITORY

OREGON

DAKOTA TERRITORY

MINNESOTA

WISCONSIN

MICHIGAN

MAINE

VT.

N.H.

NEW YORK

MASS.

R.I.

NEVADA TERRITORY

UTAH TERRITORY

NEBRASKA TERRITORY

IOWA

ILLINOIS

OHIO

PENNSYLVANIA

CONN.

NEW JERSEY

MD.

DEL.

CALIFORNIA

COLORADO TERRITORY

KANSAS

MISSOURI

INDIANA

KENTUCKY

WEST VA.

VIRGINIA
APRIL 1861

NEW MEXICO TERRITORY

INDIAN TERRITORY

ARKANSAS
MAY 1861

TENNESSEE
MAY 1861

NORTH CAROLINA
MAY 1861

SOUTH CAROLINA
DEC. 1860

Fort Sumter, surrendered April 1861

TEXAS
FEB. 1861

MISS.
JAN. 1861

ALABAMA
JAN. 1861

GEORGIA
JAN. 1861

ATLANTIC OCEAN

PACIFIC OCEAN

LOUISIANA
JAN. 1861

FLORIDA
JAN. 1861

MEXICO

Gulf of Mexico

Free states

Slave states not in the Confederacy (border states)

Slave states in the Confederacy after war began

Slave states in the Confederacy by February 1861

Territories under Union control

Territories aligned with the Confederacy

MAY 1861 Month and year state seceded

0   200   400 Km.

0   200   400 Mi.

1860
Lincoln elected

Battle of Bull Run

1863
Emancipation Proclamation

Battle of Gettysburg

Gettysburg Address

1864
Sherman's March to the Sea

Grant invades Virginia

1865
Lee surrenders at Appomattox Courthouse

Lincoln assassinated

1860   1861   1862   1863   1864   1865

1861
Russia abolishes serfdom

Pasteur proves germ theory of disease

1862
France invades Mexico

1864
Red Cross founded in Geneva

Russia completes conquest of Central Asia

A Violent Choice: Civil War, 1861–1865

15

The United States and the Confederate States of America

Compare the map on the facing page to the opening maps for Chapters 10, 11, and 12 in terms of population, transportation systems, and industrial capacity. Given all of this information, why was the Confederacy at a distinct disadvantage at the beginning of the war? How was the conduct of the war influenced by these geographical factors, and what long-term consequences did this have on American history?

Individual Choices

MARY ASHTON RICE LIVERMORE

Having dedicated her life to women's education and national reform, Mary Ashton Rice Livermore and her husband, a crusading journalist, moved to Kansas in 1857 to lend their voices and votes to the antislavery effort in the new territory. Stalled in Chicago by their daughter's illness, they eventually founded an abolitionist newspaper in that city. When Civil War broke out in 1861, Mary immediately volunteered to create a local commission devoted to collecting medical supplies and other relief items to send to the battlefront. She also worked with other crusading women to raise public consciousness about sanitary conditions, eventually becoming a key official in Dorothea Dix's U.S. Sanitary Commission. Choices she made throughout her life convinced Livermore that women could and should assume expanding roles in American society and demand equality with men. *Chicago Historical Society.*

Mary Ashton Rice Livermore

Mary Ashton Rice was the daughter of strict Calvinists, but growing up in the heady intellectual atmosphere that permeated antebellum Boston, she soon joined many of her contemporaries in rejecting predestination and adopting a commitment to individual improvement and universal reform. With grudging support from her father, she attended several schools in Boston and finally took a job as a teacher to support herself while attending the Female Seminary in Charlestown, Massachusetts. After graduation, she took a position as a resident teacher on a Virginia plantation, where she learned firsthand about slavery and hated what she saw. After three years in the South, Rice made a choice to devote the balance of her life to two missions: personal involvement in reform movements such as temperance and abolition, and educating a new generation of young women to be reforming activists. She acted on the second of these by returning to Massachusetts to take charge of a female seminary in Duxbury. At the same time, she became active in the Boston-area temperance movement, where she met Universalist minister and reform editor Daniel P. Livermore, whom she married in 1845. Over the next ten years she and Daniel contributed regularly to local-area reform newspapers and magazines and became more and more active in increasingly radical organizations.

The Kansas-Nebraska Act and the subsequent outbreak of violence in Kansas proved to be a major turning point in the young couple's lives. Like many New Englanders and others who opposed the extension of slavery, the Livermores decided to move to Kansas in 1857 to lend their voices and votes to the struggle to make Kansas free. They got as far as Chicago; their daughter became ill, and the family decided to halt its journey. Still burning with reform fever, they decided to start a magazine, *The New Covenant,* to bring New England–style radical journalism to the Midwest.

When war broke out in 1861, Mary was no longer satisfied to apply herself exclusively in print. She immediately formed a female society devoted to "the relief of sick and wounded soldiers, and for the care of soldiers' families." Gathering a number of like-minded women into a tight organization, she and her lieutenants traveled to cities throughout the Midwest, even into hotly contested Missouri, gathering medical supplies and morale-raising cartons filled with home-made food, personal-care items, and often encouraging notes from sympathetic women addressed to anonymous soldiers in the field.

Over the next two years, women throughout the Midwest formed similar organizations and began to coordinate their efforts. In 1863 these various societies finally merged into the Northwestern Sanitary Commission, a major arm of reformer Dorothea Dix's national U.S. Sanitary Commission, with Livermore at its head. In that same year, she and her chief lieutenant, Jane C. Hoge, sponsored the first Sanitary Fair in Chicago, a four-month-long effort to raise money and educate the public about the deplorable health conditions in army camps. The crusade brought in over $70,000, demonstrating the efficacy of fairs for raising funds as well as the public consciousness. This triumph also led communities around the country to begin giving formal recognition to female relief organizations and to their leaders as effective executives. In the years to come, Sanitary Fairs would become a regular part of the wartime environment, and women like Hoge and Livermore would gain the ear of both political leaders and military commanders.

Mary Livermore's choice to be an activist carried with it the realization that women were fully capable of performing the organizational work that many believed only men could do. Reflecting on popular writings about women, Livermore commented, "One would suppose in reading them that women possess but one class of physical organs, and that these are always diseased. Such teaching is pestiferous, and tends to cause and perpetuate the very evils it professes to remedy." Never shy about sharing her views with men—whether military camp commanders whose ignorance of public health endangered soldiers' lives or politicians who were slow to fund relief efforts—Livermore resolved after the war to work toward gaining for women the recognition that their efforts during the war had proved they deserved. As a feminist editor and activist, Livermore spent the rest of her life as it began, laboring for justice. As she advised her followers, "Courage, then, for the end draws near! A few more years of persistent, faithful work and the women of the United States will be recognized as the legal equals of men." She clearly had come a long way from her Boston Calvinist roots. A series of choices by this one woman not only changed her life but also contributed greatly to changing the country and the world.

INTRODUCTION

The outbreak of war between the states shocked many in the already deeply troubled nation. Many considered it a dire tragedy. Lying in a sickbed in Boston, Mary Livermore's father declared that he would rather die than see the nation divided. But for his daughter, this was a moment of triumph and opportunity. For years she and her husband had worked to bring about the end of slavery, and now it appeared that the time was at hand.

Many shared Livermore's enthusiasm. Over the previous decade, increasing numbers of people in the North had come to loathe the South and everything it stood for. Though many had no great love for slaves, they had grown to detest slavery, which they associated with a power-mad aristocracy bent on imposing their power, and their culture, on the entire nation. People in the South were also enthusiastic. Likening themselves to the American colonists of old standing

up to a haughty empire, southerners were eager to reenact a war for independence.

It did not take long, however, for virtually everyone to become disillusioned. The South would find it more and more difficult to withstand the superior manpower and resources controlled by the Union. And the North would suffer frustrations of its own as President Lincoln's generals let opportunity after opportunity slip by. In desperation, Lincoln would finally redefine the war by issuing the Emancipation Proclamation, making it a struggle to end slavery as well as to prevent southern secession. From that point forward, hopes for a peaceful resolution evaporated: both sides would demand total victory or total destruction.

The war would affect many people in many different ways. For some, like Mary Livermore, it would afford great opportunities for advancement. For others, it would be a long, torturous ordeal. But one thing was true for everyone and for the nation at

"It is easy to understand how men catch the contagion of war," civilian relief worker Mary Ashton Rice Livermore asserted. Many on both sides certainly caught it during the opening days of the Civil War. These two Union cavalrymen (*left*) and Confederate infantrymen (*right*), father and son, volunteered for service and obviously were eager to fight. Such enthusiasm seldom lasted long as days and weeks of boredom, often accompanied by disease, punctuated by brief but heated battles caused enormous anxiety that eroded their fighting spirit. *Left: Richard Carlile; right: Bill Turner.*

large: nothing would be the same after the conflagration was over.

The Politics of War

■ What problems did Abraham Lincoln and Jefferson Davis face as they led their respective nations into war?

■ How did each chief executive deal with those problems?

■ What role did European nations play during the opening years of the war?

Running the war posed complex problems for both Abraham Lincoln and Jefferson Davis. At the outset, neither side had the experience, soldiers, or supplies to wage an effective war, and foreign diplomacy and international trade were vital to both. But perhaps the biggest challenge confronting both Davis and Lincoln

was internal politics. Lincoln had to contend not only with northern Democrats and southern sympathizers but also with divisions in his own party. Not all Republicans agreed with the president's war aims. Davis also faced internal political problems. The Confederate constitution guaranteed a great deal of autonomy to the Confederate states, and each state had a different opinion about war strategy and national objectives.

Union Policies and Objectives

Abraham Lincoln took the oath of office in March 1861, but Congress did not convene until July. This delay placed Lincoln in an awkward position. The Constitution gives Congress, not the president, the power "to declare war" and "to provide for calling forth the militia to execute the laws of the Union, sup-

Chronology

War Between the States

1861 Lincoln takes office and runs Union by executive
authority until July
Fort Sumter falls
Battle of Bull Run
McClellan organizes the Union army
Union naval blockade begins

1862 Grant's victories in Mississippi Valley
Battle of Shiloh
U.S. Navy captures New Orleans
Peninsular Campaign
Battle of Antietam
African Americans permitted in Union army

1863 Emancipation Proclamation takes effect
Union enacts conscription

Battle of Chancellorsville and death of
Stonewall Jackson
Union victories at Gettysburg and Vicksburg
Draft riots in New York City

1864 Grant invades Virginia
Sherman captures Atlanta
Lincoln reelected
Sherman's March to the Sea
Congress passes the Thirteenth Amendment

1865 Sherman's march through the Carolinas
Lee abandons Petersburg and Richmond
Lee surrenders at Appomattox Courthouse
Lincoln proposes a gentle reconstruction policy
Lincoln is assassinated

press insurrection, and repel invasions." The secession of the southern states and the imminent threat to federal authority at Fort Sumter, however, required an immediate response.

In effect, Lincoln ruled by executive proclamation for three months, vastly expanding the wartime powers of the presidency. Lincoln called for seventy-five thousand militiamen from the states to put down the rebellion. And ignoring specific constitutional provisions, he suspended the civil rights of citizens in Maryland when it appeared likely that the border state would join the Confederacy (see page 416). At various times during the war, Lincoln would resort to similar invasions of civil liberties when he felt that dissent threatened either domestic security or the Union cause.

Having assumed nearly absolute authority, Lincoln faced the need to rebuild an army in disarray. When hostilities broke out, the Union had only sixteen thousand men in uniform, and nearly one-third of the officers resigned to support the Confederacy. What military leadership remained was aged: seven of the eight heads of army bureaus had been in the service since the War of 1812, including General in Chief Winfield Scott, who was 74 years old. Only two Union officers had ever commanded a brigade, and both were in their seventies. Weapons were old, and supplies were low. On May 3, Lincoln again exceeded his con-

stitutional authority by calling for regular army recruits to meet the crisis. "Whether strictly legal or not," he asserted, such actions were based on "a popular demand, and a public necessity," and he expected "that Congress would readily ratify them."

Lincoln had also ordered the U.S. Navy to stop all incoming supplies to the states in rebellion. The naval blockade became an integral part of Union strategy. Though the Union navy had as few resources as the army, leadership in the Navy Department quickly turned that situation around. Navy Secretary Gideon Welles, whom Lincoln called "Father Neptune," purchased ships and built an effective navy that could both blockade the South and support land forces. By the end of 1861, the Union navy had 260 warships on the seas and a hundred more under construction.

The aged Winfield Scott drafted the initial Union military strategy. He ordered that the blockade of southern ports be combined with a strong Union thrust down the Mississippi River, the primary artery in the South's transportation system. This strategy would break the southern economy and split the Confederacy into two isolated parts. Like many northerners, Scott believed that economic pressure would bring southern moderates forward to negotiate a settlement and perhaps return to the Union. However, this passive, diplomacy-oriented strategy did not appeal to

Though many northerners thought it was too passive, General Winfield Scott's "anaconda plan" was actually very well conceived. As this 1861 lithograph shows, Scott called for a naval blockade of the South and seizure of the Mississippi River, shutting down transportation routes to ruin the Confederate economy. Scott retired at the end of the war's first year, but his plan continued to shape the Union's overall strategy. *Library of Congress.*

war-fevered northerners who hungered for complete victory over those "arrogant southerners." The northern press ridiculed what it called the **anaconda plan.**

When Congress finally convened on July 4, 1861, Lincoln explained his actions and reminded congressmen that he had neither the constitutional authority to abolish slavery nor any intention of doing so. Rebellion, not slavery, had caused the crisis, he said, and the seceding states must be brought back into the Union, regardless of the cost. "Our popular government has been called an experiment," he argued, and the point to be settled now was "its successful maintenance against a formidable internal attempt to overthrow it." On July 22 and 25, 1861, both houses of Congress passed resolutions validating Lincoln's actions.

This seemingly unified front lasted only a short time. Viewing vengeance as the correct objective, **Radical Republicans** pressured Congress to create a special committee to oversee the conduct of the war. Radical leader Thaddeus Stevens (see page 287) of Pennsylvania growled, "If their whole country must be laid waste, and made a desert, in order to save this union, so let it be." Stevens and the Radicals pressed for and passed a series of confiscation acts that inflicted severe penalties against individuals in rebellion. Treason was punishable by death, and anyone aiding the Confederacy was to be punished with imprisonment, attachment of property, and confiscation

of slaves. All persons living in the eleven seceding states, whether loyal to the Union or not, were declared enemies of the Union and subject to the provisions of the law.

The Radicals splintered any consensus Lincoln might have achieved in his own party, and northern Democrats railed against his accumulation of power. To keep an unruly Congress from undermining his efforts, Lincoln shaped early Union strategy to appease all factions and used military appointments to smooth political feathers. His attitudes frequently enraged radical abolitionists, but Lincoln maintained his calm in the face of their criticism and merely reinforced his intentions. "What I do about slavery and the colored race," he stated in 1862, "I do because it helps to save the Union; and what I forbear, I forbear because I do not believe it would help to save the

anaconda plan Winfield Scott's plan (named after a snake that smothers prey in its coils) to blockade southern ports and take control of the Mississippi River, thus splitting the Confederacy, cutting off southern trade, and causing an economic collapse.

Radical Republicans Republican faction that tried to limit presidential power and enhance congressional authority during the Civil War; Radicals opposed moderation toward the South or any toleration of slavery.

TABLE 15.1   Comparison of Union and Confederate Resources

	Union (23 States)	Confederacy (11 States)
Total population	20,700,000	9,105,000[a]
Manufacturing establishments	110,000	18,000
Manufacturing workers	1,300,000	110,000
Miles of railroad	21,973	9,283
Troop strength (est.)	2,100,000	850,000

Source: Data from *Battles and Leaders of the Civil War* (1884–1888; reprinted ed., 1956).
[a]Includes 3,654,000 blacks, most of them slaves and not available for military duty.

Union." Such words, however, did not mend the ongoing divisiveness that hindered his efforts to run the war.

Nevertheless, Lincoln had far greater physical and human resources at his command than did the Confederates (see Table 15.1). The Union was home to more than twice as many people as the Confederacy, had vastly superior manufacturing and transportation systems, and enjoyed almost a monopoly in banking and foreign exchange. Lincoln also had a well-established government structure and formal diplomatic relations with other nations of the world. Still, these advantages could not help the war effort unless properly harnessed.

Confederate Policies and Objectives

At the start of the war, the Confederacy had no army, no navy, no war supplies, no government structure, no foreign alliances, and a political situation as ragged as the Union's. Each Confederate state had its own ideas about the best way to conduct the war. After the attack on Fort Sumter, amassing supplies, troops, ships, and war materials was the main task for Davis and his cabinet. Politics, however, influenced southern choices about where to field armies and who would direct them, how to run a war without offending state leaders, and how to pursue foreign diplomacy.

The Union naval blockade posed an immediate problem. The Confederacy had no navy and no capacity to build naval ships. But it did have the extremely resourceful Stephen Mallory as secretary of the navy. Under Mallory's direction, southern coastal defenders converted river steamboats, tugboats, and **revenue cutters** into harbor patrol gunboats, and they developed and placed explosive mines at the entrances to southern harbors.

Confederates pinned their main hope of winning the war on the army. Fighting for honor was praiseworthy behavior in the South, and southerners strongly believed they could "lick the Yankees" despite their disadvantage in manpower and resources. Southern boys rushed to enlist to fight the northern "popinjays," expecting a quick and glorious victory. Thousands volunteered before the Confederate war department was even organized. By the time Lincoln issued his call for seventy-five thousand militiamen, the Confederates already had sixty thousand men in uniform.

Despite this rush of fighting men, the South faced major handicaps. Even with the addition of the four Upper South states (Virginia, North Carolina, Tennessee, and Arkansas), the South built only 4 percent of all locomotives and only 3 percent of all firearms manufactured in the United States in 1860. The North produced almost all of the country's cloth, **pig iron,** boots, and shoes. Early in the war, the South could produce enough food but lacked the means to transport it where it was needed. Quartermaster General Abraham Myers drew the mammoth task of producing

revenue cutter   A small, lightly armed boat used by government customs agents to apprehend merchant ships violating customs laws.

pig iron   Crude iron, direct from a blast furnace, that is cast into rectangular molds called pigs in preparation for conversion into steel, cast iron, or wrought iron.

and delivering tents, shoes, uniforms, blankets, horses, and wagons. All were in short supply.

The miracle worker in charge of supplying southern troops with weapons and ammunition was Josiah Gorgas, who became chief of **ordnance** in April 1861. Gorgas purchased arms from Europe while his ordnance officers bought or stole copper pots and tubing to make **percussion caps,** bronze church bells to make cannon, and lead weights to make bullets. He built factories and foundries to manufacture small arms. But despite his extraordinary skill, he could not supply all of the Confederate troops. When the Confederate congress authorized the enlistment of four hundred thousand additional volunteers in 1861, the war department had to turn away more than half of the enlistees because it lacked equipment for them.

Internal politics also plagued the Davis administration. Despite the shortage of arms, state governors hoarded weapons seized from federal arsenals for their own state militias and then criticized Confederate strategies, particularly the actions of the war department. Although the South had many more qualified officers at the beginning of the war than did the North, powerful state politicians with little military experience—such as Henry A. Wise of Virginia and Robert A. Toombs of Georgia—received appointments as generals. That practice may have made good political sense, but it was military folly.

Going into the conflict, Davis favored waging a defensive war. He felt that by counterattacking and yielding territory when necessary to buy time, the Confederacy could prolong the war and make it so costly that the Union would finally give up. Although defensive strategies ran counter to southern notions of pride and honor, each state's leaders demanded that their state's borders be protected, ignoring that such a strategy would spread troops so thin that no state would be safe. In any case, most southerners preferred an aggressive policy. As one southern editor put it, the "idea of waiting for blows, instead of inflicting them is altogether unsuited to the genius of our people."

The Diplomatic Front

Perhaps the biggest challenge facing the Confederacy was gaining international recognition and foreign aid. The primary focus of Confederate foreign policy was Great Britain. For years, the South had been exporting huge amounts of cotton to Britain, and many southerners felt that formal recognition of the Confederate States of America as an independent nation would immediately follow secession. Political, diplo-

matic, and economic realities doomed them to disappointment. After all, the United States, divided as it was, was still an important player in international affairs, and the British were not going to risk offending the emerging industrial power without good cause. Also, many English voters were morally opposed to slavery and would have objected to an open alliance with the slaveholding Confederacy. Thus, while the British allowed southern agents to purchase ships and goods, they crafted a careful policy. On May 13, 1861, Queen Victoria proclaimed official neutrality but granted **belligerent status** to the South. This meant that Britain recognized the Confederates not as rebels but as responsible parties in a legitimate war for independence. But it also meant that they did not recognize the Confederate States of America as yet ready to enter the international community.

The British pronouncement set the tone for other European responses and was much less than southerners had hoped for. It was also a major blow to the North, however, for Britain rejected Lincoln's position that the conflict was rebellion against duly authorized government. Lincoln could do little but accept British neutrality, for to provoke Britain might lead to full recognition of the Confederacy or to calls for arbitration of the conflict. At the same time, he cautiously continued efforts to block all incoming aid to the Confederacy. In November 1861, however, an incident at sea nearly scuttled British-American relations. James Murray Mason, the newly appointed Confederate emissary to London, and John Slidell, the Confederate minister to France, were traveling to their posts aboard the *Trent,* a British merchant ship bound for London. After the *Trent* left Havana, the U.S. warship *San Jacinto,* under the command of Captain Charles Wilkes, stopped the British ship. Wilkes had Mason, Slidell, and their staffs removed from the *Trent* and taken to Boston for confinement at Fort Warren.

Northerners celebrated the action and praised Wilkes, but the British were not pleased. They viewed the *Trent* affair as aggression against a neutral government, a violation of international law, and an af-

---

ordnance   Weapons, ammunition, and other military equipment.

percussion cap   A thin metal cap containing an explosive compound, needed to fire the guns used in the Civil War.

belligerent status   Recognition that a participant in a conflict is a nation engaged in warfare rather than a rebel against a legally constituted government; full diplomatic recognition is one possible outcome.

front to their national honor. President Lincoln, Secretary of State William Seward, and U.S. Ambassador to England Charles Francis Adams (son of former president John Quincy Adams) calmed the British by arguing that Wilkes had acted without orders. They ordered the release of the prisoners and apologized to the British, handling the incident so adroitly that the public outcry was largely forgotten when Mason and Slidell arrived in London.

The Union's First Attack

Like most southerners, northerners were confident that military action would bring the war to a quick end. General Irvin McDowell made the first move when his troops crossed into Virginia to engage troops led by General P. G. T. Beauregard (see Map 15.1 and Table 15.2). McDowell's troops, though high-spirited, were poorly trained and undisciplined. They ambled along as if they were on a country outing, allowing Beauregard enough time to position his troops in defense of a vital rail center near Manassas Junction along a creek called **Bull Run.**

McDowell attacked on Sunday, July 21, and maintained the offensive most of the day. He seemed poised to overrun the Confederates until southern reinforcements under **Thomas J. Jackson** stalled the Union advance. Jackson's unflinching stand at Bull Run earned him the nickname "Stonewall," and under intense cannon fire, Union troops panicked and began fleeing into a throng of northern spectators who had brought picnic lunches and settled in to watch the battle. Thoroughly humiliated before a hometown crowd, Union soldiers retreated toward Washington. Jefferson Davis immediately ordered the invasion of the Union capital, but the Confederates were also in disarray and made no attempt to pursue the fleeing Union forces.

This battle profoundly affected both sides. In the South, the victory stirred confidence that the war would be short and victory complete. Northerners, disillusioned and embarrassed, pledged that no similar retreats would occur. Under fire for the loss and hoping to improve both the management of military affairs and the competence of the troops, Lincoln fired McDowell and appointed **George B. McClellan.** McClellan was assigned to create the **Army of the Potomac** to defend the capital from Confederate attack and spearhead any offensives into Virginia. Lincoln also replaced Secretary of War Simon Cameron with Edwin Stanton, a politician and lawyer from Pennsylvania. Scott remained in place as general in chief until his retirement at the end of the year.

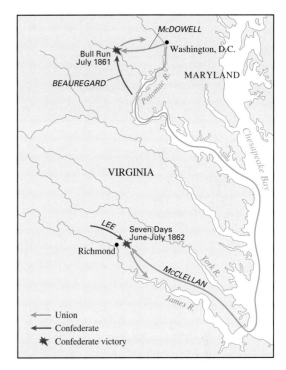

MAP 15.1 Union Offensives into Virginia, 1861–1862
This map shows two failed Union attempts to invade Virginia: the Battle of Bull Run (July 1861) and the Peninsular Campaign (August 1862). Confederate victories embarrassed the richer and more populous Union.

General McClellan's strengths were in organization and discipline. Both were sorely needed. Before Bull Run, Union officers had lounged around Washington while largely unsupervised raw recruits in army camps received no military instruction. Under

Bull Run   A creek in Virginia not far from Washington, D.C., where Confederate soldiers forced federal troops to retreat in the first major battle of the Civil War, fought in July 1861.

Thomas J. Jackson   Confederate general nicknamed "Stonewall"; he commanded troops at both battles of Bull Run and was mortally wounded by his own soldiers at Chancellorsville in 1863.

George B. McClellan   U.S. general tapped by Lincoln to organize the Army of the Potomac; a skillful organizer but slow and indecisive as a field commander. He eventually replaced Winfield Scott as general in chief of Union forces.

Army of the Potomac   Army created to guard the U.S. capital after the Battle of Bull Run in 1861; it became the main Union army in the East.

TABLE 1 5 . 2   Battle of Bull Run, July 22, 1861

	Union Army	Confederate Army
Commanders	Irvin McDowell	P. G. T. Beauregard
Troop strength	17,676	18,053
Losses		
Killed	460	387
Wounded	1,124	1,582
Captured	1,312	13
Total Losses	2,896	1,982

Source: Data from *Battles and Leaders of the Civil War* (1884–1888; reprinted ed., 1956).

McClellan, months of training turned the 185,000-man army into a well-drilled and efficient unit. Calls to attack Richmond began anew, but McClellan, seemingly in no hurry for battle, continued to drill the troops and remained in the capital. Finally on January 27, 1862, Lincoln called for a broad offensive, but his general in chief ignored the order and delayed for nearly two months. Completely frustrated, Lincoln removed McClellan as general in chief on March 11 but left him in command of the Army of the Potomac. Even so, Union forces in the East mounted no major offensives.

From Bull Run to Antietam

■ How did military action during the opening years of the war affect the people's perceptions of the war in the North and South?

■ In what ways did international diplomacy play into Lincoln's decision making as the war unfolded?

■ Why did Lincoln issue the Emancipation Proclamation when and in the way he did? What sorts of responses did it elicit?

Reorganizing the military and forming the Army of the Potomac did not accomplish Lincoln's and the nation's goal of toppling the Confederacy quickly and bringing the rebellious South back into the Union. In the second year of the war, frustration followed frustration as Confederate forces continued to outwit and outfight numerically superior and better-equipped federal troops. After Bull Run it was clear that the war would be neither short nor glorious. Military, political, and diplomatic strategies became increasingly entan-

gled as both North and South struggled for the major victories that would end the war.

The War in the West

While the war in the East slid into inactivity, events in the West seemed almost as futile for the Union forces. In the border state of Missouri, the conflict rapidly degenerated into guerrilla warfare. Confederate William Quantrill's Raiders matched atrocities committed by Unionist guerrilla units called Jayhawkers. Union officials seemed unable to stop the ambushes, arson, theft, and murder, and Missouri remained a lawless battleground throughout the war.

Both the United States and the Confederacy coveted the western territories nearly as much as they did the border states. In 1861 Confederate Henry Hopkins Sibley attempted to gain control of New Mexico and Arizona. Bearing authority directly from Jefferson Davis, Sibley recruited thirty-seven hundred Texans and marched into New Mexico. He defeated a Union force at Valverde, but his losses were high. Needing provisions to continue the operation, he sent units to raid abandoned Union storehouses at Albuquerque and Santa Fe, but withdrawing federal troops had burned whatever supplies they could not carry. The small Confederate force at Santa Fe encountered a much larger federal force and won a miraculous victory, but the effort left the Confederates destitute of supplies. Under constant attack, the starving Confederate detachment evaded Union troops and retreated back into Texas.

As the war intensified, leaders on both sides were forced to concentrate on regional defenses and focus

Angered by years of systematic mistreatment at the hands of federal authorities, many Native Americans in Indian Territory were eager to enlist for service with the Confederacy. Confederate president Jefferson Davis chose his Indian agents carefully in order to take advantage of this much-needed source of aid: his ambassador to Indian Territory, General Albert Pike, for example, had represented the Creeks in their battle against removal in the 1830s. As this daguerreotype illustrates, Davis's diplomacy was highly successful; many young Indians flocked to Confederate recruitment rallies to join the army. *Wisconsin Historical Society.*

on potential confrontations with enemy armies. Union officers pulled most of their troops back into the areas of concentrated fighting, leaving vast areas of the sparsely settled West with no military protection. In 1862 the Santee Sioux took advantage of the situation by attacking and killing more than eight hundred settlers in the Minnesota River valley. An army of fourteen hundred volunteers finally put down the uprising, but the lack of federal troops in frontier regions created severe anxiety in western communities.

Confederate leaders sought alliances with several Indian tribes at the onset of war, particularly tribes in the newly settled Indian Territory south of Kansas. Many of the residents there had endured the Trail of Tears (see page 296) and had no particular love for the Union. If these Indian tribes aligned with the Confederacy, they not only could supply troops but might also form a buffer between Union forces in Kansas and the thinly spread Confederate defenses west of the Mississippi River. Davis appointed General Albert Pike, an Arkansas lawyer who had represented the Creeks in court, as special commissioner for the Indian Territory in March 1861. Pike negotiated with several tribes and on October 7 signed a treaty with John Ross, chief of the Cherokee Nation (see pages 295–296). The treaty, which applied to some members of the Cherokee, Choctaw, Creek, Chickasaw, and Seminole tribes, granted the Indians more nearly equal status—at least on paper—than any previous federal treaty, and it guaranteed that Indians would be asked to fight only to defend their own territory. One Cherokee leader, Stand Watie, became a Confederate general and distinguished himself in battle, leading his Confederate troops in guerrilla warfare against Union forces.

Struggle for the Mississippi

While McClellan stalled in the East, one Union general finally had some success in the western theater of the war. Following the strategy outlined in General Scott's anaconda plan, **Ulysses S. Grant** moved against southern strongholds in the Mississippi Valley in 1862. On February 6, he took Fort Henry along the Tennessee River and ten days later captured Fort Donelson on the Cumberland River near Nashville, Tennessee (see Map 15.2). As Union forces approached Nashville, the Confederates retreated to Corinth, Mississippi. In this one swift stroke, Grant successfully penetrated Confederate western defenses and brought Kentucky and most of Tennessee under federal control.

At Corinth, Confederate general Albert Sidney Johnston finally reorganized the retreating southern troops while Grant was waiting for reinforcements. Early on April 6, to Grant's surprise, Johnston attacked at Pittsburg Landing, Tennessee, near a small country meetinghouse called Shiloh Church (see Table 15.3). Some

Ulysses S. Grant U.S. general who became general in chief of the Union army in 1864 after the Vicksburg campaign; he later became president of the United States.

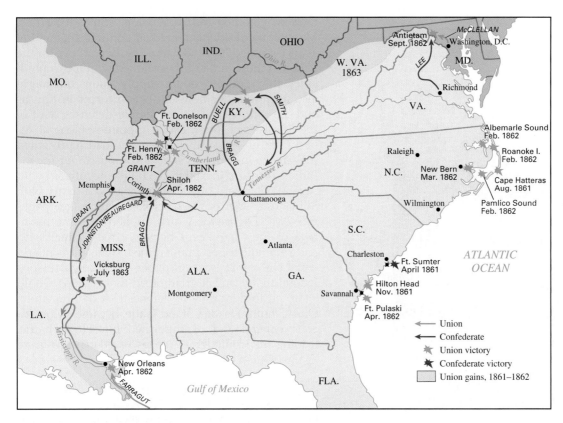

MAP 15.2 The Anaconda Plan and the Battle of Antietam This map illustrates the anaconda plan at work. The Union navy closed southern harbors while Grant's troops worked to seal the northern end of the Mississippi River. The map also shows the Battle of Antietam (September 1862), in which Confederate troops under Robert E. Lee were finally defeated by the Union army under General George McClellan.

Union forces under General **William Tecumseh Sherman** were driven back, but the Confederate attack soon lost momentum as Union defenses stiffened. The **Battle of Shiloh** raged until midafternoon. When Johnston was mortally wounded, General Beauregard took command and by day's end believed the enemy defeated. But Union reinforcements arrived during the night, and the next morning Grant counterattacked, pushing the Confederates back to Corinth.

The losses on both sides were staggering. The Battle of Shiloh made the reality of war apparent to everyone but made a particularly strong impression on the common soldier. After Shiloh, one Confederate wrote: "Death in every awful form, if it really be death, is a pleasant sight in comparison to the fearfully and mortally wounded." Few people foresaw that the horrible carnage at Shiloh was but a taste of what was to come.

Farther south, Admiral David G. Farragut led a fleet of U.S. Navy gunboats against New Orleans, the commercial and banking center of the South, and on April 25 forced the city's surrender. Farragut then sailed up the Mississippi, hoping to take the well-fortified city of **Vicksburg,** Mississippi. He scored several vic-

William Tecumseh Sherman U.S. general who captured Atlanta in 1864 and led a destructive march to the Atlantic coast.

Battle of Shiloh Battle in Tennessee in April 1862 that ended with an unpursued Confederate withdrawal; both sides suffered heavy casualties for the first time, but neither side gained ground.

Vicksburg Confederate-held city on the Mississippi River that surrendered on July 4, 1863, after a lengthy siege by Grant's forces.

TABLE 15.3 Battle of Shiloh, April 6–7, 1862

	Union Army	Confederate Army
Commanders	William Tecumseh Sherman Ulysses S. Grant	Albert Sidney Johnston (killed) P. G. T. Beauregard
Troop strength	75,000	44,000
Losses		
Killed	1,754	1,723
Wounded	8,408	8,012
Captured, missing	2,885	959
Total Losses	13,047	10,694

Source: Data from *Battles and Leaders of the Civil War* (1884–1888; reprinted ed., 1956).

tories until he reached Port Hudson, Louisiana, where the combination of Confederate defenses and shallow water forced him to halt. Meanwhile, on June 6, Union gunboats destroyed a Confederate fleet at Memphis, Tennessee, and brought the upper Mississippi under Union control. Vicksburg remained the only major obstacle to Union control over the entire river (see Map 15.2).

Realizing the seriousness of the situation in the West, the Confederates regrouped and invaded Kentucky. Union forces under General William S. Rosecrans stopped Confederate general Braxton Bragg's force on December 31 at Stone's River and did not pursue when the Confederates retreated. Back in Mississippi, Grant launched two unsuccessful attacks against Vicksburg in December, but then Union efforts stalled. Nevertheless, northern forces had wrenched control of the upper and lower ends of the river away from the Confederacy.

Lee's Aggressive Defense of Virginia

The anaconda plan was well on its way to cutting the Confederacy in two, but the general public in the North thought that the path to real victory led to Richmond, capital of the Confederacy. Thus, to maintain public support for the war, Lincoln needed victories over the Confederates in the East, and campaigns there were given higher priority than campaigns in the West. Confederate leaders, realizing that Richmond would be an important prize for the North, took dramatic steps to keep their capital city out of

enemy hands. In fact, defending Richmond was the South's primary goal: more supplies and men were assigned to campaigns in Virginia than to defending Confederate borders elsewhere.

Hoping to clear Virginia's coastline of Union blockaders and protect their capital from amphibious invasion, Confederate naval architects had redesigned a captured Union ship named the *Merrimac*. They encased the entire ship in iron plates and renamed it the *Virginia*. Learning of Confederate attempts to launch an armored ship, the Union navy began building the *Monitor*, a low-decked ironclad vessel with a revolving gun turret. In March the *Virginia* and the *Monitor* shelled each other for five hours. Both were badly damaged but still afloat when the *Virginia* withdrew, making its way back to Norfolk, never to leave harbor again.

With the *Virginia* out of service, McClellan devised precisely the amphibious assault that Virginians had been fearing. Expecting to surprise the Confederates by attacking Richmond from the south, he transported the entire Army of the Potomac by ship to Fort Monroe, Virginia. Initiating what would be called the **Peninsular Campaign,** the army marched up the peninsula between the York and James Rivers (see Map 15.1). In typical fashion, McClellan proceeded

Peninsular Campaign McClellan's attempt in the spring and summer of 1862 to capture Richmond by advancing up the peninsula between the James and York Rivers; Confederate forces under Robert E. Lee drove his troops back.

Desperate to break the grip of the Union anaconda, the Confederate navy converted the captured Union ship U.S.S. *Merrimac* into the ironclad C.S.S. *Virginia*. Virtually immune to any weapon carried by Union frigates, the *Virginia* dominated the sea-lanes out of Norfolk Harbor. Though the *Virginia* carried cannon, its iron hull was its most effective weapon, as illustrated by this painting of the Confederate ironclad ramming the Union blockade vessel *Cumberland*. The Union navy eventually completed construction of its own ironclad, the U.S.S. *Monitor,* which defeated the *Virginia* in a dramatic sea battle, eliminating that weapon from the Confederate arsenal. *"Ramming of the* U.S.S. Cumberland *and the* U.S.S. Virginia*" by Alexander Charles Stuart. Courtesy of the Charleston Renaissance Gallery, Robert M. Hicklin Jr. Inc., Charleston, SC.*

cautiously. The outnumbered Confederate forces took advantage of his indecision and twice slipped away, retreating toward Richmond while McClellan followed. Hoping to overcome the odds by surprising his opponent, General Joseph E. Johnston, commander of the Confederate Army of Northern Virginia, wheeled about and attacked at Seven Pines on May 31. Though the battle was indecisive—both sides claimed victory—it halted McClellan's progress and disabled Johnston, who was seriously wounded.

With McClellan stalled, Confederate stalwart Stonewall Jackson staged a brilliant diversionary thrust down the Shenandoah Valley toward Washington. Jackson, who had grown up in the region, seemed to be everywhere at once. In thirty days, he and his men (who became known as the "foot cavalry") marched 350 miles, defeated three Union armies in five battles, captured and sent back to Richmond a fortune in provisions and equipment, inflicted twice as many casualties as they received, and confused and immobilized Union forces in the region.

Meanwhile, Union forces were marking time near Richmond while McClellan waited for reinforcements. Determined to remove this threat, Confederate forces launched a series of attacks to drive McClellan away from the Confederate capital. Though his army had already proved itself against the Confederates at Seven Pines, a new factor weighed in against McClelland. With Johnston wounded, Davis had been forced to re-

place him, choosing Robert E. Lee. Lee was probably the Confederacy's best general. Daring, bold, and tactically aggressive, he enjoyed combat, pushed his troops to the maximum, and was well liked by those serving under him. Lee had an uncanny ability to read the character of his opponents, predict their maneuvers, and exploit their mistakes. In a move that became typical of his generalship, Lee split his forces and attacked from all sides over a seven-day period in August, forcing McClellan into a defensive position. The Peninsular Campaign was over. The self-promoting Union general had been beaten in part by his own indecisiveness.

Fed up with McClellan, Lincoln transferred command of the Army of the Potomac to General John Pope, but Pope's command was brief. Union forces encountered Lee's army again at the Manassas rail line on August 30. The Confederates pretended to retreat, and when Pope followed, Lee soundly defeated Lincoln's new general in the **Second Battle of Bull Run.** Thoroughly disappointed with Pope's performance, but lacking any other viable replacement, Lincoln once again named McClellan commander of the Army of the Potomac.

Second Battle of Bull Run Union defeat near Bull Run in August 1862; Union troops led by John Pope were outmaneuvered by Lee.

Lee's Invasion of Maryland

Feeling confident after the second victory at Bull Run, Lee devised a bold offensive against Maryland. His plan had three objectives. First, he wanted to move the fighting out of war-torn Virginia so that farmers could harvest food. Second, he hoped that he might attract volunteers from among the many slaveowners and southern sympathizers in Maryland to beef up his undermanned army. Third, he believed that a strong thrust against Union forces might gain diplomatic recognition for the Confederacy from Europe. In the process, he hoped to win enough territory to force the Union to sue for peace. On September 4, Lee crossed the Potomac into Maryland, formulating an intricate offensive by dividing his army into three separate attack wings. But someone was careless— Union soldiers found a copy of Lee's detailed instructions wrapped around some cigars at an abandoned Confederate campsite.

If McClellan had acted swiftly on this intelligence, he could have crushed Lee's army piece by piece, but he waited sixteen hours before advancing. By then, Lee had learned of the missing orders and quickly withdrew. Lee reunited some of his forces at Sharpsburg, Maryland, around **Antietam Creek** (see Map 15.2). There, on September 17, the Army of the Potomac and the Army of Northern Virginia engaged in the bloodiest single-day battle of the Civil War.

The casualties in this one battle were more than double those suffered in the War of 1812 and the War with Mexico combined. "The air was full of the hiss of bullets and the hurtle of grapeshot," one Union soldier said, and "the whole landscape turned red." The bitter fighting exhausted both armies. After a day of rest, Lee retreated across the Potomac. Stonewall Jackson, covering Lee's retreat, soundly thrashed a force that McClellan sent in pursuit. But for the first time, General Lee experienced defeat.

Although Lee's offensive had been thwarted, Lincoln was in no way pleased with the performance of his army and its leadership. He felt that McClellan could have destroyed Lee's forces if he had attacked earlier or, failing that, had pursued the fleeing Confederate army with all haste. He fired McClellan again, this time for good, and placed Ambrose E. Burnside in command of the Army of the Potomac.

Burnside moved the Army of the Potomac to the east bank of the Rappahannock River overlooking **Fredericksburg,** Virginia (see Map 15.3), where he delayed for almost three weeks. Lee used the time to fortify the heights west of the city with men and artillery. On December 13, in one of the worst mistakes of the war, Burnside ordered a day-long frontal assault. The results were devastating. Federal troops, mowed down from the heights, suffered tremendous casualties, and once again the Army of the Potomac retreated to Washington.

Diplomacy and the Politics of Emancipation

The first full year of the war ended with mixed results for both sides. Union forces in the West had scored major victories, breaking down Confederate defenses and taking Memphis and New Orleans. But the failure of the Army of the Potomac under three different generals and against Lee and Jackson's brilliant maneuvers seemed to outweigh those successes. Lee's victories, however, carried heavy casualties, and the South's ability to supply and deploy troops was rapidly diminishing. A long, drawn-out conflict favored the Union unless Jefferson Davis could secure help for the Confederacy from abroad.

The Confederacy still expected British aid, but nothing seemed to shake Britain's commitment to neutrality. To a large extent, this obstinacy was due to the efforts of Charles Francis Adams, Lincoln's ambassador in London, who demonstrated his diplomatic skill repeatedly during the war. Also, Britain possessed a surplus of cotton and did not need southern supplies, neutralizing the South's only economic lever and frustrating Davis's diplomatic goals.

Radical Republicans were also frustrated. No aspect of the war was going as they had expected. They had hoped that the Union army would defeat the South in short order. Instead the war effort was dragging on. More important from the Radicals' point of view, nothing was being done about slavery. They pressed Lincoln to take a stand against slavery, and they pushed Congress for legislation to prohibit slavery in federal territories.

Politically astute as always, Lincoln acted to appease the Radical Republicans, foster popular support in the North for the war effort, and increase favorable sentiment for the Union cause abroad. During the

Antietam Creek   Site of a battle that occurred in September 1862 when Lee's forces invaded Maryland; both sides suffered heavy losses, and Lee retreated into Virginia.

Fredericksburg   Site in Virginia of a Union defeat in December 1862, which demonstrated the incompetence of the new Union commander, Ambrose E. Burnside.

Many soldiers entered the Civil War expecting excitement and colorful pageantry, but the realities of war were harsh and ugly. This photograph by Union cameraman Andrew J. Russell shows a line of southern soldiers who were killed while defending a position at Fredericksburg. Even after Union soldiers had breached the wall, the Confederates fought on, using their rifles as clubs until they were all mowed down. Scenes like this became so common that veterans reported that they became numb to the shock of death. *Library of Congress.*

summer of 1862, he drafted a proclamation freeing the slaves in the Confederacy and submitted it to his cabinet. Cabinet members advised that he postpone announcing the policy until after the Union had achieved a military victory. In August, **Horace Greeley,** founder of the *New York Tribune,* called for the immediate emancipation of all slaves, but Lincoln reiterated that his objective was "to save the Union," not "to save or destroy slavery." On September 22, however, five days after the Battle of Antietam, Lincoln unveiled the **Emancipation Proclamation,** which abolished slavery in the states "in rebellion" and would go into effect on January 1, 1863.

Although the Emancipation Proclamation was a major step toward ending slavery, it actually freed no slaves. The proclamation applied only to slavery in areas controlled by the Confederacy, not in any area controlled by the Union. Some found this exception troubling, labeling the proclamation an empty fraud, but the president's reasoning was sound. He could not afford to alienate the four slave states that had remained in the Union, nor could he commit any manpower to enforce emancipation in the areas that had been captured from the Confederacy. Lincoln made emancipation entirely conditional on a Union military victory, a gambit designed to force critics of the war, whether in the United States or Great Britain, to rally behind his cause.

Whether or not it was successful as a humanitarian action, issuing the Emancipation Proclamation at the time he did and in the form he did was a profoundly successful political step for Lincoln. Although a handful of northern Democrats and a few Union military leaders called it an "absurd proclamation of a political coward," more joined Frederick Douglass in proclaiming, "We shout for joy that we live to record this righteous decree." Meanwhile, some in Britain pointed to the paradox of the proclamation: it declared an end to slavery in areas where Lincoln could not enforce it, while having no effect on slavery in areas where he could. But even there, most applauded the document and rallied against recognition of the Confederacy.

Still, Lincoln's new general in chief, Henry Halleck, was chilled by the document. As he explained to Grant, the "character of the war has very much changed within the last year. There is now no possible hope of reconciliation." The war was now about slavery as well as secession, and the Emancipation Proclamation committed the Union to conquering the enemy. As Lincoln told one member of his cabinet, the war would now be "one of subjugation."

Horace Greeley Journalist and politician who helped found the Republican Party; his newspaper, the *New York Tribune,* was known for its antislavery stance.

Emancipation Proclamation Lincoln's order abolishing slavery as of January 1, 1863, in states "in rebellion" but not in border territories still loyal to the Union.

The Human Dimensions of the War

■ How did the burdens of war affect society in the North and the South during the course of the fighting?

■ How did individuals and governments in both regions respond to those burdens?

The Civil War imposed tremendous stress on American society. As the men marched off to battle, women faced the task of caring for families and property alone. As casualties increased, the number of voluntary enlistments decreased, and both sides searched for ways to find replacements for dead and wounded soldiers. The armies consumed vast amounts of manufactured and agricultural products—constantly demanding not only weapons and ammunition but also food, clothing, and hardware. Government spending was enormous, hard currency was scarce, and inflation soared as both governments printed paper money to pay their debts. Industrial capability, transportation facilities, and agricultural production often dictated when, where, and how well armies fought. Society in both North and South changed to meet an array of hardships as individuals facing unfamiliar conditions attempted to carry on their lives amid the war's devastation.

Instituting the Draft

By the end of 1862, heavy casualties, massive desertion, and declining enlistments had depleted both armies. Although the North had a much larger population pool than the South to draw from, its enlistments sagged with its military fortunes during 1862. More than a hundred thousand Union soldiers were absent without official leave. Most volunteers had enlisted in 1861 for limited terms, which would soon expire. Calling on state militias netted few replacements because the Democrats, who made tremendous political gains at the state level in 1862, openly criticized Republican policies and at times refused to cooperate. In March 1863, Congress passed the **Conscription Act,** trying to bypass state officials and ensure enough manpower to continue the war. The law in effect made all single men between the ages of 20 and 45 and married men between 20 and 35 eligible for service. Government agents collected names in a house-to-house survey, and draftees were selected by lottery.

The conscription law did offer "escape routes." Drafted men could avoid military service by providing—that is, hiring—an "acceptable substitute" or by paying a $300 fee to purchase exemption. The burden of service thus fell on farmers and urban workers—a large proportion of whom were immigrants—who were already suffering from the economic burden of high taxation and inflation caused by the war. Added to that was workers' fears that multitudes of former slaves freed by the Emancipation Proclamation would pour into the already crowded job market, further lowering the value of their labor. Together, conscription and emancipation created among the urban poor a sense of alienation, which exploded in the summer of 1863.

The trouble started on July 13 in New York City. Armed demonstrators protesting unfair draft laws engaged in a spree of violence, venting their frustration over the troubles plaguing working people. During three nights of rioting, white workingmen beat many African Americans and lynched six. The Colored Orphan Asylum and several homes owned by blacks were burned. Mobs ransacked businesses owned by African Americans and by people who employed them. Irish men and women and members of other groups that seemed to threaten job security also felt the fury as mobs attacked their churches, businesses, and homes. The rioters also expressed their frustration against Republican spokesmen and officials. Republican journalist Horace Greeley was **hanged in effigy,** and the homes of other prominent Republicans and abolitionists were vandalized. Protesting draft exemptions for the rich, rioters also set upon well-dressed strangers on the streets. After four days of chaos, federal troops put down the riot. Fearful of future violence, the city council of New York City voted to pay the $300 exemption fee for all poor draftees who chose not to serve in the army.

The Confederacy also instituted a draft after the first wave of enlistments dried up. Conscription in the South, as in the North, met with considerable resentment and resistance. Believing that plantations were necessary to the war effort and that slaves would not work unless directly overseen by masters, in 1862 Confederate officials passed the **Twenty Negro Law,**

Conscription Act   Law passed by Congress in 1863 that established a draft but allowed wealthy people to escape it by hiring a substitute or paying the government a $300 fee.

hang in effigy   To hang, as if on a gallows, a crude likeness or dummy—an effigy—representing a hated person.

Twenty Negro Law   Confederate law that exempted planters owning twenty or more slaves from the draft on the grounds that overseeing farm labor done by slaves was necessary to the war effort.

Angered by the fact that rich men were virtually exempt from the draft, frightened by the prospect of job competition from freed southern slaves, and frustrated by the lack of resolution on the battlefield, workingmen took to the streets in New York City during the summer of 1863 to protest against the war. Well-dressed men, African Americans, and leading war advocates were the main targets of mob violence during three nights of uncontrolled rioting. As this illustration shows, federal troops finally put down the rioting in a series of battles around the city. An unknown number of people were killed and injured. *Collection of Picture Research Consultants & Archives.*

which exempted planters owning twenty or more slaves from military service. Like the exemptions in the North, the southern policy fostered the feeling that the poor were going off to fight while the rich stayed safely at home. The law was modified in 1863, requiring exempted planters to pay $500, and in 1864, the number of slaves required to earn an exemption was lowered to fifteen. Nevertheless, resentment continued to smolder.

Confederate conscription laws also ran afoul of states' rights advocates, who feared that too much power was centered in Richmond. Southerners developed several forms of passive resistance to the draft laws. Thousands of draftees simply never showed up, and local officials, jealously guarding their political autonomy, made little effort to enforce the draft.

Wartime Economy in the North and South

Although riots, disorder, and social disruption plagued northern cities, the economy and industry of the Union actually grew stronger as the war progressed. In his 1864 message to Congress, Abraham Lincoln stated that the war had not depleted northern resources. Although the president exaggerated a bit, the statement con-

tained some truth. Northern industry and population did grow during the Civil War. Operating in cooperation with government, manufacturing experienced a boom. Manufacturers of war supplies benefited from government contracts. Textiles and shoemaking boomed as new labor-saving devices improved efficiency and increased production. Congress stimulated economic growth by means of subsidies and land grants to support a transcontinental railroad, higher tariffs to aid manufacturing, and land grants that states could use to finance higher education. In 1862 Congress passed the **Homestead Act** to make land available to more farmers. The law granted 160 acres of the public domain in the West to any citizen or would-be citizen who lived on, and improved, the land for five years.

Of course the economic picture was not entirely positive. The Union found itself resorting to financial

Homestead Act   Law passed by Congress in 1862 that promised ownership of 160 acres of public land to any citizen or would-be citizen who lived on and cultivated the land for five years.

tricks to keep the economy afloat. Facing a cash-flow emergency in 1862, Congress passed the Legal Tender Act, authorizing Treasury Secretary Salmon Chase to issue $431 million in paper money, known as **greenbacks,** that was backed not by specie but only by the government's commitment to redeem the bills. Financial support also came through selling bonds. In the fall of 1862, Philadelphia banker Jay Cooke started a bond drive. More than $2 billion worth of government bonds were sold, and most of them were paid for in greenbacks. These emergency measures helped the Union survive the financial pressures created by the war, but the combination of bond issues and paper money not backed by gold or silver set up a highly unstable situation that came back to haunt Republicans after the war.

The South, an agrarian society, began the war without an industrial base. In addition to lacking transportation, raw materials, and machines, the South lacked managers and skilled industrial workers. The Confederate government intervened more directly in the economy than did its Union counterpart, offering generous loans to new or existing companies that would produce war materials and agree to sell at least two-thirds of their production to the government. Josiah Gorgas started government-owned production plants in Alabama, Georgia, and South Carolina. These innovative programs, however, could not compensate for inadequate prewar industrialization.

The supply of money was also a severe problem in the South. Like the North, the South tried to ease cash-flow problems by printing paper money, eventually issuing more than $1 billion in unbacked currency. The outcome was runaway inflation. By the time the war ended, southerners were paying more than $400 for a barrel of flour and $10 a pound for bacon.

Southern industrial shortcomings severely handicapped the army. During Lee's Maryland campaign, many Confederate soldiers were barefoot because shoes were in such short supply. Ordnance was always in demand. Northern plants could produce more than five thousand muskets a day; Confederate production never exceeded three hundred. The most serious shortage, however, was food. Although the South was an agricultural region, most of its productive acreage was devoted to cotton, tobacco, and other crops that were essential to its overall economy but not suitable to eat. Corn and rice were the primary food products, but supplies were continually reduced by military campaigns and Union occupation of farmlands. Hog production suffered from the same disruptions as rice and corn growing, and while Southern cattle were abundant, most were range stock grown for hides and

tallow rather than for food. Hunger became a miserable part of daily life for the Confederate armies.

Civilians in the South suffered from the same shortages as the army. Because of prewar shipping patterns, the few rail lines that crossed the Confederacy ran north and south. Distribution of goods became almost impossible as invading Union forces cut rail lines and disrupted production. The flow of cattle, horses, and food from the West diminished when Union forces gained control of the Mississippi. Imported goods had to evade the Union naval blockade. Southern society, cut off from the outside world, consumed its existing resources and found no way to obtain more.

Women in Two Nations at War

Because the South had fewer men than the North to send to war, a larger proportion of southern families were left in the care of women. Some women worked farms, herded livestock, and supported their families. Others found themselves homeless, living in complete poverty, as the ravages of war destroyed the countryside. One woman wrote to the Confederacy's secretary of war, pleading that he "discharge" her husband so that "he might do his children some good" rather than leaving them "to suffer." Some tried to persuade their husbands to desert, to come home to family and safety. One woman shouted to her husband, who was being drafted for the second time, "Desert again, Jake." The vast majority, however, fully supported the war effort despite the hardships at home and at the front.

Women became responsible for much of the South's agricultural and industrial production, overseeing the raising of crops, working in factories, managing estates, and running businesses. As one southern soldier wrote, women bore "the greatest burden of this horrid war." Indeed, the burden of a woman was great—working the fields, running the household, and waiting for news from loved ones at the front or for the dreaded message that she was now a widow or childless.

Women in the North served in much the same capacity as their southern counterparts. They maintained families and homes alone, working to provide income and raise children. Although they did not face the shortages and ravages of battle that made life so hard for southern women, they did work in factories, run family businesses, teach school, and supply soldiers. Many served in managerial capacities or as

greenbacks   Paper money issued by the Union; it was not backed by gold.

As Mary Ashton Rice Livermore pointed out, many women served in many different capacities during the Civil War. An unknown number of them actually dressed as men to join the fighting. Frances Clayton was one of the few documented cases of such Civil War gender-bending. *Left and right: Trustees of the Boston Public Library.*

writers and civil servants. Even before the war ended, northern women were going south to educate former slaves and help them find a place in American society. Women thus assumed new roles that helped prepare them to become more involved in social and political life after the war.

Women from both South and North actively participated in the war itself. Many women on both sides served as scouts, couriers, and spies, and more than four hundred disguised themselves as men and served as active soldiers until they were discovered. General William S. Rosecrans expressed dismay when one of his sergeants was delivered of "a bouncing baby boy," which was, the general complained, "in violation of all military regulations." Army camps frequently included officers' wives, female employees, camp followers, and women who came to help in whatever way they could. One black woman served the 33rd U.S. Colored Troops for four years and three months without pay, teaching the men to read and write and binding up their wounds.

Free Blacks, Slaves, and War

The changes the Civil War brought for African Americans, both free and slave, were radical and not always for the better. At first, many free blacks attempted to enlist in the Union army but were turned away. In 1861 General Benjamin F. Butler began using runaway slaves, called contrabands, as laborers. Several other northern commanders quickly adopted the practice. As the number of contrabands increased, however, the Union grappled with problems of housing and feeding them.

In the summer of 1862, Congress authorized the acceptance of "persons of African descent" into the armed forces, but enlistment remained low. After the Emancipation Proclamation, Union officials actively recruited former slaves, raising troops from among the freedmen and forming them into regiments known as the U.S. Colored Troops. Some northern state governments sought free blacks to fill state draft quotas; agents offered generous bonuses to those who signed up. By the end of the war, about 180,000 African Americans had enlisted in northern armies.

Army officials discriminated against African American soldiers in a variety of ways. Units were segregated, and until 1864, blacks were paid less than whites. All black regiments had white commanders; the government refused to allow blacks to lead blacks. Only one hundred were commissioned as officers, and no African American soldier ever received a commission higher than major.

Eager to fill constantly depleting army ranks, Union officials appealed to African Americans to volunteer for military service. This recruiting poster, which bore the legend "Come Join Us, Brothers," presents a highly glorified vision of what conditions were like for black units. One accurate detail is that the only officer in the scene is white; in fact, no African Americans were permitted to command troops during the Civil War. *Chicago Historical Society.*

At first, African American regiments were used as laborers or kept in the rear rather than being allowed to fight. But several black regiments, when finally allowed into battle, performed so well that they won grudging respect. These men fought in 449 battles in every theater of the war and had a casualty rate 35 percent higher than white soldiers. Still, acceptance by white troops was slow, and discrimination was the rule, not the exception.

As the war progressed, the number of African Americans in the Union army increased dramatically. By 1865, almost two-thirds of Union troops in the Mississippi Valley were black. Some southerners violently resented the Union's use of these troops, and African American soldiers suffered atrocities because some Confederate leaders refused to take black prisoners. At Fort Pillow, Tennessee, for example, Confederate soldiers massacred more than a hundred African American soldiers who were trying to surrender.

About sixty-eight thousand black Union soldiers were killed or wounded in battle, and twenty-one were awarded the Congressional Medal of Honor. Probably no unit acquitted itself better in the field than the **54th Massachusetts.** On July 18, 1863, it led a frontal assault on Confederate defenses at Charleston Harbor. Despite sustaining grievous casualties, the African American troops captured the fort's front wall and held it for nearly an hour before being forced to retreat. Their conduct in battle had a large impact on changing attitudes toward black soldiers and emancipation.

The war effort in the South relied heavily on the slave population, mostly as producers of food and as military laborers. Slaves constituted more than half of the work force in armament plants and military hospitals. Though crucial to the southern war effort, slaves suffered more than other southerners in the face of food shortages and other privations. And after Lincoln issued the Emancipation Proclamation, fears of slave revolts prompted whites to institute harsh security procedures. Hungry and even less free than usual, slaves became the greatest unsung casualties of the war.

Life and Death at the Front

Many volunteers on both sides in the Civil War had romantic notions about military service. Most were disappointed. Life as a common soldier was anything but glorious. Letters and diaries written by soldiers most frequently tell of long periods of boredom in

54th Massachusetts   Regiment of African American troops from Massachusetts commanded by abolitionist Colonel Robert Gould Shaw; it led an assault on Fort Wagner at Charleston Harbor.

In this photograph, taken outside an army hospital in Fredericksburg, Virginia, one of the many women who served as nurses during the Civil War sits with some of her wounded charges. Despite the efforts of women like her, medical facilities and treatment for the wounded were woefully inadequate—most of those who were not killed outright by the primitive surgical practices of the day died from their wounds or from secondary infections. *Library of Congress.*

overcrowded camps punctuated by furious spells of dangerous action.

Though life in camp was tedious, it could be nearly as dangerous as time spent on the battlefield. Problems with supplying safe drinking water and disposing of waste constantly plagued military leaders faced with providing basic services for large numbers of people, often on short notice. Diseases such as dysentery and **typhoid fever** frequently swept through unsanitary camps. And in the overcrowded conditions that often prevailed, smallpox and other contagious diseases passed rapidly from person to person. At times, as many as a quarter of the uninjured people in camps were disabled by one or another of these ailments.

Lacking in resources, organization, and expertise, the South did little to upgrade camp conditions. In the North, however, women drew on the organizational skills they had gained as antebellum reformers and created voluntary organizations to address the problem. At the local level, women like Mary Livermore and Jane Hoge created small relief societies designed to aid soldiers and their families. Gradually these merged into regional organizations that would take the lead in raising money and implementing large-scale public health efforts, both in the army camps and at home. Mental health advocate and reformer Dorothea Dix (see page 348) was also one of these crusaders. In June 1861, President Lincoln responded to their concerns by creating the **United States Sanitary Commission,** a government agency responsible for advising the military on public health issues and investigating sanitary problems. Gradually enfolding many of the local and regional societies into its structure, "The Sanitary," as it was called, put hundreds of nurses into the field, providing much-needed relief for overburdened military doctors. Even with this official organization in place, many women continued to labor as volunteer nurses in the camps and in hospitals behind the lines.

Nurses on both sides showed bravery and devotion. Often working under fire at the front and with almost no medical supplies, these volunteers nursed sick and wounded soldiers, watched as they died not only from their wounds but also from infection and disease, and offered as much comfort and help as they could. **Clara Barton,** a famous northern nurse known as the "Angel of the Battlefield," recalled "speaking to and feeding with my own hands each soldier" as she attempted to nurse them back to health. Hospitals were unsanitary, overflowing, and underfunded.

The numbers of wounded who filled the hospital tents was unprecedented, largely because of technological innovations that had taken place during the antebellum period. New **rifled** muskets had many

typhoid fever An infectious disease transmitted through contact with contaminated water, milk, or food; causes severe intestinal distress and high fever.

United States Sanitary Commission Government commission established by Abraham Lincoln to improve public health conditions in military camps and hospitals.

Clara Barton Organizer of a volunteer service to aid sick and wounded Civil War soldiers; she later founded the American branch of the Red Cross.

rifled Having a series of spiral grooves inside the barrel of a gun that cause the bullet to spin, giving it greater range and accuracy.

times the range of the old smooth-bore weapons used during earlier wars—the effective range of the Springfield rifle used by many Union soldiers was 400 yards, and a stray bullet could still kill a man at 1,000 yards. Waterproof cartridges, perfected by gunsmith Samuel Colt, made these weapons much less prone to misfire and much easier to reload. And at closer range, the revolver, also perfected by Colt, could fire six shots without any reloading. Rifled artillery also added to the casualty count, as did exploding artillery shells, which sent deadly shrapnel ripping through lines of men.

Many surgeons at the front lines could do little more than amputate limbs to save lives. Hospitals, understaffed and lacking supplies and medicines, frequently became breeding grounds for disease. The war exacted a tremendous emotional toll on everyone, even on those who escaped physical injury. As one veteran put it, soldiers had seen "so many new forms of death" and "so many frightful and novel kinds of mutilation."

Conditions were even worse in prison camps. Throughout much of the war, an agreement provided for prisoner exchanges, but that did not prevent overcrowding and unsanitary conditions. And as the war dragged on, the exchange system stopped working effectively. In part the program collapsed because of the enormity of the task: moving and accounting for the large numbers of prisoners presented a serious organizational problem. Another contributing factor, though, was the refusal by Confederate officials to exchange African American prisoners of war—those who were not slaughtered like the men at Fort Pillow were enslaved. Also, late in the war, Union commanders suspended all prisoner exchanges in hopes of depriving the South of much-needed replacement soldiers.

The most notorious of the Civil War prison camps was **Andersonville,** in northern Georgia, where thousands of Union captives languished in an open stockade with only a small creek for water and virtually no sanitary facilities. Without enough food to feed its own armies and civilian population, the Confederacy could allocate little food for its overcrowded prison camps. Designed to house 10,000 men, Andersonville held more than 33,000 prisoners during the summer of 1864. As many as 100 men died of disease and malnutrition within its walls each day; estimates put the death toll at that one prison at nearly 14,000 over the course of the war.

Even death itself came to be redefined, as 8 percent of the white male population in the United States between the ages of 13 and 43 died in such a short time and in such grisly ways. People at the front reported being numbed by the horror. One army surgeon reported, "I pass over the putrefying bodies of the dead . . . and feel as . . . unconcerned as though they were two hundred pigs." Nor was distance any insulation from the horrors of death. The new art of photography brought graphic images of the gruesome carnage directly into the nation's parlors. "Death does not seem half so terrible as it did long ago," one Texas woman reported. "We have grown used to it."

Waging Total War

■ What factors contributed to the Union's adoption of a total war strategy after 1863?

■ Was total war a justifiable option in light of the human and property damage it inflicted and the overall consequences it achieved? Why or why not?

As northerners anticipated the presidential election of 1864, Lincoln faced severe challenges on several fronts. The losses to Lee and Jackson in Virginia and the failure to catch Lee at Antietam had eroded public support. Many northerners resented the war, conscription, and abolitionism. Others feared Lincoln's powerful central government.

Northern Democrats advocated a peace platform and turned to George B. McClellan, Lincoln's ousted general, as a potential presidential candidate. Lincoln also faced a challenge from within his own party. Radical Republicans, who felt he was too soft on the South and unfit to run the war, began planning a campaign to win power. They championed the candidacy of John C. Frémont (see page 404), who had become an ardent advocate of the complete abolition of slavery.

Lincoln's Generals and Southern Successes

The surest way for Lincoln to stop his opponents was through military success. Lincoln had replaced McClellan with Burnside, but the results had been disastrous. Lincoln tried again, demoting Burnside and elevating General Joseph Hooker. Despite Hooker's reputation for bravery in battle—his nickname was "Fighting Joe"—Lee soundly defeated his forces at **Chancellorsville** in May 1863 (see Map 15.3 and

Andersonville   Confederate prisoner-of-war camp in northern Georgia where some fourteen thousand Union prisoners died of disease and malnutrition.

Chancellorsville   Site in Virginia where in May 1863 Confederate troops led by Lee defeated a much larger Union force.

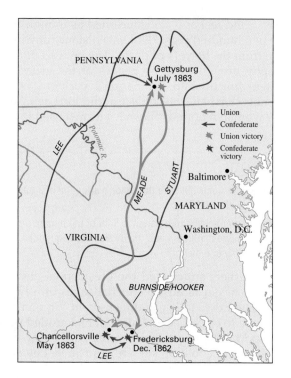

MAP 15.3 Fredericksburg, Chancellorsville, and Gettysburg This map shows the campaigns that took place during the winter of 1862 and spring of 1863, culminating in the Battle of Gettysburg (July 1863). General Meade's victory at Gettysburg may have been the critical turning point of the war.

Table 15.4). After Hooker had maneuvered Lee into a corner, Stonewall Jackson unleashed a vicious attack, and Fighting Joe simply "lost his nerve," according to one of his subordinates. Hooker resigned, and Lincoln replaced him with General George E. Meade.

Chancellorsville was a devastating loss for the North, but it was perhaps more devastating for the Confederates. They lost Stonewall Jackson. After he led the charge that unnerved Hooker, Jackson's own men mistakenly shot him as he rode back toward his camp in the darkness. Doctors amputated Jackson's arm in an attempt to save his life. "He has lost his left arm," moaned Lee, "but I have lost my right." Eight days later, Jackson died of pneumonia.

In the West too, Union forces seemed mired during the first half of 1863. General Rosecrans was bogged down in a costly and unsuccessful campaign to take the vital rail center at Chattanooga, Tennessee. Grant had settled in for a long siege at Vicksburg (see Map 15.2). Nowhere did there seem to be a prospect for the dramatic victory Lincoln needed.

The summer of 1863, however, turned out to be a major turning point in the war. Facing superior northern resources and rising inflation, Confederate leaders met in Richmond to consider their options. Lee proposed another major invasion of the North, arguing that such a maneuver would allow the Confederates to gather supplies and might encourage the northern peace movement, revitalize the prospects of foreign recognition, and perhaps capture the Union capital. Confederate leaders agreed and approved Lee's plan.

Lee's advance met only weak opposition as the Army of Northern Virginia crossed the Potomac River and marched into Union territory (see Map 15.3). In Maryland and Pennsylvania the troops seized livestock, supplies, food, clothing, and shoes. Union forces had been converging on the area of **Gettysburg,** Pennsylvania, since early June, anticipating Lee's move but unsure of his exact intention. Learning that the Federals were waiting and believing them to be weaker than they were, on June 29 Lee moved to engage the Union forces. Meade, who had been trailing Lee's army as it marched north from Chancellorsville, immediately dispatched a detachment to reinforce Gettysburg. On the following day, the two armies began a furious three-day battle.

Arriving in force on July 1, Meade took up an almost impregnable defensive position on the hills along Cemetery Ridge. The Confederates hammered both ends of the Union line but could gain no ground. On the third day, Lee ordered a major assault on the middle of the Union position. Eleven brigades, more than thirteen thousand men, led by fresh troops under Major General George E. Pickett, tried to cross open ground and take the hills held by Meade while Major J. E. B. "Jeb" Stuart's cavalry attacked from the east. Lee made few strategic mistakes during the war, but Pickett's charge was foolhardy. Meade's forces drove off the attack. The whole field was "dotted with our soldiers," wrote one Confederate officer. Lee met his retreating troops with the words "It's all my fault, my fault." Losses on both sides were high (see Table 15.5), but Confederate casualties exceeded twenty-eight thousand men, more than half of Lee's army. Lee retreated, his invasion of the North a failure.

On the heels of this major victory for the North came news from Mississippi that Vicksburg had fallen to

Gettysburg   Site in Pennsylvania where in July 1863 Union forces under General George Meade defeated Lee's Confederate forces, turning back Lee's invasion of the North.

TABLE 15.4   Battle of Chancellorsville, May 1–4, 1863

	Union Army	Confederate Army
Commanders	Joseph Hooker	Robert E. Lee
Troop strength	75,000	50,000
Losses		
Killed	1,606	1,665
Wounded	9,762	9,081
Captured, missing	5,919	2,018
Total Losses	17,287	12,764

Source: Data from *Battles and Leaders of the Civil War* (1884–1888; reprinted ed., 1956).

TABLE 15.5   Battle of Gettysburg, July 1–3, 1863

	Union Army	Confederate Army
Commanders	George E. Meade	Robert E. Lee
Troop strength	75,000	50,000
Losses		
Killed	3,155	3,903
Wounded	14,529	18,735
Captured, missing	5,365	5,425
Total Losses	23,049	28,063

Source: Data from *Battles and Leaders of the Civil War* (1884–1888; reprinted ed., 1956).

Grant's siege on July 4. Sherman had been beating back Confederate forces in central Mississippi, and Union guns had been shelling the city continuously for nearly seven weeks, driving residents into caves and barricaded shelters. But it was starvation and disease that finally subdued the defenders. Then on July 9, after receiving news of Vicksburg's fate, **Port Hudson,** the last Confederate garrison on the Mississippi River, also surrendered. The Mississippi River was totally under Union control. The "Father of Waters," said Lincoln, "again goes unvexed to the sea."

Despite jubilation over the recent victories, Lincoln and the North remained frustrated. Northern newspapers proclaiming Gettysburg to be the last gasp of the South had anticipated an immediate southern surrender, but Meade, like McClellan, acted with extreme caution and failed to pursue Lee and his retreating troops. Back in Washington, Lincoln waited for word of Lee's capture, believing it would signal the end of the rebellion. When he learned of Lee's escape, the president said in disbelief, "Our Army held the war in the hollow of their hand and they would not close it."

Disappointment in Tennessee also soon marred the celebration over Gettysburg and Vicksburg. Rosecrans had taken Chattanooga, but on September 18, Bragg's forces attacked Rosecrans at Chickamauga Creek. Rosecrans scurried in retreat to take refuge

Port Hudson   Confederate garrison in Louisiana that surrendered to Union forces in July 1863, thus giving the Union unrestricted control of the Mississippi River.

During the summer of 1863, Confederate General Robert E. Lee proposed a daring invasion into Pennsylvania in hopes that it might force the Union to end the war. It proved to be a turning point, but not the one Lee anticipated. At Gettysburg, a series of battles like the one shown here—this one on the first day of the fighting—cost Lee more than half of his entire army, and he was forced to retreat into Virginia. President Lincoln hoped that the Union army would pursue the fleeing Confederates and destroy the remnants of Lee's force, but he was disappointed when he learned that Lee had escaped. "Our Army held the war in the hollow of their hand," Lincoln complained, "and they would not close it." *West Point Museum, United States Military Academy, West Point, NY.*

back in Chattanooga, leaving part of his troops in place to cover his retreat. This force, under the command of George H. Thomas, delayed the Confederate offensive and, in the words of one veteran, "saved the army from defeat and rout." Bragg nonetheless was able to follow and laid siege to Chattanooga from the heights of Missionary Ridge and Lookout Mountain, overlooking the city.

With Lee and his army intact and Rosecrans pinned down in Tennessee, the war, which in July had appeared to be so nearly over, was, in Lincoln's words, "prolonged indefinitely." Lincoln needed a new kind of general.

Grant, Sherman, and the Invention of Total War

Among the available choices, Grant had shown the kind of persistence and boldness Lincoln thought

necessary. Lincoln placed him in charge of all Union forces in the West on October 16. Grant immediately replaced Rosecrans with the more intrepid and decisive Thomas. Sherman's troops joined Thomas under Grant's command on November 14. This united force rid the mountains above Chattanooga of Confederate strongholds and drove Bragg's forces out of southern Tennessee. Confederate forces also withdrew from Knoxville in December, leaving the state under Union control.

While fighting raged in Tennessee, Lincoln took a break from his duties in the White House to participate in the dedication of a national cemetery at the site where, just months before, the Battle of Gettysburg had taken the lives of thousands. In the speech he delivered on November 19, 1863, Lincoln dedicated not only the cemetery but the war effort itself to the fallen soldiers, and also to a principle. "Fourscore and seven years ago," Lincoln said, "our fathers brought forth on this continent a new nation, con-

The Gettysburg Address

When the war began, Lincoln made it clear that his purpose in pursuing a military course was simply the defense of the Constitution. But when he spoke on the Gettysburg battlefield two years later, he gave voice to a broader vision that seems to have evolved as the bloodshed and horror escalated. Interestingly, Lincoln referenced the Declaration of Independence as the founding document for the republic, *not* the Constitution. Though the Declaration was an important document in American history, it was never a binding legal instrument; it had no power in law. Yet through this speech, Lincoln transformed Thomas Jefferson's stirring announcement of enlightenment principle into a central element in American legal thinking. When the war was over, and after Lincoln's death, Congress acted on this sentiment by framing the Fourteenth Amendment, which codified the central principle that "all men are created equal." Though enforced inconsistently through the years, this principle would become the foundation for all of the civil rights that Americans enjoy and continue to fight for.

ceived in liberty and dedicated to the proposition that all men are created equal." Though delivered in a low voice that most of the crowd could not hear, the **Gettysburg Address** was circulated in the media and galvanized many Americans who had come to doubt the war's purpose.

The president was delighted with Grant's successes in Tennessee. Lincoln promoted him again on March 10, 1864, this time to general in chief. Grant immediately left his command in the West to prepare an all-out attack on Lee and Virginia, authorizing Sherman to pursue a campaign into Georgia.

In Grant and Sherman, Lincoln had found what he needed. On the surface, neither seemed a likely candidate for a major role in the Union army. Both were West Point graduates but left the army after the War with Mexico to seek their fortunes. Neither had succeeded in civilian life: Grant was a binge drinker who had accomplished little, and Sherman had failed as a banker and a lawyer. Both were "political generals,"

owing their Civil War commissions to the influence of friends or relatives. Despite their checkered pasts, these two men invented a new type of warfare that eventually brought the South to its knees. Grant and Sherman were willing to wage **total war** in order to destroy the South's will to continue the struggle.

Preparing for the new sort of war he was about to inaugurate, Grant suspended prisoner-of-war exchanges. Realizing that the Confederates needed soldiers badly, he understood that one outcome of this policy would be slow death by starvation for Union prisoners. Cruel though his policy was, Grant reasoned that victory was his primary goal and that suffering and death were unavoidable in war. Throughout the remainder of the war, this single-mindedness pushed Grant to make decisions that cost tens of thousands of lives on both sides.

On May 4, Grant and Meade moved toward Richmond and Robert E. Lee. The next day, Union and Confederate armies collided in a tangle of woods called **The Wilderness,** near Chancellorsville (see Map 15.4). Two days of bloody fighting followed, broken by a night during which hundreds of the wounded burned to death in brushfires that raged between the two lines. Grant decided to skirt Lee's troops and head for Richmond, but Lee anticipated the maneuver and blocked Grant's route at Spotsylvania. Twelve days of fighting ensued. Grant again attempted to move around Lee, and again Lee anticipated him. On June 1, the two armies met at **Cold Harbor,** Virginia. After each side had consolidated its position, Grant ordered a series of frontal attacks against the entrenched Confederates on June 3. Lee's veteran troops waited patiently in perhaps the best position they had ever defended, while Union soldiers expecting to die marched toward them. The assault failed amid unspeakable slaughter.

Gettysburg Address   A speech given by Abraham Lincoln on November 19, 1863, dedicating a national cemetery in Gettysburg, Pennsylvania; it enunciated Lincoln's maturing view of the war and its purpose.

total war   War waged with little regard for the welfare of troops on either side or for enemy civilians; the objective is to destroy both the human and the economic resources of the enemy.

The Wilderness   Densely wooded region of Virginia that was the site in May 1864 of a devastating but inconclusive battle between Union forces under Grant and Confederates under Lee.

Cold Harbor   Area of Virginia, about 10 miles from Richmond, where Grant made an unsuccessful attempt to drive his forces through Lee's center.

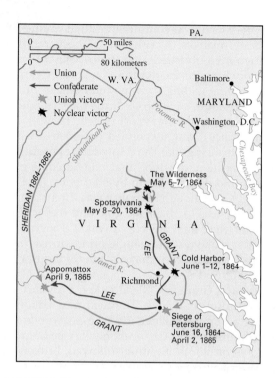

MAP 15.4　**Grant's Campaign Against Lee**　This map shows the series of battles during the late spring of 1864 in which Grant's army suffered staggering casualties but finally drove Lee into retreat. After holding up for months behind heavy fortifications in Petersburg, Lee made a daring attempt to escape in April 1865 but was headed off by General Philip Sheridan's troops. Grant quickly closed in on the greatly weakened Confederate army, forcing Lee's surrender.

Disliked by most of his fellow officers because of his coarse behavior and binge drinking, Ulysses S. Grant had the right combination of daring, unconventionality, and ruthlessness to wear down Robert E. Lee's forces in Virginia and finally defeat the Confederate army. *National Archives.*

One southerner described Grant's assaults as "inexplicable and incredible butchery." The wounded were left to die between the lines while the living fell back exhausted into their trenches. Many of the young federal attackers at Cold Harbor had pinned their names on their shirts in the hope that their shattered bodies might be identified after the battle. Casualties on both sides at Spotsylvania and Cold Harbor were staggering, but Union losses were unimaginably horrible. As one Confederate officer put it, "We have met a man, this time, who either does not know when he is whipped, or who cares not if he loses his whole army." During the three encounters, Grant lost a total of sixty thousand troops, more than Lee's entire army. Said Lee, "This is not war, this is murder." But Grant's seeming wantonness was calculated, for the Confederates lost more than twenty-five thousand troops. And Grant knew, as did Lee, that the Union could afford the losses but the Confederacy could not.

After Cold Harbor, Grant guessed that Lee would expect him to try to assault nearby Richmond next. This time, though, he steered the Union army south of Richmond for Petersburg to try to take the vital rail center and cut off the southern capital. Once again, Lee reacted quickly: he rapidly shifted the **vanguard** of his troops, beat back Grant's advance, and occupied Petersburg. Grant bitterly regretted this failure, feeling that he could have ended the war. Instead, the campaign settled into a siege that neither side wanted. Lee and the Confederates could ill afford a siege that ate up supplies and munitions. And elections were rapidly approaching in the Union.

vanguard　The foremost position in any army advancing into battle.

The Election of 1864 and Sherman's March to the Sea

Lincoln was under fire from two directions. On May 31, 1864, Radical Republicans met in Cleveland and officially nominated John C. Frémont as their presidential candidate. Lincoln's wing of the party, which began calling itself the Union Party, held its nominating convention in June and renominated Lincoln. To attract Democrats who still favored fighting for a clear victory, Union Party delegates dumped Vice President Hannibal Hamlin and chose **Andrew Johnson,** a southern Democrat, as Lincoln's running mate. Then, in August, the Democratic National Convention met at Chicago. The Democrats pulled together many **Copperheads** and other northerners who were so upset by the heavy casualties that they were determined to stop the war even at the cost of allowing slavery to continue. The Democrats selected McClellan as their presidential candidate and included a peace plank in their platform. Thus Lincoln sat squarely in the middle between one group that castigated him for pursuing the war and another group that rebuked him for failing to punish the South vigorously enough.

Confederate president Jefferson Davis did not face an election in 1864, but he too had plenty of political problems. As deprivation and military losses mounted, some factions began to resist the war effort. The Confederate congress called for a new draft, but several states refused to comply. Governors in Georgia, North Carolina, and South Carolina, who controlled their state's militia, kept troops at home and defied Davis to enforce conscription.

Eager to solve their problems, Lincoln and Confederate vice president Alexander H. Stephens had conversations about negotiating a settlement. Lincoln stated his terms: reunion, abolition, and amnesty for Confederates. Southern officials balked, pointing out that "amnesty" applied to criminals and that the South had "committed no crime." The only possible outcomes of the war for the South, they concluded, were independence or extermination, even if it meant enduring the sight of "every Southern plantation sacked and every Southern city in flames." The words proved prophetic.

Grant had instructed Sherman "to get into the interior of the enemy's country as far as you can, inflicting all the damage you can against their war resources." Sherman responded with a vengeance. Slowly and skillfully his army advanced southward from Tennessee toward Atlanta, one of the South's few remaining industrial centers, against Confederate armies under the command of General Joseph E. Johnston (see Map 15.5). Only Johnston's skillful retreats kept Sherman from annihilating his army. President Davis then replaced Johnston with John Bell Hood, who vowed to take the offensive. Hood attacked, but Sherman inflicted such serious casualties that Hood had to retreat to Atlanta.

For days Sherman shelled Atlanta and wrought havoc in the surrounding countryside. When a last-ditch southern attack failed, Hood evacuated the city on September 1. The victorious Union troops moved in and occupied Atlanta on the following day. Sherman's victory caused tremendous despair among Confederates but gave great momentum to Lincoln's reelection campaign.

Also boosting Lincoln's reelection efforts was General Philip Sheridan's campaign in the Shenandoah Valley, an important source of food for Lee's army. Adopting the same sort of devastating tactics that Sherman used so successfully, Sheridan's men lived off the land and destroyed both military and civilian supplies whenever possible. Accepting high casualties, Sheridan drove Confederate forces from the region in October, laying waste to much of Lee's food supply in the process.

These victories proved the decisive factor in the election of 1864. Sherman's and Sheridan's successes defused McClellan's argument that Lincoln was not competent to direct the Union's military fortunes and quelled much antiwar sentiment in the North. Equally discredited, the Radical Republican platform and the Frémont candidacy disappeared before election day. As late as August, Lincoln had been expecting to lose the election in November, but the victory in Atlanta gave him some hope. When the votes were counted, Lincoln learned that he had defeated McClellan—by half a million popular votes and by a landslide margin of 212 to 21 in the Electoral College.

The southern peace movement had viewed a Democratic victory as the last chance to reach a settlement. Without it, all hope of negotiation appeared lost. Amid the bleak prospects, animosity toward Jefferson Davis increased in the South. But Lee's forces still remained in Petersburg, as did Hood's in Georgia. Southern hopes were dimmed but not extinguished.

Andrew Johnson   Tennessee senator who became Lincoln's running mate in 1864 and who succeeded to the presidency after Lincoln's assassination.

Copperheads   Derogatory term (the name of a poisonous snake) applied to northerners who supported the South during the Civil War.

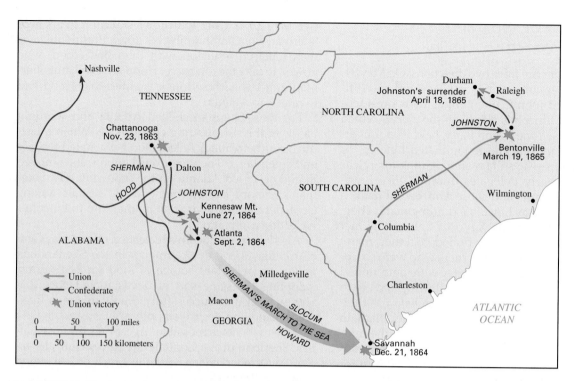

MAP 15.5 Sherman's Campaign in the South This map shows how William Tecumseh Sherman's troops slashed through the South, destroying both civilian and military targets and reducing the South's will to continue the war.

Sherman soon grew bored with the occupation of Atlanta and posed a bold plan to Grant. He wanted to ignore Hood, leave the battered Confederates loose at his rear, go on the offensive, and "cut a swath through to the sea." "I can make Georgia howl," he promised. Despite some misgivings, Grant agreed and convinced Lincoln.

A week after the election, Sherman began preparing for his 300-mile **March to the Sea** (see Map 15.5). His intentions were clear. "We are not only fighting hostile armies, but a hostile people," he stated. By devastating the countryside and destroying the South's ability to conduct war, he intended to break down southerners' will to resist. "We cannot change the hearts of those people of the South," he concluded, but we can "make them so sick of war that generations would pass away before they would again appeal to it." With that, he burned most of Atlanta and then set out on his march to Savannah, on the coast. His troops plundered and looted farms and towns on the way, foraging for food and supplies and destroying everything in their path.

While Sherman headed toward Savannah, Confederate general Hood turned north and attacked General George Thomas's Union forces at Franklin, Tennessee, on November 30. Hood lost convincingly in a bloody battle. The Confederate Army of Tennessee fragmented, and all opposition to Sherman's onslaught dissolved. Sherman entered Savannah unopposed on December 21.

The March to the Sea completed, Sherman turned north. In South Carolina, the first state to secede and fire shots, Sherman's troops took special delight in ravaging the countryside. When they reached Columbia, flames engulfed the city. Whether Sherman's men or retreating Confederates started the blaze was not clear, but African American regiments in Sher-

March to the Sea Sherman's march through Georgia from Atlanta to Savannah from November 15 to December 21, 1864, during which Union soldiers carried out orders to destroy everything in their path.

Determined to "make Georgia howl," William Tecumseh Sherman and his band of "bummers" slashed their way through the South during the winter of 1864, destroying military and civilian property along the way. This painting shows Sherman astride a white horse looking on while his men rip up a rail line and burn bridges and homes. *"Sherman's March to the Sea," engraving after F.O.C. Darley. Photo by Ben Lourie. Collection of David H. Sherman.*

man's command helped to put out the fires after Sherman occupied the South Carolina capital on February 17, 1865.

With the capital in flames, Confederate forces abandoned their posts in South Carolina, moving north to join with Joseph E. Johnston's army in an effort to stop Sherman from crossing North Carolina and joining Grant in Virginia. Union forces quickly moved into abandoned southern strongholds, including Charleston, where Major Robert Anderson, who had commanded Fort Sumter in April 1861, returned to raise the Union flag over the fort that he had surrendered four years earlier.

The Fall of Lee and Lincoln

Under increasing pressure from Sherman, the Confederacy's military situation was deteriorating rapidly. In a last-ditch effort to keep the Confederacy alive, Lee advised Davis to evacuate Richmond—the army intended to abandon the capital, moving west as rapidly as possible toward Lynchburg (see Map 15.4). From there Lee hoped to use surviving rail lines to move his troops south to join with Johnston's force in North Carolina. The unified armies might then halt Sherman's advance and wheel around to deal with Grant.

Suffering none of his predecessors' indecisiveness, Grant ordered an immediate assault as Lee's forces retreated from Petersburg. Lee had little ammunition, almost no food, and only thirty-five thousand men. As they retreated westward, under constant pressure from harassing attacks, hundreds of southern soldiers collapsed from hunger and exhaustion. By April 9, Union forces had surrounded Lee's broken army. Saying, "There is nothing left for me to do but go and see General Grant," Lee sent a note offering surrender.

The two generals met at a private home in the little village of Appomattox Courthouse, Virginia. Grant offered generous terms, allowing Confederate officers and men to go home "so long as they observe their paroles and the laws in force where they reside." This guaranteed them immunity from prosecution

The nation's mood shifted from celebration to shock when it learned that President Lincoln had fallen to an assassin's bullet. His funeral provided an occasion for the entire country to mourn, not only his death but also the deaths of hundreds of thousands of Americans who had fallen in the Civil War. A specially constructed rail car pulled by an armored military locomotive carried the president's body on a route that retraced his 1860 campaign throughout the North. In large cities, Lincoln's body was paraded through the streets in mourning processionals. Throughout the countryside, however, people consulted published schedules of the train's route and lined the tracks at all hours of the day and night waiting for the train to pass so they could pay tribute to their fallen leader. *Left and right: Picture History.*

for treason and became the model for surrender. Grant sent the starving Confederates rations and let them keep their horses.

On the following day, Lincoln addressed a crowd outside the White House about his hopes and plans for rebuilding the nation. He talked about the need for flexibility in pulling the nation back together after the long and bitter conflict. He had already taken steps to bring southerners back into the Union. In December 1863, he had issued a Proclamation of Amnesty and Reconstruction offering pardons to any Confederates who would take a loyalty oath. After his re-election in 1864, Lincoln had begun to plan for the Confederacy's eventual surrender, and he pushed for a constitutional ban on slavery, which passed on January 31, 1865.

With victory at hand and a peace plan in place, on April 14 after an exhausting day in conference with his cabinet and with General Grant, Lincoln chose to relax by attending a play at Ford's Theater in Washington. At about ten o'clock, **John Wilkes Booth,** an actor and a southern sympathizer, entered the president's box and shot him behind the ear. Meanwhile, one of Booth's accomplices entered the home of Sec-

John Wilkes Booth Actor and southern sympathizer who on April 14, 1865, five days after Lee's surrender, fatally shot President Lincoln at Ford's Theater in Washington.

retary of State Seward, who was bedridden as a result of a carriage accident, and stabbed him several times before being driven out by Seward's son and a male nurse. Another accomplice was supposed to assassinate Vice President Johnson but apparently lost his nerve. Although the conspiracy had failed, one of its main objectives succeeded: the following morning, Lincoln died of his wound.

Even though Lincoln was dead and Lee had fallen, the war continued. Joseph E. Johnston, whose forces succeeded in preventing Sherman from joining Grant, did not surrender until April 18. And although most of his forces had been defeated, Jefferson Davis remained in hiding and called for guerrilla warfare and continued resistance. But one by one, the Confederate officers surrendered to their Union opponents. On May 10, Davis and the Confederate postmaster general were captured near Irwinville, Georgia, and placed in prison. Andrew Johnson, who had assumed the presidency upon Lincoln's death, issued a statement to the American people that armed rebellion against legitimate authority could be considered "virtually at an end." The last Confederate general to lay down his arms was Cherokee leader Stand Watie, who surrendered on June 23, 1865.

The price of victory was high for both the winner and the loser. More than 350,000 Union soldiers had been killed in action. No exact figures exist for the Confederacy, but southern casualties probably equaled or exceeded those of the Union. The war had wrecked the economy of the South, for most of the fighting had occurred there. Union military campaigns had wiped out most southern rail lines, destroyed the South's manufacturing capacity, and severely reduced agricultural productivity. Both sides had faced rising inflation during the war, but the Confederacy's actions to supply troops and keep the war effort going had bled the South of most of its resources and money. Secession had been defeated, but reunion remained a distant and difficult objective.

Individual Voices

Examining a Primary Source

Mary Ashton Rice Livermore Depicts Women's War Efforts

When Civil War broke out, women in both the North and South rallied in support of the war effort. An unknown number actually dressed up as men to enter the ranks as combat soldiers. Others carried on volunteer work, both at home and in the field, becoming fundraisers, nurses, and public health advocates. Mary Livermore served a short stint as a battlefield nurse but spent most of the war as a soldiers' relief worker. She urged other women to act on their patriotism by becoming involved in ways that would draw on the peculiar skills and affinities that nineteenth-century Americans believed belonged exclusively to women. After the war, she wrote a book recounting her experiences and presenting her perspectives. The following excerpt is taken from that 1888 publication.

It is easy to understand how men catch the contagion of war, especially when they feel their quarrel to be just. One can comprehend how, fired with enthusiasm, and

■ How does Livermore characterize the differences between men and women in terms of their response to the appeals of war? What does this reflect about general attitudes toward gender in mid-nineteenth-century America?

■ What is Livermore suggesting here about the role of women during wartime? Does she portray this role as inferior, superior, or equal to that played by men?

■ In light of this eloquent description of women's efforts during the war, what would Livermore probably suggest about appropriate peacetime employment for women? Would you characterize this as a "feminist" or a "traditionalist" statement? What leads you to this conclusion?

inspired by martial music, they march to the cannon's mouth, where the iron hail rains heaviest, and the ranks are mowed down like grain in harvest. But for women to send forth their husbands, sons, brothers and lovers to the fearful chances of the battle-field, knowing well the risks they run,—this involves exquisite suffering, and calls for another kind of heroism. . . . ■

The number of women who actually bore arms and served in the ranks during the war was greater than is supposed. . . . Such service was not the noblest that women rendered the country during its four years' struggle for life, and no one can regret that these soldier women were exceptional and rare. It is better to heal a wound than to make one. And it is to the honor of American women, not that they led hosts to the deadly charge, and battled amid contending armies, but that they confronted the horrid aspects of war with mighty life and earnestness. ■ They kept up their own courage and that of their households. They became ministering angels to their countrymen who periled health and life for the nation. They sent the love and impulses of home into the extended ranks of the army, through the unceasing correspondence they maintained with "the boys in blue." They planned largely, and toiled untiringly, and with steady persistence to the end, that the horrors of the battle-field might be mitigated, and the hospitals abound in needed comforts. ■

Summary

Both the Union and the Confederacy entered the war in 1861 with glowing hopes. Jefferson Davis pursued a defensive strategy, certain that northerners would soon tire of war and let the South withdraw from the Union. Abraham Lincoln countered by using the superior human, economic, and natural resources of the North to strangle the South into submission. But both leaders became increasingly frustrated during the first year of the war.

For Lincoln, the greatest frustration was military leadership. Beginning with the first Battle of Bull Run, Union forces seemed unable to win any major battles despite their numerical superiority. Although Union forces under Ulysses S. Grant's command scored victories in the Mississippi Valley, the Federals were stalemated. Robert E. Lee and Thomas "Stone-wall" Jackson seemed able to defeat any Union general that Lincoln sent to oppose them.

The war's nature and direction changed after the fall of 1862, however. Lee invaded Maryland and was defeated at Antietam. Despite this crushing loss, Union generals still failed to capture Lee or to subdue Confederate forces in Virginia. Still vexed by military blundering, political attacks, and popular unrest, Lincoln issued the Emancipation Proclamation in an effort to undermine southern efforts and unify northern ones. After the proclamation, the only option for either side was total victory or total defeat.

After further reversals in the spring of 1863, Union forces turned the tide in the war by defeating Lee's army at Gettysburg and taking Vicksburg to gain full control of the Mississippi. With an election drawing near, Lincoln spurred his generals to deal the death blow to the Confederacy, and two in particular rose to the occasion. During the last half of 1864, William

Tecumseh Sherman wreaked havoc, making Georgia "howl." And Grant, in a wanton display of disregard for human life, drove Lee into a defensive corner. In November, buoyed by Sherman's victories in Georgia, Lincoln was reelected.

Suffering was not confined to those at the front. Governments in both the North and the South had to dig deep into depleting economic resources to keep the war effort going. Inflation plagued both nations, and common people faced hunger, disease, and insufficient police protection. Riots broke out in major cities, including New York. But throughout the country many people responded heroically to their own privations and to suffering at the front. Women such as Mary Livermore and others faced up to epidemics, enemy gunfire, and gender bias to institute public health standards and bring solace to suffering civilians and soldiers alike.

As hope dwindled for the South in the spring of 1865, Lee made a final desperate effort to keep the flagging Confederacy alive, racing to unify the last surviving remnants of the once-proud southern army. But Grant closed a net of steel around Lee's troops, forcing surrender. Lincoln immediately promoted a gentle policy for reunion, but his assassination ended this effort. The saintly American hero was gone, leaving a southern Democrat—Andrew Johnson—as president and a nation reeling in shock. The war was over, but the issues were still unresolved. Both the North and the South were beset with uncertainty about what would follow four years of suffering and sacrifice.

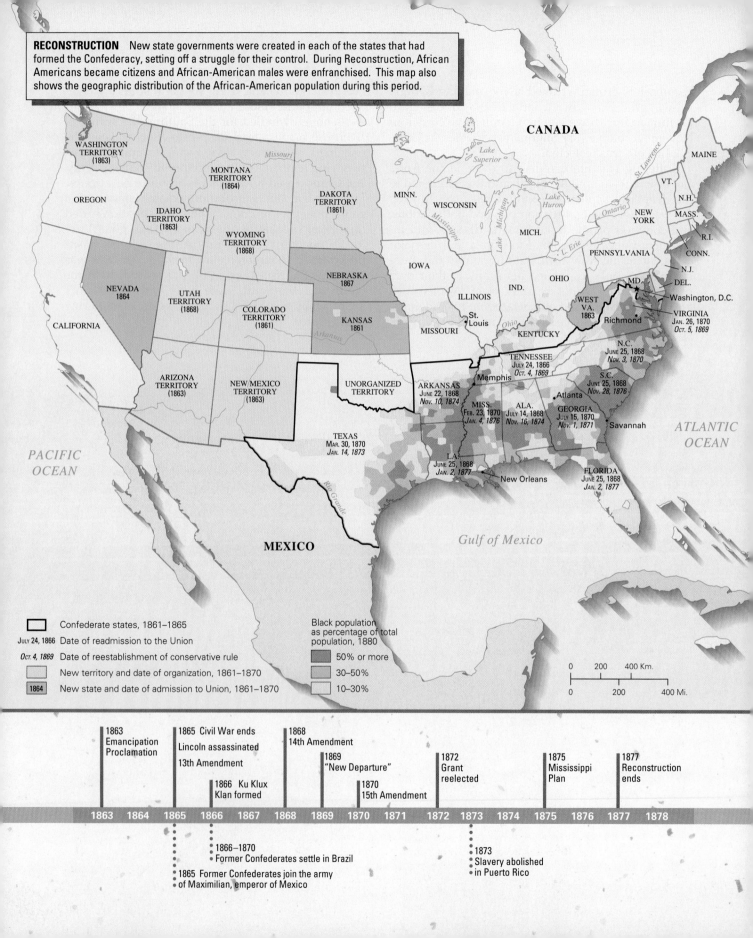

RECONSTRUCTION New state governments were created in each of the states that had formed the Confederacy, setting off a struggle for their control. During Reconstruction, African Americans became citizens and African-American males were enfranchised. This map also shows the geographic distribution of the African-American population during this period.

CANADA

WASHINGTON TERRITORY (1863)

OREGON

MONTANA TERRITORY (1864)

IDAHO TERRITORY (1863)

DAKOTA TERRITORY (1861)

MINN.

WISCONSIN

MAINE

VT.

N.H.

MASS.

NEW YORK

R.I.

CONN.

WYOMING TERRITORY (1868)

IOWA

MICH.

PENNSYLVANIA

N.J.

NEVADA 1864

UTAH TERRITORY (1868)

NEBRASKA 1867

ILLINOIS

IND.

OHIO

WEST VA. 1863

MD.

DEL.

Washington, D.C.

CALIFORNIA

COLORADO TERRITORY (1861)

KANSAS 1861

St. Louis

MISSOURI

KENTUCKY

Richmond

VIRGINIA
Jan. 26, 1870
Oct. 5, 1869

N.C.
June 25, 1868
Nov. 3, 1870

ARIZONA TERRITORY (1863)

NEW MEXICO TERRITORY (1863)

UNORGANIZED TERRITORY

ARKANSAS
June 22, 1868
Nov. 10, 1874

TENNESSEE
July 24, 1866
Oct. 4, 1869

Memphis

MISS.
Feb. 23, 1870
Jan. 4, 1876

ALA.
July 14, 1868
Nov. 16, 1874

Atlanta

S.C.
June 25, 1868
Nov. 28, 1876

GEORGIA
July 15, 1870
Nov. 1, 1871

Savannah

PACIFIC OCEAN

TEXAS
Mar. 30, 1870
Jan. 14, 1873

LA.
June 25, 1868
Jan. 2, 1877

New Orleans

FLORIDA
June 25, 1868
Jan. 2, 1877

ATLANTIC OCEAN

Rio Grande

MEXICO

Gulf of Mexico

Legend

Confederate states, 1861–1865

July 24, 1866 Date of readmission to the Union

Oct. 4, 1869 Date of reestablishment of conservative rule

New territory and date of organization, 1861–1870

1864 New state and date of admission to Union, 1861–1870

Black population as percentage of total population, 1880

50% or more

30–50%

10–30%

0   200   400 Km.

0   200   400 Mi.

Timeline

1863 Emancipation Proclamation

1865 Civil War ends
Lincoln assassinated
13th Amendment

1866 Ku Klux Klan formed

1868 14th Amendment

1869 "New Departure"

1870 15th Amendment

1872 Grant reelected

1875 Mississippi Plan

1877 Reconstruction ends

1863 1864 1865 1866 1867 1868 1869 1870 1871 1872 1873 1874 1875 1876 1877 1878

1866–1870 Former Confederates settle in Brazil

1865 Former Confederates join the army of Maximilian, emperor of Mexico

1873 Slavery abolished in Puerto Rico

Reconstruction: High Hopes and Shattered Dreams, 1865–1877

Reconstruction
What does the map on the facing page suggest regarding the connection between the proportion of the population that was African American and the length of time that each southern state experienced Black Reconstruction? Compare this map with Map 16.1 and consider which southern whites were most likely to vote Republican.

Individual Choices

Andy Anderson

ANDY ANDERSON

Andy Anderson was 94 years old when he was interviewed in 1937. Unfortunately, no photo of him has been found. This photo depicts an African American family from East Texas, the area where Anderson was born and grew up and where he began to farm. The photo shows what Anderson's home may have looked like in the 1880s or 1890s. *East Texas Research Center, Stephen F. Austin State University.*

Andy Anderson was born into slavery in East Texas in 1843. In 1937, when he was 94 years old, he told an interviewer about the day when he made the decision to be free. The interview was one of more than two thousand conversations with former slaves that the Federal Writers Project (a New Deal agency for unemployed professionals) collected between 1936 and 1938. Interviewers were instructed to record the interviews exactly, word for word.

Anderson explained that he had been born on the plantation of Jack Haley. Anderson remembered Haley as "kind to his cullud folks" and "kind to ever'body." Haley rarely whipped his slaves, Anderson recalled, and he had been "reasonable" when he did apply the lash. Anderson remembered that Haley treated his slaves so well that neighboring whites called them "petted niggers." With the coming of the Civil War, however, conditions changed. Haley sold Anderson to W. T. House, whom Anderson remembered as a man that "hell am too good fo'," and who whipped Anderson for a minor accident with a wagon.

> De overseer ties me to de stake an' ever' ha'f hour, fo' four hours, deys lay 10 lashes on my back. Aftah I's stood dat fo' a couple of hours, I's could not feel de pain so much an' w'en dey took me loose, I's jus' ha'f dead. I's could not feel de lash 'cause my body am numb, an' my mind am numb. De last thing I's 'membahs am dat I's wishin' fo' death. I's laid in the de bunk fo' two days gittin' over dat whuppin'. Dat is, gittin' over it in de body but not in de heart. No Sar! I's have dat in de heart 'til dis day.

Soon after the whipping, Anderson was sold again, to House's brother John, who, to Anderson's knowledge, had never struck a slave.

As the Civil War was winding down to its end, Anderson remembered the day when House called his slaves together and told them that they were free and that the official order would soon be given. He offered any who wished to stay the choice to work for wages or work the land as sharecroppers, and he urged the freed people to "stay with me." Anderson was standing near House and said to himself, not expecting anyone to hear, "Lak hell I's will." He meant only that he intended to take his freedom, but House heard him, took it as a challenge, and promised that he would "tend to yous later." Anderson recalled that he was sure to keep his lips closed when he thought, "I's won't be heah."

Toward sundown, Anderson left the House plantation for good. He traveled at night to avoid the patrollers, who were always on the lookout for African Americans on the road without passes, and hid in the brush during the day. Though he was 21 years old, he'd never been farther from home than a neighbor's house, and he was uncertain of his way. Nonetheless he managed to locate the Haley plantation and to find his father, who hid Anderson. Haley permitted Anderson to stay on his place until the final proclamation of freedom.

Sheldon Cauthier of the Federal Writers Project interviewed Andy Anderson on September 16, 1937, and Anderson gave him this account of his decision to take his freedom. By then, Anderson was living in Fort Worth, Texas. Anderson provided only limited information on his later life. He left Haley's farm soon after emancipation to work on another farm for $2 a month plus clothing and food, and he continued to do farm work until his old age. He married in 1883, when he was about 40, an indication, perhaps, that his labor did not provide enough income to support a family until then. He and his first wife had two children, but both children and his wife died. He married again in 1885, and he and second his wife had six children, of whom four were still living in 1937. His second wife died in 1934, and he married a third time in 1936. He joked with the interviewer that "dere am no chilluns yet f'om my third mai'age." Though we know little of what Anderson experienced during the years of Reconstruction, we do have his dramatic account of how he claimed his freedom.

INTRODUCTION

Andy Anderson was not the only African American who claimed freedom while the war was raging. Anderson's experience was repeated time and time again, with many variations, all across the South. Those decisions were made legal by the Emancipation Proclamation, the presence of Union armies, and later the Thirteenth Amendment to the Constitution. The **freed people** now faced a wide range of new decisions—where to live, where to work, how to create their own communities.

The war was a momentous event for nearly all Americans. By 1865, when the war ended, some 2.6 million men—and a few hundred women—had served in the Union or Confederate armies, equal to almost 40 percent of all the men ages 15 to 40 in the United States in 1860. More than a half-million had died—more deaths than in any other American war—and many others were permanently disabled. By 1865, the war had touched the lives of nearly every person living in the nation.

Nearly all the major battles occurred in the South or in the border states. Toward the end of the war, Union armies swept across the South, leaving havoc behind them: burned and shelled buildings, ravaged fields, twisted railroad tracks. This destruction, and the collapse of the region's financial system, devastated the southern economy.

More distressing for many white southerners than the ravaged countryside was the **emancipation** of 4 million slaves. In 1861 fears for the future of slavery under Republicans had caused the South to attempt to **secede** from the Union. With the end of the war, fears became reality. The end of slavery forced southerners of both races to develop new social, economic, and political patterns.

Historians identify the years between 1865 and 1877 as **Reconstruction.** Although the period was a time of physical rebuilding throughout the South, Reconstruction refers primarily to the rebuilding of the federal Union and to the political, economic, and social changes that came to the South as it was restored to the nation. Reconstruction involved some of the most momentous questions in American history. How was the defeated South to be treated? What was to be the future of the 4 million former slaves? Should key decisions be made by the federal government or in state capitols and county courthouses throughout the South? Which branch of the government was to establish policies?

freed people Former slaves; *freed people* is the term used by historians to refer to former slaves, whether male or female.

emancipation Release from slavery.

secede To withdraw from membership in an organization; in this case, the attempted withdrawal of eleven southern states from the United States in 1860–1861, giving rise to the Civil War.

Reconstruction Term applied by historians to the years 1865–1877, when the Union was restored from the Civil War; important changes were made to the federal Constitution; and social, economic, and political relations between the races were transformed in the South.

As the dominant Republicans turned their attention from waging war to reconstructing the Union, they wrote into law and the Constitution new definitions of the Union itself. They also defined the rights of the former slaves and the terms on which the South might rejoin the Union. And they permanently changed the definition of American citizenship.

Most white southerners disliked the new rules emerging from the federal government, and some resisted. Disagreement over the future of the South and the status of the former slaves led to conflict between the president and Congress. A temporary result of this conflict was a more powerful Congress and a less powerful executive. A lasting outcome of these events was a significant increase in the power of the federal government and new limits on local and state governments.

Reconstruction significantly changed many aspects of southern life. In the end, however, Reconstruction failed to fulfill many African Americans' hopes for their lives as free people.

Presidential Reconstruction

■ What did Presidents Lincoln and Johnson seek to accomplish through their Reconstruction policies? How did their purposes differ? In what ways were their policies similar?

■ How did white southerners respond to the Reconstruction efforts of Lincoln and Johnson? What does this suggest about the expectations of white southerners?

On New Year's Day 1863, the Emancipation Proclamation took effect. More than four years earlier, Abraham Lincoln had insisted that "this government cannot endure permanently half slave and half free. . . . It will become all one thing, or all the other." With the Emancipation Proclamation, President Lincoln began the legal process by which the nation became all free. At the time, however, the Proclamation did not affect any slave because it abolished slavery only in territory under Confederate control, where it was unenforceable. But every advance of a Union army after January 1, 1863, brought the law of the land—and emancipation—to the Confederacy.

Republican War Aims

For Lincoln and the Republican Party, freedom for the slaves became a central concern partly because **abolitionists** were an influential group within the party. The Republican Party had promised only to prohibit slavery in the territories during their 1860 electoral

This engraving celebrating the Emancipation Proclamation first appeared in 1863. While it places a white Union soldier in the center, it also portrays the important role of African American troops and emphasizes the importance of education and literacy. *The Library Company of Philadelphia.*

campaign, and Lincoln initially defined the war only as one to maintain the Union. Some leading Republicans, however, favored abolition of slavery everywhere in the Union. As Union troops moved into the South, some slaves took matters into their hands by walking away from their owners and seeking safety with the advancing army. Within a year, former slaves had become an important part of the Union army's work force. Abolitionists throughout the North—including Frederick Douglass, an escaped slave and an important leader of the abolition movement—began to argue that emancipation would be meaningless unless the government guaranteed the civil and political rights of the former slaves. Thus some Republicans expanded their definition of war objectives to include not just preserving the Union but also abolishing slavery, extending citizenship for the former slaves, and guaranteeing the equality of all citizens before the law. At the time, these were extreme views

Chronology

Reconstruction

1863	Emancipation Proclamation The Ten Percent Plan	**1869–1870**	Victories of "New Departure" Democrats in some southern states
1864	Abraham Lincoln reelected	**1870**	Fifteenth Amendment (guaranteeing voting rights) ratified
1865	Freedmen's Bureau created Civil War ends Lincoln assassinated Andrew Johnson becomes president Thirteenth Amendment (abolishing slavery) ratified	**1870–1871**	Ku Klux Klan Acts
		1872	Grant reelected
		1875	Civil Rights Act of 1875 Mississippi Plan ends Reconstruction in Mississippi
1866	Ku Klux Klan formed Congress begins to assert control over Reconstruction Civil Rights Act of 1866 Riots by whites in Memphis and New Orleans	**1876**	Disputed presidential election: Hayes versus Tilden
1867	Military Reconstruction Act Command of the Army Act Tenure of Office Act	**1877**	Compromise of 1877 Rutherford B. Hayes becomes president End of Reconstruction
1868	Impeachment of President Johnson Fourteenth Amendment (defining citizenship) ratified Ulysses S. Grant elected president		

on abolition and equal rights, and the people who held them were called **Radical Republicans,** or simply Radicals.

Thaddeus Stevens, 73 years old in 1865 and perhaps the leading Radical in the House of Representatives, had made a successful career as a Pennsylvania iron manufacturer before he won election to Congress in 1858. Born with a clubfoot, he always seemed to identify with those outside the social mainstream. He became a compelling spokesman for abolition and an uncompromising advocate of equal rights for African Americans. A masterful parliamentarian, he was known for his honesty and his sarcastic wit. From the beginning of the war, Stevens urged that the slaves be not only freed but also armed, to fight the Confederacy. By the end of the war, some 180,000 African Americans, the great majority of them freedmen, had served in the Union army and a few thousand in the Union navy. Many more worked for the army as laborers.

Charles Sumner of Massachusetts, a prominent Radical in the Senate, had argued for **racial integration** of Massachusetts schools in 1849 and won election to the U.S. Senate in 1851. Immediately establishing himself as the Senate's foremost champion of abolition, he became a martyr to the cause after a severe beating he suffered in 1856 because of an antislavery speech. After emancipation, Sumner, like

abolitionist An individual who condemns slavery as morally wrong and seeks to abolish (eliminate) slavery.

Radical Republicans A group within the Republican Party during the Civil War and Reconstruction who advocated abolition of slavery, citizenship for the former slaves, and sweeping alteration of the South.

racial integration Equal opportunities to participate in a society or organization by people of different racial groups; the absence of race-based barriers to full and equal participation.

President Andrew Johnson was initially seen by the Radical Republicans as a potential ally. Instead he proved to be unsympathetic to most Radical goals. His self-righteous and uncompromising personality led to conflict that eventually produced an unsuccessful effort to remove him from office in 1868. *Library of Congress.*

Stevens, fought for full political and civil rights for the freed people.

Stevens, Sumner, and other Radicals demanded a drastic restructuring not only of the South's political system but also of its economy. They opposed slavery not only on moral grounds but also because they believed free labor was more productive. Slaves worked to escape punishment, they argued, but free workers worked to benefit themselves. Eliminating slavery and instituting a free-labor system in its place, they claimed, would benefit everyone by increasing the productivity of the nation's work force. Free labor not only contributed centrally to the dynamism of the North's economy, they argued, but was crucial to democracy itself. "The middling classes who own the soil, and work it with their own hands," Stevens once proclaimed, "are the main support of every free government." For the South to be fully democratic, the Radicals concluded, it had to elevate free labor to a position of honor.

Not all Republicans agreed with the Radicals. All Republicans had objected to slavery, but not all Republicans were abolitionists. Similarly, not all Republicans wanted to extend full citizenship rights to the former slaves. Some favored rapid restoration of the South to the Union so that the federal government could concentrate on stimulating the nation's economy and developing the West. Republicans who did not immediately endorse severe punishment for the South or citizenship for the freed people are usually referred to as **moderates.**

Lincoln's Approach to Reconstruction: "With Malice Toward None"

After the Emancipation Proclamation, President Lincoln and the congressional Radicals agreed that the abolition of slavery had to be a condition for the return of the South to the Union. Major differences soon appeared, however, over other terms for reunion and the roles of the president and Congress in establishing those terms. In his second inaugural address, a month before his death, Lincoln defined the task facing the nation:

> With malice toward none; with charity for all; with firmness in the right, as God gives us to see the right, let us strive on to finish the work we are in: to bind up the nation's wounds; to care for him who shall have borne the battle, and for his widow and orphan, to do all which may achieve and cherish a just and lasting peace among ourselves, and with all nations.

Lincoln began to rebuild the Union on the basis of these principles. He hoped to hasten the end of the war by encouraging southerners to renounce the Confederacy and to accept emancipation. As soon as Union armies occupied portions of southern states, he appointed temporary military governors for those regions and tried to restore civil government as quickly as possible.

Drawing on the president's constitutional power to issue **pardons** (Article II, Section 2), Lincoln issued

moderates People whose views are midway between two more-extreme positions; in this case, Republicans who favored some reforms but not all the Radicals' proposals.

pardon A governmental directive canceling punishment for a person or people who have committed a crime.

a Proclamation of **Amnesty** and Reconstruction in December 1863. Often called the "Ten Percent Plan," it promised a full pardon and restoration of rights to those who swore their loyalty to the Union and accepted the abolition of slavery. Only high-ranking Confederate leaders were not eligible. Once those who had taken the oath in a state amounted to 10 percent of the number of votes cast by that state in the 1860 presidential election, the pardoned voters were to write a new state constitution that abolished slavery, elect state officials, and resume self-government. Some congressional Radicals disagreed with Lincoln's lenient approach. When they tried to set more stringent standards, however, Lincoln blocked them, fearing their plan would slow the restoration of civil government and perhaps even lengthen the war.

Under Lincoln's Ten Percent Plan, new state governments were established in Arkansas, Louisiana, and Tennessee during 1864 and early 1865. In Louisiana, the new government denied voting rights to men who were one-quarter or more black. Radicals complained, but Lincoln urged patience, suggesting the reconstructed government in Louisiana was "as the egg to the fowl, and we shall sooner have the fowl by hatching the egg than by smashing it." Events in Louisiana and elsewhere convinced Radicals that freed people were unlikely to receive equitable treatment from state governments formed under the Ten Percent Plan. Some moderates agreed and moved toward the Radicals' position that only **suffrage** could protect the freedmen's rights and that only federal action could secure black suffrage.

Abolishing Slavery Forever: The Thirteenth Amendment

Amid questions about the rights of freed people, congressional Republicans prepared the final destruction of slavery. The Emancipation Proclamation had been a wartime measure, justified partly by military necessity, and it never applied in Union states. State legislatures or conventions abolished slavery in West Virginia, Maryland, Missouri, and the reconstructed state of Tennessee. In early 1865, however, slavery remained legal in Delaware and Kentucky, and old, prewar state laws—which might or might not be valid—still permitted slavery in the states that had seceded. To destroy slavery forever, Congress in January 1865 approved the **Thirteenth Amendment,** which read simply, "Neither slavery nor involuntary servitude, except as a punishment for crime whereof the party shall have been duly convicted, shall exist within the United States, or any place subject to their jurisdiction."

The Constitution requires any amendment to be ratified by three-fourths of the states—then 27 of 36. By December 1865, only 19 of the 25 Union states had ratified the amendment. The measure passed, however, when 8 of the reconstructed southern states approved it. In the end, therefore, the abolition of slavery hinged on action by reconstructed state governments in the South.

By abolishing slavery, the United States followed the lead of most of the nations of Europe and Latin America. Table 16.1 summarizes information on the abolition of slavery elsewhere in the world.

Andrew Johnson and Reconstruction

After the assassination of Lincoln in mid-April 1865, Vice President Andrew Johnson became president. Born in North Carolina, he never had the opportunity to attend school and spent his early life in a continual struggle against poverty. As a young man in Tennessee, he worked as a tailor and then turned to politics. After he married, his wife, Eliza McCardle Johnson, tutored him in reading, writing, and arithmetic. A Democrat, Johnson relied on his oratorical skills to win several terms in the Tennessee legislature. He was elected to Congress and afterward served as governor before winning election to the U.S. Senate in 1857. His political support came primarily from small-scale farmers and working people. The state's elite of plantation owners usually opposed him. Johnson, in turn, resented their wealth and power and blamed them for secession and the Civil War.

Johnson was the only southern senator who rejected the Confederacy. Early in the war, Union forces captured Nashville, the capital of Tennessee, and Lincoln appointed Johnson as military governor. Johnson dealt harshly with Tennessee secessionists, especially wealthy planters, and Radical Republicans thought that Johnson's severe treatment of former Confederates was exactly what the South needed. Johnson was

amnesty A general pardon granted by a government, especially for political offenses.

suffrage The right to vote.

Thirteenth Amendment Constitutional amendment, ratified in 1865, that abolished slavery in the United States and its territories.

TABLE 16.1   Abolition of Slavery Around the World

1772	Slavery abolished in England
1807	British navy begins operations to end the international slave trade
1808	United States prohibits the importation of slaves
1820s	Slavery abolished in most Spanish-speaking Latin American nations
1833	Slavery abolished within the British Empire
1848	Slavery abolished within the French Empire
1861	Abolition of serfdom in Russia
1863	Emancipation Proclamation (United States); abolition of slavery within the Dutch Empire
1865	Thirteenth Amendment abolishes slavery everywhere in the United States
1888	Slavery abolished in Brazil
1926	Thirty-five states sign a Convention to Suppress the Slave Trade and Slavery
1948	United Nations adopts the Universal Declaration of Human Rights, which includes a call for the abolition of slavery and the slave trade
1962	Abolition of slavery in Saudi Arabia
2004	International Year to Commemorate the Struggle against Slavery and its Abolition, proclaimed by the United Nations General Assembly

Though illegal throughout the world, chattel slavery still exists in some parts of Africa, notably Mauritania and Sudan, and in some parts of Asia, especially the Middle East. In other places throughout the world, people are still forced to work in conditions approaching that of slavery, through forced prostitution, debt bondage, and forced-labor camps.

elected vice president in 1864, receiving the nomination for vice president in part because Lincoln wanted to appeal to Democrats and to Unionists in border states.

When Johnson became president, Radicals hoped he would join their efforts to transform the South. Johnson, however, soon made clear that he was strongly committed to **states' rights** and opposed the Radicals' objective of a powerful federal government. "White men alone must manage the South," Johnson told one visitor, although he recommended limited political roles for the freedmen. Self-righteous and uncompromising, Johnson saw the major task of Reconstruction as **empowering** the region's white middle class and excluding the wealthy planters from power.

Johnson's approach to Reconstruction differed little from Lincoln's. Like Lincoln, he relied on the president's constitutional power to grant pardons. His desire for a quick restoration of the southern states to the Union apparently overcame his bitterness toward the southern elite, and he granted amnesty to most former Confederates who pledged loyalty to the Union and support for emancipation. In one of his last actions as president, he granted full pardon and amnesty to all southern rebels, although after 1868 the Fourteenth Amendment prevented him from restoring their right to hold office.

Johnson appointed **provisional** civilian governors for the southern states not already reconstructed. He instructed them to reconstitute functioning state administrations and to call constitutional conventions of delegates elected by pardoned voters. Some provisional governors, however, appointed former Confederates to state and local offices, outraging those who expected Reconstruction to bring to power loyal Unionists committed to a new southern society.

states' rights   A political position favoring limitation of the federal government's power and the greatest possible self-government by the individual states.

empower   To increase the power or authority of some person or group.

provisional   Temporary.

Before Emancipation, slaves typically made their own simple and rough clothing or they received the cast-off clothing of their owners and overseers. With Emancipation, those freed people who had an income could afford to dress more fashionably. The Harry Stephens family probably put on their best clothes for a visit to the photographer G. Gable in 1866. *Gilman Paper Company, NY.*

The Southern Response: Minimal Compliance

Johnson expected the state constitutional conventions to abolish slavery within each state, ratify the Thirteenth Amendment, renounce secession, and **repudiate** the states' war debts. The states were then to hold elections and resume their places in the Union. State conventions during the summer of 1865 usually complied with these requirements, though some did so grudgingly. Johnson had specified nothing about the rights of the freed people, and every state rejected black suffrage.

By April 1866, a year after the close of the war, all the southern states had fulfilled Johnson's requirements for rejoining the Union and had elected legislators, governors, and members of Congress. Their choices troubled Johnson. He had hoped for the emergence of new political leaders in the South and was dismayed at the number of rich planters and former Confederate officials who won state contests.

Most white southerners, however, viewed Johnson as their protector, standing between them and the Radicals. His support for states' rights and his opposition to federal determination of voting rights led white southerners to expect that they would shape the transition from slavery to freedom—that they, and not Congress, would define the status of the former slaves.

Freedom and the Legacy of Slavery

■ How did the freed people respond to freedom? What seem to have been the leading objectives among freed people as they explored their new opportunities?

■ How did southern whites respond to the end of slavery?

■ How do the differing responses of freed people and southern whites show different understandings of the significance of emancipation?

As state conventions wrote new constitutions and politicians argued in Washington, African Americans throughout the South set about creating new, free lives for themselves. In the antebellum South, all slaves and most free African Americans had led lives tightly constrained by law and custom. They were permitted few social organizations of their own. Eric Foner, in his comprehensive study *Reconstruction* (1988), described the central theme of the black response to emancipation as "a desire for independence from white control, for autonomy both as individuals and as members of a community." The prospect of **autonomy** touched every

repudiation   The act of rejecting the validity or authority of something; to refuse to pay.
autonomy   Control of one's own affairs.

aspect of life—family, churches, schools, newspapers, and a host of other social institutions. From this ferment of freedom came new black institutions that provided the basis for southern African American communities. At the same time, the economic life of the South had been shattered by the Civil War and was being transformed by emancipation. Thus white southerners also faced drastic economic and social change.

Defining the Meaning of Freedom

At the most basic level, freedom came every time an individual slave stopped working for a master and claimed the right to be free. Thus freedom did not come to all slaves at the same time or in the same way. For some, freedom came before the Emancipation Proclamation, when they walked away from their owners, crossed into Union-held territory, and asserted their liberty. Toward the end of the war, as civil authority broke down throughout much of the South, many slaves declared their freedom and left the lands they had worked when they were in bondage. Some left for good, but many remained nearby, though with a new understanding of their relationship to their former masters. For some, freedom did not come until ratification of the Thirteenth Amendment.

Across the South, the approach of Yankee troops set off a joyous celebration—called a Jubilee—among those who knew that their enslavement was ending. As one Virginia woman remembered, "Such rejoicing and shouting you never heard in your life." A man recalled that, with the appearance of the Union soldiers, "We was all walking on golden clouds. Hallelujah!" Once the celebrating was over, however, the freed people had to decide how best to use their freedom.

The freed people expressed their new status in many ways. Some chose new names to symbolize their new beginning. Andy Anderson (see page 456), for example, had been called Andy Haley, after the last name of his owner. On claiming his freedom, he changed his name to Anderson, the last name of his father. Many freed people changed their style of dress, discarding the cheap clothing provided to slaves. Some acquired guns. A significant benefit of freedom was the ability to travel without a pass and without being checked by the **patrollers** who had enforced the **pass system.**

Many freed people took advantage of this new opportunity to travel. Indeed, some felt they had to leave the site of their enslavement to experience full freedom. Andy Anderson refused to work for his last owner, not because he had anything against him but because he wanted "to take my freedom." One freed woman said, "If I stay here I'll never know I'm free." Most did not move, however. Those who did generally traveled only short distances, usually to find work or land to farm, to seek family members separated from them by slavery, or for other well-defined reasons.

The towns and cities of the South attracted some freed people. The presence of Union troops and officials promised protection from the random violence against freed people that occurred in many rural areas. A new federal program, the **Freedmen's Bureau,** offered assistance with finding work and necessities. Cities and towns also offered black churches, schools (which before the war had usually operated in secret), and other social institutions begun by free blacks before the war. Many African Americans also came to towns and cities looking for work. With little housing available, however, most crowded into hastily built shanties. Sanitation was poor and disease a common scourge. In September 1866, for example, more than a hundred people died of **cholera** in Vicksburg, Mississippi. Such conditions improved only very slowly.

Creating Communities

During Reconstruction, African Americans created their own communities with their own social institutions, beginning with family ties. Joyful families were reunited after years of separation caused by the sale of a spouse or children. Some people spent years searching for lost family members.

The new freedom to conduct religious services without white supervision was especially important. Churches quickly became the most prominent social organizations in African American communities.

---

patrollers During the era of slavery, white guards who made the rounds of rural roads to make certain that slaves were not moving about the countryside without written permission from their masters.

pass system Laws that forbade slaves from traveling without written authorization from their owners.

Freedmen's Bureau Agency established in 1865 to aid former slaves in their transition to freedom, especially by administering relief and sponsoring education.

cholera Infectious and often fatal disease associated with poor sanitation.

Churches were the first institutions in America to be completely controlled by African Americans, and ministers were highly influential figures in the African American communities that emerged during Reconstruction. This photograph shows the Reverend John Qualls at the pulpit of his church in New Orleans in the 1880s. *Historic New Orleans Collection.*

Churches were, in fact, among the very first social institutions that African Americans fully controlled. During Reconstruction, black denominations, including the African Methodist Episcopal, African Methodist Episcopal Zion, and several Baptist groups (all founded well before the Civil War), grew rapidly in the South. Black ministers helped to lead congregation members as they adjusted to the changes that freedom brought, and many ministers became key leaders within developing African American communities.

Throughout the cities and towns of the South, African Americans—especially ministers and church members—worked to create schools. Setting up a school, said one, was "the first proof" of independence. Many new schools were for both children and adults, whose literacy and learning had been restricted by state laws prohibiting education for slaves. The desire to learn was widespread and intense. One freedman in Georgia wrote to a friend: "The Lord has sent books and teachers. We must not hesitate a moment, but go on and learn all we can."

Before the war, free public education had been rudimentary in much of the South, and wholly absent in many places. When African Americans set up schools, they faced severe shortages of teachers, books, and schoolrooms—everything but students. As abolitionists and northern reformers tried to assist the transition from slavery to freedom, many of them focused first on education.

In March 1865, Congress created the Freedmen's Bureau to assist the freed people in their transition to freedom. It played an important role in organizing and equipping schools. Freedmen's Aid Societies also sprang up in most northern cities and, along with northern churches, collected funds and supplies for the freed people. Teachers—mostly white women, often from New England and often acting on religious impulses—came from the North. Northern aid societies and church organizations, together with the Freedmen's Bureau, established schools to train black teachers. Some of those schools evolved into black colleges. By 1870, the Freedmen's Bureau supervised more than 4,000 schools, with more than 9,000 teachers and 247,000 students. Still, in 1870, the schools had room for only one black child in ten of school age.

In addition to churches and schools, other African American social institutions emerged and grew, including **fraternal orders, benevolent societies,** and newspapers. By 1866, the South had ten black newspapers, led by the *New Orleans Tribune,* and black newspapers played important roles in shaping African American communities.

In politics, African Americans' first objective was recognition of their equal rights as citizens. Spokesman Frederick Douglass insisted, "Slavery is not abolished until the black man has the ballot." Political conventions of African Americans attracted hundreds of leaders of the emerging black communities. They called for equality and voting rights and pointed to black contributions in the American Revolution and the Civil War as evidence of patriotism

fraternal order   An organization of men, often with a ceremonial initiation, that typically provided rudimentary life insurance; many fraternal orders also had auxiliaries for the female relatives of members.

benevolent society   An organization of people dedicated to some charitable purpose.

During Reconstruction, the freed people gave a high priority to the establishment of schools, often with the assistance of the Freedmen's Bureau and northern missionary societies. This teacher and her barefoot pupils were photographed in the 1870s, in Petersburg, Virginia. In a school like this, one teacher typically taught grades 1–8. Note the daylight coming through the wall of the school behind the teacher's right shoulder, the gaps in the floorboards, and the benches for the students which seem to have been constructed from logs. *Clayton Lewis, William L. Clements Library, University of Michigan.*

and devotion. They also appealed to the nation's republican traditions, in particular the Declaration of Independence and its dictum that "all men are created equal."

Land and Labor

Former slaveowners reacted to emancipation in many ways. Some tried to keep their slaves from learning of their freedom. A very few white southerners welcomed the end of slavery—Mary Chesnut, for example, a plantation mistress from South Carolina, believed that the power of male slaveholders over female slaves led to sexual coercion and adultery, and she was glad to see the end of slavery. Few former slaveowners provided any compensation to assist their former slaves. One freedman later recalled, "I do know some of dem old slave owners to be nice enough to start der slaves off in freedom wid somethin' to live on . . . but dey wasn't in droves, I tell you."

Many freed people looked to Union troops for assistance. When General William T. Sherman led his victorious army through Georgia in the closing months of the war, thousands of African American men, women, and children claimed their freedom and followed in the Yankees' wake. Their leaders told Sherman that what they wanted most was to "reap the fruit of our own labor." In January 1865, Sherman issued Special Field Order No. 15, setting aside the Sea Islands and land along the South Carolina coast for

freed families. Each family, he specified, was to receive 40 acres and the loan of an army mule. By June, the area had filled with forty thousand freed people settled on 400,000 acres of "Sherman land."

Sherman's action encouraged many African Americans to expect that the federal government would redistribute land throughout the South. "Forty acres and a mule" became a rallying cry. Only land, Thaddeus Stevens proclaimed, would give the freed people control of their own labor. "If we do not furnish them with homesteads," Stevens said, "we had better left them in bondage."

By the end of the war, the Freedmen's Bureau controlled some 850,000 acres of land abandoned by former owners or confiscated from Confederate leaders. In July 1865, General Oliver O. Howard, head of the bureau, directed that this land be divided into 40-acre plots to be given to freed people. However, President Johnson ordered Howard to halt **land redistribution** and to reclaim land already handed over and return it to its former owners. Johnson's order displaced thousands of African Americans who had already taken their 40 acres. They and others who had hoped for land felt disappointed and betrayed. One later re-

land redistribution The division of land held by large landowners into smaller plots that are turned over to people without property.

called that they had expected "a heap from freedom dey didn't git."

The congressional act that created the Freedmen's Bureau also authorized it to assist white refugees. In a few places, white recipients of aid outnumbered the freed blacks. The vast majority of southern whites had never owned slaves, and some opposed secession, but the outcome of the war meant that some lost their livelihood, and many feared that they would now have to compete with the freed people for farmland or wage labor. Like the freed people, many southern whites lacked the means to farm on their own. With the collapse of the Confederate government, Confederate money—badly devalued by rampant inflation—became worthless. This currency fiasco, together with the failure of southern banks and the devastation of the southern economy, meant that even many whites with large landholdings lacked the cash to hire farm workers.

Sharecropping slowly emerged across much of the South as an alternative both to land redistribution and to wage labor on the plantations. Sharecropping derived directly from the central realities of southern agriculture. Much of the land was in large holdings, but the landowners had no one to work it. Many families, black and white, wanted to raise their own crops with their own labor but had no land, no supplies, and no money. The entire region was short of **capital.** Under sharecropping, an individual—usually a family head—signed a contract with a landowner to rent land as home and farm. The tenant—the sharecropper—was to pay, as rent, a share of the harvest. The share might amount to half or more of the crop if the landlord provided mules, tools, seed, and fertilizer as well as land. Many landowners thought that sharecropping encouraged tenants to be productive, to get as much value as possible from their shares of the crop. The rental contract often allowed the landlord to specify what crop would be planted, and most landlords chose cotton so that their tenants would not hold back any of the harvest for personal consumption. Thus sharecropping helped to perpetuate the dependency of the South on cotton.

Southern farmers—black or white, sharecroppers or owners of small plots—often found themselves in debt to a local merchant who advanced supplies on credit. In return for credit, the merchant required a lien (a legal claim) on the growing crop. Many landlords ran stores that they required their tenants to patronize. Often the share paid as rent and the debt owed the store exceeded the value of the entire harvest. Furthermore, many rental contracts and **crop liens** were automatically renewed if all debts were not paid at the end of a year. Thus, in spite of their ef-

Sharecropping gave the African Americans more control over their labor than did labor contracts. But sharecropping also contributed to the South's dependence on one-crop agriculture and helped to perpetuate widespread rural poverty. This family of sharecroppers near Aiken, South Carolina, was photographed picking cotton around 1870. © *Collection of the New York Historical Society.*

forts to achieve greater control over their lives and labor, many southern farm families, black and white alike, found themselves trapped by sharecropping and debt. Still, sharecropping gave freed people more control over their daily lives than had slavery.

Landlords often exercised political as well as economic power over their tenants. Until the 1890s, the act of casting a ballot on election day was an open process, and any observer could see how an individual voted (see page 474). Thus, when a landlord or merchant advocated a particular candidate, the unspoken message was often an implicit threat to cut off credit at the store or to evict a sharecropper if he did

sharecropping A system for renting farmland in which tenant farmers give landlords a share of their crops, rather than cash, as rent.

capital Money, especially the money invested in a commercial enterprise.

crop lien A legal claim to a farmer's crop, similar to a mortgage, based on the use of crops as collateral for extension of credit by a merchant.

not vote accordingly. Such forms of economic **coercion** had the potential to undercut voting rights.

The White South: Confronting Change

The Civil War and the end of slavery transformed the lives of white southerners as well as black southerners. For some, the changes were nearly as profound as for the freed people. Savings vanished. Some homes and other buildings were destroyed. Thousands left the South.

Before the war, few white southerners had owned slaves, and even fewer owned large numbers. Distrust or even hostility had always existed between the privileged planter families and the many whites who farmed small plots by themselves. Some regions populated by small-scale farmers had resisted secession, and some of them welcomed the Union victory and supported the Republicans during Reconstruction. Some southerners also welcomed the prospect of the economic transformation that northern capital might bring.

Most white southerners, however, shared what one North Carolinian described in 1866 as "the bitterest hatred toward the North." Even people with no attachment to slavery detested the Yankees who so profoundly changed their lives. For many white southerners, the "lost cause" of the Confederacy came to symbolize their defense of their prewar lives, not an attempt to break up the nation or protect slavery. During the early phases of Reconstruction, most white southerners apparently expected that, except for slavery, things would soon be put back much as they had been before the war.

As civil governments began to function in late 1865 and 1866, state legislatures passed **black codes** defining the new legal status of African Americans. These regulations varied from state to state, but every state placed significant restraints on black people. Various black codes required African Americans to have an annual employment contract, limited them to agricultural work, forbade them from moving about the countryside without permission, restricted their ownership of land, and provided for forced labor by those found guilty of **vagrancy**—which usually meant anyone without a job. Some codes originated in prewar restrictions on slaves and free blacks. Some reflected efforts to ensure that farm workers would be on hand for planting, cultivating, and harvesting. Taken together, however, the black codes represented an effort by white southerners to define a legally subordinate place for African Americans.

In this picture, the artist has portrayed a Republican leader, John Campbell, pleading for mercy from a group of bizarrely dressed Klansmen in Moore County, North Carolina, on August 10, 1871. Campbell was a white grocery store owner who was active in the local Republican Party; the Klansmen flogged him before releasing him. Those responsible were captured and photographed in their Klan costumes, providing the basis for this drawing. Curiously, the artist has depicted Campbell as an African American. *The Granger Collection, New York.*

Some white southerners also used violence to coerce freed people into accepting a subordinate status within the new southern society. Clara Barton, who had organized women as nurses for the Union army, visited the South from 1866 to 1870 and observed "a condition of lawlessness toward the blacks" and "a

coercion   Use of threats or force to compel action.
black codes   Laws passed by the southern states after the Civil War to define the status of freed people as subordinate to whites.
vagrancy   The legal condition of having no fixed place of residence or means of support.

disposition . . . to injure or kill them on slight or no provocation."

Violence and terror became closely associated with the **Ku Klux Klan,** a secret organization formed in 1866 and led by a former Confederate general. Most Klan members were small-scale farmers and workers, but the leaders were often prominent within their own communities. As one Freedmen's Bureau agent observed about the Klan, "The most respectable citizens are engaged in it." Klan groups existed throughout the South, but operated with little central control. Their major goals were to restore **white supremacy** and to destroy the Republican Party. Other, similar organizations also formed and adopted terrorist tactics.

Klan members were called ghouls. Officers included cyclops, night-hawks, and grand dragons, and the national leader was called the grand wizard. Klan members covered their faces with hoods, wore white robes, and rode horses draped in white as they set out to intimidate black Republicans and their Radical white allies. Klan members also attacked less politically prominent people, whipping African Americans accused of not showing sufficient deference to whites. Nightriders also burned black churches and schools. By such tactics, the Klan devastated Republican organizations in many communities.

In 1866 two events dramatized the violence that some white southerners were inflicting on African Americans. In early May, in Memphis, Tennessee, black veterans of the Union army came to the assistance of a black man being arrested by white police, setting off a three-day riot in which whites, including police, indiscriminately attacked African Americans. Forty-five blacks and three whites died. In late July, in New Orleans, some forty people died, most of them African Americans, in an altercation between police and a largely black prosuffrage group. General Philip Sheridan, the military commander of the district, called it "an absolute massacre by the police." Memphis and New Orleans were unusual only in the numbers of casualties. Local authorities often seemed uninterested in stopping such violence, and federal troops were not always available when they were needed.

The black codes, violence against freed people, and the failure of southern authorities to stem the violence turned northern opinion against President Johnson's lenient approach to Reconstruction. Increasing numbers of moderate Republicans accepted the Radicals' arguments that the freed people required greater federal protection, and congressional Republicans moved to take control of Reconstruction. When Johnson's stubborn and uncompromising personality ran up against the equally stubborn and uncompromising Thaddeus Stevens, the nation faced a constitutional crisis.

Challenging Presidential Reconstruction

In December 1865, the Thirty-ninth Congress (elected in 1864) met for the first time. Republicans outnumbered Democrats by more than three to one. The president's annual message proclaimed Reconstruction complete and the Union restored. Few Republicans agreed. Events in the South had convinced most moderate Republicans of the need to protect free labor in the South and to establish basic rights for the freed people. Most also agreed that Congress could withhold representation from the South until reconstructed state governments met these conditions.

On the first day of the Thirty-ninth Congress, moderate Republicans joined Radicals to exclude newly elected congressmen from the South. Citing Article I, Section 5, of the Constitution (which makes each house of Congress the judge of the qualifications of its members), Republicans set up a Joint Committee on Reconstruction to evaluate the qualifications of the excluded southerners and to determine whether the southern states were entitled to representation. Some committee members wanted to launch an investigation of presidential Reconstruction. In the meantime, the former Confederate states had no representation in Congress.

Congressional Republicans also moved to provide more assistance to the freed people. Moderates and Radicals approved a bill extending the Freedmen's

Congressional Reconstruction

■ Why did congressional Republicans take control over Reconstruction policy? What did they seek to accomplish? How successful were they?

■ How did the Fourteenth and Fifteenth Amendments change the nature of the federal Union?

Ku Klux Klan A secret society organized in the South after the Civil War to resurrect white supremacy by means of violence and intimidation.

white supremacy The racist belief that whites are inherently superior to all other races and are therefore entitled to rule over them.

These white southerners are shown taking the oath of allegiance to the United States in 1865, as part of the process of restoring civil government in the South. The Union soldiers and officers are administering the oath. *Library of Congress.*

Bureau and giving it more authority against racial discrimination. When Johnson vetoed it, Congress drafted a slightly revised version. Similar Republican unity produced a **civil rights** bill, a far-reaching measure that extended citizenship to African Americans and defined some of the rights guaranteed to all citizens. Johnson vetoed both the civil rights bill and the revised Freedmen's Bureau bill, but Congress passed both over his veto. With creation of the Joint Committee on Reconstruction and passage of the Civil Rights and Freedmen's Bureau Acts, Congress took control of Reconstruction.

The Civil Rights Act of 1866

The Civil Rights Act of 1866 defined all persons born in the United States (except Indians not taxed) as citizens. It also listed certain rights of all citizens, including the right to testify in court, own property, make contracts, bring lawsuits, and enjoy "full and equal benefit of all laws and proceedings for the security of person and property." This was the first effort to define in law some of the rights of American citizenship. It placed significant restrictions on state actions on the grounds that the rights of national citizenship

took precedence over the powers of state governments. The law expanded the power of the federal government in unprecedented ways and challenged traditional concepts of states' rights. Though the law applied to all citizens, its most immediate consequence was to benefit African Americans.

Much of the debate in Congress over the measure focused on the situation of the freed people. Some supporters saw the Civil Rights Act as a way to secure the freed people's basic rights. Some northern Republicans hoped the law would encourage freed people to stay in the South. For other Republicans, the bill carried broader implications because it empowered the federal government to force states to abide by the principle of equality before the law. They applauded its redefinition of federal-state relations. Senator Lot Morrill of Maine described it as "absolutely revolutionary" but added, "Are we not in the midst of a revolution?"

---

civil rights The rights, privileges, and protections that are a part of citizenship.

When President Johnson vetoed the bill, he argued that it violated states' rights. By defending states' rights and taking aim at the Radicals, Johnson may have hoped to generate enough political support to elect a conservative Congress in 1866 and to win the presidency in 1868. He probably expected the veto to appeal to voters and to turn them against the Radicals. Instead, the veto led most moderate Republicans to give up all hope of cooperation with him. In April 1866, when Congress passed the Civil Rights Act over Johnson's veto, it was the first time ever that Congress had overridden a presidential veto of major legislation.

Defining Citizenship: The Fourteenth Amendment

Leading Republicans, though pleased that the Civil Rights Act was now law, worried that it could be amended or repealed by a later Congress or declared unconstitutional by the Supreme Court. Only a constitutional amendment, they concluded, could permanently safeguard the freed people's rights as citizens.

The **Fourteenth Amendment** began as a proposal made by Radicals seeking a constitutional guarantee of equality before the law. But the final wording—the longest of any amendment—resulted from many compromises. Section 1 of the amendment defined American citizenship in much the same way as the Civil Rights Act of 1866, then specified that

> *No State shall make or enforce any law which shall abridge the privileges or immunities of citizens of the United States; nor shall any State deprive any person of life, liberty, or property, without due process of law; nor deny to any person within its jurisdiction the equal protection of the laws.*

The Constitution and Bill of Rights prohibit federal interference with basic civil rights. The Fourteenth Amendment extends this protection against action by state governments.

The amendment was vague on some points. For example, it penalized states that did not **enfranchise** African Americans by reducing their congressional and electoral representation, but it did not specifically guarantee to African Americans the right to vote.

Some provisions of the amendment stemmed from Republicans' fears that a restored South, allied with northern Democrats, might try to undo the outcome of the war. One section barred from public office anyone who had sworn to uphold the federal Constitution and then "engaged in insurrection or rebellion against the same." Only a two-thirds vote of Con-

It Matters

The Fourteenth Amendment

The Fourteenth Amendment is one of the most important amendments to the Constitution, next to the Bill of Rights (the first ten amendments). One key change was the definition of American citizenship. The Constitution had no provisions regarding citizenship until the Fourteenth Amendment. The Fourteenth Amendment cleared up any confusion about who was, and who was not, a citizen.

The amendment also specified that no state could abridge the liberties of a citizen "without due process of law." Until this time, the Constitution and the Bill of Rights restricted action by the *federal* government to restrict individual liberties. The Fourteenth Amendment extends many of these restrictions to *state* governments. For example, the Supreme Court has interpreted the Fourteenth Amendment to mean that the restrictions placed on Congress by the First Amendment also restrict state governments—that no state government could abridge the freedom of speech, press, assembly, and religion. The Supreme Court continues to interpret these provisions when it is presented with new cases. For example, the Supreme Court cited this provision to conclude that states may not prevent residents from buying contraceptives, and also cited the due process clause, among others, in *Roe v. Wade*, to conclude that state laws may not prevent women from having abortions.

gress could override this provision. (In 1872 Congress passed a blanket measure pardoning nearly all former Confederates.) The amendment also prohibited federal or state governments from assuming any of the Confederate debt or from paying any claim arising from emancipation.

Fourteenth Amendment Constitutional amendment, ratified in 1868, defining American citizenship and placing restrictions on former Confederates.

enfranchise To grant the right to vote to an individual or group.

Not everyone approved of the final wording. Charles Sumner condemned the provision that permitted a state to deny suffrage to male citizens if it accepted a penalty in congressional representation. Stevens wanted to bar former Confederates not just from holding office but also from voting. Woman suffrage advocates, led by **Susan B. Anthony** and **Elizabeth Cady Stanton,** complained that the amendment, for the first time, introduced the word *male* into the Constitution in connection with voting rights.

Despite such concerns, Congress approved the Fourteenth Amendment by a straight party vote in June 1866 and sent it to the states for ratification. Johnson protested that Congress should not propose constitutional amendments until all representatives of the southern states had taken their seats. Tennessee promptly ratified the amendment, became the first reconstructed state government to be recognized by Congress, and was exempted from most later Reconstruction legislation.

Although Congress adjourned in the summer of 1866, the nation's attention remained fixed on Reconstruction. In May and July, the bloody riots in Memphis and New Orleans turned more moderates against Johnson's Reconstruction policies. Some interpreted the congressional elections that fall as a referendum on Reconstruction and the Fourteenth Amendment, pitting Johnson against the Radicals. Johnson undertook a speaking tour to promote his views, but one of his own supporters calculated that Johnson's reckless tirades alienated a million voters. Republicans swept the 1866 elections, outnumbering Democrats 143 to 49 in the new House of Representatives, and 42 to 11 in the Senate. Lyman Trumbull, senator from Illinois and a leading moderate, voiced the consensus of congressional Republicans: Congress should now "hurl from power the disloyal element" in the South.

Radicals in Control

As congressional Radicals struggled with Johnson over control of Reconstruction, it became clear that the Fourteenth Amendment might fall short of ratification. Rejection by ten states could prevent its acceptance. By March 1867, the amendment had been rejected by twelve states—Delaware, Kentucky, and all the former Confederate states except Tennessee. Moderate Republicans who had expected the Fourteenth Amendment to be the final Reconstruction measure now became more receptive to other proposals that the Radicals put forth.

The Military Reconstruction Act of 1867, passed on March 2 over Johnson's veto, divided the Confederate states (except Tennessee) into five military districts. Each district was to be governed by a military commander authorized by Congress to use military force to protect life and property. The ten states were to hold constitutional conventions, and all adult male citizens were to vote, except former Confederates barred from office under the proposed Fourteenth Amendment. The constitutional conventions were to create new state governments that permitted black suffrage, and the new governments were to ratify the Fourteenth Amendment. Congress would then evaluate whether those state governments were to regain representation in Congress.

Congress had wrested a major degree of control over Reconstruction from the president, but it was not finished with him. On the same day, March 2, Congress further limited Johnson's powers. The Command of the Army Act specified that the president could issue military orders only through the General of the Army, then Ulysses S. Grant, considered an ally of Congress. It also specified that the General of the Army could not be removed without Senate permission. Congress thereby blocked Johnson from direct communication with military commanders in the South. The Tenure of Office Act specified that officials appointed with the Senate's consent were to remain in office until the Senate approved a successor, thereby preventing Johnson from removing federal officials who opposed his policies. Johnson understood both measures as invasions of presidential authority.

Early in 1867, some Radicals began to consider impeaching President Johnson. The Constitution (Article I, Sections 2 and 3) gives the House of Representatives exclusive power to **impeach** the president—that is, to charge the chief executive with misconduct. The Constitution specifies that the Senate shall hold trial on those charges, with the chief justice of the Supreme Court presiding. If found guilty by a two-thirds vote of the Senate, the president is removed from office.

In January 1867, the House Judiciary Committee investigated charges against Johnson but found no convincing evidence of misconduct. Johnson, however, challenged Congress over the Tenure of Office Act by

---

Susan B. Anthony   Tireless campaigner for woman suffrage and close associate of Elizabeth Cady Stanton.

Elizabeth Cady Stanton   A founder and leader of the American woman suffrage movement from 1848, and the Seneca Falls Conference, until her death in 1902.

impeach   To charge a public official with improper, usually criminal, conduct.

Tickets such as these were in high demand, for they permitted the holder to watch the historic proceedings as the Radical leaders presented their evidence to justify removing Andrew Johnson from the presidency. *Collection of Janice L. and David J. Frent.*

removing Edwin Stanton as secretary of war. This provocation gave Johnson's opponents something resembling a violation of law by the president. Still, an effort to secure impeachment through the House Judiciary Committee failed. The Joint Committee on Reconstruction, led by Thaddeus Stevens, then took over and developed charges against Johnson. On February 24, 1868, the House adopted eleven articles, or charges, nearly all based on the Stanton affair. The actual reasons the Radicals wanted Johnson removed were clear to all: they disliked him and his actions.

To convict Johnson and remove him from the presidency required a two-thirds vote by the Senate. Johnson's defenders argued that he had done nothing to warrant impeachment. The Radicals' legal case was weak, but they urged senators to vote on whether they wished Johnson to remain as president. Republican unity unraveled when some moderates, fearing a precedent of removing a president for such flimsy reasons, joined with Democrats to defeat the Radicals. The vote, on May 16 and 26, 1868, was 35 in favor of conviction and 19 against, one vote short of the required two-thirds. By this tiny margin, the Congress maintained the principle that it should not remove the president from office simply because they disagreed with or disliked each other.

Political Terrorism and the Election of 1868

The Radicals' failure to unseat Johnson left him with less than a year remaining in office. As the election

approached, the Republicans nominated Ulysses S. Grant for president. A war hero, popular throughout the North, Grant had fully supported Lincoln and Congress in implementing emancipation. By 1868, he had committed himself to the congressional view of Reconstruction. The Democrats nominated Horatio Seymour, a former governor of New York, and focused their energies on denouncing Reconstruction.

In the South, the campaign stirred up fierce activity by the Ku Klux Klan and similar groups. **Terrorists** assassinated an Arkansas congressman, three members of the South Carolina legislature, and several other Republican leaders. Throughout the South, mobs attacked Republican offices and meetings, and sometimes attacked any black person they could find. Such coercion had its intended effect at the ballot box. For example, as many as two hundred blacks were killed in St. Landry Parish, Louisiana, where the Republicans previously had a thousand-vote majority. On election day, not a single Republican vote was recorded from that parish.

Despite such violence, many Americans may have been anticipating a calmer political future. In June 1868 Congress had readmitted seven southern states that met the requirements of congressional Reconstruction. In July, the secretary of state declared the Fourteenth Amendment ratified. In November, Grant easily won the presidency, carrying twenty-six of the thirty-four states and 53 percent of the vote.

Voting Rights and Civil Rights

With Grant in the White House, Radical Republicans now considered pressing for voting rights for all African Americans. In 1867 Congress had removed racial barriers to voting in the District of Columbia and in the territories, but elsewhere the states still defined voting rights. Congress had required southern states to enfranchise black males as the price of readmission to the Union, but only seven northern states had taken that step by 1869. Further, any state that had enfranchised African Americans could change its law to reverse the policy. In addition to the principled arguments of Douglass and other Radicals, many Republicans concluded that they needed to guarantee black suffrage in the South if they were to continue to win presidential elections and enjoy majorities in Congress.

terrorists   Those who use threats and violence to achieve ideological or political goals.

This engraving appeared on the cover of *Harper's Weekly* in November 1867. It shows black men lined up to cast their ballots in that fall's elections. Note that the artist has shown first an older black workingman, with his hammer in his pocket; and next a well-dressed young black man, probably a city-dweller and perhaps a leader in the emerging black community; and next a black Union soldier. Note, too, the open process of voting. Voters received a ballot (a "party ticket") from a party campaigner and deposited that ballot in a ballot box, in full sight of all. Voting was not secret until much later. *Harper's Weekly, Nov. 16, 1867. Granger Collection.*

moderates and Radicals. Some African American leaders argued for language guaranteeing voting rights to all male citizens, because prohibiting some grounds for **disfranchisement** might imply the legitimacy of other grounds. Some Radicals tried, unsuccessfully, to add "**nativity,** property, education, or religious beliefs" to the prohibited grounds. Democrats condemned the Fifteenth Amendment as a "revolutionary" change in the rights of states to define voting rights.

Elizabeth Cady Stanton, Susan B. Anthony, and other advocates of woman suffrage opposed the amendment because it ignored restrictions based on sex. For nearly twenty years, the cause of women's rights and the cause of black rights had marched together. Once black male suffrage came under discussion, however, this alliance began to fracture. When one veteran abolitionist declared it to be "the Negro's hour" and called for black male suffrage, Anthony responded that she "would sooner cut off my right hand than ask the ballot for the black man and not for woman." The break between the women's movement and the black movement was eventually papered over, but the wounds never completely healed.

Despite such opposition, within thirteen months the proposed amendment received the approval of enough states to take effect. Success came in part because Republicans, who might otherwise have been reluctant to impose black suffrage in the North, concluded that the future success of their party required black suffrage in the South.

The Fifteenth Amendment did nothing to reduce the violence—especially at election time—that had become almost routine in the South after 1865. When Klan activity escalated in the elections of 1870, southern Republicans looked to Washington for support. In 1870 and 1871, Congress adopted several Enforcement Acts—often called the Ku Klux Klan Acts—to enforce the Fourteenth and Fifteenth Amendments.

Despite a limited budget and many obstacles, the prosecution of Klansmen began in 1871. Across the South many hundreds were indicted, and many were convicted. In South Carolina, President Grant de-

To secure suffrage rights for all African Americans, Congress approved the **Fifteenth Amendment** in February 1869. Widely considered to be the final step in Reconstruction, the amendment prohibited both federal and state governments from restricting a person's right to vote because of "race, color, or previous condition of servitude." Like the Fourteenth Amendment, the Fifteenth marked a compromise between

Fifteenth Amendment   Constitutional amendment, ratified in 1870, that prohibited states from denying the right to vote because of a person's race or because a person had been a slave.

disfranchisement   The taking away of an individual's or group's right to vote.

nativity   Place of birth.

clared martial law. By 1872, federal intervention had broken much of the strength of the Klan.

Congress eventually passed one final Reconstruction measure. Charles Sumner introduced a bill prohibiting **discrimination** in 1870 and in each subsequent session of Congress until his death in 1874. On his deathbed, Sumner urged his visitors to "take care of the civil-rights bill," begging them, "Don't let it fail." Passed after Sumner's death, the **Civil Rights Act of 1875** prohibited racial discrimination in the selection of juries and in public transportation and **public accommodations.**

Black Reconstruction

▪ What major groups made up the Republican Party in the South during Reconstruction? Compare their reasons for being Republicans, their relative size, and their objectives.

▪ What were the most lasting results of the Republican state administrations?

Congressional Reconstruction set the stage for new developments at state and local levels throughout the South, as newly enfranchised black men organized for political action. African Americans never completely controlled any state government, but they did form a significant element in the governments of several states. The period when African Americans participated prominently in state and local politics is usually called **Black Reconstruction.** It began with efforts by African Americans to take part in politics as early as 1865 and lasted for more than a decade. A few African Americans continued to hold elective office in the South long after 1877, but they could do little to bring about significant political change.

The Republican Party in the South

Not surprisingly, nearly all African Americans who participated actively in politics did so as Republicans. African Americans formed the large majority of those who supported the Republican Party in the South. Nearly all black Republicans were new to politics, and they often braved considerable personal danger by participating in a party that many white southerners equated with the conquering Yankees. In the South, the Republican Party also included some southern whites along with a smaller number of transplanted northerners—both black and white.

Suffrage made politics a centrally important activity for African American communities. The state con-

This lithograph from 1883 depicts prominent African American men, several of whom had leading roles in Black Reconstruction. *Library of Congress.*

stitutional conventions that met in 1868 included 265 black delegates. Only in Louisiana and South Carolina were half or more of the delegates black. With suffrage established, southern Republicans began to elect African Americans to public office. Between 1869 and 1877, fourteen black men served in the national House of Representatives, and Mississippi sent

discrimination   Denial of equal treatment based on prejudice or bias.

Civil Rights Act of 1875   Law passed by Congress in 1875 prohibiting racial discrimination in selection of juries and in transportation and other businesses open to the general public.

public accommodations   Hotels, bars and restaurants, theaters, and other places set up to do business with anyone who can pay the price of admission.

Black Reconstruction   The period of Reconstruction when African Americans took an active role in state and local government.

two African Americans to the U.S. Senate: Hiram R. Revels and Blanche K. Bruce.

Across the South, six African Americans served as lieutenant governors, and one of them, P. B. S. Pinchback, succeeded to the governorship of Louisiana for forty-three days. More than six hundred black men served in southern state legislatures during Reconstruction, but only in South Carolina did African Americans have a majority in the state legislature. Elsewhere they formed part of a Republican majority but rarely held key legislative positions. Only in South Carolina and Mississippi did legislatures elect black presiding officers.

Although politically inexperienced, most African Americans who held office during Reconstruction had some education. Of the eighteen who served in statewide offices, all but three are known to have been born free. P. B. S. Pinchback, for example, was educated in Ohio and served in the army as a captain before entering politics in Louisiana. Most black politicians first achieved prominence through service with the army, the Freedmen's Bureau, the new schools, or the religious and civic organizations of black communities.

Throughout the South, Republicans gained power only by securing some support from white voters. These white Republicans are usually remembered by the names fastened on them by their political opponents: "carpetbaggers" and "scalawags." Both groups included idealists who hoped to create a new southern society, but both also included opportunists expecting to exploit politics for personal gain.

Southern Democrats applied the term *carpetbagger* to northern Republicans who came to the South after the war, regarding them as second-rate schemers—outsiders with their belongings packed in a carpet bag. In fact, most northerners who came south were well-educated men and women from middle-class backgrounds. Most men had served in the Union army and moved south before blacks could vote. Some were lawyers, businessmen, or newspaper editors. Whether as investors in agricultural land, teachers in the new schools, or agents of the Freedmen's Bureau, most hoped to transform the South by creating new institutions based on northern models, especially free labor and free public schools. Few in number compared with southerners, transplanted northerners nonetheless took leading roles in state constitutional conventions and state legislatures. Some were also prominent advocates of economic modernization.

Southern Democrats reserved their greatest contempt for those they called *scalawags,* slang for

Bags made of carpeting, like this one, were inexpensive luggage for traveling. Southern opponents of Reconstruction fastened the label "carpetbaggers" on northerners who came south to participate in Reconstruction, suggesting that they were cheap opportunists. *Collection of Picture Research Consultants.*

someone completely unscrupulous and worthless. Scalawags were white southerners who became Republicans. They included many southern Unionists, who had opposed secession, and others who thought the Republicans offered the best hope for economic recovery. Scalawags included merchants, artisans, and professionals who favored a modernized South. Others were small-scale farmers who saw Reconstruction as a way to end political domination by the plantation owners.

The freedmen, carpetbaggers, and scalawags who made up the Republican Party in the South hoped to inject new ideas into that region. They tried to modernize state and local governments and make the postwar South more like the North. They repealed outdated laws and established or expanded schools, hospitals, orphanages, and penitentiaries.

carpetbagger Derogatory term for the northerners who came to the South after the Civil War to take part in Reconstruction.

scalawag Derogatory term for white southerners who aligned themselves with the Republican Party during Reconstruction.

The Hampton Normal and Agricultural Institute was founded in 1868 with financial assistance from the Freedmen's Bureau and the American Missionary Association. Its purpose was to provide education for African Americans to prepare males for jobs in agriculture or industry, and to prepare women as homemakers. As a normal school, it also trained teachers. One of Hampton's most prominent graduates was Booker T. Washington, who attended shortly after this picture was taken around 1870. *Archival and Museum Collection, Hampton University.*

Creating an Educational System and Fighting Discrimination

Free public education was perhaps the most permanent legacy of Black Reconstruction. Reconstruction constitutions throughout the South required tax-supported public schools. Implementation, however, was expensive and proceeded slowly. By the mid-1870s, only half of southern children attended public schools.

In creating public schools, Reconstruction state governments faced a central question: would white and black children attend the same schools? Many blacks favored racially integrated schools. On the other hand, southern white leaders, including many southern white Republicans, argued that integration would destroy the fledgling public school system by driving whites away. In consequence, no state required school integration. Similarly, southern states set up separate black normal schools (to train schoolteachers) and colleges.

On balance, most blacks probably agreed with Frederick Douglass that separate schools were "infinitely superior" to no public education at all. Some found other reasons to accept segregated schools: separate black schools gave a larger role to black parents, and they hired black teachers.

Funding for the new schools was rarely adequate. Creating and operating two educational systems, one white and one black, was costly. The division of limited funds posed an additional problem, and black schools almost always received less support per student than white schools. Despite their accomplishments, the segregated schools institutionalized discrimination.

Reconstruction state governments moved toward protection of equal rights in areas other than education.

In the period after the Civil War, political leaders of all parties eagerly sought to encourage railroad construction because railroads were equated with economic development and prosperity. This advertisement for the Savannah and Charleston Railroad appeared in 1878. *Charleston City Directory for 1878, South Carolina Historical Society.*

As Republicans gained control in the South, they often wrote into the new state constitutions prohibitions against discrimination and protections for civil rights. Some Reconstruction state governments enacted laws guaranteeing **equal access** to public transportation and public accommodations. Elsewhere efforts to pass equal access laws foundered on the opposition of southern white Republicans, who often joined Democrats to favor **segregation.** Such conflicts pointed up the internal divisions within the southern Republican Party. Even when equal access laws were passed, they were often not enforced.

Railroad Development and Corruption

Across the nation, Republicans sought to use the power of government to encourage economic growth and development. Efforts to promote economic development—North, South, and West—often focused on encouraging railroad construction. In the South, as elsewhere in the nation, some state governments granted state lands to railroads, or lent them money, or committed the state's credit to **underwrite** bonds for construction. Sometimes they promoted railroads without adequate planning or determining whether companies were financially sound. Some efforts to promote railroad construction failed as companies squandered funds without building rail lines. During the 1870s, only 7,000 miles of new track were laid in the South, compared with 45,000 miles elsewhere in the nation. Even that was a considerable accomplishment for the South, given its dismal economic situation.

Railroad companies sometimes sought favorable treatment by bribing public officials. All too many officeholders—North, South, and West—accepted their offers. Given the excessive favoritism that most public officials showed to railroads, revelations and allegations of corruption became common from New York City to Mississippi to California.

Conditions in the South were ripe for political corruption as government responsibilities expanded rapidly and created new opportunities for scoundrels. Many Reconstruction officials—white and black—had only modest holdings of their own and wanted more. One South Carolina legislator bluntly described his attitude toward electing a U.S. senator: "I was pretty hard up, and I did not care who the candidate was if I got two hundred dollars." Corruption was usually nonpartisan, but it seemed more prominent among Republicans because they held the most important offices. One Louisiana Republican claimed, "Corruption is the fashion." Charges of corruption became

equal access   The right of any person to use a public facility, such as streetcars, as freely as other people in the society.

segregation   Separation on account of race or class from the rest of society, such as the separation of blacks from whites in most southern school systems.

underwrite   To assume financial responsibility for; in this case, to guarantee the purchase of bonds so that a project can go forward.

common everywhere in the nation as politicians sought to discredit their opponents.

The End of Reconstruction

▪ What major factors brought about the end of Reconstruction? Evaluate their relative significance.

▪ Many historians began to reevaluate their interpretations of Reconstruction during the 1950s and 1960s. Why do you suppose that happened?

From the beginning, most white southerners resisted the new order that the conquering Yankees imposed on them. Initially, resistance took the form of black codes and the Klan. Later, some southern opponents of Reconstruction developed new strategies, but terror remained an important instrument of resistance.

The "New Departure"

By 1869, some leading southern Democrats had abandoned their last-ditch resistance to change, deciding instead to accept some Reconstruction measures and African American suffrage. At the same time, they also tried to secure restoration of political rights for former Confederates. Behind this **New Departure** for southern Democrats lay the belief that continued resistance would only cause more regional turmoil and prolong federal intervention.

Sometimes southern Democrats supported conservative Republicans for state and local offices instead of members of their own party, hoping to defuse concern in Washington and dilute Radical influence in state government. This strategy was tried first in Virginia, the last southern state to hold an election under its new constitution. There William Mahone, a former Confederate general, railroad promoter, and leading Democrat, forged a broad political **coalition** that accepted black suffrage. In 1869 Mahone's organization elected as governor a northern-born banker and moderate Republican. In this way, Mahone got state support for his railroad plans, and Virginia successfully avoided Radical Republican rule.

Coalitions of Democrats and moderate Republicans won in Tennessee in 1869 and in Missouri in 1870. Elsewhere leading Democrats endorsed the New Departure, accepted black suffrage, and attacked Republicans more for raising taxes and increasing state spending than for their racial policies. And Democrats almost always charged Republicans with corruption. Such campaigns brought a positive response

from many taxpayers because southern tax rates had risen drastically to support the new educational systems, railroad subsidies, and other modernizing programs. In 1870 Democrats won the governorship in Alabama and Georgia. For Georgia, it meant the end of Reconstruction.

The victories of so-called **Redeemers** and New Departure Democrats in the early 1870s coincided with renewed terrorist activity aimed at Republicans. The worst single incident occurred in 1873. A group of armed freedmen fortified the town of Colfax, Louisiana, to hold off Democrats who were planning to seize the county government. After a three-week siege, well-armed whites overcame the black defenders and killed 280 African Americans. Leading Democrats rarely endorsed such bloodshed, but they reaped political advantages from it.

The 1872 Presidential Election

The New Departure movement, at its peak in 1872, coincided with a division within the Republican Party in the North. The Liberal Republican movement grew out of several elements within the Republican Party. Some were moderates, concerned that the Radicals had gone too far, especially with the Enforcement Acts, and had endangered federalism. Others opposed Grant on issues unrelated to Reconstruction. All were appalled by growing evidence of corruption in Washington. Liberal Republicans found allies among Democrats by arguing against further Reconstruction measures.

Horace Greeley, editor of the *New York Daily Tribune*, won the Liberal nomination for president. An opponent of slavery before the Civil War, Greeley had given strong support to the Fourteenth and Fifteenth Amendments. But he had sometimes taken puzzling positions, including a willingness to let the South secede. His unkempt appearance and whining voice conveyed little of a presidential image. One political

---

New Departure Strategy of cooperation with some Reconstruction measures adopted by some leading southern Democrats in the hope of winning compromises favorable to their party.

coalition An alliance, especially a temporary one of different people or groups.

Redeemers Southern Democrats who hoped to bring the Democratic Party back into power and to suppress Black Reconstruction.

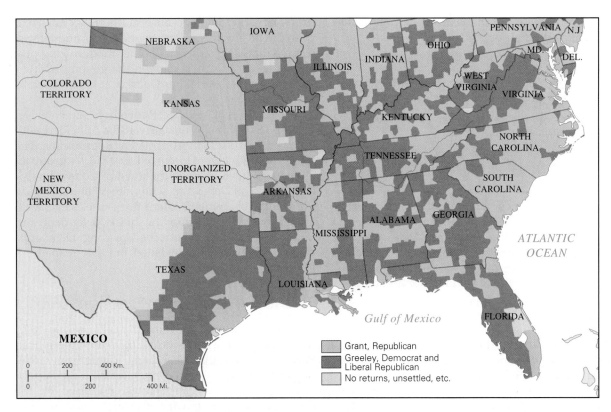

MAP 16.1 **Popular Vote for President in the South, 1872** This map shows which candidate carried each county in the southeastern United States in 1872. Looking at both this map and the chapter-opening map, you can see the relation between Republican voting and African American population in some areas, as well as where the southern Republican Party drew strong support from white voters.

observer described him as "honest, but . . . conceited, fussy, and foolish."

Greeley had long ripped the Democrats in his newspaper columns. Even so, the Democrats nominated him in an effort to defeat Grant. Many saw the Democrats' action as desperate opportunism, and Greeley alienated many northern Democrats by favoring restrictions on the sale of alcohol. Grant won convincingly, carrying 56 percent of the vote and winning every northern state and ten of the sixteen southern and border states (see Map 16.1).

The Politics of Terror: The "Mississippi Plan"

By the 1872 presidential race, nearly all southern whites had abandoned the Republicans, and Black Reconstruction had ended in several states. African

Americans, however, maintained their Republican loyalties. As Democrats worked to unite all southern whites behind their banner of white supremacy, the South polarized politically along racial lines. Elections in 1874 proved disastrous for Republicans: Democrats won more than two-thirds of the South's seats in the House of Representatives and "redeemed" Alabama, Arkansas, and Texas.

Terrorism against black Republicans and their remaining white allies played a role in some victories by Democrats in 1874. Where the Klan had worn disguises and ridden at night, by 1874 in many places Democrats openly formed rifle companies, put on red-flannel shirts, and marched and drilled in public. In some areas, armed whites prevented African Americans from voting or terrorized prominent Republicans, especially African American Republicans.

Republican candidates in 1874 also lost support in the North because of scandals within the Grant administration and because a major economic **depression** that had begun in 1873 was producing high unemployment. Before the 1874 elections, the House of Representatives included 194 Republicans and 92 Democrats. After those elections, Democrats outnumbered Republicans by 169 to 109. Now southern Republicans could no longer look to Congress for assistance. Even though Republicans still controlled the Senate, the Democratic majority in the House of Representatives could block any new Reconstruction legislation.

During 1875 in Mississippi, political violence reached such levels that the use of terror to overthrow Reconstruction became known as the **Mississippi Plan.** Democratic rifle clubs broke up Republican meetings and attacked Republican leaders in broad daylight. One black Mississippian described the election of 1875 as "the most violent time we have ever seen." When Mississippi's carpetbagger governor, Adelbert Ames, requested federal help, President Grant declined, fearful that the southern Reconstruction governments had become so discredited that further federal military intervention might endanger the election prospects of Republican candidates in the North.

The Democrats swept the Mississippi elections, winning four-fifths of the state legislature. When the legislature convened, it impeached and removed from office Alexander Davis, the black Republican lieutenant governor, on grounds no more serious than those brought against Andrew Johnson. The legislature then brought similar impeachment charges against Governor Ames, who resigned and left the state. Ames had foreseen the result during the campaign when he wrote, "A revolution has taken place—by force of arms."

The Compromise of 1877

In 1876, on the centennial of American independence, the nation stumbled through a deeply troubled—and potentially dangerous—presidential election. As revelations of corruption multiplied, the issue of reform took center stage. The Democratic Party nominated Samuel J. Tilden, governor of New York, as its presidential candidate. A wealthy lawyer and businessman, Tilden had earned a reputation as a reformer by fighting political corruption in New York City. The Republicans selected **Rutherford B. Hayes,** a Civil War general and governor of Ohio, whose unblemished reputation proved to be his greatest asset. Not well known outside Ohio, he was a candidate nobody could object to. During the campaign in the South, intimidation of Republicans, both black and white, continued in many places.

First election reports indicated a victory for Tilden (see Map 16.2). In addition to the border states and South, he also carried New York, New Jersey, and Indiana. Tilden received 51 percent of the popular vote versus 48 percent for Hayes. Leading Republicans quickly realized that their party still controlled the counting and reporting of ballots in South Carolina, Florida, and Louisiana, and that those three states could change the Electoral College majority from Tilden to Hayes. Charging **voting fraud,** Republican election boards in those states rejected enough ballots so that the official count gave Hayes narrow majorities and thus a one-vote margin of victory in the Electoral College. Crying fraud in return, Democratic officials in all three states submitted their own versions of the vote count.

Angry Democrats vowed to see Tilden inaugurated, by force if necessary, and some Democratic newspapers ran headlines that read "Tilden or War." For the first time, Congress faced the problem of disputed electoral votes that could decide the outcome of an election. To resolve the challenges, Congress created a commission: five senators, chosen by the Senate, which had a Republican majority; five representatives, chosen by the House, which had a Democratic majority; and five Supreme Court justices, chosen by the justices. Initially, the balance was seven Republicans, seven Democrats, and one independent from the Supreme Court. The independent withdrew, however, and the remaining justices (all but one of whom had been appointed by Republican presidents) chose a Republican to replace him. The Republicans now had a one-vote majority on the commission.

This body needed to make its decision before the constitutionally mandated deadline of March 4. Some Democrats and Republicans worried over the potential for violence. However, as commission hearings droned on through January and into February 1877, informal discussions took place among leading

depression A period of economic contraction, characterized by decreasing business activity, falling prices, and high unemployment.

Mississippi Plan Use of threats, violence, and lynching by Mississippi Democrats in 1875 to intimidate Republicans and bring the Democratic Party to power.

Rutherford B. Hayes Ohio governor and former Union general who won the Republican nomination in 1876 and became president of the United States in 1877.

voting fraud Altering election results by illegal measures to bring about the victory of a particular candidate.

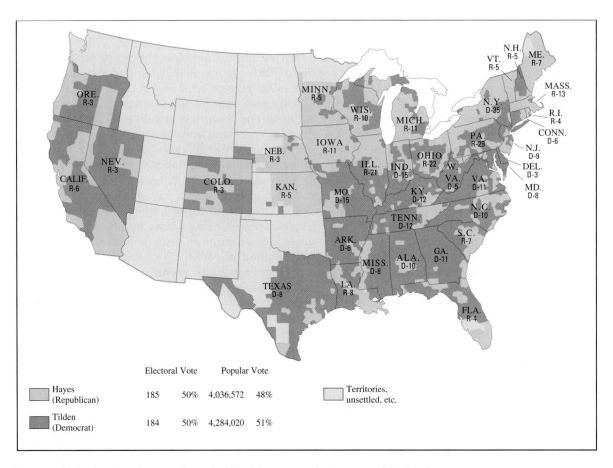

MAP 16.2 **Election of 1876**   The end of Black Reconstruction in most of the South combined with Democratic gains in the North to give a popular majority to Samuel Tilden, the Democratic candidate. The electoral vote was disputed, however, and was ultimately resolved in favor of Rutherford B. Hayes, the Republican.

Republicans and Democrats. The result was often called the **Compromise of 1877.**

Southern Democrats demanded an end to federal intervention in southern politics but insisted on federal subsidies for railroad construction and waterways in the South. And they wanted one of their own as postmaster general because that office held the key to most federal patronage. In return, southern Democrats seemed willing to abandon Tilden's claim to the White House.

Although the Compromise of 1877 was never set down in one place or agreed to by all parties, most of its conditions were met. By a straight party vote, the commission confirmed the election of Hayes. Soon after his peaceful inauguration, the new president ordered the last of the federal troops withdrawn from

occupation duties in the South. The Radical era of a powerful federal government pledged to protect "equality before the law" for all citizens was over. The last three Republican state governments fell in 1877. The Democrats, the self-described party of white supremacy, now held sway in every southern state. One Radical journal bitterly concluded that African Americans had been forced "to relinquish the artificial right to vote for the natural right to live." In parts

Compromise of 1877   Name applied by historians to the resolution of the disputed presidential election of 1876; it gave the presidency to the Republicans and made concessions to southern Democrats.

of the South thereafter, election fraud and violence became routine. One Mississippi judge acknowledged in 1890 that "since 1875 . . . we have been preserving the ascendancy of the white people by . . . stuffing ballot boxes, committing perjury and here and there in the state carrying the elections by fraud and violence."

The Compromise of 1877 marked the end of Reconstruction. The Civil War was more than ten years in the past. Many moderate Republicans had hoped that the Fourteenth and Fifteenth Amendments and the Civil Rights Act would guarantee black rights without a continuing federal presence in the South. Southern Democrats tried hard to persuade northerners—on paltry evidence—that carpetbaggers and scalawags were all corrupt and self-serving, that they manipulated black voters to keep themselves in power, that African American officeholders were ignorant and illiterate and could not participate in politics without guidance by whites, and that southern Democrats wanted only to establish honest self-government. The truth of the situation made little difference.

Northern Democrats had always opposed Reconstruction and readily adopted the southern Democrats' version of reality. Such portrayals found growing acceptance among other northerners too, for many had shown their own racial bias when they resisted black suffrage and kept their public schools segregated. In 1875, when Grant refused to use federal troops to protect black rights, he declared that "the whole public are tired out with these . . . outbreaks in the South." He was quoted widely and with approval throughout the North.

In addition, a major depression in the mid-1870s, unemployment and labor disputes, the growth of industry, the emergence of big business, and the development of the West focused the attention of many Americans, including many members of Congress, on economic issues.

Some Republicans, to be certain, kept the faith of their abolitionist and Radical forebears and hoped the federal government might again protect black rights. After 1877, however, though Republicans routinely condemned violations of black rights, few Republicans showed much interest in using federal power to prevent such outrages.

After Reconstruction

Southern Democrats read the events of 1877 as permission to establish new systems of politics and race relations. Most Redeemers worked to reduce taxes, dismantle Reconstruction legislation and agencies, and grab political influence away from black citizens. They also began the process of turning the South into a one-party region, a situation that reached its fullest development around 1900 and persisted until the 1950s and in some areas later.

Voting and officeholding by African Americans did not cease in 1877, but the context changed profoundly. Without federal enforcement of black rights, the threat of violence and the potential for economic retaliation by landlords and merchants sharply reduced meaningful political involvement by African Americans. Black political leaders soon understood that efforts to mobilize black voters posed dangers to candidates and voters, and they concluded that their political survival depended on favors from influential white Republicans or even from Democratic leaders. The public schools survived, segregated and underfunded, but presenting an important opportunity. Many Reconstruction-era laws remained on the books. Through much of the 1880s, many theaters, bars, restaurants, hotels, streetcars, and railroads continued to serve African Americans without discrimination.

Not until the 1890s did black disfranchisement and thoroughgoing racial segregation become widely embedded in southern law. From the mid-1870s to the late 1890s, African Americans exercised some constitutional rights. White supremacy had been established by force of arms, however, and blacks exercised their rights at the sufferance of the dominant whites. Such a situation bore the seeds of future conflict.

After 1877, Reconstruction was held up as a failure. Although far from accurate, the southern version of Reconstruction—that conniving carpetbaggers and scalawags had manipulated ignorant freedmen—appealed to many white Americans throughout the nation, and it gained widespread acceptance among many novelists, journalists, and historians. William A. Dunning, for example, endorsed that interpretation in his history of Reconstruction, published in 1907. Thomas Dixon's popular novel *The Clansman* (1905) inspired the highly influential film *The Birth of a Nation* (1915). Historically inaccurate and luridly racist, the book and the movie portrayed Ku Klux Klan members as heroes who rescued the white South, and especially white southern women, from domination and debauchery at the hands of depraved freedmen and carpetbaggers.

Against this pattern stood some of the first black historians, notably George Washington Williams, a Union army veteran whose two-volume history of African

Americans appeared in 1882. *Black Reconstruction in America,* by W. E. B. Du Bois, appeared in 1935. Both presented fully the role of African Americans in Reconstruction and pointed to the accomplishments of the Reconstruction state governments and black leaders. Not until the 1950s and 1960s, however, did large numbers of American historians begin to reconsider their interpretations of Reconstruction. Historians today recognize that Reconstruction was not the failure that had earlier been claimed. The creation of public schools was the most important of the changes in southern life pro-duced by the Reconstruction state governments. At a federal level, the Fourteenth and Fifteenth Amendments eventually provided the constitutional leverage to restore the principle of equality before the law that so concerned the Radicals. Historians also recognize that Reconstruction collapsed partly because of internal flaws, partly because of divisions within the Republican Party, and partly because of the political terrorism unleashed in the South and the refusal of the North to commit the force required to protect the constitutional rights of African Americans.

Individual Voices

Examining a Primary Source

A Freedman Offers His Former Master a Proposition

This letter appeared in the *New York Daily Tribune* on August 22, 1865, with the notation that it was a "genuine document," reprinted from the *Cincinnati Commercial*. At that time, all newspapers had strong connections to political parties, and both of these papers were allied to the Republicans. By then, battle lines were being drawn between President Andrew Johnson and Republicans in Congress over the legal and political status of the freed people.

> DAYTON, Ohio, August 7, 1865
> To my Old Master, Col. P. H. Anderson, Big Spring, Tennessee
> Sir: I got your letter and was glad to find that you had not forgotten Jordan, and that you wanted me to come back and live with you again, promising to do better for me than anybody else can. . . .
> I want to know particularly what the good chance is you propose to give me. I am doing tolerably well here; I get $25 a month, with victuals and clothing; have a comfortable home for Mandy (the folks here call her Mrs. Anderson), and the children, Milly[,] Jane and Grundy, go to school and are learning well. . . . Now, if you will write and say what wages you will give me, I will be better able to decide whether it would be to my advantage to move back again. ■
> As to my freedom, which you say I can have, there is nothing to be gained on that score, as I got my free-papers in 1864 from the Provost-Marshal-General of the Department at Nashville. Mandy says she would be afraid to go back without some proof that you are sincerely disposed to treat us justly and kindly—and we have concluded to test your sincerity by asking you to send us our wages for the time we served you. This will make us forget and forgive old sores, and rely on

■ How does the author indicate that the lives of these freed people have changed by leaving Tennessee for Ohio?

■ *Anderson's monthly wages of $25 in 1865 would be equivalent to about $2,280 today. The amount he asks for as compensation for his slave labor, $11,680, in 1865 would be equivalent to more than $130,000 today.*

■ *How does the author use this letter to raise a wide range of issues about the nature of slavery and about the uneasiness of freed people about life in the South in 1865?*

■ *Evaluate the likelihood that this letter was actually written by a former slave. What are the other possibilities? Why do you think this letter appeared in newspapers in August of 1865?*

your justice and friendship in the future. I served you faithfully for thirty-two years, and Mandy twenty years, at $25 a month for me and $2 a week for Mandy. Our earnings would amount to $11,680. ■ *Add to this the interest for the time our wages has been kept back and deduct what you paid for our clothing and three doctor's visits to me, and pulling a tooth for Mandy, and the balance will show what we are in justice entitled to. . . . If you fail to pay us for faithful labors in the past we can have little faith in your promises in the future. We trust the good Maker has opened your eyes to the wrongs which you and your fathers have done to me and my fathers, in making us toil for you for generations without recompense. . . .*

In answering this letter please state if there would be any safety for my Milly and Jane, who are now grown up and both good looking girls. You know how it was with poor Matilda and Catherine. I would rather stay here and starve and die if it had to come to that than have my girls brought to shame by the violence and wickedness of their young masters. You will also please state if there has been any schools opened for the colored children in your neighborhood, the great desire of my life now is to give my children an education, and have them form virtuous habits. ■

From your old servant, ■   *JOURDAN ANDERSON.*

P.S.—Say howdy to George Carter, and thank him for taking the pistol from you when you were shooting at me.

Summary

At the end of the Civil War, the nation faced difficult choices regarding the restoration of the defeated South and the future of the freed people. Committed to ending slavery, President Lincoln nevertheless chose a lenient approach to restoring states to the Union, partly to persuade southerners to accept emancipation and abandon the Confederacy. When Johnson became president, he continued Lincoln's approach.

The end of slavery brought new opportunities for African Americans, whether or not they had been slaves. Taking advantage of the opportunities that freedom opened, they tried to create independent lives for themselves, and they developed social institutions that helped to define black communities. Because few were able to acquire land of their own, most became either sharecroppers or wage laborers. White southerners also experienced economic dislocation, and many also became sharecroppers. Most white southerners expected to keep African Americans in a subordinate role and initially used black codes and violence toward that end.

In reaction against the black codes and violence, Congress took control of Reconstruction away from President Johnson and passed the Civil Rights Act of 1866, the Fourteenth Amendment, and the Reconstruction Acts of 1867. An attempt to remove Johnson from the presidency was unsuccessful. Additional federal Reconstruction measures included the Fifteenth Amendment, laws directed against the Ku Klux Klan, and the Civil Rights Act of 1875. Several of these measures strengthened the federal government at the expense of the states.

Enfranchised freedmen, white and black northerners who moved to the South, and some southern whites created a southern Republican Party that governed most southern states for a time. The most lasting contribution of these state governments was the creation of public school systems. Like government officials elsewhere in the nation, however, some southern politicians fell prey to corruption.

In the late 1860s, many southern Democrats chose a "New Departure": they grudgingly accepted some features of Reconstruction and sought to recapture control of state governments. By the mid-1870s, however, southern politics turned almost solely on race. The 1876 presidential election was very close and hotly disputed. Key Republicans and Democrats developed a compromise: Hayes took office and ended the final stages of Reconstruction. Without federal protection for their civil rights, African Americans faced terrorism, violence, and even death if they challenged their subordinate role. With the end of Reconstruction, the South entered an era of white supremacy in politics and government, the economy, and social relations.

SUGGESTED READING

CHAPTER 1 Making a "New" World, to 1588

Marvin B. Becker. *Civility and Society in Western Europe, 1300–1600* (1988).

A brief but comprehensive look at social conditions in Europe during the period leading up to and out of the exploration of the New World.

Alfred W. Crosby. *The Columbian Exchange: Biological and Cultural Consequences of 1492* (1972).

The landmark book that brought the Columbian impact into focus for the first time. Parts of the book are technical, but the explanations are clear and exciting.

Alvin M. Josephy. *America in 1492: The World of the Indian Peoples before the Arrival of Columbus* (1992).

An overview of American civilizations prior to Columbus's and subsequent European intrusions. Nicely written, comprehensive, and engaging.

Kupperman, Karen Ordahl, ed. *America in European Consciousness, 1493–1750* (1995).

A collection of essays by leading scholars tracing the impact of America on the European intellectual world from the time of discovery through the colonization period.

William H. McNeill. *Plagues and Peoples* (1976).

A fascinating history of disease and its impact on people throughout the period of European expansion and New World colonization.

Roland Oliver and J. D. Fage. *A Short History of Africa* (1988).

The most concise and understandably written comprehensive history of Africa available.

CHAPTER 2 A Continent on the Move, 1400–1725

Peter N. Moogk. *La Nouvelle France: The Making of French Canada—A Cultural History* (2000).

An excellent overview of French activities in Canada during the colonial era.

Oliver A. Rink. *Holland on the Hudson: An Economic and Social History of Dutch New York* (1986).

A comprehensive overview of Dutch colonial activities in New Netherland with an emphasis on both the activities of the Dutch West India Company and private traders in creating the culture of Dutch New York.

Daniel H. Usner, Jr. *Indians, Settlers, and Slaves in a Frontier Exchange Economy: The Lower Mississippi Valley before 1783* (1992).

A highly acclaimed study of the complex world of colonial Louisiana.

David Weber. *The Spanish Frontier in North America* (1992).

A broad synthesis of the history of New Spain by the foremost scholar in the field.

Richard White. *The Middle Ground: Indians, Empires, and Republics in the Great Lakes Region, 1650–1815* (1991).

Although it covers material far beyond the chronological scope of this chapter, students interested in the relations between Indians and Europeans in the colonial era will find this book extraordinarily rich.

CHAPTER 3 Founding the English Colonies in the Eighteenth Century, 1585–1732

Philip Barbour. *Pocahontas and Her World* (1970).

A factual account of the life of an American Indian princess celebrated in folklore.

Elaine G. Breslaw. *Tituba, Reluctant Witch of Salem: Devilish Indians and Puritan Fantasies* (1996).

The author reconstructs the life of the Caribbean-born Indian slave who was a central figure in the Salem witch trials.

John Demos. *A Little Commonwealth: Family Life in Plymouth Colony* (1970).

A beautifully written and very engaging portrait of family and community life in Plymouth Plantations.

Kai T. Erikson. *Wayward Puritans: A Study in the Sociology of Deviance* (1966).

The author discovers the values and ideals of Massachusetts Puritan society by examining the behavior and ideas these Puritans condemned, including witchcraft and Quakerism.

Mary Beth Norton. *In the Devil's Snare* (2003).

Unlike earlier scholars of the Salem witch trials, Norton places the events of 1692 in the context of European imperial rivalries, especially the intense struggles between England and France for control of North America.

CHAPTER 4 The English Colonies in the Eighteenth Century, 1689–1763

Bernard Bailyn. *Voyagers to the West: A Passage in the Peopling of America on the Eve of the Revolution* (1986).

Bailyn won a Pulitzer Prize for this survey of the character of, and motives for, emigration from the British Isles to America during the eighteenth century.

Patricia Bonomi. *Under the Cope of Heaven: Religion, Society, and Politics in Colonial America* (1986).

Bonomi provides an overview of the role of religion in colonial society and a close look at the leaders of the Great Awakening and the impact of that religious revival movement on pre-Revolutionary politics in the 1760s and 1770s.

Richard Hofstadter. *America at 1750: A Social Portrait* (1971).

This highly accessible work includes chapters on indentured servitude, the slave trade, the middle-class world of the colonies, the Great Awakening, and population growth and immigration patterns.

Thomas A. Lewis. *For King and Country: The Maturing of George Washington, 1748–1760* (1993).

This look at the early career of George Washington follows him as a colonial soldier of the Crown, a Virginia planter, and a young man of ambition.

Jane T. Merritt. *At the Crossroads: Indians and Empires on a Mid-Atlantic Frontier, 1700–1763* (2003).

Merritt takes a close look at the interaction between Indians and colonists in the backcountry of Pennsylvania and narrates the growing tensions between settlers and Native Americans.

Betty Wood. *The Origins of American Slavery* (1998).

This is a brief but excellent look at the use of enslaved labor in the West Indies and in the English mainland colonies and at the laws that arose to institutionalize slavery.

CHAPTER 5 Deciding Where Loyalties Lie, 1763–1776

Carol Berkin. *Revolutionary Mothers: Women in the Struggle for America's Independence* (2005).

This book recounts the role of colonial women in the boycotts of the 1760s and 1770s. In separate chapters it tells the story of Indian, African American, and Loyalist women as

A-1

well as the stories of camp followers, generals' wives, spies, and female soldiers during the Revolution.

Colin G. Calloway. *The American Revolution in Indian Country: Crisis and Diversity in Native American Communities* (1995).
>   A well-written account of the variety of Indian experiences during the American revolutionary era.

Edward Countryman. *The American Revolution* (1985).
>   An excellent narrative of the causes and consequences of the Revolutionary War.

David Hackett Fischer. *Paul Revere's Ride* (1994).
>   This lively account details the circumstances and background of the efforts to rouse the countryside in response to the march of British troops toward Lexington.

Woody Holton. *Forced Founders: Indians, Debtors, Slaves and the Making of the American Revolution in Virginia* (1999).
>   Holton provides a new interpretation of the factors that went into transforming wealthy planters into revolutionaries. He examines the importance of mounting debts, fear of slave revolts and Indian attacks, and pressures from small farmers in radicalizing the men we often think of as leading "founding fathers."

"Liberty!" PBS series on the American Revolution.
>   Using the actual words of revolutionaries, loyalists, and British political leaders, this six-hour series follows events from the Stamp Act to the Constitution.

Pauline Maier. *American Scripture: Making the Declaration of Independence* (1998).
>   This path-breaking book points out that the ideas expressed in the Declaration of Independence were widely accepted by Americans, and proclaimed in state declarations of independence before Jefferson set them down in July 1776. Maier also traces the history of the Declaration in the decades following the revolution.

Edmund Morgan. *Benjamin Franklin* (2002).
>   A distinguished historian of colonial America draws a compelling portrait of Benjamin Franklin, following the printer-writer-scientist-diplomat through major crises and turning points in his life and the life of his country.

CHAPTER 6   Recreating America: Independence and a New Nation, 1775–1783

Sylvia Frey. *Water From a Rock: Black Resistance in a Revolutionary Age* (1991).
>   This scholar of African American religion and culture examines the experiences of African Americans during the Revolution and the repression that followed in the Southern states that continued to rely on slave labor.

Joseph Plumb Martin. *Ordinary Courage: The Revolutionary War Adventures of Joseph Plumb Martin,* ed. James Kirby Martin (1993).
>   The military experiences of a Massachusetts soldier who served with the Continental Army during the American Revolution.

William Nelson. *The American Tory* (1961).
>   An account of those who chose to align themselves with the British during the war.

Charles Royster. *A Revolutionary People at War: The Continental Army and American Character, 1775–1783* (1996).
>   Royster's in-depth account of military life during the Revolution provides insights into both the American character and the changing understanding of the political ideals of the war among the common soldiers.

Alfred Young. *The Shoemaker and the Tea Party: Memory and the American Revolution* (2000).
>   Young looks at the memories of an aging shoemaker who witnessed the Boston Tea Party. These memories reveal the meaning of the Revolution to ordinary Americans.

CHAPTER 7   Competing Visions of the Virtuous Republic, 1770–1796

Carol Berkin. *A Brilliant Solution: Inventing the American Constitution* (2002).
>   A highly readable account of the crises that led to the constitutional convention and the men who created a new national government.

Lyman Butterfield, et al., eds. *The Book of Abigail and John: Selected Letters of the Adams Family, 1762–1784* (1975).
>   The editors of the Adams Papers have collected part of the extensive correspondence between John and Abigail Adams during the critical decades of the independence movement.

Joseph Ellis. *Founding Brothers: The Revolutionary Generation* (2002).
>   An award-winning study of the most notable leaders of the American Revolution, and an examination of their political ideas and actions.

Richard B. Morris. *Witness at the Creation* (1985).
>   A distinguished scholar re-creates the drama of the Constitutional Convention by focusing on the personalities and motives of the framers.

Thomas P. Slaughter. *The Whiskey Rebellion* (1986).
>   A vivid account of the major challenge to the Washington government.

Gary Wills. *Cincinnatus: George Washington and the Enlightenment* (1984).
>   A beautifully written intellectual biography of America's first president and his times.

CHAPTER 8   The Early Republic, 1796–1804

Stephen E. Ambrose. *Undaunted Courage: Meriwether Lewis, Thomas Jefferson, and the Opening of the American West* (1996).
>   A critically acclaimed and highly readable narrative exploring the relationship between Jefferson and Lewis and their efforts to acquire and explore Louisiana.

Alexander DeConde. *This Affair of Louisiana* (1976).
>   Dated, but still the best overview of the diplomacy surrounding the Louisiana Purchase.

Joseph J. Ellis. *American Sphinx: The Character of Thomas Jefferson* (1996).
>   Winner of the National Book Award, this biography focuses on Jefferson's personality seeking to expose his inner character; highly readable.

Joanne B. Freeman. *Affairs of Honor: National Politics in the New Republic* (2001).

Jeffrey L. Pasley. *"The Tyranny of Printers": Newspaper Politics in the Early American Republic* (2001).
>   Taken together, these two groundbreaking studies of political culture in the Early Republic bring a whole set of new perspectives to the topic. Freeman concentrates on honor as a political force, while Pasley illustrates the power of an increasingly self-conscious press in shaping the political landscape.

Richard Hofstadter. *The Idea of a Party System* (1969).
>   The classic account of the rise of legitimate opposition in the American party system.

David McCullough. *John Adams* (2001).
>   A highly acclaimed and extremely readable biography of one of America's true founding fathers.

Gary B. Nash. *Forging Freedom: The Formation of Philadelphia's Black Community, 1720–1840* (1990).
>   A brilliant and exciting exploration of how African Americans in early Philadelphia created their own urban community.

James Ronda. *Lewis and Clark Among the Indians* (1984).

A bold retelling of the expedition's story, showcasing the Indian role in both Lewis and Clark's and the nation's successful expansion into the Louisiana Territory and beyond.

CHAPTER 9 Increasing Conflict and War, 1805–1815

Gregory E. Dowd. *A Spirited Resistance: The North American Indian Struggle for Unity, 1745–1815* (1992).
> Hailed by many as one of the best works on Native American history, this well-written study covers the efforts by Indians to unite in defense of their lands and heritages, culminating in the struggles during the War of 1812.

R. David Edmunds. *The Shawnee Prophet* (1983); *Tecumseh and the Quest for Indian Leadership* (1984).
> Each of these biographies is a masterpiece, but taken together, they present the most complete recounting of the lives and accomplishments of these two fascinating Shawnee brothers and their historical world.

John Denis Haeger. *John Jacob Astor; Business and Finance in the Early Republic* (1991).

William E. Foley and C. David Rice. *The First Chouteaus: River Barons of Early St. Louis* (1983).
> Taken together, these two books provide a comprehensive overview of the fur trade during its early years, showcasing the importance of business tycoons like Astor and the Chouteaus and demystifying this huge business enterprise.

Donald Hickey. *The War of 1812: A Forgotten Conflict* (1989).
> Arguably the best single-volume history of the war, encyclopedic in content, but so colorfully written that it will hold anyone's attention.

Robert A. Rutland. *Madison's Alternatives: The Jeffersonian Republicans and the Coming of War, 1805–1812* (1975).
> An interesting review of the events leading up to the outbreak of war in 1812 and the various alternatives Jefferson and Madison had to choose from in facing the evolving diplomatic and political crises.

CHAPTER 10 The Rise of a New Nation, 1815–1836

George Dangerfield. *The Era of Good Feelings* (1952).
> An older book, but so well written and informative that it deserves its status as a classic. All students will enjoy this grand overview.

Angie Debo. *And Still the Waters Run: The Betrayal of the Five Civilized Tribes* (1940; reprint, 1972).
> A classic work by one of America's most talented and sensitive historical writers, a truly engaging history of this tragic sequence of events.

Richard E. Ellis. *The Union at Risk: Jacksonian Democracy, States' Rights, and the Nullification Crisis* (1987).
> An invigorating reconsideration of the Nullification Crisis set in context with the other problems that beset the Jackson administration, suggesting how close the nation came to civil war in the 1830s.

Theda Perdue and Michael D. Green. *The Cherokee Removal* (2005).
> Designed for classroom use, this brief history with selected documents is an excellent and interesting resource for students who wish to know more about this tragedy in American history. The new Second Edition has expanded coverage and additional documents.

Charles G. Sellers. *The Market Revolution: Jacksonian America, 1815–1846* (1991).
> A far-reaching reassessment of economics and politics during this period focusing on the rise of the market economy and the responses, both positive and negative, that led to the rise of Jacksonian democracy.

John William Ward. *Andrew Jackson: Symbol for an Age* (1955).
> More a study of American culture during the age of Jackson than a biography of the man himself, Ward seeks to explain Old Hickory's status as a living myth during his own time and as a continuing monument in American history.

CHAPTER 11 The Great Transformation, 1828–1840

Ira Berlin. *Slaves Without Masters* (1975).
> A masterful study of a forgotten population: free African Americans in the Old South. Lively and informative.

Stuart M. Blumin. *The Emergence of the Middle Class: Social Experience in the American City, 1760-1900* (1989).
> Considered by many to be the most comprehensive overview of the emergence of the middle class in America during the nineteenth century.

Bill Cecil-Fronsman. *Common Whites: Class and Culture in Antebellum North Carolina* (1992).
> A pioneering effort to describe the culture, lifestyle, and political economy shared by the antebellum South's majority population: nonslaveholding whites. Though confined in geographical scope, the study is suggestive of conditions that may have prevailed throughout the region.

Nancy M Cott. *The Bonds of Womanhood: "Woman's Sphere" in New England, 1780–1835* (1977).
> A classic work on the ties that held the woman's world together, but collectively bound them into a secondary position in American life.

Thomas Dublin. *Women at Work: The Transformation of Work and Community in Lowell, Massachusetts, 1826–1860* (1979).
> An interesting look at the way in which the nature of work changed and the sorts of changes that were brought to one manufacturing community.

Elizabeth Fox-Genovese. *Within the Plantation Household* (1988).
> A look at the lives of black and white women in the antebellum South. This study is quite long, but is well written and very informative.

Isabel Lehuu. *Carnival on the Page: Popular Print Media in Antebellum America* (2000).
> An overview of the explosion in print media during the early nineteenth century and its role in shaping national culture.

Margaret Mitchell. *Gone With the Wind* (1936).
> Arguably the most influential book in conveying a stereotyped vision of antebellum southern life. The film version, directed by Victor Fleming in 1939, was even more influential.

Mary P. Ryan. *Cradle of the Middle Class: The Family in Oneida County, New York, 1790–1865* (1981).
> A marvelous synthesis of materials focusing on the emergence of a new social and economic class in the midst of change from a traditional to a modern society.

George Rogers Taylor. *The Transportation Revolution, 1815–1860* (1951).
> The only comprehensive treatment of changes in transportation during the antebellum period and their economic impact. Nicely written.

CHAPTER 12 Responses to the Great Transformation, 1828–1840

Eugene D. Genovese. *From Rebellion to Revolution: Afro-American Slave Revolts in the Making of the Modern World* (1979).
> Although it focuses somewhat narrowly on confrontation, as opposed to more subtle forms of resistance, this study traces the emergence of African American political organization from its roots in antebellum slave revolts.

Karen Haltunen. *Confidence Men and Painted Women: A Study of Middle-Class Culture in America, 1830–1870* (1982).

A wonderfully well-researched study of an emerging class defining and shaping itself in the evolving world of early nineteenth-century urban space.

Edward Pessen. *Most Uncommon Jacksonians: The Radical Leaders of the Early Labor Movement* (1967).

A look at early labor movements and reform by one of America's leading radical scholars.

Anthony F. C. Wallace. *Rockdale: The Growth of an American Village in the Early Industrial Revolution* (1978).

A noted anthropologist's reconstruction of a mill town and the various class, occupational, and gender cultures that developed there during its transition from a traditional village to a mill town.

Ronald G. Walters. *American Reformers, 1815–1860* (1978).

The best overview of the reform movements and key personalities who guided them during this difficult period in American history.

Sean Wilentz. *Chants Democratic: New York City and the Rise of the American Working Class, 1788–1850* (1984).

An insightful view of working-class culture and politics in the dynamic setting of Erie Canal–era New York City.

Susan Zaeske. *Signatures of Citizenship: Petitioning, Antislavery, and Women's Political Identity* (2003).

A fascinating study of how participation in reform campaigns helped lead early nineteenth-century women into a new sense of political identity.

CHAPTER 13   Westward Expansion and Manifest Destiny, 1841–1848

Ray Allen Billington. *America's Frontier Heritage* (1966).

A broad overview of America's Western experience from a Turnerian point of view.

Thomas R. Hietala. *Manifest Design* (1985).

An interesting and well-written interpretation of the Mexican War and the events leading up to it.

Patricia Nelson Limerick. *The Legacy of Conquest* (1988).

Considered by many to be the Bible of the New Western History, this wonderfully written interpretation of events in the West challenges many assumptions and stereotypes.

Donald W. Meinig. *Imperial Texas* (1969).

A descriptive look at Texas history by a leading historical geographer.

Christopher L. Miller. *Prophetic Worlds* (2003).

This new edition includes commentary that helps to define the debates that this book has sparked about the history of the Pacific Northwest during the pioneer era.

Kenneth N. Owens, ed. *Riches for All: The California Gold Rush and the World* (2002).

A collection of essays by leading scholars about the California Gold Rush and its impact on both national and international life.

Wallace E. Stegner. *The Gathering of Zion* (1964).

A masterfully written history of the Mormon Trail by one of the West's leading literary figures.

John David Unruh. *The Plains Across* (1979).

Arguably the best one-volume account of the overland passage to Oregon. The many pages melt as the author captures the reader in the adventure of the Oregon Trail.

CHAPTER 14   Sectional Conflict and Shattered Union, 1848–1860

Don E. Fehrenbacher. *Prelude to Greatness* (1962).

A well-written and interesting account of Lincoln's early career.

Don E. Fehrenbacher. *Slavery, Law, and Politics: The Dred Scott Case in Historical Perspective* (1981).

An excellent interpretive account of this landmark antebellum legal decision, placing it firmly into historical context.

William E. Gienapp, et al. *Essays in American Antebellum Politics, 1840–1860* (1982).

A collection of essays by the rising generation of new political scholars. Exciting and challenging reading.

Michael F. Holt. *The Political Crisis of the 1850s* (1978).

Arguably the best single-volume discussion of the political problems besetting the nation during this critical decade.

Stephen B. Oates. *To Purge This Land with Blood* (1984).

The best biography to date on John Brown, focusing on his role in the emerging sectional crisis during the 1850s.

David Potter. *The Impending Crisis, 1848–1861* (1976).

An extremely long and detailed work but beautifully written and informative.

James Rawley. *Race and Politics: "Bleeding Kansas" and the Coming of the Civil War* (1969).

An interesting look at the conflicts in Kansas, centering upon racial attitudes in the West. Insightful and captivating reading.

Harriet Beecher Stowe. *Uncle Tom's Cabin* (1852; reprint, 1982).

This edition includes notes and chronology by noted social historian Kathryn Kish Sklar, making it especially informative. See also the one-hour film version produced by the Program for Culture at Play, available from Films for the Humanities and Sciences.

CHAPTER 15   A Violent Choice: Civil War, 1861–1865

Annie Heloise Abel. *The Slaveholding Indians*, 3 vols. (1919–1925; reprint, 1992–1993).

This long-ignored classic work focuses on Indians as slaveholders, participants in the Civil War, and subjects of Reconstruction. Its three volumes have recently been updated by historians Theda Purdue and Michael Green. Each volume can stand on its own and will reward the patient reader.

Bruce Catton. *This Hallowed Ground: The Story of the Union Side of the Civil War* (1956).

Catton is probably the best in the huge company of popular writers on the Civil War. This is his most comprehensive single-volume work. More detailed but still very interesting titles by Catton include *Glory Road: The Bloody Route from Fredericksburg to Gettysburg* (1952), *Mr. Lincoln's Army* (1962), *A Stillness at Appomattox* (1953), and *Grant Moves South* (1960).

Paul D. Escott. *After Secession: Jefferson Davis and the Failure of Confederate Nationalism* (1978).

An excellent overview of internal political problems in the Confederacy by a leading Civil War historian.

Ann Giesberg. *Civil War Sisterhood: The U.S. Sanitary Commission and Women's Politics in Transition* (2000).

A study of how women's activism in forming the sanitary movement during the Civil War recast their view of themselves as political figures and helped shape an emerging women's movement.

Alvin M. Josephy. *The Civil War in the American West* (1991).

A former editor for *American Heritage*, Josephy writes an interesting and readable story about this little-known chapter in Civil War history.

William Marvel. *The Alabama & the Kearsarge: The Sailor's Civil War* (1996).

Military and social historians have compared this new study favorably with *The Life of Billy Yank* (1952) and *The Life of Johnny Reb* (1943), Bell Irvin Willey's classic studies of life for the common soldier, calling it an insightful narrative of the Civil War experience for the common sailor.

James McPherson. *Battle Cry of Freedom: The Civil War Era* (1988).
Hailed by many as the best single-volume history of the Civil War era; comprehensive and very well written.

Emory M. Thomas. *The Confederate Nation* (1979).
A classic history of the Confederacy by an excellent southern historian.

Garry Wills. *Lincoln at Gettysburg: The Words That Remade America* (1992).
A prize-winning look at Lincoln's rhetoric and the ways in which his speeches, especially his Gettysburg Address, recast American ideas about equality, freedom, and democracy. Exquisitely written by a master biographer.

Gettysburg (the movie)
Ronald Maxwell directed this four-hour epic detailing one of the Civil War's most famous battles. Based on Michael Shaara's Pulitzer Prize–winning novel *The Killer Angels,* this ambitious film seeks to capture not only the historical events but also the atmosphere and personalities of the era.

CHAPTER 16 Reconstruction: High Hopes and Shattered Dreams, 1865–1877

David Donald. *Charles Sumner and the Rights of Man* (1970).
Deals both with this important Radical leader and with Reconstruction issues.

W. E. B. Du Bois. *Black Reconstruction in America: An Essay Toward a History of the Part Which Black Folk Played in the Attempt to Reconstruct Democracy in America, 1860–1880* (1935; reprint, 1999).
Written more than a half-century ago, Du Bois's book is a classic and still useful for both information and insights.

Carol Faulkner. *Women's Radical Reconstruction: The Freedmen's Aid Movement.* (2004).
A new study of the role of women in the Freedmen's Bureau and in federal Reconstruction policy more generally.

Eric Foner. *Reconstruction: America's Unfinished Revolution, 1863–1877* (1988; reprint, 2002).
The most thorough of recent treatments, incorporating insights from many historians who have written on the subject during the past fifty years.

Leon F. Litwack. *Been in the Storm So Long: The Aftermath of Slavery* (1979).
An account that focuses especially on the experience of the freed people.

William S. McFeely. *Frederick Douglass* (1991).
A highly readable biography of the most prominent black political leader of the nineteenth century.

Michael Perman. *Emancipation and Reconstruction*, 2nd ed. (2003).
Short, readable, and recently revised.

C. Vann Woodward. *Reunion and Reaction: The Compromise of 1877 and the End of Reconstruction,* rev. ed. (1956; reprint, 1991).
The classic account of the Compromise of 1877.

Declaration of Independence in Congress, July 4, 1776

When, in the course of human events, it becomes necessary for one people to dissolve the political bonds which have connected them with another, and to assume, among the powers of the earth, the separate and equal station to which the laws of nature and of nature's God entitle them, a decent respect to the opinions of mankind requires that they should declare the causes which impel them to the separation.

We hold these truths to be self-evident: That all men are created equal; that they are endowed by their Creator with certain unalienable rights; that among these are life, liberty, and the pursuit of happiness; that, to secure these rights, governments are instituted among men, deriving their just powers from the consent of the governed; that whenever any form of government becomes destructive of these ends, it is the right of the people to alter or to abolish it, and to institute new government, laying its foundation on such principles, and organizing its powers in such form, as to them shall seem most likely to effect their safety and happiness. Prudence, indeed, will dictate that governments long established should not be changed for light and transient causes; and accordingly all experience hath shown that mankind are more disposed to suffer, while evils are sufferable, than to right themselves by abolishing the forms to which they are accustomed. But when a long train of abuses and usurpations, pursuing invariably the same object, evinces a design to reduce them under absolute despotism, it is their right, it is their duty, to throw off such government, and to provide new guards for their future security. Such has been the patient sufferance of these colonies; and such is now the necessity which constrains them to alter their former systems of government. The history of the present King of Great Britain is a history of repeated injuries and usurpations, all having in direct object the establishment of an absolute tyranny over these states. To prove this, let facts be submitted to a candid world.

He has refused his assent to laws, the most wholesome and necessary for the public good.

He has forbidden his governors to pass laws of immediate and pressing importance, unless suspended in their operation till his assent should be obtained; and, when so suspended, he has utterly neglected to attend to them.

He has refused to pass other laws for the accommodation of large districts of people, unless those people would relinquish the right of representation in the legislature, a right inestimable to them, and formidable to tyrants only.

He has called together legislative bodies at places unusual, uncomfortable, and distant from the depository of their public records, for the sole purpose of fatiguing them into compliance with his measures.

He has dissolved representative houses repeatedly, for opposing, with manly firmness, his invasions on the rights of the people.

He has refused for a long time, after such dissolutions, to cause others to be elected; whereby the legislative powers, incapable of annihilation, have returned to the people at large for their exercise; the state remaining, in the mean time, exposed to all the dangers of invasions from without and convulsions within.

He has endeavored to prevent the population of these states; for that purpose obstructing the laws for naturalization of foreigners; refusing to pass others to encourage their migration hither, and raising the conditions of new appropriations of lands.

He has obstructed the administration of justice, by refusing his assent to laws for establishing judiciary powers.

He has made judges dependent on his will alone, for the tenure of their offices, and the amount and payment of their salaries.

He has erected a multitude of new offices, and sent hither swarms of officers to harass our people and eat out their substance.

He has kept among us, in times of peace, standing armies, without the consent of our legislatures.

He has affected to render the military independent of, and superior to, the civil power.

He has combined with others to subject us to a jurisdiction foreign to our constitution, and unacknowledged by our laws, giving his assent to their acts of pretended legislation:

For quartering large bodies of armed troops among us;

For protecting them, by a mock trial, from punishment for any murders which they should commit on the inhabitants of these states;

For cutting off our trade with all parts of the world;

For imposing taxes on us without our consent;

For depriving us, in many cases, of the benefits of trial by jury;

For transporting us beyond seas, to be tried for pretended offenses;

For abolishing the free system of English laws in a neighboring province, establishing therein an arbitrary government, and enlarging its boundaries, so as to render it at once an example and fit instrument for introducing the same absolute rule into these colonies;

For taking away our charters, abolishing our most valuable laws, and altering fundamentally the forms of our governments;

For suspending our own legislatures, and declaring themselves invested with power to legislate for us in all cases whatsoever.

He has abdicated government here, by declaring us out of his protection and waging war against us.

He has plundered our seas, ravaged our coasts, burned our towns, and destroyed the lives of our people.

He is at this time transporting large armies of foreign mercenaries to complete the works of death, desolation, and tyranny already begun with circumstances of cruelty and perfidy scarcely paralleled in the most barbarous ages, and totally unworthy the head of a civilized nation.

He has constrained our fellow-citizens, taken captive on the high seas, to bear arms against their country, to become the executioners of their friends and brethren, or to fall themselves by their hands.

He has excited domestic insurrection among us, and has endeavored to bring on the inhabitants of our frontiers the merciless Indian savages, whose known rule of warfare is an undistinguished destruction of all ages, sexes, and conditions.

In every stage of these oppressions we have petitioned for redress in the most humble terms; our repeated petitions have been answered only by repeated injury. A prince, whose character is thus marked by every act which may define a tyrant, is unfit to be the ruler of a free people.

Nor have we been wanting in our attentions to our British brethren. We have warned them, from time to time, of attempts by their legislature to extend an unwarrantable jurisdiction over us. We have reminded them of the circumstances of our emigration and settlement here. We have appealed to their native justice and magnanimity; and we have conjured them, by the ties of our common kindred, to disavow these usurpations, which would inevitably interrupt our connections and correspondence. They, too, have been deaf to the voice of justice and of consanguinity. We must, therefore, acquiesce in the necessity which denounces our separation, and hold them, as we hold the rest of mankind, enemies in war, in peace friends.

We, therefore, the representatives of the United States of America, in General Congress assembled, appealing to the Supreme Judge of the world for the rectitude of our intentions, do, in the name and by the authority of the good people of these colonies, solemnly publish and declare, that these United Colonies are, and of right ought to be, FREE AND INDEPENDENT STATES; that they are absolved from all allegiance to the British crown, and that all political connection between them and the state of Great Britain is, and ought to be, totally dissolved; and that, as free and independent states, they have full power to levy war, conclude peace, contract alliances, establish commerce, and do all other acts and things which independent states may of right do. And for the support of this declaration, with a firm reliance on the protection of Divine Providence, we mutually pledge to each other our lives, our fortunes, and our sacred honor.

JOHN HANCOCK
and fifty-five others

Articles of Confederation

Whereas the Delegates of the United States of America in Congress assembled did on the fifteenth day of November in the Year of our Lord One Thousand Seven Hundred and Seventy seven, and in the Second Year of the Independence of America agree to certain articles of Confederation and perpetual Union between the States of Newhampshire, Massachusetts-bay, Rhode-island and Providence Plantations, Connecticut, New-York, New-Jersey, Pennsylvania, Delaware, Maryland, Virginia, North-Carolina, South-Carolina and Georgia in the Words following, viz. "Articles of Confederation and perpetual Union between the states of Newhampshire, Massachusetts-bay, Rhodeisland and Providence Plantations, Connecticut, New-York, New-Jersey, Pennsylvania, Delaware, Maryland, Virginia, North-Carolina, South-Carolina and Georgia.

Article I The Stile of this confederacy shall be "The United States of America."

Article II Each state retains its sovereignty, freedom and independence, and every Power, Jurisdiction and right, which is not by this confederation expressly delegated to the United States, in Congress assembled.

Article III   The said states hereby severally enter into a firm league of friendship with each other, for their common defence, the security of their Liberties, and their mutual and general welfare, binding themselves to assist each other, against all force offered to, or attacks made upon them, or any of them, on account of religion, sovereignty, trade, or any other pretence whatever.

Article IV   The better to secure and perpetuate mutual friendship and intercourse among the people of the different states in this union, the free inhabitants of each of these states, paupers, vagabonds and fugitives from Justice excepted, shall be entitled to all privileges and immunities of free citizens in the several states; and the people of each state shall have free ingress and regress to and from any other state, and shall enjoy therein all the privileges of trade and commerce, subject to the same duties, impositions and restrictions as the inhabitants thereof respectively, provided that such restriction shall not extend so far as to prevent the removal of property imported into any state, to any other state of which the Owner is an inhabitant; provided also that no imposition, duties or restriction shall be laid by any state, on the property of the united states, or either of them.

If any Person guilty of, or charged with treason, felony, or other high misdemeanor in any state, shall flee from Justice, and be found in any of the united states, he shall upon demand of the Governor or executive power, of the state from which he fled, be delivered up and removed to the state having jurisdiction of his offence.

Full faith and credit shall be given in each of these states to the records, acts and judicial proceedings of the courts and magistrates of every other state.

Article V   For the more convenient management of the general interests of the united states, delegates shall be annually appointed in such manner as the legislature of each state shall direct, to meet in Congress on the first Monday in November, in every year, with a power reserved to each state, to recall its delegates, or any of them, at any time within the year, and to send others in their stead, for the remainder of the Year.

No state shall be represented in Congress by less than two, nor by more than seven Members; and no person shall be capable of being a delegate for more than three years in any term of six years; nor shall any person, being a delegate, be capable of holding any office under the united states, for which he, or another for his benefit receives any salary, fees or emolument of any kind.

Each state shall maintain its own delegates in a meeting of the states, and while they act as members of the committee of the states.

In determining questions in the united states, in Congress assembled, each state shall have one vote.

Freedom of speech and debate in Congress shall not be impeached or questioned in any Court, or place out of Congress, and the members of congress shall be protected in their persons from arrests and imprisonments, during the time of their going to and from, and attendance on congress, except for treason, felony, or breach of the peace.

Article VI   No state without the Consent of the united states in congress assembled, shall send any embassy to, or receive any embassy from, or enter into any conference, agreement, or alliance or treaty with any King, prince or state; nor shall any person holding any office of profit or trust under the united states, or any of them, accept of any present, emolument, office or title of any kind whatever from any king, prince or foreign state; nor shall the united states in congress assembled, or any of them, grant any title of nobility.

No two or more states shall enter into any treaty, confederation or alliance whatever between them, without the consent of the united states in congress assembled, specifying accurately the purposes for which the same is to be entered into, and how long it shall continue.

No state shall lay any imposts or duties, which may interfere with any stipulations in treaties, entered into by the united states in congress assembled, with any king, prince or state, in pursuance of any treaties already proposed by congress, to the courts of France and Spain.

No vessels of war shall be kept up in time of peace by any state, except such number only, as shall be deemed necessary by the united states in congress assembled, for the defence of such state, or its trade; nor shall any body of forces be kept up by any state, in time of peace, except such number only, as in the judgment of the united states, in congress assembled, shall be deemed requisite to garrison the forts necessary for the defence of such state; but every state shall always keep up a well regulated and disciplined militia, sufficiently armed and accoutred, and shall provide and constantly have ready for use, in public stores, a due number of field pieces and tents, and a proper quantity of arms, ammunition and camp equipage.

No state shall engage in any war without the consent of the united states in congress assembled, unless such state be actually invaded by enemies, or shall have received certain advice of a resolution being formed by some nation of Indians to invade such state, and the danger is so imminent as not to admit of a delay, till the united states in congress assembled can be consulted: nor shall any state grant commissions to any ships or vessels of war, nor letters of marque or reprisal, except it be after a declaration of war by the united states in congress assembled, and then only against the kingdom or state and the subjects thereof, against which war has been so declared, and under such regulations as shall be established by the united states in congress assembled, unless such state be infested by pirates, in which case vessels of war may be fitted out for that occasion, and kept so long as the danger shall continue, or until the united states in congress assembled shall determine otherwise.

Article VII   When land-forces are raised by any state for the common defence, all officers of or under the rank of colonel, shall be appointed by the legislature of each state respectively by whom such forces shall be raised, or in such manner as such state shall direct, and all vacancies shall be filled up by the state which first made the appointment.

Article VIII   All charges of war, and all other expences that shall be incurred for the common defence or general welfare, and allowed by the united states in congress assembled, shall be defrayed out of a common treasury, which shall be supplied by the several states, in proportion to the value of all land within each state, granted to or surveyed for any Person, as such land and the buildings and improvements thereon shall be estimated according to such mode as the united states in congress assembled, shall from time to time direct and appoint. The taxes for paying that proportion shall be laid and levied by the authority and direction of the legislatures of the several states within the time agreed upon by the united states in congress assembled.

Article IX   The united states in congress assembled, shall have the sole and exclusive right and power of determining on peace and war, except in the cases mentioned in the sixth article—of sending and receiving ambassadors—entering into treaties and alliances, provided that no treaty of commerce shall be made whereby the legislative power of the respective states shall be restrained from imposing such imposts and duties on foreigners, as their own people are subjected to, or from prohibiting the exportation or importation of any species of goods or commodities whatsoever—of establishing rules for deciding in all cases, what captures on land or water shall be legal, and in what manner prizes taken by land or naval forces in the service of the united states shall be divided or appropriated.—of granting letters of marque and reprisal in times of peace—appointing courts for the trial of piracies and felonies committed on the high seas

and establishing courts for receiving and determining finally appeals in all cases of captures, provided that no member of congress shall be appointed a judge of any of the said courts.

The united states in congress assembled shall also be the last resort on appeal in all disputes and differences now subsisting or that hereafter may arise between two or more states concerning boundary, jurisdiction or any other cause whatever; which authority shall always be exercised in the manner following. Whenever the legislative or executive authority or lawful agent of any state in controversy with another shall present a petition to congress, stating the matter in question and praying for a hearing, notice thereof shall be given by order of congress to the legislative or executive authority of the other state in controversy, and a day assigned for the appearance of the parties by their lawful agents, who shall then be directed to appoint by joint consent, commissioners or judges to constitute a court for hearing and determining the matter in question: but if they cannot agree, congress shall name three persons out of each of the united states, and from the list of such persons each party shall alternately strike out one, the petitioners beginning, until the number shall be reduced to thirteen; and from that number not less than seven, nor more than nine names as congress shall direct, shall in the presence of congress be drawn out by lot, and the persons whose names shall be so drawn or any five of them, shall be commissioners or judges, to hear and finally determine the controversy, so always as a major part of the judges who shall hear the cause shall agree in the determination: and if either party shall neglect to attend at the day appointed, without shewing reasons, which congress shall judge sufficient, or being present shall refuse to strike, the congress shall proceed to nominate three persons out of each state, and the secretary of congress shall strike in behalf of such party absent or refusing; and the judgment and sentence of the court to be appointed, in the manner before prescribed, shall be final and conclusive; and if any of the parties shall refuse to submit to the authority of such court, or to appear to defend their claim or cause, the court shall nevertheless proceed to pronounce sentence, or judgment, which shall in like manner be final and decisive, the judgment or sentence and other proceedings being in either case transmitted to congress, and lodged among the acts of congress for the security of the parties concerned: provided that every commissioner, before he sits in judgment, shall take an oath to be administered by one of the judges of the supreme or superior court of the state, where the cause shall be tried, "well and truly to hear and determine the matter in question, according to the best of his judgment, without favour, affection or hope of reward:" provided also that no state shall be deprived of territory for the benefit of the united states.

All controversies concerning the private right of soil claimed under different grants of two or more states, whose jurisdictions as they may respect such lands, and the states which passed such grants are adjusted, the said grants or either of them being at the same time claimed to have originated antecedent to such settlement of jurisdiction, shall on the petition of either party to the congress of the united states, be finally determined as near as may be in the same manner as is before prescribed for deciding disputes respecting territorial jurisdiction between different states.

The united states in congress assembled shall also have the sole and exclusive right and power of regulating the alloy and value of coin struck by their own authority, or by that of the respective states—fixing the standard of weights and measures throughout the united states.—regulating the trade and managing all affairs with the Indians, not members of any of the states, provided that the legislative right of any state within its own limits be not infringed or violated—establishing and regulating post-offices from one state to another, throughout all the united states, and exacting such postage on the papers passing thro' the same as may be requisite to defray the expences of the said office—appointing all officers of the land forces, in the service of the united states, excepting regimental officers.—appointing all the officers of the naval forces, and commissioning all officers whatever in the service of the united states—making rules for the government and regulation of the said land and naval forces, and directing their operations.

The united states in congress assembled shall have authority to appoint a committee, to sit in the recess of congress, to be denominated "A Committee of the States," and to consist of one delegate from each state; and to appoint such other committees and civil officers as may be necessary for managing the general affairs of the united states under their direction—to appoint one of their number to preside, provided that no person be allowed to serve in the office of president more than one year in any term of three years; to ascertain the necessary sums of Money to be raised for the service of the united states, and to appropriate and apply the same for defraying the public expences—to borrow money, or emit bills on the credit of the united states, transmitting every half year to the respective states an account of the sums of money so borrowed or emitted,—to build and equip a navy—to agree upon the number of land forces, and to make requisitions from each state for its quota, in proportion to the number of white inhabitants in such state; which requisition shall be binding, and thereupon the legislature of each state shall appoint the regimental officers, raise the men and cloath, arm and equip them in a soldier like manner, at the expence of the united states, and the officers and men so cloathed, armed and equipped shall march to the place appointed, and within the time agreed on by the united states in congress assembled: But if the united states in congress assembled shall, on consideration of circumstances judge proper that any state should not raise men, or should raise a smaller number than its quota, and that any other state should raise a greater number of men than the quota thereof, such extra number shall be raised, officered, cloathed, armed and equipped in the same manner as the quota of such state, unless the legislature of such state shall judge that such extra number cannot be safely spared out of the same, in which case they shall raise, officer, cloath, arm and equip as many of such extra number as they judge can be safely spared. And the officers and men so cloathed, armed and equipped, shall march to the place appointed, and within the time agreed on by the united states in congress assembled.

The united states in congress assembled shall never engage in a war, nor grant letters of marque and reprisal in time of peace, nor enter into any treaties or alliances, nor coin money, nor regulate the value thereof, nor ascertain the sums and expences necessary for the defence and welfare of the united states, or any of them, nor emit bills, nor borrow money on the credit of the united states, nor appropriate money, nor agree upon the number of vessels of war, to be built or purchased, or the number of land or sea forces to be raised, nor appoint a commander in chief of the army or navy, unless nine states assent to the same: nor shall a question on any other point, except for adjourning from day to day be determined, unless by the votes of a majority of the united states in congress assembled.

The congress of the united states shall have power to adjourn to any time within the year, and to any place within the united states, so that no period of adjournment be for a longer duration than the space of six Months, and shall publish the Journal of their proceedings monthly, except such parts thereof relating to treaties, alliances or military operations as in their judgment require secresy; and the yeas and nays of the delegates of each state on any question shall be entered on the Journal, when it is desired by any delegate; and the delegates of a state, or any of them, at his or their request shall be furnished with a transcript of the said Journal, except such parts as are above excepted, to lay before the legislatures of the several states.

Article X   The committee of the states, or any nine of them, shall be authorised to execute, in the recess of congress, such of the powers of congress as the united states in congress assembled, by the consent of nine states, shall from time to time think expedient to vest them with; provided that no power be delegated to the said committee, for the exercise of which, by the articles of confederation, the voice of nine states in the congress of the united states assembled is requisite.

Article XI   Canada acceding to this confederation, and joining in the measures of the united states, shall be admitted into, and entitled to all the advantages of this union: but no other colony shall be admitted into the same, unless such admission be agreed to by nine states.

Article XII   All bills of credit emitted, monies borrowed and debts contracted by, or under the authority of congress, before the assembling of the united states, in pursuance of the present confederation, shall be deemed and considered as a charge against the united states, for payment and satisfaction whereof the said united states, and the public faith are hereby solemnly pledged.

Article XIII   Every state shall abide by the determinations of the united states in congress assembled, on all questions which by this confederation are submitted to them. And the Articles of this confederation shall be inviolably observed by every state, and the union shall be perpetual; nor shall any alteration at any time hereafter be made in any of them; unless such alteration be agreed to in a congress of the united states, and be afterwards confirmed by the legislatures of every state.

AND WHEREAS it hath pleased the Great Governor of the World to incline the hearts of the legislatures we respectively represent in congress, to approve of, and to authorize us to ratify the said articles of confederation and perpetual union. Know Ye that we the under-signed delegates, by virtue of the power and authority to us given for that purpose, do by these presents, in the name and in behalf of our respective constituents, fully and entirely ratify and confirm each and every of the said articles of confederation and perpetual union, and all and singular the matters and things therein contained: And we do further solemnly plight and engage the faith of our respective constituents, that they shall abide by the determinations of the united states in congress assembled, on all questions, which by the said confederation are submitted to them. And that the articles thereof shall be inviolably observed by the states we respectively represent, and that the union shall be perpetual. In Witness whereof we have hereunto set our hands in Congress. Done at Philadelphia in the state of Pennsylvania the ninth Day of July in the Year of our Lord one Thousand seven Hundred and Seventy-eight, and in the third year of the independence of America.

Constitution of the United States of America and Amendments*

Preamble

We the people of the United States, in order to form a more perfect union, establish justice, insure domestic tranquillity, provide for the common defense, promote the general welfare, and secure the blessings of liberty to ourselves and our posterity, do ordain and establish this Constitution for the United States of America.

Article I

Section 1   All legislative powers herein granted shall be vested in a Congress of the United States, which shall consist of a Senate and a House of Representatives.

Section 2   The House of Representatives shall be composed of members chosen every second year by the people of the several States, and the electors in each State shall have the qualifications requisite for electors of the most numerous branch of the State Legislature.

No person shall be a Representative who shall not have attained to the age of twenty-five years, and been seven years a citizen of the United States, and who shall not, when elected, be an inhabitant of that State in which he shall be chosen.

Representatives and direct taxes shall be apportioned among the several States which may be included within this Union, according to their respective numbers, *which shall be determined by adding to the whole number of free persons, including those bound to service for a term of years and excluding Indians not taxed, three-fifths of all other persons.* The actual enumeration shall be made within three years after the first meeting of the Congress of the United States, and within every subsequent term of ten years, in such manner as they shall by law direct. The number of Representatives shall not exceed one for every thirty thousand, but each State shall have at least one Representative; *and until such enumeration shall be made, the State of New Hampshire shall be entitled to choose three, Massachusetts eight, Rhode Island and Providence Plantations one, Connecticut five, New York six, New Jersey four, Pennsylvania eight, Delaware one, Maryland six, Virginia ten, North Carolina five, South Carolina five, and Georgia three.*

When vacancies happen in the representation from

---

* Passages no longer in effect are printed in italic type.

any State, the Executive authority thereof shall issue writs of election to fill such vacancies.

The House of Representatives shall choose their Speaker and other officers; and shall have the sole power of impeachment.

Section 3 The Senate of the United States shall be composed of two Senators from each State, *chosen by the legislature thereof,* for six years; and each Senator shall have one vote.

Immediately after they shall be assembled in consequence of the first election, they shall be divided as equally as may be into three classes. The seats of the Senators of the first class shall be vacated at the expiration of the second year, of the second class at the expiration of the fourth year, and of the third class at the expiration of the sixth year, so that one-third may be chosen every second year; *and if vacancies happen by resignation or otherwise, during the recess of the legislature of any State, the Executive thereof may make temporary appointments until the next meeting of the legislature, which shall then fill such vacancies.*

No person shall be a Senator who shall not have attained to the age of thirty years, and been nine years a citizen of the United States, and who shall not, when elected, be an inhabitant of that State for which he shall be chosen.

The Vice-President of the United States shall be President of the Senate, but shall have no vote, unless they be equally divided.

The Senate shall choose their other officers, and also a President *pro tempore,* in the absence of the Vice-President, or when he shall exercise the office of President of the United States.

The Senate shall have the sole power to try all impeachments. When sitting for that purpose, they shall be on oath or affirmation. When the President of the United States is tried, the Chief Justice shall preside: and no person shall be convicted with-out the concurrence of two-thirds of the members present.

Judgment in cases of impeachment shall not extend further than to removal from the office, and disqualification to hold and enjoy any office of honor, trust or profit under the United States: but the party convicted shall nevertheless be liable and subject to indictment, trial, judgment and punishment, according to law.

Section 4 The times, places and manner of holding elections for Senators and Representatives shall be prescribed in each State by the legislature thereof; but the Congress may at any time by law make or alter such regulations, except as to the places of choosing Senators.

The Congress shall assemble at least once in every year, and such meeting *shall be on the first Monday in December, unless they shall by law appoint a different day.*

Section 5 Each house shall be the judge of the elections, returns and qualifications of its own members, and a majority of each shall constitute a quorum to do business; but a smaller number may adjourn from day to day, and may be authorized to compel the attendance of absent members, in such manner, and under such penalties, as each house may provide.

Each house may determine the rules of its proceedings, punish its members for disorderly behavior, and with the concurrence of two-thirds, expel a member.

Each house shall keep a journal of its proceedings, and from time to time publish the same, excepting such parts as may in their judgment require secrecy; and the yeas and nays of the members of either house on any question shall, at the desire of one-fifth of those present, be entered on the journal.

Neither house, during the session of Congress, shall, without the consent of the other, adjourn for more than three days, nor to any other place than that in which the two houses shall be sitting.

Section 6 The Senators and Representatives shall receive a compensation for their services, to be ascertained by law and paid out of the treasury of the United States. They shall in all cases except treason, felony and breach of the peace, be privileged from arrest during their attendance at the session of their respective houses, and in going to and returning from the same; and for any speech or debate in either house, they shall not be questioned in any other place.

No Senator or Representative shall, during the time for which he was elected, be appointed to any civil office under the authority of the United States, which shall have been created, or the emoluments whereof shall have been increased, during such time; and no person holding any office under the United States shall be a member of either house during his continuance in office.

Section 7 All bills for raising revenue shall originate in the House of Representatives; but the Senate may propose or concur with amendments as on other bills.

Every bill which shall have passed the House of Representatives and the Senate, shall, before it become a law, be presented to the President of the United States; if he approve he shall sign it, but if not he shall return it with objections to that house in which it originated, who shall enter the objections at large on their journal, and proceed to reconsider it. If after such reconsideration two-thirds of that house shall agree to pass the bill, it shall be sent, together with the objections, to the other house, by which it shall likewise be reconsidered, and, if approved by two-thirds of that house, it shall become a law. But in all such cases the votes of both houses shall be determined by yeas and nays, and the names of the persons voting for and against the bill shall be entered on the journal of each house respectively. If any bill shall not be returned by the President within ten days (Sundays excepted) after it shall have been presented to him, the same shall be a law, in like manner as if he had signed it, unless the Congress by their adjournment prevent its return, in which case it shall not be a law.

Every order, resolution, or vote to which the concurrence of the Senate and House of Representatives may be necessary (except on a question of adjournment) shall be presented to the President of the United States; and before the same shall take effect, shall be approved by him, or being disapproved by him, shall be repassed by two-thirds of the Senate and House of Representatives, according to the rules and limitations prescribed in the case of a bill.

Section 8   The Congress shall have power

To lay and collect taxes, duties, imposts, and excises, to pay the debts and provide for the common defense and general welfare of the United States; but all duties, imposts and excises shall be uniform throughout the United States;

To borrow money on the credit of the United States;

To regulate commerce with foreign nations, and among the several States, and with the Indian tribes;

To establish an uniform rule of naturalization, and uniform laws on the subject of bankruptcies throughout the United States;

To coin money, regulate the value thereof, and of foreign coin, and fix the standard of weights and measures;

To provide for the punishment of counterfeiting the securities and current coin of the United States;

To establish post offices and post roads;

To promote the progress of science and useful arts by securing for limited times to authors and inventors the exclusive right to their respective writings and discoveries;

To constitute tribunals inferior to the Supreme Court;

To define and punish piracies and felonies committed on the high seas and offenses against the law of nations;

To declare war, grant letters of marque and reprisal, and make rules concerning captures on land and water;

To raise and support armies, but no appropriation of money to that use shall be for a longer term than two years;

To provide and maintain a navy;

To make rules for the government and regulation of the land and naval forces;

To provide for calling forth the militia to execute the laws of the Union, suppress insurrections, and repel invasions;

To provide for organizing, arming, and disciplining the militia, and for governing such part of them as may be employed in the service of the United States, reserving to the States respectively the appointment of the officers, and the authority of training the militia according to the discipline prescribed by Congress;

To exercise exclusive legislation in all cases whatsoever, over such district (not exceeding ten miles square) as may, by cession of particular States, and the acceptance of Congress, become the seat of government of the United States, and to exercise like authority over all places purchased by the consent of the legislature of the State, in which the same shall be, for erection of forts, magazines, arsenals, dockyards, and other needful buildings; — and

To make all laws which shall be necessary and proper for carrying into execution the foregoing powers, and all other powers vested by this Constitution in the government of the United States, or in any department or officer thereof.

Section 9   *The migration or importation of such persons as any of the States now existing shall think proper to admit shall not be prohibited by the Congress prior to the year 1808; but a tax or duty may be imposed on such importation, not exceeding $10 for each person.*

The privilege of the writ of habeas corpus shall not be suspended, unless when in cases of rebellion or invasion the public safety may require it.

No bill of attainder or ex post facto law shall be passed.

No capitation, or other direct, tax shall be laid, unless in proportion to the census or enumeration herein before directed to be taken.

No tax or duty shall be laid on articles exported from any State.

No preference shall be given by any regulation of commerce or revenue to the ports of one State over those of another; nor shall vessels bound to, or from, one State, be obliged to enter, clear, or pay duties in another.

No money shall be drawn from the treasury, but in consequence of appropriations made by law; and a regular statement and account of the receipts and expenditures of all public money shall be published from time to time.

No title of nobility shall be granted by the United States: and no person holding any office of profit or trust under them, shall, without the consent of the Congress, accept of any present, emolument, office, or title, of any kind whatever, from any king, prince, or foreign state.

Section 10   No State shall enter into any treaty, alliance, or confederation; grant letters of marque and reprisal; coin money; emit bills of credit; make anything but gold and silver coin a tender in payment of debts; pass any bill of attainder, ex post facto law, or law impairing the obligation of contracts, or grant any title of nobility.

No State shall, without the consent of Congress, lay any imposts or duties on imports or exports, except what may be absolutely necessary for executing its inspection laws: and the net produce of all duties and imposts, laid by any State on imports or exports, shall be for the use of the treasury of the United States; and all such laws shall be subject to the revision and control of the Congress.

No State shall, without the consent of Congress, lay any duty of tonnage, keep troops or ships of war in time of peace, enter into any agreement or compact with another State, or with a foreign power, or engage in war, unless actually invaded, or in such imminent danger as will not admit of delay.

Article II

Section 1   The executive power shall be vested in a President of the United States of America. He shall hold his office during the term of four years, and, together with the Vice-President, chosen for the same term, be elected as follows:

Each State shall appoint, in such manner as the legislature thereof may direct, a number of electors, equal to the whole number of Senators and Representatives to which the State may be entitled in the Congress; but no Senator or Representative, or person holding an office of trust or profit under the United States, shall be appointed an elector.

The electors shall meet in their respective States, and vote by ballot for two persons, of whom one at least shall not be an inhabitant of the same State with themselves. And they shall make a list of all the persons voted for, and of the number of votes for each; which list they shall sign and certify, and transmit sealed to the seat of government of the United States, directed to the President of the Senate. The President of the Senate shall, in the presence of the Senate and House of Representatives, open all the certificates, and the votes shall then be counted. The person having the greatest number of votes shall be the President, if such number be a majority of the whole number of electors appointed; and if there be more than one who have such majority, and have an equal number of votes, then the House of Representatives shall immediately choose by ballot one of them for President; and if no person have a majority, then from the five highest on the list said house shall in like manner choose the President. But in choosing the President the votes shall be taken by States, the representation from each State having one vote; a quorum for this purpose shall consist of a member or members from two-thirds of the States, and a majority of all the States shall be necessary to a choice. In every case, after the choice of the President, the person having the greatest number of votes of the electors shall be the Vice-President. But if there should remain two or more who have equal votes, the Senate shall choose from them by ballot the Vice-President.

The Congress may determine the time of choosing the electors and the day on which they shall give their votes; which day shall be the same throughout the United States.

No person except a natural-born citizen, *or a citizen of the United States at the time of the adoption of this Constitution*, shall be eligible to the office of President; neither shall any person be eligible to that office who shall not have attained to the age of thirty-five years, and been fourteen years a resident within the United States.

In cases of the removal of the President from office or of his death, resignation, or inability to discharge the powers and duties of the said office, the same shall devolve on the Vice-President, and the Congress may by law provide for the case of removal, death, resignation, or inability, both of the President and Vice-President, declaring what officer shall then act as President, and such officer shall act accordingly, until the disability be removed, or a President shall be elected.

The President shall, at stated times, receive for his services a compensation, which shall neither be increased nor diminished during the period for which he shall have been elected, and he shall not receive within that period any other emolument from the United States, or any of them.

Before he enter on the execution of his office, he shall take the following oath or affirmation:—"I do solemnly swear (or affirm) that I will faithfully execute the office of the President of the United States, and will to the best of my ability preserve, protect and defend the Constitution of the United States."

Section 2   The President shall be commander in chief of the army and navy of the United States, and of the militia of the several States, when called into the actual service of the United States; he may require the opinion, in writing, of the principal officer in each of the executive departments, upon any subject relating to the duties of their respective offices, and he shall have power to grant reprieves and pardons for offenses against the United States, except in cases of impeachment.

He shall have power, by and with the advice and consent of the Senate, to make treaties, provided two-thirds of the Senators present concur; and he shall nominate, and by and with the advice and consent of the Senate, shall appoint ambassadors, other public ministers and consuls, judges of the Supreme Court, and all other officers of the United States, whose appointments are not herein otherwise provided for, and which shall be established by law: but Congress may by law vest the appointment of such inferior officers, as they think proper, in the President alone, in the courts of law, or in the heads of departments.

The President shall have power to fill up all vacancies that may happen during the recess of the Senate, by granting commissions which shall expire at the end of their next session.

Section 3   He shall from time to time give to the Congress information of the state of the Union, and recommend to their consideration such measures as he shall judge necessary and expedient; he may, on extraordinary occasions, convene both houses, or either of them, and in case of disagreement between them, with respect to the time of adjournment, he may adjourn them to such time as he shall think proper; he shall receive ambassadors and other public ministers; he shall take care that the laws be faithfully executed, and shall commission all the officers of the United States.

Section 4   The President, Vice-President and all civil officers of the United States shall be removed from office on impeachment for, and on conviction of, treason, bribery, or other high crimes and misdemeanors.

Article III

Section 1   The judicial power of the United States shall be vested in one Supreme Court, and in such inferior courts as the Congress may from time to time ordain and establish. The judges, both of the Supreme and inferior courts, shall hold their offices during good behavior, and shall, at stated times, receive for their services a compensation which shall not be diminished during their continuance in office.

Section 2   The judicial power shall extend to all cases, in law and equity, arising under this Constitution, the laws of the United States, and treaties made, or which shall be made, under their authority;—to all cases affecting ambassadors, other public ministers and consuls;—to all cases of admiralty and maritime jurisdiction;—to controversies to which the United States shall be a party;—to controversies between two or more States;—*between a State and citizens of another State;*—between citizens of different States;—between citizens of the same State claiming lands under grants of different States, and between a State, or the citizens thereof, and foreign states, citizens or subjects.

In all cases affecting ambassadors, other public ministers and consuls, and those in which a State shall be party, the Supreme Court shall have original jurisdiction. In all the other cases before mentioned, the Supreme Court shall have appellate jurisdiction, both as to law and fact, with such exceptions, and under such regulations, as the Congress shall make.

The trial of all crimes, except in cases of impeachment, shall be by jury; and such trial shall be held in the State where said crimes shall have been committed; but when not committed within any State, the trial shall be at such place or places as the Congress may by law have directed.

Section 3   Treason against the United States shall consist only in levying war against them, or in adhering to their enemies, giving them aid and comfort. No person shall be convicted of treason unless on the testimony of two witnesses to the same overt act, or on confession in open court.

The Congress shall have power to declare the punishment of treason, but no attainder of treason shall work corruption of blood, or forfeiture except during the life of the person attainted.

Article IV

Section 1   Full faith and credit shall be given in each State to the public acts, records, and judicial proceedings of every other State. And the Congress may by general laws prescribe the manner in which such acts, records, and proceedings shall be proved, and the effect thereof.

Section 2   The citizens of each State shall be entitled to all privileges and immunities of citizens in the several States.

A person charged in any State with treason, felony, or other crime, who shall flee from justice, and be found in another State, shall on demand of the executive authority of the State from which he fled, be delivered up, to be removed to the State having jurisdiction of the crime.

No person held to service or labor in one State, under the laws thereof, escaping into another, shall, in consequence of any law or regulation therein, be discharged from such service or labor, but shall be delivered up on claim of the party to whom such service or labor may be due.

Section 3   New States may be admitted by the Congress into this Union; but no new State shall be formed or erected within the jurisdiction of any other State; nor any State be formed by the junction of two or more States, or parts of States, without the consent of the legislatures of the States concerned as well as of the Congress.

The Congress shall have power to dispose of and make all needful rules and regulations respecting the territory or other property belonging to the United States; and nothing in this Constitution shall be so construed as to prejudice any claims of the United States, or of any particular State.

Section 4 The United States shall guarantee to every State in this Union a republican form of government, and shall protect each of them against invasion; and on application of the legislature, or of the executive (when the legislature cannot be convened), against domestic violence.

Article V

The Congress, whenever two-thirds of both houses shall deem it necessary, shall propose amendments to this Constitution, or, on the application of the legislatures of two-thirds of the several States, shall call a convention for proposing amendments, which, in either case, shall be valid to all intents and purposes, as part of this Constitution, when ratified by the legislatures of three-fourths of the several States, or by conventions in three-fourths thereof, as the one or the other mode of ratification may be proposed by the Congress; provided *that no amendments which may be made prior to the year one thousand eight hundred and eight shall in any manner affect the first and fourth clauses in the ninth section of the first article;* and that no State, without its consent, shall be deprived of its equal suffrage in the Senate.

Article VI

All debts contracted and engagements entered into, before the adoption of this Constitution, shall be as valid against the United States under this Constitution, as under the Confederation.

This Constitution, and the laws of the United States which shall be made in pursuance thereof; and all treaties made, or which shall be made, under the authority of the United States, shall be the supreme law of the land; and the judges in every State shall be bound thereby, anything in the Constitution or laws of any State to the contrary notwithstanding.

The Senators and Representatives before mentioned, and the members of the several State legislatures, and all executive and judicial officers, both of the United States and of the several States, shall be bound by oath or affirmation to support this Constitution; but no religious test shall ever be required as a qualification to any office or public trust under the United States.

Article VII

The ratification of the conventions of nine States shall be sufficient for the establishment of this Constitution between the States so ratifying the same.

Done in Convention by the unanimous consent of the States present, the seventeenth day of September in the year of our Lord one thousand seven hundred and eighty-seven and of the Independence of the United

States of America the twelfth. In witness whereof we have hereunto subscribed our names.

GEORGE WASHINGTON
and thirty-seven others

Amendments to the Constitution*

Amendment I

Congress shall make no law respecting an establishment of religion, or prohibiting the free exercise thereof; or abridging the freedom of speech, or of the press; or the right of the people peaceably to assemble, and to petition the government for a redress of grievances.

Amendment II

A well-regulated militia being necessary to the security of a free State, the right of the people to keep and bear arms shall not be infringed.

Amendment III

No soldier shall, in time of peace, be quartered in any house without the consent of the owner, nor in time of war, but in a manner to be prescribed by law.

Amendment IV

The right of the people to be secure in their persons, houses, papers, and effects, against unreasonable searches and seizures, shall not be violated, and no warrants shall issue but upon probable cause, supported by oath or affirmation, and particularly describing the place to be searched, and the persons or things to be seized.

Amendment V

No person shall be held to answer for a capital, or otherwise infamous crime, unless on a presentment or indictment of a grand jury, except in cases arising in the land or naval forces, or in the militia, when in actual service in time of war or public danger; nor shall any person be subject for the same offense to be twice put in jeopardy of life or limb; nor shall be compelled in any criminal case to be a witness against himself, nor be deprived of life, liberty, or property, without due process of law; nor shall private property be taken for public use without just compensation.

Amendment VI

In all criminal prosecutions, the accused shall enjoy the right to a speedy and public trial, by an impartial jury of

---

* The first ten Amendments (the Bill of Rights) were adopted in 1791.

the State and district wherein the crime shall have been committed, which district shall have been previously ascertained by law, and to be informed of the nature and cause of the accusation; to be confronted with the witnesses against him; to have compulsory process for obtaining witnesses in his favor, and to have the assistance of counsel for his defense.

Amendment VII

In suits at common law, where the value in controversy shall exceed twenty dollars, the right of trial by jury shall be preserved, and no fact tried by a jury shall be otherwise reexamined in any court of the United States, than according to the rules of the common law.

Amendment VIII

Excessive bail shall not be required, nor excessive fines imposed, nor cruel and unusual punishments inflicted.

Amendment IX

The enumeration in the Constitution, of certain rights, shall not be construed to deny or disparage others retained by the people.

Amendment X

The powers not delegated to the United States by the Constitution, nor prohibited by it to the States, are reserved to the States respectively, or to the people.

Amendment XI

[Adopted 1798]

The judicial power of the United States shall not be construed to extend to any suit in law or equity, commenced or prosecuted against one of the United States by citizens of another State, or by citizens or subjects of any foreign state.

Amendment XII

[Adopted 1804]

The electors shall meet in their respective States, and vote by ballot for President and Vice-President, one of whom, at least, shall not be an inhabitant of the same State with themselves; they shall name in their ballots the person voted for as President, and in distinct ballots the person voted for as Vice-President, and they shall make distinct lists of all persons voted for as President, and of all persons voted for as Vice-President, and of the number of votes for each, which lists they shall sign and certify, and transmit sealed to the seat of government of the United States, directed to the President of the Senate;—the President of the Senate shall, in the presence of the Senate and House of Representatives, open all the certificates and the votes shall then be counted;—the person having the great-

est number of votes for President shall be the President, if such number be a majority of the whole number of electors appointed; and if no person have such majority, then from the persons having the highest numbers not exceeding three on the list of those voted for as President, the House of Representatives shall choose immediately, by ballot, the President. But in choosing the President, the votes shall be taken by States, the representation from each State having one vote; a quorum for this purpose shall consist of a member or members from two-thirds of the States, and a majority of all the States shall be necessary to a choice. And if the House of Representatives shall not choose a President whenever the right of choice shall devolve upon them, before the fourth day of March next following, then the Vice-President shall act as President, as in the case of the death or other constitutional disability of the President.

The person having the greatest number of votes as Vice-President shall be the Vice-President, if such number be a majority of the whole number of electors appointed; and if no person have a majority, then from the two highest numbers on the list the Senate shall choose the Vice-President; a quorum for the purpose shall consist of two-thirds of the whole number of Senators, and a majority of the whole number shall be necessary to a choice. But no person constitutionally ineligible to the office of President shall be eligible to that of Vice-President of the United States.

Amendment XIII

[Adopted 1865]

Section 1   Neither slavery nor involuntary servitude, except as a punishment for crime whereof the party shall have been duly convicted, shall exist within the United States, or any place subject to their jurisdiction.

Section 2   Congress shall have power to enforce this article by appropriate legislation.

Amendment XIV

[Adopted 1868]

Section 1   All persons born or naturalized in the United States, and subject to the jurisdiction thereof, are citizens of the United States and of the State wherein they reside. No State shall make or enforce any law which shall abridge the privileges or immunities of citizens of the United States; nor shall any State deprive any person of life, liberty, or property, without due process of law; nor deny to any person within its jurisdiction the equal protection of the laws.

Section 2   Representatives shall be apportioned among the several States according to their respective numbers, counting the whole number of persons in each State, excluding Indians not taxed. But when the right to vote at any election for the choice of Electors for President and Vice-President of the United States, Representatives in Congress, the executive and judicial officers of a State, or the members of the legislature thereof, is denied to any of the male inhabitants of such State, being twenty-one years of age and citizens of the United States, or in any way abridged, except for participation in rebellion, or other crime, the basis of representation therein shall be reduced in the proportion which the number of such male citizens shall bear to the whole number of male citizens twenty-one years of age in such State.

Section 3 No person shall be a Senator or Representative in Congress, or Elector of President and Vice-President, or hold any office, civil or military, under the United States, or under any State, who, having previously taken an oath, as a member of Congress, or as an officer of the United States, or as a member of any State legislature, or as an executive or judicial officer of any State, to support the Constitution of the United States, shall have engaged in insurrection or rebellion against the same, or given aid or comfort to the enemies thereof. Congress may, by a vote of two-thirds of each house, remove such disability.

Section 4 The validity of the public debt of the United States, authorized by law, including debts incurred for payment of pensions and bounties for services in suppressing insurrection or rebellion, shall not be questioned. But neither the United States nor any State shall assume or pay any debt or obligation incurred in aid of insurrection or rebellion against the United States, or any claim for the loss or emancipation of any slave; but all such debts, obligations, and claims shall be held illegal and void.

Section 5 The Congress shall have power to enforce, by appropriate legislation, the provisions of this article.

Amendment XV

[Adopted 1870]

Section 1 The right of citizens of the United States to vote shall not be denied or abridged by the United States or by any State on account of race, color, or previous condition of servitude.

Section 2 The Congress shall have power to enforce this article by appropriate legislation.

Amendment XVI

[Adopted 1913]

The Congress shall have power to lay and collect taxes on incomes, from whatever source derived, without apportionment among the several States, and without regard to any census or enumeration.

Amendment XVII

[Adopted 1913]

Section 1 The Senate of the United States shall be composed of two Senators from each State, elected by the people thereof, for six years; and each Senator shall have one vote. The electors in each State shall have the qualifications requisite for electors of [voters for] the most numerous branch of the State legislatures.

Section 2 When vacancies happen in the representation of any State in the Senate, the executive authority of such State shall issue writs of election to fill such vacancies: Provided, that the Legislature of any State may empower the executive thereof to make temporary appointments until the people fill the vacancies by election as the Legislature may direct.

Section 3 This amendment shall not be so construed as to affect the election or term of any Senator chosen before it becomes valid as part of the Constitution.

Amendment XVIII

[Adopted 1919; Repealed 1933]

Section 1 After one year from the ratification of this article the manufacture, sale, or transportation of intoxicating liquors within, the importation thereof into, or the exportation thereof from the United States and all territory subject to the jurisdiction thereof, for beverage purposes, is hereby prohibited.

Section 2 The Congress and the several States shall have concurrent power to enforce this article by appropriate legislation.

Section 3 This article shall be inoperative unless it shall have been ratified as an amendment to the Constitution by the legislatures of the several States, as provided by the Constitution, within seven years from the date of the submission thereof to the States by the Congress.

Amendment XIX

[Adopted 1920]

Section 1 The right of citizens of the United States to vote shall not be denied or abridged by the United States or by any State on account of sex.

Section 2 The Congress shall have power to enforce this article by appropriate legislation.

Amendment XX

[Adopted 1933]

Section 1 The terms of the President and Vice-President shall end at noon on the 20th day of January, and the terms of Senators and Representatives at noon on the 3rd day of January, of the years in which such terms would have ended if this article had not been ratified; and the terms of their successors shall then begin.

Section 2 The Congress shall assemble at least once in every year, and such meeting shall begin at noon on the 3d day of January, unless they shall by law appoint a different day.

Section 3 If, at the time fixed for the beginning of the term of the President, the President-elect shall have died, the Vice-President-elect shall become President. If a President shall not have been chosen before the time fixed for the beginning of his term, or if the President-elect shall have failed to qualify, then the Vice-President-elect shall act as President until a President shall have qualified; and the Congress may by law provide for the case wherein neither a President-elect nor a Vice-President-elect shall have qualified, declaring who shall then act as President, or the manner in which one who is to act shall be selected, and such persons shall act accordingly until a President or Vice-President shall have qualified.

Section 4 The Congress may by law provide for the case of the death of any of the persons from whom the House of Representatives may choose a President whenever the right of choice shall have devolved upon them, and for the case of the death of any of the persons from whom the Senate may choose a Vice-President whenever the right of choice shall have devolved upon them.

Section 5 Sections 1 and 2 shall take effect on the 15th day of October following the ratification of this article.

Section 6 This article shall be inoperative unless it shall have been ratified as an amendment to the Constitution by the Legislatures of three-fourths of the several States within seven years from the date of its submission.

Amendment XXI

[Adopted 1933]

Section 1 The eighteenth article of amendment to the Constitution of the United States is hereby repealed.

Section 2 The transportation or importation into any State, Territory, or Possession of the United States for delivery or use therein of intoxicating liquors, in violation of the laws thereof, is hereby prohibited.

Section 3 This article shall be inoperative unless it shall have been ratified as an amendment to the Constitution by conventions in the several States, as provided in the Constitution, within seven years from the date of submission thereof to the States by the Congress.

Amendment XXII

[Adopted 1951]

Section 1 No person shall be elected to the office of President more than twice, and no person who has held the office of President, or acted as President, for more than two years of a term to which some other person was elected President shall be elected to the office of President more than once. But this article shall not apply to any person holding the office of President when this article was proposed by the Congress, and shall not prevent any person who may be holding the office of President, or acting as President, during the term within which this article becomes operative from holding the office of President or acting as President during the remainder of such term.

Section 2 This article shall be inoperative unless it shall have been ratified as an amendment to the Constitution by the legislatures of three-fourths of the several States within seven years from the date of its submission to the States by the Congress.

Amendment XXIII

[Adopted 1961]

Section 1 The District constituting the seat of Government of the United States shall appoint in such manner as the Congress may direct:

A number of electors of President and Vice-President equal to the whole number of Senators and Representatives in Congress to which the District would be entitled if it were a State, but in no event more than the least populous State; they shall be in addition to those appointed by the States, but they shall be considered for the purposes of the election of President and Vice-President, to be electors appointed by a State; and they shall meet in the District and perform such duties as provided by the twelfth article of amendment.

Section 2 The Congress shall have the power to enforce this article by appropriate legislation.

Amendment XXIV

[Adopted 1964]

Section 1 The right of citizens of the United States to vote in any primary or other election for President or Vice-President, for electors for President or Vice-President, or for Senator or Representative in Congress, shall not be denied or abridged by the United States or any State by reason of failure to pay any poll tax or other tax.

Section 2 The Congress shall have the power to enforce this article by appropriate legislation.

Amendment XXV

[Adopted 1967]

Section 1 In case of the removal of the President from office or of his death or resignation, the Vice-President shall become President.

Section 2 Whenever there is a vacancy in the office of the Vice-President, the President shall nominate a Vice-President who shall take office upon confirmation by a majority vote of both Houses of Congress.

Section 3 Whenever the President transmits to the President pro tempore of the Senate and the Speaker of the House of Representatives his written declaration that he is unable to discharge the powers and duties of his office, and until he transmits to them a written declaration to the contrary, such powers and duties shall be discharged by the Vice-President as Acting President.

Section 4 Whenever the Vice-President and a majority of either the principal officers of the executive departments or of such other body as Congress may by law provide, transmit to the President pro tempore of the Senate and the Speaker of the House of Representatives their written declaration that the President is unable to discharge the powers and duties of his office, the Vice-President shall immediately assume the powers and duties of the office as Acting President.

Thereafter, when the President transmits to the President pro tempore of the Senate and the Speaker of the House of Representatives his written declaration that no inability exists, he shall resume the powers and duties of his office unless the Vice-President and a majority of either the principal officers of the executive department[s]

or of such other body as Congress may by law provide, transmit within four days to the President pro tempore of the Senate and the Speaker of the House of Representatives their written declaration that the President is unable to discharge the powers and duties of his office. Thereupon Congress shall decide the issue, assembling within forty-eight hours for that purpose if not in session. If the Congress, within twenty-one days after receipt of the latter written declaration, or, if Congress is not in session, within twenty-one days after Congress is required to assemble, determines by two-thirds vote of both Houses that the President is unable to discharge the powers and duties of his office, the Vice-President shall continue to discharge the same as Acting President; otherwise, the President shall resume the powers and duties of his office.

Amendment XXVI

[Adopted 1971]

Section 1 The right of citizens of the United States, who are eighteen years of age or older, to vote shall not be denied or abridged by the United States or by any State on account of age.

Section 2 The Congress shall have power to enforce this article by appropriate legislation.

Amendment XXVII

[Adopted 1992]

No law, varying the compensation for the services of the Senators and Representatives, shall take effect, until an election of Representatives shall have intervened.

Territorial Expansion of the United States

Territory	Date Acquired	Square Miles	How Acquired
Original states and territories	1783	888,685	Treaty with Great Britain
Louisiana Purchase	1803	827,192	Purchase from France
Florida	1819	72,003	Treaty with Spain
Texas	1845	390,143	Annexation of independent nation
Oregon	1846	285,580	Treaty with Great Britain
Mexican Cession	1848	529,017	Conquest from Mexico
Gadsden Purchase	1853	29,640	Purchase from Mexico
Alaska	1867	589,757	Purchase from Russia
Hawai`i	1898	6,450	Annexation of independent nation
The Philippines	1899	115,600	Conquest from Spain (granted independence in 1946)
Puerto Rico	1899	3,435	Conquest from Spain
Guam	1899	212	Conquest from Spain
American Samoa	1900	76	Treaty with Germany and Great Britain
Panama Canal Zone	1904	553	Treaty with Panama (returned to Panama by treaty in 1978)
Corn Islands	1914	4	Treaty with Nicaragua (returned to Nicaragua by treaty in 1971)
Virgin Islands	1917	133	Purchase from Denmark
Pacific Islands Trust (Micronesia)	1947	8,489	Trusteeship under United Nations (some granted independence)
All others (Midway, Wake, and other islands)		42	

Admission of States into the Union

State	Date of Admission	State	Date of Admission
1. Delaware	December 7, 1787	26. Michigan	January 26, 1837
2. Pennsylvania	December 12, 1787	27. Florida	March 3, 1845
3. New Jersey	December 18, 1787	28. Texas	December 29, 1845
4. Georgia	January 2, 1788	29. Iowa	December 28, 1846
5. Connecticut	January 9, 1788	30. Wisconsin	May 29, 1848
6. Massachusetts	February 6, 1788	31. California	September 9, 1850
7. Maryland	April 28, 1788	32. Minnesota	May 11, 1858
8. South Carolina	May 23, 1788	33. Oregon	February 14, 1859
9. New Hampshire	June 21, 1788	34. Kansas	January 29, 1861
10. Virginia	June 25, 1788	35. West Virginia	June 20, 1863
11. New York	July 26, 1788	36. Nevada	October 31, 1864
12. North Carolina	November 21, 1789	37. Nebraska	March 1, 1867
13. Rhode Island	May 29, 1790	38. Colorado	August 1, 1876
14. Vermont	March 4, 1791	39. North Dakota	November 2, 1889
15. Kentucky	June 1, 1792	40. South Dakota	November 2, 1889
16. Tennessee	June 1, 1796	41. Montana	November 8, 1889
17. Ohio	March 1, 1803	42. Washington	November 11, 1889
18. Louisiana	April 30, 1812	43. Idaho	July 3, 1890
19. Indiana	December 11, 1816	44. Wyoming	July 10, 1890
20. Mississippi	December 10, 1817	45. Utah	January 4, 1896
21. Illinois	December 3, 1818	46. Oklahoma	November 16, 1907
22. Alabama	December 14, 1819	47. New Mexico	January 6, 1912
23. Maine	March 15, 1820	48. Arizona	February 14, 1912
24. Missouri	August 10, 1821	49. Alaska	January 3, 1959
25. Arkansas	June 15, 1836	50. Hawai`i	August 21, 1959

Presidential Elections

Year	Number of States	Candidates	Parties	Popular Vote	% of Popular Vote	Electoral Vote	% Voter Participation[a]
1789	11	**George Washington**	No party			69	
		John Adams	designations			34	
		Other candidates				35	
1792	15	**George Washington**	No party			132	
		John Adams	designations			77	
		George Clinton				50	
		Other candidates				5	
1796	16	**John Adams**	Federalist			71	
		Thomas Jefferson	Democratic-Republican			68	
		Thomas Pinckney	Federalist			59	
		Aaron Burr	Democratic-Republican			30	
		Other candidates				48	
1800	16	**Thomas Jefferson**	Democratic-Republican			73	
		Aaron Burr	Democratic-Republican			73	
		John Adams	Federalist			65	
		Charles C. Pinckney	Federalist			64	
		John Jay	Federalist			1	
1804	17	**Thomas Jefferson**	Democratic-Republican			162	
		Charles C. Pinckney	Federalist			14	
1808	17	**James Madison**	Democratic-Republican			122	
		Charles C. Pinckney	Federalist			47	
		George Clinton	Democratic-Republican			6	
1812	18	**James Madison**	Democratic-Republican			128	
		DeWitt Clinton	Federalist			89	
1816	19	**James Monroe**	Democratic-Republican			183	
		Rufus King	Federalist			34	
1820	24	**James Monroe**	Democratic-Republican			231	
		John Quincy Adams	Independent-Republican			1	
1824	24	**John Quincy Adams**	Democratic-Republican	108,740	30.5	84	26.9
		Andrew Jackson	Democratic-Republican	153,544	43.1	99	

Presidential Elections (continued)

Year	Number of States	Candidates	Parties	Popular Vote	% of Popular Vote	Electoral Vote	% Voter Participation[a]
		Henry Clay	Democratic-Republican	47,136	13.2	37	
		William H. Crawford	Democratic-Republican	46,618	13.1	41	
1828	24	**Andrew Jackson**	Democratic	647,286	56.0	178	57.6
		John Quincy Adams	National Republican	508,064	44.0	83	
1832	24	**Andrew Jackson**	Democratic	688,242	54.5	219	55.4
		Henry Clay	National Republican	473,462	37.5	49	
		William Wirt	Anti-Masonic	101,051	8.0	7	
		John Floyd	Democratic			11	
1836	26	**Martin Van Buren**	Democratic	765,483	50.9	170	57.8
		William H. Harrison	Whig			73	
		Hugh L. White	Whig			26	
		Daniel Webster	Whig	739,795	49.1	14	
		W. P. Mangum	Whig			11	
1840	26	**William H. Harrison**	Whig	1,274,624	53.1	234	80.2
		Martin Van Buren	Democratic	1,127,781	46.9	60	
1844	26	**James K. Polk**	Democratic	1,338,464	49.6	170	78.9
		Henry Clay	Whig	1,300,097	48.1	105	
		James G. Birney	Liberty	62,300	2.3		
1848	30	**Zachary Taylor**	Whig	1,360,967	47.4	163	72.7
		Lewis Cass	Democratic	1,222,342	42.5	127	
		Martin Van Buren	Free-Soil	291,263	10.1		
1852	31	**Franklin Pierce**	Democratic	1,601,117	50.9	254	69.6
		Winfield Scott	Whig	1,385,453	44.1	42	
		John P. Hale	Free-Soil	155,825	5.0		
1856	31	**James Buchanan**	Democratic	1,832,955	45.3	174	78.9
		John C. Frémont	Republican	1,339,932	33.1	114	
		Millard Fillmore	American	871,731	21.6	8	
1860	33	**Abraham Lincoln**	Republican	1,865,593	39.8	180	81.2
		Stephen A. Douglas	Democratic	1,382,713	29.5	12	
		John C. Breckinridge	Democratic	848,356	18.1	72	
		John Bell	Constitutional Union	592,906	12.6	39	
1864	36	**Abraham Lincoln**	Republican	2,206,938	55.0	212	73.8
		George B. McClellan	Democratic	1,803,787	45.0	21	
1868	37	**Ulysses S. Grant**	Republican	3,013,421	52.7	214	78.1
		Horatio Seymour	Democratic	2,706,829	47.3	80	
1872	37	**Ulysses S. Grant**	Republican	3,596,745	55.6	286	71.3
		Horace Greeley	Democratic	2,843,446	43.9	[b]	
1876	38	**Rutherford B. Hayes**	Republican	4,036,572	48.0	185	81.8

Presidential Elections *(continued)*

Year	Number of States	Candidates	Parties	Popular Vote	% of Popular Vote	Electoral Vote	% Voter Participation[a]
		Samuel J. Tilden	Democratic	4,284,020	51.0	184	
1880	38	**James A. Garfield**	Republican	4,453,295	48.5	214	79.4
		Winfield S. Hancock	Democratic	4,414,082	48.1	155	
		James B. Weaver	Greenback-Labor	308,578	3.4		
1884	38	**Grover Cleveland**	Democratic	4,879,507	48.5	219	77.5
		James G. Blaine	Republican	4,850,293	48.2	182	
		Benjamin F. Butler	Greenback-Labor	175,370	1.8		
		John P. St. John	Prohibition	150,369	1.5		
1888	38	**Benjamin Harrison**	Republican	5,477,129	47.9	233	79.3
		Grover Cleveland	Democratic	5,537,857	48.6	168	
		Clinton B. Fisk	Prohibition	249,506	2.2		
		Anson J. Streeter	Union Labor	146,935	1.3		
1892	44	**Grover Cleveland**	Democratic	5,555,426	46.1	277	74.7
		Benjamin Harrison	Republican	5,182,690	43.0	145	
		James B. Weaver	People's	1,029,846	8.5	22	
		John Bidwell	Prohibition	264,133	2.2		
1896	45	**William McKinley**	Republican	7,102,246	51.1	271	79.3
		William J. Bryan	Democratic	6,492,559	47.7	176	
1900	45	**William McKinley**	Republican	7,218,491	51.7	292	73.2
		William J. Bryan	Democratic; Populist	6,356,734	45.5	155	
		John C. Wooley	Prohibition	208,914	1.5		
1904	45	**Theodore Roosevelt**	Republican	7,628,461	57.4	336	65.2
		Alton B. Parker	Democratic	5,084,223	37.6	140	
		Eugene V. Debs	Socialist	402,283	3.0		
		Silas C. Swallow	Prohibition	258,536	1.9		
1908	46	**William H. Taft**	Republican	7,675,320	51.6	321	65.4
		William J. Bryan	Democratic	6,412,294	43.1	162	
		Eugene V. Debs	Socialist	420,793	2.8		
		Eugene W. Chafin	Prohibition	253,840	1.7		
1912	48	**Woodrow Wilson**	Democratic	6,296,547	41.9	435	58.8
		Theodore Roosevelt	Progressive	4,118,571	27.4	88	
		William H. Taft	Republican	3,486,720	23.2	8	
		Eugene V. Debs	Socialist	900,672	6.0		
		Eugene W. Chafin	Prohibition	206,275	1.4		
1916	48	**Woodrow Wilson**	Democratic	9,127,695	49.4	277	61.6
		Charles E. Hughes	Republican	8,533,507	46.2	254	
		A. L. Benson	Socialist	585,113	3.2		
		J. Frank Hanly	Prohibition	220,506	1.2		
1920	48	**Warren G. Harding**	Republican	16,143,407	60.4	404	49.2
		James M. Cox	Democratic	9,130,328	34.2	127	

Presidential Elections *(continued)*

Year	Number of States	Candidates	Parties	Popular Vote	% of Popular Vote	Electoral Vote	% Voter Participation[a]
		Eugene V. Debs	Socialist	919,799	3.4		
		P. P. Christensen	Farmer-Labor	265,411	1.0		
1924	48	**Calvin Coolidge**	Republican	15,718,211	54.0	382	48.9
		John W. Davis	Democratic	8,385,283	28.8	136	
		Robert M. La Follette	Progressive	4,831,289	16.6	13	
1928	48	**Herbert C. Hoover**	Republican	21,391,993	58.2	444	56.9
		Alfred E. Smith	Democratic	15,016,169	40.9	87	
1932	48	**Franklin D. Roosevelt**	Democratic	22,809,638	57.4	472	56.9
		Herbert C. Hoover	Republican	15,758,901	39.7	59	
		Norman Thomas	Socialist	881,951	2.2		
1936	48	**Franklin D. Roosevelt**	Democratic	27,752,869	60.8	523	61.0
		Alfred M. Landon	Republican	16,674,665	36.5	8	
		William Lemke	Union	882,479	1.9		
1940	48	**Franklin D. Roosevelt**	Democratic	27,307,819	54.8	449	62.5
		Wendell L. Wilkie	Republican	22,321,018	44.8	82	
1944	48	**Franklin D. Roosevelt**	Democratic	25,606,585	53.5	432	55.9
		Thomas E. Dewey	Republican	22,014,745	46.0	99	
1948	48	**Harry S Truman**	Democratic	24,179,345	49.6	303	53.0
		Thomas E. Dewey	Republican	21,991,291	45.1	189	
		J. Strom Thurmond	States' Rights	1,176,125	2.4	39	
		Henry A. Wallace	Progressive	1,157,326	2.4		
1952	48	**Dwight D. Eisenhower**	Republican	33,936,234	55.1	442	63.3
		Adlai E. Stevenson	Democratic	27,314,992	44.4	89	
1956	48	**Dwight D. Eisenhower**	Republican	35,590,472	57.6	457	60.6
		Adlai E. Stevenson	Democratic	26,022,752	42.1	73	
1960	50	**John F. Kennedy**	Democratic	34,226,731	49.7	303	62.8
		Richard M. Nixon	Republican	34,108,157	49.5	219	
1964	50	**Lyndon B. Johnson**	Democratic	43,129,566	61.1	486	61.7
		Barry M. Goldwater	Republican	27,178,188	38.5	52	
1968	50	**Richard M. Nixon**	Republican	31,785,480	43.4	301	60.6
		Hubert H. Humphrey	Democratic	31,275,166	42.7	191	
		George C. Wallace	American Independent	9,906,473	13.5	46	
1972	50	**Richard M. Nixon**	Republican	47,169,911	60.7	520	55.2
		George S. McGovern	Democratic	29,170,383	37.5	17	
		John G. Schmitz	American	1,099,482	1.4		
1976	50	**Jimmy Carter**	Democratic	40,830,763	50.1	297	53.5
		Gerald R. Ford	Republican	39,147,793	48.0	240	
1980	50	**Ronald Reagan**	Republican	43,899,248	50.8	489	52.6
		Jimmy Carter	Democratic	35,481,432	41.0	49	
		John B. Anderson	Independent	5,719,437	6.6	0	
		Ed Clark	Libertarian	920,859	1.1	0	

Presidential Elections *(continued)*

Year	Number of States	Candidates	Parties	Popular Vote	% of Popular Vote	Electoral Vote	% Voter Participation[a]
1984	50	**Ronald Reagan**	Republican	54,455,075	58.8	525	53.1
		Walter Mondale	Democratic	37,577,185	40.6	13	
1988	50	**George Bush**	Republican	48,901,046	53.4	426	50.2
		Michael Dukakis	Democratic	41,809,030	45.6	111[c]	
1992	50	**Bill Clinton**	Democratic	44,908,233	43.0	370	55.0
		George Bush	Republican	39,102,282	37.4	168	
		Ross Perot	Independent	19,741,048	18.9	0	
1996	50	**Bill Clinton**	Democratic	47,401,054	49.2	379	49.0
		Robert Dole	Republican	39,197,350	40.7	159	
		Ross Perot	Independent	8,085,285	8.4	0	
		Ralph Nader	Green	684,871	0.7	0	
2000	50	**George W. Bush**	Republican	50,456,169	47.88	271	50.7
		Albert Gore, Jr.	Democratic	50,996,116	48.39	267	
		Ralph Nader	Green	2,783,728	2.72	0	
2004	50	George W. Bush	Republican	59,668,401[d]	51	286	58[e]
		John F. Kerry	Democratic	56,170,687[d]	48	252	
		Ralph Nader	Independent	400,706[d]	1	0	

Candidates receiving less than 1 percent of the popular vote have been omitted. Thus the percentage of popular vote given for any election year may not total 100 percent.

Before the passage of the Twelfth Amendment in 1804, the Electoral College voted for two presidential candidates; the runner-up became vice president.

Before 1824, most presidential electors were chosen by state legislatures, not by popular vote.

[a]Percent of voting-age population casting ballots (eligible voters).

[b]Greeley died shortly after the election; the electors supporting him then divided their votes among minor candidates.

[c]One elector from West Virginia cast her Electoral College presidential ballot for Lloyd Bentsen, the Democratic Party's vice-presidential candidate.

[d]At press time.

[e]Estimate at press time.

Presidents, Vice Presidents, and Cabinet Members

The Washington Administration

President	George Washington	1789–1797
Vice President	John Adams	1789–1797
Secretary of State	Thomas Jefferson	1789–1793
	Edmund Randolph	1794–1795
	Timothy Pickering	1795–1797
Secretary of Treasury	Alexander Hamilton	1789–1795
	Oliver Wolcott	1795–1797
Secretary of War	Henry Knox	1789–1794
	Timothy Pickering	1795–1796
	James McHenry	1796–1797
Attorney General	Edmund Randolph	1789–1793
	William Bradford	1794–1795
	Charles Lee	1795–1797
Postmaster General	Samuel Osgood	1789–1791
	Timothy Pickering	1791–1794
	Joseph Habersham	1795–1797

The John Adams Administration

President	John Adams	1797–1801
Vice President	Thomas Jefferson	1797–1801
Secretary of State	Timothy Pickering	1797–1800
	John Marshall	1800–1801
Secretary of Treasury	Oliver Wolcott	1797–1800
	Samuel Dexter	1800–1801
Secretary of War	James McHenry	1797–1800
	Samuel Dexter	1800–1801
Attorney General	Charles Lee	1797–1801
Postmaster General	Joseph Habersham	1797–1801
Secretary of Navy	Benjamin Stoddert	1798–1801

The Jefferson Administration

President	Thomas Jefferson	1801–1809
Vice President	Aaron Burr	1801–1805
	George Clinton	1805–1809
Secretary of State	James Madison	1801–1809
Secretary of Treasury	Samuel Dexter	1801
	Albert Gallatin	1801–1809
Secretary of War	Henry Dearborn	1801–1809
Attorney General	Levi Lincoln	1801–1805
	Robert Smith	1805
	John Breckinridge	1805–1806
	Caesar Rodney	1807–1809

Postmaster General	Joseph Habersham	1801
	Gideon Granger	1801–1809
Secretary of Navy	Robert Smith	1801–1809

The Madison Administration

President	James Madison	1809–1817
Vice President	George Clinton	1809–1813
	Elbridge Gerry	1813–1817
Secretary of State	Robert Smith	1809–1811
	James Monroe	1811–1817
Secretary of Treasury	Albert Gallatin	1809–1813
	George Campbell	1814
	Alexander Dallas	1814–1816
	William Crawford	1816–1817
Secretary of War	William Eustis	1809–1812
	John Armstrong	1813–1814
	James Monroe	1814–1815
	William Crawford	1815–1817
Attorney General	Caesar Rodney	1809–1811
	William Pinkney	1811–1814
	Richard Rush	1814–1817
Postmaster General	Gideon Granger	1809–1814
	Return Meigs	1814–1817
Secretary of Navy	Paul Hamilton	1809–1813
	William Jones	1813–1814
	Benjamin Crowninshield	1814–1817

The Monroe Administration

President	James Monroe	1817–1825
Vice President	Daniel Tompkins	1817–1825
Secretary of State	John Quincy Adams	1817–1825
Secretary of Treasury	William Crawford	1817–1825
Secretary of War	George Graham	1817
	John C. Calhoun	1817–1825
Attorney General	Richard Rush	1817
	William Wirt	1817–1825
Postmaster General	Return Meigs	1817–1823
	John McLean	1823–1825
Secretary of Navy	Benjamin Crowninshield	1817–1818
	Smith Thompson	1818–1823
	Samuel Southard	1823–1825

The John Quincy Adams Administration

President	John Quincy Adams	1825–1829
Vice President	John C. Calhoun	1825–1829

Presidents, Vice Presidents, and Cabinet Members *(continued)*

Secretary of State	Henry Clay	1825–1829
Secretary of Treasury	Richard Rush	1825–1829
Secretary of War	James Barbour	1825–1828
	Peter Porter	1828–1829
Attorney General	William Wirt	1825–1829
Postmaster General	John McLean	1825–1829
Secretary of Navy	Samuel Southard	1825–1829

The Jackson Administration

President	Andrew Jackson	1829–1837
Vice President	John C. Calhoun	1829–1833
	Martin Van Buren	1833–1837
Secretary of State	Martin Van Buren	1829–1831
	Edward Livingston	1831–1833
	Louis McLane	1833–1834
	John Forsyth	1834–1837
Secretary of Treasury	Samuel Ingham	1829–1831
	Louis McLane	1831–1833
	William Duane	1833
	Roger B. Taney	1833–1834
	Levi Woodbury	1834–1837
Secretary of War	John H. Eaton	1829–1831
	Lewis Cass	1831–1837
	Benjamin Butler	1837
Attorney General	John M. Berrien	1829–1831
	Roger B. Taney	1831–1833
	Benjamin Butler	1833–1837
Postmaster General	William Barry	1829–1835
	Amos Kendall	1835–1837
Secretary of Navy	John Branch	1829–1831
	Levi Woodbury	1831–1834
	Mahlon Dickerson	1834–1837

The Van Buren Administration

President	Martin Van Buren	1837–1841
Vice President	Richard M. Johnson	1837–1841
Secretary of State	John Forsyth	1837–1841
Secretary of Treasury	Levi Woodbury	1837–1841
Secretary of War	Joel Poinsett	1837–1841
Attorney General	Benjamin Butler	1837–1838
	Felix Grundy	1838–1840
	Henry D. Gilpin	1840–1841
Postmaster General	Amos Kendall	1837–1840
	John M. Niles	1840–1841
Secretary of Navy	Mahlon Dickerson	1837–1838
	James Paulding	1838–1841

The William Harrison Administration

President	William H. Harrison	1841
Vice President	John Tyler	1841
Secretary of State	Daniel Webster	1841
Secretary of Treasury	Thomas Ewing	1841
Secretary of War	John Bell	1841
Attorney General	John J. Crittenden	1841
Postmaster General	Francis Granger	1841
Secretary of Navy	George Badger	1841

The Tyler Administration

President	John Tyler	1841–1845
Vice President	None	
Secretary of State	Daniel Webster	1841–1843
	Hugh S. Legaré	1843
	Abel P. Upshur	1843–1844
	John C. Calhoun	1844–1845
Secretary of Treasury	Thomas Ewing	1841
	Walter Forward	1841–1843
	John C. Spencer	1843–1844
	George Bibb	1844–1845
Secretary of War	John Bell	1841
	John C. Spencer	1841–1843
	James M. Porter	1843–1844
	William Wilkins	1844–1845
Attorney General	John J. Crittenden	1841
	Hugh S. Legaré	1841–1843
	John Nelson	1843–1845
Postmaster General	Francis Granger	1841
	Charles Wickliffe	1841
Secretary of Navy	George Badger	1841
	Abel P. Upshur	1841
	David Henshaw	1843–1844
	Thomas Gilmer	1844
	John Y. Mason	1844–1845

The Polk Administration

President	James K. Polk	1845–1849
Vice President	George M. Dallas	1845–1849
Secretary of State	James Buchanan	1845–1849
Secretary of Treasury	Robert J. Walker	1845–1849
Secretary of War	William L. Marcy	1845–1849
Attorney General	John Y. Mason	1845–1846
	Nathan Clifford	1846–1848
	Isaac Toucey	1848–1849

Presidents, Vice Presidents, and Cabinet Members *(continued)*

Postmaster General	Cave Johnson	1845–1849
Secretary of Navy	George Bancroft	1845–1846
	John Y. Mason	1846–1849

The Taylor Administration

President	Zachary Taylor	1849–1850
Vice President	Millard Fillmore	1849–1850
Secretary of State	John M. Clayton	1849–1850
Secretary of Treasury	William Meredith	1849–1850
Secretary of War	George Crawford	1849–1850
Attorney General	Reverdy Johnson	1849–1850
Postmaster General	Jacob Collamer	1849–1850
Secretary of Navy	William Preston	1849–1850
Secretary of Interior	Thomas Ewing	1849–1850

The Fillmore Administration

President	Millard Fillmore	1850–1853
Vice President	None	
Secretary of State	Daniel Webster	1850–1852
	Edward Everett	1852–1853
Secretary of Treasury	Thomas Corwin	1850–1853
Secretary of War	Charles Conrad	1850–1853
Attorney General	John J. Crittenden	1850–1853
Postmaster General	Nathan Hall	1850–1852
	Sam D. Hubbard	1852–1853
Secretary of Navy	William A. Graham	1850–1852
	John P. Kennedy	1852–1853
Secretary of Interior	Thomas McKennan	1850
	Alexander Stuart	1850–1853

The Pierce Administration

President	Franklin Pierce	1853–1857
Vice President	William R. King	1853–1857
Secretary of State	William L. Marcy	1853–1857
Secretary of Treasury	James Guthrie	1853–1857
Secretary of War	Jefferson Davis	1853–1857
Attorney General	Caleb Cushing	1853–1857
Postmaster General	James Campbell	1853–1857
Secretary of Navy	James C. Dobbin	1853–1857
Secretary of Interior	Robert McClelland	1853–1857

The Buchanan Administration

President	James Buchanan	1857–1861
Vice President	John C. Breckinridge	1857–1861
Secretary of State	Lewis Cass	1857–1860
	Jeremiah S. Black	1860–1861
Secretary of Treasury	Howell Cobb	1857–1860
	Philip Thomas	1860–1861
	John A. Dix	1861
Secretary of War	John B. Floyd	1857–1861
	Joseph Holt	1861
Attorney General	Jeremiah S. Black	1857–1860
	Edwin M. Stanton	1860–1861
Postmaster General	Aaron V. Brown	1857–1859
	Joseph Holt	1859–1861
	Horatio King	1861
Secretary of Navy	Isaac Toucey	1857–1861
Secretary of Interior	Jacob Thompson	1857–1861

The Lincoln Administration

President	Abraham Lincoln	1861–1865
Vice President	Hannibal Hamlin	1861–1865
	Andrew Johnson	1865
Secretary of State	William H. Seward	1861–1865
Secretary of Treasury	Salmon P. Chase	1861–1864
	William P. Fessenden	1864–1865
	Hugh McCulloch	1865
Secretary of War	Simon Cameron	1861–1862
	Edwin M. Stanton	1862–1865
Attorney General	Edward Bates	1861–1864
	James Speed	1864–1865
Postmaster General	Horatio King	1861
	Montgomery Blair	1861–1864
	William Dennison	1864–1865
Secretary of Navy	Gideon Welles	1861–1865
Secretary of Interior	Caleb B. Smith	1861–1863
	John P. Usher	1863–1865

The Andrew Johnson Administration

President	Andrew Johnson	1865–1869
Vice President	None	
Secretary of State	William H. Seward	1865–1869
Secretary of Treasury	Hugh McCulloch	1865–1869
Secretary of War	Edwin M. Stanton	1865–1867
	Ulysses S. Grant	1867–1868

Presidents, Vice Presidents, and Cabinet Members *(continued)*

	Lorenzo Thomas	1868
	John M. Schofield	1868–1869
Attorney General	James Speed	1865–1866
	Henry Stanbery	1866–1868
	William M. Evarts	1868–1869
Postmaster General	William Dennison	1865–1866
	Alexander Randall	1866–1869
Secretary of Navy	Gideon Welles	1865–1869
Secretary of Interior	John P. Usher	1865
	James Harlan	1865–1866
	Orville H. Browning	1866–1869

The Grant Administration

President	Ulysses S. Grant	1869–1877
Vice President	Schuyler Colfax	1869–1873
	Henry Wilson	1873–1877
Secretary of State	Elihu B. Washburne	1869
	Hamilton Fish	1869–1877
Secretary of Treasury	George S. Boutwell	1869–1873
	William Richardson	1873–1874
	Benjamin Bristow	1874–1876
	Lot M. Morrill	1876–1877
Secretary of War	John A. Rawlins	1869
	William T. Sherman	1869
	William W. Belknap	1869–1876
	Alphonso Taft	1876
	James D. Cameron	1876–1877
Attorney General	Ebenezer Hoar	1869–1870
	Amos T. Ackerman	1870–1871
	G. H. Williams	1871–1875
	Edwards Pierrepont	1875–1876
	Alphonso Taft	1876–1877
Postmaster General	John A. J. Creswell	1869–1874
	James W. Marshall	1874
	Marshall Jewell	1874–1876
	James N. Tyner	1876–1877
Secretary of Navy	Adolph E. Borie	1869
	George M. Robeson	1869–1877
Secretary of Interior	Jacob D. Cox	1869–1870
	Columbus Delano	1870–1875
	Zachariah Chandler	1875–1877

The Hayes Administration

President	Rutherford B. Hayes	1877–1881
Vice President	William A. Wheeler	1877–1881
Secretary of State	William B. Evarts	1877–1881

Secretary of Treasury	John Sherman	1877–1881
Secretary of War	George W. McCrary	1877–1879
	Alex Ramsey	1879–1881
Attorney General	Charles Devens	1877–1881
Postmaster General	David M. Key	1877–1880
	Horace Maynard	1880–1881
Secretary of Navy	Richard W. Thompson	1877–1880
	Nathan Goff, Jr.	1881
Secretary of Interior	Carl Schurz	1877–1881

The Garfield Administration

President	James A. Garfield	1881
Vice President	Chester A. Arthur	1881
Secretary of State	James G. Blaine	1881
Secretary of Treasury	William Windom	1881
Secretary of War	Robert T. Lincoln	1881
Attorney General	Wayne MacVeagh	1881
Postmaster General	Thomas L. James	1881
Secretary of Navy	William H. Hunt	1881
Secretary of Interior	Samuel J. Kirkwood	1881

The Arthur Administration

President	Chester A. Arthur	1881–1885
Vice President	None	
Secretary of State	F. T. Frelinghuysen	1881–1885
Secretary of Treasury	Charles J. Folger	1881–1884
	Walter Q. Gresham	1884
	Hugh McCulloch	1884–1885
Secretary of War	Robert T. Lincoln	1881–1885
Attorney General	Benjamin H. Brewster	1881–1885
Postmaster General	Timothy O. Howe	1881–1883
	Walter Q. Gresham	1883–1884
	Frank Hatton	1884–1885
Secretary of Navy	William H. Hunt	1881–1882
	William E. Chandler	1882–1885
Secretary of Interior	Samuel J. Kirkwood	1881–1882
	Henry M. Teller	1882–1885

The Cleveland Administration

President	Grover Cleveland	1885–1889
Vice President	Thomas A. Hendricks	1885–1889
Secretary of State	Thomas F. Bayard	1885–1889

Presidents, Vice Presidents, and Cabinet Members *(continued)*

Secretary of Treasury	Daniel Manning	1885–1887
	Charles S. Fairchild	1887–1889
Secretary of War	William C. Endicott	1885–1889
Attorney General	Augustus H. Garland	1885–1889
Postmaster General	William F. Vilas	1885–1888
	Don M. Dickinson	1888–1889
Secretary of Navy	William C. Whitney	1885–1889
Secretary of Interior	Lucius G. C. Lamar	1885–1888
	William F. Vilas	1888–1889
Secretary of Agriculture	Norman J. Colman	1889

The Benjamin Harrison Administration

President	Benjamin Harrison	1889–1893
Vice President	Levi P. Morton	1889–1893
Secretary of State	James G. Blaine	1889–1892
	John W. Foster	1892–1893
Secretary of Treasury	William Windom	1889–1891
	Charles Foster	1891–1893
Secretary of War	Redfield Proctor	1889–1891
	Stephen B. Elkins	1891–1893
Attorney General	William H. H. Miller	1889–1891
Postmaster General	John Wanamaker	1889–1893
Secretary of Navy	Benjamin F. Tracy	1889–1893
Secretary of Interior	John W. Noble	1889–1893
Secretary of Agriculture	Jeremiah M. Rusk	1889–1893

The Cleveland Administration

President	Grover Cleveland	1893–1897
Vice President	Adlai E. Stevenson	1893–1897
Secretary of State	Walter Q. Gresham	1893–1895
	Richard Olney	1895–1897
Secretary of Treasury	John G. Carlisle	1893–1897
Secretary of War	Daniel S. Lamont	1893–1897
Attorney General	Richard Olney	1893–1895
	James Harmon	1895–1897
Postmaster General	Wilson S. Bissell	1893–1895
	William L. Wilson	1895–1897
Secretary of Navy	Hilary A. Herbert	1893–1897
Secretary of Interior	Hoke Smith	1893–1896
	David R. Francis	1896–1897
Secretary of Agriculture	Julius S. Morton	1893–1897

The McKinley Administration

President	William McKinley	1897–1901
Vice President	Garret A. Hobart	1897–1901
	Theodore Roosevelt	1901
Secretary of State	John Sherman	1897–1898
	William R. Day	1898
	John Hay	1898–1901
Secretary of Treasury	Lyman J. Gage	1897–1901
Secretary of War	Russell A. Alger	1897–1899
	Elihu Root	1899–1901
Attorney General	Joseph McKenna	1897–1898
	John W. Griggs	1898–1901
	Philander C. Knox	1901
Postmaster General	James A. Gary	1897–1898
	Charles E. Smith	1898–1901
Secretary of Navy	John D. Long	1897–1901
Secretary of Interior	Cornelius N. Bliss	1897–1899
	Ethan A. Hitchcock	1899–1901
Secretary of Agriculture	James Wilson	1897–1901

The Theodore Roosevelt Administration

President	Theodore Roosevelt	1901–1909
Vice President	Charles Fairbanks	1905–1909
Secretary of State	John Hay	1901–1905
	Elihu Root	1905–1909
	Robert Bacon	1909
Secretary of Treasury	Lyman J. Gage	1901–1902
	Leslie M. Shaw	1902–1907
	George B. Cortelyou	1907–1909
Secretary of War	Elihu Root	1901–1904
	William H. Taft	1904–1908
	Luke E. Wright	1908–1909
Attorney General	Philander C. Knox	1901–1904
	William H. Moody	1904–1906
	Charles J. Bonaparte	1906–1909
Postmaster General	Charles E. Smith	1901–1902
	Henry C. Payne	1902–1904
	Robert J. Wynne	1904–1905
	George B. Cortelyou	1905–1907
	George von L. Meyer	1907–1909
Secretary of Navy	John D. Long	1901–1902
	William H. Moody	1902–1904
	Paul Morton	1904–1905
	Charles J. Bonaparte	1905–1906
	Victor H. Metcalf	1906–1908
	Truman H. Newberry	1908–1909

Presidents, Vice Presidents, and Cabinet Members *(continued)*

Secretary of Interior	Ethan A. Hitchcock	1901–1907
	James R. Garfield	1907–1909
Secretary of Agriculture	James Wilson	1901–1909
Secretary of Labor and Commerce	George B. Cortelyou	1903–1904
	Victor H. Metcalf	1904–1906
	Oscar S. Straus	1906–1909
	Charles Nagel	1909

The Taft Administration

President	William H. Taft	1909–1913
Vice President	James S. Sherman	1909–1913
Secretary of State	Philander C. Knox	1909–1913
Secretary of Treasury	Franklin MacVeagh	1909–1913
Secretary of War	Jacob M. Dickinson	1909–1911
	Henry L. Stimson	1911–1913
Attorney General	George W. Wickersham	1909–1913
Postmaster General	Frank H. Hitchcock	1909–1913
Secretary of Navy	George von L. Meyer	1909–1913
Secretary of Interior	Richard A. Ballinger	1909–1911
	Walter L. Fisher	1911–1913
Secretary of Agriculture	James Wilson	1909–1913
Secretary of Labor and Commerce	Charles Nagel	1909–1913

The Wilson Administration

President	Woodrow Wilson	1913–1921
Vice President	Thomas R. Marshall	1913–1921
Secretary of State	William J. Bryan	1913–1915
	Robert Lansing	1915–1920
	Bainbridge Colby	1920–1921
Secretary of Treasury	William G. McAdoo	1913–1918
	Carter Glass	1918–1920
	David F. Houston	1920–1921
Secretary of War	Lindley M. Garrison	1913–1916
	Newton D. Baker	1916–1921
Attorney General	James C. McReynolds	1913–1914
	Thomas W. Gregory	1914–1919
	A. Mitchell Palmer	1919–1921
Postmaster General	Albert S. Burleson	1913–1921
Secretary of Navy	Josephus Daniels	1913–1921
Secretary of Interior	Franklin K. Lane	1913–1920
	John B. Payne	1920–1921

Secretary of Agriculture	David F. Houston	1913–1920
	Edwin T. Meredith	1920–1921
Secretary of Commerce	William C. Redfield	1913–1919
	Joshua W. Alexander	1919–1921
Secretary of Labor	William B. Wilson	1913–1921

The Harding Administration

President	Warren G. Harding	1921–1923
Vice President	Calvin Coolidge	1921–1923
Secretary of State	Charles E. Hughes	1921–1923
Secretary of Treasury	Andrew Mellon	1921–1923
Secretary of War	John W. Weeks	1921–1923
Attorney General	Harry M. Daugherty	1921–1923
Postmaster General	Will H. Hays	1921–1922
	Hubert Work	1922–1923
	Harry S. New	1923
Secretary of Navy	Edwin Denby	1921–1923
Secretary of Interior	Albert B. Fall	1921–1923
	Hubert Work	1923
Secretary of Agriculture	Henry C. Wallace	1921–1923
Secretary of Commerce	Herbert C. Hoover	1921–1923
Secretary of Labor	James J. Davis	1921–1923

The Coolidge Administration

President	Calvin Coolidge	1923–1929
Vice President	Charles G. Dawes	1925–1929
Secretary of State	Charles E. Hughes	1923–1925
	Frank B. Kellogg	1925–1929
Secretary of Treasury	Andrew Mellon	1923–1929
Secretary of War	John W. Weeks	1923–1925
	Dwight F. Davis	1925–1929
Attorney General	Henry M. Daugherty	1923–1924
	Harlan F. Stone	1924–1925
	John G. Sargent	1925–1929
Postmaster General	Harry S. New	1923–1929
Secretary of Navy	Edwin Derby	1923–1924
	Curtis D. Wilbur	1924–1929
Secretary of Interior	Hubert Work	1923–1928
	Roy O. West	1928–1929
Secretary of Agriculture	Henry C. Wallace	1923–1924
	Howard M. Gore	1924–1925
	William M. Jardine	1925–1929

Presidents, Vice Presidents, and Cabinet Members (continued)

Secretary of Commerce	Herbert C. Hoover	1923–1928
	William F. Whiting	1928–1929
Secretary of Labor	James J. Davis	1923–1929

The Hoover Administration

President	Herbert C. Hoover	1929–1933
Vice President	Charles Curtis	1929–1933
Secretary of State	Henry L. Stimson	1929–1933
Secretary of Treasury	Andrew Mellon	1929–1932
	Ogden L. Mills	1932–1933
Secretary of War	James W. Good	1929
	Patrick J. Hurley	1929–1933
Attorney General	William D. Mitchell	1929–1933
Postmaster General	Walter F. Brown	1929–1933
Secretary of Navy	Charles F. Adams	1929–1933
Secretary of Interior	Ray L. Wilbur	1929–1933
Secretary of Agriculture	Arthur M. Hyde	1929–1933
Secretary of Commerce	Robert P. Lamont	1929–1932
	Roy D. Chapin	1932–1933
Secretary of Labor	James J. Davis	1929–1930
	William N. Doak	1930–1933

The Franklin D. Roosevelt Administration

President	Franklin D. Roosevelt	1933–1945
Vice President	John Nance Garner	1933–1941
	Henry A. Wallace	1941–1945
	Harry S Truman	1945
Secretary of State	Cordell Hull	1933–1944
	Edward R. Stettinius, Jr.	1944–1945
Secretary of Treasury	William H. Woodin	1933–1934
	Henry Morgenthau, Jr.	1934–1945
Secretary of War	George H. Dern	1933–1936
	Henry A. Woodring	1936–1940
	Henry L. Stimson	1940–1945
Attorney General	Homer S. Cummings	1933–1939
	Frank Murphy	1939–1940
	Robert H. Jackson	1940–1941
	Francis Biddle	1941–1945
Postmaster General	James A. Farley	1933–1940
	Frank C. Walker	1940–1945
Secretary of Navy	Claude A. Swanson	1933–1940
	Charles Edison	1940
	Frank Knox	1940–1944
	James V. Forrestal	1944–1945

Secretary of Interior	Harold L. Ickes	1933–1945
Secretary of Agriculture	Henry A. Wallace	1933–1940
	Claude R. Wickard	1940–1945
Secretary of Commerce	Daniel C. Roper	1933–1939
	Harry L. Hopkins	1939–1940
	Jesse Jones	1940–1945
	Henry A. Wallace	1945
Secretary of Labor	Frances Perkins	1933–1945

The Truman Administration

President	Harry S Truman	1945–1953
Vice President	Alben W. Barkley	1949–1953
Secretary of State	Edward R. Stettinius, Jr.	1945
	James F. Byrnes	1945–1947
	George C. Marshall	1947–1949
	Dean G. Acheson	1949–1953
Secretary of Treasury	Fred M. Vinson	1945–1946
	John W. Snyder	1946–1953
Secretary of War	Robert P. Patterson	1945–1947
	Kenneth C. Royall	1947
Attorney General	Tom C. Clark	1945–1949
	J. Howard McGrath	1949–1952
	James P. McGranery	1952–1953
Postmaster General	Frank C. Walker	1945
	Robert E. Hannegan	1945–1947
	Jesse M. Donaldson	1947–1953
Secretary of Navy	James V. Forrestal	1945–1947
Secretary of Interior	Harold L. Ickes	1945–1946
	Julius A. Krug	1946–1949
	Oscar L. Chapman	1949–1953
Secretary of Agriculture	Clinton P. Anderson	1945–1948
	Charles F. Brannan	1948–1953
Secretary of Commerce	Henry A. Wallace	1945–1946
	W. Averell Harriman	1946–1948
	Charles W. Sawyer	1948–1953
Secretary of Labor	Lewis B. Schwellenbach	1945–1948
	Maurice J. Tobin	1948–1953
Secretary of Defense	James V. Forrestal	1947–1949
	Louis A. Johnson	1949–1950
	George C. Marshall	1950–1951
	Robert A. Lovett	1951–1953

The Eisenhower Administration

President	Dwight D. Eisenhower	1953–1961
Vice President	Richard M. Nixon	1953–1961

Presidents, Vice Presidents, and Cabinet Members *(continued)*

Secretary of State	John Foster Dulles	1953–1959
	Christian A. Herter	1959–1961
Secretary of Treasury	George M. Humphrey	1953–1957
	Robert B. Anderson	1957–1961
Attorney General	Herbert Brownell, Jr.	1953–1958
	William P. Rogers	1958–1961
Postmaster General	Arthur E. Summerfield	1953–1961
Secretary of Interior	Douglas McKay	1953–1956
	Fred A. Seaton	1956–1961
Secretary of Agriculture	Ezra T. Benson	1953–1961
Secretary of Commerce	Sinclair Weeks	1953–1958
	Lewis L. Strauss	1958–1959
	Frederick H. Mueller	1959–1961
Secretary of Labor	Martin P. Durkin	1953
	James P. Mitchell	1953–1961
Secretary of Defense	Charles E. Wilson	1953–1957
	Neil H. McElroy	1957–1959
	Thomas S. Gates, Jr.	1959–1961
Secretary of Health, Education, and Welfare	Oveta Culp Hobby	1953–1955
	Marion B. Folsom	1955–1958
	Arthur S. Flemming	1958–1961

The Kennedy Administration

President	John F. Kennedy	1961–1963
Vice President	Lyndon B. Johnson	1961–1963
Secretary of State	Dean Rusk	1961–1963
Secretary of Treasury	C. Douglas Dillon	1961–1963
Attorney General	Robert F. Kennedy	1961–1963
Postmaster General	J. Edward Day	1961–1963
	John A. Gronouski	1963
Secretary of Interior	Stewart L. Udall	1961–1963
Secretary of Agriculture	Orville L. Freeman	1961–1963
Secretary of Commerce	Luther H. Hodges	1961–1963
Secretary of Labor	Arthur J. Goldberg	1961–1962
	W. Willard Wirtz	1962–1963
Secretary of Defense	Robert S. McNamara	1961–1963
Secretary of Health, Education, and Welfare	Abraham A. Ribicoff	1961–1962
	Anthony J. Celebrezze	1962–1963

The Lyndon Johnson Administration

President	Lyndon B. Johnson	1963–1969
Vice President	Hubert H. Humphrey	1965–1969

Secretary of State	Dean Rusk	1963–1969
Secretary of Treasury	C. Douglas Dillon	1963–1965
	Henry H. Fowler	1965–1969
Attorney General	Robert F. Kennedy	1963–1964
	Nicholas Katzenbach	1965–1966
	Ramsey Clark	1967–1969
Postmaster General	John A. Gronouski	1963–1965
	Lawrence F. O'Brien	1965–1968
	Marvin Watson	1968–1969
Secretary of Interior	Stewart L. Udall	1963–1969
Secretary of Agriculture	Orville L. Freeman	1963–1969
Secretary of Commerce	Luther H. Hodges	1963–1964
	John T. Connor	1964–1967
	Alexander B. Trowbridge	1967–1968
	Cyrus R. Smith	1968–1969
Secretary of Labor	W. Willard Wirtz	1963–1969
Secretary of Defense	Robert S. McNamara	1963–1968
	Clark Clifford	1968–1969
Secretary of Health, Education, and Welfare	Anthony J. Celebrezze	1963–1965
	John W. Gardner	1965–1968
	Wilbur J. Cohen	1968–1969
Secretary of Housing and Urban Development	Robert C. Weaver	1966–1969
	Robert C. Wood	1969
Secretary of Transportation	Alan S. Boyd	1967–1969

The Nixon Administration

President	Richard M. Nixon	1969–1974
Vice President	Spiro T. Agnew	1969–1973
	Gerald R. Ford	1973–1974
Secretary of State	William P. Rogers	1969–1973
	Henry A. Kissinger	1973–1974
Secretary of Treasury	David M. Kennedy	1969–1970
	John B. Connally	1971–1972
	George P. Shultz	1972–1974
	William E. Simon	1974
Attorney General	John N. Mitchell	1969–1972
	Richard G. Kleindienst	1972–1973
	Elliot L. Richardson	1973
	William B. Saxbe	1973–1974
Postmaster General	Winton M. Blount	1969–1971
Secretary of Interior	Walter J. Hickel	1969–1970
	Rogers Morton	1971–1974
Secretary of Agriculture	Clifford M. Hardin	1969–1971
	Earl L. Butz	1971–1974

Presidents, Vice Presidents, and Cabinet Members *(continued)*

Secretary of Commerce	Maurice H. Stans	1969–1972
	Peter G. Peterson	1972–1973
	Frederick B. Dent	1973–1974
Secretary of Labor	George P. Shultz	1969–1970
	James D. Hodgson	1970–1973
	Peter J. Brennan	1973–1974
Secretary of Defense	Melvin R. Laird	1969–1973
	Elliot L. Richardson	1973
	James R. Schlesinger	1973–1974
Secretary of Health, Education, and Welfare	Robert H. Finch	1969–1970
	Elliot L. Richardson	1970–1973
	Casper W. Weinberger	1973–1974
Secretary of Housing and Urban Development	George Romney	1969–1973
	James T. Lynn	1973–1974
Secretary of Transportation	John A. Volpe	1969–1973
	Claude S. Brinegar	1973–1974

The Ford Administration

President	Gerald R. Ford	1974–1977
Vice President	Nelson A. Rockefeller	1974–1977
Secretary of State	Henry A. Kissinger	1974–1977
Secretary of Treasury	William E. Simon	1974–1977
Attorney General	William Saxbe	1974–1975
	Edward Levi	1975–1977
Secretary of Interior	Rogers Morton	1974–1975
	Stanley K. Hathaway	1975
	Thomas Kleppe	1975–1977
Secretary of Agriculture	Earl L. Butz	1974–1976
	John A. Knebel	1976–1977
Secretary of Commerce	Frederick B. Dent	1974–1975
	Rogers Morton	1975–1976
	Elliot L. Richardson	1976–1977
Secretary of Labor	Peter J. Brennan	1974–1975
	John T. Dunlop	1975–1976
	W. J. Usery	1976–1977
Secretary of Defense	James R. Schlesinger	1974–1975
	Donald Rumsfeld	1975–1977
Secretary of Health, Education, and Welfare	Casper Weinberger	1974–1975
	Forrest D. Mathews	1975–1977
Secretary of Housing and Urban Development	James T. Lynn	1974–1975
	Carla A. Hills	1975–1977
Secretary of Transportation	Claude Brinegar	1974–1975
	William T. Coleman	1975–1977

The Carter Administration

President	Jimmy Carter	1977–1981
Vice President	Walter F. Mondale	1977–1981
Secretary of State	Cyrus R. Vance	1977–1980
	Edmund Muskie	1980–1981
Secretary of Treasury	W. Michael Blumenthal	1977–1979
	G. William Miller	1979–1981
Attorney General	Griffin Bell	1977–1979
	Benjamin R. Civiletti	1979–1981
Secretary of Interior	Cecil D. Andrus	1977–1981
Secretary of Agriculture	Robert Bergland	1977–1981
Secretary of Commerce	Juanita M. Kreps	1977–1979
	Philip M. Klutznick	1979–1981
Secretary of Labor	F. Ray Marshall	1977–1981
Secretary of Defense	Harold Brown	1977–1981
Secretary of Health, Education, and Welfare	Joseph A. Califano	1977–1979
	Patricia R. Harris	1979
Secretary of Health and Human Services	Patricia R. Harris	1979–1981
Secretary of Education	Shirley M. Hufstedler	1979–1981
Secretary of Housing and Urban Development	Patricia R. Harris	1977–1979
	Moon Landrieu	1979–1981
Secretary of Transportation	Brock Adams	1977–1979
	Neil E. Goldschmidt	1979–1981
Secretary of Energy	James R. Schlesinger	1977–1979
	Charles W. Duncan	1979–1981

The Reagan Administration

President	Ronald Reagan	1981–1989
Vice President	George Bush	1981–1989
Secretary of State	Alexander M. Haig	1981–1982
	George P. Shultz	1982–1989
Secretary of Treasury	Donald Regan	1981–1985
	James A. Baker III	1985–1988
	Nicholas F. Brady	1988–1989
Attorney General	William F. Smith	1981–1985
	Edwin A. Meese III	1985–1988
	Richard L. Thornburgh	1988–1989
Secretary of Interior	James G. Watt	1981–1983
	William P. Clark, Jr.	1983–1985
	Donald P. Hodel	1985–1989

Presidents, Vice Presidents, and Cabinet Members *(continued)*

Secretary of Agriculture	John Block	1981–1986
	Richard E. Lyng	1986–1989
Secretary of Commerce	Malcolm Baldridge	1981–1987
	C. William Verity, Jr.	1987–1989
Secretary of Labor	Raymond J. Donovan	1981–1985
	William E. Brock	1985–1987
	Ann Dore McLaughlin	1987–1989
Secretary of Defense	Casper Weinberger	1981–1987
	Frank C. Carlucci	1987–1989
Secretary of Health and Human Services	Richard S. Schweiker	1981–1983
	Margaret Heckler	1983–1985
	Otis R. Bowen	1985–1989
Secretary of Education	Terrel H. Bell	1981–1984
	William J. Bennett	1985–1988
	Lauro F. Cavazos	1988–1989
Secretary of Housing and Urban Development	Samuel R. Pierce, Jr.	1981–1989
Secretary of Transportation	Drew Lewis	1981–1982
	Elizabeth Hanford Dole	1983–1987
	James H. Burnley IV	1987–1989
Secretary of Energy	James B. Edwards	1981–1982
	Donald P. Hodel	1982–1985
	John S. Herrington	1985–1989

The George Bush Administration

President	George Bush	1989–1993
Vice President	Dan Quayle	1989–1993
Secretary of State	James A. Baker III	1989–1992
	Lawrence Eagleburger	1992–1993
Secretary of Treasury	Nicholas F. Brady	1989–1993
Attorney General	Richard L. Thornburgh	1989–1992
	William P. Barr	1992–1993
Secretary of Interior	Manuel Lujan, Jr.	1989–1993
Secretary of Agriculture	Clayton K. Yeutter	1989–1991
	Edward Madigan	1991–1993
Secretary of Commerce	Robert A. Mosbacher	1989–1992
	Barbara Hackman Franklin	1992–1993
Secretary of Labor	Elizabeth Hanford Dole	1989–1991
	Lynn Martin	1991–1993
Secretary of Defense	Richard B. Cheney	1989–1993
Secretary of Health and Human Services	Louis W. Sullivan	1989–1993

Secretary of Education	Lauro F. Cavazos	1989–1991
	Lamar Alexander	1991–1993
Secretary of Housing and Urban Development	Jack F. Kemp	1989–1993
Secretary of Transportation	Samuel K. Skinner	1989–1992
	Andrew H. Card	1992–1993
Secretary of Energy	James D. Watkins	1989–1993
Secretary of Veterans Affairs	Edward J. Derwinski	1989–1993

The Clinton Administration

President	Bill Clinton	1993–2000
Vice President	Albert Gore, Jr.	1993–2000
Secretary of State	Warren M. Christopher	1993–1997
	Madeleine K. Albright	1997–2000
Secretary of Treasury	Lloyd Bentsen	1993–1995
	Robert E. Rubin	1995–2000
Attorney General	Janet Reno	1993–2000
Secretary of the Interior	Bruce Babbitt	1993–2000
Secretary of Agriculture	Mike Espy	1993–1995
	Daniel R. Glickman	1995–2000
Secretary of Commerce	Ronald H. Brown	1993–1996
	Mickey Kantor	1996–1997
	William Daley	1997–2000
Secretary of Labor	Robert M. Reich	1993–1997
	Alexis M. Herman	1997–2000
Secretary of Defense	Les Aspin	1993–1994
	William J. Perry	1994–1997
	William S. Cohen	1997–2000
Secretary of Health and Human Services	Donna E. Shalala	1993–2000
Secretary of Education	Richard W. Riley	1993–2000
Secretary of Housing and Urban Development	Henry G. Cisneros	1993–1996
	Andrew Cuomo	1997–2000
Secretary of Transportation	Federico F. Peña	1993–1997
	Rodney E. Slater	1997–2000
Secretary of Energy	Hazel O'Leary	1993–1997
	Federico F. Peña	1997–1998
Secretary of Veterans Affairs	Jesse Brown	1993–2000

Presidents, Vice Presidents, and Cabinet Members *(continued)*

The George W. Bush Administration

President	George W. Bush	2001–
Vice President	Richard Cheney	2001–
Secretary of State	Colin Powell	2001–2005
Secretary of Treasury	Paul O'Neill	2001–2002
	John Snow	2003–
Attorney General	John Ashcroft	2001–2005
Secretary of Interior	Gale Norton	2001–
Secretary of Agriculture	Ann Veneman	2001–2005
Secretary of Commerce	Donald Evans	2001–2005
Secretary of Labor	Elaine Chao	2001–
Secretary of Defense	Donald Rumsfeld	2001–
Secretary of Health and Human Services	Tommy Thompson	2001–
Secretary of Education	Rodney Paige	2001–2005
Secretary of Housing and Urban Development	Melvin Martinez	2001–2003
	Alphonso Jackson	2003–
Secretary of Transportation	Norman Mineta	2001–
Secretary of Energy	Spencer Abraham	2001–2005
Secretary of Veterans Affairs	Anthony Principi	2001–
Secretary of Homeland Security	Tom Ridge	2001–

Party Strength in Congress, 1789–2004

Year	President and vice president	Party of president	Congress	House Majority party	House Minority party	Senate Majority party	Senate Minority party
1789–1797	George Washington John Adams	None	1st 2d 3d 4th	38 Admin 37 Fed 57 Dem-Rep 54 Fed	26 Opp 33 Dem-Rep 48 Fed 52 Dem-Rep	17 Admin 16 Fed 17 Fed 19 Fed	9 Opp 13 Dem-Rep 13 Dem-Rep 13 Dem-Rep
1797–1801	John Adams Thomas Jefferson	Federalist	5th 6th	58 Fed 64 Fed	48 Dem-Rep 42 Dem-Rep	20 Fed 19 Fed	12 Dem-Rep 13 Dem-Rep
1801–1809	Thomas Jefferson Aaron Burr (to 1805) George Clinton (to 1809)	Dem-Rep	7th 8th 9th 10th	69 Dem-Rep 102 Dem-Rep 116 Dem-Rep 118 Dem-Rep	36 Fed 39 Fed 25 Fed 24 Fed	18 Dem-Rep 25 Dem-Rep 27 Dem-Rep 28 Dem-Rep	13 Fed 9 Fed 7 Fed 6 Fed
1809–1817	James Madison George Clinton (to 1813) Elbridge Gerry (to 1817)	Dem-Rep	11th 12th 13th 14th	94 Dem-Rep 108 Dem-Rep 112 Dem-Rep 117 Dem-Rep	48 Fed 36 Fed 68 Fed 65 Fed	28 Dem-Rep 30 Dem-Rep 27 Dem-Rep 25 Dem-Rep	6 Fed 6 Fed 9 Fed 11 Fed
1817–1825	James Monroe Daniel D. Tompkins	Dem-Rep	15th 16th 17th 18th	141 Dem-Rep 156 Dem-Rep 158 Dem-Rep 187 Dem-Rep	42 Fed 27 Fed 25 Fed 26 Fed	34 Dem-Rep 35 Dem-Rep 44 Dem-Rep 44 Dem-Rep	10 Fed 7 Fed 4 Fed 4 Fed
1825–1829	John Quincy Adams John C. Calhoun	Nat-Rep	19th 20th	105 Admin 119 Jack	97 Jack 94 Admin	26 Admin 28 Jack	20 Jack 20 Admin
1829–1837	Andrew Jackson John C. Calhoun (to 1833) Martin Van Buren (to 1837)	Democratic	21st 22d 23d 24th	139 Dem 141 Dem 147 Dem 145 Dem	74 Nat Rep 58 Nat Rep 53 AntiMas 98 Whig	26 Dem 25 Dem 20 Dem 27 Dem	22 Nat Rep 21 Nat Rep 20 Nat Rep 25 Whig
1837–1841	Martin Van Buren Richard M. Johnson	Democratic	25th 26th	108 Dem 124 Dem	107 Whig 118 Whig	30 Dem 28 Dem	18 Whig 22 Whig
1841	William H. Harrison[*] John Tyler	Whig					
1841–1845	John Tyler (VP vacant)	Whig	27th 28th	133 Whig 142 Dem	102 Dem 79 Whig	28 Whig 28 Whig	22 Dem 25 Dem
1845–1849	James K. Polk George M. Dallas	Democratic	29th 30th	143 Dem 115 Whig	77 Whig 108 Dem	31 Dem 36 Dem	25 Whig 21 Whig

NOTES: Only members of two major parties in Congress are shown; omitted are independents, members of minor parties, and vacancies.

Party balance as of beginning of Congress.

Congresses in which one or both houses are controlled by party other than that of the president are shown in color.

During administration of George Washington and (in part) John Quincy Adams, Congress was not organized by formal parties; the split shown is between supporters and opponents of administration.

ABBREVIATIONS: **Admin** = Administration supporters; **AntiMas** = Anti-Masonic; **Dem** = Democratic; **Dem-Rep** = Democratic-Republican; **Fed** = Federalist; **Jack** = Jacksonian Democrats; **Nat-Rep** = National Republican; **Opp** = Opponents of administration; **Rep** = Republican; **Union** = Unionist; **Whig** = Whig.

[*]Died in office.

Party Strength in Congress, 1789–2004 *(continued)*

Year	President and vice president	Party of president	Congress	House Majority party	House Minority party	Senate Majority party	Senate Minority party
1849–1850	**Zachary Taylor**[*] Millard Fillmore	Whig	31st	112 Dem	109 Whig	35 Dem	25 Whig
1850–1853	**Millard Fillmore** (VP vacant)	Whig	32d	140 Dem	88 Whig	35 Dem	24 Whig
1853–1857	**Franklin Pierce** William R. King	Democratic	33d 34th	159 Dem 108 Rep	71 Whig 83 Dem	38 Dem 40 Dem	22 Whig 15 Rep
1857–1861	**James Buchanan** John C. Breckinridge	Democratic	35th 36th	118 Dem 114 Rep	92 Rep 92 Dem	36 Dem 36 Dem	20 Rep 26 Rep
1861–1865	**Abraham Lincoln**[*] Hannibal Hamlin (to 1865) Andrew Johnson (1865)	Republican	37th 38th	105 Rep 102 Rep	43 Dem 75 Dem	31 Rep 36 Rep	10 Dem 9 Dem
1865–1869	**Andrew Johnson** (VP vacant)	Republican	39th 40th	149 Union 143 Rep	42 Dem 49 Dem	42 Union 42 Rep	10 Dem 11 Dem
1869–1877	**Ulysses S. Grant** Schuyler Colfax (to 1873) Henry Wilson (to 1877)	Republican	41st 42d 43d 44th	149 Rep 134 Rep 194 Rep 169 Dem	63 Dem 104 Dem 92 Dem 109 Rep	56 Rep 52 Rep 49 Rep 45 Rep	11 Dem 17 Dem 19 Dem 29 Dem
1877–1881	**Rutherford B. Hayes** William A. Wheeler	Republican	45th 46th	153 Dem 149 Dem	140 Rep 130 Rep	39 Rep 42 Dem	36 Dem 33 Rep
1881	**James A. Garfield**[*] Chester A. Arthur	Republican	47th	147 Rep	135 Dem	37 Rep	37 Dem
1881–1885	**Chester A. Arthur** (VP vacant)	Republican	48th	197 Dem	118 Rep	38 Rep	36 Dem
1885–1889	**Grover Cleveland** Thomas A. Hendricks	Democratic	49th 50th	183 Dem 169 Dem	140 Rep 152 Rep	43 Rep 39 Rep	34 Dem 37 Dem
1889–1893	**Benjamin Harrison** Levi P. Morton	Republican	51st 52d	166 Rep 235 Dem	159 Dem 88 Rep	39 Rep 47 Rep	37 Dem 39 Dem
1893–1897	**Grover Cleveland** Adlai E. Stevenson	Democratic	53d 54th	218 Dem 244 Rep	127 Rep 105 Dem	44 Dem 43 Rep	38 Rep 39 Dem
1897–1901	**William McKinley**[*] Garret A. Hobart (to 1901) Theodore Roosevelt (1901)	Republican	55th 56th	204 Rep 185 Rep	113 Dem 163 Dem	47 Rep 53 Rep	34 Dem 26 Dem
1901–1909	**Theodore Roosevelt** (VP vacant, 1901–1905) Charles W. Fairbanks (1905–1909)	Republican	57th 58th 59th 60th	197 Rep 208 Rep 250 Rep 222 Rep	151 Dem 178 Dem 136 Dem 164 Dem	55 Rep 57 Rep 57 Rep 61 Rep	31 Dem 33 Dem 33 Dem 31 Dem

[*]Died in office.

Party Strength in Congress, 1789–2004 *(continued)*

Year	President and vice president	Party of president	Congress	House Majority party	House Minority party	Senate Majority party	Senate Minority party
1909–1913	**William Howard Taft** James S. Sherman	Republican	61st 62d	219 Rep 228 Dem	172 Dem 161 Rep	61 Rep 51 Rep	32 Dem 41 Dem
1913–1921	**Woodrow Wilson** Thomas R. Marshall	Democratic	63d 64th 65th 66th	291 Dem 230 Dem 216 Dem 240 Rep	127 Rep 196 Rep 210 Rep 190 Dem	51 Dem 56 Dem 53 Dem 49 Rep	44 Rep 40 Rep 42 Rep 47 Dem
1921–1923	**Warren G. Harding**[*] Calvin Coolidge	Republican	67th	301 Rep	131 Dem	59 Rep	37 Dem
1923–1929	**Calvin Coolidge** (VP vacant, 1923–1925) Charles G. Dawes (1925–1929)	Republican	68th 69th 70th	225 Rep 247 Rep 237 Rep	205 Dem 183 Dem 195 Dem	51 Rep 56 Rep 49 Rep	43 Dem 39 Dem 46 Dem
1929–1933	**Herbert Hoover** Charles Curtis	Republican	71st 72d	267 Rep 220 Dem	167 Dem 214 Rep	56 Rep 48 Rep	39 Dem 47 Dem
1933–1945	**Franklin D. Roosevelt**[*] John N. Garner (1933–1941) Henry A. Wallace (1941–1945) Harry S Truman (1945)	Democratic	73d 74th 75th 76th 77th 78th	310 Dem 319 Dem 331 Dem 261 Dem 268 Dem 218 Dem	117 Rep 103 Rep 89 Rep 164 Rep 162 Rep 208 Rep	60 Dem 69 Dem 76 Dem 69 Dem 66 Dem 58 Dem	35 Rep 25 Rep 16 Rep 23 Rep 28 Rep 37 Rep
1945–1953	**Harry S Truman** (VP vacant, 1945–1949) Alben W. Barkley (1949–1953)	Democratic	79th 80th 81st 82d	242 Dem 245 Rep 263 Dem 234 Dem	190 Rep 188 Dem 171 Rep 199 Rep	56 Dem 51 Rep 54 Dem 49 Dem	38 Rep 45 Dem 42 Rep 47 Rep
1953–1961	**Dwight D. Eisenhower** Richard M. Nixon	Republican	83d 84th 85th 86th	221 Rep 232 Dem 233 Dem 283 Dem	211 Dem 203 Rep 200 Rep 153 Rep	48 Rep 48 Dem 49 Dem 64 Dem	47 Dem 47 Rep 47 Rep 34 Rep
1961–1963	**John F. Kennedy**[*] Lyndon B. Johnson	Democratic	87th	263 Dem	174 Rep	65 Dem	35 Rep
1963–1969	**Lyndon B. Johnson** (VP vacant, 1963–1965) Hubert H. Humphrey (1965–1969)	Democratic	88th 89th 90th	258 Dem 295 Dem 247 Dem	177 Rep 140 Rep 187 Rep	67 Dem 68 Dem 64 Dem	33 Rep 32 Rep 36 Rep
1969–1974	**Richard M. Nixon**[†] Spiro T. Agnew[††] Gerald R. Ford[§]	Republican	91st 92d	243 Dem 254 Dem	192 Rep 180 Rep	57 Dem 54 Dem	43 Rep 44 Rep

[*]Died in office.   [†]Resigned from the presidency.   [††]Resigned from the vice presidency.   [§]Appointed vice president.

Party Strength in Congress, 1789–2004 *(continued)*

Year	President and vice president	Party of president	Congress	House Majority party	House Minority party	Senate Majority party	Senate Minority party
1974–1977	Gerald R. Ford Nelson A. Rockefeller[§]	Republican	93d 94th	239 Dem 291 Dem	192 Rep 144 Rep	56 Dem 60 Dem	42 Rep 37 Rep
1977–1981	Jimmy Carter Walter Mondale	Democratic	95th 96th	292 Dem 266 Dem	143 Rep 157 Rep	61 Dem 58 Dem	38 Rep 41 Rep
1981–1989	Ronald Reagan George Bush	Republican	97th 98th 99th 100th	243 Dem 269 Dem 253 Dem 257 Dem	192 Rep 165 Rep 182 Rep 178 Rep	53 Rep 54 Rep 53 Rep 54 Dem	46 Dem 46 Dem 47 Dem 46 Rep
1989–1993	George Bush Dan Quayle	Republican	101st 102d	262 Dem 267 Dem	173 Rep 167 Rep	55 Dem 56 Dem	45 Rep 44 Rep
1993–2000	Bill Clinton Albert Gore, Jr.	Democratic	103d 104th 105th 106th	258 Dem 230 Rep 228 Rep 223 Rep	176 Rep 204 Dem 206 Dem 211 Dem	57 Dem 53 Rep 55 Rep 54 Rep	43 Rep 47 Dem 45 Dem 46 Dem
2000	George W. Bush Richard Cheney	Republican	107th 108th***	221 Rep 230 Rep	212 Dem 201 Dem	50 Rep* 55 Rep	50 Dem** 44 Dem

[§]Appointed vice president.

*On June 6, 2001, Republican John Jeffords become an Independent, reducing the Republican total in the Senate to 49. In the November 5, 2002, election, the Republicans gained a seat, bringing the final total of Republicans in this session again to 50.

**On October 25, 2002, Democrat Paul Wellstone died; an Independent was appointed as his replacement, reducing the Democrat total in the Senate to 49. In the November 5, 2002, election, the Democrats lost a seat, bringing the final total of Democrats in this session to 48.

***At press time, two seats in Louisiana had not yet been decided.

GLOSSARY

A

Aaron Burr New York lawyer and vice-presidential candidate in 1796; he became Thomas Jefferson's vice president in 1801 after the House of Representatives broke a deadlock in the Electoral College.

abolitionist An individual who supported national legislation outlawing slavery, either gradually or immediately, with or without compensation to slave owners.

Abraham Lincoln Illinois lawyer and politician who argued against popular sovereignty in debates with Stephen Douglas in 1858; he lost the senatorial election to Douglas but was elected president in 1860.

absentee planters An estate owner who collects profits from farming or rent but does not live on the land or help cultivate it.

absolute monarch The ruler of a kingdom in which every aspect of national life—including politics, religion, the economy, and social affairs—comes under royal authority.

acculturation Changes in the culture of a group or an individual as a result of contact with a different culture.

Ácoma pueblo Pueblo Indian community that resisted Spanish authority in 1598 and was subdued by the Spanish.

acquired immunity Resistance or partial resistance to a disease; acquired immunity develops in a population over time as a result of exposure to harmful bacteria and viruses.

ad hoc Created for, or concerned with, one specific purpose; Latin for "to this [end]."

Adams-Onís Treaty Treaty between the United States and Spain in 1819 that ceded Florida to the United States, ended any Spanish claims in Oregon, and recognized Spanish rights in the American Southwest.

Adena culture An early nonagricultural American Indian society centered in the Ohio River Valley and spreading as far as West Virginia; it is known for having built large trading centers, where artifacts from all over North America have been found.

African Methodist Episcopal Church African American branch of Methodism established in Philadelphia in 1816 and in New York in 1821.

agrarian capitalism A system of agriculture based on the efficient, specialized production of crops intended to generate profits rather than subsistence.

agribusiness A large-scale farming operation typically involving considerable land holdings, hired labor, and extensive use of machinery; may also involve processing and distribution as well as growing.

Alamo A fortified Franciscan mission at San Antonio; rebellious Texas colonists were besieged and annihilated there by Santa Anna's forces in 1836.

Albert Gallatin Treasury secretary in Jefferson's administration; he favored limited government and reduced the federal debt by cutting spending.

Alexis de Tocqueville French traveler and historian who toured the United States in 1831 and wrote *Democracy in America*, a classic study of American institutions and the American character.

Alien and Sedition Acts Collectively, the four acts—Alien Act, Alien Enemies Act, Naturalization Act, and Sedition Act—passed by Congress in 1798 designed to prevent immigrants from participating in politics and to silence the anti-Federalist press.

Allegheny Portage Railroad A rail line that carried canal boats over the Allegheny Mountains as part of the Main Line Canal system.

allegory A story in which characters and events stand for abstract ideas and suggest a deep, symbolic meaning.

almshouse A public shelter for the poor.

amenities Conveniences, comforts, and services.

American Colonization Society Organization founded in 1817 to end slavery gradually by assisting individual slave owners to liberate their slaves and then transporting them to Africa.

American Prohibitory Act British law of 1775 that authorized the royal navy to seize all American ships engaged in trade; it amounted to a declaration of war

American System An economic plan sponsored by nationalists in Congress following the War of 1812; it was intended to capitalize on regional differences to spur U.S. economic growth and the domestic production of goods previously bought from foreign manufacturers.

Amerigo Vespucci Italian explorer of the South American coast; Europeans named America after him.

amnesty A general pardon granted by a government, especially for political offenses.

anaconda plan Winfield Scott's plan (named after a snake that smothers prey in its coils) to blockade southern ports and take control of the Mississippi River, thus splitting the Confederacy, cutting off southern trade, and causing an economic collapse.

Andersonville Confederate prisoner-of-war camp in northern Georgia where some fourteen thousand Union prisoners died of disease and malnutrition.

Andrew Jackson General who defeated the Creeks at Horseshoe Bend in 1814 and the British at New Orleans in 1815; he later became the seventh president of the United States.

Andrew Johnson Tennessee senator who became Lincoln's running mate in 1864 and who succeeded to the presidency after Lincoln's assassination.

Anglo A term applied in the Southwest to English-speaking whites.

Anne Hutchinson A religious leader banished from Massachusetts in 1637 because of her criticism of the colonial government and what were judged to be heretical beliefs.

annexation The incorporation of a territory into an existing political unit such as a neighboring country.

annuity An allowance or income paid annually.

annul To declare a law or contract invalid.

antebellum The decades before the Civil War, the period from 1815 to 1860; Latin for "before the war."

anthropologist A scholar who studies human behavior and culture in the past or the present.

Antietam Creek Site of a battle that occurred in September 1862 when Lee's forces invaded Maryland; both sides suffered heavy losses, and Lee retreated into Virginia.

anti-expansionist Opposed to the policy of expanding a country by acquiring new territory.

Antifederalists Opponents of the ratification of the Constitution; they believed a strong central government was a threat to American liberties and rights.

Antimasonic Party Political party formed in 1827 to capitalize on popular anxiety about the influence of the Masons; it opposed politics-as-usual without offering any particular substitute.

Antonio López de Santa Anna Mexican general who was president of Mexico when he led an attack on the Alamo in 1836; he again led Mexico during its war with the United States in 1846–1848.

apprentice A person who is bonded to a craftsman, providing labor in exchange for learning the skills associated with the craft.

appropriation Public funds authorized for a specific purpose.

aqueduct An elevated structure raising a canal to bridge rivers, canyons, or other obstructions.

armada A fleet of warships.

Army of the Potomac Army created to guard the U.S. capital after the Battle of Bull Run in 1861; it became the main Union army in the East.

Articles of Confederation The first constitution of the United States; it created a central government with limited powers, and it was replaced by the Constitution in 1788.

artisan A person whose primary employment is the specialized production of hand-manufactured items; a craftsperson.

ascetic Practicing severe abstinence or self-denial, generally in pursuit of spiritual awareness.

astrolabe An instrument for measuring the position of the sun and stars; using these readings, navigators could calculate their latitude—their distance north or south of the equator.

autonomy Control of one's own affairs.

Aztecs An Indian group living in central Mexico; the Aztecs used military force to dominate nearby tribes; their civilization was at its peak at the time of the Spanish conquest.

B

Bahamas A group of islands in the Atlantic Ocean east of Florida and Cuba.

balance of payments The difference between a nation's total payments to foreign countries and its total receipts from abroad.

Baltimore and Ohio Railroad First steam railroad commissioned in the United States; it resorted to using horse-drawn cars after a stagecoach horse beat its pioneer locomotive in a race.

Bank War The political conflict that occurred when Andrew Jackson tried to destroy the Second Bank of the United States, which he thought represented special interests at the expense of the common man.

Barbary pirates Pirates along the Barbary Coast of North Africa who attacked European and American vessels engaged in Mediterranean trade.

Baron Friedrich von Steuben Prussian military officer who served as Washington's drillmaster at Valley Forge.

battery An army artillery unit, usually supplied with heavy guns.

Battle of Buena Vista Battle in February 1847 during which U.S. troops led by Zachary Taylor forced Santa Anna's forces to withdraw into the interior of Mexico.

Battle of Bunker Hill British assault on American troops on Breed's Hill near Boston in June 1775; the British won the battle but suffered heavy losses.

Battle of Fallen Timbers 1794 battle in which Kentucky riflemen defeated Indians of several tribes, helping to end Indian resistance in the Northwest.

Battle of Horseshoe Bend Battle in 1814 in which Tennessee militia massacred Creek Indians in Alabama, ending Red Stick resistance to white westward expansion.

Battle of King's Mountain Battle fought in October 1780 on the border between the Carolinas in which revolutionary troops defeated loyalists.

Battle of Monmouth New Jersey battle in June 1778 in which Charles Lee wasted a decisive American advantage.

Battle of New Orleans Battle in the War of 1812 in which American troops commanded by Andrew Jackson destroyed the British force attempting to seize New Orleans.

Battle of Shiloh Battle in Tennessee in April 1862 that ended with an unpursued Confederate withdrawal; both sides suffered heavy casualties for the first time, but neither side gained ground.

Battle of Tippecanoe Battle near Prophetstown in 1811, where American forces led by William Henry Harrison defeated the followers of the Shawnee Prophet and destroyed the town.

Battle of Trenton Battle on December 26, 1776, when Washington led his troops by night across the Delaware River and captured a Hessian garrison wintering in New Jersey.

Battles of Lexington and Concord Two confrontations in April 1775 between British soldiers and patriot Minutemen; the first recognized battles of the Revolution.

belligerent status Recognition that a participant in a conflict is a nation engaged in warfare rather than a rebel against a legally constituted government; full diplomatic recognition is one possible outcome.

Benedict Arnold Pharmacist-turned-military-leader whose bravery and daring made him an American hero and a favorite of George Washington until he committed treason in 1780.

benevolent society An organization of people dedicated to some charitable purpose.

Benjamin Franklin American writer, inventor, scientist, and diplomat instrumental in bringing about a French alliance with the United States in 1778 and who later helped negotiate the treaty ending the war.

Berlin Decree Napoleon's order declaring the British Isles under blockade and authorizing the confiscation of British goods from any ship found carrying them.

bicameral Having a legislature with two houses.

bill of rights A formal statement of essential rights and liberties under law.

Bill of Rights The first ten amendments to the U.S. Constitution, added in 1791 to protect certain basic rights of American citizens.

black codes Laws passed by the southern states after the Civil War to define the status of freed people as subordinate to whites.

Black Hawk Sauk leader who brought his people back to their homeland in Illinois; he was captured in 1832 when U.S. troops massacred his followers.

black market The illegal business of buying and selling goods that are banned or restricted.

Black Reconstruction The period of Reconstruction when African Americans took an active role in state and local government.

blandishments The use of flattery or manipulation to convince others to support a particular project or point of view.

bloc A group of people united for common action.

block voting The practice by organized groups of people to coordinate their voting so that all members vote the same way, thereby enhancing the group's political influence.

blue laws Local legislation designed to enforce Christian morality by forbidding certain activities, including traveling, on Sunday.

blue-collar workers Workers who wear work clothes, such as coveralls and jeans, on the job; their work is likely to involve manual labor.

border states The slave states of Delaware, Maryland, Virginia, Kentucky, and Missouri, which shared a border with states in which slavery was illegal.

bosch loopers Dutch term meaning "woods runners"; independent Dutch fur traders.

boycott An organized political protest in which people refuse to buy goods from a nation or group of people whose actions they opposed.

Brigham Young Mormon leader who took over in 1844 after Joseph Smith's death and guided the Mormons from Illinois to Utah, where they established a permanent home for the church.

broad constructionist A person who believes the government can exercise any implied powers that are in keeping with the spirit of the Constitution.

broadside An advertisement, public notice, or other publication printed on one side of a large sheet of paper. Also, the simultaneous discharge of all the guns on one side of a warship.

Brook Farm An experimental farm based on cooperative living; established in 1841, it first attracted transcendentalists and then serious farmers before fire destroyed it in 1845.

buffalo The American bison, a large member of the ox family, native to North America and the staple of the Plains Indian economy between the fifteenth and mid-nineteenth centuries.

Bull Run A creek in Virginia not far from Washington, D.C., where Confederate soldiers forced federal troops to retreat in the first major battle of the Civil War, fought in July 1861.

bureaucrat A government official, usually appointed, who is deeply devoted to the details of administrative procedures.

burghers Town-dwellers who were free from feudal obligations and were responsible for civic government during the medieval period in Europe; in New Amsterdam these were men who were not Dutch West India Company officials, but who governed civic affairs through their political influence.

cabildo secular Secular municipal council that provided local government in Spain's New World empire.

C

cabinet A body of officials appointed by the president to run the executive departments of the government and to act as the president's advisers.

Caddoan A family of languages spoken by the Wichitas, Pawnees, Arikaras, and other Plains Indians.

Californios Spanish colonists in California in the eighteenth and nineteenth centuries.

Calvinists   Protestant followers of John Calvin, whose theology emphasizes the absolute power of God, human sinfulness, and people's inability to effect salvation.

canvass   A survey that is taken.

Cape of Good Hope   A point of land projecting into the Atlantic Ocean at the southern tip of Africa; to trade with Asia, European mariners had to sail around the cape to pass from the South Atlantic into the Indian Ocean.

capital   Money needed to start or sustain a commercial enterprise.

caricature   An exaggerated image of a person, usually enhancing their most uncomplimentary features.

carpetbagger   Derogatory term for the northerners who came to the South after the Civil War to take part in Reconstruction.

carrying trade   The business of transporting goods across the Atlantic or to and from the Caribbean.

cash crop   A crop raised in large quantities for sale rather than for local or home consumption.

censure   To issue an official rebuke, as by a legislature to one of its members.

Chancellorsville   Site in Virginia where in May 1863 Confederate troops led by Lee defeated a much larger Union force.

charismatic   Having a spiritual power or personal quality that stirs enthusiasm and devotion in large numbers of people.

Charles Cornwallis   British general who was second in command to Henry Clinton; his surrender at Yorktown in 1781 brought the American Revolution to a close.

Charles Cotesworth Pinckney   Federalist politician and brother of Thomas Pinckney; he was sent on a diplomatic mission to Paris in 1796 during a period of unfriendly relations between France and the United States.

Charles Lee   Revolutionary general who tried to undermine Washington's authority on several occasions; he was eventually dismissed from the military.

Charles Maurice de Talleyrand-Périgord   French foreign minister appointed by the revolutionary government in 1797; he later aided Napoleon Bonaparte's overthrow of that government and served as his foreign minister.

Charles Sumner   Massachusetts senator who was brutally beaten by a southern congressman in 1856 after delivering a speech attacking the South.

chattel slavery   The bondage of people who are considered to be the movable personal property of their owners.

cheap money   Paper money that is readily available but has declined in value.

Cherokee Nation v. Georgia   Supreme Court case (1831) concerning Georgia's annulment of all Cherokee laws; the Supreme Court ruled that Indian tribes did not have the right to appeal to the federal court system.

Chesapeake   The Chesapeake was the common term for the two colonies of Maryland and Virginia, both of which border on the Chesapeake Bay.

chivalry   The code of honor among medieval knights that was central to the romantic self-image among southern planters.

Choctaw Indians   A mound-building people who became a society of hunters after 1400; they were steadfast allies of the French in wars against the Natchez and Chickasaws.

cholera   Infectious and often fatal disease associated with poor sanitation.

Christian benevolence   A tenet in some Christian theology teaching that the essence of God is self-sacrificing love and that the ultimate duty for Christians is to perform acts of kindness with no expectation of reward in return.

Christopher Columbus   (Cristoforo Colombo) Italian explorer in the service of Spain who attempted to reach Asia by sailing west from Europe, thereby arriving in America in 1492.

Church of England   The Protestant church established in the sixteenth century by King Henry VIII as England's official church; also known as the Anglican Church.

circuit court   A court of appeals that has the power to review and either uphold or overturn decisions made by lower courts; in terms of authority, these stand between federal district courts and the Supreme Court.

circulation   The number of copies of a publication sold or distributed.

civil chiefs   In many Native American societies, leadership was shared among different classes of chiefs, each of which was responsible for specific political tasks; civil chiefs generally were responsible for overseeing domestic affairs, while war chiefs were responsible for diplomacy.

civil court   Any court that hears cases regarding the rights of private citizens.

civil liberties   Fundamental individual rights such as freedom of speech and religion, protected by law against interference from the government.

Civil Rights Act of 1875   Law passed by Congress in 1875 prohibiting racial discrimination in selection of juries and in transportation and other businesses open to the general public.

civil rights   The rights, privileges, and protections that are a part of citizenship.

Clara Barton   Organizer of a volunteer service to aid sick and wounded Civil War soldiers; she later founded the American branch of the Red Cross.

coalition   An alliance, especially a temporary one, of different people or groups.

coercion   Use of threats or force to compel action.

Cold Harbor   Area of Virginia, about 10 miles from Richmond, where Grant made an unsuccessful attempt to drive his forces through Lee's center.

Columbian Exchange   The exchange of people, plants, and animals between Europe, Africa, and North America that occurred after Columbus's arrival in the New World.

Common Sense Revolutionary pamphlet written by Thomas Paine in 1776; it attacked George III, argued against monarchy, and advanced the patriot cause.

Commonwealth The republic established after the victory of Oliver Cromwell in the English civil war; the Commonwealth lasted from 1649 until the monarchy was restored in 1660.

Community of Habitants of New France Company chartered by Anne of Austria to make operations in New France more efficient and profitable; it gave significant political power to local officials in Canada.

Company of New France Company established by Cardinal Richelieu to bring order to the running of France's North American enterprises.

Company of the West Company chartered by Colbert after New France became a royal colony; modeled on the Dutch West India Company, it was designed to maximize profits to the Crown.

company town A town built and owned by a single company; its residents depend on the company not only for jobs but for stores, schools, and housing.

Compromise of 1850 Plan intended to reconcile North and South on the issue of slavery; it recognized the principle of popular sovereignty and included a strong fugitive slave law.

Compromise of 1877 Name applied by historians to the resolution of the disputed presidential election of 1876; it gave the presidency to the Republicans and made concessions to southern Democrats.

concession In diplomacy, something given up during negotiations.

conciliatory Striving to overcome distrust or to regain good will.

Confederate States of America Political entity formed by the seceding states of South Carolina, Georgia, Florida, Alabama, Mississippi, and Louisiana in February 1861; Texas, Virginia, Arkansas, Tennessee, and North Carolina joined later.

Congregationalism A form of Protestant church government in which the local congregation is independent and self-governing; in the colonies, the Puritans were Congregationalists.

Congress of Vienna Conference between ambassadors from the major powers in Europe to redraw the continent's political map after the defeat of Napoleon; it also sought to uproot revolutionary movements and restore traditional monarchies.

conquistadors Spanish soldiers who conquered Indian civilizations in the New World.

conscience Whigs Members of the Whig Party who supported moderate abolitionism, as opposed to cotton Whigs, members who opposed abolitionism.

Conscription Act Law passed by Congress in 1863 that established a draft but allowed wealthy people to escape it by hiring a substitute or paying the government a $300 fee.

Constitutional Union Party Political party that organized on the eve of the Civil War with no platform other than preservation of the Constitution, the Union, and the law.

constitutionality Accordance with the principles or provisions of the Constitution.

consumer revolution The rising market for manufactured goods, particularly luxury items, that occurred in the early eighteenth century in the colonies.

cooper A person who makes or repairs wooden barrels.

Copperheads Derogatory term (the name of a poisonous snake) applied to northerners who supported the South during the Civil War.

corporate colony A self-governing colony, not directly under the control of proprietors or the Crown.

Cotton Belt The region in the southeastern United States in which cotton is grown.

cotton boll The pod of the cotton plant; it contains the plant's seeds surrounded by the fluffy fiber that is spun into yarn.

coureurs de bois Literally, "runners of the woods"; independent French fur traders who lived among the Indians and sold furs to the French.

courier A messenger carrying official information, sometimes secretly.

Covenant Chain An alliance of Indian tribes established to resist colonial settlement in the Ohio Valley and Great Lakes region and to oppose British trading policies.

Creek Confederacy Alliance of Indians living in the Southeast; formed after the lethal spread of European diseases to permit a cooperative economic and military system among survivors.

creole In colonial times, a term referring to anyone of European or African heritage who was born in the colonies; in Louisiana, refers to the ethnic group resulting from intermarriage by people of mixed languages, races, and cultures.

crop lien A legal claim to a farmer's crop, similar to a mortgage, based on the use of crops as collateral for extension of credit by a merchant.

Crusades Military expeditions undertaken by European Christians in the eleventh through the thirteenth centuries to recover the Holy Land from the Muslims.

cult of domesticity The belief that women's proper role lies in domestic pursuits.

Cumberland Road A national highway built with federal funds; it eventually stretched from Cumberland, Maryland, to Vandalia, Illinois, and beyond.

cupidity The extreme desire for wealth; greed.

Currency Act British law of 1764 banning the printing of paper money in the American colonies.

customs service A government agency authorized to collect taxes on foreign goods entering a country.

Cyrus McCormick Virginia inventor and manufacturer who developed and mass-produced the McCormick reaper, a machine that harvested grain.

D

dandyism Dressing and behaving in an overly ornate and flamboyant fashion.

Daniel Shays Revolutionary War veteran considered the leader of the farmers' uprising in western Massachusetts called Shays's Rebellion.

Daniel Webster Massachusetts senator and lawyer who was known for his forceful speeches and considered nullification a threat to the Union.

dark horse A political candidate who has little organized support and is not expected to win.

Dartmouth College v. Woodward Supreme Court case (1819) in which the majority ruled that private contracts are sacred and cannot be modified by state legislatures.

Declaration of Independence A formal statement, adopted by the Second Continental Congress in 1776, that listed justifications for rebellion and declared the American mainland colonies to be independent of Britain.

Deep South The region of the South farthest from the North, usually said to be the states of Alabama, Florida, Georgia, Louisiana, Mississippi, and South Carolina.

deference Yielding to the judgment or wishes of a social or intellectual superior.

deism The belief that God created the universe in such a way that it could operate without any further divine intervention.

delusion A false belief strongly held in spite of evidence to the contrary.

demilitarization The removal of military forces from a region and the restoration of civilian control.

Democratic-Republican societies Political organizations formed in 1793 and 1794 to demand greater responsiveness by the state and federal governments to the needs of the citizens.

Democrats Political party that brought Andrew Jackson into office; it recalled Jeffersonian principles of limited government and drew its support from farmers, craftsmen, and small businessmen.

demographic disaster The outcome of a high death rate and an unbalanced ratio of men to women in the seventeenth-century Chesapeake colonies.

demographics The statistical distribution of subpopulations (ethnic groups, for example) among the larger population of a community or nation.

denomination A group of religious congregations that accept the same doctrines and are united under a single name.

deploy To position military resources (troops, artillery, equipment) in preparation for action.

depression A period of drastic economic decline, marked by decreased business activity, falling prices, and high unemployment.

despotism Rule by a tyrant.

direct tax A tax imposed to raise revenue rather than to regulate trade.

discretion The power or right to act according to one's own judgment.

discretionary powers Powers to be used at one's own judgment; in government, powers given to an administrative official to be used without outside consultation or oversight.

discrimination Treatment based on class, gender, or racial category rather than on merit; prejudice.

disfranchisement The taking away of an individual's or group's right to vote.

dissenter A person who does not accept the doctrines of an established or national church.

divine right The idea that monarchs derive their authority to rule directly from God and are accountable only to God.

Dominion of New England A megacolony created in 1686 by James II that brought Massachusetts, Plymouth Plantations, Connecticut, Rhode Island, New Jersey, and New York under the control of one royal governor; William and Mary dissolved the Dominion when they came to the throne in 1689.

Don Juan de Oñate Spaniard who conquered New Mexico and claimed it for Spain in the 1590s.

Dorothea Dix Philanthropist, reformer, and educator who was a pioneer in the movement for specialized treatment of the mentally ill.

Dred Scott Slave who sued for his liberty in the Missouri courts, arguing that four years on free soil had made him free; the Supreme Court's 1857 ruling against him negated the Missouri Compromise.

Duke of Wellington The most respected military leader in Great Britain in the early nineteenth century, Wellington was responsible for the defeat of Napoleon.

Dutch Reform Church Calvinistic Protestant denomination; the established church in the Dutch Republic and the official church in New Netherland.

Dutch West India Company Dutch investment company formed in 1621 to develop colonies for the Netherlands in North America.

E

Ebenezer McIntosh Boston shoemaker whose workingman's organization, the South End "gang," became the core of the city's Sons of Liberty in 1765.

Ecology Relating to the interactive relationships between organisms (animals, plants, microorganisms, etc.) and the physical environment in which they are found.

Edmund Genêt Diplomat sent by the French government to bring the United States into France's war with Britain and Spain.

egalitarianism A belief in human equality.

Elect, the According to Calvinism, the people chosen by God for salvation.

Electoral College A body of electors chosen by the states to elect the president and vice president; each state may select a number of electors equal to the number of its senators and representatives in Congress.

electorate The portion of the population that possesses the right to vote.

electric telegraph Device invented by Samuel F. B. Morse in 1836 that transmits coded messages along a wire over long distances; the first electronic communications device.

Eli Whitney American inventor and manufacturer; his perfecting of the cotton gin revolutionized the cotton industry.

Elizabeth Cady Stanton Pioneering woman suffrage leader, co-organizer of the first Women's Rights Convention, held in Seneca Falls, New York, in 1848.

Elizabeth I Queen of England (r. 1558–1603); she succeeded the Catholic Mary I and reestablished Protestantism in England; her reign was a time of domestic prosperity and cultural achievement.

Emancipation Proclamation Lincoln's order abolishing slavery as of January 1, 1863, in states "in rebellion" but not in border territories still loyal to the Union.

emancipation Release from slavery.

Embargo Act Embargo (a government-ordered trade ban) announced by Jefferson in 1807 in order to pressure Britain and France to accept neutral trading rights; it went into effect in 1808 and closed down all U.S. foreign trade.

Embargo of 1813 An absolute embargo on all American trade and British imports.

empower To increase the power or authority of some person or group.

***encomienda* system** A system of bonded labor in which Indians were assigned to Spanish plantation and mine owners in exchange for a tax payment and an agreement to "civilize" and convert them to Catholicism.

endemic Present among a particular group or groups of people or geographical area.

enfranchise To grant the right to vote to an individual or group.

Enlightenment An eighteenth-century intellectual movement that stressed the pursuit of knowledge through reason and challenged the value of religious belief, emotion, and tradition.

entail A legal limitation that prevents property from being divided, sold, or given away.

entrepreneur A person who organizes and manages a business enterprise that involves risk and requires initiative.

enumerate To count.

envoy A government representative charged with a special diplomatic mission.

equal access The right of any person to use a public facility, such as streetcars, as freely as other people in the society.

Era of Good Feelings The period from 1816 to 1823, when the decline of the Federalist Party and the end of the War of 1812 gave rise to a time of political cooperation.

Erie Canal A 350-mile canal stretching from Buffalo to Albany; it revolutionized shipping in New York State.

Esquire A term used to indicate that a man was a gentleman.

Essex Junto Junto—A group of political conspirators who seek power outside of the regular political process—composed of radical Federalists in Essex County, Massachusetts, who at first advocated constitutional changes that would favor New England politically and later called for New England and New York to secede from the United States.

established church The official church of a nation or colony, usually supported by taxes collected from all citizens, no matter what their religious affiliation.

ethnic cleansing An effort to eradicate an ethnic or religious group from a country or region, often through mass killings.

evangelical sects Protestant groups that emphasized the sole authority of the Bible and the necessity of actively striving to convert others.

evangelicalism A Protestant religious persuasion that emphasizes the literal truth of the Gospels and salvation through faith alone; in the early nineteenth century it became infused with increasing amounts of romantic emotionalism and an emphasis on converting others.

excise A tax on the production, sale, or consumption of a commodity or on the use of a service within a country.

excise men Men who collected taxes on an article of trade or sale.

executive powers Powers given to the president by the Constitution.

extended family A family group consisting of various close relatives as well as the parents and children.

external taxation Revenue raised in the course of regulating trade with other nations.

extractive industry An industry, such as fur trapping, logging, or mining, that removes natural resources from the environment.

F

faction A political group with shared opinions or interests.

factionalism In politics, the emergence of various self-interested parties (factions) that compete to impose their own views onto either a larger political party or the nation at large.

fait accompli An accomplished deed or fact that cannot be reversed or undone.

Far West In North America, the lands west of the Mississippi River.

farthing A British coin worth one-fourth of a penny and thus a term used to indicate something of very little value.

favorite son A candidate nominated for office by delegates from his or her own region or state.

federal Indian agents Government officials who were responsible for negotiating treaties with Native American groups; in the nineteenth century they were employed by the War Department.

Federalist Papers Essays written by Alexander Hamilton, John Jay, and James Madison in support of the Constitution.

Federalists Supporters of the Constitution; they desired a strong central government.

femme couverte From the French for "covered woman"; a legal term for a married woman; this legal status limited women's rights, denying them the right to sue or be sued, own or sell property, or earn wages.

femme sole From the French for "woman alone"; a legal term for an unmarried, widowed, or divorced woman with the legal right to own or sell property, sue or be sued, or earn wages.

Ferdinand and Isabella Joint rulers of Spain (r. 1469–1504); their marriage in 1469 created a united Spain from the rival kingdoms of Aragon and Castile.

feudal Relating to a system in which landowners held broad powers over peasants or tenant farmers, providing protection in exchange for loyalty and labor.

fictive ancestor A mythical figure believed by a social group to be its founder and from whom all members are believed to be biologically descended.

field hands People who do agricultural work such as planting, weeding, and harvesting.

Fifteenth Amendment Constitutional amendment, ratified in 1870, that prohibited states from denying the right to vote because of a person's race or because a person had been a slave.

54th Massachusetts Civil War regiment of African American troops from Massachusetts commanded by abolitionist Colonel Robert Gould Shaw; it led an assault on Fort Wagner at Charleston Harbor.

filibuster To use obstructionist tactics, especially prolonged speechmaking, in order to delay legislative action.

First Organic Laws A constitution adopted by American settlers in the Oregon Country on July 5, 1843, establishing a government independent from Great Britain and requesting annexation by the United States.

fiscal Relating to finances.

Five Civilized Tribes Term used by whites to describe the Cherokee, Choctaw, Seminole, Creek, and Chickasaw Indians, many of whom were planters and merchants.

flagship The ship that carries the fleet commander and bears the commander's flag.

Fletcher v. Peck Supreme Court case (1810) growing out of the Yazoo affair in which the majority ruled that the original land sale contract rescinded by the Georgia legislature was binding, establishing the superiority of contracts over legislation.

Fort Orange Dutch trading post established near present-day Albany, New York, in 1614.

Fort Sumter Fort at the mouth of the harbor of Charleston, South Carolina; it was the scene of the opening engagement of the Civil War in April 1861.

forty-niners Prospectors who streamed into California in 1849, after the discovery of gold at New Helvetia in 1848.

Fourierism Social system advanced by Frenchman Charles Fourier, who argued that people were capable of living in perfect harmony under the right conditions, which included communal life and republican government.

Fourteenth Amendment Constitutional amendment, ratified in 1868, defining American citizenship and placing restrictions on former Confederates.

Frances (Fanny) Wright Nineteenth-century reformer who advocated what at the time were considered radical causes, including racial equality, equality for women, birth control, and open sexuality.

Francis Marion South Carolina leader of guerrilla forces during the Revolutionary War; known as the "Swamp Fox," he harassed British forces during the second southern campaign.

Francis Scott Key Author of "The Star-Spangled Banner," which chronicles the British bombardment of Fort McHenry in 1814; Key's poem, set to music, became the official U.S. national anthem in 1931.

François Dominique Toussaint L'Ouverture Black revolutionary who liberated the island of Santo Domingo in 1791, only to see it reinvaded by the French in 1802.

Franklin Pierce New Hampshire lawyer and Democratic politician nominated as a compromise candidate and elected president in 1852.

fraternal Describes a group of people with common purposes or interests.

fraternal order An organization of men, often with a ceremonial initiation, that typically provided rudimentary life insurance; many fraternal orders also had auxiliaries for the female relatives of members.

Frederick Douglass Abolitionist and journalist who escaped from slavery in 1838 and became an influential lecturer in the North and abroad.

Fredericksburg Site in Virginia of a Union defeat in December 1862, which demonstrated the incompetence of the new Union commander, Ambrose E. Burnside.

free trade Trade between nations without any protective tariffs.

freed people Former slaves; *freed people* is the term used by historians to refer to former slaves, whether male or female.

Freedmen's Bureau Agency established in 1865 to aid former slaves in their transition to freedom, especially by administering relief and sponsoring education.

Freeport Doctrine   Stephen Douglas's belief, stated at Freeport, Illinois, that a territory could exclude slavery by writing local laws or regulations that made slavery impossible to enforce.

Free-Soil Party   A political party that opposed the extension of slavery into any of the territories newly acquired from Mexico.

French Revolution   Political rebellion against the French monarchy and aristocratic privileges; it began in 1789 and ended in 1799.

Fries's Rebellion   A tax revolt by Pennsylvania citizens in 1799 that was suppressed by federal forces; leader John Fries was condemned to death for treason but received a presidential pardon from John Adams.

frigate   A very fast warship, rigged with square sails and carrying from thirty to fifty cannon on two gun decks.

frontier line   The outer limit of agricultural settlement bordering on areas still under Indian control or unoccupied.

frugality   An unwillingness to spend money for unnecessary things; by stereotype, New Englanders (Yankees) supposedly have an ingrained tendency to frugality.

fugitive slave law   Law providing for the return of escaped slaves to their owners.

G

Gadsden Purchase   A strip of land in present-day Arizona and New Mexico that the United States bought from Mexico in 1853 to secure a southern route for a transcontinental railroad.

gag rule   A rule that limits or prevents debate on an issue.

genteel   The manner and style associated with elite classes, usually characterized by elegance, grace, and politeness.

gentry   The class of English landowners ranking just below the nobility.

George B. McClellan   U.S. general who replaced Winfield Scott as general in chief of Union forces; a skillful organizer, but slow and indecisive as a field commander.

George Grenville   British prime minister who sought to tighten controls over the colonies and to impose taxes to raise revenues.

George Guess (Sequoyah)   Cherokee silversmith and trader who created an alphabet that made it possible to transcribe the Cherokee language according to the sounds of its syllables.

George III   King of England (r. 1760–1820); his government's policies produced colonial discontent that led to the American Revolution in 1776.

George Rogers Clark   Virginian who led his troops to successes against the British and Indians in the Ohio Territory in 1778.

George Washington   Commander in chief of the Continental Army; he led Americans to victory in the Revolution and later became the first president of the United States.

George Whitefield   English evangelical preacher of the Great Awakening whose charismatic style attracted huge crowds during his preaching tours of the colonies.

Gettysburg Address   A speech given by Abraham Lincoln on November 19, 1863, dedicating a national cemetery in Gettysburg, Pennsylvania; it enunciated Lincoln's maturing view of the war and its purpose.

Gettysburg   Site in Pennsylvania where in July 1863 Union forces under General George Meade defeated Lee's Confederate forces, turning back Lee's invasion of the North.

Gibbons v. Ogden   Supreme Court case (1824) in which the majority ruled that the authority of Congress is absolute in matters of interstate commerce.

Glorious Revolution   A term used to describe the removal of James II from the English throne and the crowning of the Protestant monarchs, William and Mary.

gradualism   The belief that slavery in the United States should be abolished gradually, by methods such as placing territorial limits on slavery or settling free blacks in Africa.

graft   Unscrupulous use of one's position for profit or advantage.

grain elevator   A building equipped with mechanical lifting devices and used for storing grain.

Great Awakening   A series of religious revivals based on fiery preaching and emotionalism that swept across the colonies during the second quarter of the eighteenth century.

Great Basin   A desert region of the western United States including most of Nevada and parts of Utah, California, Idaho, Wyoming, and Oregon.

Great Compromise   A proposal calling for a bicameral legislature with equal representation for the states in one house and proportional representation in the other.

Great Migration   The movement of Puritans from England to America in the 1630s, caused by political and religious unrest in England.

Great Salt Lake   A shallow, salty lake in the Great Basin near which the Mormons established a permanent settlement in 1847.

greenbacks   Paper money issued by the Union; it was not backed by gold.

guerrilla tactics   A method of warfare in which small bands of fighters in occupied territory harass and attack their enemies, often in surprise raids; the Indians used these tactics during King Philip's War.

guild   An association of craftspeople with the same skills who join together to protect their mutual interests.

H

Half-Way Covenant   An agreement (1662) that gave partial membership in Puritan churches to the children of church members even if they had not had a "saving faith" experience.

hang in effigy   To hang, as if on a gallows, a crude likeness or dummy—an effigy—representing a hated person.

Harpers Ferry Town in present-day West Virginia and site of the U.S. arsenal that John Brown briefly seized in 1859.

Harriet Beecher Stowe American novelist and abolitionist whose novel *Uncle Tom's Cabin* fanned antislavery sentiment in the North.

Harriet Tubman One of the most famous and most effective of the many African American "conductors" on the Underground Railroad in the years before the Civil War; she is thought to have been personally responsible for leading at least three hundred slaves into freedom.

head right system The grant of 50 acres of land for each settler brought over to Virginia by a colonist.

Henry David Thoreau Writer and naturalist and friend of Ralph Waldo Emerson; his best-known work is *Walden* (1854).

Henry Hudson Dutch ship captain and explorer who sailed up the Hudson River in 1609, giving the Netherlands a claim to the area now occupied by New York.

Henry the Navigator Prince who founded an observatory and school of navigation and directed voyages that helped build Portugal's colonial empire.

Henry VIII King of England (r. 1509–1547); his desire to divorce his first wife led him to break with Catholicism and establish the Church of England.

Henry Ware Liberal Congregationalist who was elected senior theologian at Harvard College in 1805, making Unitarianism the dominant religious view at the previously Calvinist stronghold.

heretic A person who does not behave in accordance with an established attitude, doctrine, or principle, usually in religious matters.

Hernando Cortés Spanish soldier and explorer who conquered the Aztecs and claimed Mexico for Spain.

Hessian troops German soldiers from the state of Hesse who were hired by Britain to fight in the American Revolution.

hierarchical A system in which people or things are ranked above one another.

Holy Land Palestine, which now is divided between Israel, Jordan, and Syria; called the Holy Land because it is the region in which the events described in the Old and New Testaments of the Bible took place; it is sacred to Christians, Jews, and Muslims.

Holy Roman Empire A political entity, authorized by the Catholic Church in 1356, unifying central Europe under an emperor elected by four princes and three Catholic archbishops.

Homestead Act Law passed by Congress in 1862 that promised ownership of 160 acres of public land to any citizen or would-be citizen who lived on and cultivated the land for five years.

Hopewell culture A successor to the Adena culture also centered in the Ohio River Valley and spreading as far as New York; Hopewell Indians introduced maize agriculture in about 200 BCE and built larger and more elaborate mound cities in which large-scale trading activities continued.

Hopewell Treaties Treaties signed by 1785 in which the Choctaws, Chickasaws, and Cherokees granted American settlement rights in the Southwest.

Hopi Indians Indians who were related to the Comanches and Shoshones and took up residence among the Pueblo Indians as agricultural town-dwellers; their name means "peaceful ones."

Horace Greeley Journalist and politician who helped found the Republican Party; his newspaper, the *New York Tribune,* was known for its antislavery stance.

Horace Mann Educator who called for publicly funded education for all children and was head of the first public board of education in the United States.

Horatio "Granny" Gates Elderly Virginia general who led the American troops to victory in the Battle of Saratoga in 1777.

House of Burgesses The elected lawmaking body of Virginia, established by the Virginia Company in 1618; the assembly first met in 1619.

house slaves People who did domestic work such as cleaning and cooking.

Hudson River school The first native school of landscape painting in the United States (1825–1875); it attracted artists rebelling against the neoclassical tradition.

I

idolater A person who worships idols.

idolatry The worship of idols, a practice forbidden in the Judeo-Christian tradition.

impeach To formally charge a public official with criminal conduct in office; once Congress has impeached a federal official, the official is then tried in the Senate on the stated charges.

implied power Power that is not specifically granted to the government by the Constitution but can be viewed as necessary to carry out the governing duties listed in the Constitution.

import duties A tax on imported goods.

impressment Procedure permitted under British maritime law that authorized commanders of warships to force English civilian sailors into military service.

indentured servants Compulsory service for a fixed period of time, usually from four to seven years, most often agreed to in exchange for passage to the colonies; a labor contract called an indenture spelled out the terms of the agreement.

Indian Removal Act Law passed by Congress in 1830 providing for the removal of all Indian tribes east of the Mississippi and the purchase of western lands for their resettlement.

indigo Shrublike plant with clusters of red or purple flowers, grown on plantations in the South; a primary source of blue dye.

inequities Unfair circumstances or proceedings.

infant depravity The idea that children are naturally sinful because they share in the original sin of the human race but have not learned the discipline to control their evil instincts.

inflation Rising prices that occur when the supply of currency or credit grows faster than the available supply of goods and services.

influence peddling Using one's influence with people in authority to obtain favors or preferential treatment for someone else, usually in return for payment.

installment Partial payments of a debt to be made at regular intervals until the entire debt is repaid.

insubordination Resistance to authority; disobedience.

insurrection An uprising against a legitimate authority or government.

internal taxes Taxes collected directly from citizens, like Alexander Hamilton's various excise taxes, as opposed to tariffs or other taxes collected in connection with foreign trade.

interpose To place a barrier between two objects or forces; to Jefferson, the principle of interposition meant that states had the right to use their sovereign power as a barrier between the federal government and the states' citizens when the natural rights of those citizens were at risk.

irreligious Hostile or indifferent to religion.

itinerant Traveling from place to place.

J

Jacob Leisler German merchant who led a revolt in New York in 1689 against royal officials representing the Dominion of New England; he was executed as a traitor when he refused to surrender control of the colony to a governor appointed by William and Mary.

Jacques Cartier French explorer who, by navigating the St. Lawrence River in 1534, gave France its primary claim to territories in the New World.

James Buchanan Pennsylvania senator who was elected president in 1856 after gaining the Democratic nomination as a compromise candidate.

James Forten African American entrepreneur with a successful sailmaking business in Philadelphia who provided leadership for black business enterprises and advocated both racial integration and equal rights during the Jeffersonian era.

James K. Polk Tennessee congressman who was a leader of the Democratic Party and the dark-horse winner of the presidential campaign in 1844.

James Madison Virginia planter and political theorist known as the "father of the Constitution"; he became the fourth president of the United States.

James Monroe Republican politician from Virginia who served in diplomatic posts under George Washington, John Adams, and Thomas Jefferson; he later became the fifth president of the United States.

James Oglethorpe English philanthropist who established the colony of Georgia in 1732 as a refuge for debtors.

Jamestown First permanent English settlement in mainland America, established in 1607 by the Virginia Company and named in honor of King James I.

Jay's Treaty Controversial 1794 treaty negotiated between the United States and Great Britain by John Jay to ensure American neutrality in the French and English war.

Jean Laffite Leader of a band of pirates in southeast Louisiana; he offered to fight for the Americans at New Orleans in return for the pardon of his men.

Jefferson Davis Secretary of war under Franklin Pierce; he later became president of the Confederacy.

John Brown Abolitionist who fought proslavery settlers in Kansas in 1855; he was hanged for treason after seizing the U.S. arsenal at Harpers Ferry in 1859 as part of an effort to liberate southern slaves.

John Burgoyne British general forced to surrender his entire army at Saratoga, New York, in October 1777.

John C. Calhoun Congressman from South Carolina who was a leader of the War Hawks and the author of the official declaration of war in 1812.

John C. Frémont Explorer, soldier, and politician who explored and mapped much of the American West and Northwest; he later ran unsuccessfully for president.

John Cabot (Giovanni Caboto) Italian explorer who led the English expedition that sailed along the North American mainland in 1497.

John Coode Leader of a rebel army, the Protestant Association, that won control of Maryland in 1691.

John Deere Nineteenth-century American industrialist who pioneered the manufacture of steel plows especially suited for working hard-packed prairie soil.

John Dickinson Philadelphia lawyer and revolutionary pamphleteer who drafted the Articles of Confederation.

John J. Crittenden Kentucky senator who made an unsuccessful attempt to prevent the Civil War by proposing a series of constitutional amendments protecting slavery south of the Missouri Compromise line.

John Jay New York lawyer and diplomat who negotiated with Great Britain and Spain on behalf of the Confederation; he later became the first chief justice of the Supreme Court and negotiated the Jay Treaty with England.

John Marshall Virginia lawyer and politician whom President John Adams made chief justice of the Supreme Court; his legal decisions helped shape the role of the Supreme Court in American government.

John Randolph Virginia Republican politician who was a cousin of Thomas Jefferson; he believed in limited government and objected to several of Jefferson's policies.

John Ross Cherokee leader who had reluctantly directed the forced removal of the Cherokees from Georgia to Oklahoma Territory in the 1830s; he signed an alliance between some groups in Indian Territory and the Confederacy.

John Sutter Swiss immigrant who founded a colony in

California; the discovery of gold on his property in Coloma Valley, northeast of New Helvetia (Sacramento), in 1848 attracted hordes of miners who seized his land, leaving him financially ruined.

John Tyler Virginia senator who left the Democratic Party after conflicts with Andrew Jackson; he was elected vice president in 1840 and became president when William Henry Harrison died in office.

John Wilkes Booth Actor and southern sympathizer who on April 14, 1865, five days after Lee's surrender, fatally shot President Lincoln at Ford's Theater in Washington.

John Winthrop One of the founders of Massachusetts Bay Colony and the colony's first governor.

joint resolution A formal statement adopted by both houses of Congress and subject to approval by the president; if approved, it has the force of law.

joint-stock company A business financed through the sale of shares of stock to investors; the investors share in both the profits and losses from a risky venture.

Joseph Smith Jr. Founder of the Church of Jesus Christ of Latter-day Saints, also known as the Mormon Church, who transcribed the Book of Mormon and led his congregation westward from New York to Illinois; he was later murdered by an anti-Mormon mob.

journeyman A person who has finished an apprenticeship in a trade or craft and is a qualified worker in the employ of another.

judicial review The power of the Supreme Court to review the constitutionality of laws passed by Congress and by the states.

Judiciary Act of 1789 Law establishing the Supreme Court and the lower federal courts; it gave the Supreme Court the right to review state laws and state court decisions to determine their constitutionality.

Judiciary Act of 1801 Law that the Federalist Congress passed to increase the number of federal courts and judicial positions; President John Adams rushed to fill these positions with Federalists before his term ended.

Junípero Serra Spanish missionary who went to California in 1769; he and his successors established near the California coast a chain of missions that depended on Indian labor.

justice of the peace The lowest level of judge in some state court systems, usually responsible for hearing small claims and minor criminal cases; because Washington, D.C., is a federal territory rather than a state, the justice of the peace for that district is a federal appointee.

K

Kansas-Nebraska Act Law passed by Congress in 1854 that allowed residents of Kansas and Nebraska Territories to decide whether to allow slavery within their borders.

katsina dolls Painted wooden models that represent important spirit beings in Pueblo beliefs, often used in ceremonies and possessing great cultural significance.

Kenniwick Man The name given to a human skeleton discovered next to the Columbia River near Kenniwick, Washington, in 1996. The skeleton is believed to be over 9,000 years old and appears to have facial features unlike those of other ancient Indian relics.

Kitchen Cabinet President Jackson's informal advisers, who helped him shape both national and Democratic Party policy.

Know-Nothings Members of anti-Catholic, anti-immigrant organizations who eventually formed themselves into a national political party.

Ku Klux Klan A secret society organized in the South after the Civil War to resurrect white supremacy by means of violence and intimidation.

L

labor glut Oversupply of labor in relation to the number of jobs available.

Lakotas/Dakotas Subgroups of the Sioux Nation of Plains Indians; Lakotas make up the western branch, living mostly on the Great Plains; Dakotas, the eastern branch, live mostly in the prairie and lakes region of the Upper Midwest.

lame duck An officeholder who has failed to win, or is ineligible for, reelection but whose term in office has not yet ended.

land redistribution The division of land held by large landowners into smaller plots that are turned over to people without property.

lay exhorter A church member who preaches but is not an ordained minister.

Lecompton constitution State constitution written for Kansas in 1857 at a convention dominated by proslavery forces; it would have allowed slavery, but Kansas voters rejected it.

Liberty Party The first antislavery political party; it was formed in Albany, New York, in 1840.

lock A section of canal with gates at each end, used to raise or lower boats from one level to another by admitting or releasing water; locks allow canals to compensate for changes in terrain.

lockjaw A popular name for tetanus, an often fatal disease resulting primarily from deep wounds.

longhouse A communal dwelling, usually built of poles and bark and having a central hallway with family apartments on either side.

long-staple cotton A variety of cotton with long and loosely packed pods of fiber that is easy to comb out and process.

Louis XVI The king of France (r. 1774–1792) when the French Revolution began; he and his wife, Marie Antoinette, were executed in 1793 by the revolutionary government.

Louisiana French colony south of New France; it included the entire area drained by the Mississippi River and all its tributary rivers.

Louisiana Purchase   The U.S. purchase of Louisiana from France for $15 million in 1803; the Louisiana Territory extended from the Mississippi River to the Rocky Mountains.

loyalist   An American colonist who remained loyal to the king during the Revolution.

Lucretia Mott   Quaker minister who founded the Philadelphia Female Anti-Slavery Society (1833) and co-organized the Seneca Falls Women's Rights Convention in 1848.

Lydia Sigourney   Nineteenth-century Romantic and sentimental author who was one of the first women in American history to make a living as a professional writer.

M

machine politics   The aggressive use of influence, favors, and tradeoffs by a political organization, or "machine," to mobilize support among its followers.

Macon's Bill No. 2   Law passed by Congress in 1810 that offered exclusive trading rights to France or Britain, whichever recognized American neutral rights first.

magistrate   A civil officer charged with administering the law.

Main Line Canal   Ambitious canal-building enterprise by the state of Pennsylvania to connect the Delaware River at Philadelphia with the Ohio River at Pittsburgh.

maize   Corn; the word *maize* comes from an Indian word for this plant.

malarial   Related to malaria, an infectious disease characterized by chills, fever, and sweating; malaria is often transmitted through mosquito bites.

Mandan Indians   A Siouan-speaking Native American group that lived in permanent villages and practiced agriculture in the Red River Valley in present-day North Dakota; they hosted the Lewis and Clark expedition during the winter of 1804.

manifest destiny   Term first used in the 1840s to describe the right and duty of the United States to expand westward.

manifesto   A written statement publicly declaring the views of its author.

manioc   Also called cassava, a root vegetable native to South America that became a staple food source throughout the tropical world after 1500.

manumit   To free from slavery or bondage; to emancipate.

Marbury v. Madison   Supreme Court decision (1803) declaring part of the Judiciary Act of 1789 unconstitutional, thereby establishing an important precedent in favor of judicial review.

March to the Sea   Sherman's march through Georgia from Atlanta to Savannah from November 15 to December 21, 1864, during which Union soldiers carried out orders to destroy everything in their path.

market economy   An economic system based on the buying and selling of goods and services, in which prices are determined by the forces of supply and demand.

martial law   Temporary rule by military authorities, imposed on a civilian population in time of war or when civil authority has broken down.

Martin Van Buren   New York politician known for his skillful handling of party politics; he helped found the Democratic Party and later became the eighth president of the United States.

Mary Ludwig Howe   Wife of a soldier at Fort Monmouth; one of many women known popularly as "Molly Pitchers" because they carried water to cool down the cannon their husbands fired in battle.

Mason-Dixon Line   The boundary between Pennsylvania and Maryland; it marked the northern division between free and slave states before the Civil War.

Masons   An international fraternal organization with many socially and politically prominent members, including a number of U.S. presidents.

materialism   Excessive interest in worldly matters, especially in acquiring goods.

mawkish   Mushy, exaggerated, and insincere sentimentality.

Maximilian   Austrian archduke appointed by France to be emperor of Mexico in 1864; later executed by Mexican republicans.

Mayflower Compact   An agreement drafted in 1620 when the Pilgrims reached America that granted political rights to all male colonists who would abide by the colony's laws.

McCulloch v. Maryland   Supreme Court case (1819) in which the majority ruled that federal authority is superior to that of individual states and that states cannot control or tax federal operations within their borders.

mechanize   To substitute machinery for human labor.

mercantile theory   The economic notion that a nation should amass wealth by exporting more than it imports; colonies are valuable in a mercantile system as a source of raw materials and as a market for manufactured goods.

merchant marine   A nation's commercial ships.

Mercy Otis Warren   Writer and historian known for her influential anti-British plays and essays during the prerevolutionary era; an active opponent of the Constitution.

Meriwether Lewis   Jefferson aide who was sent to explore the Louisiana Territory in 1803; he later served as its governor.

Metacomet   A Wampanoag chief, known to the English as King Philip, who led the Indian resistance to colonial expansion in New England in 1675.

middle passage   The transatlantic voyage of indentured servants or African slaves to the Americas.

midwifery   The practice of assisting women in childbirth.

Milan Decree   Napoleon's order authorizing the capture of any neutral vessels sailing from British ports or submitting to British searches.

militiamen   Soldiers who were not members of a regular army but ordinary citizens called out in case of an emergency.

millennia The plural of *millennium*, a period of one thousand years.

millet A large family of grain grasses that produce nutritious, carbohydrate-rich seeds used for both human and animal feed.

milliner A maker or designer of hats.

millrace The channel for the fast-moving stream of water that drives a mill wheel.

millwright A person who designs, builds, or repairs mills or mill machinery.

minstrel show A variety show in which white actors made up as blacks presented jokes, songs, dances, and comic skits.

Minutemen Nickname first given to the Concord militia because of their speed in assembling and later applied generally to colonial militia during the Revolution.

Mississippi Plan Use of threats, violence, and lynching by Mississippi Democrats in 1875 to intimidate Republicans and bring the Democratic Party to power.

Mississippian tradition A culture shared by a number of American Indian societies centered in the southern Mississippi River Valley; influenced by Mexican culture, it is known for its pyramid building and urban centers.

Missouri Compromise Law proposed by Henry Clay in 1820 admitting Missouri to the Union as a slave state and Maine as a free state and banning slavery in the Louisiana Territory north of latitude 36°30′.

moderates People whose views are midway between two more extreme positions; in this case, Republicans who favored some reforms but not all the Radicals' proposals.

Mohammed Born ca. 570 into an influential family in Mecca, on the Arabian Peninsula; around 610 Mohammed began having religious visions in which he was revealed as "the Messenger of God." The content of his various visions was recorded as the Qur'an, the sacred text that is the foundation for the Islamic religion.

Mohicans Algonquin-speaking Indians who lived along the Hudson River, were dispossessed in a war with the Iroquois confederacy, and eventually were all but exterminated.

Monroe Doctrine President Monroe's 1823 statement declaring the Americas closed to further European colonization and discouraging European interference in the affairs of the Western Hemisphere.

Moors Natives of northern Africa who converted to Islam in the eighth century, becoming the major carriers of the Islamic religion and culture both to southern Africa and to the Iberian Peninsula (Spain and Portugal), which they conquered and occupied from the eighth century until their ouster in the late fifteenth century.

mortar A portable, muzzle-loading cannon that fires large projectiles at high trajectories over a short range; traditionally used by mobile troops against fixed fortifications.

mound builder Name applied to a number of Native American societies, including the Adena, Hopewell, and Mississippian cultures, that constructed massive earthen mounds as monuments and building foundations.

Muslims People who practice the religion of Islam, a monotheistic faith that accepts Mohammed as the chief and last prophet of God.

N

Napoleon Bonaparte General who took control of the French government in November 1799, at the end of France's revolutionary period; he eventually proclaimed himself emperor of France and conquered much of the continent of Europe.

Napoleonic wars Wars in Europe waged by or against Napoleon Bonaparte between 1803 and 1815.

Natchez Indians An urban, mound-building Indian people who lived on the lower Mississippi River until they were destroyed in a war with the French in the 1720s; survivors joined the Creek Confederacy.

Natchez Trace A road connecting Natchez, Mississippi, with Nashville, Tennessee; it was commercially and strategically important in the late eighteenth and early nineteenth centuries.

Nathanael Greene American general who took command of the Carolinas campaign in 1780.

National Trades' Union The first national association of trade unions in the United States; it was formed in 1834.

nationalists Americans who preferred a strong central government rather than the limited government prescribed in the Articles of Confederation.

nativist Favoring native-born inhabitants of a country over immigrants.

nativity Place of birth.

naturalized Granted full citizenship (after having been born in a foreign country).

neoclassicism A revival in architecture and art in the eighteenth and nineteenth centuries inspired by Greek and Roman models and characterized by order, symmetry, and simplicity of style.

Netherlands, the/Holland/Dutch Often used interchangeably, the first two terms refer to the low-lying area in western Europe north of France and Belgium and across the English Channel from Great Britain; the Dutch are the inhabitants of the Netherlands.

neutrality The policy of treating both sides in a conflict the same way and thus favoring neither.

New Departure Strategy of cooperation with some Reconstruction measures adopted by some leading southern Democrats in the hope of winning compromises favorable to their party.

New France The colony established by France in what is now Canada and the Great Lakes region of the United States.

New Harmony Utopian community that Robert Owen established in Indiana in 1825; economic problems and discord among members led to its failure two years later.

New Jersey Plan A proposal submitted by the New Jersey delegation at the Constitutional Convention for creating a government in which the states would have equal representation in a unicameral legislature.

New Netherland The colony founded by the Dutch West India Company in present-day New York; its capital was New Amsterdam on Manhattan Island.

New World A term that Europeans used during the period of early contact and colonization to refer to the Americas, especially in the context of their discovery and colonization.

Nicholas Biddle President of the Second Bank of the United States; he struggled to keep the bank functioning when President Jackson tried to destroy it.

Ninety-five Theses A document prepared by Martin Luther in 1517 protesting certain Roman Catholic practices that he believed were contrary to the will of God as revealed in Scripture.

noblesse oblige The belief that members of the elite are duty-bound to treat others charitably, especially those of lower status than themselves.

noncompliance Failure or refusal to obey a law or request.

nonconformity Refusal to accept or conform to the beliefs and practices of the majority.

Non-Intercourse Act Law passed by Congress in 1809 reopening trade with all nations except France and Britain and authorizing the president to reopen trade with them if they lifted restrictions on American shipping.

nonliterate Lacking a system of reading and writing, relying instead on storytelling and mnemonic (memory-assisting) devices such as pictures.

Northwest Ordinances Three laws (1784, 1785, 1787) that dealt with the sale of public lands in the Northwest Territory and established a plan for the admission of new states to the Union.

Northwest Passage The rumored and much-hoped-for water route from Europe to Asia by way of North America sought by early explorers.

nullification Refusal by a state to recognize or enforce a federal law within its boundaries.

O

Ohio Canal A canal connecting Cleveland to Portsmouth, completing a network of waterways linking the Hudson River, the Great Lakes, and the Mississippi River system.

Old Ironsides Nickname of the U.S.S. *Constitution*, the forty-four-gun American frigate whose victory over the *Guerrière* bolstered sagging national morale during the War of 1812.

Old Northwest The area of the United States referred to at the time as the Northwest Territory, it would eventually be broken into the states of Indiana, Illinois, Michigan, and Wisconsin.

oligarchy A small group of people or families who hold power.

Olive Branch Petition Resolution, adopted by the Second Continental Congress in 1775 after the Battles of Lexington and Concord, that offered to end armed resistance if the king would withdraw his troops and repeal the Intolerable Acts.

Oliver Hazard Perry American naval officer who led the fleet that defeated the British in the Battle of Put-in-Bay during the War of 1812.

omnibus Including or covering many things; an omnibus bill is a piece of legislation with many parts.

Oneida Community A religious community established in central New York in 1848; its members shared property, practiced group marriage, and reared children under communal care.

opposition party A political party opposed to the party or government in power.

oratorical Related to the art of persuasive and eloquent public speaking.

ordnance Weapons, ammunition, and other military equipment.

Oregon Country The region to the north of Spanish California extending from the crest of the Rocky Mountains to the Pacific Coast.

Oregon Question The question of the national ownership of the Pacific Northwest; the United States and England renegotiated the boundary in 1846, establishing it at 49° north latitude.

Oregon Trail The overland route from St. Louis to the Pacific Northwest followed by thousands of settlers in the 1840s.

original sin In Christian doctrine, the condition of sinfulness that all humans share because of Adam and Eve's disobedience to God in the Garden of Eden.

Osceola Seminole leader in Florida who opposed removal of his people to the West and led resistance to U.S. troops; he was captured by treachery while bearing a flag of truce.

Ostend Manifesto Declaration by American foreign ministers in 1854 that if Spain refused to sell Cuba, the United States might be justified in taking it by force.

P

pacifism Opposition to war or violence of any kind.

Panic of 1819 A financial panic that began when the Second Bank of the United States tightened credit and recalled government loans.

Panic of 1837 An economic collapse that came as the result of Andrew Jackson's fiscal policies and led to an extended national economic depression.

pardon A governmental directive canceling punishment for a person or people who have committed a crime.

Parliament The lawmaking branch of the English government, composed of the House of Lords, representing England's nobility, and the House of Commons, an elected body of untitled English citizens.

parochial school   A school supported by a church parish; in the United States, the term usually refers to a Catholic school.

partisan   Taking a strong position on an issue out of loyalty to a political group or leader.

party caucus   A meeting of members of a political party to decide on questions of policy or leadership or to register preferences for candidates running for office.

party platform   A formal statement of the principles, policies, and promises on which a political party bases its appeal to the public.

pass system   Laws that forbade slaves from traveling without written authorization from their owners.

passive resistance   Resistance by nonviolent methods.

patent   A government grant that gives the creator of an invention the sole right to produce, use, or sell that invention for a set period of time.

paternalistic   Treating social dependents as a father treats his children, providing for their needs but denying them rights or responsibilities.

Patrick Henry   Member of the Virginia House of Burgesses and American revolutionary leader noted for his oratorical skills.

patrollers   During the era of slavery, white guards who made the rounds of rural roads to make certain that slaves were not moving about the countryside without written permission from their masters.

patronage   Jobs or favors distributed on a political basis, usually as rewards for loyalty or service.

patroonship   A huge grant of land given to any Dutch West India Company stockholder who, at his own expense, brought fifty colonists to New Netherland; the colonists became the tenants of the estate owner, or patroon.

paupers   A term popular in the eighteenth and nineteenth centuries to describe poor people; cities like New York and Boston often registered paupers so as to provide local relief.

Paxton Boys   Settlers in Paxton, Pennsylvania, who massacred Conestoga Indians in 1763 and then marched on Philadelphia to demand that the colonial government provide better defense against the Indians.

payload   The part of a cargo that generates revenue, as opposed to the part needed to fire the boiler or supply the crew.

Peninsular Campaign   McClellan's attempt in the spring and summer of 1862 to capture Richmond by advancing up the peninsula between the James and York Rivers; Confederate forces under Robert E. Lee drove his troops back.

Pequot War   Conflict in 1636 between the Pequot Indians inhabiting eastern Connecticut and the colonists of Massachusetts Bay and Connecticut: the Indians were destroyed and driven from the area.

percussion cap   A thin metal cap containing an explosive compound, needed to fire the guns used in the Civil War.

pet banks   State banks into which Andrew Jackson ordered federal deposits to be placed to help deplete the funds of the Second Bank of the United States.

philosophe   Any of the popular French intellectuals or social philosophers of the Enlightenment, such as Voltaire, Diderot, or Rousseau.

piedmont   Land lying at the foot of a mountain range.

Piegan Indians   The branch of the Blackfoot Indians who resided in areas of what is now Montana during the late eighteenth and early nineteenth centuries.

pig iron   Crude iron, direct from a blast furnace, that is cast into rectangular molds called pigs in preparation for conversion into steel, cast iron, or wrought iron.

Pilgrims   A small group of separatists who left England in search of religious freedom and sailed to America on the *Mayflower* in 1620.

plank   One of the articles of a political platform.

plurality   In an election with three or more candidates, the number of votes received by the winner when the winner receives less than half of the total number of votes cast.

policy   A course of action taken by a government or a ruler.

Pontiac   Ottawa chief who led the unsuccessful resistance against British policy in 1763.

popular sovereignty   The doctrine that the people of a territory had the right to determine whether slavery would exist within their territory.

Port Hudson   Confederate garrison in Louisiana that surrendered to Union forces in July 1863, thus giving the Union unrestricted control of the Mississippi River.

portage   The carrying of boats or supplies overland between two waterways.

posse   A group of people usually summoned by a sheriff to aid in law enforcement.

postmillennialism   The tenet in some Christian theology teaching that Christ will return to Earth after religious activists have succeeded in converting all people to Christianity and following a thousand years under their godly rule.

power of the purse   The political power that is enjoyed by the branch of government that controls taxation and the use of tax monies.

preamble   An introductory paragraph in a formal document setting out its underlying justification and purpose.

precedent   An event or decision that may be used as an example in similar cases later on.

pre-Columbian   Existing in the Americas before the arrival of Columbus.

preemption bill   A temporary law that gave squatters the right to buy land they had settled on before it was offered for sale at public auction.

Presbyterians   Members of a Protestant sect that eventually became the established church of Scotland but which in the seventeenth century was sometimes persecuted by Scotland's rulers.

primogeniture The legal right of the eldest son to inherit the entire estate of his father.

privateer A ship captain who owned his own boat, hired his own crew, and was authorized by his government to attack and capture enemy ships.

probate court A court that establishes the validity of wills and administers the estates of people who have died.

Proclamation Line of 1763 Temporary boundary that Britain established in the Appalachian Mountains, west of which white settlement was banned; it was intended to reduce conflict between Indians and colonists.

property requirement The limitation of voting rights to citizens who own certain kinds or amounts of property.

Prophet, The Shawnee religious visionary who called for a return to Indian traditions and founded the community of Prophetstown on Tippecanoe Creek in Indiana.

proportional representation Representation in the legislature based on the population of each state.

proprietor A person who owns something.

protective tariff Tax on imported goods intended to make them more expensive than similar domestic goods, thus protecting the market for goods produced at home.

protégé An individual whose welfare or career is promoted by an influential person.

Protestantism From the root word *protest,* the beliefs and practices of Christians who broke with the Roman Catholic Church; rejecting church authority, the doctrine of "good works," and the necessity of the priesthood, Protestants accepted the Bible as the only source of revelation, salvation as God's gift to the faithful, and a direct, personal relationship with God as available to every believer.

provincialism The limited and narrow perspective thought to be characteristic of people in rural areas.

provisional Temporary.

proviso A clause making a qualification, condition, or restriction in a document.

Prussia A northern European state that became the basis for the German Empire in the late nineteenth century.

public accommodations Hotels, bars and restaurants, theaters, and other places set up to do business with anyone who can pay the price of admission.

public domain Land owned and controlled by the federal government.

public prosecutor A lawyer appointed by the government to prosecute criminal actions on behalf of the state.

Pueblo Revolt Indian rebellion against Spanish authority in 1680 led by Popé; succeeded in driving the Spanish out of New Mexico for nearly a decade.

putting-out system Manufacturing system through which machine-made components were distributed to individual families who used them to craft finished goods.

Q

Quakers Members of the Society of Friends, a radical Protestant sect that believed in the equality of men and women, pacifism, and the presence of a divine "inner light" in every individual.

Quasi-War Diplomatic crisis triggered by the XYZ affair; fighting occurred between the United States and France between the early summer of 1798 and the official end of the conflict in September 1800, but neither side issued a formal declaration of war.

quill pen A pen made from the shaft of a feather; the end of the quill is sharpened with a knife and then dipped in ink.

R

racial integration Equal opportunities to participate in a society or organization by people of different racial groups; the absence of race-based barriers to full and equal participation.

Radical Republicans Republican faction that tried to limit presidential power and enhance congressional authority during the Civil War; Radicals opposed moderation toward the South or any toleration of slavery.

rail gauge The distance between train tracks.

Ralph Waldo Emerson Philosopher, writer, and poet whose essays and poems made him a central figure in the transcendentalist movement and an important figure in the development of literary expression in the United States.

ratification The act of approving or confirming a proposal.

ratifying conventions A meeting of delegates in each state to determine whether that state would ratify the Constitution.

rationalism The theory that the exercise of reason, rather than the acceptance of authority or spiritual revelation, is the only valid basis for belief and the best source of spiritual truth.

rebellion Open, armed, and organized resistance to a legally constituted government.

reciprocal trade A system of trading in which the objective is equal exchange of commodities rather than profit.

Reconquista The campaign undertaken by European Christians to recapture the Iberian Peninsula from the Moors.

Reconstruction Term applied by historians to the years 1865–1877, when the Union was restored from the Civil War; important changes were made to the federal Constitution; and social, economic, and political relations between the races were transformed in the South.

redeem To pay a specified sum in return for something; in this case, to make good on paper money issued by the government by exchanging it for hard currency, silver or gold.

Redeemers Southern Democrats who hoped to bring the Democratic Party back into power and to suppress Black Reconstruction.

re-exports Products shipped from one nation to another by way of a third; during wartime, neutral nations can be used as third parties to carry goods to combatants.

Reformation The sixteenth-century rise of Protestantism, with the establishment of state-sponsored Protestant churches in England, the Netherlands, parts of Germany and Switzerland, and elsewhere.

regionalism Loyalty to the interests of a particular region of the country.

Regulators Frontier settlers in the Carolinas who protested the lack or abuse of government services in their area; the North Carolina Regulators were suppressed by government troops in 1771.

Reign of Terror The period from 1793 to 1794 in the French Revolution when thousands of people were executed as enemies of the state.

repossession The reclaiming of land or goods by the seller or lender after the purchaser fails to pay installments due.

republic A nation in which supreme power resides in the citizens, who elect representatives to govern them.

Republican Party Political party formed in 1854 that opposed the extension of slavery into the western territories.

"Republican womanhood" A role for mothers that became popularized following the Revolution; it stressed women's importance in instructing children in republican virtues such as patriotism and honor.

Republicans Political group formed during Washington's first administration; led by Thomas Jefferson and James Madison, they favored limited government involvement in encouraging manufacturing and the continued dominance of agriculture in the national economy.

repudiate To refuse to acknowledge or pay.

repudiation The act of rejecting the validity or the authority of something.

requisition To demand for military use.

Restoration The era following the return of monarchy to England, beginning in 1660 with King Charles II and ending in 1688 with the exile of King James II.

retaliatory tariff A tariff on imported goods imposed neither to raise revenue nor control commerce but to retaliate against tariffs charged by another nation.

retrenchment In government, the elimination of unnecessary jobs or functions for reform or cost-cutting purposes.

return on capital The yield on money that has been invested in an enterprise or product.

revenue cutter A small, lightly armed boat used by government customs agents to apprehend merchant ships violating customs laws.

revenue stamps Stickers affixed to taxed items by government officials indicating that the tax has been paid.

revival meeting A meeting for the purpose of reawakening religious faith, often characterized by impassioned preaching and emotional public testimony by converted sinners.

Richard Howe British admiral who commanded British naval forces in America; he was General William Howe's brother.

Richmond Port city on the James River in Virginia; already the state capital, it became the capital of the Confederacy.

rifled Having a series of spiral grooves inside the barrel of a gun that causes the bullet to spin, giving it greater range and accuracy.

Rio Bravo The Spanish and then Mexican name for the river that now forms the border between Texas and Mexico; the Rio Grande.

Roanoke Island Island off North Carolina that Raleigh sought to colonize beginning in 1585.

Robert Cavelier, Sieur de La Salle French explorer who followed the Mississippi River from its origin in present-day Illinois to the Gulf of Mexico in 1683, giving France a claim to the entire river way and adjoining territory.

Robert E. Lee A Virginian with a distinguished career in the U.S. Army who resigned to assume command of the Confederate army in Virginia when the Civil War began.

Robert Morris Pennsylvania merchant and financial expert who advised the Continental Congress during the Revolution and served as a fundraiser for the Confederation government.

Roger Williams Puritan minister banished from Massachusetts for criticizing its religious rules and government policies; in 1635, he founded Providence, a community based on religious freedom and the separation of church and state.

romanticism Artistic and intellectual movement characterized by interest in nature, emphasis on emotion and imagination over rationality, and rebellion against social conventions.

runoff election A final election held to determine a winner after an earlier election has eliminated the weakest candidates.

Rutherford B. Hayes Ohio governor and former Union general who won the Republican nomination in 1876 and became president of the United States in 1877.

S

Sacajawea Shoshone woman who served as guide and interpreter on the Lewis and Clark expedition.

Saint Augustine First colonial city in the present-day United States; located in Florida and founded by Pedro Menéndez de Aviles for Spain in 1565.

sainthood Full membership in a Puritan church.

salutary neglect The British policy of relaxed enforcement of most colonial trade regulations as long as the mainland colonies remained loyal to the government and profitable within the British economy.

Sam Houston American general and politician who fought in the struggle for Texas's independence from Mexico and became president of the Republic of Texas.

Samuel Adams Massachusetts revolutionary leader and propagandist who organized opposition to British policies after 1764.

Samuel de Champlain French explorer who traced the St. Lawrence River inland to the Great Lakes, founded the city of Quebec, and formed the French alliance with the Huron Indians.

sanctity Saintliness or holiness; the quality of being sacred or beyond reproach.

Santa Fe Spanish colonial town established in 1609; eventually the capital of the province of New Mexico.

Santo Domingo Caribbean island (originally named Hispaniola by Christopher Columbus and also known as Saint Domingue) shared by the modern nations of Haiti and the Dominican Republic.

scalawag Derogatory term for white southerners who aligned themselves with the Republican Party during Reconstruction.

Scots-Irish Protestant Scottish settlers in British-occupied northern Ireland, many of whom migrated to the colonies in the eighteenth century.

seasoning A period during which slaves from Africa were held in the West Indies so they could adjust to the climate and disease environment of the American tropics.

secede To withdraw formally from membership in a political union; threats of secession were used frequently during the early nineteenth century to bring attention to political issues.

secession Withdrawal from the United States.

Second Battle of Bull Run Union defeat near Bull Run in August 1862; Union troops led by John Pope were outmaneuvered by Lee.

Second Great Awakening An upsurge in religious fervor that began around 1800 and was characterized by revival meetings.

sectionalism Excessive concern for local or regional interests.

sedition Conduct or language inciting rebellion against the authority of a state.

segregation Separation on account of race or class from the rest of society, such as the separation of blacks from whites in most southern school systems.

separatists English Protestants who chose to leave the Church of England because they believed it was corrupt.

serfs Peasants who were bound to a particular estate but, unlike slaves, were not the personal property of the estate owner and received traditional feudal protections.

Shakers A mid-eighteenth-century offshoot of the Quakers, founded in England by Mother Ann Lee; Shakers engaged in spirited worship, including dancing and rhythmic shaking, hence their name, and practiced communal living and strict celibacy.

shaman A person who acts as a link between the visible material world and an invisible spirit world; a shaman's duties include healing, conducting religious ceremonies, and foretelling the future.

sharecropping A system for renting farmland in which tenant farmers give landlords a share of their crops, rather than cash, as rent.

short-staple cotton A variety of cotton with short and tightly packed pods of fiber in which the plant's seeds are tangled.

Sir Henry Clinton General who replaced William Howe as commander of the British forces in America in 1778 after the British surrender at Saratoga.

Sir Walter Raleigh English courtier, soldier, and adventurer who attempted to establish the Virginia Colony.

Slave Coast A region of coastal West Africa adjacent to the Gold Coast; it was the principal source of the slaves taken out of West Africa from the sixteenth to the early nineteenth century.

slave codes Laws that established the status of slaves, denying them basic rights and classifying them as the property of slaveowners.

social contract A theoretical agreement between the governed and the government that defines and limits the rights and obligations of each.

socialist Practicing socialism, the public ownership of manufacturing, farming, and other forms of production so that they benefit society rather than produce individual or corporate profits.

Sojourner Truth Abolitionist and feminist who was freed from slavery in 1827 and became a leading preacher against slavery and for the rights of women.

Songhai Empire A large empire in West Africa whose capital was Timbuktu; its rulers accepted Islam around the year 1000.

Sons of Liberty A secret organization first formed in Boston to oppose the Stamp Act.

sovereignty The ultimate power in a nation or a state.

special interest A person or organization that seeks to benefit by influencing legislators.

specie Coins minted from precious metals.

Specie Circular Order issued by President Jackson in 1836 stating that the federal government would accept only specie—gold and silver—as payment for public land; one of the causes of the Panic of 1837.

speculator A person who buys and sells land or some other commodity in the hope of making a profit.

spendthrift A person who spends money recklessly or wastefully.

spiritual A religious folk song originated by African Americans, often expressing a longing for deliverance from the constraints and hardships of their lives.

spoils Jobs and other rewards for political support.

Squanto A Patuxet Indian who taught the Pilgrims survival techniques in America and acted as translator for the colonists.

squatter A person who settles on unoccupied land to which he or she has no legal claim.

Stamp Act British law of 1765 that directly taxed a variety of items, including newspapers, playing cards, and legal documents.

standard-bearer The recognized leader of a movement, organization, or political party.

staple crop A basic or necessary agricultural item, produced for sale or export.

states' rights The political position in favor of limiting federal power to allow the greatest possible self-government by the individual states.

statesman A political leader who acts out of concern for the public good and not out of self-interest.

stay laws Laws suspending the right of creditors to foreclose on debtors; they were designed to protect indebted farmers from losing their land.

Stephen A. Douglas Illinois senator who tried to reconcile northern and southern differences over slavery through the Compromise of 1850 and the Kansas-Nebraska Act.

Stephen F. Austin American colonizer in Texas and leading voice in the Texas Revolution.

Stono Rebellion Slave revolt in South Carolina in 1739; it prompted the colony to pass harsher laws governing the movement of slaves and the capture of runaways.

strict constructionist A person who believes the government has only the powers specifically named in the Constitution.

Stuart kings The dynasty of English kings who claimed the throne after the death of Elizabeth I, who left no heirs.

subpoena A writ, or order, requiring an individual to appear in court to give testimony.

sub-Saharan Africa The region of Africa south of the Sahara Desert.

subsidy Financial assistance that a government grants to an enterprise considered to be in the public interest.

subsistence farming Farming that produces enough food for survival but no surplus that can be sold.

subsistence society A society that produces the food and supplies necessary for its survival but which does not produce a surplus that can be marketed.

suffrage The right to vote.

Sugar Act British law of 1764 that taxed sugar and other colonial imports to pay for some of Britain's expenses in protecting the colonies.

supply and demand The two factors that determine price in an economy based on private property: (1) how much of a commodity is available (supply) and (2) how many people want it (demand).

survey To determine the area and boundaries of land through measurement and mathematical calculation.

Susan B. Anthony Tireless campaigner for woman suffrage and close associate of Elizabeth Cady Stanton.

syphilis An infectious disease usually transmitted through sexual contact; if untreated, it can lead to paralysis and death.

T

Table Action taken by a legislative body (Congress, for example) to postpone debate on an issue until a positive vote to remove the topic from the table is taken.

tallow Hard fat obtained from the bodies of cattle and other animals and used to make candles and soap.

Tallmadge Amendment An amendment to a statehood bill for Missouri proposed by New York congressman James Tallmadge Jr. that would have banned slavery from the new state; it created a deadlock in Congress that necessitated the Missouri Compromise.

tariff A tax on imported or exported goods.

Tariff of 1816 First protective tariff in U.S. history; its purpose was to protect America's fledgling textile industry.

Tariff of Abominations Tariff package designed to win support for anti-Adams forces in Congress; its passage in 1828 discredited Adams but set off sectional tension over tariff issues.

Tecumseh Shawnee leader and brother of The Prophet; he established an Indian confederacy along the frontier that he hoped would be a barrier to white expansion.

Tejanos Mexican settlers in Texas in the nineteenth century.

temperance Moderation or abstinence in the consumption of alcoholic drinks.

tenement An urban apartment house, usually with minimal facilities for sanitation, safety, and comfort.

terrorists Those who use threats and violence to achieve ideological or political goals.

Tertium Quid Republican faction formed by John Randolph in protest against Jefferson's plan for acquiring Florida from Spain; the name is Latin and means a "third thing," indicating Randolph's rejection of both the Federalist and Republican Parties.

Texas Revolution A revolt by American colonists in Texas against Mexican rule; it began in 1835 and ended with the establishment of the Republic of Texas in 1836.

Texians Non-Hispanic settlers in Texas in the nineteenth century.

Thaddeus Stevens Pennsylvania congressman who was a leader of the Radical Republicans during the Civil War and Reconstruction.

Thayendanegea Mohawk chief known to the Americans as Joseph Brant; his combined forces of loyalists and Indians defeated John Sullivan's expedition to upstate New York in 1779.

Thirteenth Amendment Constitutional amendment, ratified in 1865, that abolished slavery in the United States and its territories.

Thomas Gage British general who was military governor of

Massachusetts and commander of the army occupying Boston in 1775.

Thomas Hart Benton U.S. senator from Missouri and legislative leader of the Democrats; he was a champion of President Jackson and a supporter of westward expansion.

Thomas Hutchinson Boston merchant and judge who served as lieutenant governor and later governor of Massachusetts; Stamp Act protesters destroyed his home in 1765.

Thomas J. Jackson Confederate general nicknamed "Stonewall"; he commanded troops at both battles of Bull Run and was mortally wounded by his own soldiers at Chancellorsville in 1863.

Thomas Pinckney South Carolina politician and diplomat who was an unsuccessful Federalist candidate for president in 1796.

Three-Fifths Compromise An agreement to count three-fifths of a state's slave population for purposes of determining a state's representation in the House of Representatives.

tidewater Low coastal land drained by tidal streams in Maryland and Virginia.

total war War waged with little regard for the welfare of troops on either side or for enemy civilians; the objective is to destroy both the human and the economic resources of the enemy.

trade union A labor organization whose members work in a specific trade or craft.

Trail of Tears Forced march of the Cherokee people from Georgia to Indian Territory in the winter of 1838, during which thousands of Cherokees died.

transcendent Lying beyond the normal range of experience.

transcendentalism A philosophical and literary movement asserting the existence of God within human beings and in nature and the belief that intuition is the highest source of knowledge.

transship The practice of shipping cargo to a secondary port and then transferring it to other ships for transport to a final destination; cargos from up the Mississippi River were shipped by barge to New Orleans and then loaded onto ocean-going vessels to be carried to American ports along the Atlantic Coast.

Treaty of Fort Stanwix Treaty signed in 1784 that opened all Iroquois lands to white settlement.

Treaty of Ghent Treaty ending the War of 1812, signed in Belgium in 1814; it restored peace but was silent on the issues over which the United States and Britain had gone to war.

Treaty of Greenville 1795 treaty in which the United States agreed to pay northwestern Indians about $10,000 for the land that later became the state of Ohio.

Treaty of Guadalupe Hidalgo Treaty (1848) in which Mexico gave up Texas above the Rio Grande and ceded New Mexico and California to the United States in return for $15 million.

Treaty of New Echota Treaty in 1835 by which a minority faction gave all Cherokee lands east of the Mississippi to the

U.S. government in return for $5 million and land in Indian Territory.

Treaty of Paris of 1763 The treaty ending the French and Indian War in 1763; it gave all of French Canada and Spanish Florida to Britain.

Treaty of Paris of 1783 Treaty that ended the Revolutionary War in 1783 and secured American independence.

Treaty of San Lorenzo Treaty between the United States and Spain, negotiated in 1795 by Thomas Pinckney; Spain granted the United States the right to navigate the Mississippi River and use the port of New Orleans as an outlet to the sea.

Treaty of Tordesillas The agreement, signed by Spain and Portugal in 1494, that moved the line separating Spanish and Portuguese claims to territory in the non-Christian world, giving Spain most of the Western Hemisphere.

Treaty of Velasco Treaty that Santa Anna signed in May 1836 after his capture at the San Jacinto River; it recognized the Republic of Texas but was later rejected by the Mexican congress.

tributary empire An empire in which subjects rule themselves but make payments, called tribute, to an imperial government in return for protection and services.

tribute A payment of money or other valuables that one group makes to another as the price of security.

trickster tales Stories that feature as a central character a clever figure who uses his wits and instincts to adapt to changing times; a survivor, the trickster is used by traditional societies, including African cultures, to teach important cultural lessons.

Trinity In Christian doctrine, the belief that God has three divine aspects—Father, Son, and Holy Spirit.

turnpike A road on which tolls are collected at gates set up along the way; private companies hoping to make a profit from the tolls built the first turnpikes.

Twelfth Amendment Constitutional amendment, ratified in 1804, that provides for separate balloting in the Electoral College for president and vice president.

Twenty Negro Law Confederate law that exempted planters owning twenty or more slaves from the draft on the grounds that overseeing farm labor done by slaves was necessary to the war effort.

typhoid fever An infectious disease transmitted through contact with contaminated water, milk, or food; causes severe intestinal distress and high fever.

U

Ulysses S. Grant U.S. general who became general in chief of the Union army in 1864 after the Vicksburg campaign; he later became president of the United States.

Underground Railroad The secret network of northerners who helped fugitive slaves escape to Canada or to safe areas in free states.

underwrite To assume financial responsibility for; for

example, to guarantee the purchase of bonds so that a project can go forward.

unicameral   Having a single legislative house.

unilateral   Undertaken or issued by only one side and thus not involving an agreement made with others.

Unionist   Loyal to the United States of America.

Unitarianism   A religion that denies the Trinity, teaching that God exists only in one person; it also stresses individual freedom of belief and the free use of reason in religion.

United States Sanitary Commission   Government commission established by Abraham Lincoln to improve public health conditions in military camps and hospitals.

unprecedented   Unheard of or novel.

urbanization   The growth of cities in a nation or region and the shifting of the population from rural to urban areas.

utopian   Idealistic reform sentiment based on the belief that a perfect society can be created on Earth and that a particular group or leader has the knowledge to actually create such a society.

V

vagrancy   The legal condition of having no fixed place of residence or means of support.

Valley Forge   Winter encampment of Washington's army in Pennsylvania in 1777–1778; because the soldiers suffered greatly from cold and hunger, the term *Valley Forge* has become synonymous with "dire conditions."

vanguard   The foremost position in any army advancing into battle.

veto   The power or right of one branch of government to reject the decisions of another branch.

vice-admiralty court   Nonjury British court in which a judge heard cases involving shipping.

vicissitudes   Sudden or unexpected changes encountered during the course of life.

Vicksburg   Confederate-held city on the Mississippi River that surrendered on July 4, 1863, after a lengthy siege by Grant's forces.

vigilance committees   Groups of armed private citizens who use the threat of mob violence to enforce their own interpretation of the law.

Vikings   Late-medieval Danish, Swedish, and Norwegian groups who responded to land shortages and climatic conditions in Scandinavia by taking to the sea and establishing communities in various parts of western Europe, Iceland, Greenland, and North America.

Virginia and Kentucky Resolutions   Statements that the Virginia and Kentucky legislatures issued in 1798 in response to the Alien and Sedition Acts; they asserted the right of states to overrule the federal government.

Virginia Dynasty   Term applied to the U.S. presidents from Virginia in the period between 1801 and 1825: Jefferson, Madison, and Monroe.

Virginia Plan   Fourteen proposals by the Virginia delegation to the Constitutional Convention for creating a more powerful central government and giving states proportional representation in a bicameral legislature.

voluntary association   An organization or club through which individuals engage in voluntary service, usually associated with charity or reform.

voting fraud   Altering election results by illegal measures to bring about the victory of a particular candidate.

W

wage slavery   The bondage of workers who, though legally free, are underpaid, trapped in debt, and living in extreme poverty.

War Hawks   Members of Congress elected in 1810 from the West and South who campaigned for war with Britain in the hopes of stimulating the economy and annexing new territory.

ward   A child who is legally put into the care of someone other than a parent.

Webster-Ashburton Treaty   Treaty that in 1842 established the present border between Canada and northeastern Maine.

West Point   Site of a fort overlooking the Hudson River, north of New York City.

Western Hemisphere   Geographers speak of the world as being divided into two halves (hemispheres). The Western Hemisphere includes North America, Mexico, Central America, and South America; the Eastern Hemisphere includes Europe, Asia, and Africa.

wheelwright   A person who makes or repairs wheels for carts, wagons, or other vehicles.

Whig Party   Political party that came into being in 1834 as an anti-Jackson coalition and that charged "King Andrew" with executive tyranny.

Whiskey Rebellion   A protest by grain farmers against the 1794 federal tax on whiskey; militia forces led by President Washington put down this Pennsylvania uprising.

white supremacy   The racist belief that whites are inherently superior to all other races and are therefore entitled to rule over them.

white-collar workers   Workers able to wear white shirts on the job because they do no grubby manual labor.

Wilderness, The   Densely wooded region of Virginia that was the site in May 1864 of a devastating but inconclusive battle between Union forces under Grant and Confederates under Lee.

William Bradford   The separatist who led the Pilgrims to America; he became the first governor of Plymouth Plantations.

William Clark   Soldier and explorer who joined Meriwether Lewis as coleader on the expedition to explore the Louisiana Territory; he was responsible for mapmaking.

William Howe   British general in command at the Battle of Bunker Hill; three years later he became commander in chief of British forces in America.

William Lloyd Garrison   Abolitionist leader who founded and published *The Liberator,* an antislavery newspaper.

William Penn   English Quaker who founded the colony of Pennsylvania in 1681.

William Tecumseh Sherman   U.S. general who captured Atlanta in 1864 and led a destructive march to the Atlantic Coast.

Wilmot Proviso   Amendment to an appropriations bill in 1846 proposing that any territory acquired from Mexico be closed to slavery; it was defeated in the Senate.

Winfield Scott   Virginia soldier and statesman who led troops in the War of 1812 and the War with Mexico; he was still serving as a general at the start of the Civil War.

Worcester v. Georgia   Supreme Court case (1832) concerning the arrest of two missionaries to the Cherokees in Georgia; the Court found that Georgia had no right to rule in Cherokee territory.

X

xenophobic   Fearful of or hateful toward foreigners or those seen as being different.

XYZ affair   A diplomatic incident in which American envoys to France were told that the United States would have to loan France money and bribe government officials as a precondition for negotiation.

Y

Yazoo affair   Corrupt deal in which the Georgia legislature sold a huge tract of public land to speculators for a low price but later overturned the sale; the basis for the Supreme Court case of *Fletcher v. Peck*, which in 1810 supported Jefferson's position favoring compensation and helped establish the sanctity of civil contracts over state legislation.

yeoman   Independent landowner entitled to suffrage.

Yorktown   Site of the last major battle of the Revolution; American and French troops trapped Cornwallis's army here, on a peninsula on the York River near the Chesapeake Bay, and forced him to surrender.

Young America movement   A political movement popular among young voters during the 1840s and early 1850s that advocated free-market capitalism, national expansionism, and American patriotism; a strong force within the Democratic Party, Young America leaders tried to avoid antislavery debates and other divisive controversies.

Z

Zachary Taylor   American general whose defeat of Santa Anna at Buena Vista in 1847 made him a national hero and the Whig choice for president in 1848.

Boldfaced terms indicate glossary terms that are defined on that page.

The History Handbook

Carol Berkin

Baruch College,
City University of New York

Betty S. Anderson

Boston University

HOUGHTON MIFFLIN COMPANY   Boston   New York

Contents

13 How Do I Make Computer Technology Work for Me? How Do I Succeed in an Online Class? A77

14 Are There Any Other Tips I Should Know? A85

Preface

The authors of this *Handbook* still remember their freshman history class with a combination of horror and humor. We both recall frantically underlining almost every sentence in the textbook. We remember the panic we felt when a professor handed out instructions for the first written assignment as well as our sweaty palms when we had to take our first in-class exam. Worst of all, perhaps, were our first stumbling efforts at doing historical research.

Watching our students go through the same traumas we did semester after semester, we wondered: Was this an inevitable rite of passage every student must endure? Did every student have to learn the hard way, by trial and error, mistake and regret? Was it really impossible for a freshman to enjoy a history course and do well in it? Our answer to all these questions was a resounding "No." And this is why we sat down to write *The History Handbook*.

Our basic premise is simple: Success in a history class is within the reach of every student. But like all specialized disciplines, history has its tricks of the trade, and mastering them is the key to that success. Thus, the *History Handbook* is, above all, a collection of practical suggestions on everything from how to tackle a textbook and study for an exam to how to turn the Internet into an effective research tool. The *Handbook* is not a theoretical collection of ideas; it is a concrete tool , providing clear definitions and helpful examples on every topic. Although the *Handbook* is primarily a no-nonsense guide to the skills you'll need in a history course, it also introduces you to the ta special feature called "Helping Hand." In these "Helping Hand" segments, we level with you. We give you the teacher's point of view on what is happening in the classroom and remind you that professors are people too. We also offer sage and sensible advice on developing good study habits. Much of what we say in the "Helping Hand" features may sound familiar—don't try to cram the night before the exam! Don't leave the research for a paper to the last minute! Don't fall behind in your assigned readings! But remember—just because you've heard it before doesn't mean it isn't excellent advice. Finally, we've added a Glossary so that even new information isn't mysterious.

The companion student web site takes advantage of the breadth of resources available to you on the World Wide Web. You can link to select web sites to get help in researching history topics, access on-line versions of a variety of style guides, and more. The site also features a Glossary of key terms and web activities.

What skills do we think are essential for success in a history course? The answer can be found by looking closely at the table of contents. The basic "how tos" of taking notes in class, getting the most out of lectures and class discussions, tackling the textbook effectively, and studying for a variety of exam types are laid out in Chapters 1 through 3. Because interpreting and understanding maps is an important part of a history course, we've included a whole chapter on how maps can help you understand history. And, because you will have to learn to recognize the difference between primary sources, secondary sources, and works of fiction as well as learn how to use each of these types of works in your history course, we've included a chapter on that subject as well. Since most history classes require you to write papers, we've devoted Chapters 6 through 8 to every aspect of the writing process from picking a topic to conducting research to organizing an essay. These chapters contain useful suggestions on using both the library and the Web. In Chapter 9, we offer a guide to oral rather than written projects such as debates or role playing. Because most colleges have developed guidelines against plagiarism, we've also included two chapters on this form of intellectual theft, carefully defining plagiarism and explaining how to cite the sources you use appropriately. We've also included a chapter on those rules of grammar that help you communicate your ideas to others. Because technology has become a critical part of the learning process, we've written a chapter on the role of the computer in the virtual, or online, classroom. The final ype of questions historians ask and the variety of sources they turn to for answers to those questions. It is a guide both to how to "do" history and how to do well in a history class.

One of our main goals was to make *The History Handbook* genuinely accessible to all students. Realizing that you're often in a hurry to find specific help on a particular topic, we open each chapter with a bulleted list of all the topics being covered within it and end each chapter with a brief "Recap," providing similar content information. These features guarantee that you won't have to read through the entire *Handbook* to find the solution to that one particular—and urgent—problem. Throughout the *Handbook*, you'll see chapter of the *Handbook*, "Are There Any Other Tips I Should Know?" allows us to share a variety of other valuable tips that come from years of being both students and professors ourselves.

You've probably noticed that we haven't attempted to provide a long defense of history or its importance, for we believe that you'll recognize the value of history as you become involved in its study. Instead, *The History Handbook* provides a guide to developing the skills you need to succeed in a college history class. Once those skills are acquired our hope is that you'll be able to relax and join in some of the fun.

Carol Berkin would like to give special thanks to Roberta McCutcheon, head of the history department at Trevor Day School in New York City, and Angelo Angelis, Assistant Professor of History at Hunter College, who both read drafts of the manuscript and offered sage advice based on their years of teaching. Both authors are also grateful to the following instructors, who read and criticized the manuscript throughout its development:

Peter K. Bacon, U.S. Military Academy at West Point
Emerson W. Baker, Salem State College
Linda Bregstein, Mercer County Community College
Jerry Cooper, University of Missouri, St. Louis
Anthony J. Heideman, U.S. Naval Academy
Randolph Hollingsworth, University of Kentucky
Toren Hudson, South Texas Community College
Earl F. Mulderink III, Southern Utah University
William H. Mulligan, Jr., Murray State University
Patrick M. Patterson, Honolulu Community College
Alice E. Reagan, Northern Virginia Community College, Woodbridge
Patrick D. Reagan, Tennessee Technological University
Denise S. Spooner, California State University, Northridge
Janet A.Thompson, Tallahassee Community College
Louise Blakeney Williams, Central Connecticut State University
Kathleen Xidis, Johnson County Community College

C.B
B.S.A.

What is History and Why Is it Important?

Here you are, in First, the study of history sharpens your reading and your writing skills. Many historians are master storytellers and their books are good examples of how to narrate a tale, describe an event, and vividly capture the character of a person so that the reader feels they know that person intimately. These are skills that you will be called upon to demonstrate in most of your other courses in college. They are also skills we all wish we had worked on when we are trying to make conversation at a party, sell a product to potential buyers, or write an evaluation of a colleague or employee. Other historians have penetrating, focused minds; they carry us, step by step, through a process of analysis that shows us how a muddle of apparently unconnected information actually has a logical thread. Like good detectives, they demonstrate how to gather clues, create the connections among them, distinguish cause and consequence from accident and coincidence. Who doesn't want to be more like Sherlock Holmes when they are analyzing stocks, putting together a legal defense, or even figuring out who stole cookies from the cookie jar? There is no way around it: history books provide models for communicating, analyzing, and organizing ideas and information. This is why many of the best lawyers, judges, corporate executives, and teachers majored in history in college.

Second, doing history yourself—writing book reviews, producing research papers, giving oral reports in class, and writing an essay that compares one event to another or explains why something happened and what results it produced—allows you to test and hone these skills for yourself. Knowing where to find information, how to evaluate it, and how to discern the connections among many pieces of information are essential talents in this era of information revolutions and cybernetics. They are also talents that will serve you well as long as you are a person who wants to make independent judgments about important issues in your personal and professional life.

Finally, history is just plain fun—and even the most serious and ambitious college students need some fun. Where else can you find so many zany or heroic characters? Open any history book and you will find con men and philosophers, women's rights advocates and dance hall girls, kings, queens, revolutionaries, and paupers who became millionaires, plus an endless assortment of assassins, murderers, madmen, and poets. Where else is there so much drama and excitement? For sheer nail-biting, edge-of-your-seat tension, what can compete with the fall of Rome, the decision to drop the atomic bomb, the voyages of Christopher Columbus, or the first humans landing on the moon? Not even the most ambitious movie director can produce the rise and fall of so many nations, bloody battles and secret peace negotiations, inventions, discoveries, horrifying acts of cruelty, and crusades for human rights. Murder, mayhem, romance—history has them all, and more.

Interested? Read on. *The History Handbook* will provide you with a step-by-step guide to developing all the skills you need to succeed in your first college history class. It will allow you to relax, and share in some of the fun.

The History Handbook is a straightforward "how-to" book designed for speedy reference. It is organized so that you can quickly find help for the problem you are facing. Each chapter begins with a preview of what will be covered, called Tips in This Chapter. Throughout each chapter you will see a feature called Helping Hand, in which the authors modestly share their experience and wisdom drawn from many years as students themselves and as professors. At the end of every chapter, you will find a brief section called Recap, which sums up the main topics that the chapter has covered.

Now, you should be ready to begin.

*H*ow Can I Succeed in My History Class?

- *What will help me most?*

- *How many notes should I take during the lecture?*

- *Why are class discussions important?*

- *Can I ask the professor for help?*

What Will Help Me Most?

The following three suggestions may seem obvious, but they are critical nevertheless.

First, go to class. Professors are frustrated when students don't come to class and then arrive at the end of the semester to complain about the heavy workload or ask for an extension. Professors will generally be more responsive to students they know and see on a regular basis.

Second, go to class prepared to participate. Most professors consider classroom participation important. To be part of any class discussion, you need to be caught up on the reading assignments. It will also help if you jot down some questions or observations about the readings or the material covered in the last lecture or class discussion. If you are a naturally shy person, arriving with notes on the reading and a provocative question or two will help you jump into the discussion. Remember, never to try to score points with your professor by making fun of another student's comments. Constructive criticism will be welcome; personal attacks on a classmate will not.

Third, keep up with the work. Don't leave everything until the night before the paper is due or the exam is scheduled. Don't fool yourself into believing the old clichés of "I do better when I'm under pressure" or "I can't write a paper until the night before it's due." If you try to cram at the last moment, you will not do well. Well-written papers don't fly out of the computer printer in the middle of the night. You need to attend class regularly, complete all the readings and assignments, and review all of your notes regularly.

How Many Notes Should I Take During the Lecture?

Unless you have mastered shorthand, you cannot hope to take down everything your professor or your classmates say. While you are furiously scribbling down the professor's first sentence, you are probably missing something important that he or she is saying in her second sentence. Is it hopeless? Not if you think before you write. Try following these six steps if you're attending a class lecture.

First, if the professor puts an outline for the day's topic on the board, copy it down immediately. (You might even want to get into the habit of arriving early so that you can transfer the outline into your notebook before the lecture begins.) If the professor hands out an outline, make sure you add it to your notebook immediately.

 HELPING HAND Make the most of the professor's outline by adding to it. Fill in examples taken from the lecture, class discussion, and/or the assigned reading that illustrate the main points on that outline. Add your own informed comments and questions. Add relevant dates and names. Define terms used on the outline.

Second, if the professor begins the lecture with a series of questions or interpretive statements to be answered or proven during the course of the lecture, use them as the heading for the day's notes. If you are lucky, the professor will end the day's lecture with a summary of what was covered. If you add this summary to your notes, you will have produced the same format as a textbook chapter.

HELPING HAND   Let the professor be your note-taking guide. If her opening question is "What were the main causes of the French Revolution?" then don't take elaborate notes on the execution of Queen Marie Antoinette (even if the gory details are exciting).

Third, listen carefully as the professor develops the day's theme or topic. He or she will probably provide several examples for each point along the way. Don't try to copy all of these examples down. Instead, choose one or two examples that you feel illustrate the point *best for you.*

Fourth, listen closely to any questions asked by classmates during or after the lecture. Record the question and the response if you feel both clarify an issue for you.

Fifth, do you have a question? Is there something you aren't sure you understood or something you are especially curious about that the professor did not cover? Ask—and then record the question and the response in your notes.

Sixth, record your own insights, comments, and questions as they occur to you during the lecture.

Seventh, develop your own catch phrases or codes that will save you time. For example, if you want to remind yourself to compare the issue being discussed in this class with one that was covered a week before, you might want to write "c/c [compare and contrast] discussion on ____ [enter date]." Or use familiar symbols from other disciplines such as math, e.g., the = sign, or the ≠ sign (the equals sign with a line drawn through it to signify "not the same as"). Or before class, list in the margins all the key people or terms likely to be mentioned often in the day's class and assign abbreviations, such as their initials, to each of them. This way, in a lecture on Progressivism, you won't have to write Theodore Roosevelt a dozen times. Finally, be creative! Make up your own codes. One of the authors of this handbook made it through a class on the U.S. Constitution by writing "Csstus" for "Constitution" at least a million times in her notes!

If the class is a discussion class, steps 1 and 2 still apply. You will still want to jot down the main issues and points raised by your classmates, and you will still want to limit yourself to one or two examples that your classmates may provide in discussing each issue.

Finally, review, review, review. As soon as possible following a day's class, review your notes. Fill in missing verbs and punctuation so that, a month from now, the sentences make sense. Write a summary at the end of the day's notes, recapping the main themes and the most interesting points made. These mini-essays will be valuable when you study for the exam. Who knows? The professor may ask for a short essay on one of these very topics.

Why Are Class Discussions Important?

Some students let their minds drift off once the professor stops lecturing and the class discussion begins. But you're too smart to make that mistake. Class discussions help in at least four ways.

First, in the give and take of discussion, the main points of the day's topic are repeated and clarified.

Second, during the discussion, your classmates will provide analogies and examples that you will find useful.

Third, one of your classmates may raise a question that you are hesitant to raise but want answered.

Fourth, participating in a class discussion tests your ability to present your own views clearly and persuasively.

 HELPING HAND   Learning to discuss a topic effectively with a diverse group of peers is a skill that will serve you well throughout your life. Remember: Don't monopolize the floor. Don't interrupt. Don't mumble. Most important, never try to make your point by insulting a classmate who disagrees with you.

Can I Ask the Professor for Help?

Some students think of the classroom as an adversarial situation—the professor against the students. Others think that the professor is too busy to be "bothered" by a visit or an email from a student. Still others think that a professor's office hours are only for students who fail an exam, want to drop out of a course, or have some life-threatening problem to relate that interferes with the course requirements. All these assumptions are wrong.

If you have a question about the assignments, the readings, or the topic of a class lecture or discussion, do talk to the professor. If you are having trouble organizing a paper for the class, ask for your professor's help. And if you did not do as well on an exam or a paper as you think you are capable of doing, ask your professor's advice on how to improve your work next time. You will not be imposing if you go during the professor's scheduled office hours. You can also ask, before or after class, if your professor would mind receiving an email from you.

Of course, there are limits. Don't ask a professor to explain a reading you haven't actually read. Don't expect her to reproduce a lecture or discussion class you missed. Don't ask for special treatment, such as getting the length of an assignment shortened or a deadline changed.

 HELPING HAND   If you have a problem or a question about the class or an assignment, discuss it with the professor immediately. Don't let it fester until after a test or after the assignment has been turned in. As those late night advertisements on television always say: "Act now, before it's too late."

RECAP

This chapter provided a strategy for note taking, getting the most out of classroom discussions, and asking your professor for help. The key advice on note taking is to listen carefully for the major themes in the professor's lecture, don't bury yourself in details, and revise and review those class notes as soon as possible. The secret to getting the most out of classroom discussions is to listen, participate, and incorporate other people's ideas into your notes. Remember that the rule of thumb in seeking a professor's help is to ask for constructive advice not special treatment. And, finally, attending class and keeping up with your work are fundamental.

There's So Much Weekly Reading Assigned for the Class... How Can I Ever Do it All?

- ■ *Why is this textbook so big?*

- ■ *How can I make this textbook manageable?*

- ■ *What do I highlight in the textbook?*

Why Is This Textbook So Big?

In most courses, the textbook is a student's main study aid. It provides the basic narrative of the historical period you will be studying, and introduces you to the "who," "what," "when," and "why" for the semester's work. Generally, a textbook is bulky, imposing, and bursting with names, dates, and descriptions of events that may be unfamiliar to you. The result is that you may feel overwhelmed.

Why is the textbook so packed with information on so many topics? The authors of the textbook try to be as inclusive as possible, providing a broad portrait of the political, social, economic, military, diplomatic, and intellectual trends and developments of each historical era because they do not know which topics your professor—and the hundreds of other professors across the country—may choose to focus on for the semester. Because the textbook is inclusive rather than selective, your professors can be selective, confident that the textbook will fill in the gaps for each student.

How Can I Make the Textbook Manageable?

First, familiarize yourself with its format. Most textbooks will have a table of contents that previews the topics you are going to encounter in the book, a list of illustrations and special features that appear in the book, and an index at the end of the volume. Every textbook divides the historical material to be covered into manageable chapters, and each chapter is likely to have the following: an introduction, which lays out the major themes of the chapter; a time line and/or a chronological chart, which lists the main events covered in the chapter; the body of the chapter, divided into topical sections; illustrations, including maps, charts, graphs, photographs, or paintings relevant to the era; a summary, which recaps the main points of the chapter; a bibliography, which lists books or web sites or films for further study of the period; and finally, one or two special features, such as a biography of a famous or typical person of the era.

Here is a sample table of contents of a chapter on the era following the Civil War, known as Reconstruction, in the textbook, *Making America*. See how many of the "clues" in the list that follows the outline you picked up as you read this table of contents.

```
Chapter 16 Reconstruction: High Hopes and Broken Dreams, 1865-1877
  Presidential Reconstruction
     Republican War Aims
     Lincoln's Approach to Reconstruction:
       "With Malice Toward None"
     Abolishing Slavery Forever: The Thirteenth Amendment
     Andrew Johnson and Reconstruction
     The Southern Response: Minimal Compliance
  Freedom and the Legacy of Slavery
    Defining the Meaning of Freedom
    Creating Communities
    Land and Labor
    The White South: Confronting Change
```

```
Congressional Reconstruction
   Challenging Presidential Reconstruction
   The Civil Rights Act of 1866
   Defining Citizenship: The Fourteenth Amendment
   Radicals in Control: Impeachment of the President
   Political Terrorism and the Election of 1868
   Voting Rights and Civil Rights
Individual Choices: Frederick Douglass
Black Reconstruction
   The Republican Party in the South
   Creating an Educational System and Fighting Discrimination
   Railroad Development and Corruption
The End of Reconstruction
   The "New Departure"
   The 1872 Election
   Redemption by Terror: The "Mississippi Plan"
   The Compromise of 1877
   After Reconstruction
Summary
Suggested Readings
```

How many of these clues did you pick up?

1. The title of the chapter provides the theme: much was expected but there were many failures during Reconstruction.
2. Reconstruction began in 1865 and ended in 1877—it will be important to know what events occurred in these twelve years [the end of the Civil War, 1865; the removal of federal troops from the South, 1877].
3. The table of contents is actually an outline of the Reconstruction era.
4. The textbook covers not only political developments of the era but social and economic ones, as in the topics "Creating Communities" and "Land and Labor."
5. Key terms that you will want to write down and learn are listed here, such as "Mississippi Plan" and "the Civil Rights Act of 1866."
6. There were three different Reconstruction plans: presidential, congressional, and African American or black.
7. The special feature, "Individual Choices," suggests that individuals shape history by the choices they make.
8. The summary will provide a review of the key points from each of the sections of the chapter.
9. If you are doing a paper on Reconstruction, the "Suggested Readings" is a good place to start for a biliography.

 HELPING HAND   Reading the table of contents for the chapter you are assigned makes good sense. The table of contents tells you what you can expect to find in the text; it introduces you to key terms and ideas. It only takes a few moments to read— time that is well spent!

What Do I Highlight in the Textbook?

Now that you know what to expect, you can move on to step two: resist the temptation to barge right in, armed with a highlighter or a pen, ready to underline every name, date, or event mentioned in the chapter. Turning the whole chapter bright yellow or pink won't help much, even though it may make you feel like you are doing something! Instead, read the assigned chapter's introduction and summary *first*. They will tell you what is important to remember, consider—and highlight. Then, read the body of the chapter.

If, for example, the chapter introduction tells you that the focus will be on the events and policies during Reconstruction, you will want to highlight the names of key political figures during the era, such as President Johnson, and key legislation, such as the Fourteenth Amendment. In this particular textbook, *Making America,* the authors have gone a long way to assist you by including a running glossary on each page, in which key figures, key terms, and key events or legislation are defined for you. Other texts help you by printing these key terms in bold or italic type for you.

The same principle applies no matter what period of history you are studying. If the chapter introduction in a European textbook tells you that the focus will be on the causes of the French Revolution, you will want to highlight the names and descriptions of those acts or political decisions that heightened tensions between the government and the people, as well as any key information on economic problems, radical organizations, or ideological challenges to the monarchical system of government.

📫 *HELPING HAND*   Always review the summary of the chapter to see if you have taken special notice—by highlighting or note taking—of all the main points recapped for you by the author.

Now you are ready for the final step: testing yourself. For example, close the book and write your own short essay on the main themes of the chapter. Afterward, check the textbook introduction and summary to see if you left out anything important. Or list as many of the important people or events from the chapter as you can recall and then define and explain the significance of each item on your list. Save these self-tests. They will make excellent review materials for the professor's tests.

RECAP

This chapter showed you how to make the textbook a tool for learning, not just a heavy load in your backpack.

*H*ow Do I Study for History Tests?

- *What kinds of tests will I take in class?*

- *How can I improve my performance on these in-class tests?*

- *How do I complete the take-home essay exam?*

- *How do I complete online tests?*

- *How do I study for any test?*

■ Identifying the many kinds of tests   ■ Learning how to study for all kinds of tests

What Kinds of Tests Will I Take in Class?

No matter what you call it—test, exam, quiz, evaluation—that moment of truth is bound to strike a little terror in the heart of any student. Perhaps it will help if you know what types of tests you are likely to encounter in a college history class.

1. **The *quiz* and its many variations:**
   a. **The map quiz.**   The professor asks you to fill in certain key items, such as national boundaries, important rivers, capital cities, mountain ranges, disputed territories, or the nations forming various political alliances.
   b. **The pop quiz on a specific reading.**   For this surprise test (one that is "popped" on you without warning) the professor requires that you answer a set of questions on the reading assigned for that day or week.
   c. **The pop quiz on basic information.**   Again, without prior warning, the professor examines you on fundamental facts, such as critical dates, names of treaties or wars, or historical events, to discover if you have mastered the basic information needed to move on to an analysis of the material.

2. **Identification:** The professor asks you to identify, define, and usually to give the significance of a term, person, event, piece of legislation, treaty, etc.

3. **Time line or chronology:** The professor asks you to place a series of events in chronological order.

4. **The multiple-choice exam:** For each question, a number of possible answers are provided. You are expected to select the answer that is correct from among these choices. For example,

```
The Declaration of Sentiments of 1848 was modeled after what earlier
landmark document in American history?
   A. The Constitution
   B. The Articles of Confederation
   C. The Virginia and Kentucky Resolves
   D. The Declaration of Independence
```

Another example would be:

```
The Magna Carta clarified the relationship between
   A. English wives and husbands.
   B. The king and the barons.
   C. The House of Commons and the House of Lords.
   D. English merchants and farmers.
```

By the way, the answer to question 1 is "D"; the answer to question 2 is "B."

5. **The in-class essay exam:** The professor requires you to write one or more essays, each with a thesis statement that is developed through examples and that has a conclusion. The question may require you, for example, to take a pro or con side in an historical debate, to compare and contrast two movements or historical events, or to explain the causes and consequences of a major historical decision. This exam can be an **open-book exam,** a test in which you are allowed to consult your texts and your own notes, or it may be a **closed-book exam,** a test in which you cannot consult any of these resources.

How Can I Improve My Performance on These In-Class Tests?

For any in-class exam or quiz, the important thing is: don't panic! Take a deep breath. Then, follow these tips:

1. Before you pick up your pen or turn on your computer, read the instructions carefully so that you understand what the professor wants you to do and how he wants it done.
2. Take a moment to read all the questions carefully.
3. Now prioritize your time. Are there questions you can answer easily? Answer them first. Are there questions you know you can answer but you will need to dig deep for the necessary information? Answer them next. Leave the questions that stump you for the end.
4. Be sure to leave yourself enough time to reread and, if necessary, revise your answers. Make sure you answered the specific question you were asked.
5. Finally, whatever you write, make it legible as well as intelligible. Tiny, cramped handwriting; messy pages filled with crossed out material and arrows pointing everywhere; and lots of curly-ques on those g's or y's are likely to alienate the professor. He's only human, after all.

How Do I Complete the Take-Home Essay Exam?

The questions are similar to those in the in-class essay exam, but the professor may set higher standards for grammar, punctuation, organization, and number of examples cited or details provided, and he may expect a longer essay because you will have more time than you have in the in-class exam. He may also require footnotes to any sources you consult because you write the essays at home.

How Do I Complete Online Tests?

Many professors now use the computer for exams and quizzes. Although you should use the same study strategies for these tests, the format will be different from in-class exams. On the day of the test, the professor will give you the URL for the web page and instructions on how to take the test. Make sure you are aware of any time limits the professor might set. Must the test be taken during certain hours? Will the computer program you're using automatically shut down when the time allotted for the test runs out? Can you go back and change something once you've hit the "Submit" or "OK" button?

For multiple-choice tests, you will probably be given a list of questions, each followed by several possible answers. Every answer will have a box next to it. When you find the right answer, click the mouse on the correct box. At the bottom of the Web page will be different kinds of hyperlinks. Some might tell you to continue to the next page, while others might say "Submit" or "OK." When you hit "Submit" or "OK," you are sending the exam to the professor and will not be able to change any answers.

For map quizzes, the professor will create some kind of mechanism for placing a name or number on the map.

For essay exams, the most common format acts much like a bulletin board. The form will have questions and then large boxes underneath them for you to type in your answer. You can either type your answers directly on the form or you can write the text on a word-processing program and then copy and paste the material into the form. To send the exam to the professor, hit the "Submit" or "OK" button at the bottom of the screen.

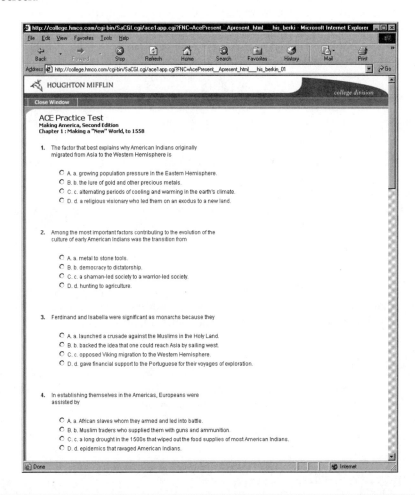

How Do I Study for Any Test?

Remember the Boy Scout motto: be prepared. It's the best advice, not only for those wilderness survival trips but also for taking a history exam.

1. **Keep current in your assignments.** This is crucial for handling pop quizzes, but it also applies to exams that are scheduled.
2. **Review your class notes regularly.** Instead of that frantic effort to memorize material the night before the exam, reading and reviewing your notes calmly each week may yield surprising results: you will actually remember more than you ever thought possible.
3. **Review the chapter introductions and summaries in your main texts before the exam.** Remember: these chapter sections contain the essentials.
4. **Familiarize yourself with typical formats for essay questions.** Professors who want analysis and evaluation rather than description are likely to ask questions in these formats:

a. *Compare and contrast.* For example, compare and contrast the way in which French colonizers and English colonizers interacted with the Native Americans in the seventeenth and eighteenth centuries. Or compare and contrast the political platforms of the Populist party and the Republican party in the election of 1896.

b. *Evaluate the pros and cons of the following statement.* For example, evaluate the claim by some historians that dropping the atomic bomb on Japan was a justifiable military strategy during World War II. Or evaluate the pros and cons of the following statement: Slavery caused the Civil War.

c. *What are the causes and/or consequences of . . . .* For example, what are the main causes for the failure of the Revolution of 1848? Or what were the causes and the consequences of the 1896 Supreme Court decision in Plessy v. Ferguson?

5. **Review old quizzes or exams to gauge your strengths and weaknesses.** Did the professor comment on the same problems in each of your earlier exams? For example, was your organization poor in several instances? Do you notice that you often lost credit for answers that were not specific enough or did not contain enough examples? Did you consistently run out of time when writing an in-class exam? Or did the professor consistently praise your writing style or organization of the essay? Now that you know your strengths and weaknesses, it's time to develop a strategy for emphasizing the former and improving the latter. Poor organization? Try outlining your answer before you begin to write. You ran out of time? Answer the questions you find easiest first. You didn't provide enough examples? Get into the habit of listing two examples for every major point you are making. Check to make sure you have included both when your read over your answer.

 HELPING HAND Until it becomes an automatic process, you might have to say in your essay, "Two examples that come to mind," or "To illustrate the point, I will offer two examples." This is perfectly acceptable.

6. **Create your own practice multiple-choice questions, your own short answers, and even your own essay questions, using the textbook, assigned readings, and your class notes.**

7. **Find a study partner.** Have him write a dozen multiple-choice questions for you; write a dozen for him. Discuss possible exam topics—and possible answers. Remember: two heads can sometimes be better than one.

8. **Create other tools, such as time lines or chronologies, to help you master the material being tested.**

 HELPING HAND Remember that some students excel when they are given an in-class exam—their adrenalin starts flowing and off they go. Others do best on take-home exams—they like to ponder, outline their thoughts, revise, and polish. Some students get a sinking feeling in the pit of their stomach when they take tests, but they really enjoy writing research papers or book critiques. Very few of us do everything well. Get to know your own preferences—learn what comes naturally and what is a struggle. Then—you guessed it—put some extra time and work into improving in the areas that aren't easy for you..

RECAP

This chapter helped ease your fears about tests. It described the various types of tests you will encounter, from simple quizzes to take-home essay exams to online tests. Then it took you step by step through the best way to prepare for these tests—and do well on them. The keys to success are to keep up with the class assignments, review your notes, and learn from your past mistakes.

*H*ow Can Maps Help Me Understand History?

- *What are the different kinds of maps?*

- *How do I read a map?*

- *How can I test my map-reading skills?*

TIPS IN THIS CHAPTER

- Recognizing types of maps
- Testing your map-reading skills
- Learning to read a map

You stuff maps in your glove compartment in case you get lost on your next trip. You check the station stops on a rumbling subway car when you travel underground in New York, San Francisco, Boston, or Washington, D.C. You follow your plane's flight path on the map you find in the airline's complimentary magazine. Trail maps guide you along the hiking path; pirate's treasure maps appear in the old movies you remember watching; and when you turn on your television, you can watch your local meteorologist draw clouds, raindrops and smiley faced suns on a weather map. In short, maps are a useful part of your daily life. Can they be useful in your college history class? The answer, of course, is yes.

The maps you find in your college history textbook are not there to help you find the best route from Houston, Texas, to Salt Lake City, Utah. They won't tell you whether to bring a raincoat to class. If you read maps correctly, however, they will help you understand historical events and developments by reinforcing visually what has been described in the text. Maps provide you with a different way of conceptualizing, a different way of taking in information. To use them well, however, you must know how to read them.

What Are the Different Kinds of Maps?

Cartographers, or mapmakers, produce several different types of maps. The most common types are described in the following paragraphs.

Physical Maps

Physical maps provide visual representations of the physical features of an area of the world, including oceans, continents, rivers, and mountains. Often the elevations of a mountain range or the depths of a valley are shown by a particular color chosen by the mapmaker to reinforce the differences in the topography, or physical features of the earth. Historians find these maps useful in illustrating a relationship between people and the natural world that they have introduced in the text. For example, you can read that Hannibal's crossing the Alps was a miraculous feat, but you may not grasp just how impressive it was until you look at a map illustrating the obstacles presented to a third-century B.C. army by this towering mountain range. Or you can read that seventeenth-century Chesapeake planters settled along riverbanks, but you may not fully appreciate the wisdom of their choices until you see a map of Virginia and Maryland's waterways and their connection to the Atlantic Ocean. You can hear a professor discuss how European explorers of the fifteenth century changed shipping patterns in the Indian Ocean, but a map showing currents and winds would more graphically illustrate how weather dictated the schedules of the earlier sailors but did not have such a hold over the Europeans, with their new technologies.

 HELPING HAND   You can use physical maps as a window into the technological and scientific limitations and advances of an historical era. After the voyages of Christopher Columbus and other European explorers, sixteenth-century cartographers attempted to re-map the globe. Without aerial photography, sophisticated computer-based measurement techniques, or other modern technological aids, they were limited to drawing maps based on first-hand and sometimes second-hand descriptions by ship captains, soldiers, and sailors. Comparing those maps with modern maps may help you appreciate the impact of modern technology on our perceptions of the world.

Political Maps

Political maps show how political decision making shapes the world in which we live. They show national, state, province, or county boundaries and the location of cities and towns within the borders of a nation. Traditionally, boundaries between countries are drawn in thick, black lines and countries are given distinctive colors. You have been using these maps since elementary school, when teachers asked you to fill in the names of the states or to mark the location of state capitals. Historians use them to provide critical visual information. For example, the location of Belgium is a key element in any discussion of German military strategy and French and English responses to it in World War I. Using a series of maps that show the changing national borders on the continent of Africa from 1900 to 2000 will open the door to understanding European colonialism and African independence movements. For a striking comparison, a history text might place a distribution map showing languages and religions next to a map showing the borders of African states created during the era of European colonization. Looking at these maps, you can begin to explore the problems that were created for the African peoples living in each of these artificially created states or nations.

 HELPING HAND   Remember that you can read political maps as just that: political. They reveal power relationships among nations, social classes, races, or political parties within a nation. The right to establish national boundaries, like the right to establish the boundaries of a voting district or to decide where a national capital will be located, provides valuable clues to who wields authority and power in an historical era.

Transportation Maps

Transportation maps show land, sea, or air routes. Imagine trying to follow European exploration of the Americas without a map showing Columbus's sea route or Magellan's voyage around the world. Or consider the advantages of seeing, on a map, the difficult overland route followed by American settlers along the Oregon Trail. Transportation maps can also help you see how the movement of people is linked to the movement of ideas and even disease. For example, a map showing the trade routes from the Mediterranean to India after the eighth century can provide important clues to the rapid spread of Islam across the Asian continent. A map showing that European trading patterns before 1492 did not cross the Atlantic Ocean will help you understand the dramatic impact of contact between the New World and the Old—a contact that brought new and often deadly diseases into the lives of both the Amerindians and the Europeans.

Distribution Maps

Distribution maps focus on the occurrence of one or two special features, for example, rainfall in various regions, population density in a nation's cities, or agricultural specialization within a state. A map showing the distribution of Democratic, Liberty Party, and Republican votes in the presidential election of 1860 is certain to help a student of the Civil War understand the impact of sectionalism and the breakdown of national party systems. Similarly, a map showing the population of major European cities before and after the Black Plague will bring home the impact of disease on the history of Late Medieval Europe. Finally, a map showing the distribution of various diseases in Africa will help you understand why it took so long for Europe to colonize that continent.

 HELPING HAND   Don't forget that many maps are a combination of types. A mapmaker assigned to illustrate the journeys of Marco Polo might include the national boundaries that this Italian adventurer crossed, the physical features he confronted along the way, and the land routes that he followed.

How Do I Read a Map?

Most maps have several standard features that you will need to understand.

First, the *scale* tells you the relationship between the size of an area on a map and the size of that same area on the earth. The scale can be indicated in various ways, but most maps in a history book have a bar or line in one corner of the map that is divided into sections that represent actual distance. One inch on that bar, for example, can equal 25 miles.

Second, *direction* is shown on the map by a grid of parallels and meridians. Many maps also have a *compass rose* that shows you north, south, east, and west. Although a map can be oriented in any direction, traditionally north is at the top.

Third, the *legend* provides a key to the symbols for all the features you will encounter on the map. For example, cities are usually indicated by dots; the larger the dot, the bigger the city. International boundaries, state or provincial boundaries, and county boundaries are indicated by broken lines of different shape or thickness. A star is often the symbol for the capital of a nation or a state.

Finally, the *title* of a historical map alerts you to the type of information that the mapmaker is illustrating.

How Can I Test My Map-Reading Skills?

Are you ready to test your map-reading skills? Below are three maps.

The first map is entitled "The Burgoyne Campaign, 1777," and illustrates one of the most important

MAP 4.1 The Burgoyne Campaign, 1777   *The defeat of General John Burgoyne and his army at Saratoga was a major turning point in the war. This map shows American and British troop movement and the locations and dates of the Saratoga battles leading to the British surrender.*

turning points in the American Revolution—the defeat of a major British army by the Americans. What is the scale of this map? What physical features are indicated on the map? What special features are indicated in the legend? What type of map would you say best describes this first example?

The second map is entitled "Presidential Election, 1828." Why did the map maker feel that a scale and a compass rose were unnecessary? What information is provided in the legend? Who won the election? How does the map make this point clearer to you?

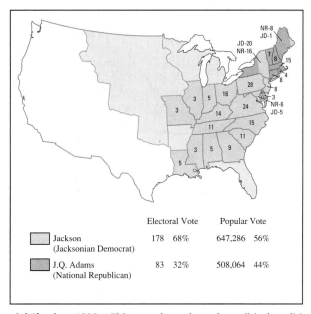

	Electoral Vote		Popular Vote	
Jackson (Jacksonian Democrat)	178	68%	647,286	56%
J.Q. Adams (National Republican)	83	32%	508,064	44%

MAP 4.2 Presidential Election, 1828   *This map shows how the political coalition between Andrew Jackson and Martin Van Buren turned the tables in the election of 1828. Jackson's Democratic Party won every region except Adams's native New England.*

The third map is entitled "The African Slave Trade, 1500–1800." In what sense could you call this a transportation map? How does the mapmaker indicate where the majority of slaves came from and where the majority were taken? Were all the slaves transported to the Americas?

Map 4.3 The African Slave Trade, 1500–1800   *After 1500 a vast new trade in slaves from sub-Saharan Africa to the Americas joined the ongoing slave trade to the Islamic states of North Africa, the Middle East, and India. The West Indies were the major destination of the Atlantic slave trade, followed by Brazil.*

 HELPING HAND   Remember that historians and history professors use maps to illustrate important points about events, developments, and human decision making in the past. Your professor will probably want you to consider the implications of the information provided on the map rather than memorize that information.

RECAP

This chapter introduced you to maps as historical tools; it described the different types of maps you are likely to encounter and it explained the common elements you will find on a map. It also provided you with some examples that allow you to test your map-reading skills.

How Can I Work Effectively with Primary, Secondary, and Fictional Sources in My History Class?

- *What is a primary source?*

- *What is a secondary source?*

- *What questions should I ask when I analyze or evaluate sources?*

- *What does the professor mean when he or she asks for the historical context of a document?*

- *Why do my sources disagree?*

- *Why did my professor assign a piece of fiction in a history class—and how do I evaluate it?*

In addition to the textbook, most professors will assign a list of specialized readings, films, or illustrative materials. The professor will often want you to do more than simply read or view these assignments; she will want you to analyze or evaluate them. To do this, you will need to ask—and answer—a few basic questions about each of them.

What Is a Primary Source?

To the historian, *primary sources* are the basic "stuff" of history. A *primary source* is any document or artifact from the period under study. It was written or created by a person who lived through the events being described. Primary sources include, but are not limited to: diaries, journals, and correspondence; government records or documents; public speeches; newspapers, pamphlets, broadsides, or books; portraits, landscape paintings, maps, photographs or films; and the records of military, religious, business, or charitable institutions. Although many primary sources have been published in collections of documents, most are held by historical societies or archives, university and public libraries, or government offices. When historians do research, they usually have to go to one of these archives to read the primary sources they need for their project.

You are probably already familiar with several famous primary sources, such as the Magna Carta, the Declaration of Independence, the Communist Manifesto, or Hammirabi's Code. In high school you may have read one of these well-known diaries or autobiographies: the autobiography of Benjamin Franklin, the journals of Marco Polo, or Anne Frank's diary. But primary sources do not have to be the work of famous figures; the correspondence between an ordinary Civil War soldier and his wife, the photo albums your grandmother creates, and the tax records your parents store in their filing cabinet are also primary sources.

Here's an excerpt from a primary source you are likely to recognize immediately.

```
We the people of the United States, in order to form a more perfect union,
establish justice, insure domestic tranquility, provide for the common
defense, promote the general welfare, and secure the blessings of liberty
to ourselves and our posterity, do ordain and establish this Constitution
for the United States of America.
```

If you said that it is the preamble to the U.S. Constitution, you are right. Here's another excerpt that you won't recognize, yet it fits the criteria for a primary source. This is a statement by a Pennsylvania delegate on the floor of the Constitutional Convention of 1787, recorded in the minutes of the convention and also in James Madison's own secret journal of the debates at that convention.

```
Life and liberty were generally said to be of more value than property. An
accurate view of the matter would, nevertheless, prove that property was
the main object of society . . . .
```

Finally, here is an excerpt from a letter by New York lawyer, and later Chief Justice of the first Supreme Court, John Jay, to George Washington, who would become the first president of the United States if the new Constitution was ratified, or approved, by nine states. Jay was a delegate to New York's ratifying convention.

There is much Reason to believe that the Majority of the Convention of this State will be composed of anti foederal [the antifederalists opposed the Constitution] Characters: but it is doubtful whether the Leaders will be able to govern the Party. Many in the opposition are Friends to the Union and mean well, but their principle Leaders are very far from being solicitous about the Fate of the Union.

Not all primary sources are written sources. Here is a portrait of Thomas Jefferson, the third president of the United States, showing Jefferson's preference for plain, informal clothing rather than the elegant dress of European aristocrats.

This 1822 portrait by Thomas Sully captures the former president in his customary greatcoat, unadorned suit, and well-worn boots. "Thomas Jefferson" by Thomas Sully, West Point Museum, United States Military Academy, West Point, N.Y.

Public documents, records of a political meeting, a private letter to a friend, paintings of Thomas Jefferson's inauguration—each of these primary sources hold clues to the motives, attitudes, and political philosophies of the people of the era. For a good historian, they are all critical pieces of the puzzle of the past.

 HELPING HAND Don't make the mistake of believing that all primary sources are old, written on faded and yellowing paper, or written with a quaint vocabulary. The first test you take in a history class on the Constitution could be a primary source document for someone, five years from now, writing a paper on students' views on the Constitutional Convention! In fact, you are creating primary sources every day: photos taken on a summer vacation, college admissions essays, tax returns, letters home to your parents asking for money, and your first college transcript.

What Is a Secondary Source?

A *secondary source* is any document or artifact that was created after the period under study has passed. It is usually an assessment or analysis of, or commentary on, events or people of the past. Secondary sources include, but are not limited to: scholarly monographs or books, scholarly articles in journals, biographies, and historical novels or films.

Again, you have probably read many secondary sources during your school career. If your high school history teacher assigned a book on the coming of the American Revolution such as Edmund Morgan's *The Stamp Act Crisis* or you did a book report on Eric Foner's biography *Tom Paine,* then you have already worked with secondary sources. Perhaps you read a biography of Queen Elizabeth, a novel about the Civil War, or an article in *American Heritage Magazine* about the battle of the Alamo. Even the textbook for this college history course qualifies as a secondary source.

Here are the concluding paragraphs of a book written in 1986 by Christopher Collier and James Lincoln Collier, entitled *Decision at Philadelphia: The Constitutional Convention of 1787.* Notice that it assesses the delegates to the convention and their achievements. The authors speak as analysts, not as participants, in the events of 1787.

```
The writers of the American Constitution were not angels. They made mis-
takes: they left out a bill of rights, they did not confront the question of
judicial review, and most tragically, they were so much people of their time
that they could not see that blacks were as human as they were. But withal,
they rose above themselves far more than most men would have done in their
place. And the generations of Americans who have grown up under the
Constitution they struggled so hard to make are eternally in their debt.
```

 HELPING HAND Sometimes a source can be either primary or secondary. It all depends on how it is being used. An historian analyzing changing attitudes of other historians toward the men who wrote the Constitution would see the Colliers' book as a primary source.

What Questions Should I Ask When I Analyze or Evaluate Sources?

Reading a primary or a secondary source intelligently requires that you be a good detective. Like Sherlock Holmes, you need to search for clues.

Some questions you might want to ask about primary sources are obvious: Who wrote it, and why? Who is the audience for this source? If it is a public document, was it a campaign speech, a policy statement, a judicial ruling? Is it a private letter? If so, is it written to a loved one, a friend, or an enemy? Is it a diary entry, intended only for the diary-keeper to read? Is the document propaganda? Is it polemical? Is it didactic; that is, is the author's intention to instruct or educate? Where did the document appear in print? In a newspaper? In a prestigious journal or a glossy magazine? In a religious publication? In a pamphlet issued by a nonprofit organization or a special interest group?

If it is a secondary source, you might want to learn the credentials of the author. Does the author have an obvious political or ideological bias—or a hidden one? Is the bogeneral audience or is it a scholarly work? And, most important of all perhaps, what claims does the author make, what interpretation does he offer, and what evidence does he provide to back up his argument?

What Does the Professor Mean When Asking for the Historical Context of a Document?

The historical context is, simply, the circumstances in which the document was generated. What was happening at the time, in the author's personal life or in the world around her, that might have prompted the document to be written or might have shaped how it was written and what was said? What was the intellectual climate of the time? That is, what were the accepted "truths" about human nature, the roles of men and women, and other fundamental issues? Did people explain events in religious terms? In scientific terms? Was the author's society prosperous or poor? Did the author live in times of crisis and war or in peace?

For example, what was the historical context for the Declaration of Independence? We know that the relationship between Great Britain and the colonies was in crisis in 1776. Over a decade of political debate and public demonstrations had occurred as colonists protested British policies and articulated their views on the proper role of government. We know also that the author of the Declaration of Independence, Thomas Jefferson, represented an elite group of educated and wealthy colonists who were widely read in Enlightenment philosophy, seventeenth-century English liberal thought, and the history of ancient republics. These elements of the historical context provide powerful clues to why the Declaration of Independence was issued, what arguments it chose to make, and why it persuaded many colonists to join the Revolution.

What was the historical context for the work of historian Eric Foner, whose prize winning study, *Reconstruction,* argued persuasively that African Americans played important roles in shaping government policy during and after the Civil War and in creating new social institutions for freedmen and -women? Important clues lie in the fact that Foner's generation, many of them political activists in the civil rights movement in the late 1950s and 1960s, produced a school of historians known as "revisionists." One of the central goals of the revisionists was to rewrite U.S. history so that bok or article intended for a minority, or "marginalized" peoples such as African Americans, Indians, women, and workers, were seen as active agents in shaping their destinies rather than as passive recipients.

Remember, understanding the historical context of a document is only the beginning of your analysis, not an end in itself. Don't ignore the content just because you have placed it and the author in their historical place and time.

 HELPING HAND   Think of yourself as a detective, ferreting out clues about the author of the document and the moment in history in which that author wrote. Every clue to the past has a history of its own!

Why Do My Sources Disagree?

Every student who has ever watched a police drama knows that people who witness the same event often have different accounts of it. The thief was tall; the thief was short; his coat was blue; his coat was gray. The first-hand accounts, or primary sources, you may deal with in a history class may disagree with one another just as dramatically. This is also true with secondary sources, because the historian's job is not only to re-create events of the past but to interpret and analyze them. Two excellent scholars may well come to different conclusions. Consider the excerpts below from two respected historians of the Nazi movement, Christopher R. Browning and Daniel Jonah Goldhagen. Both scholars seek to explain why ordinary men and women supported Hitler and, in particular, why these ordinary people were capable of acts of atrocity.

Browning examines the actions of a reserve police battalion who participated in the massacre of Jews at Jozefow. He concludes:

. . . [T]he collective behavior of Reserve Police Battalion 101 has deeply disturbing implications. There are many societies afflicted by traditions of racism and caught in the siege mentality of war or threat of war. Everywhere society conditions people to respect and defer to authority, and indeed could scarcely function otherwise. Everywhere people seek career advancement. In every modern society, the complexity of life and the resulting bureaucratization and specialization attenuate the sense of personal responsibilities of those implementing official policy. Within virtually every social collective, the peer group exerts tremendous pressures on behavior and sets moral norms. If the men of Reserve Police Battalion 101 could become killers under such circumstances, what group of men cannot?

Goldhagen disagrees. He believes that a unique set of values and attitudes shared by the German people led to Nazism and the Holocaust, or mass murder of Jewish citizens. He writes:

The beliefs that were already the common property of the German people upon Hitler's assumption of power and which led the German people to assent and contribute to the eliminationist measures of the 1930's [the concentration camps, for example] were the beliefs that prepared not just the Germans who by circumstances, chance or choice ended up as perpetrators but also the vast majority of the German people to understand, assent to, and, when possible, do their part to further the extermination, root and branch, of the Jewish people. German political culture had evolved to the point where an enormous number of ordinary, representative Germans became—and most of the rest of their fellow Germans were fit to be—Hitler's willing executioners.

Both scholars examine the evidence, yet they come to dramatically different conclusions. If you look closely, you will see that, behind their conclusions, are a set of assumptions about human behavior. Browning assumes that all societies require certain attitudes— respect for authority and obedience to those in command—to function properly and that, under certain stressful conditions, people of any nation would have behaved as the German people behaved. Goldhagen argues that societies develop quite different sets of values and attitudes and that, over time, they develop distinctive cultures. He feels that there were elements in the German culture that made the German citizens accept and even embrace the racism of Nazism.

Was Germany unique or typical? Scholars have been asking this question for decades and coming up with different answers. You may not come up with the final answer, but you can subject the work of these two scholars to some of the useful questions covered above. What is the historical context for the two works? Did one write immediately after the war and one many decades later? Did either of these men fight in the war? Is one of them part of a revisionist movement in his field? Many of the questions raised in the section of this handbook that discussed how to evaluate your sources might help as well.

Why Did My Professor Assign a Piece of Fiction in a History Class—and How Do I Evaluate It?

You may ask yourself, What's a novel doing in a class assignment on the Industrial Revolution? Or perhaps you ask yourself, Why am I being asked to read a collection of poems when the topic on the syllabus is the Civil War? History professors often assign fiction or poetry related to the era under discussion because novelists or poets can provide rich, compelling descriptions of an era and its people. The characters created by a novelist or a poet can dramatize and personalize many of the changes, crises, or problems faced by the real people of an era. For example, you might understand the impact of European ideas and values on African society by reading *Things Fall Apart,* Chinua Achebe's richly detailed story of life in a traditional Nigerian village before and after the arrival of Christian missionaries. Or you and your classmates might understand more fully the rise of chivalry and its rituals in medieval Europe by reading *The Song of Roland.*

> ### RECAP
>
> This chapter introduced you to the two types of sources you and all other historians use while conducting research—primary sources and secondary sources—and it walked you through the questions you need to ask as you evaluate those sources, especially questions about the historical context in which the document was produced. Finally, it explained what that novel was doing on a history reading list and why it can be an important source for understanding the past.

*H*ow Do I Manage Written Assignments?

■ *What sample assignments might I find in my history class?*

TIPS IN THIS CHAPTER

- Keeping a journal
- Writing a critical essay
- Writing a book review
- Participating in bulletin board discussions

Like most people, professors know the value of variety. During the course of the semester, your professor may ask you to grapple with other kinds of assignments besides papers, presentations, and exams. His goal is not to throw you off guard; he is simply trying to bring history to life by allowing you to act the part of different historical characters or debate different political positions.

 HELPING HAND   For any of the assignments listed below, consider showing your professor a rough draft of your work a few days before the due date. This gives you time to get, and make use of, valuable assistance that will probably translate into a better final grade. Remember: the professor cannot help you if you do not ask for help.

What Sample Assignments Might I Find in My History Class?

Journals

Professors assign weekly or monthly journals to illustrate more vividly the importance of journal writing for the study of history. In the computer and telephone age, people rarely write diaries or journals. For centuries, however, this was a common means by which people organized their thoughts and described their lives.

Journals written by historical figures such as Abigail Adams, Marco Polo, or Christopher Columbus will appear in class syllabi. Reading them provides you with an invaluable insight into their thoughts and their activities at pivotal moments in world history. But writing your own journal will give you added insight into the experiences and motivations of these men and women. You will discover that it is more difficult to articulate your opinions on paper than in your own mind. As you write your own journal, going through the same process as these other journal writers, you will be better equipped to analyze their words and deeds. You will recognize, for example, how opinions change as external circumstances change. Did Marco Polo's views of non-Europeans change during the course of his travels? If so, why did they change? What were the circumstances surrounding his change of opinion?

The first step in journal writing is to do the assignment required by the professor. Even if he collects the journals only once or twice during the semester, you have to keep up with the work. If the professor requires you to write in your journal once a week, write in it once a week. Don't wait until the deadline to write out three or four quick entries. The professor wants to see the progression of your views, which may change dramatically as new information comes to light in the classroom and the class readings.

The second step is to think of the journal in the same way you think of any other written assignment. In other words, you should follow all grammar and spelling rules. Finally, make sure you follow the professor's instructions. Some journal assignments require that you give personal insights about your own life; some ask you to analyze the different readings and topics in class. If you do not understand the assignment, ask the professor to clarify what he wants.

Book Reviews

Book reviews are not the same as book reports. Book reviews analyze the main themes of a book rather than simply providing summaries of the plot. Avoid the book report pitfall by remembering that the professor has read the book and doesn't need you to describe what happened in it. He has given you this assignment because he wants to know if you are capable of picking out the most important aspects of the story and analyzing them. A book review of *The Diary of Anne Frank* should *not* look like this:

```
Anne, her family, and a few of their friends had to hide in an attic because
the Nazis were trying to arrest and deport all the Jews living in Amsterdam.
In the attic, they had to remain quiet all day so no-one would detect them.
At night, they had quiet conversations and Anne wrote in her diary. Friends
brought them food and the news every day.
```

Read the Book   You will not be able to write a credible book review unless you read the book. Crib notes and the film version (if available) are *never* a substitute for actually reading the book yourself.

While reading, take notes about the major plot points, and the themes and views expressed by each of the characters, making sure to write down the pertinent page numbers. If you do not take organized notes, you will have a much harder time trying to put together an analysis later. You do not want to waste time flipping through the pages trying to find that quote that you "distinctly" remember was somewhere in the middle of the book.

When you have finished reading the book, write down a short, one- or two-paragraph summary of the plot. This brief summary should help draw out the main themes, not just serve as a chronological list of events.

Now you are ready to write an outline or list of the major themes that will help you identify the thesis of the book review. For *The Diary of Anne Frank*, three possible themes might be:

1. Nazi Persecution of the Jews throughout Europe
2. Psychological and material survival techniques used by the inhabitants of the attic
3. Anne's own problems with adolescence, compounded by the problems presented by living in an attic

The list above highlights Anne's particular problems, but it also addresses the larger question of how people coped with the Holocaust. Your thesis, then, might be the importance of case studies in analyzing larger historical phenomena.

Before you begin to develop your thesis further, you should do some research on Anne Frank herself. Knowing who the author is and why she wrote the book will provide insight into the themes the author raises and his or her perspective. Anne Frank actually lived through the events of the Holocaust, so her insights are probably very different from those of an author in the United States who had friends or relatives fighting in World War II but did not experience the war or persecution first-hand. Be sure to include any relevant information about the author in your review.

You might decide you need to do additional research for your review. Anne Frank's diary, for example, includes very little about the policies of the Nazis during World War II that led to her life in the attic. To place Anne's story within the historical context of World War II, you will need to read some secondary sources on this subject.

The next step is to write a thesis paragraph that sets out the main argument of your review. The thesis should make use of the themes you identified in your outline. You will probably need to provide a brief summary of the book, stressing the points that relate to your thesis. Don't just fill in paper space with details! End the review with a concluding paragraph that restates the thesis and the main themes that support it.

Critical Essays

It has finally happened: your instructor has given you your first big writing assignment: an essay analyzing an important historical figure, event, or topic. Is that panic or anticipation you feel in the pit of your stomach? Don't worry. There are some easy, sure-fire steps to success.

Imagine that the assigned topic is "Why Did American Political Leaders Call for a Constitutional Convention in 1787?" Here are the steps for writing a good essay on this topic:

1. **Review what you know.** If your class has already discussed the political ideology behind the Articles of Confederation, the successes and failures of that government, the problems that first constitution of the new nation could solve, and those it could not, then review your notes. Reread the chapters in the textbook that cover this topic, and look once again at any other reading assignments you have been given on these issues and events. Perhaps your instructor has given you a bibliography of books and articles on the subject that will help. Use these materials as resources also.

2. **Develop a thesis, or main argument.** The question being asked is "why?" The answer you develop should focus on motive, circumstances, and precipitating events. For example, your thesis might be: "These political leaders believed that the nation was in danger of total collapse and concluded that the Articles government lacked the powers that were necessary to rescue it."

3. **Write a clear statement of your thesis.** Refer to it as you proceed; don't wander off onto topics or issues that do not reinforce your thesis.

4. **Make an argument that explains and supports your thesis.** Given your thesis, the body of your essay should do the following:

   a. Summarize the powers the Articles of Confederation did give the central government; summarize the powers that were purposely denied the central government. Quote, when necessary, from the document itself. (Note: Most textbooks carry a copy of the Articles, the Declaration of Independence, and the Constitution in their appendices. These documents are also readily available on the Internet.)

   b. Give several examples of the results of the limitations placed on the Articles government that created major problems. Devote at least a paragraph to each of these limitations. You could write, for example:

```
This government could not raise taxes and thus it had to rely on the gen-
erosity of the states. The decision not to allow the government to tax
was based on a fear of creating a new tyrannical government like the one
the nation had just rebelled against. But the result was that the gov-
ernment could not pay its debts to its own citizens or to foreign
nations, and it could not borrow money it needed because of its poor
credit reputation.
```

Here is a second example:

```
The Articles government could not control interstate trade among the
thirteen states. Each state could set tariffs, or import duties, on goods
coming in from other states; each state could charge the others for nec-
essary goods imported from Europe and England. The result was constant
rivalry, exploitation, and resentment.
```

   c. Describe a crisis that might have prompted these political leaders to believe that the nation was on the verge of collapse. For example, you can discuss news of Shays' Rebellion in 1786, a farmers' revolt in New England, that set armed citizens against the government of Massachusetts. Men like George Washington feared that anarchy was about to replace law and order in the nation.

5. **Always enliven your essay, where you can, with quotes from the historical figures themselves.** Do you have a letter from George Washington that describes how concerned he was about the nation's

growing debt? Do you have a pamphlet or a newspaper article attacking the Articles for their weakness? Often textbooks and other secondary sources will include quotes or documents you can use.

6. **Write a conclusion.** Bring all the examples you have provided together to demonstrate the basis for the belief that the nation was in danger of collapse. You may also want to offer your own interpretation of the crisis. Do you agree with the "founding fathers" that the nation was in danger of collapse?

7. **Reread your essay.** Make sure you are convinced by your own argument. Ask yourself: Have I made my point effectively? Have I offered enough examples? Do I want to say that some concerns expressed by these political leaders were more important than others?

8. **Reread your essay—again.** Check for spelling errors. Check for grammatical errors. Make sure you have provided footnotes for all quotes. Make sure you have cited the sources you have paraphrased or quoted.

9. **Add a bibliography (a listing of the books, articles, and other sources you have used in the preparation of this assignment).** Your instructor may want an "annotated bibliography." In this case, you must provide a few sentences on each source, evaluating its quality and its value to you in writing the paper. For example:

Carol Berkin, *A Brilliant Solution: Inventing the American Constitution.* New York: Harcourt, Fall 2002. This book tells the story of the Constitutional Convention, its conflicts, goals, and concerns about the dangers of putting power in the hands of a central government.

> ☞ *HELPING HAND* Make sure you follow the instructor's directions regarding length of your paper, types of sources that must be used, and which citation format you should use for footnotes and bibliography.

> ☞ *HELPING HAND* In reviews and critiques, follow the advice of the best public speakers: tell the reader or audience what you plan to talk about (your introductory paragraph). Talk about it (the body of your paper), and then recap what you just talked about (your concluding paragraph).

Bulletin Board Discussions

With bulletin boards, professors can organize discussions outside the scheduled class period. Your professor might post a question about the assigned readings and ask you to respond. An assignment could include splitting you into groups of five or six students and asking each group to debate a certain question. This is a good tool for analyzing the readings because you get to ask questions and post your views as you are reading. This process can also help you learn more from each of the readings because your fellow students and the professor may have insights you did not consider on your own.

If your professor wants to assign a bulletin board discussion, he will give you the URL at the beginning of the semester and then announce the office hours for each week. You use your web browser to access the bulletin board. Typically, bulletin boards include a form where you can type in your name, possibly your email address, and your comments. When you are done typing in these boxes, hit the "Submit" or "OK" button, depending on how the form is organized. Your message will then be sent to the professor who can then respond. You will see not only your own message and the professor's response, but also comments from the other students. A debate can take place among you, your fellow students, and the professor, and you can respond or ask questions of anyone involved. These messages can also stay up on the Web throughout the semester, so you may read the messages at any time.

HELPING HAND   When using a bulletin board, be aware that you will not see new messages instantaneously. Most web browsers require that you hit the "Refresh" or "Reload" button to see the new messages.

RECAP

This chapter gave you tips about writing a journal entry, book review, critical essay, and bulletin board entries.

How Do I Pick a Research Topic and Find Information for it?

- *How do I choose a topic?*

- *How do I choose a note-taking system?*

- *How is research conducted?*

- *What sources should I use?*

- *How do I find sources in the library?*

- *How do I conduct research on the web?*

- *How do I find historical information in the library and on the web?*

A research paper assignment can ask you to write five pages or twenty-five pages. Regardless of the size, a few tips will help you complete the assignment with a minimum of trouble.

How Do I Choose a Topic?

The first step in writing any paper is to choose an appropriate, manageable topic. Often, the professor will make this choice easier by providing the topic and narrowing it for you. In this case, your job will be to answer the question posed by the professor.

If you are asked to choose your own topic, you will find that this task involves both emotional and practical considerations. At a very basic level, you need to find a topic that interests you. The semester will be very long if you are struggling to write a research paper about an issue that bores you. Take the time to look through the syllabus, read some of the assignments for the class, and talk to the professor so that you can find a topic that truly engages you. Usually, what makes a topic interesting is finding a question you want to answer. "Why was the fur trade so important to the French in colonial Canada?" "What led to the success of the Haitian revolution?" "How was slave labor organized in the English tobacco colonies?" But enthusiasm and curiosity about a topic are not enough.

In choosing your subject, you will have to use common sense. Can the topic be researched and written about in one semester? Can you find the resources you will need in your school library or on the Web? In other words, is your topic manageable? You will never be able to write a paper that explains the whole history of America's westward migration and settlement in the nineteenth century, but you can explain how the extension of the railroad system aided the settlement movement, or you can examine the role women played in this migration. Making sure you have the proper resources is the second key to success. You may want to write about the social and political consequences of the Iranian Revolution of 1979, but you should not pursue the idea if your library does not contain enough books and articles on this topic.

Finding a narrowed-down topic that interests you and making sure that your library has many resources on this topic can be painful, but it is critical. In narrowing the subject, you need to calculate how many points you want to make in the given number of pages. A five-page paper usually involves proving a thesis with four or five pieces of evidence; a twenty-five-page paper also proves a thesis, but here you can use more pieces of evidence and additional sections of background information. For example, the role of the railroad in western expansion could be written in five pages that discuss in brief terms the three or four major ways the railroad facilitated the process economically, socially, and physically. A twenty-five-page paper about this topic could include these same pieces of evidence, but provide personal stories about settlers or government documents about land grants to the railway companies, as well as a number of pages of historical data.

In the example given in Chapter 6 for the critical essay, the question posed was: "Why Did American Political Leaders Call for a Constitutional Convention in 1787?" In a research paper, you can ask the same question, but discuss in more depth the political opinions of the leaders involved and the crises that forced them to revisit the whole debate about what kind of government the new country should have.

You should follow the same format that you used for the essay but provide more historical data as background information. You must also supply primary source material so that you and your reader can gain a better understanding about what the different actors in the story felt and believed. This chapter, and the following one, will cover some of the steps you should take to write a research paper answering this question ("Why did American political leaders call for a constitutional convention in 1787?").

How Do I Choose a Note-Taking System?

Before you start doing the research, you need to think about a note-taking system. Without a system, you will face a disorganized mess on the day you start writing your paper. You will waste precious hours if you wait until the last minute to organize the information you have gathered. You will have trouble figuring out what information is missing and what you may still need to research.

 HELPING HAND   If you start researching a topic and find that the library and the Web do not have enough information or have too much (i.e., the topic is too broad), you need to alter your topic. This could involve merely changing the focus a little bit or changing the entire topic itself. Talk to your professor and your school librarian; they can help redirect your work.

. Choosing a note-taking system:

  a. One common system is to use index cards. Write only one piece of information on each card. When you start writing your paper, you have an instant organizational system because you can put all the cards containing similar information in one pile and continue until all the cards are organized.

  b. You can also use an outline system. In this case, you divide the outline into the different sections of your paper and place relevant information under each of your outline headings.

 HELPING HAND   Regardless of the system you choose, you must keep track of where you found each piece of information. Make sure that every card or outline entry includes information about the source, including the page number. You might also want to include the call number of a book or journal you used, in case you have to return to it.

2. Mastering the note-taking process itself:

  a. Don't rewrite every line in every book you read. This will slow your research and could lead you down the road to plagiarism. (See Chapter 10 for an explanation of plagiarism.)

  b. Write out individual quotes you know you want to use, and make sure that you write the entire quote correctly (or make a photocopy of that page).

  c. For other pieces of information, write in a kind of shorthand. Write down only key words and phrases, not complete sentences.

 HELPING HAND   Make sure that you can understand the words and phrases later. Don't cut corners so much that the notes are worthless on the day you finally sit down to write the paper.

How Is Research Conducted?

Research requires utilizing as many resources as you can find. Begin scouring your school library because it contains primary and secondary books and journals, and possibly even tapes and videos that you can use for your research paper. (See Chapter 5 for a definition of primary and secondary sources.) Don't forget to use the Web, not only for printed sources but to find people in your neighborhood who have special insights into your topic. You need to do the leg work to find as many of the relevant sources as possible.

HELPING HAND For almost all research papers, your professor will require that you utilize primary sources. Rarely will a professor assign a research paper without them because they provide the real building-blocks of any historical writing. Your professor wants you to serve as a junior historian, analyzing the raw data for yourself and not relying solely on the words of others.

What Sources Should I Use?

A good rule of thumb is to start with sources containing a broad analysis of your topic and gradually move toward sources with a more focused analysis. What does this rule mean for you? Start with a few secondary sources to get an historical overview of your topic. Once you have a strong understanding of your topic, you can start reading more specialized sources. These will often be primary sources because they give a hands-on narrative and opinion about the events you're describing and analyzing. Don't limit yourself when it comes to primary sources. Personal diaries, government documents, treaties, letters, and published interviews may all be helpful, but you might also find novels and poetry helpful for your analysis because they give alternative views about your subject. In general, it is best to move from the general to the particular, from books that set the broad historical context to books that focus on specific issues or events that relate directly to the question you have raised in your thesis.

 HELPING HAND Your professor will often require that you use certain types of sources and answer a certain type of question. Make sure you understand the assignment before you start your research so that you won't waste a lot of time looking for the wrong kinds of information.

 HELPING HAND While the Web is a wonderful tool for getting information quickly, do not rely on it exclusively when writing a research paper. Push yourself away from the computer screen and go to the library. The best resources will be at the library, both in terms of the written documents stored there and the personal help you will receive. Librarians are in the library to help you; take advantage of their assistance and expertise.

How Do I Find Sources in the Library?

Probably by now, every library in the country has a computer database program that allows you to access the materials. Every database program is slightly different, so you need either to find an instruction sheet somewhere near the computer terminal or to ask a librarian how to use your school's program. Many libraries also allow you to access the database from your home computer. Ask your librarian or computer department for instructions.

All books are not created equal, as the saying goes. The books available range from secondary sources to autobiographies of famous people, to government documents, to novels. For example, the autobiography of a politician involved in a major policy decision will probably provide a very different account of that decision-making process than a scholar who studied it years later. This is why Chapter 5 reminded you that not all secondary sources arrive at the same conclusion, even when the same facts are used. And that's why you can't rely on a single source—or even two or three—to tell your tale in a research paper. Make every effort to find as many different perspectives on your topic as you can.

How Do I Conduct Research on the Web?

The Web literally becomes a more useful source for historical writing every day. You can use it to get a biography of someone, check on that date you need to include in your paper, get a wide range of opinions about a given issue, and so on. Since library books are so expensive, many schools are now asking their students to rely on Web research whenever possible. Even in cases when the library is well stocked, the

Web is now an invaluable source for finding pieces of information that were previously found only in dark and dank archives.

The Web is a completely unregulated medium, however, so any person, in any country, can post information to it. What does this lack of regulation mean for you? Even more than when you do research in the library, you must question the source of *all* the information you obtain on the Web. You must evaluate a web source just as you do a book, journal, or magazine by making every effort to find out who wrote the piece, who its target audience is likely to be, and what its political slant or opinion is. Without this process of evaluation, you can not be sure you are using valid data in your paper. Here are some examples of web sites that must be evaluated and used with care:

1. Groups like Amnesty International and Human Rights Watch post reports about human rights abuses perpetrated by countries around the the world. These reports provide information often unavailable in books, but the reports are also controversial because the countries under examination frequently disagree with the findings. To use these sources, you should always indicate the organization issuing the report and any information you can find about how the data was obtained. For example, the data could have come from interviews with political prisoners or from newspaper reports.

2. As crises develop around the world, more people are writing first-hand accounts and sending them via email or list-serves to those outside the affected area. These insights can be invaluable if they are used correctly, but be careful not to claim that this information is undisputed truth. Provide some background information on the author in your paper and explain that this is a subjective, eyewitness account.

3. Groups like the Ku Klux Klan post their racial views on the Web. You might want to use this kind of source if you're writing about racial politics in America. If you write about this group's views, always indicate the source; do not write as if the majority of people in the country agree with them.

4. Governments, politicians, and political organizations around the world are beginning to use the web to put forward their opinions. For example, Hizbollah, a military and political organization stationed in southern Lebanon, and the current president of Iran both have specialized web sites. These sites contain information and quotes unavailable anywhere else, but here too you should indicate the author of the site and the fact that these organizations and politicians have political motives for getting this information out to the world.

5. Many people—outside the university system and the political world—have posted sites discussing the activities and writings of major historical and literary figures and major historical events. A small number of sites might be of value, but generally the analysis presented is not at a university level and should be avoided. These are amateur sites, so you have no way of guaranteeing the information they contain.

6. News outlets such as CNN and the Associated Press have web sites. If you're writing about a contemporary event, these web sites can be useful because they often provide articles and reports from many different news sources. However, the very nature of the news industry necessitates that you use these sources with caution. Newspapers and cable stations always want to be the first to publish a piece of information, to "get the scoop" on their competitors. In the rush to get the information to the public, many of the facts may be left out of the story or they may be completely wrong. To avoid this problem, follow the story over a few days, or even a few months, to see how the story evolves over time. Also, try to use a number of different news sources as a way of backing up your own facts. One news source might ignore information that another source uncovered.

Although you must use the Web with care, there is no doubt that it has become a great source for all kinds of information, including material that is also available in your own school library. The advantage of the Web in this case is that it makes these sources easier to access. Check the Web for the following:

HELPING HAND   Instead of the old saying "innocent until proven guilty," think in terms of "guilty until proven innocent" when dealing with information on the Web. Initially assume that all the information you find on the Web is questionable. Only after you do the research to find out who the author is and what his or her motivation is for creating the site may you consider using the information obtained.

1. Major newspapers and academic and political journals like *The New York Times, The Nation,* and *American Historical Review* post articles to the Web. In addition, foreign newspapers, often in English, appear on the Web every day. You may use these as you would the hard copies.

2. Many historical essays and articles have been written by university classes like your own or by professors themselves. In this case, the URL will usually include the identification *.edu* as an indicator. Generally, these sources will be secondary sources because the class and the professor have done their own research, similar to your own. You may quote from the analysis they have included, but you should go to the original sources for the more substantive facts. A good paper will always cite all the sources and a bibliography, so this search should be an easy process. Think of a page like this as a guide to finding more information.

3. Historical societies and research institutes post historical essays about any number of issues. You may use these sources as secondary sources, but be sure to indicate in your paper the source of the information, and always try to find the original sources of the information obtained.

4. More and more often, universities and libraries are posting primary source material to the Web. Three of the most famous are the Victorian Web at Brown University, the Chicago Fire site, and Yale University's Avalon Project. Web sites also have collected the writings and papers of famous historical figures. You may use these documents in your paper as you would primary documents you found in the library.

5. Governments all over the world post parliamentary, congressional, and diplomatic documents to the Web. You may use these as primary documents.

6. International organizations like the United Nations post resolutions and laws on their web sites. You may use these sources as you would the hard copies generally available in government depositories.

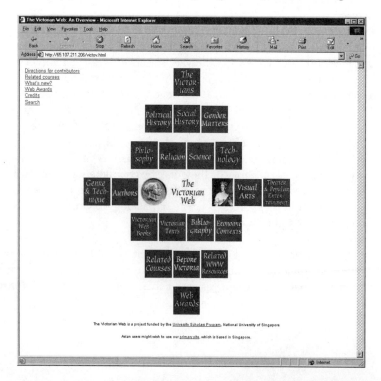

7. Online encyclopedias have also proliferated on the Web. Microsoft Encarta and Britannica Online are the two largest, but they should be used with caution by any university student. The analysis presented in them is at a high school rather than a university level. You may use these sources, but only for simple background information such as names and dates, not for analyses or quotes.

How Do I Find Historical Information in the Library and on the Web?

With the enormous number of sources available to you on the Web and in your library, you may ask yourself: How do I find information quickly and efficiently? It helps to think in terms of peeling an onion. Merely cutting off the skin shows very little of the onion. Layer by layer must be peeled away for the center to appear. In doing research, each layer will provide a different piece of the story. Also some layers are more important than others for a given project.

Layer 1

The best way to start finding information in the library and on the Web is by typing broad phrases into the library database program or the most popular search engines on the Web—www.yahoo.com, www.google.com, www.hotbot.com, etc. All of these programs and sites provide a box for typing in the search criteria.

For example, for information about the American Civil War, type that phrase in the box. In your library database, the names of the different books will be shown. On the Web, a short description appears under each URL. Read them to see which sources are closest to the topic you are actually researching. Also, remember that the search engines rate each of the sites to determine which are more important for this search. Thus, the sites that appear near the top of the screen will probably be more useful, but you cannot take this for granted. These searches are really a hit-or-miss process. For example, asking about the country of Jordan will bring up not only a number of sites about the Hashemite Kingdom of Jordan, but many more about the basketball star Michael Jordan.

For the sample research paper, try:

Articles of Confederation
Constitutional Convention
George Washington
James Madison
Alexander Hamilton

If too many sites appear after a broad search, try narrowing down the search parameters. To use the American Civil War example, try typing "Women in the American Civil War" or "Battles in the American Civil War" to bring up sites and book lists more closely related to your particular topic. In other words, the more specific the phrase, the better the response will be from the database and/or the search engine.

For the sample research paper, now try:

Shays' Rebellion
Northwest Ordinances
Federalist Papers
Federalists
Antifederalists
John Dickinson (the man who wrote the initial draft of the Articles of Confederation)

In the Library   Once you have a list of books in the library, write down the call numbers of the books you want to see or ask the librarian if there is a way to print out or email to yourself a list of the most important books.

On the Web Most search engines are better for one type of search than for another.

Don't stick with just one, Yahoo, for example; try several. Over time, you will discover which search engines are best suited for one project or another.

Once the search engine has generated a number of sites, enter them by clicking on the URL provided. Searching from page to page on the site can be slow, so look for any internal search engine the site might provide. Usually a "search" button of some kind will be on the top of the page or in a frame to the side. If not, surf around the site to see if one is available on another page. If no search option is available, you will have to surf around the site yourself. If the information you want does not appear quickly, go back to the search-engine results and try another web page.

 HELPING HAND The Web contains too many pages and options to spend too much time looking on just one site. If the information is not on the first site, move on to another.

Layer 2

Use these initial searches to dig deeper into the resources of both the library and the Web.

In the Library Once you've located a book through the library database system, hyperlinks for related topics will appear at the bottom of the page. These are Library of Congress subject headings. Every book in the library is stored by its title and its author, and also by the topics it covers. If you don't find enough books via a search for specific titles, try using different subject headings.

You can also use Boolean phrases to narrow your search. Boolean phrases use words like *and* to tell the computer that you want to find titles that contain only the words that you've stated. Ask your librarian about all the different Boolean options available in your library's database.

Most libraries in the United States use the Library of Congress reference system. In this system, books with similar themes are placed on the same shelves. Once you've found a few books or journals via the computer database, check the whole shelf and section to see if any other useful books are located there.

 HELPING HAND   Once you've found books that are useful, be sure to look at the bibliography at the back of each one. Remember: The authors have already done some of the work for you.

On the Web   Once you have found a site that appears useful, look through it to see if the authors suggest more sites on the same topic. For example, a number of sites on the author J. R. R. Tolkien not only give information about his life and books but also recommend other sites to visit. Hyperlinks will be provided to navigate you to the other sites.

The Web can become addictive quickly. It is so easy to use and has so much information to offer. Make sure you do not get mired down, moving from one worthless page to another. Remember that the Web is only useful for a class if it gives you the information you need. Do not surf for hours hoping you'll discover the data somewhere in cyberspace. If the information is hidden too deeply, turn off your computer and head back to the library instead.

For the sample research paper, some good secondary sources would be:

Charles Beard. *An Economic Interpretation of the Constitution*. New York: Free Press, 1986.

Carol Berkin. *A Brilliant Solution: Inventing American Constitution*. New York: Harcourt, 2002.

Forrest McDonald. *E Pluribus Unum: Formation of the American Republic, 1776-1790*. Boston: Houghton Mifflin, 1965.

Richard B. Morris. *Witnesses at the Creation: Hamilton, Madison, Jay, and the Constitution*. New York: Holt, Rinehart, and Winston, 1985.

Jack Rakove. *Original Meanings: Politics and Ideas in the Making of the Constitution*. New York: Knopf, 1996.

For the sample research paper, some good primary sources would be:

Avalon Project at the Yale Law School, http://www.yale.edu/lawweb/avalon/ avalon.htm (Posted to the site are many primary sources surrounding the Articles of Confederation and the U.S. Constitution)

Lyman Butterfield et al., eds. *The Book of Abigail and John: Selected Letters of the Adams Family, 1762-1784* (1975). Cambridge: Harvard University Press, 1975

The Federalist Papers

The Articles of Confederation

The U.S. Constitution

Layer 3

In the last few years, a new type of electronic index has appeared in library databases. It directs users to newspaper and journal articles, as well as to government documents. These are important new tools because the regular database searches do not uncover the same kinds of sources. These indexes will find keywords in articles. For example, a search for Thomas Jefferson in a regular library database will probably list only the books about him. An electronic index will list all articles with his name in the title as well as any articles where his name appears in the body of the text.

The indexes are generally accessible only through a university or college Internet connection. In other words, you must log on to the Web using a school log-in program or access the indexes while at school. If you are using AOL, Microsoft Network, or another private service, you will not be able to use these indexes. Schools must pay for the right to use them, unlike search engines like Yahoo, so only enrolled students may access them. Ask the librarian at your school or check the school's web site to find out which indexes you can use. A few examples follow:

JSTOR: This index searches for journal articles and allows the user to download full-text versions of them in different formats.

Lexis-Nexis: This index directs the user to newspaper and journal articles published in the last twenty years. Not only are the citations listed, but many of the articles can be downloaded for free or a small fee. This site is useful for papers covering current events.

Public Affairs Information Service (PAIS): This index provides citation information for books and articles, but does not provide full-text versions of any of them.

Libraries also collect bibliographical databases, like *Historical Abstracts* and *America: History and Life*, which provide lists of articles and books written about a given subject. Ask your school librarian to see which bibliographical databases your school owns.

Layer 4

Government agencies and departments throughout the country and the world provide copies of the documents they produce.

In the Library   Most large libraries in the country have collections of U.S. government documents. You find these documents by using the library database program. If your library is too small, find out how to gain the right to use a larger one in your area.

On the Web   The U.S. government, as well as many other governments around the world, have increasingly begun to place documents on the Web, which makes them accessible to all users. On many of these, documents, laws, maps, census data, and additional documents may be downloaded to the user's computer.

A good starting point for U.S. government documents is: http://www.firstgov.gov/.

Layer 5

Local governments and private individuals have established research centers, tourist sites, museums, and lobbying organizations all over the country. They look at local, national, and international issues, as well gender, class, and historical items, to mention just a few topics. If you want information from them, write, call, or visit their centers. Most of them now have web pages so you can easily obtain their contact information. These institutions are often loaded with information that you can't find anywhere else.

Layer 6

The Web has also spawned an enormous number of listservs where you can discuss thousands of different topics, from Revolutionary War battles to environmental concerns. While a lot of junk passes around the various listservs, they do highlight current events and publish articles pertinent to a particular topic. Two different types of listservs appear on the Internet.

1. Some listservs allow you to view a discussion taking place on a given subject from a web browser. To find one, use a search engine to search for a particular topic. The listserv will appear as a URL; click on it and you will be able to view the most recent discussion. One particularly good web site is H-Net: Social Sciences and the Humanities, found at http://www2.h-net.msu.edu/.
2. Some listservs require you to sign up to receive the information via email. Again, a search-engine will find pages discussing different topics. When you click on a site that states that it has a listserv, look at the instructions on the page.

Typically, you will have to send an email message to the listserv. In the body of the letter, you will have to type a specific line (as instructed on the web page).

You will then receive dozens, if not hundreds, of letters a day. Remain on the listserv if interesting issues are discussed, but remove yourself from the list (by following the instructions on the web page) if you do not find it useful. You do not want to waste precious time reading through worthless emails.

Downloading Information from the Web

Most pages have automated the process of downloading information from the Web, but here are two methods for completing this process.

Automated: When downloading an article or file from the Web, check to see if a button or hyperlink labeled "download" appears somewhere on the page. If so, click on it and then follow the directions on the screen. The biggest decision you will have to make will be where the file should be saved. After clicking on the particular "download" button, a box will appear asking for the location of the desired file. Go to the top of the box, to the line that says "Look in:" and click on the down arrow. Search through the folders on the computer until the correct one is open. Then hit "OK" or "Save," depending on which program you are using.

Manual: If the program has not provided a download option, then you must save the file manually. Open up the page you want to save and click on "File" and "Save" or "Save frame" (depending on which program you are using). You will then be prompted to pick a folder in which to save the file. Use the instructions above to find the appropriate folder and then save the file.

The files saved by these methods will probably be in an HTML or word-processing format. To avoid having to guess the format, the best method is to open the file manager on your computer. In Windows, this will appear as "Windows Explorer." If you are using a different type of operating system, you must search your computer for a similar program.

Once you have opened the file manager, search until you have opened the folder with the appropriate file. Click on the file two times and the computer should open the appropriate program. If it does not, then you will not be able to view the file because you do not have the right kind of program.

Adobe Acrobat Reader Many web pages have created Adobe Acrobat files to ease the process of reading long, complicated files. For example, the U.S. government uses the Adobe format for almost all of its tax files. Files written in languages that do not use Latin letters (Arabic, Hebrew, Russian, for example) often appear in the Adobe format.

To read these files, you must have the Adobe Acrobat Reader program installed on your computer. This program is free and can be obtained in many different places. The easiest place to look is on the web page where you want to read an Adobe file. Often the producers of the page will place a button, a hyperlink, somewhere on the page saying something like "Download Adobe Reader Now." If the web page contains this button, click on it and follow the instructions.

If no hyperlink appears, go to the Adobe Acrobat Reader home page at http://www.adobe.com/products/acrobat/readstep.html and click on the hyperlink that says "Get Acrobat Reader Free!" and follow the instructions.

Layer 7

Be creative about choosing your sources; not everything is within the covers of a history book.

Depending on your topic, you can, for example, interview people involved in the events you're describing. If you're writing a paper about migration to the United States, find someone who arrived here via Ellis Island in New York. That could be your very own grandmother!

Or you can utilize photographs or stills from movies and documentaries to enhance your analysis. Jacob Riis took photographs of immigrants in New York City at the end of the nineteenth century. If you were writing that same paper on immigration, you could show his pictures as examples of how the immigrants worked and lived in the city. At the same time, you need to be aware of the fact that Riis often put his subjects into posed positions so that he could represent their lives as he imagined them.

> ☞ *HELPING HAND*   The fact that Jacob Riis rigged some of his photographs to show what he imagined was the truth should remind you that you should always check who the author of a source is, regardless of the type of source. Photographs can display a bias just as easily as a written article.

Fictional sources, such as poems, short stories, and novels, provide a unique glimpse into historical eras. For that same immigration paper, you could quote Emma Lazarus's famous poem, engraved on the Statue of Liberty today. "Give us your tired/your poor . . . ." A novel by Charles Dickens could add flavor to a paper on nineteenth-century working conditions in London.

In other words, use your imagination! These additional sources will improve your research paper and make the whole process more interesting for you.

RECAP

This chapter gave you tips about choosing a research topic and conducting the research. The key to this process is to find a topic that interests you and that can be researched using the resources at your disposal. It also means that you need to use your imagination as you conduct your research. Don't take the easy route; try to find unique sources that bring your topic to life.

*H*ow Do I Write a Research Paper?

■ *What is the difference between an analysis and narrative?*

■ *What steps should I follow when writing my paper?*

TIPS IN THIS CHAPTER

■ Writing an analysis versus writing a narrative ■ Writing a rough draft
■ Making final revisions to the research paper

What Is the Difference Between an Analysis and a Narrative?

One of the most common problems students encounter when starting to write any kind of paper is recognizing the difference between an analysis and a narrative. An analysis looks at different pieces of evidence and presents a thesis. In other words, an analysis proves a point or answers a question. A narrative describes the event, usually in a chronological manner. A narrative of World War II would look something like this:

```
In 1939, the German army invaded Poland and thus started World War II. The
Germans then conquered the Netherlands and France through its blitzkrieg
offense. The United States entered the war after the Japanese attack on
Pearl Harbor, on December 7, 1941.
```

An analysis would answer a question, such as the following:

```
How did the Germans successfully conquer Poland, the Netherlands, and
France?
Why did the United States enter the war?
```

Most research papers combine analysis and narrative. The problem for the student is to find the right mixture of these two styles. Research papers should always be constructed around an analytical framework, with narrative sections used only to prove the different points.

What Steps Should I Follow When Writing My Paper?

Step 1: Write the Thesis Paragraph

The thesis paragraph is the cornerstone of your paper. You must present your thesis as clearly as possible so that the reader will know the direction you plan to take. The thesis sentence itself—the question you plan to answer—can appear anywhere in the thesis paragraph, but it is most often placed at the beginning or the end of the paragraph. You must also detail the most important points you plan to make in the paper, so that you give the reader a guideline to follow.

HELPING HAND   The thesis paragraph is so important because it's your chance to tell the professor what you plan to prove in the paper. You have all the power in this situation: you tell the professor exactly what you want to say and the professor checks to see if you've done it effectively.

A thesis paragraph for the question, "Why Did American Political Leaders Call for a Constitutional Convention in 1787?" could look like this:

American political leaders believed that the nation was in danger of total collapse and concluded that the Articles of Confederation government lacked the powers necessary to rescue it. Financial concerns, diplomatic crises, and a farmers' revolt highlighted how weak and ineffective the Articles government had become. These problems confirmed for many of the country's political leaders the need to create a stronger central government, while at the same time recognizing the political rights of the states. The provisions of the U.S. Constitution ultimately reflect the historical context in which they were written because they established the strong central government the country clearly needed at the time, while providing a system of checks and balances to supervise the powers newly granted.

Step 2: Write an Outline for the Whole Paper

Don't start writing immediately; make an outline of the main points you plan to present. Each section of the paper should analyze a different aspect of your paper. In other words, each section of your paper should answer a different aspect of your question.

Organize your notes according to the outline. If you've used note cards, pile them in different areas of the room, depending on where they go in the outline. If they're in the computer, collect them under the relevant outline heading. For the sample research paper, the outline could look like this:

I. Introduction (Thesis)
II. Short History of the Revolutionary War and the Writing of the
    Articles of Confederation
  A. Victory in the Revolutionary War
  B. Political Opinions of the Political Leaders
    1. Fear of Creating an Authoritarian Government
    2. Power of the States
    3. Different Views of Citizenship, Political Rights, Democracy
      a. John Adams
      b. John Dickinson
  C. Provisions of the Articles of Confederation
III. Financial Problems Under the Articles of Confederation
  A. Postwar Depression
    1. Costs of Rebuilding After the War
    2. Speculators
    3. Destruction of Markets During the War
  B. Problems of Tax Collection
  C. War Debts Owed by the Articles
      Government
  D. The Articles Government's Inability to Impose Federal Tariffs
  E. Economic Problems and the Northwest Ordinances

IV. Diplomatic Crises Under the Articles of Confederation

   A. British Support for Indian Resistance in the Ohio Valley

   B. Spanish Concerns with American Settlers in Mississippi, Kentucky, and Tennessee

   C. Barbary Pirates in the Mediterranean

V. Shays' Rebellion

   A. Causes of the Rebellion

     1. Land Rights Issues

     2. Economic Problems in the Postwar Period

     3. Inflation

   B. "Stay" Laws

   C. Failures of the State and Federal Governments

VI. Constitutional Convention

   A. Members

   B. Political Differences of the Members

     1. States' Rights Versus the Power of the Central Government

     2. Slavery Issues

   C. U.S. Constitution

VII. Conclusion (Reiterate the Thesis)

This outline highlights the *reasons why the Articles of Confederation had to be revised*; it does not provide a narrative of events.

Throughout the paper, utilize both primary and secondary sources. Use secondary sources for analysis and primary sources to highlight the real voices of the people concerned with these events. For the sample research paper, the primary sources could include:

The papers of all the political leaders   Libraries all over the country and sites now on the Web have collected the writings of just about every major figure involved in writing the Articles of Confederation and the Constitution. Use them throughout your paper to show why these men felt the Articles had failed. If a secondary source gives a quote from, say, James Madison, don't use that source; find the primary source. Use the secondary source only if you can't find the original.

Government documents   When writing about a specific document, like the U.S. Constitution, always quote from the original.

Historical sites and museums   Cities up and down the East Coast have museums and historical sites designed to highlight the early years of this country's history. Contact them to get additional information for your paper.

> ☞ *HELPING HAND*   Always keep your thesis in mind while you're organizing the paper so that every part of the outline answers part of your question. If a point in the outline has nothing to do with your thesis, delete it.

Step 3: Write a Rough Draft

The old cliché that claims, "I always write better under pressure," is not true. Actually, you just write under pressure because you know you have a deadline. Papers written the night before the due date generally look like rough drafts and receive much lower grades than they would have if they had been written progressively over a few days. The best option is to write a rough draft a few days before the due date and show it to the professor or to one of your friends. You can then incorporate their suggestions into your final draft. At the same time, this break will allow you to step away from the paper for a couple of days. You can then read the paper over and bring fresh ideas to it.

 HELPING HAND   Caffeine is not a substitute for a good night's sleep. Don't put yourself in the position of having to "pull an all-nighter," because you will not be able to take the time to write a rough draft, you will not be able to get the advice of your professor, and you will not be able to find grammatical or thematic problems.

Go through your notes, concentrating on one section at a time. Always keep in mind the question you're trying to answer; don't give information that has nothing to do with your thesis. Every paragraph in the paper must add some key piece to the puzzle.

You must cite the sources of your information. See Chapter 11 for tips on citing sources.

When you finish writing the paper, read it through a number of times, to check for grammatical errors and to make sure that you successfully proved your point.

 HELPING HAND   The act of writing generates the process of analysis and might very well make you rethink your ideas about the topic. If you get to the end of the paper and find that your evidence proves a different point than you initially wrote in the thesis, change the thesis.

Step 4: Edit the Final Draft

Once you've shown your paper to your professor or to a friend, make sure you consider all of their suggestions and make the appropriate changes. It's often difficult to identify problems with your own writing; outside readers are invaluable in this process.

 HELPING HAND   Don't forget to add a bibliography to the end of the paper. The professor needs to know what sources you used. You can't take any shortcuts in this process.

RECAP

This chapter discussed all the steps necessary for writing a research paper. You must utilize several skills in the process, from hunting down the right sources to organizing an analytical paper. You should ask your professor for advice about sources, your topic, and the writing of the paper itself.

*H*ow Do I Join Class Presentation Assignments and Debates Successfully?

- *What is involved in a class presentation?*

- *What is role playing?*

- *What is a class debate?*

Most history assignments involve writing, but many professors like to assign individual or group oral presentations too because they help you hone speaking skills that will serve you well in your future career. Doctors, lawyers, administrators, and real estate brokers, for example, all find themselves standing up in front of a group and presenting data they have collected and analyzed. So think of these class presentations as invaluable opportunities to improve your job prospects after graduation.

What Is Involved in a Class Presentation?

A class presentation involves both preparation and then the actual presentation.

Preparation

The best way to get over the stage fright associated with giving talks in front of a group of people is to come to the class as fully prepared as possible. If you have done your research thoroughly, written a couple of drafts of your talk, put together useful materials for the class, and rehearsed the whole presentation in front of the mirror, a lot of that fear will disappear. In the following section, part of a sample twenty-minute presentation entitled "The Influence of European Imperialism on Africa" will be prepared.

Group Work If the assignment requires that you work with another person in the class, meet together as soon as possible and divide the workload. The best way to do this is to divide the topic into segments so that each person covers a different theme or a different period of historical time. Ask the professor for advice if you do not know how to divide the work fairly and economically. These assignments can always be changed later as the research brings out new aspects of the topic, but this is a good step because it provides a solid foundation for each section that you will discuss in the final presentation.

In addition, at the first meeting, make a schedule for all future meetings so you can work at a steady pace. Get everyone's phone numbers and email addresses so you can contact each other whenever you need to do so.

 HELPING HAND   The biggest problem with group work is making sure that everyone carries his or her share of the load. Avoid problems by meeting at regular intervals and supervising each other's work. If one person still does not do enough work, talk to the professor as soon as possible.

Research   Approach the presentation as you would a paper: get the topic from the professor or come up with one of your own (depending on how the assignment is worded in the syllabus), narrow it down, and then find the necessary sources. As early as possible in the semester, consult with the professor about the topic and discuss the sources available at the school.

 HELPING HAND   Don't wait until the last minute to start the research process. Calculate how much time you think the project should take— and add a bit more for good measure. You don't want to be frantically hunting down sources in the library the night before your presentation is due.

Writing   Until this point, the process has been the same as writing a paper for the class. Now, however, you need to think about the best format for presenting the information orally. Writing a paper and reading it, line by line, for twenty minutes will be boring for you, the professor, and your classmates. To give a successful presentation, you need to find a livelier way to present the information.

Step 1: Make an outline of the major themes you want to present. Since the average student presentation lasts about ffteen to thirty minutes, you should think in terms of having three to six major points to discuss, depending on the assigned time for yours. For the sample presentation, the major points include the following:

```
I.   Economic Imperialism
II.  Cultural Imperialism
III. Colonial Imperialism
IV.  Changes in Africa as a Result of European Imperialism.
```

Step 2: Under each of these points, write complete sentences discussing them, either in paragraphs or in an outline form. Paragraphs work well when you want to connect the information in your own mind. This format is closer to writing a normal paper. The outline format saves a little time, but it is helpful only when you already know the key points you want to discuss and do not need to think through your analysis in quite the same way. Samples of both are shown below.

```
I. Economic Imperialism (Paragraph Style)

European sailors began to trade along the West African coast at the end of
the fifteenth century. European merchants had traded with Africa for cen-
turies, but the goods had come across the Sahara Desert and the
Mediterranean Sea. To increase their profits, the Europeans wanted to find
a more direct way to tap into the ivory and gold available for sale in
Africa. In the last decades of the fifteenth century, as shipping technol-
ogy improved and sailors could explore the West Coast of Africa, European
merchants came along to make the necessary trading contacts. When they
arrived on the coast, these merchants began to barter European manufac-
tured goods for the raw materials available in Africa. During the next cen-
tury, the Europeans solidified their positions along the coast by build-
ing their own trading forts and by making strategic alliances with the dif-
ferent kingdoms trading in the region.

II. Cultural Imperialism (Outline Style)

   A. Catholic and Protestant missionaries arrived in West Africa almost
      immediately after the sailors first touched on the shore.
   B. From the coast, they quickly worked their way further inland.
   C. In small villages, they set up churches and schools.
   D. As part of the process of converting Africans to Christianity, the
      missionaries taught European languages and incorporated Africans
      into their church as workers.
   E. The first converts were Africans who were alienated by their own
      religious or societal beliefs.
```

F. Others converted to obtain jobs with European merchants.

Step 3:   After putting together the main points of the topic, you must organize them into a presentation. You do not want to read the paper, line by line. A more natural approach works better for oral presentations. To organize a successful presentation, you now need to put together an outline of key words and phrases. These phrases and words should be descriptive enough to trigger your memory about the larger topics to be presented. Write longer sentences if you need additional clues about the information.

I. Economic Imperialism

   A. Europeans Discovered West Africa in the Fifteenth Century.

   B. Changed Trade Routes—Sahara to Coast

   C. Traded Ivory and Gold

   D. Shipping Technology Improved (This technology allowed the Europeans
       to sail along the whole coast for the first time.)

   E. European Forts Dotted Coastline

   F. Europeans Directly Involved in Trade in Africa

 HELPING HAND   To give a good presentation, you must know your key words and phrases as thoroughly as possible. These words and phrases will mean nothing to you on the day of the presentation if you have not read through the information several times. You must practice your presentation to guarantee that you understand and remember the information.

Step 4:   Type out a clear copy of your outline or write the phrases and words on a series of index cards. If you have to fumble through your notes during the presentation, the students and the professor will lose interest. It is very important that you organize the outline or the index cards as efficiently as possible. For example, use different colors and fonts so you can easily distinguish the different topics.

Step 5:   In addition to the task of putting together a well-researched presentation, many professors will ask you to provide supplementary materials to highlight the most important aspects of the topic. These supplementary materials could be outlines, maps, images, or even food.

The computer programs discussed below only help you present the information to the class. You should still write the talk itself on a separate outline or on index cards.

Word-Processing Program   If you want the students and the professor to have a broad outline of the topics you plan to discuss, you can type this outline using any word-processing program. To distribute it to the class, print the page and make a copy for everyone or print it out on a transparency.

Economic Imperialism

1. European Discovery of West Africa

2. Trade

3. Technology

4. European Forts

Power Point   You can also use a program called Power Point, which creates presentations very easily. The program automatically provides outlines and allows you to insert pictures or images between the lines of text.

Web Page   You may also create your own web page for a presentation. The advantage of this is that the Web allows you to construct permanent documents.

For example, a Power Point presentation is good for the twenty minutes you are actually speaking, but a web page can be put up on the Internet and the students can re-examine it at any time, twenty-four hours a day, while the semester continues.

Images   Pictures and maps can add a visual image to the topic you are presenting. You can get images by downloading them from the Web or by scanning them into your computer from books. You can then put them into your web page or Power Point presentation or print them out as transparencies or hard copies. See Chapter 13 for instructions about how to perform these functions.

Examples of images to be used in the sample presentation:

Portuguese caravels (ships)
European trading forts
Missionary villages and churches
A map of West Africa
A map showing European exploration routes

Depending on your topic, you might find that other items are important to show to the class. You can prepare or buy food from a given geographical or cultural area. In the sample presentation, you could bring

 HELPING HAND   Even if the professor does not require these additional materials, try to come up with some ideas of your own. Make sure, however, that these materials enhance your presentation. Do not show a lot of pictures just because you can find them; show only those items that help explain your topic.

in yams because much of West Africa subsisted on yams. You could also bring in clothing from the region. Try to be creative.

Step 6:   Organize all your cards, transparencies, outlines, and images into the format needed for the presentation.

Step 7:   Practice your presentation in front of a friend or a mirror. If you are doing a group project, make sure you practice the whole presentation together. Only by going through a practice-run (or two or three) will you know if the presentation runs for the right length of time and if your trigger words are good enough to allow you to discuss all the information you have put together. In the practice runs, go through your additional material as well to make sure all of it is organized sufficiently.

If you find, after a couple of practice runs, that the phrases and words written on your outline or index cards do not trigger enough information in your mind, change them. Write out longer phrases or add a few more words. The thing to remember is that these cards are your guide. You need to make them as useful as possible. What works for one person will not necessarily work for another. By practicing the talk ahead of time, you can find your own system.

HELPING HAND   You may be surprised to know that many professors experience stage fright. So if you are still afraid, even after following all these steps, go to the professor to discuss the problem. He will probably give you tips for overcoming the fear because (1) he wants you to succeed, and (2) chances are he understands the problem all too well.

Presentation

If you have followed the steps listed above, the presentation should go off without a problem. In the end, the key to the presentation itself is practice, practice, practice. If you know your information and your materials well enough, the presentation will be easy.

What Is Role Playing?

Role playing involves stepping into the shoes of a historical character and putting voice to his or her words. The reason professors use this device is to encourage students to look closely at the opinions expressed in different countries and by different historical figures. While other assignments certainly serve this function as well, role playing adds a new component to the process. Role playing requires that you speak in someone else's voice, defend another's position. To do this, you must know that person's ideas well enough to uphold them, regardless of your own particular views. You should come away from a role-playing session with a new perspective on how hard it is to negotiate treaties, determine policy decisions, and decide who to support in a given debate, to name only a few instances. Role playing allows you to step inside the mind of an historical figure you have studied merely on paper.

A common role-playing device is to act out a mock session of the United Nations, or another international or regional organization, and have students represent the different countries involved. The professor will typically present the forum with a problem—the status of Northern Ireland or the issue of economic sanctions against Iraq, for example—and ask that the students negotiate and debate as if they were the Prime Minister of England or Saddam Hussein.

Another example of role playing is a military re-enactment. By representing the soldiers who fought at the Battle of Gettysburg, for example, you will better understand how the North won that battle and why geography and the amount of supplies held by each side can easily change the balance of power on the battlefield.

You could be asked to act out a play that may be a work of fiction but that highlights some of the historical themes of the period. An example would be a Shakespearean tragedy. You could also be asked to act the roles of some of the characters involved in European imperialism in Africa, people like an African king, a European missionary, or a European adminisrator.

How do you study for something like this? As with any assignment, the answer is to complete the homework and do any extra research the professor requires. You will not be able to represent that African king if you do not understand his religious views or the alliances he has possibly made with the new European arrivals. If the information is not included in the regular reading for the class, talk to the professor about the extra research you should conduct.

What Is a Class Debate?

Like role playing, debates require that you defend a particular political or moral position and persuade others to support your side. Debates typically involve two opposing sides—each represented by either one person or a group of people—and a moderator. The moderator asks the questions, and each side then has a specified time to state its positions. After each side has done this, the first group usually gets to respond to the other side's views. The professor will lay out the rules for the debate beforehand so you will understand the format.

A debate can cover just about any issue in history. Some debates might re-enact a political debate, such as the John Kennedy–Richard Nixon debates in the presidential elections of 1960. Others might debate the pros and cons of capitalism and communism; still others might debate the merits of the American Constitution.

The key to success, as always, is to research and study your materials thoroughly because debates delve deeply into the issues. That debate about the American Constitution would cover diverse issues such as states' rights, equality of the individual, and the bases of power in the new state. To be successful, you must do the required readings for the class and then any additional research the professor assigns. Like the presentation and role-playing examples above, you could be asked to take different sides in the debate over whether European imperialism ultimately helped or harmed Africa. Issues in the debate might include economic benefits from increased trade, African dependence on European products, religious benefits from conversion to Christianity, and the loss of indigenous religious traditions.

To prepare for the debate itself:

Step 1:   Debates move very quickly, so you do not want to waste time shuffling through your notes. You must prepare a series of index cards or an outline of the key topics to be debated. Regardless of the format you choose (index cards or an outline) do not write long sentences detailing the different positions. Write short phrases or key words that will trigger your memory about the larger pieces of information.

Step 2:   The best policy is to follow the practice, practice, practice philosophy. While you might not know every question the moderator plans to ask, you can make a good guess and pretend to answer the questions in front of the mirror. By doing this, you make sure you really understand the issues and that your notes have the right trigger words. If you forget some of the facts, write longer phrases on your notes, to guarantee that they trigger your memory on the day of the debate. If you are working within a group, get the whole group together one or two times to practice the debate together. One person can act as moderator while the others debate the issues.

Step 3:   On the day of the debate, get to class a little early to prepare your notes. You might want to bring in a glass of water. Most people get very thirsty while they speak before a group. During the debate, try to look at your audience. People instinctively trust someone who looks them in the eyes (and the goal of a debate is to convince the audience that your position is the correct one). If you get nervous, try to look just at the professor or one of your friends. They want you to succeed just as much as you do. If you start to get nervous or confused, stop and take a look at your notes or index cards. Take another deep breath and give yourself a little time to think about the next piece of information you want to discuss.

 HELPING HAND   Every in-class presentation gets easier. The stage fright really does diminish each time you successfully complete a presentation.

RECAP

This chapter walked you through all the steps necessary for a successful presentation, debate, and role-playing exercise. The key to success is preparation. You need to conduct the research, prepare any necessary multimedia programs, and practice, practice, practice before you step in front of the class. If you have followed all the advice in this handbook, you'll discover that these kinds of presentations are easy.

*W*hat Is Plagiarism and When Would I Be Cheating on My Paper?

- *What is plagiarism?*

- *How can I recognize the different kinds of plagiarism and cheating?*

- *How can I avoid plagiarism?*

TIPS IN THIS CHAPTER

- Definition of plagiarism   ▪ Types of plagiarism and cheating
- Facts

What Is Plagiarism?

Plagiarism is the intellectual theft of someone else's ideas and words. When you plagiarize, you are taking someone else's work and attempting to pass it off as your own. This seems straightforward enough, but when you are writing a research paper you may find yourself saying: "All the information I have collected is new to me. How can I tell what is unique enough that it must be cited?" If you are in doubt, ask yourself the following: Are these words unique to this author? Have I seen this idea anywhere else? Have I really put this into my own words?

 HELPING HAND   If you are tempted to plagiarize, consider this: Your professor is not stupid; you will rarely be able to fool her. The reasons? (1) The books and articles you use for your research, and from which you might consider plagiarizing, contain more sophisticated analyses than the average student can produce. As a result, she'll have no trouble spotting material taken from a published article. (2) Your professor reads many more books and articles than most students do, so she might very well recognize the original source immediately . If she does not, she can contact friends in the field who can probably point her in the right direction. (3) Your professor knows how to use Internet search engines as well as her students; she can find the same paper you can.

How Can I Recognize the Different Kinds of Plagiarism and Cheating?

Plagiarism comes in all sizes and colors, sometimes blatant and sometimes more subtle. Several different types of plagiarism are described below.

Word-for-Word Transcription   This example is the easiest to define. Plagiarism rules are very explicit on this point. It is forbidden to copy someone else's work, word for word, and present it as your own. If only one sentence in the paper contains a word-for-word transcription, the paper is plagiarized. Word-for-word transcriptions must be placed within quotation marks and the source cited.

Unique Terms   Authors often invent their own terms to make a given point. These invented words or phrases are often combinations of two words or a merger of an English word and a foreign one. Sometimes, the word has been given a new definition by the author. Frequently, the word or combination will be contained within quotes. If you do not see this term in another article or book, you can assume that it is unique to the author. You must cite the source of any such terms.

Paraphrasing   A common misconception is that if you change a few words in a text, the text is now your own. This is not true.

- If you copy the same basic sentence structure as the original text, you are plagiarizing, regardless of how many nouns and verbs you change.
- If you present your evidence in the same order as the original text, you are plagiarizing.

In other words, if you retain the same stylistic and analytical framework of the original text, you are plagiarizing.

Despite these potential pitfalls, paraphrasing can be part of your paper. You may begin a section of paraphrasing by saying something like, "Author X states . . ." or "To paraphrase author X's work . . ." and then provide a citation at the end of the section.

> *HELPING HAND*   The best way to avoid crossing the line into plagiarism is to work solely from your own notes and your own interpretations of the data and not directly from the book.

Papers on the Web   Thousands of web sites selling and giving away prewritten papers have been created in the past decade. Without any doubt, it is plagiarism to copy or buy a paper from the Internet and present it as your own work.

Papers Written by Your Friends   Fraternities, sororities, campus organizations, and your own friends often keep old papers on file. Copying these papers represents plagiarism because you did not do the work and the words are not your own.

Papers You Wrote for Another Class   Many students have an interest in a particular topic or region of the world and so they take a number of courses covering it. As a result, students may find themselves writing papers on similar subjects. You are cheating if you submit a paper to more than one class.

Citing Works You Have Never Read or Data You Haven't Collected   The following group of offenses are loosely connected and constitute cheating.

- Padding your bibliography with materials you have never read.
- Changing the results of your data to better fit your thesis.
- Citing a source you did not actually consult.

> *HELPING HAND*   If you're not sure if a piece of information should be cited, ask the professor. If the professor isn't available, err on the side of caution and cite the source. It's always better to use too many citations than too few.

How Can I Avoid Plagiarism?

Several options for avoiding plagiarism are available to you. Some of these options are described below.

1. Conduct sufficient research to have an understanding of what material is unique to a particular author and what information is not. This sounds like a heavy burden, but this is the goal of a research paper—to find enough information to present your case and to prove your thesis.

With each source you find, you'll have a better understanding about what information is unique to a particular author. If you do a shoddy research job, your paper will not be good, even if you don't plagiarize.

2. Never write your paper with a book or an article open in your lap or propped up on the desk. Always take notes while reading your sources, placing the ideas and facts into your own words. Only exact quotes should be written word for word and, in those cases, you should place quotes around the passage and indicate the source of the quotation. If you try to take a shortcut and highlight your sources with a marker, you're setting the stage for plagiarism later. It's much too tempting to use the original author's words if the book is right in front of you. If you write out notes in your own words from the very beginning, you're working from your own statements, not the original author's.

When you start to write the paper, place all the original sources (the books, the articles, whatever you've used) away from the computer or your writing pad. You should work only from your notes. At this point, your job is to write sentences and paragraphs that best present your analysis of the various pieces of information you've compiled. You are now reworking and rewriting your notes, not the original author's.

3. Don't copy and paste information from the Web. The procedure for copying text from a web page and pasting it into a document is so easy that you may be tempted to do so. *This is plagiarism.* Students cannot take a section of someone else's work and pass it in to a professor as their own. Plagiarism rules apply to the Web as stringently as they do to traditional sources found in books, journals, and magazines. Quotes and pieces of information may be taken from web pages but the sources must be properly identified in the paper.

This information is so important that it needs to be repeated: *Do not be lulled by how easy it is to get information from the Web; copying and pasting someone else's words constitutes plagiarism.*

The Web should be considered a tool for research, just as a book or a magazine has always been. The Web offers thousands of newspapers, analyses, and critiques that can add to the quality of a student's paper; but only as the stepping-stones to a good paper, not as the body of that paper.

 HELPING HAND   Professors have access to the same web sites as the students. This means that professors can easily surf the Web and find the sources when they suspect plagiarism has occurred.

After reading about all these problems, you may be asking yourself, when can I use the copy and paste function on the Web? Since the Web can be considered a source for research, it is acceptable to copy and paste small pieces of text from the Web into a document of research notes. Next to the text, the URL of the web page, the writer of the text (if identifiable on the page), and the date the text was obtained should all be included. In the final paper, the text must then be cited in a footnote or endnote to identify it as someone else's words and ideas.

 HELPING HAND   If you do not heed the advice offered in this chapter, your professor and your school administration will bring you before an academic conduct board. Every school in the country has a clearly stated plagiarism policy that may differ slightly from the wording presented in this book but that covers the same general issues. The punishments for plagiarism include probation, suspension, and expulsion from the college or university.

RECAP

This chapter illustrated the many types of plagiarism so that you can avoid the pitfalls they present. Plagiarism is a serious offense because stealing intellectual property is the same as stealing a stereo. School is a time for you to learn how to think and how to write. If you steal the work of others, you're destroying the benefits of your own school experience.

*W*hat Information Do I Have to Cite?

- *What kind of information must be cited?*

- *What kind of information does not have to be cited?*

- *What citation system should I use?*

- *What information must be included in footnotes, endnotes, parenthetical citations, and bibliographies?*

- *What is the proper form for the second citation of any source?*

- *How do I cite web sites in my paper?*

TIPS IN THIS CHAPTER

- Information to be cited
- Citation styles
- Information that does not need to be cited

To grade your paper, your professor will, among other things, look to see if you've used good quality sources to support your thesis. The citations you place throughout the paper and the bibliography you supply at the end provide that information. Think of these sources as the building blocks of your entire paper. Your professor needs to know what sources were primary and which were secondary, when they were published, who published them, and so on. You need to investigate your sources before you use them (as described in Chapter 5), and your professor will do the same when you turn in your paper. In that way, the professor can determine if some sources are better for your particular topic than others, and if you've used a sufficient number of sources to construct your thesis.

Two issues present themselves when you think about citing sources in your paper:

1. What information do I cite?

2. What citation system should I use?

What Kind of Information Must Be Cited?

The following list describes several kinds of information that must be cited in a scholarly work, including your research papers.

1. **Quotes.** By citing quotes, you're acknowledging the uniqueness of people's words.
2. **Ideas, analyses, and opinions.** Identifying a unique idea, analysis, or opinion is probably the hardest aspect of deciding what to cite. The goal of most authors is to present a unique analysis of a given event. Your job is to find that analysis and to acknowledge that it is "owned" by the original author. Here are some guidelines.

   - Every paper you read will have a thesis, often presented in the first or second paragraph. The thesis of a book usually appears in the introductory chapter. You must cite the source of this thesis.
   - If you read an analysis in one source that does not appear in any other, you must cite the source of that idea.
   - A good rule is to cite any statement that includes objective terms such as "he believed," "she felt," or "they thought," because only the original author can voice such an opinion.

3. **Unique words or phrases created by the author.** Often, historians create new words to express a given phenomenon because they don't feel that regular vocabulary words truly articulate their ideas. Cite any words or phrases that seems a little strange to you because they're used in a unique way or if they seem to be a combination of two or more words.
4. **Disputed facts.** If you encounter a debate about a given date, then cite the different sources and explain, in your paper, why the date is disputed. If historians question the facts of a given event, you must cite the source you choose to use.
5. **Paraphrasing.** *Paraphrasing, without citation, is plagiarism.* You may not copy the bulk of a sentence or paragraph, change a word or two, and present it as your own work. For that matter, you can't change a few words and present it as your own work. As long as you retain the basic structure and ideas of the sentence or the paragraph, it doesn't matter how many words you change; you are still stealing some-one else's work if you don't include a citation. You *may* paraphrase another author's words if you iden-tify the author, by stating his name in the text and by citing his work at the end of the passage.

☞ *HELPING HAND*   Since plagiarism rules often vary at different colleges and universities, the best course of action is to ask your professor whenever you're confused about citing sources

What Kind of Information Does Not Have to Be Cited?

1. Generally, you do not have to provide a citation for a date.
2. Generally, information you find in your textbooks can be considered "common knowledge" and so it does not need to be cited.
3. Many analyses that appear in your sources can be considered "common knowledge" because historians do not question them. These analyses could include statements such as "The U.S. antiwar movement grew during the course of the Vietnam War" and "The nineteenth century witnessed an explosion in railway building throughout the world."
4. Avoid citing every sentence in a given paragraph. You can state near the beginning of the paragraph that you will be discussing a person's words and then you can put one citation at the end of the paragraph.
5. You don't have to cite your own words. You shouldn't be afraid to present your own analyses in a paper. Students often feel that they have to rely solely on the historians' works they find printed in books or on the Web. Use that information to construct your own thesis.

What Citation System Should I Use?

Various citation systems have been devised. The most familiar being the *Chicago Manual of Style* and the *MLA Handbook for Writers of Research Papers (MLA)*. Ask your professor which system she prefers. Your options include footnotes, endnotes, or parenthetical citations. If the professor does not have a preference, choose the system you want. You must also include a full bibliography at the end of each paper, unless otherwise directed by the professor.

This handbook is too small to discuss in detail all the different citation styles. Only a general overview

☞ *HELPING HAND*   Regardless of the citation system you choose, be consistent. Do not use parenthetical citations for half the paper and footnotes for the second half. Do not use the Chicago system sometimes and the MLA system at other times.

will be provided. For an exact list of citations, buy the Chicago Manual or the MLA guide, or access either one on the Web.

What Information Must Be Included in Footnotes, Endnotes, Parenthetical Citations, and Bibliographies?

In both systems (Chicago and MLA), depending on the type of source, you must include the following kinds of information.

Books
Author(s) of the book
Title of the book
City of publication
Publisher
Date of publication

Here is an example of a footnote or endnote in the Chicago system:

[1]Adam Hochschild, *King Leopold's Ghost: A Story of Greed, Terror, and Heroism in Colonial Africa* (Boston: Houghton Mifflin Co., 1999), 125.

The MLA system recommends the parenthetical style for documentation. An example of a parenthetical note in the MLA system is shown here:

(Hochschild 202)

An example of a bibliographic entry in both the Chicago and MLA systems appears as shown here:

Hochschild, Adam. *King Leopold's Ghost: A Story of Greed, Terror, and Heroism in Colonial Africa*. Boston: Houghton Mifflin Co., 1999.

Edited Volumes
Editor(s) of the book
Title of the book
City of publication
Publisher
Date of publication

If you are citing a chapter in an edited volume, you must also cite:

Author(s)
Title of the chapter

An example of a footnote or endnote in the Chicago system is shown here:

[1]Ainslee Embree, "Imperialism and Decolonization," in *The Columbia History of the 20th Century*, ed. Richard W. Bulliet (New York: Columbia University Press, 1998), 150.

The MLA system recommends the parenthetical style for documentation, an example of which is shown below:

(Ainslee 150)

The following is an example of a bibliographic entry in the Chicago system:

Embree, Ainslee. "Imperialism and Decolonization." In *The Columbia History of the 20th Century*, edited by Richard W. Bulliet. New York: Columbia University Press, 1998.

The following is an example of a bibliographic entry in the MLA system:

Embree, Ainslee. "Imperialism and Decolonization." *The Columbia History of the 20th Century*. Ed. Richard W. Bulliet. New York: Columbia University Press, 1998, 147-171.

Journal Articles
Author(s)
Title of article
Title of journal
Publication information (volume number, date of publication)

Page numbers

Here is an example of a footnote or endnote in the Chicago system:

[1]Samira Aghacy, "Lebanese Women's Fiction: Urban Identity and the Tyranny
of the Past," *International Journal of Middle East Studies* 33, no. 4
(November 2001): 505.

And this is an example of the parenthetical style recommended by the MLA system:

(Aghacy 505)

Here is an example of a bibliographic entry in the Chicago system:

Aghacy, Samira. "Lebanese Women's Fiction: Urban Identity and the Tyranny
of the Past." *International Journal of Middle East Studies* 33, no. 4
(November 2001): 503-523.

This is an example of a bibliographic entry in the MLA system:

Aghacy, Samira. "Lebanese Women's Fiction: Urban Identity and the Tyranny
of the Past." *International Journal of Middle East Studies* 33: 4
(November 2001): 503-523.

What Is the Proper Form for the Second Citation of Any Source?

You do not need to provide a full citation every time you cite the same source. A number of different styles can be used when you cite the same source more than once.

1. You can provide a shortened version of the citation by writing the author's last name and the page number, or the author's last name, a shortened version of the title, and the page number. (The latter style should be used if you use more than one source from the same author.)

2. Another shortened version of the citation is created by writing "Ibid.," followed by the page number. This style should be used if you are citing from the same source two times in a row, but from two different pages.

How Do I Cite Web Sites in My Paper?

You must cite the source of any information you find on the Web. The various citation styles (such as *Chicago* and *MLA*) have slightly different forms, but all require the same basic information. Always include in both a bibliographical and citation note the following information:

■ Author/editor
■ Title of the web page
■ Publication date and/or the date you retrieved the page from the Web (because pages change so rapidly, you need to indicate the date when you found the information)
■ URL
■ Include any other information pertinent to that particular article/page, for example, the volume number, issue number, etc.

The *Chicago Manual of Style* has not yet clarified a system for citing web sites, so use the *MLA* system for parenthetical citations:

(Victorian Web)

An example of a bibliographic entry in the *MLA* system would appear as follows:

Victorian Web. Ed. George Landow. 1994. Brown University. 6 Sept. 1998
  <http://www.stg.brown.edu/projects/hypertext/landow/victorian/
  victov.html>.

 HELPING HAND   Always provide enough information so that your readers can find the web site again. It is particularly important that you type the correct (and complete) URL and the date when you accessed the site.

RECAP

This chapter outlined some of the occasions when you must cite the sources in your papers and provided you with a short style guide outlining how the citations should actually be written.

This Isn't English Class, So Why do I have to Correct My Grammar?

- *Why is grammar important?*

- *What are the most common grammatical errors?*

TIPS IN THIS CHAPTER

- Keep a good grammar book by your side
- Edit carefully
- Avoid common mistakes

Why Is Grammar Important?

A famous historian is fond of recounting the day a student raised his hand and asked, "Do grammar count?" Without skipping a beat, the professor replied, "Yes, grammar do." Why do all professors agree that grammar counts? Because grammar is a tool for communication. It helps writers express themselves clearly and it helps readers follow what is being said. It eliminates barriers to understanding between the two. So that often-asked question, "Why do I have to correct my grammar?" really translates into "Why do I have to worry about being understood?"

If you were stranded on a desert island, a good guide to grammar and proper writing style would still be a necessity. Fortunately, many good guides are available. The style guides most commonly recommended by college professors include *The Chicago Manual of Style* and the *MLA Handbook for Writers of Research Papers (MLA)*. Keep the guide you chose handy, along with a thesaurus and a dictionary. All three are essential tools in academic life.

What Are the Most Common Grammatical Errors?

Here is a list of do's and don'ts, including some of the most common grammatical errors and problems of style. This list is by no means exhaustive. But if you avoid these errors and stylistic mistakes, you will have made a lot of headway toward writing a history exam or paper that communicates well.

1. **Avoid the passive tense.** Make the subject of your sentence a "doer" not someone or something "done to." Good narrative is propelled along, not dragged behind. Instead of "The repeal of the Corn Laws was discussed in the nineteenth century" you will want to write "The British Parliament discussed the repeal of the Corn Laws in the nineteenth century."
2. **Don't leave those participles dangling.** How do you know if you have dangled a participle? That's easy: insert the phrase immediately after the subject of your sentence. For example, test the sentence "Walking across the field, a rock stuck in Joe's shoe" by putting the dependent clause directly after the subject: "A rock, walking across the field, stuck in Joe's shoe." Can a rock actually walk? Shouldn't the sentence say: "Walking across the field, Joe got a rock stuck in his shoe"? Or take another example: "If handled properly, you should be able to pass this exam easily." Do you really need to be handled properly—or does the exam? "If handled properly, the exam should be easy to pass."
3. **Don't split those infinitives.** An infinitive, as in "to sit," "to read," "to go," should not be divide by the insertion of another form of speech.
   Right: I had to sit quickly or I would be forced to stand for the whole trip.
   Wrong: I had to quickly sit or I would be forced to stand for the whole trip.
4. **Make certain the noun and the verb agree.** Singular noun, singular verb; plural noun, plural verb.
   Right: The Constitution and the Declaration of Independence *are* fundamental documents in American history.
   Wrong: The kings and queens of England *is* important figures in history.
   Right: The fall of Rome *is* a major historical event.
   Wrong: Some Americans *comes* from southern Europe.
5. **Do not fall into the habit of calling a country "they."** If you use a pronoun to describe a country, use a singular pronoun, not a plural one. If you discuss the officials in a given country, then you can use the plural pronoun. (And, by the way, a country is not a "she.")

Right: Egypt *is* a country containing a Muslim majority and a Christian minority. As a result, *it* must be tolerant of both Muslim and Christian laws.

Right: The leaders in a democratic nation know *they* must answer to the people through regular elections.

6. **Don't shift point of view.**

   Wrong: *We* all want to study history because *you* can apply the skills you learn in other subjects.

   Right: We all want to study history because *we* can apply the skills *we* learn in other subjects.

7. **Make certain each sentence is a complete sentence, not a phrase.**

   Wrong: Lincoln had many goals as president. *Especially to preserve the union.*

   The first sentence is a sentence; the second is a phrase without a subject or a verb.

   Right: Lincoln had many goals as president. He was especially eager to preserve the union.

8. **Don't construct a sentence that is really several sentences combined.**

   Wrong: Louis XIV of France was a proud man he thought he was above the law.

   There are two sentences here, pretending to be one.

   Right: Louis XIV of France was a proud man. He thought he was above the law.

   Or you could create one sentence.

   Right: Louis XIV of France was a proud man who thought he was above the law.

9. **Don't shift tenses suddenly.**

   If you choose to write in the present tense, stick with the present tense. Don't confuse your readers by shifting to the past tense.

   Wrong: Some colonists *want* to rebel. Other colonists *did* not.

   Right: Some colonists want to rebel. Other colonists *do* not.

10. **Have you used the correct word?**

    a. *There* refers to location; *their* means in the possession of several people; *they're* means "they are."

    b. *Its* is a possessive pronoun; *It's* is a contraction of "it is."

    c. *Your* is a possessive pronoun; *you're* is a contraction of "you are."

    d. *Lie* means "to recline"; *lay* means "to put" or "to place."

    e. *To* is a preposition; *too* means "also" or "excessively."

    f. "Ain't" isn't correct in formal written English.

    g. To "affect" something is to have an impact on it; an "effect" is the result of an action taken.

11. **Don't end a sentence with a preposition.**

    Wrong: He had a lot of problems to contend with.

    Right: He had to contend with a lot of problems.

12. **Use your apostrophes properly.**

    Don't confuse plurals with possessives. Plurals don't require apostrophes; possessives do.

👉 *HELPING HAND*   Never sit down to write without a good dictionary by your side. If you are a terrible speller, look for one of those dictionaries that enter the word in several of the most commonly misspelled forms and then give you the proper spelling. Most computer word-processing programs alert you to a misspelled word and then offer you the chance to correct your mistake.

   Right: The queen's robe is elegant.

   Wrong: The queen's of England were powerful.

13. **You're repeating yourself.**

    a. "The reason is because" really translates to "the reason is the reason"; instead, write "the reason is that."

    b. "Revert back" really means "go back back" because *revert* means "to go back."

14. **Pronouns need nouns.**

    A pronoun takes the place of a noun. For example, Mary took a history test. *She* made an "A" on it. *She* stands for Mary; *it* stands for the history test. But if you start a new paragraph in your test or essay or paper, you can't start it with a pronoun. The pronoun needs an antecedent, or a noun that comes in an earlier sentence. So a paragraph that begins with "He" is like a ship lost at sea.

15. **Here is a short list of the most common mistakes.**
    a. Don't write "a revolution is when"; *when* signals time.
    b. Don't write "a revolution is where"; *where* signals a location.
    c. Don't confuse "woman"—one female person—with "women"—two or more female persons.
    d. Don't write "between you and I"; write "between you and me" because "you and me" are the objects of the preposition, not the subject of the sentence.
    e. Don't confuse "who" and "whom." *Who* is the subjective case; *whom* is the objective case.
    Right: Halt! Who goes there?
    Right: To whom are you speaking?
    Wrong: To who is that addressed?
    Wrong: Whom is the new president?

Is your head spinning? Don't worry. There are scores of excellent grammar books available, some of them with a good sense of humor and most of them inexpensive.

RECAP

This chapter pointed out that writing is a form of communication. To communicate well, you must master a set of grammatical rules that are not designed to torment you or trick you but to help you say what you mean, say it clearly, and say it with some grace and style. Fortunately, you can find several books that set out the rules of grammar for you—clearly and gracefully.

*H*ow Do I Make Computer Technology Work for Me? How Do I Succeed in an Online Class?

- *What are the technical issues?*

- *What is email etiquette?*

- *What are my professor's virtual office hours?*

- *Does my professor have a web page for this class?*

- *How can I use the computer to create different kinds of presentations and papers?*

- *What must I know to succeed in an online class?*

TIPS IN THIS CHAPTER

- Critiquing sources on the Web
- Downloading information from the Web
- Adding images to your presentations and papers
- Finding information on the Web
- Preparing transparencies
- Online courses

Computer technology brings exciting new tools into the classroom. It helps you and your professor interact more easily and it allows both of you to present materials in a multimedia format. But computer technology changes on an almost daily basis, and *The History Handbook* can't cover all the different programs that exist or those that will come into existence while you are reading this book! What this chapter can do, however, is give you some tips on how to use these new computer programs.

What Are the Technical Issues?

For technical questions, consult your school's Information Technology office or the Help menu in each program. You can also access the Web for more detailed information about each program. For example, if you have any questions about Microsoft programs, you can try the http://www.microsoft.com web site. If you still can't find an answer to your question, call the help lines (these telephone lines are often toll free) provided with most programs.

If you have technical problems, you should let the professor know right away. Other students may be having the same problems, and the professor will be able to work with all of you to resolve them. If the problems continue, he may want to reschedule your assignment. Like you, the professor is mastering new computer technologies and experimenting with their usefulness. He may not be certain which ones will actually help in the classroom, so your input will be invaluable.

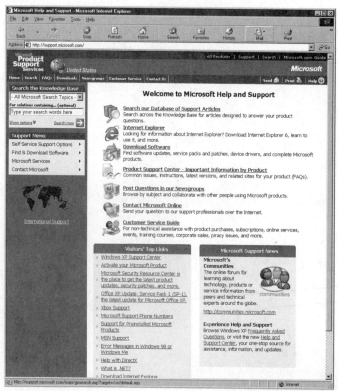

What Is Email Etiquette?

Email has certainly changed the way professors and students communicate with each other; professors can easily send out messages to the entire class and students can ask quick questions without checking for the professor's office hours.

However, email should not be considered a substitute for personal interaction between the professor and the student. Email is a fabulous technology, but its design allows for quick statements and answers, not in-depth debates. Questions concerning problems in the class or drafts of papers, or anything that requires a discussion between the professor and the student, should take place in the professor's office.

 HELPING HAND   Professors have entered this profession in part because they like to work with students and hear their opinions of the world around them. Thus, students who take the time to visit their professors during scheduled office hours to talk about the class will generally receive a better reception than those who choose to ask their questions only through email.

 HELPING HAND   When writing an email to a professor, check your spelling and grammar. Email will never be part of the final grade, but a poorly spelled or worded email gives a bad impression of your writing abilities.

What Are My Professor's Virtual Office Hours?

A number of professors are starting to hold virtual office hours (meaning that you can contact the professor via the computer, not in his or her office) in addition to or in contrast to regular, in-the-office hours.

One example of virtual office hours occurs when the professor promises to answer all the email he receives in a given hour during the day. If that is the case, send your questions and requests during the allotted time. As with regular office hours, this is the time the professor sets aside every week to talk to students. Respect that time and contact the professor accordingly. Otherwise, the professor might be away from the computer at other times or might not be able to answer your questions immediately.

Another means of offering virtual office hours occurs when the professor sets up a bulletin board for the class. If the professor has done this, he will give you the URL at the beginning of the semester and then announce the office hours for each week. On the appointed day, instead of sending an email to your professor, you can use your web browser to access the bulletin board. Typically, bulletin boards include a form where you can type in your name, possibly your email address, and your comments. When you are done typing in these boxes, hit the "Submit" or "OK" button, depending on how the form is organized. Your message will then be sent to the professor and he can then respond. The difference between a computer bulletin board and email is that you see not only your own message and the professor's response, but also the questions of the other students. A debate can take place among you, your fellow students, and the professor, in which you can respond or ask questions of anyone involved. These messages can also stay up on the Web throughout the semester, so you may read the messages at any time.

 HELPING HAND   When using a bulletin board, you will not see new messages instantaneously. Most web browsers require that you hit the "Refresh" or "Reload" button to see the new messages.

A number of computer programs also mimic the chat rooms that are so popular on the Web. If the professor has set up a chat room, he will give you the URL and explain how the program works. Usually, everybody entering the chat room will be able to see all the comments made by the other participants. On the screen will be a section allowing you to type your own comments and your message will appear instantaneously on the screen, along with the others.

Does My Professor Have a Web Page for This Class?

More and more often, professors are creating individualized web pages for each class. Professors post class information, such as the syllabus, course outlines, and study guides, and also any images that are relevant to the week's lecture, to these class web pages. You will probably also find a number of hyperlinks to other programs that the professor wants to use, such as bulletin boards, virtual office hours, and the posting of student web pages. Two common courseware programs are WebCT and Blackboard/Courseinfo. They contain some areas for uploading documents and images, and others that allow for interaction between students and professors.

 HELPING HAND　The professor has gone to a lot of work to construct a class web page. This page is a tool for you. Professors would not take the effort to do all this work if the site were not important. Make sure you check the site at least once every week or before every class to read announcements or any other material the professor wants you to have.

How Can I Use the Computer to Create Different Kinds of Presentations and Papers?

Many professors now require that students prepare multimedia presentations and papers for their classes. These assignments not only enhance your knowledge of the class topics but also prepare you for similar presentations that you might have to give in a future job.

You can find images and maps on the World Wide Web and in books. However, the rules of copyright apply to these images, just as plagiarism laws apply to the text.

Unless otherwise indicated (and some web pages do say that images in a particular area are free), assume that all images seen on the Web or printed in books are owned by someone.

Class work falls under the "fair-use" policies followed by most colleges and universities. If you are showing an image one time in a class or adding it to a research paper, you usually can do so without obtaining the copyright. Make sure you indicate the source for the image, just as you would cite any quote in the text. Also, check with the professor to see what rules your specific college or university follows concerning copyright.

The following paragraphs describe programs and supplementary materials that will aid you in preparing these kinds of assignments.

World Wide Web　Millions of maps and photographs are available on the Web. To use a map or photograph in a presentation or paper, open the web page containing it and save the image on your own computer.

Books　To use an image in a book, you must either copy the image directly to a copier or scan it into the computer. To scan an image, you must use a scanner. Many university computer labs have scanners for students to use. If not, ask the professor how you should copy the image that you want to use.

You may insert images into your word-processing document, Power Point presentation, or web page. In this way, you can intersperse the images that illustrate the major themes you are discussing in the presentation and paper.

Word-Processing Programs　While you probably use your word-processing program only to type papers, it can actually do many more things. You can insert maps and images into your text, create outlines of your presentation, and highlight the text in various font sizes and colors.

Power Point　A program called Power Point creates presentations very easily. The program automatically provides outlines and allows you to insert pictures or images between the lines of text. When you open a new Power Point session, it will ask you which style you would prefer. From that point, it is very easy to follow the instructions on the page.

Web Page You may also create your own web page for a presentation. The advantage of this process is that the Web allows you to construct permanent documents. For example, a Power Point presentation is good for the twenty minutes you are actually speaking, but a web page can be posted to the Internet, and your classmates can re-examine it at any time, twenty-four hours a day, while the semester continues.

Newer versions of Netscape and Internet Explorer also have areas where you can construct your own web page. Go to the web browser that you prefer and look for a compose function. Create a web page as you would in a word-processing program. It will automatically save it in an HTML format.

WebCT and Blackboard/Courseinfo provide guidance about creating web pages. Consult your professor and the program documentation to find out how to create your own web sites with these programs.

Both word-processing programs and web browsers generally come free with most new computers. You may also choose to spend a little more money and buy a web page composer. This program allows you to create complex web pages. It is your decision whether a class presentation necessitates the extra expense.

To post your web page to the World Wide Web, you must consult with your professor because you need to send the page to a computer attached to the Internet.

To present the web page in class, you have several different options:

1. You can bring your laptop into class and show your web pages by connecting the computer to an LCD projector.
   a. If the classroom is wired for the Web, you can connect to the Web and then the site where your web pages are housed. To do this, you must contact your Information Technology office to find out how to post your web pages to the Internet and then how to access them via that particular classroom. Be warned: Web access through these classroom lines is tricky at best and rarely works smoothly.
   b. A better method is to save your web pages on the hard drive of the laptop and to display them from the computer itself.
2. Bring students into a computer lab and show them your site using a web browser.
3. Print the pages on transparencies, and show the site as you would a Power Point presentation.

If you need to show an outline or an image on a transparency in class, the process for creating the transparency is the same as printing a piece of paper. All printers—from inkjet to laser printers—will take transparency sheets. Buy the transparencies at any office supply store, and make sure you buy the kind used by your printer. Read the instructions contained in the transparency box to learn how to place the transparency into the printer.

 HELPING HAND Transparencies work best if you remember to use large font sizes so everyone can see what you have written. If you rely on phrases instead of long sentences, everyone has time to read what you have written. Most important, make sure that the projector is in place and ready to be used on the day when you make your presentation.

What Must I Know to Succeed in an Online Class?

With daily improvements in computer technology, colleges and universities are moving toward virtual classrooms, where professors and students interact via the computer and not in person. This type of distance learning is a wonderful opportunity that did not exist just a few years ago. To get the most of this type of class takes a little bit of organizational skill on your part. For one thing, the relationship between the professor and the student changes. In some ways, the connection is stronger because your email lets you spend more time in one-on-one contact with the professor. But emails sometimes don't convey all the feelings and concerns that you can express when you talk them out, face-to-face. A classroom is a much better setting for that. Because of the realities of the online connection, you need to schedule your time carefully and you need to go the extra mile to maintain contact with your professor, both face-toface and in writing.

While all online classes are designed differently, a few tips can help you succeed. The following paragraphs describe some tips for success in an online class.

Keep in Contact with the Professor   Even though the course is online, try to visit the professor in his office at the beginning of the semester and if you need help throughout the semester. If you meet the professor, he will then be able to attach a face to any emails, papers, and tests he receives from you. This personal contact will be invaluable when he sits down to determine your final grade.

If you live too far away from the school to visit the professor, consider calling him to talk about the requirements for the course at the beginning of the semester. Maintain this contact throughout the semester if you need further explanations about the coursework. If telephone contact isn't possible, email the professor whenever you have a problem or if you want to discuss any of the topics posed in the class in more detail.

Follow the Rules of Email Etiquette When Contacting Your Professor   Since email will be your primary contact with the professor all semester, remember that a kind, well-written email will receive a much warmer response than a rude, poorly written one. You will never be graded on your email etiquette directly, but you make an impression with the professor every time you contact him, and he will carry that impression with him as he calculates your grade.

Make Sure You Have Access to the Right Computer Technology   If you are using a home computer, make sure it has all the programs required by the online course. You can get a list of the programs from your university or your professor. Also, make sure that your connection is fast enough and stable enough that you won't find yourself waiting hours for documents to download, or have the connection break just as you are taking a test.

If you need to use a public computer, make sure you can get access to it during class periods and then for long periods of time when class assignments are due. Check with your school's computer office to find out what rights you have to use the computers. Ask about time limits and printing quotas.

Follow All the Instructions Given by the Professor   Just like any course assignment, make sure you read the instructions. For example, if the professor tells you to utilize a certain kind of source in a paper, use it. Read the exam questions carefully to make sure that you have answered them properly.

The fact that you're taking the course online presents you with new ways of scheduling your time. Frequently, professors will give you online tests. If that's the case, remember that you are probably being timed. If you take too much time, the program might shut down. Also be aware that once you send your test (probably by hitting a "Submit" button), you will not be able to retrieve the test. Always make sure that you understand all the instructions before you start taking an online test.

Stick to All the Deadlines   You should not think of deadlines as only those associated with papers and exams. Online classes have virtual office hours and virtual class periods. You must attend all of them, even though you are sitting at home at your computer. At the beginning of the semester, write a schedule of all the deadlines and display it prominently on your desk. Passing in an assignment late for an online class or being absent from a virtual class session will incur the same penalties as those for a regular class.

Discipline Yourself to Do the Work   Students in regular classes have the professor in front of them two, three, or four times a week as a reminder that they have work to do. For at least that time period, the students have very few distractions. At home, you do not have the same luxury. You need to find a place as far away from any distractions as possible. You also need to allot a certain number of hours every week to your class work. You should not try to get the work done between other jobs. You should make an actual schedule to guarantee that you work, for example, every Monday and Wednesday, from 1:00 to 3:00, on the online class work.

An Online Course Does Not Mean You Should Avoid Campus Completely   Just because the course is online doesn't mean that all the information you'll need will be on the Web. If the course requires that you conduct research, do not focus just on the Web. Follow all the rules laid out in Chapter 7 on conducting research: go to the library, interview relevant people, find photographs, etc. The online course allows you to schedule only some of the class time; consider yourself a regular student for all the other assignments during the semester.

If you absolutely can't get to campus, investigate what libraries and archives exist in your own town. You can then utilize both library and online research for any papers you need to write.

Make Arrangements with Your Professor for the Return of Any Materials   The best way to arrange for the return of your materials is to send a self-addressed stamped envelope to the professor with any work assignments. If the professor has set up a system whereby you pass in every assignment via email or the Web, send the self-addressed stamped envelope separately or drop it off in the professor's office. Most professors don't have a budget for sending papers and tests to everyone in a class.

RECAP

This chapter outlined the most common uses of computer technology in the classroom. The computer allows for a give-and-take relationship: you can take information and images from the Web, and then you can use the computer to put together multimedia presentations and to contact your professor and fellow students. Computers are even allowing you to access your courses. The key to remember is that computer elements should be utilized intelligently to enhance your class work.

Are There Any Other Tips I Should Know?

- *Why should I go to class?*

- *How can I contact my professor?*

- *How can I avoid problems in this class?*

TIPS IN THIS CHAPTER

■ Attending class   ■ Contacting the professor   ■ Solving problems

Why Should I Go to Class?

Professors are frustrated when students don't come to class, and then arrive at the end of the semester to complain about the heavy workload or ask for an extension. Professors will generally be more responsive to students who they know and see on a regular basis.

How Can I Contact My Professor?

Email and the Web provide several ways to communicate with the professor, but they do not replace the professor. If you have a question about a lecture, a paper, or an assignment, try to see the professor during her office hours or make a special appointment.

If you have a question or a problem, discuss it with the professor immediately. Don't let the problem fester until the end of the semester, when you either do badly on an assignment or have to ask for an extension.

How Can I Avoid Problems in This Class?

Keep up with the work; do not leave everything until the night before the paper is due or the exam is scheduled. Do *not* go by the old adage, "I do better when I'm under pressure. I can't write a paper until the night before it's due." If you cram at the last moment, you will not do well. You need to attend class regularly, complete all the readings and assignments, and keep reviewing all your notes.

RECAP

This chapter examined the important relationship between you and your professor. To do well in class, you must attend each class session and, if you have a problem or a question, you should seek out the professor for help.

Glossary

bulletin boards Provide a means for online communication between professors and students. If a professor has set up a bulletin board, then go to the designated web page and type or copy and paste the information you wish to send. At the bottom of the page will be a "Submit" button. Hit the "Refresh" button in the menu button to see your entry.

button Used on web pages to indicate a hyperlink. You can identify a hyperlink by placing the mouse arrow on top of the button. If the mouse arrow changes to a hand, then the hyperlink will take you to a new area of the site.

cartographer A person who makes maps.

chat rooms Instantaneous discussion areas on the Web. Once you access the web page, you can type your message, submit it, and see it appear on the screen automatically. Other people in the chat room may then respond to you just as quickly.

copyright The legal right to intellectual property or a creative work. Someone owns the right to every page on the Web. You may not sell or benefit financially from images or maps you retrieve from the Web. Generally, you may use an image or map from the Web in a class but you must always indicate the source.

cursor The flashing line indicating where text can be inserted on a computer screen. The mouse can also be utilized to move the cursor to desired areas of the document.

database The organization of information into fields. An address database, for example, would have fields for first name, last name, street address, town, state, and zip code. To access the database, search for a person's last name or a street address. Many historical web sites are supported by databases that you can search for a particular historical event or figure.

download Copying an image, map, or piece of text found on the Web and saving it to your computer. For a PC, place the mouse on top of an image and click the right button. A menu will appear asking you if you want to download or copy the image. Follow the menus on the screen. For a Mac, hold the mouse button down until a similar menu appears. To download or save a piece of text, hit the File and then Save commands on the menu bar at the top of the screen. Sometimes the web page will give instructions for downloading a file or a program. Follow these instructions when they are available.

electronic index Indexes, like the Social Sciences Citation Index, that can be accessed on your own library database via the Web. Check your school library to see what the URL is for the web page and follow the instructions. While library databases generally direct you only to books or journals, indexes are more specialized and can provide information about articles and book reviews. Often, these indexes focus on a particular subject, like American history or the history of science.

folder All computers place programs and files into different folders, which organize the data.

HTML A computer language that tells the browser to center a picture, for example, or place a hyperlink on a specific word.

hyperlink Used on web pages to allow the user to travel from one page on the Internet to another. Hyperlinks frequently appear as underlined text on the screen or as buttons. When the mouse is moved over a hyperlink, its symbol changes from an arrow to a hand.

icon Small pictures and buttons on the Web and in computer programs.

Internet The whole network of computers that connect your home computer to the world. The Internet works something like a telephone network: you dial into your university computer and it routes your request to the appropriate computer.

LCD projector   The device used to project web pages from your computer to a large screen.

listserv   A list of a group of people who would like to receive email about a given subject. To add your email address to a given list, you must subscribe to it. This usually involves sending a blank email to a designated address. From that point, you will receive all the email sent to that list and may send your email to the entire list as well.

Mac (Macintosh)   A computer that uses the Macintosh operating system. Power Macs, built in the latter half of the 1990s, are able to read both Mac and PC files.

menu   At the top of most computer programs appears a list of commands, for example, "File," "Edit," etc. Click on any of them with the mouse and a menu will appear with more choices.

operating system (OS)   Every computer has an operating system running behind the scenes to allow users to turn on the computer and access the different programs saved onto it. PCs generally use Microsoft Windows; Macs use their own system.

personal computer (PC)   A computer that uses the Microsoft Windows operating system and cannot read files created on a Mac.

Pine   A Telnet-based email program that provides only the simplest of commands. It is useful, however, for accessing email while you are away from your home computer.

plagiarism   The intellectual theft of someone else's ideas and words. When you plagiarize, you are taking someone else's work and attempting to pass it off as your own.

Power Point   A program that creates presentations on the computer. The program already has a series of templates, so all you need to do is fit your images and text into the boxes provided. You can then display your presentation to a group using a laptop computer and an LCD projector.

primary source   A document or artifact from the historical period under study.

scanner   A machine that "scans," or enters, images and text into your computer.

search engines   Allow you to ask questions of the Web. Examples include Yahoo! and Google. Pose your question by typing in a word or a phrase about your topic and then search engine generates a list of web pages where you will find that word or phrase.

secondary source   A document or artifact created after the historical period under study has passed.

Telnet   A program that allows a computer user to access email from a computer other than the user's own. When email is sent from one person to another it actually travels along a series of lines, taking it from one computer to the next. When someone reads email, he or she is actually taking it from the last computer (in the case students, from the university's main email computer). To access that mail while away from town or a home computer, a person can use Telnet to make a phone call to that email computer. A person is actually looking at another computer while viewing his or her email.

URL   An address for a web page and every web page has one. You may use a URL to access a web page by typing it into the box provided at the top of the browser and hitting "Enter."

web browser   A gateway to the Web. The most common web browsers are Netscape Communicator and Internet Explorer.

web page   The Web is comprised of millions of pages of text and images. Each individual page that appears on your screen is called a web page.

word-processing programs   Programs allow you to type letters and papers. The two most common are Microsoft Word and Corel WordPerfect.

World Wide Web (the Web)   The whole collection of pages people have posted to the Internet.

Index